PHILIP'S

STREET ATLAS

UNRIVALLED DETAIL FROM THE BEST-SELLING ATLAS RANGE*

NAVIGATOR® DERBYSHIRE

www.philips-maps.co.uk
Published Philip's, a division of
Octopus Publishing Group Ltd
www.octopusbooks.co.uk
Carmelite House
50 Victoria Embankment
London EC4Y 0DZ
www.hachette.co.uk

First edition 2023
First impression 2023
DBYFA

978-1-84907-637-1 (spiral)

© Philip's 2023

CONTENTS

T0319297

III Major administrative and Postcode boundaries

IV **Key to map pages**

VI **Route planning**

X **Key to map symbols**

1 **Street maps** at 3½ inches to 1 mile

266 **Street maps** of Chesterfield and Derby at 7 inches to 1 mile

268 **Index** of towns, villages, streets, hospitals, industrial estates, railway stations, schools, shopping centres, universities and places of interest

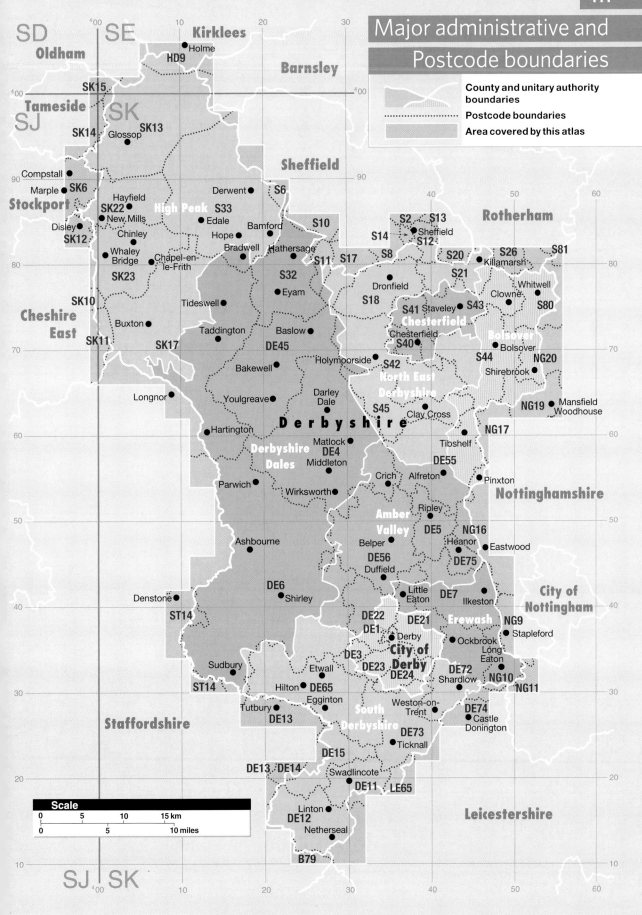

III

Major administrative and
Postcode boundaries

County and unitary authority boundaries

Postcode boundaries

Area covered by this atlas

SD
Oldham
SE
Kirklees
Holme
HD9
Barnsley

Tameside
SK15
SJ
SK
SK14
Glossop
SK13
Sheffield

Compstall
Marple
SK6
Derwent
S6
Stockport
Disley
SK12
SK22
Hayfield
New Mills
Chinley
High Peak
S33
Edale
Hope
Bamford
Bradwell
Hathersage
S10
S2
S13
S14
Sheffield
S12
Rotherham
Whaley
Bridge
Chapel-en-le-Frith
S11
S17
S8
S20
S26
S81
Killamarsh
SK23
S32
Eyam
S18
S21
Whitwell
Clowne
S80
Cheshire
East
Tideswell
Dronfield
S41
Staveley
S43
SK10
Buxton
DE45
S40
Chesterfield
Chesterfield
Bolsover
Bolsover
SK11
SK17
Holmoorside
S42
S44
NG20
Shirebrook
Longnor
Bakewell
North East
Derbyshire
Youlgreave
Darley
Dale
S45
Clay Cross
NG19
Mansfield
Woodhouse
Hartington
Derbyshire
Dales
Matlock
DE4
Middleton
Derbyshire
Crich
Alfreton
Tibshelf
NG17
Parwich
Wirksworth
Amber
Valley
Ripley
DE55
Pinxton
Nottinghamshire
Ashbourne
Belper
DE5
NG16
Heanor
Eastwood
DE56
Duffield
DE75
Denstone
ST14
DE6
Shirley
Little
Eaton
DE7
Ilkeston
City of
Nottingham
Etwall
DE22
DE1
DE21
Erewash
NG9
Stapleford
Sudbury
DE3
Derby
City of
Derby
Ockbrook
Long
Eaton
ST14
Hilton
DE65
DE23
DE24
DE72
Shardlow
NG10
NG11
Tutbury
Egginton
Weston-on-Trent
DE74
Castle
Donington
Staffordshire
DE13
South
Derbyshire
DE73
Ticknall
DE15
DE13
DE14
Swadlincote
DE11
LE65
Linton
DE12
Netherseal
Leicestershire
B79
SJ
SK

Scale

| 0 | 5 | 10 | 15 km |
| 0 | | 5 | 10 miles |

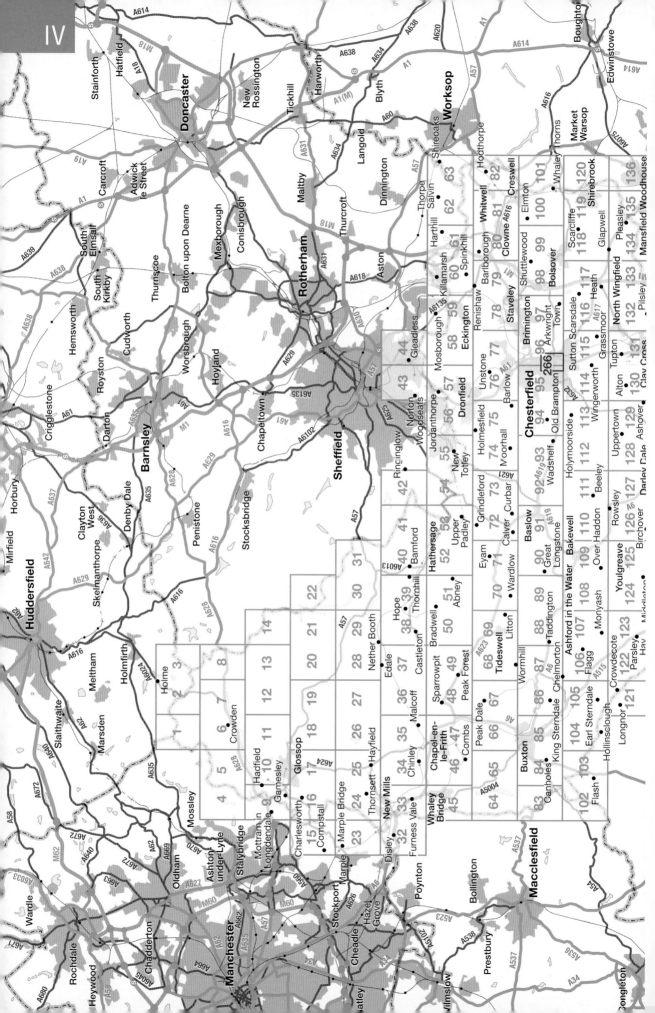

IV

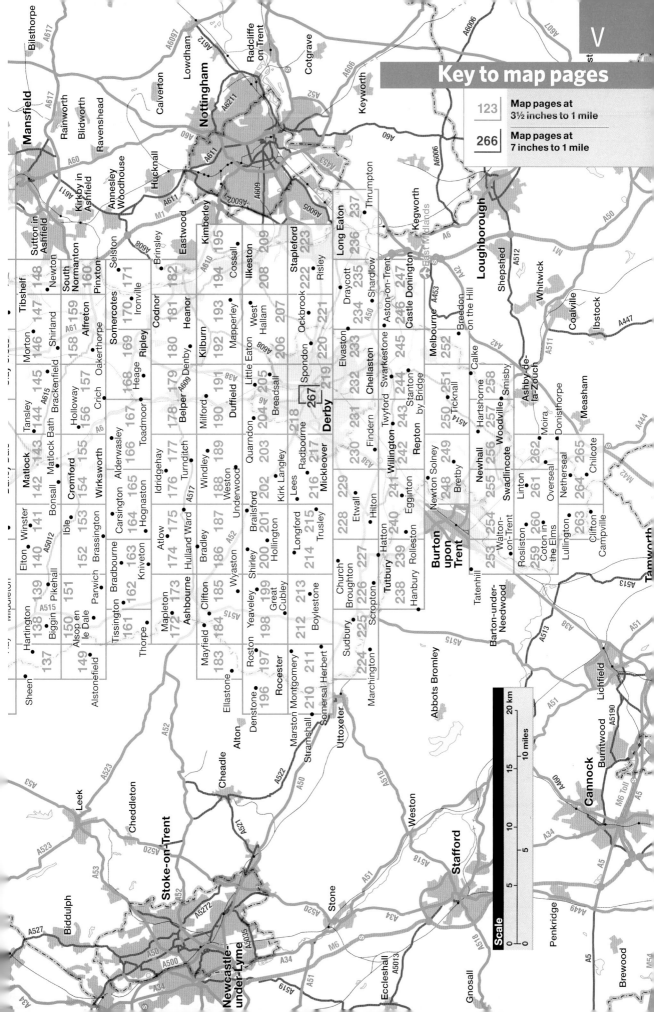

V

Key to map pages

| 123 | Map pages at 3½ inches to 1 mile |
| 266 | Map pages at 7 inches to 1 mile |

Scale

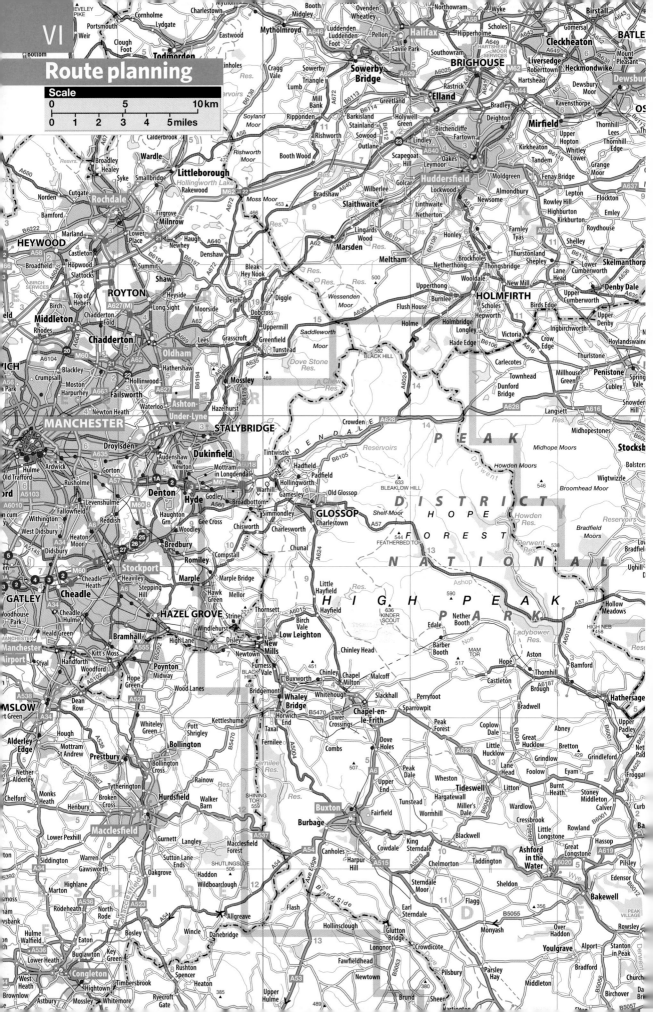

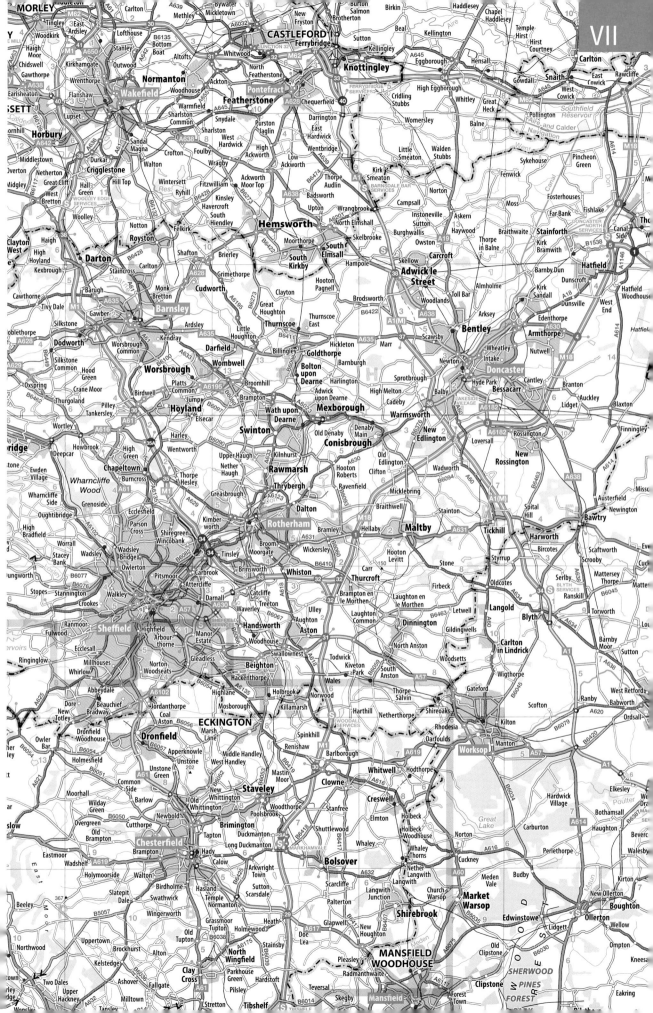

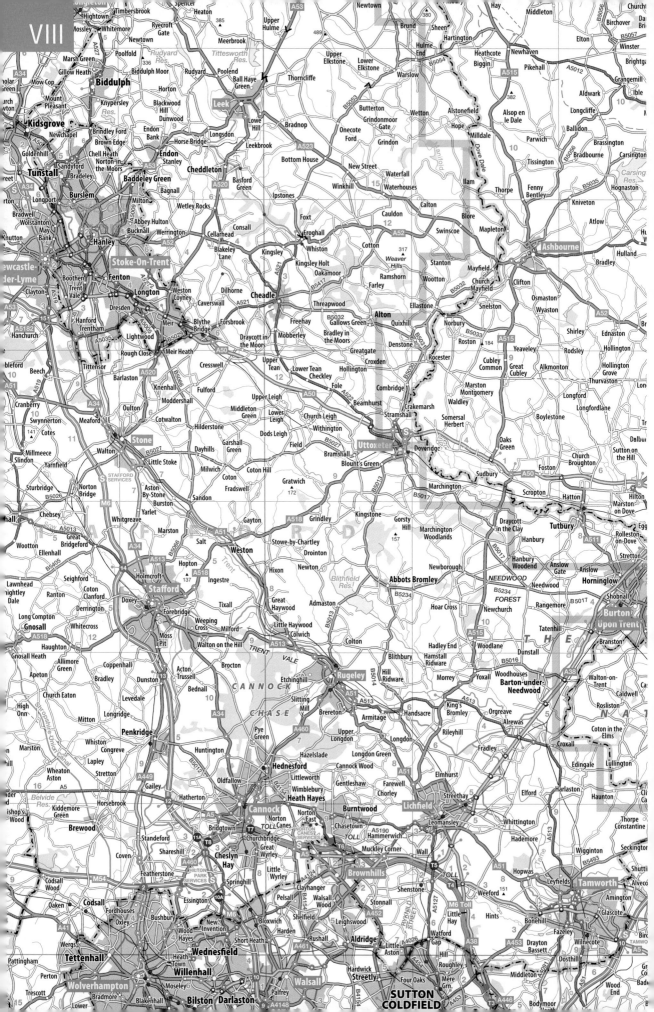

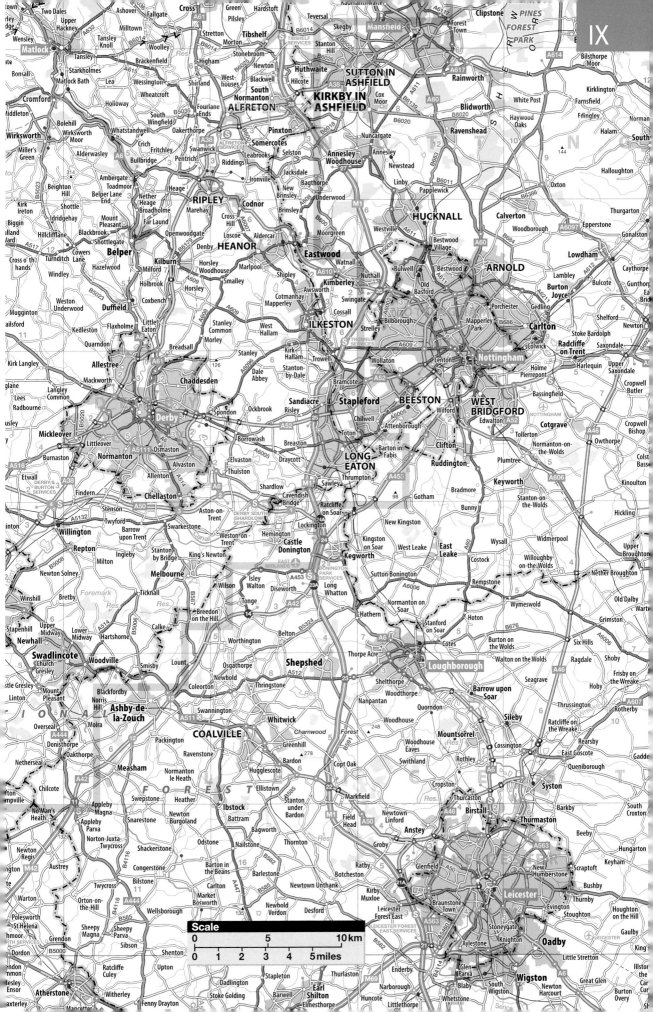

Key to map symbols

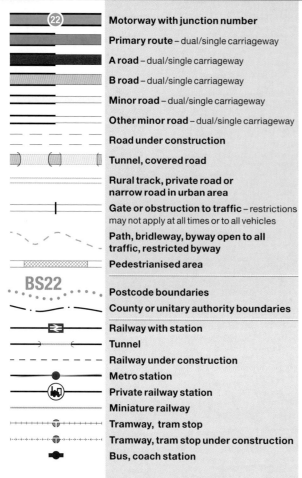

Motorway with junction number

Primary route – dual/single carriageway

A road – dual/single carriageway

B road – dual/single carriageway

Minor road – dual/single carriageway

Other minor road – dual/single carriageway

Road under construction

Tunnel, covered road

Rural track, private road or narrow road in urban area

Gate or obstruction to traffic – restrictions may not apply at all times or to all vehicles

Path, bridleway, byway open to all traffic, restricted byway

Pedestrianised area

BS22   Postcode boundaries

County or unitary authority boundaries

Railway with station

Tunnel

Railway under construction

Metro station

Private railway station

Miniature railway

Tramway, tram stop

Tramway, tram stop under construction

Bus, coach station

Ambulance station

Coastguard station

Fire station

Police station

Accident and Emergency entrance to hospital

H   Hospital

Place of worship

i   Information centre – open all year

P   Shopping centre, parking

P&R   PO   Park and Ride, Post Office

Camping site, caravan site

Golf course, picnic site

Church   ROMAN FORT   Non-Roman antiquity, Roman antiquity

Univ   Important buildings, schools, colleges, universities and hospitals

Woods, built-up area

River Medway   Water name

River, weir

Stream

Canal, look, tunnel

Water

Tidal water

58   87   Adjoining page indicators and overlap bands – the colour of the arrow and band indicates the scale of the adjoining or overlapping page (see scales below)

246

The dark grey border on the inside edge of some pages indicates that the mapping does not continue onto the adjacent page

The small numbers around the edges of the maps identify the 1-kilometre National Grid lines

Enlarged maps only

Railway or bus station building

Place of interest

Parkland

Abbreviations

Acad	Academy	Meml	Memorial
Allot Gdns	Allotments	Mon	Monument
Cemy	Cemetery	Mus	Museum
C Ctr	Civic centre	Obsy	Observatory
CH	Club house	Pal	Royal palace
Coll	College	PH	Public house
Crem	Crematorium	Recn Gd	Recreation ground
Ent	Enterprise		
Ex H	Exhibition hall	Resr	Reservoir
Ind Est	Industrial Estate	Ret Pk	Retail park
IRB Sta	Inshore rescue boat station	Sch	School
		Sh Ctr	Shopping centre
Inst	Institute	TH	Town hall / house
Ct	Law court	Trad Est	Trading estate
L Ctr	Leisure centre	Univ	University
LC	Level crossing	W Twr	Water tower
Liby	Library	Wks	Works
Mkt	Market	YH	Youth hostel

The map scale on the pages numbered in blue is 3½ inches to 1 mile
5.52 cm to 1 km • 1:18 103

0	¼ mile	½ mile	¾ mile	1 mile
0	250m	500m	750m	1km

The map scale on the pages numbered in red is 7 inches to 1 mile
11.04 cm to 1 km • 1:9 051

0	220yds	440yds	660yds	½ mile
0	125m	250m	375m	500m

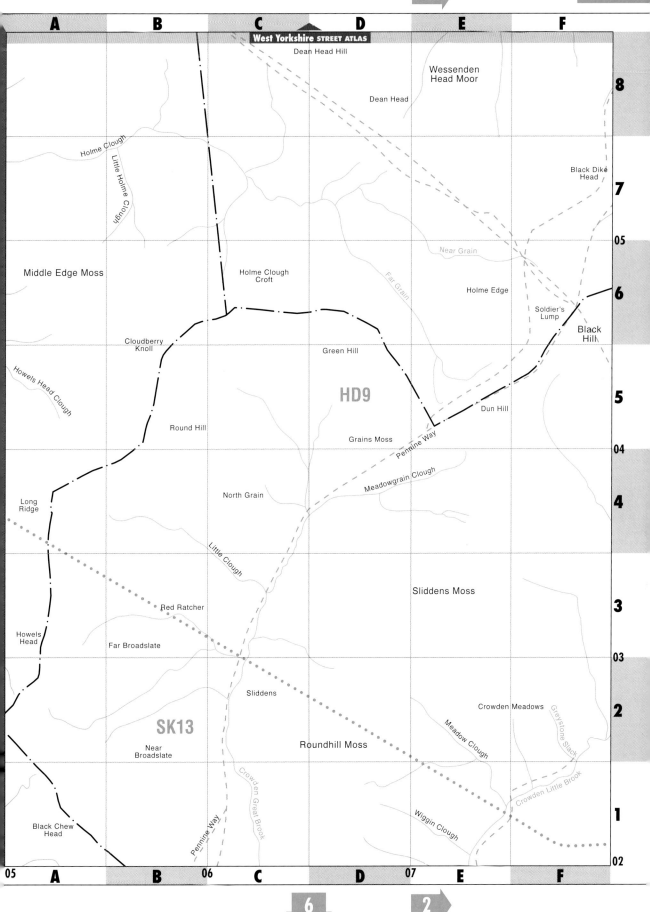

West Yorkshire STREET ATLAS

Dean Head Hill

Wessenden
Head Moor

Dean Head

Holme Clough

Little Holme Clough

Black Diké
Head

Near Grain

Middle Edge Moss

Holme Clough
Croft

Far Grain

Holme Edge

Soldier's
Lump

Black
Hill

Cloudberry
Knoll

Green Hill

Howels Head Clough

HD9

Round Hill

Dun Hill

Grains Moss

Pennine Way

Long
Ridge

North Grain

Meadowgrain Clough

Little Clough

Sliddens Moss

Red Ratcher

Howels
Head

Far Broadslate

Crowden Meadows

Greystone Slack

Sliddens

SK13

Meadow Clough

Near
Broadslate

Roundhill Moss

Crowden Great Brook

Crowden Little Brook

Black Chew
Head

Pennine Way

Wiggin Clough

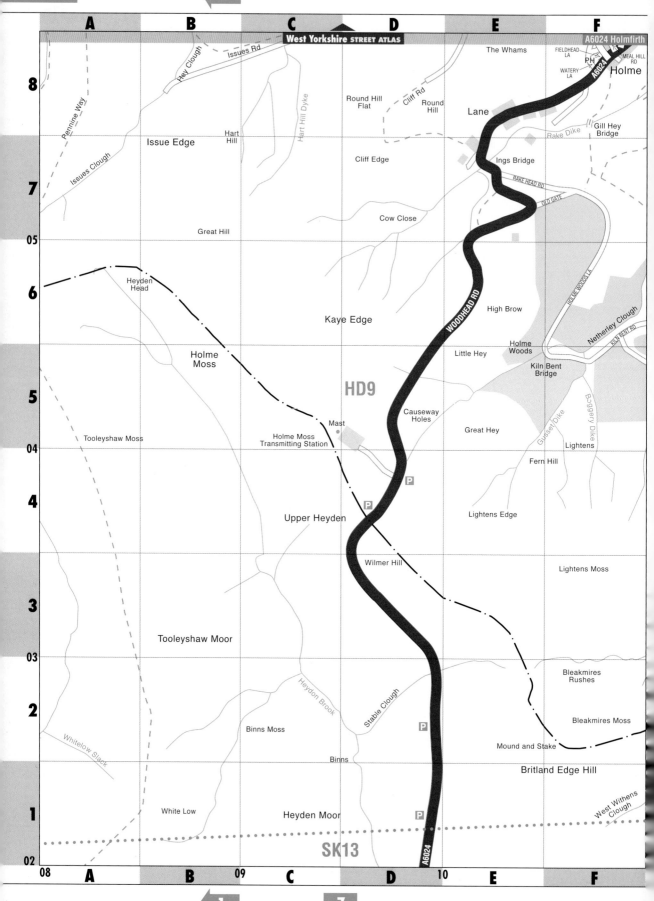

A   B   C   D   E   F

West Yorkshire STREET ATLAS

A6024 Holmfirth

The Whams

FIELDHEAD LA

PH

WATERY LA

MEAL HILL RD

A6024

Holme

Hey Clough

Issues Rd

Round Hill Flat

Cliff Rd

Round Hill

Lane

8

Pennine Way

Hart Hill Dyke

Hart Hill

Issue Edge

Rake Dike

Gill Hey Bridge

Issues Clough

Cliff Edge

Ings Bridge

RAKE HEAD RD

7

Great Hill

Cow Close

OLD GATE

05

Heyden Head

HOLME WOODS LA

6

Kaye Edge

High Brow

Netherley Clough

KILN BENT RD

Holme Moss

WOODHEAD RD

Little Hey

Holme Woods

Tooleyshaw Moss

HD9

Causeway Holes

Kiln Bent Bridge

Guyset Dike

Baggery Dike

5

Mast

Great Hey

Lightens

04

Holme Moss Transmitting Station

Fern Hill

Upper Heyden

P

P

Lightens Edge

4

Wilmer Hill

Lightens Moss

Tooleyshaw Moor

3

03

Heydon Brook

Bleakmires Rushes

Stable Clough

Bleakmires Moss

2

Binns Moss

P

Mound and Stake

Whitelow Slack

Binns

Britland Edge Hill

White Low

Heyden Moor

P

West Withens Clough

1

SK13

A6024

02

08   A   B   09   C   D   10   E   F

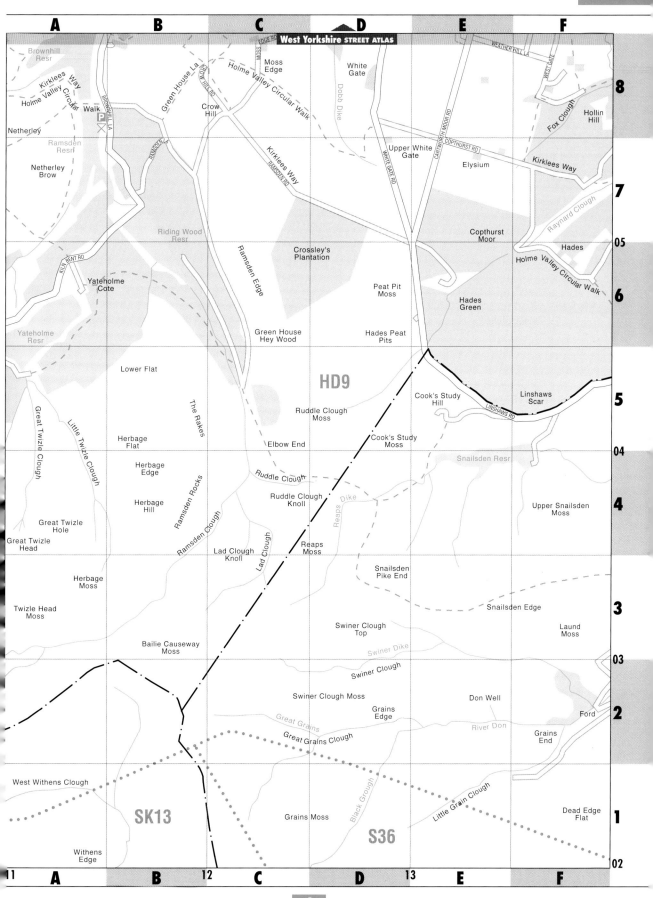

Brownhill
Resr

Kirklees Way

Holme Valley Circular Walk

Netherley

Ramsden
Resr

Netherley
Brow

Green House La

Crow
Hill

Moss
Edge

White Gate

Holme Valley Circular Walk

Dobb Dike

WEATHER HILL LA

WEST GATE

Fox Clough

Hollin
Hill

Upper White
Gate

Elysium

Kirklees Way

Killa Bent Rd

Yateholme
Cote

Riding Wood
Resr

Ramsden Edge

Kirklees Way

Crossley's
Plantation

Copthurst
Moor

Raynard Clough

Hades

Holme Valley Circular Walk

05

Yateholme
Resr

Peat Pit
Moss

Hades
Green

6

Green House
Hey Wood

Hades Peat
Pits

Lower Flat

HD9

Cook's Study
Hill

Linshaws
Scar

5

LINSHAWS RD

Great Twizle Clough

Little Twizle Clough

The Rakes

Ruddle Clough
Moss

Ruddle Clough

Cook's Study
Moss

Snailsden Resr

04

Herbage
Flat

Elbow End

Herbage
Edge

Ramsden Rocks

Ruddle Clough
Knoll

Reaps Dike

Upper Snailsden
Moss

4

Herbage
Hill

Ramsden Clough

Great Twizle
Hole

Great Twizle
Head

Lad Clough
Knoll

Lad Clough

Reaps
Moss

Snailsden
Pike End

Herbage
Moss

Twizle Head
Moss

Snailsden Edge

Laund
Moss

3

Bailie Causeway
Moss

Swiner Clough
Top

Swiner Dike

03

Swiner Clough

Don Well

Ford

2

Swiner Clough Moss

Grains
Edge

River Don

Grains
End

West Withens Clough

Great Grains

Great Grains Clough

Black Grough

Little Grain Clough

Dead Edge
Flat

1

SK13

Grains Moss

S36

02

Withens
Edge

Buckton Moor

Broken Ground

Hare Hill

Far Harehill Clough

8

Buckton Vale
Quarry

Hoarstone
Edge

7

CARR
LA

PRINTERS DR

01

CALICO CRES

Iron Tongue

6

Shire Clough
Farm

Slatepit Moor

SK15

Irontongue Hill

5

Wicken
Spring

Swineshaw
Moor

Turf Pits

00

Harridge
Pike

Tameside Trail

Higher
Swineshaw
Resr

Boar Flat

4

Harridge

3

BRUSHES

BRUSHES
RD

Brushes
Resr

Swineshaw Brook

Lower
Swineshaw
Resr

Lees Hill

SK13

Ogden Clough

Walkerwood
Resr

99

Higher
Bank

Ford

Cock
Wood

Stalybridge
Country Park

Pack
Saddle

Arnfield
Low Moor

2

Cock Knarr

Middle
Bank

Ogden Brook

1

Lower
Bank

SK14

HORSON MOOR RD

Devil's
Bridge

98

Arnfield
Farm

ARNFIELD
LANE

99

A

B

00

C

D

01

E

F

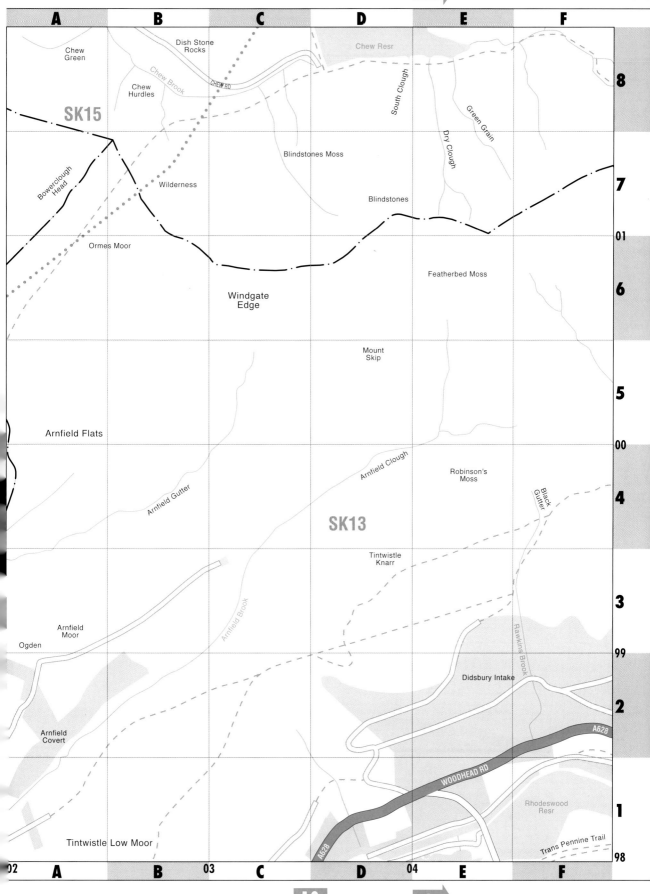

A   B   C   D   E   F

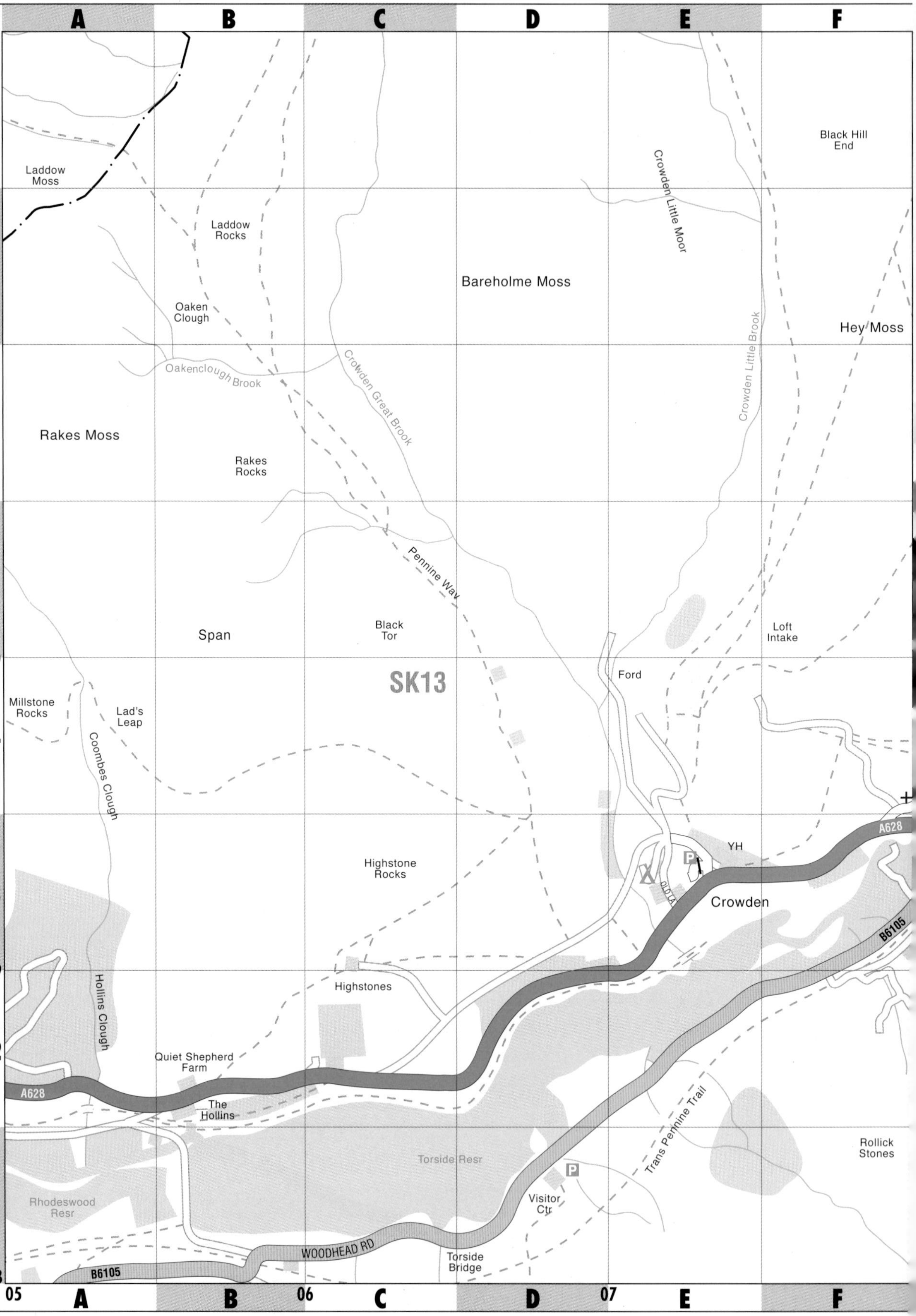

8

Laddow
Moss

Laddow
Rocks

Bareholme Moss

Crowden Little Moor

Black Hill
End

7

Oaken
Clough

Hey Moss

01

Oakenclough Brook

Crowden Great Brook

Crowden Little Brook

6

Rakes Moss

Rakes
Rocks

5

Span

Black
Tor

Pennine Way

Loft
Intake

00

SK13

Ford

Millstone
Rocks

Lad's
Leap

4

Coombes Clough

Highstone
Rocks

YH

P

A628

X

Crowden

3

B6105

99

Hollins Clough

Highstones

2

Quiet Shepherd
Farm

A628

The
Hollins

Torside Resr

Trans Pennine Trail

Rollick
Stones

1

Rhodeswood
Resr

P

Visitor
Ctr

98

B6105

WOODHEAD RD

Torside
Bridge

05   A   06   B   C   06   D   07   E   F

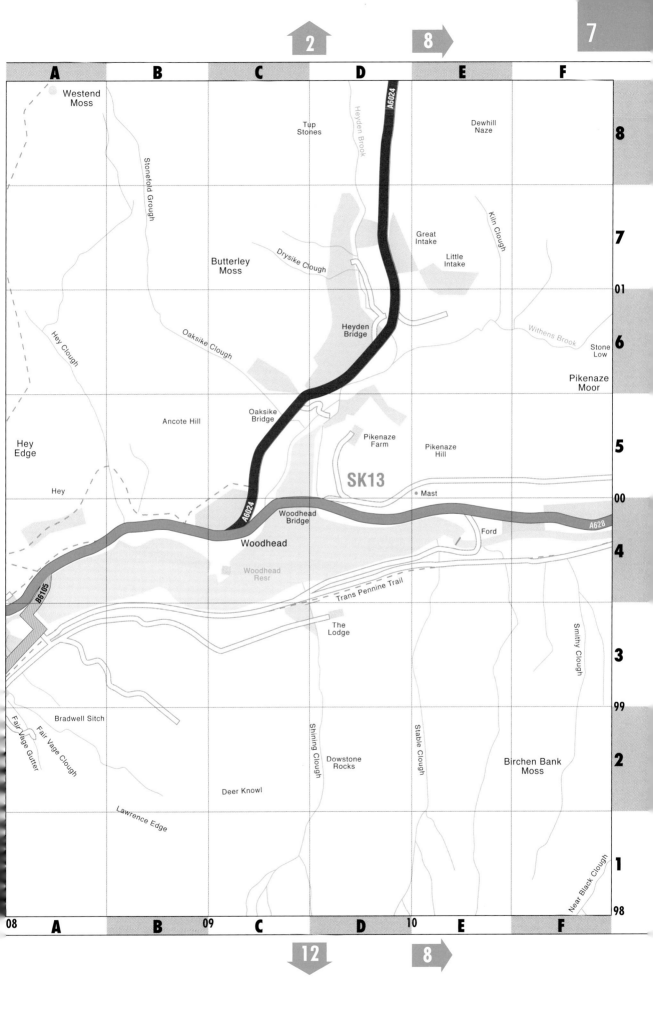

A B C D E F

Westend
Moss

Tup
Stones

Heyden Brook

A6024

Dewhill
Naze

8

Stonefold Grough

Great
Intake

Kiln Clough

7

Butterley
Moss

Drysike Clough

Little
Intake

01

Oaksike Clough

Heyden
Bridge

Withens Brook

Stone
Low

6

Hey Clough

Pikenaze
Moor

Oaksike
Bridge

Ancote Hill

Pikenaze
Farm

Pikenaze
Hill

5

Hey
Edge

SK13

Hey

A6024

Mast

00

Woodhead
Bridge

Ford

A628

4

Woodhead

B6105

Woodhead
Resr

Trans Pennine Trail

The
Lodge

Smithy Clough

3

Bradwell Sitch

99

Fair Vage Gutter

Fair Vage Clough

Shining Clough

Dowstone
Rocks

Stable Clough

Birchen Bank
Moss

2

Deer Knowl

Lawrence Edge

Near Black Clough

1

98

08 A B 09 C D 10 E F

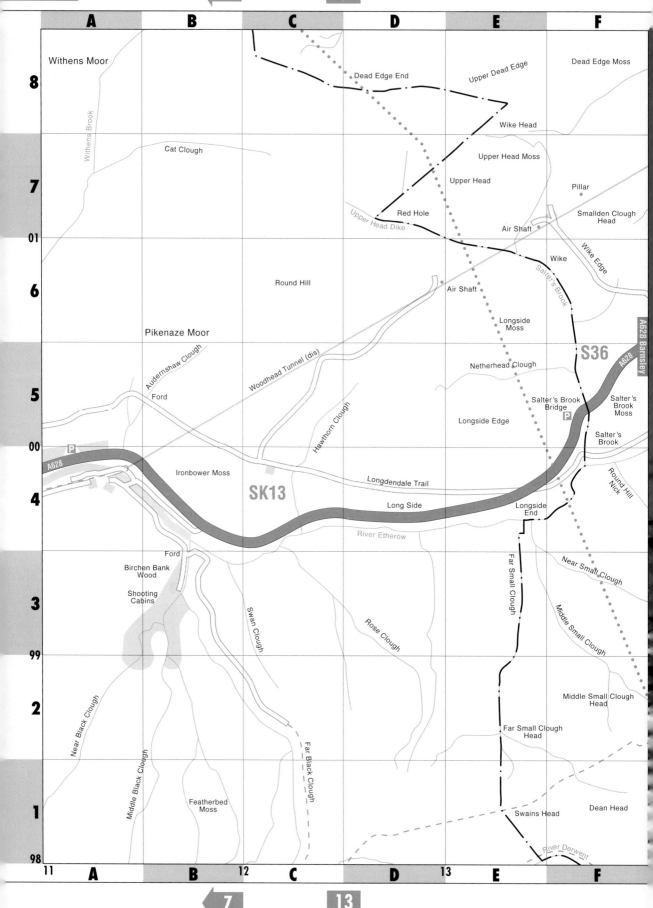

A B C D E F

Withens Moor

8

Cat Clough

7

01

Round Hill

6

Pikenaze Moor

Audernshaw Clough

5

Ford

Woodhead Tunnel (dis)

00

A628

P

Ironbower Moss

SK13

4

Ford

Birchen Bank Wood

Shooting Cabins

Swan Clough

Rose Clough

River Etherow

3

99

Near Black Clough

Middle Black Clough

Featherbed Moss

Far Black Clough

2

1

98

Withens Brook

Dead Edge End

Upper Dead Edge

Dead Edge Moss

Wike Head

Upper Head Moss

Upper Head

Pillar

Smallden Clough Head

Red Hole

Upper Head Dike

Air Shaft

Wike

Wike Edge

Air Shaft

Salter's Brook

Longside Moss

S36

A628 Barnsley

A628

Netherhead Clough

Salter's Brook Bridge

P

Salter's Brook Moss

Longside Edge

Salter's Brook

Longdendale Trail

Round Hill Nick

Long Side

Longside End

Near Small Clough

Far Small Clough

Middle Small Clough

Middle Small Clough Head

Far Small Clough Head

Swains Head

Dean Head

River Derwent

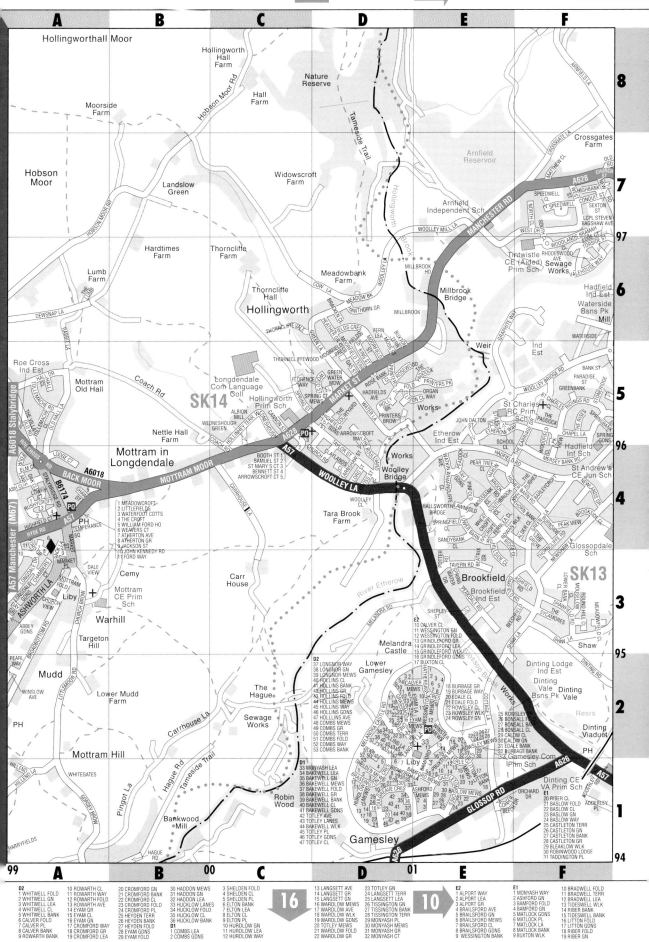

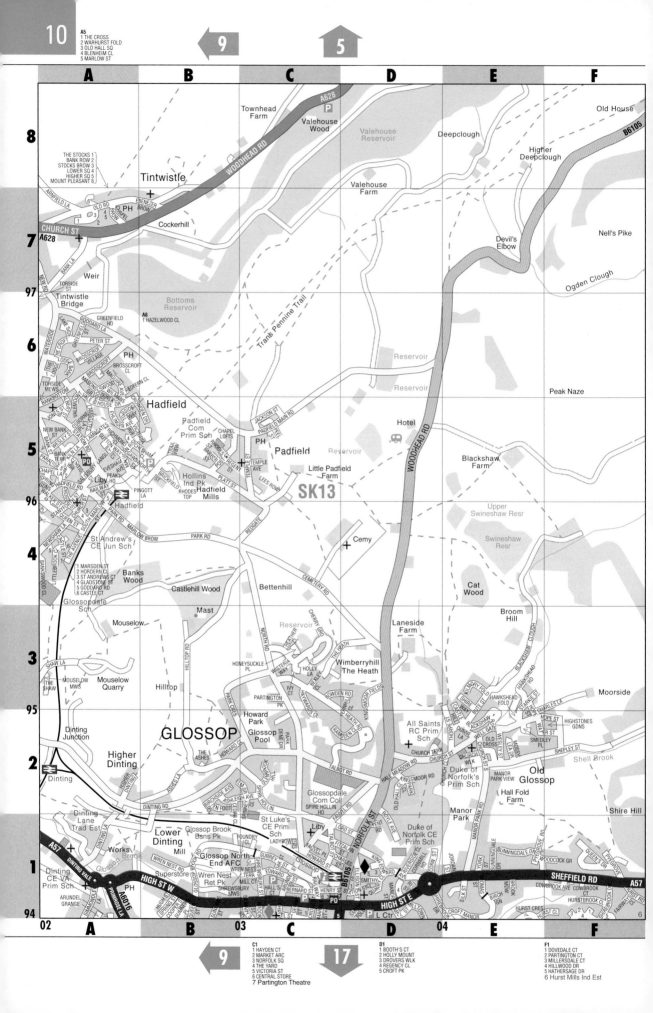

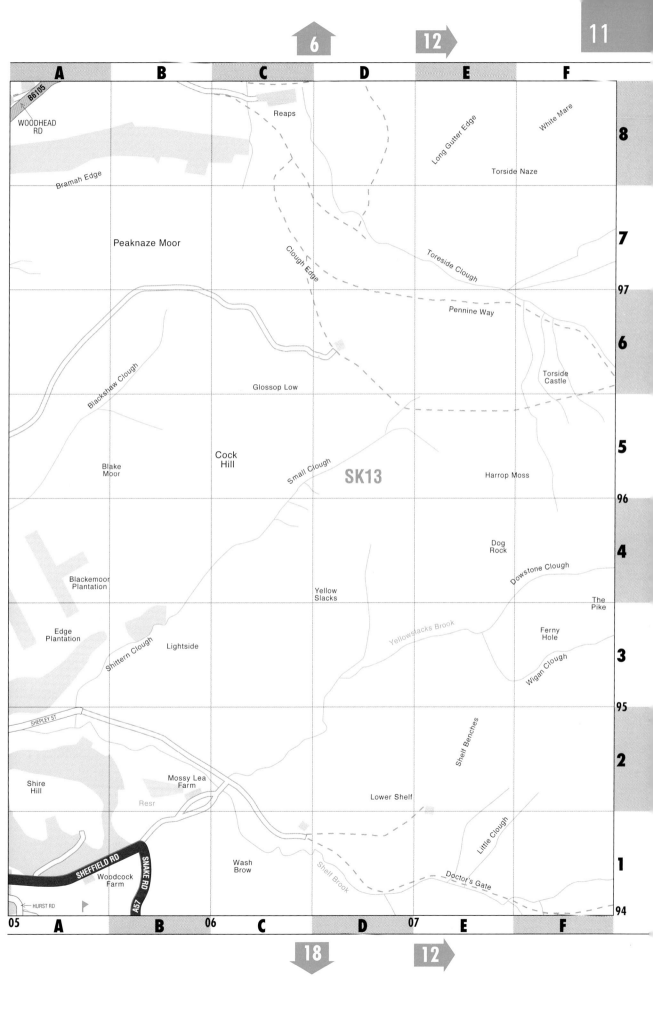

11
7

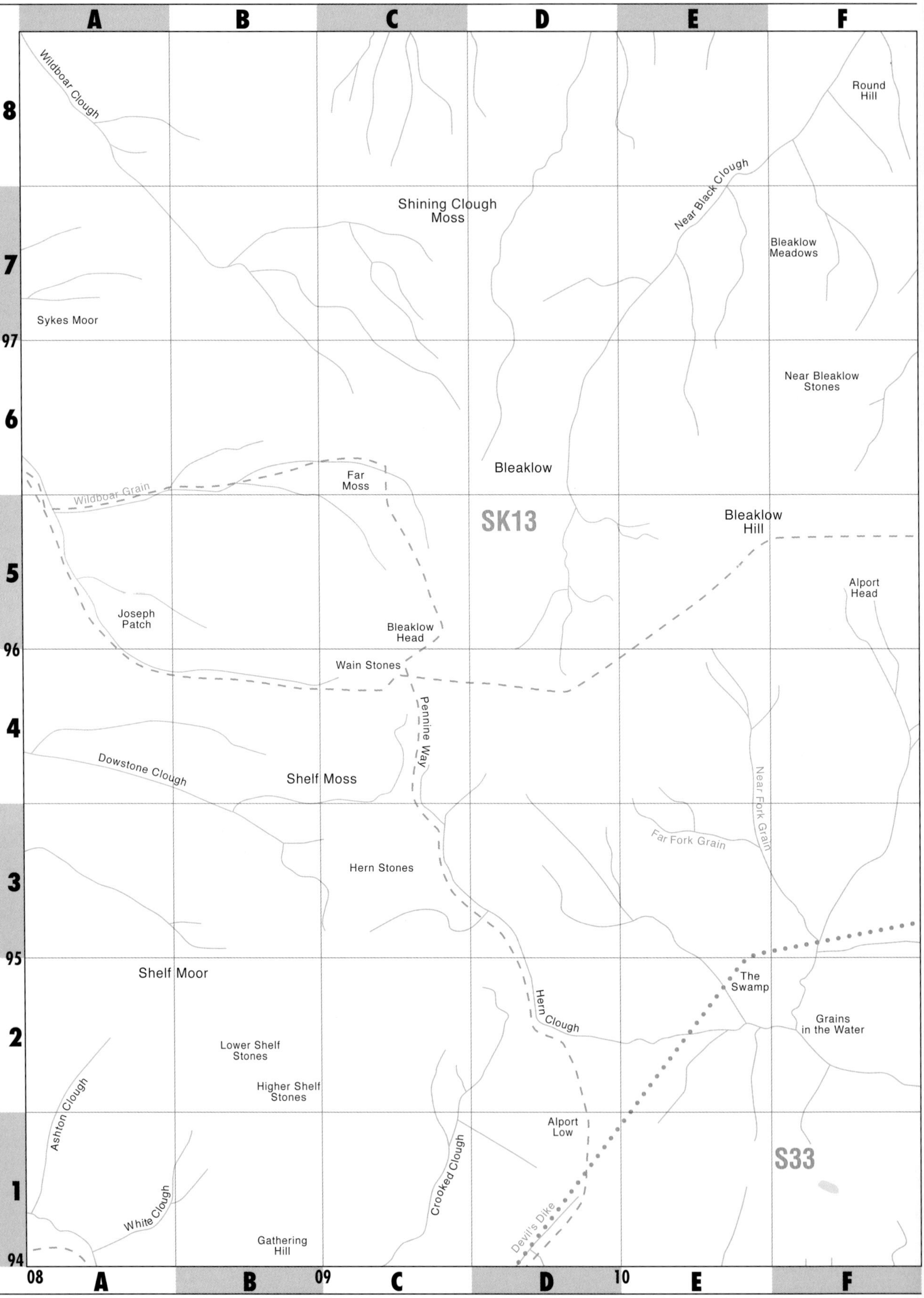

A **B** **C** **D** **E** **F**

Wildboar Clough

Round Hill

8

Shining Clough Moss

Near Black Clough

7

Bleaklow Meadows

Sykes Moor

97

Near Bleaklow Stones

6

Far Moss

Bleaklow

Wildboar Grain

SK13

Bleaklow Hill

5

Joseph Patch

Bleaklow Head

Alport Head

96

Wain Stones

4

Pennine Way

Dowstone Clough

Shelf Moss

Near Fork Grain

Far Fork Grain

Hern Stones

3

95

The Swamp

Shelf Moor

Hern Clough

Grains in the Water

2

Lower Shelf Stones

Higher Shelf Stones

Ashton Clough

Alport Low

S33

1

White Clough

Crooked Clough

Devil's Dike

Gathering Hill

94

08 **A** **B** 09 **C** **D** 10 **E** **F**

11
19

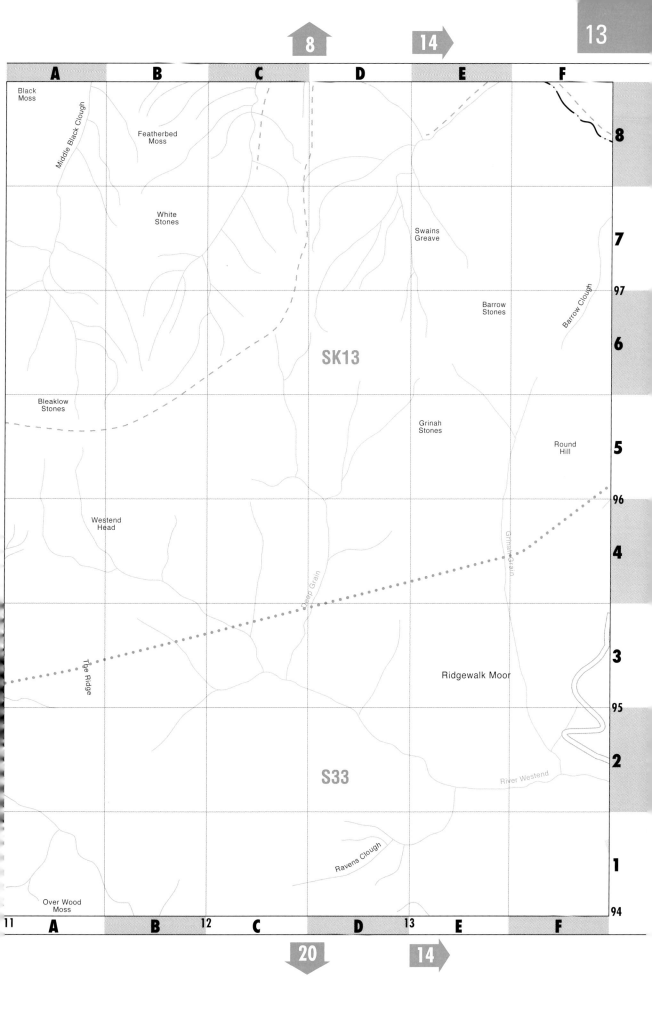

A **B** **C** **D** **E** **F**

Black
Moss

Middle Black Clough

Featherbed
Moss

White
Stones

Swains
Greave

8

7

97

Barrow
Stones

Barrow Clough

6

SK13

Bleaklow
Stones

Grinah
Stones

Round
Hill

5

96

Westend
Head

Grinah Grain

4

Deep Grain

The Ridge

Ridgewalk Moor

3

95

2

S33

River Westend

Ravens Clough

1

Over Wood
Moss

94

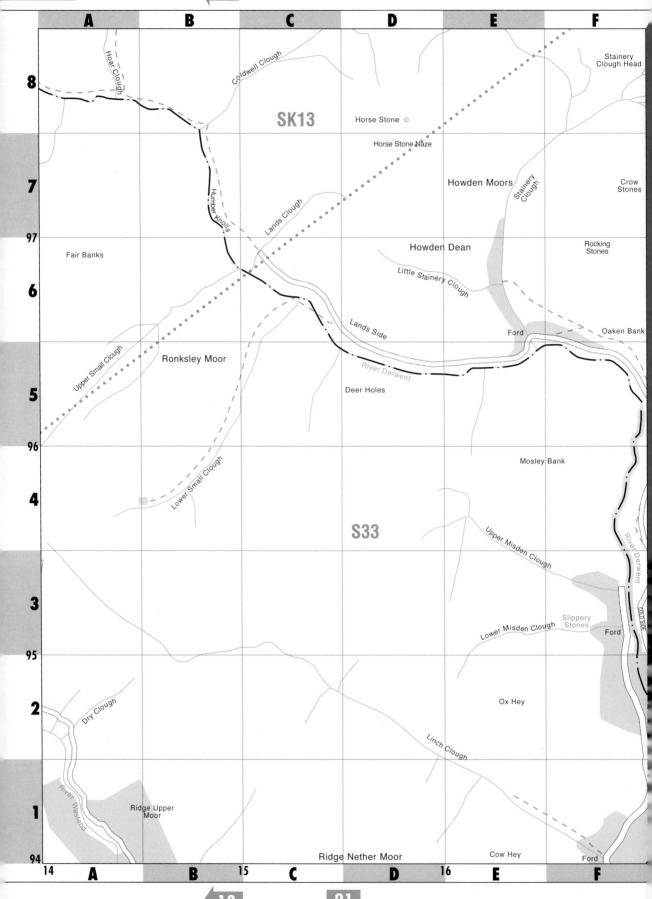

A B C D E F

Hoar Clough

Coldwell Clough

SK13

Horse Stone ○

Horse Stone Naze

Stainery Clough Head

Howden Moors

Crow Stones

7

Humber Knolls

Lands Clough

Howden Dean

Stainery Clough

Rocking Stones

97

Fair Banks

Little Stainery Clough

6

Upper Small Clough

Ronksley Moor

Lands Side

Ford

Oaken Bank

River Derwent

Deer Holes

5

Mosley Bank

96

Lower Small Clough

4

S33

Upper Misden Clough

River Derwent

3

Lower Misden Clough

Slippery Stones

Ford

COLD SIDE

95

Dry Clough

Ox Hey

2

Linch Clough

River Westend

1

Ridge Upper Moor

94

Ridge Nether Moor

Cow Hey

Ford

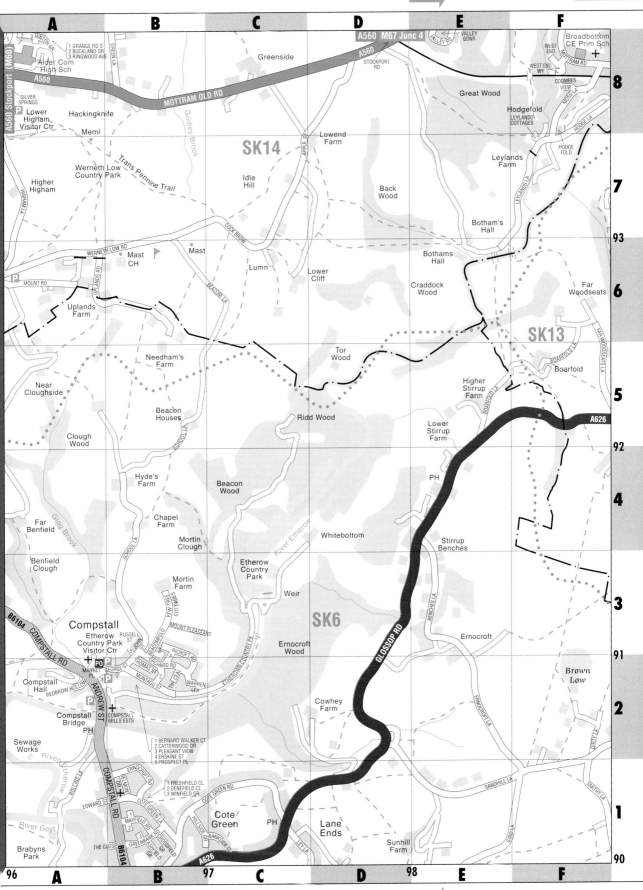

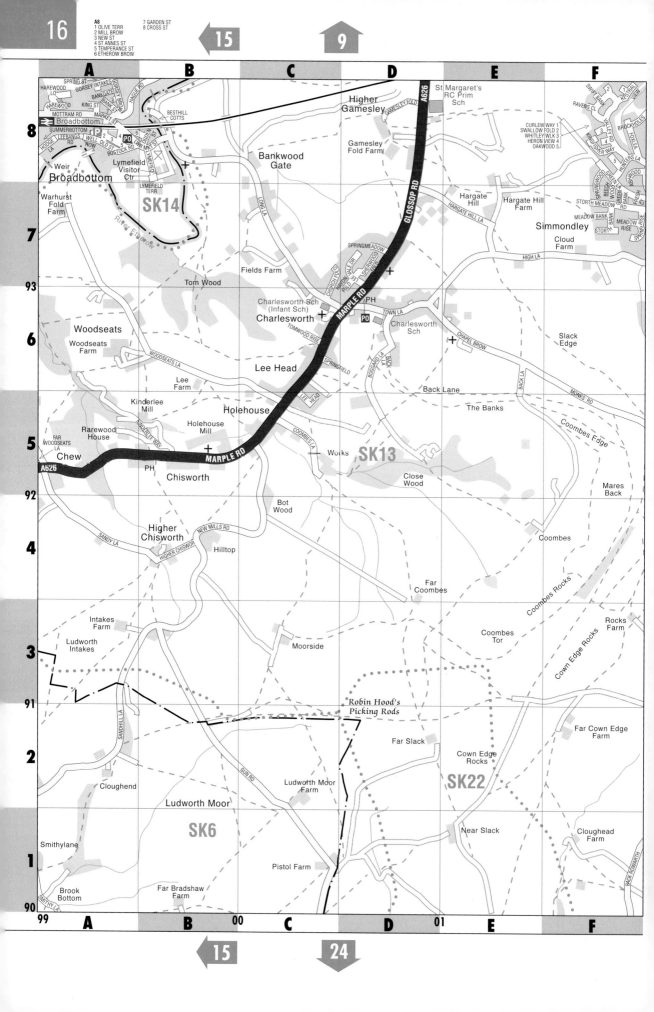

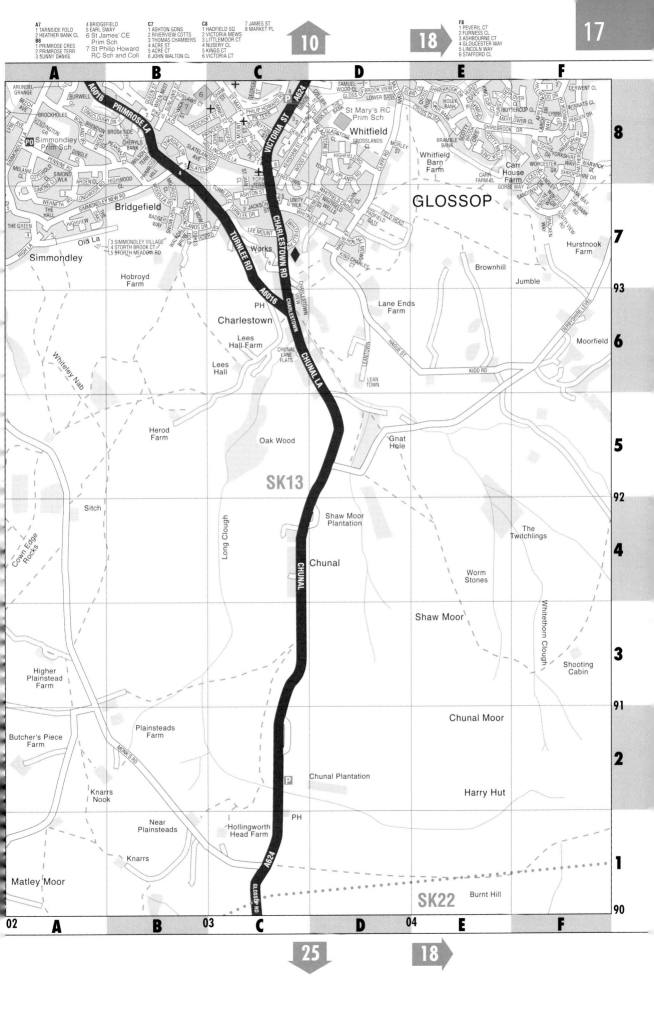

A   B   C   D   E   F

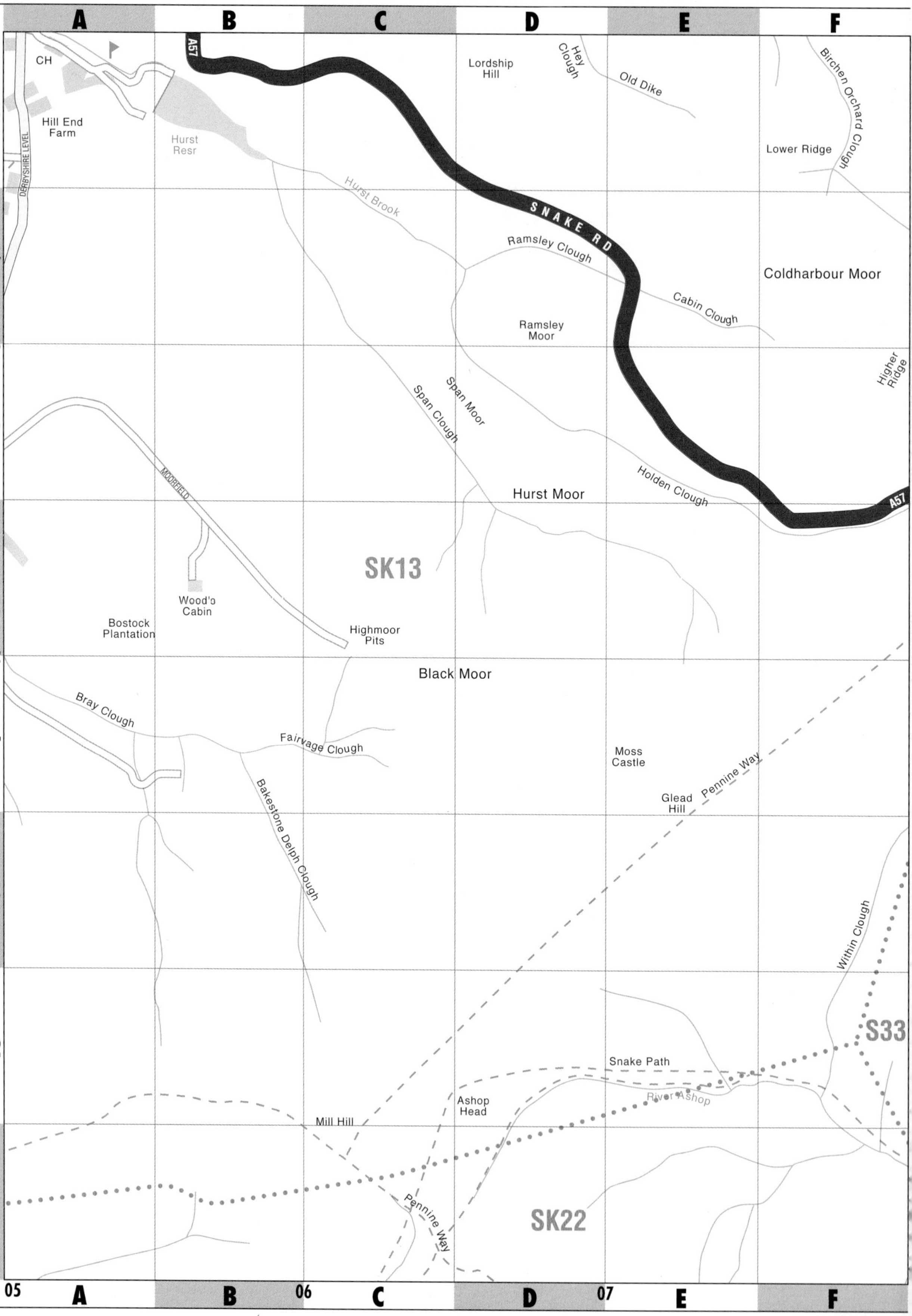

CH

Hill End
Farm

Hurst
Resr

A57

Lordship
Hill

Hey
Clough

Old Dike

Birchen Orchard Clough

Lower Ridge

8

Hurst Brook

SNAKE RD

Ramsley Clough

Coldharbour Moor

7

Ramsley
Moor

Cabin Clough

93

Span Moor

Span Clough

Higher
Ridge

6

MOORFIELD

Hurst Moor

Holden Clough

A57

Wood's
Cabin

Bostock
Plantation

Highmoor
Pits

SK13

5

Black Moor

92

Bray Clough

Fairvage Clough

Moss
Castle

Pennine Way

4

Bakestone Delph Clough

Glead
Hill

3

Within Clough

91

S33

2

Snake Path

River Ashop

Mill Hill

Ashop
Head

1

Pennine Way

SK22

90

05   A   B   06   C   D   07   E   F

A B C D E F

8

Rose Clough

Crooked Clough

Devil's Dike

Upper North Grain

Urchin Clough

Doctor's Gate

Pennine Way

SK13

Old Woman

7

93

Snake Pass

Doctor's Gate
Culvert

SNAKE RD

Nether North Grain

6

Thomason's Hollow

Featherbed
Moss

Lady Clough Moor

5

Within Clough

Featherbed
Top

Salvin Ridge

Lady Clough

92

S33

4

Upper Gate Clough

Snake
Woodland
Forest Walk

P

3

Snake
Plantations

Red Clough

Nether Gate Clough

91

Saukin Ridge

A57

2

Ashop Clough

Urchin Clough

Rough Bank

Snake Path

River Ashop

Black Ashop Moor

1

SK22

90

A   B   C   D   E   F

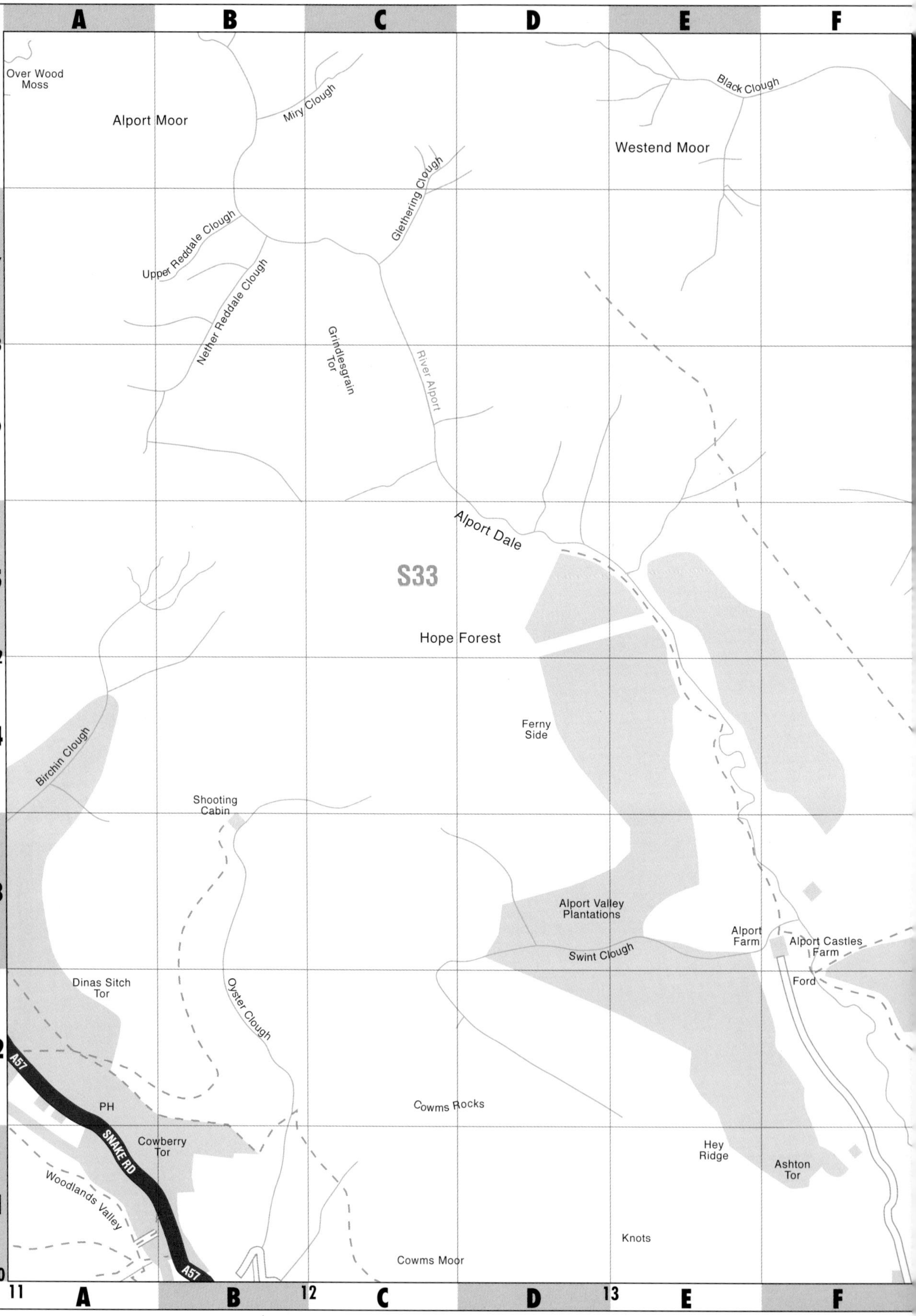

8   Over Wood Moss

Alport Moor

Miry Clough

Black Clough

Westend Moor

Glethering Clough

7   Upper Reddale Clough

Nether Reddale Clough

Grindlesgrain Tor

93

River Alport

6

Alport Dale

5   **S33**

Hope Forest

92

Ferny Side

4   Birchin Clough

Shooting Cabin

Alport Valley Plantations

3   Alport Farm

Alport Castles Farm

Swint Clough

91   Dinas Sitch Tor

Oyster Clough

Ford

2   **A57**

PH

SNAKE RD

Cowberry Tor

Cowms Rocks

Hey Ridge

Ashton Tor

1   Woodlands Valley

A57

Cowms Moor

Knots

90

11   A   B   12   C   D   13   E   F

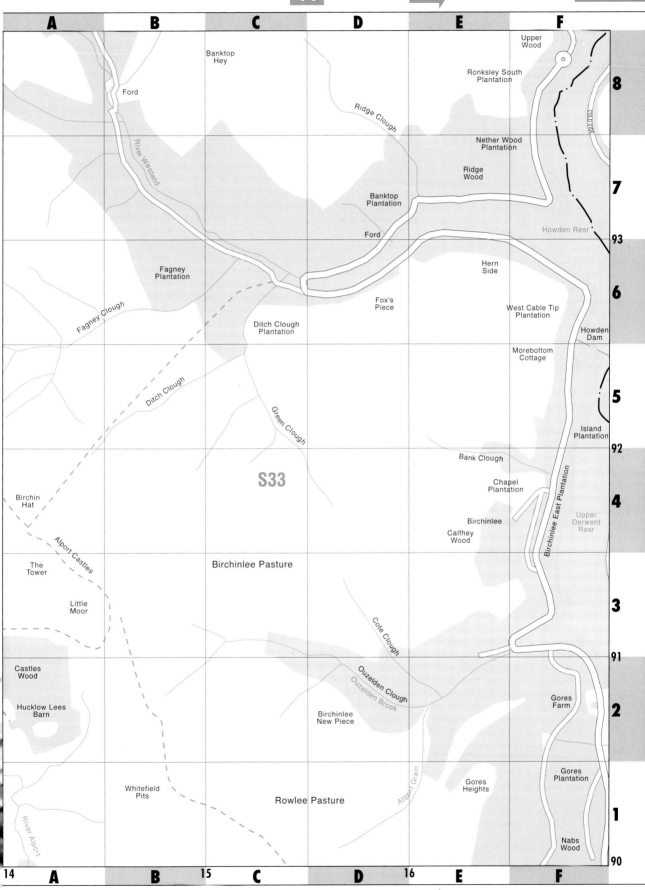

Upper Wood

Banktop Hey

Ronksley South Plantation

8

Ford

COLD SIDE

Ridge Clough

River Westland

Nether Wood Plantation

Ridge Wood

7

Banktop Plantation

Fagney Plantation

Ford

Howden Resr

93

Hern Side

6

Fox's Piece

West Cable Tip Plantation

Fagney Clough

Ditch Clough Plantation

Howden Dam

Morebottom Cottage

Ditch Clough

Green Clough

5

Island Plantation

Bank Clough

92

S33

Chapel Plantation

Birchin Hat

Birchinlee East Plantation

Upper Derwent Resr

4

Birchinlee

Calfhey Wood

Alport Castles

The Tower

Birchinlee Pasture

Little Moor

3

Cote Clough

Castles Wood

91

Ouzelden Clough

Ouzelden Brook

Gores Farm

Hucklow Lees Barn

Birchinlee New Piece

2

Gores Plantation

Allport Grain

Gores Heights

Whitefield Pits

Rowlee Pasture

1

River Alport

Nabs Wood

90

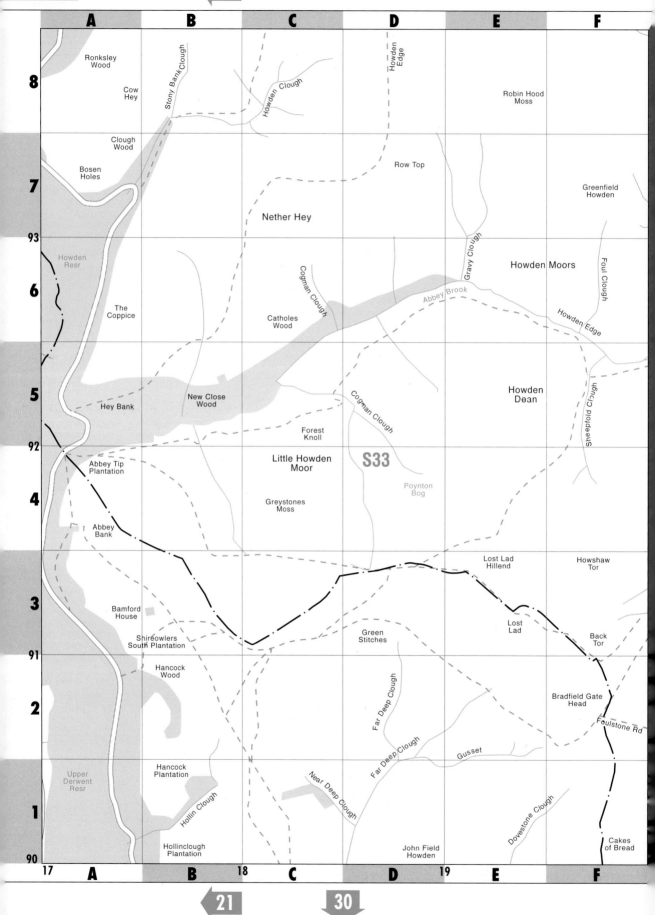

A **B** **C** **D** **E** **F**

8 — Ronksley Wood, Cow Hey, Stony Bank Clough, Howden Clough, Howden Edge, Robin Hood Moss

7 — Clough Wood, Bosen Holes, Row Top, Greenfield Howden

93

6 — Howden Resr, Cogman Clough, Abbey Brook, Gravy Clough, Howden Moors, Foul Clough, Howden Edge

The Coppice, Catholes Wood

5 — Hey Bank, New Close Wood, Cogman Clough, Howden Dean, Shepherd Clough

92 — Forest Knoll

Abbey Tip Plantation, Little Howden Moor, S33, Poynton Bog

4 — Abbey Bank, Greystones Moss

Bamford House, Lost Lad Hillend, Howshaw Tor

3 — Shireowlers South Plantation, Green Stitches, Lost Lad, Back Tor

91 — Hancock Wood, Far Deep Clough, Bradfield Gate Head

2 — Far Deep Clough, Gusset, Foulstone Rd

Hancock Plantation, Near Deep Clough, Dovestone Clough

1 — Upper Derwent Resr, Hollin Clough, John Field Howden, Cakes of Bread

90

Hollinclough Plantation

A **B** 18 **C** **D** 19 **E** **F**

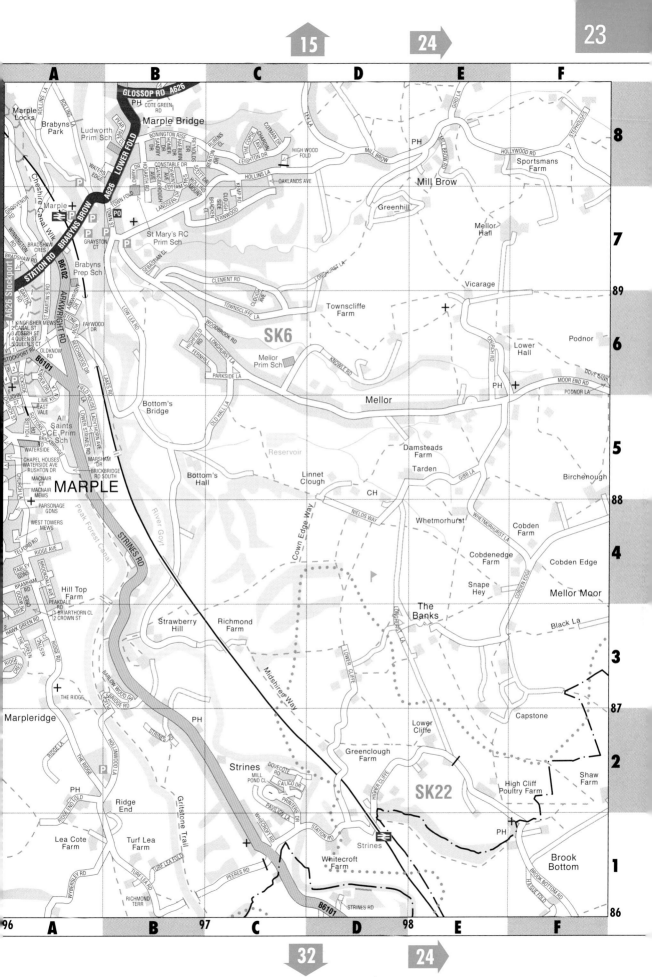

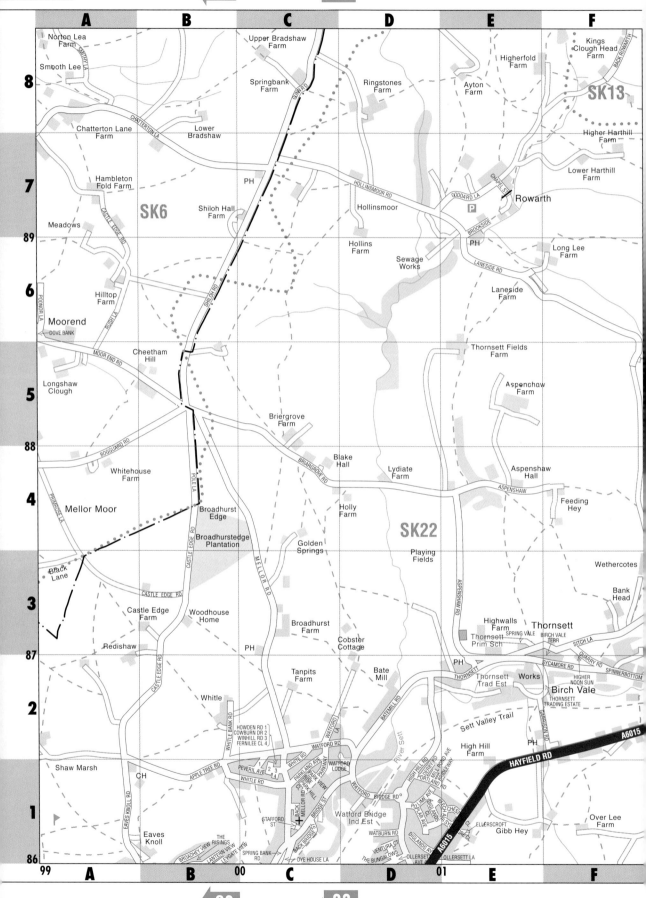

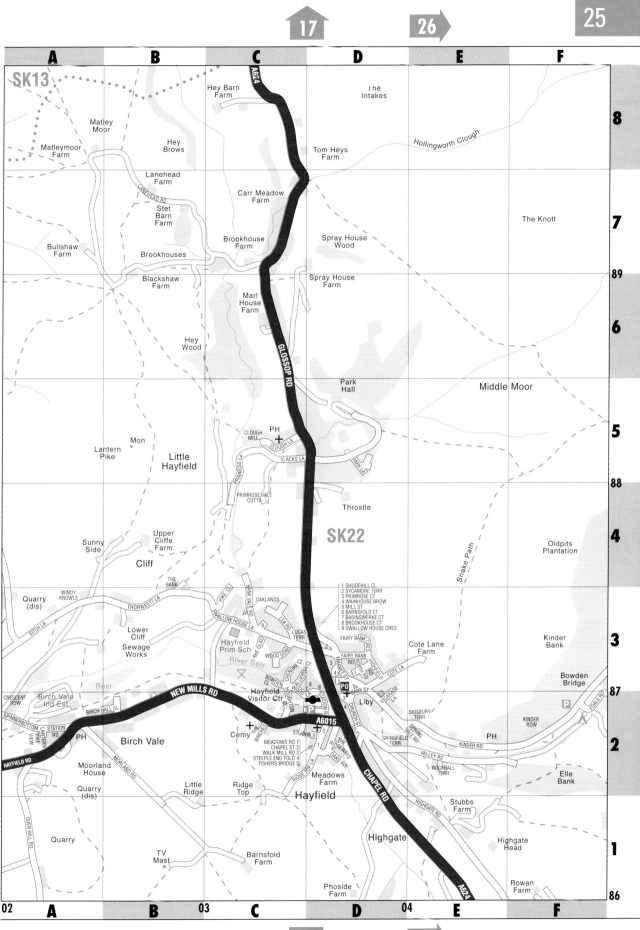

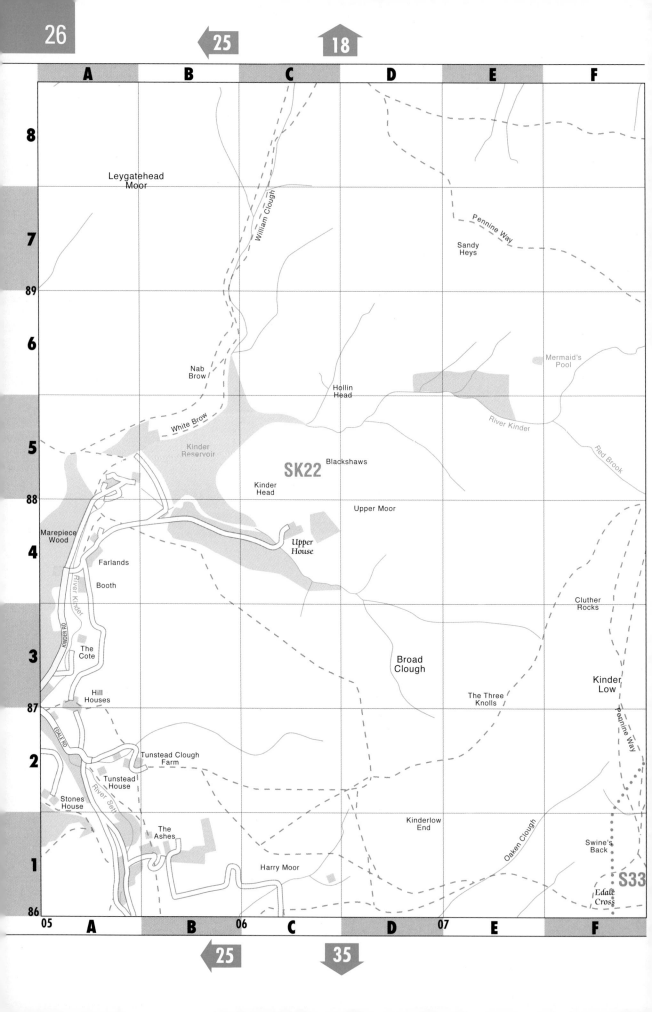

A **B** **C** **D** **E** **F**

8

Leygatehead
Moor

7

William Clough

Pennine Way

Sandy
Heys

89

6

Mermaid's
Pool

Nab
Brow

Hollin
Head

River Kinder

White Brow

5

Red Brook

Kinder
Reservoir

Blackshaws

SK22

Kinder
Head

88

Upper Moor

Marepiece
Wood

Upper
House

4

Farlands

Booth

Cluther
Rocks

River Kinder

The
Cote

3

Broad
Clough

Kinder
Low

KINDER RD

Hill
Houses

The Three
Knolls

87

Pennine Way

EDALE RD

2

Tunstead Clough
Farm

Tunstead
House

River Sett

Stones
House

Kinderlow
End

Oaken Clough

Swine's
Back

The
Ashes

S33

1

Harry Moor

Edale
Cross

86

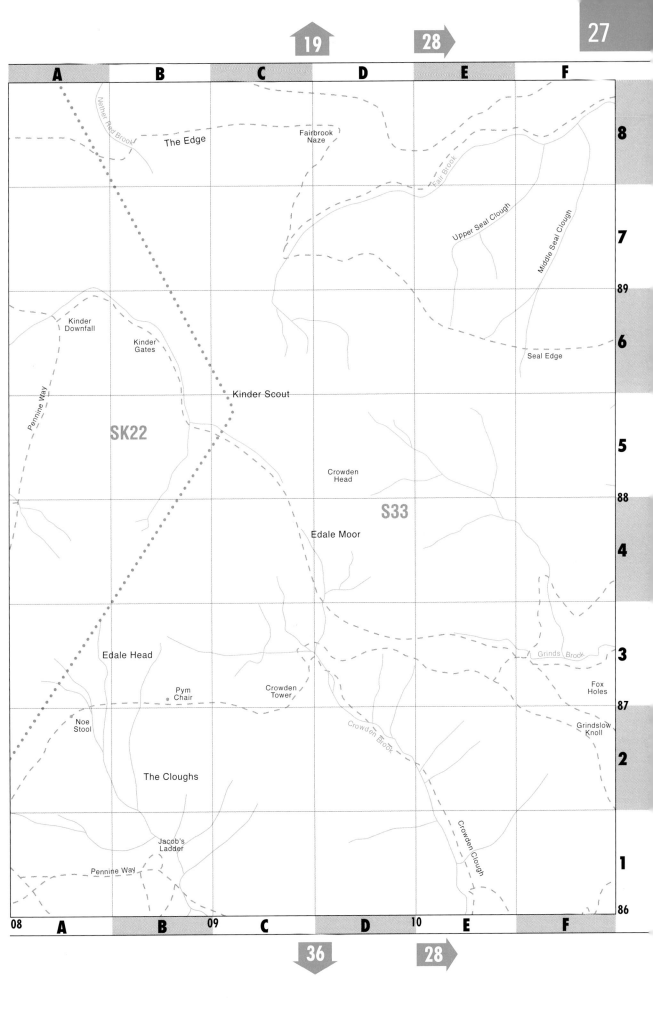

A   B   C   D   E   F

8

Nether Red Brook

The Edge

Fairbrook
Naze

Fair Brook

7

Upper Seal Clough

Middle Seal Clough

89

Kinder
Downfall

Kinder
Gates

6

Seal Edge

Pennine Way

Kinder Scout

SK22

Crowden
Head

5

S33

88

Edale Moor

4

Grinds Brook

3

Edale Head

Fox
Holes

Pym
Chair

Crowden
Tower

87

Noe
Stool

Crowden Brook

Grindslow
Knoll

2

The Cloughs

Jacob's
Ladder

Crowden Clough

1

Pennine Way

86

08   A   B   09   C   D   10   E   F

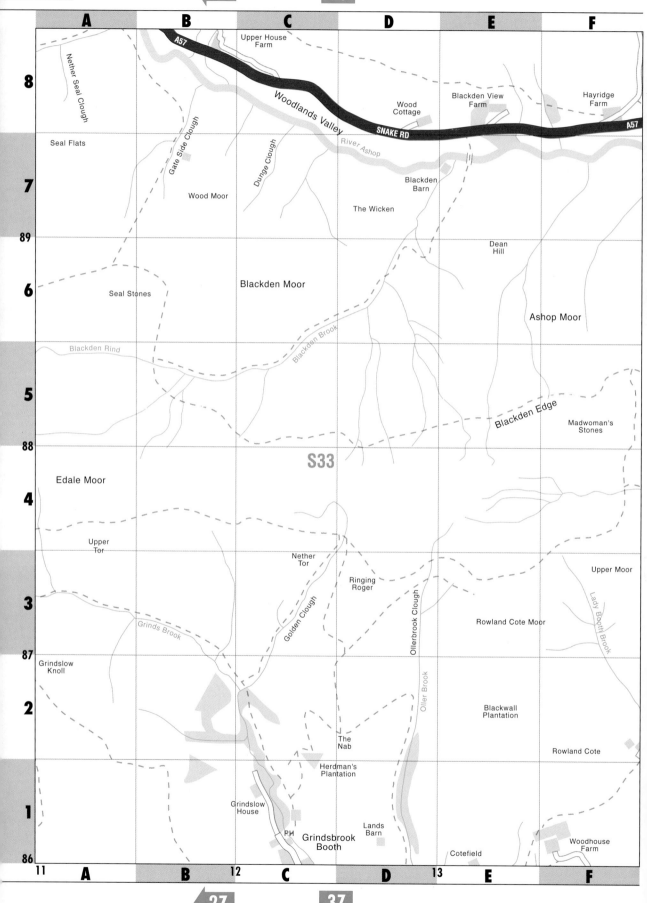

8

Nether Seal Clough

Upper House Farm

Woodlands Valley

Wood Cottage

Blackden View Farm

Hayridge Farm

A57

SNAKE RD

A57

Seal Flats

Gate Side Clough

Dunge Clough

River Ashop

Blackden Barn

7

Wood Moor

The Wicken

89

Dean Hill

Seal Stones

Blackden Moor

6

Blackden Brook

Ashop Moor

Blackden Rind

5

Blackden Edge

Madwoman's Stones

88

S33

Edale Moor

4

Upper Tor

Nether Tor

Upper Moor

Ringing Roger

3

Grinds Brook

Golden Clough

Ollerbrook Clough

Rowland Cote Moor

Lady Booth Brook

87

Grindslow Knoll

Oller Brook

2

Blackwall Plantation

Rowland Cote

The Nab

Herdman's Plantation

1

Grindslow House

Lands Barn

Woodhouse Farm

PH

Grindsbrook Booth

Cotefield

86

Ashton
Clough

Lockerbrook
Heights

Rowlee Pasture

Gillott Hey
Coppice

Alport
Bridge

Gillott Hey
Farm

Pasture
Tor

Lockerbrook
Farm

Lockerbrook
Coppice

Locker Brook

Rowlee
Farm

Bellhagg
Barn

Upper
Ashop

Bellhagg
Wood

Rowlee
Bridge

SNAKE RD

Hagg
Farm

River Ashop

Haggtor
Coppice

Open
Hagg

Woodlands Valley

Blackley
Hey

Haggwater
Bridge

Crookstone
Knoll

Hagglee

Longley
Bank

Blackley Clough

Crookstone Out Moor

Crookstone
Hill

S33

Great
Wood

Crookstone
Barn

Jaggers Clough

Nether Moor

Hope
Cross

Ladybower Resr

A57

Backside Wood

Ridge
Wood

Slack Barn

Carr
House

YH

Carr House
Farm

Edale End

Clough
Farm

River Noe

Upper Fulwood
Farm

Nether
Booth

HOPE RD

Vale of Edale

EDALE RD

Bagshaw Bridge

Lady Booth
Hall
Farm

Nether Booth
Farm

Fiddle Clough

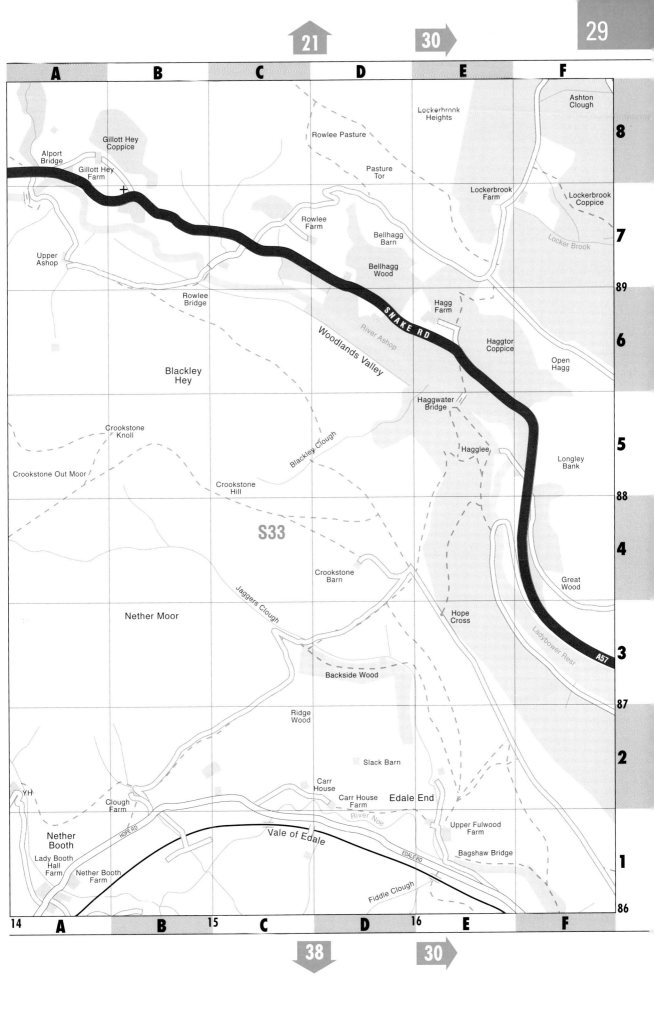

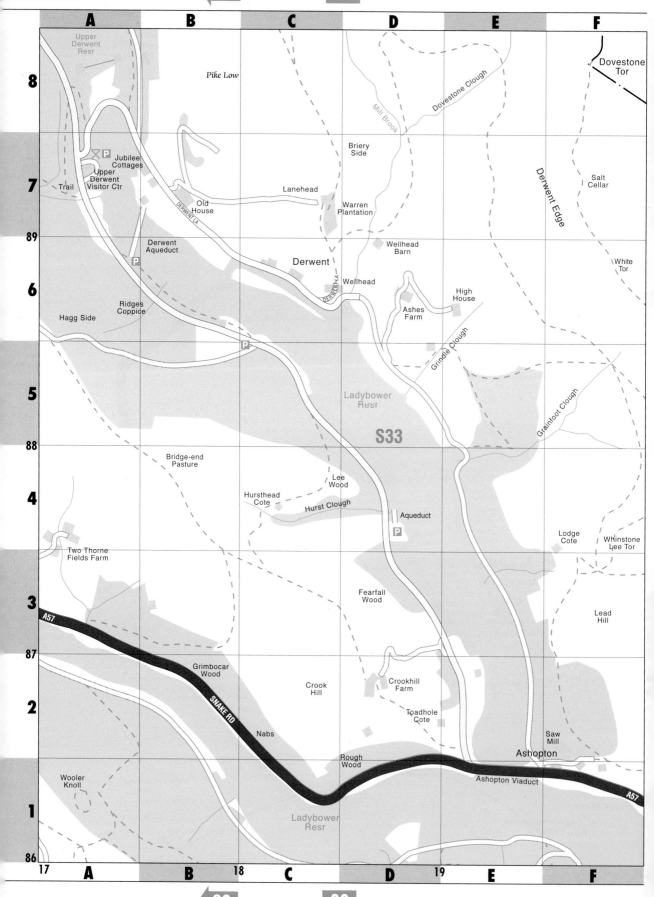

A B C D E F

8

Upper Derwent Resr

Pike Low

Dovestone Tor

Briery Side

Mill Brook

Dovestone Clough

Jubilee Cottages

7 Upper Derwent Visitor Ctr

Trail

Lanehead

Old House

Warren Plantation

DERWENT LA

Derwent Edge

Salt Cellar

89

Derwent Aqueduct

Wellhead Barn

White Tor

Derwent

6 Hagg Side

Ridges Coppice

Wellhead

DERWENT LA

Ashes Farm

High House

Grindle Clough

5

Ladybower Resr

Grainfoot Clough

88

S33

Bridge-end Pasture

Lee Wood

4 Hursthead Cote

Hurst Clough

Aqueduct

Lodge Cote

Whinstone Lee Tor

Two Thorne Fields Farm

Fearfall Wood

Lead Hill

3 A57

Grimbocar Wood

87

SNAKE RD

Crook Hill

Crookhill Farm

2 Nabs

Toadhole Cote

Saw Mill

Ashopton

Rough Wood

Ashopton Viaduct

A57

1 Wooler Knoll

Ladybower Resr

86

17 A 18 B C 19 D E F

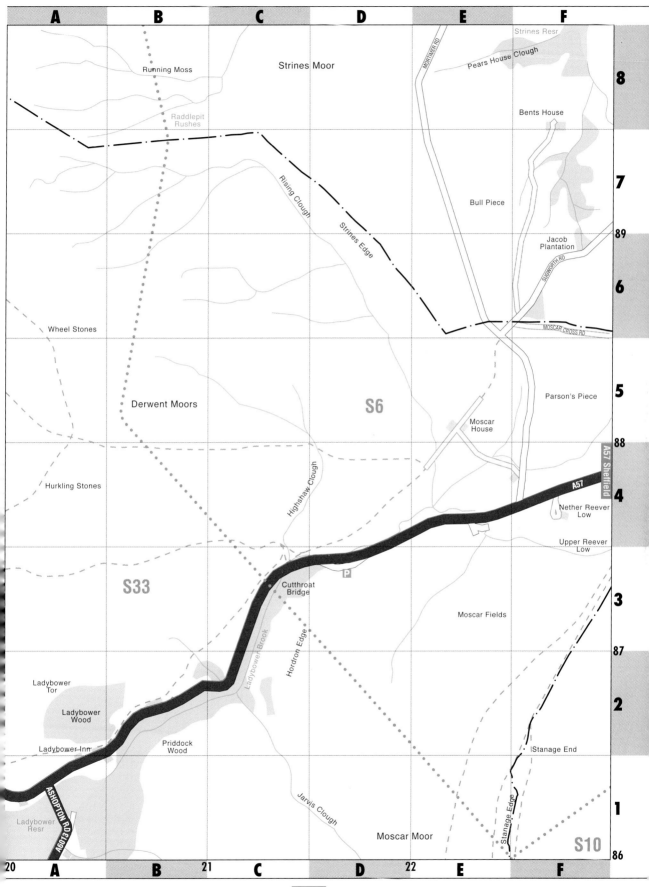

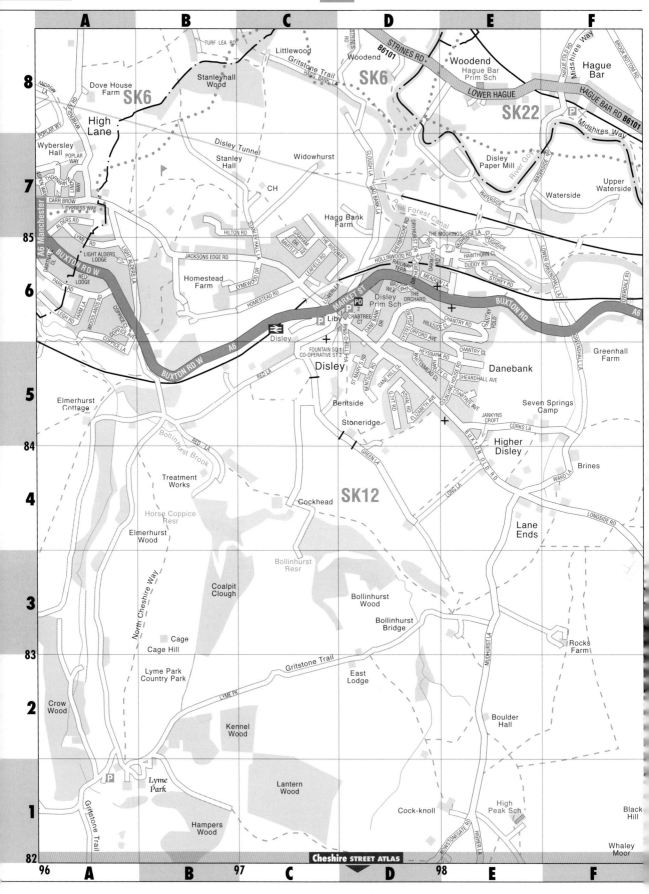

C7
1 FOUNDRY CT
2 LOWER ROCK ST
3 BACK UNION RD
4 LEES MILL

C8
1 New Mills Sch
and Sixth From Ctr

24

34

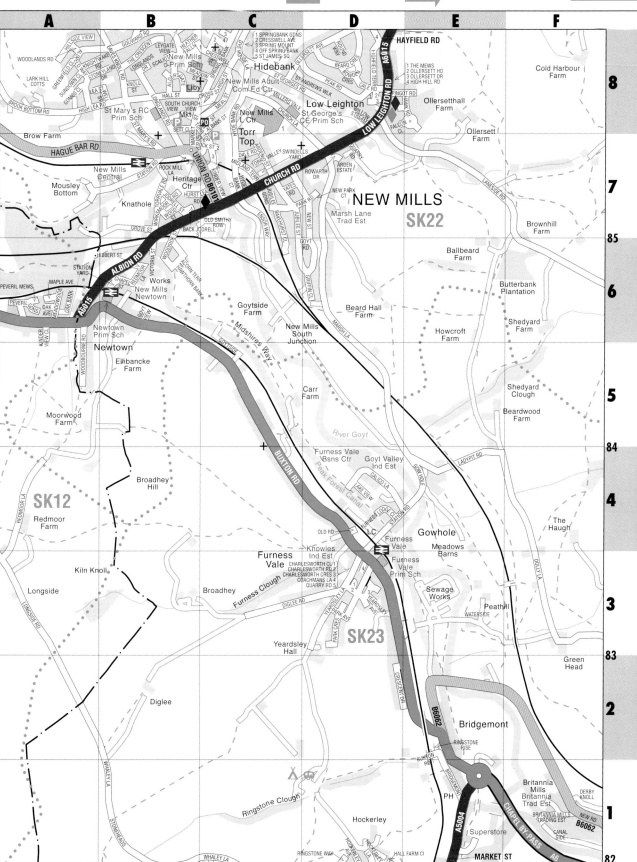

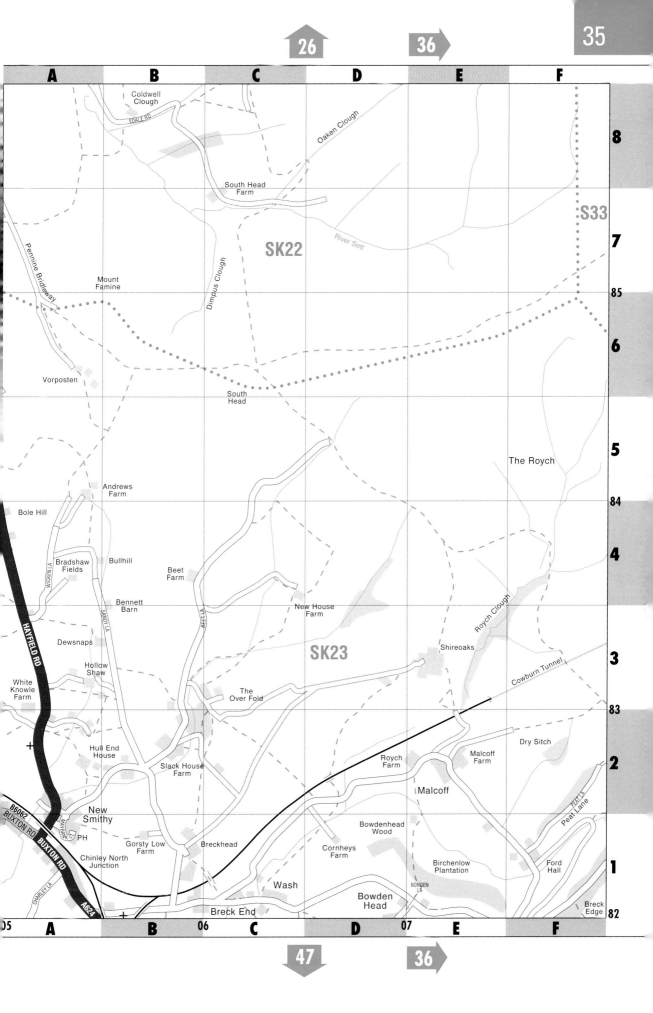

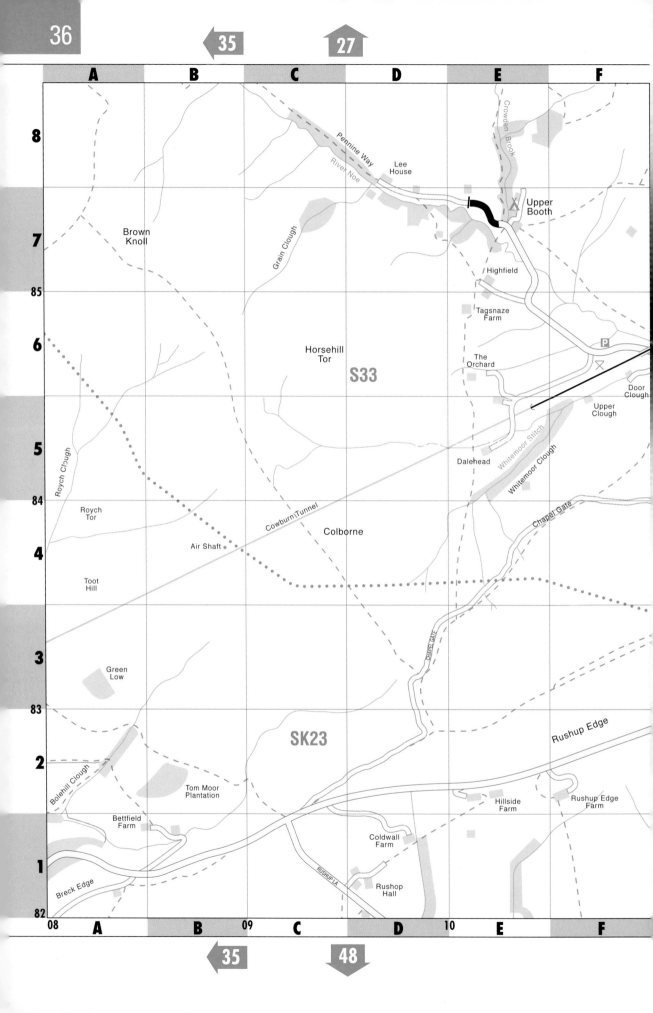

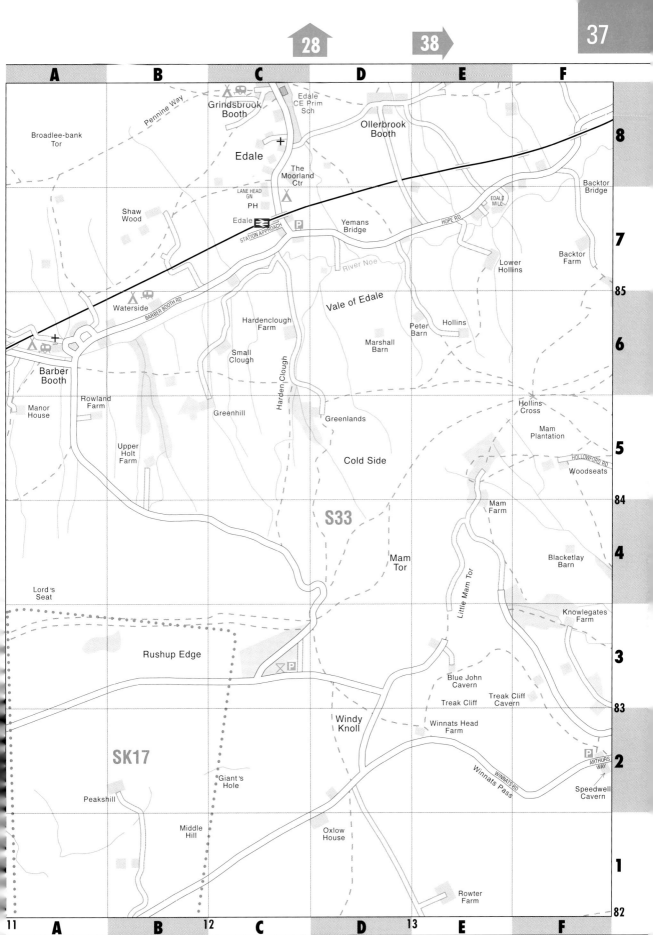

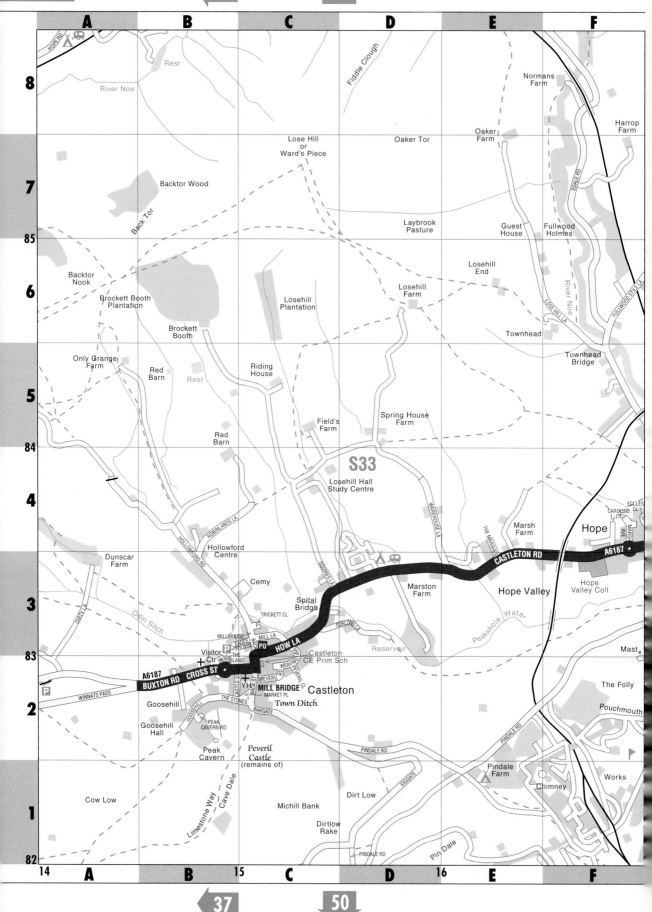

37
29

A B C D E F

8

Normans
Farm

River Noe

Resr

Harrop
Farm

Fiddle Clough

Oaker Tor

Oaker
Farm

Edale Rd

7

Lose Hill
or
Ward's Piece

Backtor Wood

Back Tor

Laybrook
Pasture

Guest
House

Fullwood
Holmes

85

River Noe

Lose Hill La

Backtor
Nook

Losehill
End

6

Brockett Booth
Plantation

Losehill
Plantation

Losehill
Farm

Townhead

Fullwood Stile La

Brockett
Booth

Townhead
Bridge

Only Grange
Farm

Red
Barn

Riding
House

Resr

Spring House
Farm

5

Red
Barn

Field's
Farm

84

S33

Robinlands La

Losehill Hall
Study Centre

4

Dunscar
Farm

Hollowford
Centre

Hollowford Rd

Warehouse La

Marsh
Farm

The Marshes

Hope

Caroline
Ct

Eccles
Cl

A6187

Marsh Ave

Hope Valley

Castleton Rd

Hope
Valley Coll

3

Odin Sitch

Cemy

Spital
Bridge

Trickett Cl

Squires La

Marston
Farm

Peakshole Water

Mast

Furlong La

Reservoir

83

Dirtl La

Visitor
Ctr

P

Millbridge

Mill La

The
Island

Back St

PO

Castle St

How La

Peveril Cl

Weaving

Red Way

Castleton
CE Prim Sch

A6187

Buxton Rd   Cross St

Mill Bridge

Market Pl

YH

The Folly

P

Winnats Pass

Goosehill

The Stones

Bargate

Castleton

Town Ditch

Pouchmouth

2

Goosehill
Hall

Goosehill

Peak
Cavern Rd

Pindale Rd

Pindale
Farm

Chimney

Works

Peak
Cavern

Peveril
Castle
(remains of)

Siggate

Cow Low

Limestone Way

Cave Dale

Michill Bank

Dirt Low

1

Dirtlow
Rake

Pin Dale

Pindale Rd

82

14   A   15   B   C   16   D   E   F

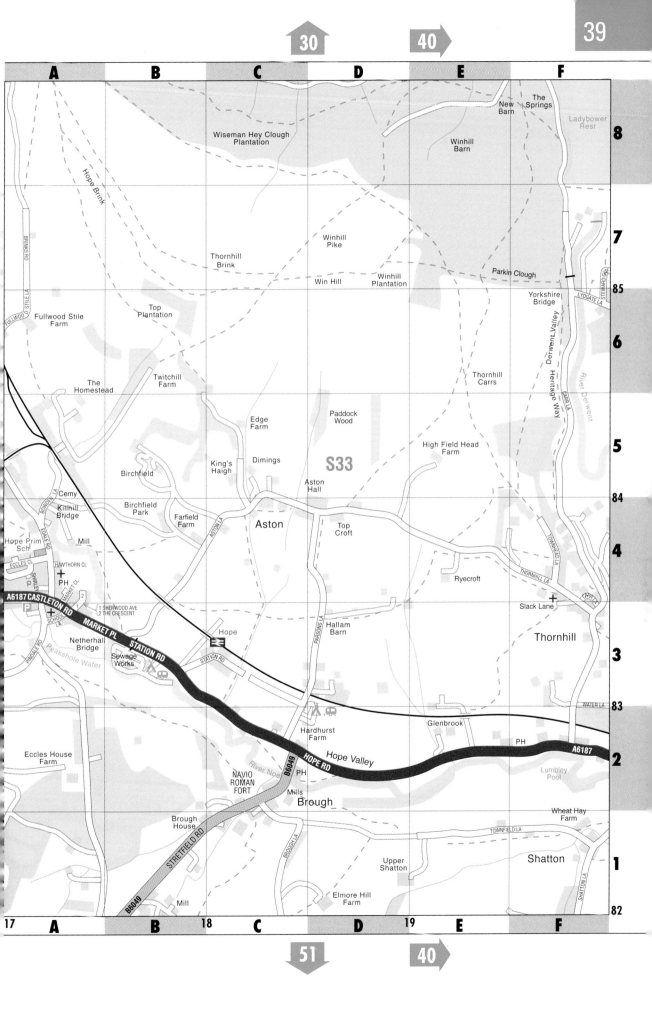

A B C D E F

8
Moscar Moor
Ladybower Resr
Derwent Valley Heritage Way
Trails
Grow Chin
S10

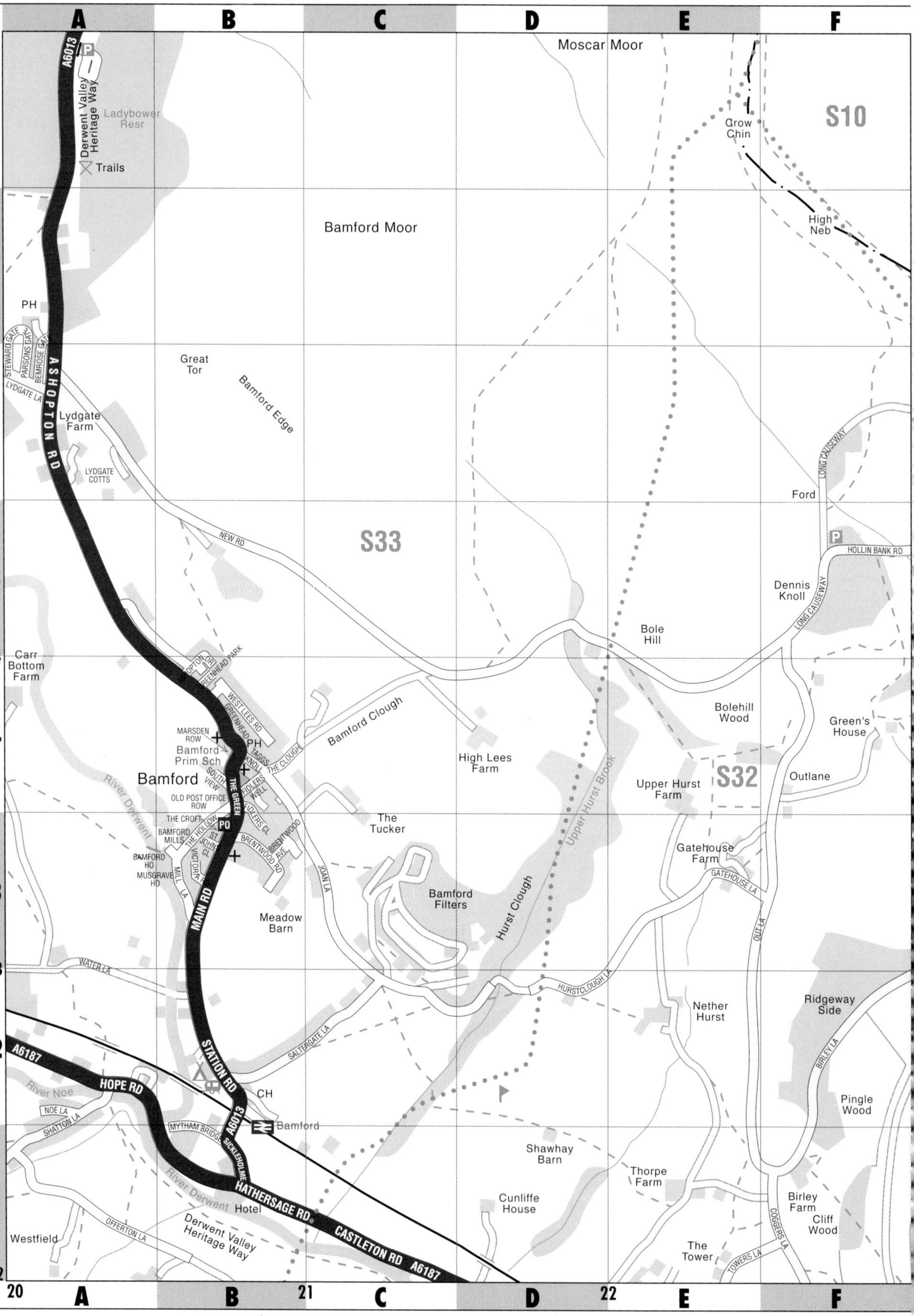

7
Bamford Moor
High Neb

85
PH
Great Tor
Bamford Edge

6
Lydgate Farm
Ashopton Rd
Long Causeway
Ford
Lydgate Cotts

5
New Rd
S33
Hollin Bank Way
Dennis Knoll

84
Carr Bottom Farm
Bole Hill
Bolehill Wood
Green's House

4
Marsden Row
Bamford Prim Sch
PH
Bamford Clough
High Lees Farm
Upper Hurst Farm
S32
Outlane

Bamford
Old Post Office Row
The Croft
The Tucker
Gatehouse Farm

3
Bamford Ho Musgrave Ho
Main Rd
Meadow Barn
Bamford Filters
Hurst Clough
Nether Hurst
Ridgeway Side

83
Water La
Hurstclough La
Pingle Wood

2
A6187
Hope Rd
Station Rd
Saltergate La
Birley La

River Noe
Noe La
Shatton La
Mytham Bridge
CH
Bamford
Shawhay Barn
Thorpe Farm
Birley Farm
Cliff Wood

1
A6013
Hathersage Rd
Castleton Rd A6187
Hotel
Cunliffe House
The Tower

Westfield
Offerton La
Derwent Valley Heritage Way
River Derwent

82
20 A B 21 C D 22 E F

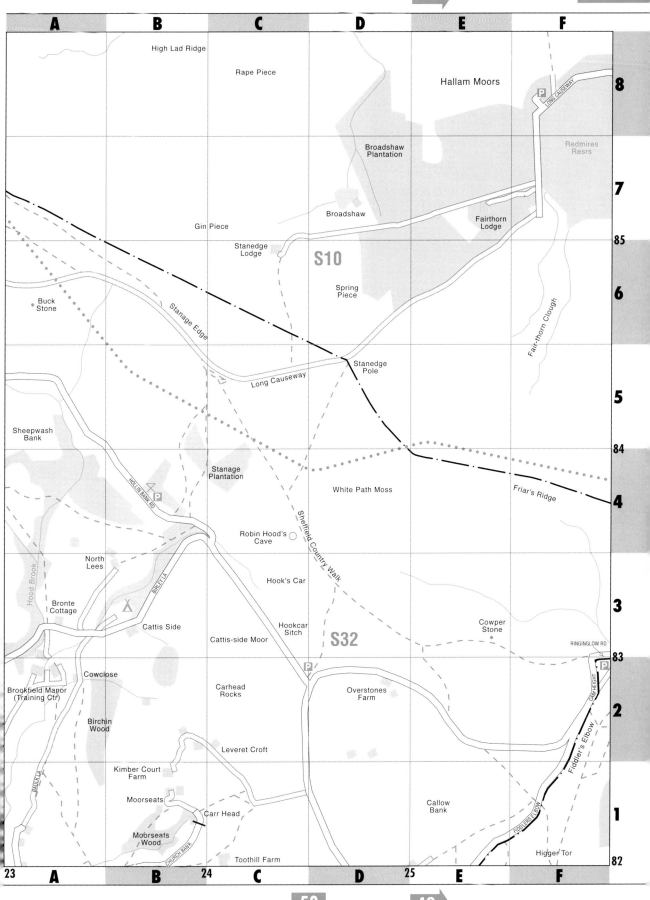

A	B	C	D	E	F

High Lad Ridge

Rape Piece

Hallam Moors

8

Broadshaw
Plantation

Redmires
Resrs

P

LONG CAUSEWAY

7

Gin Piece

Broadshaw

Fairthorn
Lodge

85

Stanedge
Lodge

S10

6

Buck
Stone

Spring
Piece

Stanage Edge

Fair-thorn Clough

Stanedge
Pole

5

Long Causeway

Sheepwash
Bank

84

Stanage
Plantation

White Path Moss

Friar's Ridge

4

Hood Brook

HOLLIN BANK RD

P

Robin Hood's
Cave

Sheffield Country Walk

North
Lees

BIRLEY LA

Hook's Car

Cowper
Stone

3

Bronte
Cottage

Cattis Side

Hookcar
Sitch

S32

RINGINGLOW RD

83

Cattis-side Moor

P

CAM HEIGHT

Cowclose

Carhead
Rocks

Overstones
Farm

P

2

Brookfield Manor
(Training Ctr)

Birchin
Wood

BAULK LA

Fiddler's Elbow

Kimber Court
Farm

Leveret Croft

Moorseats

Callow
Bank

FIDDLERS ELBOW

1

Carr Head

Moorseats
Wood

CHURCH BANK

Toothill Farm

Higger Tor

82

41

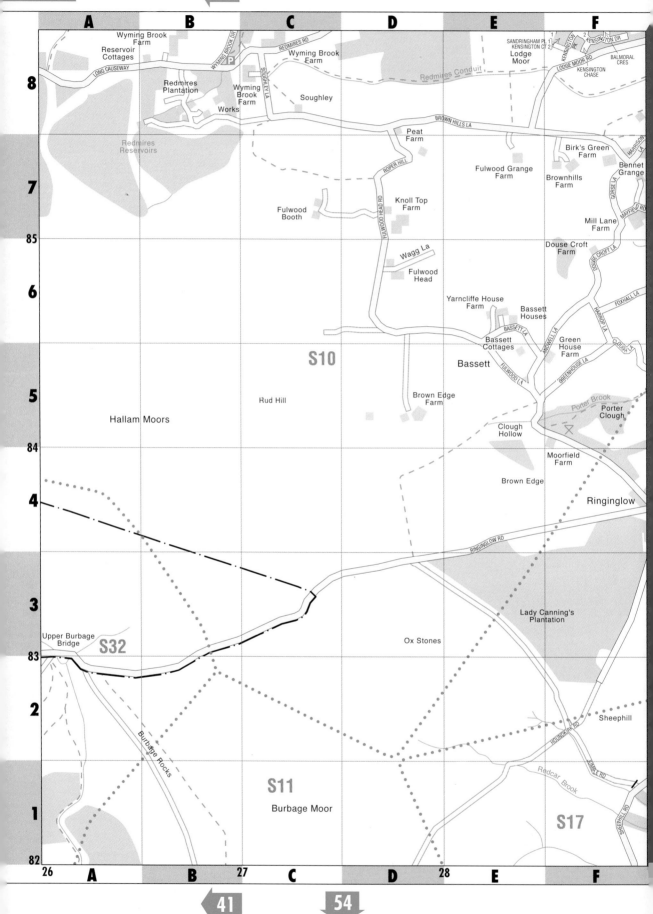

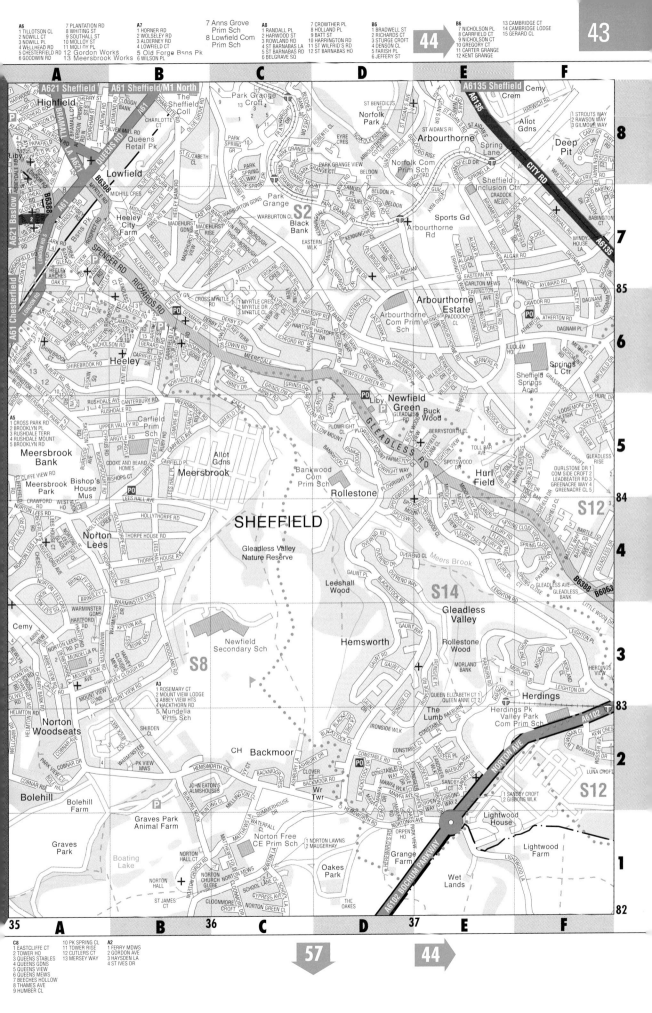

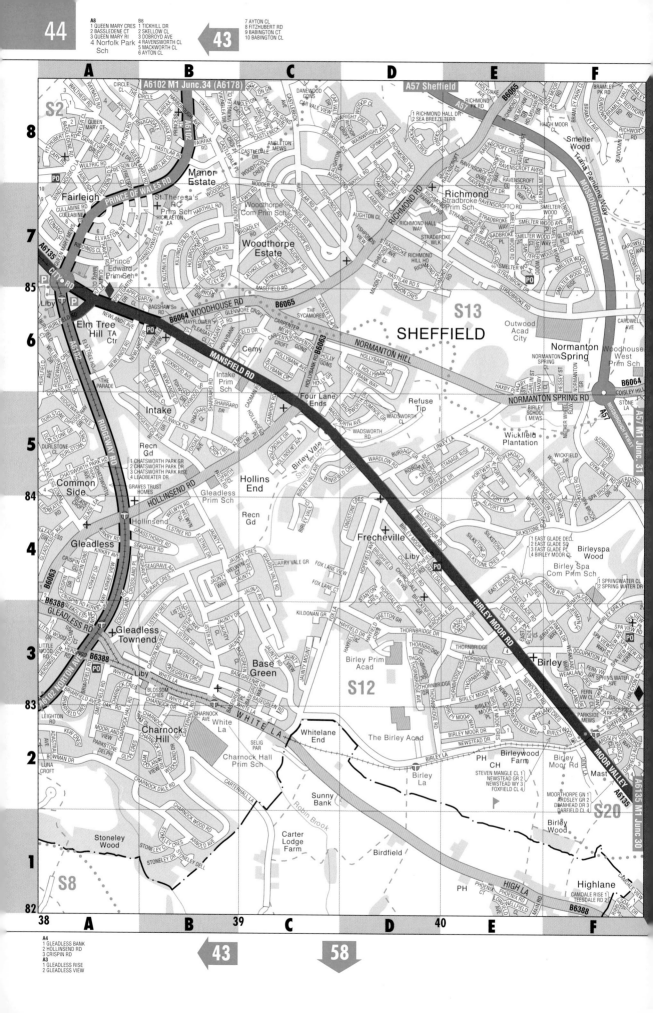

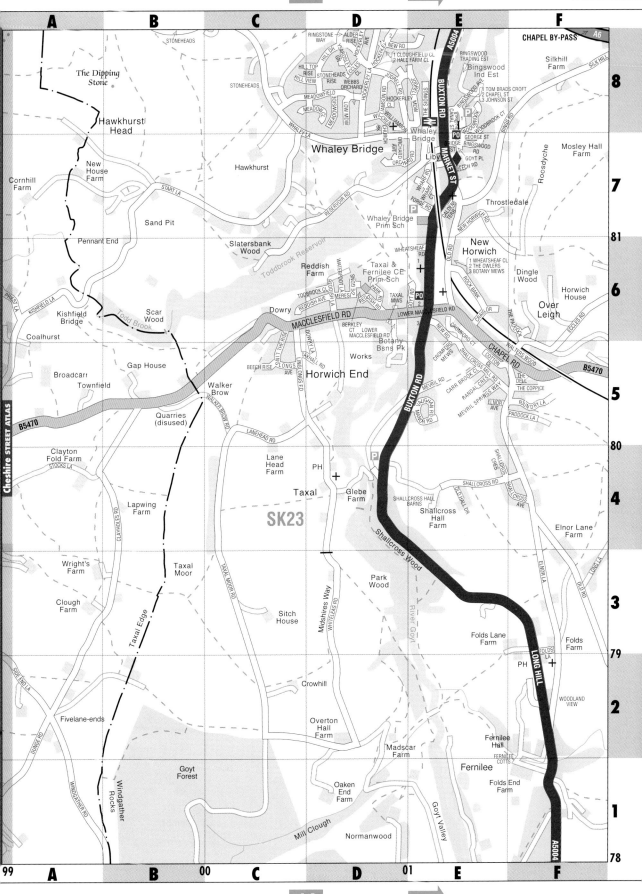

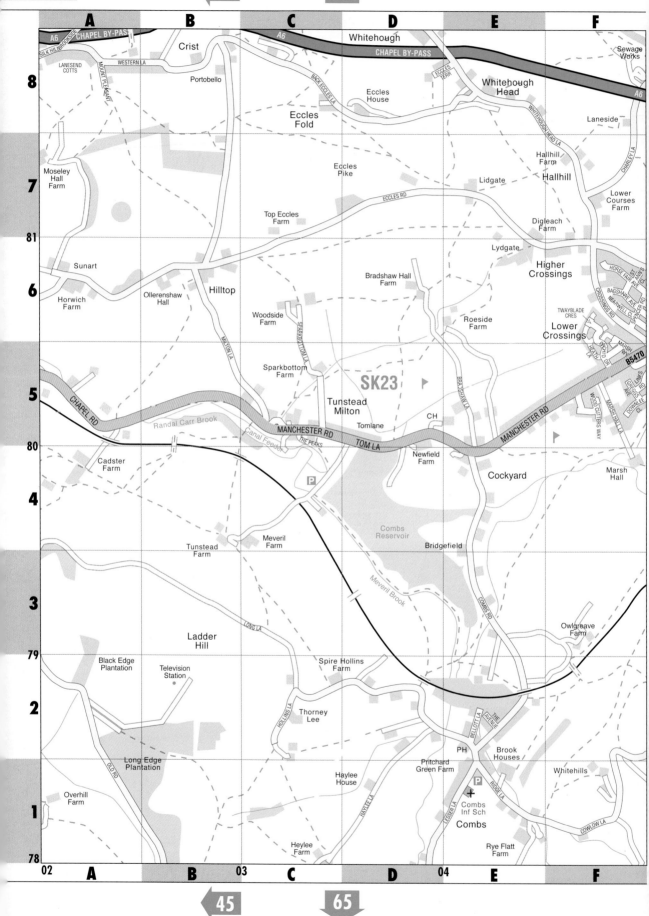

A   B   C   D   E   F

8

Chapel By-Pass
A6
Silk Hill Broadside
Lanesend Cotts
Western La
Mount Pleasant
Crist
Portobello
A6
Chapel By-Pass
Whitehough
Eccles Terr
Sewage Works
Eccles House
Eccles Fold
Whitehough Head
Whitehough Head La
Laneside

7

Moseley Hall Farm
Eccles Pike
Eccles Rd
Hallhill Farm
Lidgate
Hallhill
Lower Courses Farm
Charley La

81

Sunart
Top Eccles Farm
Digleach Farm
Lydgate
Higher Crossings

6

Horwich Farm
Ollerenshaw Hall
Hilltop
Woodside Farm
Bradshaw Hall Farm
Roeside Farm
Lower Crossings
Horse Fair Ave
Bagshaw Ave
Nearwell Close
Spencer St
Twayblade Cres
Crossings Rd
Marsh Ave
Heath La
Orchid Dr

Milton La
Sparkbottom La
Sparkbottom Farm
SK23
Bradshaw La
Manchester Rd
B5470
Marshall La
Downlee Close
Wood Cutters Way
Gregg St
Aspenshaw Close

5

Chapel Rd
Randal Carr Brook
Tunstead Milton
Tomlane
CH
Manchester Rd

80

Canal Feeder
The Peaks
Manchester Rd
Tom La
Newfield Farm
Cockyard
Marsh Hall

4

Cadster Farm
P
Combs Reservoir
Bridgefield

3

Tunstead Farm
Meveril Farm
Meveril Brook
Combs Rd
Long La
Owlgreave Farm

79

Black Edge Plantation
Ladder Hill
Spire Hollins Farm

2

Television Station
Hollins La
Thorney Lee
The Avenue
Bellott La
PH
Brook Houses
Whitehills

Long Edge Plantation
Old Rd
Pritchard Green Farm
P
Ridge La

1

Overhill Farm
Haylee House
Haylee La
Lesser La
Combs Inf Sch
Combs
Rye Flatt Farm
Conlow La

78

Heylee Farm

02   A   B   03   C   D   04   E   F

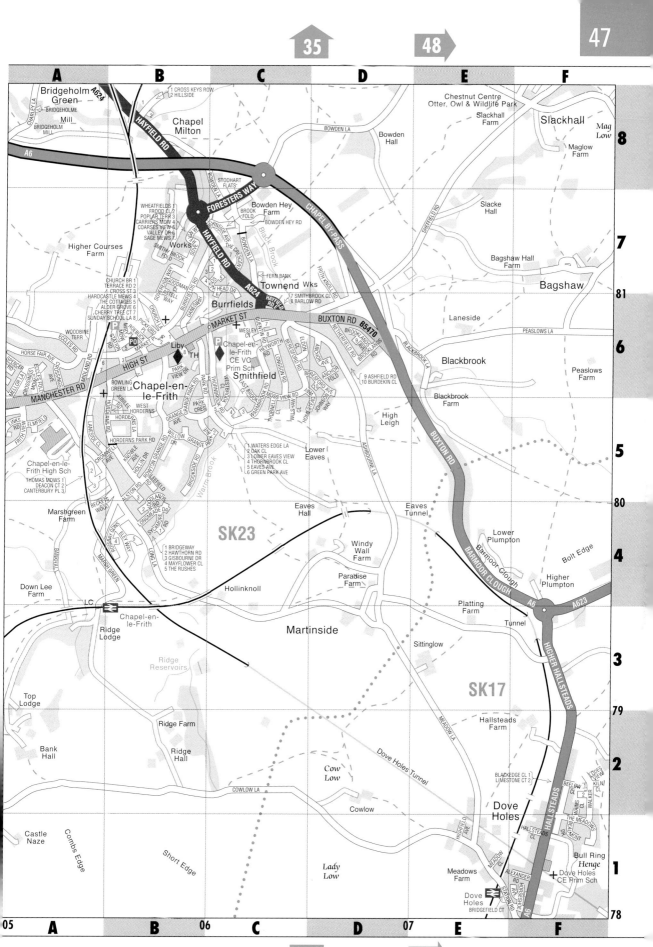

A   B   C   D   E   F

8
7
81
6
5
80
4
79
2
1
78

Bridgeholm Green
BRIDGEHOLME MILL
Chapel Milton
1 CROSS KEYS ROW
2 HILLSIDE
Chestnut Centre Otter, Owl & Wildlife Park
Slackhall Farm
Slackhall
Mag Low
Maglow Farm
BOWDEN LA
Bowden Hall
Slacke Hall
HAYFIELD RD
FORESTERS WAY
A624
A6
Higher Courses Farm
WHEATFIELDS 1
FROOD CL 2
POPLAR TERR 3
CARRIERS MDW 4
COARSES VIEW 5
VALLEY DR 6
SAGE MEWS 7
Works
STODHART FLATS
Bowden Hey Farm
BROOK FOLD
Bowden Hey Rd
Black Brook
CHAPEL BY-PASS
Bagshaw Hall Farm
FERN BANK
Townend
Wks
7 SMITHBROOK CL
8 BARLOW RD
FRITH KNOLL
Bagshaw
CHURCH BR 1
TERRACE RD 2
CROSS ST 3
HARDCASTLE MEWS 4
THE COTTAGES 5
ALDER GROVE 6
CHERRY TREE CT 7
SUNDAY SCHOOL LA 8
Burrfields
HAYFIELD RD
Laneside
PEASLOWS LA
WOODBINE TERR
HORSE FAIR AVE
ECCLES RD
MARKET ST
BUXTON RD
B5470
BROOKLANDS
Blackbrook
BLACKBROOK LA
Peaslows Farm
HIGH ST
Liby
TH
Chapel-en-le-Frith CE VC Prim Sch
WESLEY CT
9 ASHFIELD RD
10 BURDEKIN CL
Blackbrook Farm
Chapel-en-le-Frith
Smithfield
PARK VIEW DR
WEST HORDERNS
WARBERTON RD
MOSS VIEW
ASHBOURNE LA
High Leigh
BUXTON RD
Chapel-en-le-Frith High Sch
THOMAS MDWS 1
DEACON CT 2
CANTERBURY PL 3
1 WATERS EDGE LA
2 OAK CL
3 LOWER EAVES VIEW
4 THORNBROOK CL
5 EAVES AVE
6 GREEN PARK AVE
Lower Eaves
Eaves Tunnel
Lower Plumpton
Bolt Edge
Marshgreen Farm
WARM BROOK
SK23
1 BRIDGEWAY
2 HAWTHORN RD
3 GISBOURNE DR
4 MAYFLOWER CL
5 THE RUSHES
Eaves Hall
Windy Wall Farm
BARMOOR CLOUGH
Higher Plumpton
A6
A623
Down Lee Farm
LC
Chapel-en-le-Frith
Ridge Lodge
Hollinknoll
Paradise Farm
Platting Farm
Tunnel
HIGHER HALLSTEADS
Ridge Reservoirs
Martinside
Sittinglow
SK17
Top Lodge
Ridge Farm
Ridge Hall
Hallsteads Farm
Bank Hall
COWLOW LA
Cow Low
Cowlow
BLACKEDGE CL 1
LIMESTONE CT 2
BEELOW CL
Dove Holes
HALLSTEADS CL
HALLSTEADS
Castle Naze
Combs Edge
Short Edge
Lady Low
Dove Holes Tunnel
Meadows Farm
HIGHFIELD AVE
MEADOW LA
STATION RD
ALEXANDER RD
Bull Ring Henge
Dove Holes CE Prim Sch
Dove Holes
BRIDGEFIELD CT
A6

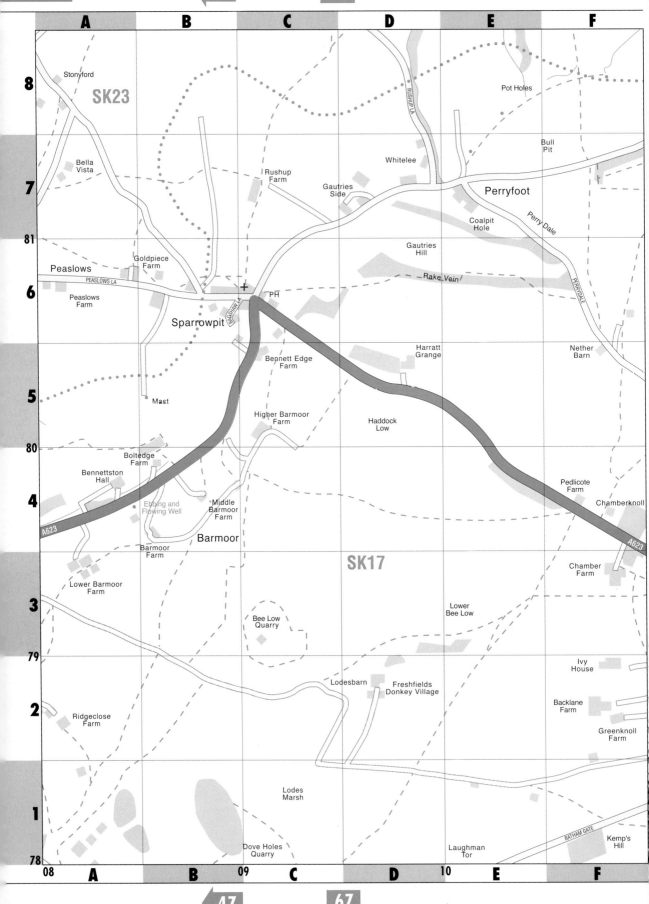

A B C D E F

8 Stonyford
SK23
Bella Vista

Pot Holes

Bull Pit

7 Rushup Farm
Gautries Side
Whitelee
Perryfoot
Coalpit Hole
Perry Dale

81
Gautries Hill
Rake Vein
PERRYDALE

Peaslows
Goldpiece Farm
PEASLOWS LA
6 Peaslows Farm
PH
Sparrowpit
BASHAW LA
Nether Barn

Bennett Edge Farm
Harratt Grange

5 Mast
Higher Barmoor Farm
Haddock Low

80 Boltedge Farm
Bennettston Hall
Pedlicote Farm
Chamberknoll

4 Ebbing and Flowing Well
Middle Barmoor Farm
A623
Barmoor
Barmoor Farm
SK17
Chamber Farm

3 Lower Barmoor Farm
Bee Low Quarry
Lower Bee Low
Ivy House

79
Lodesbarn
Freshfields Donkey Village
Backlane Farm

2 Ridgeclose Farm
Greenknoll Farm

1 Lodes Marsh
BATHAM GATE
Kemp's Hill

78
Dove Holes Quarry
Laughman Tor

08 A B 09 C D 10 E F

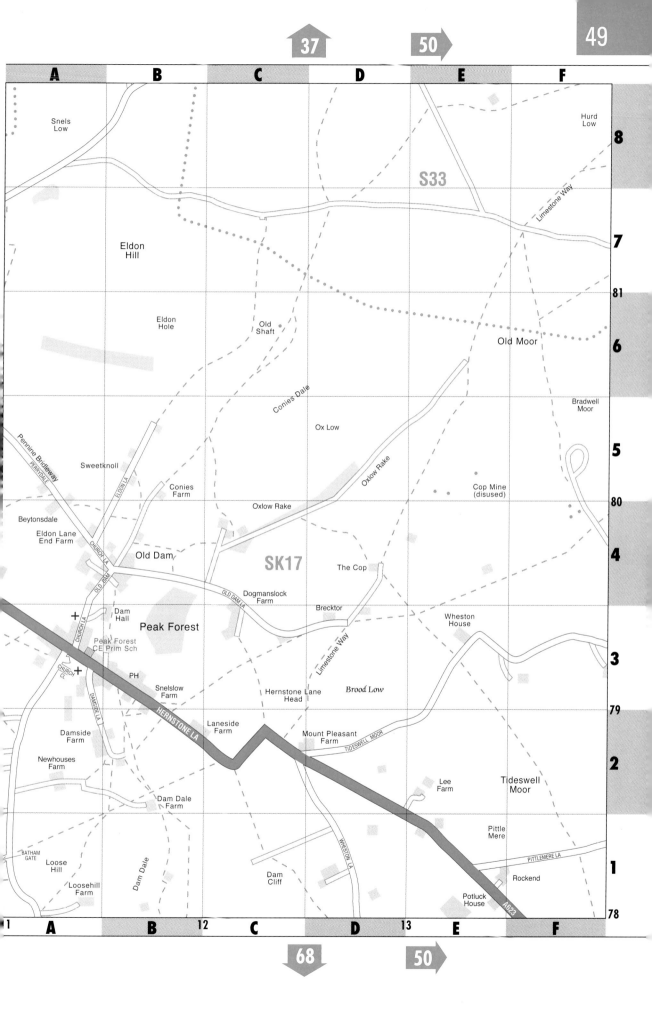

A B C D E F

8

Snels
Low

Hurd
Low

S33

7

Eldon
Hill

Limestone Way

81

Eldon
Hole

Old
Shaft

Old Moor

6

Conies Dale

Bradwell
Moor

Ox Low

5

Pennine Bridleway

PERRYDALE

Sweetknoll

Conies
Farm

Oxlow Rake

Cop Mine
(disused)

ELDON LA

80

Beytonsdale

Oxlow Rake

Eldon Lane
End Farm

SK17

The Cop

4

CHURCH LA

Old Dam

Dogmanslock
Farm

Wheston
House

OLD DAM

OLD DAM LA

Dam
Hall

Brecktor

+

Peak Forest

CHURCH LA

Peak Forest
CE Prim Sch

Limestone Way

3

+

CHURCH CL

PH

Snelslow
Farm

Hernstone Lane
Head

Brood Low

DAMSIDE LA

HERNSTONE LA

79

Laneside
Farm

Mount Pleasant
Farm

TIDESWELL MOOR

Damside
Farm

2

Newhouses
Farm

Lee
Farm

Tideswell
Moor

Dam Dale
Farm

Pittle
Mere

BATHAM
GATE

Loose
Hill

Dam Dale

WHESTON LA

PITTLEMERE LA

1

Loosehill
Farm

Dam
Cliff

Rockend

Potluck
House

A623

78

A B C D E F

1 12 13

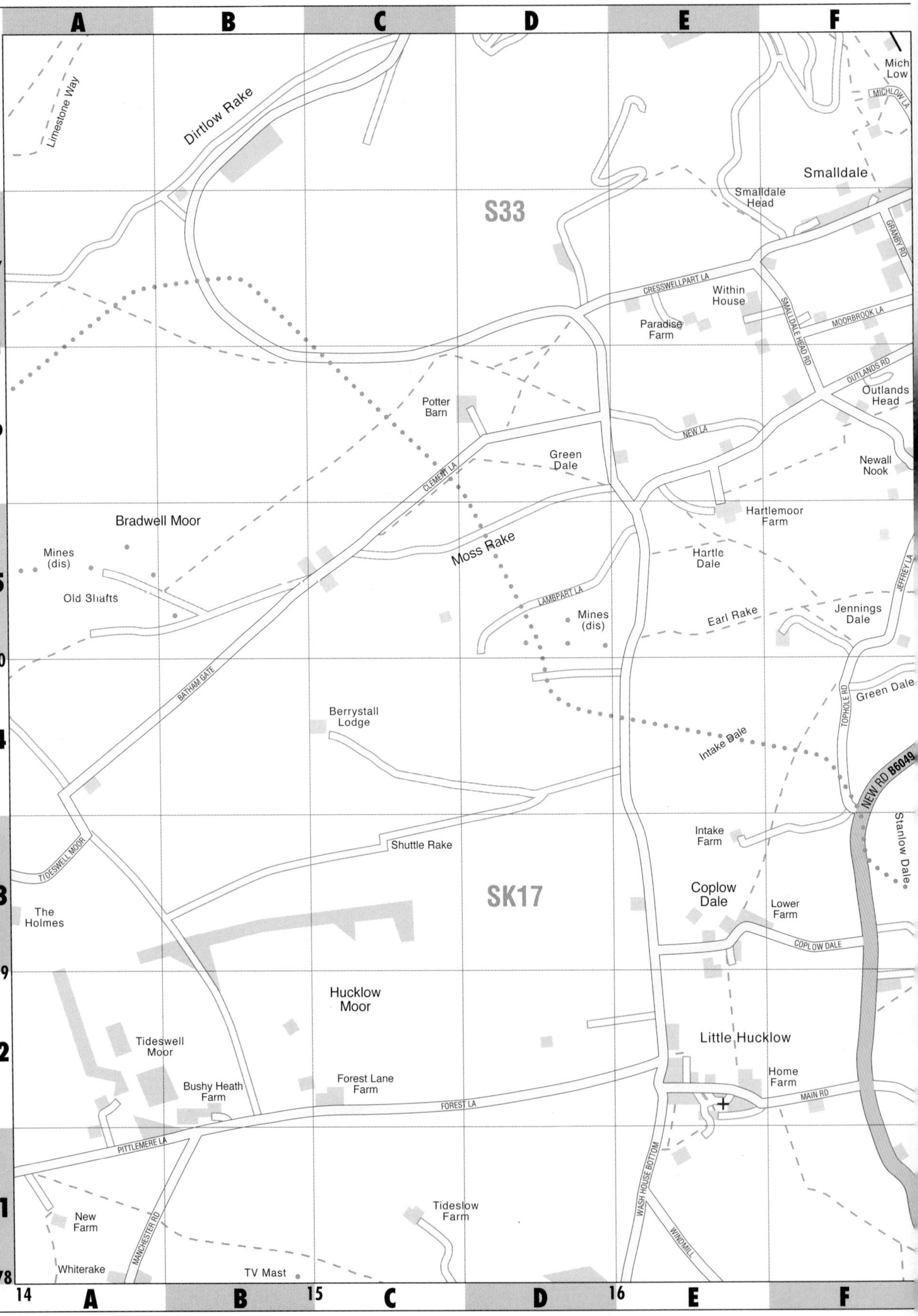

A B C D E F

8

7

81

6

5

80

4

3

79

2

1

78

14 A B 15 C D 16 E F

Limestone Way

Dirtlow Rake

S33

Smalldale

Smalldale Head

MICHLOW LA

Mich Low

GRANBY RD

Cresswellpart La

Within House

SMALLDALE HEAD RD

MOORBROOK LA

Paradise Farm

OUTLANDS RD

Outlands Head

Potter Barn

NEW LA

Green Dale

Newall Nook

CLEMENT LA

Hartlemoor Farm

Bradwell Moor

Moss Rake

Hartle Dale

Mines (dis)

LAMBPART LA

Earl Rake

JEFFREY LA

Jennings Dale

Old Shafts

Mines (dis)

TOPHOLE RD

Green Dale

80

BATHAM GATE

Intake Dale

NEW RD B6049

Berrystall Lodge

Stanlow Dale

Intake Farm

Shuttle Rake

Coplow Dale

Lower Farm

SK17

The Holmes

TIDESWELL MOOR

COPLOW DALE

79

Hucklow Moor

Little Hucklow

Tideswell Moor

Home Farm

Bushy Heath Farm

Forest Lane Farm

MAIN RD

FOREST LA

WASH HOUSE BOTTOM

PITTLEMERE LA

MANCHESTER RD

WINDMILL

New Farm

Tideslow Farm

Whiterake

TV Mast

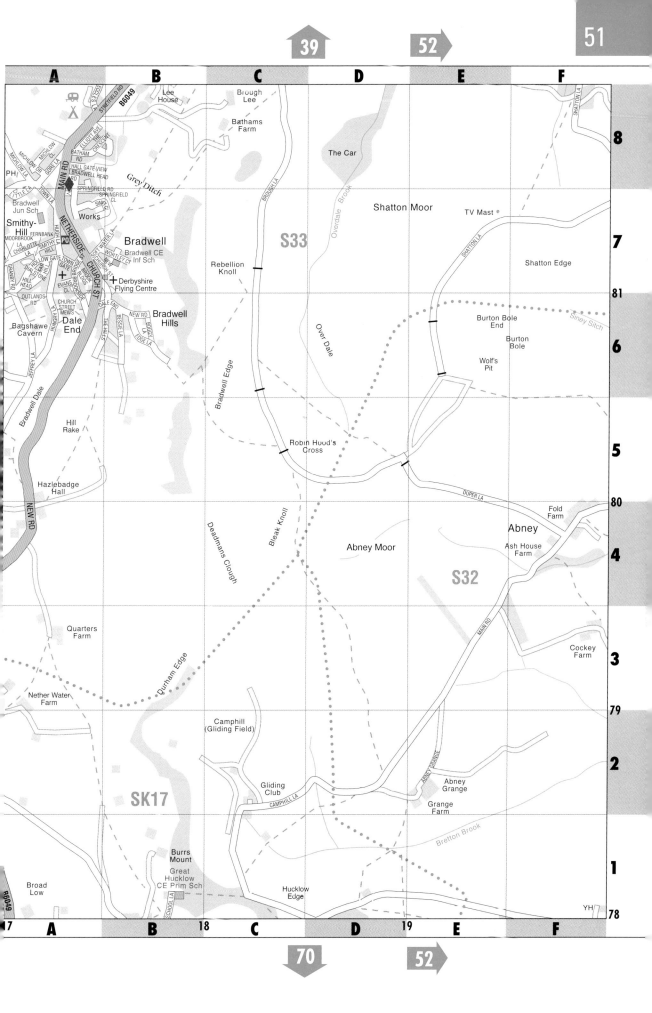

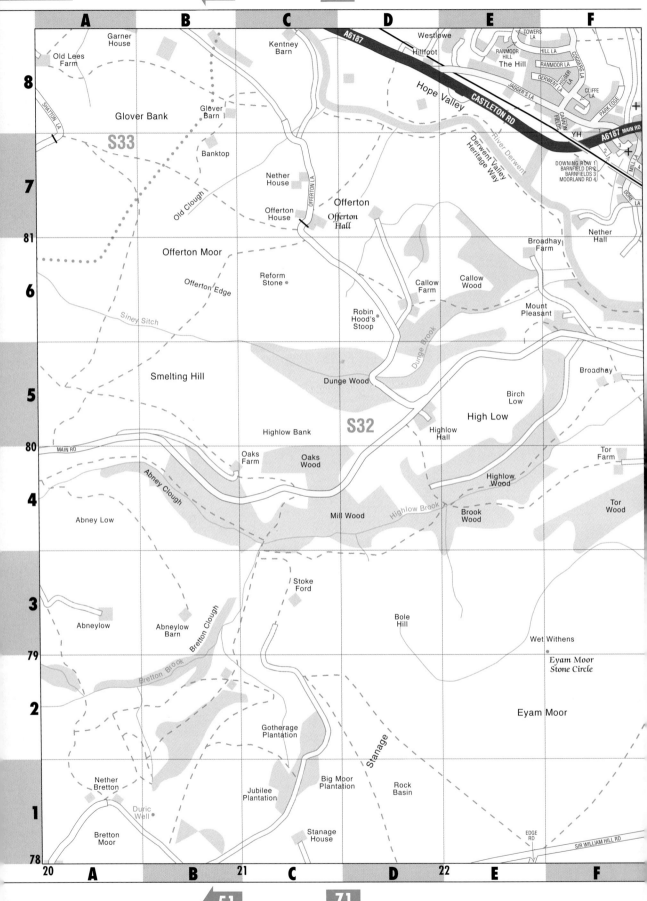

A **B** **C** **D** **E** **F**

8

Old Lees Farm

Garner House

Glover Bank

S33

Kentney Barn

Westlowe

Hillfoot

Hope Valley

A6187

CASTLETON RD

TOWERS LA

RANMOOR HILL

The Hill

RANMOOR LA

HILL LA

COGGERS LA

DERWENT LA

HIGHER LA

CLIFFE LA

JAGGER'S LA

CANYON FIELDS

PARK EDGE

A6187 MAIN RD

YH

DORE LA

MILL LA

Glover Barn

Banktop

7

Old Clough

Nether House

Offerton House

OFFERTON LA

Offerton

Offerton Hall

River Derwent

Derwent Valley Heritage Way

DOWNING ROW 1
BARNFIELD DR 2
BARNFIELDS 3
MOORLAND RD 4

Nether Hall

Broadhay Farm

81

Offerton Moor

6

Offerton Edge

Reform Stone

Siney Sitch

Robin Hood's Stoop

Callow Farm

Dunge Brook

Callow Wood

Mount Pleasant

5

Smelting Hill

Dunge Wood

S32

Highlow Bank

Highlow Hall

Birch Low

High Low

Broadhay

80

MAIN RD

Oaks Farm

Oaks Wood

Highlow Wood

Tor Farm

4

Abney Low

Abney Clough

Mill Wood

Highlow Brook

Brook Wood

Tor Wood

3

Abneylow

Abneylow Barn

Bretton Clough

Stoke Ford

Bole Hill

Wet Withens

79

Bretton Brook

Eyam Moor Stone Circle

2

Gotherage Plantation

Eyam Moor

1

Nether Bretton

Duric Well

Jubilee Plantation

Big Moor Plantation

Stanage

Rock Basin

EDGE RD

78

Bretton Moor

Stanage House

SIR WILLIAM HILL RD

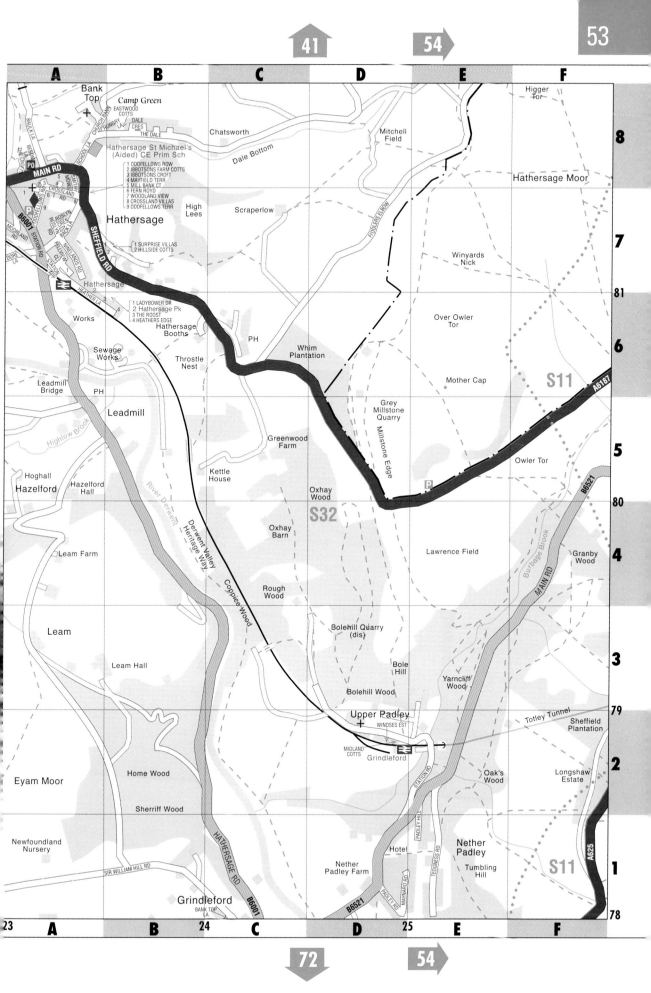

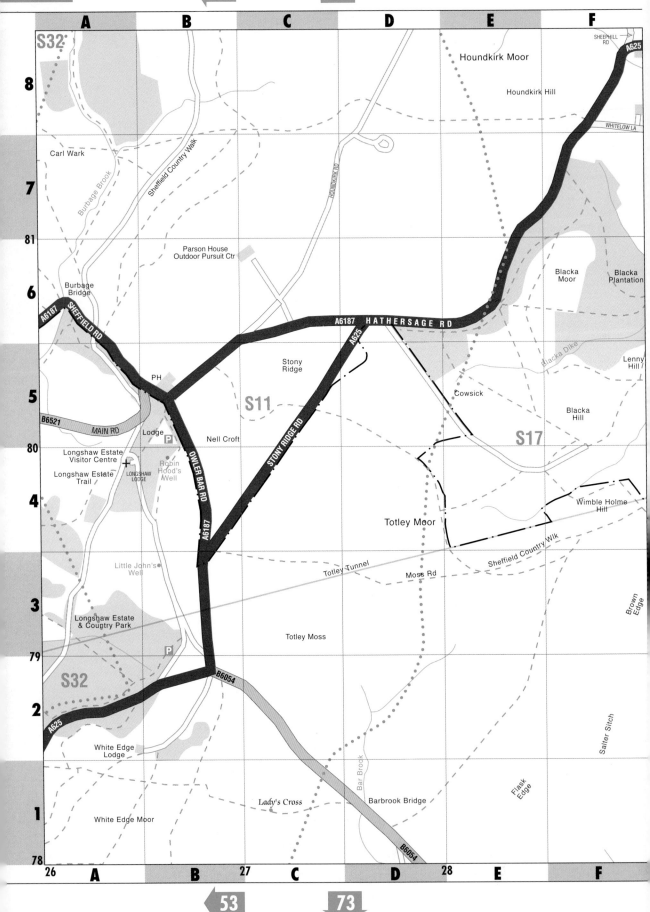

S32

A **B** **C** **D** **E** **F**

8

Carl Wark

Houndkirk Moor

Houndkirk Hill

SHEEPHILL RD

A625

WHITELOW LA

7

Burbage Brook

Sheffield Country Walk

HOUNDKIRK RD

81

Parson House
Outdoor Pursuit Ctr

Blacka
Moor

Blacka
Plantation

6

A6187

SHEFFIELD RD

Burbage
Bridge

A6187 HATHERSAGE RD

A625

Blacka Dike

Lenny
Hill

PH

Stony
Ridge

Cowsick

Blacka
Hill

5

S11

B6521

MAIN RD

Lodge

P

Nell Croft

STONY RIDGE RD

S17

80

Longshaw Estate
Visitor Centre

Longshaw Estate
Trail

LONGSHAW
LODGE

Robin
Hood's
Well

OWLER BAR RD

A6187

4

Little John's
Well

Totley Moor

Wimble Holme
Hill

Sheffield Country Wlk

Brown
Edge

3

Longshaw Estate
& Country Park

Totley Tunnel

Moss Rd

P

Totley Moss

79

B6054

S32

2

A625

White Edge
Lodge

B6054

Bar Brook

Salter Sitch

1

White Edge Moor

Lady's Cross

Barbrook Bridge

Flask
Edge

B6054

78

26 **A** **B** 27 **C** **D** 28 **E** **F**

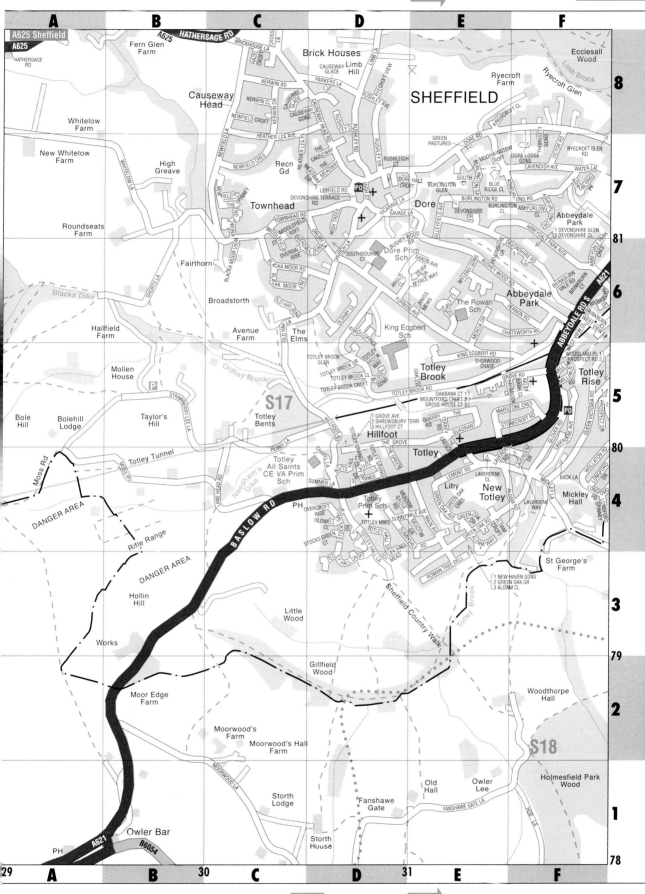

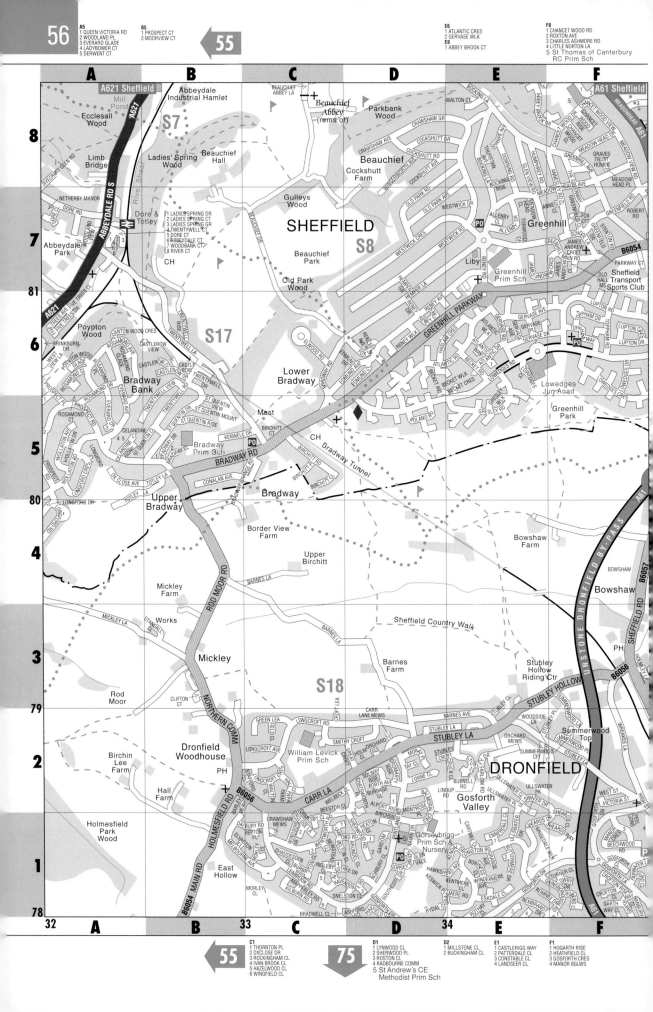

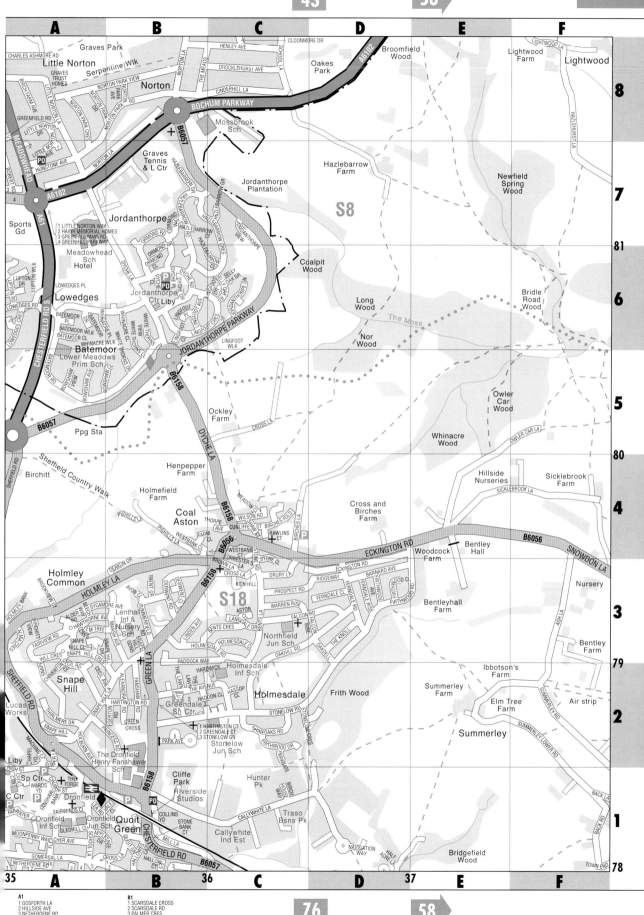

A B C D E F

8 7 81 6 5 80 4 3 79 2 1 78

Little Norton
Graves Park
Norton
Jordanthorpe
Lowedges
Batemoor
Coal Aston
Holmley Common
Snape Hill
Dronfield
Quoit Green
Holmesdale
Summerley
Lightwood

BOCHUM PARKWAY
JORDANTHORPE PARKWAY
ECKINGTON RD
SNOWDON LA
CHESTERFIELD RD
SHEFFIELD RD

S8
S18

A B C D E F

A1
1 GOSFORTH LA
2 HILLSIDE AVE
3 NETHERDENE RD
4 PEMBROKE RD
5 UPPER SCHOOL LA
6 HIGHDALE FOLD

B1
1 SCARSDALE CROSS
2 SCARSDALE RD
3 PALMER CRES

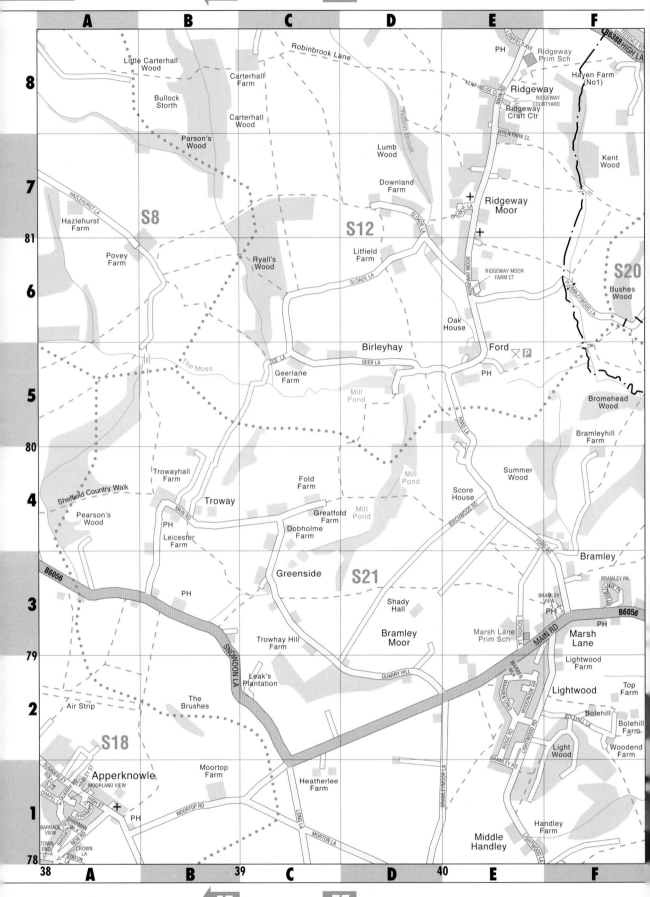

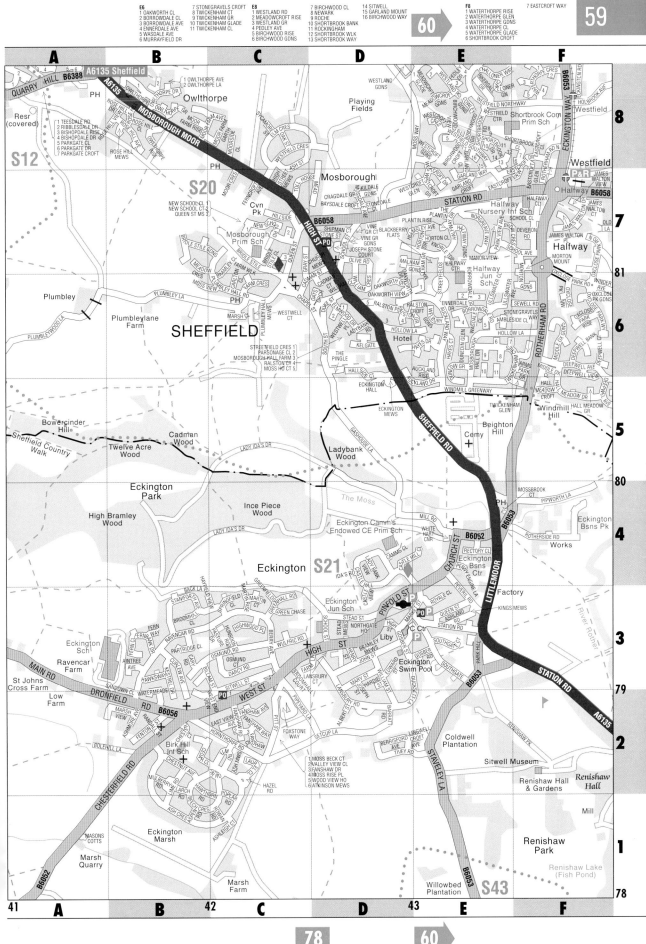

E6
1 OAKWORTH CL
2 BORROWDALE CL
3 BORROWDALE AVE
4 ENNERDALE AVE
5 WASDALE AVE
6 MURRAYFIELD DR

7 STONEGRAVELS CROFT
8 TWICKENHAM CT
9 TWICKENHAM GR
10 TWICKENHAM GLADE
11 TWICKENHAM CL

E8
1 WESTLAND RD
2 MEADOWCROFT RISE
3 WESTLAND GR
4 PEDLEY AVE
5 BIRCHWOOD RISE
6 BIRCHWOOD GDNS

7 BIRCHWOOD CL
8 NEWARK
9 ROCHE
10 SHORTBROOK BANK
11 ROCKINGHAM
12 SHORTBROOK WLK
13 SHORTBROOK WAY

14 SITWELL
15 GARLAND MOUNT
16 BIRCHWOOD WAY

60 →

F8
1 WATERTHORPE RISE
2 WATERTHORPE GLEN
3 WATERTHORPE GDNS
4 WATERTHORPE CL
5 WATERTHORPE GLADE
6 SHORTBROOK CROFT

7 EASTCROFT WAY

59

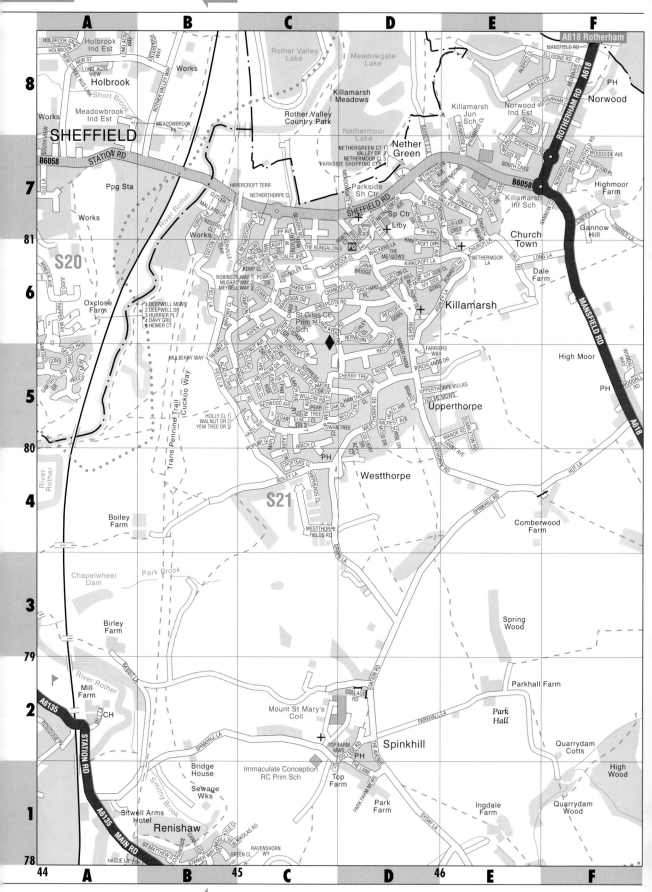

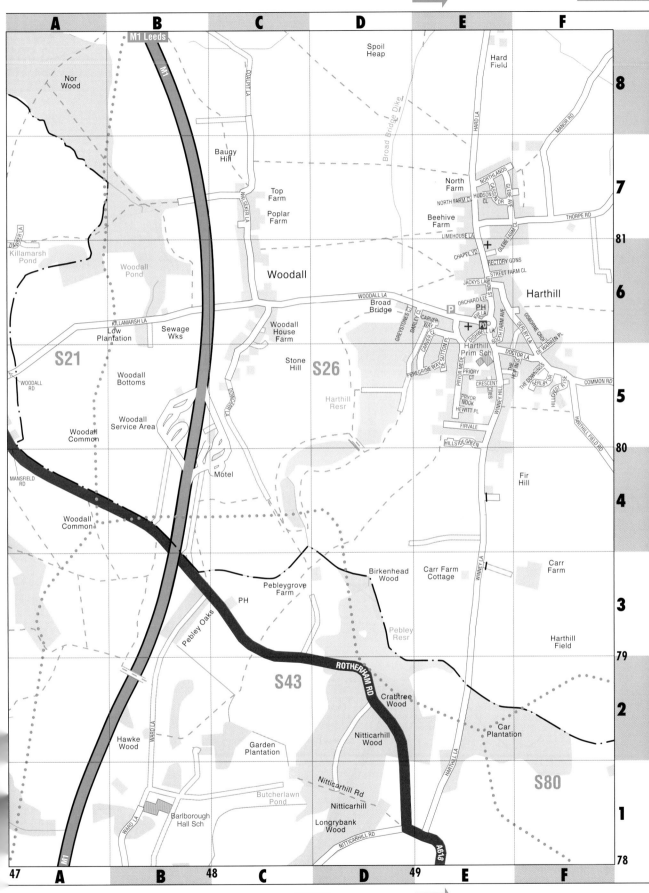

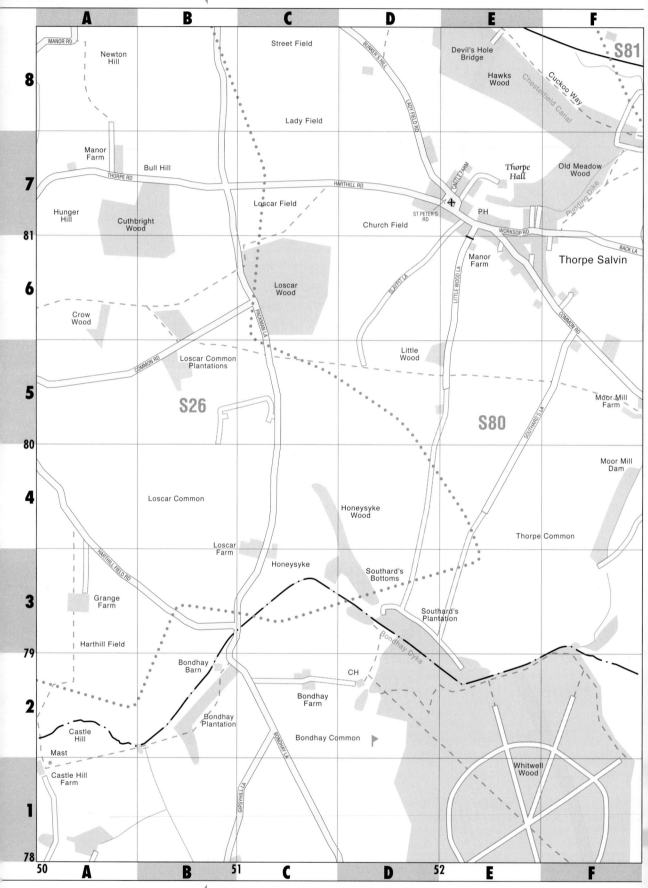

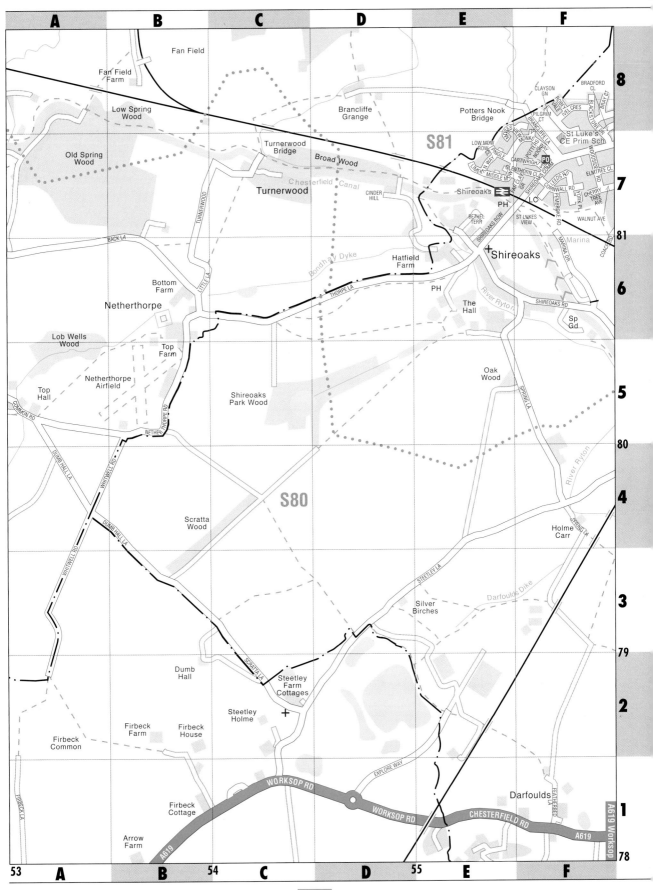

A B C D E F

8
7
81
6
5
80
4
3
79
2
1
78

Fan Field

Fan Field Farm

Low Spring Wood

Old Spring Wood

Turnerwood Bridge

Broad Wood

Brancliffe Grange

Chesterfield Canal

Turnerwood

CINDER HILL

Potters Nook Bridge

S81

CLAYSON GN

BRADFORD CL

PILGRIM CT

St Luke's CE Prim Sch

LOW MDW ROW

CARTWRIGHT

Shireoaks

PH

LC

BETHEL TERR

ST LUKES VIEW

SHIREOAKS ROW

+ Shireoaks

Marina

MARINA DR

COACH RD

BACK LA

Bondhay Dyke

Hatfield Farm

PH

THORPE LA

LITTLE LA

TURNERWOOD

Bottom Farm

Netherthorpe

The Hall

River Ryton

SHIREOAKS RD

Sp Gd

6

Lob Wells Wood

Top Farm

Oak Wood

5

Top Hall

Netherthorpe Airfield

THORPE RD

NETHER

Shireoaks Park Wood

SPRING LA

River Ryton

80

COMMON RD

DUMB HALL LA

WHITWELL RD

S80

4

Scratta Wood

Holme Carr

SPRING LA

DUMB HALL LA

STEETLEY LA

Darfoulds Dike

3

Silver Birches

79

WHITWELL RD

SCRATTA LA

Dumb Hall

Steetley Farm Cottages

2

FIRBECK LA

Firbeck Common

Firbeck Farm

Firbeck House

Steetley Holme +

EXPLORE WAY

Darfoulds

1

Firbeck Cottage

WORKSOP RD

WORKSOP RD

CHESTERFIELD RD

FEATHERBED

A619 Worksop

78

Arrow Farm

A619

A619

53 A B 54 C D 55 E F

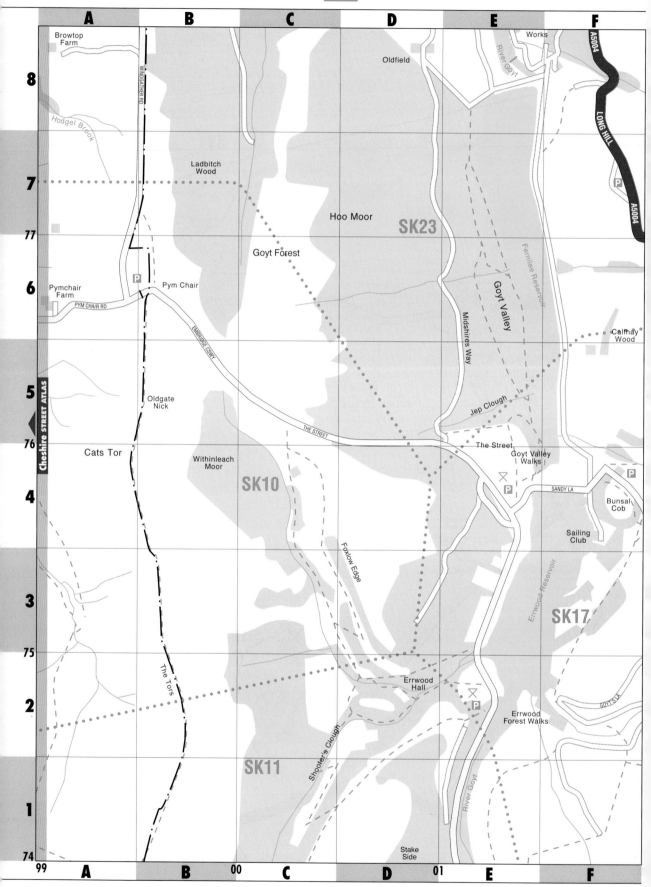

Cheshire STREET ATLAS

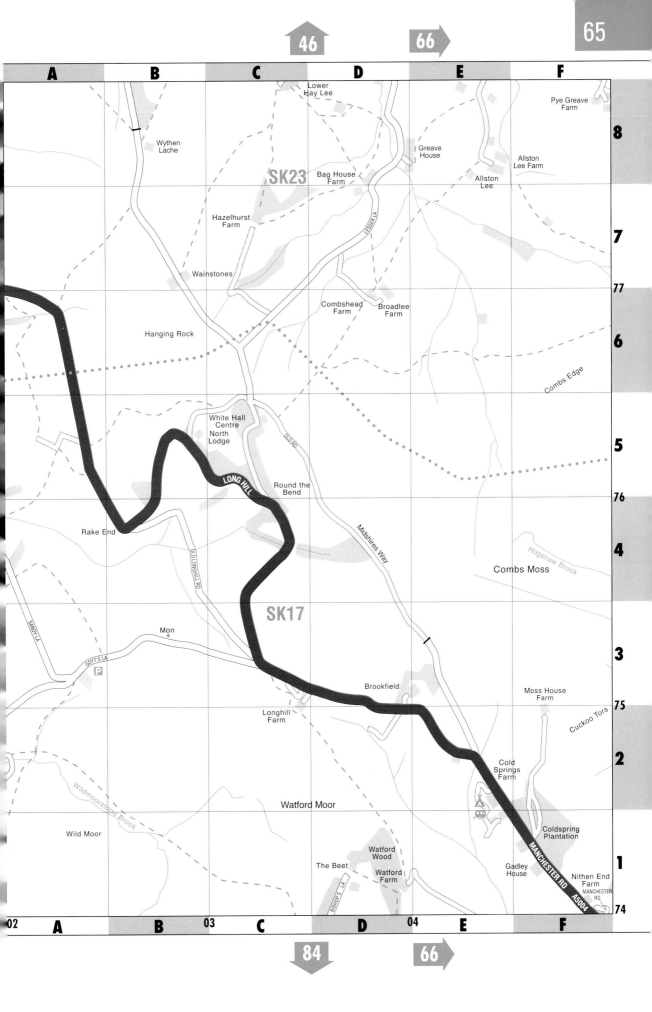

A B C D E F

8

7

77

6

5

76

4

3

75

2

1

74

A B C D E F

Pye Greave
Farm

Wythen
Lache

SK23

Lower
Hay Lee

Greave
House

Allston
Lee Farm

Bag House
Farm

Allston
Lee

Hazelhurst
Farm

LESSER LA

Wainstones

Combshead
Farm

Broadlee
Farm

Hanging Rock

Combs Edge

White Hall
Centre
North
Lodge

OLD RD

LONG HILL

Round the
Bend

Rake End

Midshires Way

Combs Moss

Hogshaw Brook

OLD LONGHILL RD

SK17

SANDY LA

Mon

GOYT'S LA

P

Brookfield

Moss House
Farm

Cuckoo Tors

Longhill
Farm

Cold
Springs
Farm

Wildmoorstone Brook

Watford Moor

Coldspring
Plantation

Wild Moor

Watford
Wood

The Beet

BISHOP'S LA

Watford
Farm

Gadley
House

Nithen End
Farm

MANCHESTER RD

MANCHESTER
RD

A5004

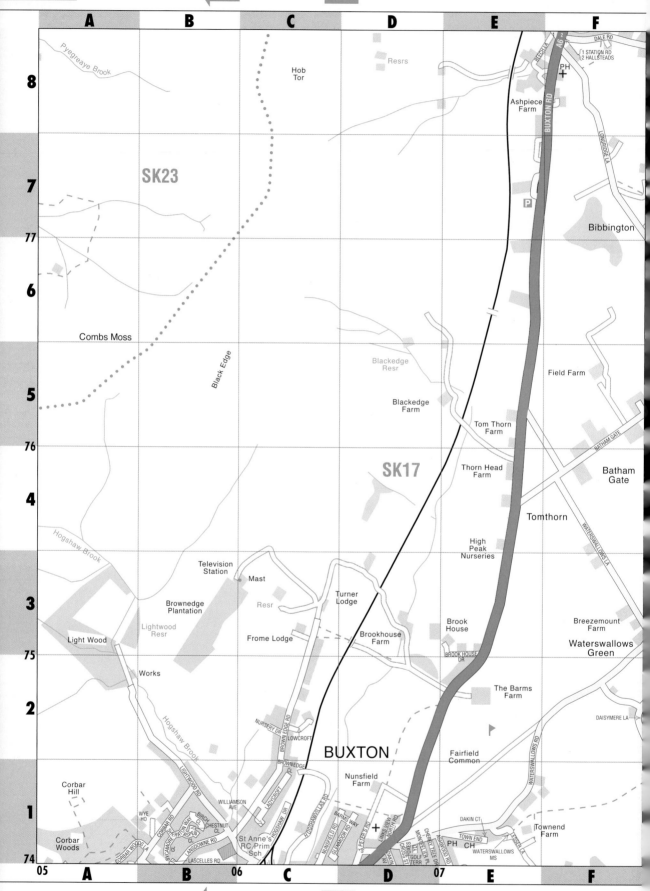

	A	B	C	D	E	F

8

Pyegreaye Brook

Hob Tor

Resrs

1 STATION RD
2 HALLSTEADS

DALE RO

PH

Ashpiece Farm

BUXTON RD

BEECHER LA

A6

LONGRIDGE LA

SK23

7

Bibbington

77

Combs Moss

Black Edge

Blackedge Resr

Field Farm

BATHAM GATE

5

Blackedge Farm

Tom Thorn Farm

76

Batham Gate

SK17

Thorn Head Farm

4

Tomthorn

Hogshaw Brook

High Peak Nurseries

WATERSWALLOWS LA

3

Television Station

Mast

Resr

Turner Lodge

Brook House

Breezemount Farm

Brownedge Plantation

Lightwood Resr

Frome Lodge

Brookhouse Farm

BROOK HOUSE DR

Waterswallows Green

75

Light Wood

Works

The Barms Farm

2

NURSERY DR

BROWN EDGE RD

LOWCROFT

WATERSWALLOWS RD

DAISYMERE LA

Hogshaw Brook

LIGHTWOOD RD

BROWNEDGE CL

BUXTON

Fairfield Common

Nunsfield Farm

Corbar Hill

WILLIAMSON AVE

LADYCROFT

HOGSHAW DR

HORSHAWDALE RD

NUNSFIELD RD

BARMS WAY

GLENMOOR RD

ST PETER'S RD

LINKS VIEW

NORTH RD

DAKIN CT

TOWN END

PH CH

Townend Farm

1

WYE HO

CORBAR RD

PERRYTON WAY

BIRCH CL

ASPEN

CHESTNUT CL

LANSDOWNE RD

St Anne's RC Prim Sch

SYCAMORE CL

DAKIN

GOLF PL

CROSS ST

MONTPELIER PL

CHERRYTREE DR

ASHWOOD RD

LESSER

WATERSWALLOWS MS

Corbar Woods

CORBAR WOODS LA

LASCELLES RD

74

| **05** | A | **06** | B | C | **06** | C | D | **07** | E | F |

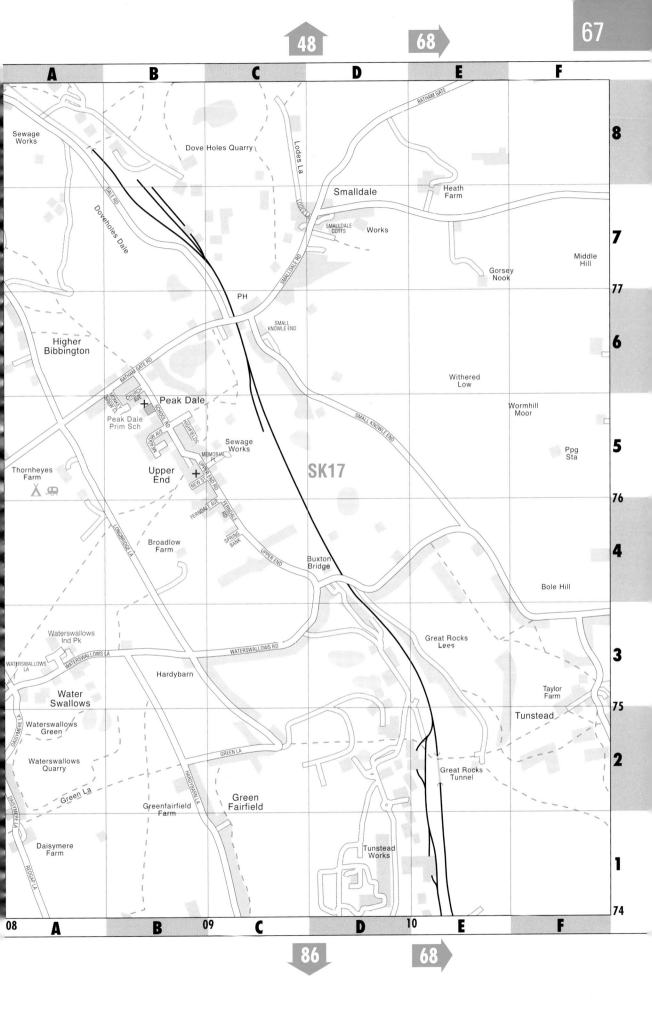

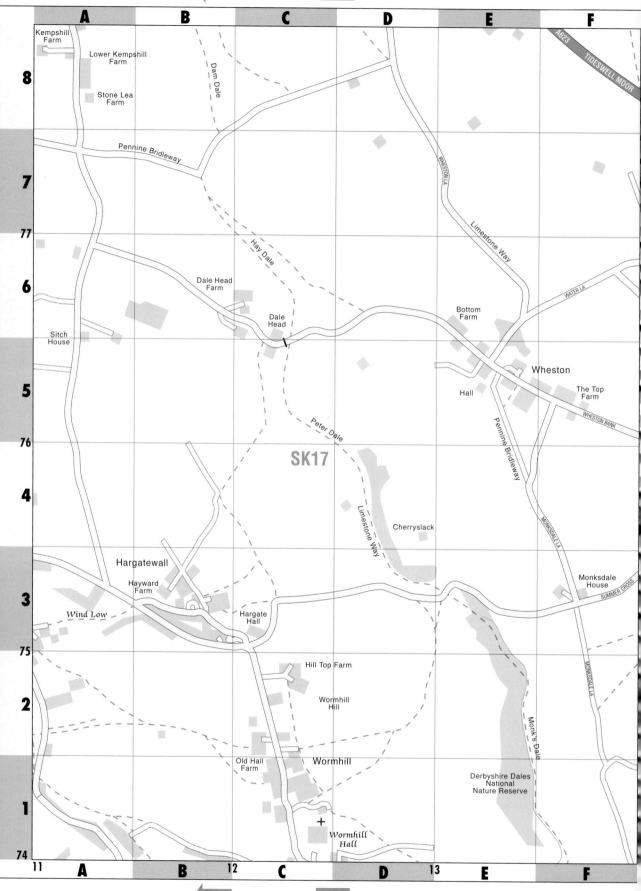

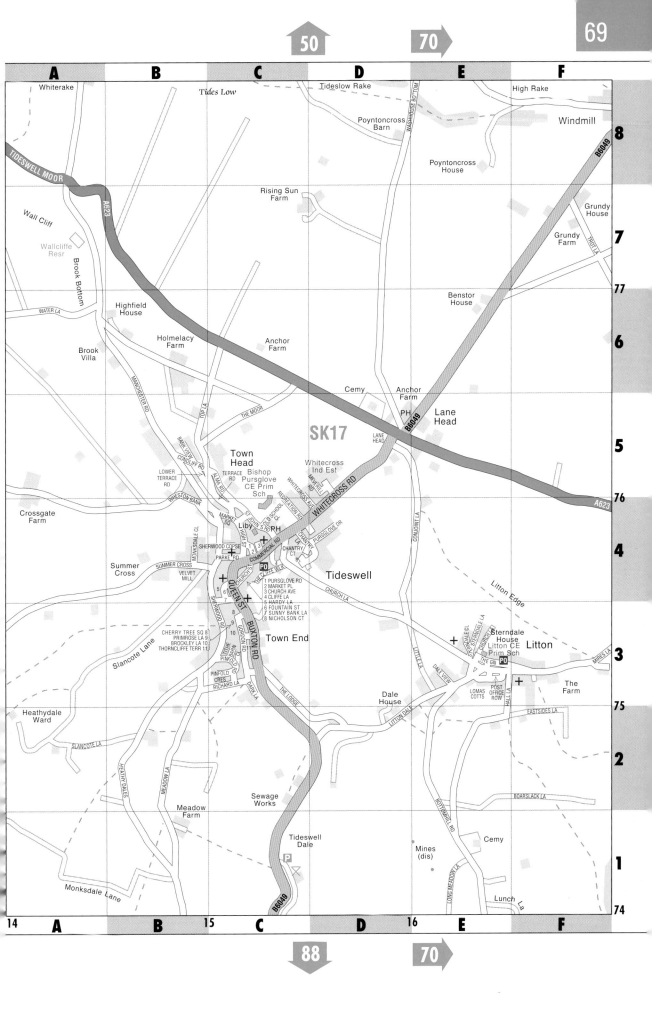

A   B   C   D   E   F

Whiterake

Tides Low

Tideslow Rake

High Rake

8

Windmill

B6049

Poyntoncross Barn

WASHHOUSE BOTTOM

Poyntoncross House

Rising Sun Farm

Grundy House

7

Wall Cliff

A623

Grundy Farm

TROIT LA

77

Wallcliffe Resr

Brook Bottom

Benstor House

Highfield House

WATER LA

Holmelacy Farm

MANCHESTER RD

TOP LA

THE MOOR

Anchor Farm

Brook Villa

Cemy

Anchor Farm

PH

B6049

Lane Head

6

Crossgate Farm

LOWER TERRACE RD

BANK VIEW

CONDLIFF RD

WHESTON BANK

Town Head

TERRACE RD

ALMA RD

Bishop Pursglove CE Prim Sch

SK17

Whitecross Ind Est

WHITECROSS AVE

NEVFELL RD

RECREATION RD

WHITECROSS RD

LANE HEAD

CONDUINT LA

A623

5

76

Liby

ST JOHN ST

OLD SCHOOL CL

CHANTRY LA

PURSGLOVE DR

MARKET SQ

COMMERCIAL RD

PH

MONKSDALE CL

Sherwood Copse

PARKE RD

CHANTRY CT

4

Summer Cross

SUMMER CROSS

VELVET MILL

PO

Pursglove Rd

1 PURSGLOVE RD
2 MARKET PL
3 CHURCH AVE
4 CLIFFE LA
5 HARDY LA
6 FOUNTAIN ST
7 SUNNY BANK LA
8 NICHOLSON CT

Tideswell

Litton Edge

QUEEN ST

SHERWOOD RD

CHURCH LA

CHURCH LA

STERNDALE LA

STERNDALE CL

CHURCH LA

Sterndale House

Litton CE Prim Sch

Litton

MIRES LA

3

CHERRY TREE SQ 8
PRIMROSE LA 9
BROCKLEY LA 10
THORNCLIFFE TERR 11

GORDON RD

BUXTON RD

Town End

THE GREEN

PINFOLD

DARK LA

LITTLE LA

DALE VIEW

PO

PINFOLD CRES

RICHARD LA

THE LODGE

GN

POST OFFICE ROW

HALL LA

The Farm

Slancote Lane

Dale House

LOMAS COTTS

EASTSIDES LA

75

Heathydale Ward

SLANCOTE LA

LITTON DALE

HEATHY DALES

MEADOW LA

Meadow Farm

Sewage Works

BOTTOMMILL RD

BOARSLACK LA

2

Tideswell Dale

P

Mines (dis)

Cemy

1

LONG MEADOW LA

Monksdale Lane

B6049

Lunch La

74

A   B   C   D   E   F

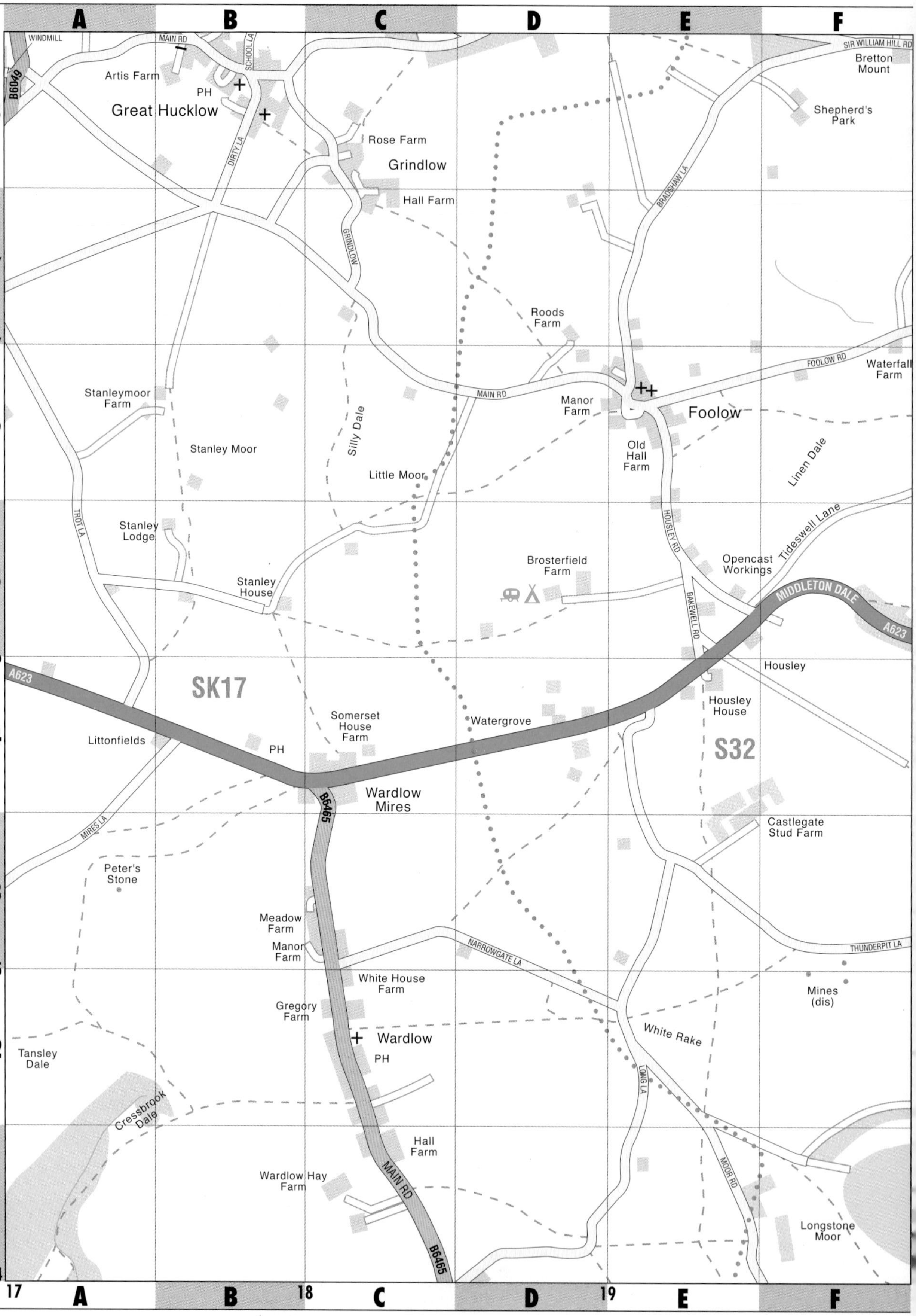

8

WINDMILL

MAIN RD

SIR WILLIAM HILL RD

Bretton
Mount

B6049

Artis Farm

SCHOOL LA

PH

Great Hucklow

DIRTY LA

Shepherd's
Park

Rose Farm

Grindlow

Hall Farm

GRINDLOW

BRADSHAW LA

7

77

Roods
Farm

FOOLOW RD

Waterfall
Farm

Stanleymoor
Farm

MAIN RD

Manor
Farm

Foolow

6

Stanley Moor

Silly Dale

Little Moor

Old
Hall
Farm

Linen Dale

TROT LA

Tideswell Lane

HOUSLEY RD

Opencast
Workings

Stanley
Lodge

Brosterfield
Farm

Housley

BAKEWELL RD

MIDDLETON DALE

5

Stanley
House

A623

76

A623

SK17

Housley
House

Littonfields

Somerset
House
Farm

PH

Watergrove

S32

4

MIRES LA

B6465

Wardlow
Mires

Castlegate
Stud Farm

3

Peter's
Stone

Meadow
Farm

NARROWGATE LA

THUNDERPIT LA

Manor
Farm

75

White House
Farm

Mines
(dis)

Gregory
Farm

White Rake

2

Tansley
Dale

Wardlow

PH

LONG LA

Cressbrook
Dale

MAIN RD

Hall
Farm

MOOR RD

Longstone
Moor

Wardlow Hay
Farm

1

74

17   A   B   18   C   D   19   E   F

B6465

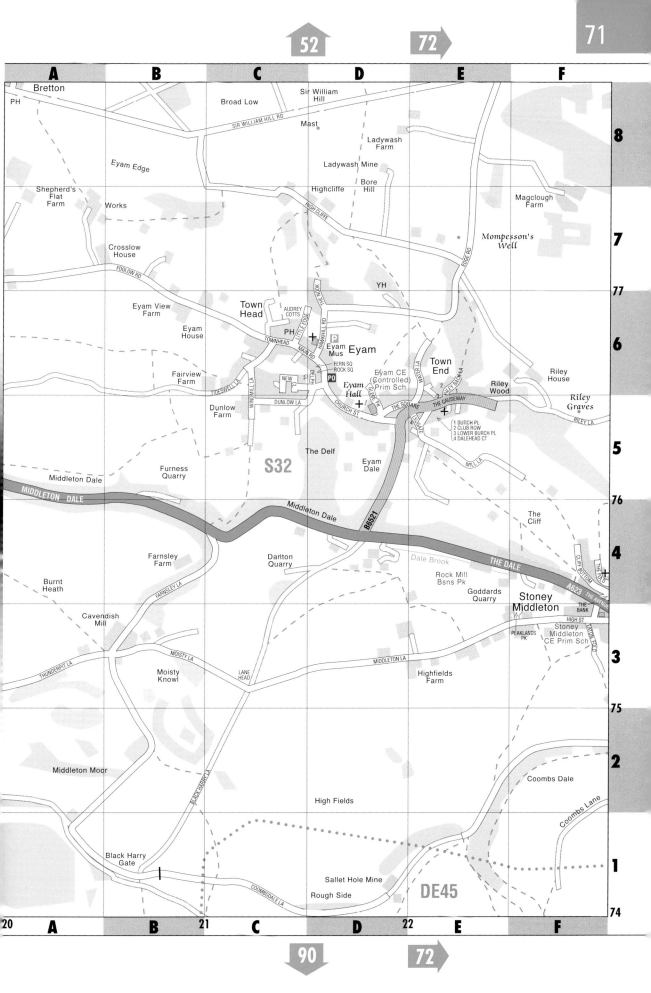

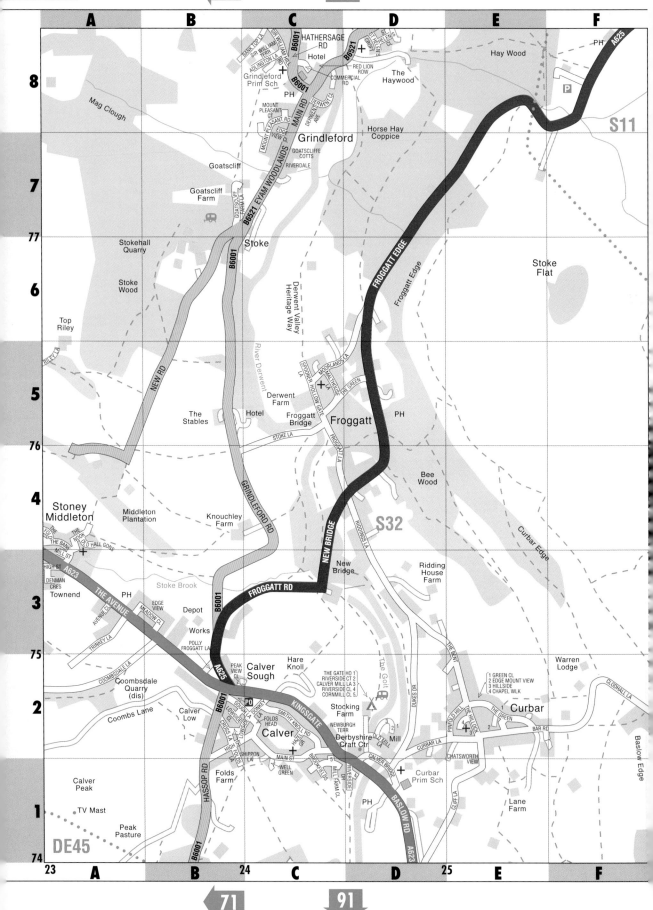

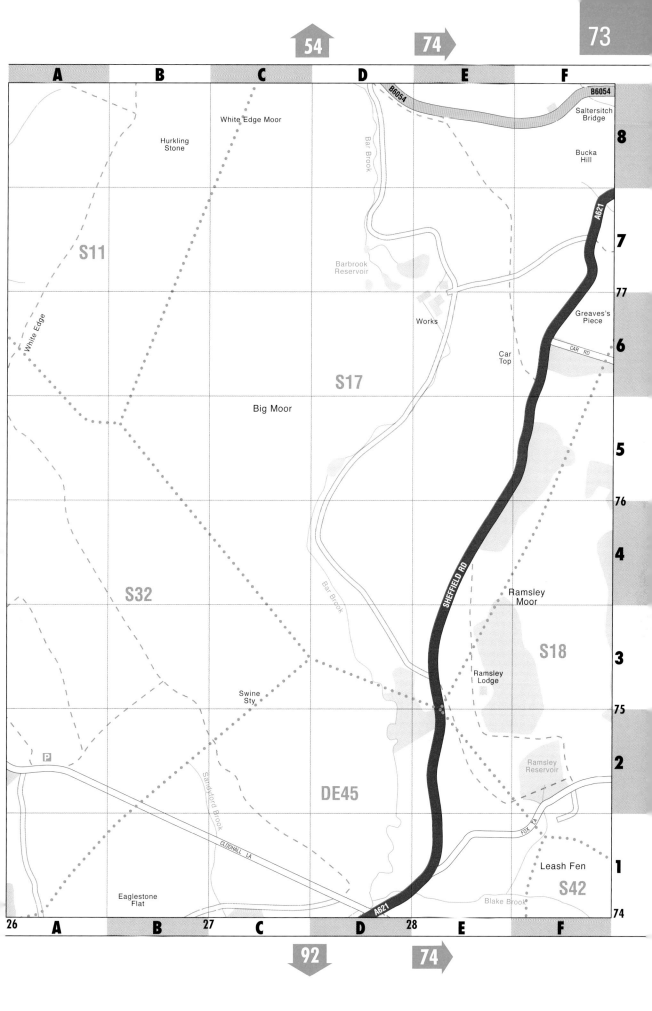

A B C D E F

B6054
B6054

Saltersitch
Bridge

White Edge Moor

8

Hurkling
Stone

Bucka
Hill

Bar Brook

S11

A621

7

White Edge

Barbrook
Reservoir

77

Works

Greaves's
Piece

6

Car
Top

CAR RD

S17

Big Moor

5

76

Bar Brook

SHEFFIELD RD

4

S32

Ramsley
Moor

S18

3

Swine
Sty

Ramsley
Lodge

75

Sandyford Brook

P

DE45

Ramsley
Reservoir

2

CLODHALL LA

FOX LA

Leash Fen

1

Eaglestone
Flat

A621

Blake Brook

S42

74

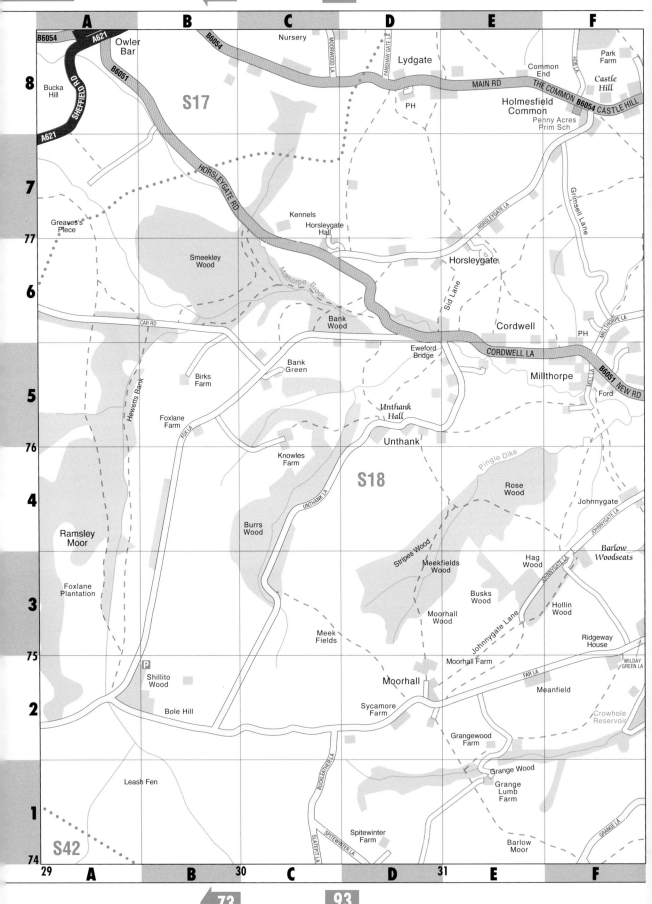

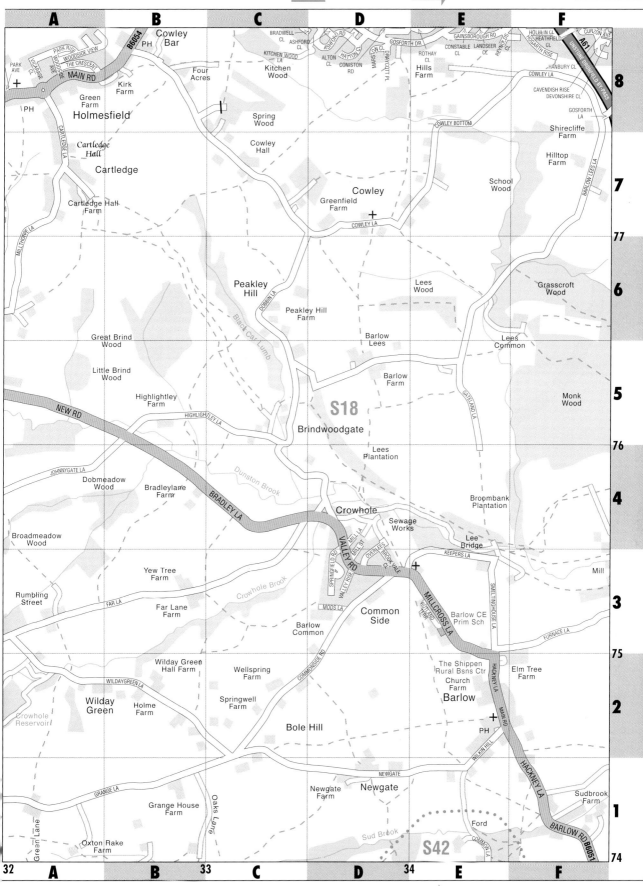

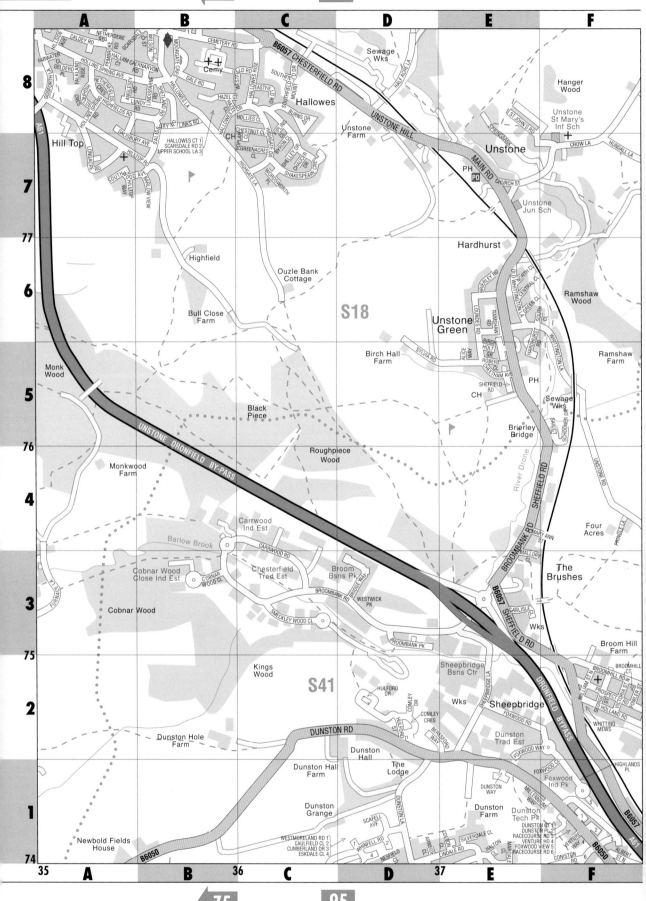

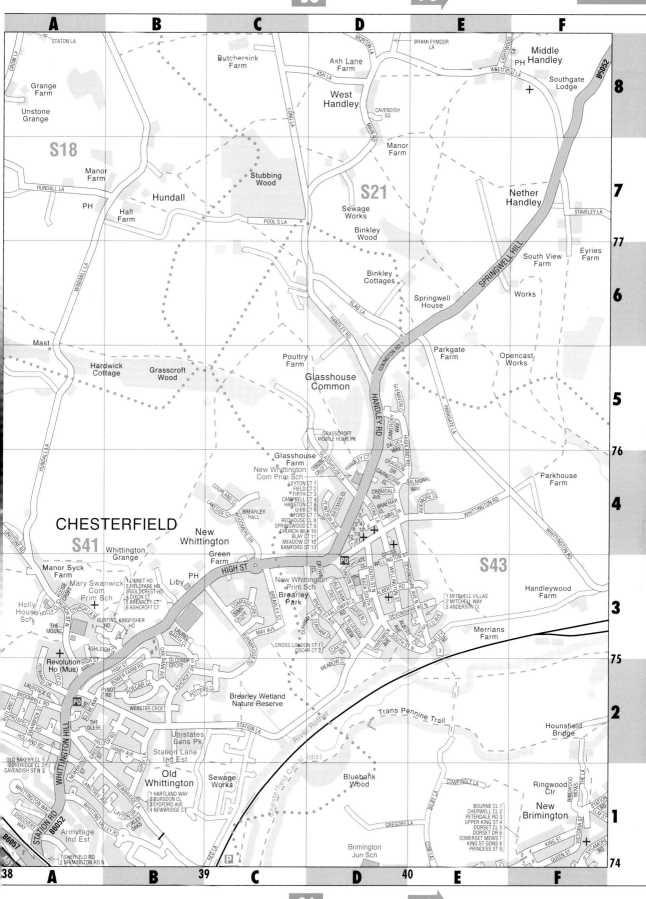

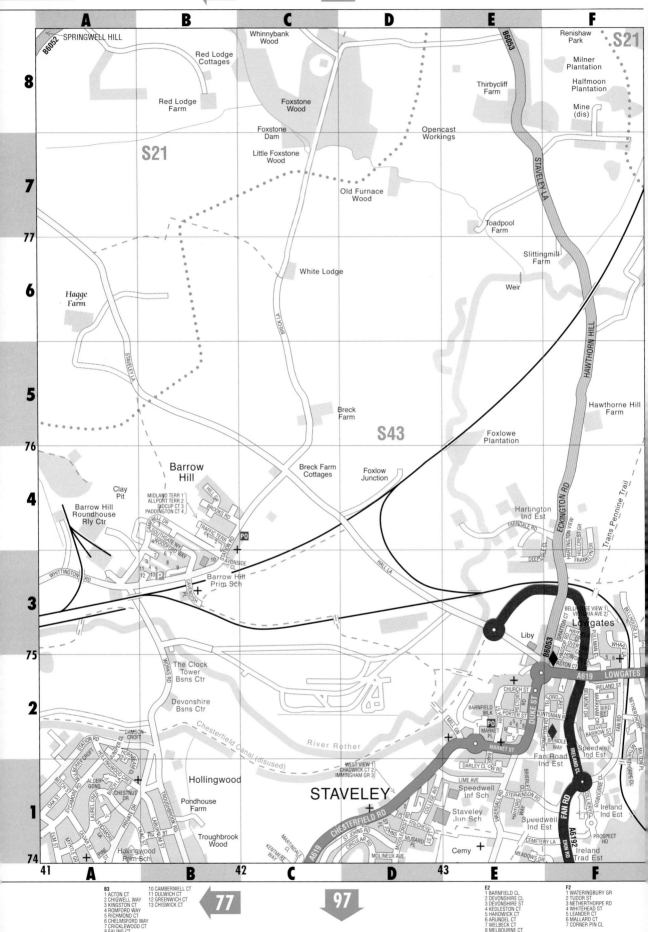

B3
1 ACTON CT
2 CHIGWELL WAY
3 KINGSTON CT
4 ROMFORD WAY
5 RICHMOND CT
6 CHELMSFORD WAY
7 CRICKLEWOOD CT
8 EALING CT
9 DUEWELL CT

10 CAMBERWELL CT
11 DULWICH CT
12 GREENWICH CT
13 CHISWICK CT

E2
1 BARNFIELD CL
2 DEVONSHIRE CL
3 DEVONSHIRE ST
4 KEDLESTON CT
5 HARDWICK CT
6 ARUNDEL CT
7 WELBECK CT
8 MELBOURNE CT
9 PORTER HO

F2
1 WATERINGBURY GR
2 TUDOR ST
3 NETHERTHORPE RD
4 WHITEHEAD ST
5 LEANDER CT
6 MALLARD CT
7 CORNER PIN CL

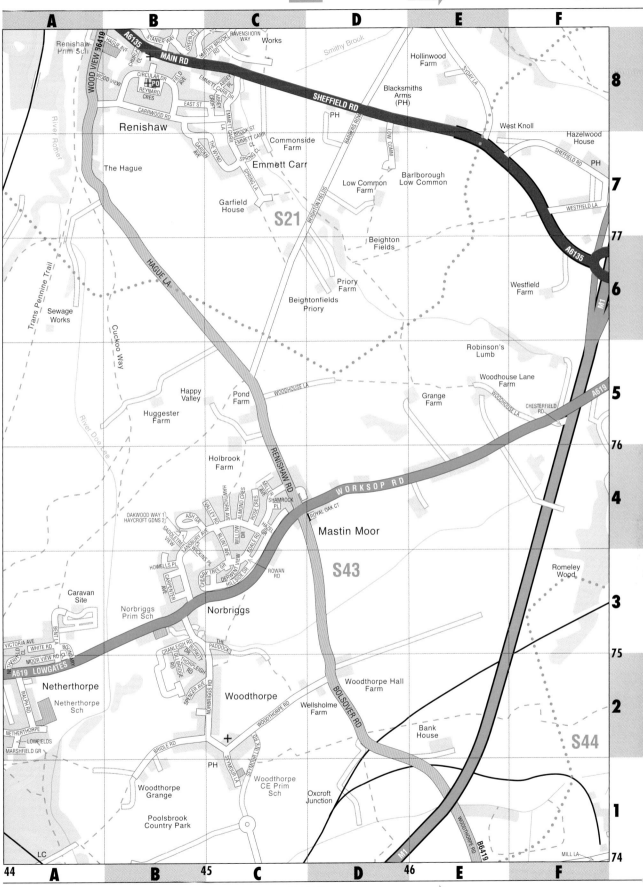

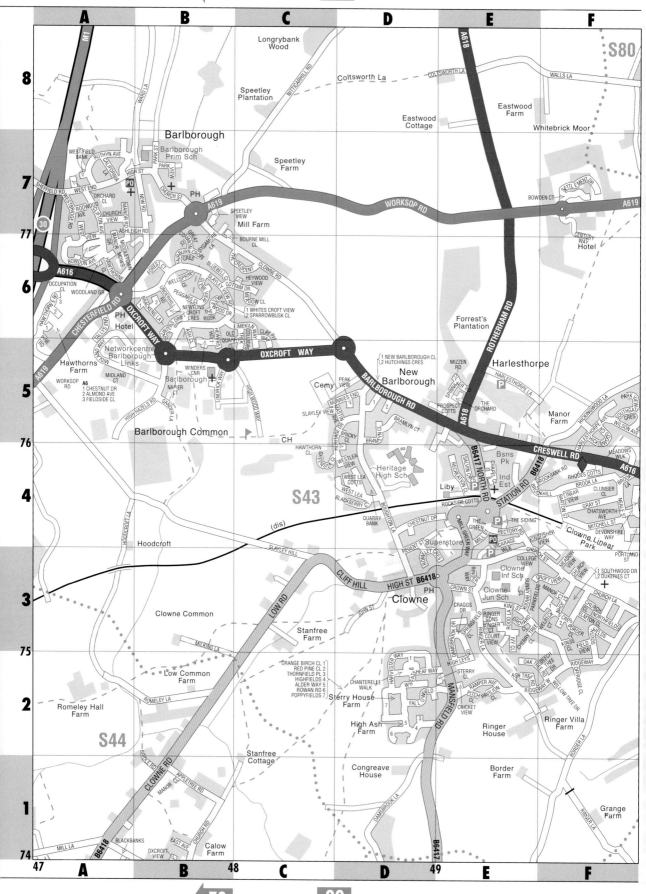

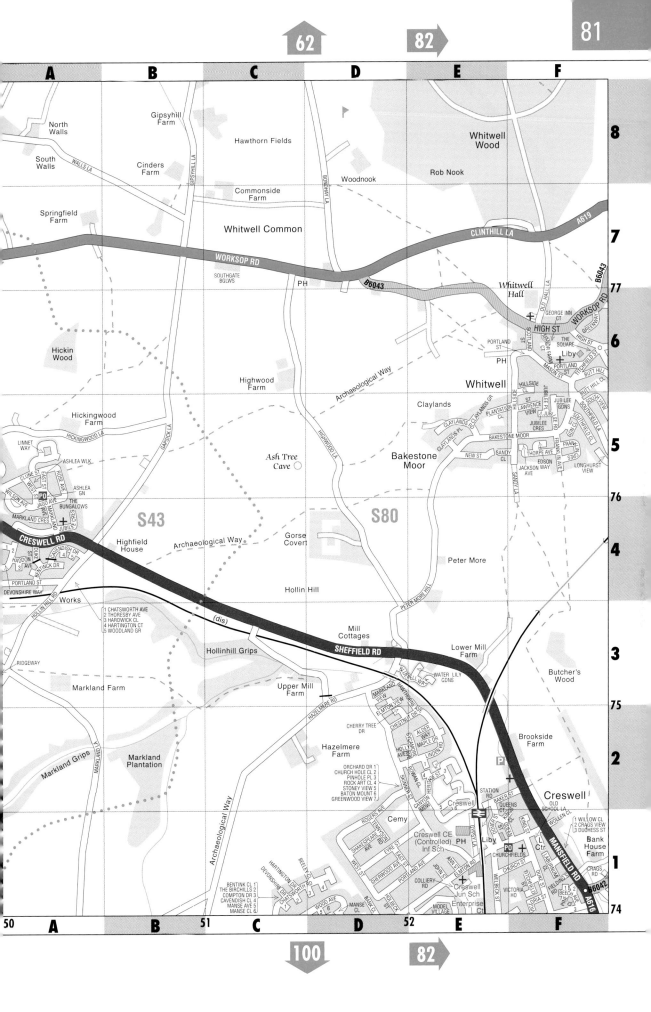

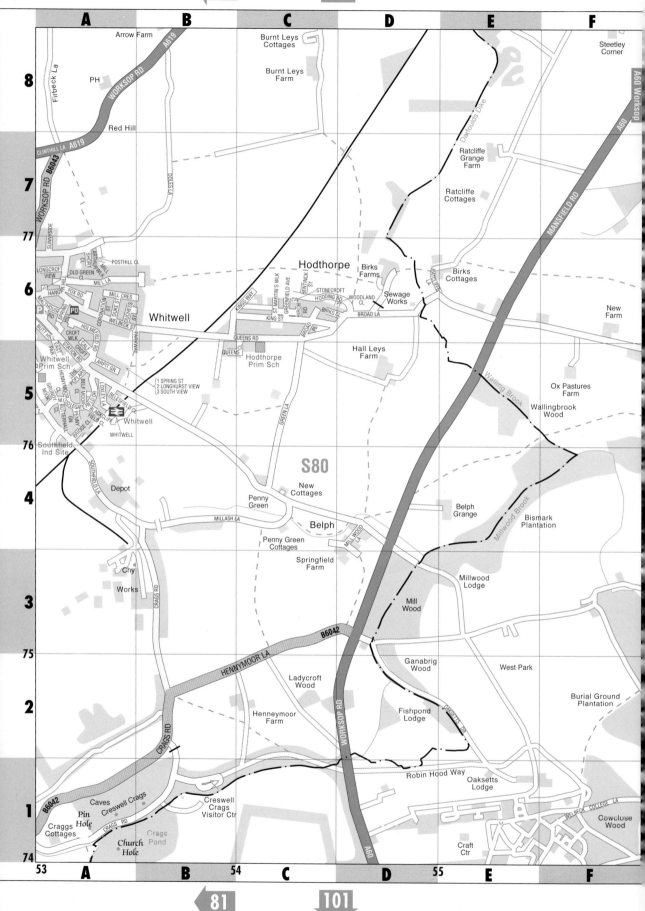

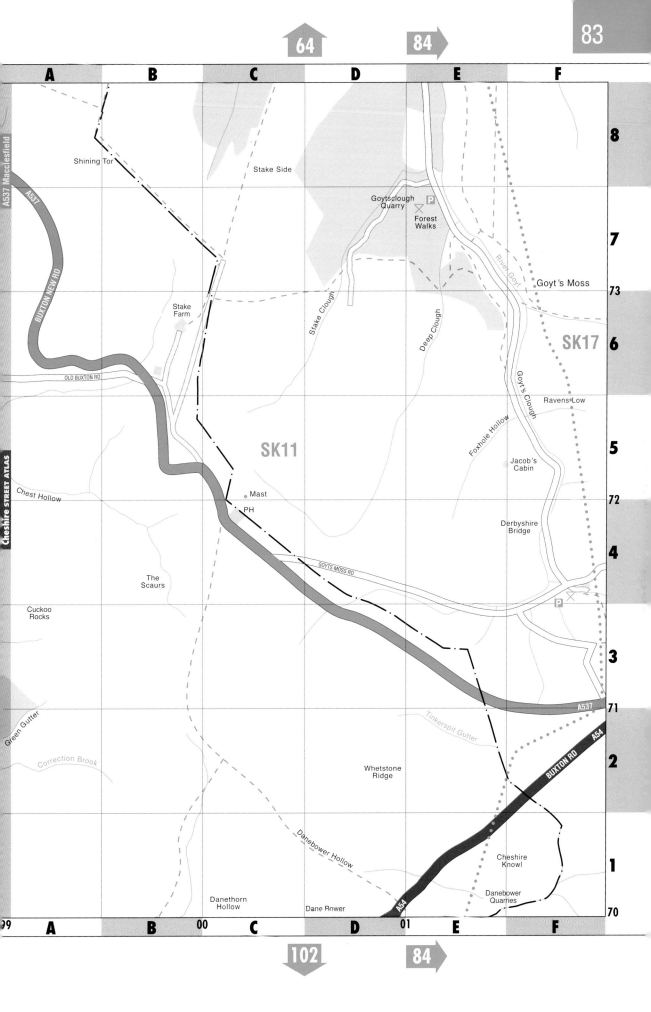

A B C D E F

8

Shining Tor

Stake Side

Goytsclough
Quarry

Forest
Walks

7

Goyt's Moss

73

SK17

Stake
Farm

Stake Clough

Deep Clough

River Goyt

6

OLD BUXTON RD

Goyt's Clough

Ravens Low

SK11

Chest Hollow

Foxhole Hollow

Jacob's
Cabin

5

Mast

PH

72

Derbyshire
Bridge

4

GOYTS MOSS RD

The
Scaurs

Cuckoo
Rocks

P

3

A537

71

Green Gutter

Tinkerspit Gutter

A54

BUXTON RD

2

Correction Brook

Whetstone
Ridge

Danebower Hollow

Cheshire
Knowl

1

Danethorn
Hollow

Dane Bower

A54

Danebower
Quarries

70

A B C D E F

A537 Macclesfield

BUXTON NEW RD

99

00

01

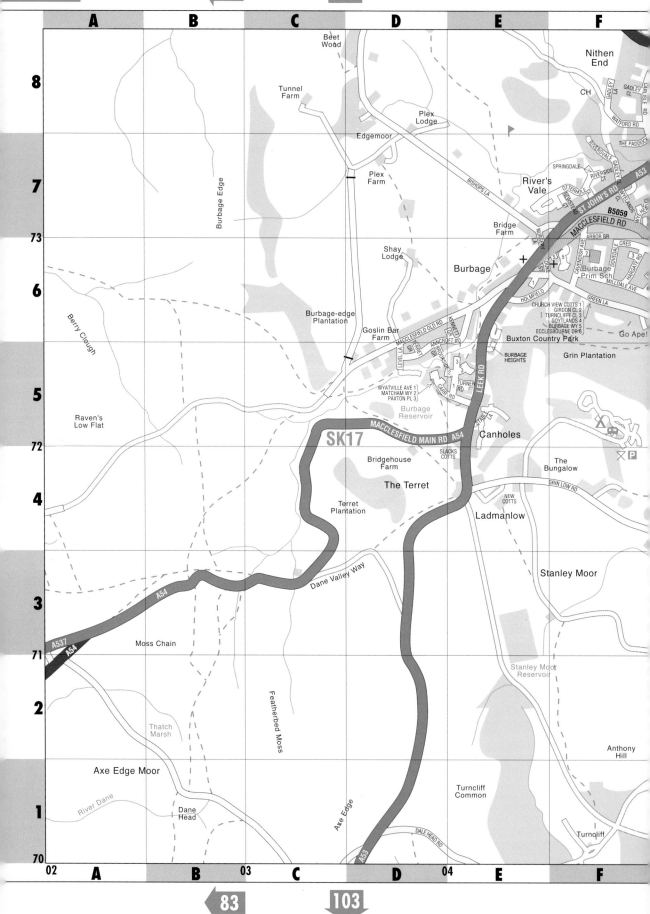

A   B   C   D   E   F

8

7

73

6

5

72

4

3

71

2

1

70

Beet Wood

Tunnel Farm

Burbage Edge

Plex Lodge

Edgemoor

Plex Farm

Shay Lodge

Burbage-edge Plantation

Goslin Bar Farm

Berry Clough

Raven's Low Flat

Macclesfield Old Rd

MACCLESFIELD MAIN RD   A54

SK17

Burbage Reservoir

Bridgehouse Farm

The Terret

Terret Plantation

Dane Valley Way

A54

Moss Chain

Featherbed Moss

Thatch Marsh

Axe Edge Moor

River Dane

Dane Head

Axe Edge

DALE HEAD RD

A53

Nithen End

CH

GADLEY LA
GADLEY CL
CARLISLE RD
WATFORD RD

RIVERSVALE GADLEY
RIVERSIDE CT
THE PADDOCK

SPRINGDALE

River's Vale

ST JOHN'S RD
A53
B5059
MACCLESFIELD RD

BISHOPS LA

Bridge Farm

Burbage

ARBOR GR
CAVENDISH AVE
DOVEDALE CRES
HARGATE RD
Burbage Prim Sch
MILLDALE AVE
GREEN LA

Go Ape!

CHURCH VIEW COTTS 1
GIRDON CL 2
TURNCLIFFE CL 3
GOYTLANDS 4
BURBAGE WY 5
ECCLESBOURNE DR 6

Buxton Country Park

Grin Plantation

LEVEL LA
TERRET GR
ANNCROFT RD
KENNETT GR
BROOKSIDE GR
CARR RD
TURNER RD
LEEK RD

WYATVILLE AVE 1
MATCHAM WY 2
PAXTON PL 3

BURBAGE HEIGHTS

Canholes

STABLE LA

SLACKS COTTS

The Bungalow

GRIN LOW RD

NEW COTTS

Ladmanlow

Stanley Moor

Stanley Moor Reservoir

Turncliff Common

Anthony Hill

Turncliff

02   A   B   03   C   D   04   E   F

A7
1 SOUTHCROFT
2 SOUTHWOOD
3 NORMANTON HO
4 ST JOHN'S

B8
1 LOWER HARDWICK ST
2 GROVE PAR
3 THE COLONNADE
4 OLD COURT HOUSE SHOPS
5 QUADRANT MEWS
6 CAVENDISH CIR

7 GEORGE ST
8 THE SAVOY
9 Buxton Baths

B6
1 BELVEDERE TERR
2 WEST ROAD HO
3 NEWSTEAD TERR

B7
1 BELMONT TERR
2 THE SAVOY
3 PAVILION MANS
4 EAGLE ST
5 HARDWICK GDNS
6 CONCERT PL

7 MARKET PL
8 SCARSDALE PL
9 EAGLE PAR
10 SOUTH MEWS
11 HARTINGTON GDNS
12 MILTON CT
13 SANDRINGHAM CT

14 ST JAMES ST
15 MARKET VIEW
16 ODDFELLOWS COTTS
17 Buxton Mus &
   Art Gall

C8
1 HOGSHAW VILLAS RD
2 HOLMWOOD TERR
3 LIGHTWOOD AVE
4 CHARLES ST
5 MARLOW ST
6 BRIAR CL

D8
1 STATION WLK
2 VICTORIA AVE
3 WESLEY HO
4 NORTHLANDS
5 MONTPELIER GDNS

66   86   **85**

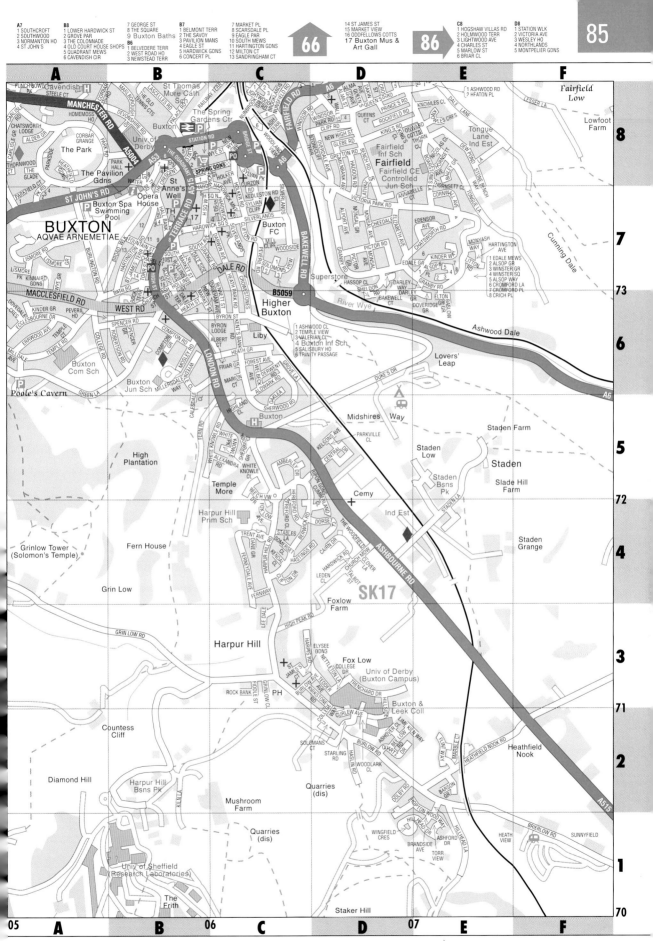

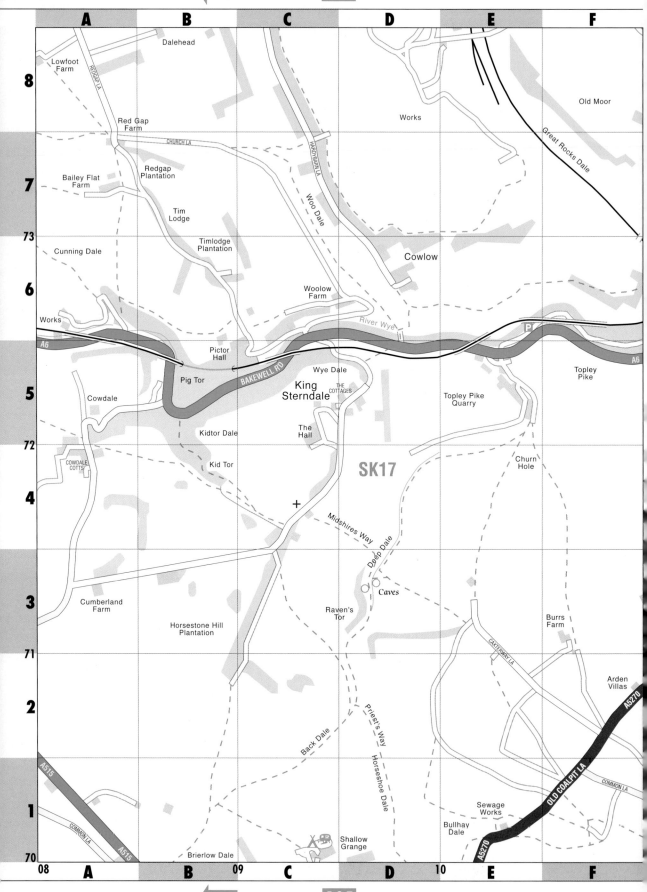

A   B   C   D   E   F

8

Lowfoot Farm

Dalehead

Old Moor

Red Gap Farm

CHURCH LA

Works

Great Rocks Dale

7

Bailey Flat Farm

Redgap Plantation

Tim Lodge

HARDYBARN LA

WOO DALE

73

Cunning Dale

Timlodge Plantation

Cowlow

6

Woolow Farm

River Wye

Works

A6

Pictor Hall

Pig Tor

BAKEWELL RD

Wye Dale

King Sterndale

THE COTTAGES

Topley Pike Quarry

Topley Pike

A6

5

Cowdale

Kidtor Dale

The Hall

72

COWDALE COTTS

Kid Tor

SK17

Churn Hole

4

+

Midshires Way

Deep Dale

Caves

3

Cumberland Farm

Horsestone Hill Plantation

Raven's Tor

CAXTERWAY LA

Burrs Farm

71

Arden Villas

A5270

2

Priest's Way

Back Dale

Horseshoe Dale

OLD COALPIT LA

COMMON LA

A515

1

COMMON LA

A515

Sewage Works

Bullhay Dale

A5270

70

Brierlow Dale

Shallow Grange

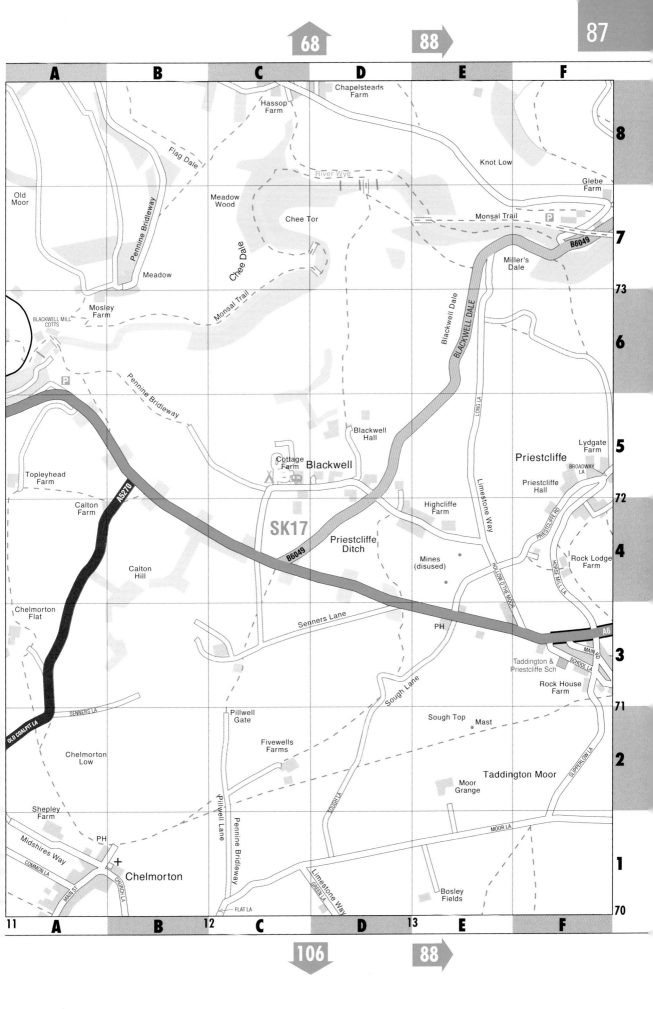

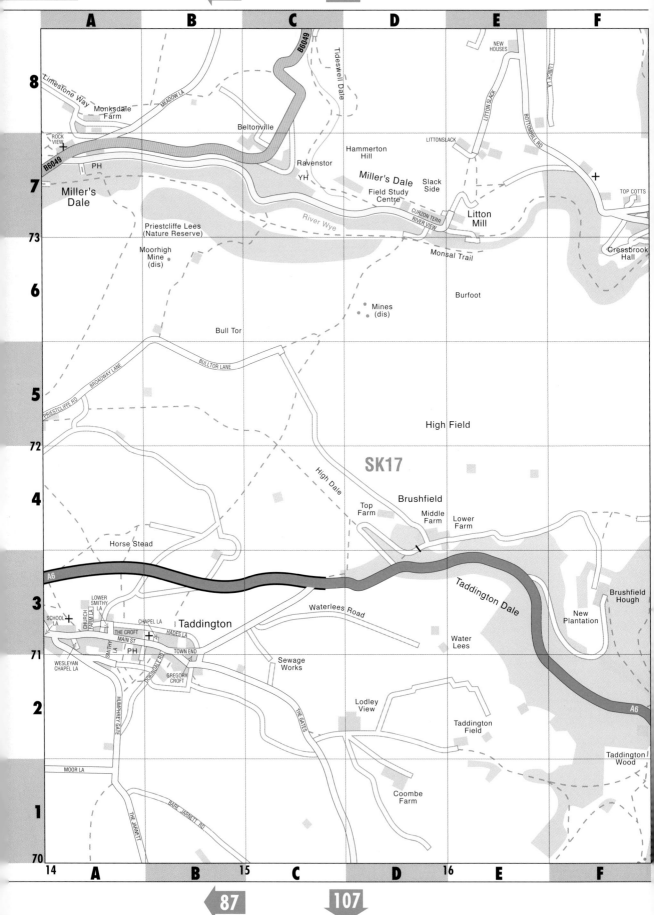

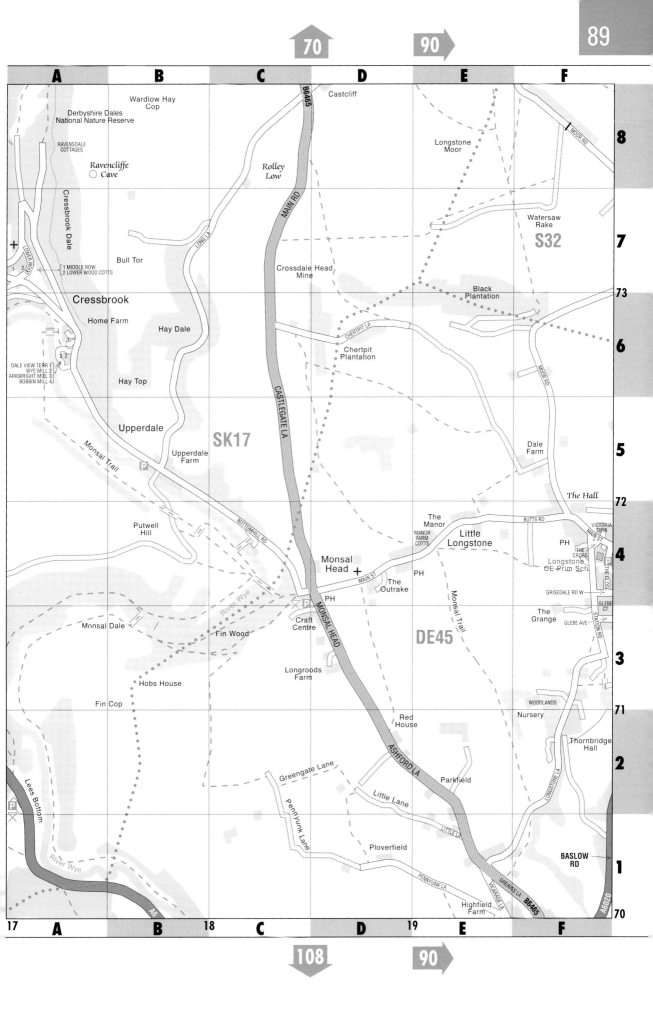

A B C D E F

17 A 18 B C 19 D E F

Wardlow Hay Cop
Derbyshire Dales National Nature Reserve
RAVENSDALE COTTAGES
Ravencliffe Cave
Rolley Low
Castcliff
Longstone Moor
MOOR RD
8
Watersaw Rake
S32
7
Cressbrook Dale
LOWER WOOD
LONG LA
Bull Tor
1 MIDDLE ROW
2 LOWER WOOD COTTS
Crossdale Head Mine
73
Cressbrook
Home Farm
Hay Dale
CHERTPIT LA
Chertpit Plantation
Black Plantation
6
DALE VIEW TERR 1
WYE MILL 2
ARKWRIGHT MILL 3
BOBBIN MILL 4
Hay Top
MOOR RD
CASTLEGATE LA
Upperdale
SK17
Dale Farm
5
Monsal Trail
Upperdale Farm
P
The Hall
72
Putwell Hill
BOTTOMHILL RD
The Manor
Little Longstone
MANOR FARM COTTS
BUTTS RD
VICTORIA TERR
MAIN ST
PH
THE CROSS
Longstone CE Prim Sch
P
THE CLOSE
4
Monsal Head
MAIN ST
PH
The Outrake
Monsal Trail
GRISEDALE RD W
GLEBE CT
STATION RD
River Wye
P
Craft Centre
MONSAL HEAD
PH
DE45
The Grange
GLEBE AVE
Monsal Dale
Fin Wood
3
Longroods Farm
WOODLANDS
Nursery
71
Hobs House
Red House
Thornbridge Hall
Fin Cop
2
Greengate Lane
Parkfield
PENNYUNK LANE
Little Lane
LONGSTONE LA
Lees Bottom
P
LITTLE LA
Ploverfield
BASLOW RD
1
River Wye
PENNYUNK LA
GREAVES LA
VICARAGE LA
B6465
Highfield Farm
A6020
70
A6
B6465
MAIN RD

89
71

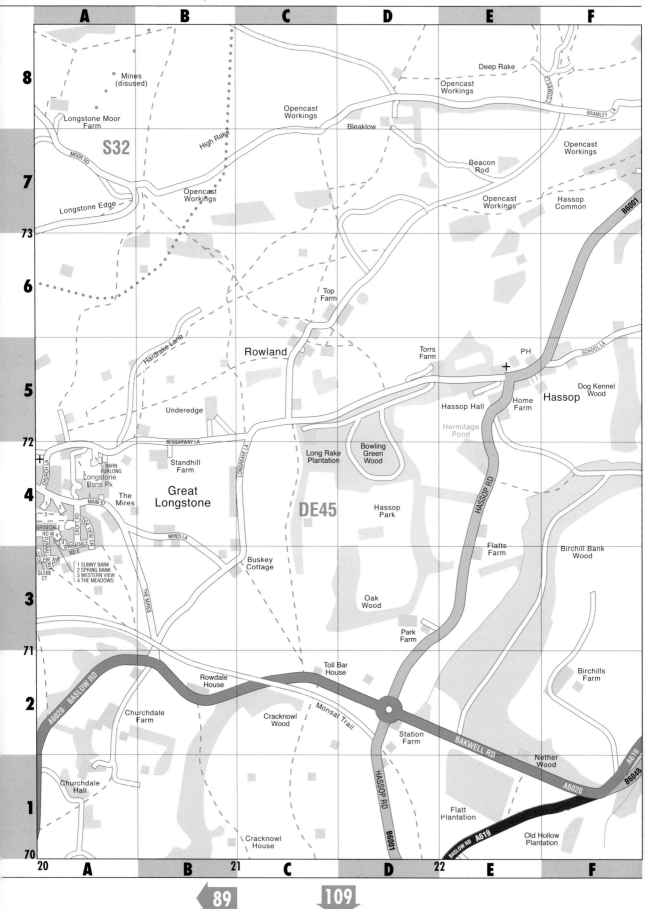

89
109

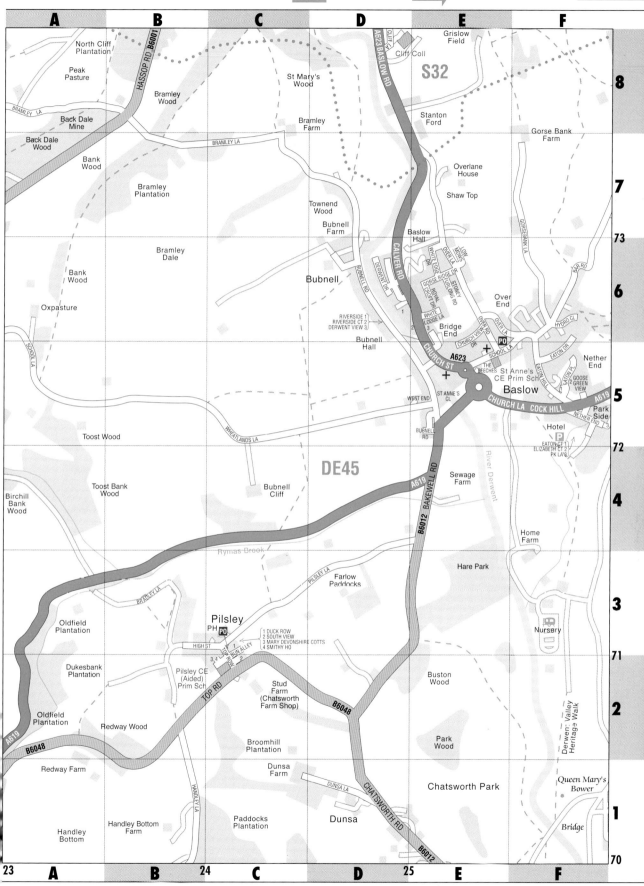

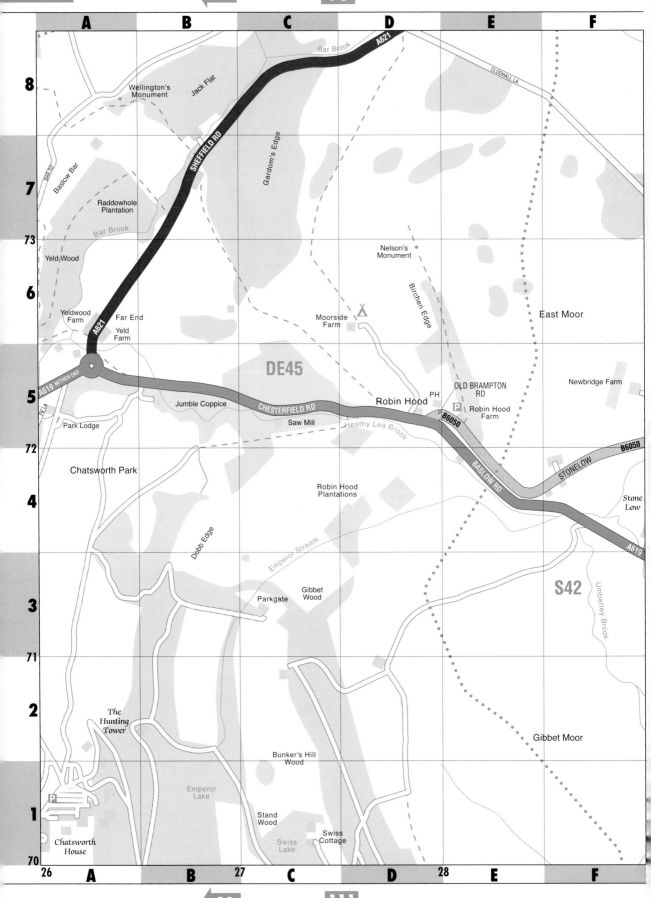

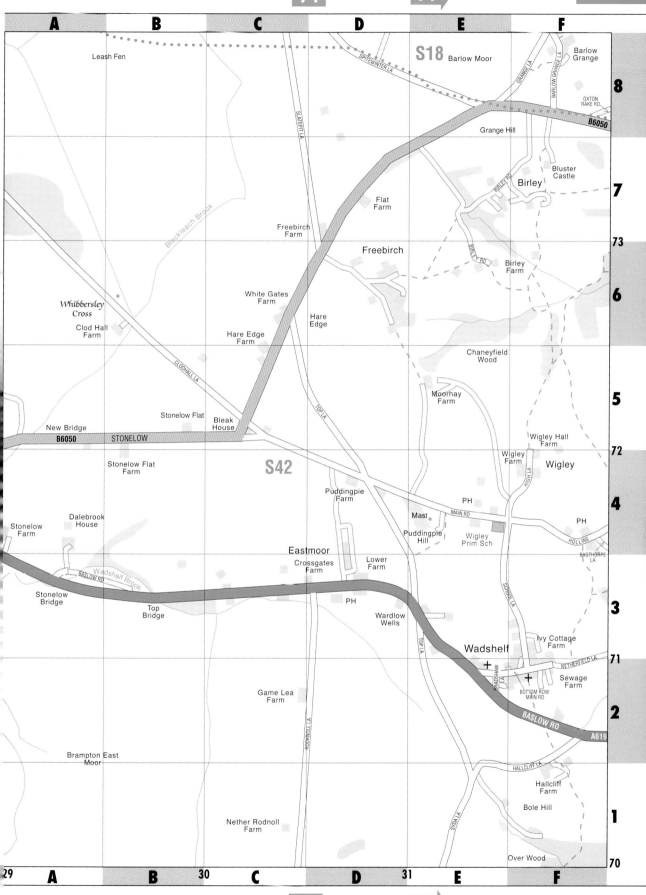

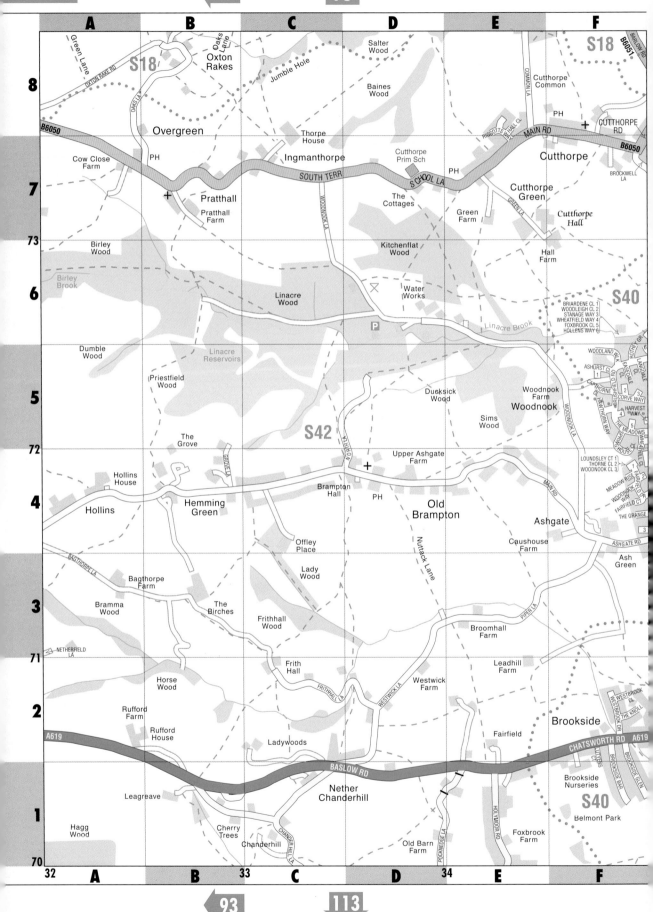

A B C D E F

S18

Green Lane

OXTON RAKE RD

Oaks Lane

8

S18

B6051

BARLOW RD

S18

Oxton Rakes

Salter Wood

CUTTHORPE RD

OAKS LA

Overgreen

Jumble Hole

Baines Wood

Cutthorpe Common

PH

B6050

Cow Close Farm

PH

Ingmanthorpe

Thorpe House

Cutthorpe Prim Sch

RIGGOTTS WAY

HALL CL

COMMON LA

MAIN RD

CUTTHORPE

B6050

PH

Cutthorpe

7

Pratthall

SOUTH TERR

SCHOOL LA

PH

Cutthorpe Green

BROCKWELL LA

Pratthall Farm

The Cottages

Green Farm

GREEN LA

Cutthorpe Hall

73

Birley Wood

WOODNOOK LA

Kitchenflat Wood

Hall Farm

6

Birley Brook

Linacre Wood

Water Works

Linacre Brook

S40

BRIARDENE CL 1
WOODLEIGH CL 2
STANAGE WAY 3
WHEATFIELD WAY 4
FOXBROOK CL 5
HOLLENS WAY 6

P

ROTHER CR

Dumble Wood

Linacre Reservoirs

WOODLAND WALK

LANGDALE

EASEDALE

Priestfield Wood

ASHURST CL

CAPTHORNE CL

CLOTHE CL

CORVE WAY

HAWTHORN WAY

HARVEST WAY

Woodnook Farm

Woodnook

WOODNOOK LA

THE MEADOWS

WHEATHILL CL

5

S42

Ducksick Wood

Sims Wood

MEADOWHEAD CL

LOUNDSLEY CT 1
THORNE CL 2
WOODNOOK CL 3

The Grove

GROVE LA

FAIRFIELD DR

72

Upper Ashgate Farm

MEADOW RISE

WOODNOOK WAY

FAIRFIELD CT

Hollins House

Brampton Hall

PH

Old Brampton

MAIN RD

THE GRANGE

4

Hollins

Hemming Green

Ashgate

Caushouse Farm

ASHGATE RD

Ash Green

BAGTHORPE LA

Offley Place

Lady Wood

Bagthorpe Farm

The Birches

3

Bramma Wood

Frithhall Wood

PIPER LA

Broomhall Farm

71

NETHERFIELD LA

Frith Hall

FRITHHALL LA

Leadhill Farm

Horse Wood

WESTWICK LA

Westwick Farm

WESTBROOK DR

WESTBROOK CL

THE KNOLL

2

Rufford Farm

Nuttack Lane

Brookside

Rufford House

Ladywoods

Fairfield

CHATSWORTH RD

A619

A619

BROOKSIDE BAR

LUMBS LA

BROOKSIDE DR

BROOKSIDE GLEN

A619

Leagreave

BASLOW RD

Nether Chanderhill

HOLYMOOR RD

Brookside Nurseries

S40

1

Hagg Wood

Cherry Trees

CHANDER HILL LA

Chanderhill

POCKNEDGE LA

Old Barn Farm

Foxbrook Farm

Belmont Park

70

32 A 33 B C 33 D 34 E F

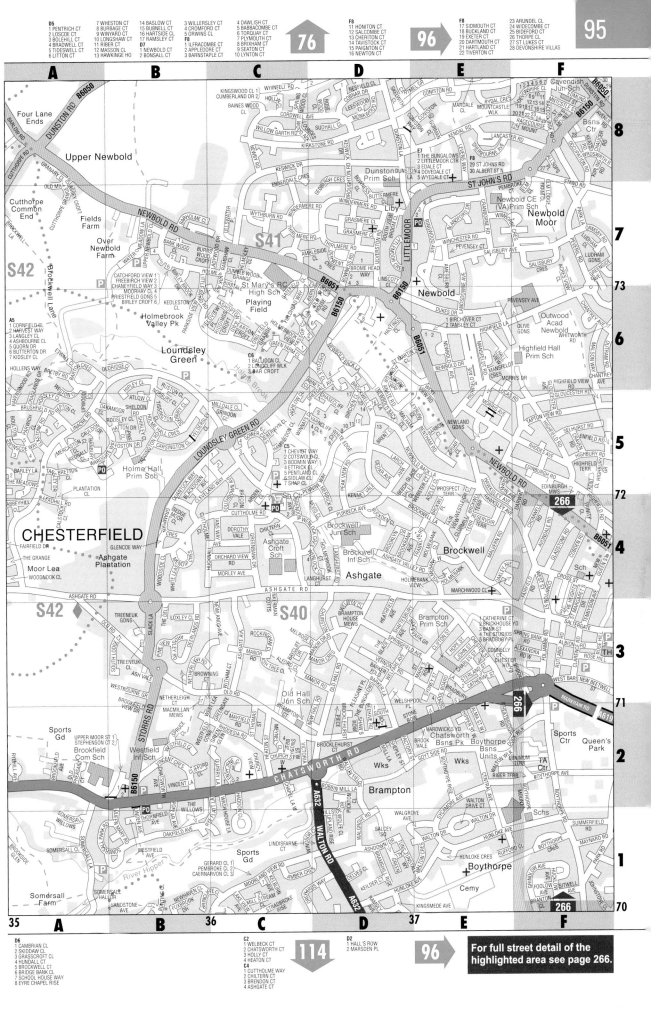

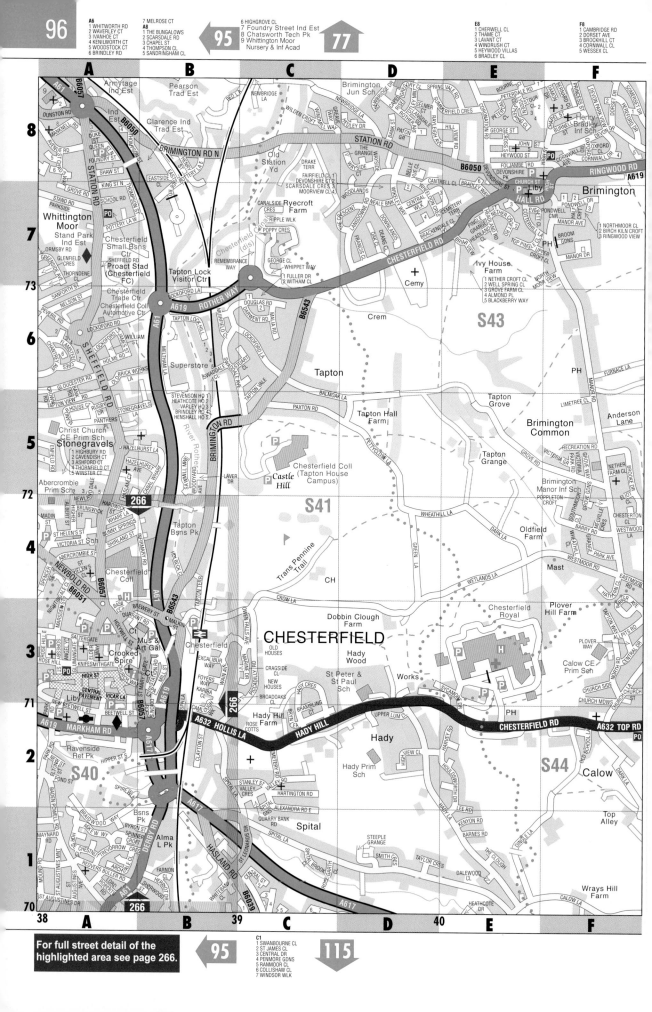

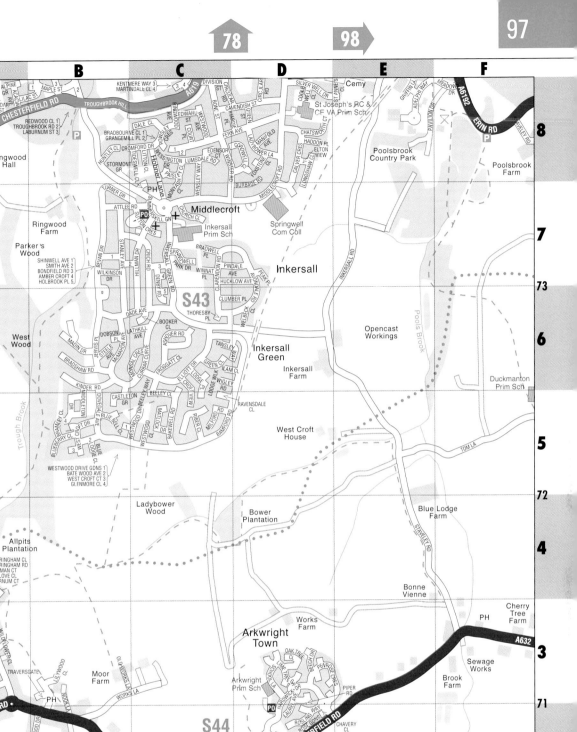

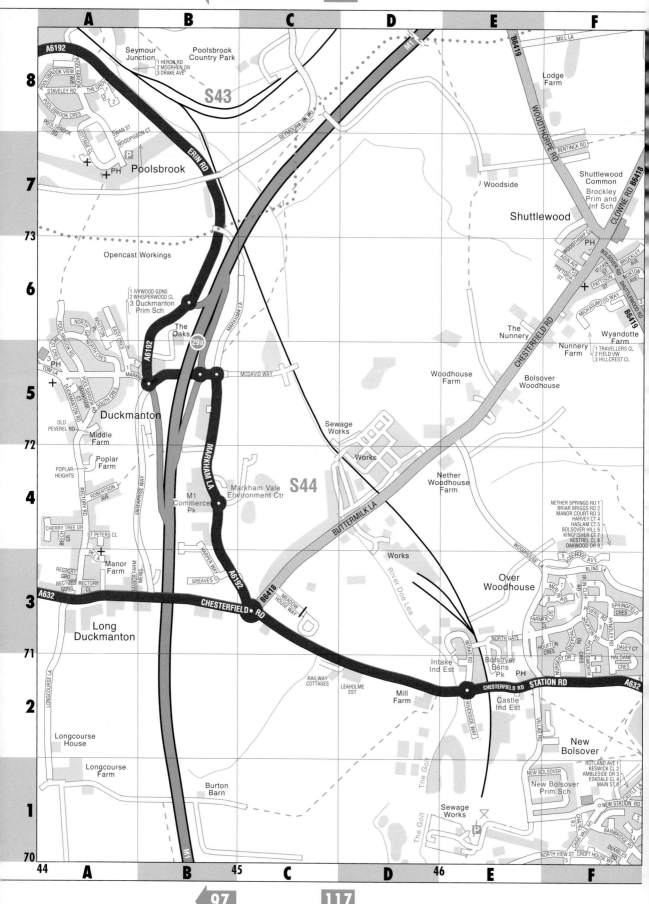

A B C D E F

RINGER LA

OXCROFT LA

Markland Farm

Grange Farm

MARKLAND LA

Elmton

+ THE SQUARE

SPRING LA

PH

MAIN RD

Elm Tree Farm

THE GREEN

Green Farm

HAZELMERE RD

WOOD LA

Camp Hill

Oaks Farm

CHATSWORTH RD

BULLMAN AVE

WOOD AVE

MANSE CL

CHASE AVE

RAILWAY AVE

CENTRAL AVE

ELMTON RD

OAKS AVE

BANK CL

ELMTON CT

WOOD LA

MODEL VILLAGE

MODEL VW

ELMTON WAY

FOX ST

FOX ST

COLLIERY RD

Creswell Bsns Pk

HAZELBY RD

WELBECK

MORVEN ST

DUCHESS ST

Crags Bsns Pk

A616

Fox Green

MANSFIELD RD

FRITHWOOD LA

S80

Archaeological Way

Frithwood Farm

FRITHWOOD LA

The Old Hag

OXPASTURE LA

Frith Wood

Whaley Hall

MAG LA

Whaley Moor

NORWOOD LA

LC

WHALEY RD

Norwood Farm

WHALEY COMM

WHALEY COMMON

Whaley Common

MOORFIELD LA

PH

Whaley

Grave Wood

Whaley Farm

WHALEY RD

NG20

Bolsover Moor Quarry

Mill Pond

Mill Farm

P

Whaley Thorns Ind Est

Langwith-Whaley Thorns

PARK VIEW

MAIN ST

BATHURST TERR

P

Poulter Country Park

S44

Scarcliffe Park

Owl Sick

WHALEY RD

PARK HILL

Apsley Grange

Owl Spring

Archaeological Way

River Poulter

P

PO

PH

A632 MAIN RD

LANGWITH MALTINGS

DEVONSHIRE DR

POULTER DR

BOUNDARY WLK

LANGWITH DALE

Scarcliffe Grange

50 A B 51 C D 52 E F

8 7 73 6 5 72 4 3 71 2 1 70

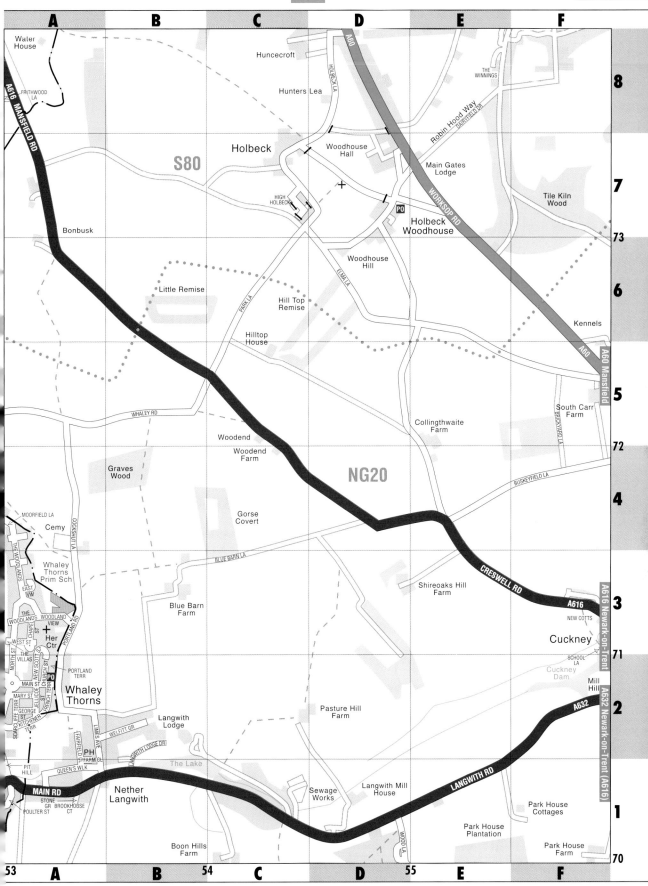

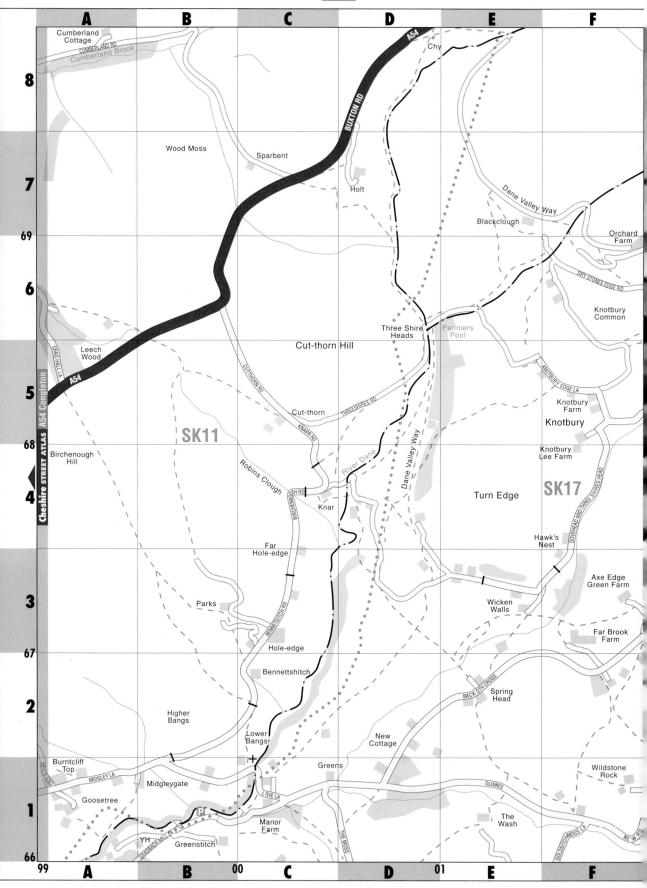

A B C D E F

8

7

69

6

5

68

4

3

67

2

1

66

99 00 01

A54

Cheshire STREET ATLAS

A54 Congleton

SK11

SK17

Cumberland Cottage

CUMBERLAND RD

Cumberland Brook

Wood Moss

Sparbent

BUXTON RD

A54

Chy

Holt

Dane Valley Way

Blackclough

Orchard Farm

DRY STONES EDGE RD

Knotbury Common

Three Shire Heads

Panniers Pool

Cut-thorn Hill

KNOTBURY EDGE LA

Knotbury Farm

Knotbury

Leech Wood

CRAG HALL LA

CUT-THORN RD

KNARR RD

Cut-thorn

THREESHIRES RD

Dane Valley Way

River Dane

Knotbury Lee Farm

Birchenough Hill

Robins Clough

BIRCHENOUGH RD

Knar

Turn Edge

Hawk's Nest

DOVEHEAD AND THREE SHIRES HEAD

Far Hole-edge

Axe Edge Green Farm

Parks

BENNETTSITCH RD

Hole-edge

Wicken Walls

Far Brook Farm

Bennettshitch

BACK O'TH CROSS

Spring Head

Higher Bangs

Lower Bangs

New Cottage

Greens

Wildstone Rock

Burntcliff Top

HELL'S KNOT

MIDGLEY LA

Midgleygate

LOVE LA

OLDIKES

THE MOSS

The Wash

NEW RD

GOLDSITCH-MOSS LA

Goosetree

P

YH

BROADRACH MILL LA

Greenstitch

Manor Farm

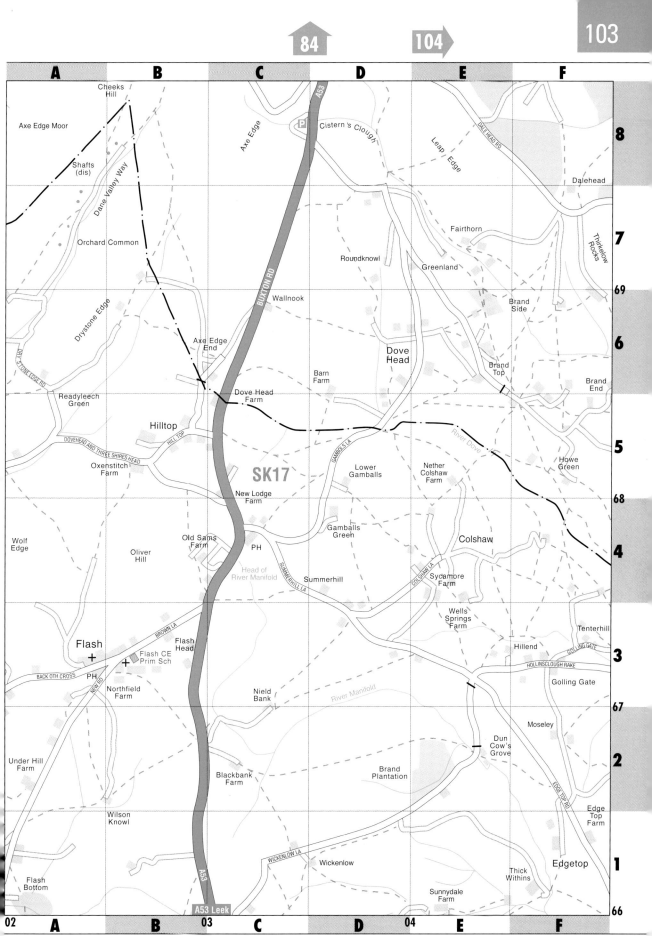

103
85

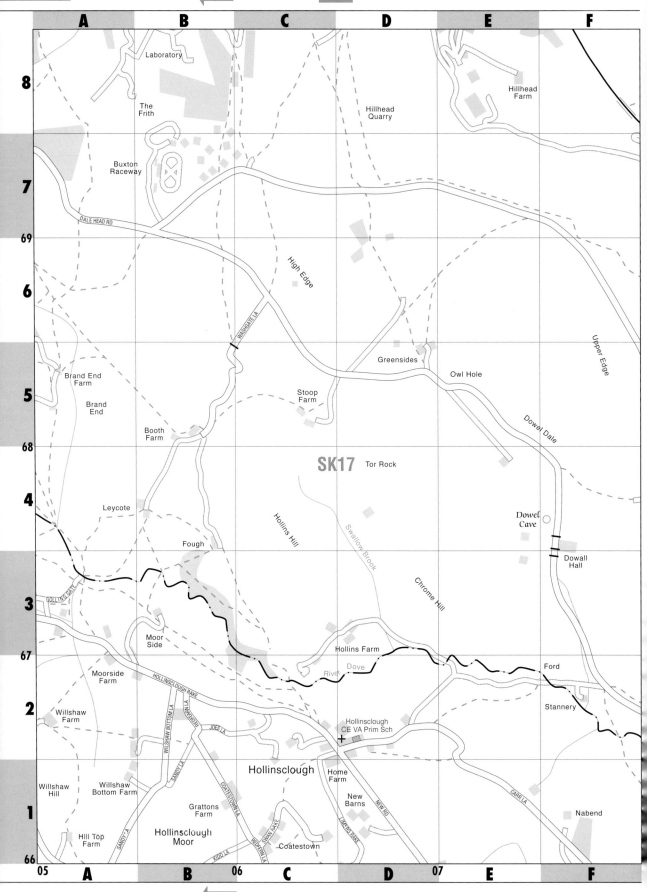

Laboratory

The Frith

Hillhead Farm

Hillhead Quarry

Buxton Raceway

DALE HEAD RD

69

High Edge

7

6

WASHGATE LA

Upper Edge

Brand End Farm

Greensides

Owl Hole

Brand End

Stoop Farm

Dowel Dale

Booth Farm

68

SK17   Tor Rock

Leycote

4

Hollins Hill

Swallow Brook

Dowel Cave

Fough

Chrome Hill

Dowall Hall

GOLLINS GATE

3

Moor Side

67

Hollins Farm

River   Dove

Ford

Moorside Farm

HOLLINSCLOUGH RAKE

Stannery

2

Willshaw Farm

WILSHAW BOTTOM LA

NEWTON LA

JOE'S LA

Hollinsclough CE VA Prim Sch

Willshaw Hill

Willshaw Bottom Farm

SANDY LA

COATESTOWN LA

Hollinsclough

Home Farm

New Barns

NEW RD

CARR LA

Nabend

Grattons Farm

SWAN GATE

LIMERS RAKE

Hill Top Farm

SANDY LA

KIDD LA

REDFERN LA

Hollinsclough Moor

Coatestown

66

05   A   B   06   C   D   07   E   F

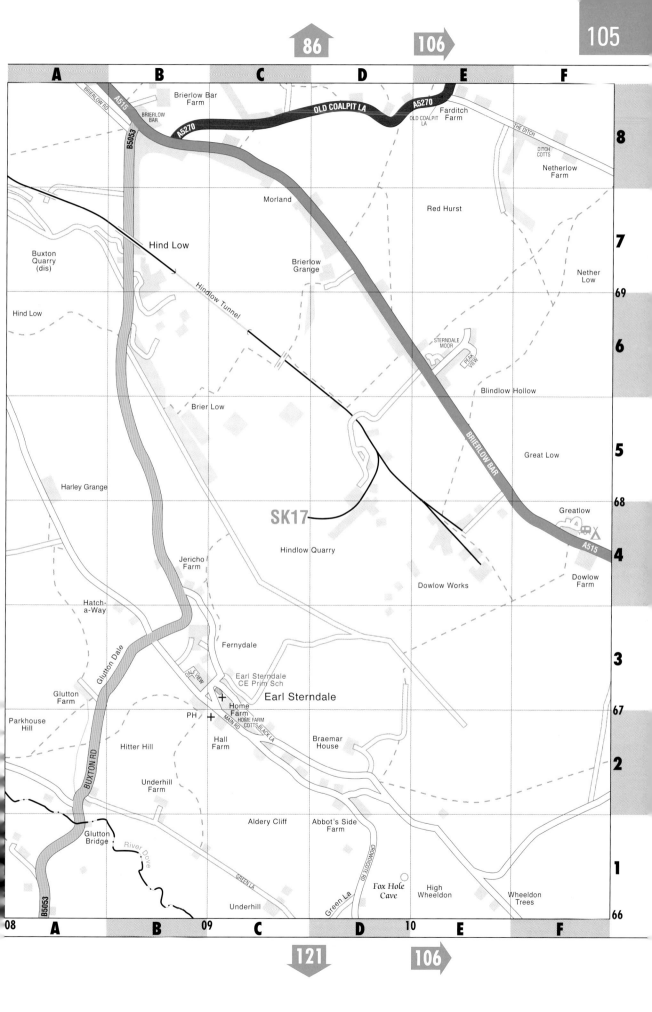

◀ 105
87 ▲

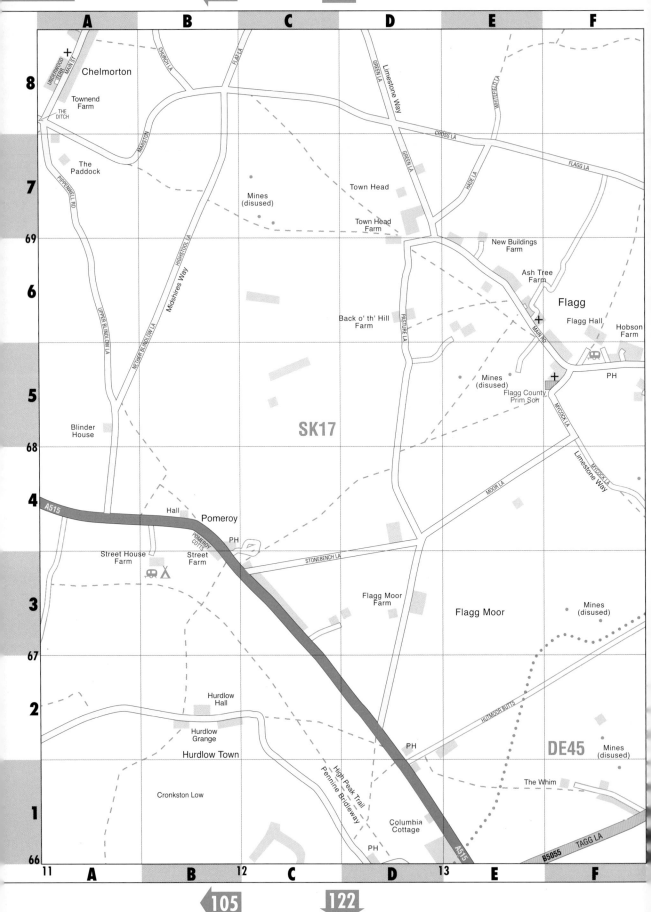

◀ 105
122 ▼

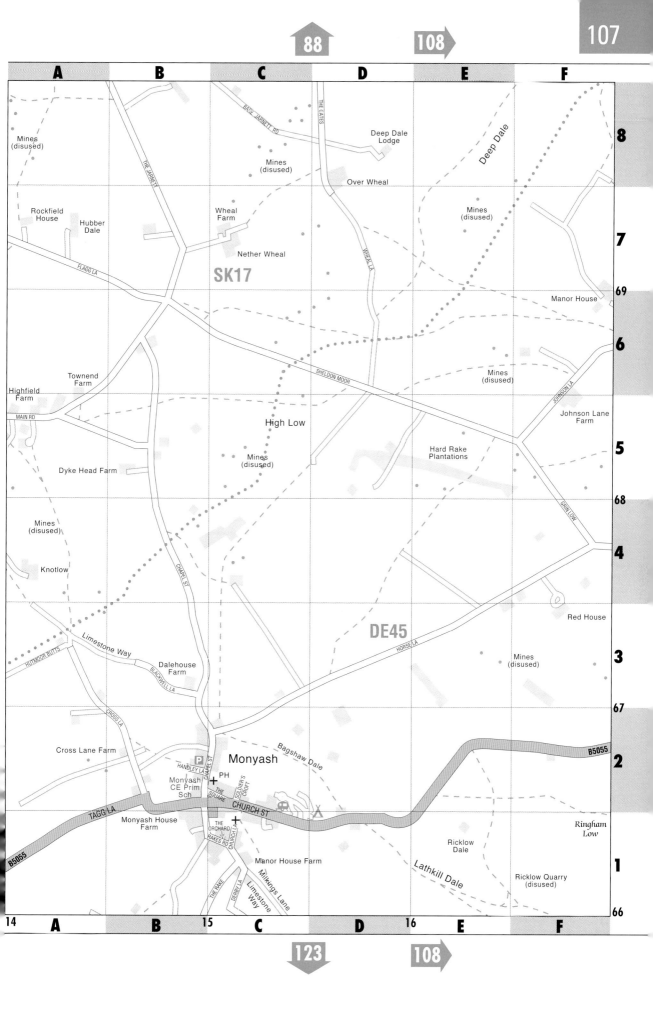

88
108
123
108

Mines (disused)

Rockfield House

Hubber Dale

FLAGG LA

THE JARNETT

BATE JARNETT RD

THE GATES

Deep Dale Lodge

Mines (disused)

Over Wheal

Deep Dale

Wheal Farm

Nether Wheal

SK17

WHEAL LA

Mines (disused)

Manor House

SHELDON MOOR

Highfield Farm

MAIN RD

Townend Farm

High Low

Mines (disused)

Hard Rake Plantations

Johnson Lane Farm

JOHNSON LA

Dyke Head Farm

Mines (disused)

GRIN LOW

Mines (disused)

Knotlow

CHAPEL ST

DE45

Red House

HORSE LA

Mines (disused)

Limestone Way

HUTMOOR BUTTS

Dalehouse Farm

BLACKWELL LA

CROSS LA

Cross Lane Farm

Bagshaw Dale

Monyash

P

HANDLEY LA

CHAPEL ST

PH

THE SQUARE

SOLDIER'S CROFT

B5055

Monyash CE Prim Sch

CHURCH ST

Ringham Low

TAGG LA

Monyash House Farm

THE ORCHARD

CHURCH LA

RAKES RD

B5055

Manor House Farm

THE RAKE

DERBY LA

Milkings Lane

Limestone Way

Ricklow Dale

Lathkill Dale

Ricklow Quarry (disused)

B5055

14   A   B   15   C   D   16   E   F   66

107
89

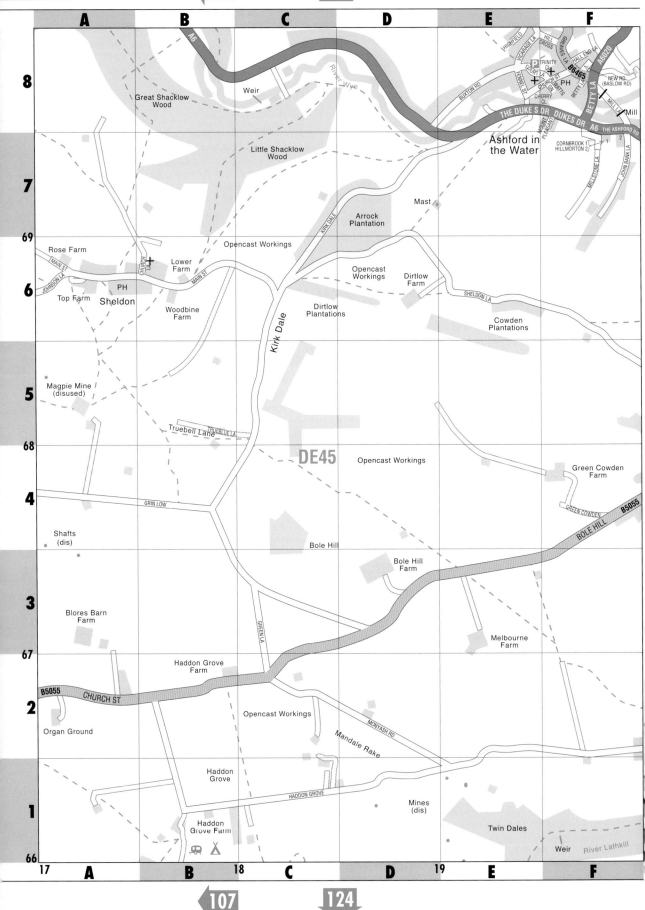

107
124

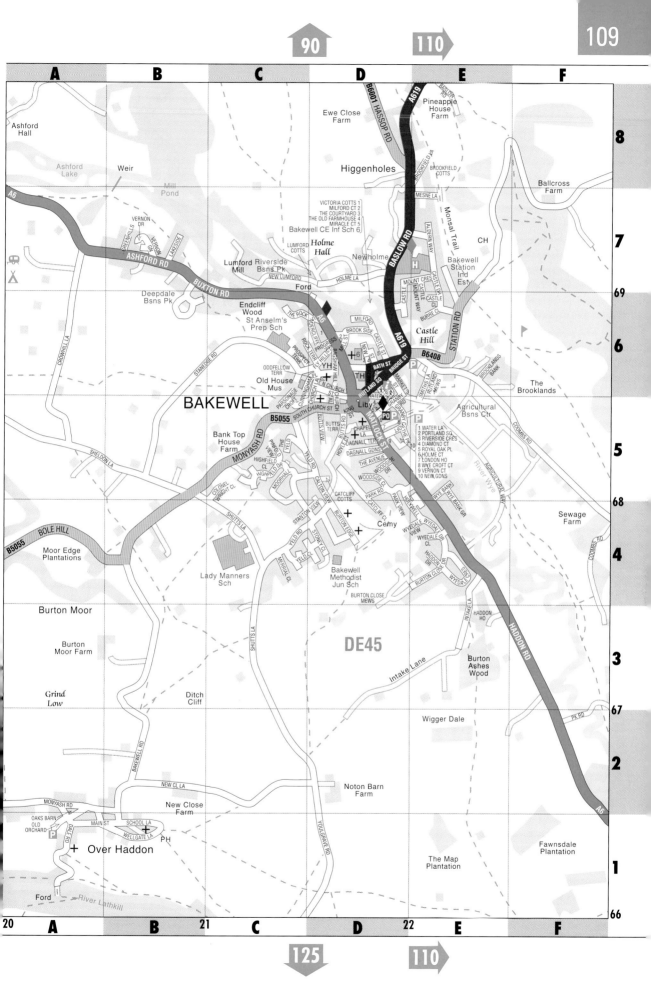

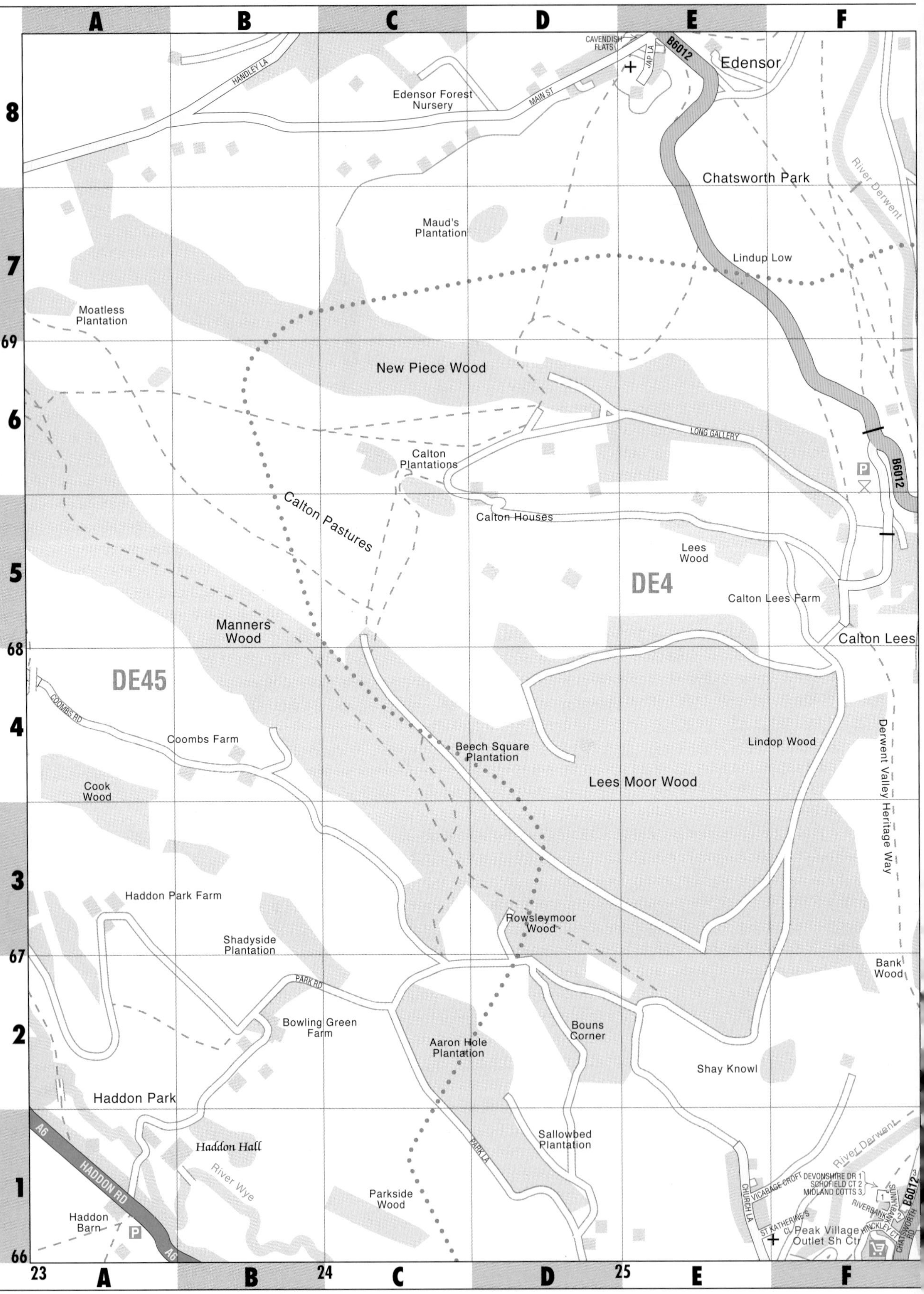

109
91

A   B   C   D   E   F

8

CAVENDISH FLATS
JAP LA
B6012
Edensor
Edensor Forest Nursery
MAIN ST
Chatsworth Park
River Derwent

Maud's Plantation
Lindup Low

7

69

Moatless Plantation
New Piece Wood

6

LONG GALLERY
Calton Plantations
B6012
Calton Pastures
Calton Houses
P

Lees Wood

DE4

5

Manners Wood
Calton Lees Farm
Calton Lees

68

DE45
Coombs Rd
Coombs Farm
Beech Square Plantation
Lindop Wood
Derwent Valley Heritage Way

4

Cook Wood
Lees Moor Wood

3

Haddon Park Farm
Rowsleymoor Wood

67

Shadyside Plantation
Bank Wood
PARK RD
Bowling Green Farm
Bouns Corner

2

Aaron Hole Plantation
Shay Knowl
PARK LA

Haddon Park
Sallowbed Plantation

1

Haddon Hall
River Wye
HADDON RD
A6
Parkside Wood
VICARAGE CROFT DEVONSHIRE DR 1
SCHOFIELD CT 2
MIDLAND COTTS 3
CHURCH LA
B6012
RIVERBANK

Haddon Barn
P
A6
St KATHERINE'S
Peak Village Outlet Sh Ctr

66

23   A   B   24   C   D   25   E   F

109
126

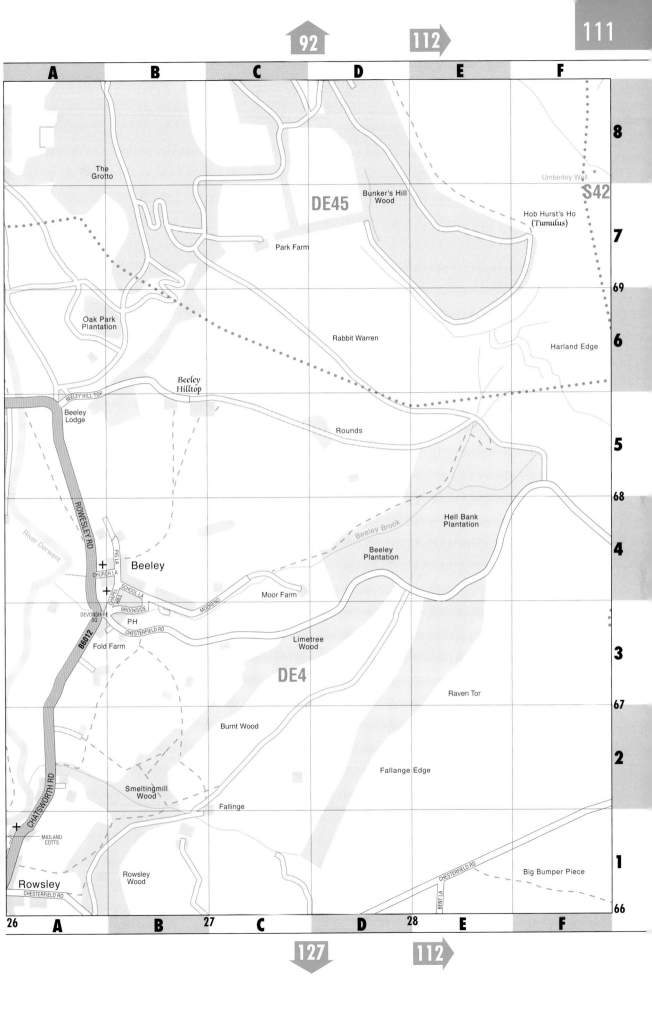

A B C D E F

8
7
69
6
5
68
4
3
67
2
1
66

The Grotto

DE45

Bunker's Hill Wood

Umberley Well

S42

Hob Hurst's Ho (Tumulus)

Park Farm

Oak Park Plantation

Rabbit Warren

Harland Edge

Beeley Hilltop

Beeley Hill Top

Beeley Lodge

Rounds

Hell Bank Plantation

River Derwent

Beeley Brook

Beeley Plantation

ROWSLEY RD

PIG LA

CHURCH LA

SCHOOL LA

Beeley

CHAPEL HILL

BROOKSIDE

MODREND

Moor Farm

DEVONSHIRE SQ

PH

CHESTERFIELD RD

B6012

Fold Farm

Limetree Wood

DE4

Raven Tor

Burnt Wood

Fallange Edge

CHATSWORTH RD

Smeltingmill Wood

Fallinge

MIDLAND COTTS

Rowsley Wood

Rowsley

CHESTERFIELD RD

CHESTERFIELD RD

BENT LA

Big Bumper Piece

26 A B 27 C D 28 E F

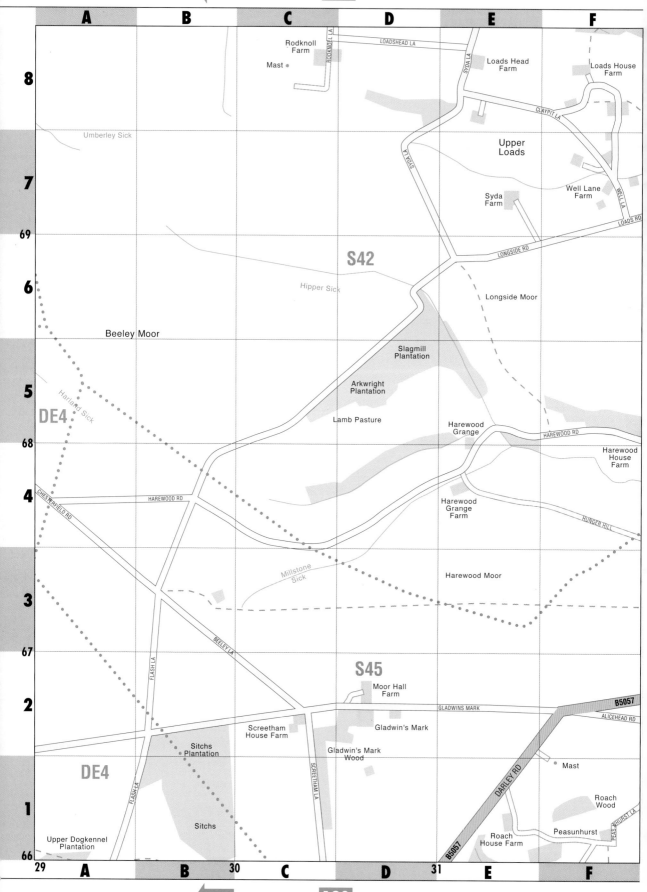

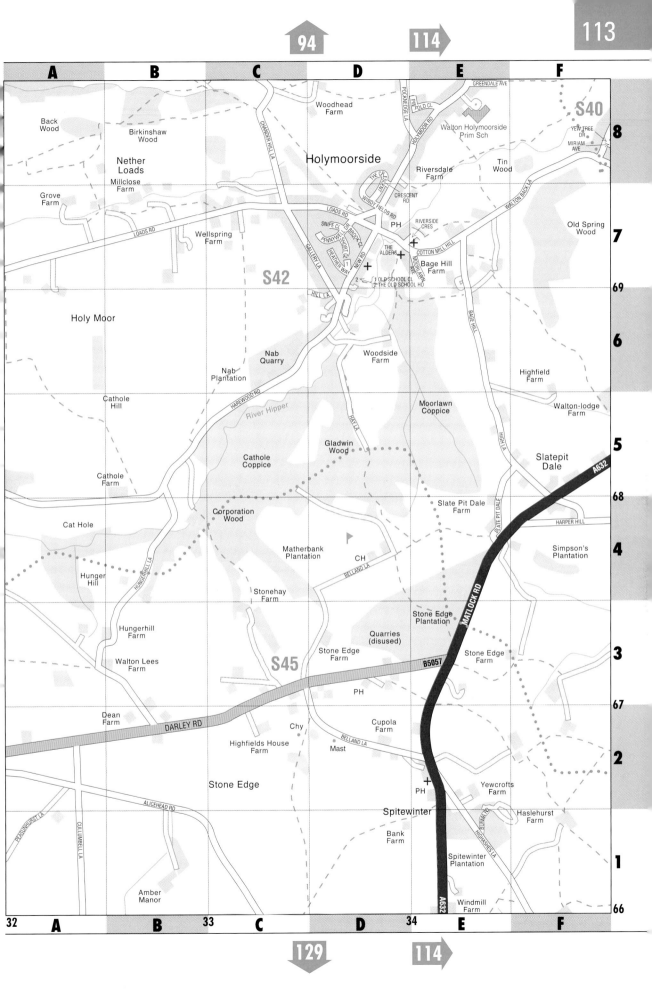

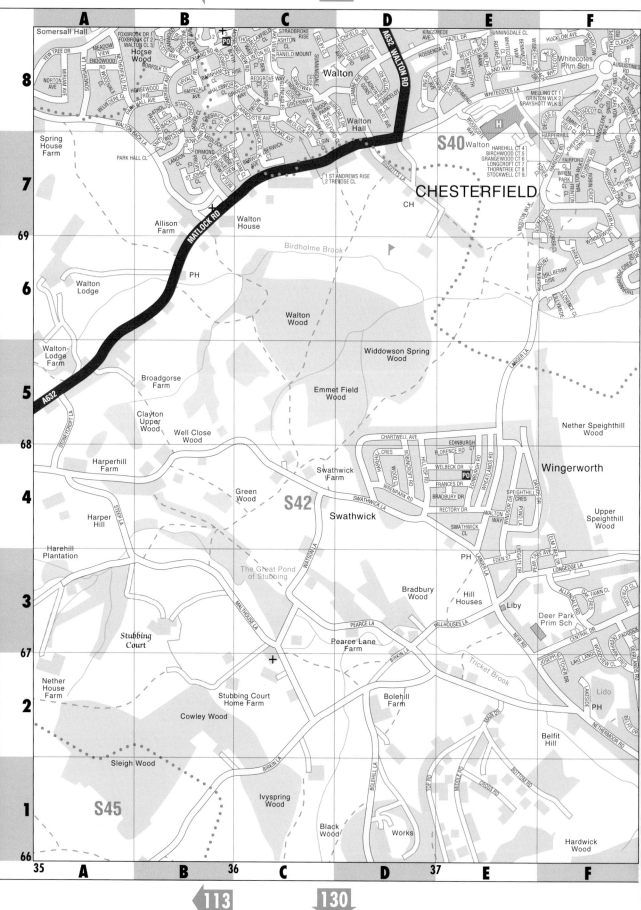

Somersall Hall

FOXBROOK DR 1
FOXBROOK CT 2
WALTON CL 3

Horse
Wood

YEW TREE DR

MEADOW VIEW
ENDOWOOD RD

NORTON
AVE

MIRIAM AVE

SOMERSALL LA

NETHERFIELD RD

WOODNALL RD

BELVEDERE CL

PALM HALL AVE

PARK HALL AVE

WALTON BACK LA

PARK HALL CL

NORFOLK CL

HORSEWOOD RD

FIRVALE RD

PATMOL CL

STANFORD

SACKVILLE

AVRO

BARBERS CL

ROYSTON

BOWER LA

MEDLOCK

MEDLOCK

BOWLAND

PRIORY

ST JOHNS

LANDON CL

ORMOND

ACORN RIDGE

LODGE

BELL
VIEW

BERWICK
CT

BERWICK AVE

SANDS CL

WOODTHORPE RD

FOXCROFT WAY

WINDSOR
BERWICK CL

BRECKLAND RD

THORNDON WAY

LINTON RD

LAXFIELD
CL

DEBEN

REDGROVE WAY

GRANSDEN
WAY

HALESWORTH

BARNHAM
RISE

FARNDALE AVE

SHALESWORTH CL

GLENEAGLES

HOLBROOK

LINDRICK

SANDYWAY

GREENWAYS

LINGROAD

STRADBROKE
RISE

RANELD MOUNT

ASHTON
CL

SELBY CL

ST DAVID
RISE

GILLFIELD

GILLFORD

LICHFIELD

HOLMEBANK
W

SUNNINGDALE
AVE

TURNBERRY

MOOR

PARK

CRESWICK

CARNOUSTIE AVE

MEDLOCK RD

HYLAKE AVE

BIRKDALE DR

FELTON CL

ELGIN

LANCELOT

RIGGOTTS LA

KINGSMEDE
AVE

HAZEL DR

SUNNINGDALE CL

BELVEDERE
BANK

ROTHER CT

FEE LANE WAY

ST
CLARKSON
ST

BOYTHORPE
RD

HUCKLOW AVE

HAROLD AVE

WHITECOTES
PRIM SCH

ST
AUGUSTINES
RD

BACON'S CL

Walton

Walton Hall

MATLOCK RD

WALTON
RD
A632

KINGSMEDE
AVE

ROSSENDALE
CL

BENNINGWOOD
WAY

DEVAN WAY

LING RD

LOVELL

RICHMOND

DEPL

DEVAN WAY

WHITECOTES LA

WISBECH CL

DELVES RD

MEULING CT 1
GRINTON WLK 2
GRAYSHOTT WLK 3

CHELTSEY

DIDCOT CL

EDEN

LINSBY

CHESTERTON

BRAMBLING

DERBY

FAIRFIELD
CL

HARPERHILL
CL

CHEPSTOW RD

STUBBING RD

GRANGEWOOD
RD

BROADWOOD
CL

CHURCH

WREN
PARK

FRINTON CL

ST
BACON'S
CL

DRYDEN AVE

S40 Walton

HAREHILL CT 4
BIRCHWOOD CT 5
GRANGEWOOD CT 6
LONGCROFT CT 7
THORNTREE CT 8
STOCKWELL CT 9

H

FISHER

CHESTERFIELD

CH

Spring
House
Farm

Allison
Farm

Walton
House

Birdholme Brook

Walton Lodge

PH

PUSHEN MOUNT

HILLBERRY
RISE

LILY MEDE

FLORENCE CL

LANGER LA

MOSTON WLK

ROCKLEY CL

BROADGROVE CL

FARM CL

WINGERFIELD

CARL RD

AVA

THORNBRIDGE CRES

Walton-
Lodge
Farm

A632

STONECROFT LA

STEEL LA

Walton
Wood

Broadgorse
Farm

Clayton
Upper
Wood

Well Close
Wood

Widdowson Spring
Wood

Emmet Field
Wood

LANGER LA

Nether Speighthill
Wood

CHARTWELL AVE

EDINBURGH
CT

Wingerworth

Harperhill
Farm

Harper
Hill

Green
Wood

S42

Swathwick
Farm

Swathwick

HAREPIT
CRES

ROBINCROFT RD

WOOD CL

WRENPARK RD

SWATHWICK LA

HILLTOP RD

FLORENCE RD

WELBECK DR

FRANCES DR

BRADBURY DR

RECTORY DR

WALTON
WAY

SWATHWICK
CL

EDINBURGH RD

WHEATLANDS RD

SPEIGHTHILL
CRES

DAVINS DR

WINDSOR DR

POND LA

PO

Upper
Speighthill
Wood

ELM TREE DR

Harehill
Plantation

The Great Pond
of Stubbing

Bradbury
Wood

Hill
Houses

PH

EDEN ST

LANGER LA

LYDGATE DR

TREE AVE

LONGEDGE LA

ALLENDALE RD

OAK CRES

FAWN CL

JOSEPH
FLETCHER DR

CENTRAL DR

Deer Park
Prim Sch

WOODTHORPE

OAK PARK CL

PADDOCK

Liby

Stubbing
Court

MALTHOUSE LA

Pearce Lane
Farm

BIRKIN LA

PEARCE LA

HILLHOUSES LA

NEW RD

Tricket Brook

LAKE LANDS DR

LAKESIDE

Lido
PH

Nether
House
Farm

Stubbing Court
Home Farm

Cowley Wood

Bolehill
Farm

BOLEHILL LA

MAIN DR

TOP RD

MIDDLE RD

CROSS RD

BOTTOM RD

NETHERMOOR RD

BELFIT DR

Belfit
Hill

Sleigh Wood

BIRKIN LA

Ivyspring
Wood

S45

Black
Wood

Works

Hardwick
Wood

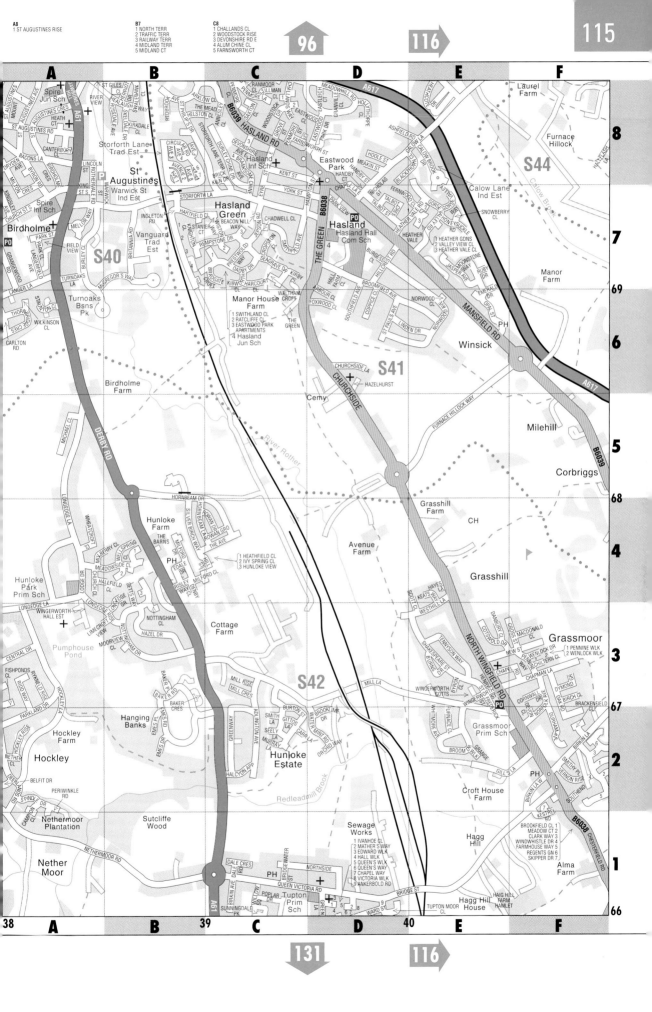

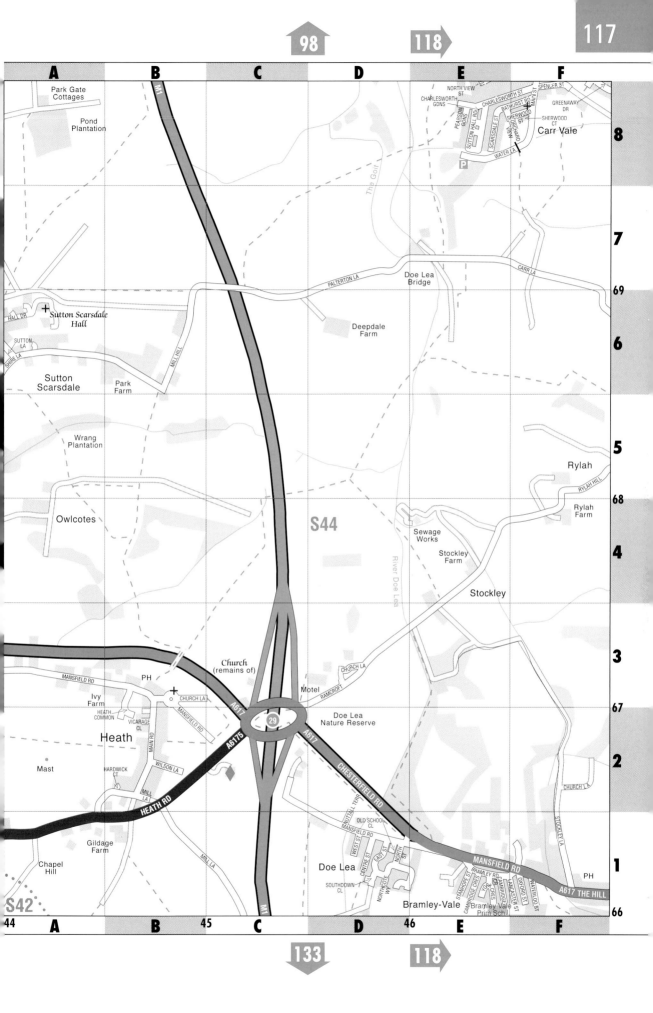

A B C D E F

8
7
69
6
5
68
4
3
67
2
1
66

Park Gate Cottages
Pond Plantation

NORTH VIEW ST
CHARLESWORTH GDNS
CHARLESWORTH ST
SPENCER ST
GREENAWAY DR
PEARSON GDNS
SUTTON HALL RD
MAIN ST
BATHURST RD
SCARSDALE ST
SHERWOOD ST
ORCHARD
SHERWOOD CT
Carr Vale
VIC RD
WATER LA
P

The Goit

M1

PALTERTON LA
Doe Lea Bridge
CARR LA

HALL DR
Sutton Scarsdale Hall
SUTTON LA
SHIRE LA

Deepdale Farm

Sutton Scarsdale
Park Farm
MILL HILL

Wrang Plantation

Rylah
RYLAH HILL
Rylah Farm

68

Owlcotes

S44

Sewage Works
Stockley Farm

Stockley

River Doe Lea

Church (remains of)
CHURCH LA
RAMCROFT
Motel
Doe Lea Nature Reserve

MANSFIELD RD
PH
Ivy Farm
HEATH COMMON
CHURCH LA
VICARAGE CL
MANSFIELD RD
A617
A6175
29
A617
CHESTERFIELD RD

Heath
MAIN RD
Mast
HARDWICK CT
WILSON LA
MILL LA

HEATH RD

Gildage Farm

Chapel Hill

NUTTALL TERR
OLD SCHOOL CL
MANSFIELD RD
WEST ST
CENTRE ST
EAST ST
NORTH ST
Doe Lea
SOUTHDOWN CL
NORTHCOTE WY

MANSFIELD RD
STANHOPE CRES
CAMBRIDGE CRES
BRAMLEY RD
CAMBRIDGE CRES
LANCASTER ST
OXFORD ST
WATERLOO ST
STOCKLEY LA
CHURCH L
PH
A617 THE HILL

Bramley-Vale
Bramley Vale Prim Sch

S42

S44

117
99

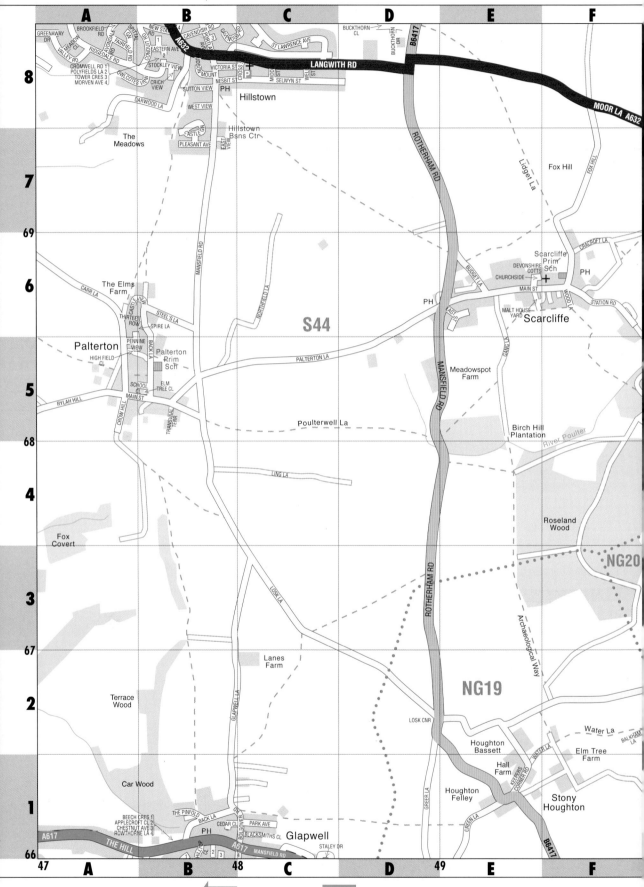

117
134

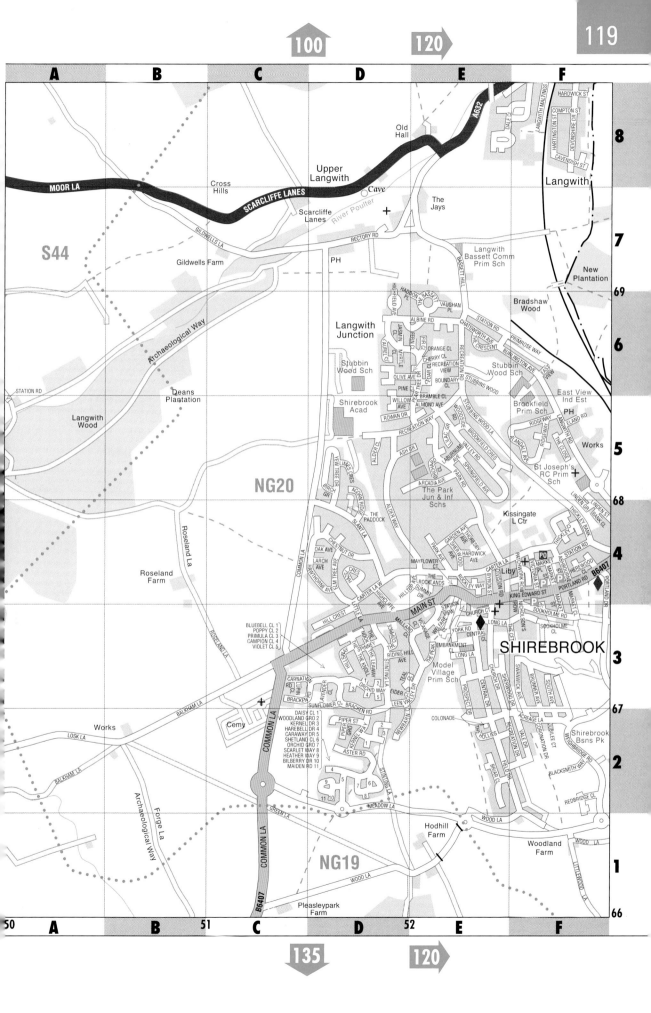

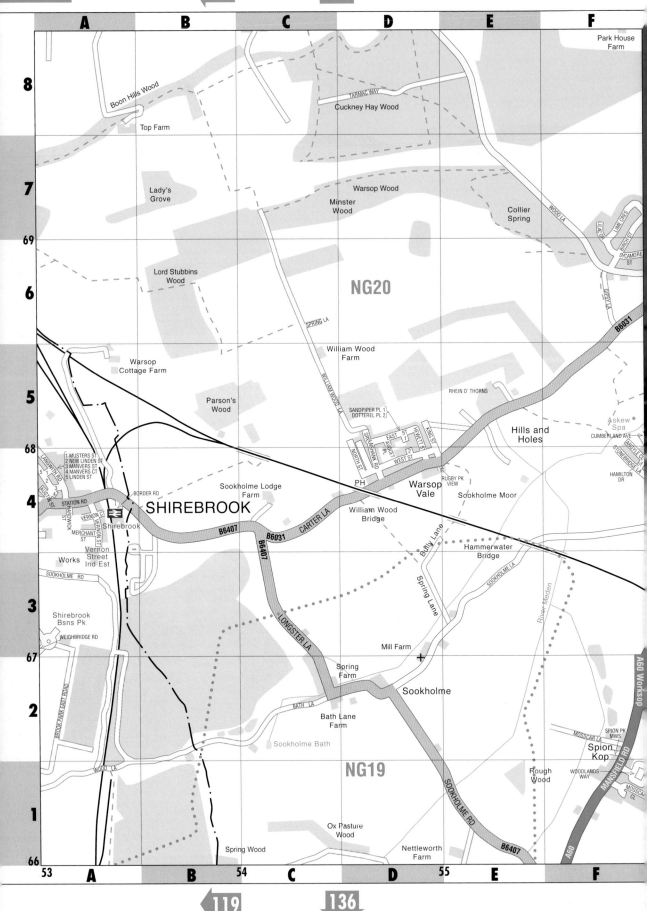

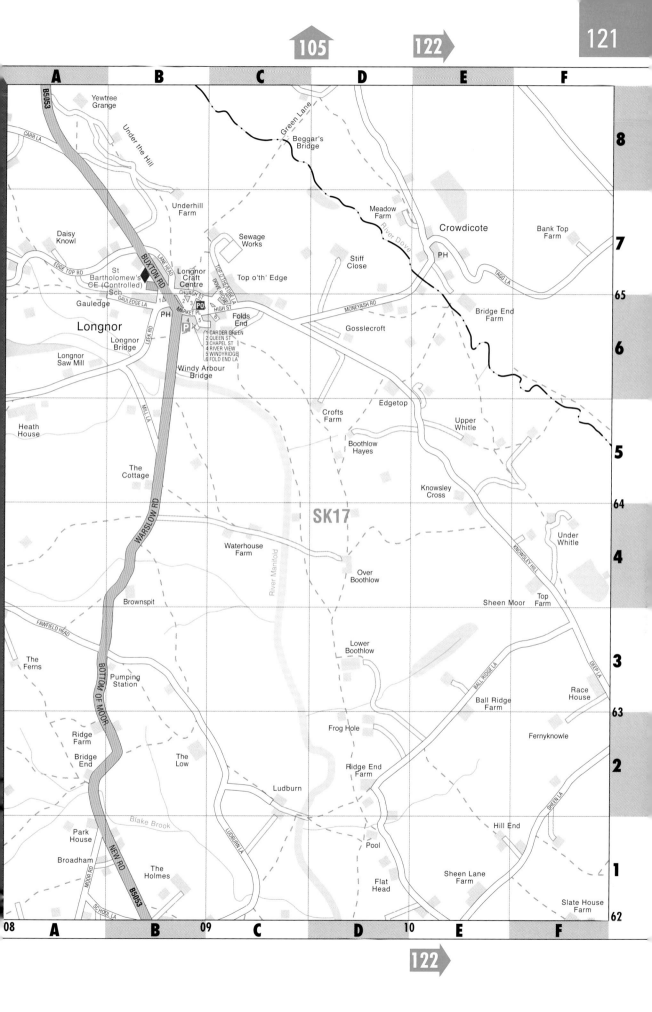

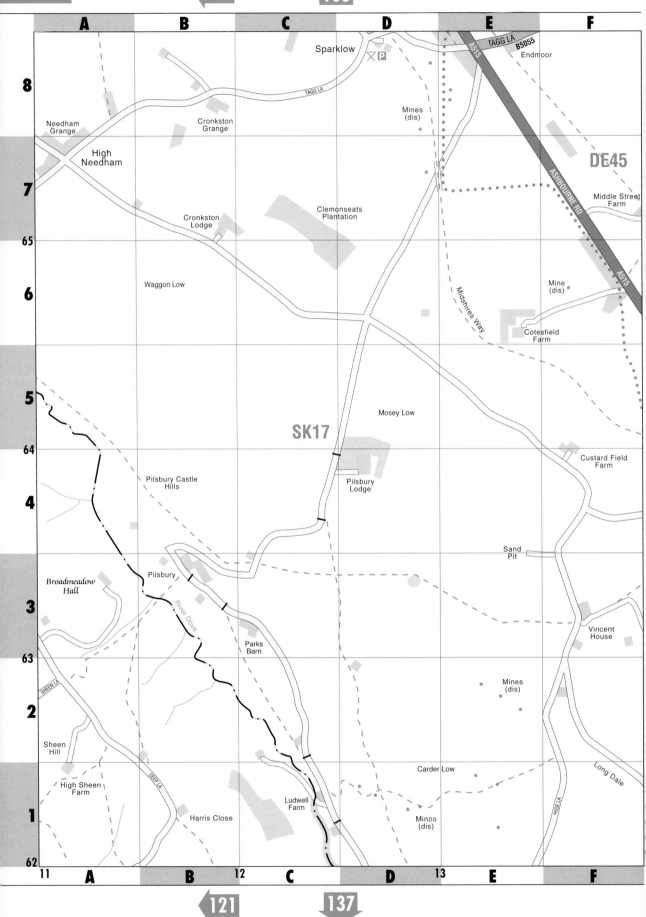

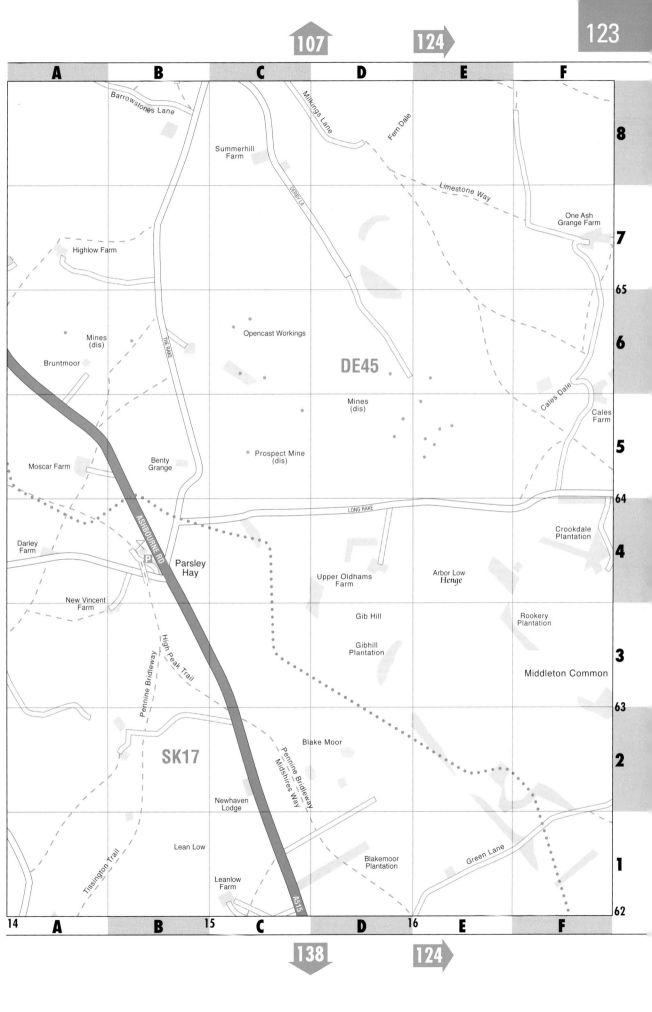

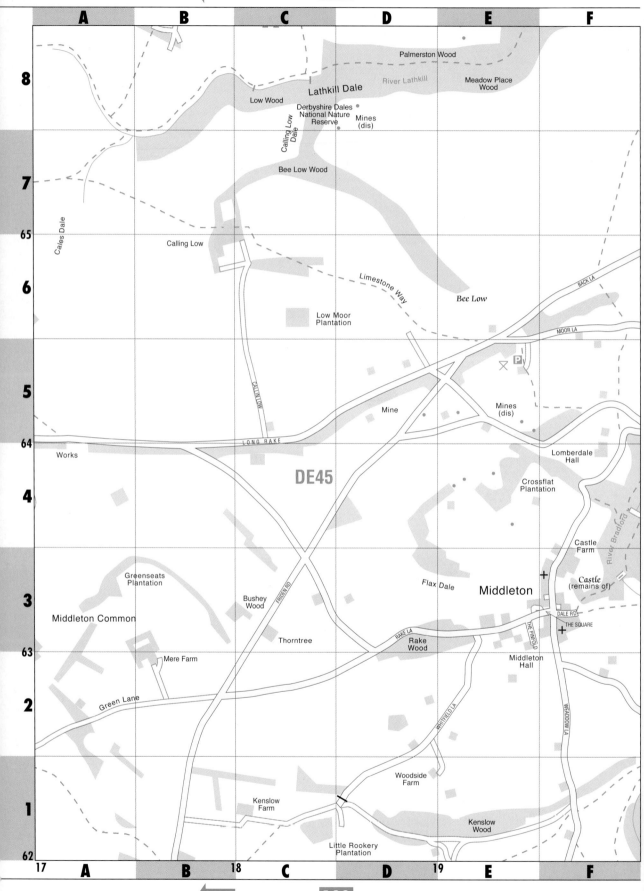

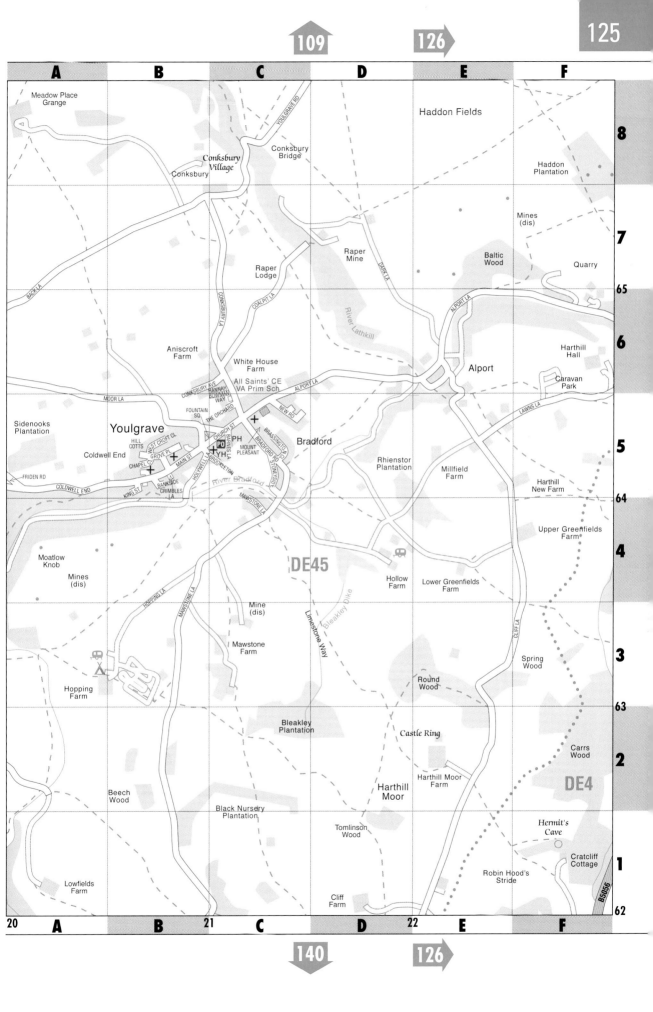

A　　B　　C　　D　　E　　F

8

Meadow Place
Grange

Haddon Fields

Conksbury
Village
Conksbury

Conksbury
Bridge

Haddon
Plantation

7

YOULGRAVE RD

Mines
(dis)

Raper
Mine

Baltic
Wood

Quarry

Raper
Lodge

65

CONKSBURY LA

COALPIT LA

DARK LA

River Lathkill

ALPORT LA

6

Aniscroft
Farm

White House
Farm

Harthill
Hall

Alport

Caravan
Park

All Saints' CE
VA Prim Sch

MOOR LA

ALPORT LA

LAWNS LA

CONKSBURY AVE

Sidenooks
Plantation

Youlgrave

HANNAH
BOWMAN
WAY

FOUNTAIN
SQ

THE ORCHARD

NEW RD

5

HILL
COTTS

CHURCH ST

PH

Bradford

Rhienstor
Plantation

Millfield
Farm

Harthill
New Farm

Coldwell End

WEST CROFT CL

GROVE PL

PO

BARNES LA

MOUNT
PLEASANT

BRASSINGTON RD

BRADFORD

STONESIDE

CHAPEL CL

MAIN ST

YHA

FRIDEN RD

BANKSIDE

KING ST

CRIMBLES
LA

HOLLWELL LA

BROOKLETGN

River Bradford

MAWSTONE LA

64

Upper Greenfields
Farm

Moatlow
Knob

4

Mines
(dis)

DE45

Hollow
Farm

Lower Greenfields
Farm

HOPPING LA

MAWSTONE LA

Mine
(dis)

Limestone Way

Bleakley Dike

CLIFF LA

Spring
Wood

3

Mawstone
Farm

Round
Wood

Hopping
Farm

63

Bleakley
Plantation

Castle Ring

Carrs
Wood

2

Beech
Wood

Harthill
Moor

Harthill Moor
Farm

DE4

Black Nursery
Plantation

Tomlinson
Wood

Hermit's
Cave

Cratcliff
Cottage

1

Lowfields
Farm

Robin Hood's
Stride

Cliff
Farm

B5056

62

20　　A　　B　　21　　C　　D　　22　　E　　F

125
110

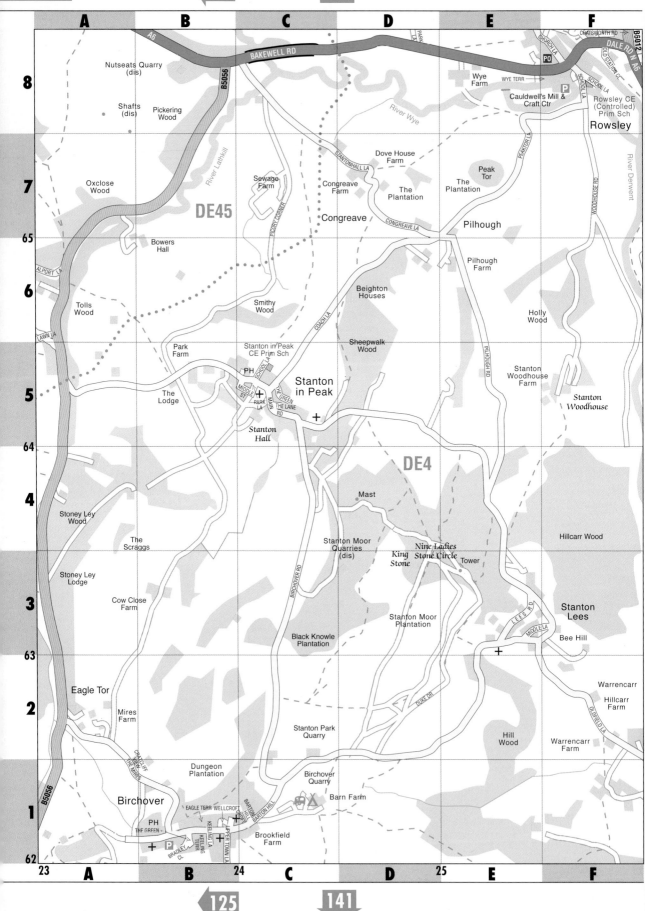

125
141

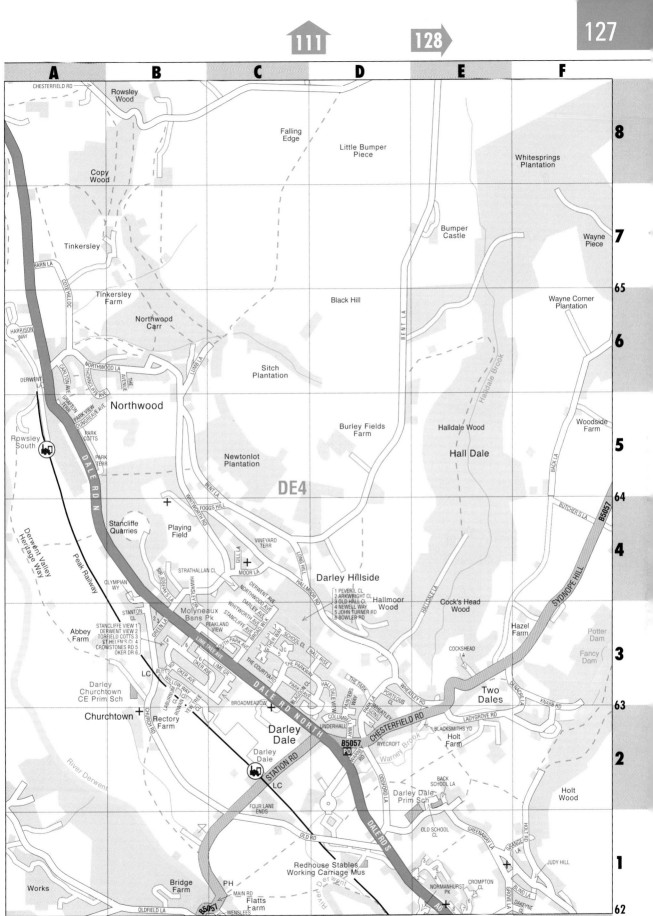

E1
1 KENNEDY CT
2 GROVE COTTS
3 POLLARD WAY
4 ROBINSON CT
5 HOPKINS CT
6 ST ELPHINS HOUSE
7 HUDSON PL
8 CHAPEL MWS

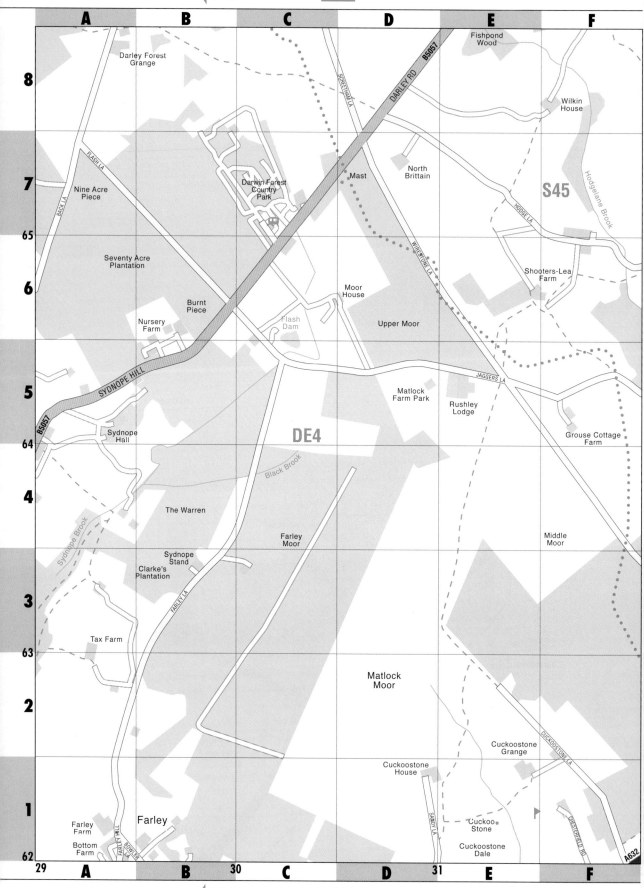

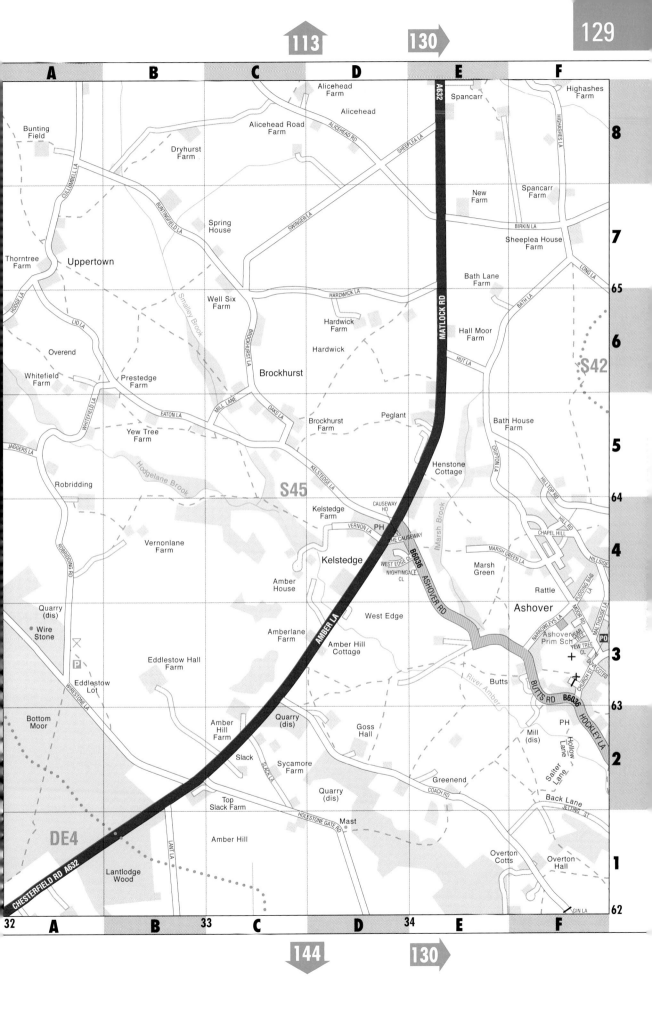

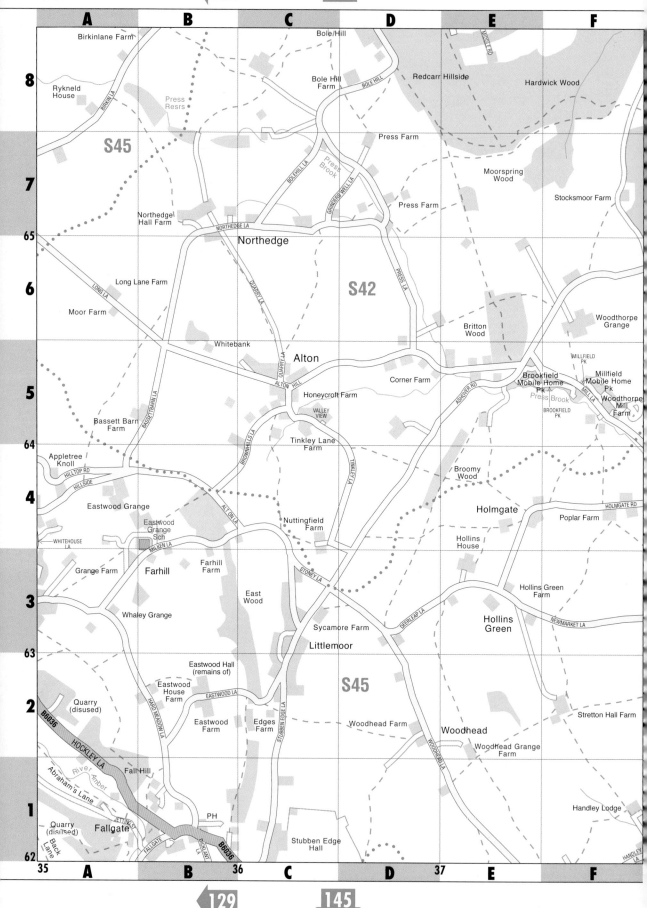

A B C D E F

8

Birkinlane Farm

Bole/Hill

Rykneld
House

BIRKIN LA

S45

Press
Resrs

Bole Hill
Farm

BOLE HILL LA

Redcarr Hillside

BOLE HILL

Hardwick Wood

MIDDLE RD

Press Farm

7

Moorspring
Wood

Stocksmoor Farm

Northedge
Hall Farm

GRINDERS WELL LA

Press
Brook

Press Farm

NORTHEDGE LA

65

Northedge

6

Long Lane Farm

LONG LA

QUARRY LA

S42

PRESS LA

Moor Farm

Woodthorpe
Grange

Whitebank

Britton
Wood

MILLFIELD
PK

Alton

Millfield
Mobile Home
Pk

5

BASSETT BARN LA

ALTON HILL

QUARRY LA

Corner Farm

ASHOVER RD

MILL LA

Brookfield
Mobile Home
Pk

Woodthorpe
Mill
Farm

Honeycroft Farm

Press Brook

BROOKFIELD
PK

Bassett Barn
Farm

VALLEY
VIEW

64

Appletree
Knoll

Tinkley Lane
Farm

BROWNHILLS LA

HILLTOP RD

HILLSIDE

TINKLEY LA

Broomy
Wood

Holmgate

HOLMGATE RD

4

Eastwood Grange

ALTON LA

Nuttingfield
Farm

Poplar Farm

WHITEHOUSE
LA

Eastwood
Grange
Sch

MILKEN LA

Hollins
House

Grange Farm

Farhill
Farm

STONEY LA

Hollins Green
Farm

Farhill

3

Whaley Grange

East
Wood

Sycamore Farm

DEERLEAP LA

Hollins
Green

NEWMARKET LA

HARD MEADOW LA

Littlemoor

63

Eastwood Hall
(remains of)

Eastwood
House
Farm

EASTWOOD LA

STUBBEN EDGE LA

S45

2

B6036

Quarry
(disused)

Eastwood
Farm

Edges
Farm

Woodhead Farm

Woodhead

Stretton Hall Farm

HOCKLEY LA

Fall Hill

WOODHEAD LA

Woodhead Grange
Farm

River Amber

Abraham's Lane

PH

1

Handley Lodge

Quarry
(disused)

JETTINGS

Fallgate

FALLGATE

DICK LANT

B6036

Stubben Edge
Hall

Back
Lane

HANDLEY

62

35 A B 36 C D 37 E F

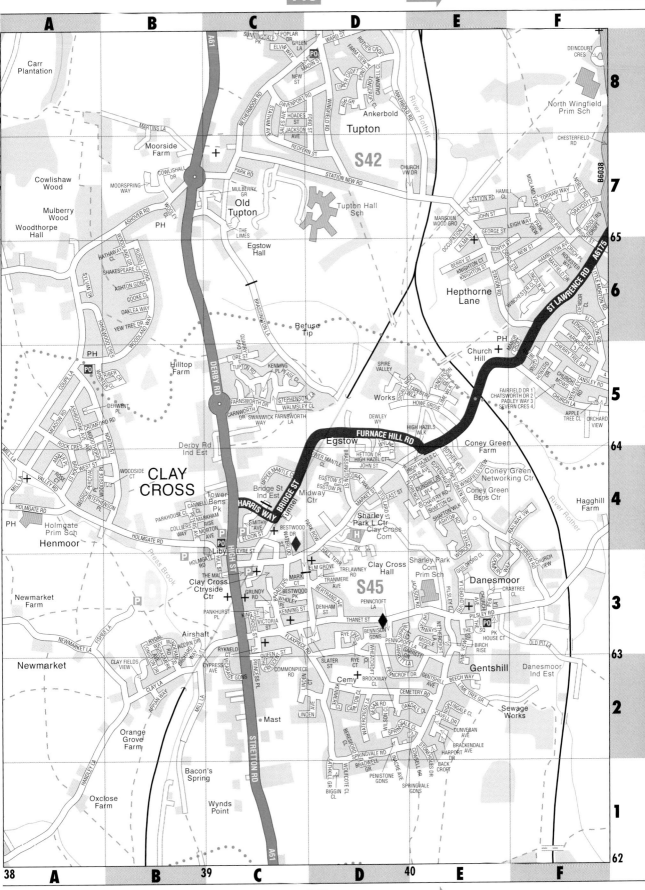

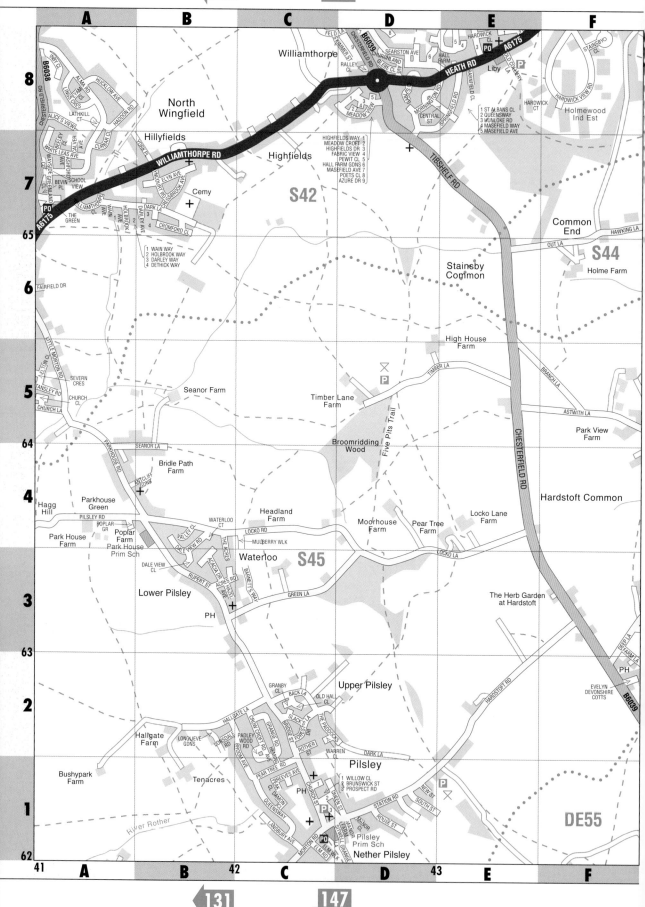

North Wingfield

Williamthorpe

Hillyfields

Highfields

S42

WILLIAMTHORPE RD

HEATH RD

TIBSHELF RD

Cemy

The Green

A6175

Liby

Holmewood Ind Est

Common End

S44

Holme Farm

Stainsby Common

High House Farm

Timber La

CHESTERFIELD RD

Park View Farm

ASTWITH LA

BRANCH LA

Seanor Farm

Timber Lane Farm

Broomridding Wood

Five Pits Trail

Fairfield Dr

Hagg Hill

Parkhouse Green

Park House Farm

Poplar Farm

Park House Prim Sch

Waterloo

Lower Pilsley

Headland Farm

S45

Moorhouse Farm

Pear Tree Farm

Locko Lane Farm

Hardstoft Common

The Herb Garden at Hardstoft

Bridle Path Farm

Seanor La

Locko La

Locko Rd

Green La

PH

Upper Pilsley

Evelyn Devonshire Cotts

B6039

PH

Hallgate Farm

Bushypark Farm

Tenacres

Pilsley

Pilsley Prim Sch

Nether Pilsley

Pilsley Grange

River Rother

DE55

1 WILLOW CL
2 BRUNSWICK ST
3 PROSPECT RD

HIGHFIELDS WAY 1
MEADOW CROFT 2
HIGHFIELDS DR 3
FABRIC VIEW 4
PEWIT CL 5
HALL FARM GDNS 6
MASEFIELD AVE 7
POETS CL 8
AZURE DR 9

1 ST ALBANS CL
2 QUEENSWAY
3 WINLOKE RD
4 MASEFIELD WAY
5 MASEFIELD AVE

1 WAIN WAY
2 HOLBROOK WAY
3 DARLEY WAY
4 DETHICK WAY

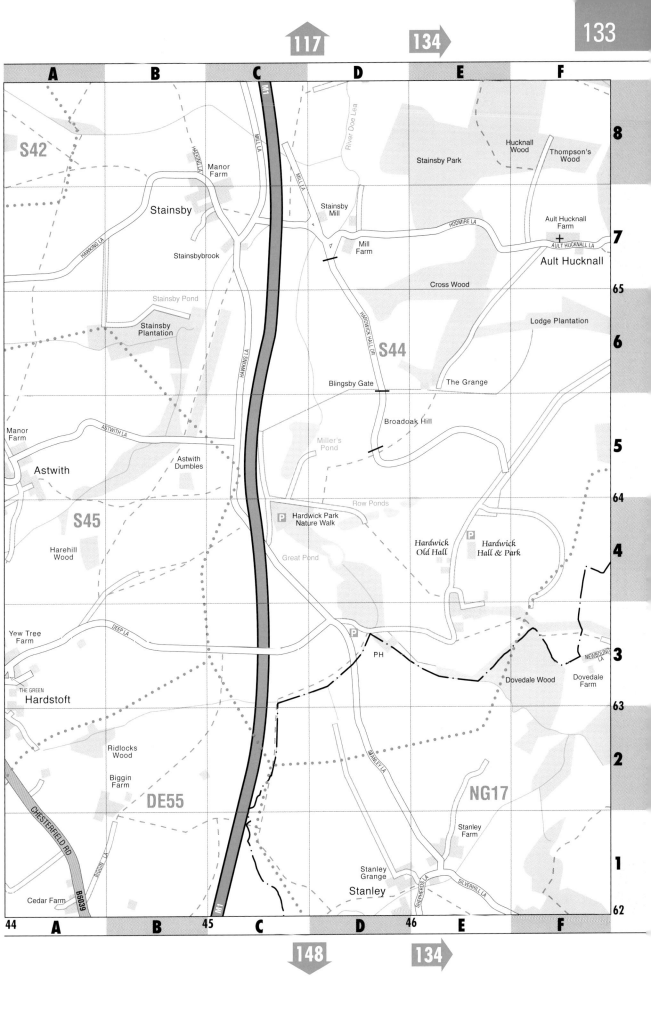

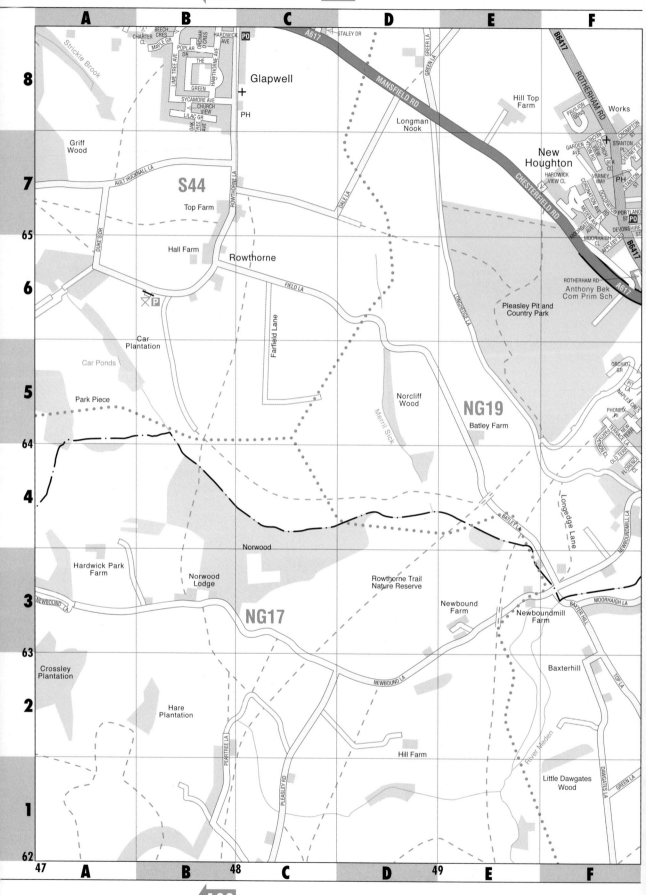

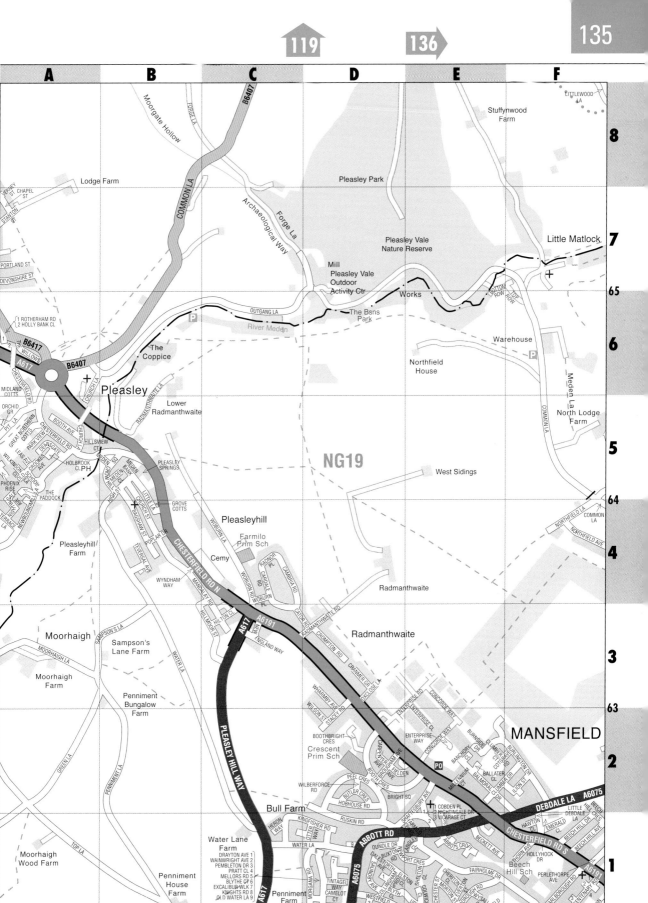

A B C D E F

8

Stuffynwood
Farm

LITTLEWOOD
LA

Lodge Farm

VERNEY ST
CHAPEL ST
STANTON ST

MOORGATE HOLLOW
FORGE LA

COMMON LA
B6407

Archaeological Way
Forge La

Pleasley Park

Pleasley Vale
Nature Reserve

Little Matlock 7

PORTLAND ST
DEVONSHIRE ST

Mill
Pleasley Vale
Outdoor
Activity Ctr

BOTTOM ROW
TOP ROW

65

1 ROTHERHAM RD
2 HOLLY BANK CL

OUTGANG LA
River Meden

The Bsns
Park

Works

Warehouse 6

B6417
A617
B6407

The
Coppice

Northfield
House

Meden La

P

CHESTERFIELD RD
MIDLAND COTTS

CHURCH LA

Pleasley

Lower
Radmanthwaite

North Lodge
Farm

COMMON LA

ORCHID GR
PIT LA
GREAT NORTHERN COTTS
PARK VIEW
LEAS AVE
CROOKES AVE
DEANGATE
WILKINSON CL
SCHOOL LA
BOOTH AVE
CHESTERFIELD RD
CHURCH
HILLSVIEW CT

RADMANTHWAITE LA

NG19

5

PHOENIX RISE
NEWBOUND LA
HOLBROOK CL PH
MEDEN BANK
NIGALS ST
LITTLE LA
PLEASLEY SPRINGS

West Sidings

NORTHFIELD LA

64

THE PADDOCK
CALF CL
TERRACE LA

BAGSHAW ST
GROVE COTTS

Pleasleyhill

Farmilo
Prim Sch

NORTHFIELD AVE
COMMON LA

4

Pleasleyhill
Farm

POPLAR DR
TEVERSAL AVE
WOBURN RD
WYNDHAM WAY
CHESTERFIELD RD N
MANDALA RD

WOBURN PL
Cemy

RADNOR PL
CARDALE RD
CAMBRIA RD
CATON RD
RADMANTHWAITE RD

Radmanthwaite

Moorhaigh

SAMPSON'S LA
WATER LA

Sampson's
Lane Farm

HILLMOOR ST
HILTON CL
A617
A6191

AVON
ENGLAND WAY
CROMPTON RD

CRANMER GR

Radmanthwaite 3

MOORHAIGH LA

Moorhaigh
Farm

Penniment
Bungalow
Farm

OXCLOSE LA
WHARNABY AVE
WILSON ST
STACEY AVE

ENTERPRISE RD
ENTERPRISE CL

CONCORDE WAY

BURNSIDE CL
LUMLEY CL
CTGB RD
BANCHORY CL

63

PENNIMENT LA

GREEN LA

Enterprise
Way

BOOTHBRIGHT
CRES

Crescent
Prim Sch

CARPENTER AVE
BROUGHAM AVE

CONCORDE WAY

PO

BALLATER CL
BALMORAL
CLIMBER DR
LUMLEY ST
BURLINGTON DR

MANSFIELD 2

MILLENNIUM WAY

WILBERFORCE
RD

PEEL CRES
BUTLER CRES
HOBHOUSE RD

BOOTH CRES

BRIGHT SQ

SHAFTESBURY AVE

COBDEN PL

HAWTON AVE
EMERALD

DEBDALE LA
A6075

LITTLE
DEBDALE
LA

BEECH HILL DR
BEECH
HILL AVE

Bull Farm

KINGFISHER RD

RUSKIN RD

ABBOTT RD

1 NIGHTINGALE DR
2 VICARAGE CT
3

CHESTERFIELD RD S

HOLLYHOCK
DR

THORN AVE

Beech
Hill Sch

A6191 1

Water Lane
Farm

DRAYTON AVE 1
WAINWRIGHT AVE 2
PEMBLETON DR 3
PRATT CL 4
MELLORS RD 5
BLYTHE CL 6
EXCALIBUR WLK 7
KNIGHTS RD 8
OLD WATER LA 9

HERON WAY
OTTER WAY
WATER LA

MORGANA RD
A6075

TINTAGEL WAY
CAMELOT CT
AVISTA

OUNDLE DR
DALE BUXTON
NORTH LINDLEY
EVERTON
SHELTON
BLYTH
CHESTER ST
MORTON CL
REDBRIDGE
FAIRHOLME DR
DRAY CL
PORT CRES
ABBOTS CROFT
BECKETT AVE

PERLETHORPE
AVE

MARLBOROUGH DR
CENTENARY RD
ALBION

PLEASLEY HILL WAY
A617

Penniment
Farm

Penniment
House Farm

Moorhaigh
Wood Farm

TOP LA

WESTFIELD LA
LUPTON CL
WOODBOROUGH PL
WY SALL
WESTFIELD DR

62

A617 Newark-on-Trent   A6075   M1 June 28 (A38)

F1
1 BROWNLOW RD
2 FLANDERS CL
3 LARK CL
4 LIBERTY

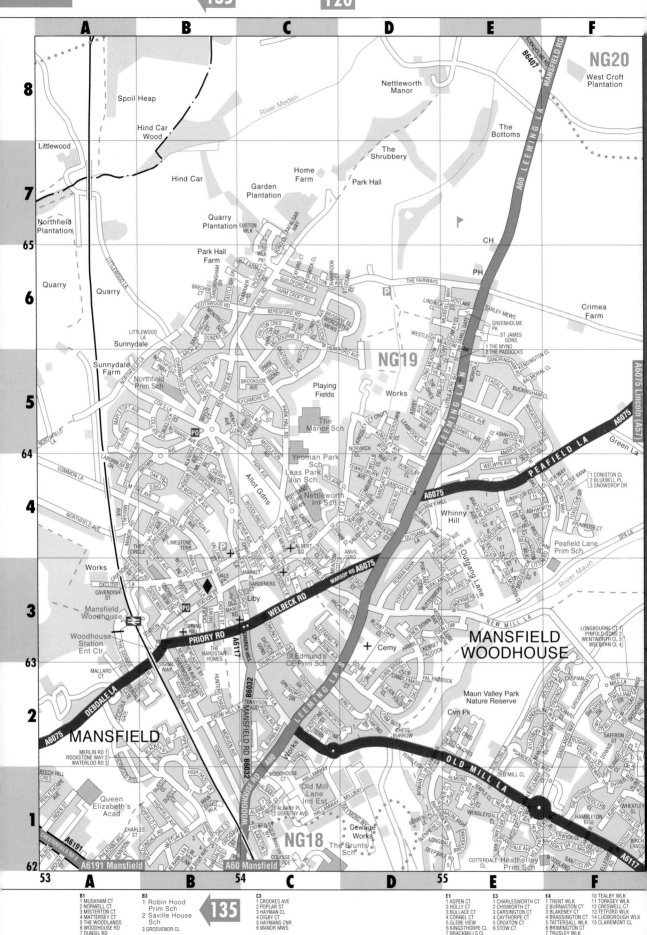

NG20
West Croft Plantation

NG19

NG18

MANSFIELD WOODHOUSE

MANSFIELD

←135

A	B	C	D	E	F

B1
1 MUSKHAM CT
2 NORWELL CT
3 MISTERTON CT
4 MATTERSEY CT
5 THE WOODLANDS
6 WOODHOUSE RD
7 DUNSIL RD
8 MAIN BRIGHT RD
	B3
	1 Robin Hood
	  Prim Sch
	2 Saville House
	  Sch
	
	3 GROSVENOR CL
		C3
		1 CROOKES AVE
		2 POPLAR ST
		3 HAYMAN ST
		4 DIGBY CT
		5 HAYMANS CNR
		6 MANOR MWS
			D1
			1 CHARLESWORTH CT
			2 CHISWORTH CT
			3 CARSINGTON CT
			4 CAYTHORPE CT
			5 CROXTON CT
			6 STOW CT
				E1
				1 ASPEN CT
				2 HOLLY CT
				3 BULLACE CT
				4 CORNEL CT
				5 GLEBE VIEW
				6 KINGSTHORPE CL
				7 BRACKMILLS CL
				
				E3
				1 CONISTON CT
				2 BLUEBELL PL
				3 SNOWDROP DR
					E4
					1 TRENT WLK
					2 BURNASTON CT
					3 BLAKENEY CT
					4 BRASSINGTON CT
					5 TATTERSALL WLK
					6 BRIMINGTON CT
					7 TRUSLEY WLK
					8 REPTON CT
					9 THURLBY CT
						F2
						10 TEALBY WLK
						11 TORKSEY WLK
						12 CRESWELL CT
						13 TETFORD WLK
						14 LUDBOROUGH WLK
						15 CLAREMONT CT

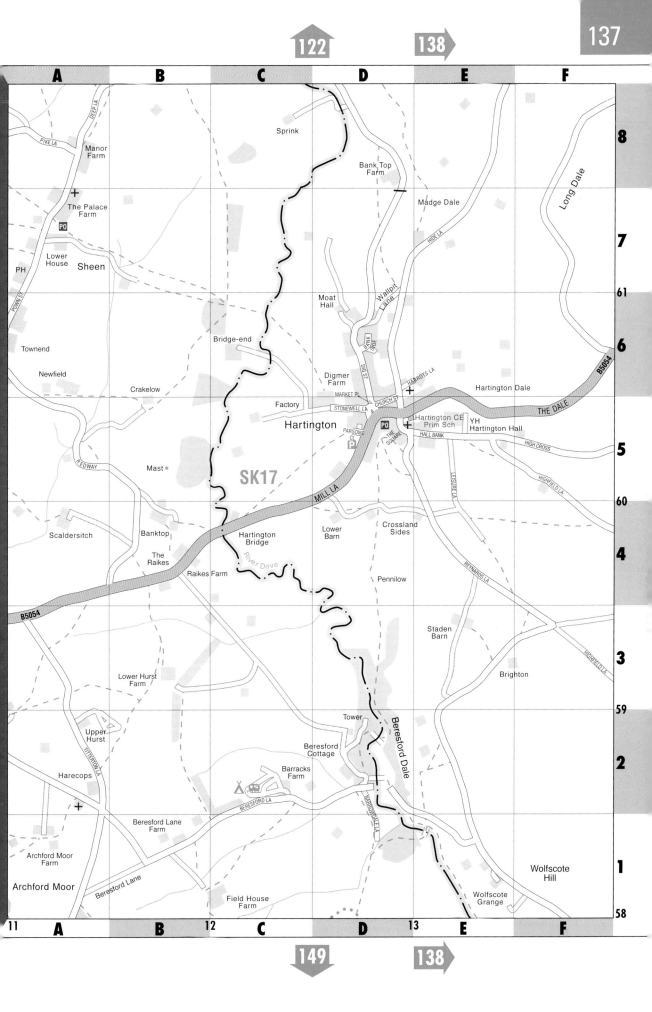

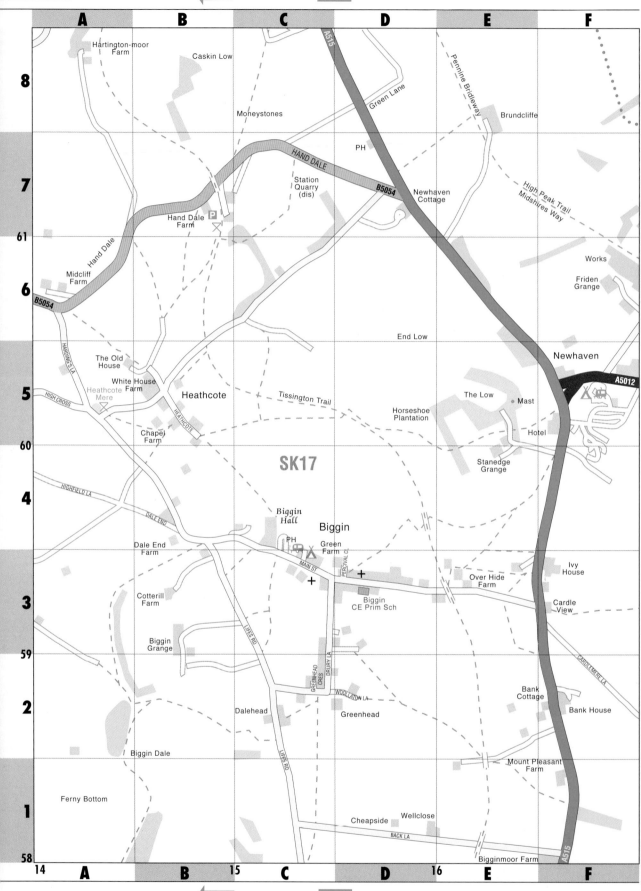

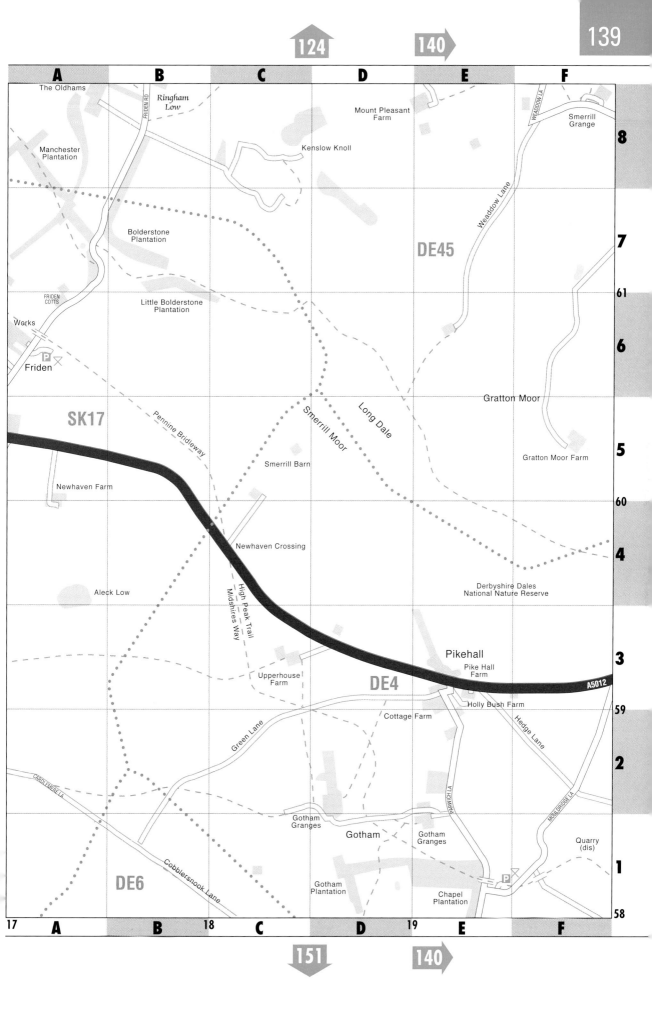

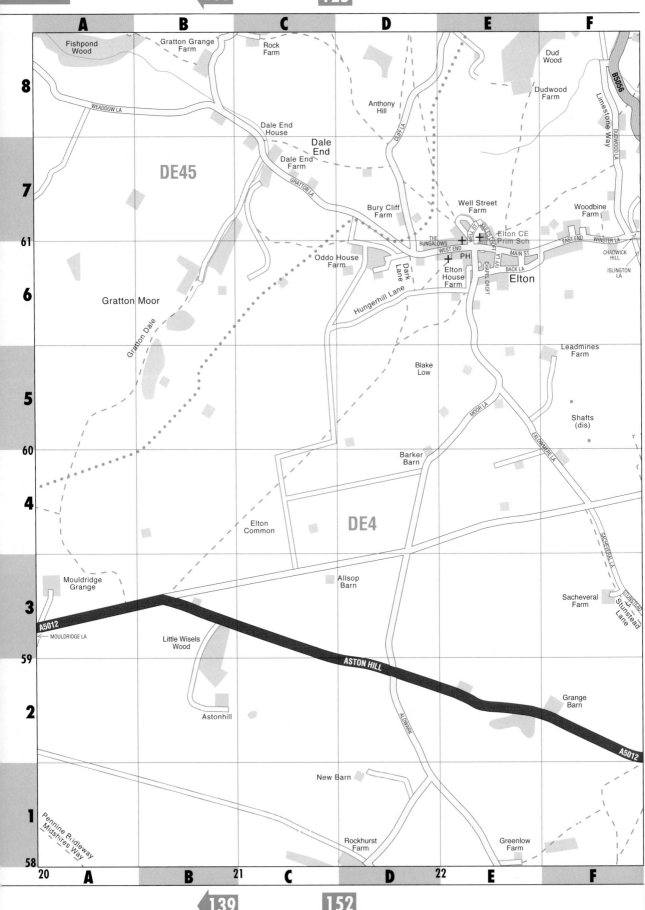

A B C D E F

8

7

61

6

5

60

4

3

59

2

1

58

20 A B 21 C D 22 E F

Fishpond Wood

Gratton Grange Farm

Rock Farm

Anthony Hill

Dud Wood

Dudwood Farm

B5056

WEADDOW LA

Dale End House

Dale End

DE45

Dale End Farm

GRATTON LA

CLIFF LA

Limestone Way

DUDWOOD LA

Well Street Farm

Woodbine Farm

Bury Cliff Farm

Elton CE Prim Sch

WELL ST

SOL'S CROFT

EAST END

WINSTER LA

CHADWICK HILL

The Bungalows

WEST END

IVY LA

MAIN ST

BACK LA

ISLINGTON LA

Oddo House Farm

PH

Elton House Farm

CHAPEL CROFT

Elton

Gratton Moor

Dark Lane

Hungerhill Lane

Leadmines Farm

Gratton Dale

Blake Low

MOOR LA

EXLOWMERE LA

Shafts (dis)

Barker Barn

DE4

Mouldridge Grange

Elton Common

Allsop Barn

SACHEVERAL LA

Sacheveral Farm

STUNSTEAD LA

Stunstead Lane

A5012

MOULDRIDGE LA

Little Wisels Wood

ASTON HILL

Grange Barn

Astonhill

ALLOWAY

A5012

New Barn

Pennine Bridleway Midshires Way

Rockhurst Farm

Greenlow Farm

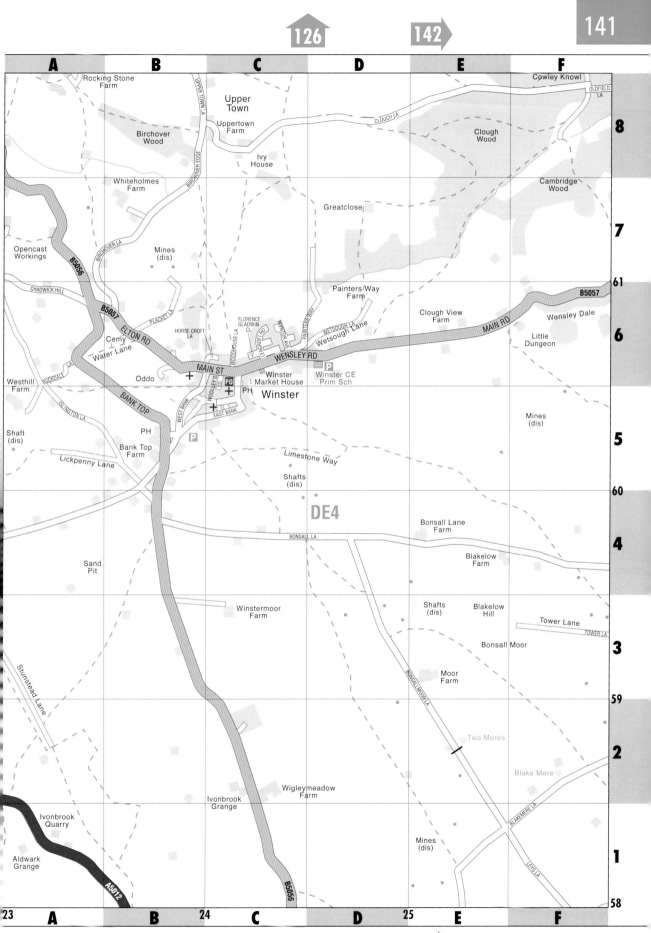

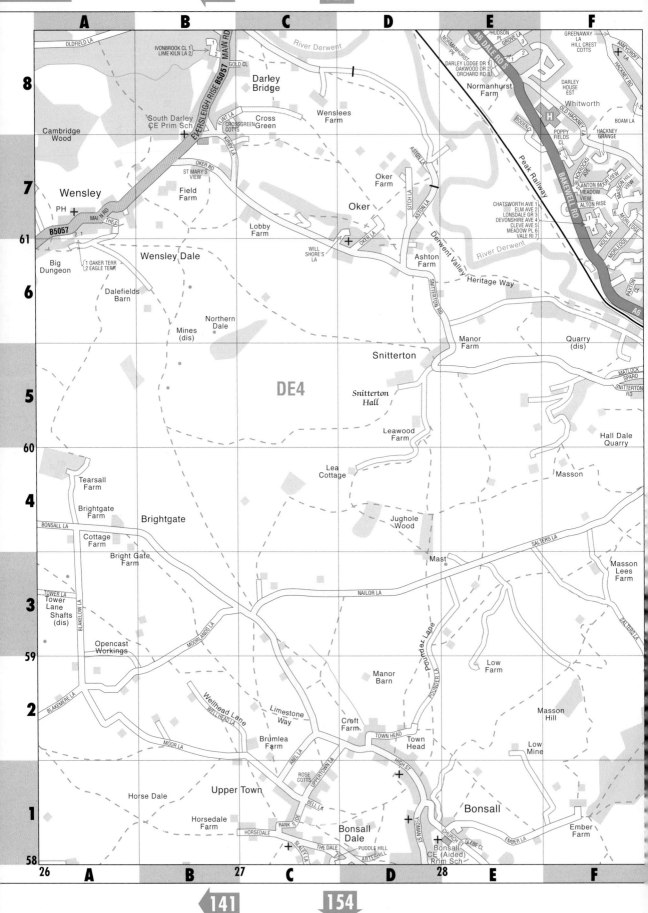

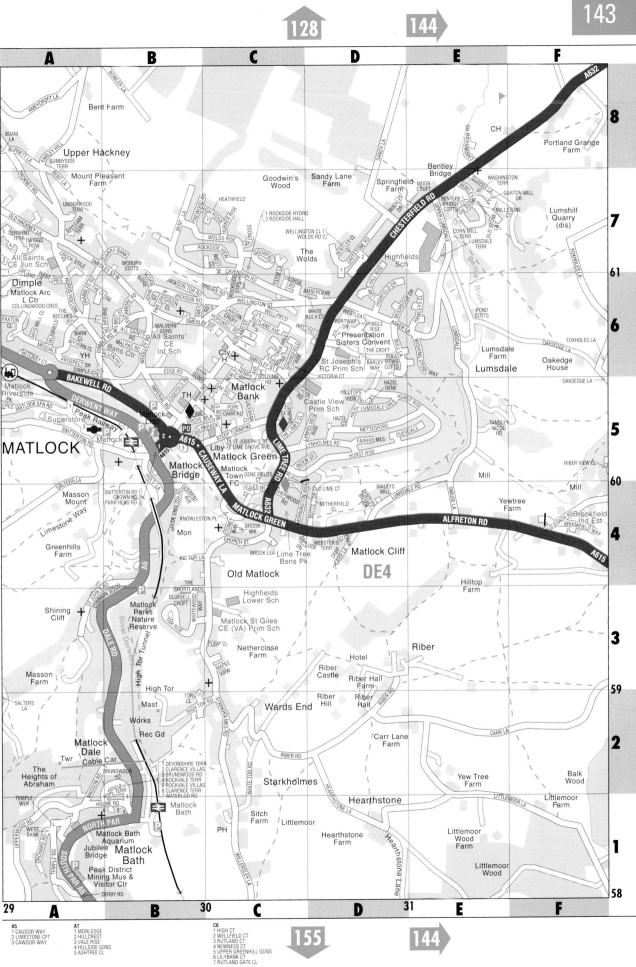

A5
1 CAUDOR WAY
2 LIMESTONE CFT
3 CAWDOR WAY

A7
1 MORLEDGE
2 HILLCREST
3 VALE RISE
4 HILLSIDE GDNS
5 ASHTREE CL

C6
1 HIGH CT
2 WELLFIELD CT
3 RUTLAND CT
4 NEWNESS CT
5 UPPER GREENHILL GDNS
6 LILYBANK CT
7 RUTLAND GATE CL

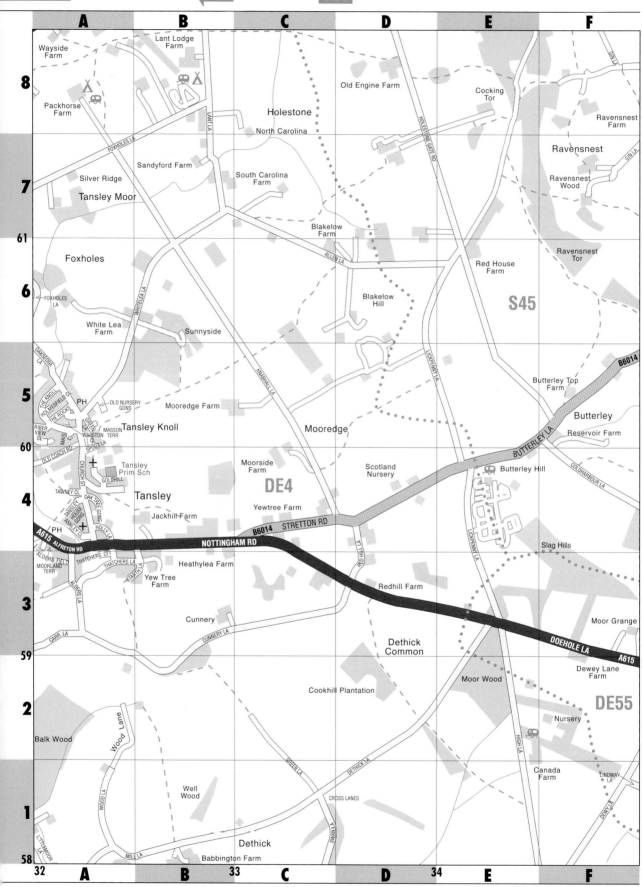

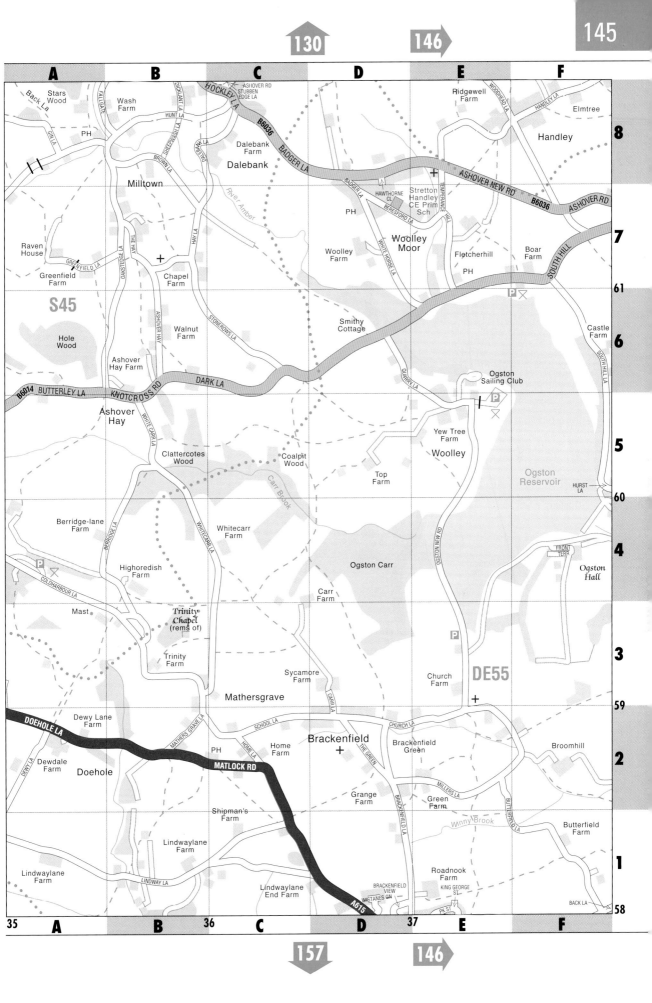

8
7
61
6
5
60
4
3
59
2
1
58

A B C D E F

Stars Wood
Back La
GIN LA
PH
FALLGATE
Wash Farm
HUNT LA
CLICKANT LA
SHEEPWASH LA
BROWN LA
OAK LA
HOCKLEY LA
Dalebank Farm
ASHOVER RD
STUBBEN EDGE LA
B6036
Dalebank
BADGER LA
Ridgewell Farm
WOODHEAD LA
HANDLEY LA
Elmtree
Handley
Milltown
HAY LA
BADGER LA
Hawthorne CL
Stretton Handley CE Prim Sch
BERESFORD LA
WHITE HORSE LA
TEMPERANCE HILL
ASHOVER NEW RD
B6036
ASHOVER RD

Raven House
GREENFIELD LA
Greenfield Farm
THE HAY
OAKSTEDGE LA
ASHOVER HAY
+
Chapel Farm
PH
Woolley Farm
Woolley Moor
Fletcherhill
PH
Boar Farm
South Hill
SOUTH HILL

S45
Hole Wood
Ashover Hay Farm
Walnut Farm
STONEROWS LA
Smithy Cottage
QUARRY LA
Ogston Sailing Club
Castle Farm
SOUTH HILL LA

B6014 BUTTERLEY LA
KNOTCROSS RD
DARK LA
Ashover Hay
WHITE CARR LA
P

Clattercotes Wood
Coalpit Wood
Carr Brook
Top Farm
Yew Tree Farm
Woolley
Ogston Reservoir
HURST LA

Berridge-lane Farm
BERRIDGE LA
WHITECARR LA
Whitecarr Farm
Ogston Carr
OGSTON MILL RD
FRONT TERR
Ogston Hall

COLDHARBOUR LA
P
Highoredish Farm
Carr Farm
P

Mast
Trinity Chapel (rems of)
Church Farm
DE55

Trinity Farm
Sycamore Farm
CARR LA
+

Mathersgrave
CHURCH LA

DOEHOLE LA
Dewy Lane Farm
MATHERS GRAVE LA
SCHOOL LA
HOME LA
PH
Home Farm
Brackenfield
+
THE GREEN
Brackenfield Green
Broomhill

DEWY LA
Dewdale Farm
Doehole
MATLOCK RD
Grange Farm
BRACKENFIELD LA
MILLERS LA
Green Farm
BUTTERFIELD LA
Butterfield Farm

Shipman's Farm
Lindwaylane Farm
LINDWAY LA
Lindwaylane End Farm
A615
Winny Brook
BRACKENFIELD VIEW
WISTANES GN
KING GEORGE ST
Roadnook Farm
PK ST
BACK LA

Lindwaylane Farm

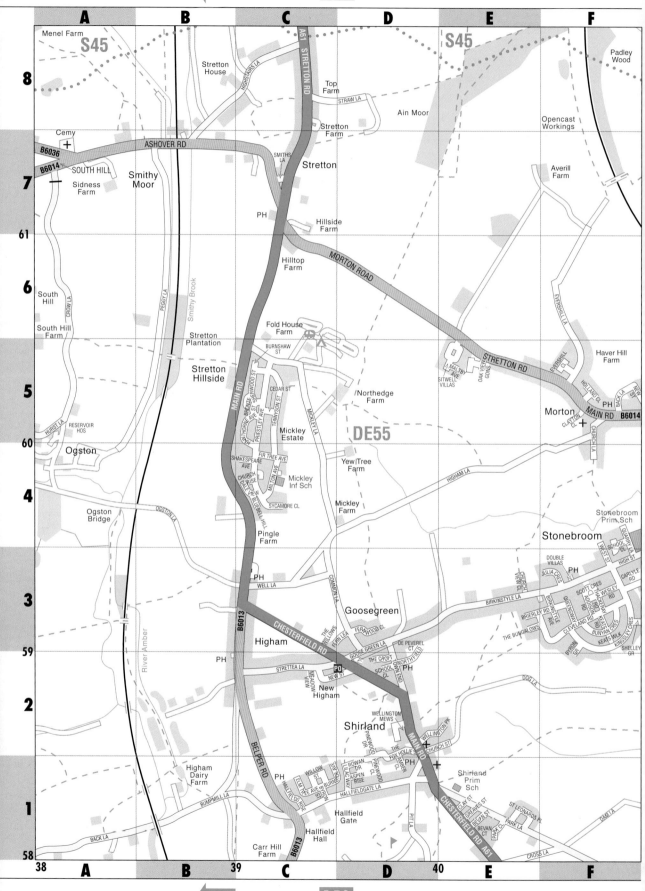

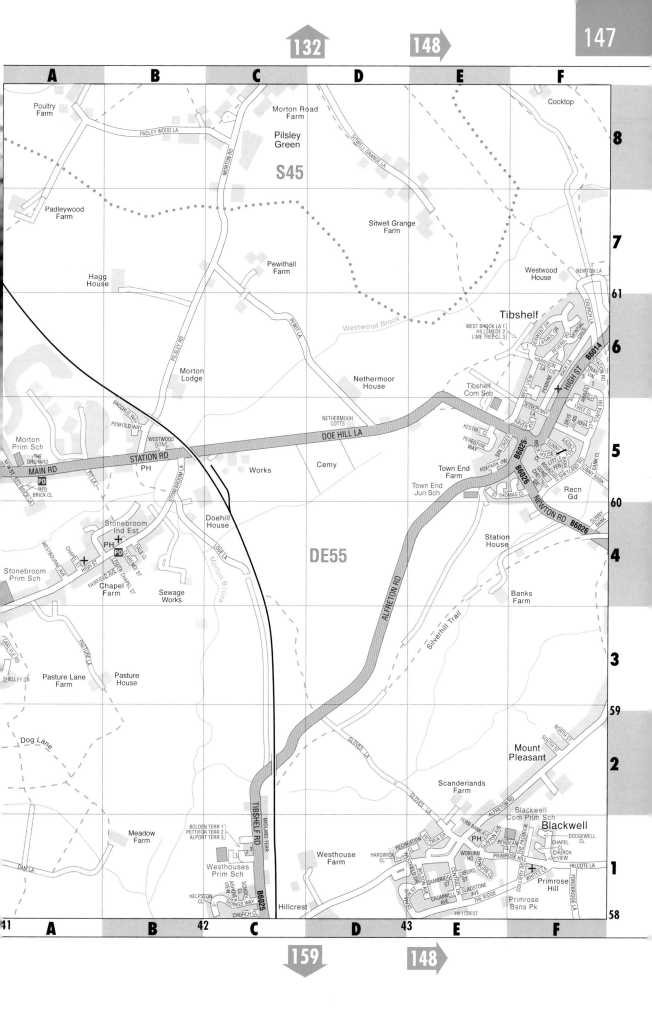

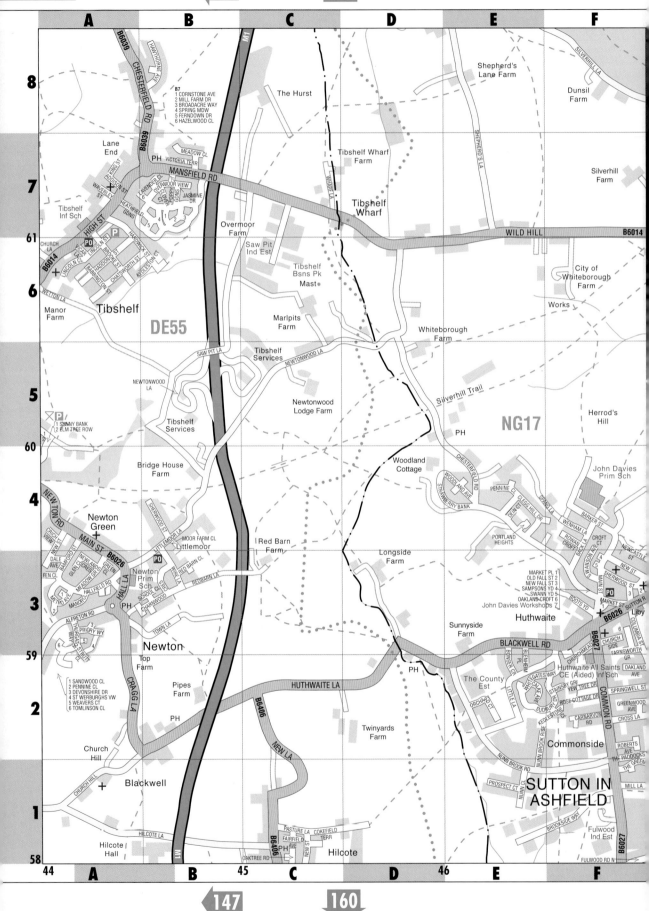

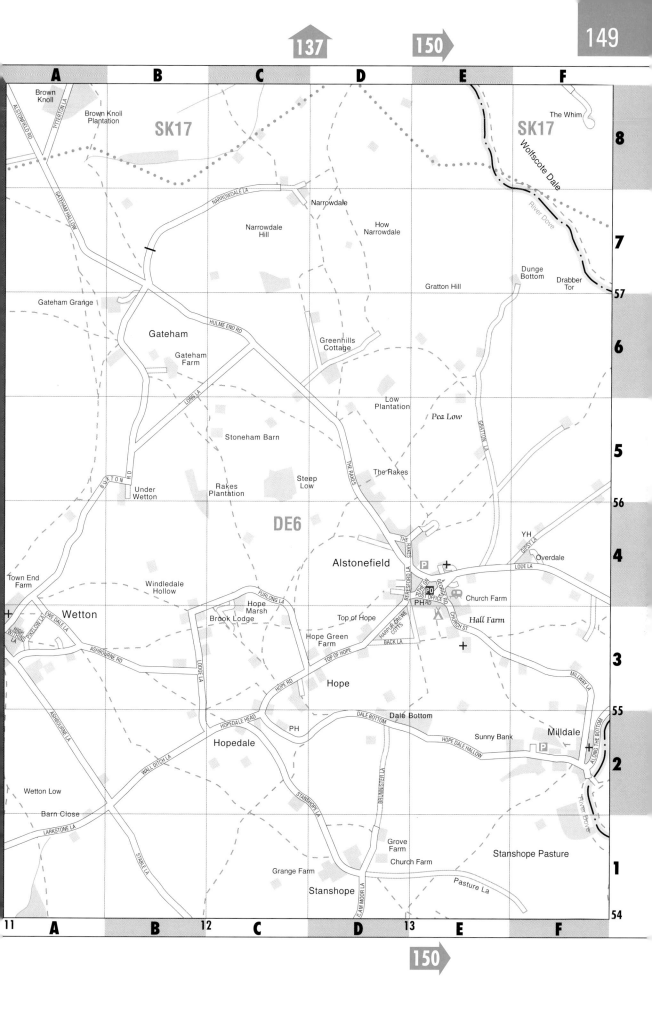

A B C D E F

Brown
Knoll

Brown Knoll
Plantation

SK17

The Whim

SK17

Wolfscote Dale

River Dove

8

Narrowdale

Narrowdale

How
Narrowdale

Narrowdale
Hill

7

Gratton Hill

Dunge
Bottom

Drabber
Tor

57

Gateham Grange

HULME END RD

Greenhills
Cottage

Gateham

6

Gateham
Farm

Low
Plantation

Pea Low

GRATTON LA

LONG LA

Stoneham Barn

Steep
Low

The Rakes

5

BUXTON RD

Rakes
Plantation

THE RAKES

56

Under
Wetton

DE6

THE RAKES

YH

GIPSY LA

Overdale

Alstonefield

P

LODE LA

4

Town End
Farm

Windledale
Hollow

Hope
Marsh

FURLONG LA

PO
POST OFFICE
GEORGE RD

Church Farm

Wetton

HIGH WETTON LA
EWE DALE LA
PIKE LOW LA

Brook Lodge

Top of Hope

PH

Hall Farm

LODE LA

HARPUR CREWE COTTS
BACK LA

BERESFORD LA
CHURCH ST
MILLWAY LA

ASHBOURNE RD

Hope Green
Farm

HOPE RD

3

Hope

TOP OF HOPE

55

ASHBOURNE LA

HOPEDALE HEAD

PH

Dale Bottom

Dale Bottom

Sunny Bank

Milldale

P

ALONG THE BOTTOM

Hopedale

WALL DITCH LA

HOPE DALE HALLOW

2

Wetton Low

BRUNNISTER LA

River Dove

STABLE LA

Barn Close

STANSHOPE LA

Grove
Farm

Stanshope Pasture

LARKSTONE LA

Church Farm

1

Grange Farm

Pasture La

CLAM MOOR LA

Stanshope

54

149
138

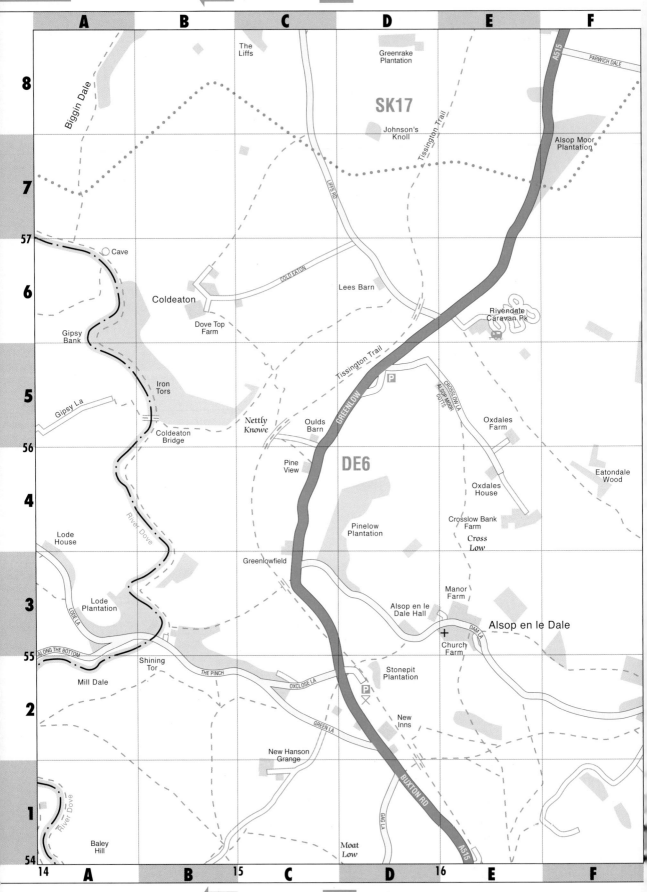

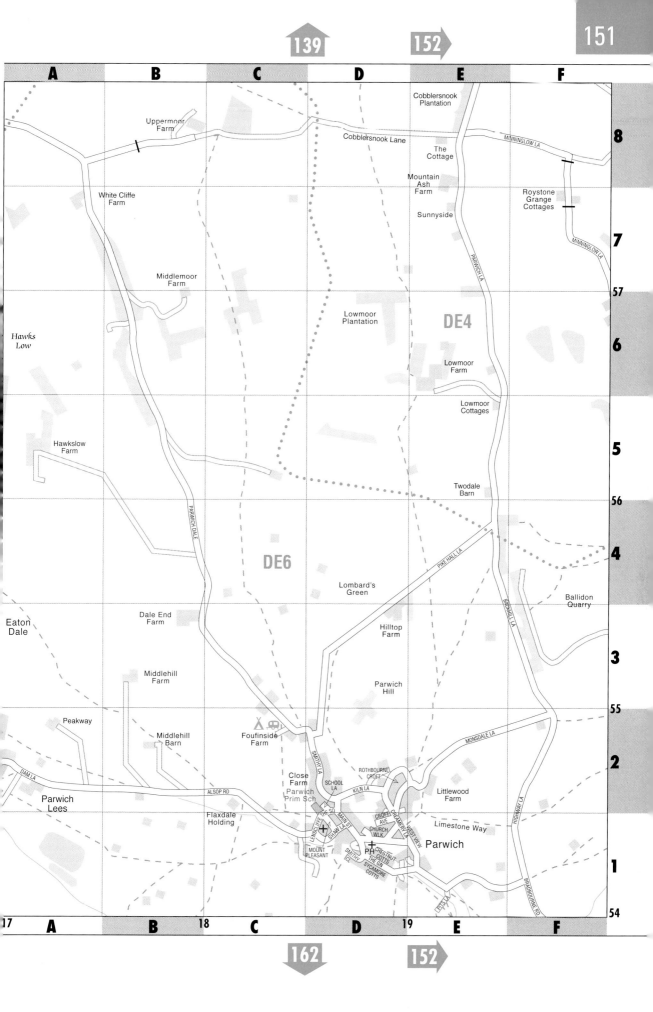

A B C D E F

8

Cobblersnook
Plantation

Uppermoor
Farm

Cobblersnook Lane

MINNINGLOW LA

The
Cottage

White Cliffe
Farm

Mountain
Ash
Farm

Roystone
Grange
Cottages

Sunnyside

7

MINNINGLOW LA

Middlemoor
Farm

57

Lowmoor
Plantation

DE4

Hawks
Low

6

Lowmoor
Farm

PARWICH LA

Lowmoor
Cottages

Hawkslow
Farm

5

56

PARWICH DALE

Twodale
Barn

DE6

4

PIKE HALL LA

Lombard's
Green

Ballidon
Quarry

Dale End
Farm

BACKHILL LA

Eaton
Dale

Hilltop
Farm

3

Middlehill
Farm

Parwich
Hill

55

Peakway

MONSDALE LA

Middlehill
Barn

2

Foufinside
Farm

ROTHBOURNE
CROFT

Littlewood
Farm

DAM LA

Close
Farm

SMITHY LA

SCHOOL
LA

KILN LA

HIGHWAY LA

Parwich
Lees

ALSOP RD

Parwich
Prim Sch

CROFT
AVE

Limestone Way

Flaxdale
Holding

LEYS CLIFFE

THE SQ

CREAMERY LA

WEST VIEW

Parwich

MAIN ST

CHURCH
WLK

MOUNT
PLEASANT

PH

THE GN

CHESTNUT
COTTS

BRADBOURNE RD

SMITHY
CL

SYCAMORE
COTTS

LEYS LA

1

17 A 18 B C 19 D E F 54

151
140

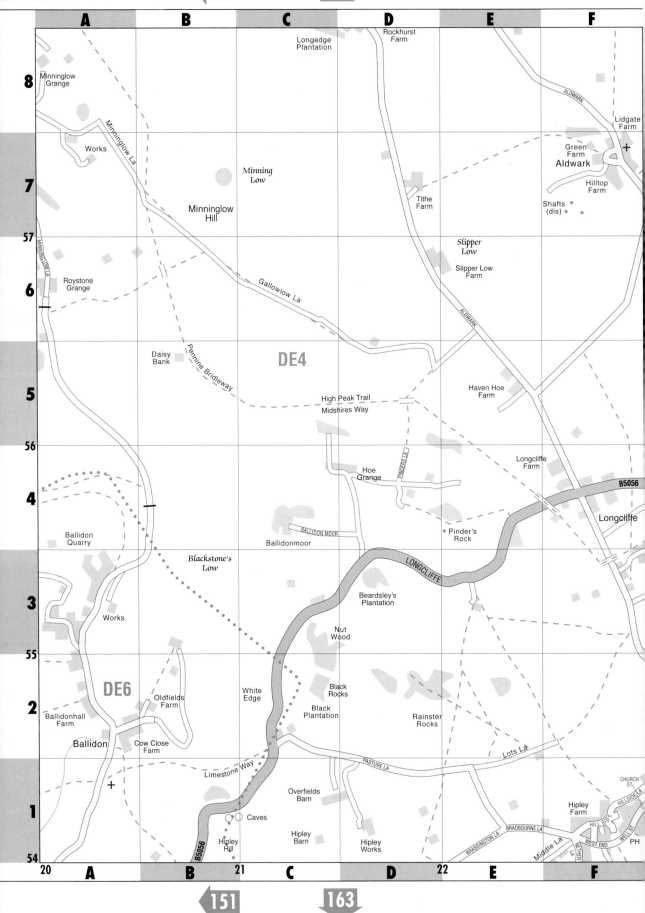

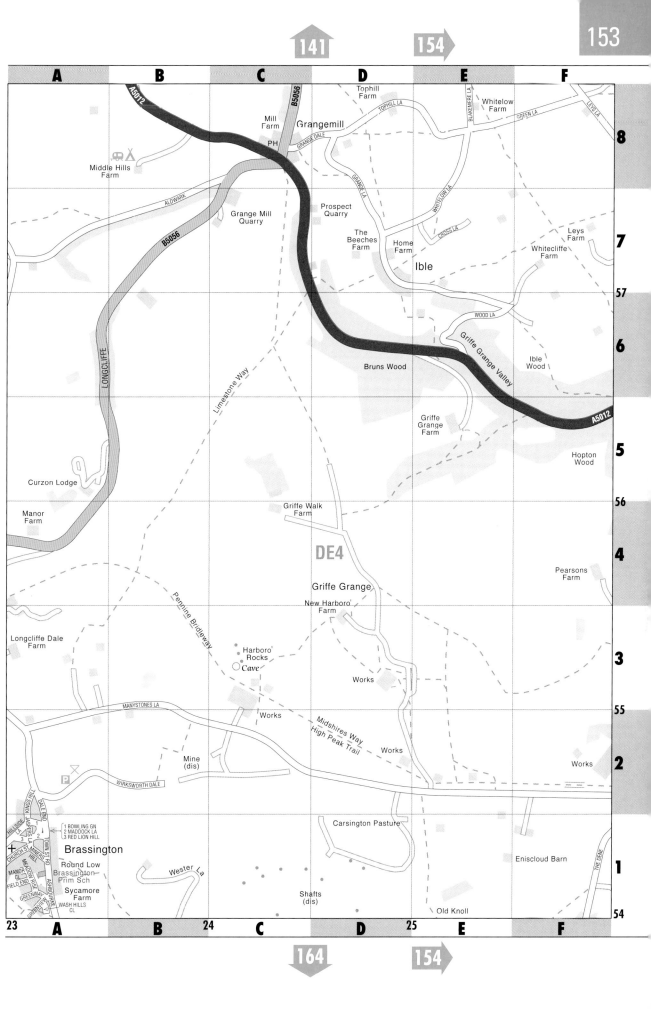

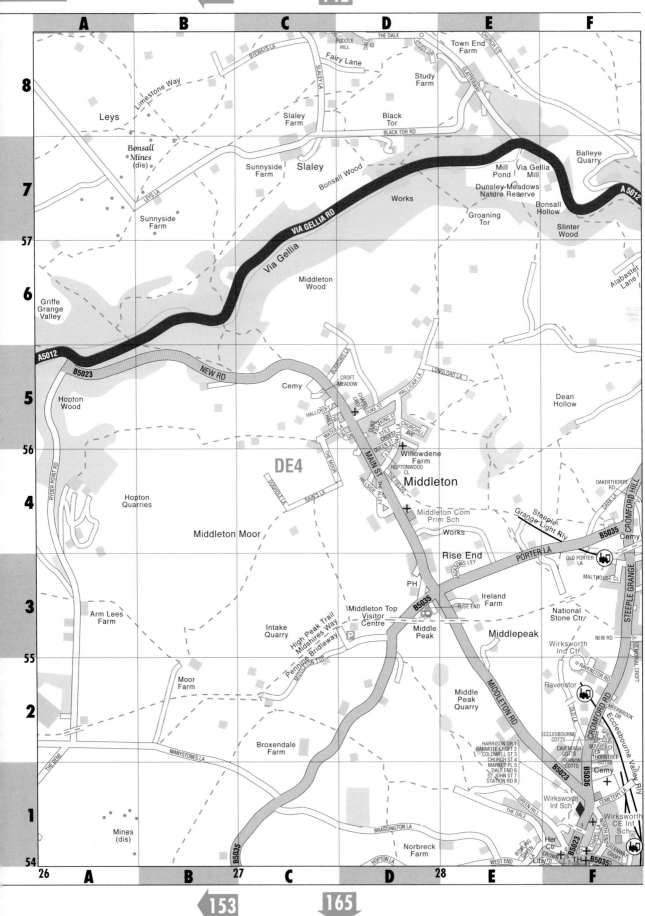

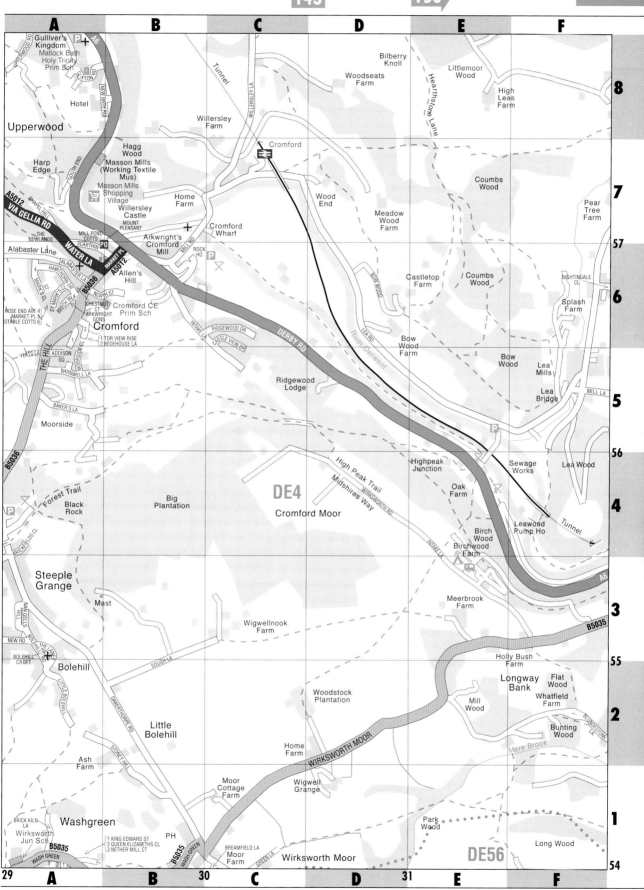

8

7

57

6

5

56

4

3

55

2

1

54

Gulliver's Kingdom
Matlock Bath Holy Trinity Prim Sch

Hotel

Upperwood

Harp Edge

Hagg Wood
Masson Mills (Working Textile Mus)
Masson Mills Shopping Village

Willersley Castle

A5012 VIA GELLIA RD

The Newlands

WATER LA

MARKET PL

A5012

Alabaster Lane

B5036

Rose End Ave
Market Pl
Stable Cotts

Cromford

Moorside

B5036

Forest Trail

Black Rock

Steeple Grange

Mast

New Rd

Bolehill

Little Bolehill

Ash Farm

Washgreen

Wirksworth Jun Sch

B5035

Brick Kiln La

Wash Green

PH

Moor Cottage Farm

Moor Farm

Breamfield La

Wirksworth Moor

Wigwell Grange

Home Farm

WIRKSWORTH MOOR

Woodstock Plantation

Sough La

Wigwellnook Farm

Big Plantation

DE4

Cromford Moor

Midshires Way

High Peak Trail

Ridgewood Lodge

Ridgewood Dr

DERBY RD

Willersley Farm

Tunnel

Willersley La

Cromford

Woodseats Farm

Bilberry Knoll

Hearthstone Lane

Littlemoor Wood

High Leas Farm

Coumbs Wood

Pear Tree Farm

Wood End

Meadow Wood Farm

Castletop Farm

Coumbs Wood

Splash Farm

Nightingale Cl

Bow Wood Farm

Bow Wood

Lea Mills

Lea Bridge

Mill La

Highpeak Junction

River Derwent

Lea Wood

Sewage Works

Leawood Pump Ho

Tunnel

A6

Oak Farm

Birch Wood

Birchwood

Meerbrook Farm

B5035

Holly Bush Farm

Longway Bank

Flat Wood

Whatfield Farm

Mill Wood

Blundestone La

Bunting Wood

Mere Brook

Park Wood

Long Wood

DE56

155
144

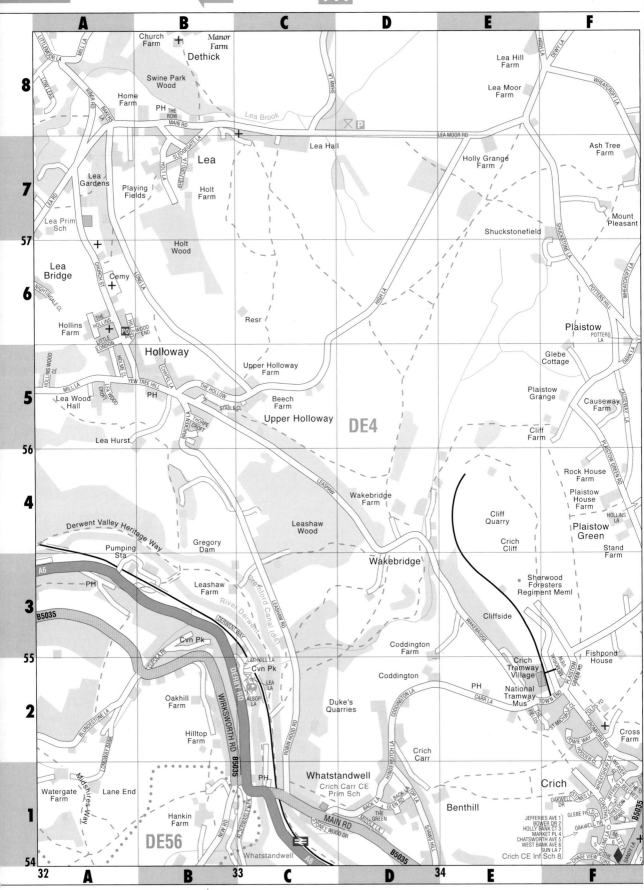

155
167

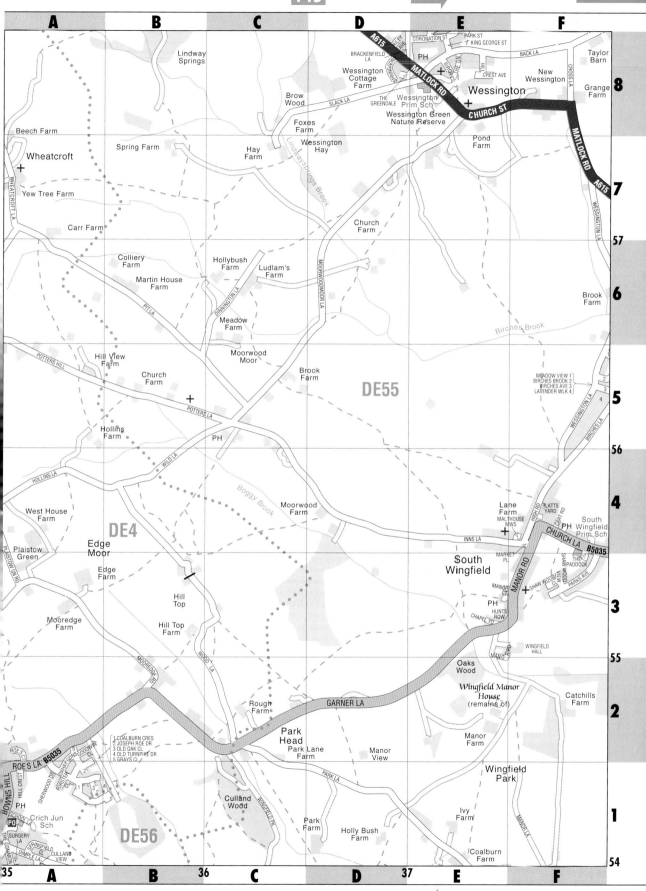

A   B   C   D   E   F

8
7
57
6
5
56
4
56
3
55
2
1
54

35   A   B   36   C   D   37   E   F

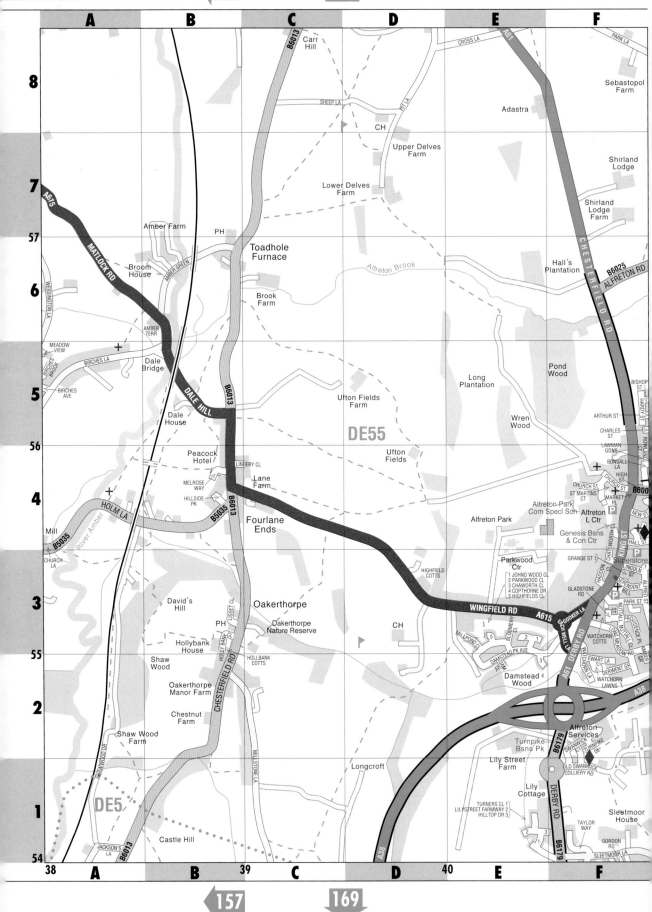

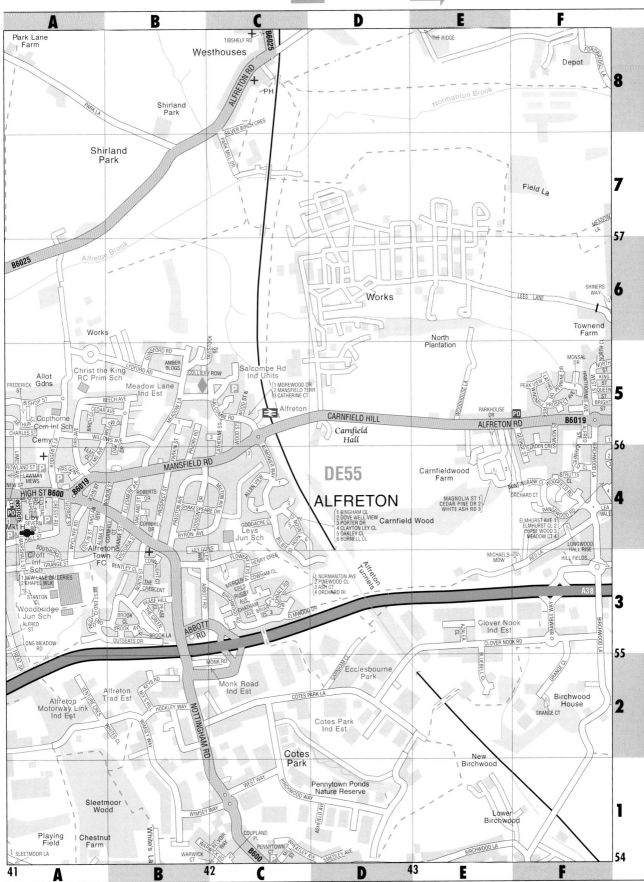

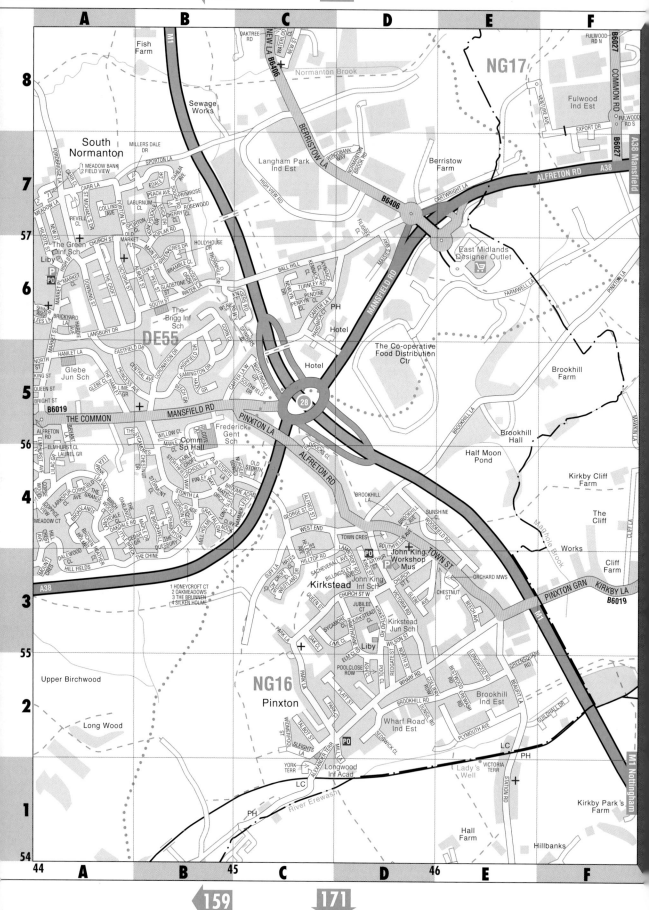

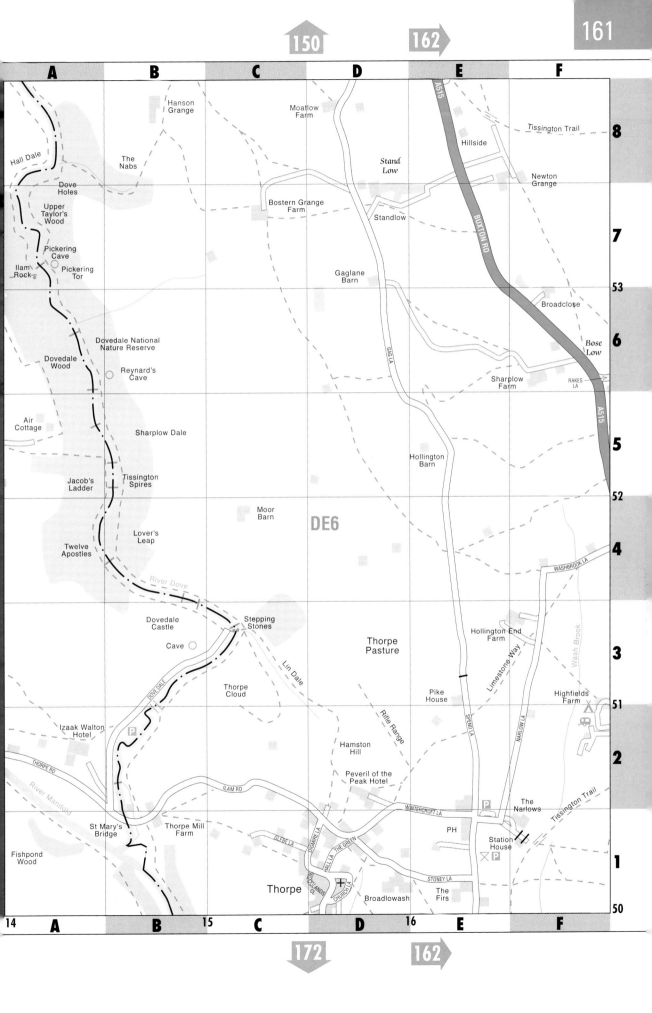

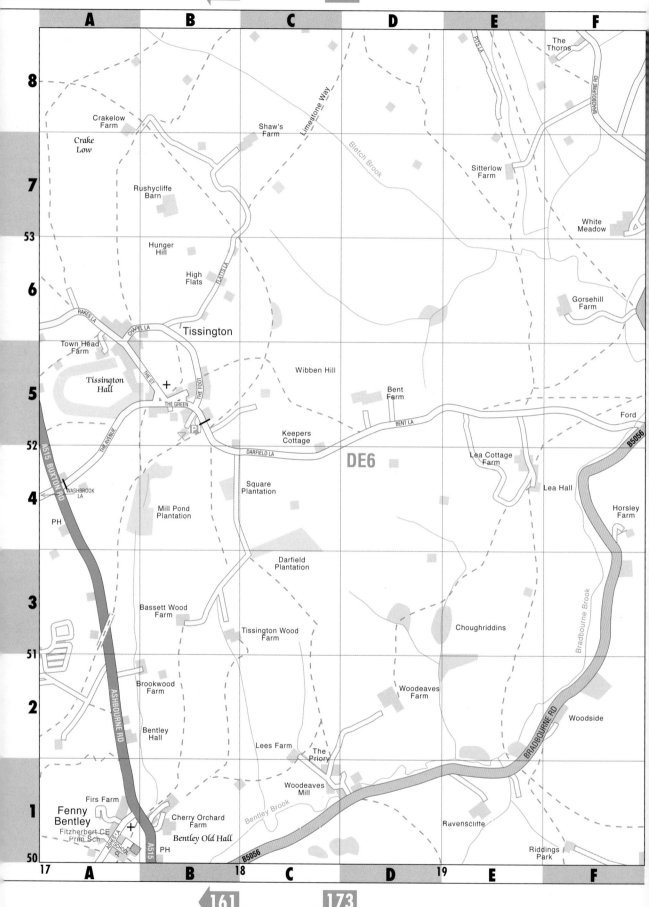

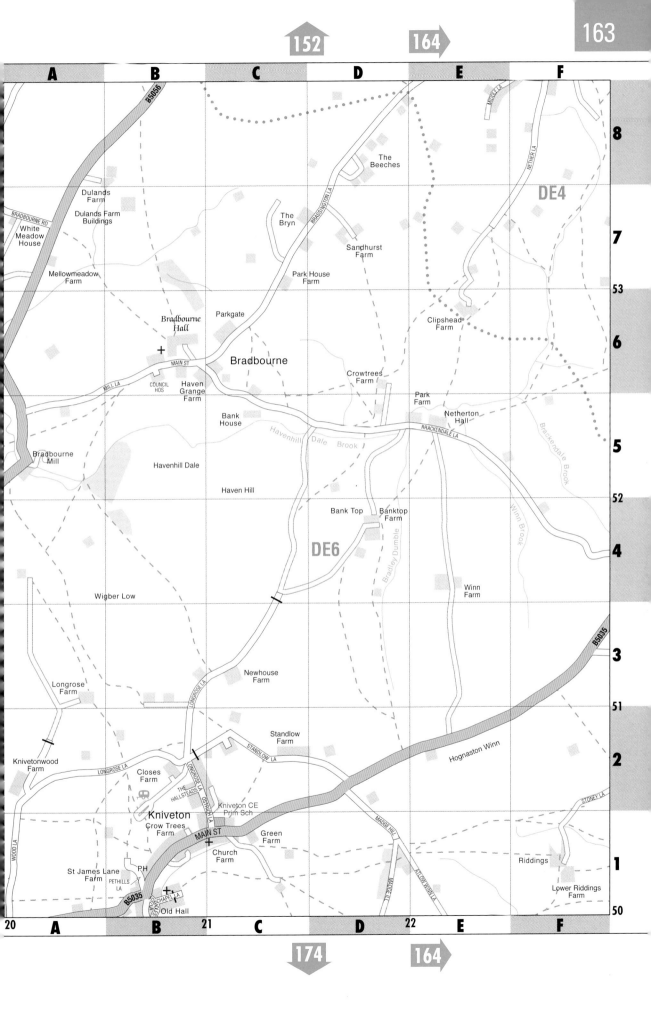

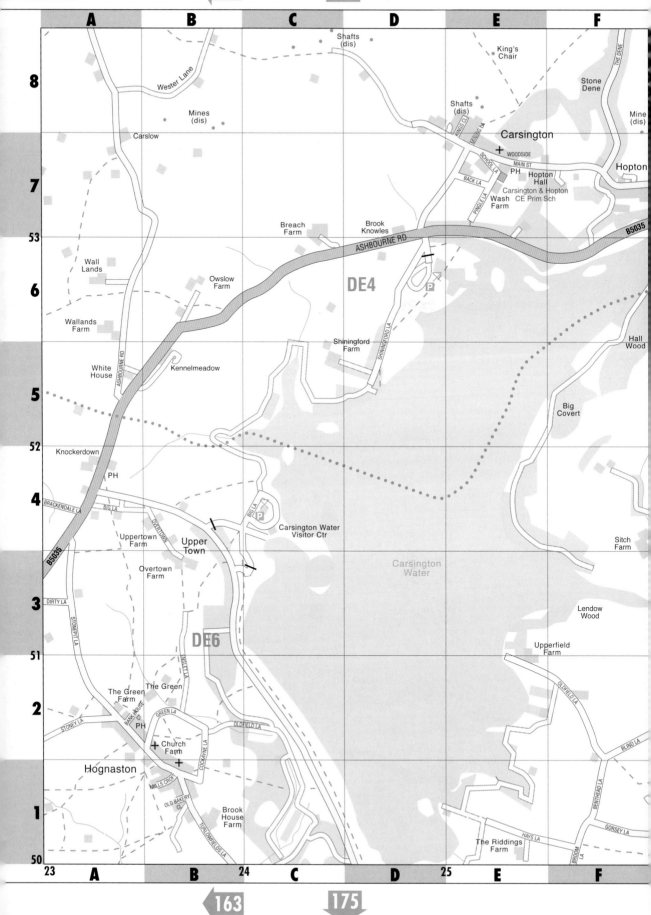

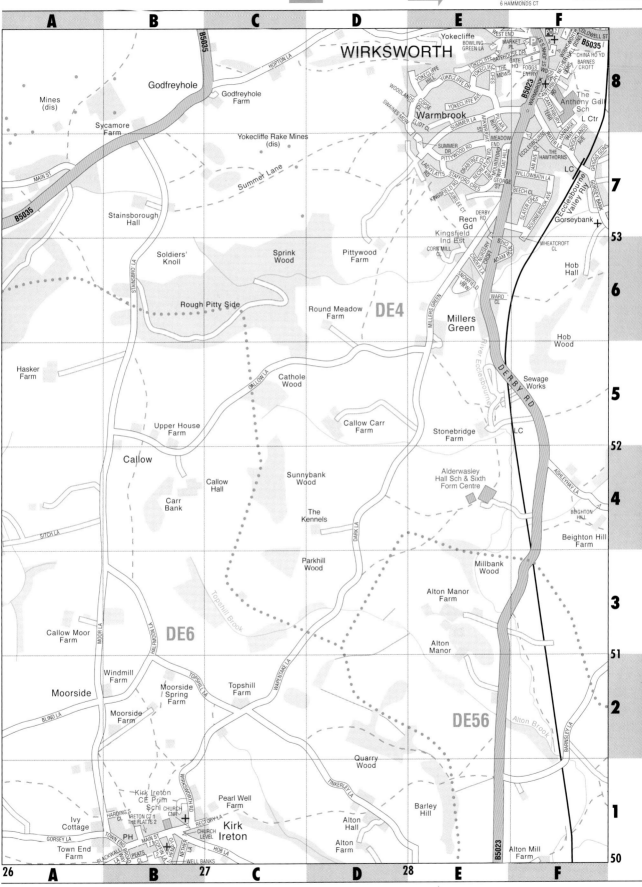

F8
1 BLIND LA
2 CHURCH ST
3 CHURCH WLK
4 ST MARY'S GATE
5 THE CAUSEWAY
6 HAMMONDS CT
7 CROWN YD

A B C D E F

8
53
7
6
5
52
4
3
51
2
1
50

Mines (dis)

Godfreyhole

Godfreyhole Farm

Sycamore Farm

B5035

Hopton La

WIRKSWORTH

Yokecliffe

West End
Market Pl
Bowling Green La

Warmbrook

Yokecliffe Rake Mines (dis)

Summer Lane

B5023

The Anthony Gell Sch
L Ctr

L C

Stainsborough Hall

Sprink Wood

Pittywood Farm

DE4

Recn Gd
Kingsfield Ind Est
CORN MILL CL

Gorseybank

Soldiers' Knoll

Rough Pitty Side

Round Meadow Farm

Millers Green

Hob Hall

Hob Wood

Hasker Farm

Cathole Wood

Callow La

Sewage Works

Callow Carr Farm

Stonebridge Farm

L C

Upper House Farm

Callow

Carr Bank

Callow Hall

Sunnybank Wood

The Kennels

Dark La

Alderwasley Hall Sch & Sixth Form Centre

Beighton Hill

Beighton Hill Farm

Ashleyhay La

Sitch La

Parkhill Wood

Millbank Wood

Alton Manor Farm

Callow Moor Farm

Moor La

Halfmoon La

DE6

Topshill Brook

Wapentake La

Alton Manor

DE56

Windmill Farm

Moorside

Moorside Spring Farm

Moorside Farm

Blind La

Topshill La

Topshill Farm

Alton Brook

Barnsley La

Quarry Wood

Ivy Cottage

Gorsey La

Town End Farm

Kirk Ireton CE Prim Sch

Pearl Well Farm

Wirksworth Rd

Rectory La

Kirk Ireton

Tinkerley La

Alton Hall

Alton Farm

Barley Hill

B5023

Alton Mill Farm

PH
Main St
Blackwall La
Nether La
Well Banks
Hob La

26 A 27 B C 28 D E F

176 166

165
155

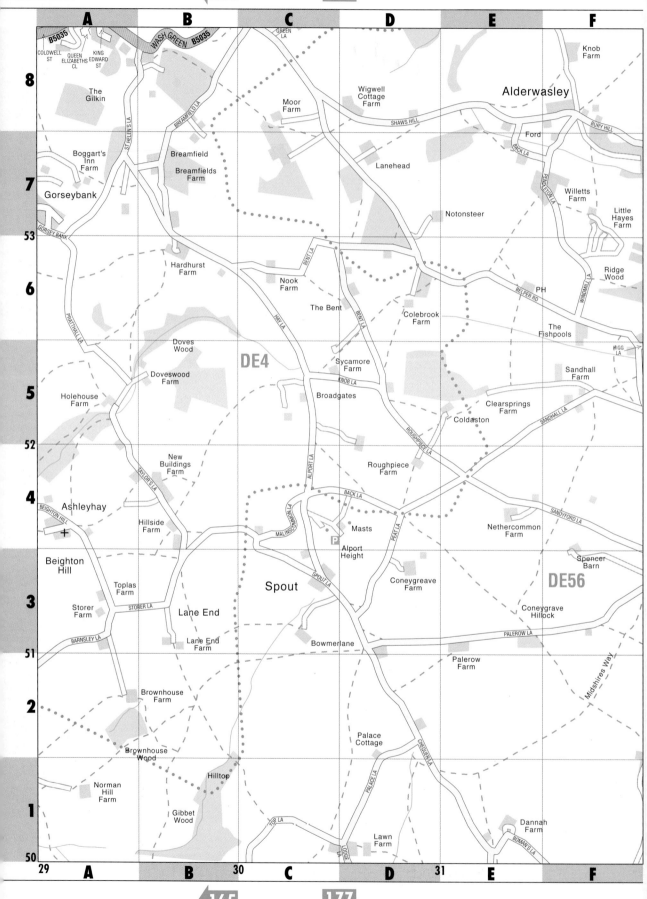

165
177

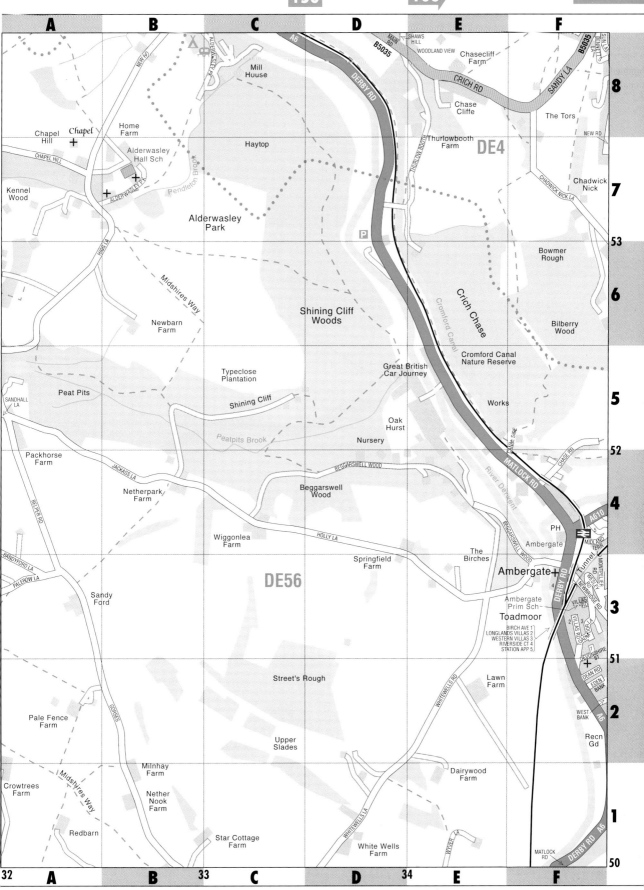

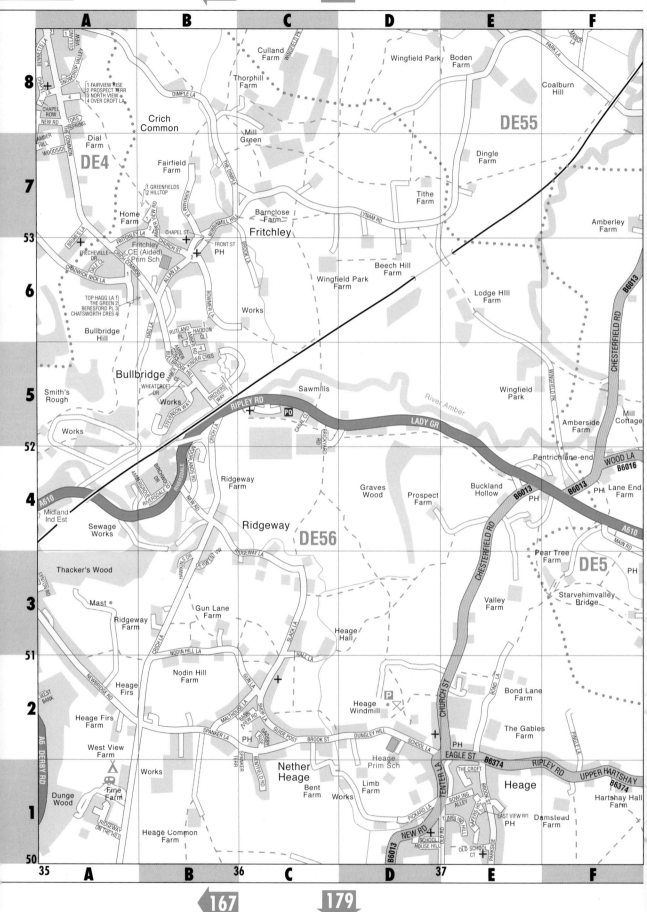

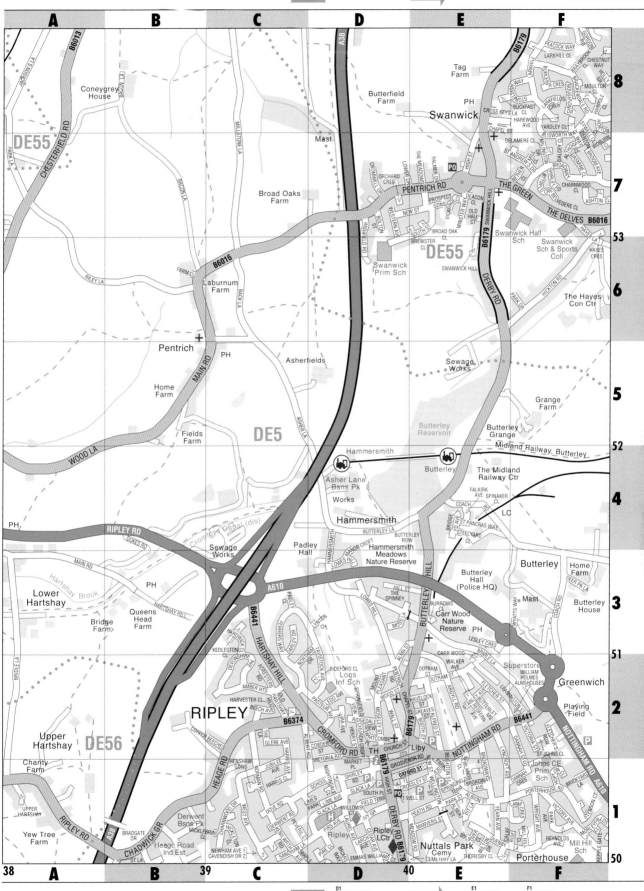

8

7

53

6

5

52

4

3

51

2

1

50

DE55

DE5

DE56

Coneygrey House

Broad Oaks Farm

Butterfield Farm

Mast

Tag Farm

Swanwick

PH

Pentrich

Home Farm

Laburnum Farm

Fields Farm

Asherfields

Swanwick Prim Sch

Swanwick Hall Sch

Swanwick Sch & Sports Coll

The Hayes Con Ctr

Grange Farm

Sewage Works

Butterley Reservoir

Butterley Grange

Midland Railway, Butterley

Hammersmith

Butterley

The Midland Railway Ctr

Asher Lane Bsns Pk

Works

Hammersmith

Padley Hall

Hammersmith Meadows Nature Reserve

Butterley Hall (Police HQ)

Butterley

Home Farm

Butterley House

Lower Hartshay

Hartshay Brook

Queens Head Farm

Bridge Farm

Upper Hartshay

Charity Farm

Yew Tree Farm

Heage Road Ind Est

Derwent Bsns Pk

RIPLEY

Lons Inf Sch

Carr Wood Nature Reserve

Superstore
WILLIAM HOLMES ALMSHOUSES

Greenwich

Playing Field

St Johns CE Prim Sch

Ripley

Ripley LCtr

Nuttals Park

Cemy
CEMETERY LA

Porterhouse

Mill Hill Sch

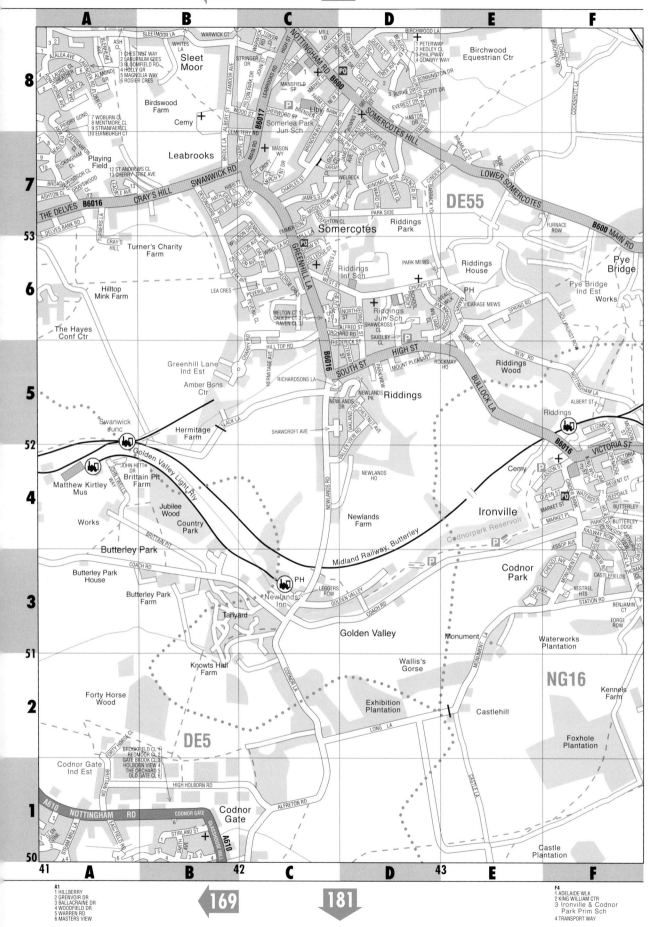

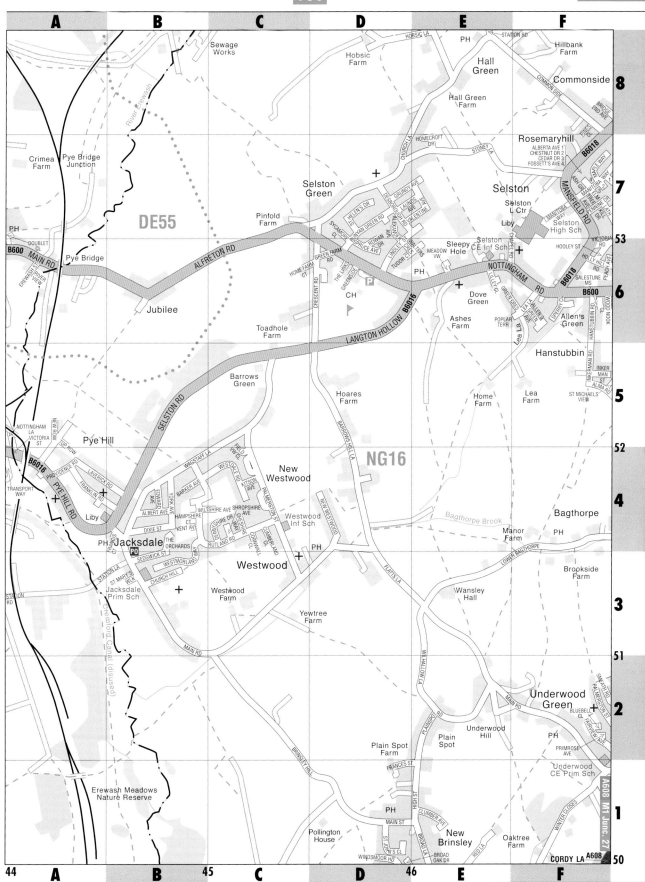

161

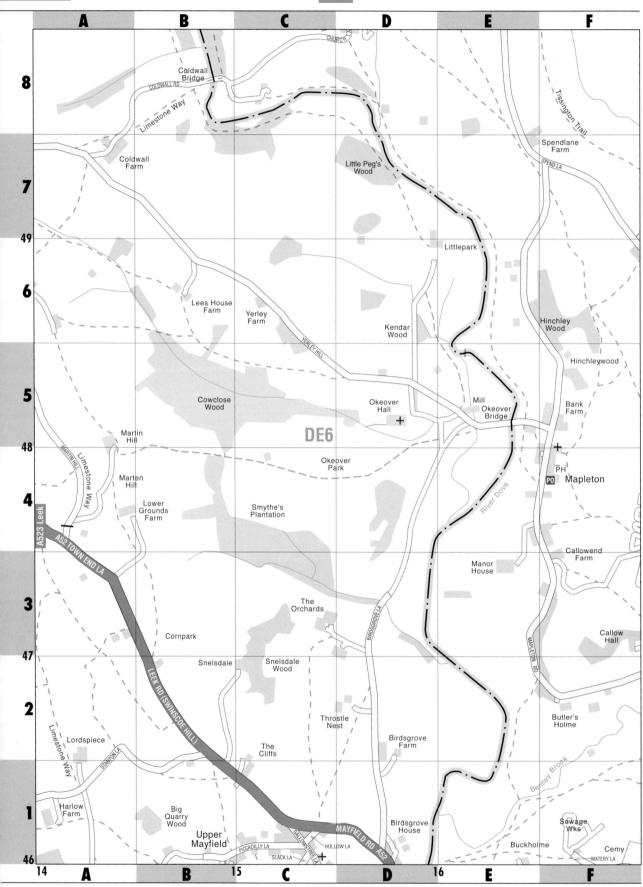

184

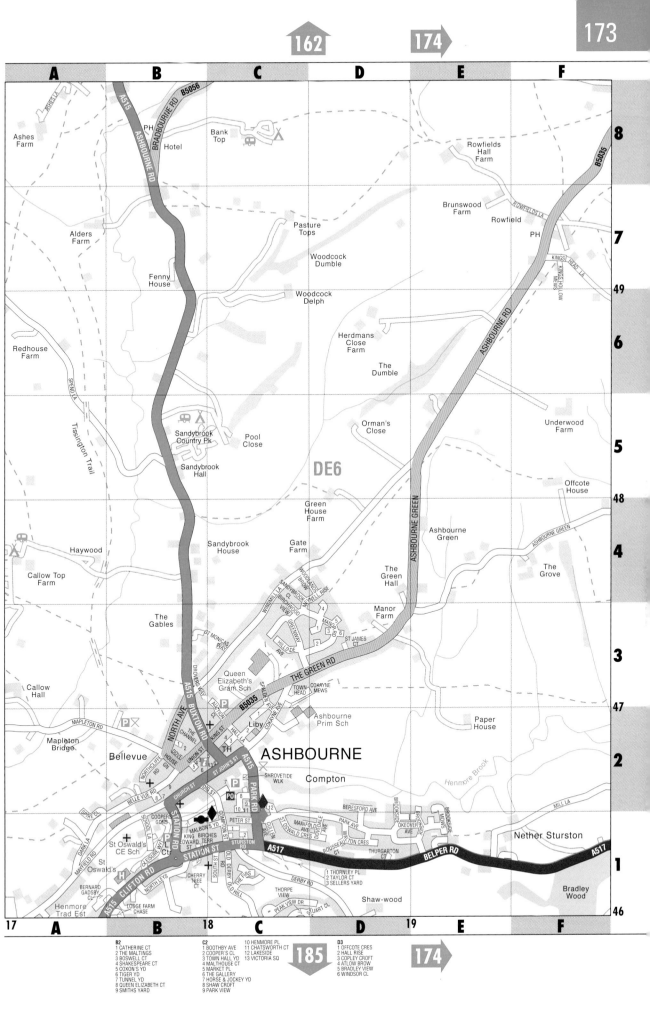

B2
1 CATHERINE CT
2 THE MALTINGS
3 BOSWELL CT
4 SHAKESPEARE CT
5 COXON'S YD
6 TIGER YD
7 TUNNEL YD
8 QUEEN ELIZABETH CT
9 SMITHS YARD

C2
1 BOOTHBY AVE
2 COOPER'S CL
3 TOWN HALL YD
4 MALTHOUSE CT
5 MARKET PL
6 THE GALLERY
7 HORSE & JOCKEY YD
8 SHAW CROFT
9 PARK VIEW
10 HENMORE PL
11 CHATSWORTH CT
12 LAKESIDE
13 VICTORIA SQ

D3
1 OFFCOTE CRES
2 HALL RISE
3 COPLEY CROFT
4 ATLOW BROW
5 BRADLEY VIEW
6 WINDSOR CL

1 THORNLEY PL
2 TAYLOR CT
3 SELLERS YARD

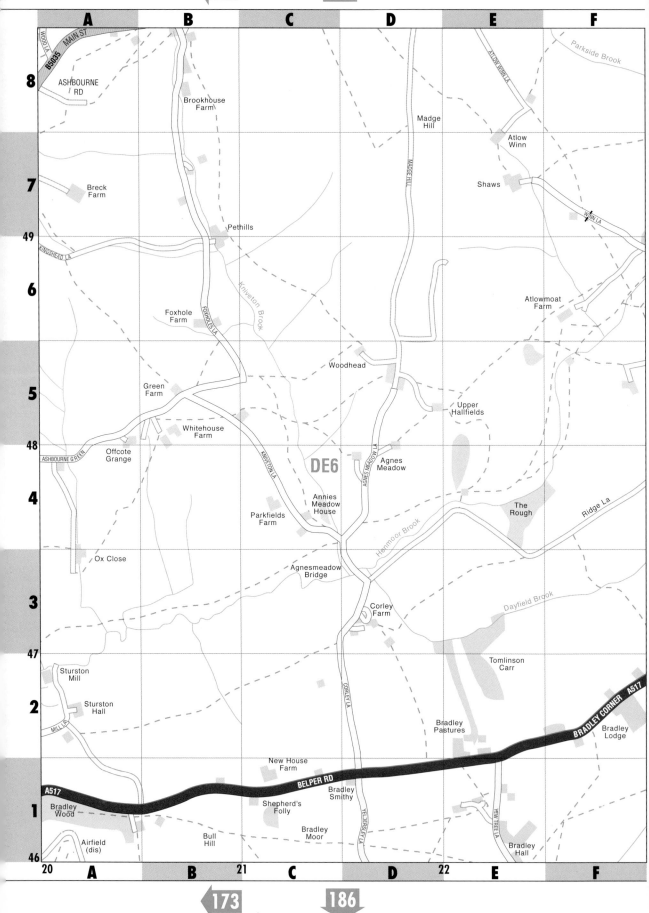

A B C D E F

8

ASHBOURNE
RD

WOOD LA
B5035
MAIN ST

Brookhouse
Farm

ATLOW WINN LA

Madge
Hill

Parkside Brook

Atlow
Winn

7

Breck
Farm

Shaws

WINN LA

49

Pethills

Kniveton Brook

KINGSHEAD LA

6

Foxhole
Farm

FOXHOLES LA

MADGE HILL

Atlowmoat
Farm

5

Green
Farm

Woodhead

Upper
Hallfields

48

Offcote
Grange

ASHBOURNE GREEN

Whitehouse
Farm

KNIVETON LA

DE6

AGNES MEADOW LA

Agnes
Meadow

4

Ox Close

Parkfields
Farm

Annies
Meadow
House

Henmoor Brook

The
Rough

Ridge La

3

Agnesmeadow
Bridge

Corley
Farm

Dayfield Brook

47

Sturston
Mill

Tomlinson
Carr

BRADLEY CORNER A517

2

Sturston
Hall

MILL LA

CORLEY LA

Bradley
Pastures

Bradley
Lodge

New House
Farm

BELPER RD

Bradley
Smithy

YELDERSLEY LA

YEW TREE LA

A517

1

Bradley
Wood

Shepherd's
Folly

Bradley
Moor

Bradley
Hall

46

Airfield
(dis)

Bull
Hill

20 A B 21 C D 22 E F

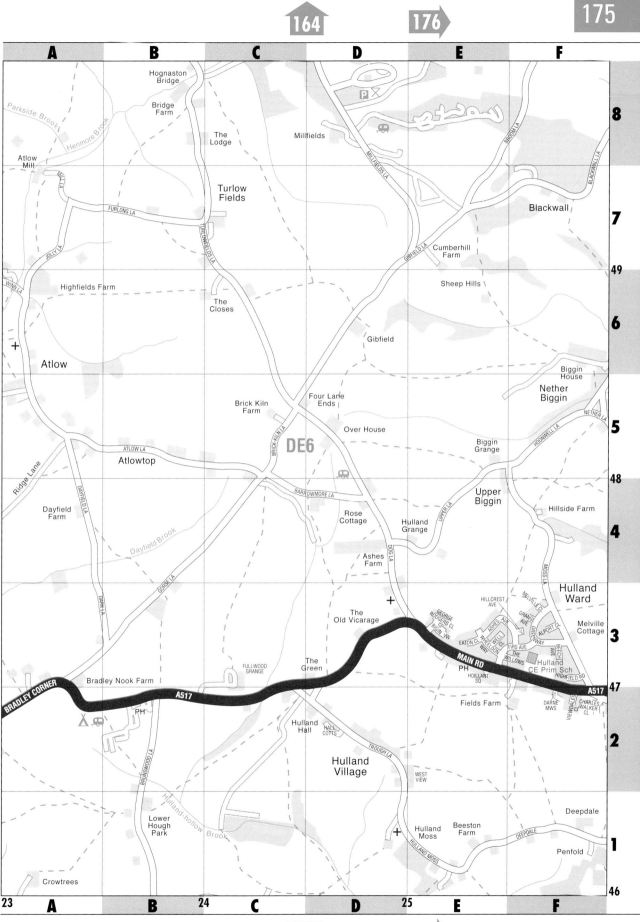

A B C D E F

8
7
49
6
5
48
4
3
47
2
1
46

Parkside Brook
Henmore Brook
Atlow Mill
WINN LA
JOLLY LA
FURLONG LA
Ridge Lane
Atlow
Dayfield Farm
DAYFIELD LA
Dayfield Brook
DARK LA
GORSE LA
BRUNSWOOD LA
Crowtrees
Lower Hough Park
Hulland-hollow Brook

Hognaston Bridge
Bridge Farm
The Lodge
Turlow Fields
ORLOWFIELDS LA
Highfields Farm
The Closes
Brick Kiln Farm
Atlowtop
ATLOW LA
BRICK KILN LA
BARROWMORE LA
DE6
Four Lane Ends
Over House
Rose Cottage
Ashes Farm
The Old Vicarage
FULLWOOD GRANGE
The Green
Bradley Nook Farm
BRADLEY CORNER
A517
PH
Hulland Hall
NALL COTTS
Hulland Village
TROUGH LA

Millfields
P
GIFIELD LA
Gibfield
MILLFIELDS LA
Cumberhill Farm
Sheep Hills
Hulland Grange
DOG LA
UPPER LA
Fullwood Grange
Hulland Moss
HULLAND MOSS
WEST VIEW

Blackwall
BROOM LA
BLACKWALL LA
Biggin House
Nether Biggin
NETHER LA
HOONWELL LA
Biggin Grange
Upper Biggin
Hillside Farm
MOSS LA
Hulland Ward
HILLCREST AVE
MELVILLE CL
Melville Cottage
ASHES AVE
GRANGE AVE
GREENWAY
ALPORT CL
BEECH AVE
Hulland CE Prim Sch
HIGHFIELD RD
GEORGE RODGERS CL
BILLIN VW
EATON CL
WHEELDON WAY
WELL
FIRS AVE
THE WILLOWS
MAIN RD
PH
HOILLANT SQ
Fields Farm
DARNE MWS
VW DALES
CHARLES WALKER CL
A517
Deepdale
DEEPDALE
Penfold
Beeston Farm

23 A B 24 C D 25 E F

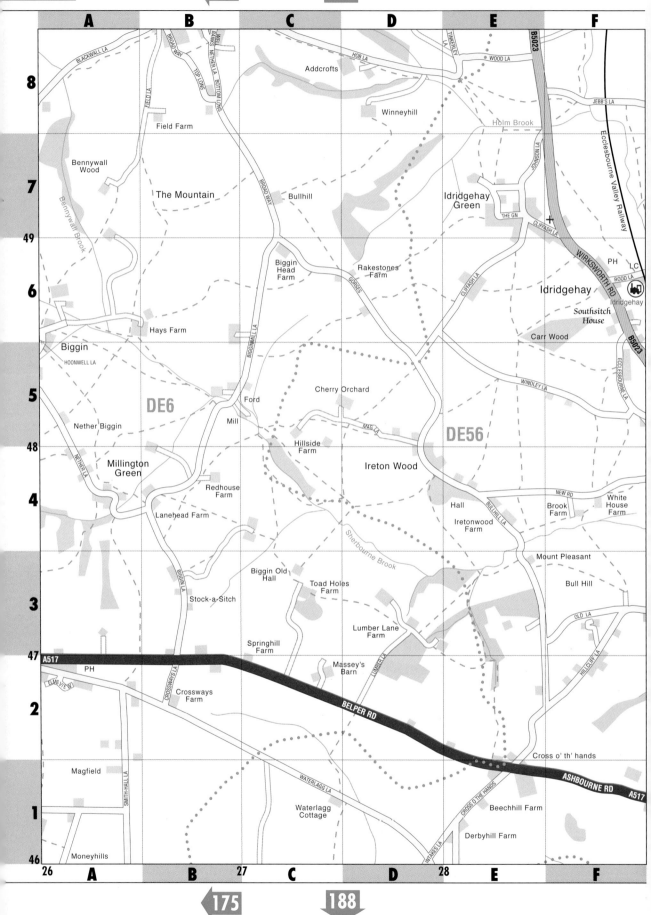

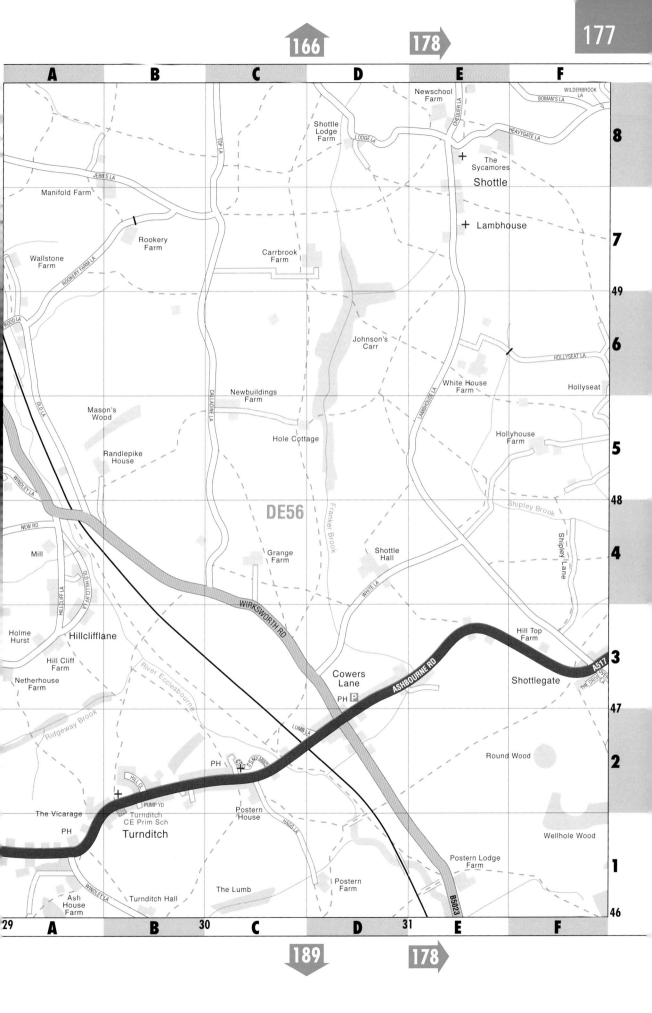

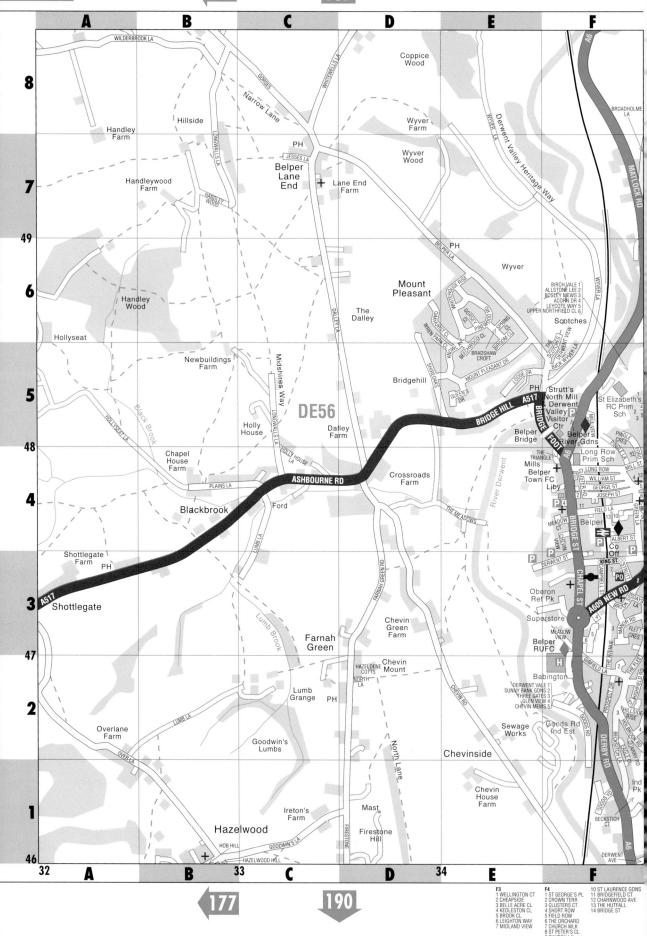

	A	B	C	D	E	F

8
7
49
6
5
48
4
47
3
2
46

32   A   B   33   C   D   34   E   F

Main place labels and streets visible:

WILDERBROOK LA, Handley Farm, Hillside, Narrow Lane, GORSES, WHITEWELLS LA, Coppice Wood, Wyver Farm, Derwent Valley Heritage Way, BROADHOLME LA, A6, MATLOCK RD, WYVER LA, PH, Belper Lane End, JESSES LA, Lane End Farm, Wyver Wood, Handleywood Farm, Handley Wood, HANDLEY WOOD, LONGWALLS LA, BELPER LA, PH, Wyver, Mount Pleasant, Scotches, BIRCH VALE 1, ALLSTONE LEE 2, BOSLEY MEWS 3, ACORN DR 4, LEYCOTE WAY 5, UPPER NORTHFIELD CL 6, Hollyseat, Newbuildings Farm, Midshires Way, The Dalley, WHITEMOOR, GORSEY CL, PINEWOOD, BROOM CL, SPRING, OAKHURST CL, WREN PARK CL, OWL AVE, BEECHWOOD CL, Bradshaw Croft, THE SCOTCHES, DERWENT VIEW, BACK WYVER LA, DE56, Bridgehill, SHIREOAKS, MOUNT PLEASANT DR, LODGE DR, PH, Strutt's North Mill & Derwent Valley Visitor Ctr, St Elizabeth's RC Prim Sch, HOLLYSEAT LA, Black Brook, Holly House, LONGWALLS LA, HOLLY HOUSE LA, Dalley Farm, QUEEN'S DR, BRIDGE HILL, A517, BRIDGE, Belper Bridge, FOOT, A6, Belper River Gdns, PINGLE CRES, Long Row Prim Sch, PINGLE, FORD, MILL ST, Chapel House Farm, PLAINS LA, ASHBOURNE RD, Crossroads Farm, River Derwent, THE TRIANGLE, Mills, Belper Town FC, LONG ROW, CLUSTER RD, WILLIAM ST, GEORGE ST, GREEN LA, Belper Liby, JOSEPH ST, FIELD LA, Blackbrook, PT LIMIT, Ford, THE MEADOWS, MEADOW CT, Belper, ALBERT ST, Co Off, Shottlegate Farm, PH, A517, Shottlegate, FARNAH GREEN RD, DERWENT ST, P, CHEVIN AVE, KING ST, CAMPBELL ST, CHAPEL ST, A609 NEW RD, PO, Oberon Ret Pk, MANOR RD, FLEET CRES, Superstore, MEADOW VIEW, Belper RUFC, H, GIBFIELD LA, Babington, Farnah Green, Chevin Green Farm, HAZELDENE COTTS, NORTH LA, Chevin Mount, CHEVIN RD, DERWENT VALE 1, SUNNY BANK GDNS 2, THREE GATES 3, GLEN VIEW 4, CHEVIN MEWS 5, Lumb Grange, PH, Lumb Brook, LUMB LA, Goodwin's Lumbs, North Lane, Sewage Works, Goods Rd Ind Est, GOODS RD, DERBY RD, A6, PROSPECT DR, BECKSITCH LA, THE BROOK, HILLSIDE RISE, EAGLE CL, Overlane Farm, OVER LA, Chevinside, Chevin House Farm, Ireton's Farm, GOODWIN'S LA, Mast, Firestone Hill, FIRESTONE, Hazelwood, HOB HILL, HAZELWOOD HILL, BECKSTICH CT, Ind Pk, GOODS YD, DERWENT AVE

F3
1 WELLINGTON CT
2 CHEAPSIDE
3 BELLE ACRE CL
4 KEDLESTON CL
5 BROOK CL
6 LEIGHTON WAY
7 MIDLAND VIEW

F4
1 ST GEORGE'S PL
2 CROWN TERR
3 CLUSTERS CT
4 SHORT ROW
5 FIELD ROW
6 THE ORCHARD
7 CHURCH WLK
8 ST PETER'S CL
9 CHURCH LA

F4
10 ST LAURENCE GDNS
11 BRIDGEFIELD CT
12 CHARNWOOD AVE
13 THE HUTFALL
14 BRIDGE ST

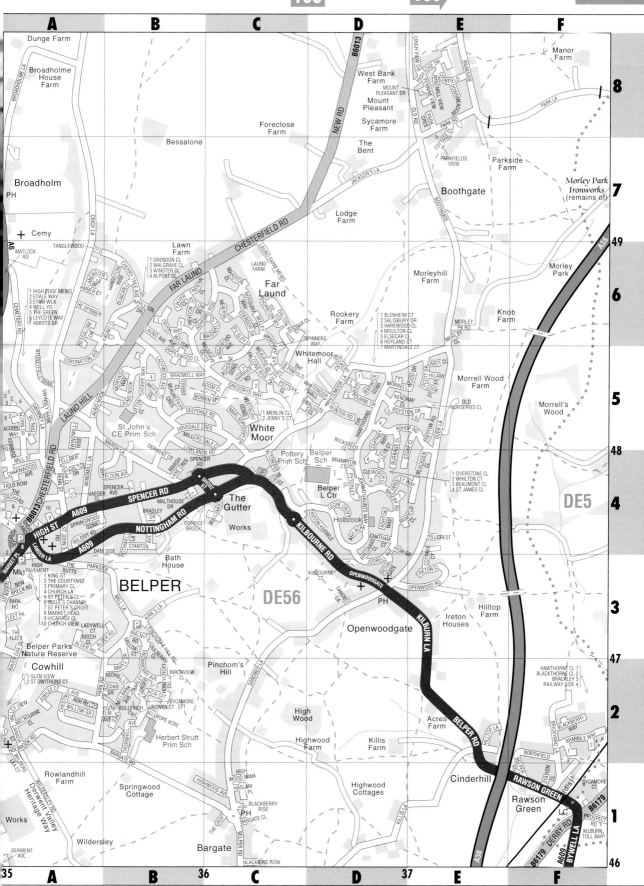

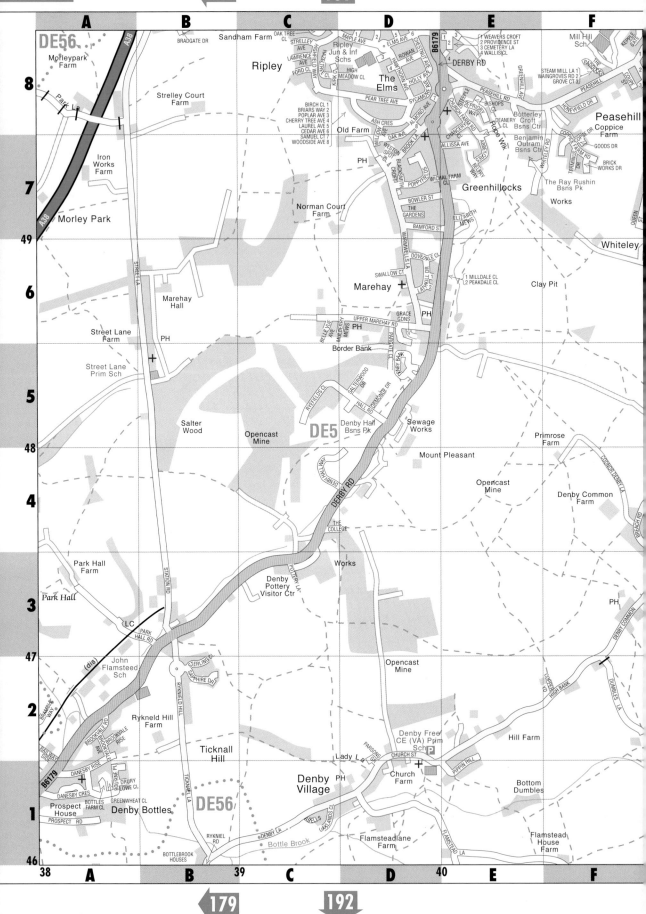

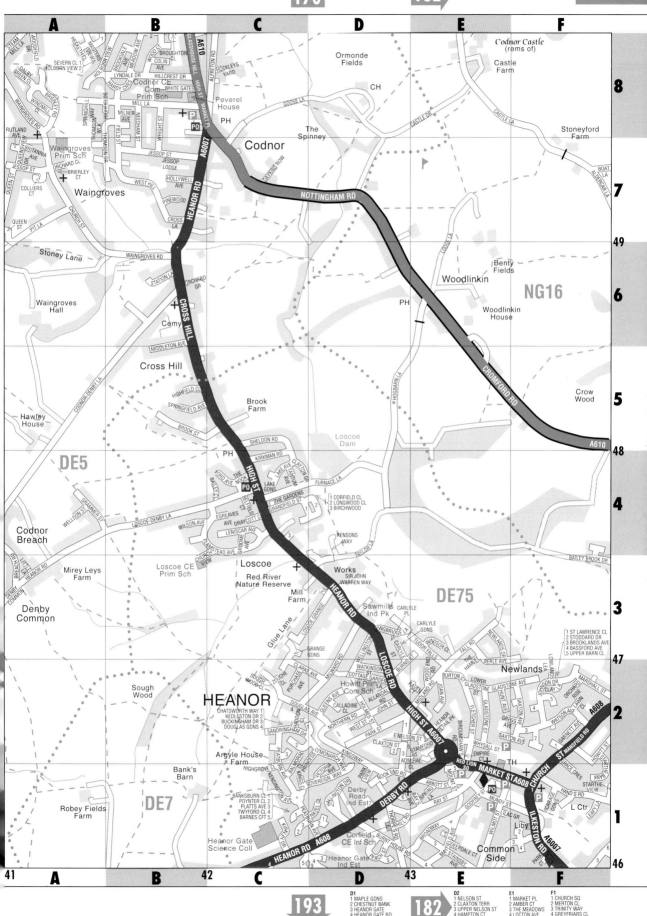

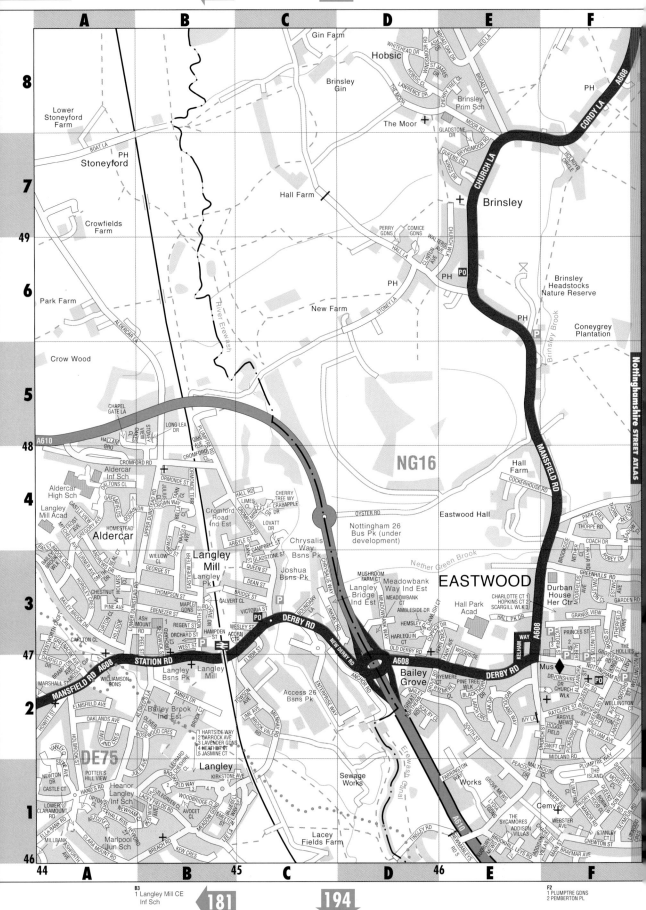

Nottinghamshire STREET ATLAS

B3
1 Langley Mill CE
  Inf Sch

◀ 181

194

F2
1 PLUMPTRE GDNS
2 PEMBERTON PL

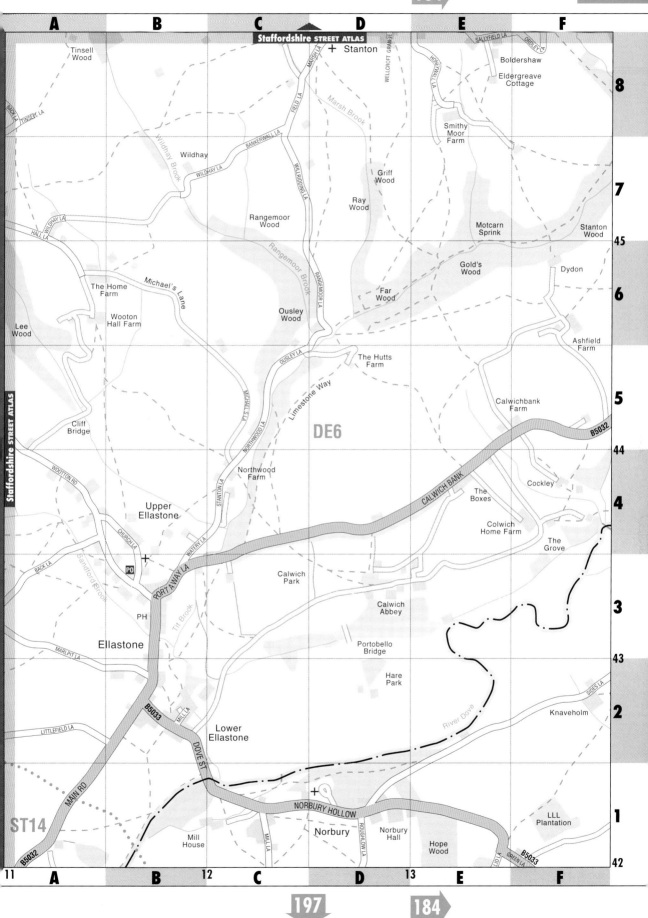

Staffordshire STREET ATLAS

Tinsell Wood

Stanton

Boldershaw

Eldergreave Cottage

8

BACK LA
TINSELL LA
Wildhay Brook
Wildhay
BANKERWALL LA
WILDHAY LA
FIELD LA
Marsh Brook
MARSH LA
WELLCROFT GRANGE
HONEYWALL LA
SALLYFIELD LA
ORDLEY LA

Smithy Moor Farm

Griff Wood

Ray Wood

7

Rangemoor Wood

HALL LA
WILDHAY LA
WILRIDING LA
RANGEMOOR LA
Rangemoor Brook

Motcarn Sprink

Stanton Wood

45

The Home Farm

Michael's Lane

Wooton Hall Farm

Ousley Wood

Gold's Wood

Far Wood

Dydon

6

Lee Wood

DE6

Ashfield Farm

OUSLEY LA
MICHAEL'S LA
NORTHWOOD LA

The Hutts Farm

Limestone Way

Calwichbank Farm

5

Cliff Bridge

B5032

44

WOOTON RD
BACK LA
Sandford Brook
CHURCH LA
WATERY LA
STANTON LA

Northwood Farm

CALWICH BANK

The Boxes

Cockley

Upper Ellastone

Colwich Home Farm

The Grove

4

PO ✚

PORT AWAY LA
Tit Brook

Calwich Park

Calwich Abbey

3

PH

Ellastone

Portobello Bridge

River Dove

43

MARLPIT LA

Hare Park

SIDES LA

Knaveholm

2

MAIN RD
B5033
MILL LA

Lower Ellastone

LITTLEFIELD LA
DOVE ST
MILL LA
ROUGHLOW LA
LID LA
GREEN LA

LLL Plantation

1

ST14

NORBURY HOLLOW

Norbury

Norbury Hall

Hope Wood

B5033

B5032

Mill House

42

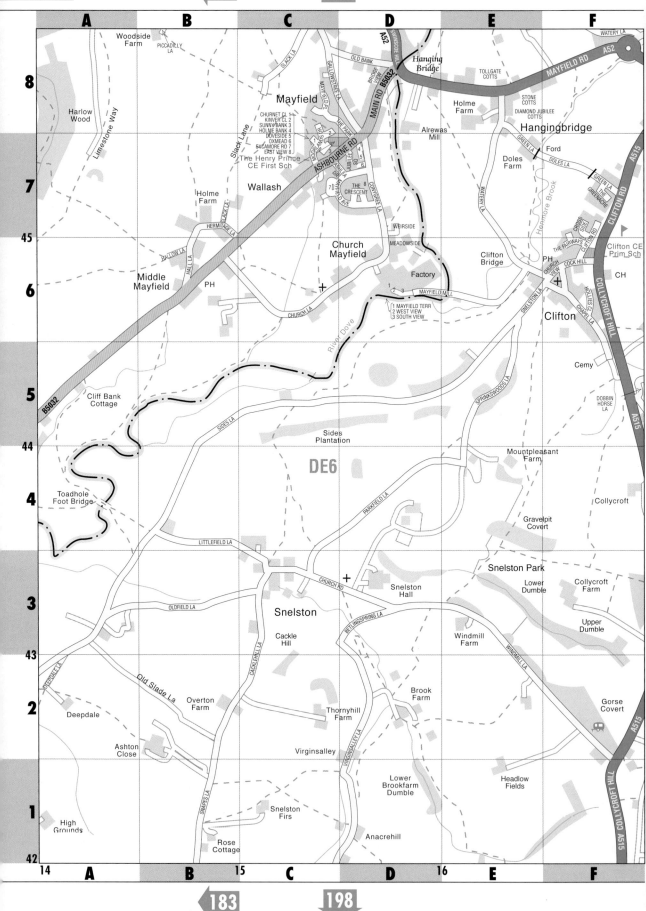

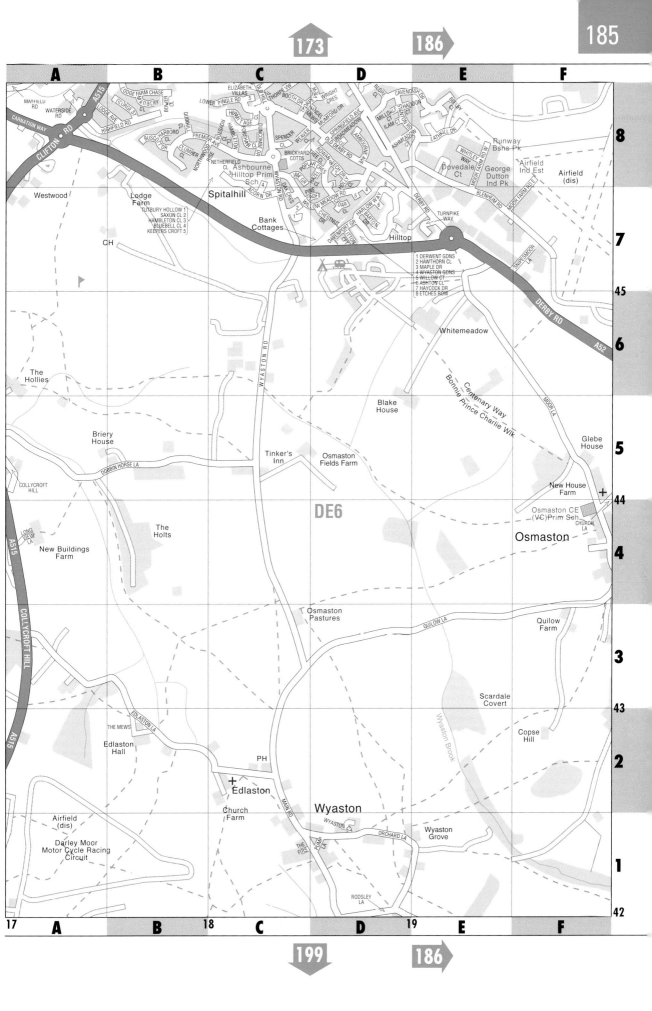

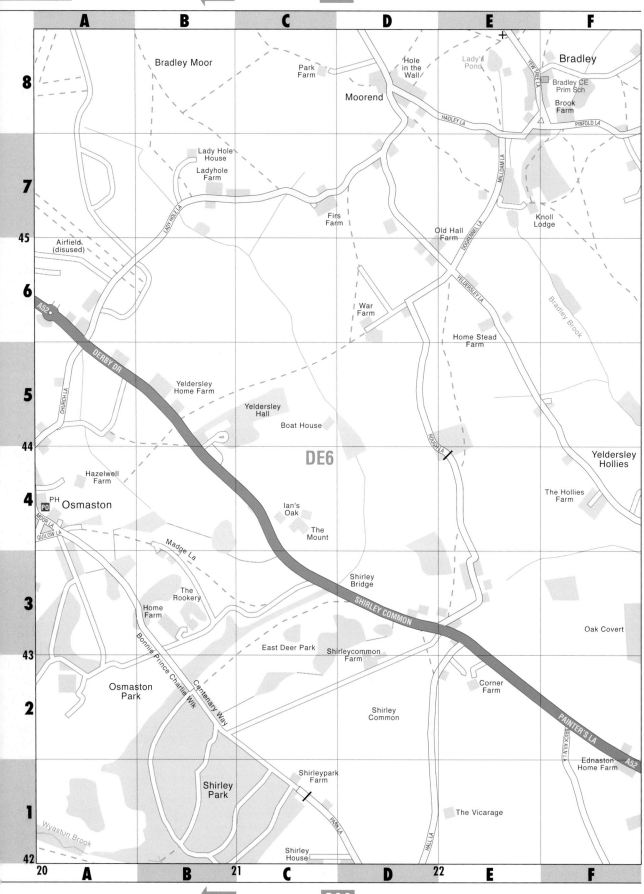

185
174
185
200

Bradley Moor

Park Farm

Hole in the Wall

Lady's Pond

Bradley

Bradley CE Prim Sch

Moorend

Brook Farm

HADLEY LA

PINFOLD LA

TEW TREE LA

Lady Hole House

Ladyhole Farm

LADY HOLE LA

Firs Farm

Old Hall Farm

DOGKENNEL LA

MILLDAM LA

Knoll Lodge

Airfield (disused)

YELDERSLEY LA

Bradley Brook

A52

DERBY DR

War Farm

Home Stead Farm

CHURCH LA

Yeldersley Home Farm

Yeldersley Hall

Boat House

DE6

ROUGH LA

Yeldersley Hollies

Hazelwell Farm

The Hollies Farm

PH
PO
Osmaston

MOOR LA

QUILOW LA

Ian's Oak

The Mount

Madge La

Shirley Bridge

SHIRLEY COMMON

Oak Covert

The Rookery

Home Farm

East Deer Park

Shirleycommon Farm

Corner Farm

Bonnie Prince Charlie Wlk

Centenary Way

Osmaston Park

Shirley Common

PAINTER'S LA

BRICK KILN LA

A52

Ednaston Home Farm

Shirley Park

Shirleypark Farm

PARK LA

The Vicarage

HALL LA

Wyaston Brook

Shirley House

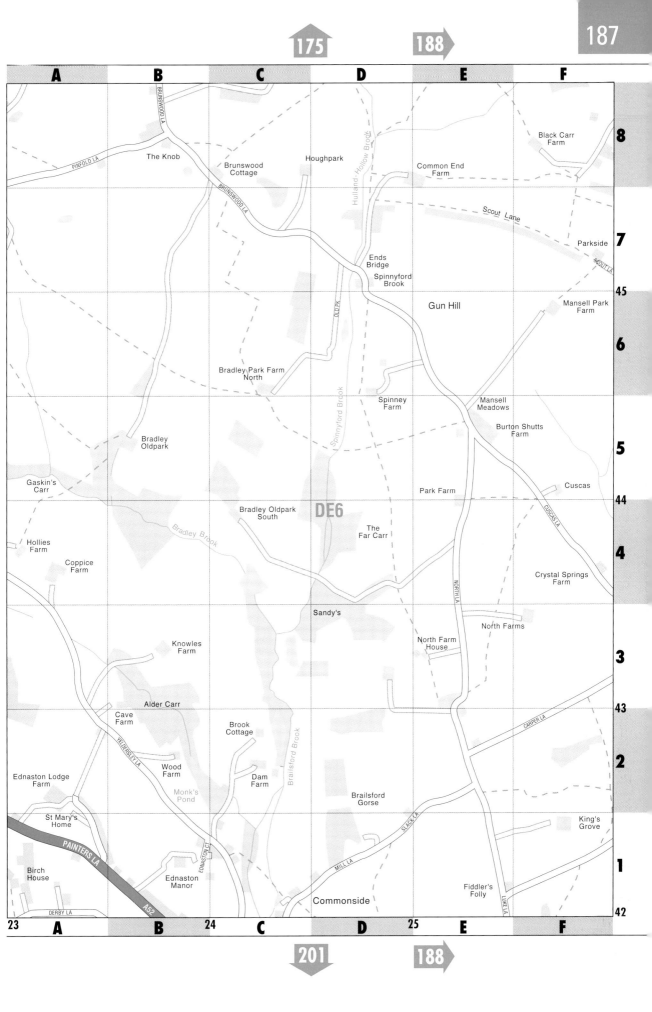

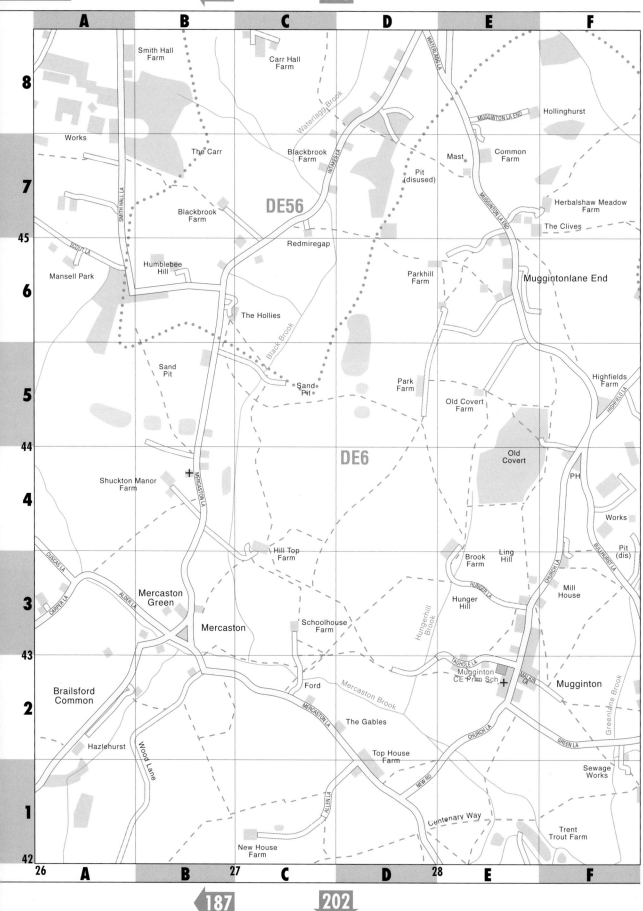

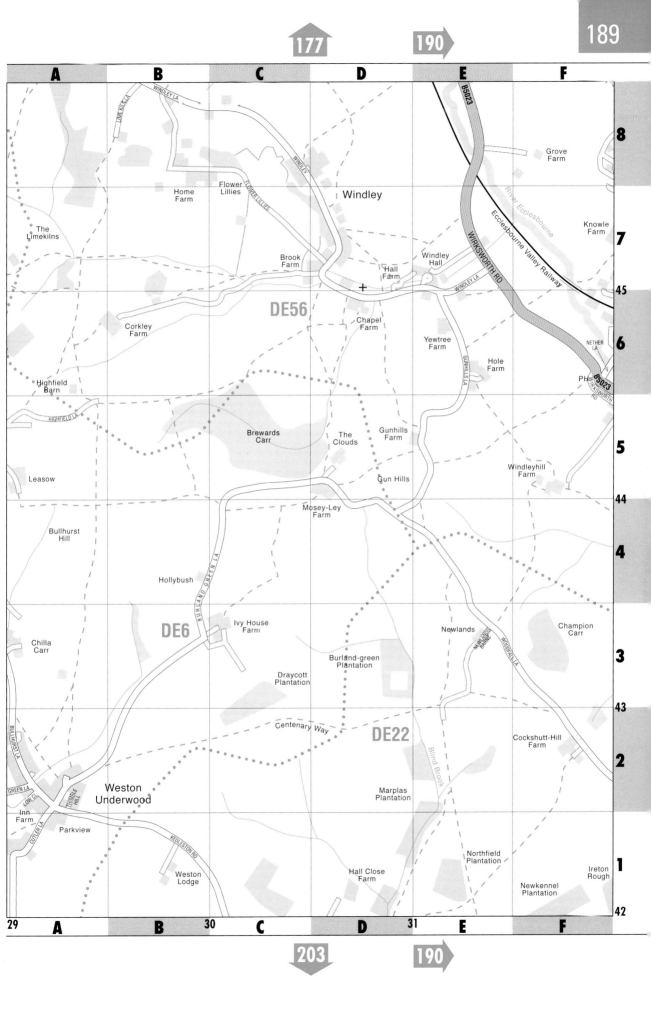

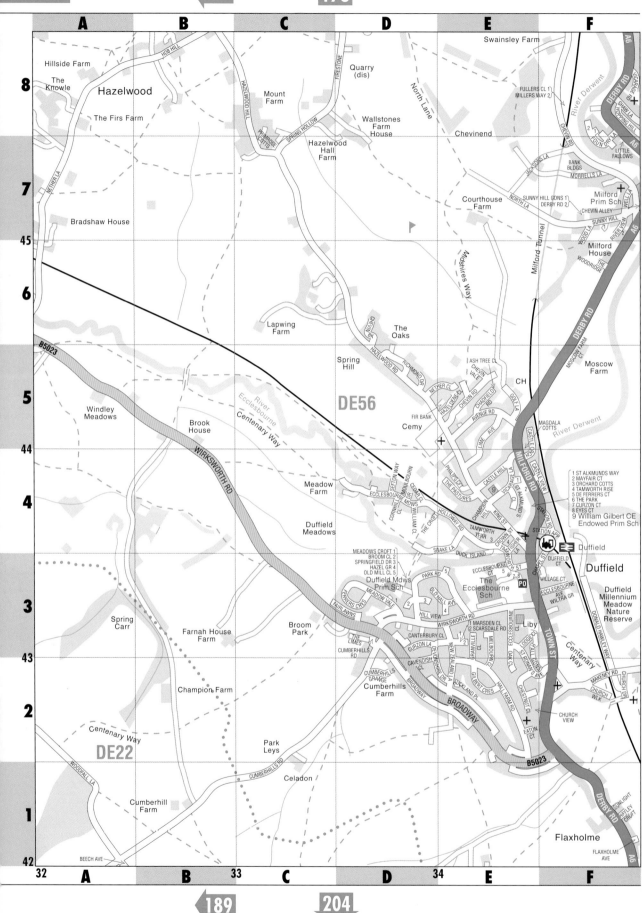

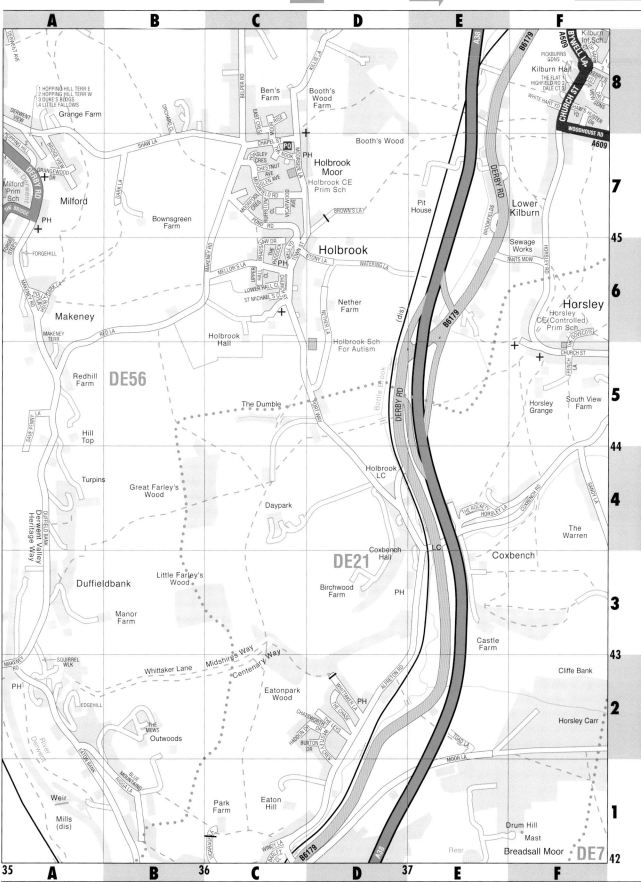

A B C D E F

8
7
45
6
5
44
4
43
3
2
1
42

35 A 36 B C 37 D E F

Kilburn Inf. Sch.
B6179
BAWELL LA.
PICKBURNS GDNS
Kilburn Hall
THE FLAT
HIGHFIELD RD 2
DALE CT 3
WHITE HART YD
CHURCH ST
SHAW'S HUNTER YD
WOODHOUSE RD
A609

DERWENT AVE
1 HOPPING HILL TERR E
2 HOPPING HILL TERR W
3 DUKE'S BLDGS
4 LITTLE FALLOWS
Grange Farm
DERWENT VIEW
ORCHARD CL
SHAW LA
Ben's Farm
Booth's Wood Farm
KILLIS LA
BELPER RD
EAST CRES
CHAPEL ST
PO
Booth's Wood

BRIDGE VIEW
GRANGEWOOD DR
PH
Milford
Milford Prim Sch
River Derwent
DERBY RD
THE BRIDGE
HOPPING HILL
DARK LA
Bownsgreen Farm
HORSLEY CRES
CHESTNUT AVE
GLEN AVE
MOORFIELD RD
MOORPOOL CRES
RUFFSTONE RD
VICARWOOD AVE
THE NOOK
MOORSIDE LA
MOORSIDE RISE
Holbrook Moor
Holbrook CE Prim Sch
Pit House
BROOKHILLOS
Lower Kilburn
HORSLEY RD
Sewage Works
TANTS MDW

PH
FORGEHILL
FORGE STEPS
MAKENEY RD
HOLLY HILL
DARK LA
MAKENEY TERR
Makeney
RED LA
MELLOR'S LA
UPPER HALL
LOWER HALL
ST MICHAEL'S CT
CHURCH ST
Holbrook Hall
POND RD
NEW DR
BRADSHAW LA
THE PADDOCK
WELL CL
TOWN ST
STONY LA
PH
Holbrook
Nether Farm
WATERING LA
Holbrook Sch For Autism
Bottle Brook
DERBY RD
B6179
(dis)
Horsley
Horsley CE (Controlled) Prim Sch
THE DOVECOTE
CHURCH ST
FRENCH LA
SANDY LA

DE56
Redhill Farm
Hill Top
Turpins
SAVE PENNY LA
The Dumble
PORT WAY
Great Farley's Wood
Daypark
Holbrook LC
Horsley Grange
South View Farm
44

Derwent Valley Heritage Way
Derwent Bank
DUFFIELD BANK
Little Farley's Wood
DE21
Coxbench Hall
LC
THE ROCKERY
HORSLEY LA
COXBENCH RD
COXBENCH LA
Coxbench
SANDY LA
The Warren

Duffieldbank
Manor Farm
MAKENEY RD
SQUIRREL WLK
EDGEHILL
Whittaker Lane
Midshires Way
Centenary Way
Eatonpark Wood
Birchwood Farm
PH
WHITTAKER LA
ALFRETON RD
Castle Farm
Cliffe Bank

PH
River Derwent
EATON BANK
THE MEWS
Outwoods
BLUE MOUNTAINS
RIGGA LA
Weir
Mills (dis)
VICARAGE LA
Park Farm
WINDY LA
BARLEY CL
B6179
Eaton Hill
Eatonpark Wood
CHATSWORTH DR
HADDON DR
BUXTON DR
THE LEYS
THE CHASE
DRYSTLEY CRES
TOAD LA
MOOR LA
A38
Horsley Carr
Drum Hill
Mast
Resr
Breadsall Moor
DE7
42

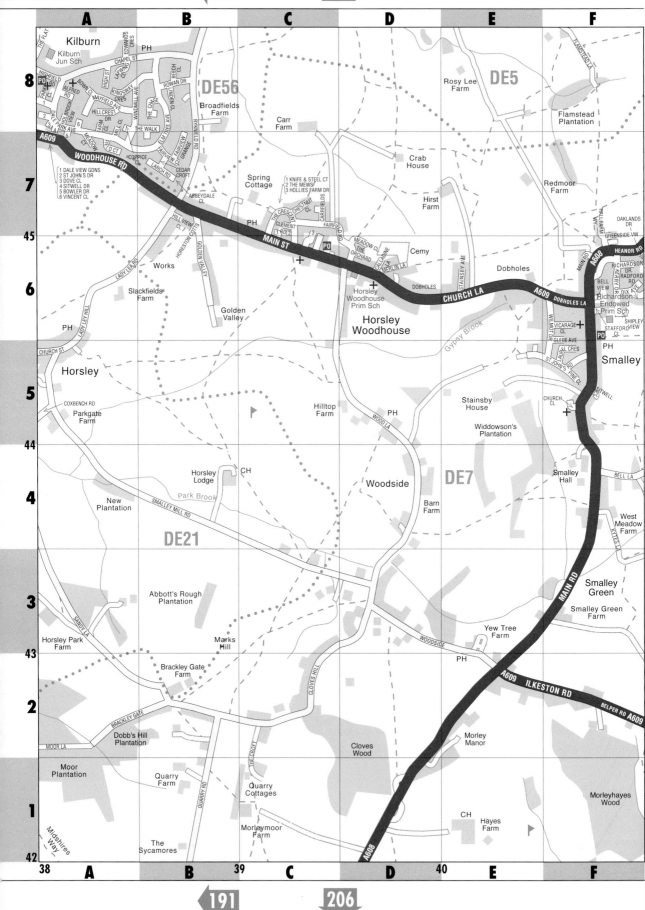

Kilburn
Kilburn
Jun Sch
PH
EDWARDS CRES
DE56
Broadfields
Farm
Carr
Farm
Crab
House
Rosy Lee
Farm
DE5
Flamstead
Plantation

THE FLAT
HIGHFIELD RD
PO
PARK RD
ALFRED RD
BOWN CL
HIGH ST
LADYCROFT
CHAPEL ST
KINGSWAY
MAYFIELD AVE
WINDMILL AVE
THE CHASE
BEECH CL
ROWAN DR
THE WALK
RYKNELD RD
LARCH RD
CEDAR CROFT
COPPICE
FAIRVIEW CL
FAIRVIEW GRANGE
ELM TREE AVE
HILLCREST DR
HILLCREST FARM CL
MILL LA
FIELD CT
MEADOW CL
DALE PARK AVE
OLD BROOK VIEW

A609
WOODHOUSE RD

1 DALE VIEW GDNS
2 ST JOHN S DR
3 DOVE CL
4 SITWELL DR
5 BOWLER DR
6 VINCENT CL

Spring
Cottage

1 KNIFE & STEEL CT
2 THE MEWS
3 HOLLIES FARM DR

ABBEYDALE CL
HILL VIEW CL
HORESTON COTTS
GOLDEN VALLEY
THE CRESCENT
CLEMENT RD
CHESTNUT CL
CARRFIELDS
FAIRFIELD RD
PH
MAIN ST
PO
MEADOW CL
THE ORCHARD
CALLADINE
MERLIN LA
Cemy
STAINSBY AVE
Hirst
Farm
Dobholes
Redmoor
Farm

Works
LADY LEA RD
Slackfields
Farm
Golden
Valley
Horsley
Woodhouse
Prim Sch
Horsley
Woodhouse
Dobholes
CHURCH LA
A609
Dobholes
DOBHOLES LA
WILMOT DR
VICARAGE CL
GLEBE AVE
DAIRY RD
ST CRES
PINE CL
ST JOHN S RD
Richardson
Endowed
Prim Sch
PO
PH
Smalley
BELL VIEW
KERRY DR
DIX AVE
STAFFORD CL
SHIPLEY VIEW
RICHARDSON DR
RADFORD RD
HEANOR RD
A608
MAIN RD
THALL FARM
GREENSIDE VW
OAKLANDS DR

PH
LADY LEY HILL
Horsley
CHURCH ST
COXBENCH RD
Parkgate
Farm
Hilltop
Farm
WOOD LA
PH
Stainsby
House
Widdowson's
Plantation
CHURCH CL
SITWELL
DE7
Smalley
Hall
BELL LA
West
Meadow
Farm
KYTES LA

Horsley
Lodge
CH
SMALLEY MILL RD
Park Brook
New
Plantation
DE21
Woodside
Barn
Farm
Smalley
Green
Smalley
Green
Farm

Abbott's Rough
Plantation
SANDY LA
Horsley Park
Farm
Marks
Hill
Brackley Gate
Farm
WOODSIDE
Yew Tree
Farm
PH
MAIN RD
A609
ILKESTON RD
BELPER RD
A609

Dobb's Hill
Plantation
BRACKLEY GATE
MOOR LA
QUARRY RD
CLOVES HILL
THE CROFT
Cloves
Wood
Morley
Manor

Moor
Plantation
Quarry
Farm
Quarry
Cottages
Morleymoor
Farm
The Sycamores
Midshires Way
A608
CH
Hayes
Farm
Morleyhayes
Wood

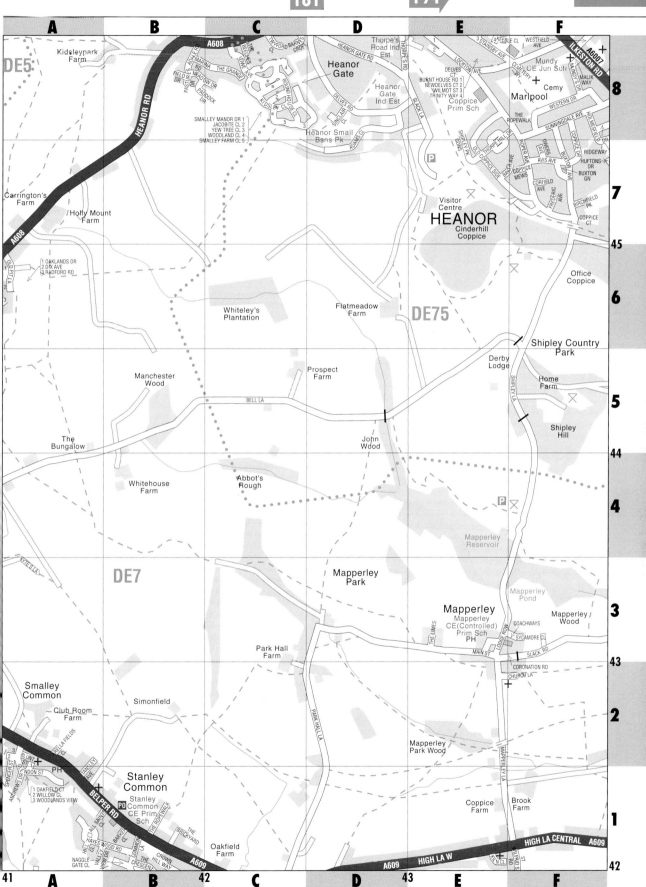

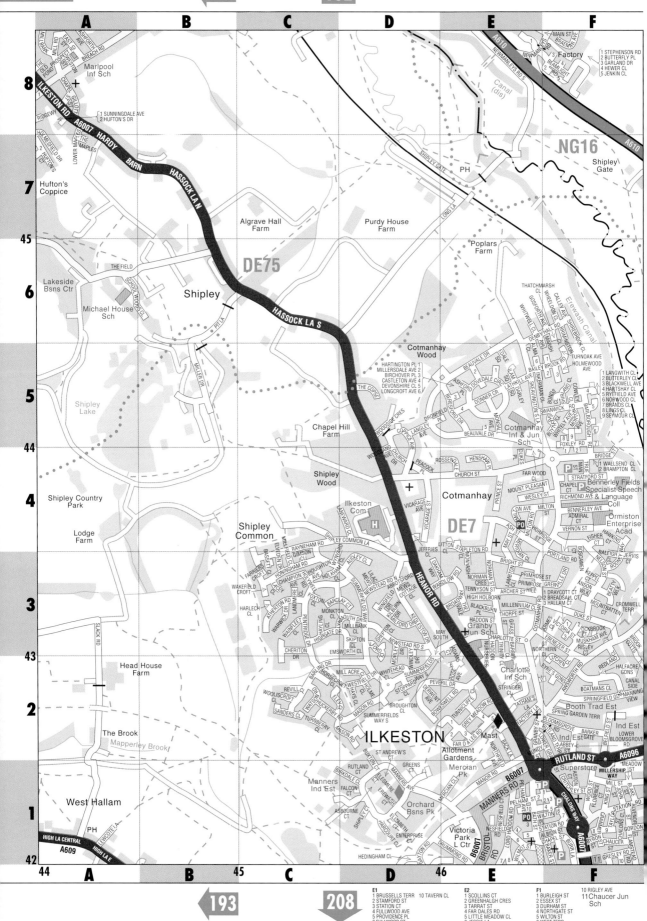

E1
1 BRUSSELLS TERR
2 STAMFORD ST
3 STATION CT
4 FULLWOOD AVE
5 PROVIDENCE PL
6 FULLWOOD ST
7 WHARNCLIFFE RD
8 JACKSON AVE
9 GREGORY ST
10 TAVERN CL

E2
1 SCOLLINS CT
2 GREENHALGH CRES
3 TARRAT ST
4 FAR DALES RD
5 LITTLE MEADOW CL
6 JESSIE LA

F1
1 BURLEIGH ST
2 ESSEX ST
3 DURHAM ST
4 NORTHGATE ST
5 WILTON ST
6 WEST TERR
7 NORTH ST
8 CHAPEL ST
9 LOWER CHAPEL ST

10 RIGLEY AVE
11 Chaucer Jun Sch

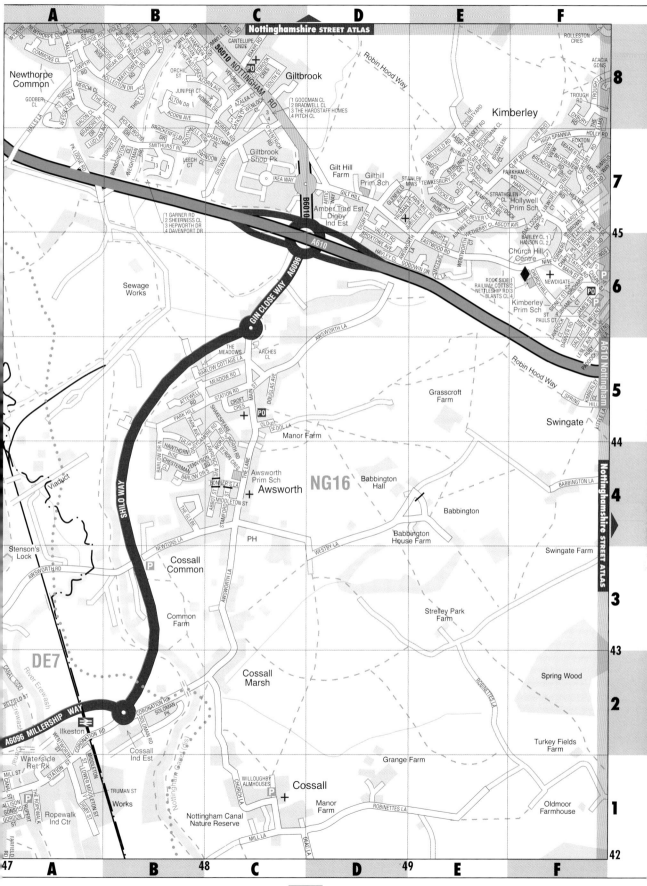

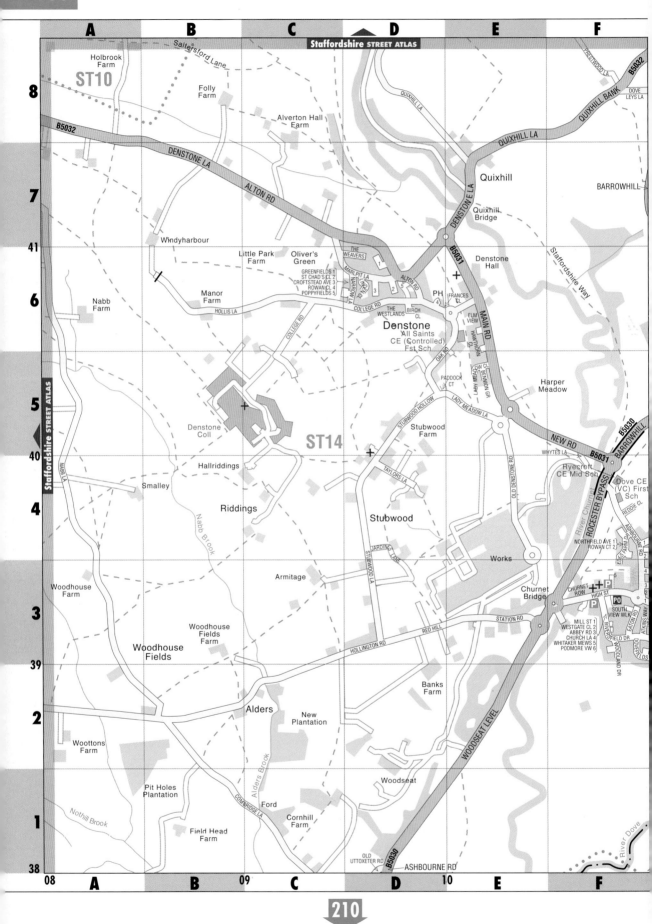

ST10

ST14

B5032

DENSTONE LA

ALTON RD

Holbrook Farm

Saltersford Lane

Folly Farm

Alverton Hall Farm

Windyharbour

Little Park Farm

Oliver's Green

THE WEAVERS

Nabb Farm

Manor Farm

HOLLIS LA

COLLEGE RD

GREENFIELDS 1
ST CHAD'S CL 2
CROFTSTEAD AVE 3
ROWAN CL 4
POPPYFIELDS 5

MARLPIT LA

NARROW LA

ALTON RD

COLLEGE RD

THE WESTLANDS

BIRCH CL

Denstone
All Saints
CE (Controlled)
Fst Sch

PH

FRANCES CL

ELM VIEW

HAWTHORN

LADY MEADOW

DOW CL

BENNION GR

OAK RD

MAIN RD

Quixhill

QUIXHILL LA

QUIXHILL LA

DENSTON E LA

DENSTON E LA

B5031

Quixhill Bridge

Denstone Hall

Staffordshire Way

BARROWHILL

QUIXHILL BANK

FIRSTWOOD LA

B5032

DOVE LEYS LA

Harper Meadow

PADDOCK CT

STURWOOD HOLLOW

Stubwood Farm

LADY MEADOW LA

NEW RD

B5031

B5030

BARROWHILL

WHYTES LA

Ryecroft CE Mid Sch

Dove CE (VC) First Sch

ROCESTER BYPASS

River Churnet

REDDIE CL

ASHBOURNE RD

ERS FARM DR

NORTHFIELD AVE 1
ROWAN CT 2

Denstone Coll

Hallriddings

Smalley

NABB LA

Nabb Brook

Riddings

TAYLORS LA

Stubwood

STUBWOOD LA

JARDINE'S LANE

Armitage

Works

Churnet Bridge

CHURNET ROW

HIGH ST

PO

P

P

SOUTH VIEW WLK

MILL ST 1
WESTGATE CL 2
ABBEY RD 3
CHURCH LA 4
WHITAKER MEWS 5
PODMORE VW 6

ATKINS WAY

EATON RD

RIVERS

WOODLAND DR

FIELDS

DOVE

ASHBOURNE RD

Woodhouse Farm

Woodhouse Fields Farm

Woodhouse Fields

Alders

New Plantation

ALDERS BROOK

Banks Farm

HOLLINGTON RD

RED HILL

STATION RD

WOODSEAT LEVEL

Woottons Farm

Pit Holes Plantation

Nothill Brook

CORNBRIDGE LA

Ford

Field Head Farm

Cornhill Farm

Woodseat

OLD UTTOXETER RD

B5030

ASHBOURNE RD

River Dove

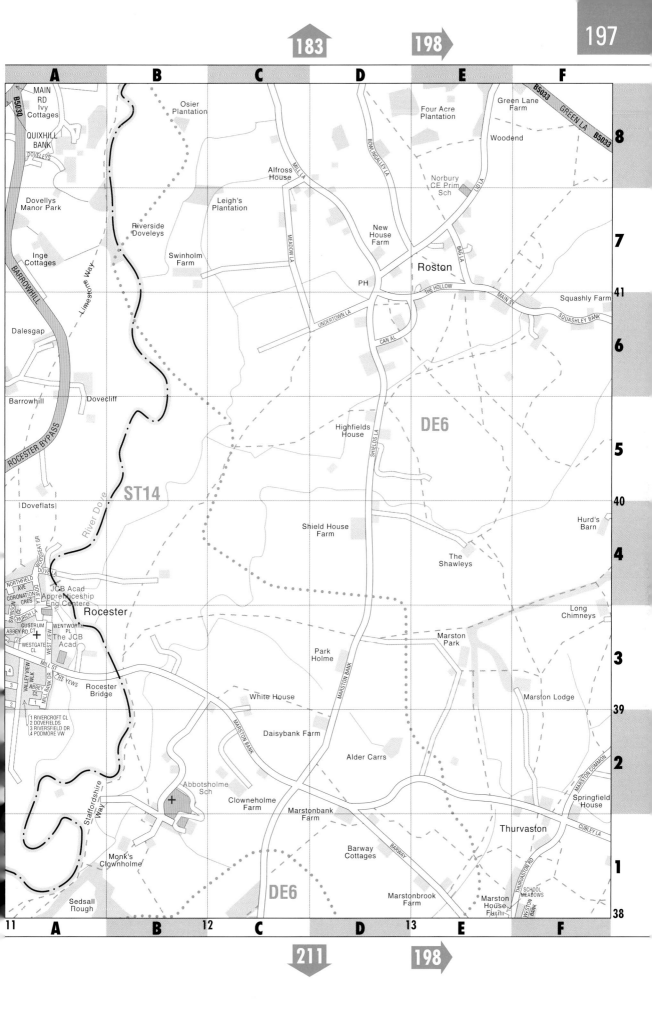

197 184

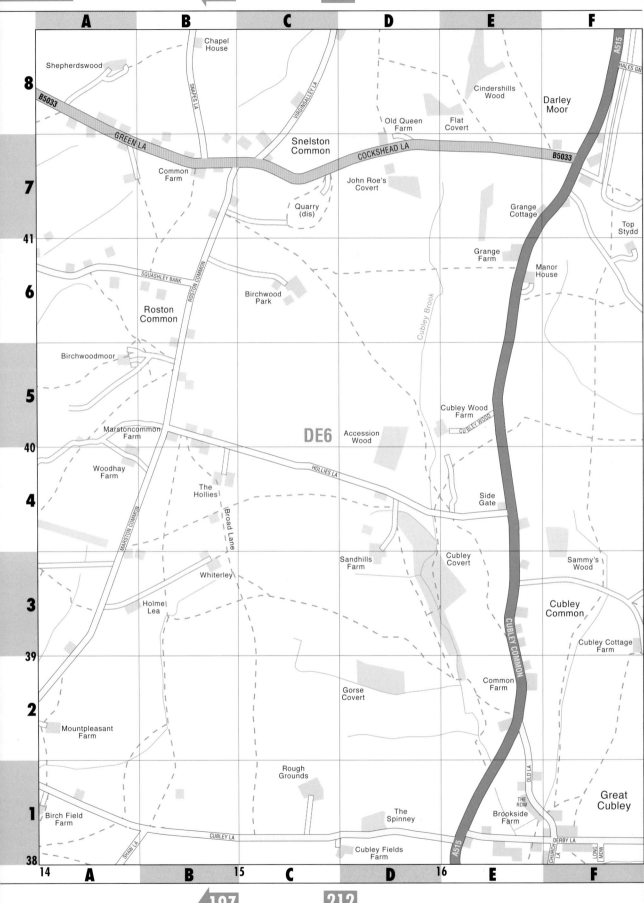

197 212

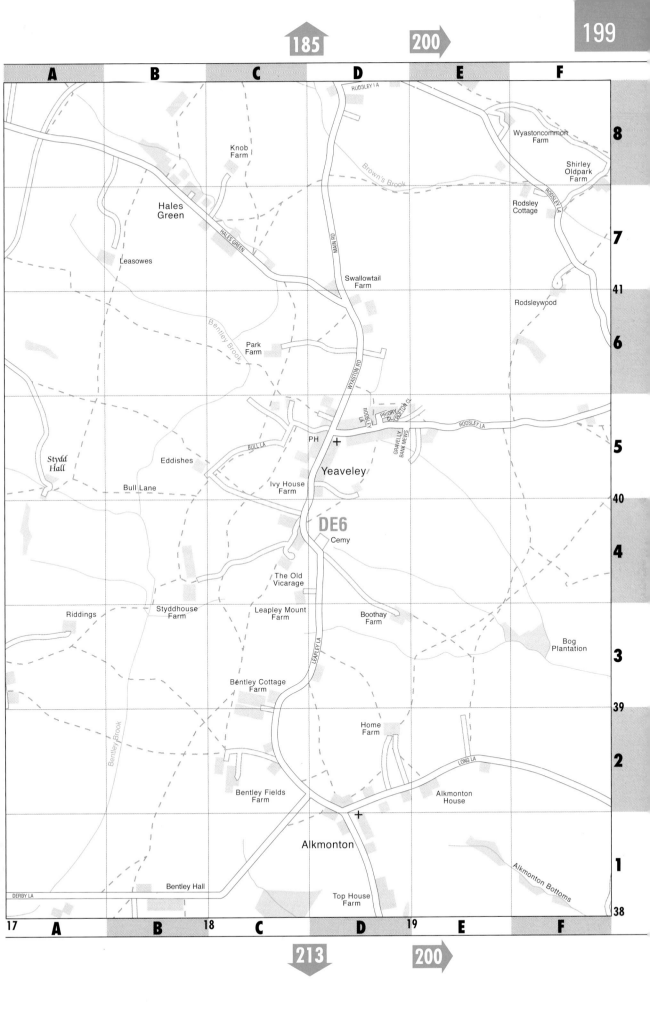

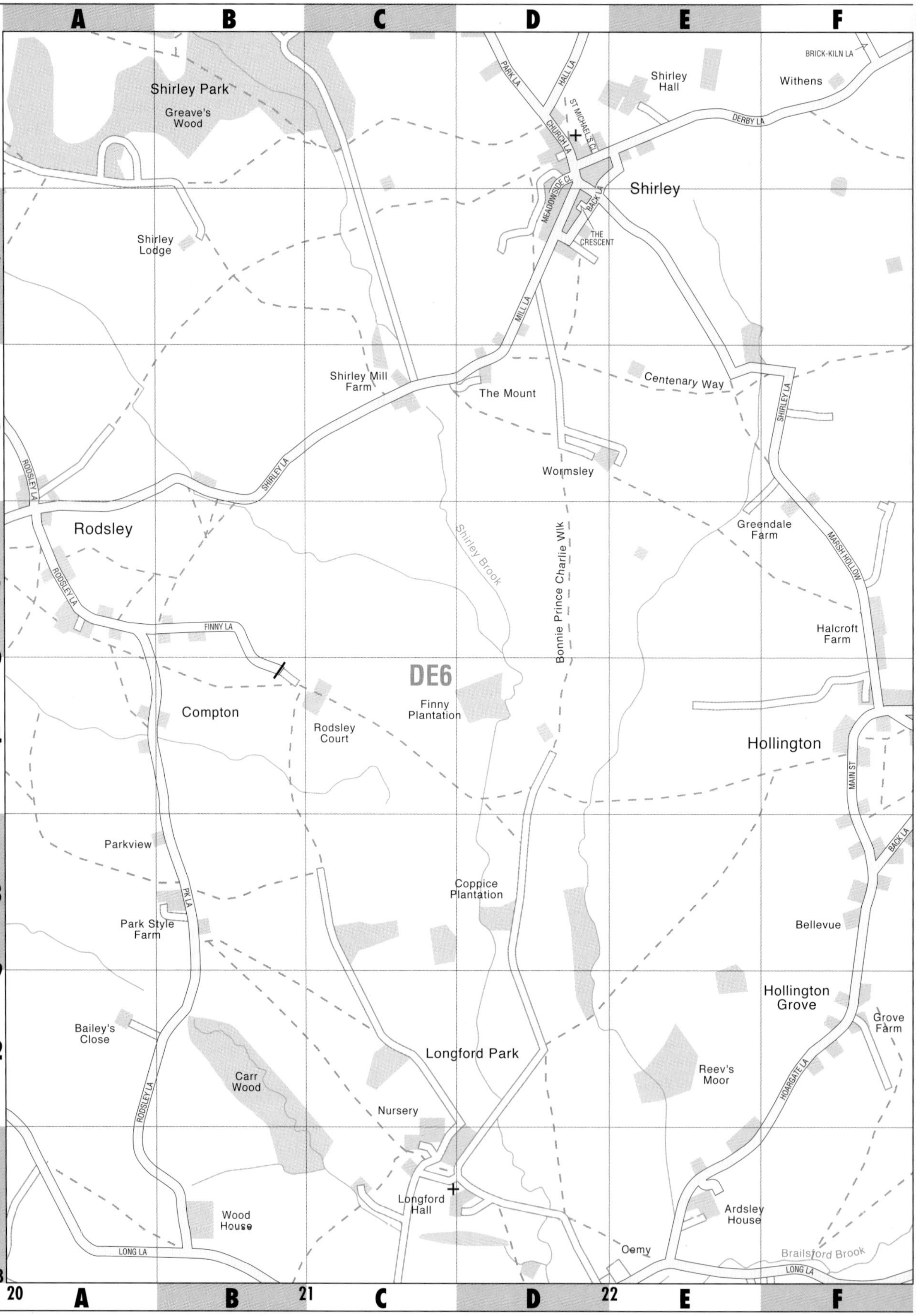

199
186

A B C D E F

8

BRICK-KILN LA

Shirley Park

Greave's Wood

PARK LA

HALL LA

Shirley Hall

Withens

DERBY LA

ST MICHAEL'S CH

CHURCH LA

Shirley

MEADOWSIDE CL

BACK LA

7

Shirley Lodge

THE CRESCENT

41

MILL LA

6

Shirley Mill Farm

The Mount

Centenary Way

SHIRLEY LA

Wormsley

Rodsley

Greendale Farm

MARSH HOLLOW

RODSLEY LA

5

Halcroft Farm

FINNY LA

40

Bonnie Prince Charlie Wlk

Shirley Brook

Compton

DE6

Rodsley Court

Finny Plantation

Hollington

4

MAIN ST

BACK LA

Parkview

Coppice Plantation

3

PK LA

Park Style Farm

Bellevue

39

Hollington Grove

Bailey's Close

Longford Park

Reev's Moor

Grove Farm

HOARGATE LA

2

RODSLEY LA

Carr Wood

Nursery

Wood House

Longford Hall

Ardsley House

1

LONG LA

Oemy

Brailsford Brook

LONG LA

38

20 A B 21 C D 22 E F

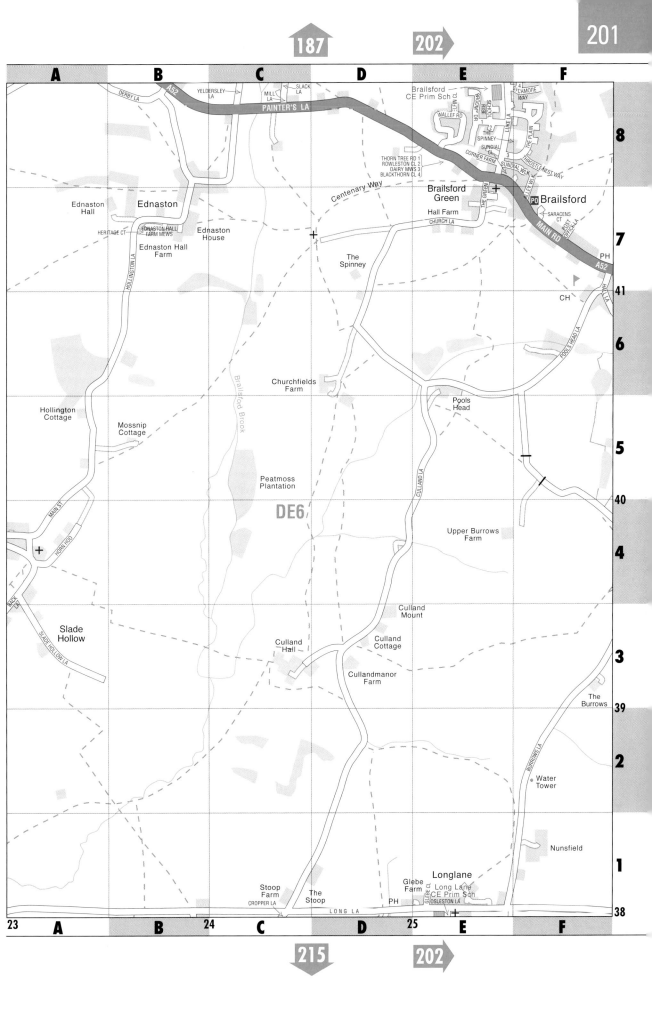

A B C D E F

8
7
41
6
5
40
4
3
39
2
1
38

DERBY LA
A52
YELDERSLEY LA
MILL LA
SLACK LA
PAINTER'S LA

Brailsford CE Prim Sch
WALLEF RD
ELM CL
JOHN LDHDS
WOODR HO
SYCAMORE WAY
THE PLAIN
THROSTLE NEST WAY
LUKE LA
SUNDIAL CL
SUNDIAL WLK
VALLEY WLK

Centenary Way
THORN TREE RD 1
ROWLESTON CL 2
DAIRY MWS 3
BLACKTHORN CL 4
CORNER FARM
THE SPINNEY

Brailsford Green
Brailsford
PO
SARACENS CT
POST OFFICE LA
MAIN RD
A52

Ednaston Hall
Ednaston
HERITAGE CT
EDNASTON HALL FARM MEWS
Ednaston House
Ednaston Hall Farm
HOLLINGTON LA

Hall Farm
CHURCH LA

The Spinney

PH
CH
HALL LA
POOLS HEAD LA

Churchfields Farm

Pools Head

Hollington Cottage
MAIN ST
HORN HOO

Mossnip Cottage

Brailsford Brook

DE6

Peatmoss Plantation

Upper Burrows Farm

Slade Hollow
SLADE HOLLOW LA
BACK LA

Culland Mount

Culland Hall
Cullandmanor Farm
Culland Cottage

CULLAND LA

The Burrows

BURROWS LA

Water Tower

Nunsfield

Stoop Farm
CROPPER LA
The Stoop

Glebe Farm
GLEBE CL
PH
Longlane
Long Lane CE Prim Sch
OSLESTON LA

LONG LA

A B C D E F
23 24 25

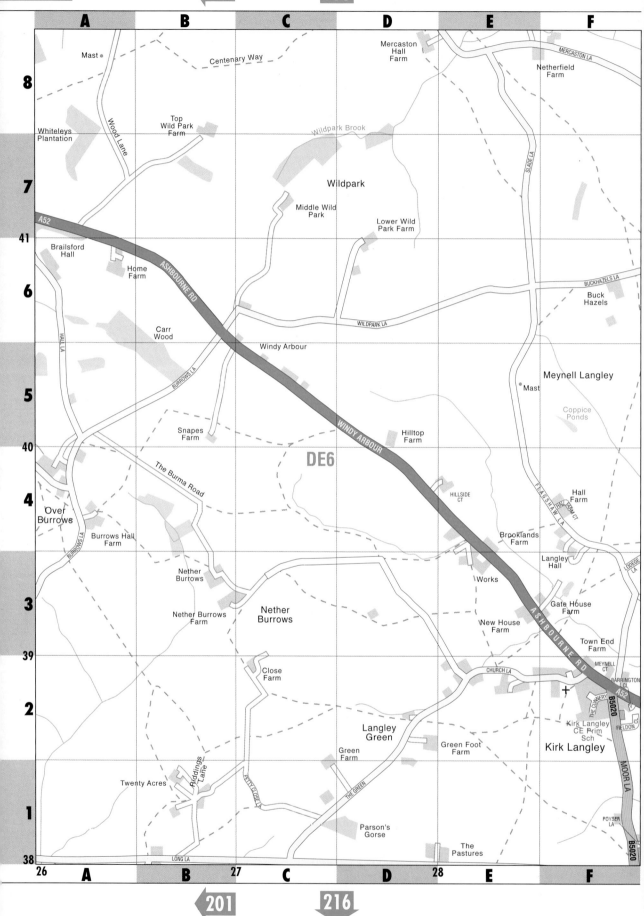

A   B   C   D   E   F

Mast

Centenary Way

Mercaston Hall Farm

MERCASTON LA

Netherfield Farm

8

Top Wild Park Farm

Wildpark Brook

Whiteleys Plantation

Wood Lane

Wildpark

SLADE LA

7

A52

Middle Wild Park

Lower Wild Park Farm

41

Brailsford Hall

ASHBOURNE RD

Home Farm

BUCKHAZELS LA

Buck Hazels

6

HALL LA

Carr Wood

WILDPARK LA

Windy Arbour

Meynell Langley

Mast

5

BURROWS LA

Coppice Ponds

Snapes Farm

WINDY ARBOUR

Hilltop Farm

40

The Burma Road

DE6

Hall Farm

FLAGSHAW LA

HALL FARM CT

4

Over Burrows

Burrows Hall Farm

HILLSIDE CT

Brooklands Farm

Langley Hall

LODGE LA

BURROWS LA

Nether Burrows

Works

Gate House Farm

3

Nether Burrows Farm

Nether Burrows

New House Farm

ASHBOURNE RD

Town End Farm

MEYNELL CT

BARRINGTON CL

39

Close Farm

CHURCH LA

A52

B5020

THE DUMERY

2

Langley Green

Green Farm

Green Foot Farm

Kirk Langley CE Prim Sch

FIELDON

Kirk Langley

Twenty Acres

Riddings Lane

PETTY CLOSE

THE GREEN

MOOR LA

1

Parson's Gorse

The Pastures

POYSER LA

B5020

38

LONG LA

26   A   B   27   C   D   28   E   F

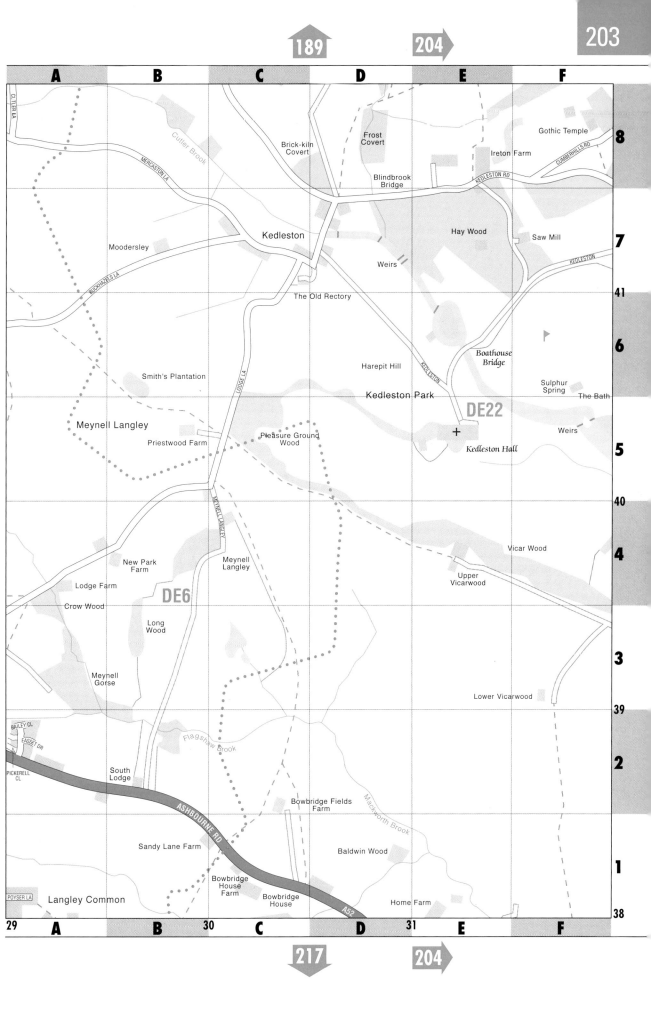

203
190

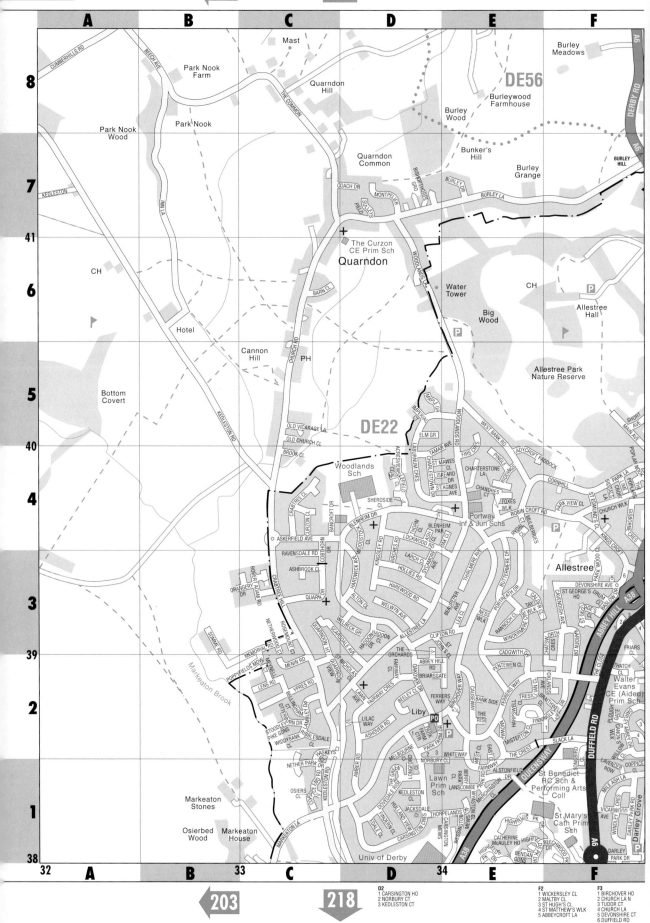

203
218

D2
1 CARSINGTON HO
2 NORBURY CT
3 KEDLESTON CT

F2
1 WICKERSLEY CL
2 MALTBY CL
3 ST HUGH'S CL
4 ST MATTHEW'S WLK
5 ABBEYCROFT LA

F3
1 BIRCHOVER HO
2 CHURCH LA N
3 TUDOR CT
4 CHURCH LA
5 DEVONSHIRE CT
6 DUFFIELD RD

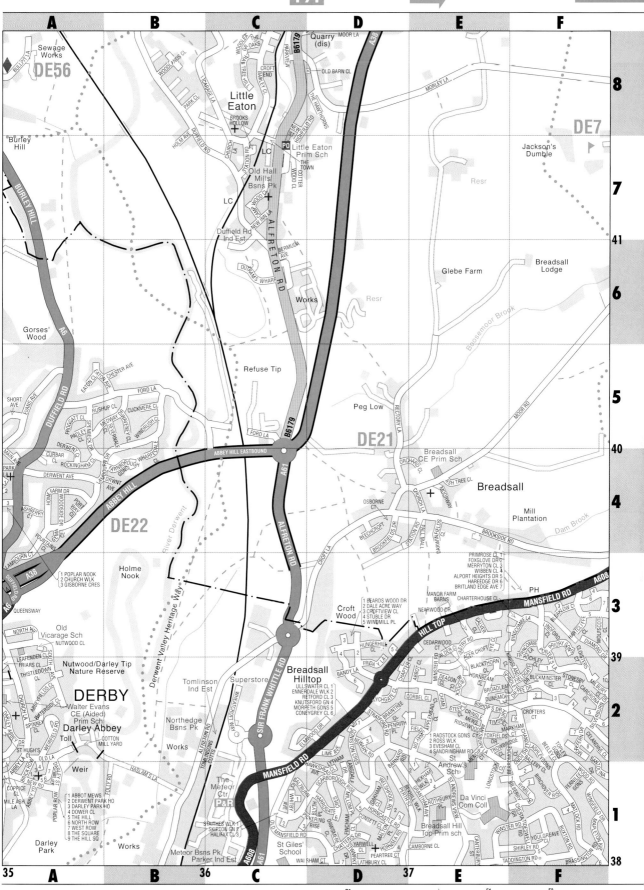

D1
1 KENDAL WLK
2 LEDBURY PL
3 MALVERN WAY
4 FILEY WLK
5 SEASCALE CL
6 REDCAR GDNS
7 WOODHURST CL

F1
1 INGLEDEW CL
2 HEATHERMEAD CL
3 BEAMWOOD CL
4 TANSLEY RISE
5 WOLLATON RD N
6 CHELMORTON PL

F2
1 CARDINAL CL
2 SEDGEBROOK CL
3 SOMERBY WAY
4 GARTHORPE CT
5 TWEEDS MUIR CL
6 PYKESTONE CL
7 HOUGHTON CT
8 RUTHERFORD RISE
9 PADDOCK CROFT
10 EMERALD CL

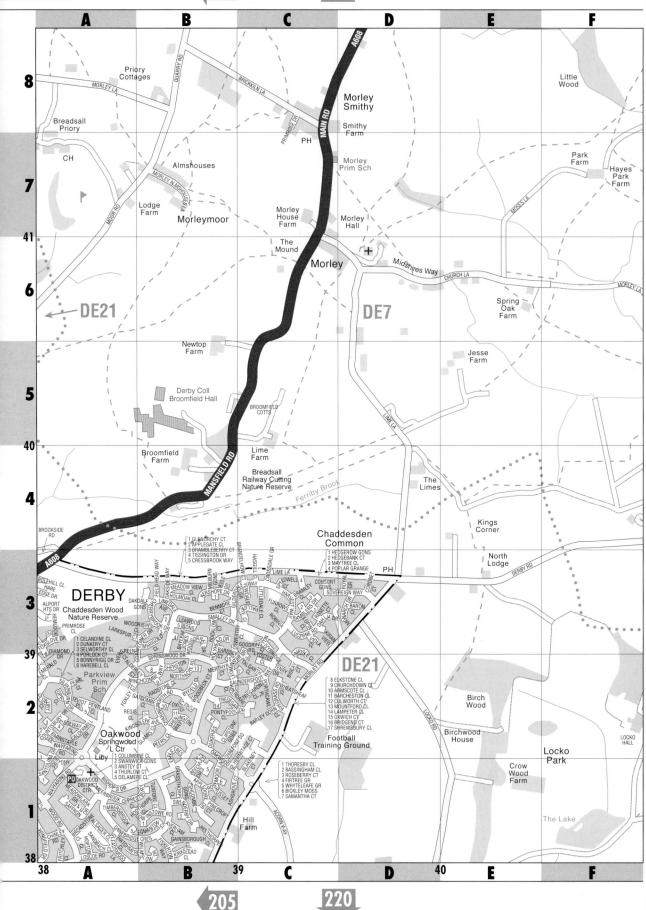

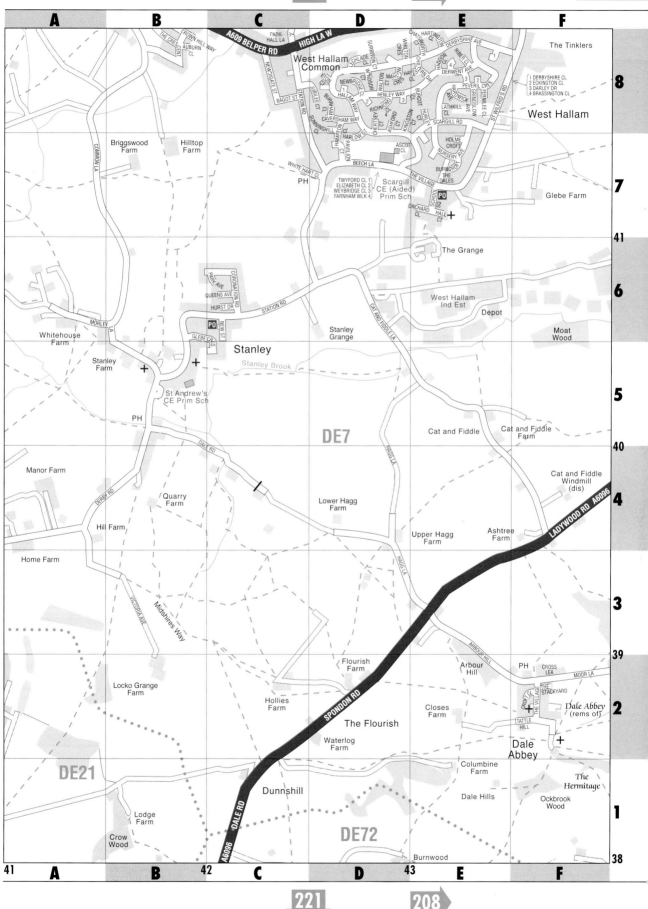

207 194

E8
1 DRUMMOND RD
2 WILMOT ST
3 CHAPEL HO

F6
1 SCHOLAR CL
2 LOWERWHITWORTH RD
3 NICHOLAS CL

F7
1 CANNING MEWS
2 HOPE ST
3 GRANGEWOOD AVE
4 OXFORD ST
5 HARGREAVES CT

F8
1 CORONATION ST
2 HALLCROFT RD
3 DERBY ST
4 PALMERSTON RD
5 RIGLEY AVE
6 Chaucer Jun Sch

Grid columns: A B C D E F
Grid rows: 8 41 7 6 40 5 4 3 39 2 1 38

A609

Paddock Farm

Whitefurrows

Centenary Walk

HIGH LA E

HIGH LA EAST

Pewitt Carr Nature Reserve

Ormiston Ilkeston Enf Acad

Rutland Sports Park

CH

TA Ctr

Derby Coll
PIMLICO
TH
Erewash Mus & Gdns Liby

KING GEORGE AVE

OAKWELL DR B6007

BELPER ST

A6096

A6007

CHALONS WAY

Chaucer Inf Sch

DERBY RD

Straw's Bridge

Kniveton Dr

ILKESTON

A6096 WHITE LION SQ

NOTTINGHAM RD A609

STANTON RD

Thacker Barn Cottages

St John Houghton Cath Voluntary Acad Sch

Kirk Hallam Com Acad

St Thomas RC Prim Sch

DERBYSHIRE DR

Field House

Thacker Barn

EARLHAM CL 1
LIMETREE CT 2
MARSHALL WAY 3
TOAD HOLE CL 4

Kirk Hallam

GODFREY DR

NURSERY HOLLOW

THE SPINNEY

Foxhole Farm

BANKFIELD DR

HIGHFIELD

RIDGEWAY

Ladywood Prim Sch

LADYWOOD RD

LITTLE HALLAM HILL

Little Hallam

LOWER STANTON RD

LITTLE HALLAM LA

Hallam Fields Jun Sch

Ladywood Lodge Farm

RIBBLESDALE 1
CHATSWORTH PL 2
HARDWICK PL 3
CROSSHILL DR 4

HILLARY PL

AVONDALE RD

Queen Elizabeth Way

Meerbrook Pl

KENILWORTH DR

VALLEY VIEW

Kirk Hallam Pupil Referral Unit

QUARRY HILL RD

A6096

SPONDON RD

A6096

Lady Wood

DE7

Ladywood Farm

MAYPOLE CL

WIRKSWORTH RD

ST NORBERT DR

DALLIMORE AVE

Dallimore Prim Sch

GOOSE NOOK CL 1
GISBEY RD 2
HARE HILL CL 3
COMERY CL 4
WASH MEADOW CL 5
UPPER WOOD CL 6
TIB MEADOW CL 7
PUDDING PLATE CL 8
THREELEYS CL 9

Quarry Hill Ind Est

MERLIN WAY

Pioneer Meadows Nature Reserve

Sow Brook

SOWBROOK LA

Sowbrook Farm

Nutbrook Canal (dis)

Stanton Bridge

ILKESTON RD

New Stanton

Works

MOOR LA

Bassett Farm

LOW S LA

Stanton Grove

Spoil Heap

WOODPECKER HILL

Dale Moor

Furnace Pond Farm

Grove Farm

Works

Hermit's Wood

MIDSHIRES WAY

POTATO PIT LA

Moorfield Farm

DALE RD

Thacker Wood

LITTLEWELL LA

Stanton-by-Dale

The Manor House

Boyah Grange

HIXON'S LA

Dalemoor Farm

PEPPER

PH

44 45 46

207 222

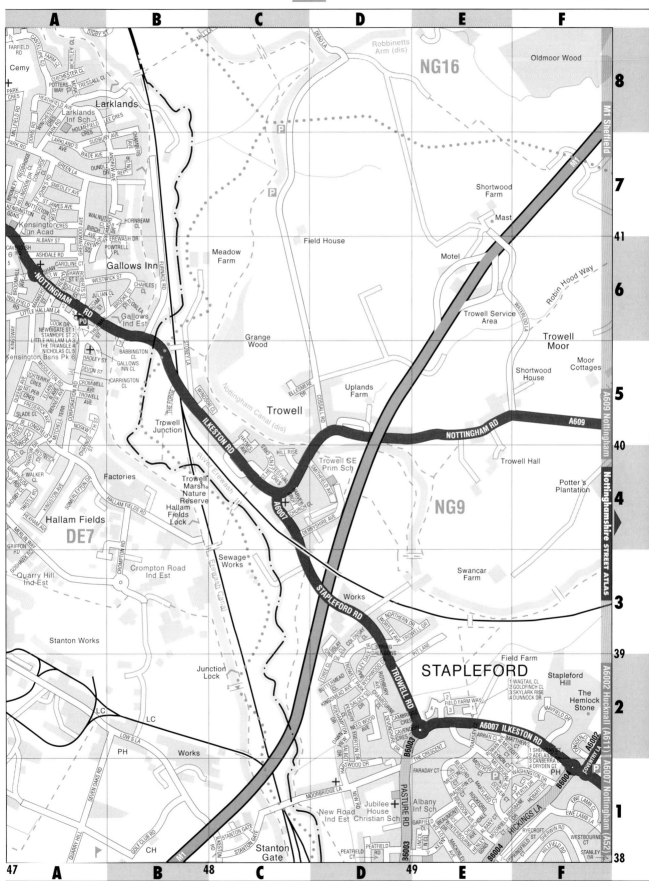

NG16

Oldmoor Wood

Robbinetts
Arm (dis)

Cemy

Larklands

Larklands
Inf Sch

Shortwood
Farm

Mast

Field House

Meadow
Farm

Motel

Kensington
Jun Acad

Gallows Inn

Robin Hood Way

Trowell Service
Area

Trowell
Moor

Gallows
Ind Est

Grange
Wood

Shortwood
House

Moor
Cottages

Nottingham Canal (dis)

Trowell

Uplands
Farm

Trowell
Junction

NG9

Trowell Hall

River Erewash

Trowell CE
Prim Sch

Potter's
Plantation

Factories

Trowell
Marsh
Nature
Reserve

Hallam
Fields
Lock

Hallam Fields

DE7

Swancar
Farm

Quarry Hill
Ind Est

Crompton Road
Ind Est

Sewage
Works

Works

Stanton Works

Field Farm

STAPLEFORD

Junction
Lock

Stapleford
Hill

The
Hemlock
Stone

1 WAGTAIL CL
2 GOLDFINCH CL
3 SKYLARK RISE
4 DUNNOCK DR

FIELD FARM WAY

PH

CAMBRIDGE
CRES

A6007 ILKESTON RD

1 SHERWIN CT
2 MEREDITH
3 ADELAIDE
4 DRYDEN CT

PH

Works

Faraday CT

New Road
Ind Est

Jubilee
House
Christian Sch

Albany
Inf Sch

Stanton
Gate

HICKINGS LA

EWE LAMB LA

EWE LAMB CL

M1 Sheffield

A609 Nottingham

Nottinghamshire STREET ATLAS

A6002 Hucknall

A6002 Nottingham (A52)

A6007

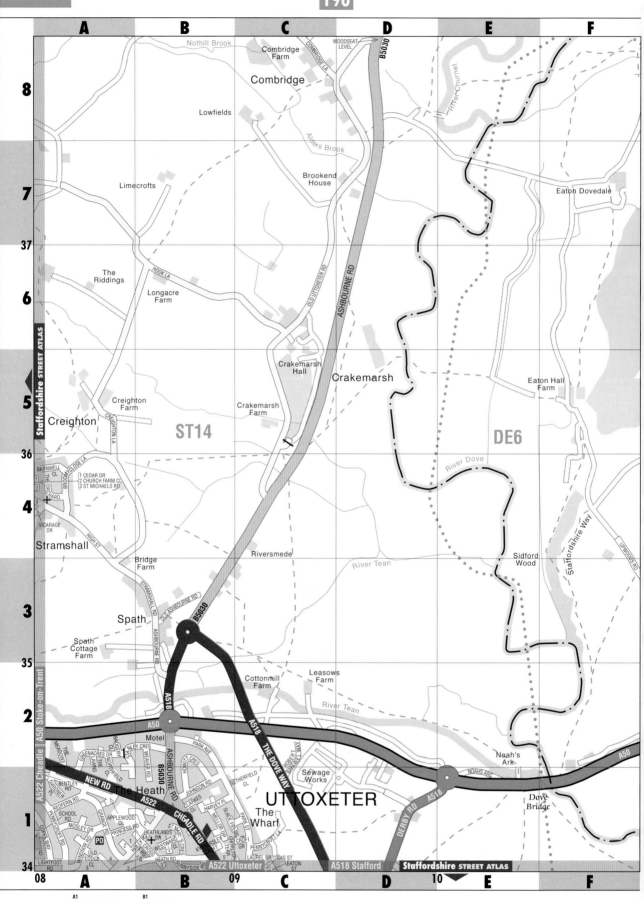

A1
1 HERMITAGE GDNS
2 THE HORNBEAMS
3 HEATH CROSS
4 SHERIDAN CT
5 MULBERRY GDNS
6 Tynsel Parkes
   CE Fst Sch

B1
1 ORCHARD CL
2 BOWLING GREEN RD
3 WINDMILL CL
4 St Mary's CE(Aided) Fst
Sch
5 THE LIMES

A B C D E F

Sedsall Farm

Morry House Farm

ST14

Marston Montgomery Prim Sch

Manor House

1 WESTON BANK
2 THURVASTON RD
3 APPLETREE LA

PEARL BANK

Marston Montgomery

8

Eaton Barn

PH

Havenhouse Farm

WALDLEY LA

Beggarsbutts

RIGGS LA

SOMERSAL LA

The Beeches

Banktop

7

Waldley

37

Waldley Farm

Marston Brook

BOWLING AL LA

Marston Woodhouse

6

Eaton Wood

Old Woodhouse Farm

Upper Eaton Farm

5

36

Upwoods Farm

DE6

4

Lady Coppice

MARSTON LA

Holmlea Farm

Somersal Farm

Hill Farm

MARSTON RD

Mount Pleasant

UPWOODS LA

Victory Farm

Woodhouse Farm

Somersal Herbert

CHURCH LA

WILLOW BANK

3

North Lodge

The Hall

35

Eaton Lodge

MARSTON LA

Field Farm

Brooksford Brook

Grove Cottages

GROVE LA

2

PICKFORD GR 1
BRACE GDNS 2
GARDNER CT 3
HINDLIP CL 4)

DERBY RD

MARSTON LA

BABBS LA

MARSTON LA

DERBY RD

Mill Cottage

Oaklea

UPWOODS RD

PH

EAST LANE DR

River Dove

Doveridge

OAK DR

HALL DR

COOK LA

MAPLE CL

SAND LA

CAVENDISH LA

BAKERS LA

Mill Farm

1

EAST PARK CRES

WEST DR

HAWTHORN CL

FLORENCE DR

DOG KENNEL LA

MILL LA

LAKE DR

LAKE SIDE

ORCHARD CT

HIGH ST

PUMP LA

PO

HALL LA

CHURCH LA

ALMS RD

1 ST CUTHBERTS RD
2 WESLEY CL
3 SADLER DR

A50

34

11 A B 12 C D 13 E F

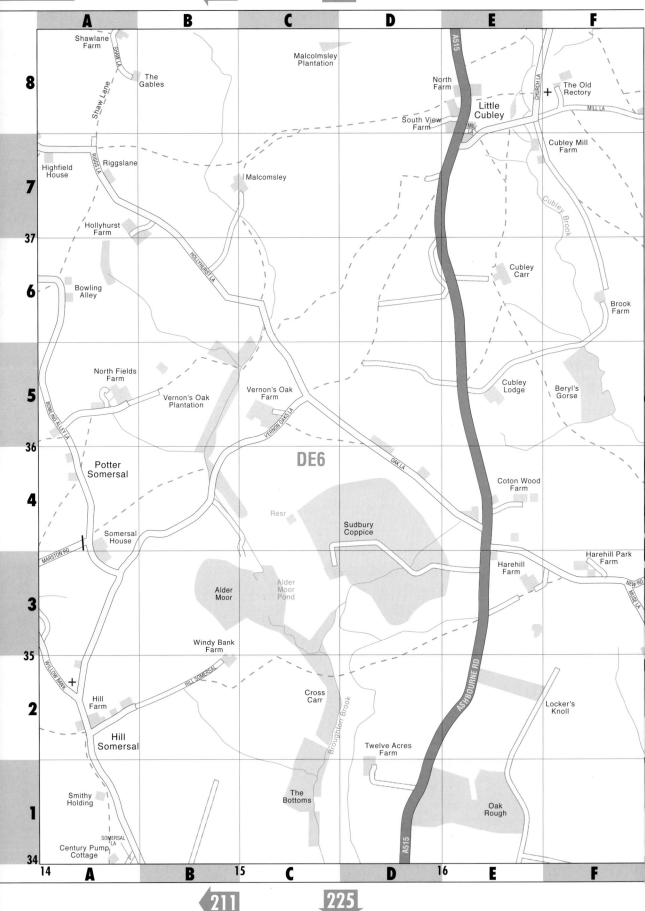

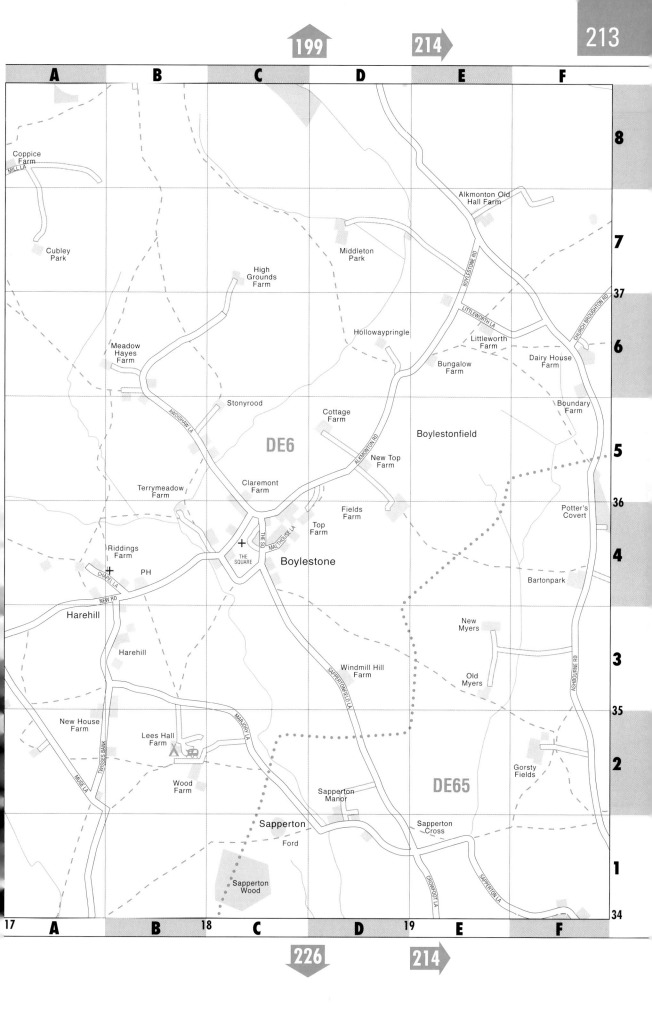

213
200

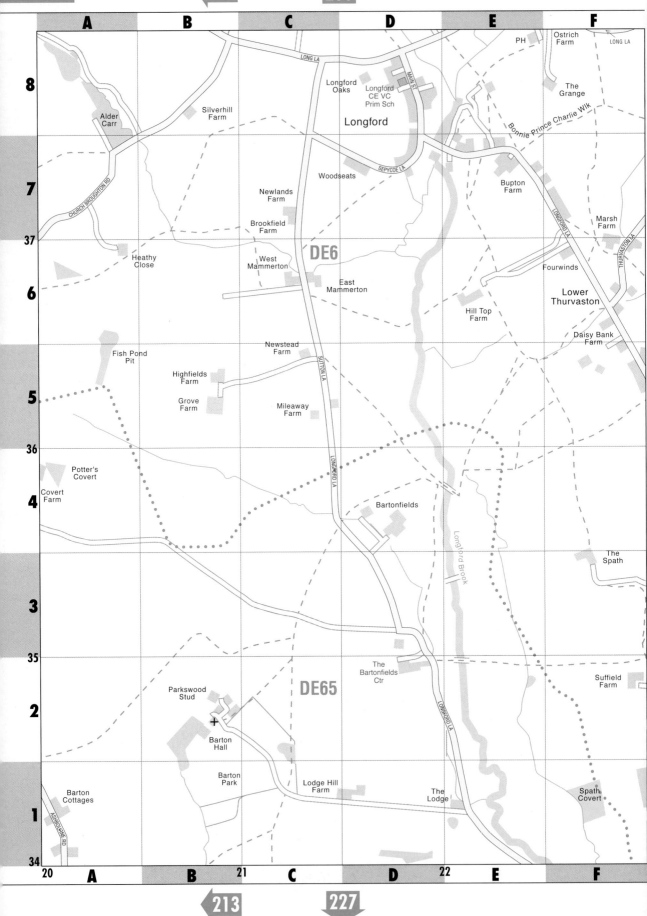

213
227

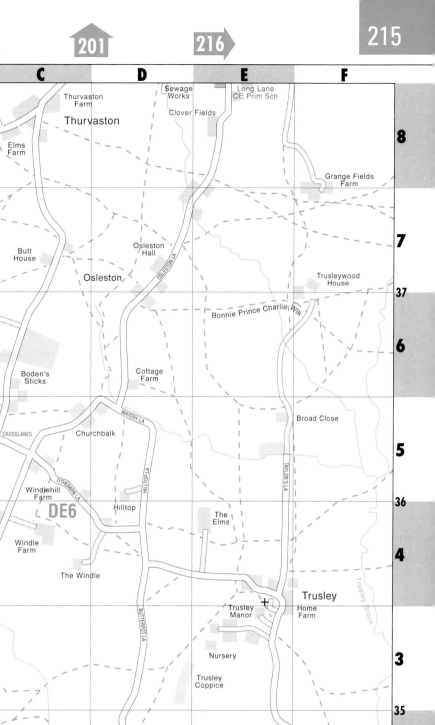

215
202

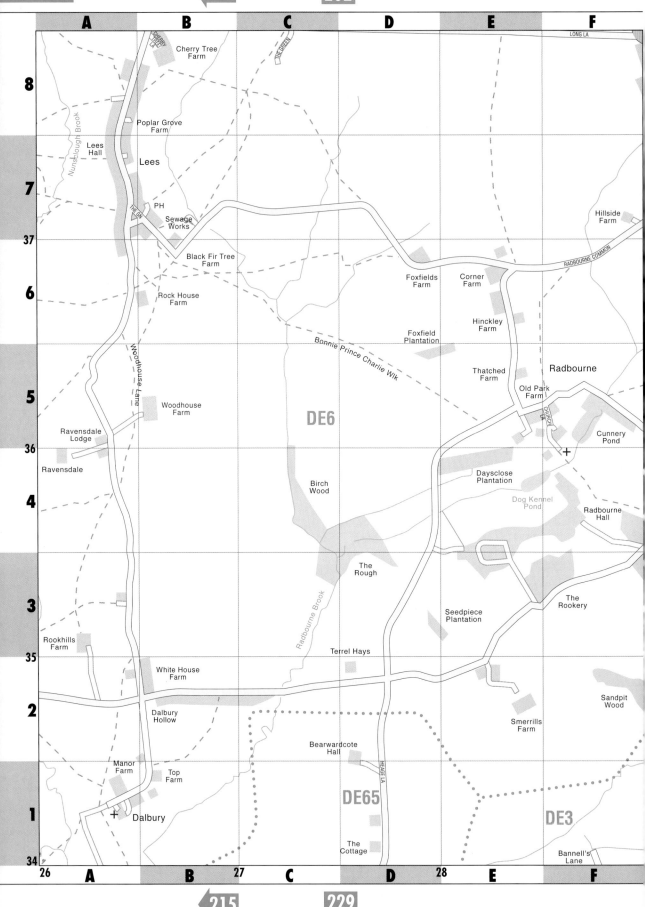

215
229

D1
1 MORLEY HO
2 BRAMBLE MEWS
3 LIMES CT
4 THE PARADE
5 MEADOW CT
6 ALL SAINTS CT
7 HOLLY END RD

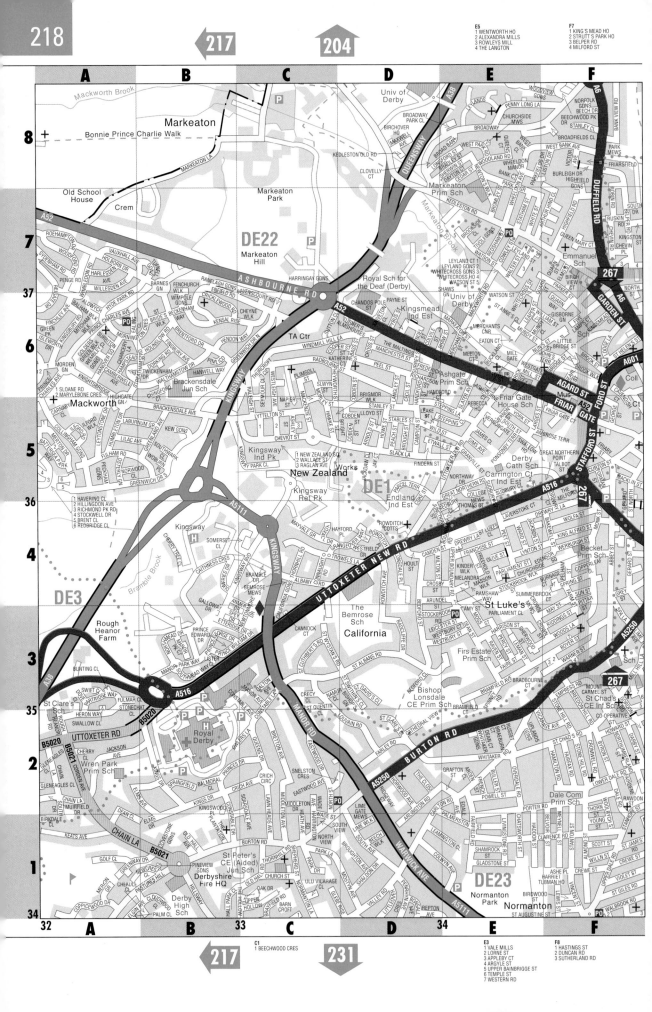

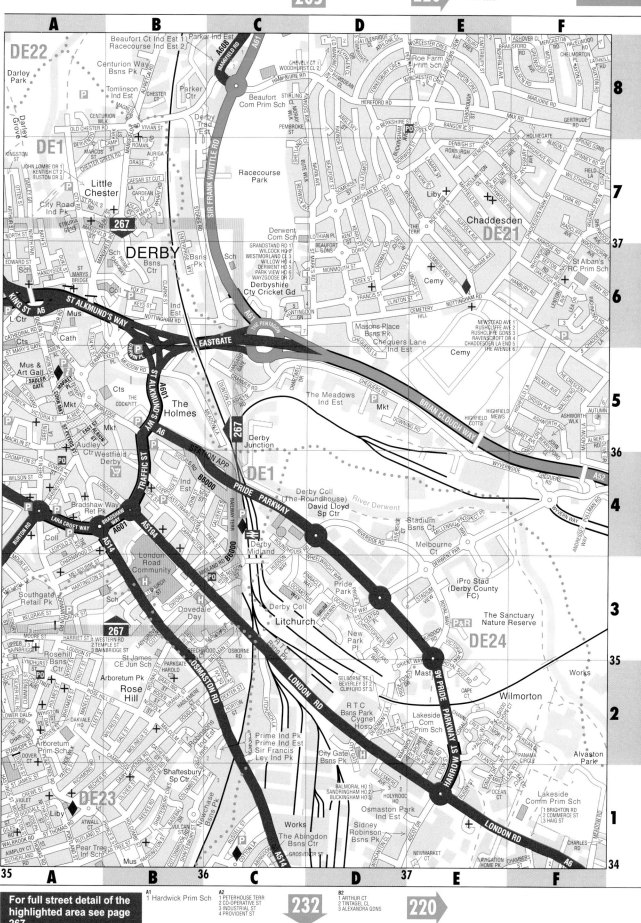

E8
1 ASHOVER RD
2 TADDINGTON CL
3 RINGWOOD CL
4 LIVERPOOL ST

DE22

Darley Park

Darley Grove

DE1

A1
1 Hardwick Prim Sch

A2
1 PETERHOUSE TERR
2 CO-OPERATIVE ST
3 INDUSTRIAL ST
4 PROVIDENT ST

B2
1 ARTHUR CT
2 TINTAGEL CL
3 ALEXANDRA GDNS

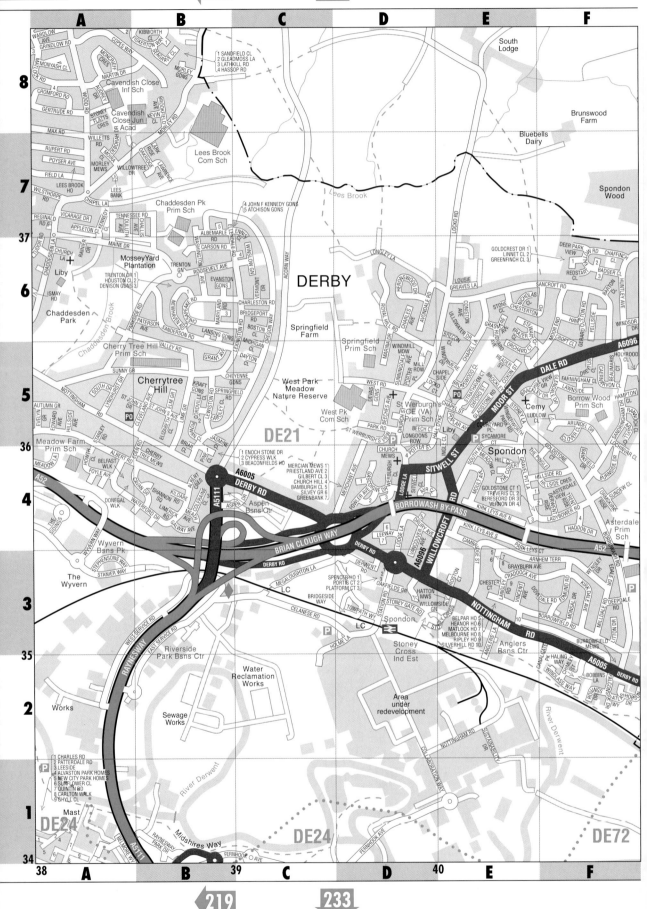

A   B   C   D   E   F

DE21

DE7

8

Bartlewood Farm
PH   Mast
The Spots

The Spots Plantation

7

Spondon Wood Farm
Moor Lane Farm
Piggin Wood
Little Hay Grange
Little London

37

Spondon Wood
MOOR LA
Fields Farm
Waterworks Plantation

6

DOVE MDW
Pheasant Field House
1 PHEASANT FIELD DR
2 LANCASTER WLK
HUNTLEY AVE
ELAND CL
DOLPHIN
BIRCH CL
DALE RD
WOOD RD
DALE RD
DEINCOURT CL
Poplar Farm
FAR LA
Toot Hills

WINDSOR DR
A6096
HOLYROOD CL
HARLECH CL
DE21
PH
HOME FARM
GREEN LA
OAK CL
ROYAL
AVE
COLUMBELL
WAY CL
PARES
1 WINDMILL CL
2 ANNE POTTER CL
3 HARGRAVE AVE
Scotland Farm
Hopwell Hall

5

Ockbrook Grange
WESLEY LA
VICARAGE
SHOP STONES
BARE LA
TOP MANOR CL
CEDAR DR
TREE LANE
THE RIDINGS
M31
Redhill Foundation Prim Sch
Ockbrook

36

Moravian Settlement
BRACKENS LA
THE PADDOCK
BACKHOUSE LA
HILLCROFT DR
CROFT
FLOOD ST
CHURCH ST
NEW ST
CROSS ST
DE72
Windmill Farm
Hopwell Nook

4

ORCHARD CL
COLLIER LA
Castle Hill

VICTORIA AVE
Birchfield
Carr Hill Farm
Hopwell House
ARBOUR HILL
Manor Farm

3

Asterdale Prim Sch
FIELD CL
GREENWAY CL
BEECH AVE
DERWENT AVE
CHESTNUT GR
HAWTHORNE AVE
PETER AVE
B5010
A52
BRIAN CLOUGH WAY

35

HOBSON DR
Borrowash House
DERBY RD
VICTORIA AVE
DEANS DR
CHEVIN AVE
HERMITAGE AVE
FAIRFIELD AVE
DEEPDALE AVE
SHERWOOD AVE
CASTLE
PRIORWAY AVE
COLE LA
Draycott House

2

Liby
LADYSMITH RD
ELM ST
NURSERY DR
PO
KIMBERLEY RD
ASHBROOK AVE
RUTLAND AVE
DEVONSHIRE AVE
HARRINGTON AVE
PRIORS BARN CL
CONWAY AVE
Covent Garden CL
Ashbrook Inf & Jun Schs
Borrowash

PRINCESS DR
DOVECOTE DR
CUMBERLAND CRES
MANOR PARK
GORDON RD
ROYAL AVE
MAYLANDS AVE
MILL CL
BRIAN CL
BALMORAL RD
CHARNWOOD AVE
B5010
RISE AVE
NOTTINGHAM RD
1 PRIORWAY GDNS
2 WINDSOR CL
3 BRADBURY CL
4 COOPERS CL
5 FAIRES CL
6 DERE CROFT

The Stryne
EVELYN CL 1
MILLSTREAM GRANGE 2
SYCAMORE CL 3
BORROWASH RD 4
STATION RD
OUTRAM CL
CENTRAL
MEADOW
WEYACRES
BORROWFIELDS
POPLARS
ROBINSCROSS
MEAR DR
SHACKLECROSS CL
PHODS WAY
OAK TREE CL
GYPS LA
WEAVERS CL
APPIAN WAY
ROMAN WAY
QUILLINGS WAY
WOODWARDS WAY
APPLETREE CT
Shacklecross
Hotel
TUDOR CT
Harris Grange Farm

1

DRAYCOTT RD
DERBY RD
A6005
WASHINGTON COTTS

34

A   B   C   D   E   F

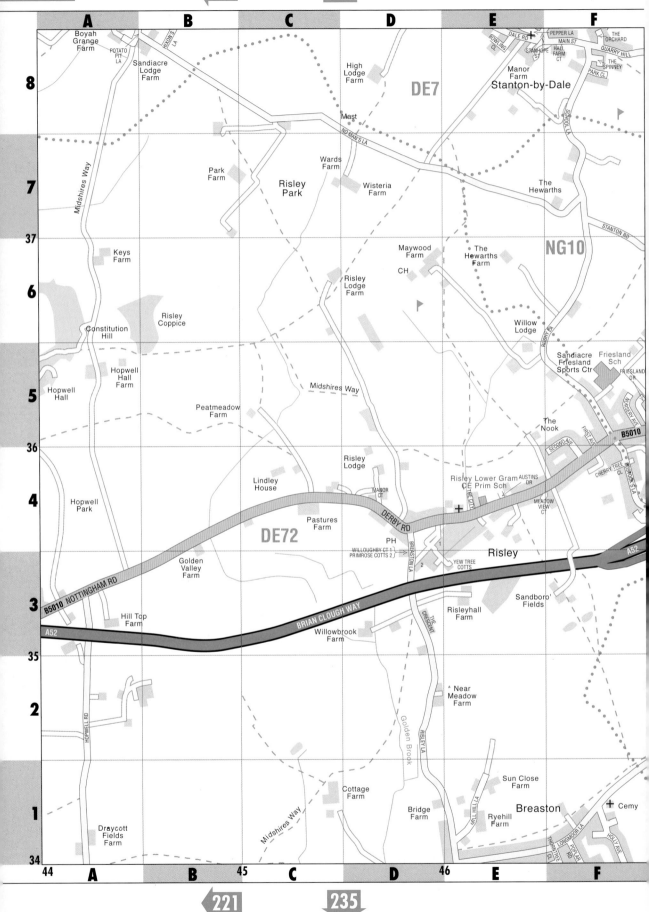

Boyah
Grange
Farm

POTATO
PIT
LA

Sandiacre Lodge
Farm

NIXON'S LA

DALE RD

BOWLING CL

STANHOPE

PEPPER LA

MAIN ST

THE
ORCHARD

QUARRY HILL

THE
SPINNEY

HALL
FARM
CT

PARK CL

Manor
Farm

Stanton-by-Dale

Midshires Way

High
Lodge
Farm

DE7

SCHOOL LA

8

Mast

NO MAN'S LA

Park
Farm

Risley Park

Wards
Farm

Wisteria
Farm

The Hewarths

STANTON RD

7

37

Keys
Farm

Maywood
Farm

CH

The
Hewarths
Farm

NG10

6

Risley
Lodge
Farm

Willow
Lodge

RABLEY LA

Constitution
Hill

Risley
Coppice

Sandiacre
Friesland
Sports Ctr

Friesland
Sch

FRIESLAND
DR

Hopwell Hall

Hopwell
Hall
Farm

Midshires Way

Peatmeadow
Farm

The Nook

FIRST AVE

SECOND AVE

NURSERY AVE

B5010

5

36

Lindley
House

Risley
Lodge

MANOR
CT

Risley Lower Gram
CE Prim Sch

AUSTINS
DR

MEADOW
VIEW
CT

CHERRY TREE
CL

BOSTOCK'S LA

4

Hopwell
Park

DE72

Pastures
Farm

DERBY RD

PH

BREASTON LA

THE CRES

Risley

3

B5010 NOTTINGHAM RD

Golden
Valley
Farm

WILLOUGHBY CT 1
PRIMROSE COTTS 2

2

YEW TREE
COTTS

1

Sandboro'
Fields

A52

BRIAN CLOUGH WAY

Hill Top
Farm

Willowbrook
Farm

THE CRESCENT

Risleyhall
Farm

A52

35

HOPWELL RD

Near
Meadow
Farm

2

Golden Brook

RISLEY LA

Cottage
Farm

Bridge
Farm

MILL HILL LA

Ryehill
Farm

Sun Close
Farm

Breaston

Cemy

1

Draycott
Fields
Farm

Midshires Way

LONGMOOR RD

THORNTREE CL

POPLAR

HOLLY AVE

34

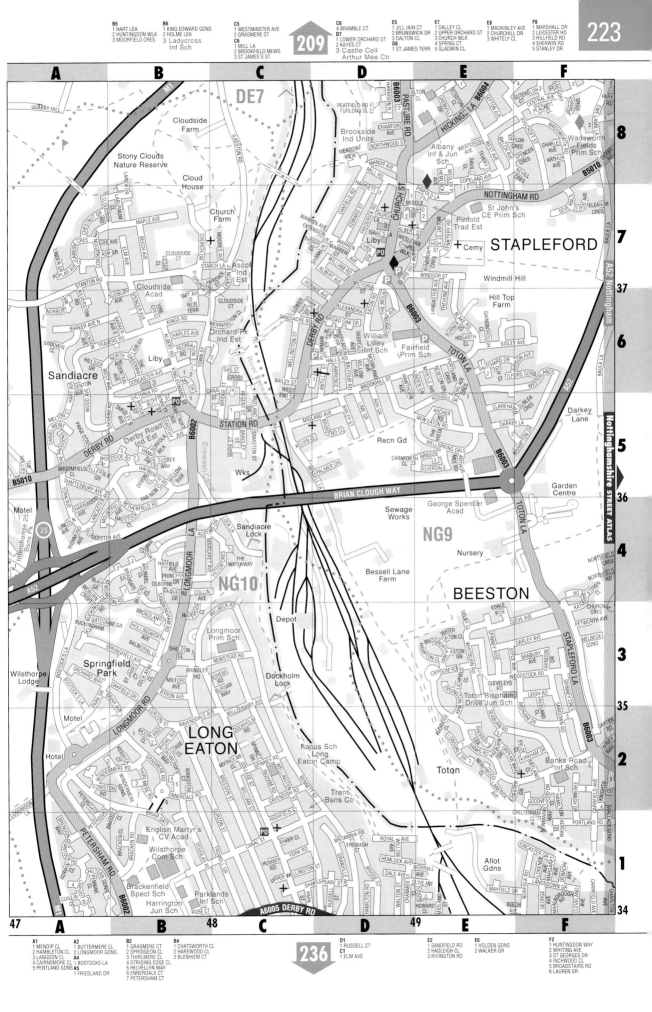

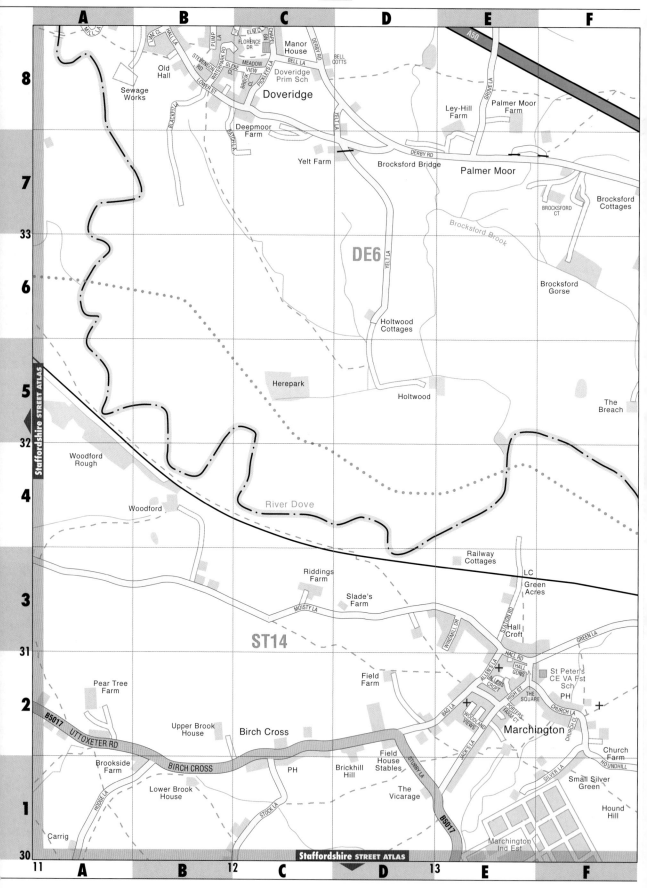

A | **B** | **C** | **D** | **E** | **F**

MILL LA
LAKE CL
HALL LA
STEVENSON RD
PUMP LA
FLORENCE DR
ELM CL
MEADOW
CHAPEL GN
BELL LA
DERBY RD
BELL COTTS

Old Hall

Sewage Works

Manor House

Doveridge Prim Sch

Doveridge

Deepmoor Farm

BLACKPIT LA
LOWER ST
WATERPARK RD
GLEBE CL
BROOK CL
PICKLEYS LA
BALL CROFT

Ley-Hill Farm

Palmer Moor Farm

GROVE LA

A50

8

7

33

Yelt Farm

Brocksford Bridge

Palmer Moor

DERBY RD

YELT LA

DE6

Brocksford Brook

BROCKSFORD CT

Brocksford Cottages

Brocksford Gorse

6

Holtwood Cottages

Herepark

Holtwood

Holtwood

The Breach

5

32

Woodford Rough

4

Woodford

River Dove

Railway Cottages

LC

Green Acres

3

ST14

Riddings Farm

Slade's Farm

MOISTY LA

WINDMILL DR

STATION RD

Hall Croft

GREEN LA

Field Farm

HALL RD

ALLEN'S LA
ALLEN'S CROFT

HALL GDNS

St Peter's CE VA Fst Sch

PH

31

2

Pear Tree Farm

Upper Brook House

Birch Cross

HIGH ST
THE SQUARE

CHURCH LA

CHURCH CL

BAG LA
PORTERS FARM CT
WOODLAND VIEWS
JACK'S LA

Marchington

Church Farm

MOUNDHILL

B5017

UTTOXETER RD

Brookside Farm

BIRCH CROSS

PH

Brickhill Hill

Field House Stables

STUBBY LA

The Vicarage

SILVER LA

Small Silver Green

1

Lower Brook House

STOCK LA

B5017

Hound Hill

HOBBLE LA

Carrig

Marchington Ind Est

30

11 | **A** | **B** | 12 | **C** | **D** | 13 | **E** | **F**

Staffordshire STREET ATLAS

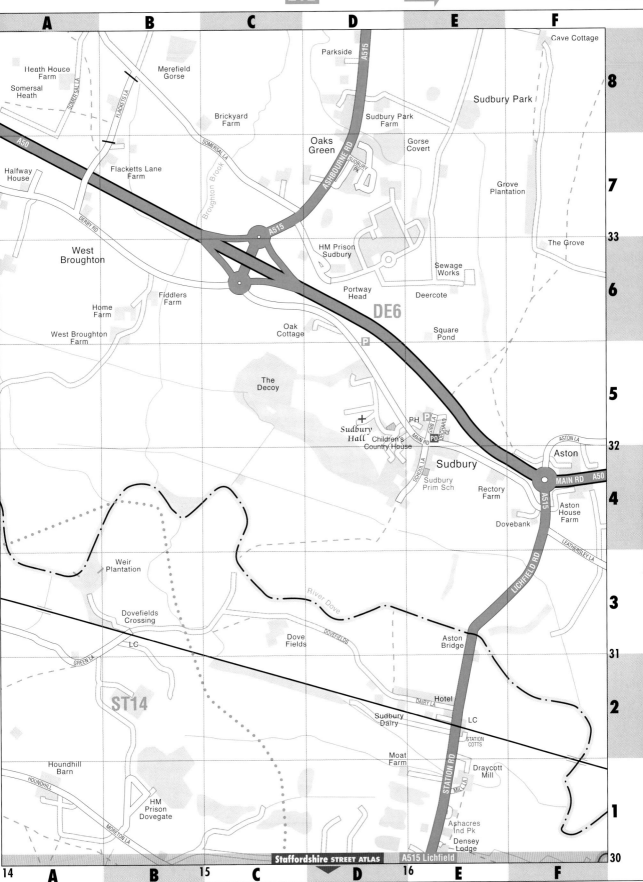

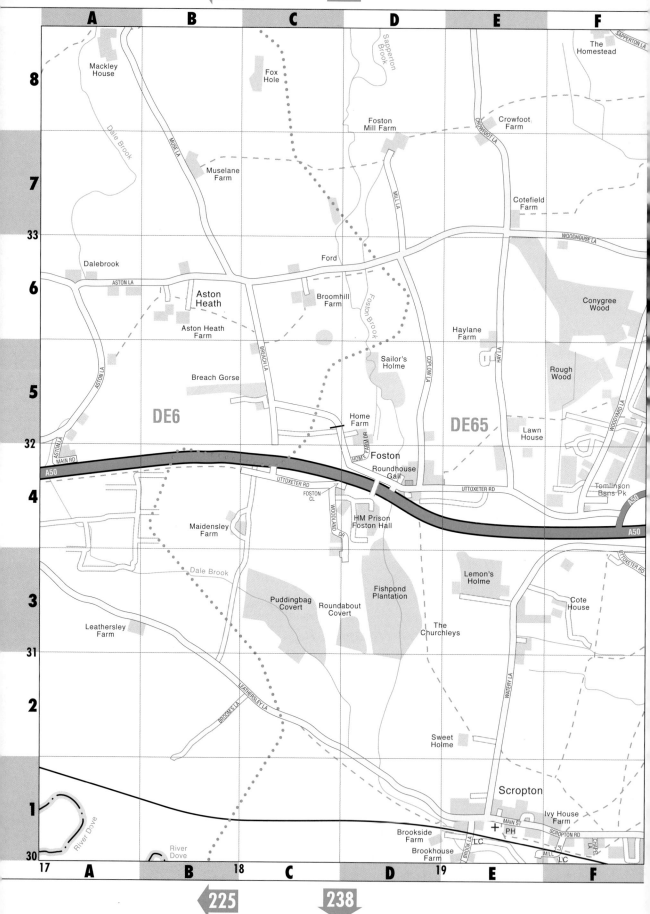

225
213

A **B** **C** **D** **E** **F**

8

Mackley
House

Fox
Hole

Sapperton
Brook

The
Homestead

Foston
Mill Farm

Crowfoot
Farm

7

Muselane
Farm

Cotefield
Farm

WOODHOUSE LA

33

Dalebrook

Ford

Conygree
Wood

ASTON LA

6

Aston
Heath

Broomhill
Farm

Aston Heath
Farm

Haylane
Farm

Foston Brook

Rough
Wood

Breach Gorse

Sailor's
Holme

BREACH LA

HAY LA

COPLOW LA

MILL LA

5

DE6

Home
Farm

Lawn
House

DE65

ASTON LA

32

Foston

MAIN RD

HOME FARM DR

Roundhouse
Gall

Tomlinson
Bsns Pk

A50

UTTOXETER RD

UTTOXETER RD

A50

4

FOSTON
CL

HM Prison
Foston Hall

UTTOXETER RD

WOODLAND DR

Maidensley
Farm

Lemon's
Holme

Cote
House

Dale Brook

Fishpond
Plantation

Puddingbag
Covert

Roundabout
Covert

3

The
Churchleys

Leathersley
Farm

WATERY LA

31

LEATHERSLEY LA

2

BROOM'S LA

Sweet
Holme

Scropton

1

Ivy House
Farm

MAIN ST

SCROPTON RD

PH

River Dove

Brookside
Farm

BROOK LA

LC

CHAPEL LA

River Dove

Brookhouse
Farm

MILL LA

LC

30

A **B** **C** **D** **E** **F**

17   18   19

225
238

A   B   C   D   E   F

8
7
33
6
5
32
4
3
31
2
1
30

Church Broughton

SAFCROFTON LA
ASHBOURNE RD
COTE BOTTOM LA
WOODYARD LA
BOGGY LA
WOODHOUSE LA
Heathtop

CHURCH RD
BROUGHTON CL
AUDEN CL
BOGGY LA
CHAPEL LA
MAIN ST
PH

1 FEARN CL
2 MEADOW RISE
3 THE ETCHELLS

TIPPER'S LA
OLD HALL LA
BADWAY LA
LITTLEFIELD RD

Church Broughton CE Prim Sch
Badder Green Farm
Badder Green
Bent Brook

Bent House
Sutton Heath
Longford Brook
COMMON LA
LONGFORD LA

Mount Pleasant

SCHOOL PIECE LA

Broughton House Farm
The Bent
SUTTON RD

Littlemeadow La
Heath Top Farm
DARK LA
BENT LA
WOODYARD LA

Claypit Hill
Limbersitch Brook
LIMBERSITCH LA
Limbersitch Farm

Birchill's Farm

PK AVE
Dove Valley Pk
PARK AVE
PARK AVE
PACKENHAM BLVD

Heath House
CH
Hatton Fields Farm
Hatton Fields
Hoon Drive Farm

DE65

MIRY LA
CHURCH BROUGHTON RD
SUTTON LA

Pennywaste Wood
Heath Cottage Farm
BROUGHTON HEATH LA
Newlands Farm

A511

Works
Hoon Mount Farm
A50

WATERY LA
UTTOXETER RD
Heath Farm

Sycamore Farm
CHURCH BROUGHTON RD
BREACH LA
Hockley Farm
Hatton House
Hoon Hall Farm

BROOK LA
MALTHOUSE LA

Guinea Farm
UTTOXETER RD
31

NETHERCLOSE LA
SAWPIT LA
PH
CROSBY DR
WINDSOR AVE
DERBY RD
2

1 BALMORAL WAY
2 CARLTON LA
3 HATFIELD LA
4 HIGHGROVE GDNS
5 SANDRINGHAM CL

ALBANY GDNS
PH
BIRCH GR
YEW TREE
THE SHIELING
LIME GR
BRADSHAW MDW
BROOK CL
COOPERS CROFT
GRANVILLE CL
YEW TREE RD
LEY CROFT
WOODMANS CROFT
FLAX CROFT
BLOSSOM WLK
RUSSET CL
HEATH WAY
HOLME CL
BRAMLEY CT
STATION RD
A511

The Firs Farm
SCROPTON RD
FIELD AVE
Heath Fields Prim Sch
FUSTON CL

ROGERS CT
PETERS CT
EATON CL
HANBURY AVE
HASSALL
CHURCH MEWS
RYE CL
RATTS LA
The Fields
Cherry Cottage

20   21   22
A   B   C   D   E   F

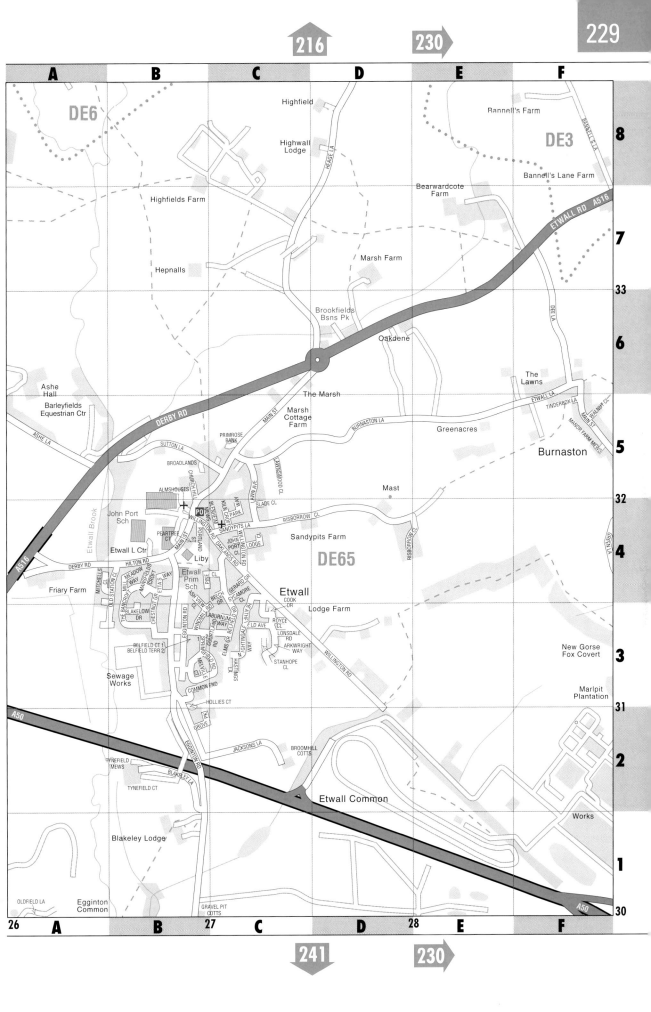

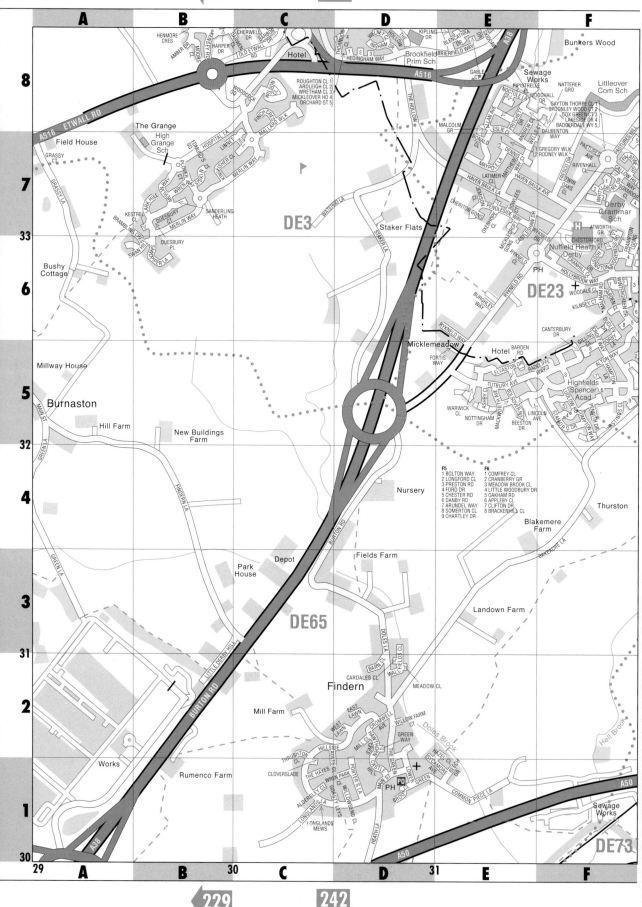

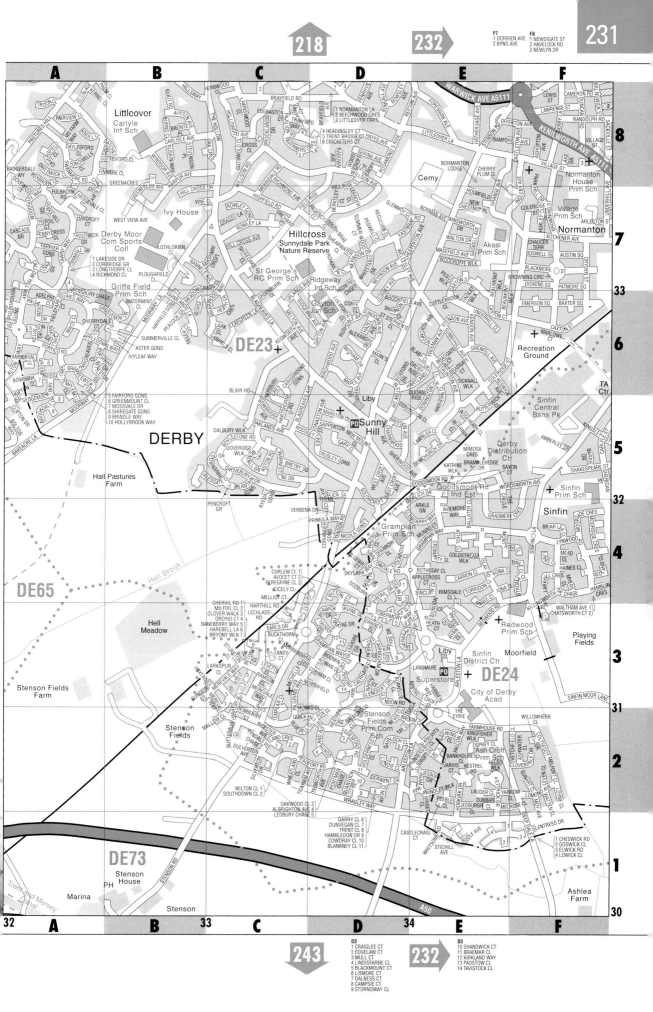

231
219

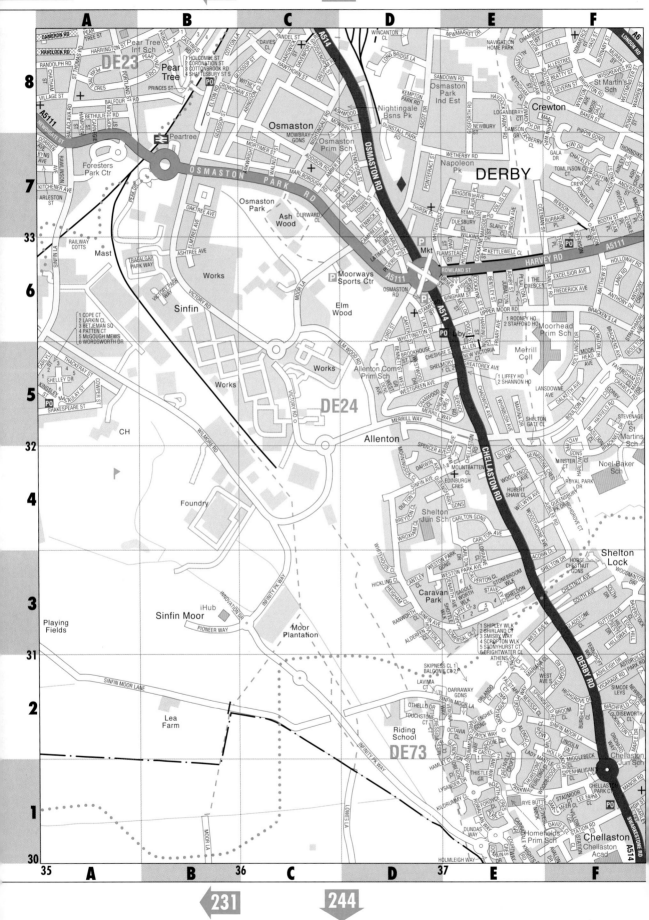

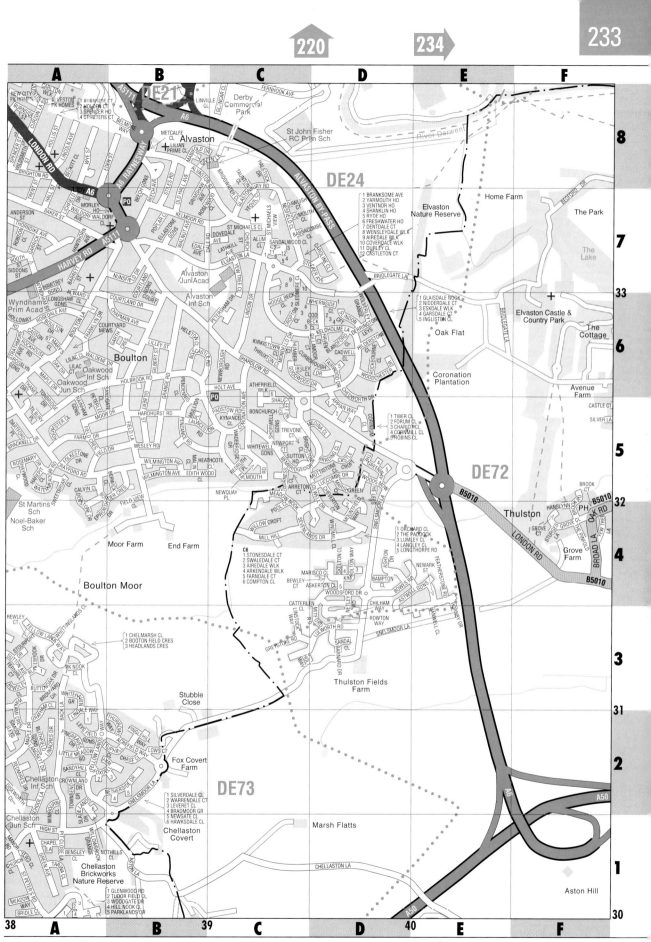

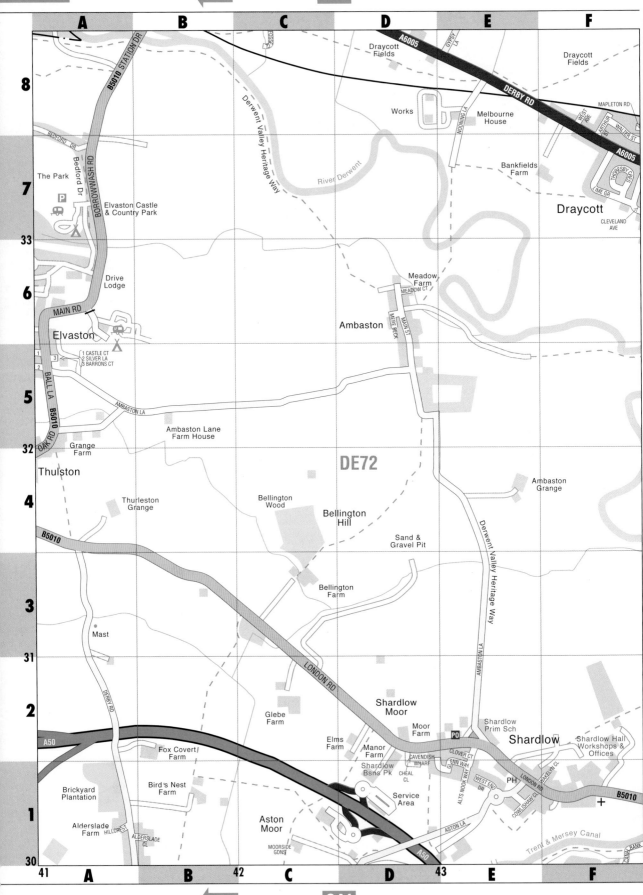

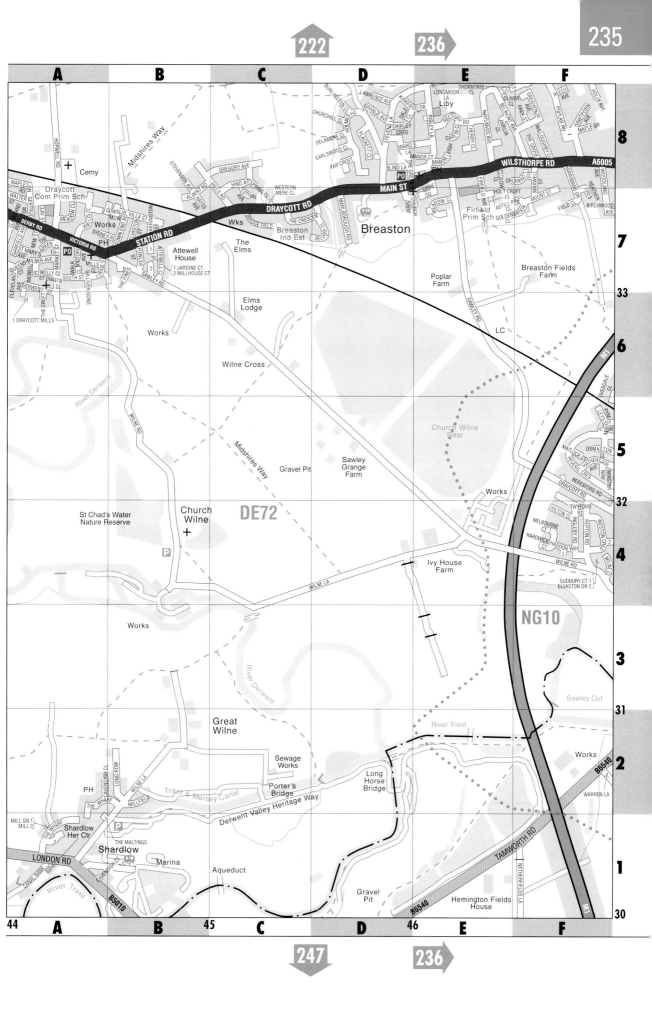

A8
1 HARTSIDE GDNS
2 PORLOCK CL
3 MICKLEDON CL
4 COTSWOLD CL
5 MALVERN GDNS
6 BRECON CL

7 BREDON CL
8 INGLEBOROUGH GDNS
9 THE PLANTATIONS
10 COPSESIDE CL

235

223

B5
1 HICKLING CL
2 WIDDOWSON RD
3 BARN CL
4 BRAMLEY RD

F8
1 CIRCUIT DR
2 INVADERS CL
3 SPEEDWAY CL
4 HONEY POT CL

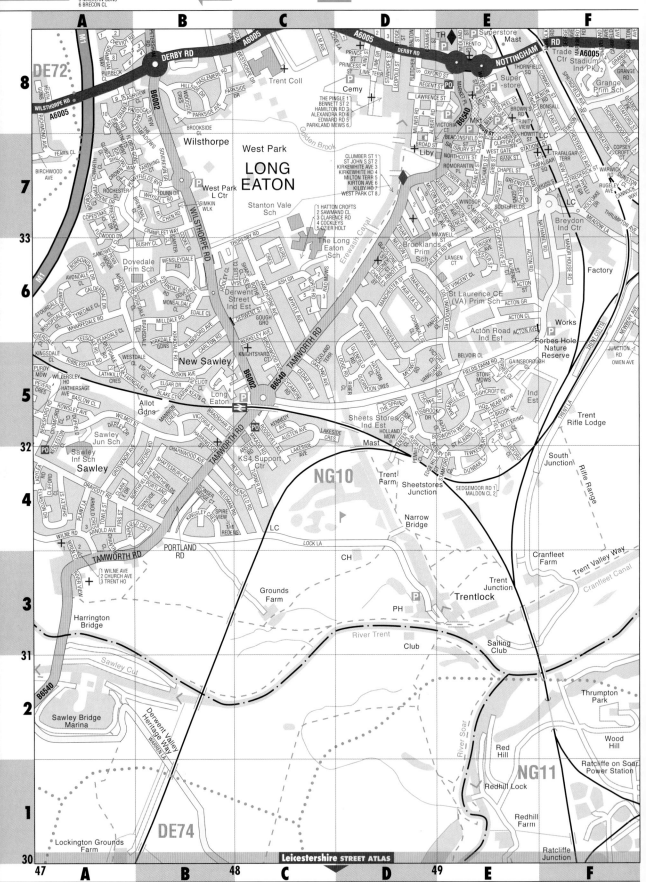

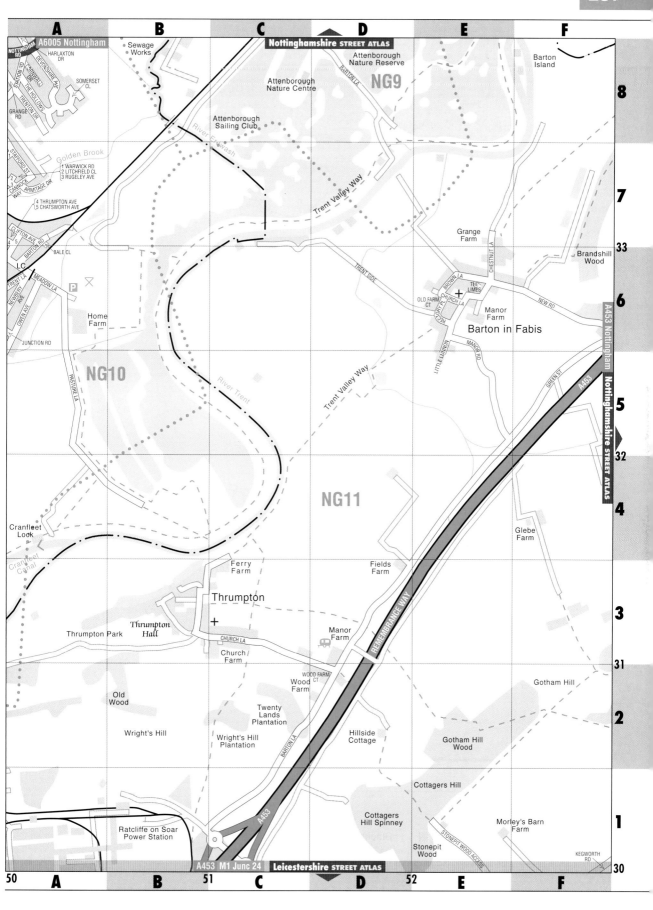

A6005 Nottingham

NOTTINGHAM RD

DEVONSHIRE AVE
HARLAXTON DR
STATION RD
CANALSIDE (?)
SOMERSET CL
THE HOLLOWS
GRANGE RD
TRENTON DR
STAFFORD ST
ARMITAGE DR
CANNOCK WAY
CLIFTON AVE
BARTON RD
BALE CL
LC

Golden Brook

1 WARWICK RD
2 LITCHFIELD CL
3 RUGELEY AVE
4 THRUMPTON AVE
5 CHATSWORTH AVE

TRENT LA
NEWBURY AVE
OWEN AVE
MEADOW LA
JUNCTION RD

PASTURE LA

Sewage Works

Attenborough Sailing Club

River Erewash

Attenborough Nature Centre

Attenborough Nature Reserve

NG9

BARTON LA

Barton Island

Trent Valley Way

Trent Side

Grange Farm

Brandshill Wood

CHESTNUT LA

BROWN LA
THE LIMES
OLD FARM CT
CHURCH LA
REDCROFT CL

NEW RD

Manor Farm

Barton in Fabis

LITTLE LUNNON
MANOR RD

A453 Nottingham

Nottinghamshire STREET ATLAS

Home Farm

NG10

River Trent

Trent Valley Way

NG11

GREEN ST
A453

Glebe Farm

Cranfleet Lock

Cranfleet Canal

Ferry Farm

Thrumpton

Thrumpton Hall

Thrumpton Park

Church Farm

CHURCH LA

Manor Farm

Fields Farm

REMEMBRANCE WAY

Old Wood

Wright's Hill

Wright's Hill Plantation

Twenty Lands Plantation

BARTON LA

WOOD FARM CT
Wood Farm

Hillside Cottage

Gotham Hill

Gotham Hill Wood

Cottagers Hill

Cottagers Hill Spinney

Morley's Barn Farm

Ratcliffe on Soar Power Station

A453

STONEPIT WOOD ACCESS

Stonepit Wood

KEGWORTH RD

50   A   B   51   C   D   52   E   F

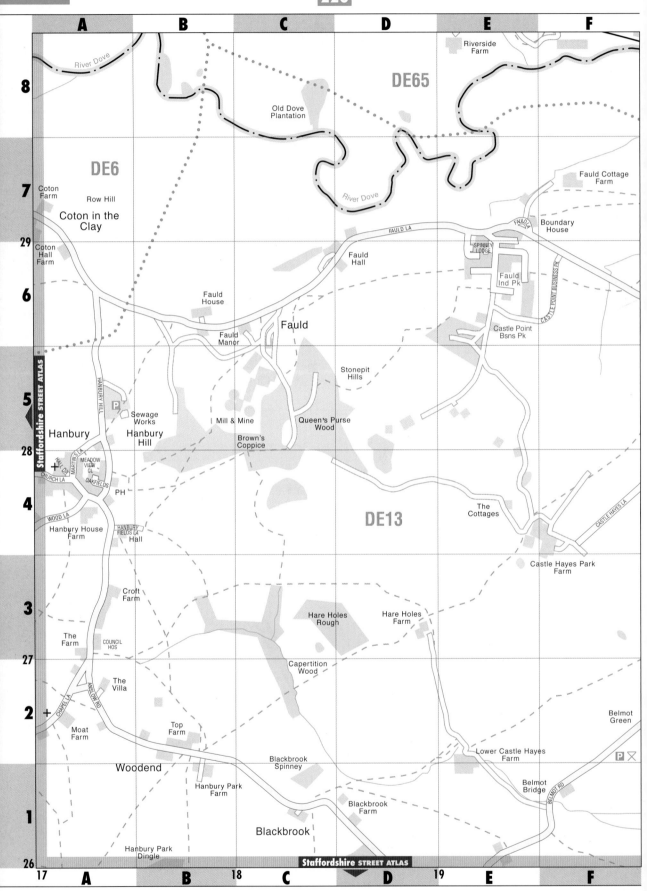

River Dove

DE65

DE6

Coton Farm

Row Hill

Coton in the Clay

Coton Hall Farm

Riverside Farm

Fauld Cottage Farm

FAULD LA

Boundary House

Spinney Lodge

Fauld Ind Pk

Fauld Hall

Fauld House

Fauld

Fauld Manor

Castle Point Bsns Pk

Castle Point Bsns Pk

CASTLE POINT BUSINESS PK

Stonepit Hills

HANBURY HILL

Sewage Works

Hanbury Hill

Mill & Mine

Queen's Purse Wood

Hanbury

MARTIN'S LA

MEADOW VIEW CL

Brown's Coppice

HALL CLOSE

OAKFIELDS

CHURCH LA

PH

WOOD LA

The Cottages

DE13

Hanbury House Farm

HANBURY FIELDS LA

Hall

Castle Hayes Park Farm

CASTLE HAYES LA

Croft Farm

The Farm

COUNCIL HOS

Hare Holes Rough

Hare Holes Farm

Capertition Wood

CHAPEL LA

ANSLOW RD

The Villa

Belmot Green

Moat Farm

Top Farm

Lower Castle Hayes Farm

Woodend

Blackbrook Spinney

Belmot Bridge

BELMOT RD

Hanbury Park Farm

Blackbrook Farm

Blackbrook

Hanbury Park Dingle

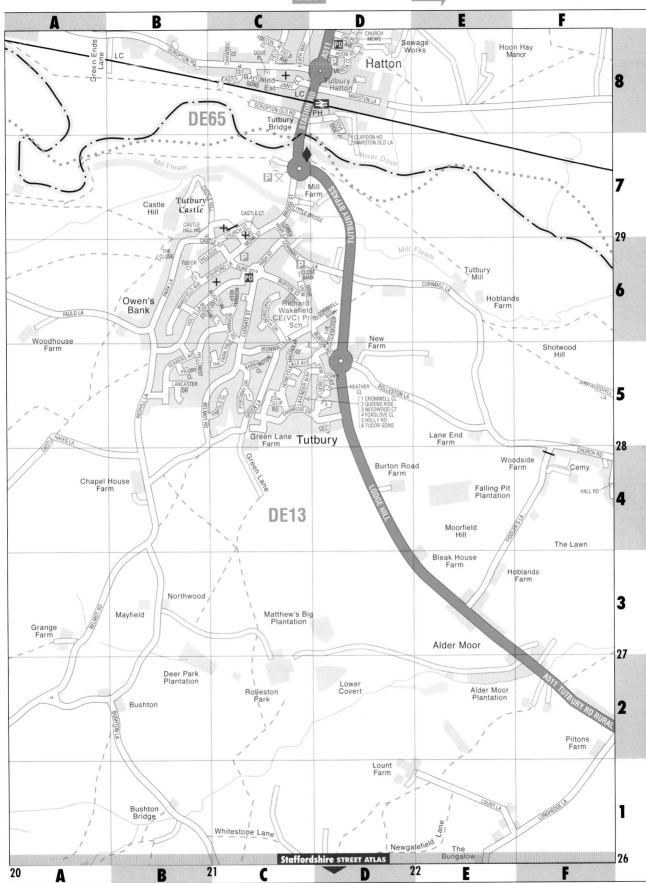

A B C D E F

8
7
29
6
5
28
4
3
27
2
1
26

Green Ends Lane
LC
SCROPTON RD
FOSTON CL
OAKWOOD
FIELD AVE
FIELD AVE
HEATH WAY
CLAYTON GDNS
CASTLE VIEW
MERCIA
JINNY
NI
CHURCH AVE
HOON RD
PO
A511
CHURCH MEWS
Sewage Works
Hoon Hay Manor
Ind Est
Tutbury & Hatton
Hatton
MARSTON LA
LC
STATION RD

DE65
SCROPTON OLD RD
Tutbury Bridge
PH
DOVE SIDE
DOVE
1 CLIFFDON HO
2 MARSTON OLD LA
River Dove

Mill Fleam
P
Mill Farm
TUTBURY BYPASS
Mill Fleam

Castle Hill
Tutbury Castle
CASTLE HILL
CASTLE CT
CASTLE HO
BRIDGE ST
LITTLE BRIDGE
CASTLE HILL HO
CHURCH ST
MONK ST
HIGH ST
LOWER
CORNMILL
CORNMILL LA
THE CLOSE
CASTLE ST
HILLSIDE
Tutbury Mill
CORNMILL LA
Hoblands Farm

FAULD LA
Owen's Bank
TUDOR CT
FISHPOND LA
DUKE ST
HIGH ST
P
CLOSE BANK
LA
CORNMILL LA
BURTON ST
DOVE
VIEW
PO
HOLTS LA
BOURNE CL
KEEPERS
PAVILION
CHRISTINA CT
Richard Wakefield CE(VC) Prim Sch
THE SYCAMORES
BURTON RD
THE BATH
New Farm
Shotwood Hill
SHOTWOODHILL LA

Woodhouse Farm
PARK LA
WAKEFIELD AVE
PUSEL END
LODGATE ST
TOWNSEND
CROWSING
MAGNOLIA CL
VALE AVE
POPPY CL
ROLLESTON LA
Lane End Farm

CASTLE HAYES LA
FERRERS AVE
PRIORY CL
HILLCREST
THE PARK PALE
PORTWAY DR
BABBINGTON CL
HONEYSUCKLE
LAVENDER WAY
BLUEBELL WAY
HEATHER CL
1 CROMWELL CL
2 QUEENS RISE
3 NEEDWOOD CT
4 FOXGLOVE CL
5 HOLLY RD
6 TUDOR GDNS

LANCASTER DR
REDHILL LA
BELMOT RD
PINFOLD CL
GREEN LA
TULIP RD
PRIMROSE DR
5
4
Tutbury
Green Lane
Green Lane Farm

Chapel House Farm
Green Lane
DE13
Burton Road Farm
Woodside Farm
Cemy
CHURCH RD
HALL RD
Falling Pit Plantation
Moorfield Hill
The Lawn
LODGE HILL
FIDDLERS LA

BELMOT RD
Northwood
Matthew's Big Plantation
Bleak House Farm
Hoblands Farm

Grange Farm
Mayfield
Alder Moor
A511 TUTBURY RD RURAL

BUSHTON LA
Deer Park Plantation
Bushton
Rolleston Park
Lower Covert
Alder Moor Plantation
Piltons Farm

Lount Farm
Bushton Bridge
Whitestone Lane
Newgatefield
LANE
LOUNT LA
LONGHEDGE LA
The Bungalow

20 A 21 B C 22 D E F

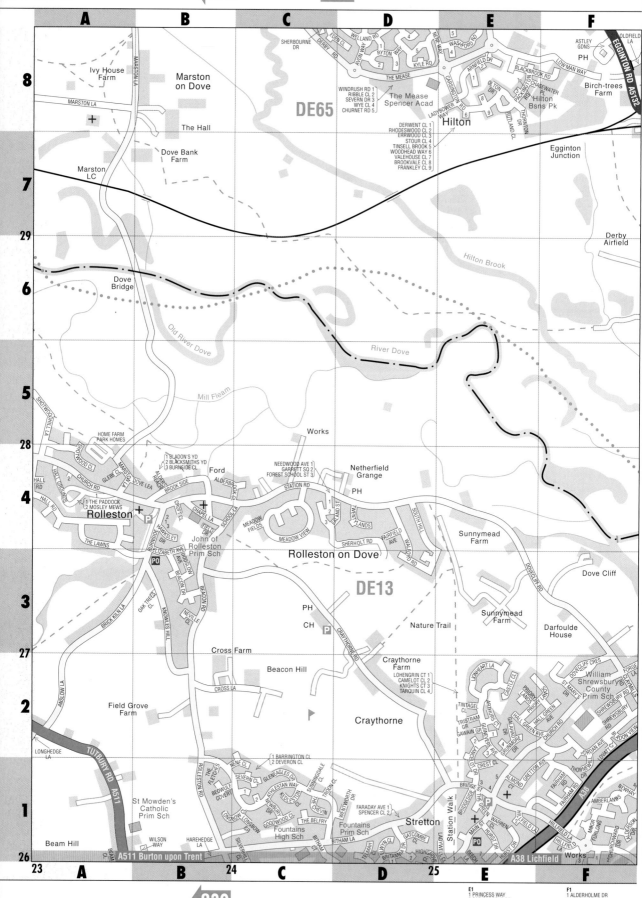

E1
1 PRINCESS WAY
2 CARISBROOKE DR
3 BRIDGE FARM
4 CHILTON CT
5 FENTON GREEN
6 BEECH GDNS

F1
1 ALDERHOLME DR
2 MANTON CL
3 JAMES BRINDLEY WAY
4 MONCREIFF DR

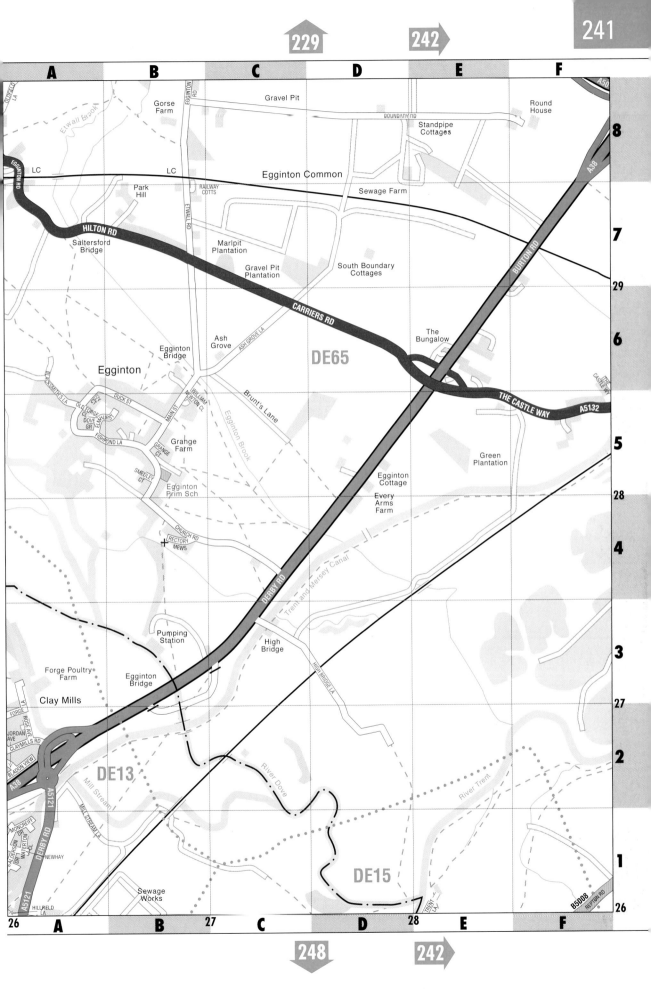

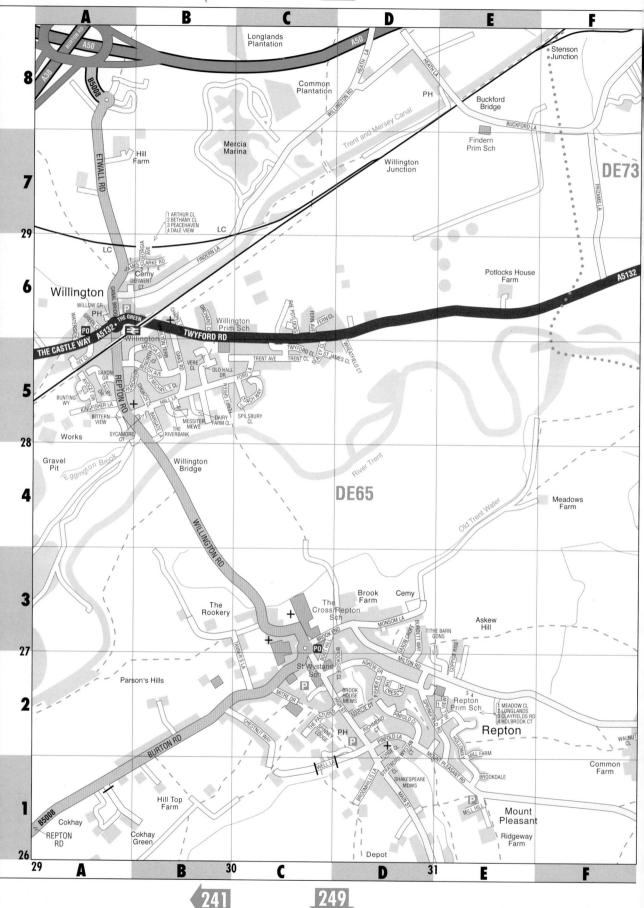

241
230

DE73

DE65

Longlands
Plantation

Common
Plantation

Trent and Mersey Canal

Willington Junction

Buckford
Bridge

Findern
Prim Sch

BUCKFORD LA

Stenson
Junction

BURTON RD   A50

A50

HEATH LA

HEATH LA

WILLINGTON RD

PH

A38

B5008

ETWALL RD

Hill
Farm

Mercia
Marina

FRIZAMS LA

A5132

Willington

1 ARTHUR CL
2 BETHANY CL
3 PEACEHAVEN
4 DALE VIEW

LC

LC

LC

JAMES CLARKE RD

GEORGIA AVE

FINDERN LA

Cemy

DERWENT CT

Potlocks House
Farm

WILLOW GR

PH

GREEN CL

WATERSIDE

PO

CANAL BRIDGE

THE GREEN

A5132

CHAPEL

THE CASTLE WAY

Willington

TWYFORD RD

Willington
Prim Sch

ORCHARD CL

CHAPEL TERR

BURTON RD

THE POTLOCKS

FERN AVE

FERN CL

TWYFORD CL

SCALEY CL

ST JAMES CT

WHEATFIELD CT

IVY CL

MERCIA DR

BEECH AVE

ST MICHAEL'S CL

OAKS RD

OLD HALL DR

FORD LA

VERE CL

TRENT AVE

TRENT CL

SS

SAXON GR

ASPEN DR

CHURCH CL

HALL LA

FERRY GREEN

CHURCH WAY

SPILSBURY CL

Works

BITTERN
VIEW

BUNTING
WY

KINGFISHER LA

REPTON RD

SYCAMORE
CT

BARGATE LA

MESSITER
MEWS

DAIRY
FARM CL

THE
RIVERBANK

Gravel
Pit

Eggington Brook

Willington
Bridge

River Trent

Old Trent Water

Meadows
Farm

WILLINGTON RD

The
Rookery

Brook
Farm

Cemy

The
Cross Repton
Sch

MONSOM LA

Askew
Hill

TITHE BARN
GDNS

TANNER'S LA

BROOK END

SCOTT HILL

PO

St Wystans
Sch

BROOKSIDE CL

ASKEW GR

BURDETT WAY

SAXON CROFT

MILTON RD

COPPICE RISE

Parson's Hills

MITRE DR

HIGH ST

MARKET CT

Brook
House
Mews

FISHER CL

THE
CRESC

PINFOLD CL

Repton
Prim Sch

1 MEADOW CL
2 LONGLANDS
3 CLAYFIELDS RD
4 HOLBROOK CT

Repton

CHESTNUT WY

THE PASTURES

THE
SPINNEY
LODGE

PH

Richmond
CL

PINFOLD LA

SPRINGER CL

WYSTAN CT

FORGE CL

MOUNT PLEASANT RD

HOLLOWAY

Mill
Farm

WALNUT
CL

Common
Farm

BURTON RD

B5008

Cokhay

Hill Top
Farm

WELL LA

BROOMHILLS LA

STRATFORD LA

MAIN ST

SHAKESPEARE
MDWS

BROOKDALE

MILL HILL

Mount
Pleasant

REPTON
RD

Cokhay
Green

Depot

Ridgeway
Farm

241
249

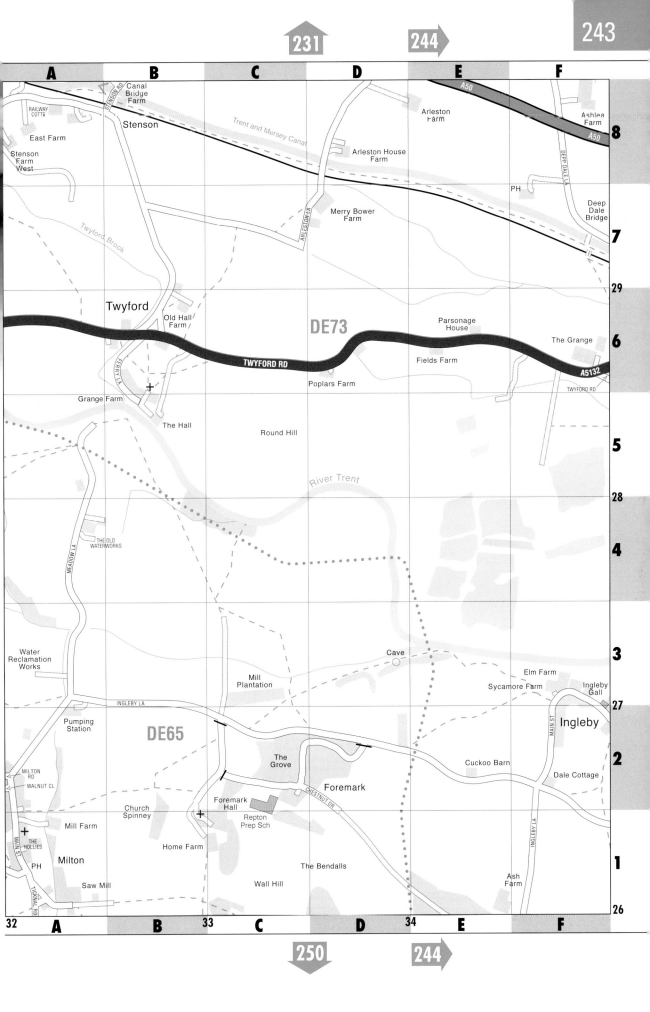

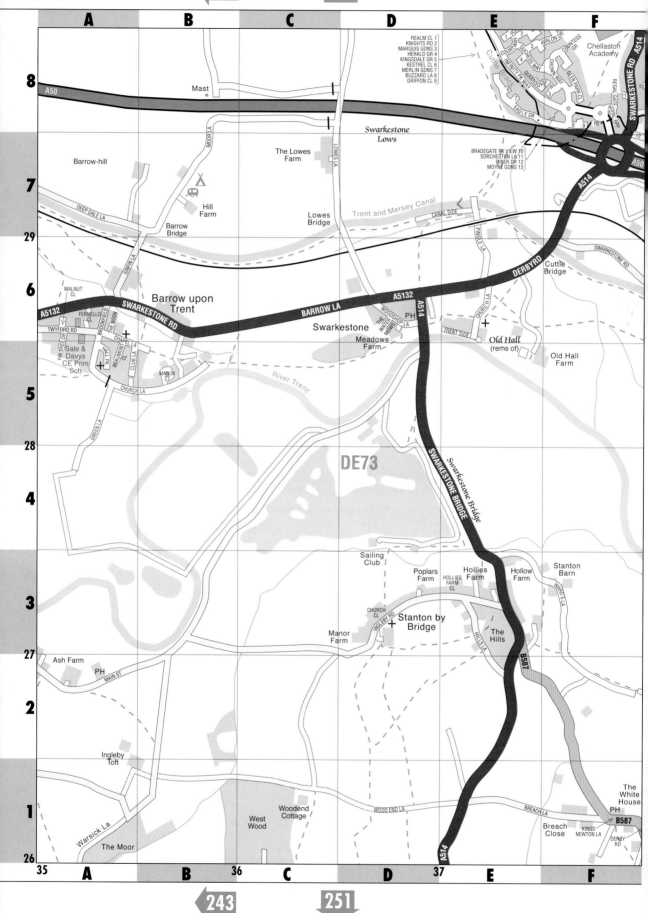

	A	B	C	D	E	F

8

A50

Mast

Swarkestone Lows

REALM CL 1
KNIGHTS RD 2
MARQUIS GDNS 3
HERALD GR 4
KINGSDALE GR 5
KESTREL CL 6
MERLIN GDNS 7
BUZZARD LA 8
GRIFFON CL 9

Chellaston Academy

Cuttle Brook

COURTNEY WAY
DUCHESS WAY
INFINITY PK WAY
CROWN WAY
QUEENS WAY
EAGLE DR
AVALON DR
COUNTESS GR
GLEN PARK CL
REGAL GATE
ROYAL APP
RIVA APP

SWARKESTONE RD

Barrow-hill

7

Hill Farm

The Lowes Farm

BRADEGATE PK VIEW 10
SORCHESTUN LA 11
RIBER DR 12
MOYNE GDNS 13

A514

DEEP DALE LA

Barrow Bridge

MOOR LA

LOWES LA

Lowes Bridge

Trent and Mersey Canal

CANAL SIDE

PINGLE LA

SWARKESTONE RD

29

SWIFT LA

DERBY RD

Cuttle Bridge

6

A5132

WALNUT CL

SWARKESTONE RD

Barrow upon Trent

BARROW LA

A5132

Swarkestone

WOODSHOP LA

A514

CHURCH LA

Old Hall (rems of)

FERNELLO CL
BROOKFIELD
THE NOOK

TWYFORD RD
FIR TREE DR
Sale & Davys CE Prim Sch

CHAPEL LA
BEAUMONT CL
CLUB LA
HALL PK

MANOR CT

THE WATER MDWS

PH

Meadows Farm

TRENT SIDE

Old Hall Farm

5

CHURCH LA

River Trent

GREEN LA

28

DE73

SWARKESTONE BRIDGE

4

Sailing Club

Poplars Farm

Hollies Farm

HOLLIES FARM CL

Hollow Farm

Stanton Barn

WARD'S LA

Stanton by Bridge

The Hills

HILLS LA

3

CHURCH CL

INGLEBY RD

Manor Farm

27

Ash Farm

PH

MAIN ST

B587

2

Ingleby Toft

Wood End La

BREACH LA

The White House PH

B587

1

Warsick La

The Moor

West Wood

Woodend Cottage

WOOD END LA

A514

Breach Close

KINGS NEWTON LA

DERBY RD

26

| 35 | A | 36 | B | C | D | 37 | E | F |

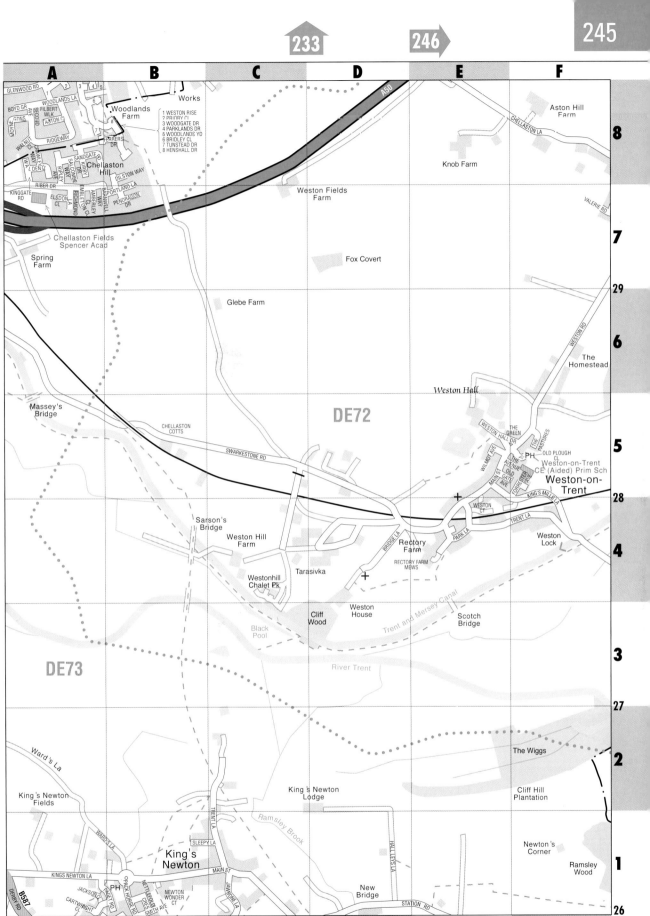

A | B | C | D | E | F

8

Glenwood Rd
Boyd Gr
AVE
FILBERT WLK
ASTON CL
Second
Woodlands La
Works
Woodlands Farm
Aston Hill Farm
Chellaston La

1 WESTON RISE
2 PRIORY CL
3 WOODGATE DR
4 PARKLANDS DR
5 WOODLANDS YD
6 BRIDLEY CL
7 TUNSTEAD DR
8 HENSHALL DR

Knob Farm

VALERIE RD

RIDGEWAY
FORRERS DR
SANDGATE CL
KIRBY
SALCOMBE
RICHMOND
EMBLETON CL
Chellaston Hill
DILSTON WAY
PORTLAND LA
PENDRAGON DR

Weston Fields Farm

RIBER DR
ELSDON CL
KINGGATE RD

Chellaston Fields Spencer Acad

7

Spring Farm

29

Fox Covert

Glebe Farm

6

WESTON RD

The Homestead

Massey's Bridge

Weston Hall

DE72

5

CHELLASTON COTTS

SWARKESTONE RD

WESTON HALL DR
THE GREEN
THE PASTURES
OLD PLOUGH CL
PH
Weston-on-Trent CE (Aided) Prim Sch

WILMOT AVE
THE AVENUE
OLD GATE AVE
FORRESTER AVE

Weston-on-Trent

28

Sarson's Bridge

Weston Hill Farm

BRIDGE LA
Rectory Farm
RECTORY FARM MEWS
PARK LA
KING'S MILLS LA
WESTON CT
TRENT LA
Weston Lock

4

Tarasivka

Westonhill Chalet PK

Weston House

Cliff Wood

Trent and Mersey Canal

Scotch Bridge

Black Pool

DE73

River Trent

3

27

Ward's La

The Wiggs

2

King's Newton Fields

WARD'S LA

King's Newton Lodge

Ramsley Brook

Cliff Hill Plantation

Newton's Corner

TRENT LA
SLEEPY LA
HALLEY'S LA
Ramsley Wood

1

KINGS NEWTON LA
King's Newton
MAIN ST
New Bridge

B587
DERBY RD
JACKSON CL
CARTWRIGHT
OPACK HORSE RD
NETTLE FOLD
SMITH AVE
NEWTON WONDER CT
JAWBONE LA
STATION RD

26

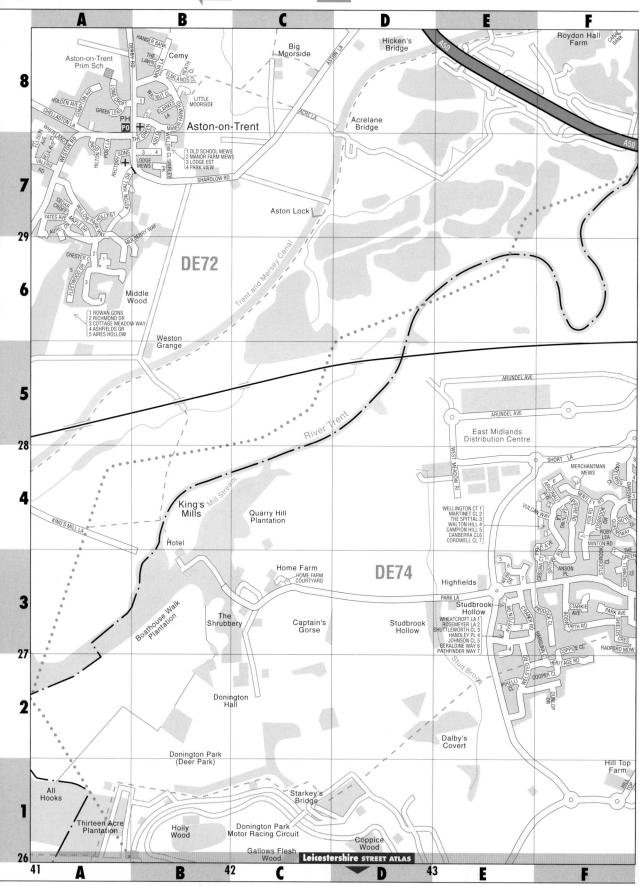

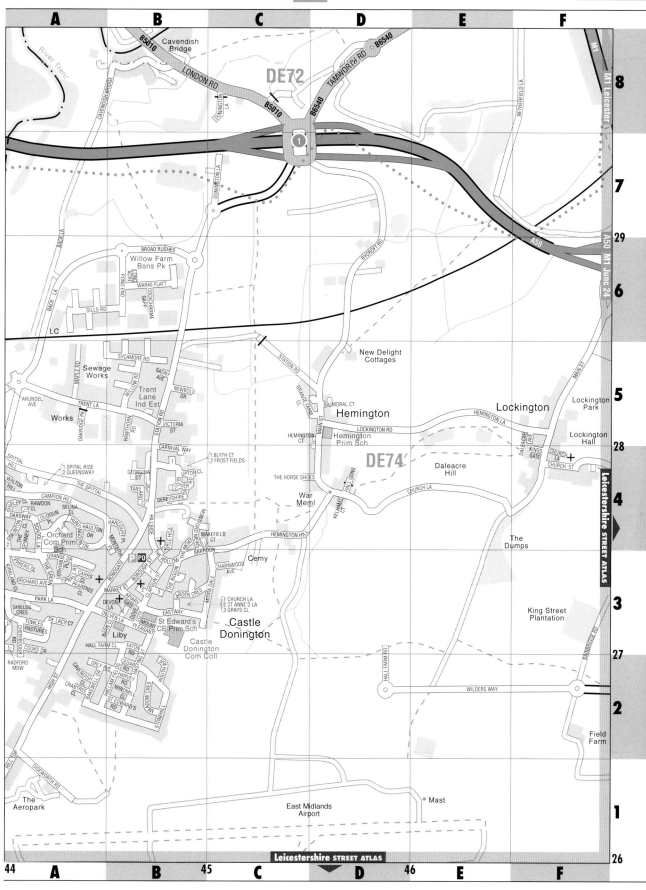

River Trent

A B C D E F

B5010
Cavendish Bridge

LONDON RD
B5010

TAMWORTH RD
B6540
B6540

DE72

8

M1

M1 Leicester

DONINGTON LA

1

7

A50

29

A50 M1 Junc 24

DONINGTON LA

BROAD RUSHES
Willow Farm Bsns Pk

BACK LA
BACK LA

LONG ACRE
POND END
WARKE FLATT
COCKCHARME
GAPP
SILLS RD

LC

New Delight Cottages

6

STATION RD

RYCROFT RD

SYCAMORE RD

Sewage Works

MAPLE RD
WILLOW RD
GASNY AVE
NEWBOLD DR

TRENT LA

Trent Lane Ind Est

ARUNDEL AVE

Works

OAKRIDGE PL

GRANGE FARM CL

BALMORAL CT

MAIN ST

Hemington

Lockington

Lockington Park

HEMINGTON LA

5

STATION RD
VICTORIA ST

HEMINGTON CT

LOCKINGTON RD

Hemington Prim Sch

Lockington Hall

DALEACRE AVE
KINGS GATE
CHURCH LA
CHURCH ST

28

SPITTAL HILL
HAWTHORN

CARNIVAL WAY

1 BLYTH CT
2 FROST FIELDS

DE74

1 SPITAL RISE
2 QUEENSWAY
THE SPITTAL

GEORGINA CT

UPTON CL
OLIVER RD

THE HORSE SHOES

Daleacre Hill

4

WALTON HILL
SHIRLEY CL
RAWDON CL
DARSWAY
SELINA CL
LOUDOUN PL
CAMPION HILL
TANY ST
DERBYSHIRE

War Meml

HALL GDNS

KELHAMS CT

CHURCH LA

The Dumps

THE SPINNEY
STANTON CL
SCHOOL LA
HUNTINGDON DR
HAULTON DR
MONTEITH PL
HARCOURT PL
HILLSIDE

MONTFORT ST
HIGH STREET
CASTLE HILL

WAKEFIELD CT

HEMINGTON HL

Orchard Com Prim Sch

GRANGE DR

THE MOAT
THE HOLLOW
BARROON

Cemy

2

CHARNWOOD AVE

3

FERRERS CL
LOTHIAN PL
TIPWALL RD
CARRS CL
PEARTREE CL
THE GREEN

BONDGATE
BOROUGH ST
CLAPGUN ST

MOIRA DALE

1 CHURCH LA
2 ST ANNE'S LA
3 GRAYS CL

ORCHARD AVE
PARK LA
SHIELDS CRES
DE LACY CT

MARKET PL

GARDEN CRES

King Street Plantation

3

TOWLES PASTURES

DEVON LA

APART

EASTWAY

Castle Donington

27

CHERBOURG RD
COOKS DR

HALL FARM CL

MOUNT PLEASANT

DELVEN LA

BARKBY CL
CLONE
DONE

St Edward's CE Prim Sch

HALL FARM RD

RADFORD MDW

HIGH ST

CAVENDISH CL
BAKEWELL CL
CRABTREE CL

ORLY AVE
HALLAM FIELDS RD
HARVEY RD
WINDMILL CL
ST EDWARD'S RD

CEDAR DR

MACON CL

WINDMILL RD
ROUTH

Liby

Castle Donington Com Coll

WILDERS WAY

2

HILL TOP

STONEHILL

Field Farm

DISEWORTH RD

The Aeropark

East Midlands Airport

Mast

1

26

44 A B 45 C D 46 E F

Leicestershire STREET ATLAS

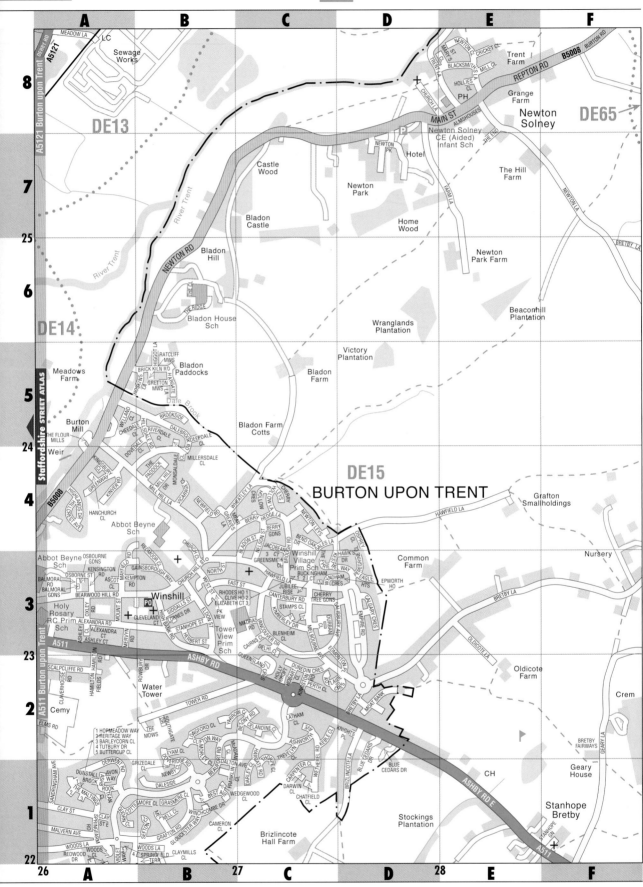

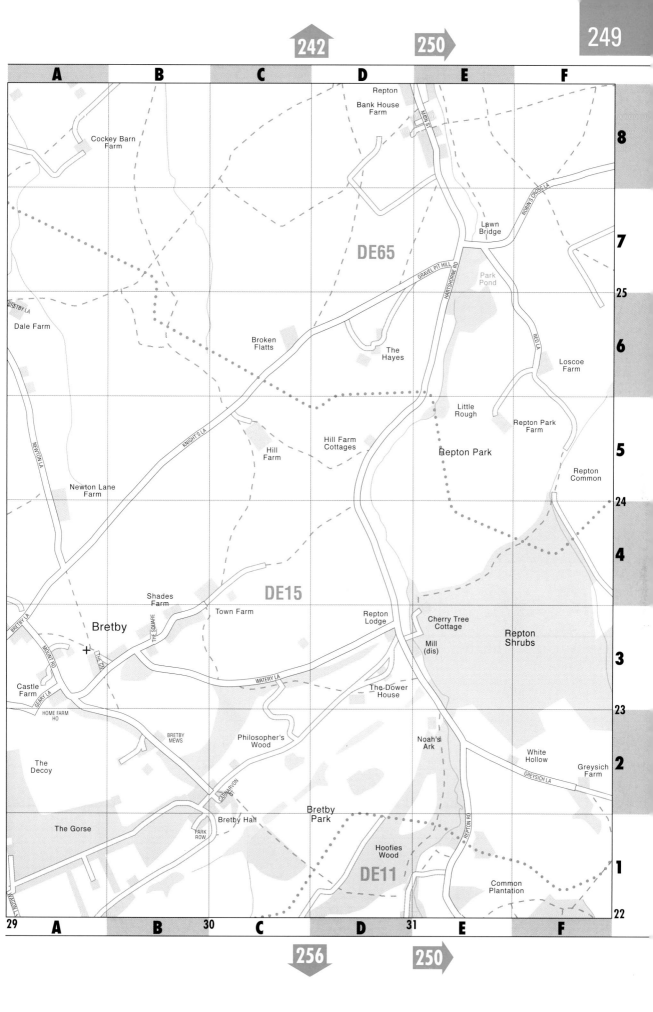

249
243

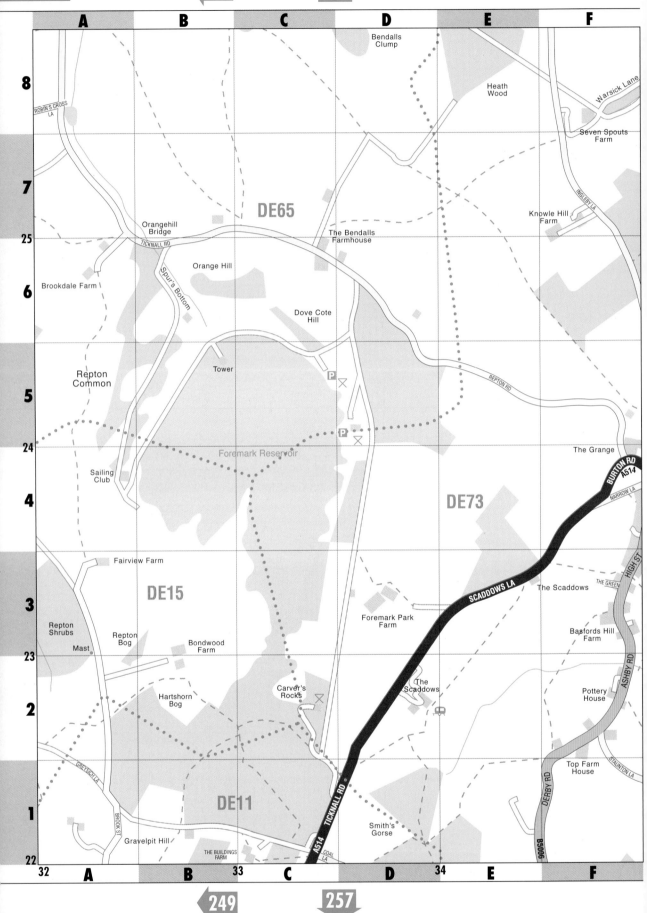

249
257

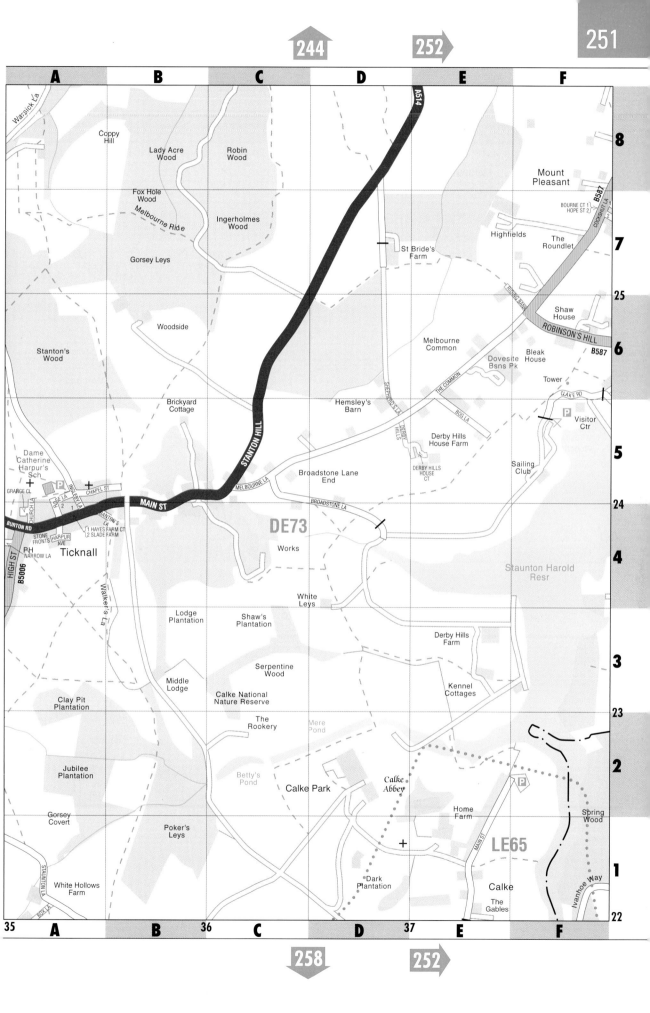

244 252 258 252

A B C D E F

8
7
25
6
5
24
4
3
23
2
1
22

Warsick La
Coppy Hill
Lady Acre Wood
Robin Wood
Fox Hole Wood
Melbourne Ride
Ingerholmes Wood
Gorsey Leys
Woodside
Stanton's Wood
Brickyard Cottage
Dame Catherine Harpur's Sch
GRANGE CL
CHURCH LA
PSE LA
INGLEBY LA
CHAPEL ST
MAIN ST
BURTON RD
STONE FRONTS
STANTON'S LA
HARPUR AVE
1 HAYES FARM CT
2 SLADE FARM
PH
NARROW LA
HIGH ST
B5006
Ticknall
Walker's La
Lodge Plantation
Shaw's Plantation
Middle Lodge
Clay Pit Plantation
Serpentine Wood
Calke National Nature Reserve
The Rookery
Jubilee Plantation
Betty's Pond
Calke Park
Gorsey Covert
Poker's Leys
STAUNTON LA
BOX LA
White Hollows Farm
Dark Plantation
MELBOURNE LA
Broadstone Lane End
BROADSTONE LA
Works
White Leys
DE73
A514
STANTON HILL
St Bride's Farm
SHEPHERD'S LA
DERBY HILLS
Hemsley's Barn
Derby Hills House Farm
DERBY HILLS HOUSE CT
Melbourne Common
THE COMMON
BOG LA
Dovesite Bsns Pk
Bleak House
Tower
CLAK'E RD
P
Visitor Ctr
Sailing Club
Derby Hills Farm
Kennel Cottages
Mere Pond
Calke Abbey
Home Farm
MAIN ST
LE65
Calke
The Gables
Staunton Harold Resr
Mount Pleasant
B587
BOURNE CT 1
HOPE ST 2
COCKSHUT LA
Highfields
The Roundlet
RIDING BANK
ROBINSON'S HILL
B587
Shaw House
P
Spring Wood
Ivanhoe Way
P

35 36 37
A B C D E F

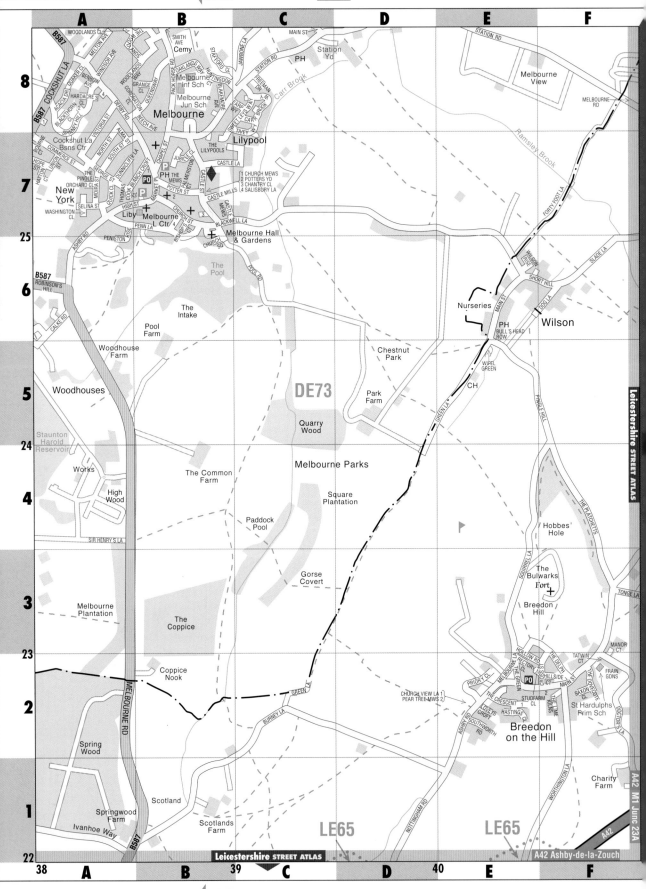

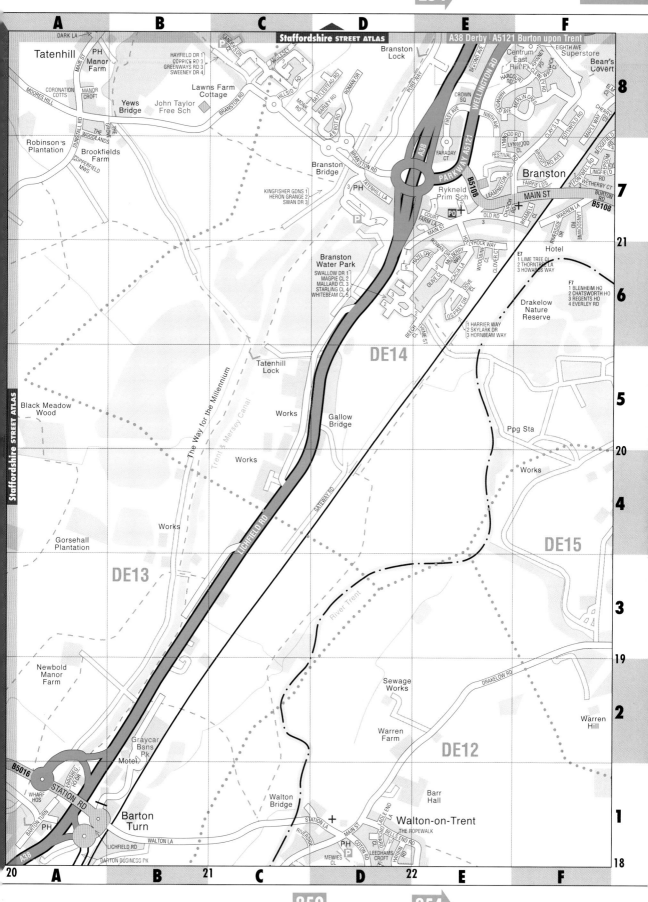

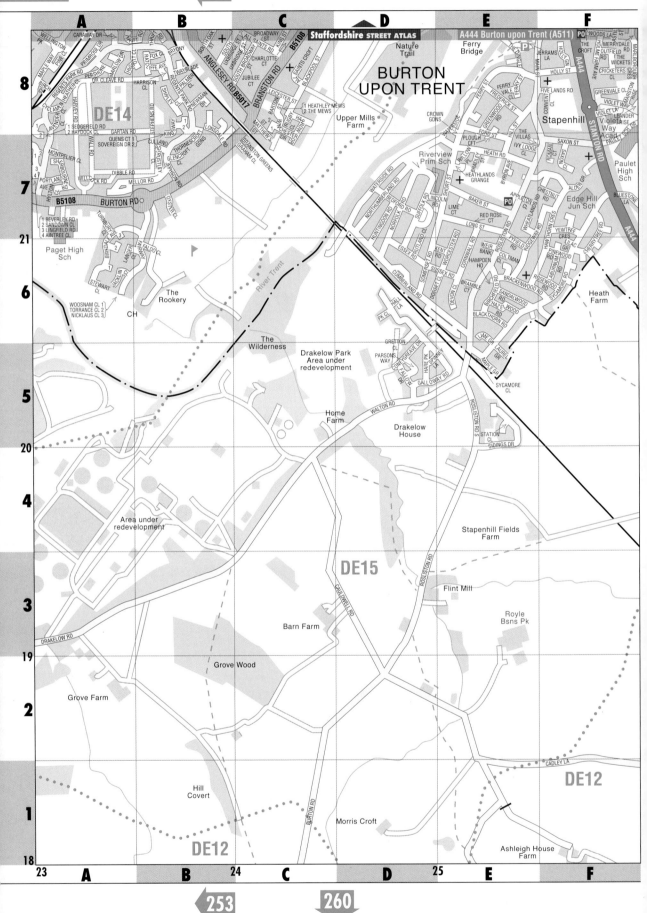

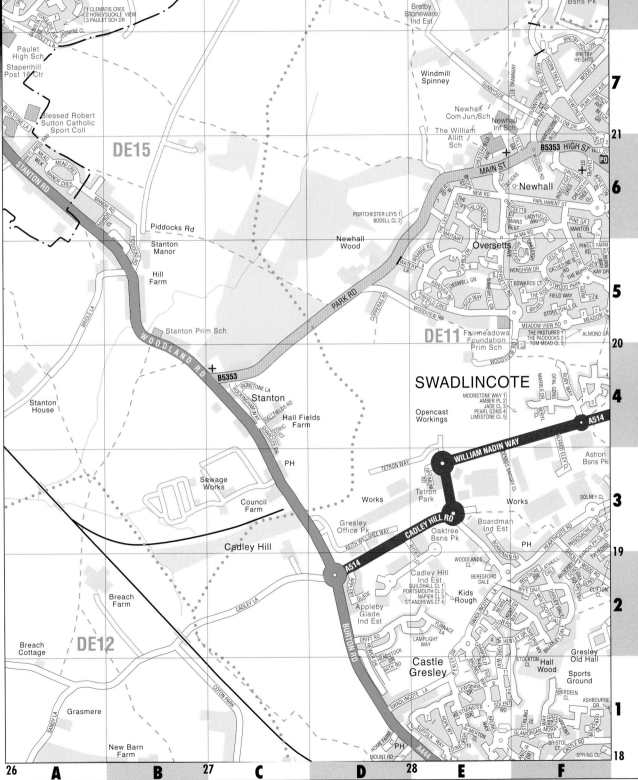

E5
1 BRAILSFORD AVE
2 BASLOW GN
3 WINSTER GN
4 DALES CL
5 THE FAIRWAY
6 THE GABLES

7 WARREN HILL
8 ARTHURRICE CL

F6
1 LABURNUM RD
2 ASH TREE CL
3 ROBINSON RD
4 PLUMMER RD
5 BRAMBLEWOOD

A B C D E F

8

GEARY LA

A511 ASHBY RD E

PH

THORN TREE LA

Bretby
Bsns Pk

Model Dairy
Farm

1 TUTBURY DR
2 RYEBACK CL
3 LUTON MWS
4 TAMWORTH CL
5 BRINDLEY CL

Works

Bretby
Stoneware
Ind Est

BRETBY HOLLOW

BRETBY
HEIGHTS

WOOD LA

7

1 CLEMATIS CRES
2 HONEYSUCKLE VIEW
3 PAULET SCH DR

Windmill
Spinney

SUNNYSIDE

THE TRAMWAY

ROSE TREE LA

THORN TREE LA

PEAR TREE AVE

VENTRE RD

LARCH RD

BIRCH
AVE

BEECH
GR

Paulet
High Sch

Newhall
Com Jun Sch

Newhall
Inf Sch

WILLOW DR

SUNNYSIDE

BRETBY RD

HAWTHORN
RISE

21

Stapenhill
Post 16 Ctr

The William
Allitt
Sch

CHESTERFIELD

TILLEY

HIGGINS RD

B5353 HIGH ST

HILL ST

CHAPEL
ST

APPLETON
ST

PO

Blessed Robert
Sutton Catholic
Sport Coll

DE15

MAIN ST

BROOK

COLVERS

Newhall

ORCHARD
CL

BOSELEY CRES

CHELMSLEY
CL

APPLETON
ST

6

STANTON RD

NEW RD

THE
CROFT

THE CRESCENT

NEW RD

OVERSETTS
RD

PARLIAMENT ST

Oversetts

PINE GR

MANTON
CL

MEAD CRES

MANOR RD

PIDDOCKS RD

Piddocks Rd

JOHN ST

THE
LEYS

ST
JOHN
ST

LADYFIELD
WAY

ALMA RD

PINGLE
FARM
RD

KILBURN

Stanton
Manor

Portchester Leys 1
Bodell Cl 2

MAYFAIR

GRANGE
RD

RALEIGH
AVE

RENSHAW DR

CECIL RD

CATHERINE ST

WESTWOOD PARK

THE BURROWS

KAY DR

5

Hill
Farm

Newhall
Wood

WATERY
LA

ASHDALE
RD

IDESWELL
GN

ST EDWARDS CT

THE RISE

BRYER CL

STONEYDALE CL

FIELD WAY

MEADOW
SIDE

BRIDLE LA

WOODLAND RD

Stanton Prim Sch

PARK RD

COPPERAS RD

FAIRFIELD CRES

CRICH WAY

WOODVIEW RD

THE RISE

MEADOW VIEW RD

THE PASTURES 1
THE PADDOCKS 2
TOM MEAD CL 3

ALMOND GR

MEADOW LA

20

DE11

Fairmeadows
Foundation
Prim Sch

WOODVIEW RD

P

B5353

IRONSTONE LA

SWADLINCOTE

MOONSTONE WAY 1
AMBER PL 2
JADE CL 3
PEARL GDNS 4
LIMESTONE CL 5

MARBLE DR

OPAL GDNS

RUBY WAY

4

Stanton
House

ROCKINGHAM WAY

Stanton

Opencast
Workings

BERYL

A514

Astron
Bsns Pk

Hall Fields
Farm

HALLFIELDS RD

CEDRIC
CL

WILLIAM NADIN WAY

DENNIS BARGBY CL

OPTIMUM RD

ALFRED ELEY CL

3

Sewage
Works

PH

TETRON WAY

Tetron
Park

Works

SOLNEY CL

19

Council
Farm

Gresley
Office Pk

CADLEY HILL RD

Oaktree
Bsns Pk

Boardman
Ind Est

HEARTHCOTE RD

HANDSACRE CL

PH

Cadley Hill

KEITH WILSHEE WAY

A514

BURTON RD

FLORIST

WOODLANDS
CL

Beresford
Dale

WYE DALE

BOARDMAN RD

WESTACRE
CL

ITHKILL
CL

DALE

ANDERBY
GDNS

GRESLEY WOOD RD

CLIFTON
CL

2

Breach
Farm

CADLEY LA

APPLEBY
GLADE

Cadley Hill
Ind Est

GUILDHALL CL 1
PORTSMOUTH CL 2
NAPIER CL 3
ST ANDREWS CT 4

Kids
Rough

FURNACE
LA

SWADLINCOTE RD

LIFTON
RD

ASHBY RD

BRAMLEY CL

TWYFORD
CL

DE12

Breach
Cottage

Appleby
Glade
Ind Est

DRIFT RD

RIVERSIDE DR

LAMPLIGHT
WAY

Castle
Gresley

OAKFIELD

BRUNEL
DR

HENLEY GR

SALFORD WAY

Hall
Wood

STOCKTON
CL

Gresley
Old Hall

Sports
Ground

1

Grasmere

SANDY LA

COTON PARK

Home Farm

PH

MOUNT RD

A444

SWADLINCOTE LA

HEADSTOCK
DR

BATH RD

WESTMINSTER
DR

SUFFOLK
WAY

HOPE WAY

MERTON
DR

EDINE

BRUNEL

ABERDEEN
CL

GLAMORGAN

MORAY

GREENAMPT
ST

ANGLIA

TILLING

ASHBOURNE
DR

BRISTOL

CASTLE RD

SPRING CL

18

New Barn
Farm

26 A 27 B C 28 D E F

E1
1 GREENWICH AVE
2 BRUNEL WAY
3 ESSEX DR
4 SUNDERLAND CL
5 GLASGOW CL
6 CROYDON CL
7 CHELMSFORD CL
8 DE MONTFORT CL
9 KEELE DR

10 NOTTINGHAM CL
11 READING AVE
12 STMARTINS CL

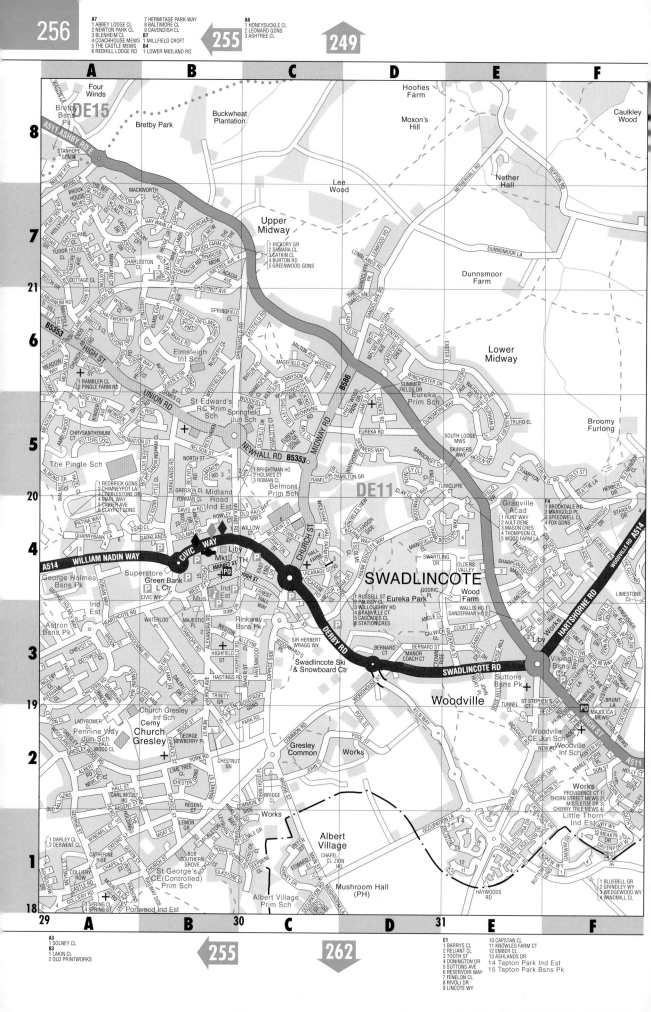

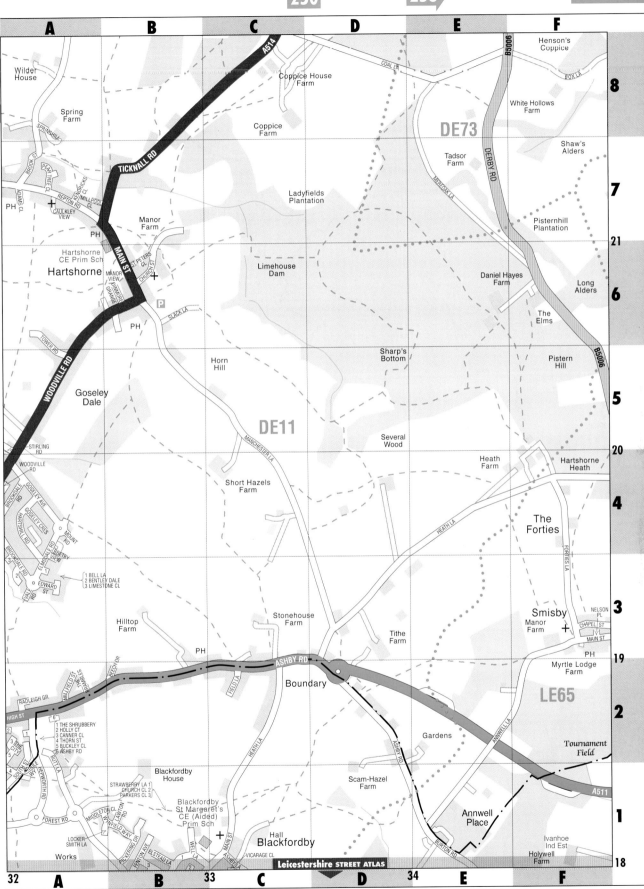

A   B   C   D   E   F

Wilder House

Spring Farm

SPRINGHILL

KILBOURNE RD

ADAMS CL

PEAR TREE CL

PH

REPTON RD

CAULKLEY VIEW

MILLPOOL CL

KENRICKS CL

PH

TICKNALL RD

A514

Coppice House Farm

COAL LA

Coppice Farm

DE73

Henson's Coppice

BOX LA

White Hollows Farm

Shaw's Alders

DERBY RD

B5006

Tadsor Farm

MEREOAK LA

Ladyfields Plantation

Pisternhill Plantation

Daniel Hayes Farm

Long Alders

Manor Farm

MAIN ST

ST PETERS CL

CHURCH ST

Hartshorne CE Prim Sch

Hartshorne

MANOR VIEW

DYMOCKE GRANGE

P

PH

SLACK LA

Limehouse Dam

The Elms

Pistern Hill

B5006

TOWER RD

WOODVILLE RD

Goseley Dale

Horn Hill

DE11

Sharp's Bottom

MANCHESTER LA

Several Wood

Heath Farm

Hartshorne Heath

STIRLING RD

WOODVILLE RD

BROOKDALE RD

GOSELEY AVE

HARTSHILL RD

GOSELEY CRES

ELMSDALE RD

BRETBY VIEW

MOUNT RD

BROOKDALE RD

DALE ST

EDWARD ST

1 BELL LA
2 BENTLEY DALE
3 LIMESTONE CL

Short Hazels Farm

HEATH LA

The Forties

FORTIES LA

Hilltop Farm

Stonehouse Farm

Tithe Farm

Smisby

Manor Farm

NELSON PL

CHAPEL ST

MAIN ST

PH

BEECH DR

PH

FIELD LA

ASHBY RD

Boundary

Myrtle Lodge Farm

LE65

RADLEIGH GR

MILLFIELD ST

BRAMBLES

HIGH ST

1 THE SHRUBBERY
2 HOLLY CT
3 CANNER CL
4 THORN ST
5 BUCKLEY CL
6 ASHBY RD

HEPWORTH RD

SOUTH ST

BUTT LA

FENTON AVE

ELSTEAD LA

PICKERING DR

WYNFIELD WAY

LAWTON CL

MIDDLETON CL

WELL LA

MAIN ST

ASHBY LA

VICARAGE CL

STRAWBERRY LA 1
CHURCH CL 2
PARKERS CL 3

Blackfordby House

Blackfordby St Margaret's CE (Aided) Prim Sch

Hall

Blackfordby

HEATH LA

ASHBY RD

Gardens

Scam-Hazel Farm

ANNWELL LA

Tournament Field

A511

Annwell Place

BURTON RD

Ivanhoe Ind Est

Holywell Farm

FOREST RD

LOCKER-SMITH LA

Works

8   7   21   6   5   20   4   3   19   2   1   18

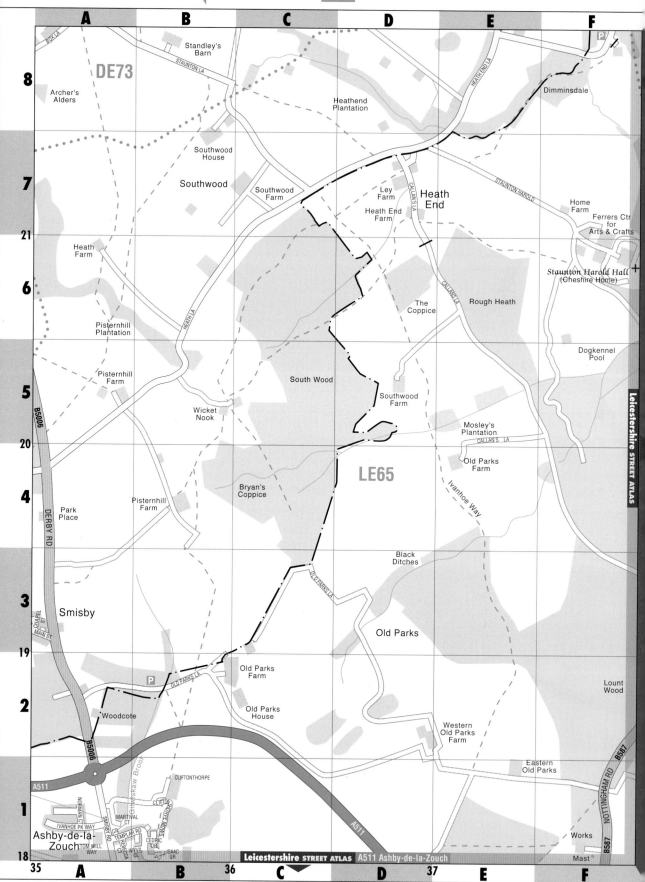

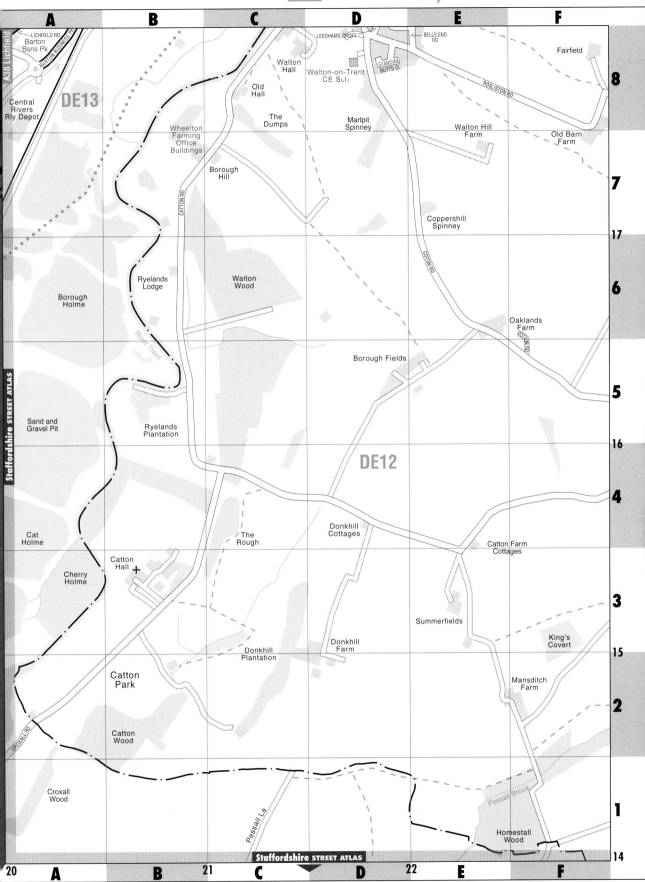

A B C D E F

8

7

17

6

5

16

4

3

15

2

1

14

A38 Lichfield

LICHFIELD RD
Barton
Bsns Pk

Barton Business Pk

Central
Rivers
Rly Depot

DE13

Walton
Hall

Old
Hall

The
Dumps

LEEDHAMS CROFT

Walton-on-Trent
CE Sch

STANDING
BUTTS CL

BELLS END
RD

Fairfield

ROSLISTON RD

Marlpit
Spinney

Walton Hill
Farm

Old Barn
Farm

Wheelton
Farming
Office
Buildings

CATTON RD

Borough
Hill

Coppershill
Spinney

COTTON RD

Ryelands
Lodge

Walton
Wood

Borough
Holme

River Trent

Oaklands
Farm

COTTON RD

Borough Fields

Sand and
Gravel Pit

Ryelands
Plantation

DE12

Cat
Holme

The
Rough

Donkhill
Cottages

Catton Farm
Cottages

Cherry
Holme

Catton
Hall

Summerfields

King's
Covert

Donkhill
Farm

Mansditch
Farm

CROXALL RD

Catton
Park

Donkhill
Plantation

Catton
Wood

Pessall La

Pessall Brook

Croxall
Wood

Homestall
Wood

Staffordshire STREET ATLAS

259
254

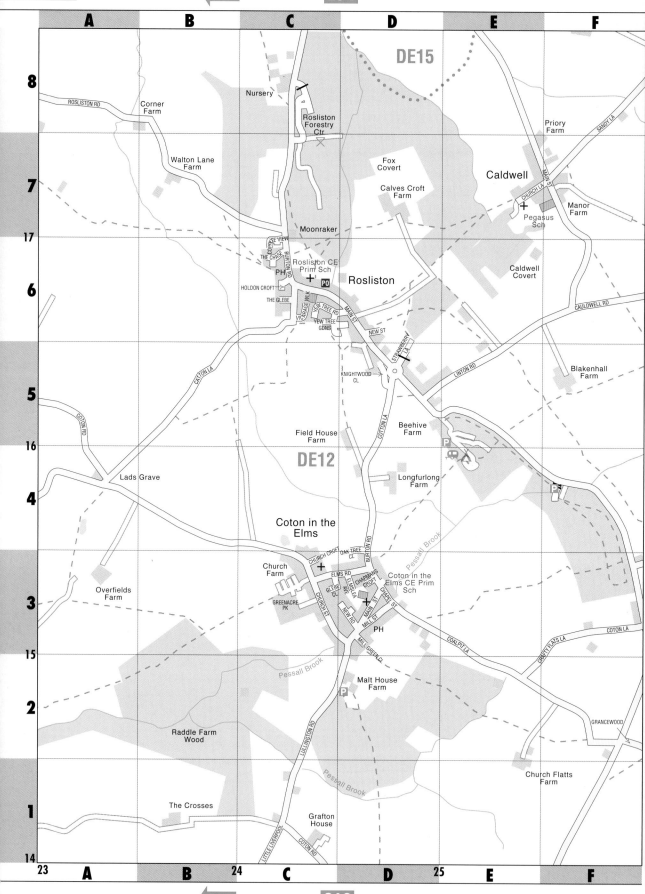

255
262

A B C D E F

8

Hill Crest Farm

Badger Wood

Coton Park

Sewage Works

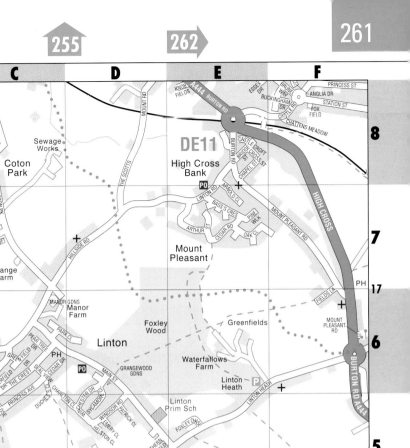

KNOB FIELDS
BURTON RD A444
MOUNT RD

PRINCESS ST
ESSEX DR
BRUNEL WAY
ANGLIA DR
BUCKINGHAM DR
STATION ST
FOX FIELD
CASTLE RD
CHATTENS MEADOW

DE11

High Cross Bank

PO

CASTLE CROFT
BURTON RD
BRIDGE CROSS ST
CHAPEL ST
ARNOLD CL
LINTON RD
BASS'S CRES
PINE WLK
ARTHUR ST
CEDAR RD
OAK RD
MOUNT PLEASANT RD

HIGH CROSS

Mount Pleasant

7

17

Coton Croft
HILLSIDE RD

Grange Farm

THE SCOTTS

MANOR GDNS
Manor Farm

Foxley Wood

Greenfields

FIELDS LA

MOUNT PLEASANT RD

6

CAULDWELL RD

PH

PEAR TREE DR
PARK CL
GREENFIELD DR
CHESTERFIELD DR
THE CREST
PRINCESS AVE
PH
Linton
GRANGEWOOD GDNS
PO
MAIN ST

Waterfallows Farm

Linton Heath

P

BURTON RD A444

VERNLEA DR
MITRE CL
MEDHAM AVE
MALCOTE MWS
MAITLAND RD
HIGH ST
WARREN DR
HIGHFIELDS DR
THE CLOSE
SEALWOOD CL
CEDAR GR
DUCHESS
CHAPLYN CL
CHESTER DR
SYCAMORE

WINDSOR RD
PATRICK CL
EMERY CL
HELSTON CL
WEATHERN FIELD

Linton Prim Sch

FOXLEY CROFT TRL
LINTON HEATH

Longlands

5

16

SEALWOOD LA

GREEN LA

DE12

Woodside Farm

Middle Hayes Farm

4

Top Wood

COLLIERY LA

SEAL WOOD LA

Sealwood Farm

Green La

Botany Bay Farm

Park Farm

3

15

Potter's Wood

LULLINGTON RD

2

Grange Wood

Gunby Lea

GUNBY HILL

P

Craft Ctr

1

Grangewood Hall

Gunby Farm

Woodfields Farm

Grangewood Lodge

Grangewood

GRANGEWOOD
SANDY LA

Woodside Farm

LODGE RD

Grenvue

14

26 A B 27 C D 28 E F

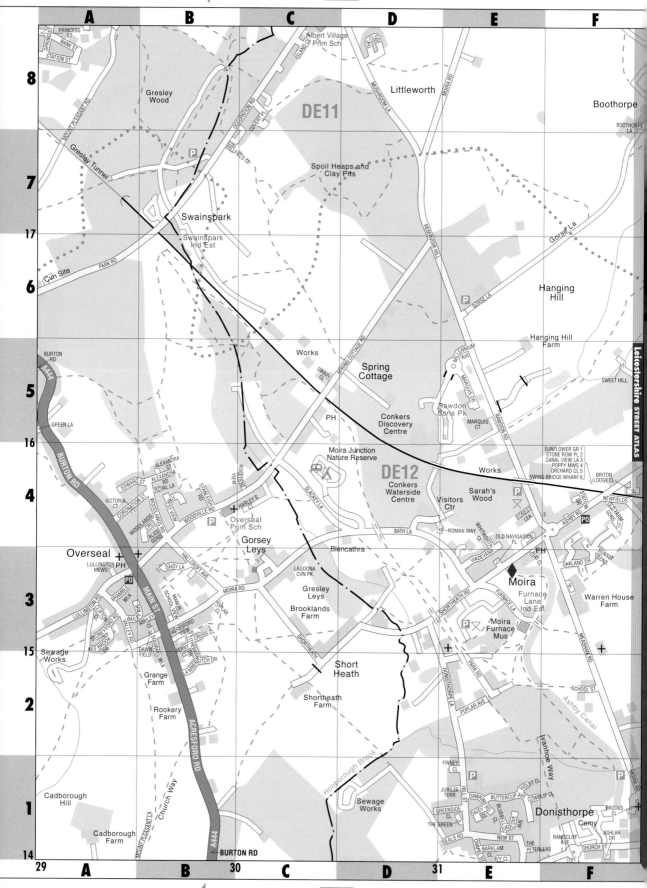

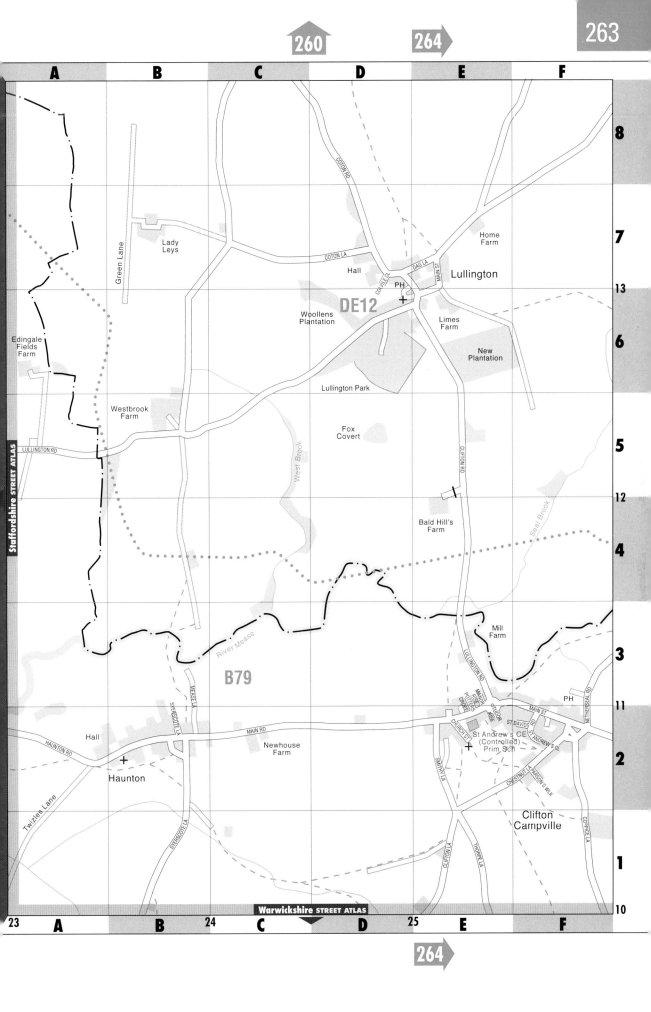

A B C D E F

8

7

Home
Farm

Green Lane

Lady
Leys

COTON RD

COTON LA

Hall

DAG LA

MAIN ST

Lullington

PH

13

DE12

Woollens
Plantation

Limes
Farm

COX VILE CL

6

New
Plantation

Edingale
Fields
Farm

Lullington Park

Fox
Covert

Westbrook
Farm

West Brook

CLIFTON RD

5

LULLINGTON RD

12

Bald Hill's
Farm

Seal Brook

4

Mill
Farm

River Mease

B79

LULLINGTON RD

PH

NETHERSEAL RD

3

11

MEASE LA

MANOR
RISE

POTTERS
CROFT

OUTDOOR
RISE

MAIN ST

SYERSCOTE LA

ST DAVIDS

ST ANDREW'S CL

Hall

MAIN RD

Newhouse
Farm

CHURCH ST

St Andrew's CE
(Controlled)
Prim Sch

2

HAUNTON RD

SMITHY LA

CHESTNUT LA

PARSON'S WLK

COPPICE LA

Haunton

Clifton
Campville

Twizies Lane

SYERSCOTE LA

CLIFTON LA

THORPE LA

1

Staffordshire STREET ATLAS

263
261

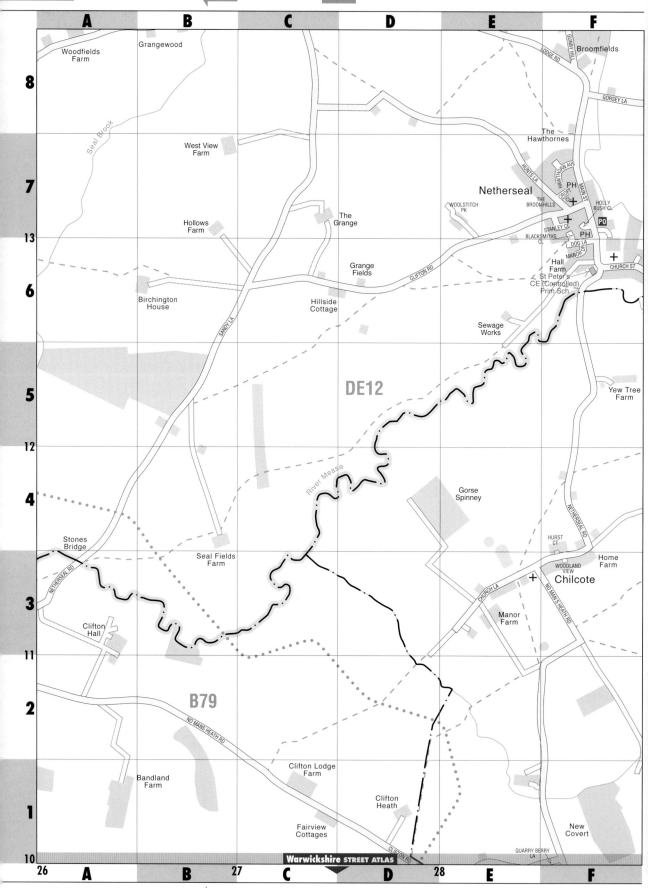

263

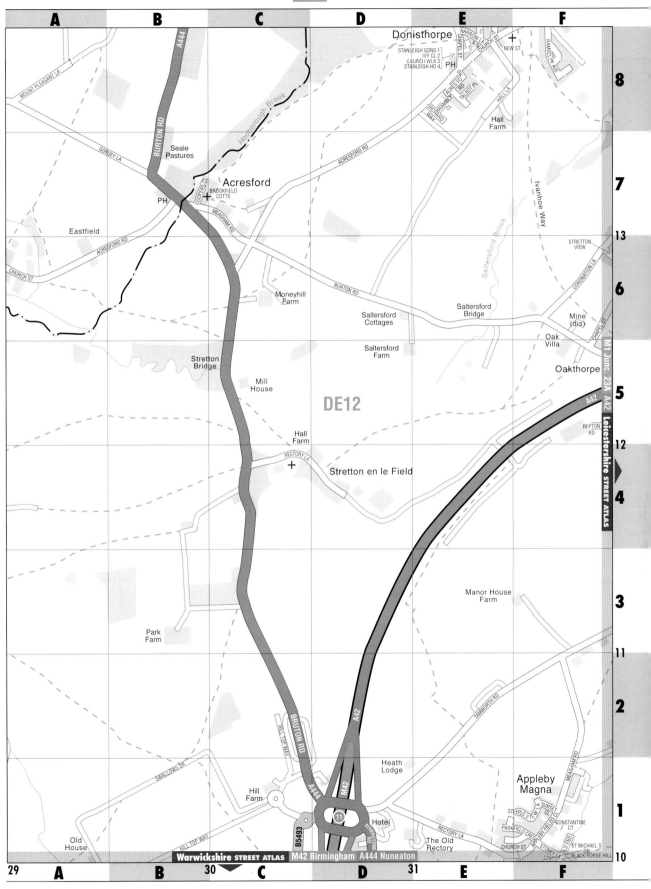

Donisthorpe

STANLEIGH GDNS 1
IVY CL 2
CHURCH WLK 3
STANLEIGH HO 4
PH

NEW ST

RAMSCLIFFE AVE

8

Seale
Pastures

BURTON RD

GORSEY LA

ACRESFORD RD

Acresford

PH

BROOKFIELD
COTTS

ACRESFORD RD

Hall
Farm

Ivanhoe Way

7

A444

Hoobrough Brook

Eastfield

CHURCH ST

ACRESFORD RD

MEASHAM RD

COOPERS CL

Saltersford Brook

13

STRETTON
VIEW

CORONATION LA

6

Moneyhill
Farm

BURTON RD

Saltersford
Cottages

Saltersford
Bridge

Mine
(dis)

CHAPEL ST

M1 Junc. 23A A42 Leicestershire STREET ATLAS

Stretton
Bridge

Saltersford
Farm

Oak
Villa

Oakthorpe

Mill
House

DE12

A42

5

REPTON
RD

12

Hall
Farm

RECTORY LA

Stretton en le Field

4

Park
Farm

Manor House
Farm

3

11

SWALLOWS DR

HILL TOP WAY

BRUTON RD

A42

TAMWORTH RD

MEASHAM RD

2

Heath
Lodge

Appleby
Magna

Hill
Farm

A444

M42

11

AIRESTONE RD

Hotel

RECTORY LA

The Old
Rectory

STEEPLE V
SUNSET CL
CONSTANTINE CT

1

Old
House

HILL TOP WAY

B5493

PARKFIELD CRES
APPLEBY FIELDS CL
STONEY LA
ST MICHAEL'S DR
BLACK HORSE HILL

CHURCH ST

OLD END

10

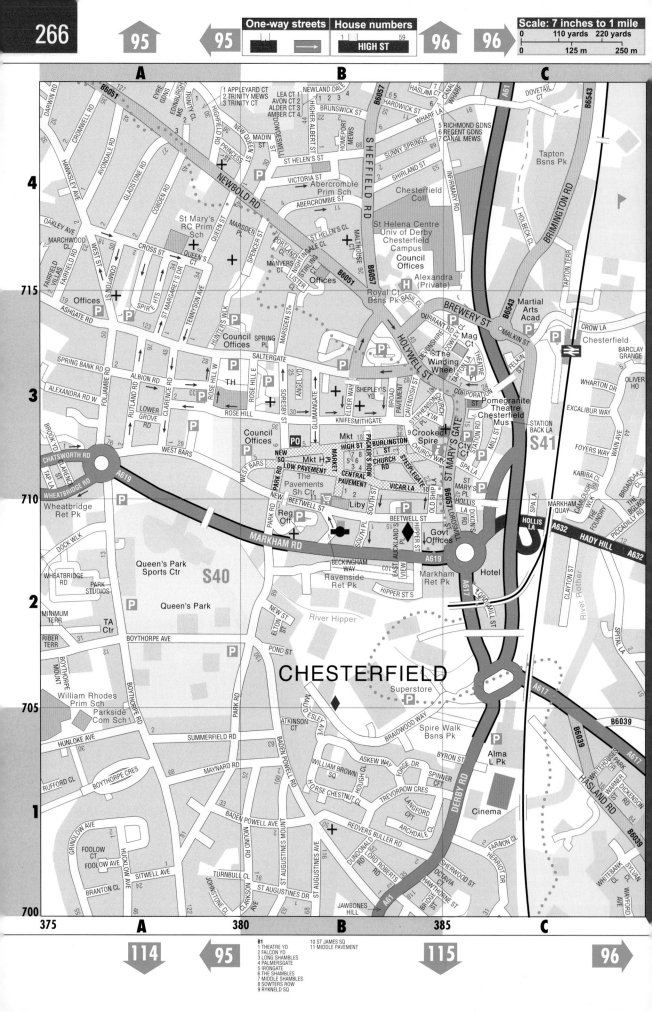

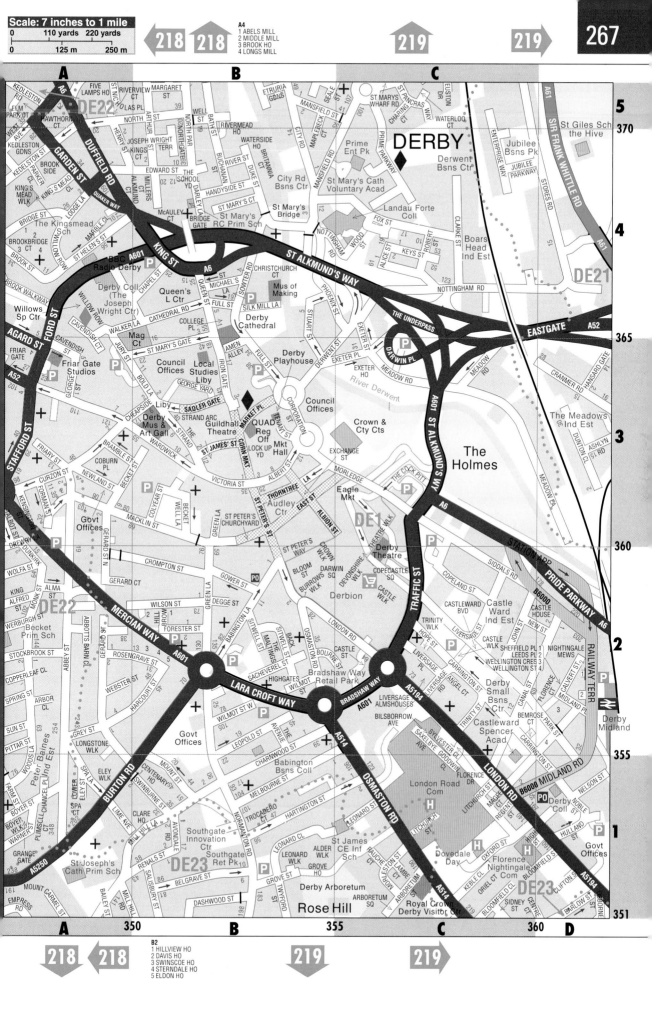

268

Index

Place name May be abbreviated on the map

Location number Present when a number indicates the place's position in a crowded area of mapping

Locality, town or village Shown when more than one place has the same name

Postcode district District for the indexed place

Page and grid square Page number and grid reference for the standard mapping

Church Rd 6 Beckenham BR2..........**53** C6

Cities, towns and villages are listed in CAPITAL LETTERS

Public and commercial buildings are highlighted in magenta **Places of interest** are highlighted in blue with a star ★

Abbreviations used in the index

Acad	Academy	Comm	Common	Gd	Ground	L	Leisure	Prom	Promenade
App	Approach	Cott	Cottage	Gdn	Garden	La	Lane	Rd	Road
Arc	Arcade	Cres	Crescent	Gn	Green	Liby	Library	Recn	Recreation
Ave	Avenue	Cswy	Causeway	Gr	Grove	Mdw	Meadow	Ret	Retail
Bglw	Bungalow	Ct	Court	H	Hall	Meml	Memorial	Sh	Shopping
Bldg	Building	Ctr	Centre	Ho	House	Mkt	Market	Sq	Square
Bsns, Bus	Business	Ctry	Country	Hospl	Hospital	Mus	Museum	St	Street
Bvd	Boulevard	Cty	County	HQ	Headquarters	Orch	Orchard	Sta	Station
Cath	Cathedral	Dr	Drive	Hts	Heights	Pal	Palace	Terr	Terrace
Cir	Circus	Dro	Drove	Ind	Industrial	Par	Parade	TH	Town Hall
Cl	Close	Ed	Education	Inst	Institute	Pas	Passage	Univ	University
Cnr	Corner	Emb	Embankment	Int	International	Pk	Park	Wk, Wlk	Walk
Coll	College	Est	Estate	Intc	Interchange	Pl	Place	Wr	Water
Com	Community	Ex	Exhibition	Junc	Junction	Prec	Precinct	Yd	Yard

Index of towns, villages, streets, hospitals, industrial estates, railway stations, schools, shopping centres, universities and places of interest

1st–Ald

1st Ave DE7........**208** F7
2nd Ave DE7........**208** F7
3rd Ave DE7........**208** F7

A

Abba Cl NG16.......**195** F7
Abbey Brook Ct 1
  S8................**56** E8
Abbey Brook Dr S8..**56** E8
Abbey Cl ST14.......**197** A3
Abbey Cres DE5....**180** E7
Abbey Croft
  Chesterfield S40......**95** A7
  Renishaw S21......**79** C8
Abbeycroft Lane 5
  DE22.............**204** F2
Abbeydale Cl DE56 .**192** B7
Abbeydale Ct S17....**56** A7
Abbeydale Industrial
  Hamlet★ S7......**56** B8
ABBEYDALE PARK ..**55** F6
Abbeydale Park Cres
  S17..............**55** F6
Abbeydale Park Rise
  S17..............**55** F6
Abbeydale Rd S7...**43** A8
Abbeydale Road S
  S17..............**56** A7
Abbeyfields Cl
  DE22............**205** A2
Abbey Gdns SK14...**9** A3
Abbey Hill
  Breadsall DE21......**205** C4
  Derby DE21, DE22 ..**205** B4
  Derby DE22.......**204** F3
Abbeyhill Cl S42.....**95** A4
Abbey Hill Rd DE22 .**204** D2
Abbey La DE22.....**205** A1
Abbey Lodge Cl 1
  DE11.............**256** A7
Abbey Pl S21.......**79** C8
Abbey St
  Derby DE1, DE22..**267** A2
  Ilkeston DE7......**194** F2
Abbey View Dr S8..**43** A3
Abbey View Hts 3
  S8...............**43** A3
Abbey View Rd S8..**43** A3

Abbey Wood Cl DE3 .**217** F5
Abbey Yd DE22......**205** A1
Abbot Beyne Sch
  DE15..............**248** A3
Abbot Cl DE21......**205** E2
Abbot Mews DE22 ..**205** A1
Abbot Rd
  Branston DE14......**253** D8
  Ilkeston DE7........**208** C6
Abbots Croft NG19..**135** E1
Abbotsford Mews
  DE7..............**194** D3
Abbots Gr DE56.....**179** A5
Abbotsholme Sch
  ST14.............**197** B2
Abbott Rd
  Alfreton DE55......**159** B3
  Mansfield NG19.....**135** D1
Abbotts Barn Cl
  DE22.............**267** A2
Abbotts Cl DE11.....**256** A6
Abbotts Rd DE11.....**256** A6
Abbott St
  Awsworth NG16......**195** C4
  Heanor DE75......**181** E1
  Long Eaton NG10....**236** D6
Abel La DE4.......**142** C2
Abells DE5........**180** C1
Abels Mill 1 DE1...**267** A4
Abercrombie Prim Sch
  Chesterfield S41......**96** A5
  Chesterfield S41....**266** B4
Abercrombie St
  S41..............**266** B4
Aberdare Cl DE21...**206** B2
Aberdeen Close
  DE11.............**255** F1
Abingdon Bsns Ctr The
  DE24.............**219** C1
Abingdon St DE24..**232** C8
ABNEY............**51** F4
Abney Cl
  Chesterfield S40......**95** D6
  Derby DE3........**217** F2
  Sheffield S14......**43** C6
Abney Dr S14......**43** C6
Abney Grange SK17..**51** E2
Abney Rd S14.....**43** C6
Acacia Ave
  Brimington S43......**97** A8
  Derby DE3........**217** E1
  Swadlincote DE11.....**256** B7
Acacia Cres S21.....**60** B5

Acacia Croft DE56..**179** B2
Acacia Ct NG19.....**136** E1
Acacia Dr
  Melbourne DE73.....**252** A8
  Pilsley S45.......**132** B3
Acacia Gdns NG16...**195** F8
Acacia La
  Branston DE14......**253** E6
  Branston DE14......**256** E6
Access 26 Bsns Pk
  NG16.............**182** C3
Acer Cl
  Killamarsh S21......**60** C5
  Pinxton NG16......**160** C3
Acer Croft DE21....**205** E3
Acorn Cl DE24......**232** E3
Acorn Ctr NG16.....**182** C3
Acorn Dr
  Ashbourne DE6......**185** C8
  Belper DE56.......**179** A5
  Clay Cross S45......**131** B3
Acorn Ridge
  Chesterfield S40......**114** B7
  Matlock DE4......**143** B6
  Shirebrook NG20.....**119** D5
Acorn Terr SK22.....**33** B6
Acorn Way
  Belper DE56.......**179** A5
  Derby DE21......**220** C6
Acreage La NG20.....**119** F2
Acre Ct 5 SK13......**17** C7
Acrefield Way DE73. **233** B2
Acre La
  Aston-on-Trent
  DE72............**246** D7
  Sutton on the Hill DE6..**228** B7
ACRESFORD........**265** C7
Acres Ford Ed DE12. **265** E8
Acresford Rd
  Donisthorpe DE12 ..**265** D7
  Netherseal DE12....**265** B6
  Overseal DE12......**262** B2
Acresford View
  DE12.............**262** B3
Acres Rd S45.......**132** B3
Acre St 4 SK13......**17** C7
Acres The S45......**132** B4
Acresview Cl DE22..**204** D4
Acres View Cl S41...**95** F7
Acton Ave NG10.....**236** E6
Acton Cl NG10......**236** E6
Acton Ct 1 S43......**78** B3

Acton Gr NG10 .....**236** E6
Acton Rd
  Derby DE22........**217** F6
  Long Eaton NG10....**236** E6
Acton Road Ind Est
  NG10.............**236** E6
Acton St NG10......**236** E6
Adale Rd DE7......**193** B8
Adam Bede Cres
  DE4..............**165** F6
Adams Cl DE75.....**193** D7
Adams Close DE11.. **257** A7
Adams Ct DE7......**194** E3
Adam's Rd DE6.....**217** A8
Adam St DE7......**209** A6
Adastral Ave S12.....**44** A2
Adderley Pl SK13.....**9** F1
Adderley Rd SK13....**9** F1
Addison Dr DE55...**159** B4
Addison Rd
  Derby DE24........**232** C7
  Stonebroom DE55...**146** F3
Addison Sq DE4 ....**155** A5
Addison St DE55....**148** A7
Addison Villas
  NG16.............**182** E1
Adelaide Cl
  Derby DE3........**217** E4
  Stapleford NG9.....**209** F1
Adelaide Cres DE15. **248** C2
Adelaide Wlk 1
  NG16.............**170** F4
Adelphi Cl DE23 ...**231** A6
Adelphi Way S43....**97** E8
Adin Ave S44......**98** F6
Adler Ct DE11......**219** B7
Adlington Ave S42...**115** C2
Adlington La S32....**72** C8
Admiral Cl DE75....**181** D2
Admiral Court DE7...**194** F4
Adrian Cl NG9......**223** F1
Adrian St DE24.....**232** D6
Adwick Cl DE3......**217** C2
Aeropark The★
  DE74.............**247** A1
Agard St DE1......**267** A4
Agnesmeadow La
  DE6..............**174** D4
Agricultural Bsns Ctr
  DE45.............**109** E5
Agricultural Way
  DE45.............**109** E5
Agrimony Pl 2 DE3 **217** C4

Aimploy Ct DE23... **219** A1
Ainley Cl DE24......**232** F7
Ainsworth Dr DE23 .**231** E7
Aintree Ave S21......**59** B3
Aintree Cl
  Burton upon Trent
  DE14.............**254** A7
  Kimberley NG16.....**195** E7
Aire Cl 7 DE65.....**228** E1
Airedale Cl NG10...**236** A6
Airedale Wlk 3
  DE24.............**233** C6
Aires Hollow 5
  DE72.............**246** A6
Airfield Industrial Est
  DE6..............**185** E7
Akaal Prim Sch
  DE23.............**231** E7
Akley Bank Cl S17....**55** F5
Alabaster La DE4 ... **155** A6
Alandale Ave NG20..**119** F5
Albany Cl NG16.....**136** C1
Albany Ct NG9......**209** E1
Albany Dr NG19....**136** C1
Albany Gdns DE65.. **227** D2
Albany Inf & Jun Schs
  NG9.............**223** E8
Albany Inf Sch NG9..**209** E1
Albany Pl NG16.....**136** C1
Albany Rd DE22 ....**218** C4
Albany St DE7......**209** A6
Albemarle Rd DE21. **220** B7
Alberta Ave NG16...**171** F7
Albert Ave
  Chesterfield S43......**77** D3
  Jacksdale S45......**171** B4
  Stapleford NG9.....**223** D7
Albert Cres DE21 ...**220** B4
Albert Ct SK17......**85** C6
Albert Rd
  Breaston DE72......**235** B7
  Chesterfield S43......**77** D3
  Derby DE21......**220** A4
  Long Eaton NG10....**236** D8
  Ripley DE5........**169** C2
  Sandiacre NG10....**223** B6
  Sheffield, Heeley S8...**43** A6
  Swadlincote DE11....**256** A2
Albert St N 30 S41...**95** F8
Albert Sq NG19....**136** C4
Albert St
  Belper DE56.......**178** F4
  Derby DE1........**267** B3

Albert St continued
  Eastwood NG16......**182** F3
  Eckington S21......**59** D2
  Glossop SK13......**10** A5
  Ilkeston DE7.......**208** E8
  Ironville NG16......**170** F5
  Mansfield Woodhouse
  NG19.............**136** C4
  Ripley DE5.........**169** E1
  Somercotes DE55...**170** B8
  South Normanton
  DE55.............**160** B6
  Swadlincote DE11 ..**223** D7
Albert Street N S41...**76** F1
ALBERT VILLAGE... **256** C1
Albert Village Prim Sch
  DE11.............**256** C1
Albine Rd NG20.....**119** E6
Albion Mill SK14.....**9** C5
Albion Rd
  Chesterfield S40.....**266** A3
  Long Eaton NG10...**236** F8
  New Mills SK22......**33** B6
Albion St
  Derby DE1........**219** A5
  Derby DE1........**267** B3
  Ilkeston DE7......**194** F1
  Mansfield NG19....**135** F1
  Ripley DE5........**169** E1
  Woodville DE11....**256** F2
Albrighton Ave
  DE24.............**231** D2
Aldam Cl S17.......**55** E4
Aldam Croft S17.....**55** E4
Aldam Rd S17......**55** E4
Aldam Way S17......**55** E4
Alder Brook SK23....**34** E2
Alderbrook Cl DE13. **256** C1
ALDERCAR.........**182** A4
Aldercar High Sch
  NG16.............**182** A4
Aldercar Inf Sch
  NG16.............**182** A4
Aldercar La NG16.. **182** A6
Alder Cl
  Derby DE21......**205** E3
  Glossop SK13......**9** F4
  Mansfield NG19....**136** E1
  Shirebrook NG20...**119** D5
Alder Com High Sch
  SK14.............**15** A8
Alder Ct S41.......**266** B4
Alderfen Cl DE24...**232** D3

Alder Gdns S43......78 A1
Alder Gr
  Burton upon Trent
  DE15..........254 F7
  Buxton SK17.....85 A8
  Mansfield Woodhouse
  NG19..........136 B5
Alder Grove SK23....47 A6
Alderholme Dr [1]
  DE13..........240 F1
Alder La DE6.....188 A3
Alderley Cl DE21....206 A2
Alderney Rd [3] S8...43 A7
Aldern Way DE45...109 E7
Alder Rd
  Belper DE56......179 A3
  Dronfield S18.......57 A3
Alder Rise SK23.....45 D8
ALDERS..........196 C2
Alders Ave SK23.....34 E1
Alders Brook DE65..228 D1
Alders Field DE4....144 A3
Aldersgate
  Derby DE22.......217 F7
  New Mills SK22......33 B8
Alders La
  Chinley SK23.......34 E2
  Tansley DE4.......144 A3
Alderslade Cl DE72..234 B1
Aldersley Cl DE65..230 C1
Alders Meadow SK23.34 E2
Alderson Dr DE13....240 F1
Alderson Pl S2......43 A8
Alderson Rd S2......43 A8
Alderson Road N S2.43 A8
Alders Rd SK12.....32 A7
Alders The S42.....113 D7
ALDERWASLEY.....166 E8
Alderwasley Hall Sch
  DE56............167 B7
Alderwasley Hall Sch
  and Sixth Form Centre
  DE4............165 E4
Alderwasley Pk
  Alderwasley DE4.....167 B7
  Alderwasley DE4.....167 C8
  Whatstandwell DE56.156 C1
Alder Way
  Clowne S43........80 D2
  Creswell S80.......81 E2
  Shirebrook NG20....119 D4
Alder Wlk DE23.....267 B1
Aldred Cl S21.......60 E8
Aldred's La DE75,
  NG16...........182 B2
Aldridge Cl NG9....223 E2
ALDWARK
  152 F7
  DE4............153 F7
Aldwark Rd SK17....85 C6
Aldwych DE22.....218 A6
Alexander Ave
  NG16...........171 D7
Alexander Rd SK17..47 F1
Alexander Terr
  NG16...........160 C1
Alexandra Ave
  NG19...........136 B5
Alexandra Ct
  Burton upon Trent
  DE15...........248 A3
  Overseal DE12.....262 B4
Alexandra Gdns [3]
  DE23...........219 B2
Alexandra Mills [2]
  DE1............218 E5
Alexandra Private Hospl
  S41............266 B4
Alexandra Rd
  Burton upon Trent
  DE15...........248 A3
  Buxton SK17......85 C5
  Dronfield S18.......57 B2
  Long Eaton NG10...236 D8
  Overseal DE12.....262 B4
  Sheffield S2........43 B7
  Swadlincote DE11..256 B3
Alexandra Road E
  S41............96 C1
Alexandra Road W
  S40............266 A3
Alexandra St
  Eastwood NG16....182 F2
  Stapleford NG9....223 D6
Alexandre Cl DE23..231 D6
Alford Cl S40.......95 C3
Alfred Eley Cl DE11.255 F4
Alfred Rd DE56.....192 A8
Alfred St
  Alfreton DE55......158 F3
  Pinxton NG16......160 C4
  Ripley DE5........169 E2
  Somercotes DE55...170 D6
  South Normanton
  DE55...........159 F5
ALFRETON........159 C4
Alfreton L Ctr DE55.158 F4
Alfreton Motorway Link
  Ind Est DE55......159 A2
Alfreton Rd
  Blackwell DE55.....147 E2
  Bradfield DE21.....205 B2
  Codnor DE5.......170 C1
  Holbrook DE21.....191 D2
  Little Eaton DE21...205 C6
  Matlock DE4.......143 C4
  Pinxton NG16......160 C4

Alfreton Rd continued
  Selston DE55, NG16..171 C6
  Shirland DE55......158 F6
  Tibshelf DE55......147 D4
Alfreton Sta DE55..159 C5
Alfreton Trad Est
  DE55............159 B2
Algar Cl S2........43 E7
Algar Cres S2.......43 F7
Algar Dr S2........43 E7
Algar Pl S2........43 E7
Algar Rd S2........43 E7
Alice Gdns DE12....262 B4
Alicehead Rd S45...113 B2
Alice St DE1.......267 C4
Alice's View S42....132 A8
Alice Way S18.......76 E5
Alison Cl DE21.....219 F7
ALKMONTON.......199 D1
Alkmonton Rd DE6..213 D5
Alkmund Ct DE1....267 B4
Allan Ave DE23.....230 E8
Allandale Rd DE75..181 D2
Allan La DE56......168 B6
Allcroft St NG19...136 C4
Allenby Cl S8.......56 E7
Allenby Dr S8.......56 E7
Allendale DE7.....208 E7
Allendale Cl S8......56 E7
Allendale Rd S42...114 F3
Allendale Way
  NG19...........136 E1
Allen Hill DE4.....143 B6
Allen La
  Ashover DE4.......144 C6
  Weston Underwood
  DE6............188 C1
Allens Croft ST14...224 E2
Allen's Green Ave
  NG16...........171 F6
Allen's La ST14....224 E2
Allen St DE24......232 E5
ALLENTON........232 D5
Allenton Com Prim Sch
  DE24...........232 D5
Allen View DE55....159 C4
Allestree Cl DE24..232 E8
Allestree Dr S18.....56 C1
Allestree La DE22..204 D3
Allestree Park Nature
  Reserve★ DE22....204 F5
Allestree St DE24..232 E8
Alley The DE4......154 D4
Alley Wlk DE6.....201 F7
Allison Ave DE11...256 B3
Allison Gdns DE7..195 A1
Allissa Ave DE5....180 E7
Allpits Rd S44.......96 F3
Allport Terr S43....78 B4
All Saints CE(Controlled)
  Fst Sch ST14......196 C6
All Saints' CE Inf Sch
  DE4............143 B6
All Saints CE Jun Sch
  DE4............143 A7
All Saints CE Prim Sch
  SK6............23 A4
All Saints' CE VA Prim
  Sch DE45........125 C5
All Saints Cl DE7...193 B1
All Saints Croft
  DE14...........254 C8
All Saints Ct [6] S43.217 D1
All Saints RC Prim Sch
  SK13............10 D2
All Saints Rd DE4..254 C8
All Saints' Rd DE4..143 B6
Allsops Pl S41.......95 F8
Allstone Lee DE56..178 F5
Alma Cl NE7.......194 E5
Alma Cres S18.......57 A3
Alma Hill NG16....195 E7
Alma Hts DE3......217 E1
Alma L Pk★ S40....266 C1
Alma Rd
  North Wingfield S42..132 A8
  Selston DE55......171 F5
  Swadlincote DE11..255 F6
  Tideswell SK17......69 C5
Alma Sq SK17.......85 D8
Alma St
  Alfreton DE55......159 A4
  Buxton SK17.......85 D8
  Derby DE22.......267 A2
  Melbourne DE73...252 A7
  North Wingfield S42..131 A6
  Ripley DE5........169 D3
Alma Street W S40..95 E2
Almshouses
  Barlborough S43....80 A6
  Ripley DE5........180 D8
  Shirebrook NG20...119 E5
Almond Cl
  Calow S44.........97 A3
  Kimberley NG16....195 E7
Almond Cres S43....79 C4
Almond Ct DE13....240 C1
Almond Dr S21......60 C5
Almond Gr
  Swadlincote DE11...256 A6
  Swanwick DE55....170 A8
Almond Pl [4] S40...96 E7
Almond Rise NG19..136 E1
Almond St DE23...218 F1

Alnwick Dr S12......44 C5
Alnwick Rd S12......44 B5
Along The Bottom
  Alstonefield DE6....150 A3
  Milldale DE6.......149 F2
Alonso Cl DE73....232 E2
Alpha Rd SK23......34 E2
Alpine Gr S43.......97 A8
Alport Ave
  Buxton SK17.......85 D7
  Sheffield S12.......44 E5
Alport Cl
  Belper DE56......179 B5
  Hulland Ward DE6..175 F3
Alport Dr S12.......44 E5
Alport Gr
  [3] Gamesley SK13....9 E2
  Sheffield S12.......44 E5
Alport Heights Dr
  DE21...........205 F3
Alport La
  Alport DE45.......125 E6
  Spout DE4, DE56...166 C4
  Stanton in Peak DE4..126 B6
  Youlgreave DE45...125 C6
Alport Lea [2] SK13...9 E2
Alport Pl S12.......44 E4
Alport Rd S12.......44 E5
Alport Rise S18......56 D2
Alport Terr DE55...147 C1
Alport Way [1] SK13..9 E2
Alsager Cl DE21....206 A1
Alsfeld Way S2......33 A8
ALSOP EN LE DALE.150 E3
Alsop La DE4......156 C2
Alsop Moor Cotts
  DE6............150 E5
Alsop Pl SK17.......85 E7
Alsop Way SK17.....85 E7
ALSTONEFIELD....149 D4
Alstonfield Dr
  DE22...........204 E1
Alstonfield Rd SK17.149 A8
Alston Rd SK23......47 B5
Althorp Cl DE55....169 F7
ALTON............130 C5
Alton Cl
  Chesterfield S40....114 B8
  Derby DE22.......204 D3
  Dronfield S18.......75 D8
Alton Dr NG16.....195 B8
Alton Hill S42......130 C5
Alton La S45......130 C4
Alton Rd
  Belper DE56......179 C4
  Denstone ST14....196 C7
  Denstone ST14....196 C7
Alton Rise DE4.....142 F7
Alton Way
  Derby DE23.......230 F5
  Derby DE23.......231 A6
Alts Nook Way
  DE72...........234 E1
Alum Chine Cl S41..115 C8
Alum Cl DE24......233 C7
ALVASTON........233 B8
Alvaston By-Pass
  DE24...........233 D7
Alvaston Inf Sch
  DE24...........233 C7
Alvaston Jun Acad
  DE24...........233 C7
Alvaston Park Homes
  DE24...........220 A1
Alvaston St DE24...233 B8
Alvenor St DE7.....194 F1
Alverton Cl DE7....217 C1
Alveston Pk Homes
  DE24...........233 A8
Alward's Cl DE24...233 A6
AMBASTON.......234 D6
Ambaston La
  Elvaston DE72.....234 A5
  Shardlow DE72....234 E2
Amber Bldgs DE55..159 B5
Amber Bsns Ctr
  DE55...........170 B5
Amber Cl
  Bullbridge DE56....168 B5
  Shirland DE55.....146 D1
Amber Croft S43....97 C7
Amber Ct
  Belper DE56......179 A6
  Chesterfield S41....266 B4
  [2] Heanor DE75...181 E1
Amberdene DE4....143 D6
Amber Dr
  Derby DE3........230 B8
  Heanor DE75......182 B2
AMBERGATE......167 F3
Ambergate Prim Sch
  DE56...........167 F3
Ambergate Sta
  DE56...........167 F4
Amber Gdns DE56..168 B5
Amber Gr DE55....158 B6
Amber Green DE55.158 B6
Ambergrove DE56..168 B4
Amber Hill DE56...168 A7
Amber Hts DE5....169 C2
Amber La S45......129 D3
Amberlands DE13..240 F1
Amberley Cl DE7...208 F6
Amberley Dr
  Buxton SK17.......85 C5
  Derby DE24.......231 F5

Amber Pl
  Clay Cross S45.....131 A4
  [2] Swadlincote DE11.255 F4
Amber Rd
  Bullbridge DE56....168 B6
  Derby DE22.......204 D1
Amber St DE24.....232 C7
Amber Terr DE55...158 B6
Amber Trad Est
  NG16...........195 D7
Ambervale Cl DE23.231 A6
Amber View Rd
  DE56...........168 B7
Amberwood DE11..256 A5
Ambleside Cl
  Chesterfield S41.....95 C7
  Sheffield S20.......59 E6
Ambleside Dr
  Bolsover S44........98 F1
  Eastwood NG16....182 D3
Ambrose Terr DE1..218 E5
Amelia Close DE7..235 E8
Amen Alley DE1....267 B3
Amesbury Cl S41....95 E7
Amesbury La DE21..205 E2
Ameycroft La DE4..143 A8
Amilda Ave DE7....208 F8
Amy St DE22......218 E4
Anchor Ave S23.....47 C6
Anchor Cl DE11....256 C4
Anchor Fold S23....47 D6
Anchor Rd NG16...182 D2
Anchor Row DE7...208 F8
Anchor Sq DE45....109 D6
Anderby Gdns
  DE11...........255 F2
Anderson Cl S43.....77 C3
Anderson St
  Derby DE24.......232 F7
  Derby DE24.......233 A7
Andressey Way
  DE21...........219 F4
Andrew Ave DE7...209 B7
Andrew Cl DE23...230 E8
Andrew La SK6......32 A8
Andrews Dr
  Langley Mill NG16..182 A3
  Stanley Common DE7.193 A1
Andrew St SK6......15 A2
Andwell La S10......42 F6
Angel Ct DE1......267 C2
Angelica Cl DE23..231 D5
Angel Yd S40......266 B3
Angerford Ave S8...43 A4
Angle Cl DE11......256 D3
Anglers Bsns Ctr
  Burton upon Trent
  DE14...........254 B8
Anglers' La DE21...220 E3
Anglesey St
  Burton upon Trent
  DE14...........253 C8
  Derby DE21.......219 D8
Anglesey St
  Burton upon Trent
  DE14...........253 C8
Angleton Ave S2.....44 C8
Angleton Cl S2......44 C8
Angleton Gdns S2...44 C8
Angleton Gn S2......44 C8
Angleton Mews S2..44 C8
Anglia Dr DE11.....255 F1
Anglo Cl S17........55 D6
Ankerbold Rd S42..131 D8
Anmer Dr DE22....218 B4
Annabelle Ct SK17..85 D7
Anncroft Rd SK17...84 D5
Anne Potter Cl
  DE72...........221 D5
Annesley Cl
  Chesterfield S41...115 C8
  Sheffield S8........56 F7
Annesley Rd S8......56 F7
Anns Grove Prim Sch [7]
  S2.............43 A7
Anns Rd S2........43 A7
Anns Road N S2....43 B7
Ann St S80.........81 E1
Annwell La LE65...257 E2
ANNWELL PLACE..257 E1
Anslow La DE13....240 A2
Anslow Rd DE13...238 B2
Anson Place DE74..246 F3
Anson Wlk DE7....194 F3
Anstee Rd NG10...236 C5
Anstey Ct DE21....206 A1
Antcliff Gdns S45..132 A8
Anthony Bek Com Prim
  Sch NG19........134 F6
Anthony Cres DE24.232 F6
Anthony Dr DE24..232 F6
Anthony Gell Sch The
  DE4............165 F8
Antill St NG9......223 D6
Anvil Gro NG19....136 D4
Apiary Gate DE74..247 B3
APPERKNOWLE....58 A1
Appian Cl DE72....221 C1
Appian Way
  Clay Cross S45.....131 B2
  Derby DE24.......233 D4
Appleby Cl
  Derby DE23.......230 F6
  Ilkeston DE7......208 F4
Appleby Fields Cl
  DE12...........265 F1
Appleby Glade
  DE11...........255 D2

Appleby Glade Ind Est
  DE11...........255 D2
APPLEBY MAGNA..265 F1
Appleby Rd NG19..134 F6
Applecroft Cl S44...118 B1
Applecross Ct DE24.231 E3
Appledore Ct [2] S41..95 F8
Appledore Dr S18...206 B1
Appledown Way
  DE15...........254 E7
Applegarth Cl S12...44 A6
Applegarth Dr S12...44 A6
Applegate Cl DE21..206 B3
Applemead Cl DE21.205 E2
Appletree Cl DE21...206 B1
Appleton Cl
  Burton upon Trent
  DE15...........254 E7
  Derby DE21.......220 A7
  Swadlincote DE11..255 F6
Appleton Dr
  Belper DE56......179 B6
  Glossop SK13.......17 F8
Appletree Ct DE7...221 C1
Apple Tree Cl S45..131 F5
Appletree Dr S18....57 A1
Appletree La [3]
  DE6............211 F8
Appletree Rd
  Bolsover S44........80 B1
  Hatton DE65......227 C1
Apple Tree Rd SK22.24 D1
Appletree Wlk DE3.217 D2
Applewood Cl
  Belper DE56......179 B5
  Uttoxeter ST14....210 A1
Appleyard Ct S41..266 A4
Arbor Cl DE22......267 A2
Arboretum Prim Sch
  DE23...........219 A2
Arboretum Sq DE23.267 C1
Arboretum St DE23.267 C1
Arbor Gr SK17......84 F7
Arbor Low (Henge)★
  DE45...........123 E4
Arbour Cl S41......115 D6
Arbour Hill
  Borrowash DE72...221 E3
  Dale Abbey DE7...207 E3
ARBOURTHORNE....43 E6
Arbourthorne Com Prim
  Sch S2...........43 D6
Arbourthorne Cotts
  S2.............43 D8
ARBOURTHORNE
  ESTATE.........43 E6
Arbourthorne Rd S2..43 E6
Arcadia Ave NG20..119 E5
Archdale Cl
  Chesterfield S40...266 B1
  Sheffield S2........44 B8
Archdale Rd S2......44 A8
Archer Dr DE3.....217 B2
Archer Rd NG9....223 E5
Archer St
  Derby DE24.......219 E2
  Ilkeston DE7......194 E3
Arches Close NG16.195 C5
Arden Cl
  Chesterfield S40.....95 C5
  Derby DE23.......218 E2
  Glossop SK13.......17 A8
Arden Est SK22......33 D7
Arden St SK22......33 C7
Ardleigh Cl DE3...230 D8
Ardsley Cl
  Heanor DE75......182 A2
  Sheffield S20.......44 F2
Ardsley Dr S20......44 F2
Ardsley Gr S20......44 F2
Ardsley Rd S40......95 B3
Arella Fields Cl
  DE7............193 A2
Argonaut Avenue
  DE74...........246 F4
Argyle Cl
  Market Warsop
  NG20...........120 F4
  Sheffield S8........43 B5
Argyle Mews NG16.182 F2
Argyle Rd S8.......43 B5
Argyle St
  Derby DE22.......218 F3
  Langley Mill NG16..182 C4
Argyll Cl DE21.....220 F5
Argyll Rd DE5......169 E2
Aria Ct NG9.......223 D6
Arkendale Wlk [4]
  DE24...........233 C6
Arkle Gn DE24.....231 E4
Arklow Cl S41......115 B8
Arkwright Ave DE56.179 C6
Arkwright Cl DE4...127 C3
Arkwright Dr SK6....23 A6
Arkwright Gdns
  DE4............155 A6
Arkwright Mill SK17.89 A4
Arkwright Prim Sch
  S44............97 D3
Arkwright Rd S6.....23 A4
Arkwright's Cromford
  Mill★ DE4.......155 B7
Arkwright St
  Derby DE24.......232 C7
  Wirksworth DE4...155 A6
ARKWRIGHT TOWN..97 D3
Arkwright Way
  DE65...........229 C3

Arleston La
  Derby DE24.......231 C7
  Twyford DE73.....243 C7
Arleston St DE23...231 F7
Arlington Ave NG19.136 E4
Arlington Dr
  Derby DE24.......232 F6
  Swanwick DE55....169 F7
Arlington Rd DE23..218 D2
Arliston Dr DE11...256 E1
Armes Cl DE7......194 F3
Armitage Dr NG10..237 A7
Armscote Cl DE21..206 B2
Arms Park Dr S20...59 F6
Armytage Ind Est
  S41.............77 A1
Arnfield Dr DE65...240 E8
Arnfield Independent
  Sch SK13..........9 E7
Arnfield La SK13.....9 F8
Arnhem Terr DE21..220 F3
Arnold Ave
  Long Eaton NG10...236 A4
  Sheffield S12.......44 B1
Arnold Cl DE11....261 E7
Arnold Cres NG10..236 A4
Arnold St DE22....218 D5
Arnside NG9.......223 E5
Arnside Cl
  Chesterfield S41.....76 D1
  Swadlincote DE11..256 C1
Arran Cl
  Derby DE24.......231 E3
  Stapleford NG9....209 E2
Arran Ct DE55.....147 F6
Arreton Ct DE24...233 C5
Arridge Rd DE21...219 F6
Arrowscroft Ct SK14..9 D5
Arrowscroft Way
  SK14............9 D4
Arthington Blgs S2..43 A6
Arthington St S8....43 A6
Arthur Ave NG9....223 F8
Arthur Cl [1] DE65..242 A6
Arthur Ct DE23....219 B2
Arthur Hind Cl DE22.218 F7
Arthur Mee Rd NG9.223 E5
Arthurrice [8]
  DE11...........255 E5
Arthurs Ct DE13...240 E2
Arthur Short Cl S80..82 A6
Arthur St
  Alfreton DE55......159 A5
  Derby DE1........267 B5
  Draycott DE72....234 F8
  Linton DE11.......261 E7
  Pinxton NG16......160 D3
Arthurs View NG16.170 F4
Artic Way NG16....195 D7
Artisan View S8.....43 A6
Arun Gale NG19...136 D2
Arundel Ave
  Castle Donington
  DE72...........246 E5
  Castle Donington
  DE74...........246 E5
  Castle Donington
  DE74...........247 A5
  Derby DE3........217 F2
Arundel Cl
  [23] Chesterfield S41..95 F8
  Dronfield S18.......56 D1
  Sandiacre NG10...223 B4
Arundel Ct [6] S43..78 E2
Arundel Dr DE21...220 F5
Arundel Grange
  SK13............17 A8
Arundel St
  Derby DE22.......218 D4
  Glossop SK13.......10 C1
Arundel Way [7]
  DE23...........230 F5
Ascot Ave NG16...195 E7
Ascot Cl
  Burton upon Trent
  DE15...........248 A3
  West Hallam DE7...207 D7
Ascot Dr DE24.....232 D8
Ascot Ind Est NG10.223 C7
Ascot Pl DE7.......208 C5
Ascott Dr DE11....256 A7
Ash Acre DE56.....179 D4
Ashacres Ind Pk
  DE6............225 E1
Ashberry Ct DE22..205 A4
ASHBOURNE......173 C2
Ashbourne Ave S45.136 A1
Ashbourne Cl [4] S40.95 A5
Ashbourne Ct
  Derby DE22.......218 E6
  [3] Glossop SK13...17 F8
Ashbourne Dr DE11.256 A1
Ashbourne Green
  Ashbourne DE6....173 D4
  Ashbourne DE6....173 F4
  Ashbourne DE6....174 A4
Ashbourne Hilltop Prim
  Sch DE6........185 C8
Ashbourne La
  Chapel-en-le-Frith
  DE6............47 D5
  Wetton DE6......149 A2
Ashbourne L Ctr
  DE6............173 B1

Ashbourne Prim Sch
DE6 . . . . 173 C2
Ashbourne Rd
Alstonefield DE6 . . . . . 149 B3
Ashbourne DE6 . . . . . . 173 E6
Belper DE56 . . . . 178 C4
Brailsford DE6 . . . . 202 B6
Buxton SK17 . . . . 85 C5
Buxton SK17 . . . . 85 A4
Carsington DE4 . . . . . . 164 D6
Carsington DE4 . . . . . . 164 A5
Church Broughton
DE65 . . . . 213 F3
Crakemarsh ST14 . . . . . 210 D6
Derby DE22 . . . . 218 C7
Fenny Bentley DE6 . . . 162 A2.
Fenny Bentley DE6 . . . 173 B8
Kirk Langley DE6 . . . . . 202 D4
Kniveton DE6 . . . . 174 A8
Mackworth DE22 . . . . 217 E8
Mayfield DE6 . . . . 184 C7
Moneyash DE45 . . . . . . 122 F7
Parsley Hay DE45 . . . . . 123 B4
Rocester ST14 . . . . 196 D1
Rocester ST14 . . . . 196 F4
Shottle DE56 . . . . 177 D3
Sudbury DE6 . . . . 212 E2
Sudbury DE6 . . . . 225 D7
Turnditch DE56 . . . . . . 176 F1
Uttoxeter ST14 . . . . . . 210 B1
Ashbourne St NG20 . . 119 F4
Ashbrook DE15 . . . . . . 248 A1
Ashbrook Ave DE72 . . 221 C2
Ashbrook Cl DE22 . . . 204 C3
Ashbrook Inf Sch
DE72 . . . . 221 B2
Ashbrook Jun Sch
DE72 . . . . 221 B2
Ashbury Dr S8 . . . . 43 C2
Ashbury La S8 . . . . 43 C2
Ashby Ave NG19 . . . . 136 D5
Ashby Cl DE3 . . . . 230 E5
ASHBY-DE-LA-
ZOUCH 258 A1
Ashby La DE11 . . . . 257 C1
Ashby Rd
Blackfordby DE11,
LE65 . . . . 257 D2
Boundary DE11 . . . . . . 257 D2
Breedon on the Hill
DE73 . . . . 252 E2
Burton upon Trent
DE15 . . . . 248 B2
Melbourne DE73 . . . . . 252 A6
Moira DE12 . . . . 262 F4
Woodville DE11 . . . . . . 257 E1
Ashby Road E DE15 . 248 E1
Ashby St DE24 . . . . . . 232 E6
Ash Cl
Aston-on-Trent
DE72 . . . . 246 B7
Barlborough S43 . . . . 80 B6
Derby DE24 . . . . 204 D4
Killamarsh S21 . . . . . . 60 C5
Mottram in Longdendale
SK14 . . . . 9 A4
Pinxton NG16 . . . . 160 D2
Somercotes DE55 . . . . 170 A8
Ashcombe Gdns
DE21 . . . . 206 B1
Ash Cres
Eckington S21 . . . . 59 B1
Mansfield Woodhouse
NG19 . . . . 136 E2
Ripley DE5 . . . . 180 D8
Ashcroft Cl DE24 . . . 232 F7
Ashcroft S41 . . . . 77 B3
Ashcroft Dr S41 . . . . . 77 B2
Ash Croft Prim Sch
DE24 . . . . 231 E2
Ash Ct DE55 . . . . 159 C3
Ashdale Cl DE15 . . . . 255 A8
Ashdale Rd DE7 . . . . 209 A6
Ashdene Gdns DE56 179 C5
Ashdown Dr S40 . . . . . 95 D1
Ashe La DE55 . . . . 229 A5
Ashe Pl DE23 . . . . 218 F1
Asher La DE5 . . . . 169 C5
Asher Lane Bsns Pk
DE5 . . . . 169 D4
Ashes Ave DE6 . . . . . 175 F3
Ashes La
Fenny Bentley DE6 . . . 162 A1
Fenny Bentley DE6 . . . 173 A8
Glossop SK13 . . . . 10 B2
Ashes The SK13 . . . . . . 10 B2
Ashfield Ave
Derby DE21 . . . . 219 E8
Somercotes DE55 . . . . 159 D4
Ashfield Cl S12 . . . . . . 43 F4
Ashfield Dr S12 . . . . . . 43 F4
Ashfield Gr SK6 . . . . . . 15 B1
Ashfield Rd
Chapel-en-le-Frith
SK23 . . . . 47 D6
Chesterfield S41 . . . . . 115 D8
Glossop SK13 . . . . 9 F3
Ash Fields DE56 . . . . . 179 A2
Ashfields Gr 4
DE72 . . . . 246 A6
Ashford Ave S42 . . . . 132 A7
Ashford Cl S18 . . . . . . 75 D8
Ashford Ct
Chesterfield S41 . . . . . . 96 A5
West Hallam DE7 . . . . 207 D8

Ashford Dr SK17 . . . . 85 E2
Ashford Gn 2 SK13 . . . . 9 E1
ASHFORD IN THE
WATER 108 E7
Ashford La DE45 . . . . . . 89 D2
Ashford Mews SK13 . . . . 9 E1
Ashford Pl DE7 . . . . . 194 E5
Ashford Rd
Bakewell DE45 . . . . . . 109 A7
Bakewell DE45 . . . . . . 109 B7
Dronfield S18 . . . . 75 D8
Ashford Rd The
DE45 . . . . 108 F8
Ashford Rise DE56 . . . 179 C6
Ashford Way DE11 . . . 255 F2
Ashforth Ave DE75 . . 194 A8
Ashfurlong Cl S17 . . . . 55 F7
Ashfurlong Dr S17 . . . 55 F7
Ashfurlong Pk S17 . . . 55 F7
Ashfurlong Rd S17 . . . 55 F7
ASHGATE
Chesterfield 95 D4
Old Brampton 94 F4
Ashgate Ave S40 . . . . 95 C3
Ashgate Croft Sch
S40 . . . . 95 C4
Ashgate Ct 4 S40 . . . 95 C4
Ashgate Prim Sch
DE22 . . . . 218 D6
Ashgate Rd
Chesterfield S40 . . . . . 94 F4
Chesterfield S40 . . . . . 95 C4
Ashgate Valley Rd
S40 . . . . 95 D4
Ash Gr
Brinsley NG16 . . . . 182 D8
Chinley SK23 . . . . 34 E1
Long Eaton NG10 . . . 236 C6
Mastin Moor S43 . . . . 79 B4
Sandiacre NG10 . . . . 223 A7
Selston NG16 . . . . 171 F7
Shirebrook NG20 . . . . 119 E5
Stapleford NG9 . . . . . . 223 D5
Tupton S42 . . . . 131 D8
Ashgrove Ct DE21 . . . 206 B1
Ash Grove La DE65 . . 241 C6
Ashiver Rd S45 . . . . . . 145 C8
Ash La
Chesterfield S21 . . . . . . 77 D8
Sutton on the Hill DE6,
DE65 . . . . 228 E7
Unstone S18 . . . . 57 F3
Ashland Rd S21 . . . . . . 59 E3
Ashlands Dr 13
DE11 . . . . 256 E1
Ashlar Dr DE12 . . . . . 262 F1
Ashlea Dr DE6 . . . . . . 184 D7
Ashlea Gn S43 . . . . 81 A4
Ashlea Wlk S43 . . . . 81 A5
Ashleigh Ave
Glossop SK13 . . . . 10 B2
Sheffield S12 . . . . 43 F5
Swadlincote DE11 . . . 255 F5
Ashleigh Cl S41 . . . . . . 77 B3
Ashleigh Croft S12 . . . 43 F5
Ashleigh Ct S21 . . . . . 59 C1
Ashleigh Dr
Chellaston DE73 . . . . 232 F2
Sheffield S12 . . . . 43 F5
Ashleigh Pl S12 . . . . . 43 F5
Ashleigh Rd S43 . . . . . 80 B7
Ashley Cl
Killamarsh S21 . . . . . . 60 D6
Overseal DE12 . . . . . . 262 B3
Tansley DE4 . . . . 144 A4
Ashley Ct DE15 . . . . . 248 A3
ASHLEYHAY 166 A4
Ashleyhay La DE4 . . . 165 F4
Ashley La S21 . . . . 60 D6
Ashley St DE22 . . . . . 218 C5
Ashlyn Rd DE21 . . . . . 219 C5
Ashmeadow DE72 . . . 221 B1
Ashmeadow Ct DE6 . 185 D8
Ashmore Ave S21 . . . . 59 B2
Ash Mount Rd
NG16 . . . . 182 B3
Ash Mws S21 . . . . 59 C2
Ashop Rd DE56 . . . . . 179 D5
ASHOPTON 39 C4
Ashopton Ave DE23 . 231 F8
Ashopton Dr S33 . . . . 40 B4
Ashopton Rd
Bamford S33 . . . . 31 A1
Bamford S33 . . . . 40 A6
Chesterfield S41 . . . . . 95 C6
ASHOVER 129 F3
Ashover Cl
Derby DE21 . . . . 219 F8
Harpur Hill SK17 . . . . . 85 B2
1 Ripley DE5 . . . . 169 F1
ASHOVER HAY 145 A4
Ashover Hay S45 . . . . 145 B6
Ashover New Rd
DE55, S45 . . . . 145 E8
Ashover Prim Sch
S45 . . . . 129 F3
Ashover Rd
Alton S45 . . . . 130 C5
Ashover S45 . . . . 129 E4
Brackenfield S45 . . . . 146 B7
Derby DE22 . . . . 204 D2
1 Derby, Chaddesden
DE21 . . . . 219 E8
Staveley S43 . . . . 97 C6
Swadlincote DE11 . . . 255 F6
Tupton S42 . . . . 131 B7
Woolley Moor S45 . . . 145 F7
Ashover View DE55 . 147 C1

Ash St
Buxton SK17 . . . . 85 B6
Ilkeston DE7 . . . . 194 E4
Sheffield, Mosborough
S20 . . . . 59 C8
Ash Terr SK17 . . . . 85 C8
Ashton Cl
6 Ashbourne DE6 . . . 185 D7
Chesterfield S40 . . . . 114 C8
Derby DE3 . . . . 217 C3
Killamarsh S21 . . . . . . 60 C6
Swanwick DE55 . . . . . 170 A7
Ashton Dr DE24 . . . . 233 D4
Ashton Gdns
Clay Cross S42 . . . . . 131 B6
1 Glossop SK13 . . . . . 17 C7
Ashton Rd S45 . . . . . 131 E4
Ashton St SK13 . . . . . . 17 C7
Ashton Way DE56 . . . 179 C8
Ashtree Ave DE24 . . . 232 B6
Ashtree Cl
3 Matlock DE4 . . . . 143 A7
5 Swadlincote DE11 . 256 A6
Ash Tree Cl
Breadsall DE21 . . . . . 205 E4
Chesterfield S40 . . . . . 95 C3
Duffield DE56 . . . . . . 190 E5
2 Swadlincote DE11 . 255 F6
Ash Tree Cres NG16 136 C5
Ash Tree Rd S43 . . . . . 80 C2
Ashurst Cl S40 . . . . . . 94 F5
Ash Vale S40 . . . . 95 B3
Ashview Cl NG10 . . . . 236 A8
Ash View Cl DE65 . . . 229 B3
Ashwater Cl DE24 . . . 231 F2
Ashwell Ave NG19 . . . 136 E5
Ashwood SK13 . . . . 16 F8
Ashwood Cl
Buxton SK17 . . . . 85 C7
Derby DE24 . . . . 232 D8
Mansfield Woodhouse
NG19 . . . . 136 E5
Ashwood Rd
Buxton SK17 . . . . 66 E1
Disley SK12 . . . . 32 D6
Ashworth Ave
Burton upon Trent
DE15 . . . . 248 C2
Derby DE21 . . . . 219 F5
Ashworth Dr NG19 . . 131 A8
Ashworth La SK14 . . . . 9 A3
Ashworth Wlk DE21 . 219 F5
Askerfield Ave
DE22 . . . . 204 C4
Asker La DE4 . . . . . . 143 D6
Askerton Cl DE24 . . . 233 D4
Askew Gr DE65 . . . . . 242 D2
Askew Way
Chesterfield S40 . . . . 266 B1
Woodville DE11 . . . . . 256 F1
Asline Rd S2 . . . . 43 A8
Aspen Bsns Ctr
DE21 . . . . 220 B4
Aspen Cl
Buxton SK17 . . . . 66 B1
Killamarsh S21 . . . . . . 60 C6
Aspen Cl 1 NG19 . . . 136 E1
Aspen Dr DE21 . . . . . 220 C4
Aspen Rd S21 . . . . 59 B1
Aspen Rise DE55 . . . 146 D1
Aspenshaw S22 . . . . . 24 E4
Aspenshaw Rd SK22 . 24 E3
Aspen Way SK6 . . . . . . 32 A7
Aspley Cl S40 . . . . 95 E5
Astbury Way DE11 . . 256 F1
Astcote Cl DE75 . . . . 182 A1
Astell Way S23 . . . . . 47 B7
Asterdale Prim Sch
Derby DE21 . . . . 220 F3
Derby DE21 . . . . 221 A3
Asterdale View
DE21 . . . . 220 F4
Aster Gdns DE23 . . . 231 B6
Aster Rd NG20 . . . . . . 119 D2
Astil St DE15 . . . . 254 F8
Astley Gdns DE65 . . 240 F8
Astlow Dr DE56 . . . . . 179 B6
ASTON
Hope 39 C4
Sudbury 225 F4
Aston Cl
Chellaston DE73 . . . . 245 A8
Dronfield S18 . . . . 57 C3
Aston Ct S43 . . . . 78 F2
Aston Dr DE11 . . . . . . 256 A7
Aston Gn NG9 . . . . . . 223 E3
Aston Hall Dr DE72 . 246 A7
Aston La
Aston DE6 . . . . 225 F5
Chellaston DE73 . . . . 233 B1
Hope S33 . . . . 39 C4
Oaker DE4 . . . . 142 D7
Shardlow DE72 . . . . . 234 E1
Sudbury DE6 . . . . 226 A5
Wensley DE4 . . . . . . 142 D7
ASTON-ON-TRENT . . 246 B8
Aston-on-Trent Prim
Sch DE72 . . . . 246 A8
Aston Rd DE23 . . . . . 231 C5
1 Derby, Chaddesden
DE21 . . . . 219 E8
Astorville Park Rd
DE73 . . . . 232 F7
Astron Bsns Pk
DE11 . . . . 256 A3
Astwell Gdns DE24 . . 233 B4
ASTWITH 133 A5
Astwith Cl S44 . . . . . . 116 F1

Astwith La
Astwith S44, S45 . . . . 133 B5
Astwith S45 . . . . 132 F5
Atchison Gdns DE21 220 B7
Athens Ct DE73 . . . . . 232 E2
Atherfield Gdns
NG16 . . . . 182 F3
Atherfield Wlk
DE24 . . . . 233 C5
Atherstone Rd
DE12 . . . . 265 D1
Atherton Ave SK14 . . . 9 A4
Atherton Cl S2 . . . . . . 43 F6
Atherton Gr SK14 . . . . 9 A4
Atherton Rd
Ilkeston DE7 . . . . 194 C3
Sheffield S8 . . . . 43 F6
Athlestan Way
DE13 . . . . 240 C1
Athlone Cl DE21 . . . . 219 D8
Athol Cl
Chesterfield S40 . . . . 114 B8
Derby DE24 . . . . 231 E4
Athol Ct
Chesterfield S40 . . . . 266 A4
Derby DE23 . . . . 267 B1
Atkin Pl S2 . . . . 43 A8
Atkinson Ct S40 . . . . 266 B1
Atkinson Mews S21 . . 59 C3
Atkins Way ST14 . . . . 196 F3
2 Swadlincote DE11 . 255 F6
Atlantic Cres 1 S8 . . 56 E6
Atlantic Dr S8 . . . . . . 56 E6
Atlantic Way
Derby DE24 . . . . 219 E2
Sheffield S8 . . . . 56 E6
Atlantic Wlk S8 . . . . . . 56 E6
Atlas Way DE21 . . . . . 220 F2
ATLOW 175 A6
Atlow Brow 4
DE6 . . . . 173 D3
Atlow Cl S40 . . . . 95 B5
Atlow La DE6 . . . . 175 A5
Atlow Rd DE21 . . . . . . 219 E7
ATLOWTOP 175 B5
Atlow Winn La DE6 . 163 E1
Attenborough Nature
Centre NG10 . . . . . . 237 C8
Attenborough Nature
Reserve* NG9 . . . . . 237 D8
Attercliffe Rd DE72 . . 235 B7
Attewell Rd NG16 . . . 195 B5
Attlebridge Cl DE21 . 219 D8
Attlee Rd S43 . . . . 97 B7
Atwall Ct DE23 . . . . . . 219 A1
Atworth Gr DE23 . . . . 230 F7
Auburn Cl DE7 . . . . . . 207 B8
Auckland Ct S43 . . . . 217 F3
Auckland Dr S20 . . . . 59 E5
Auckland Pl DE56 . . 190 E2
Auckland Rise S20 . . . 59 E6
Auckland's Pl S40 . . . 266 B2
Auckland Way S20 . . . 59 E6
Auction Cl DE6 . . . . . 173 C2
Auden Cl DE65 . . . . . . 227 A8
Audens Way DE11 . . 256 C6
Audley Cl DE7 . . . . . . 194 D3
Audley Cl DE7 . . . . . . 267 B3
Audrey Cotts S32 . . . . 71 C6
Audrey Cres NG19 . . 136 C5
Audrey Dr DE21 . . . . 220 A8
Audrey Rd S13 . . . . . . 44 C7
Aughton Cl S13 . . . . . . 44 D7
Aughton Cres S13 . . . 44 D7
Aughton Dr S13 . . . . . 44 C8
Augusta St DE23 . . . 219 B2
Ault Dene DE11 . . . . . 256 E4
Ault Hucknall La
Glapwell S44 . . . . 134 A7
North Wingfield S44 . 131 F7
Aults Cl DE55 . . . . . . 230 C1
Aumonier Way
DE55 . . . . 159 C4
Auriga Ct DE1 . . . . . 219 B7
Austen Ave
Derby DE23 . . . . 231 B8
Long Eaton NG10 . . . 236 C5
Austin Ct DE72 . . . . . 222 E4
Austins Dr NG10 . . . . 223 B4
Austin Sq DE23 . . . . . 231 F7
Austin St NG20 . . . . . 120 A4
Autumn Gr DE21 . . . 219 F5
Avalon Dr DE73 . . . . 244 F8
Avenue 1 S41 . . . . . . 115 B8
Avenue 2 S41 . . . . . . 115 B8
Avenue 3 S41 . . . . . . 115 B8
Avenue 4 S41 . . . . . . 115 B8
Avenue 5 S41 . . . . . . 115 B8
Avenue 6 S41 . . . . . . 115 B8
Avenue 7 S41 . . . . . . 115 B8
Avenue 8 S41 . . . . . . 115 B8
Avenue Cl S32 . . . . . . 72 A3
Avenue Rd
Chesterfield S41 . . . . . 96 A8
Duffield DE56 . . . . . . 190 E5
Avenue The
Bakewell DE45 . . . . . 109 D5
Belper DE56 . . . . 178 F2
Chapel-en-le-Frith
SK23 . . . . 46 E2
Derby DE1 . . . . 267 B2
Derby, Chaddesden
DE21 . . . . 219 F5
Dronfield S18 . . . . 57 B2
Glossop SK13 . . . . 10 A4
Northwood DE4 . . . . . 127 B6
Spinkhill S21 . . . . 60 D2
Stoney Middleton S32 . . 72 A3
Tissington DE6 . . . . . 162 A5
Weston-on-Trent
DE72 . . . . 245 E5

Averham Cl
Derby DE21 . . . . 206 B1
Swadlincote DE11 . . . 256 A3
Ave The
Derby DE1 . . . . 219 A4
Wingerworth S42 . . . 115 C4
Aviemore Cl S43 . . . . . 77 E4
Aviemore Way DE24 231 E4
Avis Ave DE75 . . . . . . 193 F7
Avocet Cl DE75 . . . . 182 B1
Avocet Ct DE24 . . . . 231 D4
Avocet Drive DE65 . . 242 A5
Avocet Pl NG20 . . . . 120 D5
Avon Cl
Derby DE24 . . . . 231 D2
Dronfield S18 . . . . 57 B3
Swadlincote DE11 . . . 256 B6
Avon Ct S41 . . . . 266 A4
Avondale Cl NG10 . . 236 A6
Avondale Rd
Bolsover S44 . . . . 118 A8
Chesterfield S40 . . . . 266 A4
Derby DE23 . . . . 267 B1
Derby, Spondon DE21 220 D6
Ilkeston DE7 . . . . 208 C5
Staveley S43 . . . . 97 C7
Avonlea Cl DE7 . . . . . 209 B6
Avonmouth Dr
DE24 . . . . 232 E8
Avonside Cl S43 . . . . . 78 B3
Avon St DE24 . . . . . . 232 E8
Avon Way
Burton upon Trent
DE15 . . . . 248 A1
Hilton DE65 . . . . 228 D1
Awdishaw La DE6 . . . 213 B5
AWSWORTH 195 C4
Awsworth La
Cossall NG16 . . . . 195 C3
Kimberley NG16 . . . . 195 D6
Awsworth Prim Sch
NG16 . . . . 195 C4
Awsworth Rd DE7 . . 194 F2
Aycliffe Gdns DE24 . 232 F4
Aylesbury Ave DE21 . 219 F7
Aylesbury Way
NG19 . . . . 136 E2
Aylward Cl S2 . . . . 43 F7
Aylward Rd S2 . . . . . . 43 F7
Ayncourt Rd S42 . . . 132 B7
Ayr Cl DE21 . . . . 220 D4
Ayrton Dr DE74 . . . . 246 E3
Ayton Cl 6 S2 . . . . . . 44 A7
Azalea Ave DE55 . . . 170 A8
Azalea Cl DE55 . . . . . 159 E3
Azalea Ct NG16 . . . . 195 C8
Azure Dr S42 . . . . 132 C8

B

Babbacombe Cl
S41 . . . . 95 F8
Babbacombe Ct 5
S41 . . . . 95 F8
Babbington Cl DE13 239 C5
Babbington Close
DE7 . . . . 209 B5
Babbington La
NG16 . . . . 195 F4
Babbington St DE55 148 A6
Babbs La DE6 . . . . . . 211 C1
Babington Bsns Coll
DE1 . . . . 267 B3
Babington Cl
Sheffield S2 . . . . 43 F7
10 Sheffield S2 . . . . . 44 A7
Babington Ct
Sheffield S2 . . . . 43 F7
9 Sheffield S2 . . . . . 44 A7
Babington Hospl
DE56 . . . . 178 F2
Babington La DE1 . . 267 B3
Bacchus Way DE55 . 147 B5
Back Bridge St SK22 . . 24 C1
Back Croft S45 . . . . . 131 E6
Back Eccles La S23 . . 46 C8
Back Jodrell St SK22 . . 33 B7
Backhill La DE6 . . . . . 151 F3
Back La
Alderwasley DE56 . . 166 E7
Alstonefield DE6 . . . . 149 E3
Biggin SK17 . . . . 138 C1
Brackenfield DE55 . . 146 A1
Calow S44 . . . . 116 B8
Castle Donington
DE74 . . . . 247 A6
Chellaston DE73 . . . . 233 A2
Darley Dale DE4 . . . 127 F4
Eckington S21 . . . . . . 59 B4
Ellastone DE6 . . . . . . 183 A3
Elton DE4 . . . . 140 E6
Glapwell S44 . . . . 118 B1
Hollington DE6 . . . . . . 200 B3
Hollington DE6 . . . . . . 201 A3
Ilkeston DE7 . . . . 194 C3
Mottram in Longdendale
SK14 . . . . 9 A4
New Totley S17 . . . . . 55 E4
Palterton S44 . . . . 118 B5
Pilsley S45 . . . . 132 C2
Ripley DE5 . . . . 169 C6
Shirley DE6 . . . . 200 D3
Spout DE4 . . . . 166 D4
Stonebroom DE55 . . 146 F3

Back La *continued*
Sutton in Ashfield
NG17 . . . . 148 F4
Thorpe Salvin S80 . . . 63 B6
Thurvaston DE6 . . . . 215 B3
Tibshelf DE55 . . . . . . 147 F6
Unstone S18 . . . . 57 F1
Wessington DE55 . . . 157 F8
Whatstandwell DE4 . 156 D1
Wootton DE6 . . . . 183 A8
Youlgreave DE45 . . . 125 A6
Back Mellor Rd SK22 24 C1
BACKMOOR 43 C2
Back Moor SK14 . . . . . 9 A4
Backmoor Cres S8 . . . 43 C2
Backmoor Rd S8 . . . . 43 D2
Back Oth Cross
Flash SK17 . . . . 102 E2
Flash SK17 . . . . 103 A3
Back Rd S18 . . . . 57 F1
Back Rowarth
New Mills SK13 . . . . . . 16 F1
Rowarth SK13 . . . . 24 F8
Back School La DE4 127 E2
Back Sitwell St DE1 . . 267 B2
Back South St S43 . . . 77 D3
Back St
Castleton S33 . . . . 38 C2
Castleton S33 . . . . 38 C3
Back Union Rd 3
SK22 . . . . 33 C7
Back Wyver La
DE56 . . . . 178 F5
Bacon Cl NG16 . . . . . 195 A8
Bacon La DE5 . . . . . . 169 D2
Bacons La S40 . . . . . . 115 A8
Baden Powell Ave
S40 . . . . 266 B1
Baden Powell Rd
S40 . . . . 266 B2
Badger Cl
Chesterfield S40 . . . . 114 B7
Derby DE21 . . . . 220 F6
Badgerdale Way
DE23 . . . . 231 A7
Badger La
Ashover S45 . . . . 145 C4
Woolley Moor S45 . . . 145 D8
Badgers Way SK13 . . . 17 B7
Badgery Cl ST14 . . . . 210 A2
Badway La DE65 . . . . 227 C8
Bage Hill S42 . . . . 113 E6
Baggaley Cres
NG16 . . . . 136 B3
Bag La
Marchington ST14 . . 224 E2
Roston DE6 . . . . 197 E2
Bagot St DE7 . . . . 207 C8
BAGSHAW 47 F7
Bagshawe Ave SK23 . . 46 F6
Bagshaw Hill DE45 . 109 D6
Bagshaw La SK17 . . . 48 B7
Bagshaw's Rd S12 . . . 44 B6
Bagshaw St
Derby DE24 . . . . 232 E8
Pleasley NG19 . . . . . . 135 B4
BAGTHORPE 171 F2
Bagthorpe La S42 . . . . 94 A3
Bailey Ave DE12 . . . . 262 A3
Bailey Brook Cres
Aldercar NG16 . . . . . 182 A4
Langley Mill NG16 . . 182 A3
Bailey Brook Dr
NG16 . . . . 182 A3
Bailey Brook Ind Est
NG16 . . . . 182 B2
Bailey Brook Rd
NE7 . . . . 194 F5
Bailey Brook Wlk
NG16 . . . . 182 A3
Bailey Cl
Heanor DE75 . . . . 181 C4
Kirk Langley DE6 . . . 203 A4
Bailey Dr S21 . . . . 60 E8
Bailey Gr SK17 . . . . . . 85 E8
BAILEY GROVE 182 D2
Bailey Grove Rd
NG16 . . . . 182 D2
Baileys Mill DE4 . . . . 143 D4
Bailey St
Derby DE23 . . . . 267 A1
Stapleford NG9 . . . . . 223 C6
Bainbridge Rd S44 . . . 98 F1
Bainbridge St DE23 . 219 A3
Bainbrigge Rd DE74 247 F3
Baines Wood Cl S41 . 95 C8
Bain Gdns DE3 . . . . . 217 B3
Bains Dr DE72 . . . . . . 221 D1
Bakeacre La DE55 . . 230 E3
Bakehouse La DE72 . 221 C5
Bakehurst Cl SK22 . . . 33 C3
Baker Ave DE75 . . . . 193 F7
Baker Cl
Long Eaton NG10 . . . 223 C1
Somercotes DE55 . . . 170 D7
Baker Cres S42 . . . . . 115 B3
Baker Dr S21 . . . . 60 C6
Baker Pl S42 . . . . 115 B3
Baker Rd
Eastwood NG16 . . . . 195 C4
Mansfield Woodhouse
NG19 . . . . 136 C6
Wingerworth S42 . . . 115 B3
Bakers Hill DE56 . . . . 168 E1
Baker's La
Cromford DE4 . . . . . . 155 A5
Doveridge DE6 . . . . . 211 C1

Baker St
Burton upon Trent DE15 254 E7
Creswell S80 81 E2
Derby DE24 232 F8
Ilkeston DE7 194 F1
Swadlincote DE11 256 C3
BAKESTONE MOOR 81 E5
Bakestone Moor S80 81 F5
BAKEWELL 109 C5
Bakewell Bank 39 SK13 9 D1
Bakewell CE Inf Sch DE45 109 D6
Bakewell Cl
Derby DE3 217 E3
40 Gamesley SK13 9 D1
Bakewell Ct SK17 85 D7
Bakewell Dr DE74 247 A2
Bakewell Fold 37 SK13 9 D1
Bakewell Gdns 41 SK13 9 D1
Bakewell Gn
35 Gamesley SK13 9 D1
Swadlincote DE11 255 E5
Bakewell Gr 38 SK13 9 D1
Bakewell Lea 34 SK13 9 D1
Bakewell Meth Jun Sch DE45 109 D4
Bakewell Mews 36 SK13 9 D1
Bakewell Rd
Baslow DE45 91 E4
Buxton SK17 85 C7
Congreave DE45 126 C8
Darley Dale DE4 142 F7
Foolow SK32 70 E5
King Sterndale SK17 86 C5
Long Eaton NG10 236 E5
Matlock DE4 143 A5
Over Haddon DE45 109 B2
Staveley S43 97 C5
Bakewell St DE22 218 F4
Bakewell Station Ind Est DE45 109 E7
Bakewell Wlk 44 SK13 9 D1
Bakwell Rd DE45 90 E2
Balaclava Rd DE23 232 A8
Bale Cl NG10 237 A6
Balfour Rd
Derby DE23 232 A8
Stapleford NG9 223 D6
Balgonie Ct DE73 232 E2
Balham Wlk DE22 218 A6
Balkham La
Mansfield NG20 119 A2
Stony Houghton NG19 118 F2
Stony Houghton NG20 119 B2
Ballacraine Dr
2 Ripley DE5 169 F1
3 Ripley DE5 170 A1
Ballards Way DE72 221 D1
Ballater Cl
Derby DE24 231 E4
Mansfield NG19 135 E2
Balleny Cl DE21 205 F2
Ball Hill DE55 160 C6
BALLIDON 152 A2
Ballidon Cl 1 S41 95 C6
Ballidon Moor DE6 152 C4
Ball La DE72 234 A5
Ball Ridge La SK17 121 E3
Balmoak La S41 96 C5
Balmoral Cl
Derby DE23 218 B2
Heanor DE75 181 C1
Mansfield Woodhouse NG19 136 E5
Sandiacre NG10 223 B3
Balmoral Cres
Dronfield S18 56 D2
Sheffield S10 42 F8
Balmoral Ct DE74 247 D5
Balmoral Dr NG19 135 E2
Balmoral Gdns DE15 248 A3
Balmoral Rd
Borrowash DE72 221 C1
Burton upon Trent DE15 248 A3
Ilkeston DE7 208 D5
Balmoral Way
Chesterfield S43 77 E4
1 Hatton DE65 227 D2
Baltic Cl DE24 219 F1
Baltimore Cl 8 DE11 256 A7
Bamburgh Cl DE21 220 D4
BAMFORD 40 B4
Bamford Ave
Derby DE23 231 F8
North Wingfield S42 131 F7
Bamford Fold 3 SK13 9 E1
Bamford Gn 4 SK13 9 E1
Bamford Ho S33 40 B3
Bamford La SK13 9 E1
Bamford Mews SK13 9 E1
Bamford Mills S33 40 B3
Bamford Prim Sch S33 40 B4
Bamford Rd S43 97 C5
Bamford St
Chesterfield S43 77 D4
Newton DE55 148 A3
Ripley DE5 180 D7
Bamford Sta S33 40 B1
Bampton Cl DE24 233 D4
Banbury Ave NG9 223 F3
Banchory Cl NG19 135 E2
Bancroft Cl DE65 228 D1
Bancroft Dr DE22 204 C4
Bancroft The DE65 229 B3
Bandy La DE21 205 D2
Baneberry Way DE24 231 C3
Bangor St DE21 219 E8
Bank Bldgs DE56 190 F7
Bankbottom SK13 10 A5
Bank Cl
Bolsover S44 99 A3
Creswell S80 100 D8
Shirebrook NG20 119 F4
Tibshelf DE55 147 F5
Bank Ct DE22 218 E8
Bankerwall La DE6 183 C7
Bankfield Dr
Derby DE21 220 F4
Ilkeston DE7 208 B6
Bankgate SK14 16 A8
Bank Gdns DE4 143 B6
Bankhall SK23 47 A4
Bankholmes Cl DE24 231 E2
Bank House Ct DE6 164 A2
Bank La SK13 10 A7
Bank Rd
Chesterfield S41 96 A6
Matlock DE4 143 C5
Bank Row SK13 10 A7
Banksburn Cl DE75 181 C1
Bankside DE45 125 B5
Bank Side
Derby DE22 204 E2
Hartington SK17 137 D6
Bankside Cl SK6 15 C1
Banks Rd NG9 223 E2
Banks Road Inf Sch NG9 223 F2
Bank St
Brimington S43 96 D8
Broadbottom SK14 16 A8
Chesterfield S40 95 E3
Glossop SK13 17 D8
Hadfield SK13 10 A5
Hayfield SK22 25 D3
Langley Mill NG16 182 C3
Long Eaton NG10 236 E7
Somercotes DE55 170 C8
Swadlincote DE11 262 A8
BANKS THE 23 E3
Bankswood Cl SK13 10 A4
Bank Terr SK13 10 A5
Bank The
Bonsall DE4 142 C1
Glossop SK13 17 D8
Hayfield SK22 25 B4
Stoney Middleton S32 71 F4
BANK TOP 53 A8
Bank Top DE4 141 A5
Bank Top La S30 72 C8
Bank Vale Rd SK22 25 C3
Bank View SK17 69 B5
Bank View Rd
Derby DE22 218 F8
Nether Heage DE56 168 C2
Bankwood Cl S14 43 D5
Bank Wood Cl S40 95 B7
Bankwood Com Prim Sch S14 43 D5
BANKWOOD GATE 16 C8
Bankwood Rd S14 43 D5
Bannels Ave DE23 231 B7
Banton's La DE73 251 A4
Banwell Cl DE3 217 C3
BARBER BOOTH 37 A6
Barber Cl DE7 194 E3
Barber's La S21 60 D7
Barbers Row S21 79 D7
Barber St SK13 10 B5
Barbon Cl S40 95 E5
Barbon Dr
Derby DE3 217 C1
Derby DE3 230 C8
Barcheston Cl DE21 206 B2
Barclay Ct DE7 194 D3
Barclay Grange S41 266 C3
Bar Croft 3 S40 95 C6
Barden Dr DE22 204 F3
Barden Rd DE3 230 E5
Bardolph Cl DE11 255 F3
Bardsey Ct DE21 206 B3
Bare Jarnett Road SK17 88 B1
Bare La DE72 221 C5
Barf Cl DE3 217 E1
BARGATE 179 C1
Bargate S33 38 C2
Bargate Cl DE56 179 C1
Bargate La DE65 242 B5
Bargate Rd DE56 179 B1
Barholme Cl S41 95 F7
Barker Ave NG16 171 B4
Barker Avenue E NG10 223 B6
Barker Avenue N NG10 223 A6
Barker Cl DE7 193 B1
Barker Fold S40 95 D3
Barker Gate DE7 194 F2
Barker La S40 95 D3
Barker St NG17 148 F4
Barklam Cl DE12 262 E1
BARLBOROUGH 80 B7
BARLBOROUGH COMMON 80 B5
Barlborough Hall Sch S43 61 B1
Barlborough Hospital S43 80 B5
Barlborough Prim Sch S43 80 B7
Barlborough Rd
Clowne S43 80 D5
Ilkeston DE7 194 F5
Barley Cft DE73 232 F1
Barley Cl
Kimberley NG16 195 F7
Little Eaton DE21 205 C8
Barleycorn Cl DE15 248 A1
Barley Corn Cl DE21 206 C2
Barleycroft SK13 9 F4
Barley Croft
Belper DE56 179 B2
South Normanton DE55 160 B4
Barley Dale Dr NG9 209 D2
Barley La S42 95 A5
Barley Mews
Dronfield S18 56 B2
Mansfield Woodhouse NG19 136 E6
Barley Rd DE14 253 D8
Barley Way DE4 143 D6
Barling Dr DE7 194 C2
BARLOW 75 E2
Barlow CE Prim Sch S18 75 E3
Barlow Cottage La NG16 195 C5
Barlow Drive N NG16 195 B4
Barlow Drive S NG16 195 B4
Barlow Grange La S18 93 F8
Barlow Lees La S18 75 F7
Barlow Rd
Chapel-en-le-Frith SK23 47 C6
Cutthorpe S18, S42 94 F8
Staveley S43 78 E1
Barlow St DE1, DE23 267 D1
Barlow View S18 76 B7
Barlow Wood Dr SK6 23 B3
Barmote Croft DE4 154 F1
Barms Way SK17 66 D1
Barnard Ave S18 57 D3
Barnard Rd DE21 205 D2
Barn Cl
Castle Donington DE74 247 B3
Chesterfield S41 95 D6
Findern DE65 230 D2
Glossop SK13 17 D7
Matlock DE4 143 A6
3 Nottingham NG10 236 C5
Quarndon DE22 204 C6
Barn Croft DE23 218 C1
Barnes Ave S18 56 E2
Barnes Croft
Heanor DE75 181 C1
Wirksworth DE4 165 F8
Barnes Gn DE22 218 B7
Barnes La
Dronfield S17 56 C4
Dronfield S18 56 C3
Youlgreave DE45 125 C5
Barnes Rd S41 96 E1
Barnetts Way S45 132 C3
Barnfield Cl
Holmewood S42 132 E8
1 Staveley S43 78 E2
Barnfield Dr S32 52 F7
Barnfields S32 52 F7
Barnfield Wlk S43 78 E2
Barn Furlong DE45 90 A4
Barnham Cl S40 114 B8
Barnhill Gr DE23 231 A7
Barn La DE4 127 A7
Barnsfold Ct SK22 25 D3
Barnsley La DE4, DE56 165 F2
Barnstaple Cl DE21 206 A2
Barnstaple Ct 3 S41 95 F8
Barns The S42 115 B4
Barnwell Cl ST14 210 A4
Barnwell La DE4 155 A5
Barnwood Cl DE3 217 C2
Baron Cl DE21 206 D3
Barrack Rd S18 58 A1
Barrack View S18 58 A1
Barrack Yd DE55 170 D7
Barratt Rd S21 59 D2
Bar Rd
Baslow DE45 91 F6
Curbar S32 72 F2
Barrett St DE24 233 A7
Barrie Dr DE24 231 F5
Barringer Rd NG19 136 D1
Barrington Cl
Burton upon Trent DE13 240 C1
Kirk Langley DE6 202 F2
Barrons Ct DE72 234 A5
Barron's Way DE72 221 C1
Barroon DE74 247 B3
Barrowhill ST14 197 A7
BARROW HILL 78 B4
Barrow Hill ST14 196 F5
Barrow Hill Prim Sch S43 78 B3
Barrow Hill Roundhouse Rly Ctr* S43 78 A4
Barrow La DE73 244 C6
Barrowmore La DE6 175 D4
Barrows Hill La NG16 171 D5
Barrow St S43 78 F2
Barrowstones La DE45 123 B8
BARROW UPON TRENT 244 B6
Barry Rd S43 96 F4
Barrys Cl 1 DE11 256 E1
Barson Gr SK17 85 E2
Bartle Ave S12 43 F4
Bartle Dr S12 43 F4
Bartle Rd S12 43 F4
Bartle Way S12 43 F4
Barton Bsns Pk DE13 259 A8
Barton Business Pk
Barton-under-Needwood DE13 259 A8
Walton-On-Trent DE14 253 A1
Barton Cl DE21 220 F6
Barton Cres S40 95 A6
Barton Dr DE6 185 D7
Bartonfields Ctr The DE65 214 D2
Barton Hill DE4 126 C1
Barton Hill Croft DE45 126 C1
BARTON IN FABIS 237 E6
Barton Knowle DE56 179 D4
Barton La
Broxtowe NG9 237 D8
Thrumpton NG11 237 C2
Barton Rd
Long Eaton NG10 237 A6
Sheffield S8 43 A6
Barton St
Burton upon Trent DE14 254 C8
Clowne S43 80 F4
BARTON TURN 253 B1
Barton Turn DE13 253 A1
Barway DE6 211 E8
Baseball Drive DE23 219 B1
Basegreen Ave S12 44 B3
Basegreen Cl S12 44 C3
Basegreen Cres S12 44 B3
Basegreen Dr S12 44 C3
Basegreen Pl S12 44 B3
Basegreen Rd S12 44 C3
Basegreen Way S12 44 C3
Basil Cl
Chesterfield S41 96 A3
Chesterfield S41 266 B3
Basildon Cl DE24 232 F5
Basil Dr DE3 217 C4
Basingwerke Ct SK22 25 D3
BASLOW 91 F5
Baslow Cl
22 Gamesley SK13 9 E1
Long Eaton NG10 236 A5
Baslow Ct 14 S40 95 D5
Baslow Dr DE22 204 F3
Baslow Fold 21 SK13 9 E1
Baslow Gn
23 Gamesley SK13 9 E1
2 Swadlincote DE11 255 E5
Baslow Gr SK17 85 E6
Baslow Mews SK13 9 E1
Baslow Rd
Ashford in the Water DE45 89 F1
Bakewell DE45 109 D7
Baslow DE45 92 E4
Curbar S32 72 D1
Holymoorside S42 94 C1
Sheffield S17 55 C4
Wadshelf S42 93 A3
Baslow Way 24 SK13 9 E1
BASSETT 42 E5
Bassettbarn La S42 130 B5
Bassett Cl
Ilkeston DE7 194 C3
Kimberley NG16 195 E7
Bassett Hill NG20 119 E7
Bassett La S10 42 E6
Bassett Rd NG16 195 E7
Bassett The NG20 119 E6
Bassford Ave DE75 181 F2
Bassingham Cl DE21 206 B1
Bassledene Ct 2 S2 44 A8
Bassledene Rd S2 44 A8
Bass's Cres DE11 261 E7
Bass St DE22 218 D6
Batch La DE6 224 B7
Bateman Cl S43 77 D4
Bateman St DE23 219 C3
Batemill Rd SK22 24 D2
BATEMOOR 57 A5
Batemoor Cl S8 57 A6
Batemoor Dr S8 57 A6
Batemoor Pl S8 57 A6
Batemoor Rd S8 57 A5
Batemoor Wlk S8 57 A6
Bate Wood Ave S43 97 B5
BATHAM GATE 66 F4
Batham Gate
Bradwell SK17 50 B4
Peak Forest SK17 48 F1
Peak Forest SK17 49 A1
Batham Gate Rd SK17 67 B6
Batham Rd S33 51 A8
Bath La
Ashover S45 129 F6
Moira DE12 262 D4
Shirebrook NG19 120 C2
Bath Rd
Buxton SK17 85 B6
Castle Gresley DE11 255 D1
Derby DE3 217 E2
Bath St
Bakewell DE45 109 D6
Derby DE1 267 B5
Ilkeston DE7 194 E1
Bathurst Rd S44 117 F8
Bathurst Terr NG20 100 F2
Batley La NG19 134 E4
Baton Mount 6 S43 81 E2
Battersea Park Way DE22 218 A5
Battlestead Rd DE14 253 D8
Batt St 9 S8 43 A8
Baulk La
Beeston NG9 223 F7
Hathersage S32 41 A1
Hathersage S32 53 A8
Baverstock Cl DE73 232 F3
Baxter Hill NG19 134 F3
Baxter Sq DE23 231 F6
Bay Cl DE3 217 D5
Baycliff Dr S40 95 C3
Bay Ct S21 60 C5
Bayleaf Cres DE21 206 B3
Baysdale Croft S20 59 D7
Baysdale Dr NG19 136 F1
Bayswater Cl DE22 217 F6
Bayswater Rd NG16 195 F7
Bazley Rd S2 43 F6
Beackden Cl DE56 179 E4
Beacomfold SK6 15 B3
Beacom La SK14 15 C6
Beacon Dr DE13 240 B3
Beaconfields Ho DE21 220 B4
Beacon Hill Way S41 115 C7
Beacon Rd DE13 240 B3
Beaconsfield St NG10 236 E7
Beam Cl DE13 240 A1
Beamlight Rd DE7 194 F8
Beamwood Cl 3 DE21 205 F1
Beard Cres SK22 33 D8
Beardmore Cl DE21 205 F2
Beards Rd DE11 256 A6
Beards Wood Dr DE21 205 D3
Bearwood Hill Rd DE15 248 A3
Beatrix Dr SK13 9 E3
Beattie La DE11 256 F5
Beatty St DE24 232 F8
Beatty Wlk DE7 194 F3
BEAUCHIEF 56 D8
Beauchief Abbey La S8 56 C8
Beauchief Abbey (rems of)* S8 56 C8
Beauchief Dr S17 56 C7
Beauchief Gdns DE55 170 D8
Beaufit La NG16 160 E2
Beaufort Com Prim Sch DE21 219 C8
Beaufort Court Ind Est DE21 219 C8
Beaufort Rd
Burton upon Trent DE15 248 B1
Derby DE24 231 D2
Beaufort St DE21 219 D7
Beaulieu Way DE55 170 A7
Beaumaris Ct DE21 220 F5
Beaumont Cl
Barrow upon Trent DE73 244 A5
Belper DE56 179 D4
Stapleford NG9 209 E1
Beaumont Dr SK17 47 F1
Beaumont Wlk DE23 231 E6
Beaurepaire Cres DE56 179 B5
Beaureper Ave DE22 204 E3
Beauvale Dr DE7 194 E5
Becher St DE23 219 A1
Beck Cl S44 99 C2
Beckenham Way DE22 218 B6
Becket Ave S8 56 D6
Becket Cres S8 56 E6
Becket Prim Sch DE22 218 F4
Becket Rd S8 56 E6
Becket St DE1 267 A3
Beckets Wood SK23 47 A4
Beckett Ave NG19 135 E1
Becket Well La DE1 267 B3
Becket Wlk S8 56 E6
Beckingham Way S40 266 B2
Beckitt Cl DE24 233 A8
Becksitch La DE56 178 F2
Beckstich Ct DE56 178 F1
Bedehouse La DE4 155 A6
Bedford Cl DE22 218 D3
Bedford Ct NG9 209 E1
Bedford Dr DE72 233 F7
Bedford Rd DE15 254 D7
Bedford St DE22 218 D3
Bedgrave Cl S21 60 F8
Beech Ave
Alfreton DE55 159 B5
Borrowash DE72 221 C3
Breaston DE72 235 F8
Creswell S80 81 F1
Derby DE24 233 B7
Glossop SK13 17 A8
Hulland Ward DE6 175 F3
Long Eaton NG10 223 E1
Melbourne DE73 252 B8
New Mills SK22 24 D1
Pinxton NG16 160 E3
Quarndon DE22 204 B8
Ripley DE5 169 C2
Sandiacre NG10 223 B7
Willington DE65 242 B5
Beech Cl
Belper DE56 179 A3
Branston DE14 256 E6
Kilburn DE56 192 B8
Wirksworth DE4 165 F7
Beech Cres
Eckington S21 59 B1
Glapwell S44 134 B8
Killamarsh S21 60 D5
Mansfield Woodhouse NG19 136 E2
Beechcroft DE21 205 D4
Beech Ct
Derby DE21 220 D5
Mansfield Woodhouse NG19 136 B5
Beechdale Cl S40 95 D5
Beechdale Rd
Alfreton DE55 159 C3
Mansfield NG19 136 F2
Beech Dr
Arkwright Town S44 97 D3
Ashbourne DE6 185 D8
Derby DE22 218 F8
Etwall DE65 229 C4
Findern DE65 230 E1
Woodville DE11 257 B2
Beeches Ave DE21 220 D5
Beeches Bank S2 43 C8
Beeches Dr S2 43 C8
Beeches Hollow S2 43 C8
Beeches The
Baslow DE45 91 E5
Crich DE4 156 F1
Heanor DE75 193 C8
Matlock DE4 143 A6
Beechfield Rd SK13 9 F3
Beech Gdns
Derby DE24 233 B7
6 Stretton DE13 240 E1
Beech Gr
Long Duckmanton S44 98 A4
South Normanton DE55 160 B5
Swadlincote DE11 255 F7
Beech Hill Ave NG19 135 F1
Beech Hill Cres NG19 135 F1
Beech Hill Dr NG19 135 F1
Beech Hill Sch NG19 135 F1
Beech La
Burton upon Trent DE13 240 E1
Dove Holes SK17 66 E8
West Hallam DE7 207 D7
Beechley Dr DE21 206 B1
Beech Rd SK23 45 E7
Beech Rise SK23 45 C5
Beech St S43 78 A1
Beech Tree Ave NG19 136 B5
Beech Tree Dr S43 80 F2
Beech View Drive SK17 85 C5
Beech Way
Clay Cross S45 131 E2
Dronfield S18 57 A3
Beech Wlk
Cromford DE4 155 A6
Derby DE23 218 D1
Beechwood SK13 16 F7
Beechwood Cl DE56 178 E5
Beechwood Cres
1 Derby DE23 218 C1
Derby DE23 231 C8
Beechwood Ct DE23 219 B3
Beechwood Dr SK6 23 A6
Beechwood Park Dr DE22 204 F1
Beechwood Rd S18 56 F1
Beehive Rd S40 95 D2
Bee Hives The DE11 256 A7
BEELEY 111 B4

Beeley Cl
Ashbourne DE6......**185** E8
Belper DE56......**179** C6
Creswell S80.......**81** D1
Derby DE22......**204** D2
Derby, Oakwood
  DE21......**205** F2
North Wingfield S42...**132** A7
Staveley S43......**97** C5
Beeley Hill Top DE4. **111** A5
Beeley La DE4......**112** B3
Beeley View S40......**114** B7
Beeley Way S43......**97** C5
Beelow Cl SK17......**47** E2
Bee Low Rd SK17...**85** D2
BEESTON......**223** E4
Beeston Cl S18......**56** C2
Beeston Dr DE3...**230** E5
Beet La SK23......**35** B3
Beetwell St S40...**266** B2
Beggarswell Wood
  DE56......**167** D4
Beggarway La DE45..**90** B5
Beighton Fields S21..**79** D7
Beighton Hill
Ashleyhay DE4.......**165** F4
Ashleyhay DE4......**166** A4
Beighton St DE5...**169** E1
Bek Cl NG19.......**134** F7
Beldon Cl S2......**43** D7
Beldon Court S2....**43** D7
Beldon Pl S2......**43** D7
Beldon Rd S2......**43** D7
Belfast Wlk DE21...**220** A4
Belfield Ct
Etwall DE65......**229** B3
Heanor DE7......**181** C4
Belfield Gdns NG10. **236** E2
Belfield Ind Est DE7.**194** F2
Belfield Rd
Etwall DE65......**229** C3
Swadlincote DE11...**256** B5
Belfield St
Ilkeston DE7......**194** F2
Ilkeston DE7......**195** A2
Belfield Terr DE65.. **229** B3
Belfit Dr
Wingerworth S42......**114** F2
Wingerworth S42...**115** A2
Belf Moor Cl S80...**82** A5
Belfry Cl DE13......**217** F1
Belfry The DE13...**240** C1
Belfry Way DE5... **180** E7
Belgrade Ave SK23...**34** E1
Belgrave Cl DE56...**179** C5
Belgrave Sq 6 S2...**43** A8
Belklane Dr S21...**60** E7
Bella Cl NG16......**182** B4
Belland La
Ashover S45......**113** D2
Holymoorside S45... **113** D4
Bell Ave DE72......**246** A7
Bell Cotts DE6......**224** C8
Belle Acre Cl 3
  DE56......**178** F3
BELLEVUE......**173** B2
Belle Vue SK23......**34** E2
Belle Vue Ave S45.. **180** C6
Belle Vue Cl S43......**96** D8
Belle Vue Rd DE6... **173** B2
Bellhouse La S43...**78** F3
Bell House La S43...**78** F3
Bellhouse View S43..**78** F3
Bellingham Ct DE22 **204** C2
Bell La
Bonsall DE4......**142** C1
Doveridge DE6......**224** C8
Hartshorne DE7......**257** A3
Heanor DE7, DE75... **193** C5
Bellott La DE4......**46** E2
Bellrope Acre DE56. **179** B2
Bells End Rd DE12.. **253** D1
Bellsfield Cl S80.....**82** A5
Bell View DE7......**192** F6
Belmont Ave DE72.. **235** E8
Belmont Cl DE3...**217** F5
Belmont Dr
Borrowash DE72...**221** B1
Marple SK6.......**15** B1
Staveley S43......**78** F2
Belmont Prim Sch
  DE11......**256** C4
Belmont St DE11... **256** C4
Belmont Terr 1
  SK17......**85** B7
Belmore Way
Alvaston DE24......**233** B8
Derby DE21......**220** A1
Belmot Rd DE13...**239** B4
Belpar Ho DE21... **220** E3
BELPER......**179** B3
Belper La DE56...**178** E6
BELPER LANE END . **178** C7
Belper L Ctr DE56... **179** D4
Belper Parks Nature
  Reserve ★ DE56. **179** A3
Belper Rd
Alderwasley DE4......**166** C6
Alderwasley DE56...**167** A4
Ashbourne DE6......**173** C1
Ashbourne DE6......**174** C1
3 Derby DE22......**218** F7
Holbrook DE56......**191** C8
Hulland Ward DE6... **176** D2

Belper Rd continued
Kilburn DE56.......**179** C1
Morley DE7......**192** F2
Shirland DE55......**146** C2
Stanley Common DE7..**193** B1
West Hallam DE7...**207** C8
Belper Sch DE56...**179** D4
Belper St DE7......**208** F7
Belper Sta DE56...**178** F4
BELPH.......**82** C4
Belsize Cl DE22...**217** F6
Belton Cl
Dronfield S18......**56** C1
Sandiacre NG10...**223** B4
Belton Dr DE5......**169** E1
Belvedere Ave S40 **114** E8
Belvedere Cl
Chesterfield S40.......**114** A8
Derby DE3......**217** D3
Swanwick DE55...**169** F7
Belvedere Rd DE11 .**256** F2
Belvedere Terr 1
  SK17......**85** B6
Belvoir Cl
Breaston DE72......**235** D7
Ilkeston DE7......**208** D6
Long Eaton NG10...**236** E5
Belvoir Cres DE11 .. **256** A6
Belvoir St DE23......**218** F1
Belvoir Way DE55...**159** C1
Bembridge Dr DE24. **233** C5
Bemrose Ct DE1...**267** C2
Bemrose Gate S33...**40** A6
Bemrose Mews
  DE22......**218** C4
Bemrose Rd DE24.. **232** E7
Bemrose Sch The
  DE22......**218** D4
Benbow Ave DE73.. **252** A8
Benches La SK6......**15** E3
Bench Rd SK17......**85** C8
Bendall Gn DE23... **231** C5
Bendan Gdns DE22. **204** D3
Bend Oak Dr DE7... **248** C4
Benjamin Ct NG16... **170** F3
Benjamin Outram Bsns
  Ctr DE5......**180** E7
Benmore Ct DE21... **206** B3
Benner Ave DE7... **209** A5
Bennerley Ave DE7 .**194** F4
Bennerley Fields
  Specialist Speech &
  Language Coll DE7 **194** F4
Bennetsitch Rd
  SK11......**102** C3
Bennetts La
Crich DE4......**167** F8
Crich DE4......**168** A8
Bennett St
Buxton SK17......**85** C6
Derby DE7......**232** D5
Hollingworth SK14...**9** C5
Long Eaton NG10... **223** C2
Sandiacre NG10...**223** B5
Bennimoor Way
  S40......**114** E8
Bennington Wlk
  NG19......**136** E4
Bennion Gr ST14... **196** E5
Bennison Gdns
  S41......**131** D3
Bensley Cl DE73... **233** A1
Benson St DE24... **232** F7
Bentfield Rd DE56.. **168** C1
Bentham Rd S40......**95** E5
Benthead La DE6... **164** F1
Bentinck Dr S43......**81** A4
Bentinck Rd S44......**98** F7
Bentinck Cl S80......**82** C6
Bentink Cl S80......**81** C1
Bent La
Ashleyhay DE4......**166** C6
Church Broughton
  DE65......**227** C6
Darley Dale DE4......**127** D6
Matlock DE4......**143** A7
Matlock DE4......**143** B7
Spout DE4, DE56... **166** C6
Staveley S43......**79** A3
Tissington DE6......**162** D5
Bentley Bridge Cotts
  DE4......**143** E7
Bentley Bridge Rd
  DE4......**143** E7
Bentley Brook
Hilton DE65......**228** D1
Matlock DE4......**143** D4
Bentley Cl
Alfreton DE55......**159** B3
Matlock DE4......**143** D7
Bentley Dale DE11.. **257** A3
Bentley Rd
Castle Donington
  DE74......**246** F4
Uttoxeter ST14......**210** A2
Bentley St DE24... **232** E6
Benton Dr SK6......**23** C8
Bents Cres S18......**57** C3
Bentside Rd SK12...**32** D5
Bents La S18......**57** C3
Bent The S32......**72** E3
Beowulf Covert
  DE13......**240** B1
Beresford Ave
Ashbourne DE6......**173** D2
Chapel-en-le-Frith
  SK23......**47** C6
Beresford Cl S45... **131** D2

Beresford Dale
  DE11......**255** F2
Beresford Dr
Derby DE21......**220** E4
Ilkeston DE7......**194** E5
Beresford La
Alstonefield DE6......**149** D4
Alstonefield SK17...**137** C2
Ashover DE55......**145** D7
Beresford Pl DE56.. **168** B6
Beresford Rd
Chapel-en-le-Frith
  SK23......**47** C6
Long Eaton NG10... **236** A5
Mansfield Woodhouse
  NG19......**136** C6
Berkeley Ave NG10. **236** C6
Berkeley Cl DE55...**169** C3
Berkley Ct SK23......**45** D6
Berkshire St DE21... **219** D8
Berle Ave DE75......**181** E2
Bermuda Ave DE21. **205** C6
Bernard Ave NG19.. **136** B5
Bernard Cl S43......**96** F8
Bernard Ct DE11... **256** D3
Bernard Gadsby Cl
  DE6......**173** A1
Bernard St
Glossop SK13......**10** C1
Swadlincote DE11... **256** D3
Bernard Walker Ct
  SK6......**15** B2
Berners Cl S2......**43** E6
Berners Dr S2......**43** E6
Berners Pl S2......**43** E6
Berners Rd S2......**43** E6
Berridge La S45......**145** B4
Berrisford Ave S21...**59** D2
Berristow La DE55.. **160** C7
Berry Ave S21......**59** C3
Berry Hedge La
  DE15......**248** C4
Berry Park Cl DE22 .**204** E1
Berry St S42......**131** E6
Berrystorth Cl S14...**43** E5
Bertrand Ave S45... **131** D3
Berwick Ave
Chesterfield S40......**114** C7
Derby DE21......**219** C7
Berwick Cl DE24... **233** B5
Berwick Ct S40......**114** C7
Berwick Dr DE24... **231** D3
Berwick Rd SK17...**85** C4
Berwin Cl NG10......**223** A1
Berwyn Cl S40......**95** C5
Beryl Cl DE11......**255** F4
Besom La S32......**53** A8
Bessalone Dr DE56. **179** A6
Bessell La NG10...**223** D5
Bessie La S33......**51** B6
Best Ave DE15......**248** B3
Besthill Cotts SK14...**16** B8
Besthorpe Cl DE21. **206** B1
Bestwick Ave DE75. **182** B1
Bestwick Cl DE7... **209** A4
Bestwood Dr S45... **131** C3
Bestwood Pk S45... **131** C3
Bethany Cl 2 DE65. **242** B6
Bethel Terr S81......**63** E7
Bethulie Rd DE23... **232** A8
Betjeman Sq DE24. **232** A5
Betlingspring La
  DE6......**184** D3
Betony Cl S21......**60** B5
Betony Close DE24. **231** C3
Betony Rd DE15... **248** C2
Betty La DE45......**108** F8
Bevan Ct DE55......**146** E1
Bevan Dr S43......**97** B7
Bevan Rd S45......**131** D2
Bevan St DE55......**146** E1
Beverley Dr NG16... **195** E7
Beverley Rd
4 Branston DE14... **253** F7
Burton upon Trent
  DE14......**254** A7
Beverleys Rd S8......**43** A4
Beverley St DE24... **219** D2
Bevin Pl S42......**132** A7
Bewdley Cl DE73... **233** A3
Bewley Cl DE24... **233** D4
Bexhill Wlk DE21... **205** E1
Bexley Cl
Derby DE3......**217** F5
Glossop SK13......**10** C3
Bexley Dr DE11... **255** E1
BIBBINGTON......**66** F7
Bicester Ave DE24. **231** C2
Bickley Moss DE21. **206** B1
Bideford Cl DE55... **169** D2
Bideford Dr DE3... **217** F5
Bidston Cl DE4......**143** C7
Bidworth La SK13...**9** D1
BIGGIN
Hartington......**138** C4
Hulland Ward......**176** A5
Biggin CE Prim Sch
  DE6......**138** D3
Biggin Cl S45......**131** D1
Biggin La
Alfreton DE55......**133** A1
Hulland Ward DE6... **176** B3
Bigginmill La DE6... **176** C5
Biggin The DE74...**247** B3

Bigin View DE6......**175** E3
Big La
Hognaston DE6......**164** A4
Hognaston DE6......**164** C4
Bilberry Cl DE21... **205** F1
Bilberry Dr NG20... **119** D2
Bilbie Cl DE55......**159** C4
Bilby La S43......**77** E1
Billam St S21......**59** B3
Billingsley Ave
  NG16......**160** D3
Bilsborrow Ave DE1 **267** C2
Bingham Cl DE55... **159** C4
Bingham St DE24... **232** E6
Bings Rd SK23......**45** F8
Bingswood Ave
  SK23......**45** E8
Bingswood Ind Est
  SK23......**45** E8
Bingswood Rd SK23 .**45** E7
Bingswood Trading Est
  SK23......**45** E8
Binscombe La DE21. **205** F3
Birch Ave
Ambergate DE56......**167** F3
Ilkeston DE7......**209** A7
Swadlincote DE11... **256** A7
Birch Cl
Alfreton DE55......**159** A5
Burton upon Trent
  DE14......**254** A8
Buxton SK17......**66** B1
Denstone ST14......**196** D6
Derby DE21......**221** A6
Grassmoor S42......**115** F3
Killamarsh S21......**60** C5
Ripley DE5......**180** D8
Wessington DE55... **157** E8
Birchall St DE73... **232** F2
Birch Cross ST14... **224** B1
Birchen Cl
Chesterfield S40......**95** D5
Dronfield S18......**56** D1
Birchen Holme
  DE55......**160** A4
Birches Ave DE55... **157** F5
Birches Brook
South Wingfield
  DE55......**157** F5
South Wingfield DE55. **158** A5
Birches Fold S18......**57** C4
Birches La
Dronfield S18......**57** C4
South Wingfield DE55. **158** A5
Birches Rd DE22... **204** D4
Birches Terr DE6... **173** B1
Birches The SK22...**25** C2
Birch Farm Ave S8...**57** A8
Birchfield Cl DE73.. **232** F2
Birchfield Pk DE75.. **193** F7
Birchfield Rd DE15. **254** E6
Birch Gn SK13......**10** C1
Birch Gr
Hatton DE65......**227** D2
Shirebrook NG20... **119** D5
Birch Hall Sch S42...**25** B2
Birch Holt Gr S18...**76** E5
Birch House Way
  S18......**57** C1
Birchills The S80......**81** C1
Birchitt Cl S17......**56** C5
Birchitt Ct S17......**56** C5
Birchitt Pl S17......**56** C5
Birchitt Rd S17......**56** C5
Birchitt View S18...**57** A3
Birch Kiln Croft S43 .**96** F7
Birch La S43......**78** A1
Birchlands S41......**146** E1
Birchlands Dr S21...**60** D5
BIRCHOVER......**140** F6
Birchover Ct S41......**95** E6
Birchover Edge DE4 **141** B8
Birchover Ho
1 Derby, Allestree
  DE22......**204** F3
Derby, Markeaton
  DE22......**218** D8
Birchover La DE4... **141** B7
Birchover Pl DE7... **194** E5
Birchover Rd DE4... **126** C3
Birchover Rise
  DE21......**205** F1
Birchover Way
  DE22......**204** E2
Birch Rd S80......**82** C6
Birch Rise S45......**131** E3
Birchside Ave SK13...**10** B2
Birch St NG20......**120** F6
BIRCH VALE......**25** B2
Birch Vale DE56... **178** F5
Birch Vale Ind Est
  SK22......**25** A2
Birch Vale Terr SK22. **24** F3
Birchview Cl DE56... **179** B2
Birch View Ct DE11. **218** F7
Birchway Gr DE23.. **231** A6
Birchwood
Heanor DE75......**181** C4
Heanor DE75......**181** D4
Birchwood Ave
Derby DE23......**231** D6
Long Eaton, Breaston
  NG10......**236** A7
Long Eaton, New Sawley
  NG10......**236** C5

Birchwood Cl
7 Sheffield S20.......**59** E8
South Normanton
  DE55......**160** A4
Birchwood Cres
Chesterfield S40......**114** F7
Somercotes DE55... **170** D8
Birchwood Croft S20 .**59** E8
Birchwood Ct S40......**114** F7
Birchwood Dr DE56. **168** B4
Birchwood Gdns 6
  S20......**59** E8
Birchwood Gr S20...**59** E8
Birchwood La DE55. **159** C3
Birchwood Rd
Alfreton DE55......**159** C3
Eckington S21......**58** D4
Birchwood Rise 5
  S20......**59** E8
Birchwood View
Ashbourne DE6......**173** C3
Sheffield S20......**59** E8
Birchwood Way
16 Sheffield S20......**59** E8
Somercotes DE55... **159** C1
Bircumshaw's Rd
  DE75......**181** E2
Birdcage Wlk DE22 .**217** F6
Birdcroft La DE7... **208** F5
BIRDHOLME......**115** A7
Birdholme Cres
  S40......**115** A8
Birding St NG19... **136** B1
Birdsgrove La
Ashbourne DE6......**172** D3
Mayfield DE6......**172** D4
Bird St S43......**78** F2
Birdwood St DE23...**218** F1
Birkbeck Close DE3. **217** F3
Birkdale Ave DE14... **254** A6
Birkdale Cl
Derby DE3......**218** A2
Ilkeston DE7......**194** D1
Birkdale Dr S40......**114** D8
Birk Hill Inf Sch S21 .**59** B2
Birkin Ave S45......**115** C1
Birkin La
Grassmoor S42......**115** B2
Holmewood S42... **116** A3
Wingerworth S40,
  S42......**114** C1
Wingerworth S40,
  S42......**114** D2
Birkin Lane W S42...**115** C2
Birkinstyle Ave
  DE55......**146** E3
Birkinstyle La S45... **146** E3
Birkland Ave NG19. **136** D3
Birks Cl S80......**82** D6
Birks The S22......**25** C2
BIRLEY......**93** F7
Birley Acad The S12 .**44** D2
Birley Brook Dr S40. **95** B7
Birley Croft S41......**95** B7
BIRLEYHAY......**58** D5
Birley La
Bamford S32......**40** F2
Hathersage S32......**41** B3
Sheffield S12......**44** D2
Birley Moor Ave S12. **44** E3
Birley Moor Cl S12...**44** E3
Birley Moor Cres S12 **44** E2
Birley Moor Dr S12...**44** E2
Birley Moor Pl S12...**44** E2
Birley Moor Rd S12...**44** E4
Birley Moor Way S12 **44** E2
Birley Prim Acad
  S12......**44** D3
Birley Rd
Birley S18......**93** E6
Birley S18......**93** E7
Birley School Mews
  S13......**44** E5
Birley Spa Com Prim Sch
  S12......**44** E4
Birley Spa La S12......**44** F3
Birley St NG9......**223** D5
Birley Vale Ave S12.. **44** C5
Birley Vale Cl S12......**44** C4
Birley Wood Dr S12.. **44** F2
Birstall Cl S41......**95** C7
Biscay Ct DE21... **206** C2
Bishopdale Cl NG10. **236** A6
Bishopdale Dr S20...**59** A8
Bishopdale Rise S20. **59** A8
Bishop Lonsdale CE Prim
  Sch DE22......**218** E3
Bishop Lonsdale Way
  DE3......**217** F3
Bishop Purslove CE
  Pirmary Sch SK17...**69** C4
Bishops Cl DE5......**180** E8
Bishopscourt Rd S8 .**43** A5
Bishops Ct
Melbourne DE73......**252** B7
Sheffield S8......**43** B5
Bishop's Ct S73...**252** B7
Bishop's Dr DE21... **205** E2
Bishops Gate DE11. **256** E2
Bishop's Gn DE11... **218** F7
Bishop's House (Mus) ★
  S8......**43** A4
Bishop's La SK17...**84** E7
Bishop St
Alfreton DE55......**159** A5
Eastwood NG16... **182** F2
Bishopthorpe Gro
  DE22......**204** D7
Bispham Dr NG9... **223** F2
Bitham Ct DE13... **240** C1

Bitham La DE13.... **240** D1
Bittern View DE65.. **242** A5
Blaby Cl DE23......**231** E6
Blacka Moor Cres
  S17......**55** C6
Blacka Moor Rd S17..**55** C6
Blacka Moor View
  S17......**55** C6
Blackbanks
Chesterfield S44......**80** A1
Stanfree S44......**99** B8
Blackberry Cl S43...**80** D4
Blackberry Flats S20. **59** E7
Blackberry Rise
  DE56......**179** C1
Blackberry Way
5 Brimington S40...**96** E7
Kilburn DE56......**179** F2
Blackbird Row
  DE56......**179** C1
BLACKBROOK
Belper......**178** B4
Chapel-en-le-Frith ..**47** E6
Tutbury......**238** C1
Blackbrook La S43...**47** E6
Blackbrook Rd
  DE65......**240** E8
Blackburn Pl DE7... **194** E3
Blackcliff Field Cl
  S80......**82** A5
Blackdown Ave S40...**95** B5
Blackedge Cl SK17...**47** F2
BLACKFORDBY **257** C1
Blackfordby St
  Margaret's CE (Aided)
  Prim Sch DE11... **257** B1
Black Harry La S32...**71** E3
Black Hills Dr DE7... **208** F6
Black La SK17......**105** C2
Blackmore St DE23. **231** F7
Blackmount Ct 5
  DE24......**231** D3
Blackpit La DE6... **224** B8
Blackpool St DE14.. **254** C8
Black Rock ★ S18... **155** A4
Blackrocks Ave DE4 .**142** F7
Blackshale Road
  NG19......**136** B2
Blackshaw Clough
  SK13......**10** E3
Blackshaw Rd SK13...**10** E3
Blacksmith Croft
  DE5......**180** D8
Blacksmith La S44...**97** A3
Blacksmiths Cl
Glapwell S44......**118** C1
Netherseal DE12... **264** F7
Blacksmith's La
Egginton DE65......**241** B6
Newton Solney DE15. **248** E8
Woodville DE11... **256** F3
Blacksmiths Yd
Darley Dale DE4......**127** E2
Rolleston DE13... **240** B4
Blacksmith Way
  NG20......**119** F2
Blackstock Cl S14...**43** D2
Blackstock Cres S14..**43** D2
Blackstock Dr S14...**43** D2
Blackstock Rd S14...**43** D4
Blackstone Cl DE55. **170** D2
Blackstone Dr S81...**63** F4
Blackthorn Cl
4 Brailsford DE6......**201** E8
Chesterfield S41...**115** D8
Derby DE21......**205** D2
Melbourne DE73... **252** A8
Blackthorn Dr NG16 **182** E2
Blackthorne Cl
  DE56......**179** F2
Blackthorn Rd DE15 **254** E6
Black Tor Rd DE4... **154** D8
BLACKWALL......**175** F7
Blackwall La DE6... **176** A4
BLACKWELL
Sutton in Ashfield......**147** F1
Taddington......**87** D5
Blackwell Ave DE7.. **194** F5
Blackwell Com Prim Sch
  DE55......**147** F1
Blackwell Dale SK17. **87** E6
Blackwell La
Melbourne DE73......**252** A7
Monyash DE45......**107** A3
Blackwell Mill Cotts
  SK17......**87** A6
Blackwell Rd NG17. **148** C3
Bladon House Sch
  DE15......**248** B6
Bladon St DE15... **248** C4
Bladon View DE13.. **241** A2
Blagdon Cl DE4......**127** C3
Blagreaves Ave
  DE23......**231** C5
Blagreaves La DE23. **231** C6
Blair Gr NG10......**223** A4
Blair Ho DE23......**231** C5
Blakebrook Dr
  DE73......**233** A3
Blake St DE11......**236** B5
Blakelow La DE65... **229** B3
Blakelow Dr DE65... **229** B3
Blakelow La DE4... **142** A3
Blakemere La DE4... **141** F2
Blakemore Ave
  DE73......**252** B6

Blakeney Ct continued
3 Mansfield Woodhouse
NG19 . . . . .136 E4
Blake Rd NG9 . . . . 223 E6
Blake St
Ilkeston DE7 . . . . .194 F1
Mansfield Woodhouse
NG19 . . . . .136 B2
Blanch Croft DE73 . . 252 B7
Blandford Ave
NG10 . . . . 236 B6
Blandford Cl DE24 . . 233 D6
Blandford Dr S41 . . . .95 E7
Blankney Cl DE24 . . 231 D2
Blants Cl NG16 . . . . .195 F6
Blay Ct S43 . . . . .77 D4
Bleaklow Cl DE21 . . . .205 F3
Bleaklow Wlk 29 SK13 . .9 E1
Blencathra Dr DE3 . . 208 F1
Blenheim Ave DE55. 170 A8
Blenheim Cl
Burton upon Trent
DE15 . . . . 248 C3
4 Glossop SK13 . . . . . .10 A5
Mansfield NG19 . . . . 136 D1
3 Swadlincote DE11 . . 256 A7
Blenheim Ct DE56 . . 179 D5
Blenheim Dr DE22 . . 204 D4
Blenheim Ho **1**
DE14 . . . . .253 F7
Blenheim Mews
DE65 . . . . 229 C4
Blenheim Par DE22 . 204 D4
Blenheim Pl NG17 . . 148 E3
Blenheim Rd DE6 . . . 185 E7
Blenheim Ct **3**
NG10 . . . . 223 B4
Blenkinsop Cl DE11 . .256 F5
**Blessed Robert Sutton
Catholic Voluntary
Acad** DE15 . . . . 255 A7
Blind La
Bolsover S44 . . . . .98 F3
Breaston DE72 . . . . . 235 D8
Darley Dale DE4 . . . . .127 F1
Kirk Ireton DE6 . . . . . 165 A2
1 Wirksworth DE4 . . 165 F8
Blisworth Way DE55 .169 F8
Blithe Cl DE6 . . . . . . 228 E1
Blithfield Gdns
DE73 . . . . 233 A2
Bloomery Cl DE55 . . 158 E3
Bloomery Way S45 . . 131 E3
Bloomfield Cl
Derby DE1 . . . . 267 C1
Hilton DE65 . . . . 228 D2
Bloomfield Rd DE55 170 A8
Bloomfield St DE1 . . 267 D1
Bloomsgrove Rd
DE7 . . . . .194 F2
Bloom St DE1 . . . . . . 267 B2
Blore Cl DE6 . . . . . . 185 D8
Blossom Cres S12 . . . .44 B3
Blossom Wlk DE65. . 227 C1
Bluebank Lane S44. . .99 A5
Bluebank View S43 . . .77 D3
Blue Barn La NG20. . 101 C3
Bluebell Cl
4 Ashbourne DE6. . . 185 C8
Barlborough S43 . . . . .80 B6
Derby DE24 . . . . 231 D2
Donisthorpe DE12 . . .262 E1
Hayfield SK22. . . . . . . .25 C3
Shirebrook NG20 . . . . 119 D3
Somercotes DE55. . . . .159 E2
Underwood Green
NG16 . . . . .171 F2
Blue Bell Cl S43 . . . . . .97 B5
Bluebell Croft DE4. . 143 B3
Bluebell Dairy ★
DE21 . . . . 220 F7
Bluebell Grove
DE11 . . . . .256 F1
Bluebell Hill DE55 . . 146 C4
Bluebell Pl NG19 . . . 136 F4
Bluebell Way
Heanor DE75 . . . . . . .182 B1
Tutbury DE13 . . . . . . 239 D5
Bluebell Wlk S80 . . . .81 E2
Blueberry Cl S43 . . . . .97 B5
Blueberry Ct S42 . . . 116 C1
Blueberry Way
DE11 . . . . .256 F3
Bluebird Ct DE24 . . 231 D4
Blue Cedars Dr
DE15 . . . . 248 D2
Blue John Cavern ★
S33 . . . . .37 E3
Blue Lodge Cl S43 . . . .97 B5
Blue Mountains
DE56 . . . . 191 B1
Blue Ridge Cl S17 . . . .55 E7
Bluestone La DE15 . . 255 A7
Blundestone La
DE4 . . . . 156 A2
Blunt Ave S43 . . . . . .79 C4
Blunt St DE7 . . . . . . 193 A2
Blyth Cl
Chesterfield S40. . . . .114 B8
Mansfield NG19 . . . . 135 D1
Blyth Ct DE74 . . . . . 247 B4
Blythe Ct NG19 . . . . 135 D1
Blyth Gdns DE3 . . . . 217 B1
Blyth Pl DE21 . . . . . 205 D1
Boam La DE4 . . . . . . 142 F8
Boardman Ind Est
DE11 . . . . .255 E3
Boardman Rd DE11 . .255 E2

Boarfold La
Chisworth SK13 . . . . . .15 F5
Tideswell SK17 . . . . . . .69 F2
Boars Head Ind Est
DE1 . . . . 267 C4
Boarslack La
Litton SK17 . . . . .69 F2
Tideswell SK17 . . . . . . .69 E2
Boarstones La SK17. . .85 E8
Boat La NG16 . . . . . . 182 A7
Boatmans Cl DE7 . . . .194 F2
Bobbin Mill SK17 . . . .89 A6
Bobbinmill Hill
DE56 . . . . 168 B7
Bobbin Mill La S40 . . .95 D2
Bobbins La DE21. . . . 220 F2
Bob Southern Grove
DE11 . . . . .256 B1
Bochum Parkway S8 .57 C8
Bocking La S8. . . . . . .56 E8
Bocking Rise S8. . . . . .56 E8
Bodell Cl **2** DE11 . . .255 E6
Boden Cl DE4 . . . . . . 142 E8
Boden St DE23 . . . . . 219 B2
Bodmin Cl DE24 . . . . 231 D3
Bodmin Way **3** S40 . .95 C5
Boggard La S43 . . . . . .11 D4
Bogguard Rd SK6. . . . .24 A4
Boggy La
Bradwell S33 . . . . .51 B6
Church Broughton, Heathtop
DE65 . . . . 227 A6
Bog La DE73 . . . . 251 E5
Bohem Rd NG10 . . . . 223 C3
Boiley La S21. . . . . . . .60 C4
Boland Rd S8 . . . . .56 D5
Bolden Terr DE55. . . . 147 C1
Bold La DE1 . . . . 267 B3
BOLEHILL
Calow 97 B1
Sheffield. 43 A2
Wirksworth 155 A2
BOLE HILL
Ashover S42 . . . . 130 D8
Barlow S18. . . . . .75 C2
Bole Hill
Bakewell DE45 . . . . . . 109 A4
Sheffield S8 . . . . .43 A2
Bole Hill Cotts S44 . . .97 A1
Bolehill Croft DE4. . . 155 A3
Bolehill Ct **3** S40 . . . .95 D5
Bolehill La
Eckington S21. . . . . . . .58 F2
Northedge S42. . . . . . 130 C7
Northedge S45. . . . . . 130 C7
Wingerworth S42. . . . 114 D1
Bolehill Rd DE4. . . . . 155 A3
BOLSOVER 99 B3
Bolsover Bsns Pk
S44. . . . . .98 E2
Bolsover Castle ★
S44. . . . . .99 A2
Bolsover CE Jun Sch
S44. . . . . .99 B2
Bolsover Cl DE5 . . . . 169 E1
Bolsover Hill S44 . . . . .99 A3
Bolsover Hospl S44 . . .99 C2
Bolsover Inf Sch S44 .99 B2
Bolsover Rd
Derby DE3 . . . . 230 E5
Glapwell S44 . . . . 118 C1
Mastin Moor S43 . . . . .79 D2
Shuttlewood S43 . . . . . .98 F6
Bolsover Sch The
S44. . . . . .99 C1
Bolton St DE55 . . . . . 169 D7
Bolton Way
1 Derby DE23. . . . . 230 F5
Derby DE23. . . . . 231 A5
Boman's La DE4. . . . . 177 F8
Bonchurch Cl DE24 . 233 C5
Bond Cl NG19 . . . . . . 136 C7
Bonden SK23. . . . . . . .35 E1
Bondfield Rd S43. . . . .97 C7
Bondgate DE74. . . . . 247 B3
Bondhay La S80 . . . . . .62 C2
Bond La DE56 . . . . . . 168 E2
Bonds Cl DE7. . . . . . . .194 F5
Bond St S43 . . . . .97 B8
Bonington Rise SK6 . .23 B8
Bonner's La NG16 . . . 195 C4
Bonnie Cl DE3. . . . . . 217 D6
Bonnington Dr
DE55. . . . . 170 D8
Bonnyrigg Dr DE21 . 206 A2
BONSALL 142 E1
Bonsall Ave DE23 . . . 231 D8
Bonsall Bank SK13 . . . .9 E2
**Bonsall CE (Aided) Prim
Sch** DE4 . . . . .142 E1
Bonsall Cl SK13. . . . . . .9 E2
Bonsall Ct
2 Chesterfield S41. . . .95 D7
Long Eaton NG10 . . . 236 F8
BONSALL DALE 142 D1
Bonsall Dr
Derby DE3 . . . . .217 E3
Somercotes DE55. . . . 170 D8
Bonsall Fold SK13 . . . . .9 E2
Bonsall La
Alfreton DE55. . . . . . .158 F4
Winster DE4 . . . . 141 C4
Bonsallmoor La
DE4. . . . . 141 E3
Bonsall St NG10 . . . . 236 E8
Bonser Cres NG17 . . 148 E2

Bonser Hedge Ct
NG10 . . . . 236 B4
Booker Cl S43. . . . . . . .97 C6
Booth Ave NG19 . . . . 135 A5
Boothbright Cres
NG19 . . . . 135 D2
Boothby Ave **1**
DE6. . . . . 173 C2
Booth Cres NG19 . . . 135 D2
Booth Dr DE6. . . . . . . 185 C8
BOOTHGATE 179 E7
Boothgate DE56 . . . . 179 E7
Boot Hill DE65. . . . . . 242 C3
BOOTHORPE 262 F8
Boothorpe La DE11 . .262 F8
Booth's St **1** SK13 . . .10 D1
Booth St
Derby DE24 . . . . .232 F7
Hollingworth SK14 . . . . .9 C5
Mansfield Woodhouse
NG19 . . . . 136 B3
Ripley DE5 . . . . .169 E2
Booth Trad Est NE7 . .194 F2
Booton Field Cres **2**
DE73 . . . . 233 A3
Boots Yd NG17 . . . . . 148 F3
Borage Gro **1** DE3 . 217 C4
Border Cl S43 . . . . . . .80 F7
Border Cres DE24. . . 233 B5
Border La S80 . . . . . . .80 F2
Border Rd NG20 . . . . 120 A4
Borlace Cres NG9 . . . 223 E6
Borough St DE74 . . . 247 B3
BORROWASH 221 C2
Borrowash By-pass
DE72. . . . . 221 C3
Borrowash Rd
4 Borrowash DE72. . . 221 A1
Derby DE21 . . . . 220 F4
Borrowdale Ave **3**
S20. . . . . .59 E6
Borrowdale Cl **2**
S20. . . . . .59 E6
Borrowdale Dr
Long Eaton NG10 . . . 236 A6
Sheffield S20 . . . . .59 E6
Borrowdale Rd S20. . .59 E6
Borrowfield Rd
DE21. . . . . 220 F3
Borrowfields DE72. . . 221 B1
Borrowwash Rd
DE72. . . . . 234 A7
Borrow Wood Prim Sch
DE21. . . . . 220 F3
Boscastle Rd DE24. . 233 B6
Boscawen Ct NE7. . . .194 F4
Boscowan Ct DE7. . . .194 F4
Bosley Mews DE56 . . .178 F5
Bostock Rd SK14 . . . . .16 A8
Bostocks La
NG10 . . . . 223 A4
Bostock's La
Long Eaton NG10 . . . 223 A3
Risley NG10, DE72 . . . 222 F4
Boston Cl DE21 . . . . . 220 C6
Boswell Ct **3** DE6 . . 173 B2
Boswell Sq DE23. . . . 231 F7
Bosworth Ave DE23 . 231 E6
Bosworth Rd DE74 . . 246 F3
Bosworth Way
NG10 . . . . 236 E5
Botany Bsns Pk SK23 .45 D6
Botany Mews SK23 . . .45 E6
Bothe Cl NG10. . . . . . 236 C6
Bottlebrook Houses
DE5. . . . . 180 B1
Bottles Farm Cl
DE5. . . . . 180 A1
Bottomhill Rd
Tideswell SK17. . . . . . .69 E1
Upperdale SK17. . . . . . .89 C4
Bottom Lons DE56 . . 176 B8
Bottom of Moor
SK17. . . . . 121 A3
Bottom Rd S42 . . . . . 114 E1
Bottom Row NG19 . . 135 E7
Bottom Row Main Rd
S42. . . . . .93 F2
Boughton Dr DE55 . .169 F8
Boughton La S43. . . . .80 D4
Boulevard The SK14 . .9 D6
BOULTON 233 B6
Boulton Cl S40 . . . . . . .95 A5
Boulton Dr DE24. . . . 233 A6
Boulton La
Derby DE24 . . . . 233 A6
Derby, Allenton DE24 . .232 F5
BOUNDARY 257 C2
Boundary Cl
Shirebrook NG20 . . . . 119 E6
Staveley S43. . . . . .79 A3
Boundary Gdns
DE55. . . . . .147 F5
Boundary La NG16. . 182 C3
Boundary Rd
Derby DE22 . . . . 218 A2
Eggington DE65 . . . . 241 D8
Boundary Wlk NG20 .100 F1
Bournebrook Ave
DE4. . . . . 165 F7
Bourne Cl
Brimington S43. . . . . . .96 C8
Tutbury DE13 . . . . . . 239 D6
Bourne Dr NG16 . . . . 182 B3
Bourne Mill Cl S43 . . .80 B6
Bourne Pl DE55 . . . . 180 A1
Bourne Sq DE72 . . . . 235 E7
Bourne St DE1 . . . . . 267 B2

Bourne Way DE11. . . 256 D1
Bowbank Cl DE23. . . . 231 A6
Bowbridge Ave
DE23. . . . . 231 C5
Bowden Cl SK22 . . . . .25 C3
Bowden Cres SK22 . . .33 D8
Bowden Ct S43 . . . . . .80 F7
BOWDEN HEAD 35 D1
Bowden Hey Rd
SK23. . . . . .47 C7
Bowden La
Chapel-en-le-Frith
SK23. . . . . .47 C7
Chapel-en-le-Frith
SK23. . . . . .47 D8
Hope S33 . . . . .39 A4
Bowden Rd SK13 . . . . .10 C3
Bowdon Ave S43 . . . . .80 A6
Bower Close DE6 . . . 185 B8
Bower Dr DE4 . . . . . . 156 F1
Bower Farm Rd S41 . .77 B2
Bower St DE24 . . . . . .232 F8
Bowes Rd DE24 . . . . 233 D4
Boweswell Rd DE7. . . 194 E2
Bowland Cl DE3 . . . . 217 E1
Bowland Dr S40 . . . . 114 B7
Bowland Rd SK13. . . . .17 A8
Bowlees Ct DE23 . . . . 230 E7
Bowler Dr DE56 . . . . .192 A7
Bowler La
Darley Dale DE4 . . . . .143 B8
Farley DE4 . . . . 128 A1
Matlock DE4 . . . . .143 B8
Bowler Rd DE4 . . . . . 127 C3
Bowler St DE5. . . . . . 180 D7
Bowling Al DE6 . . . . . 211 E7
Bowling Alley DE56. . 168 E1
Bowlingalley La
DE6 . . . . .197 D8
Bowling Alley La
DE6 . . . . 212 A5
Bowling Cl DE7 . . . . . 222 E8
Bowling Gn DE4 . . . . 153 A1
Bowling Green La
Chapel-en-le-Frith
SK23. . . . . .47 B6
Wirksworth DE4. . . . . 154 E1
Wirksworth DE4. . . . . 165 E8
Bowling Green Rd **2**
ST14. . . . . 210 B1
Bowman Cl S12 . . . . . .43 F7
Bowmer La DE56 . . . 168 B6
Bowmer Rd DE24 . . . 219 E1
Bown Cl DE56 . . . . . . 192 A8
Bowness Cl
Chesterfield S41. . . . . . .95 D7
Dronfield S18 . . . . .56 E1
Bowness Rd S41 . . . . .95 D7
Bowns Hill DE4 . . . . . 157 A1
Bowns Yd DE55. . . . . 170 D8
BOWSHAW 56 F4
Bowshaw S18 . . . . . . .56 F4
Bowshaw Ave S8 . . . . .57 A5
Bowshaw Cl S8 . . . . . .57 A5
Bowshaw View S8. . . .57 A5
Bow St NG19 . . . . 136 E4
Bowstonegate Rd
SK12. . . . . .32 E1
Box Cl DE11 . . . . 256 E3
Box La
Ticknall DE7 . . . . .257 F7
Ticknall DE73 . . . . . . 251 A1
Ticknall DE73 . . . . . . 258 A8
Boxmoor Cl DE23 . . . 230 F7
Boyd Gr DE73. . . . . . . 245 A8
Boyer St DE22 . . . . . . 267 A1
Boyer Wlk DE22 . . . . 267 A1
BOYLESTONE 213 C4
Boylestone Rd
Alkmonton DE6. . . . . .213 E7
Derby DE23 . . . . 231 C5
BOYLESTONFIELD . . 213 E5
BOYTHORPE 95 E1
Boythorpe Ave S40 . 266 A2
Boythorpe Bsns Units
S40. . . . . 266 A2
Boythorpe Cl DE7. . . .194 F5
Boythorpe Cres S40 266 A1
Boythorpe Mount
S40. . . . . 266 A2
Boythorpe Rd S40 . . 266 A2
Boythorpe Rise S40. . .95 E2
Brabyns Brow SK6. . . .23 A7
Brabyns Prep Sch
SK6. . . . . .23 A7
Brace Gdns **2** DE6 . 211 A1
Bracken Ave S44 . . . . 116 F1
Bracken Cl
Hollingworth SK14 . . . . .9 D6
Long Eaton NG10 . . . 223 B1
Marple SK6 . . . . .23 C7
Brackendale Ave
S45. . . . . 131 E2
Brackendale Cl S43. . .96 D7
Brackendale La
DE6 . . . . 163 C5
Brackendale Rd
DE55. . . . . 169 E6
BRACKENFIELD 145 D2
Brackenfield Ave
NG19 . . . . 136 E4
Brackenfield Close
S42. . . . . 115 F2
Brackenfield Dr
NG16 . . . . 195 B7
Brackenfield Gr S12 . .44 D3
Brackenfield La
Brackenfield DE55 . . . 145 D1

Brackenfield La continued
Wessington DE55. . . . .157 D8
Brackenfield Specl Sch
NG10 . . . . 223 B1
Brackenfield View
DE55. . . . . 145 D2
Brackenhill Cl **8**
DE23. . . . . 230 F6
Bracken La DE4 . . . . 156 B5
Bracken Rd
Long Eaton NG10 . . . 223 B1
Shirebrook NG20 . . . . 119 D3
Brackens Ave DE24 . 232 F5
Brackensdale Ave
DE22. . . . . 218 B5
Brackensdale Jun Sch
DE22. . . . . 218 B5
Brackens La S43. . . . . .80 B6
Bracken's La DE24. . .232 F6
Bracken Way SK13. . . .17 C7
Brackenwood Rd
DE15. . . . . 254 E6
Brackley DE56. . . . . . .179 F2
Brackley Dr DE21 . . . 220 B5
Brackley Gate DE7. . 192 A4
Brackmills **7**
NG19 . . . . 136 E1
Bracknell Dr DE24 . .232 F5
BRADBOURNE 163 C6
Bradbourne Cl S43 . . .97 C8
Bradbourne Ct
DE22. . . . . 218 E2
Bradbourne La DE6 . 152 E1
Bradbourne Rd
Bradbourne DE6 . . . . 163 A7
Fenny Bentley DE6 . . .162 E1
Fenny Bentley DE6 . . .173 B8
Parwich DE6. . . . . . . .162 F8
Bradbury Cl
Borrowash DE72 . . . . 221 C1
Chesterfield S40. . . . . . .95 E3
Bradbury Dr S42. . . . 114 E4
Bradbury Pl S40. . . . . .95 E3
Bradbury St S43 . . . . .43 A6
Braddon Ave NG9. . . 209 E1
Bradford Cl S81 . . . . . .63 F8
Bradford Rd DE45 . . 125 C5
Bradgate Cl NG10. . . 223 B4
Bradgate Croft S41 . 115 C7
Bradgate Ct DE23. . . 231 E6
Bradgate Dr
Ripley DE5 . . . . .169 B1
Ripley DE5 . . . . 180 B8
Bradgate Pk View **10**
DE73. . . . . 244 F8
Brading Cl DE24 . . . . 233 D5
BRADLEY 186 F6
Bradley CE Prim Sch
DE6. . . . . 186 F6
Bradley Cl
Birchover DE4 . . . . . . 126 B1
6 Brimington S43. . . . .96 E8
Bradley Corner
Bradley DE6 . . . . .174 F2
Bradley DE6 . . . . 175 A2
Bradley Dr DE56 . . . . 179 B4
Bradley La
Barlow S18. . . . . .75 C4
Pilsley DE45 . . . . .91 B3
Bradley St
Burton upon Trent
DE15. . . . . 254 E7
Derby DE22 . . . . 218 A2
Sandiacre NG10 . . . . 223 C5
Bradley View **5**
DE6. . . . . 173 D2
Bradley Way S43 . . . . .96 E7
Bradmoor Gr DE73 . . 233 B2
Bradshaw Ave DE55 170 E6
Bradshaw Cres SK6 . .23 A7
Bradshaw Croft
DE56 . . . . .178 E6
Bradshaw Dr DE56 . . 191 C6
Bradshaw La
Old Brampton S42 . . . .93 E2
Stoney Middleton S32. . .70 E8
Tunstead Milton SK23. . .46 D5
Bradshaw Mdw
DE65. . . . . 227 C1
Bradshaw Rd
Marple SK6 . . . . .23 A7
Staveley S43. . . . . .97 B6
Bradshaw St NG10 . 236 B5
Bradshaw Way DE1 . 267 C2
Bradshaw Way Ret Pk
DE1. . . . . 267 B2
BRADWAY 56 C5
BRADWAY BANK 56 A6
Bradway Dr S17 . . . . . .56 B5
Bradway Dr S17 . . . . . .56 B5
Bradway Grange Rd
S17. . . . . .56 C5
Bradway Prim Sch
S17. . . . . .56 B5
Bradway Rd
Sheffield, Bradway
S17. . . . . .56 B5
Sheffield, Lower Bradway
S17. . . . . .56 C6
BRADWELL 51 B7
Bradwell CE Inf Sch
S33. . . . . .51 B7
Bradwell Cl
Derby DE3 . . . . .217 E1
Dronfield S18 . . . . .56 C1
Eastwood NG16. . . . . 195 C8
Bradwell Fold **10** SK13 . .9 E1

Bradwell Gr S45 . . . . 131 D2
Bradwell Head Rd
S33. . . . . .51 A8
BRADWELL HILLS 51 B6
Bradwell Jun Sch
S33. . . . . .51 A7
Bradwell Lea **12** SK13 . .9 E1
Bradwell Pl S43 . . . . . .97 C7
Bradwell St **1** S2 . . . .43 B6
Bradwell Terr **11** SK13 . .9 E1
Bradwell Way DE56 . .179 B5
Braeburn Ct DE23 . . 218 E2
Braefield Cl DE7. . . . 208 C5
Braemar Ave NG16 . .182 F1
Braemar Cl
Chesterfield S43. . . . . . .77 D4
11 Derby DE24. . . . . 231 D3
Brafield Cl DE56 . . . . 179 D4
Braidwood Way
Chesterfield S40. . . . . . .96 A1
Chesterfield S41. . . . . 266 E1
BRAILSFORD 201 F7
Brailsford Ave
4 Gamesley SK13. . . . . .9 E2
1 Swadlincote DE11 . 255 E5
Brailsford CE Prim Sch
DE6. . . . . 201 E7
Brailsford Cl **7** SK13 . .9 E2
Brailsford Gdns **8**
SK13. . . . . .9 E2
Brailsford Gn **5** SK13 . .9 E2
Brailsford Mews **6**
SK13. . . . . .9 E2
Brailsford Rd DE21 . .219 F8
Braintree Cl DE21. . . 205 D2
Braithwell Cl DE22. . 204 F2
Bramah Edge Ct SK13 . .9 F7
Bramall La S2 . . . . . . .43 A8
Bramall La S2 . . . . . . .43 A8
Bramble Bank SK13. . .17 E8
Brambleberry Ct
DE21. . . . . 206 B3
Bramble Cl
Holmewood S44. . . . . 116 F1
Long Eaton NG10 . . . 223 B2
Shirebrook NG20 . . . . 119 E6
South Normanton
DE55. . . . . 160 B6
Bramble Ct
Burton upon Trent
DE15. . . . . 254 E6
4 Nottingham NG10 . 223 C6
Bramble Dr DE22 . . . 218 C4
Bramblehedge Dr
DE23. . . . . 231 E5
Bramble Mews **2**
DE3. . . . . 217 D1
Bramble St DE1 . . . . 267 A3
Brambles The DE11. . 257 B1
Bramble Way
Denby Bottles DE56 . . 180 A2
Kilburn DE56. . . . . . . 179 F4
South Normanton
DE55. . . . . 159 F3
Bramblewick Dr
DE23. . . . . 231 A6
Bramble Wlk DE12. . 262 A3
Bramblewood **5**
DE11. . . . . .255 F6
Brambling Cres
DE3. . . . . 230 B6
Brambling Ct S41. . . . .96 C2
Brambly Cl DE12. . . . 265 E8
Bramell Cl DE14 . . . . .253 F7
Bramfield Ave DE22 . 218 E3
Bramfield Ct DE22 . . 218 E4
Bramham Rd SK6. . . . .23 A4
BRAMLEY 58 F3
Bramley Cl
Derby DE21 . . . . 206 C3
Sheffield S20 . . . . .59 C7
Staveley S43. . . . . .97 B5
Bramley Ct
Hatton DE65 . . . . 227 C1
Kimberley NG16 . . . . .195 F6
Bramley Dale DE11. . 255 F2
Bramley Hall Rd S13. .44 F8
Bramley La
Baslow DE45 . . . . .91 C7
Sheffield S13 . . . . .44 F8
Bramley Mews S21 . . .59 D3
Bramleymoor La S21. .58 E1
Bramley New Pk S21 . .58 F3
Bramley Park S13 . . . .44 F8
Bramley Pk S21 . . . . . .58 F3
Bramley Pk Rd S13 . . .44 F8
Bramley Rd
Bramley-Vale S44. . . . .117 E1
Eckington S21. . . . . . . .58 E1
4 Nottingham NG10 . 236 B5
BRAMLEY-VALE 117 E1
Bramley Vale Prim Sch
S44. . . . . .117 E1
Bramley View S21 . . . .58 F3
Bramlyn Cl S43. . . . . .80 D5
Bramlyn Ct S43. . . . . .80 D5
BRAMPTON 95 E2
Brampton Ave DE75 182 A2
Brampton Cl
Derby DE3 . . . . .217 C3
Ilkeston DE7. . . . . . . .194 F4
Brampton Ct
Belper DE56 . . . . 179 D4

Brampton Ct continued
Chesterfield S40........95 C2
Brampton Dr NG9 ....223 F5
Brampton House Mews
S40...................95 D3
Brampton Prim Sch
S40...................95 E3
Bramshill Rise S40 ....95 D1
Branch La S45.......132 F5
Brancliffe La S81......63 F8
Brandelhow Ct
DE21..............206 C3
Brandene Cl S44.......97 A3
Brandreth Dr NG16..195 A8
Brands Cl DE7......194 F5
Brandside Ave SK17..85 E1
Branklene Cl NG16..195 E7
Branksome Ave
DE24...............233 C7
Branksome Chine Ave
S41.................115 C8
Bransdale Ave
NG19..............136 E1
Bransdale Cl NG10...236 B6
BRANSTON..........253 F7
Branston Greens
DE16...............254 C7
Branston Rd
Branston DE14.....253 D7
Burton upon Trent
DE14................254 C8
Tatenhill DE13, DE14 .253 C8
Branton Cl S40.......266 A1
BRASSINGTON.......153 A1
Brassington Cl
Eastwood NG16.....195 B7
West Hallam DE7 ....207 E8
Youlgreave DE45 ....125 C5
Brassington Cres
SK13....................9 D1
Brassington Ct 4
NG19..............136 E4
Brassington La
Bradbourne DE4......163 D7
Brassington DE6......152 E1
Clay Cross S42, S45..131 C6
Wirksworth DE4.......154 D1
Brassington Prim Sch
DE4.................153 A1
Brassington Rd
DE21................205 F1
Brassington St S45...131 D4
Braybrook Cl DE55..169 F8
Brayfield Ave DE23..231 D8
Brayfield Rd DE23...231 C8
Breach La
Barrow upon Trent
DE73...............244 E1
Hatton DE65........227 D3
Scropton DE6.......226 C5
Breach Rd
Denby DE5..........181 A4
Heanor DE75........194 A8
BREADSALL.........205 E4
Breadsall CE Prim Sch
DE21................205 E4
Breadsall Cl DE11....256 A2
Breadsall Ct DE7....194 F3
BREADSALL
HILLTOP...........205 D2
Breadsall Hill Top Prim
Sch DE21...........205 E1
Breadsall Rly Cutting
Nature Reserve★
DE7.................206 C3
Breamfield La
Washgreen DE4.......155 C1
Wirksworth DE4.......166 B8
Brearley Ave S43.....77 B3
Brearley Ct S41.......77 B3
Brearley Hall S41....77 C4
Brearley St S41.......77 C3
Brearley Wetland Nature
Reserve★.............77 C2
BREASTON.........235 D7
Breaston Ind Est
DE72................235 C7
Breaston La DE72....222 D3
Brechin Ct NG19.....136 B6
Breckbank NG19......136 E1
BRECK END...........35 C1
Breck La S21, S43....78 C6
Breckland Rd S40,
S42.................114 B8
Brecknock Dr NG10..236 A7
Brecon Cl
Chesterfield S40......95 C5
Derby DE21.........220 E6
6 Long Eaton NG10..236 A8
Bredon Cl 7 DE11....256 A8
Breedon Ave DE23..231 D5
Breedon Hill Rd
DE23................218 F3
BREEDON ON THE
HILL...............252 F2
Breedon St NG10...223 C2
Brenden Ave DE55...170 C2
Brenden Ct DE55....170 C8
Brenden Ave S40.....95 C4
Brendon Cl SK13.......17 A8
Brendon Ct 3 S40....95 C4
Brendon Dr NG16....195 F7
Brendon Way NG10..223 A1
Brent Cl
Chesterfield S40......95 D5

Brent Cl continued
5 Derby DE22........218 A5
Brentford Dr DE22...218 B6
Brentnall Cl NG10....236 B7
Brentwood Ave S33...40 B3
Brentwood Rd S33....40 B3
Bren Way DE65.......228 E2
BRETBY............249 A3
Bretby Bsns Pk
DE15................255 F8
Bretby Fairways
DE15................248 F2
Bretby Heights
DE11................255 F7
Bretby Hollow DE11.255 F7
Bretby Hts DE11.....256 A8
Bretby La
Bretby DE15........248 E3
Burton upon Trent
DE15................248 D2
Burton upon Trent
DE15................248 F6
Newton Solney DE15 .249 A6
Bretby Rd
Chesterfield S40......95 A6
Swadlincote DE11....255 F7
Bretby Sq DE23.....231 C5
Bretby Stoneware Ind
Est DE11............255 E8
Bretby View DE11....257 A4
Bretlands Way
DE15................255 A6
BRETTON.............71 A8
Bretton Ave
Bolsover S44.........99 C2
Derby DE23.........218 A4
Bretton Cl S40........95 A5
Bretton Gr S12........44 D3
Bretton Rd DE56....179 E5
Brewery St
Chesterfield S41.....266 C3
Kimberley NG16.....195 F6
Brewster Cl DE55....169 E7
Breydon Cl DE24....232 D4
Breydon Ind Ctr
NG10...............236 F7
Brian Clough Way
Derby DE21.........220 C4
Risley DE72..........222 C3
Stapleford NG9.......223 D5
Briar Ave NG10......223 C1
Briar Briggs Rd S44...98 F3
Briar Cl
Alfreton DE55.......159 C3
Borrowash DE72....221 C2
6 Buxton SK17.......85 C8
Chesterfield S41......95 E5
Derby DE21.........220 B5
Shirebrook NG20....119 E2
Swadlincote DE11....255 F5
Briardene Cl S40.....94 F5
Briarfield Ave S12....44 A3
Briarfield Cres S12 ...44 A2
Briarfield Rd S12.....44 A3
Briar Gate NG10.....223 B1
Briargrove Rd SK22...24 C4
Briar Lea Cl DE24....231 F4
Briar Rd NG16......195 B8
Briars Cl S21..........60 D5
Briarsgate DE22.....204 D2
Briar's La DE4........168 A7
Briars Way DE5.....180 D8
Briarthorn Cl SK6.....23 A3
Briar View S43........96 E7
Briarwood Cres SK6...23 A3
Briarwood Way
DE23................231 C6
Brickbridge Rd SK6...23 A3
Brickbridge Rd South
SK6..................23 A5
Brickfields Cl DE4 ...155 A4
Brickfield St SK13.....10 B5
Brickhouse La S17....55 C8
BRICK HOUSES......55 D8
Brickhouse Yd S40...95 E3
Brick St DE1.........218 E6
Brick Works Dr DE5 .180 F7
Brickyard Cotts
DE6.................185 D8
Brickyard La
Cuckney NG20.......101 F5
Kilburn DE56........179 F2
Ripley DE5...........169 F1
South Normanton
DE55...............160 A6
Brickyard Rd DE56...168 C5
Brickyard The DE7...193 B1
Bricky Cl S43.........80 D5
Bridge Bank Cl 6
S40...................95 D6
Bridge Cl
Swadlincote DE11 ...256 C2
Whitwell S80.........82 A5
Bridge End Ave
NG16................171 F8
Bridge Farm 3
DE13................240 E1
BRIDGEFIELD.......17 B7

Bridgefield 4 SK13...17 B8
Bridge Field DE72...235 C7
Bridgefield Ct
11 Belper DE56.....178 F4
Dove Holes SK17.....47 E1
Bridge Foot DE56...178 F5
Bridge Gate DE1....267 B4
Bridge Hill DE56....178 E5
Bridgeholme SK23...47 A8
BRIDGEHOLM
GREEN.............47 A8
Bridgeholm Mill
SK23.................47 A8
BRIDGEMONT.......33 E1
Bridgemont SK23....33 E1
Bridgend Cl NG9....223 D5
Bridgend Ct DE21...206 C2
Bridgeness Rd DE23.230 F6
Bridgeport Rd DE21 220 C6
Bridge St Ind Est
S45.................131 C4
Bridgeside DE13.....240 E1
Bridgeside Way
DE21................220 D3
Bridge St
Bakewell DE45.......109 D6
Belper DE56........178 F4
Bradwell S33.........51 A7
Burton upon Trent, Stretton
DE13................240 E1
Buxton SK17.........85 C8
Chesterfield S40....266 B1
Clay Cross S45......131 C3
Derby DE1..........267 A4
Ilkeston DE7........194 F4
Killamarsh S21.......60 D6
Langley Mill NG16...182 C3
Linton DE11.........261 E8
New Mills SK22.......24 C1
Pilsley S45..........132 C2
Sandiacre NG10.....223 C5
Swadlincote DE11....256 C2
Tupton S42..........115 D1
Tutbury DE13........239 C7
Whaley Bridge SK23...45 E7
Bridge The DE56....191 A7
Bridge View
Belper DE56........191 A7
Mayfield DE6........184 D8
Bridgewater St S42..115 C1
Bridgeway SK23......47 B4
Bridge Way S41......76 D3
Bridge Yd Ave S45...169 E4
Bridgford Ave DE14..253 F7
Bridgnorth Way
NG9.................223 E3
Bridgwater Cl DE24..232 F7
Bridle Cl DE73.......233 A1
Bridlegate La
Derby DE24.........233 D7
Elvaston DE24.......233 E6
Bridle La
Ripley, Greenwich
DE5.................169 C5
Ripley, Lower Hartshay DE5,
DE56................169 A2
Somercotes DE55....170 D7
Swadlincote DE15....255 A5
Bridle Rd
Bolsover S44.........80 B1
Staveley S43.........79 B2
Bridle Stile S20......59 C7
Bridle Stile Cl S20....59 C7
Bridle Stile Gdns S20 59 D7
Bridleway The
NG19...............136 F1
Brierfield Way DE3 .230 B8
Brierley Cl S43........78 E1
BRIERLEY GREEN...34 B2
Brierley Pk SK23......34 B1
Brierley Rd
Ripley DE5..........181 A8
Stonebroom DE55...146 F3
Unstone Green S18...76 S6
Brierlow Bar
Chelmorton SK17....105 B8
Sterndale Moor SK17 .105 E5
Brierlow Bar
Brierlow Bar SK17 ...105 A8
Harpur Hill SK17.....85 F1
Brigden Ave DE24...232 E7
Brigg Inf Sch The
DE55...............160 B6
Brighstone Cl
DE24................233 C5
BRIGHTGATE.......127 A5
Brightman Ho DE11 256 B5
Bright Mdw S20.....60 A5
Brighton Rd DE24...232 F8
Bright Sq NG19......135 D2
Bright St
Derby DE22.........218 D5
Ilkeston DE7........194 E3
Kimberley NG16.....195 E6
North Wingfield S42 .131 F5
South Normanton
DE55...............159 F5
Brightwater Cl
DE24................232 E3
Brigmor Wlk DE22...218 F5
BRIMINGTON........96 F7
Brimington Cl NE7..194 F6
BRIMINGTON
COMMON..........96 F5
Brimington Ct 6
NG19...............136 E4

Brimington Jun Sch
S43.................96 D8
Brimington Manor Inf
Sch S43.............96 F5
Brimington Rd S41...96 B5
Brimington Road N
S41.................96 B8
Brimmesfield Cl S2...43 F7
Brimmesfield Dr S2 .43 E8
Brimmesfield Rd S2 .43 E7
Brincliffe Cl S40......95 B1
Brindle Way DE23...231 A5
Brindley Cl
Derby DE72........245 B8
Sheffield S8.........43 A4
Brindley Cres S8......43 A4
Brindley Ct S17......60 C6
Brindley Ho
Chesterfield S41......96 B6
Long Eaton NG10....223 B3
Brindley Rd 6 S41 ..96 A6
Brindley Way S43....78 F2
Brindley Wlk DE24...231 E2
BRINDWOODGATE...75 D5
Brinkburn Cl S17.....55 F6
Brinkburn Ct S17.....55 F6
Brinkburn Dr S17.....55 F6
Brinkburn Vale Rd
S17..................55 F6
Brinks Road S33......39 A7
BRINSLEY..........182 E7
Brinsley Headstocks
Nature Reserve★
NG16................182 F6
Brinsley Hill NG16...171 C2
Brinsley Prim Sch
NG16................182 E8
Brisbane Cl NG19....136 C6
Brisbane Dr NG9....209 F1
Brisbane Rd DE3....217 F3
Briset Cl DE24.......231 E2
Bristol Cl DE11......255 F1
Bristol Dr DE3.......217 E2
Bristol Rd DE7......194 E1
Britannia Ave DE5 ..181 A7
Britannia Ct DE1.....267 B4
Britannia Dr DE13...240 D1
Britannia Mills Trading
Est SK23.............33 F1
Britannia Rd
Chesterfield S40.....115 B7
Long Eaton NG10....223 D1
Britannia Trad Est
SK23.................33 F1
Britland Edge Ave
DE21................205 F3
Briton Lodge Cl
DE12................262 F4
Brittain Dr DE5......170 A1
Brittain Pit DE5......170 B4
Brittain Pit Farm★
DE5.................170 A4
Brixham Ct 8 S41...95 D7
Brizlincote La DE15..248 D1
Broadacre Way 3
DE55................148 B7
Broad Bank DE22...218 E8
BROADBOTTOM.....16 A8
Broadbottom Prim Sch
SK14.................15 E8
Broadbottom Rd SK14 .9 A3
Broadbottom Sta
SK14.................16 A8
Broadfield Rd S2.....43 A7
Broadfields DE7......218 F8
Broadgorse Cl S40...95 B1
Broadhey View SK22..24 B1
BROADHOLM........179 A7
Broadholme La
DE56................179 A8
Broad La
Brinsley NG16......182 E8
Creswell S80.........82 D6
Elvaston DE72.......233 F4
Broadlands
Etwall DE65.........229 B5
Sandiacre NG10.....223 B3
South Normanton
DE55................160 A4
Broadleaf Cl DE21..205 E2
Broadley Rd S13......44 C7
Broadleys S45.......131 C3
Broadmeadow DE7...194 E3
Broad Oak Cl DE55..169 E7
Broad Oak Dr
Brinsley NG16......182 E8
New Brinsley NG16..171 D1
Stapleford NG9......223 D6
Broadoaks Cl S41...266 C3
Broad Pavement
S40.................266 B3
Broad Pl S80.........82 C6
Broad Rushes DE74 247 B6
Broad St NG10......236 D7
Broadstairs Rd 5
NG9.................223 F2
Broadstone Cl DE21 206 A1
Broadstone La
DE73................251 D4
Broadway
Derby DE22.........218 E8
Duffield DE56.......190 E2
Heanor DE75........181 E1
Ilkeston DE7........194 E3
Ripley DE5..........169 E1
Swanwick DE55.....169 F5
Broad Way
Kirk Ireton DE6.....176 B8

Broad Way continued
Kirk Ireton DE6.....176 C7
Broadway Ave DE5 .169 E1
Broadway Ct 4
DE5.................169 E1
Broadway Dr 5
DE5.................169 E1
Broadway La SK17....87 F5
Broadway Lane SK17..88 A5
Broadway Park Cl
DE22................218 E8
Broadway St DE14 ..254 C8
Broad Wlk
Buxton SK17.........85 B7
Darley Dale DE4.....127 C3
Brockhall Rise
DE75................182 A1
Brockhill Ct 3 S43 ..96 F8
Brockholes
Glossop SK13........16 F8
Glossop SK13........17 A8
BROCKHURST.......129 C6
Brockhurst La S45 ..129 C6
Brockhurst Ct S40...95 D2
Brockhurst Piece
S40..................95 D2
Brockley DE21.......220 E5
Brockley Ave S44.....98 F6
Brockley La SK17.....69 C3
Brockley Prim and Inf
Sch S44..............98 F7
Brocksford St S41....96 B6
Brockway Cl S45....131 D2
BROCKWELL.........95 D4
Brockwell Ct 5 S41..95 D5
Brockwell Inf Sch
S40..................95 D4
Brockwell Jun Sch
S40..................95 D4
Brockwell La
Chesterfield S40......95 A4
Cutthorpe S42........94 F7
Cutthorpe S42........95 A7
Brockwell Pl S40......95 E4
Brockwell Terr S40...95 E4
Brockwell The S40...95 D4
Brodie Cl DE73......232 E2
Brome Head Way
S41..................95 D7
Bromley Ct DE7.....209 A7
Bromley St DE22....218 E7
Brompton Rd DE22..217 F6
Bromyard Dr DE73...233 A3
Bronte Cl NG10......236 A7
Bronte Pl DE23......231 B8
Bronte St DE55......146 C5
Brook Ave DE55.....159 B3
Brookbank Ave S40..95 D6
Brookbank Rd S43....80 F4
Brook Bldgs S33.....51 A7
BROOK BOTTOM...23 E1
Brook Bottom Rd
SK22.................33 A8
Brookbridge Ct
DE1.................267 A4
Brook Cl
Alfreton DE55......159 B3
5 Belper DE56.....178 F3
Doveridge DE6......224 C8
Findern DE65.......230 D1
Hatton DE65........227 D2
Long Eaton NG10...236 E5
Quarndon DE22.....204 C4
Brook Cotts DE7....194 F3
Brook Ct
Elvaston DE72......233 F4
Heanor NG16........182 B2
Brookdale DE65.....242 E1
Brookdale Ave SK6...23 A4
Brookdale Dr DE23..231 A5
Brookdale Rd
Hartshorne DE11....257 A4
Swadlincote DE11....256 F4
Brooke Dr S43........96 F5
Brook End DE65.....242 D3
Brooke St
Ilkeston DE7........209 B6
Sandiacre NG10.....223 B5
Tibshelf DE55.......148 A6
BROOKFIELD..........9 E3
Brookfield DE73.....244 A6
Brookfield Ave
Chesterfield S40......95 A2
Derby, Chaddesden
DE21................220 B8
Derby, Littleover
DE23................231 D6
Brookfield Cl
Codnor DE5.........170 B1
1 Grassmoor S41..115 C7
Brookfield Com Sch
S40..................95 A2
Brookfield Cotts
Acresford DE12.....265 C7
Bakewell DE45......109 E8
Brookfield Cres
NG20...............119 E5
Brookfield Ind Est
Glossop SK13.........9 E3
Tansley DE4........143 F4
Brookfield La DE45 .109 E8
Brookfield Mews 2
NG10................223 C6
Brookfield Mobile Home
Pk S42..............130 F5
Brookfield Pk S42...130 F5

Brookfield Prim Sch
Derby DE3..........217 D1
Shirebrook NG20....119 F5
Brookfield Rd
Bolsover S44.........99 A1
Bolsover S44........118 A8
Brookfields
Calver S32...........72 C1
Horsley DE56.......191 E7
Brookfields Bsns Pk
DE65................229 D6
Brookfields Dr
DE21................205 D4
Brookfield View Dr
S40..................95 B3
Brookfield Way
Heanor DE75........182 B1
Tansley DE4........143 F4
Brook Fold SK23......47 C7
Brookhill S43.........80 B4
Brookhill Ave NG16..160 D4
Brookhill Ind Est
NG16................160 E2
Brookhill La
Pinxton NG16......160 D4
Pinxton NG16......160 E5
Brookhill Leys Rd
NG16................182 E1
Brookhill Rd NG16...160 D2
Brookhill St NG9....223 D6
Brook Ho 3 DE1....267 A4
Brookhouse Ct
Hayfield SK22........25 D3
Whaley Thorns NG20 .101 A1
Brook House Dr
SK17.................66 E3
Brook House Mews
Repton DE65........242 D2
Swadlincote DE11...256 A7
Brookhouse St
DE24................232 D5
Brook La
Alfreton DE55......159 B3
Clowne S43..........80 F4
Crich DE56.........168 C6
Hatton DE65........227 C3
Ripley DE5..........180 D7
Scropton DE6.......226 E1
Sutton on the Hill
DE6.................228 A4
Brooklands SK17.....85 C8
Brooklands Ave
Chapel-en-le-Frith
SK23.................47 D6
Heanor DE75........181 F2
Wirksworth DE4.....165 F7
Brooklands Bank
DE45................109 E6
Brooklands Dr
Derby DE23.........231 C8
Glossop SK13.......17 B7
Brooklands Prim Sch
NG10................236 D6
Brooklands Rd SK23..47 D6
Brook Lea DE4.......143 C4
Brookleton DE45....125 C5
Brooklime Dr S40...115 D2
Brooklyn Dr S40......95 D4
Brooklyn Pl 2 S8.....43 A5
Brooklyn Rd 5 S8....43 A5
Brook Mdw SK13.....10 C1
Brook Park East Road
NG20...............120 A2
Brook Rd
Borrowash DE72....221 B1
Elvaston DE72......233 F4
Sheffield S8.........43 A5
Brooks Cl DE12......262 F1
Brooks Hollow
DE21................205 C7
BROOKSIDE..........94 F2
Brookside
Ashbourne DE6......173 D1
Beeley DE4.........111 B3
Bradwell S33.........51 A7
Burton upon Trent
DE15................248 B5
Buxworth SK23......46 A8
Derby DE1..........267 A4
Eastwood NG16.....182 F4
Glossop SK13.......17 B8
New Mills SK22......24 E7
Whaley Bridge SK23 .34 A1
Brook Side
Bakewell DE45......109 D6
Belper DE56........178 F4
Rolleston DE13.....240 B4
Brookside Ave
NG19...............136 C5
Brookside Bar S40...94 F1
Brookside Cl
Derby DE1..........218 E7
Glossop SK13.........9 F4
Long Eaton NG10...236 B8
Repton DE65.......242 D2
Brookside Glen
Chesterfield S40......94 F1
Chesterfield S40......95 A1
Brookside Gr SK17....84 D5
Brookside Ind Units
NG9.................223 D8
Brookside Meadows
DE6.................173 D1
Brookside Rd
Breadsall DE21......205 D4
Chapel-en-le-Frith
SK23.................47 B5

Brookside Way NG17.........148 F1
Brooks Rd S43.......78 B4
Brook St
Clay Cross S45.....131 A4
Derby DE1.........267 A4
Glossop SK13.......10 C1
Hartshorne DE11.....250 A1
Hartshorne DE11....257 A7
Heage DE56........168 E1
Heanor DE75......181 B5
Nether Heage DE56..168 C2
Renishaw S21.......79 C8
Swadlincote DE11...256 A3
Swadlincote, Newhall
DE11...........255 E6
Brook Vale S40......95 C2
Brookvale Ave
Codnor DE5.......181 B8
Denby Village DE5..180 A2
Brookvale Cl 8
DE65...........240 E8
Brook Vale Cl S18...75 D3
Brookvale Rd DE5..180 A2
Brook Vale Rd
NG16...........182 C2
Brookvale Rise DE5.180 A2
Brookview Ct S18...57 A3
Brook Walkway
DE1............267 A4
Brook Wlk DE4......143 C4
Brook Yd S40.......266 A3
Broom Ave
Pilsley S45........132 C2
Swanwick DE55....169 F7
Broombank Pk S41..76 C3
Broombank Rd S41..76 C3
Broom Bsns Pk S41.76 D3
Broom Cl
Belper DE56.......178 E6
Chellaston DE73....232 F2
Chesterfield S41.....95 D7
Derby, Sinfin DE73..231 E2
Duffield DE56......190 D3
Broom Dr S42......115 E2
Broome Acre DE55..160 C4
Broomfield Ave
S41............115 D7
Broomfield Cl
NG10...........223 A5
Broomfield Cotts
DE7............206 C5
Broom Gdns S43....96 F7
Broomhall Court S21.59 C3
Broomhill Ave DE7..209 A6
Broomhill Cl
Derby DE3........217 D3
Eckington S21......59 B3
Broomhill Cotts
DE65...........229 C2
Broomhill Ct S41...76 F2
Broomhill Rd S41...76 F2
Broomhills La DE65..242 D1
Broomhills The
DE12...........264 F1
Broom La DE6......175 E7
Broom's La DE6....226 B2
Broomyclose La
ST14...........210 A4
Broomy Dr DE6.....201 E8
Brosscroft SK13.....10 A6
Brosscroft Cl
Glossop SK13.......10 A6
Hadfield SK13......10 A6
Brosscroft Village
SK13...........10 A6
BROUGH............39 D2
Brougham Ave
NG19...........135 D2
Brough La S33......51 C7
Brough Rd DE15...248 C3
Brough St DE22....218 D5
Broughton Ave
DE23...........218 D1
Broughton Cl
Church Broughton
DE65...........227 A8
Ilkeston DE7......194 D2
Somercotes DE55...170 C7
Broughton Close
DE5............181 B8
Broughton Heath La
DE65...........227 D4
Broughton Rd S41...95 D7
Brow Cres S20......59 F7
Brown Ave NG19...136 B4
Brown Edge Close
SK17...........66 C1
Brown Edge Rd SK17.66 C2
Brownhill La HD9.....3 B8
Brownhills La S42...130 C4
Brown Hills La S10..42 E8
Browning Cir DE23..231 F7
Browning Ct S40....95 B3
Browning Rd DE11..256 C5
Browning St DE23..231 F7
Brown La
Ashover S45.......145 B8
Barton in Fabis NG11.237 E6
Dronfield S18.......57 C3
Flash SK17........103 R3
Brownlow Rd NG19.135 F1
Brown's Flats NG16..195 F6
Brown's La DE56...191 D7
Brown's Rd NG10...236 E8
Broxtowe Ave NG16.195 D6
Brunel Parkway
DE24...........219 D3

Brunel Way
2 Castle Gresley
DE11...........255 E1
Church Gresley DE11..261 F8
Brun La DE6, DE22...217 B8
Brunnen The DE55..160 B4
Brunner Ave NG20..119 F3
Brunnister La DE6..149 D2
Brunswick Dr 2
NG9............223 E5
Brunswick St
Chesterfield S41....266 B4
Derby DE23.......231 F8
Pilsley S45........132 C1
Brunswood Cl DE21.220 E5
Brunswood Ho DE4..143 B2
Brunswood La
Bradley DE6.......187 B8
Bradley DE6.......187 C7
Hulland Ward DE6..175 D3
Brunswood Rd DE4..143 B1
Brunt La DE6......256 F3
Brunton Cl DE3....217 C1
Brunts Sch The
NG19...........136 C1
Brushes SK15........4 A3
Brushes Rd SK15....4 A3
BRUSHES THE.......76 F3
BRUSHFIELD.......88 D4
Brushfield Gr S12...44 D4
Brushfield Rd S40...94 F5
Brussells Terr 1
DE7............194 E1
Bryant La DE55....160 A5
Bryn Lea S41.......96 C2
Brynsmoor Rd
NG16...........182 E7
Bryony DE14.......254 B8
Bryony Cl
Derby DE21.......206 A1
Killamarsh S21......60 B6
Bryony Way NG19...136 F4
Bryony Wlk 7 DE24.231 C3
BUBNELL...........91 D6
Bubnell Cl 15 S40..95 D5
Bubnell Rd
Baslow DE45.......91 D6
Dronfield S18.......56 E2
Buchanan St DE1...267 B4
Buchan St DE24....232 D7
Buckdale La DE4...141 A6
Buckden Cl S40.....95 D4
Buckfast Cl DE55...169 E8
Buckford La DE65,
DE73...........242 E8
Buckhazels La
Kedleston DE6.....202 F6
Mackworth DE6,
DE22...........203 B7
Buckingham Ave
DE21...........219 D8
Buckingham Cl
2 Dronfield S18....56 D2
Mansfield Woodhouse
NG19...........136 E5
Swanwick DE55....170 A7
Buckingham Ct
Burton upon Trent
DE15...........248 C3
Sandiacre NG10....223 A3
Buckingham Dr
Church Gresley
DE11...........261 F8
Heanor DE75......181 C2
Buckingham Ho
DE65...........228 D1
Buckingham Rd
NG10...........223 A4
Buckland Cl DE1...218 E6
Buckland Ct 18 S41..95 F8
Buckland Gr SK14....15 A8
Buckleather La S18..74 C1
Buckley Cl
Woodville DE11....256 F2
Woodville DE11....257 B1
Buckley Dr DE4....143 D7
Buckminster Cl
DE21...........205 F2
Buckminster Rd
DE7............208 C4
Buckthorn Cl
Derby DE24.......231 C3
Hillstown S44.....118 D8
Buckthorn Dr
Bolsover S44.......99 D1
Hillstown S44.....118 D8
Buck Wood View
S14............43 D5
Buddleia Gro 2
DE3............217 D5
Budget La S44.....118 E6
Budle Ave DE23....231 E1
Bullace Ct 3 NG19..136 E1
BULLBRIDGE.......168 B5
Bullbridge Hill
DE56...........168 B5
Buller St
Derby DE23.......218 E2
Ilkeston DE7......209 A6
BULL FARM.......135 C2
Bullfinch Cl DF56..179 B2
Bullhill La DE56....176 E3
Bullhurst La DE6...156 F1
Bulling La DE4.....156 F1
Bullivant Ave S80..100 C8
Bull La
Matlock DE4......143 D6
Yeaveley DE6......199 C5

Bull Mews Cotts
DE4............143 C5
Bullock Cl NG19...136 B5
Bullock La NG16,
DE55...........170 E5
Bullpit La DE56....205 A8
Bull's Head Row
DE73...........252 E6
Bullsmoor DE56....179 C4
Bulltor Lane SK17...88 B5
Bumpmill La DE55..146 B1
Bun Alley DE45......91 C3
Bungalows The
Chesterfield, Brampton
S40............95 D3
Chesterfield, Hady
S41............266 C2
1 Chesterfield, Newbold
S41............95 E7
1 Chesterfield, Whittington
Moor S41.........96 A8
Clowne S43........81 A4
Elton DE4........140 D6
Killamarsh S21......60 C6
New Mills SK22.....24 D1
Stonebroom DE55..146 E3
Bunkers Hill S21....60 E6
Bunker's Hill S80...62 D8
Buntingbank Cl
DE55...........159 F4
Bunting Cl
Chesterfield S42.....95 B1
Derby DE3........218 A3
Ilkeston DE7......208 C6
Sheffield S8.......43 B2
Buntingfield La S45.129 B7
Bunting Ho S41.....77 A3
Bunting Nook S8....43 B1
Bunting Way DE65..242 A5
Bunyan Cres DE55..146 F3
Bunyan Green Rd
NG16...........171 D7
BURBAGE..........84 E6
Burbage Bank SK13..9 E2
Burbage Cl
Belper DE56.......179 D5
Dronfield S18.......56 D2
Burbage Ct 8 S40..95 D5
Burbage Gr
Gamesley SK13......9 E2
Sheffield S12......44 D5
Burbage Heights
SK17...........84 B3
Burbage Pl DE7....232 F7
Burbage Prim Sch
SK17...........84 F6
Burbage Rd S43....97 D8
Burbage Way
Buxton SK17.......84 F6
Gamesley SK13......9 E2
Burch Pl S32.......71 E6
Burcot Cl DE7.....207 E8
Burdekin Cl SK23...47 C6
Burdett Way DE65..242 D3
Burdock Cl DE21...205 E2
Burgess Cl S41....115 D7
Burghley Cl DE73..232 F2
Burghley Way DE23.230 F6
Burke Dr DE55.....170 D8
Burland Green La
DE6............189 B4
Burleigh Cres DE55.169 F8
Burleigh Dr DE22..218 F8
Burleigh St 1 DE7..194 F1
Burley Cl S40......115 A7
Burley Dr DE22....204 E7
Burley Hill
Allestree DE22....204 F7
Duffield DE22.....205 A7
Burley La DE22....204 E7
Burlington Ave
NG20...........119 F6
Burlington Cl
Breaston DE72....235 D8
Sheffield S17......55 E7
Burlington Dr NG19.135 F2
Burlington Glen S17.55 E7
Burlington Gr S17...55 E7
Burlington Rd
Buxton SK17.......85 A7
Derby DE22.......217 F6
Sheffield S17......55 E7
Burlington St S40..266 B3
Burlington Way
DE3............217 D1
Burlow Ave SK17....85 C3
Burlow Rd SK17....85 D2
Burma Rd S45......113 F1
Burnaby St DE24...232 F8
Burnage Ct DE22..218 F4
BURNASTON.......229 F5
Burnaston Cl S18...56 C1
Burnaston Ct 2
NG19...........136 E4
Burnaston La DE65.229 D5
Burnbridge Rd S41..77 C3
Burncroft DE7.....207 E7
Burnell Cl DE55....159 C4
Burnell St S43.......96 F8
Burnett La DE4....143 A8
Burney La DE73....252 C2
Burnham Cl DE7...208 C6
Burnham Dr DE3...217 C2
Burns Ave NG19....136 C2
Burns Cl
Chesterfield S40...114 F7
Derby DE23.......231 B8

Burns Dr
Dronfield S18.......76 C8
Grassmoor S42....115 E3
Burnshaw St DE55..146 C5
Burnside
Glossop SK13........9 F4
Rolleston DE13....240 B4
Burnside Ave
Chapel-en-le-Frith
SK23...........47 C7
Sheffield S8.......43 A5
Shirland DE55.....146 D1
Burnside Cl DE24..231 D3
Burnside Close
DE13...........240 B4
Burnside Ct DE24..233 A8
Burnside Dr
Derby DE21.......220 F4
Mansfield NG19...135 E2
Burnside St DE24..233 A8
Burns St
Heanor DE75......181 D2
Ilkeston DE7......208 E8
BURNTHEATH.......228 C4
Burntheath La DE65.228 C4
Burnt House Rd
Heanor DE75......181 D1
1 Heanor DE75....193 E8
Burnt Oaks Cl NG19.136 D3
Burn Wood Cl DE3..217 D6
Burre Cl DE45.....109 E6
BURRFIELDS.......47 C6
Burrfields Rd SK23...47 B6
Burr La DE7.......194 F1
Burrowfield Mews
DE21...........220 F2
Burrows Cl DE5....169 E4
Burrows La
Brailsford DE6....201 F2
Middleton DE4....154 D5
Over Burrows DE6..202 B5
Burrows The DE11..255 F5
Burrows Wlk DE1...267 B2
Burrs Wood Croft
S41............95 B7
Bursar Way NG10..223 C3
Bursdon Cl S41......77 A1
Burton Close Dr
DE45...........109 E4
Burton Close Mews
DE45...........109 D4
Burton Edge DE45..109 D4
Burton Rd
Ashby-de-la-Zouch
LE65...........257 E1
Burnaston DE65...230 B2
Burton upon Trent
DE14...........254 B7
Castle Gresley DE11.255 D2
Coton in the Elms
DE12...........260 D3
Derby DE23.......218 C1
Findern DE3......230 D4
Findern DE65.....230 D4
Oakthorpe DE12...265 D6
Overseal DE11....262 B1
Overseal DE12....262 A4
Overseal DE12....262 A5
Repton DE15, DE65.242 B2
Rosliston DE12....260 C6
Rosliston DE16....254 C1
4 Swadlincote DE11.256 B7
Swadlincote DE11..256 D6
Ticknall DE73.....250 F4
Willington DE65...241 F7
Burton St
Heanor DE75......181 E2
Tutbury DE13.....239 C6
Wingerworth S42...115 C2
**BURTON UPON
TRENT**..........254 D8
Burwell Cl SK13.....17 A8
Burwell Ct NG19...136 E4
Bury Hill DE4......166 F8
Buscott Dr DE6....185 B8
Bushey Wood Gr
S17............55 D7
Bushey Wood Rd
S17............55 E6
Bushton La DE13...239 B2
Bushy Cl NG10....236 B6
Business Pk The
NG19...........135 D6
Buskeyfield La
NG20...........101 F4
Butcher's La DE4...127 F4
Bute St SK13.......10 E3
Butler Cres NG19..135 D2
Butler Way S21.....60 C6
Butterbur Close
DE24...........231 C2
Buttercup Ave DE12.262 E1
Buttercup Cl
5 Burton upon Trent
DE15...........248 A1
Glossop SK13......17 E8
Butterfield Cres
DE55...........169 F7
Butterfield La S45..145 E1
Butterfly Gardens
DE11...........256 F1
Butterfly Pl 2 DE7..194 F8
Butterhall Cl S80...82 A5
BUTTERLEY
Ripley...........169 F3
Tansley..........144 F5
Butterley Cl NE7...194 F6

Butterley Croft Bsns Ctr
DE5............180 E8
Butterley Ct NG16..170 F4
Butterley Hill DE5..169 D3
Butterley La
Ashover DE4, S45..144 E5
Ripley DE5.......169 D4
Butterley Lodge
NG16...........170 F1
Butterley Mews
DE5............169 E2
Butterley Row DE5..169 E4
Buttermead Cl NG9..209 D2
Buttermere Cl
1 Long Eaton NG10..223 A2
Buttermere Ct
NG19...........136 D3
Buttermere Dr
Derby DE22.......204 E3
Dronfield S18......56 E1
Buttermilk La S44...98 D4
Butterpot La DE6...215 D3
Butterton Cl DE7...209 A7
Butterton Dr 6 S40..95 A5
Butterwick Cl
Derby DE23.......231 E5
Forest Town NG19..136 F1
Butt Hill S80......81 F6
Butt Hill Cl S80....81 F6
Butt La
Blackfordby DE11...257 A1
Mansfield Woodhouse
NG19...........136 C2
Buttonoak Dr DE73.233 A3
Butts Cl DE7......209 A4
Butts Dr DE4......143 D4
Butts Hill S17......55 D4
Butts Rd
Ashover S45.......129 F3
Bakewell DE45....109 D5
Darley Dale DE4...127 B3
Great Longstone DE45.89 F4
Butt St NG10......223 B5
Butts Terr DE45....109 D5
Butts The DE56....179 A3
Butts View DE45...109 D5
BUXTON............85 A7
Buxton and Leek Coll
SK17...........85 D3
Buxton Ave DE75..193 F7
Buxton Baths 9
SK17...........85 B8
Buxton Cl
17 Gamesley SK13...9 E2
Swadlincote DE11..256 A7
Buxton Com Sch
SK17...........85 A6
Buxton Ct DE7....194 D1
Buxton Ctry Pk ★
SK17...........84 E6
Buxton Dr
Derby DE3........217 E3
Little Eaton DE21..191 D2
Buxton Gn DE75...193 F7
Buxton Hospl SK17..85 C5
Buxton Inf Sch SK17.85 C4
Buxton Jun Sch SK17.85 B6
Buxton Mews SK13...9 E2
Buxton Mus & Art Gall ★
17 SK17.........85 B7
Buxton New Rd SK11.83 A6
Buxton Old Rd SK12..32 E4
**Buxton Opera
House** ★ SK17.....85 B7
Buxton Raceway ★
SK17...........104 B7
Buxton Rd
Alsop en le Dale
DE6............150 D1
Alstonefield DE6..149 B5
Ashbourne DE6....173 B2
Ashford in the Water
DE45...........108 C8
Bakewell DE45....109 B7
Bridgemont SK23...33 E2
Castleton S33......38 B2
Chapel-en-le-Frith SK23,
SK23...........47 C5
Chinley SK23......34 F2
Dove Holes SK17...66 F8
Earl Sterndale SK17..105 A2
Flash SK17........102 D1
Hartington upper Quarter
SK11...........83 F2
Hartington upper Quarter
SK17...........103 C6
High Lane SK12....32 A4
Horwich End, New Horwich
SK23...........45 A6
Longnor SK17.....121 B7
Mansfield NG19...135 D1
New Mills SK22, SK23..33 C4
New Whaley SK23...35 A1
Tideswell SK17.....69 C3
Tissington DE6....161 E7
Tissington DE6....162 A4
Whaley Bridge SK23.33 E1
Buxton Road W
SK12...........32 B5
**Buxton Spa Swimming
Pool** SK17........85 A7
Buxton Sta SK17...85 B8
Buxton Terr SK14....9 C5
Buxton Wlk 9 SK13..9 E1
BUXWORTH.........34 A1

Buxworth Prim Sch
SK23...........34 A1
Buzzard La 8 DE73.244 F8
Byeways La DE4....154 C8
Byfield Cl DE21....206 B2
Byng Ave 2 DE23..231 F7
Byron Ave
Alfreton DE55.....159 B4
Burton upon Trent
DE15...........254 E7
Long Eaton NG10..223 B3
Mansfield Woodhouse
NG19...........136 C2
Byron Cl
Dronfield S18.......76 C7
Grassmoor S42....115 E3
Byron Cres NG16..195 C4
Byron Ct NG9.....209 E2
Byron Gr DE55....146 F3
Byron Lodge SK17...85 C6
Byron Rd
Chesterfield S40...115 A8
Swadlincote DE11..256 C6
Byron St
Buxton SK17.......85 C6
Chesterfield S40...266 C1
Derby DE23.......218 F2
Ilkeston DE7......194 F1
Shirebrook NG20..119 E4
Shirland DE55.....146 C1
Bywell La DE56....179 F1

C

Cabot Cl DE56.....179 E5
Cacklehill La DE6...184 C2
Cadeby Ct DE55...170 C6
Cadgwith Dr DE22..204 E3
Cadley Hill Ind Est
DE11...........255 E2
Cadley Hill Rd DE11.255 E3
Cadley La
Castle Gresley DE11.255 C2
Cauldwell DE16....254 F1
Cadman Ct S20.....59 D6
Cadman Rd S12....44 C6
Cadman St S20.....59 D6
Cadwell Cl DE24...233 D6
Caerhays Ct DE24..231 D3
Caernarfon Cl DE55.170 A7
Caernarvon Cl
Chesterfield S40....95 C1
Derby DE21.......220 F5
Caernarvon Rd S18..76 B8
Caesar St DE1.....219 B7
Cairn Dr
Buxton SK17.......85 D4
Chesterfield S43....77 D4
Cairngorm Cl S43...77 D4
Cairngorm Dr DE24.231 D3
Cairns Cl
Burton upon Trent
DE15...........248 C3
DE15...........217 E3
Cairnsmore Cl 4
NG10...........223 A1
Caithness Cres
DE22...........218 B4
Caldene Terr SK23...45 C7
Calder Cl
Derby DE22.......204 E3
Hilton DE65......228 D1
Calderdale Dr
NG10...........236 A6
Caldermill Dr DE21.206 A2
Caldey Rd S18......76 A8
CALDWELL.........260 E7
Cale Rd SK22.......33 D8
Calesdale Cl SK17...85 B5
Calf Croft S80......82 A5
Calgary Cres DE15..248 D3
Calico Cres SK15....4 A6
Calico Drive SK6....23 C2
Calico La SK23......33 D4
CALIFORNIA........218 D3
California Gdns
DE22...........218 C4
California La S43....80 A7
CALKE............251 E1
Calke Abbey ★ LE65.251 D2
Calke Ave NG17....148 E2
**Calke National Nature
Reserve** ★ DE73...251 C3
Calke Rd DE73....252 A6
Calke Rise DE5....169 F1
Calladine Cl DE75...181 D2
Calladine La
Horsley Woodhouse
DE7............192 D6
Shottle DE56......177 C5
Callan's La
Ashby-de-la-Zouch
LE65...........258 E5
Heath End LE65...258 D7
Calley Ave NE7....194 F6
Callin Low DE45...124 C5
CALLOW...........165 B4
Callow Dr S14......43 D5
Callow Hill Way
DE23...........231 A7
Callow La DE6....165 C5
Callow Mount S14..43 D5
Callow Pl S14......43 D5
Callow Rd S14......43 C5

Callywhite Ind Est
S18. . . . . .57 C1
Callywhite La S18 . . . .57 C1
CALOW. 96 F1
Calow Brook Dr
S41. . . . . 115 E8
Calow CE Prim Sch
S44. . . . . .96 F3
Calow Cl SK13. . . . . . . .9 E2
Calow Gn SK13 . . . . . . .9 E2
CALOW GREEN. 116 A8
Calow La
Calow S41, S44. . . . . . . .96 F1
Chesterfield S41. . . . . . 115 E8
Calow Lane Ind Est
S41. . . . . 115 E8
Calstock Cl S40. . . . . . .95 A4
CALTON LEES. 110 F5
Calton View DE45. . . 109 D5
CALVER. 72 C2
Calver Ave S42 . . . . . 132 A7
Calver Bank 8 SK13. . .9 D2
Calver Bridge S32 . . .72 D2
Calver Cl
Belper DE56. . . . . 179 B6
Derby DE21 . . . . 205 E3
10 Gamesley SK13. . . . . .9 E2
Calver Cres S43 . . . . .97 D8
Calver Fold 6 SK13 . . .9 D2
Calver Mews SK13 . . . .9 E2
Calver Mill La S32. . . .72 C2
Calver Pl 7 SK13. . . . .9 D2
Calver Rd DE45. . . . . .91 F8
CALVER SOUGH. 72 C2
Calver St NG16 . . . . . 136 E4
Calvert Cl DE24. . . . . 232 B3
Calverton Cl DE24 . . 232 B3
Calvert St
Derby DE1 . . . . 219 B4
Derby DE1 . . . . 267 D2
Calvin Cl DE24. . . . . . 233 A5
Calwich Bank ST14 . . 183 E4
Calwich Cl DE11. . . . . 256 D1
Camberwell Ave
DE22. . . . . 218 A6
Camberwell Ct 10
S43 . . . . .78 B3
Camborne Cl DE21. . . 205 E1
Cambrian Cl 1 S40. . .95 D6
Cambrian Way
DE11. . . . . 256 A3
Cambria Rd NG19. . . . 135 C4
Cambridge Cres
Bramley-Vale S44. . . . . 117 E1
Stapleford NG9. . . . . . . 209 D2
Cambridge Ct 13 S8 . .43 B6
Cambridge Lodge 14
S8. . . . . .43 B6
Cambridge Rd
1 Brimington S43. . . . . .96 F8
Sheffield S8 . . . . .43 B6
Cambridge St
Blackwell DE55. . . . . . . 147 E1
Derby, Rose Hill DE23. . 219 B2
Derby, Spondon DE21 . . 220 E3
Camdale Rise S12. . . . .44 F1
Camdale View S12. . . .44 F1
Camden St DE22. . . . . 218 D4
Camellia Cl DE3 . . . . . 217 D3
Camelot Cl DE13. . . . . 240 E2
Camelot Ct NG19 . . . . 135 D1
Cameron Cl DE15. . . . 248 B1
Cameron Rd DE23 . . . 231 F8
Camerory Way S43 . . .77 D5
Cam Height S32. . . . . .41 F2
Camlough Wlk S41. . . 266 C2
Camms Cl S21. . . . . . . .59 D4
Campbell Ct S43. . . . . .77 D4
Campbell Dr S43 . . . . .78 B4
Campbell St
Belper DE56. . . . . 178 F3
Derby DE24 . . . . 232 D7
Langley Mill NG16. . . . . 182 C4
Camphil La SK17 . . . . .51 E2
Campion Cl
Shirebrook NG20 . . . . . 119 D3
Wingerworth S42. . . . . 115 A1
Campion Dr S21. . . . . .60 C6
Campion Hill
5 Castle Donington
DE74. . . . . 246 F4
Castle Donington
DE74. . . . . 247 A4
Campion Rd DE11. . . . 256 F4
Campion St DE22 . . . . 218 D5
Campsie Ct 8
DE24. . . . . 231 D3
Camp St DE1 . . . . 219 B7
Camp Wood Cl
DE21. . . . . 205 C2
Canada St DE56. . . . . 179 A2
Canal Bank DE72. . . . 235 A1
Canal Bridge
Killamarsh S21. . . . . . . .60 D6
Willington DE65 . . . . . . 242 A6
Canal Cl DE56 . . . . . . 168 C5
Canalgate Pk DE21 . . 220 F3
Can Alley DE21. . . . . . 197 D6
Canal Mews S41. . . . 266 B4
Canalside S21. . . . . . . .60 B1
Canal Side
Ambergate DE56. . . . . . 167 F5
Ilkeston DE7. . . . . 194 F2
Ilkeston DE7. . . . . 195 A2
Swarkestone DE73. . . . 244 E7

Canal Side *continued*
Whaley Bridge SK23. . . .33 F1
Canalside Cres S40. . .96 C7
Canal St
Derby DE1 . . . . 267 C2
Ilkeston DE7. . . . . 195 A1
Long Eaton NG10 . . . . . 223 C1
Marple SK6. . . . . .23 A4
Sandiacre NG10 . . . . . . 223 C6
Whaley Bridge SK23. . . .45 E8
Canal View La DE12. .262 F3
Canal Wharf S41. . . . .96 B5
Canberra Cl
6 Castle Donington
DE74. . . . . 246 F4
Derby DE3 . . . . 217 E2
Stapleford NG9. . . . . . . 209 F1
Candlemass Ct
NG19 . . . . 136 D2
CANHOLES. 84 E5
Cannell Cl S45. . . . . . 131 B4
Canner Cl DE11. . . . . . 257 A2
Canning Mews 1
DE7. . . . . 208 F7
Cannock Ct DE22 . . . . 218 C3
Cannock Way NG10 . . 237 A7
Cannon Fields S32. . . .52 E8
Cannon St SK14 . . . . . .9 C5
Canon's Wlk DE22 . . . 204 F2
Cantelupe Gdns
NG16 . . . . 195 C7
Cantelupe Rd DE7 . . . 209 A8
Canterbury Cl
Chesterfield S40. . . . . . 115 A8
Duffield DE56. . . . . 190 E3
Mansfield Woodhouse
NG19 . . . . 136 C5
Canterbury Dr S23 . . . 230 F5
Canterbury Pl SK23. . .47 A5
Canterbury Rd
Burton upon Trent
DE15. . . . . 248 C3
Sheffield S8 . . . . .43 B5
Wirksworth DE4. . . . . . 165 F8
Canterbury St DE21. . 219 E8
Canterbury Terr
DE4. . . . . 165 F8
Cantley Cl DE24. . . . . 232 D3
Cantley Rd DE55. . . . . 170 C6
Cantrell Cl S43. . . . . . .96 D8
Canyon Mdw S43. . . . .81 E2
Cape Court DE24 . . . . 219 F2
Capel Rise S43 . . . . . . .96 D8
Capstan Cl
Swadlincote DE11. . . . . 256 E1
10 Woodville DE11. . . . 256 E1
Capthorne Cl S40. . . . .94 F5
Caraway Dr
Burton upon Trent
DE14. . . . . 254 A8
Shirebrook NG20 . . . . . 119 D2
Cardale Rd NG19 . . . . 135 C4
Cardales Cl DE65. . . . 230 D2
Cardean Cl DE1. . . . . . 219 B7
Carder Gn SK17 . . . . . 121 B6
Cardigan St DE21 . . . . 219 D7
Cardinal Cl 1 DE21 . . 205 F2
Cardinshaw Rd DE4. . 143 E8
Cardlemere La
SK17. . . . . .138 F2
Cardrona Cl DE21. . . . 205 F2
Cardwell Ave S13. . . . .44 F7
Cardwell Dr S13. . . . . .44 F7
Carfield Ave S8. . . . . . .43 B5
Carfield La S8. . . . . . . .43 C5
Carfield Pl S8. . . . . . . .43 B5
Carfield Prim Sch S8 .43 B5
Carisbrooke Dr 2
DE13. . . . . 240 E1
Carisbrooke Gdns
DE23. . . . . 231 C6
Carlin Cl DE72. . . . . . . 235 E8
Carlin St S13. . . . . .44 E6
Carlisle Ave DE23. . . . 231 B8
Carlisle Cl S41. . . . . . . .76 C1
Carlisle Gr SK17. . . . . .85 A8
Carlisle Rd SK17. . . . . .84 F8
Carl Moult Ho DE11. . 256 A2
Carlton Ave
Derby DE24 . . . . 232 E4
Northwood DE4. . . . . . 127 A6
Carlton Cl
Clay Cross S45. . . . . . . 131 D2
Heanor DE75 . . . . 182 A3
Sheffield S20 . . . . .59 C6
Carlton Dr DE24 . . . . . 232 E3
Carlton Gdns DE24. . . 232 E4
Carlton La 2 DE65 . . . 227 D2
Carlton Mews S2. . . . .43 E7
Carlton Rd
Chesterfield S40. . . . . . 115 A6
Derby DE23 . . . . 218 E2
Long Eaton NG10 . . . . . 236 B5
Carlton St NG19 . . . . . 136 C1
Carlton Walk DE24. . . 220 A1
Carlton Wlk DE24. . . . 233 A8
Carlyle Gdns DE75 . . . 181 C3
Carlyle Inf Sch
DE23. . . . . .231 B8
Carlyle Pl DE75. . . . . . 181 D3
Carlyle Rd
Stonebroom DE55. . . . . 146 F3
Stretton DE55. . . . . 147 A3
Carlyle St
Derby DE24 . . . . 231 F5
Heanor DE75 . . . . 181 D3
Carlyon Gdns S40 . . . 114 F8
Carnaby Cl DE22. . . . . 218 A5

Carnarvon Ct DE15 . . 249 C2
Carnarvon Rd NG17. . 148 F2
Carnation Rd NG20 . . 119 C3
Carnation Way DE6. . 185 A8
Carnegie St DE23. . . . 232 A8
Carnfield Cl DE55. . . . 159 F4
Carnfield Hall ★
DE55. . . . . 159 D5
Carnfield Hill DE55. . 159 D5
Carnforth Cl
Derby DE3 . . . . 217 E1
Stapleford NG9. . . . . . . 223 D5
Carnival Way DE74. . . 247 B4
Carnoustie Ave S40. . 114 C8
Carnoustie Cl DE3 . . . 217 F2
Carnworth Dr S45 . . . 131 C5
Carol Cres DE21 . . . . . 219 F5
Caroline Cl DE24 . . . . 233 D7
Caroline Ct
Hope S33. . . . . .38 F4
Ilkeston DE7. . . . . 209 A6
Carpenter Ave
Mansfield NG19 . . . . . . 135 D2
Mastin Moor S43. . . . . . .79 B3
Carpenter Cl DE15. . . 248 C2
Carpenter Croft S12 . .44 C6
Carpenter Gdns S12 . .44 C6
Carpenter Mews S12. .44 C6
Carper La DE6. . . . . . . 187 F2
Carradale Gr DE73. . . 232 E1
Carr Bank SK13. . . . . . .17 E8
Carr Brook Cl SK23 . . .45 C5
Carr Brook Way
DE73. . . . . 252 C8
Carr Brow SK6. . . . . . . .32 A7
Carr Cl DE55. . . . . 160 A7
Car Rd S18. . . . . .74 B6
Carr Farm Close
SK13. . . . . .17 E8
Carrfield Ave
Beeston NG9. . . . . 223 F2
Long Eaton NG10 . . . . . 223 F1
Carrfield Ct 8 S8 . . . . .43 B6
Carrfield Dr S8. . . . . . .43 B6
Carrfield La S8. . . . . . . .43 B6
Carrfield Rd S8. . . . . . .43 B6
Carrfields DE7. . . . . . . 192 C7
Carrfield St S8. . . . . . . .43 B6
Carrhouse La SK14 . . . .9 C4
Carriage Dr The SK13. .9 F5
Carriers Mdw SK23 . . .47 B7
Carriers Rd DE65 . . . . 241 D6
Carrington Cl NG9. . . . 209 A5
Carrington Court Ind Est
DE1. . . . . 218 E5
Carrington St
Derby DE1 . . . . 219 B4
Derby DE1 . . . . 267 C2
Carr La
Brackenfield DE55 . . . . 145 D3
Crich DE4 . . . . 156 E2
Dronfield S18. . . . . .56 C2
Hollinsclough SK17. . . . 104 E1
Longnor SK17. . . . . 121 A8
Matlock DE4. . . . . 143 E2
Scarcliffe S44. . . . . 117 F7
South Normanton
DE55. . . . . 160 A7
Stalybridge SK15 . . . . . . .4 A7
Thornhill S33 . . . . .39 F5
Wingerworth S42. . . . . 115 D2
Carr Lane Mews S18. .56 C2
Carrock Ave DE75 . . . 182 B1
Carron Cl DE24 . . . . . . 231 E4
Carr Rd SK17 . . . . .84 D5
Carrs Cl DE74. . . . . 247 A3
CARR VALE. 117 F8
Carr Vale Rd S44 . . . . .98 F1
Carr Wood S26. . . . . . 169 E2
Carrwood Ind Est
S41. . . . . .76 C4
Carr Wood Nature
Reserve ★ DE5. . . . . 169 E3
Carrwood Rd
Chesterfield S41. . . . . . .76 C4
Renishaw S21. . . . . .79 B8
CARSINGTON. 164 E7
Carsington Cl S40. . . . .95 B5
Carsington Cres
DE22. . . . . 204 D1
Carsington Ct 3
NG19 . . . . 136 E3
Carsington Ho 1
DE22. . . . . 204 D2
Carsington & Hopton CE
Prim Sch DE4 . . . . . 164 E7
Carsington Mews
DE22. . . . . 204 E1
Carsington Rd DE65 . 240 E8
Carsington Water Visitor
Ctr ★ DE6 . . . . 164 C4
Carson Croft DE4. . . . 143 C6
Carson Mount S12. . . .44 B3
Carson Rd DE21 . . . . . 220 B6
Carter Cl NG10 . . . . . . 236 B6
Carter Grange 11 S8. .43 B6
Carterhall La S12. . . . .44 C2
Carterhall Rd S12 . . . . .44 B2
Carter La
Shirebrook NG20 . . . . . 119 E4
South Normanton
DE55. . . . . 160 C5
Carter Lane E DE55 . . 160 C6
Carter Lane W
Shirebrook NG20 . . . . . 119 D4
South Normanton
DE55. . . . . 160 C5
Carter Pl S8. . . . . .43 B6

Carter Rd
Beeston NG9. . . . . 223 F2
Sheffield S8 . . . . .43 A6
Carter St DE24. . . . . . 232 D6
CARTLEDGE. 75 B7
Cartledge La S18. . . . . .75 A7
Cartmel Cl S18 . . . . . . .56 E1
Cartmel Cres S41. . . . .95 E8
Cartmel Place DE3 . . . 217 F3
Cart Rd DE55 . . . . 157 F4
Cartworth Moor Rd
HD9 . . . . .3 E8
Cartwrightcl DE73. . . 245 A1
Cartwright La DE55 . . 160 E7
Cartwright St S81 . . . .63 F7
Car Vale Dr S13. . . . . . .44 C8
Car Vale View S13. . . . .44 C8
Carver Cl S26. . . . . .61 E6
Carver Way S26. . . . . . .61 E6
Cary Gr S2. . . . . .43 F8
Cary Rd
Eckington S21. . . . . .59 B3
Sheffield S2 . . . . .44 A8
Cascade Gr DE23 . . . . 231 A7
Cascades Cl 5
DE11. . . . . 256 C4
Caspian Close NG19 . 136 F2
Casson Ave DE24 . . . . 233 A6
Casson Dr S26. . . . . . . .61 E7
Casson St NG16 . . . . . 170 A4
Castings Rd DE23. . . . 232 B8
Castlebeck Ave S2. . . .44 C8
Castlebeck Dr S2. . . . .44 C8
Castle Cl
Bakewell DE45 . . . . 109 E6
Borrowash DE72 . . . . . 221 D2
Stretton DE13. . . . . 240 E2
Castle Coll Arthur Mee
Ctr 3 NG9 . . . . 223 D7
Castlecraig Ct DE24. . 231 E2
Castle Croft
Derby DE24 . . . . 233 D5
Linton DE11 . . . . 261 E8
Castle Ct
Eastwood NG16 . . . . . . 182 A1
Elvaston DE72 . . . . 234 A5
Glossop SK13. . . . . .10 A4
Tutbury DE13. . . . . 239 C7
Castledale Croft S2. . .44 B8
Castledale Gr S2. . . . . .44 C8
Castledale Pl S2. . . . . .44 B8
Castle Dr
Bakewell DE45 . . . . 109 C7
Codnor NG16 . . . . 181 E8
Somercotes DE55. . . . . 170 D8
Castle Edge Rd
New Mills SK22. . . . . . . .24 B2
Stockport SK6. . . . . .24 A7
Castle Farm S81. . . . . .62 E7
Castlefields S45. . . . . . 170 F3
Castlegate La SK17,
DE45. . . . . .89 C5
Castle Gn S44 . . . . 118 B7
CASTLE GRESLEY . . . 255 E1
Castle Hayes La
DE13. . . . . 239 A5
Castle Hill
Castle Donington
DE74. . . . . 247 B4
Duffield DE56. . . . . 190 E4
Eckington S21. . . . . .59 D4
Findern DE65 . . . . 230 D1
Glossop SK13. . . . . .10 A4
Castle Hill Cl S21. . . . .59 D4
Castle Hill Ho DE13 . . 239 B7
Castle Ho DE1 . . . . 267 D2
Castle Ind Est S44. . . .98 E2
Castle La
Bolsover S44 . . . . .99 A1
Ironville NG16 . . . . 170 E1
Melbourne DE73. . . . . . 252 B7
Castleland Way
DE73. . . . . 232 E2
Castle Mews
Mansfield Woodhouse
NG19 . . . . .136 D2
Melbourne DE73. . . . . . 252 B7
Castle Mews The 5
DE11. . . . . 256 A7
Castle Mills DE73 . . . . 252 B7
Castle Mount Cres
DE45. . . . . 109 D7
Castle Mount Way
DE45. . . . . 109 E7
Castle Orch DE56 . . . . 190 E4
Castle Point Bsns Pk
DE13. . . . . .238 E6
Castle Point Business Pk
DE13. . . . . 238 F6
Castle Rd DE11 . . . . . . 255 F1
Castlerigg Way 1
S18. . . . . .56 E1
Castle Row S17. . . . . . .56 B6
Castlerow Cl S17. . . . . .56 B6
Castlerow Dr S17. . . . . .56 B6
Castlerow View S17. . .56 B6
Castleshaw Dr DE23 . 230 E7
Castle St
Bakewell DE45 . . . . 109 D6
Bolsover S44 . . . . .99 A2
Castleton S33. . . . . .38 B2

Castle St *continued*
Derby DE1 . . . . 267 C2
Glossop SK13. . . . . .10 A4
Mansfield Woodhouse
NG19 . . . . 136 B3
Melbourne DE73. . . . . . 252 B7
Tutbury DE13. . . . . 239 C6
CASTLETON. 38 C2
Castleton Ave
Derby DE23 . . . . 231 F8
Ilkeston DE7. . . . . 194 E5
Somercotes DE55. . . . . 170 C6
Castleton Bank 27
SK13. . . . . .9 E1
Castleton CE Prim Sch
S33. . . . . .38 C2
Castleton Cl NG19 . . . 136 C4
Castleton Cres SK13 . . .9 E1
Castleton Ct 12
DE24. . . . . 233 C7
Castleton Gn 26 SK13 . .9 E1
Castleton Gr
28 Gamesley SK13. . . . . .9 E1
Staveley S43. . . . . .97 B5
Castleton Rd
Hathersage S32. . . . . . .52 E8
Hope S33. . . . . .38 E3
Castleton Terr 25
SK13. . . . . .9 E1
Castleton Visitor Ctr ★
S33. . . . . .38 B2
Castle View
Aldercar NG16 . . . . 182 A4
Duffield DE56. . . . . 190 E4
Eckington S21. . . . . .59 D3
Hatton DE65 . . . . 239 C7
Palterton S44. . . . . 118 B6
Castle View Dr S13. . . .44 C8
Castle View Prim Sch
DE4. . . . . 143 D5
Castle Ward Ind Est
DE1. . . . . 267 C2
Castleward Bvd
Derby DE1 . . . . 219 B4
Derby DE1 . . . . 267 C2
Castleward Spencer
Acad DE1 . . . . 267 C2
Castle Way The
DE65. . . . . 241 F5
Castle Wlk DE1 . . . . . . 267 C2
Cat and Fiddle La
DE7. . . . . 207 C5
Catchford View S40. . .95 B7
Catcliff Cl DE45. . . . . . 109 D5
Catcliff Cotts DE45. . . 109 D5
CATCLIFFE. 61 E7
Cathedral Rd DE1. . . . 267 B4
Cathedral View
DE22. . . . . 218 D2
Catherine Ave
Ilkeston DE7. . . . . 208 F6
Mansfield Woodhouse
NG19 . . . . 136 C3
Catherine Ct
Alfreton DE55. . . . . 159 C5
1 Ashbourne DE6. . . . . 173 B2
Chesterfield S40. . . . . . .95 E3
Catherine McAuley Ho
DE22. . . . . 204 E1
Catherine Rise
DE11. . . . . 256 A1
Catherine St
Alfreton DE55. . . . . 159 C4
Chesterfield S40. . . . . . .95 A3
Derby DE23 . . . . 219 B2
Cath of All Saints,
Derby ★
S17. . . . . .74 B7
Catkin Cl 3 DE11. . . . 256 F1
Catkin Dr NG16 . . . . . 195 C8
Cat La S2, S8. . . . . .43 C5
Cator Rd NG19. . . . . . . 135 D3
Catterick Dr DE3 . . . . 217 C1
Catterlen Cl DE24. . . . 233 C4
Catterwood Dr SK6. . .15 B2
Catton La DE12. . . . . . 260 B5
Catton Rd DE13. . . . . . 259 B7
Caudor Way 1 DE4. . . 143 C6
Caudwell Cl S42. . . . . . 131 D8
Caudwell's Mill & Craft
Ctr ★ DE4. . . . . 126 F8
Cauldon Dr S40 . . . . . . .95 A5
Cauldwell Rd
Caldwell DE12 . . . . 261 B6
Drakelow DE16. . . . . . . 254 D3
Caulfield Cl S41. . . . . . .76 D1
Caulkley View DE11. . 257 A7
Causeway DE22. . . . . . 204 C2
Causeway Gdns S17 . .55 D8
Causeway Glade
Sheffield S17. . . . . .55 C8
CAUSEWAY HEAD. . . .55 C8
Causeway Head Rd
S17. . . . . .55 D8
Causeway Ho S45 . . . 129 D4
Causeway La
Crich DE4 . . . . 156 F5
Matlock DE4. . . . . 143 C5
Causeway The
Ashover S45. . . . . 129 D4
Eyam S32. . . . . .71 E5
5 Wirksworth DE4 . . . 165 F8
Cavan Dr DE21 . . . . . . 220 B4
Cavell Dr S45. . . . . 131 E2
Cavendish Ave
Buxton SK17. . . . . .84 F6

Cavendish Ave *continued*
Derby DE22 . . . . 204 F3
Sheffield, Abbeydale Park
S17. . . . . .55 F7
CAVENDISH BRIDGE
DE72. . . . . 247 A8
Cavendish Cir 6
SK17. . . . . .85 B8
Cavendish Cl
Castle Donington
DE74. . . . . 247 A2
Creswell S80 . . . . .81 D1
Doveridge DE6 . . . . 211 C1
Duffield DE56. . . . . 190 D2
Holmewood S42. . . . . . 116 E1
Shardlow DE72. . . . . . . 235 B2
9 Swadlincote DE11. . 256 A7
Cavendish Close Inf Sch
DE21. . . . . 220 B8
Cavendish Close Jun
Acad DE21 . . . . 220 B8
Cavendish Cotts
DE4. . . . . 154 F2
Cavendish Cres
NG9 . . . . 209 D2
Cavendish Ct
Chesterfield S41. . . . . . .96 A5
Derby DE1 . . . . 267 A4
Shardlow DE72. . . . . . . 235 A1
Cavendish Dr
Ashbourne DE6. . . . . . . 185 D8
Clowne S43. . . . . .81 A4
Ripley DE5 . . . . 169 C1
Cavendish Flats
DE45. . . . . 110 E8
Cavendish Hospl The
SK17. . . . . .85 A8
Cavendish Jun Sch
S41. . . . . .95 F8
Cavendish Pl S43. . . . .78 B3
Cavendish Rd
Bolsover S44 . . . . .99 B1
Ilkeston DE7. . . . . 208 F6
Long Eaton NG10 . . . . . 223 C2
Matlock DE4. . . . . 143 C7
Cavendish Rise S18. . .75 F8
Cavendish Sq S21 . . . . .77 D8
Cavendish St
Chesterfield S40. . . . . . 266 B3
Derby DE1 . . . . 267 A3
Langwith NG20. . . . . . . 119 F8
Mansfield Woodhouse
NG19 . . . . 136 A3
Cavendish Street N
S41. . . . . .77 A2
Cavendish Way DE3 . . 217 E2
Cavendish Wharf
DE72. . . . . 235 A1
Cavendish Wlk S44 . . . .99 A2
Caversfield Cl DE23. . 231 A6
Caversham Way
DE7. . . . . 207 D8
Cavill Rd S8. . . . . .43 A3
Cawdor Rd S2. . . . . . . .43 F6
Caxterway La SK17 . . .86 E3
Caxton Cl S43 . . . . .77 D3
Caxton Ct DE23. . . . . . 231 E6
Caxton St DE23 . . . . . . 231 E7
Caythorpe Ct 4
NG19 . . . . 136 E3
Ceal The SK6. . . . . .15 B2
Cecil Ave S18 . . . . .57 A2
Cecil Rd
Dronfield S18. . . . . .57 A2
Swadlincote DE11. . . . . 255 F5
Cecil St DE22. . . . . 218 D6
Cedar Ave
Alfreton DE55. . . . . 159 A5
Chesterfield S40. . . . . . .95 D5
Long Eaton NG10 . . . . . 236 C5
Mansfield Woodhouse
NG19 . . . . 136 C5
Ripley DE5 . . . . 169 D1
Cedar Cl
Ashbourne DE6. . . . . . . 185 D7
Duffield DE56. . . . . 190 D4
Eckington S21. . . . . .59 B2
Glapwell S44. . . . . 118 B1
Glossop SK13. . . . . .10 B2
Killamarsh S21. . . . . . . .60 C5
Sandiacre NG10 . . . . . . 223 B7
Shirebrook NG20 . . . . . 119 E6
Cedar Croft
Aston-on-Trent
DE72. . . . . 246 A7
Kilburn DE56. . . . . 192 B7
Cedar Dr
Ockbrook DE72. . . . . . . 221 C4
Selston NG16. . . . . 171 F7
Uttoxeter ST14. . . . . . . 210 A4
Cedar Gr
Belper DE56. . . . . 179 B2
Linton DE12 . . . . 261 C6
South Normanton
DE55. . . . . 160 B4
Swadlincote DE11. . . . . 256 A7
Cedar Park Dr S44. . . . .99 C2
Cedar Pine Dr DE7. . . 159 E4
Cedar Pk DE7 . . . . 208 C7
Cedar Rd
Castle Donington
DE74. . . . . 247 B2
Linton DE11 . . . . 261 C9
Cedar St
Brimington S43. . . . . . . .78 A1
Derby DE22 . . . . 218 E8
Hollingwood S43. . . . . . .97 A8

Cedar St *continued*
Shirland DE55 146 C5
Cedarwood Ct DE21 205 E2
Cedric Cl DE15 255 C4
Cedric Drive LE66 258 B1
Celandine Cl
Burton upon Trent DE15 248 C2
Derby DE21 206 A2
Celandine Ct S17 56 A5
Celandine Gdns S17 56 A5
Celandine Pl DE11 256 E4
Celanese Rd DE21 220 C3
Cemetery Hill DE21 219 E6
Cemetery La
Ripley DE5 169 E1
3 Ripley DE5 180 E8
Staveley S43 78 E1
Wirksworth DE4 154 F1
Cemetery Rd
Belper DE56 179 A5
Chesterfield S41 96 C2
Clay Cross S45 131 E2
Dronfield S18 76 B8
Glossop SK13 10 C4
Somercotes DE55 170 C7
Stapleford NG9 223 E7
Cemetery Terr S43 96 E7
Cemetery Way DE75 193 F8
Centenary Ho DE1 267 B1
Centenary Rd NG19 135 F1
Central Area L Ctr DE4 143 A6
Central Ave
Borrowash DE72 221 B1
Chesterfield S40 95 E2
Creswell S80 100 D8
Sandiacre NG10 223 B6
South Normanton DE55 160 B5
Stapleford NG9 223 F8
Central Cl
Shirebrook NG20 119 E3
Unstone Green S18 76 E6
Central Dr
Blackwell DE55 147 E1
Buxton SK17 85 D5
Calow S44 96 F3
3 Chesterfield S41 96 C1
Shirebrook NG20 119 E3
Wingerworth S42 114 F3
Central Pavement S40 266 B3
Central Rd DE55 159 A4
Central St
Chesterfield S41 96 C1
Holmewood S42 132 E8
Central Store 6 SK13 10 C1
Central Wlk S43 96 D7
Centre Ct DE1 267 C1
Centre St S44 117 D1
Centro Pl DE24 219 D3
Centrum East Ret Pk DE14 253 F8
Centurion Way Bsns Pk DE21 219 B8
Century Way S43 80 F7
Cessna Court DE74 246 F3
CHADDESDEN 219 E7
Chaddesden Cl S18 56 C1
Chaddesden La DE21 220 A6
Chaddesden Lane End DE21 219 F6
Chaddesden Park Prim Sch DE21 220 B7
Chaddesden Park Rd DE21 219 F7
Chaddesden Wood Nature Reserve★ DE21 206 A3
Chadfield Rd DE56 190 E5
Chadwell Cl S41 115 C7
Chadwick Ave DE24 232 E5
Chadwick Ct S43 78 D1
Chadwick Gr DE5 169 B1
Chadwick Hill
Elton DE4 140 F7
Elton DE4 141 A6
Chadwick Nick La
Crich DE4 167 F7
Fritchley DE4 168 A6
Chadwick Rd S13 44 C7
Chadwick St SK13 17 B8
Chaffinch Cl DE21 220 F6
Chain La DE3 218 A2
Chalfont Sq DE21 206 B2
Chalkley Cl DE24 232 F7
Challands Cl 1 S41 115 C8
Challands Way S41 115 C8
Challis Ave DE21 220 B7
Challoner Gn S20 59 E8
Challoner Way S20 59 E8
Chalons Cl DE7 194 F1
Chalons Way DE7 208 F8
Chambers Ave DE7 209 B7
Chambers Ct SK14 9 A3
Chambers St DE24 219 F1
Chamomile Pl 4 DE3 217 C4
Champion Ave DE7 194 C3
Champion Hill DE56 190 E4
Chancel Pl DE22 267 A1
Chancery Cl DE5 180 E7
Chancery La DE22 218 A6
Chancet Wood Cl S8 56 F8
Chancet Wood Dr S8 56 F8
Chancet Wood Rd 1 S8 56 F8
Chancet Wood Rise S8 56 F8
Chancet Wood View S8 56 F8
Chander Hill La S42 113 C8
Chandlers Ford DE21 205 F2
Chandos Cres S21 60 D6
Chandos Pole St DE22 218 D6
Chandres Ct DE22 204 E4
Chaneyfield Way S40 95 B7
Channel Cres DE24 219 E2
Channel The DE6 173 B2
Chanterelle Walk S43 80 D2
Chantrey Ave S41 96 A6
Chantrey Rd S8 43 A3
Chantry Cl
Derby DE3 217 C1
Disley SK12 32 E5
Long Eaton NG10 236 A4
Melbourne DE73 252 B7
Chantry Ct SK17 69 C4
Chantry Fold SK12 32 E6
Chantry La SK17 69 D4
Chantry Rd SK12 32 E6
Chapel Brow
Broadbottom SK13 16 E6
Glossop SK13 10 A7
Chapel By-Pass
Bridgemont SK23 33 F1
Buxworth SK23 46 A8
Chapel-en-le-Frith SK23 47 D7
Whaley Bridge SK23 45 F8
Whitehough SK23 46 D8
Chapel Cl
Blackwell DE55 147 F1
Clowne S43 80 E4
Moira DE11 256 C1
Willington DE65 242 B6
Youlgreave DE45 125 B5
Chapel Croft
Elton DE4 140 E6
Middleton DE4 154 D5
Chapel Ct DE7 194 F4
CHAPEL-EN-LE-FRITH 47 B6
Chapel-en-le-Frith CE VC Prim Sch SK23 47 C6
Chapel-en-le-Frith High Sch SK23 47 A5
Chapel-en-le-Frith Sta SK23 47 B3
Chapel Gate
Chapel-en-le-Frith 36 D3
Chapel Gate La NG16 182 A5
Chapel Gn DE6 224 C8
Chapel Hill
Alderwasley DE4 167 A7
Ashover S45 129 F4
Beeley DE4 111 B4
Cromford DE4 155 A7
Chapel Ho 3 DE7 208 E8
Chapel Houses SK6 23 A5
Chapel La
Apperknowle S18 58 A1
Bakewell DE45 109 D5
Barrow upon Trent DE73 244 A6
Boylestone DE6 213 B4
Chellaston DE73 233 A1
Church Broughton DE65 227 B8
Clifton DE6 184 F6
Crich DE4 168 A8
Derby, Chaddesden DE21 220 A7
Derby, Spondon DE21 220 E5
Glossop SK13 9 F5
Hanbury DE13 238 A2
Holloway DE4 156 B5
Kniveton DE6 163 B1
Middleton DE4 154 D5
Rolleston DE13 240 B4
Scropton DE65 226 F1
Sheffield, Hillfoot S17 55 D4
Taddington SK17 88 B3
Thurvaston DE6 215 B8
Tissington DE6 162 B6
Wirksworth DE4 154 F1
Chapel Lane E S41 115 D7
Chapel Lane W S40 95 C2
Chapel Lofts SK13 10 B5
CHAPEL MILTON 47 B8
Chapel Mws 8 DE4 116 E1
Chapel Pl NG16 195 F6
Chapel Rd
Bolsover S44 98 F1
Grassmoor S42 115 F3
Hayfield SK22 25 D2
Horwich End SK23 45 E5
Selston NG16 171 E6
Chapel Row
Borrowash DE72 221 B2
Crich DE4 168 A8
Chapel Side DE21 220 E5
Chapel St
Alfreton DE55 159 A4
Belper DE56 178 F3
Brimington S43 96 F8
Buxton SK17 85 B7
3 Chesterfield S41 96 A8
Chapel St *continued*
Coton in the Elms DE12 260 D3
Derby DE1 267 B4
Derby, Spondon DE21 220 E5
Donisthorpe DE12 265 E8
Donisthorpe, Oakthorpe DE12 265 F6
Duffield DE56 190 F3
Eastwood NG16 182 F1
Fritchley DE56 168 B6
Glossop SK13 10 C1
Hayfield SK22 25 D2
Heanor DE75 194 A8
Holbrook DE56 191 C7
8 Ilkeston DE7 194 F1
Kilburn DE56 192 A8
Kimberley NG16 195 F6
Linton DE11 261 E8
Long Eaton NG10 236 E7
Longnor SK17 121 B6
Melbourne DE73 252 B7
Monyash DE45 107 B2
Monyash SK17 107 B4
New Houghton NG19 135 A7
New Mills SK22 33 B6
New Mills, Rowarth SK22 24 E7
Ripley DE5 169 D2
Sheffield S20 59 C6
Smisby LE65 257 F3
Somercotes DE55 170 C7
Stonebroom DE55 147 A4
Swadlincote, Church Gresley DE11 256 A1
Swadlincote, Newhall DE11 255 F6
Swanwick DE55 169 E8
Ticknall DE73 251 A5
Whaley Bridge SK23 45 E8
Whaley Thorns NG20 101 A3
Woodville DE11 256 F2
Chapel Way S42 115 D1
Chapel Wlk
Alfreton DE55 159 A4
Curbar S32 72 E2
Chapel Yd
Dronfield S18 57 A2
Harthill S26 61 E6
South Wingfield DE55 157 E3
Chapman Ave DE24 233 B6
Chapman La S42 115 F3
Chapmans Croft DE12 260 D3
Chapter Cl DE21 205 D2
Chardin Ave SK6 23 C8
Charing Ct DE1 267 C5
Charingworth Rd DE21 206 B2
Chariot Cl DE24 233 D5
Charity Rd DE55 170 C5
Charlbury Cl DE23 231 A8
Charles Ashmore Rd S8 57 A8
Charles Ave
Derby DE21 220 D6
Sandiacre NG10 223 B6
Stapleford NG9 223 F8
Charles Cl DE7 209 B6
Charles La SK13 10 E3
Charles Rd DE24 220 A1
Charles St
Alfreton DE55 159 A5
4 Buxton SK17 85 C8
Chesterfield S40 95 E3
Glossop SK13 10 C1
Long Eaton NG10 236 D6
Mansfield NG19 136 A1
Somercotes DE55 170 C7
Swadlincote DE11 256 B2
Charleston Cl DE11 256 A7
Charleston Rd DE21 220 C6
CHARLESTOWN 17 C6
Charlestown SK13 17 C6
Charlestown Dr DE22 204 D4
Charlestown Rd SK13 17 C7
Charlestown View SK13 16 C6
Charles Walker Cl DE6 175 F2
CHARLESWORTH 16 C6
Charlesworth Cl SK23 33 D3
Charlesworth Cres SK23 33 D3
Charlesworth Ct 1 NG19 136 E3
Charlesworth Gdns S44 117 E8
Charlesworth Rd SK23 33 D3
Charlesworth Sch SK13 16 D6
Charlesworth Sch (Infant Sch) SK13 16 C6
Charlesworth St S44 117 E8
Charley La SK23 47 A8
Charlotte Ct
Burton upon Trent DE14 254 C8
Eastwood NG16 182 F3
Sheffield S2 43 B8
Swadlincote DE11 256 C5
Charlotte Inf Sch DE7 194 E2
Charlotte La S33 51 A7
Charlotte Rd S2 43 B8
Charlotte St
Derby DE23 219 A2
Ilkeston DE7 194 E3
Charlton Ave NG10 223 F1
Charlton Cl DE12 261 D5
Charnock Ave S12 44 B2
Charnock Cres S12 44 A3
Charnock Dale Rd S12 44 B2
Charnock Dr S12 44 B3
Charnock Gr S12 44 B2
Charnock Hall Prim Sch S12 44 B2
Charnock Hall Rd S12 44 A2
Charnock View Rd S12 44 B2
Charnock Wood Rd S12 44 B1
Charnos Street DE7 209 A4
Charnwood Ave
12 Belper DE56 178 F4
Belper DE56 179 A4
Borrowash DE72 221 C2
Castle Donington DE74 247 C3
Derby DE23 231 D5
Long Eaton NG10 236 B4
Sandiacre NG10 223 A4
Charnwood Cl DE55 169 F7
Charnwood Cres DE55 148 B3
Charnwood Dr DE5 169 C1
Charnwood Gr NG19 136 B5
Charnwood St DE1 267 B2
Charter Cl S44 134 B8
Charterhouse Cl DE21 205 F3
Charter Pk DE7 208 E7
Charterstone La DE22 204 E4
Chartley Dr 9 DE23 230 F5
Chartley Road DE24 231 C2
Chartwell Ave S42 114 D5
Chartwell Dr DE21 219 C5
Chase Cl DE73 233 B2
Chasecliff Cl S40 95 D5
Chase Rd DE56 167 F4
Chase The
Derby DE24 231 F4
Kilburn DE56 192 B8
Little Eaton DE21 191 D2
Rosliston DE12 260 C6
Chase View DE4 156 F1
Chasewater Pl DE65 240 E8
Chatfield Cl DE15 248 C1
Chatham Ave DE55 159 C3
Chatham Ct DE56 179 D4
Chatham St DE23 232 A8
Chatsworth Ave
Chesterfield S40 95 C2
Clowne S43 80 F4
Crich DE4 156 F1
Darley Dale DE4 142 F7
Long Eaton NG10 237 A6
Shirebrook NG20 119 E6
Chatsworth Bsns Pk S40 95 E2
Chatsworth Cl
Alfreton DE55 158 F3
Bolsover S44 99 C2
1 Sandiacre NG10 223 B4
Chatsworth Cres
Bullbridge DE56 168 B5
Derby DE22 204 F3
Chatsworth Ct
11 Ashbourne DE6 173 C2
2 Chesterfield S40 95 C2
Derby DE24 231 F4
Staveley S43 97 D8
West Hallam DE7 207 E8
Chatsworth Dr
Derby DE3 217 E3
Little Eaton DE21 191 D2
North Wingfield S42 131 F6
Tutbury DE13 239 C6
Chatsworth Farm Shop★ DE45 91 C2
Chatsworth Ho★ DE45 92 A1
Chatsworth Ho 2 DE14 253 F7
Chatsworth Lodge SK17 85 A8
Chatsworth Park Ave S12 44 A5
Chatsworth Park Dr S12 44 A5
Chatsworth Park Gr S12 44 A5
Chatsworth Park Rd S12 44 A5
Chatsworth Park Rise S12 44 A5
Chatsworth Pl
Dronfield S18 56 D2
Ilkeston DE7 208 B5
Chatsworth Rd
Buxton SK17 85 E7
Creswell S80 81 C1
Pilsley DE45 91 D1
Rowsley DE4 111 A2
Sheffield S17 55 F6
Swadlincote DE11 256 A6
Chatsworth St
Derby DE23 218 E1
Tibshelf DE55 148 A6
Chatsworth Tech Pk 8 S41 96 A8
Chatsworth View S32 72 E1
Chatsworth Way DE75 181 C2
Chattens Meadow DE11 261 F8
Chatteris Dr DE21 205 D1
Chatterton La
Marple SK6 24 A8
Mellor SK6 24 B8
Chaucer Dr S18 76 C7
Chaucer Inf Sch DE7 208 F8
Chaucer Jun Sch
11 Ilkeston DE7 194 F1
Ilkeston DE7 208 D8
Chaucer Rd S41 95 F8
Chaucer St DE7 194 F1
Chaucer Terr DE23 231 F7
Chavery Close S44 97 D2
Chavery Rd S45 131 E4
Chaworth Cl 3 DE55 158 E2
Cheadle Cl DE23 218 B1
Cheadle Rd ST14 210 B1
Cheal Cl DE72 234 D2
Cheam Cl DE22 217 E6
Cheapside
2 Belper DE56 178 F3
Derby DE1 267 B3
Chedworth Dr DE24 233 D6
Cheedale SK17 85 D7
Cheedale Ave S40 95 D6
Cheedale Cl
Burton upon Trent DE15 248 B5
Chesterfield S40 95 D6
Cheetham Ave S18 76 E5
CHELLASTON 233 A1
Chellaston Acad DE73 232 F1
Chellaston Academy DE73 244 F8
Chellaston Brickworks Nature Reserve★ DE73 233 A1
Chellaston Cotts DE72 245 B5
Chellaston Fields Spencer Acad DE72 245 A7
Chellaston Inf Sch DE73 233 A2
Chellaston Jun Sch
Chellaston DE73 232 F1
Derby DE24 233 A1
Chellaston La DE72, DE73 233 D1
Chellaston Park Ct DE73 232 F1
Chellaston Rd DE24 232 E4
Chelmarsh Cl
Chellaston DE73 233 A3
1 Derby DE73 233 A3
CHELMORTON 87 B1
Chelmorton Cl NG19 136 E3
Chelmorton Pl
6 Derby DE21 205 F1
Derby DE21 219 F8
Chelmsford Cl DE3 217 C3
Chelmsford Close 7 DE11 255 E1
Chelmsford Way 6 S43 78 B3
Chelsea Cl DE22 217 F6
Cheltenham Cl NG9 223 F2
Chelwood Rd DE73 232 F2
Chendre Cl SK22 25 C3
Chepstow Cl S40 114 F8
Chepstow Gdns S42 114 F7
Chequer La DE56 166 D2
Chequers La DE21 219 D6
Chequers Lane Ind Est DE21 219 D6
Chequers Rd
Derby DE21 219 D5
Derby DE21 219 F4
Cheribough Rd DE74 247 A3
Cheriton Cl NG19 135 E1
Cheriton Ct 13 S41 95 F8
Cheriton Dr DE7 194 C3
Cheriton Gdns DE23 230 E7
Cherry Bank Rd S8 43 A3
Cherrybrook Dr DE21 206 B3
Cherry Cl
Ashford in the Water DE45 108 F8
Breaston DE72 235 E8
Derby DE3 218 A2
Shirebrook NG20 119 E6
South Normanton DE55 160 B7
Cherry Ct DE14 253 F8
Cherrydale Ct DE23 231 A6
Cherry Garth DE65 228 D2
Cherry Gro SK13 10 C3
Cherry Leys DE15 248 C4
Cherry Plum Cl DE23 231 E7
Cherry St S2 43 B8
Cherry Street S S2 43 A8
Cherry Tree Ave
Belper DE56 179 B6
Ripley DE5 180 D8
Shireoaks S81 63 F7
Swanwick DE55 170 A7
Cherry Tree Cl
Bolsover S44 99 C1
Brinsley NG16 182 E8
Clowne S43 80 E3
Derby DE22 218 B4
Hilton DE65 228 D2
Ilkeston DE7 208 D6
Mansfield Woodhouse NG19 136 B4
Risley DE72 222 F4
Swadlincote DE11 255 F6
Cherry Tree Ct
Ashbourne DE6 173 B1
Chapel-en-le-Frith SK23 47 A6
Cherry Tree Dr
Buxton SK17 66 D1
Creswell S80 81 D2
Killamarsh S21 60 D5
Long Duckmanton S44 98 A4
Cherry Tree Gdns DE15 248 C3
Cherry Tree Gr
Mastin Moor S43 79 C3
North Wingfield S42 131 F5
CHERRYTREE HILL 220 B5
Cherry Tree Hill Prim Sch DE21 220 B5
Cherry Tree La DE6 216 B8
Cherry Tree Mews
Derby DE21 220 B4
Woodville DE11 256 F2
Cherrytree Rd DE15 254 F6
Cherry Tree Sq SK17 69 C3
Cherry Tree Way NG16 182 C4
Chertpit La SK17, DE45 89 D6
Chertsey Cl S40 114 F8
Chertsey Ct DE7 207 D8
Chertsey Rd DE3 217 C2
Chervil Road DE24 231 C3
Cherwell Cl 1 S43 96 E8
Cherwell Dr
Derby DE3 217 C1
Derby DE3 230 C8
Cheryls Bank SK13 16 B8
Chesapeake Rd DE21 220 B6
Chesham Cl
Glossop SK13 10 B5
Hadfield SK13 10 B5
Cheshire St DE24 232 E5
Cheshire Way NG16 171 C4
Chess Burrow NG19 136 D2
Chessel Cl S8 43 A4
Chester Ave DE22 205 B5
Chester Cl DE72 246 A6
Chester Ct
Derby, Little Chester DE21 219 B8
Derby, Spondon DE21 220 E3
Eckington S21 59 B2
CHESTERFIELD 266 B2
Chesterfield Ave
Chesterfield S43 77 E3
Long Eaton NG10 236 F7
Swadlincote DE11 255 E6
Chesterfield Coll S41 266 B4
Chesterfield Coll Automotive Ctr S41 96 A6
Chesterfield Coll (Tapton House Campus) S41 96 C5
Chesterfield Dr DE12 261 C6
Chesterfield Mus★ S41 266 C3
Chesterfield Rd
Alfreton DE55 158 F5
Astwith S45 132 E5
Barlborough S43 79 F5
Barlborough S43 80 A5
Baslow DE45 92 C5
Beeley DE4 111 B3
Beeley DE4 112 A4
Belper DE56 179 A4
Belper DE56 179 C6
Bolsover S44 98 E2
Bramley-Vale S44 117 D2
Brimington, Middlecroft S43 97 B8
Brimington, Tapton S41, S43 96 D7
Calow S41, S44 96 E2
Calow S44 97 C2
Darfoulds S80 63 E1
Darley Dale DE4 111 E1
Darley Dale DE4 127 D2
Dronfield S18 57 B1
Eckington S21 59 B2
Farley DE4 128 F1
Fritchley DE5 168 F5
Grassmoor S42 115 F1
Heage DE56 168 E3
Holmewood S42 116 C2
Long Duckmanton S44 98 C3
Matlock DE4 143 D7

Chesterfield Rd continued
New Houghton NG19 . .134 F7
North Wingfield S42 . . . 132 A8
Oakerthorpe DE55 . . .158 B2
Pentrich DE5 . . . . 169 A7
Pilsley DE55, S45 . . . 133 A1
Pleasley NG19 . . . . . . 135 A6
Rowsley DE4. . . . . 111 A1
5 Sheffield S8. . . . . . . .43 A6
Shirland DE55. . . . . . 146 C3
Shirland DE55. . . . . . .146 E1
Shuttlewood S44 . . . . . 98 E5
Sutton in Ashfield
NG17 . . . . .148 E4
Chesterfield Road N
NG19 . . . . 135 D3
Chesterfield Road S
S8. . . . . .57 A6
Chesterfield Royal Hospl
S44. . . . . .96 E3
Chesterfield Small Bsns
Ctr S41 . . . . .96 A7
Chesterfield Sta
S41. . . . . 266 C3
Chesterfield Trade Ctr
S41. . . . . .96 A6
Chesterfield Trad Est
S41. . . . . .76 C3
Chesterford Ct
DE23. . . . . .230 F6
Chester Gdns DE11 . 256 B2
Chester Gn NG9 . . . .223 F2
Chester Green Rd
DE1. . . . . 219 A7
Chester Ho S40. . . . . .95 E3
Chesterman Cl
NG16 . . . . 195 B4
Chester Rd 5 DE23. .230 F6
Chester St
Chesterfield S40. . . . . .95 E3
Mansfield NG19 . . . . . 135 E1
Chesterton Ave
DE23. . . . . 231 E7
Chesterton Cl S43 . . . .96 F4
Chesterton Rd DE21 220 E6
Chestnut Ave
Belper DE56. . . . . . . 179 A2
Chellaston DE73. . . . .232 F3
Derby DE3 . . . . 217 D3
Derby, Rose Hill
DE23. . . . . 219 A2
Eckington S21. . . . . . . .59 B2
Glapwell S44 . . . . . . 118 C1
Holbrook DE56. . . . . 191 C7
Killamarsh S21. . . . . . .60 C5
Repton DE65. . . . . . . 243 D2
Ripley DE5 . . . . 180 D8
Somercotes DE55. . . . 170 D5
Swadlincote DE11 . . .256 B6
Chestnut Bank 2
DE75. . . . . .181 D1
Chestnut Centre Otter,
Owl & Wildlife Pk*
SK23. . . . . .47 E8
Chestnut Cl
Buxton SK17. . . . . . . .66 B1
Dronfield S18. . . . . . . .76 C8
Duffield DE56 . . . . . . 190 E2
Horsley Woodhouse
DE7. . . . . 192 C7
New Mills SK22. . . . . . .24 C1
Chestnut Cotts DE6 . 151 D1
Chestnut Ct
Cromford DE4. . . . . . 155 A6
Pinxton NG16 . . . . . . 160 C3
Chestnut Dr
Ashbourne DE6. . . . . 185 D7
Barlborough S43 . . . . .80 A6
Clowne S43. . . . . .80 D4
Creswell S80 . . . . .81 D2
Selston NG16 . . . . . . 171 F7
Shirebrook NG20 . . . . 119 D4
South Normanton
DE55. . . . . 160 B4
Chestnut Drive S43 . .78 A1
Chestnut Gn DE11 . . 256 B2
Chestnut Gr
Borrowash DE72 . . . . 221 C3
Etwall DE65. . . . . 229 B3
Mansfield Woodhouse
NG19 . . . . 136 B5
Sandiacre NG10. . . . . 223 A7
Tibshelf DE55. . . . . . . 147 F5
Chestnut La
Barton in Fabis
NG11 . . . . .237 E6
Clifton Campville B79 . .263 F2
Chestnut Rd
Burton upon Trent
DE15. . . . . .254 F7
Langley Mill NG16. . . . 182 A3
Chestnuts The
NG10 . . . . 236 A8
Chestnut Way
Repton DE65. . . . . . .242 C2
Swanwick DE55 . . . . 170 A8
Cheswick Rd 1
DE23. . . . . 231 E1
Chevely Ct DE21 . . .219 D8
Cheverton Cl DE24. . 233 D5
Chevin Alley DE56 . .190 F7
Chevin Ave
Borrowash DE72 . . . . 221 C2
Derby DE3 . . . . .217 F2
Chevin Bank DE56 . . 190 D6

Chevin Mews DE56 . .178 F2
Chevin Pl DE1 . . . . . . .218 F7
Chevin, Chevinside
DE56. . . . . .178 E2
Belper, Milford DE56 . . .190 F8
Derby DE1 . . . . .218 F7
Duffield DE56 . . . . .190 F8
CHEVINSIDE 178 E2
Chevin The DE13 . . .240 C1
Chevin Vale DE56. . . 190 E5
Chevin View DE56 . . .178 F4
Cheviot Ave NG16 . . .170 F3
Cheviot Cl DE11 . . . 256 A3
Cheviot Rd NG10 . . .223 A1
Cheviot St DE22 . . . 218 C5
Cheviot Way 1 S40 . .95 C5
CHEW. 16 A5
Chew Rd SK15. . . . . . .5 C8
Chewton St NG16. . .182 F1
Cheyenne Gdns
DE21. . . . . 220 C5
Cheyne Wlk DE22. . . 218 C6
Chichester Cl DE7 . .209 A8
Chicory Cl 3 DE3 . . 217 D5
Chigwell Way 2 S43 .78 B3
CHILCOTE. 264 F3
Children's Country
House at Sudbury,
The * DE6. . . . . 225 D5
Chilham Way DE24 . 233 D4
Chilson Dr DE3 . . . . 217 C3
Chiltern Cl
Chesterfield S40. . . . . .95 C4
Grassmoor S42 . . . . . 115 F3
Chiltern Ct 2 S40 . . .95 C4
Chiltern Dr DE7 . . . . 207 E8
Chiltern Gdns NG10. 223 A1
Chiltern Rd DE11 . . . 256 A3
Chilton Cres NG16 . . 136 C6
Chilton Ct 4 DE13. . 240 E1
Chime Cl DE21 . . . . . 205 E2
Chimley St DE21 . . .220 F2
Chimneypot La
DE11. . . . . 256 A4
China House Yd
DE4. . . . . .165 F8
Chine The DE55 . . . . 160 B3
Chingford Ct DE22 . . 218 B6
CHINLEY. 34 F1
CHINLEY HEAD 34 F5
Chinley Lodge SK23 . .34 E2
Chinley Prim Sch
SK23. . . . . .34 F1
Chinley Rd DE21 . . . 206 A1
Chinley Sta SK23 . . . .34 D2
Chippinghouse Rd
S2. . . . . .43 A7
Chiswick Cl DE21 . . .217 F6
Chiswick Ct 13 S43 . .78 B3
CHISWORTH. 16 B5
Chisworth Ct 2
NG19 . . . . 136 E3
Chiverton Cl S18 . . . .57 A2
Chorlton Terr ST14 . . 210 B1
Christ Church CE Prim
Sch S41. . . . . .96 A5
Christchurch Ct
DE1. . . . . .267 B4
Christ the King RC Prim
Sch DE55. . . . . 159 A5
Chrysalis Way NG16 182 D3
Chrysalis Way Bsns Pk
NG16 . . . . 182 C4
Chrysanthemum Ct
DE11. . . . . 256 A5
CHUNAL. 17 D4
Chunal SK13. . . . . . . .16 C4
Chunal La SK13. . . . . .17 D5
Chunal Lane Flats
SK13. . . . . .17 C6
Church Al DE45. . . . . 109 D5
Church Alley DE45. . . 109 D5
Church Ave
Buxton SK17. . . . . . . .67 B5
Clay Cross S45 . . . . . . 131 E3
Hatton DE65. . . . . . . 239 D8
Long Eaton NG10 . . . . 236 A4
Swadlincote DE11 . . .256 B3
Tideswell SK17. . . . . . .69 C4
Church Bank
Hathersage S32 . . . . . . 41 B1
Hathersage S32 . . . . . . .53 A8
Whaley Bridge SK23. . . .45 D7
CHURCH
BROUGHTON. 227 B8
Church Broughton CE
Prim Sch DE65 . . . . .227 B8
CHURCH BROUGHTON,
HEATHTOP. 227 A6
Church Broughton Rd
Alkmonton DE6. . . . . . 213 F6
Alkmonton DE6. . . . . . 214 A7
Hatton DE65. . . . . . . 227 C3
Church Brow
Chapel-en-le-Frith
SK23. . . . . .47 B6
Mottram in Longdendale
SK14. . . . . .9 A3
Church Cl
Barrow upon Trent
DE73. . . . . 244 C3
Blackfordby DE11 . . . .257 B1
Blackwell DE55. . . . . 147 C1
Burton upon Trent
DE15. . . . . .248 B3
Chellaston DE73. . . . . 233 A1
Clowne S43. . . . . .80 F3

Church Cl continued
Glossop SK13 . . . . .10 E2
Marchington ST14 . . . . .224 F2
North Wingfield S45. . . . 132 A5
Peak Forest SK17 . . . . . .49 A3
Renishaw S21. . . . . . . .79 B8
Smalley DE7. . . . . . . 192 F5
Staveley S43. . . . . . . .97 C7
Trowell NG9 . . . . .209 C4
Willington DE65 . . . . . .242 B5
Wingerworth S42. . . . . 115 A4
Church Cnr DE21 . . . 165 B1
Church Cres NG9 . . . .223 F3
Church Croft
Coton in the Elms
DE12. . . . . 260 C3
Ripley DE5 . . . . 169 D2
Church Ct NG20 . . . . 119 E3
Churchdale Ave
NG9 . . . . 209 E1
Churchdale Mews
S12. . . . . .44 D4
Churchdale Rd S12. . .44 D4
Churchdown Cl
DE21. . . . . .206 B2
Church Dr
Duffield DE56. . . . . . . 190 F2
Ilkeston DE7. . . . . . . 194 D4
Sandiacre NG10. . . . . .223 B7
Shirebrook NG20 . . . . 119 E3
Church Farm Cl
ST14. . . . . 210 A4
Church Farm La
SK17. . . . . .88 A3
Church Farm Mews
S42. . . . . 116 B3
Church Farm Rd
DE5. . . . . 180 E8
Churchfields S80. . . .81 E1
Church Fold SK13 . . . .16 C7
Church Gdns NG19 . . 136 C3
CHURCH GRESLEY . . 256 B2
Church Gresley Inf Sch
DE11. . . . . .256 B2
Church Hill
Derby DE21 . . . . 220 D4
Etwall DE65. . . . . . . .229 B5
Jacksdale NG16 . . . . . . 171 B3
Kimberley NG16. . . . . 195 F6
Mansfield Woodhouse
NG19 . . . . 136 C3
Newton DE55. . . . . . . 148 A1
Church Hill Ave
NG19 . . . . 136 C3
Church Hill Centre
NG16 . . . . 195 F6
Church Hill St DE15. 248 B3
Church Hole Cl 2
S43. . . . . .81 E2
Churchill Ave DE4 . . 154 D5
Churchill Cl DE72. . . 235 D8
Churchill Dr
Hilton DE65. . . . . . . .228 E2
2 Stapleford NG9. . . .223 E8
Church La
Bakewell DE45. . . . . . 109 D6
Barrow upon Trent
DE73. . . . . 244 A5
Barton in Fabis NG11 . .237 E6
Baslow DE45. . . . . . . .91 E5
Beeley DE4 . . . . 111 A4
Belper DE56. . . . . . . 179 A4
Brackenfield DE55 . . . 145 D2
Brailsford DE6 . . . . . . 201 E7
Bramley-Vale S44. . . . . 117 F2
Breadsall DE21. . . . . . .205 E4
Brinsley NG16 . . . . . . 182 E7
Buxton SK17. . . . . . . .86 B7
Caldwell DE12. . . . . . 260 E7
Calow S44. . . . . .97 A3
Castle Donington
DE74. . . . . .247 B3
Chapel-en-le-Frith
SK23. . . . . .47 B6
Chelmorton SK17. . . . . 106 B8
Chesterfield S40. . . . . .266 B3
Chilcote DE12. . . . . . .264 E3
Clowne S43. . . . . .80 F3
Cossall NG16 . . . . . . 195 C1
Cubley DE6. . . . . 198 F1
Cubley DE6. . . . . 212 E8
4 Derby DE22. . . . . . .204 F3
Derby, Chaddesden
DE21. . . . . 220 A6
Derby, Darley Abbey
DE22. . . . . 205 A2
Doveridge DE6. . . . . . 211 B1
Eckington S12. . . . . . . .58 E7
Ellastone DE6. . . . . . . 183 B4
Great Longstone DE45 . .90 A4
Hanbury DE13 . . . . . . 238 A4
Heath S44. . . . . 117 B3
Heath, Stockley S44 . . . 117 D3
Hemington DE74 . . . . 247 C4
Holmewood S42. . . . . 116 B3
Horsley Woodhouse
DE7. . . . . 192 E6
Killamarsh S21. . . . . . .60 E6
Kirk Langley DE6. . . . . .202 E2
Little Eaton DE21 . . . . 205 C7
Litton SK17. . . . . .69 F3
Lockington DE74. . . . . .247 F4
Mackworth DE22 . . . . .217 F7
Mapperley DE7. . . . . . 193 F3
Marchington ST14 . . . . .224 F2
Marple SK6. . . . . .23 A5
Mayfield DE6 . . . . . . 184 C6
Monyash DE45 . . . . . .107 C1

Church La continued
Morley DE7. . . . . .206 E6
Mugginton DE6. . . . . . 188 F3
New Mills SK22. . . . . . .33 C8
Newton Solney DE15 . . 248 D8
North Wingfield S42. . . . 131 F5
Osmaston DE6 . . . . . . 186 A5
Peak Forest SK17. . . . . .49 A3
Pleasley NG19 . . . . . . 135 A5
Rocester ST14 . . . . . . 197 A3
Rowsley DE4. . . . . 110 E1
Selston NG16 . . . . 171 D7
Sheffield, Townhead
S17. . . . . .55 D6
Sheldon DE45. . . . . . . 108 B6
Shirley DE6. . . . . 200 D8
Somersal Herbert
DE6. . . . . 211 F3
South Wingfield DE55 . . 157 F4
Stanton-by-Dale DE7 . . 208 F1
Stapleford NG9. . . . . . 223 D7
Stonebroom DE55 . . . . 146 F5
Sutton on the Hill DE6. . 215 B1
Sutton On The Hill
DE6. . . . . 228 A8
Swarkestone DE73. . . . .244 E6
Thorpe DE6. . . . . 161 D1
Thrumpton NG11 . . . . 237 C3
Tibshelf DE55. . . . . . . 147 F6
Ticknall DE73. . . . . . . 251 A4
Tideswell SK17. . . . . . . .69 D4
Trusley DE6. . . . . 215 F5
Weston Underwood
DE6. . . . . 188 E2
Churchland Ave
S42. . . . . 132 D8
Church Lane N
Chesterfield S41. . . . . .77 A3
2 Derby DE22. . . . . . .204 F3
Church Level DE6. . . 165 B1
CHURCH
MAYFIELD. 184 D6
Church Mdw SK17 . . .85 D4
Church Mdws
Calow S44. . . . . .96 F3
North Wingfield S42. . . . 131 F5
Churchmead NG17. . 148 F3
Church Mews
Derby DE21 . . . . 220 D4
Hatton DE65. . . . . . . 227 D1
Killamarsh S21. . . . . . .60 E7
Melbourne DE73. . . . . .252 B7
Sheffield S20. . . . . . . .59 D7
Church Rd
Branston DE14. . . . . . .253 E7
Burton upon Trent
DE13. . . . . 240 F2
Church Broughton
DE65. . . . . 227 A8
Darley Dale DE4. . . . . . 127 B2
Egginton DE65 . . . . . . 241 B4
Hollingworth SK14 . . . . .9 D4
Marple SK6. . . . . .23 A6
New Mills SK22. . . . . . .33 C7
Quarndon DE22 . . . . . 204 C5
Rolleston DE13. . . . . . 239 F4
Rolleston DE13. . . . . . 240 A4
Shuttlewood S44 . . . . . .99 A6
Shuttlewood, Stanfree
S44. . . . . .99 B8
Snelston DE6 . . . . 184 C3
Swadlincote DE11 . . . 256 A6
Church Rise DE55 . . 146 C4
Churchside
Grassmoor S41 . . . . . 115 D5
Scarcliffe S44. . . . . . . 118 E6
Willington DE65 . . . . . .242 A5
Church Side
Calow S44. . . . . .96 F3
Sutton in Ashfield
NG17 . . . . .148 F3
Churchside La S41. . 115 D6
Churchside Mws
DE22. . . . . 218 E8
Churchside Wlk
DE22. . . . . 218 E4
Church Sq
1 Heanor DE75. . . . . . 181 F1
Melbourne DE73. . . . . .252 B6
Church St
Alfreton DE55. . . . . . . 158 F4
Alstonefield DE6. . . . . 149 E3
Appleby Magna DE12 . .265 F1
Ashbourne DE6. . . . . . 173 B2
Ashford in the Water
DE45. . . . . 108 F8
Ashover S45. . . . . 129 F3
Barlborough S43 . . . . . .80 B7
Baslow DE45. . . . . . . .91 E5
Belper DE56. . . . . . . 179 A3
Bolsover S44 . . . . .99 A1
Bonsall DE4 . . . . 142 E1
Bradwell S33 . . . . .51 A7
Brassington DE4. . . . . 153 A1
Brimington S43. . . . . . .96 E8
Buxton SK17. . . . . . . .85 B6
Calow S44. . . . . .96 F3
Clifton Campville B79 . .263 E2
Clowne S43. . . . . .80 E3
Coton in the Elms
DE12. . . . . 260 C3
Creswell S80 . . . . .81 F1
Denby Village DE5 . . . . 180 D1
Derby DE23 . . . . 218 C1
Derby, Alvaston DE24. . 233 C7
Derby, Rose Hill
DE23. . . . . 219 A2
Derby, Spondon DE21. . 220 D5

Church St continued
Donisthorpe DE12 . . . .262 F1
Dronfield S18. . . . . .57 A1
Eastwood NG16 . . . . . . 182 F2
Eckington S21. . . . . . . .59 E4
Eyam S32. . . . . .71 D5
Fritchley DE56. . . . . . . 168 B6
Glossop SK13 . . . . .10 D2
Hadfield SK13. . . . . .10 A4
Hartington DE11 . . . . . 137 D5
Hartshorne DE11 . . . . . 257 B6
Hayfield SK22. . . . . .25 D2
Heage DE56. . . . . 168 E2
Holbrook DE56 . . . . . . 191 C6
Holloway DE4. . . . . . . 156 A6
Horsley DE21 . . . . 191 F5
Ilkeston DE7. . . . . 194 E4
Kilburn DE56. . . . . . . 191 F8
Lockington DE74. . . . . .247 F4
Longnor SK17. . . . . . . 121 B6
Mansfield Woodhouse
NG19 . . . . 136 C3
Marple SK6. . . . . .23 A5
Matlock DE4. . . . . 143 C4
Melbourne DE73. . . . . .252 B7
Monyash DE45 . . . . . .107 C2
Monyash DE45 . . . . . . 108 A2
Netherseal DE12 . . . . . 264 F6
Ockbrook DE72. . . . . . 221 C4
Pilsley S45 . . . . 132 C1
Pleasley NG19 . . . . . . 135 B4
Ripley DE5 . . . . 169 D2
Ripley, Waingroves
DE5. . . . . 181 A7
Sandiacre NG10. . . . . .223 B7
Shirland DE55. . . . . . 146 D2
Somercotes DE55. . . . . 170 D6
South Normanton
DE55. . . . . 160 A6
Stapleford NG9. . . . . . 223 D7
Staveley S43. . . . . . . .78 E2
Swadlincote DE11 . . . 256 B1
Swadlincote, Lower Medway
DE11. . . . . 256 C4
Swadlincote, Newhall
DE11. . . . . 256 A6
Tansley DE4 . . . . 144 A4
Tideswell SK17. . . . . . . .69 C4
Tintwistle SK13 . . . . . . .10 A7
Tintwistle SK14 . . . . . . .9 F7
Tutbury DE13 . . . . 239 C7
Unstone S18. . . . . .76 E7
Wessington DE55. . . . . 157 E8
Whaley Thorns NG20 . . 101 A2
Wirksworth DE4. . . . . . 165 F8
Youlgreave DE45 . . . . . 125 C5
Church Street E
NG16 . . . . 160 D3
Church Street Mews
S33. . . . . .51 A7
Church Street N S41. 77 A3
Church Street S
Chesterfield S40. . . . . 115 A7
Glossop SK13 . . . . .10 E2
Church Street W
Chesterfield S40. . . . . .95 C2
Pinxton NG16 . . . . . . 160 D3
Church Terr SK13. . . .10 C2
CHURCHTOWN. 127 B2
CHURCH TOWN. 60 E6
Church View
Alfreton DE55. . . . . . . 147 F1
Barlborough S43 . . . . . .80 A7
Belper DE56. . . . . . . 179 A4
Blackwell DE55. . . . . 147 F1
Breaston DE72 . . . . . . 235 D7
Chesterfield S40. . . . . .95 C2
Clay Cross S45 . . . . . . 131 F3
Clifton DE6. . . . . 184 F6
Clowne S43. . . . . .80 F3
Duffield DE56. . . . . . . 190 E2
Glapwell S44 . . . . . . 134 B8
Heanor DE75 . . . . 181 B4
Ilkeston DE7. . . . . . . .208 E7
Killamarsh S21. . . . . . .60 E7
Mottram in Longdendale
SK14. . . . . .9 A3
New Houghton NG19 . .134 F7
New Mills SK22. . . . . . .33 C8
Church View Cl
DE55. . . . . 146 E1
Church View Cotts
SK17. . . . . .84 E6
Church View Dr
Baslow DE45. . . . . . . .91 E6
Tupton S42. . . . . 131 E7
Church View La
DE73. . . . . 252 E2
Churchward Dr
DE13. . . . . 240 F1
Church Way S40. . . . 266 B3
Church Wlk
7 Belper DE56. . . . . . 178 F4
Brinsley NG16 . . . . . . 182 E6
Chesterfield S40. . . . . . 266 B3
Chesterfield, Glasshouse
Common S43 . . . . .77 D4
Derby DE22 . . . . 204 F4
Donisthorpe DE12 . . . . 265 E8
Duffield DE56. . . . . . . 190 F2
Eastwood NG16 . . . . . . 182 F2
Glossop SK13 . . . . .10 E2
Parwich DE6. . . . . . . 151 D1
3 Stapleford NG9 . . . . 223 D7
4 Wirksworth DE4. . . 165 F8
Churnet Cl DE6. . . . . 184 C7
Churnet Rd DE65 . . . 240 D8
Churnet Row ST14. . . 196 F4

Churston Rd S40 . . . . .95 D3
Cicely Cl DE23. . . . . . 231 D4
Cinder Ave DE11 . . . . 256 A4
Cinder Bank NG16. . . 170 F4
CINDERHILL. 179 E1
Cinder Hill S81. . . . . . .63 D7
Cinderhill La S8. . . . . .57 C8
Cinder La
Killamarsh S21. . . . . . .60 F7
Wirksworth DE4. . . . . . 165 E6
Cinder Rd DE55. . . . . 170 D7
Circle Cl S2. . . . . .44 B8
Circle The
Derby DE24 . . . . 231 E5
Mansfield Woodhouse
NG19 . . . . 136 B4
Sheffield S2 . . . . .44 A8
Circuit Drive NG10. . 236 F8
Circular Dr S21. . . . . . .79 B8
Circular Rd
Chesterfield S40. . . . . 115 B8
Staveley S43. . . . . . . .78 D1
City Gate DE24 . . . . . 219 D2
City Gate Bsns Pk
DE24. . . . . 219 D2
City of Derby Acad
DE24. . . . . 231 E3
City Rd
Derby DE1 . . . . 219 A7
Sheffield S12, S2. . . . . .43 F8
City Rd Bsns Ctr
DE1. . . . . .267 B4
City Road Ind Pk
DE1. . . . . 219 A7
City The
Blackfordby DE11 . . . . 257 A2
Risley DE72 . . . . 222 E4
Woodville DE11 . . . . . .256 F2
Civic Ctr S18. . . . . . . .57 A1
Civic Way DE11. . . . . 256 B4
Clake Rd DE73. . . . . . .251 F6
Clamp Dr DE11 . . . . . 256 B3
Clapgun St DE74. . . . 247 B3
Clara Mount Rd
DE75. . . . . 182 A1
Clarehaven NG9 . . . . 223 E5
Clare Ho DE1. . . . . . . 267 B1
Claremont Cl 15
NG19 . . . . 136 E4
Clarence Ind Trad Est
S41. . . . . .96 B8
Clarence Rd
Chesterfield S40. . . . . 266 A3
Derby DE23 . . . . 218 F1
Long Eaton NG10 . . . . 236 C6
Clarence St
Chesterfield S40. . . . . 266 A3
Stonebroom DE55 . . . . 147 B4
Clarence Terr DE4 . . . 143 A1
Clarence Villas DE4. 143 B2
Clarendon Rd S43 . . . .97 C7
Clarke Ave DE75. . . . 181 C2
Clarke Dr NG10. . . . . 236 A4
Clarkes Cl ST14. . . . . 210 B1
Clarkes La DE72. . . . . 246 B8
Clarke St DE1 . . . . . . 267 C4
Clarkson Ave S40. . . . 266 B1
Clark Way
3 Grassmoor S41. . . . .115 F2
Grassmoor S42 . . . . . 116 A2
Clatterway DE4. . . . . 154 E8
Claverhouse Rd
DE15. . . . . .248 A2
Claxton St DE75 . . . . 181 D2
Claxton Terr 2
DE75. . . . . 181 D2
Clay Cl DE11. . . . . 256 D5
CLAY CROSS 131 B4
Clay Cross Com Hospl
S45. . . . . 131 D4
Clay Cross Countryside
Ctr* S45. . . . . 131 C3
Claydon St DE3. . . . . 217 B1
Claye St NG10 . . . . . . 236 E7
Clayfields Rd 3
DE65. . . . . 242 E2
Clay Fields View
S45. . . . . 131 B2
Clayholes Rd SK23. . . .45 B4
Clay La
Clay Cross S45. . . . . . 131 B2
Heanor DE75 . . . . .181 F2
Claylands Cl SK14 . . . .9 D4
Claylands Gr S80 . . . .81 E5
Claylands Pl S80. . . . .81 E5
Claylands Rd S80. . . . .81 E5
Claymar Dr DE11 . . . . 256 A7
CLAY MILLS. 241 A3
Claymills Cl DE15. . . 248 B1
Claymills Rd DE13 . . . 241 A2
Claypit La S42. . . . . . . 112 F8
Clay Pit Way S43 . . . . .80 C6
Claypot Gdns DE11 . .256 A4
Clay's La DE14. . . . . . .253 F2
Clayson Gn S81. . . . . . .63 F8
Clay St
Burton upon Trent
DE15. . . . . .248 A1
Draycott DE72 . . . . . . 235 A7
Shirland DE55. . . . . . 146 C1
Clay Street E DE15. . 248 A1
Clayton Cl DE55 . . . . 146 E1
Clayton Gardens
DE65. . . . . 239 C8
Clayton Gr DE75 . . . . .181 C4
Clayton Ley Cl DE55 159 C4
Clayton St S41. . . . . . 266 C4
Cleave Rd DE14. . . . . 254 A8

Clegg Hill Dr NG17.. 148 E4
Clematis Cres DE15. 255 A8
Clement La SK17/S33 .50 C6
Clement Rd
  Horsley Woodhouse
  DE7............... 192 C7
  Marple SK6...........23 C7
Cleve Ave
  Beeston NG9.......223 F3
  Darley Dale DE4....142 F7
Cleveland Ave
  Derby DE21.........220 B5
  Draycott DE72..... 235 A7
  Long Eaton NG10 .....223 F1
Cleveland Cl DE11 .. 256 B3
Cleveland Ct DE15.. 248 B3
Cleveland Rd DE55 ..146 F3
Cleveland Way S40 ....95 C5
Cleveleys Rd NG9... 223 E3
Clewley Rd DE14... 253 F8
Cliffash La DE56.... 176 E6
Cliff Bottom S32.... 71 F4
Cliff Bvd NG16.......195 F7
Cliff Coll S32..........91 D8
Cliffdon Ho DE65 .. 239 D8
Cliffefield Rd S8.......43 A3
Cliffe Field Rd S8..... 43 A4
Cliffe Hill Ave NG9 .. 223 D7
Cliffe La
  Hathersage S32.......52 F8
  Tideswell SK17........69 C4
Cliffe Rd SK13.........17 C2
Cliffe View Rd S8.... 43 A4
Cliffe Wlk The SK17...69 C4
Cliff Hill S43..........80 D3
Cliff La
  Alport DE45.........125 F3
  Curbar S32...........72 E1
  Elton DE45 ....140 D8
  Kirkby-in-Ashfield
  NG16...............160 F4
Cliff Nook DE55.... 160 B4
Clifford Cl
  Chesterfield S40.......95 B2
  Long Eaton NG10 ... 236 A4
Clifford St
  Derby DE24 ....219 D2
  Long Eaton NG10 .....236 E7
Cliff Rd SK17..........85 D8
CLIFTON............184 F6
Clifton Ave
  Barlborough S43 ......80 A7
  Long Eaton NG10 .....237 A7
CLIFTON
  CAMPVILLE........263 F1
Clifton CE Prim Sch
  DE6...............184 F6
Clifton Cl
  Overseal DE12 ...... 262 A3
  Swadlincote DE11 ... 256 A2
Clifton Ct S17.........56 B3
Clifton Dr
  Buxton SK17..........85 C4
  [7] Derby DE23.......230 F6
  Derby DE23.........231 A5
  Derby DE3...........217 E3
Clifton La B79........ 263 E1
Clifton Rd
  Ashbourne DE6......185 A8
  Buxton SK17..........85 C7
  Clifton Campville B79 . 264 D1
  Derby DE22.........204 D1
  Lullington DE12 .....263 E5
  Matlock Bath DE4....155 A8
  Nethersea! DE12 ....264 D6
Clifton St
  Chesterfield S40......95 E3
  Derby DE1...........267 D1
Cliftonthorpe LE65.. 258 B1
Clifton Thorpe Mdws
  LE65..............258 B1
Clifton Way DE15 ... 248 B2
Clinthill La S80........81 E7
Clinton Ave NG19 .. 182 D6
Clinton St DE21..... 219 D6
Clipstone Gdns
  DE21..............206 B2
Clive Ho DE15 .... 248 C3
Clock Tower Bsns Ctr
  The S43..............78 B2
Clodhall La
  Baslow DE45.........73 C1
  Baslow DE45.........92 E8
  Curbar S32...........72 F2
  Old Brampton S42....93 B5
Cloisters The DE5 ..205 F2
Cloonmore Croft S8..43 C1
Cloonmore Dr S8.....43 C1
Close Bank DE13 ... 239 C6
Close The
  Derby, Allestree
  DE22.............204 F2
  Derby, Normanton Park
  DE23..............218 D2
  Great Longstone DE45 ..89 F4
  Linton DE12 ....261 C5
  Marple SK6...........15 B1
  Matlock DE4.........143 B6
  Moira DE11.........262 D8
  Newton Solney DE15 ..248 B6
  Shirebrook NG20 ....119 F5
  Tutbury DE13........239 B6
Cloud Ave NG16.....223 B7
Cloudside Acad
  NG10..............223 B7
Cloudside Ct NG10...223 B7
Cloudside Rd NG10..223 A7
Cloudwood Cl DE23. 218 B1

Clough Ave SK6.......23 C6
Clough Bank S2.......43 B8
Cloughfield Cl SK23 ..45 D8
Clough La
  Disley SK12..........32 D7
  Hayfield SK22........25 C5
  Sheffield S10.........42 F5
  Wensley DE4........141 D8
Clough Mill SK22.....25 C5
Cloughside SK12 .....32 E6
Clough Side SK6......23 C7
Clough St SK17........85 B7
Clough The
  Bamford S33.........40 C4
  Chesterfield S41......96 E1
Clovelly Ct DE22 ...218 D8
Clover Cl DE21 ......220 F5
Clover Ct
  Branston DE14......253 E6
  Shardlow DE72......234 E2
  Sheffield S8..........43 C2
  Tibshelf DE55......148 B7
Cloverdale DE11.....256 B7
Cloverdale Dr DE24..231 F2
Clover La SK17........85 D4
Clover Nook Ind Est
  DE55..............159 E3
Clover Nook Rd
  DE55..............159 E3
Clover Rise NG16.....195 B8
Cloverslade DE65....230 C1
Clover Walk DE24...231 C3
Clover Way NG19 ....136 F4
Cloves Hill DE7......192 C2
CLOWNE...............80 D3
Clowne Jun & Inf Schs
  S43................80 E3
Clowne Rd
  Barlborough S43 ....80 C6
  Shuttlewood S44 .....99 A8
Club La DE73........244 A5
Clubmill Terr S40......95 E4
Club Row S32.........71 E6
Clulow Cl DE72 .....235 E8
Clumber Ave NG16...171 E1
Clumber Cl
  Ashbourne DE6......185 B8
  Clowne S43...........80 E4
  [3] Ripley DE5......169 E1
Clumber Ct NG19....135 E2
Clumber Dr NG19....135 E2
Clumber Pl S43........97 E6
Clumber St NG10....236 D7
Clun Ct NG19.........136 D2
Clune St S43...........81 A5
Cluster Rd DE56.....178 F4
Clusters Ct [3] DE56..178 F4
Clyde St DE65.......228 D1
Coach Dr
  Eastwood NG16......182 F4
  Quarndon DE22......204 D7
Coachhouse Mews [4]
  DE11..............256 A7
Coachmans Sq SK23 ..33 D3
Coach Rd
  Hollingworth SK14.....9 C5
  Ironville DE55.......170 D3
  Ripley DE5...........169 E4
  Ripley DE5...........170 B3
  Shireoaks S81.........63 F6
Coach Way DE65 ...242 C5
Coachways DE7......193 F3
COAL ASTON...........57 B4
Coalburn Cres DE4..157 A1
Coal La DE11, DE73..257 D8
Coalpit La
  Coton in the Elms
  DE12..............260 E3
  Youlgreave DE45.....125 C6
Coarses View SK23 ...47 C7
Coasthill DE4.......156 F1
Coatestown La
  SK17...............104 B1
Coatsby Rd NG16...195 F7
Cobblersnook La
  DE4...............151 D8
Cobblestone Dr
  DE11..............256 A4
Cobden Edge SK6....23 F4
Cobden Pl NG19.....135 E2
Cobden Rd
  Chesterfield S40.....266 A4
  Matlock DE4........143 C6
Cobden St
  Derby DE22.........218 D5
  Long Eaton NG10 ....236 E7
  Ripley DE5...........169 D2
Cobham Cl DE24.....231 D3
Cobnar Ave S8........43 A2
Cobnar Dr
  Chesterfield S41......95 D8
  Sheffield S8..........43 A2
Cobnar Rd S8..........43 A2
Cobnar Wood Cl S18..76 B3
Cobnar Wood Close Ind
  Est S41..............76 B3
Cobthorn Dr DE22 ..204 C3
Coburn Pl DE1........267 A3
COCK ALLEY...........97 A1
Cock Ayne Cl DE24...232 E6
Cockayne La DE6.....164 B2
Cockayne Street N
  DE24...............232 E6
Cockayne Street S
  DE24...............232 E6
Cock Brow SK14.......15 C7
Cockcharme Gapp
  DE74...............247 B6

Cockerhouse Rd
  NG16..............182 E4
Cock Hill
  Baslow DE45.........91 F5
  Clifton DE6.........184 F6
Cockleys NG10 .....236 C6
Cock Pitt The DE1 .. 267 C3
Cockshead La
  Holmewood DE4.....116 E3
  Snelston DE6........198 D7
Cockshut La
  Melbourne DE73......251 F7
  Whaley Thorns NG20 . 101 A3
Cockshut Lane Bsns Ctr
  DE73..............252 A7
Cockshutt Ave S8.....56 D8
Cockshutt Dr S8......56 D8
Cockshutt La DE55...170 F8
Cockshutt Rd S8......56 D8
COCKYARD..............46 E4
Cod Beck Cl DE24...233 D6
Coddington La
  Crich DE4..........156 E2
  Whatstandwell DE4 ..156 D1
CODNOR..............181 C7
CODNOR BREACH...181 A4
Codnor CE Com Prim
  Sch DE5............181 B8
Codnor Denby La
  DE5...............180 F4
Codnor-Denby La
  DE5...............181 A5
CODNOR GATE......170 B1
Codnor Gate DE5....170 B1
Codnor Gate Ind Est
  DE5...............170 A1
Codnor La DE5.......170 C3
CODNOR PARK......170 E3
Coffin La DE5........165 B1
Coggers La S32........52 F8
Coisley Hill S13........44 F6
Cokayne Ave DE6....173 C2
Cokayne Mews DE6..173 C3
Cokefield Terr
  DE55...............148 C1
Coke St DE22.........218 D5
COLDEATON............150 B6
Cold Eaton DE6......150 C6
Coldharbour La
  S45...............145 A4
Cold Side
  Bradfield S33.........21 F8
  Bradfield S33.........22 A8
  Glossop S33...........14 F3
Coldstream Wlk
  DE24...............231 E4
Coldwall Rd DE6.....172 B8
Coldwell End DE45 ..125 A5
Coldwell St DE4 .....165 F8
Cole La DE72........221 D3
Coleman St DE24....232 E7
Coleraine Cl DE21 ..220 B4
Coleridge St
  Derby, Littleover
  DE23..............231 E6
  Derby, Normanton
  DE23..............231 F7
Colin Ave DE5.......181 B8
Colin St DE55........159 A4
Collaboration Way
  DE21..............220 D1
Collage Rd S21........60 D2
Colledge St DE55....170 C6
College Ave S43......78 D1
College Dr SK17......85 D3
College Mews DE1...218 E5
College Rd
  Buxton SK17.........85 A6
  Denstone ST14.....196 C6
  Spinkhill S21.........60 D2
College Side NG18...136 C1
College St NG10......223 C2
College The DE5.....180 C4
College View S43.....80 E3
College Way SK17....85 D2
Collier Ave NG19 ...136 B5
Collier La DE21 ......221 C4
Colliers Cl DE11 .....255 E6
Colliers Ct S43.......181 A7
Collier St SK13........17 C8
Colliers Trek S43......80 C5
Colliers Way S45.....131 B4
Colliery Cl S43.........78 C1
Colliery Ct S43.......116 C1
Colliery Drive S21.....60 D5
Colliery La DE12.....261 D4
Colliery Rd
  Blackwell DE55.......147 F1
  Creswell S43.........81 E1
  Creswell S00.........100 C8
  Swadlincote DE11 ...256 A1
Colliery Row
  Alfreton DE55........159 B5
  Pinxton NG16.......160 D2
  Swadlincote DE11 ...256 A1
Collin Ave NG10 ....223 B4
Collingham Gdns
  DE22..............218 A5
Collingham Rd
  NG19..............135 D1
Collingwood Cres
  DE4...............143 A6
Collingwood Rd
  NG10..............236 E6
Collins Ave DE55....160 A7
Collins Yd S18........57 B1
Collis Cl DE24.......232 E7
Collishaw Cl [6] S41..96 C1

Collumbell Ave
  DE72..............221 C5
Collycroft Hill
  Clifton DE6.........184 F6
  Snelston DE6.........184 F1
  Wyaston DE6........185 A3
  Wyaston DE6........185 A5
Colne Cl NG19......136 D2
Colombo St DE23....219 B1
Colonade NG20.....119 F2
Colonel Wright Cl
  DE45..............109 C5
Colonnade The [3]
  SK17...............85 B8
Colonsay Cl NG9....209 D3
COLSHAW............103 E4
Colshaw La S17......103 E4
Coltman Cl DE16....254 E6
Colton Cl S41..........76 E1
Coltsfoot Cl DE11...256 F4
Coltsfoot Dr DE24 ..231 F2
Coltsworth La S43....80 E8
Columbell Way DE4. 127 D2
Columbia St NG17 ..148 F3
Columbine Cl DE21. 206 A1
Colver Rd S2..........43 A8
Colvile Cl DE12......263 D7
Colvile St DE22......218 D6
Colwell Dr DE24.....233 D5
Colwick Cl NG19....135 E1
Colwick Way S9.......43 B2
Colwyn Ave DE23 ...218 D1
Colyear St DE1......267 B3
COMBRIDGE..........210 C8
Cambridge La
  Alders ST14.........196 B1
  Combridge ST14.....210 C8
COMBS..................46 E1
Combs Bank [53] SK13 ...9 D2
Combs Cl S42..........33 A8
Combs Fold [51] SK13 ...9 D1
Combs Gdns [2] SK13 ...9 D1
Combs Gr [49] SK13 ...9 D1
Combs Inf Sch SK23 ..46 E1
Combs Lea [1] SK13 ...9 D1
Combs Mews [48] SK13..9 D1
Combs Rd SK23.......46 E3
Combs Terr [50] SK13 ...9 D1
Combs Way [52] SK13 ...9 D2
Comery Cl [4] DE7 ..208 E5
Comfrey Cl [1] DE23..230 E2
Comice Gdns NG16..182 D6
Comley Cres S41.....76 D2
Commerce St
  Derby DE24.........232 F8
  Melbourne DE73.....252 A7
Commercial Rd
  Grindleford S32......72 C8
  Tideswell SK17.......69 C4
COMMON END.........132 F7
Common End DE65 .229 B3
Common La
  Chelmorton SK17......87 A1
  Cutthorpe S42........94 E8
  King Sterndale SK17...86 A1
  Mansfield NG19 .....135 F5
  Mansfield Woodhouse
  NG19..............136 A4
  Newgate S18..........75 E1
  Shirebrook NG20 ....119 C2
  Shirebrook NG20 ....119 C4
  Shirland DE55.......146 C3
  Stanley DE7..........207 A7
  Sutton on the Hill
  DE6...............228 A8
Commonpiece La
  DE6...............215 B2
Common Piece La
  DE65..............230 E1
Commonpiece Rd
  S45...............131 C3
Common Rd
  Harthill S26..........62 B5
  Sutton in Ashfield
  NG17..............148 E2
  Swadlincote DE11 ...256 C2
  Thorpe Salvin S80.....62 F6
Commons Cl NG16...195 A8
COMMONSIDE
  Brailsford..........187 D1
  Selston.............171 F8
  Sutton in Ashfield....148 F2
COMMON SIDE
  Barlow.............75 D3
  Heanor.............181 E1
Common Side
  Selston NG16.......171 F8
  Swadlincote DE11 ...256 C2
Commonside Rd S18 .75 D2
Common The
  Crich DE4..........168 A7
  Holmesfield Common
  S17...............74 E8
  Melbourne DE73.....251 E6
  Quarndon DE22 ....204 C8
  South Normanton
  DE55..............160 A5
Common Wood
  DE4...............143 B3
Compass Cres S41....77 C3
COMPSTALL.............15 A3
Compstall Mills Ests
  SK6...............15 B2
Compstall Rd
  Compstall SK6........15 A3
  Marple SK6...........15 A2
COMPTON.............173 D2
Compton Ave DE72 . 246 A8

Compton Cl [6]
  DE24..............233 C6
Compton Dr S80......81 D7
Compton Gr SK17....85 B6
Compton Rd SK17...85 B6
Compton St
  Ashbourne DE6......173 C2
  Chesterfield S40.....266 A4
  Holmewood S42......116 E1
  Langwith NG20......119 F8
Compton Way DE23.230 F5
Com Side Croft S12...43 F5
Concert Pl [6] SK17 ...85 B7
Concorde Cl DE7 ....209 A7
Concorde Way
  NG19..............135 E3
Condliff Rd SK17.....69 B5
Condor Rd DE7......208 F4
Conduit Rd S44......118 B8
Conduit Road S44.....99 A1
Conduit St
  Glossop SK13.........9 F7
  Tintwistle SK13........9 F7
Coneygreave Dr
  DE16..............179 B4
Coney Green Bsns Ctr
  S45...............131 E4
Coney Green Networking
  Ctr S45...........131 E4
Coney Green Rd
  S45...............131 E4
Coneygrey Cl DE21 ..205 D2
CONGREAVE.........126 D7
Congreave La DE45. 126 D7
Coniston Ave DE21 . 220 E6
Coniston Cl NG19....136 C4
Coniston Cres DE21. 205 D2
Coniston Dr
  Clay Cross S45......131 B2
  Ilkeston DE7.........208 D5
Coniston Rd
  Chesterfield S41......95 E8
  Dronfield S18.........56 E1
  Long Eaton NG10 ...223 A2
Coniston Way S41.....95 E8
Conjoint La S17........69 E4
Conkers Discovery Ctr*
  DE12..............262 D5
Conkers Waterside Ctr*
  DE12..............262 D4
Conksbury Ave
  DE45..............125 C6
Conksbury La DE45...125 C6
Connaught Ct DE55..159 B3
Connaught Rd DE22 218 C4
Connelly Ct S40.......95 E3
Consett Cl DE21.....205 D1
Consort Gdns DE21 . 206 C3
Constable Ave
  DE23..............218 C2
Constable Cl
  [3] Dronfield S18.....56 E1
  Sheffield S14........43 E2
Constable Dr
  Derby DE23..........218 B1
  Marple SK6...........23 B8
  Sheffield S14........43 E2
Constable La DE23.. 218 C3
Constable Pl S14......43 E2
Constable Rd S14.....43 E2
Constable Way S14...43 E2
Constantine Ct
  DE12..............265 F1
Convent Cl DE15.....254 F8
Conway Ave DE72 ..221 D2
Conway Rd NG10....236 E8
Conway St NG10....236 F8
Conygree La DE6....184 D7
Cook Cl DE56.........179 E5
Cook Dr
  Etwall DE65.........229 C3
  Ilkeston DE7.........209 A6
Cooke & Beard Homes
  S8................43 B5
Cooke Cl
  Clay Cross S42......131 B6
  Long Eaton NG10 ....236 B2
Cookfield DE56......179 E8
Cookham Cl DE3 ....217 C2
Cook La DE6..........211 B1
Cooks Dr DE74......247 A3
Coole Well Cl S43.....97 D8
Coombes La S43......15 C5
Coombes View SK14..15 C5
Coombsdale La
  Calver S32...........72 A2
  Stoney Middleton DE45 .71 C1
Coombs La S32........90 F8
Coombs Rd DE45....109 F5
Co-operative St
  Derby DE23..........218 C2
  Disley SK12..........32 D6
  Long Eaton NG10 ....236 E6
Cooper Cl DE74.....246 F2
Coopers Cl
  Acresford DE12 .....265 B7
  Borrowash DE72.....221 C1
Cooper's Cl [2] DE6..173 C2
Coopers Croft DE65..227 C1
Coopers Gdns DE21..173 B1
Cooper St
  Derby DE22.........218 D6
  Glossop SK13........10 D1

Cle-Cor 279

Copenhagen Rd
  S45...............131 E4
Copestake Cl NG10 .236 A7
Copes Way
  Derby DE21.........220 A8
  Uttoxeter ST14......210 A1
Copley Croft [3]
  DE6...............173 D3
COPLOW DALE........50 F3
Coplow Dale SK17....50 F3
Coplow La DE65 .....226 D5
Copperas Rd DE11...255 D5
Copper Beech Dr
  SK13...............9 E1
Copper Beeches
  DE56..............169 C2
Copperfield Mws
  DE14..............253 A7
Copperleaf Cl DE22..267 A2
Copper Yd DE5......180 F2
Coppice Ave
  High Lane SK12.......32 A6
  Ilkeston DE7.........194 D5
Coppice Brook
  DE56..............179 B4
Coppice Cl
  Castle Donington
  DE74..............246 F3
  Chesterfield S41.....115 D6
  Derby DE22.........204 F1
  High Lane SK12.......32 A6
  Kilburn DE56........192 A7
Coppice Ct DE75....193 F7
Coppice Dr
  Eastwood NG16.....182 D3
  Heanor DE75........193 F7
Coppice End Rd
  DE22..............204 C1
Coppice Farm Rd
  DE5...............180 F7
Coppice La
  Clifton Campville
  B79...............263 F1
  High Lane SK12.......32 A5
Coppice Mews
  DE75..............193 F7
Coppice Prim Sch
  DE75..............193 E8
Coppice Rd DE14 ...253 C8
Coppice Rise DE65..242 F2
Coppice Side DE11 . 256 C3
Coppice The
  Horwich End SK23....45 F5
  Shirebrook NG20 ....119 D3
Coppice View DE55..160 A4
Coppicewood Dr
  DE23..............218 A1
Copse Cl DE4.........165 E8
Copse Dr DE5........180 F7
Copse Gr DE23.......231 A7
Copse Rise DE11....256 B7
Copseside Cl [10]
  NG10..............236 A8
Copse The
  Ilkeston DE7........194 D5
  Marple SK6...........23 C8
Copsewood DE55....160 A4
Copsey Croft Ct
  NG10..............236 F3
Copthorne Com Inf Sch
  DE55..............159 E3
Copthorne Dr [4]
  DE55..............158 E2
Copthurst Rd HD9 ....3 E7
Coral Cl DE24.......219 E2
Coral Way S45.......131 D4
Corbar Grange SK17 .85 B8
Corbar Rd SK17.......66 B1
Corbar Woods La
  SK17...............66 A1
Corbel Cl DE24......253 C8
Corbridge Gr DE23..231 A7
CORBRIGGS.........115 F5
Corby Cl DE24.......232 F5
Corby La DE23.......230 F6
Cordelia Way DE73 . 232 F2
Corden Ave DE3.....218 A2
Corden St DE23......219 A2
Cordville Cl DE21....220 B5
CORDWELL.............74 E6
Cordwell Ave S41....95 C8
Cordwell Cl
  Castle Donington
  DE74..............246 F3
  [7] Castle Donington
  DE74..............246 F4
  Staveley S43..........97 D8
Cordwell La S18.......74 E5
Cordy La
  Brinsley NG16......182 F8
  New Brinsley NG16...171 F1
  Selston NG16.......182 F8
Corfe Cl DE23.......231 D6
Corfield Ave DE75...193 F7
Corfield CE Inf Sch
  DE75..............181 D1
Corfield Cl DE75.....181 D4
Coriander Gdns
  DE23..............231 D4
Corinium Cl DE24...233 D5
Corker Rd S12........44 A6
Corley La DE6........174 D2
Cornbrook DE45.....108 F7
Corn Cl DE55........160 B6

Cornel Ct **4** NG19 . . 136 E1
Corner Farm DE6 . . 201 E8
Corner Pin Ct **7** S43 . . 78 F2
Cornfield Ave DE55 . 160 A4
Cornfield Cl **1** S42. . . . .95 A5
Cornfield Rd NG16. . 195 E7
Cornflower Dr DE21 206 B3
Cornhill DE22. . . . . . . .204 F4
Cornhill Cl DE56. . . . 190 D4
Cornhill Dr DE55. . . 159 B4
Cornmill Bank
DE13. . . . . 239 D6
Cornmill Cl
Bolsover S44 . . . . .99 B2
Calver S32. . . . . 72 C1
Derby DE22 . . . . 233 D5
Corn Mill Cl DE4 . . . 165 E6
Cornmill Ho SK13. . . .10 D1
Cornmill La DE13. . . 239 E6
Corn Mill Terr DE4. . 143 E7
Corn Mkt DE1 . . . . . . 267 B3
Corn St SK13 . . . . .10 D1
Cornstone Ave **1**
DE55. . . . . 148 B7
Cornwall Ave
Brimington S43. . . . . . .96 F8
Buxton SK17. . . . . .85 E7
Cornwall Cl
4 Brimington S43. . . . .96 F8
Westwood NG16 . . . . 171 C4
Cornwall Dr
Brimington S43. . . . . . .96 F8
Grassmoor S42 . . . . . 115 F3
Long Eaton NG10 . . . 237 A8
Cornwallis Cl NG10 . 236 D6
Cornwall Rd
Burton upon Trent
DE15. . . . . 254 E6
Derby DE21 . . . . 219 D6
Shireoaks S81 . . . . .63 F7
Coronation Ave
Belper DE56 . . . . 179 A5
Derby DE24 . . . . 233 C5
New Houghton NG19 . 134 F7
Sandiacre NG10 . . . . 223 A7
Coronation Cl DE73. 252 B8
Coronation Cotts
DE13. . . . . 253 A8
Coronation Cres
ST14. . . . . 197 A4
Coronation Dr
Shirebrook NG20 . . . . 119 F2
South Normanton
DE55. . . . . 160 B5
Coronation La
DE12. . . . . 265 F6
Coronation Rd
Brimington S43. . . . . . .96 E8
Cossall DE7, NG16 . . 195 A2
Mapperley DE7. . . . . 193 F3
Stanley DE7 . . . . 207 C6
Coronation St
Derby DE23 . . . . 232 B8
1 Ilkeston DE7. . . . . 208 F8
Overseal DE12 . . . . . 262 A4
Swadlincote DE11 . . . 256 A5
Whitwell S80 . . . . .82 A6
Coronet Ct DE21. . . . 206 D3
Corporation Rd
DE7. . . . . 209 A5
Corporation St
Chesterfield S41. . . . 266 C3
Derby DE1 . . . . 267 B3
Corve Way S40. . . . . . .94 F5
COSSALL 195 C1
COSSALL
COMMON. 195 B3
Cossall Ind Est DE7. . 195 B2
COSSALL MARSH . . . 195 C2
Cossall Rd NG9 . . . . 209 D5
Cote Bottom La
DE65. . . . . 227 A7
COTE GREEN. 15 C1
Cote Green La SK6. . . .15 B1
Cote Green Rd SK6. . . .15 C1
Cote Hilloc DE4 . . . . 127 A6
Cote La SK22 . . . . .25 D3
COTES PARK 159 C2
Cotes Park Ind Est
DE55. . . . . 159 D2
Cotes Park La DE55 . 159 C2
Cotgrave Rd NG19 . . 135 F2
Cotman Dr SK6. . . . . . .23 C8
COTMANHAY 194 E4
Cotmanhay Inf & Jun
Sch DE7. . . . . 194 E5
Cotmanhay Rd DE7. . 194 F3
Coton Cl NG19. . . . . . 136 E4
COTON IN THE
CLAY. 238 A7
COTON IN THE
ELMS. 260 C4
Coton in the Elms CE
Prim Sch DE12 . . . . 260 D3
Coton La
Coton in the Elms
DE12. . . . . 260 F3
Lullington DE12 . . . . 263 D7
Rosliston DE12 . . . . 260 D5
COTON PARK 261 C8
Coton Pk DE12 . . . . 255 C1
Coton Rd
Coton in the Elms
DE12. . . . . 260 D1
Lullington DE12 . . . . 263 D8

Coton Rd continued
Walton-on-Trent
DE12. . . . . 259 E6
Walton upon Trent
DE12. . . . . 259 F5
Cotswold Cl
2 Chesterfield S40. . .95 C5
Derby DE23 . . . . 231 C8
Glossop SK13. . . . . .17 A8
4 Long Eaton NG10. . 236 B8
Swadlincote DE11 . . . 256 A3
Cotswold Dr S42 . . . 115 E3
Cotswold Rd DE14 . . 253 F8
Cottage Cl
Heage DE56 . . . . 179 E8
Ilkeston DE7. . . . . . . 194 D3
Poolsbrook S43 . . . . . .98 A7
Swadlincote DE11 . . . 256 A7
Cottage Ct DE56 . . . 179 E3
Cottage Garden La
DE75. . . . . 181 D2
Cottage La SK13 . . . . . . .9 E2
Cottage Meadow Way **3**
DE72. . . . . 246 A6
Cottages The SK23 . . . .47 B6
Cottam Cres SK6 . . . . .23 B7
Cottam Dr S43 . . . . . . .80 C6
Cotterdale Cl NG19. . 136 E1
Cotterhill La S43 . . . . .96 F7
Cotter Wood Cl
DE21. . . . . 205 C7
Cottesmore Cl DE15 248 B1
Cottesmore Rd
DE15. . . . . 248 A1
Cottisford Cl DE23 . . 231 A8
Cottonbrook Rd
DE23. . . . . 232 B8
Cotton Cl S23 . . . . . . .45 E5
Cotton La DE24. . . . . 219 C1
Cotton Lace Cl DE7 . 208 F6
Cotton Mill Hill S42. 113 F2
Cotton Mill Yard
DE21. . . . . 205 A2
Cotton St S44 . . . . . . .99 A1
Cotts The SK17 . . . . . .86 D5
Council Hos
Bradbourne DE6. . . . . 163 B6
Hanbury DE13 . . . . . 238 A3
Countess Gr DE73. . . 244 F8
Counting House Rd
SK12. . . . . .32 E5
Countisbury Dr
DE21. . . . . 206 A2
County Est The
NG17. . . . . 148 E2
Coupe La S42, S45 . . 131 A5
Coupe St DE5 . . . . . . 180 F8
Coupland Cl S41. . . . . .77 C4
Coupland Pl DE55 . . . 159 C1
Court Farm La DE14 253 E7
Court La DE45 . . . . . . 108 E8
Courtland Dr DE24. . 233 B6
Courtland Gdns
DE24. . . . . 233 B7
Courtland Rd DE65 . 229 C3
Courtney Way DE56. 179 D5
Court Pl S43 . . . . .97 C8
Court St DE11 . . . . . . 256 E3
Court The DE24. . . . . 233 B6
Court View S43. . . . . . .80 E3
Courtway Cres
DE73. . . . . 244 E8
Courtyard Mews
DE24. . . . . 233 A6
Courtyard Pl DE21. . . 220 E5
Courtyard The
Bakewell DE45 . . . . . 109 D6
Belper DE56 . . . . 179 A4
Darley Dale DE4 . . . . 127 C3
Hollingworth SK14 . . . . .9 D5
Kimberley NG16. . . . . 195 E8
Covent Garden Close
DE72. . . . . 221 B2
Coventry Cl DE11 . . . 256 D6
Coventry La NG9. . . . 209 F2
Coverdale Wlk
DE24. . . . . 233 C7
Covert Pl DE11 . . . . . 262 C8
Covert The DE21 . . . . 220 E4
Cowbrook Ave SK13 . .10 F1
Cowbrook Ct SK13. . . .10 F1
Cowburn Dr SK22. . . . .24 C1
Cowdale Cotts SK17 . .86 A4
Cowdray Cl DE24 . . . 231 D2
COWERS LANE. 177 D3
Cowham Cl DE55 . . . 159 C3
COWHILL 179 A2
Cow La
Brimington S43. . . . . . .77 E1
Hyde SK14 . . . . .9 D6
COWLEY. 75 D7
COWLEY BAR 75 B8
Cowley Bottom S18. . .75 B8
Cowley Cl
Chesterfield S41. . . . 266 C3
Ilkeston DE7. . . . . . . 194 F5
Cowley Gdns S20. . . . .59 E8
Cowley La S18. . . . . . . .75 D7
Cowley St DE22. . . . . 218 E7
Cowlishall Dr S43 . . . 131 B7
Cowlishaw Cl DE72 . 234 E1
Cowlow La SK17,
SK23. . . . . .47 C2
Cowper Rd NG16 . . . . 195 A8
Cowper St DE24 . . . . 232 A7
Cowpingle La S43 . . . .77 E1
Cowsell Dr S45. . . . . 131 E2
Cowsley Rd DE21 . . . 219 D7

Cowslip Cl DE12 . . . . 262 E1
Cowslip Mdw DE72 . . 235 B7
COXBENCH 191 F3
Coxbench Rd DE21. . . 191 F4
Cox Green Ct DE23 . . 230 F7
Coxon St DE21. . . . . . 220 E5
Coxon's Yd **6** DE6. . 173 B2
Cox's La NG19. . . . . . . 136 B5
Crabapple Dr NG16. . 182 C4
Crabtree Ave SK12. . . .32 E5
Crabtree Cl
Castle Donington
DE74. . . . . 247 A2
Clay Cross S45. . . . . . 131 E3
Derby DE22 . . . . 204 C4
Wirksworth DE4. . . . . 165 E7
Crabtree Ct S41. . . . . .32 D6
Crabtree Hill DE22. . 204 C3
Crab Tree Hill DE21. 205 C8
Cracken Cl SK23. . . . . .34 C2
Cracroft La S44. . . . . 118 F6
Craddock Ave DE21. . 220 E3
Cradock Mews S2 . . . .43 E7
Cradock Rd S2 . . . . . . .43 F7
Crafty Flats La DE12 260 F3
Cragdale Gr S20. . . . . .59 D7
Cragg La DE55. . . . . . 148 A2
Craggon Dr S43 . . . . . .77 D4
Craggs Dr S43 . . . . . . .80 E3
Craggs Rd S44 . . . . . . .99 A2
Crag Hall La S11 . . . 102 A5
Craglands Gr S40. . . . .95 A5
Crags Bsns Pk S80 . . 100 E8
Cragside Cl S41 . . . . . .96 C3
Crags Rd
Belph S80 . . . . .82 B3
Creswell S43 . . . . .81 F1
Creswell S80 . . . . .82 A1
Crags View S80. . . . . . .81 F1
Craig Dr SK23 . . . . . . .45 E6
Craiglee Ct **1** DE24. 231 D3
Craig St NG10 . . . . . . 236 E7
CRAKEMARSH 210 D5
Crampton Cl DE11 . . 256 E5
Cranberry Gr **2**
DE23. . . . . 230 F6
Cranborne Rd S41. . . .95 E7
Cranbourne Cl NG9. 209 D2
Cranbrook Cl NG19. . 136 C6
Craner Rd DE74 . . . . 246 E3
Cranfield Ave DE11 . 255 E2
Cranfleet Way NG10 236 B7
Cranhill Cl DE23 . . . . 230 F6
Cranleigh Rd S43 . . . . .79 B3
Cranmer Gr NG19. . . . 135 D3
Cranmer Rd DE21. . . . 267 D3
Cranmer St
Ilkeston DE7. . . . . . . 194 F1
Long Eaton NG10 . . . 223 D1
Cranwood Cl DE24. . . 232 D5
Cratcliff View DE4 . . 126 A1
Craven Rd S41 . . . . . . .95 F5
Crawford Ave NG9. . . 223 D8
Crawford Rd S8 . . . . . .43 A4
Crawley Rd DE24 . . . 232 F5
Crawley Way DE72. . . 245 A8
Crawshaw Ave S8 . . . .56 D8
Crawshaw Gr S8. . . . . .56 D8
Crawshaw Mews S18 .56 C1
Crayford Rd DE24. . . 233 A5
Cray's Hill
Swanwick DE55 . . . . . 170 A6
Swanwick DE55. . . . . 170 B7
CRAYTHORNE. 240 D2
Craythorne Cl DE11. 256 A7
Craythorne Rd
DE13. . . . . 240 D3
Creamery La DE6 . . . 151 D1
Crecy Cl DE22. . . . . . . 218 C3
CREIGHTON. 210 A5
Creighton La ST14. . 210 A5
Cres S26 . . . . .61 E5
Crescent Dr SK23. . . . .33 D2
Crescent Prim Sch
NG19 . . . . 135 D2
Crescent Rd
Ashover S42. . . . . 113 D7
Selston NG16 . . . . . . 171 D6
Crescent Row SK22. . .25 A2
Crescent The
Alfreton DE55. . . . . . . 159 B3
Barlborough S43. . . . . .80 C6
Bradwell S33 . . . . .51 A8
Breaston DE72. . . . . 235 C7
Breedon on the Hill
DE73. . . . . 252 E2
Brimington S43. . . . . . .96 C7
Buxton SK17. . . . . .85 B8
Chapel-en-le-Frith
SK23. . . . . .47 C7
Clay Cross S45. . . . . . 131 C2
Derby, Boulton DE24 . .232 E6
Derby, Chaddesden
DE21. . . . . 219 F5
Holmesfield S18. . . . . .75 A8
Holymoorside S42 . . 113 D8
Hope S33 . . . . .39 A4
Horsley Woodhouse
DE7. . . . . 192 C7
Mayfield DE6 . . . . . . 184 D7
New Mills SK22. . . . . . .33 B8
Repton DE65. . . . . . . 242 D2
Risley DE72 . . . . 222 D3
Sheffield S17 . . . . .55 E5
Shirebrook NG20 . . . . 119 E6
Shirley DE6. . . . . 200 D7
Stanley DE7. . . . . . . 207 B8

Crescent The continued
Stapleford NG9. . . . . 209 E2
Swadlincote DE11 . . . 255 E6
CRESSBROOK. 89 A6
Cressbrook Ave
S42. . . . . 132 B7
Cressbrook Way
DE21. . . . . 206 B3
Cressida Ct DE73 . . . 232 D2
Cresswell Ave S42. . . .33 C8
Cresswellpart La S33 .50 E7
Cresswell St SK22 . . . .33 C8
Cressy Rd DE55. . . . . 159 A4
Cresta Gr DE21. . . . . 205 F1
Crest Cl DE13. . . . . . . 240 E1
Crest The
Derby DE22 . . . . 204 E2
Linton DE12 . . . . 261 C6
CRESWELL. 81 F2
Creswell Bsns Pk
S80. . . . . 100 E8
Creswell CE (Controlled)
Inf Sch S80 . . . . .81 E1
Creswell Crags ★
S80. . . . . .82 A1
Creswell Ct **12**
NG19 . . . . 136 E4
Creswell Jun Sch
S80. . . . . .81 E1
Creswell L Ctr S80. . . .81 F1
Creswell Rd
Clowne S43. . . . . .80 F4
Cuckney NG20 . . . . . 101 E3
Creswell Sta S80. . . . . .81 E1
Creswick Cl S40. . . . . 114 B8
Crewe St S23 . . . . 218 F1
CREWTON. 232 F8
Crewton Way DE24 . . 232 F7
CRICH. 156 F1
Crich Ave DE23 . . . . . 218 C2
Crich Carr CE Prim Sch
DE4. . . . . 156 C1
Crich CE Inf Sch
DE4. . . . . 156 F1
Crich Cir DE23 . . . . . 218 C2
CRICH COMMON . . . 168 B8
Crich Common
DE56. . . . . 168 A6
Crich Jun Sch DE4 . 157 A1
Crich La
Belper DE56 . . . . 179 A7
Ridgeway DE56 . . . . . 168 B3
Crich Pl
Buxton SK17. . . . . .85 E7
North Wingfield S42 . 131 F6
Crich Rd
Crich DE4 . . . . 167 E8
Staveley S43. . . . . .97 C7
Crich Tramway Village ★
DE4. . . . . 156 E2
Crich View
Bolsover S44 . . . . 118 B8
Newton DE55 . . . . . . 148 A4
Crich View Dr DE56. 179 E8
Heanor NG16 . . . . . . 181 E5
Ripley DE5 . . . . 169 C2
Wirksworth DE4. . . . . 154 F1
Cricket Cl DE15 . . . . 248 E8
Cricket View S43 . . . . .80 E2
Cricklewood Ct **7**
S43. . . . . .78 B3
Cricklewood Rd
DE22. . . . . 218 B6
Crimbles La DE45. . . 125 B5
Cringle Mews DE21. . 205 E2
Cripton La S45 . . . . . 129 E5
Crispin Cl S12. . . . . . . .44 A4
Crispin Dr S12. . . . . . . .44 A4
Crispin Gdns S12. . . . . .44 A4
Crispin Rd **3** S12. . . . .44 A4
CRIST. 46 B8
Critchley St DE7 . . . . 194 F1
Critch's Flats NG16. . 195 F5
Croft Ave DE6 . . . . . . 151 D1
Croft Cl
Dale Abbey DE7 . . . . . 207 F2
Derby DE21 . . . . 220 F5
Netherseal DE12 . . . . 264 F7
Ockbrook DE72. . . . . 221 C4
Pinxton NG16 . . . . . . 160 C3
Rolleston DE13 . . . . 240 B4
Croft Cres NG16 . . . . 195 C5
Croft Ct NG17 . . . . . . 148 F4
Croft End DE21 . . . . . 205 C8
Crofters Cl S21. . . . . . .60 C4
Crofters Ct DE21. . . . 205 E2
Croft Gr ST14. . . . . . . 210 C1
Croft House Way S44 98 F1
Croft Inf Sch DE55. . 159 A3
Croft La DE21. . . . . . . 205 D3
Croft Lea S18. . . . . .56 C2
Croft Manor SK13 . . . .10 E1
Croft Meadow DE4 . 154 C5
Crofton Cl
Dronfield S18. . . . . . . .56 F1
Yeaveley DE6 . . . . . . 199 D5
Crofton Rise S18. . . . . .56 F1
Croft Pk SK13 . . . . .10 D1
Croft Rd
Great Longstone
DE45. . . . . .90 A4
Sheffield, Intake S12 . . 44 B5
Croftstead Ave
ST14. . . . . 196 D6
Crofts The S32 . . . . . . .53 A8
Croft The
Bamford S33 . . . . .40 B3
Belper DE56 . . . . 179 C1

Croft The continued
Burton upon Trent
DE15. . . . . 254 F8
Derby DE23 . . . . 231 D8
Draycott DE72 . . . . . 235 A6
Duffield DE56 . . . . . . 190 D4
Glossop SK13. . . . . .10 A6
Heage DE56 . . . . 168 E1
2 Melbourne DE73 . . 252 A8
Morley DE7. . . . . 192 C2
Mottram in Longdendale
SK14. . . . . .9 A4
Shirebrook NG20 . . . . 119 F3
Shirland DE55 . . . . . 146 D2
Somercotes DE55. . . 170 C7
South Normanton
DE55. . . . . 160 A6
Swadlincote DE11 . . . 255 E6
Taddington SK17 . . . . .88 A3
Croft View
Clowne S43. . . . . .80 F3
Staveley S43. . . . . .97 C6
Croftview Cl DE21 . . . 205 D3
Croft Way DE23. . . . . 230 F6
Croft Wlk S80 . . . . .82 A6
Cromarty Cl DE24. . . 231 E4
Cromarty Rise S18. . . .56 D2
Cromdale Ave S43. . . .77 D4
Cromer Cl DE3 . . . . . 217 C1
CROMFORD. 155 A6
Cromford Bank **21**
SK13. . . . . .9 D2
Cromford Canal Nature
Reserve ★ DE56. . . . 167 E5
Cromford CE Prim Sch
DE4. . . . . 155 B6
Cromford Cl
Aldercar NG16 . . . . . 182 B4
22 Gamesley SK13. . . . .9 D2
Long Eaton NG10 . . . 236 A5
North Wingfield S42 . 132 B7
Cromford Ct
4 Chesterfield S41. . . .95 D7
Horwich End SK23 . . . .45 E6
Cromford Dr
Derby DE3 . . . . 217 E4
Staveley S43. . . . . .97 C8
Cromford Fold **23**
SK13. . . . . .9 D2
Cromford Gn **20** SK13 . .9 D2
Cromford Hill **18** SK13 . .9 D2
Cromford La S45 . . . . .87 E7
Cromford Lea **19** SK13 . .9 D2
Cromford Mews
SK23. . . . . .45 E5
Cromford Pl
Buxton SK17. . . . . .85 E7
24 Gamesley SK13. . . . .9 D2
Cromford Rd
Aldercar NG16 . . . . . 182 B4
Clay Cross S45. . . . . . 131 A5
Crich DE4 . . . . 156 F2
Derby DE21 . . . . 220 A8
Heanor NG16 . . . . . . 181 E5
Ripley DE5 . . . . 169 C2
Wirksworth DE4. . . . . 154 F1
Cromford Road Ind Est
NG16 . . . . 182 B4
Cromford Sta DE4. . . 155 C7
Cromford Way **17**
SK13. . . . . .9 D2
Cromford Wharf ★
DE4. . . . . 155 C7
Crompton Cl DE4. . . 127 E1
Crompton Rd
Ilkeston DE7. . . . . . . 209 A4
Mansfield NG19 . . . . 135 D3
Staveley S43. . . . . .97 C8
Crompton Road Ind Est
DE7. . . . . 209 B3
Crompton St
Derby DE1 . . . . 267 B2
New Houghton NG19 . 134 F8
Cromwell Ave
Blackwell DE55. . . . . 147 E1
Chapel-en-le-Frith
SK23. . . . . .47 A5
Findern DE65 . . . . . . 230 D2
Ilkeston DE7. . . . . . . 209 A5
Cromwell Cl DE13 . . 239 C5
Cromwell Dr DE55 . . 169 D7
Cromwell Rd
Bolsover S44 . . . . 118 B8
Chesterfield S40. . . . 266 A4
Derby DE23 . . . . 218 F2
Cromwell St NG16 . . 195 C8
Cromwell Terr DE7 . . 194 F3
Crooked Spire (St Mary
& All Saints Church) ★
S40. . . . . 266 B4
Crookes Ave
1 Mansfield Woodhouse
NG19 . . . . 136 C3
Pleasley NG19 . . . . . 135 A5
Crook Stile DE4 . . . . 143 A7
CROPPER. 215 B4
Cropper La
Sutton on the Hill
DE6. . . . . 215 B4
Thurvaston DE6 . . . . 201 C1
Cropston Cl S41. . . . . 115 C4
Cropton Cl DE24 . . . 233 C6
Crosby Dr DE5 . . . . . 227 D2
Crosby St DE22 . . . . 218 D4
Cross Chantrey Rd
S8. . . . . .43 A3
Cross Cl
Derby DE23 . . . . 231 C8

Cross Cl continued
Overseal DE12 . . . . . 262 B3
Cross Cliffe SK13 . . . . .17 E8
Crossdale Gr DE21. . . 206 C3
Crossfield Gr SK6. . . . .15 B1
Crossgate La SK13. . . . .9 F7
Crossgreen Cotts
DE4. . . . . 142 B8
Crosshill DE5. . . . . . . 181 B6
CROSS HILL. 181 B5
Crosshill Dr DE7. . . . 208 C5
Crossings Ave SK23. . .47 A6
Crossings Mdw SK23 .47 A6
Crossings Rd SK23. . . .46 F6
Cross Key Mws
DE56. . . . . 177 C2
Cross Keys La DE55. 169 E7
Cross Keys Row
SK23. . . . . .47 B8
Cross La
Calver S32. . . . . 72 B2
Codnor DE5 . . . . 181 B7
Dronfield S18. . . . . . . .57 C5
Dronfield, Coal Aston
S18. . . . . .57 C3
Dronfield, Quoit Green
S18. . . . . .57 B1
Flagg SK17. . . . . 106 E7
Ible DE4 . . . . 153 E7
Monyash DE45 . . . . . 107 B2
Rolleston DE13 . . . . 240 B2
Sheffield S17 . . . . .55 C8
Shirland DE55 . . . . . 158 E8
Sutton in Ashfield
NG17. . . . . 148 F2
Wessington DE55. . . . 158 F8
Crossland Dr S12. . . . .44 A3
Crossland Pl S12 . . . . .44 A4
Crossland Rd S32. . . . .53 A7
Crosslands Cl SK13 . . .17 E8
Crossland Villas S32. .53 A7
Crosslanes DE6. . . . . 215 C5
Cross Lanes DE4. . . . 144 C1
Cross Lea DE7. . . . . . 207 F2
Crossley St DE5 . . . . 169 E8
Cross London St S43. .77 D3
Crosslow La DE6 . . . . 150 E5
Cross Myrtle Rd S2. . .43 B7
CROSS O' THE HANDS
DE56. . . . . 176 E1
Cross Park Rd **1** S8. . 43 A5
Cross Rd DE4. . . . . . . 210 B1
Cross/Repton Sch The
DE65. . . . . 242 C3
Cross Rise SK13 . . . . . .17 E8
Crossroads Bsns Pk
S43. . . . . .80 E4
Cross Side DE6 . . . . . 184 F7
Cross St
Bolsover S44 . . . . 118 C8
Breedon on the Hill
DE73. . . . . 252 F2
Brimington S43. . . . . . .96 E8
8 Broadbottom SK14 . .16 A8
Buxton SK17. . . . . .85 D8
Castleton S33. . . . . . . .38 B2
Chapel-en-le-Frith
SK23. . . . . .47 B6
Chesterfield S40. . . . 266 A4
Clay Cross S45. . . . . . 131 C3
Derby DE22 . . . . 218 D6
Glossop SK13. . . . . .10 C1
Grassmoor S42 . . . . . 115 F3
Hadfield SK13. . . . . . . .10 A5
Hollingworth SK14 . . . . .9 D4
Killamarsh S21. . . . . . .60 F7
Linton DE11 . . . . 261 E4
Long Eaton NG10 . . . 236 E8
Mansfield Woodhouse
NG19 . . . . 136 B2
New Mills SK22. . . . . . .33 C8
North Wingfield S42 . 131 E6
Sandiacre NG10 . . . . 223 C6
Cross The
1 Glossop SK13 . . . . . .10 A5
Great Longstone DE45 . .89 F4
Crossways La DE6 . . . 176 B2
Cross Wellington St
S43. . . . . .77 D3
Crow Croft Rd S45. . . 132 C2
Crowcroft Way
NG10 . . . . 223 B2
CROWDEN. 6 E3
Crowden Dr SK13. . . . .10 B5
CROWDICOTE 121 E7
Crowdicote Rd
SK17. . . . . 105 D1
Crowestones SK17. . . .85 C1
Crowfoot La DE65 . . 226 B8
Crow Hill
Palterton S44 . . . . . . 118 A5
Pleasley NG19 . . . . . 135 B5
Crowhill La DE45 . . . 109 A6
Crow Hill La NG19 . . 136 B2
Crow Hill Rd HD9. . . . . .3 B8
CROWHOLE. 75 D4
Crow La
Brackenfield DE55 . . 146 A6
Chesterfield S41. . . . . .96 C3
Unstone S18. . . . . .76 F7
Crown Cl
Chesterfield S43. . . . . .77 C1
Long Eaton NG10 . . . 236 E8
Crown Gdns DE16 . . . 254 C8
Crown Hill Way
Stanley Common
DE7. . . . . 193 B1
West Hallam DE7 . . . 207 B8

Crown La S18 . . . . 58 A1
Crownland Dr DE73. 233 A2
Crown Mews DE22. . 218 E3
Crown Rd S41 . . . . 96 A5
Crown Rise DE11 . . 256 D3
Crown Sq
 Branston DE14 . . . . . . 253 E8
 Matlock DF4 . . . . 143 B5
Crown St
 Clowne S43. . . . . 80 E3
 Derby DE22 . . . . 218 E3
 Duffield DE56 . . . . . . 190 E4
 Marple SK6. . . . . 23 A3
Crown Terr [2] DE56 . 178 F4
Crown Way
 Aldercar NG16 . . . . . . 182 B4
 Chellaston DE73. . . . . 244 F8
Crown Wlk DE1. . . . . . 267 B2
Crowshaw St DE24. . 232 B8
Crowstones Rd DE4. 127 B3
Crowther Pl [7] S7. . . 43 A8
Croxall Rd DE12 . . . . 259 D2
Croxton Ct [5] NG19. 136 E3
Croydon Close [6]
 DE11. . . . . 255 E1
Croydon Wlk DE22. . 217 F6
Cruck Cl S18 . . . . 56 E2
Crystal Cl DE3 . . . . . . 217 D4
Cubley Common
 DE6. . . . . 198 E3
Cubley La DE6. . . . . . 198 B1
Cubley Wood DE6 . . 198 E5
Cuckmere Cl DE22. . 205 B5
CUCKNEY. 101 F3
Cuckoostone La
 DE4. . . . . 128 F2
Cuillin Cl NG10 . . . . 223 A1
Cullabine Ct S2. . . . 44 A7
Cullabine Rd S2. . . . 44 A7
Culland La DE6. . . . . . 201 E5
Culland Rd DE14. . . . 254 B7
Culland View DE4 . . 168 A8
Cullen Ave DE6. . . . . 173 C1
Cullumbell La S45. . 129 A7
Culworth Cl DE56. . . 179 D4
Culworth Ct DE21. . 206 B2
Cumberhills Grange
 DE56. . . . . 190 D2
Cumberhills Rd
 Duffield DE56, DE56. . 190 C1
 Duffield DE56. . . . . . . 190 D3
 Quarndon DE22. . . . . 204 A8
 Weston Underwood
 DE22. . . . . 203 F8
Cumberland Ave
 Derby DE21 . . . . 219 E6
 Market Warsop NG20. 120 F5
Cumberland Cl
 Buxton SK17. . . . . . . 85 D4
 Westwood NG16. . . . 171 C4
Cumberland Cres
 DE72. . . . . 221 B2
Cumberland Dr
 Chesterfield S41. . . . . 76 D1
 Chesterfield S41. . . . . 95 C8
Cumberland Rd
 Burton upon Trent
 DE15. . . . . 254 D6
 Wildboarclough SK11. 102 A8
Cumbria Wlk DE3. . 217 C1
Cummings St DE23. 219 A2
Cundy Rd S44 . . . . . . 99 A3
Cunliffe St S18 . . . . . 57 C4
Cunnery La DE4 . . . . 144 B3
Cunnery The DE6. . . 202 F2
Cunningham Pl
 DE45. . . . . 109 D6
Cupola Pk DE4 . . . . 156 B2
CURBAR. 72 E2
Curbar Cl
 Little Eaton DE22 . . . . 205 A4
 North Wingfield S42. . 132 B7
Curbar Curve S43 . . . 97 C6
Curbar La S32. . . . . . 72 D2
Curbar Prim Sch S32 72 D1
Curborough Dr
 DE24. . . . . 233 D6
Curlew Ave
 Eckington S21. . . . . . 59 B3
 Harpur Hill SK17. . . . . 85 D2
Curlew Cl DE24. . . . . 231 D4
Curlew Way SK13. . . 16 F8
Curtis Gr SK13. . . . . . 10 A5
Curzon Ave S18 . . . . 75 F8
Curzon CE Prim Sch The
 DE22. . . . . 204 D6
Curzon Cl
 Derby DE22 . . . . 204 C4
 Killamarsh S21. . . . . 60 D6
Curzon Ct DE56. . . . 190 E3
Curzon La
 Derby DE24 . . . . 233 A8
 Duffield DE56. . . . . . . 190 D3
Curzon Rd
 Buxton SK17. . . . . . . 85 C7
 Derby DE21 . . . . 219 F7
Curzon St
 Derby DE1 . . . . 267 A3
 Long Eaton NG10 . . . 223 B2
Curzon Terr SK17. . . 88 D7
Cuscas La DE6. . . . . . 187 F4
Cut La DE1, DE6. . . . 219 B7
Cutler Cl S21. . . . . . . 60 B7
Cutler La
 Weston Underwood
 DE22. . . . . 203 A8

Cutler La continued
 Weston Underwood
 DE6. . . . . 189 A1
Cutlers Ct [12] S2. . . . 43 C8
Cutler Way DE3. . . . 217 D4
Cuttholme Cl S40. . . . 95 B4
Cuttholme Rd S40. . . 95 C4
Cuttholme Way [1]
 S40. . . . . 95 C4
Cutthorn Rd SK11. . . 102 C5
CUTTHORPE. 94 F7
Cutthorpe Grange
 S40. . . . . 95 A7
CUTTHORPE GREEN . . 94 E7
Cutthorpe Prim Sch
 S42. . . . . 94 D7
Cutthorpe Rd
 Chesterfield S40. . . . . 95 A8
 Cutthorpe S18 . . . . . . 94 F7
Cutting The DE11. . . 256 F4
Cuttlebrook Cl
 DE23. . . . . 231 E6
Cyclamen Cl DE14 . . 254 A8
Cygnet Fold NG19 . . 136 C4
Cygnet Hosp DE24. . 219 D2
Cypress Ave
 Clay Cross S45 . . . . . 131 B3
 Sheffield S8 . . . . 43 C1
Cypress Cl S21. . . . . 60 C5
Cypress Way SK6. . . 32 A7
Cypress Wlk DE21 . . 220 B5
Cyprus Rd S8. . . . . . . 43 A5
Cyril Ave NG9 . . . . . . 223 D7

D

Dade Ave S43. . . . . . . 97 C6
Daffodil Dr [1] DE3 . . 217 D5
Dag La DE12. . . . . 263 E7
Dagnall Gdns DE45 . 109 D5
Dagnall Terr DE45 . . 109 D5
Dagnam Cl S2. . . . . . . 43 F6
Dagnam Cres S2 . . . . 43 F6
Dagnam Dr S2 . . . . . . 43 F7
Dagnam Pl S2. . . . . . . 43 F6
Dagnam Rd S2. . . . . . 43 F6
Dahlia Ave DE55. . . . 160 B7
Dahlia Dr DE21 . . . . 206 C3
Dairy Farm Cl DE65. 242 B5
Dairyfield Dr S80. . . 101 E8
Dairy House Rd
 DE23. . . . . 219 B1
Dairy La ST14. . . . . . 225 E2
Dairy Mws [3] DE6 . . 201 E8
Daisy Cl
 Donisthorpe DE12 . . . 262 E1
 Shirebrook NG20 . . . . 119 D2
Daisy Farm Rd
 NG16. . . . . 195 B8
Daisy Gro DE3. . . . . . 217 C5
Daisy La DE12 . . . . . . 262 B3
Daisymere La SK17 . . 67 A2
Dakeyne Cl DE4 . . . . 127 F1
Dakin Ave SK17. . . . . 85 D8
Dakin Ct SK17. . . . . . 66 E1
DALBURY. 216 B1
Dalbury Rd S18. . . . . 56 C1
Dalbury Wlk DE3 . . . 231 C5
Dalby Green Cl
 DE5. . . . . 181 A8
DALE ABBEY. 207 F2
Daleacre Ave DE74. . 247 F5
Dale Acre Way
 DE21. . . . . 205 D3
Dale Ave
 Long Eaton NG10 . . . 223 D1
 Newton DE55 . . . . . . 148 A3
 Somercotes DE55. . . . 170 C6
DALEBANK. 145 C8
Dale Bank Cres S43. . 77 D3
Dalebank La S45 . . . . 145 B8
Dale Bottom DE6 . . . 149 D2
Dale Brook DE65 . . . 228 E1
Dalebrook Rd DE15. 248 B5
Dale Cl
 Breaston DE72 . . . . . 235 D8
 Fritchley DE56. . . . . . 168 A6
 Langwith NG20. . . . . 119 E8
 Matlock DE4 . . . . 154 D8
 Staveley S43. . . . . . . 97 C8
 Stonebroom DE55 . . . 147 B4
 Whaley Thorns NG20 . 100 F1
Dale Com Prim Sch
 DE23. . . . . 218 F2
Dale Cres
 Hathersage S32 . . . . . 53 B8
 Tupton S42. . . . . 115 C1
Dale Ct DE56 . . . . . . 191 F8
DALE END. 140 C7
Dale End
 Biggin SK17 . . . . 138 B4
 Brassington DE4. . . . . 153 A1
 Wirksworth DE4. . . . . 154 F1
Dale End Rd DE65 . . 228 C2
Dalefield Dr DE11. . 256 B3
Dalehead Ct S32. . . . 71 E5
Dale Head Rd
 Dove head SK17. . . . . 103 E8
 Hartington upper Quarter
 SK17. . . . . 84 D1
 Hartington upper Quarter
 SK17. . . . . 104 A8
Dale Hill DE55. . . . . . 158 B5
Dale La
 Buxton SK17. . . . . . . 85 E8
 Glapwell S44. . . . . . . 134 D7
Dale Park Ave DE56. 192 A8

Dale Rd
 Buxton, Higher Buxton
 SK17. . . . . 85 C7
 Buxton, Peak Dale
 SK17. . . . . 67 B7
 Derby DE21 . . . . 221 A6
 Derby DE21, DE72 . . . 221 A6
 Derby, Alvaston DE24. 233 B7
 Derby, Normanton
 DE23. . . . . 218 F2
 Dronfield S18 . . . . . . 76 B8
 Killamarsh S21. . . . . 60 E6
 Kimberley NG16. . . . . 195 F6
 Matlock Bath DE4. . . . 143 B3
 Middleton DE45 . . . . . 124 F3
 New Mills SK22. . . . . . 33 C7
 Over Haddon DE45. . . 109 A1
 Stanley DE7 . . . . 207 C4
 Stanton-by-Dale DE7 . 208 C1
 Thurvaston DE7 . . . . . 201 C1
 Tupton S42. . . . . 115 C1
Dale Rd North DE4. . 116 C3
Dale Road N DE4 . . . 127 A5
Dale Road S DE4 . . . 127 D1
Dales Cl [4] DE11 . . . 255 E5
Dalesfield DE4 . . . . . 143 A6
Dalesgate Cl DE23 . . 231 C5
Daleside DE15. . . . . . 248 B1
Dale Side SK17 . . . . . 85 B7
Dale St
 Ilkeston DE7. . . . . . . 208 F7
 Mansfield NG19 . . . . . 136 B1
Dales The DE7. . . . . . 207 E7
Dalestorth Ave
 NG19 . . . . 135 D1
Dale Terr SK17 . . . . . 85 B6
Dale The
 Bonsall DE4 . . . . 142 D1
 Hathersage S32 . . . . . 53 B8
 North Wingfield SK17. . 131 F5
 Stoney Middleton S32. . 71 E4
 Wirksworth DE4. . . . . 154 E1
Dale View
 Earl Sterndale SK17. . 105 B3
 Ilkeston DE7. . . . . . . 208 E7
 Litton SK17. . . . . 69 E3
 Mottram in Longdendale
 SK14. . . . . 9 A3
 Shirland DE55. . . . . . 146 C4
 [4] Willington DE65. . 242 B6
Dale View Cl S45 . . . 132 B3
Dale View Gdns
 DE56. . . . . 191 F8
Dale View Rd S45. . . 132 B4
Dale View Terr SK17. 89 A6
Dalewood Cl
 Chesterfield S41. . . . . 96 E1
 South Normanton
 DE55. . . . . 160 A3
Dalkeith Ave DE24. . 232 F5
Dalley Cl [1] NG9. . . 223 E7
Dalley La DE56 . . . . . 178 C6
Dallimore Prim Sch
 DE7. . . . . 208 D4
Dallimore Rd DE7 . . 208 D4
Dalness Ct [7] DE4 . . 231 D3
Dalston Rd DE11. . . . 256 A5
Dalton Ave
 Burton upon Trent
 DE15. . . . . 248 B5
 Derby DE22 . . . . 218 C3
Dalton Cl [3] NG9 . . . 223 E5
Dalton Dr DE56 . . . . 179 A4
Dalton Road DE56 . . 179 C6
Daltons Cl NG16 . . . . 182 A4
Dalvey Way S43 . . . . . 77 C5
Dam Cl DE55 . . . . 158 E3
Dame Catherine Harpur's
 Sch DE73. . . . . 251 A5
Dam La
 Alsop en le Dale
 DE6. . . . . 150 E3
 Shirland DE55. . . . . . 146 F1
Damon Cl S45. . . . . . 132 C1
Damon Dr S43. . . . . . 96 F8
Damsbrook Dr S43. . 80 E3
Damsbrook La
 Bolsover S80. . . . . . . 99 D8
 Clowne S43. . . . . 80 D1
Dam Side S43 . . . . . . 79 A4
Damside La SK17. . . . 49 A3
Damson Croft S43. . . 78 A2
Damson Gr DE24 . . . 232 E8
Damstead Pk Ave
 DE55. . . . . 158 E3
Danbury Cl S42. . . . . 115 E3
Danby Ave S41 . . . . . . 77 B2
Danby Rd [6] DE23 . . 230 F5
DANEBANK. 32 E5
Danebridge Cres
 DE21. . . . . 206 A1
Dane Gr SK17 . . . . . . 85 C4
Dane Hill Cl SK12. . . 32 D5
Danesby Cres DE5. . 180 A1
Danesby Rise DE5. . 180 A1
DANESMOOR. 131 E3
Danesmoor Ind Est
 S45. . . . . 131 F2
Danesway SK23. . . . . 47 B6
Danewood Gdns S13. . 44 E7
Daniel Mews NG10 . . 223 A5
Dannah Cres DE5. . . 169 F1
Dannah St DE5 . . . . . 169 F2
Darby St DE23 . . . . . 218 F2
Darcy Rd S21. . . . . . . 59 C3
Daresbury Cl S2. . . . 43 D6
Daresbury Dr S2 . . . 43 D6

Daresbury Pl S2. . . . 43 D6
Daresbury Rd S2 . . . 43 D6
Daresbury View S2 . . 43 D6
Darfield Ave S20. . . . 44 F2
Darfield Cl S20. . . . . 44 F2
Darfield Cl DE75 . . . 182 A2
Darfield La DE6. . . . . 162 C4
DARFOULDS. 63 F1
Darkey La NG9 . . . . . 223 E5
Dark La
 Ashbourne DE6. . . . . 173 A1
 Ashover DE55. . . . . . 145 C6
 Bradley DE6 . . . . 175 B3
 Calow S44. . . . . 96 F2
 Chesterfield S44. . . . . 96 A4
 Church Broughton
 DE65. . . . . 227 B6
 Cich DE4 . . . . 156 F5
 Cromford DE4. . . . . . 154 F4
 Holbrook DE56 . . . . . 191 F7
 North Wingfield S42. . 132 B7
 Pilsley S45 . . . . 132 D2
 Tatenhill DE13 . . . . . 253 A8
 Tideswell SK17. . . . . . 69 C3
 Wirksworth DE4,
 DE56. . . . . 165 D3
 Youlgreave DE45 . . . . 125 D7
Darklands La DE11. . 256 A4
Darklands Rd DE11 . . 256 B5
DARLEY ABBEY. 205 A2
Darley Abbey Dr
 DE22. . . . . 204 F2
Darley Ave
 Beeston NG9 . . . . 223 F3
 Darley Dale DE4 . . . . 127 C3
 North Wingfield S42. . 132 B7
DARLEY BRIDGE . . . 142 C8
Darley Churchtown CE
 Prim Sch DE4 . . . . . . 127 B3
Darley Cl
 Burton upon Trent
 DE15. . . . . 248 C1
 Harthill S26 . . . . 61 E6
 Staveley S43. . . . . . . 78 E1
 Swadlincote DE11 . . . 256 A1
DARLEY DALE. 127 C2
Darley Dale DE11. . . 255 F2
Darley Dale Prim Sch
 DE4. . . . . 127 E2
Darley Dale Sta★
 DE4. . . . . 127 C2
Darley Dr
 Long Eaton NG10 . . . 236 A5
 Ripley DE5 . . . . 169 C3
 West Hallam DE7 . . . . 207 E8
Darley Gr
 Buxton SK17. . . . . . . 85 C6
 Derby DE1 . . . . 219 A7
DARLEY HILLSIDE. . 127 D4
Darley House Est
 DE4. . . . . 142 E8
Darley La DE1 . . . . . . 267 B4
Darley Lodge Dr
 DE4. . . . . 142 E8
Darley Moor Motor Cycle
 Racing Circuit
 DE6. . . . . 185 A1
Darley Park★ DE22. 205 A1
Darley Park Dr
 DE22. . . . . 204 F2
Darley Park Ho
 DE22. . . . . 205 A1
Darley Park Rd
 DE22. . . . . 204 F2
Darley Rd
 Ashover S45. . . . . . . 113 B2
 Ashover S45. . . . . . . 128 C8
 Ashover S45. . . . . . . 112 C1
Darley Sq DE7. . . . . . 194 E5
Darley St DE22 . . . . . 205 A1
Darley Way
 Buxton SK17. . . . . . . 85 E7
 North Wingfield S42. . 132 B7
Darne Mws DE6 . . . . 175 F2
Darnley Dr S2 . . . . . . 44 A8
Darraway Gdns
 DE73. . . . . 232 D2
Darsway DE74. . . . . . 246 F4
Dartford Pl DE24 . . . 233 A5
Dartmouth Ct [20]
 S41. . . . . 95 F8
Dartnall Cl SK12. . . . 32 A6
Darwen Cl DE3 . . . . . 230 C8
Darwent Rd S41. . . . . 96 C6
Darwin Ave
 Buxton SK17. . . . . . . 85 C7
 Chesterfield S40. . . . . 95 E5
 Derby DE24 . . . . 232 D4
 Ilkeston DE7. . . . . . . 208 E7
Darwin Cl DE15. . . . . 248 C1
Darwin Fields Close
 DE21. . . . . 205 A4
Darwin Forest Ctry
 Park★ DE4 . . . . 128 C7
Darwin Pl DE1. . . . . . 267 C3
Darwin Rd
 Chesterfield S40. . . . . 266 A4
 Derby DE3 . . . . 217 E3
 Long Eaton NG10 . . . 236 B5
Darwin Sq DE1 . . . . . 267 C3
Darwood La S44. . . . . 118 B8
Dashwood St DE23 . . 267 B1
Datchet Cl DE23 . . . . 231 A8
Daubenton Way
 S42. . . . . 114 F3
Daveham Ave SK17. . 85 C6
Davenport Dr NG16. 195 B7
Davenport Gr DE6 . . 185 D7

Davenport Rd
 Derby DE24 . . . . 232 C8
 Tupton S42. . . . . 131 C8
Davenport Way
 DE11. . . . . 256 F1
Daventry Cl DE21 . . . 217 C3
Davey Ct S44. . . . . 98 F3
Davian Way S40 . . . . 114 E8
David Lloyd Sp Ctr
 DE24. . . . . 219 D4
David Nieper Acad
 DE55. . . . . 159 A3
David's Cl DE73. . . . . 232 F1
Davids Dr S42. . . . . . 114 E4
Davies Close DE24. . 232 C8
Da Vinci Com Coll
 DE21. . . . . 205 E1
Davis Ho [2] DE1. . . 267 B2
Davis Rd DE11. . . . . . 256 B4
Davy Gro S20 . . . . . . 60 A6
Dawber La S21. . . . . . 60 F7
Dawgates La NG19. . 134 F2
Dawkins Rd DE12. . . 262 E1
Dawlish Ct
 [4] Chesterfield S41. . 95 F8
 Derby DE24 . . . . 233 C7
 Eastwood NG16. . . . . 182 D3
Dawn Field DE12 . . . 262 B3
Dawn View NG9 . . . . 209 D2
Dawsmere Cl DE21. . 205 D3
Dawver Rd NG16. . . . 195 F6
Dayfield La DE6 . . . . 175 A4
Daykins Row DE5. . . 181 C7
Daylesford Cl DE23. 231 A8
Days La DE56. . . . . . . 178 F3
Days Mill Cl DE4. . . . 143 A6
Dayton Cl DE21. . . . . 220 C5
Dayton Ct DE22. . . . . 218 E8
Deacon Cl
 Derby DE21 . . . . 205 E2
 Swanwick DE55 . . . . . 169 E7
Deacon Ct S23. . . . . . 47 A5
Dead La NG16 . . . . . . 195 D1
Deadman's La DE24. 219 D2
Deakon Dr S18 . . . . . 57 B3
Deamon St DE55. . . . 147 E1
Dean Cl DE23. . . . . . . 218 A2
Dean Ct DE23. . . . . . . 218 E2
Deanery Close DE5. 168 E2
Deanhead Dr S20. . . 44 F2
Dean Rd DE56 . . . . . . 167 F2
Deans Cl S40. . . . . 96 D7
Deans Dr DE72 . . . . . 221 B2
Deansgate NG19. . . . 135 A5
Dean St
 Derby DE22 . . . . 218 E3
 Langley Mill NG16. . . . 182 C3
Debdale La NG19 . . . 136 A2
Debdale Way DE21 . . 136 B2
Deben Cl S40. . . . . . . 114 C8
Deben Down NG19. . 136 B2
Deborah Dr DE21. . . 220 A7
Dee Cl
 Derby DE24 . . . . 231 E3
 Sheffield S20. . . . . . . 228 E1
Dee La DE65. . . . . 229 F6
Deep Carr La DE4. . . 143 D4
Deepdale
 Hulland Ward DE6 . . . 175 F1
 Ironville NG16 . . . . . . 170 F4
Deepdale Ave
 Borrowash DE72 . . . . 221 C3
 Stapleford NG9. . . . . . 223 D6
Deepdale Bsns Pk
 DE45. . . . . 109 B6
Deepdale Cl
 Burton upon Trent
 DE15. . . . . 248 B5
 Staveley S43. . . . . . . 78 E1
Deepdale Ct DE75 . . 181 E1
Deepdale La DE6 . . . 184 A2
Deep Dale La
 Barrow upon Trent
 DE73. . . . . 243 F7
 Barrow upon Trent
 DE73. . . . . 244 A7
 Derby DE24, DE73 . . . 231 F1
Deepdale Rd
 Belper DE56. . . . . 179 B5
 Bolsover S44. . . . . . . 98 F3
 Derby DE21 . . . . 220 F3
 Long Eaton NG10 . . . 236 A5
 Mansfield NG19 . . . . . 136 A2
Deepdene Cl DE11. . 256 C1
Deep La
 Hardstoft S44, S45. . . 133 B3
 Sheen SK17 . . . . 121 C3
 Sheen SK17 . . . . 122 B1
DEEP PIT. 43 F8
Deepsick La S44. . . . . 97 C1
Deepwell Ave S20 . . 59 F6
Deepwell Bank S20. 59 F6
Deepwell Ct S20. . . . 59 F6
Deepwell Dr S20 . . . 60 A6
Deepwell Mews
 Killamarsh S20. . . . . 60 A6
 Sheffield S20 . . . . 59 F6
Deepwell View S20. . 59 F6
Deerlands Rd
 Chesterfield S40. . . . . 95 B3
 Wingerworth S42. . . . 114 F2
Deerleap La S42. . . . 130 D3
Deerpark Cres S42 . . 114 F3
Deer Park Prim Sch
 S42. . . . . 114 F3
Deer Park View
 DE21. . . . . 220 F4

Deer Pk La DE55. . . . 169 F3
De Ferrers Ct DE56 . 190 E3
Degge St DE1 . . . . . . 267 B2
Dein Court NG17 . . . 148 E4
Deincourt Cl DE22. . 221 A6
Deincourt Cres S42. . 131 E4
Deira Dr S17 . . . . 55 E6
De Lacy Ct DE74 . . . 247 A3
Delamere Cl
 Breaston DE72 . . . . . 235 D8
 Derby DE21 . . . . 206 A1
 Swanwick DE55 . . . . . 169 F7
Delf St S2. . . . . 43 B7
Delhi Cl DE15. . . . . . 248 C3
Dell The
 Chesterfield S40. . . . . 95 B3
 Horwich End SK23 . . . 45 F5
Delph Bank S40 . . . . 114 E8
Delph Cl S32. . . . . 71 D6
Delph The DE73 . . . . 252 F2
Delven La DE74. . . . . 247 B3
Delves Bank Rd
 DE55. . . . . 170 A7
Delves Cl S40 . . . . . . 95 D1
Delves Ct DE75 . . . . 193 E8
Delves Rd
 [9] Heanor DE75. . . . . 181 D1
 Heanor DE75. . . . . . . 193 D8
 Killamarsh S21. . . . . 60 C6
Delves The DE55. . . . 169 F7
De Montfort Close [8]
 DE11. . . . . 255 E1
Denacre Ave NG10. . 223 F1
Denacre La DE4 . . . . 127 C3
Denarth Ave DE24 . . 232 E3
Denbigh St DE21 . . . 219 E7
Denby Bank DE5. . . . 180 D5
DENBY BOTTLES. . . . 180 A1
Denby Cl S42. . . . . . . 115 B4
Denby Comm DE5 . . 180 F3
DENBY COMMON. . . . 181 A3
Denby Free CE (VA)
 Prim Sch DE5 . . . . . . 180 D1
Denby Hall Bsns Pk
 DE5. . . . . 180 D5
Denby Hall Rd NE7 . . 194 F6
Denby Hall Way
 DE5. . . . . 180 C4
Denby Pottery Visitor
 Ctr★ DE5 . . . . 180 C3
Denby Rd S43 . . . . . . 97 C7
DENBY VILLAGE. 180 C1
Denefield Cl SK6 . . . 15 B1
Dene Fields Ct DE4 . 143 C6
Dene The
 Hopton DE4. . . . . 153 F1
 Hopton DE4. . . . . 154 A1
 Hopton DE4. . . . . 164 F8
Denham St S45. . . . . 131 D3
Denison Gdns
 DE21. . . . . 220 B6
Denman Cres S32 . . . 72 A3
Denmark Rd S2 . . . . . 43 B6
Dennis Barsby Cl
 DE11. . . . . 255 E3
Dennis Cl DE23 . . . . 230 E7
Dennor Dr NG19. . . . 136 E5
Denson Cl [4] S2. . . . 43 B6
DENSTONE. 196 C7
Denstone Coll ST14. 196 B5
Denstone Dr DE24. . 233 A4
Denstone La
 Denstone ST14. . . . . . 196 C7
 Denstone ST14. . . . . . 196 E7
Dentdale Ct DE24 . . 233 C7
Dent La S12. . . . . 44 F2
Denton Ave NG10. . . 223 A6
Denton Cl NG19 . . . . 136 E1
Denton Way DE55 . . 169 F7
Denver Cl NG9 . . . . . 209 E1
Denver Rd DE3 . . . . . 217 D3
Depedale Ave DE7. . 208 D5
De Peverel Ct DE55 . 146 D2
Depot St DE23 . . . . . 219 A2
DERBY. 267 C4
Derby Arboretum★
 DE23. . . . . 267 B1
Derby Cath★ DE1. . . 267 B3
Derby Cathedral Sch
 DE1. . . . . 218 E1
Derby Coll Broomfield
 Hall DE7 . . . . 206 B5
Derby Coll (Ilkeston
 Campus) DE7 . . . . . . 208 E8
Derby Coll Sp Ctr
 DE22. . . . . 217 F5
Derby Coll (The Joseph
 Wright Ctr) DE1 . . . . 267 A4
Derby Coll (The
 Quantum Ctr) DE1 . . 267 D1
Derby Coll (The
 Roundhouse)
 DE24. . . . . 219 C4
Derby Commercial Pk
 Derby DE21 . . . . 220 D2
 Derby DE24 . . . . 233 E8
Derby Distribution Ctr
 DE24. . . . . 231 E5
Derby Gram Sch
 DE23. . . . . 230 F7
Derby High Sch
 DE23. . . . . 218 B1
Derby Hills DE73. . . . 251 E6

Derby Hills House Ct
DE73.............251 E5
Derby Knoll SK23.....33 F1
Derby La
Brailsford DE6 ....201 B8
Derby DE23 ....231 F8
Great Cubley DE6.....198 F1
Monyash DE45 ....123 C7
Shirley DE6..........200 E8
Derby Midland Sta
DE1................219 C4
Derby Moor Com Sports
Coll DE23........231 B7
Derby Mus & Art Gall★
DE1...............267 B3
Derby Pl S2........43 C6
Derbyrd DE73 ....244 E6
Derby Rd
Alfreton DE55......158 F3
Ambergate DE56....167 F3
Ashbourne DE6......185 E7
Ashbourne DE6......185 F6
Aston-on-Trent DE72...234 A2
Borrowash DE21,
DE72............221 A4
Burton upon Trent
DE13............241 A1
Chellaston DE73....232 F2
Clay Cross S45, S42..131 C5
Crich DE4.........167 D8
Cromford DE4......155 C6
Dale Abbey DE7,
DE21...........206 E3
Derby, Spondon DE21.220 C3
Doveridge DE6.....211 B1
Doveridge DE6.....224 D7
Draycott DE72.....234 E8
Duffield DE56.......190 F6
Duffield, Flaxholme
DE56..........190 F1
Eastwood NG16.....182 E2
Egginton DE65 .....241 C4
Etwall DE65 ....229 A4
Hatton DE65.......227 E2
Heanor DE75 ......181 D1
Hilton DE65 ....228 E3
Hilton DE65 ....228 F3
Hilton DE65 ....240 C8
Horsley DE21, DE56.191 D5
Ilkeston DE7.......208 D7
Kilburn DE56......179 F1
Langley Mill NG16..182 C3
Long Eaton NG10...236 B8
Lower Kilburn DE56.191 E7
Marston on Dove
DE65...........228 B2
Melbourne DE73....244 F1
Melbourne DE73....252 A8
2 Milford DE56......190 F7
New Mills SK22......24 D1
Ripley DE5 ....180 C3
Ripley DE5 ....180 E8
Risley DE72.......222 D4
Sandiacre NG10....223 A5
Smisby LE65 ......258 A4
Stanley DE7.......207 B4
Stapleford NG9....223 D6
Swadlincote DE11 ..256 C3
Swanwick DE5, S169 E5
Ticknall DE11, DE73..257 F7
Uttoxeter ST14......210 D1
West Broughton DE6..225 A7
Whatstandwell DE4..156 B2
Wingerworth S42....115 A6
Wirksworth DE4.....165 E6
Derby Road Ind Est
Clay Cross S45......131 B5
Heanor DE75 ......181 D1
Sandiacre NG10.....223 B5
Derbyshire Ave
Trowell NG9.......209 D4
West Hallam DE7...207 E8
Derbyshire Cl DE7..207 E8
Derbyshire Craft Ctr★
S32.............72 D2
Derbyshire Cty Cricket
Gd DE21 ....219 C6
Derbyshire Dales
National Nature
Reserve★ SK17....89 A3
Derbyshire Dr
Castle Donington
DE74............247 B4
Ilkeston DE7......208 E6
Westwood NG16 ....171 C4
Derbyshire Flying Ctr★
S33............51 A7
Derbyshire La S8....43 A3
Derbyshire Level
SK13.............17 F6
Derby Small Bsns Ctr
Derby DE1........267 C2
Derby, Pear Tree
DE23...........219 B1
Derby St
Glossop SK13.......17 C8
3 Ilkeston DE7......208 F8
Sheffield S2.......43 C6
Derby Terr S2........43 C6
Derby Theatre★
DE1...........267 B2
Derby Trad Est
DE21............219 B8
Dere Croft 6
DE72............221 C4

Derrington Leys
DE24.............233 D6
Derventio Cl DE1 ..219 A7
DERWENT.........30 C6
Derwent Ave
Belper DE56 ....179 A1
Borrowash DE72 ...221 C3
Darley Dale DE4....127 C4
Derby DE72 ....205 A4
Grindleford S32 .....72 C8
Ilkeston DE7.......194 D2
West Hallam DE7...207 E8
Derwent Bsns Ctr
DE1.............267 C4
Derwent Bsns Pk
DE5.............169 B1
Derwent Cl
Derby DE22 ....205 A4
Dronfield S18.......57 B3
Glossop SK13.......17 F8
Grindleford S32 .....72 C8
1 Hilton DE65 ......240 E8
Swadlincote DE11 ..256 A1
Derwent Com Sch
DE21............219 C7
Derwent Cres S41....95 D7
Derwent Ct
Belper DE56 ....179 B4
5 Sheffield S17.......56 A5
Willington DE65 ...242 B6
Derwent Dr
Baslow DE45......91 D6
Chinley SK23.......34 E1
Derby DE24 ....231 D2
Tibshelf DE55......147 F6
Derwent Gdns DE6.185 D8
Derwent Gr DE55...158 F2
Derwent Ho DE21...219 C6
Derwent La
Derwent S33.......30 B7
Derwent S33.......30 C6
Hathersage S32.....52 F8
Northwood DE4....127 A6
Derwent Par DE21,
DE24............219 E3
Derwent Park Ho
DE22 ....205 A1
Derwent Pl S45....131 A5
Derwent Rd
Burton upon Trent
DE15...........248 A2
Buxton SK17.......85 C6
Derby DE21 ....220 D3
Dronfield S18.......57 B3
Ripley DE5 ....169 C1
Derwent Rise DE21 .220 F4
Derwentside Ind Pk
DE56............178 F1
Derwent Sq SK23...34 E1
Derwent St
Belper DE56 ....178 F3
Derby DE1 ....267 C4
Draycott DE72.....235 A7
Derwent Street Ind Est
NG10............236 C6
Derwent Terr DE4 ..143 A7
Derwent Vale DE56.178 F2
Derwent Valley Visitor
Ctr★ DE56 ......178 F5
Derwent View
Baslow DE45 ....91 E6
Belper, Milford DE56.191 A8
Belper, Mount Pleasant
DE56...........178 F5
Darley Dale DE4....127 B3
Mastin Moor S43 ....79 C3
Ridgeway DE56.....168 B3
Derwent Way
Matlock DE4 ......143 A7
Whatstandwell DE4.156 B3
Desborough Rd
NG16 ....171 D7
De Sutton Pl S26....61 E5
DETHICK..........156 B8
Dethick La DE4.....144 D1
Dethick Way DE4...132 B7
Devas Gdns DE21...220 D5
Deveron Cl DE13...240 C1
Deveron Rd S20 ....59 F7
Devizes Cl S40....114 F8
Devon Cl
Burton upon Trent
DE15...........254 A6
Grassmoor S42....115 F2
Sandiacre NG10....223 B5
Devon Dr S43 ....96 F8
Devon La DE74....247 B3
Devon Park View
S43.............96 F8
Devonshire Ave
Borrowash DE72...221 C2
Darley Dale DE4...142 F7
Long Eaton NG10...237 A8
Ripley DE5 ....169 C2
Devonshire Avenue E
S41............115 C8
Devonshire Avenue N
S43.............77 E3
Devonshire Bsns Ctr
S43.............78 B2
Devonshire Cl
Chesterfield S41.....95 F8
Dronfield S18.......75 F8
Ilkeston DE7......194 E6
Sheffield S17.......55 F6
2 Staveley S43.......78 E2

Devonshire Cotts
S44..............118 E6
Devonshire Ct
Brimington S43.......96 D7
5 Derby DE22.......204 F3
Devonshire Dr
Chinley SK23........34 E2
Creswell S80 ....81 C1
Derby DE3 ....217 E3
Duffield DE56......190 D2
Eastwood NG16....182 F2
Langwith NG20.....119 F8
Rowsley DE4......110 F1
Sheffield S17.......55 E7
Somercotes DE55...170 B7
Stapleford NG9.....209 D2
Devonshire Drive
DE55.............148 A3
Devonshire Glen
S17..............55 F6
Devonshire Gr S17...55 E6
Devonshire Pk S43...96 E8
Devonshire Rd
Buxton SK17.......85 B8
Sheffield S17.......55 F6
Devonshire Rd E 3
S41..............115 C8
Devonshire Road E
S41..............115 C8
Devonshire Road N
S43.............77 D3
Devonshire Sq DE4 .111 A3
Devonshire St
Ambergate DE56 ....167 F3
Brimington S43.......96 E8
Chesterfield S41......266 B3
New Houghton NG19..135 A7
3 Staveley S43.......78 E2
Devonshire Terr
Holmewood S42.....116 E1
Matlock Bath DE4...148 A4
Devonshire Terrace Rd
S17.............55 D7
Devonshire Villas 28
S41..............115 C8
Devonshire Way S43..81 A4
Devonshire Wlk
DE1.............267 C2
Devon St DE7.......209 A5
De Warren Pl S26....61 F5
Dewberry Court
DE24.............143 B5
Dewchurch Dr DE23 231 E5
Dewint Ave SK6.....23 B8
Dewley Way S45....131 D5
Dew Pond La SK17....85 E8
Dewsnap La S14.....9 A6
Dewy La DE4, DE55..144 F1
Dexter St DE23 .....219 F3
DH Lawrence Birthplace
Mus★ NG16.......182 F2
Dialstone S18.......51 A7
Diamond Ct DE45...109 D5
Diamond Dr DE11....114 F8
Diamond Jubilee Cotts
DE6.............184 E8
Dibble Rd DE14....254 A7
Dickens Dr
Holmewood S42.....116 D1
Swadlincote DE11 ..256 C5
Dickenson Rd S41...266 C1
Dickens Sq DE23...231 F7
Dickinson's La DE6.215 B1
Dickinson St DE24...219 D2
Dicklant La S45......145 B8
Didcot Cl S40......114 F8
Didsbury Terr SK22...25 E2
Digby Ct 4 NG19..136 C3
Digby Ind Est NG16..195 D7
Digby St
Cossall DE7.......195 A1
Ilkeston DE7......209 A8
Kimberley NG16.....195 D7
Diglands Ave SK22...24 D1
Diglands Cl SK22....24 D1
Diglee Rd SK23......33 C3
Digmire La DE6......161 D1
Dig St
Ashbourne DE6......173 B2
Hartington SK17....137 D6
Dilston Way DE72...245 A8
DIMPLE...........143 A6
Dimple Cres DE4 ...143 B5
Dimple La DE56....168 B8
Dimple Rd DE4 ....143 A6
Dimple Road Bsns Ctr
DE4.............143 B6
Dimple The DE56...168 B7
Dingle Cl SK13.....17 A8
Dingle La S41, S44...96 E5
Dingle The DE15...254 E8
Dingley Cl NG19....136 E5
Dinmore Grange
DE11............257 B6
Dinnington La DE55. 157 C6
Dinting CE Prim Sch
SK13.............10 A1
Dinting CE VA Prim Sch
Glossop SK13........10 A4
Glossop SK14........9 F1
Dinting La SK13......10 A1
Dinting Lane Trad Est
SK13.............10 B2
Dinting Lodge Ind Est
SK13.............10 A1
Dinting Rd SK13.....10 B2
Dinting Sta SK13....10 A2
Dinting Vale SK13...10 A1

Dinting Vale Bsns Pk
SK13..............9 F2
Dirty La
Castleton S33.......38 A3
Great Hucklow SK17...70 B8
Hognaston DE6......164 A3
Stockport SK6.......15 F2
Discovery Way S41...77 A1
Diseworth Cl DE73...232 F2
Diseworth Rd DE74..247 A1
Dish La DE6 ....228 B6
Dishwell La S26......61 E6
DISLEY............32 C5
Disley Prim Sch
SK12.............32 D6
Disley Sta SK12.....32 C6
Disraeli Cres DE7...208 F8
Ditch Cotts SK17....105 F8
Ditch The
Chelmorton SK17....105 F8
Chelmorton SK17....106 A8
Division Rd NG20...119 E4
Division St S43......97 C8
Dix Ave
Smalley DE7........192 F6
2 Smalley DE7........193 A6
Dixie St NG16.......171 B4
Dixon Croft S43......77 C4
Dixon Ct S41........77 B3
Dixon's Rd S41.....266 C2
Dobbinhorse La
DE6.............185 B5
Dobbin La S18.......75 C6
Dobbs Cl S21........60 C6
Dobholes La DE7...192 D6
Dobholes La DE7...192 F6
Dobroyd Ave S2.....44 A7
Dobson Pl S43 ......97 B6
Dockholm Rd NG10. 223 C2
Dock Wlk S40......266 A2
Doctor La S26........61 F5
Doctor's La DE73 ...252 F2
Dodburn Ct DE24 ...231 D4
Dodgewell Cl DE55 .147 F1
Dodslow Ave DE13...240 B3
Doe Hill La DE55....147 D5
DOEHOLE.........145 A2
Doehole La
Ashover DE4, DE55...144 F3
Brackenfield DE55...145 A2
Doe La S12.........58 C5
DOE LEA..........117 D1
Doe Lea Nature
Reserve★ S44.....117 D2
Doghole La DE4 ....154 C4
Dogkennel La DE6...186 E7
Dog Kennel La DE6..211 B1
Dog La
Hulland Ward DE6...175 D4
Nethersear DE12....264 F6
Stonebroom DE55...146 E2
Wilson DE73.......252 E6
Dokindale Rd SK17...88 B2
Dolby Rd SK17.......85 D2
Doles La
Clifton DE6.......184 F7
Findern DE65......230 D3
Whitwell S80 ....82 B7
Dolly La
Chinley SK23.......34 A2
Furness Vale SK23...33 F3
Dolly Wood Cl SK23...34 B1
Dolphin Cl DE21 ....221 A6
Domain Dr DE73.....232 E1
Dominion Rd DE11...256 B5
Dominoe Gr S12....44 D5
Donald Hawley Way
DE56............190 F3
Doncaster Ave
NG10.............223 B6
Doncaster Gr NG10.223 F1
Donegal Wlk DE21...220 A4
Donington Cl DE23 .231 E5
Donington Dr
Derby DE23 ....231 E5
4 Woodville DE11....256 E1
Donington La DE72,
DE74............247 C7
Donington Park Motor
Racing Circuit★
DE74............246 C1
DONISTHORPE....262 F1
Donisthorpe La
DE12.............262 E2
Donkey La S32......72 C2
Donner Cres DE7...194 E5
Dorchester Ave
DE21............219 F7
Dorchester Rd
NG16.............195 F7
DORE.............55 E7
Dore Cl S17........56 A7
Dore Ct S17........56 A7
Dore Hall Croft S17...55 D7
Dore La S32........53 A7
Dore Lodge Gardens
S17.............55 F7
Dore Prim Sch S17...55 D6
Dore Rd S17........55 E8
Dore & Totley Sta
S17.............56 A7
Doris Rd DE7.......209 A7
Dorking Rd DE22 ...218 B8
Dormy Cl NG19....136 E5
Dorothy Ave
Mansfield Woodhouse
NG19...........136 C1
Sandiacre NG10....223 B5

Dorothy Dr NG16....136 F1
Dorothy Vale S40....95 C4
Dorrien Ave DE23...232 A7
Dorset Ave 2 S43...96 F8
Dorset Cl
Burton upon Trent
DE15...........254 E6
Buxton SK17.......85 D4
Dorset Dr S43 ....96 F8
Dorset St DE21 ....219 D6
Dorterry Cres DE7..209 A5
Dotterel Place
NG20.............120 D4
Doublet Close S18. 171 A6
Double Villas DE55 .146 F3
Douglas Ave
Awsworth NG16....195 C5
Heanor DE75 ......181 C2
Douglas Gdns S81 .181 C2
Douglas Rd
Chesterfield S41......96 C6
Long Eaton NG10...223 B1
Somercotes DE55...170 D8
Douglas St
Derby DE23 ....219 B2
Derby DE23 ....219 C2
Douse Croft La S10...42 F6
Dove Bank SK6......24 A6
Dove Bk S46.........23 F6
Dove CE Academy
ST14.............196 F4
Dove Cl
Branston DE14.....253 E6
Branston DE14.....256 E6
Derby DE3 ....218 A3
Kilburn DE56......192 A8
Woodville DE11....256 F3
Dovecliff Cres DE13.240 F2
Dovecliff Rd DE13 ..240 E3
Dovecote DE74 .....247 B3
Dovecote Dr DE72...221 B2
Dovecote Rd SK6....23 C2
Dovecotes S45......129 F3
Dovecote The
Breedon on the Hill
DE73............252 F2
Horsley DE21 .....191 F6
Dovedale Ave
Ashbourne DE6......173 D1
Derby DE24 ....233 C7
Long Eaton NG10...236 B6
Staveley S43.......97 B5
Dovedale Circ DE7..194 E5
Dovedale Cl
Burton upon Trent
DE15...........248 B5
Ripley DE5 ....180 D6
Dovedale Cres
Belper DE56 ....179 B5
Buxton SK17.......84 F6
Dovedale Ct DE6 ...185 E8
Dovedale Ct
4 Chesterfield S41.....95 F2
1 Glossop SK13.......10 F1
Long Eaton NG10...236 B6
Dovedale Day Hospl
DE1.............267 C1
Dovedale National
Nature Reserve★
DE6.............161 A6
Dovedale Prim Sch
NG10.............236 B6
Dovedale Rd DE21...220 F3
Dovedale Rise DE22 204 D1
Dovedales The DE3. 217 D2
Dovefields
Draycott in the Clay
ST14............225 D3
Rocester ST14......196 F3
Dove Fst Sch ST14..197 A3
Dove Gr DE65 ......241 A5
DOVE HEAD.......103 D6
Dovehead and Three
Shires Head
Flash SK17........102 F4
Flash SK17........103 A5
DOVE HOLES.......47 E2
Dove Holes CE Prim Sch
SK17.............47 F1
Dove Holes Sta SK17..47 E1
Dove House Gn DE6 173 B2
Dove La
Long Eaton NG10...236 C8
Rocester ST14......197 A4
Dove Lea DE13.....240 B4
Doveleys ST14......197 A8
Dove Leys La S14...196 F8
Dove Meadow DE21 221 A6
Dove Pl DE65.......239 C8
Dover Ct DE23.......219 A2
DOVERIDGE........211 A1
Dove Ridge SK17...121 C6
Doveridge Cl S41.....77 A2
Doveridge Gr SK17...85 C6
Doveridge Prim Sch
DE6.............224 C8
Doveridge Rd DE15.248 B1
Doveridge Wlk
DE23.............231 C5
Dove Rise DE65....228 C2
Dover St
Creswell S80 ....81 C1
Derby DE23 ....219 A1
Doveside DE6 .....184 D7
Dove Side DE65 ...239 D8

Dovesite Bsns Pk
DE73.............251 E6
Dove St DE6.........183 B2
Dovestone Gdns
DE23.............218 B1
Dovetail Ct S41.....266 C4
Dove Valley Pk
DE65.............227 A5
Dove View DE13 ...239 C6
Dove Way The ST14. 210 C2
Dove Well View
DE55.............159 C4
Dovewood Ct DE23 .231 A7
Dowcarr La S26......61 C5
Dowdeswell St S41..266 B4
Dower Cl DE22 ....205 A1
Dowie Way DE4 ....156 F2
Downham Cl DE3...217 E1
Downing Cl DE22...217 F6
Downing Ho DE22 ..217 F6
Downing Rd
Derby DE21 ....219 D5
Sheffield S8.........56 E8
Downing Row S32...52 F8
Downing St DE55...160 A6
Downings The S26...61 F5
Downlea S43.........96 D7
Downlee Cl S43.....46 F5
Downmeadow DE56 179 E8
Downs The NG19...136 F1
Dowry La S23.......45 D5
Drabbles Rd DE4 ...143 A6
Drage St DE1.......219 B7
Drake Ave S43......98 A8
Drakelow Nature
Reserve★ DE14...253 F6
Drakelow Rd
Walton-On-Trent
DE12...........256 E2
Walton-on-Trent
DE16...........254 A3
Walton upon Trent
DE12...........253 E2
Drake Terr S43......96 C8
DRAYCOTT........234 F7
Draycott Cl DE75...181 C4
Draycott Com Prim Sch
DE72.............235 A7
Draycott Ct DE7 ...194 F3
Draycott Dr DE3 ...217 C3
Draycott Mills DE72.235 A7
Draycott Pl S18.....75 C8
Draycott Rd
Borrowash DE72 ...221 C1
Breaston DE72.....235 C7
Long Eaton NG10...236 A4
North Wingfield S42..131 F3
Drayton Ave
Derby DE22 ....217 F6
Mansfield NG19 ....135 D1
Drayton St DE11....256 C4
Dresden Cl DE3.....217 C2
Drewry Ct DE1......218 F5
Drewry La DE22 ...218 F4
Dreyfus Cl DE21....220 F5
Drift Road DE11 ....255 D2
Drive The DE56....177 F3
DRONFIELD........56 E2
Dronfield Bypass S41 76 F2
Dronfield Henry
Fanshawe Sch The
S18..............57 B2
Dronfield Inf Sch
S18..............57 A1
Dronfield Jun Sch
S18..............57 A1
Dronfield Pl DE7 ...194 E5
Dronfield Rd S21....59 B2
Dronfield Sp Ctr S18 .57 A1
Dronfield Sta S18....57 A1
Drovers Way
Ashbourne DE6.......173 B3
Bullbridge DE56.....168 B5
Drovers Wlk 3 SK13..10 D1
Drum Cl DE22 .....204 F3
Drummond Rd DE7..194 E1
Drummond Way
DE73.............232 E2
Drury Ave DE21.....220 D4
Drury La
Biggin SK17 ....138 C2
Dronfield S18.......57 C3
Sheffield S17.......55 D7
Drury Lowe Cl DE5 . 180 A1
Dryden Ave S40....115 A6
Dryden Ct NG9 ....209 E4
Dryden St DE23.....231 F7
Dryhurst Dr SK12....32 D6
Dryhurst La S12....32 D6
Drysdale Rd DE3...217 D3
Dry Stone Edge Rd
SK17.............103 A6
Dry Stones Edge Rd
SK17............102 F7
Duchess St
Creswell S80 ....81 F1
Whitwell S80 ....82 A6
Duchess Way DE73 . 244 E8
Duck Island DE56...190 E4
DUCKMANTON....98 A5
Duckmanton Prim Sch
Duckmanton S43.....97 F6
Duckmanton Rd S44..98 A5
Duck Row DE45 ....91 C3
Ducksett La S21.....59 C2
Duck St DE65.......241 B5
Duddy Road SK12....32 E6

Dudley Dr DE23.........**230** F6
Dudwood La DE4.....**140** F7
Duesbury Cl DE24 ... **232** E7
Duesbury Ct DE3 ... **230** B7
Duesbury Pl DE3 ... **230** B7
Duesbury The DE55. **160** B4
DUFFIELD **190** F3
DUFFIELDBANK.....**191** A3
Duffield Bank DE56. **191** A4
Duffield Cl NG10.... **236** A5
Duffield Ct DE56....**190** F3
Duffield Meadows Prim
Sch DE56..........**190** D3
Duffield Millennium
Mdw Nature Reserve★
DE56............**190** F3
Duffield Rd
6 DE22.....**204** F3
Derby DE22 .... **205** A5
Duffield Rd Ind Est
DE21............**205** C7
Duffield Sta DE56....**190** F4
Duke Dr DE45 ......**126** D2
Duke Field DE4....**154** D5
Duke of Norfolk CE Prim
Sch SK13...........**10** D1
Duke of Norfolk's Prim
Sch SK13..........**10** A1
Dukeries Ct S43......**80** F3
Dukeries La DE21.... **206** B2
Duke's Bldgs DE56.. **191** A7
Dukes Cl S42........**116** E1
Dukes Dr
Ashford in the Water
DE45...........**108** F8
Chesterfield S41......**95** E6
Curbar S32.........**72** D2
Duke's Dr
Buxton SK17.......**85** C5
Glapwell S44 ...... **134** A7
Duke's Dr The DE45 **108** E8
Dukes Fold SK13 .... **17** C8
Dukes Pl DE7.... **194** E4
Dukes Rd DE5 ...... **169** B4
Dukes St SK13......**17** C8
Duke St
Buxton SK17.......**84** E6
Chesterfield S41......**96** A8
Clowne S43.........**81** A4
Creswell S80 ....**81** F1
Derby DE1 ....**267** B4
Ilkeston DE7.......**194** F3
Middleton DE4 ..... **154** D5
Sheffield S20 ....**59** D6
South Normanton
DE55..........**160** B6
Staveley S43.........**78** E2
Tutbury DE13 ...... **239** C6
Whitwell S80 ....**82** A6
Duluth Ave DE21.... **220** A7
Dulverton Ave
DE24.........**231** C2
Dulwich Ct **11** S43....**78** B3
Dulwich Rd DE22 ... **217** C6
Dumb Hall La S80 ....**63** B4
Dumbles Cl DE7 ... **208** C6
Dumbles La DE55....**180** F2
Dumbles Rd S44....**98** F1
Dumbleton Rd S21....**60** E5
Dumble Wood Grange
S41............**95** C7
Dumfries Dr DE22 .. **218** B4
Dunbar Cl
Derby DE24 .... **231** E2
Nottingham NG10...**236** E4
Dunbar Close NG10. **236** E4
Duncan Cl DE56 .... **179** B6
Duncan Rd
2 Derby DE23....**218** F8
Derby DE23 ......**231** F8
Duncombe Dr DE6.. **185** C8
Dundas Way DE73.. **232** E1
Dundee Dr NG19.... **136** B6
Dundee Rd DE11.... **256** D5
Dundonald Rd S40.. **266** B1
Dunedin Cl DE3 .... **217** E3
Dunedin Cres DE15 . **248** C3
Dunedin Glen S20 .... **59** E6
Dunedin Gr S20 ....**59** E6
Dunge Rd SK23......**45** A2
Dungley Hill S40 ... **168** D2
Dungreave Ave DE4. **127** A5
Dunkery Ct DE21 .... **206** A2
Dunkirk DE22.......**267** A2
Dunlop Dr DE4......**246** F2
Dunlow La S32.......**71** C5
Dunn Brigg NG19... **136** D2
Dunn Dr NG10 ...... **236** B7
Dunne La SK13 ......**10** E2
Dunnicliffe La DE73. **252** A7
Dunn La DE3 ...... **217** B2
Dunnock Dr **4** NG9. **209** C2
DUNNSHILL.........**207** C1
Dunnsmoor La
DE11.........**256** E7
Dunoon Cl DE24 ....**231** E3
Dunsa La DE45 ......**91** F1
Dunsford Rd DE55.. **159** B5
Dunshill Wlk S45 ... **131** E4
Dunsil Cl NG19 ...... **136** B1
Dunsil Ct NG19 ...... **136** B1
Dunsil Rd
7 Mansfield NG19..**136** B1
Pinxton NG16 .... **160** D2
Dunsley Mdws Nature
Reserve★ DE4....**154** E7
Dunsmore Dr DE21 .**205** F2

Dunsmore Way
DE11............**256** D5
Dunstall Brook
DE15.........**248** A1
Dunstall Park Rd
DE24..........**232** D8
Dunstall Rd DE13... **253** A7
Dunston Cl NG10 ...**236** F7
Dunston Ct S41......**76** F1
Dunston La S41 .....**95** D8
Dunston Pl S41 .....**76** F1
Dunston Prim Sch
S41............**95** D8
Dunston Rd S41......**76** D2
Dunston Tech Pk
S41............**76** E1
Dunston Trad Est
S41...........**76** E2
Dunston Way S41.....**76** E1
Dunton Cl DE21...**267** D3
Dunvegan Ave S45...**131** E2
Dunvegan Cl DE24 .. **231** D2
Duper La S32.........**51** E5
Durban Cl DE15.... **248** C3
Durban House Her Ctr★
NG16.........**182** F3
Durham Ave
Chesterfield S43......**77** D3
Derby DE21 ...... **219** E6
Grassmoor S42 ....**115** F2
Durham Cl
Chesterfield S43......**77** D3
Mansfield Woodhouse
NG19 .... **136** D4
Swadlincote DE11 .. **256** E5
Durham St **3** DE7 .. **194** F1
Durley Chine Dr
S41............**115** C8
Durley Cl DE24 ... **233** C2
Durlstone Cl S12 .....**44** A5
Durlstone Cres S12...**44** A5
Durlstone Dr
Sheffield S12.......**43** F5
Sheffield S12.......**44** A5
Durlstone Gr S12.....**44** A5
Durrant Rd S41....**266** B3
Durvale Ct S17 ......**55** E6
Durward Cl DE24 ... **232** C7
Dyche Cl S8.........**57** B6
Dyche Dr S8.........**57** B6
Dyche La S8, S18....**57** B5
Dyche Pl S8.........**57** B6
Dyche Rd S8 ....**57** B6
Dye House La SK22 ...**33** C8
Dykes Cl S44........**99** A2
Dyke Vale Rd S12.....**44** F5
Dymond Gr S42 .... **115** F3
Dystelegh Rd SK12 ...**32** D6

E

Each Well La DE55..**158** F3
Eades Fold S33.......**38** C3
Eagle Cl DE56 .....**178** F2
Eagle Dr DE73......**244** E8
Eagle Hts DE15 .... **248** D3
Eagle Par **9** SK17 ...**85** B7
Eagle Rd DE7.......**208** F4
Eagle St
4 Buxton SK17....**85** B7
Heage DE56 ....**168** E2
Eagle Terr
Birchover DE4 ......**126** B1
Wensley DE4 ...... **142** A7
EAGLE TOR **126** A2
Eagle Way NG19....**136** F2
Ealand St DE13 .... **240** D4
Ealing Cl DE22......**218** B6
Ealing Ct **8** S43......**78** B3
Eames Cl **6** DE75 .. **181** D1
Eardley Cl DE21 .... **220** B5
Earlham Cl DE7.... **208** C6
Earls Cres DE21 ... **206** B2
Earls Drive DE4.... **231** C3
EARL STERNDALE .. **105** C3
Earl Sterndale CE Prim
Sch SK17.......**105** C3
Earl Sway **5** S43....**17** B8
Earlswood Cl DE72 . **235** D8
Earlswood Dr DE3.. **217** F4
Earnshaw St SK14 ....**9** D4
Earp Way DE73 ....**252** C8
Easedale Cl S40 ....**94** F5
Easset Dr DE6 ......**203** A2
East Ave
Derby DE3 ....**217** E3
Stanfree S44 ....**80** B1
East Bank Cl DE4....**141** C5
East Bank Pl S2 ......**43** D6
East Bank Rd S2.....**43** D6
East Bank Way S2....**43** D6
Eastbrae Rd DE23..**231** D7
East Brook Cl SK23 ...**47** C6
East Cl DE22.......**204** E2
Eastcliffe Ct S2.......**43** C8
East Cres
Holbrook DE56 .... **191** C8
Long Duckmanton S44 ..**98** A6
East Croft Ave DE23 **231** D5
Eastcroft Cl S20 ....**59** F8
Eastcroft Dr S20....**59** F8
Eastcroft Glen S20...**59** F8
Eastcroft View S20...**59** F7
Eastcroft Way **7** S20 **59** F8
East Dr DE6........**211** B1
East End DE4........**140** F7
East End Dr DE11... **256** C4

Eastern Ave
Bolsover S44 ....**118** B8
Sheffield S2 ....**43** E7
Eastern Cres S2 ......**43** D6
Eastern Dr S2 ....**43** D7
Eastern Wlk S2.......**43** D7
Eastfield Dr DE55... **160** A5
Eastfield Rd
Dronfield S18........**76** B4
Ripley DE5 .... **170** A1
Swadlincote DE11 .. **256** C6
Eastgate DE1, DE21.. **267** D4
East Glade Ave S12...**44** E3
East Glade Cl S12....**44** E3
East Glade Cres S12 ..**44** E3
East Glade Dell S12...**44** E4
East Glade Pl S12.....**44** E3
East Glade Rd S12....**44** E3
East Glade Sq S12....**44** E3
East Glade Way S12 ..**44** E4
East Lawn DE65 ....**230** D2
East Lawn Dr DE6... **211** B1
Eastleigh Ct S41....**115** C8
Eastleigh Dr
Derby DE3 ....**217** B1
Mansfield Woodhouse
NG19 .... **136** B6
East Midlands Airport
DE74.........**247** C1
East Midlands Designer
Outlet (Sh Ctr)
DE55..........**160** E6
East Midlands
Distribution Ctr
DE74.........**246** E5
EASTMOOR **93** D4
Eastmoor Rd S43....**96** F4
East Nelson St
DE75..........**181** D2
East Par S80 ....**82** A5
East Rd S2 ....**43** B7
East Service Rd
DE21.........**220** B3
Eastside Cl S41......**96** B8
Eastside Rd S41 .....**96** B8
Eastsides La SK17 ....**69** F2
East St
Bramley-Vale S44.... **117** D1
Burton upon Trent
DE15..........**248** C3
Clay Cross S45 ..... **131** D4
Clowne S43.........**81** A5
Creswell S80 ....**81** D1
Derby DE1 ....**267** B3
Heanor DE75 ..... **194** A8
Ilkeston DE7.......**208** F8
Long Eaton NG10 .. **236** F8
Renishaw S21.......**79** B8
Scarcliffe S44.......**118** E6
Warsop Vale NG20 .. **120** D5
East Vale SK6 ....**23** A5
East View
Chesterfield S40....**266** B2
Hillstown S44.......**118** B7
Mayfield DE6 ...... **184** D7
Shirebrook NG20 ... **119** F6
Whaley Thorns NG20 . **101** A3
East View Ave S21....**59** C2
East View Ind Est
NG20 .... **119** F6
East View Rd DE56.. **168** E1
Eastview Terr
NG16 .... **182** B3
Eastway DE74 ..... **247** B3
EASTWOOD.........**182** E3
Eastwood Ave DE23. **218** C2
Eastwood Cl S41 ... **115** D8
Eastwood Cotts S32 . .**53** B8
Eastwood Dr
Calow S44..........**97** B2
Derby DE23 .... **218** C2
Eastwood Grange Sch
S45...........**130** B4
Eastwood La S45 ... **130** B2
Eastwood Park
Apartments S41... **115** C7
Eastwood Park Dr
S41...........**115** D8
Eastwood Rd NG16 . **195** E6
Eather Ave NG19 ... **136** C4
Eaton Ave
Derby DE22 ....**205** B5
Ilkeston DE7.......**208** D6
Eaton Bank DE56 ... **191** A1
Eaton Cl
Derby DE22 ....**205** A5
Hatton DE65.......**227** D1
Hulland Ward DE6 .. **175** E3
Eaton Ct
Baslow DE45 ....**91** F5
Derby DE1 ....**218** E6
Duffield DE56 ......**190** E2
Eaton Dr DE45.......**91** F5
Eaton Fold S32.......**71** F3
Eaton Grange Dr
NG10 ....**236** A8
Eaton Hill DE45.......**91** F5
Eaton La S45 ......**129** B5
Eaton Pl DE45.......**91** F5
Eaton Rd
Castle Donington
DE74..........**247** B3
Rocester ST14 .... **196** F3
Eatons Rd NG9 .... **223** D6
Eaton St S14 ......**210** C1
Eaves Ave SK23......**47** C5
Eaves Knoll Rd SK22 ..**33** B8
Ebenezer Brow SK13..**10** B7

Ebenezer St
Glossop SK13........**17** D7
Ilkeston DE7........**194** F3
Langley Mill NG16...**182** B3
Ecclesbourne Ave
DE56..........**190** F3
Ecclesbourne Cl
Duffield DE56......**190** E3
Wirksworth DE4....**165** F7
Ecclesbourne Cotts
DE4...........**154** F2
Ecclesbourne Ct
DE56..........**190** E3
Ecclesbourne Dr
Buxton SK17........**84** F6
Buxton SK17........**85** A6
Ecclesbourne La
Derby DE3 ....**217** B1
Idridgehay DE56....**176** F5
Ecclesbourne Mdws
DE56..........**190** D4
Ecclesbourne Pk
DE55..........**159** D2
Ecclesbourne Sch The
DE56..........**190** E3
Ecclesbourne Valley
Rly★ DE4 ......**154** F2
Eccles Cl
Hope S33 ....**39** A4
Whaley Bridge SK23 ..**45** D8
ECCLES FOLD **46** C8
Eccles Fold SK23 ....**47** A6
Eccles La S33 ....**51** A8
Eccles Rd
Chapel-en-le-Frith, Higher
Crossings SK23 .....**47** A6
Chapel-en-le-Frith, Hilltop
SK23...........**46** C7
Eccles Terr SK23......**46** D8
ECKINGTON **59** C4
Eckington Bsns Ctr
S21...........**59** E4
Eckington Camm's
Endowed CE Prim Sch
S21...........**59** D4
Eckington Cl DE7....**207** E8
Eckington Hall S20 ...**59** D5
Eckington Jun Sch
S21...........**59** D3
Eckington Mews S20 **59** D5
Eckington Rd
Chesterfield S43......**77** D5
Dronfield S18.......**57** D4
Sheffield S20 ......**59** F8
Staveley S43.........**78** F4
Eckington Sch S21...**59** A3
Eckington Swimming
Pool S21...........**59** D3
Eckington Way S20...**59** F8
EDALE.............**37** C8
Edale Ave
Derby DE23 ....**218** E2
Derby, Alvaston DE24.. **233** B7
Derby, Markeaton
DE3...........**217** D2
Edale Bank S33 ......**9** E2
Edale CE Prim Sch
S33...........**37** C8
Edale Cl
Derby DE22 ....**204** D1
Gamesley SK13 ....**9** E2
Long Eaton NG10 .. **236** B6
Edale Cres SK13 ......**9** E1
Edale Ct **3** S41......**95** E7
Edale Dr
Derby DE21 ....**220** F3
South Normanton
DE55..........**160** B7
Wingerworth S42....**115** B4
EDALE END **29** D2
Edale Fold SK13 ......**9** E2
Edale Mews SK13 .....**9** E7
Edale Mill S33.......**37** E7
Edale Rd
Edale S33...........**29** D1
Hayfield SK22........**26** A2
Hayfield SK22........**35** B8
Hope S33 ....**38** F7
Mastin Moor S43.....**79** C4
Edale Rise NG9 .....**223** E3
Edale Sq DE7 ......**194** E5
Edale Sta S33........**37** C7
Edale Way DE56 ....**179** A5
Eden Bank DE56....**167** F2
Eden Cl DE65 ......**240** C8
Edenhall Rd S2.......**43** F7
Eden Low NG19.....**136** E3
Eden Rd DE21 ......**220** B4
Eden St S40 ....**266** B3
EDENSOR..........**110** E8
Edensor Ave SK17 ....**85** E7
Edensor Cl S42......**131** F6
Edensor Ct S43.......**97** C8
Edensor Dr DE56 ... **179** C6
Edensor Sq DE22 .. **218** F4
Eden St
Derby DE24 .... **233** A8
Wingerworth S42....**114** E3
Edes Farm Dr ST14. **196** F4
Edgbaston Ct DE21 . **206** B3
Edgecote Dr DE11 .. **256** A7
Edgefold Rd DE4 ... **143** B5
Edgehill DE56 ......**191** A2
Edge Hill DE73 ....**232** F3
Edgehill Gr NG19 ... **136** C2
Edge Hill Jun Sch
DE15..........**254** F7

Edge La S33..........**51** B6
Edgelaw Ct **2** DE24 **231** D3
Edge Mount View
S32...........**72** E2
Edge Rd
Eyam S32 ....**71** E7
Eyam Moor S32 ..... **52** E1
Matlock DE4 ......**143** B6
EDGETOP.........**103** F1
Edge Top Rd
Longnor SK17 ...... **121** A7
Moseley SK17......**103** F2
Edge View S32.......**72** B3
Edge View Cl S32....**72** C7
Edge View Dr DE45 ...**90** A4
Edgware Rd DE22...**217** F6
Edgwood Rd NG16..**195** F6
Edinboro Row NG16 **195** E7
Edinburgh Cres
DE24.........**232** E4
Edinburgh Ct
Chesterfield S42....**114** E4
Swanwick DE55 ... **170** A7
Edinburgh Mews
S41...........**266** A4
Edinburgh Mws S40 ..**95** F5
Edinburgh Rd
Chesterfield S41.....**95** F5
Wingerworth S42....**114** E4
Edinburgh Road
S41...........**255** E1
Edith Wood Cl DE24 **233** B5
EDLASTON...........**185** C2
Edlaston La DE6 ... **185** B3
Edmonton Pl DE15.. **248** D2
Edmund Ave S17 ....**56** D6
Edmund Cl S17......**56** D6
Edmund Dr S17 .....**56** D6
Edmund Rd
Derby DE21 ....**220** F3
Sheffield S2 ....**43** B8
Edmund's Sq DE3...**230** B7
Edmund St S41......**95** F8
Ednaston Ave DE23 . **231** D5
Ednaston Hall Farm
Mews DE6 ....**201** B3
Edson Way S43......**81** F5
Edward Ave
Derby DE21 ....**220** A5
Jacksdale NG16....**171** B4
Edward Rd NG10 ... **236** D8
Edwards Cres DE56. **192** A8
Edward St
Aldercar NG16 .....**182** B4
Belper DE56 ......**179** A4
Derby DE1 ....**267** B4
Eckington S21.......**59** D3
Glossop SK13 ....**10** C1
Hartshorne DE11 ... **257** A3
Marple SK6.........**15** B1
Moira DE11.........**256** C1
Overseal DE12 ..... **262** A4
Stapleford NG9.....**223** D7
Staveley S43.........**97** C8
Edward Wlk S42 ... **115** C1
Edwin Ave S40 .....**114** D8
Edwin Rd S2 ....**43** C6
Edwinstowe Rd
DE21.........**206** B1
Egerton Dr NG9 ...**209** D2
Egerton Rd S18.......**57** B2
Eggesford Rd DE24 . **231** D2
Eggington Rd
Etwall DE65 ....**229** B3
Hilton DE65 ...... **240** F8
EGGINTON **241** B6
Egginton Prim Sch
DE65..........**241** B5
Egginton Rd
Etwall DE65 ....**229** B2
Hilton DE65 ...... **228** D2
Egmanton Cl DE21.. **206** B1
Egreaves Ave DE75 . **181** C4
EGSTOW **131** D5
Egstow Pl S45......**131** D4
Egstow St S45......**131** D4
Ehlinger Ave SK13 ...**10** A5
Eider Cl NG20 .....**119** D3
Eighth Ave DE14....**253** F8
Eland Cl DE21 .....**221** A6
Eland Rd NG20 ....**119** F5
Elder Cl DE55......**170** A8
Elder Ct S21........**60** C5
Elderflower Cl **4**
DE3...........**217** D5
Elder Way S40......**266** B3
Eldon Cl SK23 ....**47** C6
Eldon Ho **5** DE1...**267** B2
Eldon La SK17 ....**49** B5
Eldon St
Burton upon Trent
DE15..........**248** B3
Clay Cross S45 .....**131** C4
Eleanor Ave DE7.... **209** A5
Eleanor Cres NG9....**223** F7
Elesmere Ct DE7 ... **194** D1
Eley Cl DE7........**194** C2
Eley Way SK23........**47** B4
Eley Wlk DE21 ......**267** A1
Elfin Cl DE6 ....**201** E8
Elgar Dr NG10 ....**236** B5
Elgin Ave DE23 ....**218** A1
Elgin Cl S40 ....**114** C7

Eliot Rd DE23......**231** B8
Elizabeth Ave
Buxton SK17........**85** D7
Disley SK12 ....**32** D5
Rolleston DE13.....**240** B3
Elizabeth Cl
Derby DE21 ....**220** B5
West Hallam DE7 ...**207** D8
Elizabeth Ct
Baslow DE45 ....**91** F5
Burton upon Trent
DE15..........**248** C3
Ilkeston DE7........**194** D1
Elizabeth Mews
DE5...........**180** E7
Elizabeth Pk NG16..**170** F5
Elizabeth Villas DE6 **185** C8
Elka Rd DE7 ....**208** E5
Elkstone Cl DE21 ... **206** B2
Elkstone Rd S40......**95** A5
Ella Bank Rd DE75 . **182** A1
ELLASTONE.........**183** B3
Ellastone Gdns
DE24.........**233** B7
Ellendale Rd DE21 . **220** B7
Ellerscroft S42......**24** E1
Ellerslie Gr NG10 .. **223** A5
Ellesmere Ave
Alfreton DE55......**159** B4
Derby DE24 .... **219** D1
Ellesmere Dr NG9 .. **209** C5
Ellesmere Rd NG19 . **136** F1
Elliott Ave S33.......**51** A8
Elliott Dr S43.......**97** C6
Ellis Cl NG10 ......**236** C6
Ellison Ave DE72.... **246** A7
Ellison Cl SK14 ....**9** D5
Ellisons Rd S21......**60** F8
Ellison St SK13......**10** D1
Elma La S80 ....**101** D6
Elm Ave
Belper DE56 ......**179** B2
Darley Dale DE4....**142** F7
1 Long Eaton NG10.. **223** C1
Long Eaton NG10 .. **236** C8
Sandiacre NG10.....**223** B7
Elm Cl
Bolsover S44 ....**99** C1
Branston DE14.....**253** F8
Chesterfield S41.....**95** F8
Doveridge DE6 .....**224** C8
Killamarsh S21......**60** C5
Mottram in Longdendale
SK14...........**9** A4
Pinxton NG16 .....**160** D3
Elm Cres S20........**59** C8
Elm Dr
Hilton DE65 ....**228** D2
Killamarsh S21......**60** C5
Elmfield SK23.......**47** A5
Elm Gr
Clay Cross S45 .....**131** D3
Derby DE22 ....**204** D5
Derby, Cherrytree Hill
DE21..........**220** B5
Glossop SK13 ....**10** C2
Elmhurst DE65 ....**241** A5
Elmhurst Ave DE55 . **160** A4
Elmhurst Cl DE55...**160** A4
Elmhurst Rd NG19 .. **136** C1
Elmlands Cl DE72 .. **246** B8
Elm Lodge Farm Cl
S41...........**95** F7
Elm Park Ct DE1...**267** A5
Elm Rd
Eckington S21.......**59** C2
Pilsley S45 ....**132** C1
Elms Ave
Alfreton DE55......**159** A4
Derby DE23 ....**218** B2
Ripley DE5 ....**180** D8
Elms Cl DE55.......**159** A4
Elmsdale Rd DE11.. **257** A4
Elms Dr DE23.......**218** B1
Elms Farm Way
DE23.........**231** A8
Elmsfield DE75.....**182** A2
Elms Gr DE65.......**229** C3
Elmslea Ave DE12 .. **260** D3
Elmsleigh Cl DE11.. **256** B6
Elmsleigh Dr DE11.. **256** B6
Elmsleigh Gr DE11.. **256** B6
Elmsleigh Inf Sch
DE11.........**256** B6
Elms Rd
Burton upon Trent
DE15..........**248** A1
Coton in the Elms
DE12..........**260** D3
Elms St DE1 ....**218** F7
Elm St
Borrowash DE72....**221** B2
Brimington S43......**97** A8
Holmewood S42....**116** B4
ELMS THE **180** D8
Elms The NG16.....**195** F7
Elms View DE6 .....**176** A2
ELMTON **100** A7
Elmton Cl
Clowne S43.........**80** F3
Creswell S80 ......**100** D8
Elmton La S44........**99** C3
Elmton Park Mews
S80...........**99** E5
Elmton Rd S80 ......**81** E1

Elmton View S80 . . . . .**81** D2
Elmton Way S80. . . .**100** E8
Elmtree Ave
Derby DE24 . . . .**232** B7
Selston NG16 . . . .**171** F7
Elm Tree Ave
Kilburn DE56. . . . .**192** B7
Mansfield Woodhouse
NG19 . . . .**136** A4
Shirebrook NG20 . . .**119** D4
Shirland DE55. . . . . .**146** C1
Elmtree Cl S81 . . . . . .**63** F7
Elm Tree Cl S44 . . . .**118** B5
Elm Tree Cres S18. . .**57** A3
Elm Tree Dr S42. . . . .**114** F4
Elm Tree Ho S12 . . . . .**44** B4
Elm Tree Row DE55.**148** A5
Elm View ST14 . . . . .**196** E6
Elm Wlk S41 . . . .**132** C1
Elmwood Dr
Alfreton DE55. . . . . . .**159** C3
Derby DE21 . . . .**205** D2
Sheffield S20 . . . .**33** C7
Elm Wood Rd DE24.**232** D5
Elnor Ave SK23. . . . . . .**45** E5
Elnor La SK23. . . . .**45** F4
Elnor St NG16 . . . . . .**182** C3
Elsdon Cl DE72 . . . . .**245** A8
Elsecar Cl DE56. . . . .**179** D5
Elstead La DE11 . . . . .**257** B1
Elston Cl NG19 . . . . .**135** D1
Elstree Dr S12. . . . .**44** B4
Elstree Rd S12 . . . .**44** B4
ELTON. **140** E6
Elton Bank 6 SK13 . . . .**9** D1
Elton CE Prim Sch
DE4. . . . .**140** E6
Elton Cl
8 Gamesley SK13. . . . .**9** D1
North Wingfield S42. .**132** A5
Stapleford NG9. . . . . .**223** D8
Elton Gr SK17 . . . .**85** E6
Elton Lea 7 SK13 . . . . .**9** D1
Elton Pl 9 SK13 . . . .**9** D1
Elton Rd
Derby DE24 . . . .**232** B8
Winster DE4. . . . .**141** B6
Elton St
Chesterfield S40. . . . . .**96** A2
Chesterfield S40. . . . .**266** B2
Elton View S43 . . . . . .**97** D8
ELVASTON. **234** A6
Elvaston Castle & Ctry
Pk★ DE21. . . . .**233** F6
Elvaston Cl S18. . . . . .**56** B1
Elvaston Dr
Derby DE3 . . . .**230** E5
Long Eaton NG10 . . . .**236** A4
Elvaston La DE24 . . . .**233** C7
Elvaston Nature
Reserve★
DE24. . . . .**233** E7
Elvaston Rd S42. . . . .**131** F6
Elvaston St DE72 . . . .**235** B7
Elvaston Way S13 . . . .**44** B7
Elveden Dr DE7. . . . . .**194** C3
Elvin Way S42 . . . . . .**131** C8
Elwick Rd 3 DE23. . . .**231** F1
Elwood Rd S17. . . . . . .**56** C6
Elwyn Cl DE13. . . . . .**240** D1
Ely Cl
Mansfield Woodhouse
NG19 . . . .**136** D4
Swadlincote DE11 . . .**256** D6
Elyn Ave S42 . . . .**132** B7
Elysee Gdns SK17. . . . .**85** C3
Embankment Cl
DE22. . . . .**217** F7
Embankment Close
NG20 . . . .**119** E3
Ember Cl 1 DE11. . . . .**256** E1
Ember La DE41 . . . . . .**142** E1
Embleton Way
DE72. . . . .**245** A8
Embridge Cswy SK10 .**64** B5
Emerald Cl
10 Derby DE21 . . . . . .**205** F2
Derby DE21 . . . .**206** A2
Mansfield NG19 . . . . .**135** F1
Emerald Dr S40 . . . . .**115** E6
Emerson Sq DE23. . . .**231** F6
Emery Cl DE12. . . . . . .**261** D5
Emes Dr S42 . . . .**115** B2
Emes Pl S42 . . . .**115** B2
Emes Rd S42 . . . .**115** B2
Emmanuel Sch
DE22. . . . .**218** F7
Emmas Williams Ct
DE5. . . . .**169** D1
Emmerson Rd DE55. .**170** C7
Emmet Field Cl S40.**114** F8
EMMETT CARR. **79** C7
Emmett Carr Cl S21 . .**79** C7
Emmett Carr Dr S21 . .**79** C8
Emmett Carr La S21 . .**79** C8
Empire Ct DE75. . . . .**181** E2
Empire Rd DE15 . . . . .**248** D3
Empress Rd DE23. . . .**267** A1
Emsworth Cl DE7. . . .**194** D3
Endland Ind Est
DE1. . . . .**218** D5
Endowood Rd S40. . . .**114** A8
Endsleigh Gdns
DE22. . . . .**217** F6
End The DE15 . . . .**248** E8

Enfield Cl DE65 . . . . .**228** E2
Enfield Rd
Chesterfield S41. . . . . .**96** A5
Derby DE22 . . . .**218** B6
England Cres DE75 .**182** A2
English Martyrs' Catholic
Voluntary Acad
NG10 . . . .**223** B1
Ennerdale Ave 4
S20. . . . .**59** E6
Ennerdale Cl S18. . . . . .**56** E1
Ennerdale Cres S41. . . .**95** C8
Ennerdale Ct 6
NG10 . . . .**223** B2
Ennerdale Dr S20. . . . . .**59** E6
Ennerdale Rd NG10. .**223** B2
Ennerdale Wlk
DE21. . . . .**205** D2
Ennis Cl DE21 . . . . . .**220** C7
Enslet La DE6 . . . .**164** B2
Ensor Cl DE11. . . . . . .**256** D5
Ensor Way S42. . . . .**33** C7
Enterprise Cl NG19 .**135** E2
Enterprise Ct S80 . . . . .**81** E1
Enterprise Ct DE7 . . .**194** D1
Enterprise Dr S42 . . .**116** D1
Enterprise Rd NG19.**135** E3
Enterprise Way
Derby DE21 . . . .**267** C4
Duckmanton S44 . . . . .**98** B4
Langley Mill NG16. . .**182** C2
Mansfield NG19 . . . . .**135** E2
Sheffield S20 . . . .**60** B8
Epping Cl DE22 . . . . .**217** E6
Epsom Cl DE14 . . . . .**253** F7
Epsom Rd NG24 . . . . .**223** E3
Epworth Dr DE24 . . . .**233** A4
Epworth Ho DE15. . . .**248** D3
Erdington Way NG9.**223** E3
Erewash Ct
Ilkeston DE7. . . . .**194** D1
Long Eaton NG10 . . . .**223** D1
Erewash Dr DE7 . . . . .**209** B6
Erewash Gr NG9. . . . .**223** F2
Erewash Mus & Gdns★
DE7. . . . .**208** F8
Erewash Rd NG16. . . .**160** E2
Erewash Sq DE7. . . . .**209** A6
Erewash St DE55 . . . .**171** A6
Erica Dr DE55 . . . . . .**160** B7
Erin Rd
Poolsbrook S43, S44 . . . .**98** B7
Staveley S43. . . . .**78** F1
Ernest Hall Way
DE11. . . . .**256** C4
Ernocroft La SK6. . . . . .**15** E2
Ernocroft Rd SK6. . . . .**15** B1
Errington Ave S2. . . . . .**43** E6
Errington Cl S2. . . . . . .**43** E6
Errington Cres S2 . . . . .**43** E6
Errington Rd
Chesterfield S40. . . . .**114** D8
Sheffield S2 . . . .**43** E6
Errington Way S2 . . . . .**43** E7
Errisbeg House Dr
DE14. . . . .**253** A1
Errwood Ave SK17. . . . .**85** A6
Errwood Cl 3 DE65.**240** E8
Errwood Forest Walks★
SK17. . . . .**64** E2
Erskine Cres S2 . . . . . .**43** C7
Erskine Rd S2. . . . .**43** C7
Erskine St SK6. . . . .**15** B3
Erskine View S2. . . . . .**43** C7
Escolme Cl DE11 . . . .**256** D4
Eskdale Cl
Bolsover S44 . . . .**98** F1
Chesterfield S41. . . . . .**76** D1
Dronfield S18. . . . .**56** E1
Long Eaton NG10 . . . .**236** B5
Eskdale Wlk DE4. . . . .**233** D6
Essendine Cres S8. . . .**43** B3
Essex Dr 3 DE11 . . . .**255** E1
Essex Rd DE15. . . . . .**254** C6
Essex St
Derby DE21 . . . .**219** D6
2 Ilkeston DE7 . . . . .**194** F1
Estwic Ave NG16. . . .**182** F3
Etchells The DE55. . . .**227** A8
Etches Row 8 DE6 .**185** D7
Etherow Brow 6
SK14. . . . .**16** A8
Etherow Ctry Pk★
SK6. . . . .**15** C3
Etherow Ctry Pk Visitor
Ctr★ SK6. . . . .**15** B2
Etherow Country Pk
SK6. . . . .**15** C3
Etherow Way SK13 . . . .**9** E5
Eton Ct DE7 . . . .**207** D8
Eton St DE24 . . . .**219** E1
Etruria Gdns DE1. . . .**267** B5
Etta's Way DE65 . . . . .**229** B4
Etteridge Dr DE22 . . .**218** B3
Ettrick Cl 4 S40. . . . . .**95** C5
Ettrick Dr DE24. . . . . .**231** E2
ETWALL. **229** C3
Etwall Cl S40. . . . .**95** A6
ETWALL COMMON. .**229** D2
Etwall La DE65 . . . . . .**229** F5
Etwall L Ctr DE65. . .**229** B4
Etwall Prim Sch
DE65. . . . .**229** B4
Etwall Rd
Burnaston DE3. . . . . .**229** F7
Derby DE3 . . . .**217** C1

Etwall Rd continued
Derby DE3 . . . .**230** A8
Egginton DE65 . . . . . .**241** B7
Willington DE65 . . . . .**242** A7
Etwall St DE22. . . . . .**218** E5
Eureka Lodge Gdns
DE11. . . . .**256** C5
Eureka Prim Sch
DE11. . . . .**256** D5
Eureka Rd DE11 . . . . .**256** D5
Euston Dr DE1. . . . . . .**219** B7
Euston Wlk NG19 . . . .**136** C7
Evans Ave DE22. . . . . .**205** A5
Evans Cl S33 . . . .**51** A7
Evanston Gdns
DE21. . . . .**220** B6
Evelyn Cl DE72 . . . . . .**221** B1
Evelyn Devonshire Cotts
S45. . . . .**132** F2
Evelyn Gr DE21 . . . . .**220** A5
Everard Ave S17. . . . . .**56** A5
Everard Dr S17. . . . .**56** A5
Everard Glade 3
S17. . . . .**56** A5
Everest Dr DE55 . . . . .**170** D8
Everett Cl S43. . . . .**96** E7
Evergreen Cl DE21. . .**206** A3
Everley Rd 4 DE14 .**256** F7
Evershill Cl DE55. . . .**146** F5
Evershill La DE55 . . .**146** F6
Eversleigh Rise DE4 .**142** B8
Everton St NG19 . . . .**135** E1
Evesham Ave SK13. . . .**10** A5
Evesham Cl DE21. . . .**205** E1
Ewart La DE55. . . . . . .**158** F3
Ewe Dale La DE6 . . . .**149** A3
Ewe Lamb Cl NG9 . . .**209** F1
Ewe Lamb La NG9 . . .**209** F1
Excalibur Way
Chesterfield S40. . . . . .**96** B3
Chesterfield S41. . . . .**266** C3
Excalibur Wlk NG19.**135** D1
Excelsior Ave DE24 .**232** F6
Excelsior Dr DE11 . . .**256** C1
Exchange St DE1 . . . .**267** B3
Exe Fold NG19. . . . . . .**136** D2
Exeter Cl DE11. . . . .**256** A3
Exeter Ct 19 S41. . . . . .**95** F8
Exeter Ho DE1. . . . . . .**267** C3
Exeter Pl
Derby DE1 . . . .**219** B5
Derby DE1 . . . .**267** C3
Exeter St DE1 . . . .**267** C4
Exford Cl NG19 . . . . .**136** D2
Exlowmere La DE4. . .**140** F5
Explore Way S80 . . . . .**63** D1
Export Dr NG17. . . . . .**160** F8
Eyre St
Clay Cross S45 . . . . . .**131** C3
Creswell S80 . . . .**81** D6
Eyre Street E S41. . . .**115** C8
Eyrie The
Burton upon Trent
DE15. . . . .**248** C3
Derby DE24 . . . .**231** E3

F

Fabis Cl DE11. . . . .**256** A3
Fabric View S41. . . . .**132** D8
Factory La DE7. . . . . . .**194** D2
Factory St S40. . . . .**95** D2
Fairbourne Dr DE3 . .**217** D4
Fairburn Croft Cres
S43. . . . .**80** B6
Faircroft Ave NG10 .**223** B6
Fairdene DE23. . . . . . .**218** F2
Faires Cl DE72. . . . . . .**221** D1
Faire St DE22. . . . .**218** E3
Fairfax Dr S2. . . . .**44** B8
Fairfax Rd
Derby DE23 . . . .**218** F2
Sheffield S2 . . . .**44** B8
Fairfax Rise
Sheffield S13 . . . .**44** B8
Sheffield S13 . . . .**44** B8
FAIRFIELD. **85** C8
Fairfield Ave
Borrowash DE72 . . . . .**221** C1
Hilcote DE55. . . . .**148** C1

Fairfield Ave continued
Rolleston DE13. . . . . .**240** D4
Stonebroom S45. . . . .**147** B4
Fairfield CE Controlled
Jun Sch SK17 . . . .**85** E7
Fairfield Cl
Brimington S43. . . . . .**96** D8
Whaley Thorns NG20 .**101** A2
Fairfield Cres
Long Eaton NG10 . . . .**236** B4
Swadlincote DE11 . . . .**255** E5
Fairfield Ct S42. . . . . . .**94** F4
Fairfield Dr
Belper DE56. . . . .**179** C4
Chesterfield S40. . . . .**114** F6
Dronfield S18. . . . .**57** B4
Hilton DE65 . . . .**228** C1
Ilkeston DE7. . . . .**209** A8
Kilburn DE56. . . . . . .**192** A8
Long Eaton NG10 . . . .**236** B5
Ripley DE5 . . . .**169** B6
Sheffield S12 . . . .**44** A2
Fairfield Inf Sch
SK17. . . . .**85** E8
Fairfield Prim Sch
NG9 . . . .**223** D6
Fairfield Rd
Bolsover S44 . . . .**118** A8
Buxton SK17 . . . .**85** C8
Chesterfield S40. . . . .**266** A4
Derby DE23 . . . .**218** E1
Horsley Woodhouse
DE7. . . . .**192** C7
Fairfields
Branston DE14. . . . . .**253** F7
Branston DE14. . . . . .**256** F7
Fairfield Terr DE11 . .**256** F3
Fairfield Villas S40 . .**266** A4
Fairford Cl S40. . . . . .**114** F7
Fairford Gdns DE23.**231** A6
Fairham Rd DE13 . . . .**240** F1
Fairholme Dr NG19 .**135** E1
Fairholmes DE4 . . . . .**143** D5
Fairisle Cl DE21 . . . . .**206** C3
Fairlawns DE56. . . . . .**190** D3
Fair Lea Cl NG10. . . . .**236** D6
Fairleigh S2. . . . .**44** A8
Fairmeadows
Foundation Prim Sch
DE11. . . . .**255** E5
Fair View S40 . . . .**95** E4
Fairview Ave NG16. . .**171** F2
Fairview Cl
Derby DE23 . . . .**231** A8
Kilburn DE56. . . . . . .**192** B7
Fairview Grange
DE56. . . . .**192** B7
Fairview Rd S18 . . . . . .**57** A3
Fairview Rise DE4 . . .**168** A8
Fairway DE14. . . . .**254** B6
Fairway Cl DE22 . . . . .**204** D2
Fairway Cres DE22. . .**204** D2
Fairways Cl SK13 . . . . .**10** F1
Fairways The
Clay Cross S45 . . . . . .**131** E3
Clifton DE6 . . . .**184** F6
Mansfield Woodhouse
NG19 . . . .**136** D6
Fairway The 5
DE11. . . . .**255** E5
Fairwinds Cl S18. . . . .**57** A1
Fairwood Dr DE24 . . .**233** D6
Fairy Bank Cres
SK22. . . . .**25** D3
Fairy Bank Rd SK22. . .**25** D3
Falaise Way DE65. . . .**228** E2
Falcon Cl SK22 . . . .**33** D8
Falcon Ct DE7 . . . .**194** D1
Falcon Rd S18. . . . .**57** C3
Falcon Rise S18. . . . . .**57** D3
Falconside Dr DE21 .**220** F2
Falcons Rise DE56 . . .**179** C5
Falcon Way
Derby DE24 . . . .**231** E2
Woodville DE11 . . . . .**256** F3
Falcon Yd S40. . . . . . .**266** B3
Faldo Cl DE14 . . . .**254** B6
Falkirk Ave DE5 . . . . .**169** E4
Falkland Rise S18 . . . . .**76** A8
FALLGATE S45. . . . . .**130** B1
Fallgate S45. . . . .**145** A4
Fallow Dr DE16. . . . . .**254** D5
Fallowfield S43. . . . . . .**80** D2
Fallowfield Rd S43 . . . .**77** D3
Fallow Rd DE21. . . . . .**220** F6
Fall Rd DE75. . . . .**181** E3
Falmouth Rd DE24. . .**233** C5
Fal Paddock NG19 . . .**136** D2
Falstaff Ct DE73 . . . . .**232** E2
Fanny Ave S21 . . . .**60** E5
Fan Rd S43. . . . .**78** F1
Fan Road Ind Est S43.**78** F2
Fanshaw Ave S21 . . . . .**59** C2
Fanshaw Bank S18 . . . .**57** A1
Fanshaw Cl S21 . . . . . .**59** C2
Fanshaw Dr S21 . . . . . .**59** C2
Fanshawe Gate La S17,
S18. . . . .**55** E1
Fanshaw Rd
Dronfield S18. . . . .**57** B2
Eckington S21. . . . .**59** C2
Fanshaw Way S21 . . . . .**59** C2
Faraday Ave DE13 . . .**240** D1
Faraday Ct
Branston DE14. . . . . .**253** E7
Stapleford NG9. . . . . .**209** E1
Far Clay Gr S81. . . . . . .**63** F7
Far Croft DE72. . . . . . .**235** D8
Far Cross S45. . . . .**143** C7
Far Dales Road DE7 .**194** E2
Farfield Rd DE7 . . . . .**209** A8
Far Green DE4. . . . . . .**143** B6
Far Hill S33 . . . .**51** A7
Farish Pl 5 S2. . . . . . .**43** B6

Far La
Barlow S18. . . . .**75** B3
Ockbrook DE72. . . . . .**221** D6
FAR LAUND. **179** C6
Far Laund DE56. . . . .**179** B6
FARLEY. **128** C3
Farley Hill DE4 . . . . .**143** A8
Farley La DE4 . . . .**128** B3
Farley Rd DE23 . . . . .**218** D2
Farlow Rd S18. . . . .**56** E2
Farm Cl
Belper DE56. . . . .**179** C4
Chesterfield S40. . . . .**114** F6
Dronfield S18. . . . .**57** B4
Hilton DE65 . . . .**228** C1
Ilkeston DE7. . . . .**209** A8
Kilburn DE56. . . . . . .**192** A8
Long Eaton NG10 . . . .**236** E5
Ripley DE5 . . . .**169** B6
Sheffield S12 . . . .**44** A2
Somercotes DE55. . . .**170** C8
Whaley Thorns NG20 .**101** A2
Farm Cres S20 . . . .**59** C6
Farm Croft Rd
NG19 . . . .**136** C6
Farm Dr DE24 . . . .**233** A5
Farmfields Cl S44 . . . .**98** E3
Farmhouse Rd
DE24. . . . .**231** E2
Farmhouse Way
5 Grassmoor S41. . . .**115** F2
Grassmoor S42 . . . . . .**116** A2
Farmilo Cres NG19 . .**135** E1
Farmilo Prim Sch
NG19 . . . .**135** C4
Farm La
Hardstoft S45. . . . . . .**132** F3
High Lane SK12 . . . . . .**32** A6
Matlock DE4 . . . .**143** C7
Newton Solney DE15 .**248** E7
Farmlands La DE23 . .**231** B6
Farm Lane S21 . . . .**59** C3
Farm Side DE11 . . . . .**255** F5
Farm St DE22. . . . .**267** A1
Farmstead Cl S14. . . . .**43** D5
Farm View S42. . . . . . .**131** D8
Farmway NG19 . . . . . .**136** C2
Farmwell La DE55 . . .**160** E6
Farm Wlk S20 . . . .**59** C7
FARNAH GREEN. . . .**178** C3
Farnah Green Rd
DE56. . . . .**178** D3
Farnborough Gdns
DE22. . . . .**205** B4
Farncombe La DE21 .**205** F3
Farndale Ave S40. . . .**114** B8
Farndale Cl NG10. . . .**236** A5
Farndale Ct 5
DE24. . . . .**233** C6
Farndale Rd
Chesterfield S43. . . . . .**78** E4
Staveley S43. . . . .**78** E4
Farndon Dr NG9. . . . .**223** F3
Far New Cl NG10 . . . .**223** B5
Farnsworth Rd DE3. .**217** D2
Farnham Cl DE3 . . . . .**217** C1
Farnham Wlk DE7. . . .**207** D8
Farningham Cl
DE21. . . . .**220** F5
Farnon Cl S40. . . . . . .**266** C1
Farnsley La S32. . . . . . .**71** B4
Farnsworth Ct 5
S41. . . . .**115** C8
Farnsworth Dr S45 . .**131** C5
Farnsworth Gr
NG17. . . . .**148** F3
Farnsworth La S45 . .**131** C5
Farnsworth St S41. . .**115** C8
Farnway DE22. . . . . . .**204** E1
Farrendale Cl NG19 .**136** D1
Farrier Gdns DE23 . .**231** A7
Farriers Croft DE7 . .**194** C3
Farriers Way S21. . . . . .**60** D5
Farringdon Cl DE22 .**217** F6
Farrington Way
NG16 . . . .**182** E1
Farthing Ct NG10. . . .**236** B7
Farwater Cl S18 . . . . . .**76** A8
Farwater La S18 . . . . . .**56** F1
Far Wood Cl DE7 . . . .**194** E4
Far Woodseats La
SK13. . . . .**15** F5
FAULD. **238** C6
Fauld Ind Pk DE13. . .**238** E6
Fauld La
Tutbury DE13 . . . .**239** A6
Tutbury, Fauld DE13 . .**238** D7
Fauvel Pl SK13 . . . .**10** C1
Fauvel Rd SK13. . . . . . .**10** C2
Faversham Cl DE24 .**232** F5
Fawfield Head SK17 .**121** A3
Fawn Cl S42. . . . .**114** F3
Fay Gdns SK13. . . . .**9** E4
Faywood Dr SK6. . . . . .**23** A6
Fearn Ave DE5. . . . . . .**169** E1
Fearn Cl
Church Broughton
DE65. . . . .**227** B8
Long Eaton DE72 . . . .**236** A7
Featherbed La
Bolsover S44 . . . .**99** A5
Darfoulds S80 . . . .**63** F1
Featherstone Rd
DE24. . . . .**233** E4
Feld La
Holmewood S42. . . . .**116** C1
Holmewood S42. . . . .**132** C8
Felkin St S41 . . . .**266** C3

Fellbrigg Rd S2 . . . . . .**43** D7
Fellow Lands Way
Chellaston DE73 . . . . .**233** A2
Derby DE73 . . . .**233** A3
Fellside
Belper DE56. . . . .**179** A4
Derby DE21 . . . .**220** F6
Fellview Cl S32. . . . . . .**53** A7
Felton Ave NG19. . . . .**136** C6
Fenchurch Wlk
DE22. . . . .**218** B7
Fen Cl DE55 . . . .**148** A3
Fenelon Pl 7 DE11 . .**256** E1
Fenland Way S40. . . .**114** E8
Fennel Ave DE3 . . . . .**217** C4
Fennel St DE45 . . . . .**108** E8
FENNY BENTLEY. . .**162** A1
Fenton Ave DE11 . . . .**257** B1
Fenton Rd DE3 . . . . . .**217** C2
Fenton Drive S12 . . . . .**44** F4
Fenton Green 5
DE13. . . . .**240** E1
Fenton Rd DE3 . . . . . .**217** C2
Fenton St S21 . . . .**59** B2
Fenwick St DE24. . . . .**232** D7
Ferguson Ave NG19.**136** B4
Fern Ave
Staveley S43. . . . .**97** D8
Willington DE65 . . . . .**242** C6
Fernbank S33 . . . .**51** A7
Fern Bank SK23. . . . . . .**47** C7
Fern Bank Ave
DE55. . . . .**147** E1
Fernbank Dr S21 . . . . .**59** B3
Fern Cl
Eckington S21. . . . .**59** B3
Holmewood S44. . . . .**116** F1
Shirebrook NG20 . . . .**119** E6
Willington DE65 . . . . .**242** C6
Fern Cres NG16. . . . . .**182** D3
Ferncroft Ave S20 . . . . .**59** C7
Ferncroft Wlk DE73 .**232** F2
Ferndale Ave SK17. . . .**67** C4
Ferndale Cl S18 . . . . . .**57** D3
Ferndale Rd
Buxton SK17 . . . .**67** C4
Dronfield S18. . . . .**57** D3
Ferndale Rise S18 . . . .**57** D3
Ferndene Dr NG10. . .**236** A7
Ferndown Dr 5
DE55. . . . .**148** B7
Fernello Cl DE73. . . . .**244** C4
Ferneydale Ave SK17 .**85** C4
Fernhill SK6. . . . .**23** C3
Fernhill Cl SK13 . . . . . .**10** D3
Fernhill Ct DE73 . . . .**233** A3
Fernhook Ave DE21.**220** D1
Fernhook Avenue
Alvaston DE21 . . . . . .**233** C8
Derby DE21 . . . .**220** B1
FERNILEE. **45** E1
Fernilee Cl
New Mills SK22. . . . . .**24** C1
West Hallam DE7 . . . .**207** E8
Fernilee Cotts SK23. . .**45** E1
Fernilee Gdns DE21.**205** F1
Fern Lea
Hollingworth SK14. . . . .**9** D1
Shirland DE55. . . . . . .**146** D3
Fernlea Cl SK13 . . . .**9** E4
Fernlea Dr DE11. . . . .**261** B6
Fernleigh Rise
NG19 . . . .**136** D1
Fern Rd SK17. . . . .**85** B5
Fern Royd S32. . . . .**53** A7
Fern Sq S32. . . . .**71** D6
Fern View Cl S12. . . . . .**44** F3
Fern View Gr S12. . . . . .**44** F3
Fernway SK17 . . . .**85** C4
Fern Way S21 . . . .**59** B3
Fernwood NG6. . . . . . .**23** C7
Fernwood Cl
Chesterfield S41. . . . .**115** E7
Derby DE23 . . . .**231** C8
Shirland DE55. . . . . . .**146** D3
Ferny Cl DE12 . . . .**262** B3
Ferrers Ave DE13 . . .**239** B5
Ferrers Cl DE74. . . . . .**247** A3
Ferrers Cres DE56 . . .**190** D3
Ferrers Ctr for Arts &
Crafts★ LE65. . . . . .**258** F7
Ferrers Way
Derby DE22 . . . .**204** D2
Derby DE22 . . . .**204** E2
Ripley DE5 . . . .**169** C3
Ferry Gn DE65 . . . . . .**242** B5
Ferry La DE73 . . . .**244** E3
Ferry Mdws 1 S8 . . . .**43** A2
Ferry St DE15. . . . . . .**254** E8
Ferry Vale DE15. . . . . .**254** E8
Festival Ave DE72. . . .**235** C7
Festival Crescent
DE7. . . . .**209** C4
Festival Rd
Branston DE14. . . . . .**253** E7
Ilkeston DE7. . . . .**208** C5
Fiddlers Elbow
Hathersage S11. . . . . . .**53** D7
Hathersage S32 . . . . . .**41** F1
Fiddler's La DE13. . . .**239** F4
Fiddle St SK17. . . . .**85** C3
Fidlers Cl S33. . . . .**40** B3
Fidlers Well S33. . . . . .**40** B4
Field Ave
Hatton DE65 . . . .**239** C8
Renishaw S21. . . . .**79** B8
Field Cl
Borrowash DE72 . . . . .**221** B3
Breaston DE72. . . . . .**235** F7

Field Cl continued
Dronfield S18 . . . .**56** C2
Hilton DE65 . . . .**228** D2
Mansfield Woodhouse
NG19 . . . .**136** D5
Field Cres DE24 . . . .**233** A5
Field Ct
Chesterfield S43. . . . . .**77** D4
Kilburn DE56 . . . .**192** A7
Field Dr
Derby DE24 . . . .**233** A5
Rolleston DE13. . . . . .**240** A3
Shirebrook NG20 . . . . .**119** E2
Field Drive DE7 . . . .**193** B8
Fielden Ave NG19 . .**135** D2
Field End DE4 . . . . . .**153** A1
Fieldfare Ct DE23. . .**231** A6
Fieldfare Ho S41 . . . .**77** B3
Field Farm Way
NG9 . . . .**209** E2
Fieldgate Dr DE21 . .**205** F2
Field Head SK13 . . . . .**16** D7
Fieldhead La HD9. . . . . .**2** F8
Fieldhead Rd S8. . . . . .**43** A7
Fieldhead Way S41 . .**95** C6
Field Head Way
DE21 . . . .**206** B3
Blackfordby DE11. . . . .**257** C2
Derby DE21 . . . .**219** F7
Derby, Boulton DE24. . .**233** B5
Derby, Chaddesden
DE21. . . . .**220** A7
Glapwell NG19, S44 . . .**134** C6
Killamarsh S20 . . . .**60** B6
Killamarsh S21. . . . . . .**60** B5
Kirk Ireton DE6 . . . . . .**176** B8
Mayfield DE6 . . . .**183** C8
Fieldon Cl DE6 . . . . .**202** F2
Field Rd DE7 . . . . . .**208** F7
Field Rise DE23. . . . .**231** C7
Field Row DE56 . . . .**178** F4
Fields Cres SK14. . . . . . .**9** D6
Fields Farm Rd
NG10 . . . .**236** E5
Fields Gr SK14. . . . .**9** D5
Fieldside Cl S43 . . . . .**80** A6
Fields La DE11. . . . . .**261** F6
Field St DE5 . . . .**181** B8
Fields The
Crich DE4 . . . .**156** E2
Middleton DE4 . . . . . .**154** D4
Fieldsway Dr DE21. . .**205** E2
Field Terr DE5 . . . . . .**169** D1
Field The DE75 . . . . .**194** A6
Field View
Chesterfield S40. . . . .**115** A7
Clowne S43. . . . .**80** F3
Shuttlewood S44 . . . . . .**98** F6
South Normanton
DE55. . . . .**160** A7
Swadlincote DE11 . . . .**256** E5
Field View Cl
Derby DE24 . . . .**233** B6
Westwood NG16 . . . . .**171** C4
Fieldview Pl S41. . . . .**95** C6
Field Way DE11. . . . .**255** F5
Fife St DE24 . . . .**232** F8
Filbert Wlk DE73 . . . .**245** A8
Filey Wlk DE21 . . . . .**205** D1
Filigree Close
DE55. . . . .**160** D7
Fincham Cl DE21 . . . .**205** D1
Finch Cl DE11 . . . . . .**256** F3
Finch Cres DF3 . . . . .**230** C8
Finchley Ave DE22. . .**217** F6
FINDERN **230** D2
Findern Cl
Belper DE56 . . . .**179** B6
Derby DE22 . . . .**204** D1
Findern La
Burnaston DE65 . . . . . .**230** B4
Willington DE65 . . . . . .**242** B6
Findern Prim Sch
DE65. . . . .**242** E8
Findern St DE22 . . . .**218** D5
Finley Way DE55. . . .**160** B4
Finmere Cl DE23. . . .**231** A8
Finney Cl DE12 . . . . .**262** E1
Finney La DE3 . . . . . .**217** B2
Finningley Dr DE22 . .**204** F2
Finny La DE6 . . . .**200** B5
Finsbury Ave DE22. . .**218** B6
Finsley Wlk DE23 . . .**231** E6
Fir Bank DE56 . . . . . .**190** D5
Firbeck La S80 . . . .**63** A1
Fir Cl NG20 . . . .**119** E6
Firestone DE56 . . . . .**178** D1
Firfield Ave DE7 . . . .**235** E8
Firfield Prim Sch
DE72. . . . .**235** E7
Fir Pl S21 . . . .**60** C5
Fir Rd S21. . . . .**59** C2
Firs Ave
Alfreton DE55. . . . . . .**159** A5
Hulland Ward DE6 . . . .**175** F3
Ripley DE5 . . . .**169** D1
Firs Cres DE22. . . . . .**204** E4
Firs Estate Prim Sch
DE22. . . . .**218** E3
Firs Gdns DE6 . . . . . .**173** C8
Firs Par DE4. . . . .**143** C5
Firs St NG10 . . . .**236** A4
Fir St S43 . . . .**78** B1

First Ave
Branston DE14 . . . . . .**253** E7
Risley NG10 . . . .**222** F5
Firs The
Ashbourne DE6. . . . . .**173** C1
Wyaston DE6 . . . .**185** C1
Firth Ct S43 . . . .**77** D4
Firthwood Ave S18 . . .**57** D3
Firthwood Cl S18. . . . .**57** D3
Firthwood Rd S18. . . .**57** D3
Fir Tree Ave DE55 . . .**146** C4
Fir Tree Dr DE73. . . .**244** A6
Firtree Gr DE21. . . . .**206** B2
Fisher Cl
Chesterfield S40. . . . . .**114** F7
Repton DE65. . . . .**242** D2
Fisher Ct DE7. . . . . . .**194** F4
Fisher La DE56 . . . . .**190** E4
Fishers Bridge SK22 . .**25** D2
Fisher St DE24. . . . . .**232** E6
Fishes La S45 . . . . . .**131** A3
Fishpond La
Egginton DE65 . . . . . .**241** A5
Tutbury DE13 . . . .**239** C6
Fishponds Cl S42. . . .**115** A3
Fishponds Rd S13 . . . .**44** C7
Fishponds Road W
S13. . . . .**44** C7
Fishponds View S13 . .**44** B7
Fiskerton Way DE21 . .**206** B1
Fitzalan St SK13 . . . . .**10** C1
Fitzherbert CE Prim Sch
DE6. . . . .**162** A1
Fitzhubert Rd
Sheffield S2. . . . .**44** A7
Sheffield S2 . . . .**44** A8
Fitzroy Rd S2. . . . .**43** B6
Fitzwilliam Dr NG19 .**136** F2
Fitzwilliam Place
DE3. . . . .**217** F3
Five Lamps Ct DE1. . .**218** F6
Five Lamps Ho DE1 . .**267** A5
Five Lands Rd DE15. .**254** F8
Five Trees Ave S17 . . . .**56** A6
Five Trees Cl S17 . . . . .**56** A6
Five Trees Dr S17 . . . .**56** A6
Flackets La
Sudbury DE6. . . . .**225** B7
Sudbury DE6. . . . .**225** B8
FLAGG. **106** F6
Flagg La SK17. . . . . . .**106** F7
Flagshaw La DE6 . . . .**202** F4
Flake La DE7 . . . .**208** E1
Flamstead Ave
DE75. . . . .**181** C4
Flamstead La
Denby Village DE5 . . . .**180** E1
Smalley DE5 . . . .**192** F8
Flamstead Rd DE7 . . .**194** F1
Flamstead St DE24. . .**232** E6
Flamsteed Cres S41 . .**96** A6
Flanders Cl NG19 . . . . .**135** F1
FLASH. **103** A3
Flash CE Prim Sch
SK17. . . . .**103** B3
Flash La
Beeley DE4. . . . .**112** B2
Darley Dale DE4 . . . . .**128** A7
Flat La SK17. . . . .**106** B8
Flat The DE56 . . . . . .**191** F8
Flatts La
Tissington DE6 . . . . . .**162** B6
Westwood NG16 . . . . .**171** D3
Flatts The DE6. . . . . .**165** B1
Flax Croft DE65 . . . . .**227** C1
FLAXHOLME. **190** F1
Flaxholme Ave
DE56. . . . .**190** F1
Flaxpiece Rd S45. . . .**131** D3
Fleet Cres DE56 . . . . .**178** F3
Fleet Pk DE56 . . . . . .**179** A3
Fleet St DE23 . . . .**219** A2
Fleet The DE56 . . . . .**178** F2
Fleetwood Dr DE72. .**246** A6
Fletcher Ave S18 . . . . .**57** A1
Fletcher's Row DE5. .**169** F2
Fletcher St
Heanor DE75 . . . .**181** E2
Long Eaton NG10 . . . .**236** D8
Ripley DE5 . . . .**169** E2
Fletches The DE13. . .**240** B1
Fleury Cl S14. . . . .**43** E4
Fleury Cres S14 . . . . . .**43** E4
Fleury Pl S14. . . . .**43** E4
Fleury Rd S14. . . . .**43** E4
Fleury Rise S14. . . . . .**43** E4
Flint Ave NG19 . . . . .**136** F1
Flint La DE4. . . . .**142** B8
Flintson Ave S43 . . . . .**77** D4
Flint St DE24 . . . .**232** D6
Flint Way SK17 . . . . . .**85** E2
Flixton Rd NG16 . . . .**195** F7
Flood St DE72 . . . . . .**221** C4
Florence Ave NG10 . .**223** F1
Florence Cl
Chesterfield S40. . . . . .**114** F6
Pleasley NG19 . . . .**134** F4
Florence Ct
Derby DE1 . . . .**267** D2
Ilkeston DE7. . . . .**194** F1
Florence Dr
Derby DE1 . . . .**267** C2
Doveridge DE6 . . . . . .**224** C8
Florence Gladwin Cl
DE4. . . . .**141** C6

Florence Rd
Clay Cross S45 . . . . . .**131** E4
Wingerworth S42 . . . . .**131** E4
Florence Way SK14. . . . .**9** D5
Florin Gdns NG10 . . .**236** B7
FLOURISH THE **207** D2
Flour Mills The
DE15. . . . .**248** A5
Flower Lillies DE56 . .**189** C7
Flowery Leys La
DE55. . . . .**159** C3
Fly Hill DE45. . . . . . .**109** A6
Focus Sch Long Eaton
Campus NG10 . . . .**223** C2
Foggs Entry DE4. . . .**165** F8
Foggs Hill DE4 . . . . .**127** C4
Fold End La SK17 . . . .**121** B6
Folds Head S32. . . . . .**72** C2
Folds La
Calver S32 . . . .**72** B2
Horwich End SK23 . . . . .**45** F3
Folds Yd DE4. . . . . . .**156** F2
Fold The S32. . . . .**71** F4
Foljambe Ave S40 . . .**114** D8
Foljambe Rd
Brimington S43. . . . . . .**96** E8
Chesterfield S40. . . . . .**266** A3
Folkestone Dr DE24. .**233** A5
Folly Rd DE22 . . . . . .**205** B1
Fontwell Rd DE14. . .**253** F7
FOOLOW **70** E6
Foolow Ave S40 . . . . .**266** A1
Foolow Ct S40. . . . . .**266** A1
Foolow Rd
Eyam S32. . . . .**71** B7
Foolow SK17 . . . .**70** F6
Foot The DE6. . . . . . .**162** B5
Foragers Way DE3. . .**217** D4
Forbes Cl NG10 . . . . .**236** E5
Forbes Hole Nature
Reserve★ NG10 . . . .**236** F5
FORD. **58** E5
Ford Ave DE75. . . . . .**181** C4
Fordbridge La DE55 .**160** A7
Ford Cl
Dronfield S18 . . . .**56** F1
Ripley DE5 . . . .**180** C8
Ford Dr DE23 . . . . . .**230** F5
Ford Gr SK14. . . . .**9** A4
Ford La
Breadsall DE21. . . . . . .**205** C5
Derby DE22 . . . .**205** B5
Eckington S12, S21. . . . .**58** E5
Willington DE65 . . . . .**242** C5
Ford Rd S21. . . . .**58** E4
Ford St
Belper DE56 . . . .**178** F4
Burton upon Trent
DE15. . . . .**254** E7
Derby DE1 . . . .**267** A4
Tupton S42 . . . .**131** D8
Ford Way SK14 . . . .**9** A4
Fordwells Cl DE23 . . .**231** A8
Fordyce Cl DE73. . . . .**232** E1
FOREMARK. **243** D2
Foremark Ave DE21. .**231** E8
Forest Ave SK17. . . . . .**85** C6
Forest Cl DE56. . . . . .**179** B5
Forest Ct S43. . . . .**80** B6
Forest Dr S45 . . . . . .**132** C2
Foresters Park Ctr
DE23. . . . .**232** A7
Foresters Rd DE5. . . .**169** C2
Forester St DE1 . . . . .**267** B2
Foresters Way S43. . . .**47** C7
Forest La SK17 . . . . . .**50** C2
Forest Lea DE12 . . . . .**262** E4
Forest Rd DE11. . . . . .**257** A1
Forest School St
DE13. . . . .**240** C4
Forest View DE12. . . .**262** B4
Forge Cl DE65 . . . . . .**242** D2
Forge Dr S40. . . . .**266** B1
Forgehill DE56 . . . . .**191** A6
Forge La
Burton upon Trent
DE13. . . . .**241** A2
Killamarsh S21. . . . . . .**60** B7
Pleasley NG19 . . . .**135** B8
Forge Rd
Chinley SK23. . . . .**34** E1
Whaley Bridge SK23. . . .**45** E7
Forge Row NG16 . . . . .**170** F3
Forge Steps DE56 . . . .**191** A6
Forge Terr SK23 . . . . . .**34** E1
Forge The
Dronfield S18 . . . .**57** A1
Trowell NG9 . . . .**209** B5
Forman Cl DE11 . . . .**256** B4
Forman St DE1,
DE22. . . . .**267** A3
Forrester Ave DE72 . .**245** F5
Forrester's La S18. . . .**57** C4
Forshaw Cl DE6 . . . . .**185** C8
Forster Cl DE4. . . . . .**157** A1
Forth Ave S18 . . . .**56** D2
Forties La LE65. . . . . .**257** F3
FORTIES THE **257** F4
Fortis Way DE3 . . . . .**230** E5
Forty Foot La DE73 . .**252** F7
Forty Horse Cl DE5 . .**170** A2
Forum Cl DE24. . . . . .**233** D5
Fossbrooke Dr NG10 .**236** D5
Fosse Cl
Borrowash DE72 . . . . .**221** D4
Borrowash DE72 . . . . .**234** C8
Fossett's Ave NG16 . .**171** F7

Foss Rd DE65 . . . . . .**228** E1
Foster Cl DE3. . . . . . .**217** B2
Foster Rd DE11 . . . . .**256** F2
FOSTON **226** D4
Foston Cl
Hatton DE65 . . . .**227** C1
Hatton DE65 . . . .**239** C8
Foston Dr S40 . . . .**95** B5
Foundry Cl SK13. . . . . .**10** C1
Foundry Ct SK22. . . . .**33** C7
Foundry La
Belper DE56 . . . .**190** F8
Horwich End SK23 . . . . .**45** F5
Foundry St S41. . . . . .**96** A8
Foundry Street Ind Est
S41 . . . .**96** A8
Foundry The S41 . . . . .**96** A8
Fountains Cl DE22 . .**205** A4
Fountains High Sch
DE13. . . . .**240** C1
Fountains Prim Sch
DE13. . . . .**240** D1
Fountain Sq
Disley SK12 . . . .**32** D6
Youlgreave DE45 . . . . .**125** B5
Fountain St
Buxton SK17. . . . .**85** B7
Tideswell SK17. . . . . . .**69** C4
FOURLANE ENDS. . . .**158** C4
Four Lane Ends
Darley Dale DE4 . . . . .**127** C1
Swadlincote DE11 . . . .**256** A6
Four Lanes SK14. . . . . . .**9** A4
Fowler Ave DE21 . . . .**220** D4
Fowler St
Chesterfield S41. . . . . .**76** F2
Derby DE22 . . . .**218** E6
Draycott DE72 . . . . . .**235** B7
Fox Cl
Greenhill S8 . . . .**56** F7
Tibshelf DE55 . . . .**147** F5
Fox Croft
Greenhill S8 . . . .**56** F7
Tibshelf DE55 . . . .**147** F5
Foxbrook Cl
Chesterfield S42. . . . . .**94** F5
Derby DE23 . . . .**231** A8
Foxbrook Ct S40. . . . .**114** B8
Foxbrook Dr S40 . . . .**114** B8
Fox Cl
Burton upon Trent
DE14. . . . .**254** D8
Derby DE24 . . . .**231** D2
Long Eaton NG10 . . . .**236** D5
Foxcote Way S40 . . . .**114** B8
Fox Croft
Greenhill S8 . . . .**56** F7
Tibshelf DE55 . . . .**147** F5
Foxcroft Chase
S21. . . . .**60** C6
Foxcroft Dr S21. . . . . .**60** C5
Foxcroft Gr S21. . . . . .**60** C6
Foxdale Ave S12. . . . .**44** E2
Foxdell Way DE73 . . .**233** A2
Foxes Wlk DE22 . . . . .**204** E4
Foxes Yd SK17. . . . . . .**66** D1
Fox Field DE11 . . . . . .**261** E5
Foxfield Close S12. . . .**44** F2
Foxfields Dr DE21 . . .**205** E2
Fox Gdns DE11 . . . . . .**256** F4
Foxglove Ave
Burton upon Trent
DE15. . . . .**255** A8
Donisthorpe DE12 . . . .**262** E1
Foxglove Cl
Bolsover S44 . . . .**99** D1
Calow S44. . . . .**97** A3
Tutbury DE13. . . . . . .**239** D5
Foxglove Dr
Bolsover S44 . . . .**99** D1
Derby DE21 . . . .**205** F3
Derby DE21 . . . .**206** A3
Foxglove Gr NG19 . . .**136** F4
Foxglove Rd NG16 . . .**195** B8
FOX GREEN. **100** F8
Foxhall La S10. . . . . . .**42** F6
Fox Hill S44 . . . .**118** F7
Foxholes DE6. . . . . . .**163** B1
Foxholes La
Kniveton DE6 . . . .**174** B6
Tansley DE4 . . . .**144** A7
Fox Hollies The
DE55. . . . .**146** D2
Fox La
Baslow DE45 . . . .**73** E1
Creswell S80 . . . .**100** D8
Creswell S80 . . . .**100** D8
Holmesfield S18. . . . . . .**74** B5
Sheffield, Base Green
S12. . . . .**44** C3
Sheffield, Lower Bradway
S17. . . . .**56** D6
Foxlands Ave DE22 . .**204** F2
Fox Lane Ct S12. . . . . .**44** C4
Fox Lane View S12 . . .**44** C4
Foxlea SK13. . . . .**16** F8
Foxley Chase DE11 . . .**261** E5
Foxley Ct DE21 . . . . . .**206** A2
Foxley Oaks S41. . . . .**77** B1
Foxley Rd DE7. . . . . . .**194** F5
Foxpark View DE55 . .**147** E5
Fox Rd
Castle Donington
DE74. . . . .**246** F4
Whitwell S80 . . . .**82** A6
Fox St DE1 . . . .**267** C4
Foxwood Ave S12 . . . .**44** B6
Foxwood Cl
Chesterfield S41. . . . . .**115** C6

Foxwood Cl continued
Chesterfield, Sheepbridge
S41. . . . .**76** F1
Foxwood Dr S12. . . . . .**44** B6
Foxwood Gr S12. . . . . .**44** B5
Foxwood Ind Pk S41. .**76** F1
Foxwood Rd
Chesterfield S41. . . . . .**76** F2
Sheffield S12 . . . .**44** B6
Foxwood View S41. . . .**76** F2
Foxwood Way S41. . . .**76** E2
Foyers Way
Chesterfield S40. . . . . .**96** B3
Chesterfield S41. . . . . .**266** C3
Foyle Ave DE21 . . . . .**220** A4
Frain Gdns DE73. . . . .**252** F2
Framingham Cl S41 . . .**96** A6
Framlingham Rd S2 . .**43** D7
Frampton Gdns
DE23. . . . .**230** F6
Frances Cl ST14. . . . .**196** E6
Frances Dr S42. . . . . .**114** E4
Frances St NG16. . . . .**171** D1
Franchise St DE22 . . .**218** E4
Francis Cl S43. . . . .**96** D7
Francis St NG16 . . . . .**171** B4
Francis St DE21. . . . . .**219** D6
Frank Bodicote Way
DE11. . . . .**256** D4
Frankley Cl DE65 . . . .**240** E8
Franklin Ave S80 . . . . .**81** F5
Franklin Cl DE15. . . . .**248** B1
Franklin Cres S80 . . . .**81** F5
Franklin Rd NG16 . . . .**171** A4
Franklyn Dr
Derby DE24 . . . .**233** A6
Staveley S43. . . . .**78** F3
Franklyn Rd S40. . . . . .**95** E4
Frankwright Dr S2. . . .**43** C8
Frazer Cl DE21 . . . . . .**220** E6
Frecheville Dr DE56 .**168** A6
Frecheville St S43 . . . .**78** D1
Frederic Ave DE75. . .**193** F7
Frederick Ave
Derby DE24 . . . .**232** F6
Ilkeston DE7. . . . .**209** A5
Frederick Gent Sch
DE55. . . . .**160** B5
Frederick Rd NG9 . . .**223** D7
Frederick St
Alfreton DE55. . . . . . .**159** A5
Burton upon Trent
DE15. . . . .**254** E8
Derby DE22 . . . .**218** D6
Grassmoor S42 . . . . . .**115** E3
Long Eaton NG10 . . . .**236** F7
Somercotes DE55. . . . .**170** D5
Woodville DE11 . . . . . .**256** E5
FREEBIRCH **93** D6
Freebirch View S40. . .**95** B7
Freeby Ave NG19 . . . .**136** D5
Freehold St DE22 . . . .**218** E4
Freeland Cl NG9. . . . .**223** F3
Freeman Ave DE23 . . .**231** A6
Freeman Dr DE73. . . .**252** C8
Freesia Cl DE3 . . . . . .**217** E1
Freetown SK13 . . . . . .**17** C8
Fremantle Rd DE3 . . .**217** E3
French La DE21. . . . . .**191** F5
French St
Derby DE23 . . . .**218** E2
Ilkeston DE7. . . . .**209** A6
French Terr NG20 . . . .**101** A2
Fresco Dr DE23. . . . . .**230** F7
Fresh Ct SK13 . . . .**16** F7
Freshfield Cl SK6. . . . .**15** B1
Freshwater Ho
DE24. . . . .**233** C7
Freshwaters S42. . . . .**116** C1
Fretson Cl S2 . . . .**44** A8
Fretson Gn S2. . . . . . .**44** A8
Fretson Rd S2. . . . .**44** A8
Fretson Rd S S2 . . . . . .**44** A8
Freydon Way S44. . . . .**97** A3
Friar Gate DE1 . . . . . .**218** F5
Friar Gate Ct DE1. . . .**218** F5
Friar Gate House Sch
DE1. . . . .**218** E6
Friar Gate Studios
DE1. . . . .**267** A3
Friar Gr SK17. . . . .**85** C6
Friars Cl DE22 . . . . . .**205** A2
Friars Ct DE7 . . . .**208** C6
Friarsfield DE22 . . . . .**218** F8
Friar St NG10. . . . . . .**236** D7
Friary Ave DE24 . . . . .**232** E6
Friary Croft DE11 . . . .**256** F2
Friary St DE1 . . . .**267** A3
Friday La DE21 . . . . . .**205** D2
FRIDEN. **139** A2
Friden Cotts SK17 . . .**139** A5
Friden Dr
Sandiacre NG10 . . . . .**222** F5
Sandiacre NG10 . . . . .**223** A5
Friesland Sch NG10 . .**222** F5
Frinton Cl S40. . . . . . .**114** F7
Frisby Ave NG10 . . . . .**236** E6
FRITCHLEY. **168** C7
Fritchley CE (Aided)
Prim Sch DE56 . . . .**168** B6
Fritchley Cl DE21 . . . .**206** A1
Fritchley La DE56. . . .**168** A7

Frith Cl S12. . . . .**44** B5
Frithhall La S42 . . . . . .**94** C2
Frith Knoll Rd SK23. . .**47** D7
Frith Rd S12. . . . .**44** B5
Frith View S43 . . . .**47** A5
Frithwood Dr S18 . . . .**57** C7
Frithwood La
Creswell S80 . . . .**100** F3
Creswell S80 . . . .**101** A8
Elmton S80. . . . .**100** D7
Frizams La DE73. . . . .**242** F7
FROGGATT. **72** C5
Froggatt Cl
Derby DE22 . . . .**205** A5
Staveley S43. . . . .**97** C6
Froggatt Edge S32. . .**72** D6
Froggatt La S32 . . . . .**72** C5
Froggatt Rd S32. . . . . .**72** C3
Froggett Cl DE55 . . . .**170** D7
Front St DE56 . . . . . .**168** B6
Front Terr DE55 . . . . .**145** F4
Frood Cl SK23 . . . .**47** C7
Frost Ave NG16. . . . . .**182** A4
Frost Fields DE74. . . .**247** B4
Fryar Rd NG16. . . . . . .**182** F4
Fulbrook Rd DE23 . . .**231** A8
Fulford Cl S40. . . . . . .**114** C8
Fulham Rd DE22. . . . .**218** A5
Fuller Dr S41. . . . .**96** C6
Fullers Cl
Belper DE56 . . . .**190** F8
Milford DE56 . . . .**190** F8
Fulleylove Ct S44. . . . .**99** B1
Full St DE1 . . . .**267** B3
Fullwood Ave
DE7. . . . .**194** E1
Fullwood Grange
DE6. . . . .**175** C3
Fullwood Ind Est
NG17. . . . .**148** F1
Fullwood St DE7. . . . .**194** E1
Fullwood Stile La
S33. . . . .**38** F6
Fulmar Cl
Derby DE3 . . . .**218** A3
Mansfield NG19 . . . . .**136** E1
Fulwood Dr NG10 . . .**236** A7
Fulwood Head Rd
S10. . . . .**42** D7
Fulwood Ind Est
NG17. . . . .**160** F8
Fulwood La S10, S11 . .**42** E5
Fulwood Rd N NG17 .**160** F8
Fulwood Road N
NG17. . . . .**148** F1
Fulwood Road S
NG17. . . . .**160** F8
Furlong Cl NG9. . . . . .**223** D8
Furlong La
Alstonefield DE6. . . . .**149** C4
Atlow DE6. . . . .**175** B7
Castleton S33. . . . .**38** C3
Furnace Cl S42. . . . . .**115** E2
Furnace Hillock Way
S41. . . . .**115** E5
Furnace Hill Rd
S45. . . . .**131** D5
Furnace La
Barlow S18. . . . .**75** F3
Brimington S40. . . . . . .**96** F6
Castle Gresley DE11. . .**255** E2
Heanor DE75 . . . .**181** D4
Moira DE12. . . . .**262** E3
Furnace Lane Ind Est
DE12. . . . .**262** E3
Furnace Rd DE7 . . . . .**209** B6
Furnace Row DE55 . . .**170** F7
Furnall Ave DE45 . . . . .**90** A3
Furness Cl SK13 . . . . . .**17** F8
Furness Lodge Cl
SK23. . . . .**33** D4
FURNESS VALE. **33** C3
Furness Vale Bsns Ctr
SK23. . . . .**33** D4
Furness Vale Prim Sch
SK23. . . . .**33** D3
Furness Vale Sta
SK23. . . . .**33** D4
Furniss Ave S17 . . . . . .**55** E6
Furniss Mews S17. . . . .**55** E6
Furrows Cl DE21. . . . .**206** C3
Fyfield Rd DE15 . . . . .**254** E6
Fylde Cl NG9 . . . .**223** F2

G

Gable Ct DE3 . . . .**230** E8
Gables Cl S42 . . . .**132** D8
Gables The
Hilton DE65 . . . .**228** D1
Swadlincote DE11. . . . .**255** E5
Gadley Cl
Buxton SK17. . . . .**84** F7
Buxton SK17. . . . .**84** F8
Gadley La SK17. . . . . .**84** F8
Gadsby Cl DE7. . . . . .**209** A4
Gadsby Rise DE56 . . .**168** C2
Gag La DE6. . . . .**161** D6
Gainsborough Ave
SK6. . . . .**23** B8
Gainsborough Cl
Derby DE21 . . . .**206** B1
Long Eaton NG10 . . . .**236** E5
Stapleford NG9. . . . . . .**223** E6

Gainsborough Rd
S18 75 E8
Gainsborough Way
DE15 248 B3
Gairloch Cl DE24 231 D2
Gala Dr DE24 232 F7
Galahad Dr DE13 240 E2
Gallery La S42 113 D7
Gallery The [6] DE6 173 C2
Galloway Dr DE22 218 B3
Galloway Rd DE16 254 D5
Gallows Ind Est DE7 209 B6
GALLOWS INN 209 B6
Gallows Inn Cl DE7 209 A5
Gallowstree La DE6 184 C8
Galway Ave DE21 220 B4
Gambols La SK17 103 D5
GAMESLEY 9 D1
Gamesley Com Prim Sch
SK13 9 E2
Gamesley Fold SK13 16 D8
Gander La S43 80 B5
Gang La S44 118 E5
Gannow Cl S21 60 F7
Gapsick La S43, S80 81 B5
Garden Ave
Ilkeston DE7 208 F5
New Houghton NG19 134 F7
Renishaw S21 79 B7
Shirebrook NG20 119 E4
Garden Cl
Chesterfield S43 77 D3
Whitwell S43 81 F5
Garden Cres
Castle Donington
DE74 247 B3
South Normanton
DE55 159 F4
Gardeners Ct
Bolsover S44 99 A2
Mansfield Woodhouse
NG19 136 C3
Garden Rd NG16 182 F3
Garden St
[7] Broadbottom
SK14 16 A8
Derby DE1 267 A4
Gardens The
Heanor DE75 181 C4
Ripley DE5 180 D7
Gardner Ct [3] DE6 211 A2
Gardner Pl ST14 210 A1
Gardom Cl S18 56 D1
Garfield Ave DE72 235 A7
Garfield Cl
Derby DE23 231 C6
Stapleford NG9 209 E1
Garland Cl S20 59 E7
Garland Croft S20 59 E7
Garland Dr [3] DE7 194 F8
Garland Mount [15]
S20 59 E8
Garland Way S20 59 E7
Garner La DE4, DE55 157 D2
Garner Rd NG16 195 B7
Garnett Ave DE75 181 F2
Garnham Cl DE55 159 D2
Garrett Gn S45 131 E3
Garrett La S45 131 D2
Garrett Sq DE13 240 C4
Garrick St DE24 233 A7
Garrison Rd SK22 24 F2
Garry Cl DE24 231 D2
Garsdale Ct DE24 233 D6
Gartan Rd DE14 254 A8
Garth Cres DE24 233 B6
Garthorpe Ct [4]
DE21 205 F2
Garth Rd SK6 23 A6
Garth Way S18 56 F1
Garth Way Cl S18 56 F1
Garton Mill Dr DE4 143 E7
Gartrice Gdns S20 60 A5
Gartrice Gr S20 60 A5
Gary Cl DE23 231 D5
Gascoigne Dr DE21 220 D4
Gashouse La S20,
S21 59 D5
Gaskell Ave DE23 231 E7
Gasny Ave DE74 247 B5
Gas St
Hollingworth SK14 9 D5
Sandiacre NG10 223 C6
Uttoxeter ST14 210 C1
Gatcombe Cl
Burton upon Trent
DE13 240 D1
Derby DE21 206 B2
Gatcombe Gr NG10 223 A3
Gate Brook Cl DE5 170 B1
Gatefield Cl S41 95 C7
Gateham Hallow
SK17 149 A7
Gate Ho DE4 165 F8
Gate Ho The S32 72 D2
Gatehouse Dr DE4 165 F8
Gatehouse La S32 40 E3
Gateland La S18 75 E5
Gates The
Taddington SK17 88 C2
Taddington SK17 107 D8
Gateway Ct DE4 143 A6
Gauledge La SK17 121 B6
Gaunt Cl
Killamarsh S21 60 C6
Gaunt Cl *continued*
Sheffield S14 43 D3
Gaunt Dr S14 43 D3
Gaunt Pl S14 43 D4
Gaunt Rd S14 43 D3
Gaunt Way S14 43 D3
Gawain Gr DE13 240 E2
Gawsworth Cl SK13 10 A5
Gayton Ave DE23 231 D6
Gayton Jun Sch
DE23 231 D6
Gayton Rd NE7 194 D1
Gayton Thorpe Cl
DE23 230 F7
Geary La DE15 248 F2
Geer La S12 58 D5
Gelderd Pl S18 76 A8
Gema Cl DE22 205 A4
Genista Cl DE15 255 A8
GENTSHILL 131 E2
Gentshill Ave S45 131 E2
George Ave NG10 223 F1
George Cl S40 96 C7
George Cres DE55 170 C6
George Dutton Ind Pk
DE6 185 E8
George Holmes Bsns Pk
DE11 256 A4
George Holmes Way
DE11 256 A3
George Inn Ct S80 81 F6
George Newberry Pl
DE11 256 B2
George Percival Pl
S45 131 A4
George Rd
Alstonefield DE6 149 E4
Matlock DE4 143 C6
George Rodgers Cl
DE6 175 E3
George Spencer Acad
NG9 223 E5
George St
Alfreton DE55 159 A4
Ashbourne DE6 185 B8
Belper DE56 178 F4
Brimington S43 96 E8
[7] Buxton SK17 85 B8
Chesterfield S41 76 F2
Compstall SK6 15 B2
Derby DE1 218 F5
Derby DE1 267 A3
Glossop SK13 17 C8
Langley Mill NG16 182 B3
Mansfield Woodhouse
NG19 136 D3
Melbourne DE73 252 A7
North Wingfield S42 131 E7
Pinxton NG16 160 C4
Somercotes DE55 170 D8
Somercotes, Riddings
DE55 170 D6
South Normanton
DE55 159 F5
Swadlincote DE11 256 A1
Whaley Bridge SK23 45 E7
Whaley Thorns NG20 101 A2
George Yard DE1 267 B3
Georgia Ave DE65 242 B6
Georgina Ct DE74 247 B4
Geraldine Way [6]
DE74 246 E3
Gerard Cl
Chesterfield S40 95 C1
Derby DE21 220 F6
[15] Sheffield S8 43 B6
Gerard Ct DE1 267 A2
Gerard Gr DE65 229 C4
Gerard St N DE1 267 A2
Gerard St North
DE1 218 F5
Gerard St
Derby DE1 267 A2
Sheffield S8 43 B6
Gertrude Rd
Derby DE21 219 F8
Derby DE21 220 A8
Draycott DE72 235 A7
Gervase Ave S8 56 E6
Gervase Dr S8 56 E6
Gervase Pl S8 56 E6
Gervase Rd S8 56 E6
Gervase Wlk [2] S8 56 E6
Ghyll Cl DE24 220 A1
Gibb Ct S43 77 D4
Gibb La
Marple SK6 23 E5
Sudbury DE6 225 E5
Gibbons Ave NG9 223 D6
Gibbons Dr S14 43 E2
Gibbons Way S14 43 E2
Gibbons Wlk S14 43 E2
Gibb St NG10 236 E7
Gibfield La
Belper DE56 178 F2
Kirk Ireton DE6 175 F7
Gifford Rd S8 43 A7
Gilbert Ave S40 114 D8
Gilbert Cl DE21 220 D4
Gilbert Cres DE56 190 E2
Gilbert St DE24 233 B6
Gilderdale Way
DE21 206 B3
Gildwells La NG20 119 B7
Gillamoor Ct DE24 233 D6
Gilleyfield Ave S17 55 E7
Gilling Cl
Derby DE23 230 F5
Gilling Cl *continued*
Derby DE23 230 F6
Gilliver Gdns DE72 235 A7
Gill La DE4 127 C4
Gillott St DE75 194 A8
Gill's La S42 115 E2
Gilmour Way S2 43 F8
GILTBROOK 195 C8
Giltbrook Cres
NG16 195 C8
Giltbrook Shopping Pk
NG16 195 C7
Gilt Hill NG16 195 D7
Gilthill Prim Sch
NG16 195 D7
Giltway NG16 195 C7
Gimson Cl DE7 194 C3
Gin Close Way
NG16 195 C6
Gin La
Ashover S45 144 F8
Ravensnest S45 144 F7
Gipsyhill La S80 81 B8
Gipsy La
Alstonefield DE6 149 F4
Apperknowle S18 58 A1
Chesterfield S41 77 B1
Market Warsop NG20 120 F6
Gird La SK6 15 E1
Girdon Cl SK17 84 F6
Girton Way DE3 217 F3
Gisbey Rd [2] DE7 208 E5
Gisborne Cl DE3 217 E3
Gisborne Cres
DE22 204 F4
Gisborne Gn DE1 218 E6
Gisbourne Cl S43 78 F1
Gisbourne Dr SK23 47 B5
Gittos La S42 115 C2
Glade Cl S40 95 E5
Glade Croft S12 44 A4
Glade Lea S12 44 A4
Glade The
Buxton SK17 85 A8
Chesterfield S40 95 D3
Hayfield SK22 25 C3
Gladstone Ave
Blackwell DE55 147 E1
Heanor DE75 181 F2
Gladstone Cl
Chellaston DE73 232 F3
Glossop SK13 17 D8
Gladstone Dr NG16 182 E7
Gladstone Rd
Alfreton DE55 158 F3
Chesterfield S40 266 A4
Derby DE21 220 E5
Gladstone St W DE7 208 F7
Gladstone St
Derby DE23 218 E1
Glossop SK13 17 D8
Hadfield SK13 10 A4
Heanor DE75 181 E2
Langley Mill NG16 182 C3
Long Eaton NG10 236 D6
Mansfield Woodhouse
NG19 136 C2
South Normanton
DE55 160 B6
Gladstone Terr
NG19 136 C2
Gladwin Cl [5] NG9 223 E7
Gladwin Gdns S40 114 D8
Gladwins Mark
SE45 112 E2
Glaisdale Nook
DE24 233 D6
Glamis Cl DE21 206 B2
Glamorgan Way
DE11 255 F1
GLAPWELL 134 C8
Glapwell La S44 118 B2
Glasgow Close [5]
DE11 255 E1
GLASSHOUSE
COMMON 77 D5
Glasshouse Hill DE5 181 B8
Glasshouse La S43 77 D4
Glastonbury Cl
NG19 136 D4
Glastonbury Rd
DE24 233 C7
Glaven Cl NG19 136 D2
Gleadless Ave S12 44 A4
Gleadless Bank S12 43 F4
Gleadless Comm S12 44 A5
Gleadless Ct S2 43 B6
Gleadless Dr S12 43 F4
Gleadless Mount S12 44 A3
Gleadless Prim Sch
S12 44 B5
Gleadless Rd
Sheffield S12, S14,
S2 43 D5
Sheffield S14 43 D5
Gleadless Rise
Sheffield S12 43 F5
[1] Sheffield, Gleadless
Townend S12 44 A3
GLEADLESS VALLEY 43 E3
Gleadless Valley Nature
Reserve★ S8 43 C4
Gleadless View
Sheffield S12 43 F5
[2] Sheffield, Gleadless
Townend S12 44 A3
Gleadsmoss La
DE21 206 A1
Glebe Ave
Great Longstone
DE45 90 A3
Harthill S26 61 E7
Pinxton NG16 160 D3
Ripley DE5 169 C2
Smalley DE7 192 F6
Glebe Cl
Bonsall DE4 142 E1
Coton in the Elms
DE12 260 C3
Doveridge DE6 224 B8
Holmewood S42 132 D8
Rolleston DE13 240 A4
South Normanton
DE55 160 A5
Thurvaston DE6 201 E1
Glebe Cres
Ilkeston DE7 209 A7
Stanley DE7 207 B6
Glebe Ct DE45 90 A3
Glebe Farm Cl S26 61 E7
Glebe Field Cl DE4 156 F1
Glebe Gdns S42 131 F5
Glebe Jun Sch
DE55 160 A5
Glebe La DE6 161 C1
Glebe Pk S32 71 D5
Glebe Rd SK17 85 D8
Glebe Rise DE23 218 D1
Glebe St DE11 256 B3
Glebe The
Awsworth NG16 195 B4
Chesterfield S41 77 A2
Rosliston DE12 260 C6
Glebe View
Barlborough S43 80 B6
[5] Forest Town
NG19 136 E1
Glebe Way The S41 77 A2
Gledhill Cl S18 57 A1
Glen Ave DE56 191 C7
Glenavon Cl S43 77 D5
Glenbrook Hill SK13 10 C2
Glencar Cl DE24 233 C8
Glen Cl DE55 148 A3
Glencoe Way S40 95 B4
Glencroft Cl DE14 254 B7
Glencroft Dr DE24 231 D3
Glendale Dr DE21 220 F5
Glendevon Way
DE73 232 E2
Glendon Rd
Derby DE24 231 D3
Ilkeston DE7 208 C4
Glendon St DE7 193 A1
Gleneagles Cl
Chesterfield S40 114 C8
Derby DE3 217 F2
Gleneagles Dr DE13 240 C1
Glenfield Ave NG16 195 D7
Glenfield Cres
Chesterfield S41 96 A7
Derby DE3 217 C2
Glenfield Rd NG10 236 D5
Glengarry Way
DE24 231 E4
Glenholme Dr S13 44 E7
Glenholme Pl S13 44 F7
Glenholme Rd S13 44 F7
Glenholme Way
S13 44 E7
Glenmoor Rd SK17 66 D1
Glenmore Cl S43 97 B5
Glenmore Croft S12 44 C6
Glenmore Dr DE24 231 D3
Glenmoy Cl DE23 231 D7
Glenn Way DE72 234 E1
Glenorchy Ct DE21 206 B3
Glen Park Cl DE73 244 F8
Glen Rd DE4 156 D1
Glenshee Gdns
DE73 232 E2
Glenthorn Cl S81 63 F7
Glenthorne Cl S40 95 C2
Glentress Dr DE23 231 E1
Glen Vale S18 56 D1
Glen View DE56 178 F2
Glen View Rd S8 56 E8
Glen Vine DE5 170 A1
Glenwood Rd DE73 245 A8
Glinton Ave DE55 147 E1
GLOSSOP 10 B2
Glossop Brook Bsns Pk
SK13 10 B1
Glossop Brook Rd
SK13 10 B1
Glossop Brook View
SK13 16 C8
Glossop Central Sta
SK13 10 C1
Glossopdale Sch
Glossop SK13 9 F4
Glossop SK13 10 A4
Glossop L Ctr SK13 10 D1
Glossop Pool SK13 10 C2
Glossop Rd
Broadbottom SK13 16 D7
Gamesley SK13 9 E1
Hayfield SK22 25 C6
Marple SK6 15 D3
Glossop's Croft S41 77 B2
Glossop St DE24 232 B8
Gloster St DE24 219 E2
Gloucester Ave
Chesterfield S41 95 F5
Sandiacre NG10 223 A4
Gloucester Rd S41 95 F5
Gloucester Way
Burton upon Trent
DE15 248 B1
[4] Glossop SK13 17 F8
Glover Rd
Castle Donington
DE74 247 B4
Sheffield, Highfield S8 43 A7
Sheffield, Totley Rise
S17 55 F5
Gloves La
Alfreton DE55 147 E2
Blackwell DE55 147 D2
Glumangate S40 266 B3
Gn The DE56 176 E7
Go Ape!★ SK17 84 F6
Goathland Rd DE24 231 D2
Goatscliffe Cotts S32 72 C7
Goatscliff Farm La
S32 72 B7
Godber Cl NG16 195 A8
Goddard La
Glossop SK13 10 A6
New Mills SK22 24 E7
Goddard Rd SK13 10 A4
Godfrey Dr DE7 208 D6
GODFREYHOLE 165 B8
Godfrey St DE75 181 E1
Godkin Dr NG16 182 A4
Godric Pl DE11 256 D4
Godward Rd SK22 33 B8
Gold Cl DE4 142 B8
Goldcrest Dr DE21 220 F6
Goldcrest Ho S41 77 B3
Goldcrest Road
NG19 136 F2
GOLDEN VALLEY 170 D3
Golden Valley
Horsley Woodhouse
DE7 192 B6
Somercotes DE55 170 D3
Golden Valley Light Rly★
DE5 170 B4
Golders Green Wlk
DE22 218 A6
Goldfinch Cl [2]
NG9 209 E2
Goldhill DE4 144 A4
Golding Ho DE4 143 C6
Gold La DE22 217 E8
Goldsitch Moss La
SK17 102 F1
Goldstone Ct DE21 220 E4
Golf Cl DE23 218 A1
Golf Club Rd DE7 209 B1
Golf La DE56 190 E5
Golf Terr SK17 66 D1
Golling Gate
Hollinsclough SK17 103 F3
Hollinsclough SK17 104 A3
Gomersal La S18 57 A1
Goodacre Cl DE55 159 C4
Goodale St DE23 219 A1
Good Hope Ct DE24 219 E2
Goodman Cl
Chapel-en-le-Frith
SK23 47 B7
Eastwood NG16 195 C8
Goodman Ct S44 97 A3
Goodricke Ct [7]
DE3 217 F3
Goodrington Rd
DE21 206 C3
Goods Dr DE5 180 F7
Goodsmoor Rd DE23,
DE24 231 E5
Goodsmoor Rd Ind Est
DE24 231 E5
Goods Rd DE56 178 F2
Goods Road Ind Est
DE56 178 F2
Goods Yd DE56 178 F1
Goodwin Cl
Crich DE4 157 A1
Derby DE1 267 C1
Sandiacre NG10 223 A6
Goodwin Dr NG16 195 E6
Goodwin Rd [6] S8 43 A6
Goodwin's La DE56 178 C1
Goodwood Cl DE13 240 C1
Goodwood Cres
DE7 208 D4
Goodwood Dr
Beeston NG9 223 F2
Derby DE24 233 C6
Gooker La DE55 158 F3
Goole Ave DE7 208 D5
GOOSEGREEN 146 D3
Goose Green La
DE55 146 D3
Goose Green View
DE45 91 F5
Goosehill S33 38 B2
Goose La DE5 181 C8
Goose Nook Cl [1]
DE7 208 E5
Gordon Ave [2] S8 43 A2
Gordon Cres DE55 160 B4
Gordondale Rd
NG19 136 B1
Gordon Rd
Borrowash DE72 221 B1
Derby DE23 218 F3
Swanwick DE55 158 F1
Swanwick DE55 169 F8
Tideswell SK17 69 C3
Gordon St DE7 195 A1
Gordon Works [12] S2 43 A6
Gore La S33 51 A8
Gorman Cl S41 95 E8
Gorse Bank S44 116 F2
Gorsebank La DE45 91 F7
Gorse Cl
Derby DE23 231 B6
Eastwood NG16 195 B8
Long Eaton NG10 223 B2
Gorse Dr S21 60 D5
Gorsehill Gr DE23 231 A7
Gorse La
Bradley DE6 175 B3
Moira DE12 262 E6
Sheffield S10 42 F7
Gorse Ridge Dr DE45 91 E6
Gorses
Alderwasley DE56 167 B2
Alderwasley DE56 178 C8
Idridgehay DE6 176 D5
Gorse Valley Rd
S41 115 E7
Gorse Valley Way
S41 115 E7
Gorse Way SK13 17 F7
GORSEYBANK 166 A7
Gorsey Bank DE4 165 F7
Gorseybrigg S18 56 D1
Gorseybrigg Prim Sch
S18 56 D1
Gorsey Brow SK14 9 A1
Gorsey Cl DE56 178 E6
Gorsey Intakes SK14 16 A8
Gorsey La
Kirk Ireton DE6 165 A1
Netherseal DE12 265 A7
GORSEY LEYS 262 C4
Gorsty Leys DE65 230 D1
Gosber Rd S21 59 E3
Gosber St S21 59 D3
Goseley Ave DE11 257 A4
Goseley Cres DE11 257 A4
Gosforth Ave NE7 194 E6
Gosforth Cl S18 56 F1
Gosforth Cres [3] S18 56 F1
Gosforth Dr S18 75 D8
Gosforth Gn S18 56 F1
Gosforth La S18 56 F1
Gosforth Rd DE24 232 E8
GOSFORTH VALLEY 56 E2
Goshawk Rd DE7 209 A3
Goswick Cl [2] DE23 231 E1
GOTHAM 139 D1
Gough Gro NG10 236 C6
Gower Cres S40 95 C5
Gower St
Derby DE1 219 A4
Derby DE1 267 B2
GOWHOLE 33 E4
Goyt Forest Walks★
SK11 83 E7
Goytlands SK17 84 F6
Goyt Pl SK23 45 E7
Goyt Rd
Disley SK12 32 D5
Horwich End SK23 45 E6
New Mills SK22 33 D6
Goytside SK23 33 C5
Goyt Side Rd S40 95 E2
Goyt's La SK17 65 A3
Goyts Moss Rd SK11 83 C4
Goyt Valley Ind Est
SK23 33 D4
Goyt Valley Walks★
SK17 64 E4
Goyt View SK22 33 B6
Grace Cres DE75 181 F2
Grace Gdns DE5 180 D6
Gradbach Mill La
SK11 102 B1
Grafham Cl DE73 233 A2
Grafton Rd DE15 248 B1
Grafton St DE23 218 E2
Grafton Terr DE4 127 A5
Graham Cl DE14 254 C7
Graham Dr SK12 32 C6
Graham St DE7 208 F7
Grammer St DE5 181 A4
Grampian Cres S40 95 B4
Grampian Prim Sch
DE24 231 D4
Grampian Way
Derby DE24 231 E4
Long Eaton NG10 236 A8
Granary Cl S40 95 A8
Granby Ave SK23 34 E1
Granby Cl S45 132 C2
Granby Croft DE45 109 D5
Granby Jun Sch
DE7 194 E3
Granby Rd
Bakewell DE45 109 D5
Bradwell S33 50 F7
Buxton SK17 85 D7
Granby St DE7 194 E2
Grandfield St DE75 181 C4
Grandison Cl DE3 217 D6
Grandstand Rd
DE21 219 C6
Grange Ave
Breaston DE72 235 D8
Chapel-en-le-Frith
SK23 47 B5
Derby DE23 231 E7
Dronfield S18 56 E1
Hulland Ward DE6 175 F3
Grange Cl
Melbourne DE73 252 B8
Somercotes DE55 159 F2

Grange Cl continued
Ticknall DE73 . . . . 251 A4
Grange Ct
Eggington DE65 . . . . . .241 B5
South Normanton
DE55. . . . . .159 F2
Grange Dale DE4 . . 153 C8
Grange Dr
Castle Donington
DE74. . . . . 247 A3
Long Eaton NG10 . . . 236 F8
Grange Farm Cl
DE74. . . . . 247 D5
Grange Gate DE22 . . 267 A1
Grange Gdns DE75.. 181 C3
Grange La
Barlow S18. . . . . .75 B1
Darley Dale DE4 . . . .127 F1
Ible DE4 . . . . 153 D7
GRANGEMILL 153 D8
Grangemill Pl S43 . . . .97 C8
Grangeover Way
DE22. . . . . 218 D4
Grange Park Ave
Calow S43. . . . . .96 F4
Chapel-en-le-Frith
SK23. . . . . .47 B5
Grange Park Rd
SK23. . . . . .47 B5
Grange Pk NG10... 236 F8
Grange Prim Sch
NG10. . . . . 236 F8
Grange Rd
Buxton SK17. . . . . .85 C7
Derby DE24 . . . . .233 B6
Derby DE3 . . . . .217 E6
Long Eaton NG10 . . . 236 F8
Long Eaton NG10 . . . 237 A8
Pilsley S45 . . . . 132 C2
Swadlincote DE11 . . . 255 E5
Uttoxeter ST14. . . . . 210 A1
Grange Road S SK14. .15 A8
Grange St
1 Alfreton DE55. . . . . .158 F3
Alfreton DE55. . . . . . 159 A3
Derby DE23 . . . . .219 B2
Grange The
Brimington S43. . . . . .96 D8
Chesterfield S42. . . . .94 F4
Chesterfield S43. . . . .95 A4
Smalley DE75 . . . . . . 193 C8
South Normanton
DE55. . . . . 160 A4
Grange View NG16. . .182 F3
Grange Wlk S42 . . . . 115 E2
Grangewood
Coton in the Elms
DE12. . . . . .260 F2
Grangewood DE12 . . . 261 C1
Grangewood Ave 3
DE7. . . . . .208 F7
Grangewood Ct S40 .114 F7
Grangewood Dr
DE56. . . . . 191 A7
Grangewood Gdns
DE12. . . . . 261 D6
Grangewood Rd
S40. . . . . .114 F7
Gransden Way S40 . 114 C8
Grant Ave DE21. . . . . 220 B5
Grantham Ave
DE21. . . . . .205 E1
Grantham Cl NG16.. 195 C7
Granville Acad
DE11. . . . . 256 E4
Granville Ave NG10 . 223 D1
Granville Cl
Chesterfield S41. . . . .115 D8
Duffield DE56. . . . . . .190 E3
Hatton DE65. . . . . . . 227 D1
Granville Ct DE11. . 256 C4
Granville Sports Coll
DE11. . . . . .256 E4
Granville St
Derby DE1 . . . . .218 E5
Woodville DE11 . . . . 256 E3
Graphite Way
Glossop SK13. . . . . 9 F6
Hollingworth SK13. . . .9 F6
Grasmere Ave
Clay Cross S45 . . . . . 131 B3
Derby DE21. . . . . . . .220 E6
Grasmere Cl
Burton upon Trent
DE15. . . . . .248 B1
Chesterfield S41. . . . . .95 D7
Grasmere Cres
DE24. . . . . 231 E4
Grasmere Ct 1
NG10. . . . . 223 B2
Grasmere Rd
Dronfield S18. . . . . . .56 D1
Long Eaton NG10 . . .223 B2
Grasmere St 2
NG10. . . . . 223 C5
Grasscroft Cl S43 S40 ..95 D6
Grasscroft Mobile Home
Pk S43 . . . . .77 D5
Grassdale View S12 . .44 F3
GRASSHILL 115 E4
GRASSMOOR 115 F3
Grassmoor Cl S12 . . . .43 F5
Grassmoor Ctry Pk* S42,
S41. . . . . 116 A4
Grassmoor Prim Sch
S42. . . . . .115 F2
Grass St DE7 . . . . . . 194 E3

Grassthorpe Cl
DE21. . . . . 206 B1
Grassthorpe Rd S12 ..44 B4
Grassy Ct DE3 . . . . . 230 A7
Grassy La DE65 . . . . . 230 A7
Gratton Ct S43 . . . . . .78 F3
Gratton La
Ashbourne DE6. . . . . .149 E5
Dale End DE45 . . . . . 140 C7
Elton DE45 . . . . 140 C7
Gravelly Bank Mews
DE6. . . . . 199 D5
Gravel Pit Cotts
DE65. . . . . 229 B1
Gravel Pit Hill DE65 . 249 E7
Gravel Pit La DE21. . 220 E4
Graves Park Animal
Farm* S8 . . . . .43 B1
Graves Tennis & L Ctr
S8. . . . . .57 B7
Graves Trust Homes
Sheffield, Common Side
S12. . . . . .44 A5
Sheffield, Greenhill S8 . .56 F8
Sheffield, Little Norton
S8. . . . . .57 B7
Grayburn Ave DE21 . 220 E3
Graycar Bsns Pk
DE13. . . . . .253 B2
Gray Fallow DE55. . . 160 B4
Grayling St DE23 . . . 219 B2
Grays Cl
Castle Donington
DE74. . . . . 247 B3
Crich DE4 . . . . .157 A1
Grayshott Wlk S40 . .114 F8
Gray St
Clowne S43. . . . . .80 F4
Sheffield, Mosborough
S20. . . . . .59 C7
Grayston Ct SK6 . . . . . .23 B7
Grayswood Cl DE55 . 170 A7
Great British Car
Journey* DE56 . . .167 E5
Great Common Cl
S43. . . . . .80 B6
Great Croft S18. . . . . 56 D2
GREAT CUBLEY 198 F1
GREAT HUCKLOW . . .70 B8
Great Hucklow CE Prim
Sch SK17. . . . . .51 B1
GREAT LONGSTONE . .90 B4
Great Northern Cl
DE7. . . . . .194 E2
Great Northern Cotts
NG19 . . . . 135 A5
Great Northern Point
DE22. . . . . .218 F4
Great Northern Rd
Derby DE1 . . . . .218 F5
Eastwood NG16 . . . . 182 D2
Greatorex Ave DE24 . 232 E5
GREAT WILNE. 235 C2
Greaves Close S44. . . .98 B3
Greaves La DE45. . . . 108 F8
Greaves St
Ripley DE5 . . . . .169 E2
Shirland DE55. . . . . . 146 E1
Greave Way S43. . . . . .96 C8
Greenacre Ave
DE75. . . . . 182 A3
Greenacre Cl S12. . . . .43 F5
Greenacre Pk DE12 . 260 C3
Greenacres DE23 . . . 231 B8
Greenacres Cl S18. . . .76 C7
Greenacres Dr
South Normanton
DE55. . . . . .160 B6
Uttoxeter ST14. . . . . 210 A2
Greenacre The DE6. .184 F7
Greenacre Way S12 . .43 F5
Green Ave DE3 . . . . . 233 A1
Greenaway Dr S44. . . 118 A8
Greenaway La DE4. . . 127 E1
Greenbank
Derby DE21. . . . . . . .220 D4
Hollingworth SK13. . . . 9 F5
Green Bank SK13. . . . .16 F7
Greenbank Dr S40. . . .95 C4
Green Bank L Ctr
DE11. . . . . .256 B4
Greenbank Rd SK6 ..15 B8
Greenburn Cl DE23 . 231 C6
Green Chase S21 . . . .59 C3
Green Cl
Curbar S32. . . . . .72 E2
Matlock DE4 . . . . . . .143 B6
Newton DE55 . . . . . . 148 A3
Renishaw S21. . . . . . .60 B1
Renishaw S21. . . . . . .79 B8
Staveley S43. . . . . . . .97 C6
Unstone Green S18 . . .76 E6
Willington DE65 . . . . 242 A6
Green Cowden
DE45. . . . . .108 F4
Green Cres NG16 . . . 171 E6
Green Cross S18. . . . . 57 B2
Greendale Ave S42 . . 113 E8
Greendale Ct S18. . . . 57 B2
Greendale Sh Ctr
S18. . . . . .57 B2
Greendale The
DE55. . . . . 157 D8
GREEN FAIRFIELD . . .67 C2
Green Farm Cl S40 . . .95 C6
Green Farm Rd
NG16 . . . . 171 D6
Greenfield Ave S80 ..82 C6

Greenfield Cl
New Mills SK22. . . . . .33 A8
Sheffield S8 . . . . .56 F7
Greenfield Dr
Linton DE12 . . . . 261 C6
Sheffield S8 . . . . .56 F7
Greenfield Ho SK13. . .10 A6
Greenfield La S45 . . . .56 F7
Greenfield Rd S8 . . . .56 F7
Greenfields
Aldercar NG16 . . . . . 182 A4
Denstone ST14. . . . . 196 D6
Eckington S21. . . . . . .59 C3
Fritchley DE56. . . . . .168 B7
Greenfields Ave
DE23. . . . . .231 B8
Greenfield St S13 . . . 170 C6
Greenfinch Cl DE21. . 220 F6
Greengate Cl S40. . . . .95 C2
Green Glen S40 . . . . . .95 C2
Greenhalgh Crescent 2
DE7. . . . . .194 E2
Greenhall Rd S21. . . . .59 C3
Greenhead Cres
SK17. . . . . .85 B7
Greenhead Pk S33. . . .40 B4
GREENHILL 56 F7
Green Hill DE4 . . . . . 154 E1
Greenhill Ave
Ripley DE5 . . . . .180 E8
Sheffield S8 . . . . .56 F8
Greenhill La DE55 . . . 170 C6
Greenhill Lane Ind Est
DE55. . . . . .170 B5
Greenhill Main Rd
S8. . . . . .56 F7
GREENHILLOCKS . . . 180 E7
Greenhill Parkway
S8. . . . . .56 D6
Greenhill Prim Sch
S8. . . . . .56 E7
Greenhills DE45 . . . . 109 B7
Green Hills DE45 . . . 109 B7
Greenhills Rd NG16 . .182 E3
Greenhill Wlk SK12 . .32 D6
Greenholme Pk
NG19 . . . . 136 E6
Greenhouse La S10.. .42 F5
Green Inf Sch The
DE55. . . . . .160 A6
Green La
Alsop en le Dale
DE6. . . . . 150 C2
Bakewell DE45 . . . . . 108 C3
Barrow upon Trent
DE73. . . . . 244 A5
Belper DE56 . . . . . . .178 F4
Bonsall DE4 . . . . 153 F8
Breedon on the Hill
DE73. . . . . 252 C2
Burnaston DE65. . . . 230 A4
Buxton SK17. . . . . . . .85 A6
Buxton, Water Swallows
SK17. . . . . .67 C2
Chelmorton SK17 . . . 106 D8
Chesterfield S41. . . . . .96 D4
Chinley SK23. . . . . . . .34 E2
Clifton DE6. . . . . .184 E7
Compstall SK14 . . . . . .15 B8
Creswell S80 . . . . . . .82 C5
Cutthorpe S42 . . . . . . .94 E7
Darley Dale DE4 . . . .127 B3
Derby DE1 . . . . .219 A5
Derby DE1 . . . . .267 B2
Derby DE1 . . . . .267 B3
Derby, Alvaston DE24. 233 C8
Dethick S45 . . . . 144 C1
Disley SK12 . . . . .32 D4
Dronfield S18. . . . . . .57 B2
Earl Sterndale SK17 . .105 C1
Flagg SK17 . . . . .106 D7
Glossop SK13. . . . . . .16 F8
Glossop, Brookfield
SK13. . . . . 9 F4
Hognaston DE6. . . . . .164 B2
Hollingworth SK14 . . . . 9 D6
Ilkeston DE7. . . . . . . 209 A7
Killamarsh S21. . . . . . .60 C3
Mansfield NG19 . . . . 135 A2
Marchington ST14 . . 225 A2
Ockbrook DE72. . . . . 221 C5
Overseal DE12 . . . . . 261 F4
Overseal DE12 . . . . . 262 A5
Pilsley S45 . . . . 132 C3
Pleasley S44. . . . . . . 134 D8
Roston DE6. . . . . .197 F8
Shirebrook NG19,
NG20 . . . . 119 C2
Tansley DE4 . . . . 144 A5
Tupton S42 . . . . 115 D1
Tutbury DE13 . . . . . . 239 C5
Washgreen DE4 . . . . 155 C1
Weston Underwood
DE6. . . . . .188 F2
Wilson DE73. . . . . . . .252 E5
Greenland Ave
DE22. . . . . .218 B5
Greenland Cl S42. . . . 132 A7
Green Lands DE11 . . 256 B7
Green Lea S18. . . . . . .56 C7
Green Leas DE72 . . . 246 A8
Greenlow DE6. . . . . . 150 D5
Greenmount Cl
DE23. . . . . .231 A6
Greenmount St
DE11. . . . . .255 F1
Green Oak Ave S17. . .55 E4

Green Oak Cres S17 ..55 E4
Green Oak Dr S17 . . . .55 E4
Green Oak Gr S17 . . . .55 E4
Green Oak Rd S17. . . .55 E4
Green Park Ave S43 .47 C6
Green Pastures S17 . .55 E7
Green Pk DE22 . . . . . 218 A6
Green Rd The DE6 . . 173 C5
Greens Ct DC7. . . . . . 194 D1
Greenshall La SK12. . .32 F5
Greenshank Rd
NG20 . . . . 120 D4
GREENSIDE. 58 C3
Greenside NG16. . . . . 171 D6
Greenside Ave S41 . . . .96 A3
Greenside Cl
Barlborough S43 . . . . .80 C4
Donisthorpe DE12 . . .262 E1
Long Eaton NG10 . . . 236 E7
Greenside Ct DE3. . . 217 C2
Greenside View
DE7. . . . . .192 F6
Greens La NG16 . . . . 195 F6
Greensmith Cl
DE15. . . . . .248 C3
Greensquare Rd
NG16 . . . . 160 E2
Green St
Barton in Fabis
NG11. . . . . .237 F5
Chesterfield S41. . . . . .77 A2
Green The
Alfreton DE55. . . . . . .159 B3
Alstonefield DE6. . . . .149 E4
Aston-on-Trent DE72 . 246 B8
Bamford S33 . . . . .40 B4
Belper DE56 . . . . . . .179 A5
Birchover DE4 . . . . . .126 B1
Brackenfield DE55 . . 145 D2
Bradwell S33 . . . . . . .51 B6
Brailsford DE6 . . . . . 201 E7
Breedon on the Hill
DE73. . . . . 252 E2
Bretby DE15. . . . . . . 249 A3
Burton upon Trent
DE13. . . . . 240 E1
Castle Donington
DE74. . . . . 247 A3
Chesterfield S41. . . . . 115 D7
Clowne S43. . . . . .80 E4
Crich DE4 . . . . .156 D1
Curbar S32. . . . . .72 E2
Derby DE22 . . . . .204 D1
Derby, Markeaton
DE3. . . . . .217 D1
Donisthorpe DE12 . . .262 E1
Draycott DE72 . . . . . 235 A7
Elmton S80 . . . . .100 B7
Findern DE65 . . . . . . 230 D1
Fritchley DE56. . . . . .168 B6
Froggatt S32. . . . . . . .72 D5
Glapwell S44 . . . . . . .134 B8
Hardstoft S45. . . . . . 133 A3
Kirk Langley DE6. . . . 202 C1
Lees DE6. . . . . 216 A7
Lees DE6. . . . . 216 C8
Litton SK17. . . . . .69 E3
Mansfield Woodhouse
NG19 . . . . 136 A5
Marple SK6. . . . . .23 A3
Matlock DE4 . . . . 154 D5
Middleton DE4 . . . . . 154 D5
North Wingfield S42. . 132 A7
Sheffield S17 . . . . . . .55 D8
Stanton in Peak DE4. 126 C5
Sutton in Ashfield
NG17 . . . . 148 F1
Swanwick DE55 . . . . .169 E7
Thorpe DE6. . . . . 161 C1
Ticknall DE73 . . . . . . .250 F3
Tissington DE6. . . . . 162 B5
Wessington DE55. . . 157 E8
Weston-on-Trent
DE72. . . . . 245 F5
Willington DE65 . . . . 242 A6
Greenvale Cl DE15.. 254 F8
Greenview DE4 . . . . . 153 A1
Greenville Croft
DE73. . . . . .232 E1
Green Water Mdw
SK14. . . . . .9 D5
Greenway
Ashbourne DE6. . . . . .173 C3
Brassington DE4. . . . 153 A1
Burton upon Trent
DE15. . . . . .248 A4
Hulland Ward DE6 . . .175 F3
Whitwell S80 . . . . . . .81 F6
Wingerworth S42. . . . 115 C2
Green Way DE65. . . . 230 D2
Greenway Cl
Borrowash DE72 . . . .221 B3
Derby DE72 . . . . .221 B3
Greenway Croft
DE4. . . . . .154 F1
Greenway Dr DE23. . 218 A1
Greenways S40. . . . . 114 D8
Greenways Rd DE14 253 C8
Greenway The
Derby DE72 . . . . .233 D5
Sandiacre NG10 . . . . 223 B6
Sheffield S8 . . . . .56 F8
Greenwheat Cl DE5. 180 A1
GREENWICH 169 F2
Greenwich Ave 1
DE11. . . . . .255 F1
Greenwich Ct 12 S43 .78 B3

Greenwich Drive N
DE22. . . . . .218 C6
Greenwich Drive S
DE22. . . . . .218 B5
Greenwood Ave
Derby DE21. . . . . . . .219 F8
Ilkeston DE7. . . . . . . 209 A7
Mansfield Woodhouse
NG19 . . . . .136 B4
Sutton in Ashfield
NG17 . . . . .148 F2
Greenwood Gdns 5
DE11. . . . . .256 B7
Greenwood Rd
DE15. . . . . .254 E8
Greenwood View 7
S43. . . . . .81 E2
Greer La S44. . . . . . . 118 D1
Gregg Ave DE75 . . . . 181 F2
Greggs Ave S23 . . . . .46 F5
Gregory Ave
Aldercar NG16 . . . . . 182 A4
Breaston DE72. . . . . . 235 C8
Gregory Cl
Brimington S43. . . . . .96 D8
Stapleford NG9. . . . . 223 F8
Gregory Croft SK17. . .88 B2
Gregory Ct 10 S8 . . . .43 B6
Gregory La S43. . . . . .77 D1
Gregory Rd S8 . . . . . .43 A6
Gregory St DE7. . . . . 208 E8
Gregorys Way DE56. 179 C5
Gregory Wlk DE23 . . 230 E7
Gregson Cl DE11.. . . 256 B5
Grendon Cl DE56 . . . 179 B6
Grenfell Ave DE23 . . 231 E6
Grenville Dr
Ilkeston DE7. . . . . . . 194 F3
Stapleford NG9. . . . . 223 E8
Gresham Rd DE24 . . 232 C8
Gresley Office Pk
DE11. . . . . .255 D3
Gresley Rd
Ilkeston DE7. . . . . . . 194 F1
Sheffield S8 . . . . .56 E5
Gresley Wlk S8 . . . . . .56 E5
Gresley Woodlands
DE11. . . . . .256 A2
Gresley Wood Rd
Swadlincote DE11 . . .255 F2
Woodville DE11 . . . . 256 A2
Gressingham Cl
NG19 . . . . 136 F2
Gretton Ave DE13. . . 240 E1
Gretton Cl DE16. . . . 254 D6
Gretton Mws DE15.. 248 B5
Gretton Rd SK17. . . . .85 D8
Greyfriars Cl 4
DE75. . . . . .181 F1
Greyfriars Place
DE3. . . . . .217 F3
Grey Meadow Road
DE7. . . . . .194 E2
Greysich La
Bretby DE11. . . . . . . 250 A1
Bretby DE65. . . . . . . 249 F2
Grey St DE22 . . . . . . 267 A2
Greystoke Rd DE75 . 233 C3
Greystones Ct S26. . .61 D6
Griffe Field Prim Sch
DE23. . . . . .231 A6
GRIFFE GRANGE . . . 153 D4
Griffin Cl
Derby DE24 . . . . .232 F7
New Mills SK22. . . . . .33 D6
Staveley S43. . . . . . . .97 E8
Griffon Cl 9 DE73..244 F8
Griffon Rd DE7. . . . . 208 F4
Griggs Gdns DE7 . . . 165 F7
Grimshaw Ave DE24 233 B7
Grinders Well La
S45. . . . . .130 C7
GRINDLEFORD 72 C7
Grindleford Gdns 16
SK13. . . . . .9 E2
Grindleford Gr 13
SK13. . . . . .9 E2
Grindleford Lea 14
SK13. . . . . .9 E2
Grindleford Prim Sch
S32. . . . . .72 C8
Grindleford Rd S32. . .72 C4
Grindleford Sta 13 S32 .53 D2
Grindleford Wlk 15
SK13. . . . . .9 E2
Grindley Way DE11 ..256 F7
GRINDLOW
70 C8
Great Hucklow SK17. . .70 C7
Grindlow Ave S40 . . . 266 A1
Grindlow Cl S43 . . . . .43 C6
Grindlow Dr S14 . . . . .43 C6
Grindlow Rd DE21. . . 220 A8
Grindon Cl S40. . . . . .95 C5
GRINDSBROOK
BOOTH 37 C8
Grindslow Ave DE7. 207 C8
Grin Low
Ashford in the Water
DE45. . . . . .108 B4
Ashford In the Water
SK17. . . . . .107 F4
Grinlow Cl SK17. . . . . .85 C3
Grin Low Rd SK17 . . . .85 B8
Grinton Wlk S40. . . . 114 F8

Grisedale Road W
DE45. . . . . .90 A4
Grisedale Wlk S18. . . .56 E1
Gritstone Rd DE4. . . 143 D7
Grizedale Cl DE15 . . 248 B1
Groombridge Cres
DE23. . . . . .231 A6
Groome Ave DE75 . . 181 C4
Grosvenor Ave
Breaston DE72. . . . . . 235 F8
Long Eaton NG10 . . . 236 A4
Grosvenor Cl 3
NG19 . . . . 136 B3
Grosvenor Dr DE23 . 231 A6
Grosvenor Rd
Eastwood NG16 . . . . 182 F2
Marple SK6. . . . . .23 A7
Ripley DE5 . . . . .169 D2
Grosvenor St
Derby DE24 . . . . .219 C1
Derby DE24 . . . . .232 C8
Grove Ave S17. . . . . . .55 D5
Grovebury Dr DE23 . 231 C5
Grove Cl DE72 . . . . . 233 F4
Grove Cotts
2 Holmewood DE4 . .116 E1
Pleasley NG19 . . . . . .135 B4
Grove Ct
Elvaston DE72. . . . . . 233 F4
Ripley DE5 . . . . .180 F8
Grove Farm Cl S43 . . .96 E7
Grove Gdns S43 . . . . .96 F5
Grove Ho DE23 . . . . . 267 B1
Grove House Ct S17 . .55 E5
Grove La
Buxton SK17. . . . . . . .85 C6
Darley Dale DE4 . . . .127 E1
Old Brampton S42 . . . .94 B4
Somersal Herbert
DE6. . . . . .211 F2
Grove Mews NG16. . .182 E1
Grove Par 2 SK17. . .85 B8
Grove Pk DE65 . . . . . 229 B2
Grove Pl DE45 . . . . . 125 B5
Grove Rd
Calow S43. . . . . .96 E5
Chesterfield S41. . . . . .96 A4
Sheffield, Totley Brook
S17. . . . . .55 F5
Groves Nook DE73. . 232 E1
Grove St
Chesterfield S41. . . . . 115 C4
Derby DE1 . . . . .219 A3
Derby DE23 . . . . .267 B1
Mansfield Woodhouse
NG19 . . . . .136 B3
New Mills SK22. . . . . .33 B3
Swadlincote DE11 . . .256 B4
Grove The
Breaston DE72. . . . . . 235 F8
Derby DE3 . . . . .217 E2
Glossop SK13. . . . . . . .9 F4
Poolsbrook S43 . . . . . .98 A8
Sheffield, Hillfoot S17. . .55 D5
Tatenhill DE13 . . . . . 253 A8
Grove Way
Calow S43. . . . . .96 F5
Mansfield Woodhouse
NG19 . . . . .136 B3
Grundy Ave NG16. . . 171 D7
Grundy Nook S80. . . . .82 A5
Grundy Rd S45 . . . . . 131 C3
Grunmore Dr DE13 . 240 E2
Guernsey Rd S2. . . . . .43 A7
Guide Post DE56. . . . 168 C2
Guildford Ave
Chesterfield S40. . . . . 114 D8
Mansfield Woodhouse
NG19 . . . . .136 C6
Sheffield S2 . . . . .43 D6
Swadlincote DE11 . . .256 E6
Guildford Cl S45. . . . 131 E3
Guildford La S45 . . . 131 E3
Guildford Rise S2 . . . .43 E8
Guildford View S2. . . .43 E7
Guildford Wlk S2 . . . .43 E8
Guildhall Cl DE11.. . 255 E2
Guildhall Dr NG16.. .160 F2
Guildhall Theatre *
DE1. . . . . .267 B3
Guinea Cl NG10. . . . 236 A7
Guinevere Ave
DE4. . . . . .240 E2
Gulliver's Kingdom*
DE4. . . . . .155 A8
Gunby Hill DE12 . . . 261 F2
Gunhills La DE56 . . . 189 E6
Gun La DE56. . . . . . . 168 C2
Gun Rd SK6 . . . . .16 C2
Gurney Ave DE23 . . . 231 D6
Gutersloh Ct NG9. . . 223 F8
GUTTER THE. 179 C4
Guy Cl NG9. . . . . 223 E6
Gypsy La
Creswell S80 . . . . . . .81 E1
Draycott DE72 . . . . . 221 E1

H

Hackney Grange
DE4. . . . . .142 F7
Hackney La
Barlow S18. . . . . .75 E2
Barlow S18. . . . . .75 F1

Hackney Rd DE4.... 143 A7
Hackthorn Rd **4** S8 . .43 A3
Hackwood Prim Acad
DE22............. 217 D5
Haddon Ave S43....81 A4
Haddon Cl
Alfreton DE55......158 F3
Bullbridge DE56....168 B6
Chesterfield S40......95 C1
Derby DE22.........204 D3
Dronfield S18.........57 B2
Heanor DE75.......181 C2
West Hallam DE7...207 E8
Haddon Ct DE6....185 D8
Haddon Dr
Bakewell DE45......109 E4
Derby DE22.........204 D3
Derby, Markeaton
DE3..............217 E3
Derby, Spondon DE21..220 F4
Little Eaton DE21....191 C2
Haddon Gn **31** SK13....9 D2
Haddon Hall★ DE45..110 B1
Haddon Ho DE45 . . 109 E3
Haddon Lea **32** SK13...9 D2
Haddon Mews **30**
SK13.............9 D2
Haddon Nurseries
DE7.............194 E3
Haddon Pl
Shirebrook NG20....119 E6
Staveley S43.........97 D8
Haddon Rd
Bakewell DE45......109 F3
Buxton SK17..........85 B8
Haddon Park DE4....110 A1
North Wingfield S42...132 A8
Haddon St
Derby DE23........218 E1
Ilkeston DE7.......194 E3
Tibshelf DE55......148 A6
Haddon Way NG10...235 F4
Hade La SK17......106 E7
Hades La SK17........88 B3
HADFIELD.............10 B5
Hadfield Dr SK23...34 F1
Hadfield Etherow Ind Est
SK13..............9 E5
Hadfield Ind Est SK13 . 9 F6
Hadfield Inf Sch SK13 . 9 F5
Hadfield Pl SK13.....17 C8
Hadfield Rd
Glossop SK13.........9 F4
Hadfield SK13........10 A1
Hadfields Ave SK14....9 D5
Hadfield Sq **1** SK13 . .17 C8
Hadfield St SK13.....17 C8
Hadfield Sta SK13....10 A5
Hadleigh Cl **2** NG9 . 223 E2
Hadley La DE6......186 E8
Hadley St DE7......209 A5
Hadstock Cl NG10 . . 223 B4
HADY.................96 D2
Hady Cres S41........96 C3
Hady Hill S41.........96 C2
Hady La S41..........96 E1
Hady Prim Sch S41....96 D2
Haeking La S41.....131 B8
Hag Bank La SK12.....32 D7
Hagg Bank La SK12....32 C8
Hagg La
Dale Abbey DE7.....207 D4
Turnditch DE56.....177 C1
Hag La DE56.......168 B6
Hague Ave S21........79 B8
HAGUE BAR..........32 F8
Hague Bar Prim Sch
SK22...............32 E8
Hague Bar Rd SK22...33 A7
Hague Fold SK6......23 F1
Hague Fold Rd SK22 .32 F8
Hague La S21, S43 . . .79 B6
Hague Rd SK14......16 A8
Hague St
Charlesworth SK13......16 D6
Glossop SK13.......17 D7
Haig Hill Farm Hamlet
S42.............115 E1
Haigh Memorial Homes
S8................57 A7
Haigh Moor S13.....44 F8
Haigh Moor Rd S13...44 F8
Haig St DE24.......232 F8
Hailsham Cl DE3....217 D3
Haines Cl DE24.....231 F4
Halcyon App S42 . . .115 C2
Halcyon Cl S12......44 F3
Haldane Cres S44.....98 F2
HALES GREEN.......199 B7
Hales Green DE6 . . .199 C7
Halesworth Cl S40...114 B8
Half Acre Gardens
DE7.............194 F2
Half Acre La
Dronfield S18.........57 D1
Dronfield S18.........76 D8
Half Croft S43........96 F7
Halfmoon La DE6...165 B3
HALFWAY............59 F7
Halfway Cl S20........59 F7
Halfway Ctr S20......59 E7
Halfway Dr S20........59 F7
Halfway Gdns S20....59 E7
Halfway Jun Sch
S20................59 E6

Halfway Nursery Inf Sch
S20................59 F7
Halifax Cl
Derby DE21........205 C1
Hilton DE65.......228 E2
Haling Way DE21...220 F2
Hallam Ct
Dronfield S18........76 A8
Ilkeston DE7.......194 F3
HALLAM FIELDS....209 A4
Hallam Fields DE74 . 247 B2
Hallam Fields Jun Sch
DE7.............208 F5
Hallam Fields Rd
DE7.............209 B4
Hallam Grove NG16 . 182 A5
HALLAM MOORS......41 E8
Hallamway NG19 . . .136 C1
Hallam Way
Langley Mill NG16....182 C3
West Hallam DE7....207 D8
Hall Bank
Buxton SK17..........85 B7
Hartington SK17.....137 E5
Hall Cl
Cutthorpe S42.......94 E8
Dronfield S18........56 C2
Mottram in Longdendale
SK14..............9 A5
Hallcliff La S42.......93 F1
Hall Cotts DE6.....175 D2
Hallcroft DE4......154 C5
Hallcroft Ave DE12...262 B3
Hallcroft Rd **2** DE7..208 F8
Halldale La DE7.....207 E7
Hall Dale View DE4. .127 D3
Hall Dr
Doveridge DE6.....211 A1
Hanbury DE13......238 A4
Mottram in Longdendale
SK14..............9 A5
Sandiacre NG10....223 B6
Sutton Scarsdale S44..116 F6
Sutton Scarsdale S44. .117 A6
Hall Dyke DE21.....220 D5
Hall End La DE45...108 F3
Hall Farm
Holmewood S42.....132 D8
Mansfield Woodhouse
NG19.............136 C6
Hall Farm Cl
Castle Donington
DE74.............247 B3
Chesterfield S41.....115 D7
Swadlincote DE11....256 C4
Whaley Bridge SK23...33 D1
Whaley Bridge SK23...45 D8
Hall Farm Ct
Kirk Langley DE6....202 F4
Stanton-by-Dale DE7 . .222 F8
Hall Farm Gdns
S42.............132 D8
Hall Farm Rd
Castle Donington
DE74.............247 D2
Duffield DE56......190 E2
Swadlincote DE11....256 C4
Hall Farm Way DE7 . .192 F6
Hallfield Cl S42.....115 A4
Hallfield Gate La
DE55.............146 D1
Hallfield Rd DE55....148 A3
Hallfields Rd DE15...255 C4
Hallfields Rise
DE55.............146 D1
Hallflash La S44.....116 A8
Hall Gardens DE56...190 E3
Hallgate Cl DE21....206 C3
Hallgate La S45.....132 B2
Hall Gate View S33...51 A8
Hall Gdns
Hemington DE74....247 D4
Marchington ST14...224 E2
HALL GREEN......171 E8
Hall Green Ave
DE13.............240 F2
Hall Grounds DE13..240 A4
HALLHILL...........46 F7
Hallicar La DE4.....154 D5
Hallington Dr DE75 . 181 D1
Hall La
Ashbourne DE6......173 C2
Brailsford DE6......202 A6
Brinsley NG16......182 D6
Burton upon Trent
DE16.............254 D6
Donisthorpe DE12...265 E8
Doveridge DE6.....211 B1
Doveridge DE6.....224 B8
Litton SK17..........69 E3
Mayfield DE6.......183 A7
Mayfield DE6.......184 B6
Nether Heage DE56 . .168 C3
Newton DE55......148 A3
Shirley DE6.........200 D8
Staveley S43.........78 D3
Thorpe DE6.........161 D1
Willington DE65....242 B5
Hall Leys La DE73...245 D1
Hall Meadow Croft
S20................59 F5
Hall Meadow Dr S20..59 F5
Hall Meadow Gr S20..59 F5
Hall Meadow Rd
SK13..............10 D2
Hallmoor Rd DE4...127 C4
HALLOWES...........76 C8

Hallowes Ct
Dronfield S18........57 B1
Dronfield S18........76 B8
Hallowes Dr S18.....76 B8
Hallowes La S18......76 B8
Hallowes Rise S18....76 C8
Hallow La DE6......184 B6
Hall Park Acad
NG16.............182 E3
Hall Park Cl DE23....218 B1
Hall Pk DE73.......244 A5
Hall Pk Rd NG16....182 E3
Hall Rd
Aldercar NG16......182 C4
Brimington S43.......96 E7
Marchington ST14...224 E2
Marehay DE5.......180 D5
Rolleston DE13.....239 F4
Hall Rise
2 Ashbourne DE6...173 D3
Darley Dale DE4....127 D3
Hall's Ct S21.........10 C1
Hallside S20..........59 C6
Halls La NG16......195 A8
Halls Rd NG9.......223 D6
Hall St
Alfreton DE55......159 A4
Derby DE24........233 A7
New Mills SK22......33 B8
Swadlincote DE11....256 A2
Hallsteads SK17......47 F1
Hallsteads S17........47 F1
Hallsteads The DE6..163 B2
Hallsworth Bridge
SK14..............9 E4
Hall Terr S45.......131 D3
Hall The
Glossop SK13........17 A7
Middleton DE4.....154 D5
Hall View S41........95 E6
Hall Wlk S42.......115 D1
Hall Wood Cl S41....256 A2
Hallworth Wlk S21....58 E2
Hallyburton Cl S2....43 C6
Hallyburton Dr S2...43 C6
Hallyburton Rd S2...43 C6
Halstead Cl NG19...136 F2
Halstock Dr DE24...233 C8
Halton Cl S41.......95 C5
Hamble Cl NG19....136 D3
Hambledon Cl S40....95 C5
Hambledon Dr
DE24.............231 D2
Hambleton Ave S42..131 F6
Hambleton Cl
Ashbourne DE6.....185 C8
2 Long Eaton NG10..223 A1
Hambleton Rise
NG19.............136 F1
Hamble Way DE65...228 C1
Hamblin Cres DE24 . 231 F4
Hamill Cl S42.......131 F7
Hamilton Cl
Beeston NG9.......223 F2
Derby DE3.........217 F3
Hamilton Dr
Market Warsop
NG20.............120 F4
Swadlincote DE11....256 C5
Hamilton Fields
DE15.............248 A2
Hamilton Gr DE21...256 D5
Hamilton Rd
Burton upon Trent
DE15.............248 A2
Derby DE23........218 F2
Derby, Spondon DE21..220 F6
Long Eaton NG10....223 D1
Hamilton Terr DE65..242 B6
Hamlet Ct DE73......232 E1
Hamlet La DE55.....160 A5
Hamlet The
Heanor DE75.......181 E3
South Normanton
DE55.............160 A5
Hammer Leys DE55..160 C4
HAMMERSMITH.....169 D4
Hammersmith S43...169 D4
Hammersmith Meadows
Nature Reserve★
DE5.............169 D3
Hammersmith Sta★
DE5.............169 D4
Hammonds Ct **6**
DE4..............165 F8
Hampden Ho DE15...254 E6
Hampden St
Derby DE23........232 A8
Eastwood NG16.....195 B8
Langley Mill NG16...182 B3
Hampshire Cl SK13....17 F8
Hampshire Dr NG10 . 223 B5
Hampshire Rd
DE21.............219 C8
Hampstead Dr
DE22.............218 A6
Hampton Cl
Beeston NG9.......223 F2
Derby DE21........220 F5
West Hallam DE7...207 D8
Hampton Ct **4**
DE75.............181 D2
Hampton La DE23...230 F5
Hampton St S41....115 D7
HANBURY..........238 A5
Hanbury Ave DE65..227 D1

Hanbury Cl
Chesterfield S40.......95 A5
Dronfield S18........56 F1
Hanbury Fields La
DE13.............238 A4
Hanbury Hill DE13 . .238 A5
Hanbury Rd DE21...219 F6
Hanchurch Ct S15 . . .248 A4
Handby Ct S41......115 D7
Handby St S41......115 D8
Handel Mews DE6...185 D8
Handel St DE24.....232 C8
Handford Ct DE22...218 D6
Handford St DE22...218 D5
HANDLEY
145 F8
S45.............130 F1
Handley Ct S43........77 D4
Handley La
Ashover S45.......145 E4
Clay Cross S45.....131 A1
Monyash SK17......107 B2
Pilsley DE45.........91 B1
Handley Pl **4** DE74..246 E5
Handley Rd
Chesterfield S43.......77 D5
Chesterfield S43.......77 D6
Handley Wood
DE56.............178 B7
Handsacre Cl DE11...255 F7
Hand's Rd DE75....182 A1
Handyside St
Derby DE1.........219 A6
Derby DE1.........267 B4
Hangar Hill S80......82 A6
Hanger Bank DE72...246 B8
HANGINGBRIDGE....184 F8
Hangthwaite Cl S13 . .44 B7
Hanley Cl SK12........32 D5
Hannage Way DE4...165 F7
Hannah Bowman
Way DE45........125 C6
Hanover Sq DE22 . . .218 A6
Hansard Gate
DE21.............267 D3
Hanslynn DE72.....233 F4
Hanson Cl NG16....195 F7
Hanston Ct S43........77 D4
HANSTUBBIN........171 F5
Hanstubbin Rd
NG16.............171 F6
Hanwell Cl DE72....233 E3
Hanwell Way DE22..218 B6
Harbin Rd DE12....253 D1
Harboro Cl DE6.....185 D8
Harby Ave NG19....136 D5
Harcourt Cl
Chesterfield S41.....115 C7
Ilkeston DE7.......194 D1
Harcourt Pl DE74...247 B4
Harcourt Rd DE14 . .253 F8
Harcourt St DE1....267 B4
Hardacre Cl DE73...252 A8
Hardcastle Mews
SK23..............47 B6
HARDHURST.........76 E6
Hardhurst Rd
Derby DE24........233 B5
Unstone Green S18....76 B6
Hardie Ave DE55....160 A6
Hardie Pl S43.........97 D8
Hardie St S21.........59 D3
Harding's Cl DE6....165 B1
Harding's La SK17...138 A5
Hard La S26..........61 E8
HARDLEY HILL......215 C2
Hard Meadow La
S45.............130 B2
Hardstaff Homes The
Eastwood NG16....195 C8
Mansfield Woodhouse
NG19.............136 B3
HARDSTOFT.........133 A3
Hardstoft Rd S45...132 E2
Hardwick Ave
Chesterfield S43.......77 D3
Derby DE24........204 D3
Glapwell S44.......134 B8
Shirebrook NG20....119 E4
West Hallam DE7...207 E8
Hardwick Cl
Blackwell DE55.....147 D1
Clowne S43.........81 A4
Dronfield S18........57 C2
Holmewood S42....132 E8
Ripley DE5.........169 C3
Hardwick Ct
Heath S44..........117 B2
Holmewood S42....132 E8
Long Eaton NG10...235 F4
South Normanton
DE55.............160 C6
5 Staveley S43.......78 E2
Hardwick Dr
Arkwright Town S44...97 D2
Arkwright Town S44...97 D3
Derby DE3.........217 E2
Hardwick Gdns **5**
SK17..............85 B7
Hardwick Hall Dr
S44.............131 D4
Hardwick Hall & Park★
S44.............131 D4
Hardwick La S45...129 D6
Hardwick Mount
SK17..............85 C7
Hardwick Old Hall★

Hardwick Park Farm★
NG17.............134 A3
Hardwick Pl DE7....208 C5
Hardwick Prim Sch **1**
DE23.............219 A1
Hardwick Rd SK17....85 D4
Hardwick Square E
SK17..............85 C7
Hardwick Square N
SK17..............85 C7
Hardwick Square S
SK17..............85 B7
Hardwick Square W
SK17..............85 B7
Hardwick St
Buxton SK17..........85 B8
Chesterfield S41....266 B4
Derby DE24........232 C8
Langwith NG20.....119 F8
Shirebrook NG20....120 A4
Tibshelf DE55......148 A7
Hardwick's Yd S40 . . .95 E2
Hardwick View Cl
NG19.............134 F7
Hardwick View Rd
Derby DE23........218 C1
10 Sheffield S2.........43 A8
Harrington St
Derby, Allenton
DE24.............232 E6
Derby, Normanton
DE23.............232 A8
Draycott DE72.....235 B7
Long Eaton NG10...236 B5
Harris Ave DE5.....169 C2
Harris Cl DE5.......169 C1
Harrison Cl DE14...254 B8
Harrison Dr DE4....154 C1
Harrison La
Sheffield S10........42 F7
Tibshelf DE55......147 F6
Harrison Rd NG9...223 D8
Harrison St DE22...218 E3
Harrison Way DE4...127 A6
Harris Rd SK17........85 C3
Harris Way S45.....131 C4
Harrogate Cres
DE21.............205 D1
Harrop La S10........42 F6
Harrots La SK17....137 D6
Harrow Dr
Burton upon Trent
DE14.............254 C8
Ilkeston DE7.......209 A4
Harrow Rd DE11...256 B7
Harrow St DE24....219 E1
Harryfields SK14......9 A1
Hart Ave NG10......223 A6
Hartcliffe Cl DE21...205 F3
Hartfield Cl S41....115 B7
Hartford Rd S8......43 A3
HARTHILL............61 F6
Harthill Field Rd S26 .62 A3
Harthill La S43......61 E1
Harthill Prim Sch
S26..............61 E5
Harthill Rd
Derby DE24........231 C3
Sheffield S13........44 B7
Thorpe Salvin S80.....62 D7
HARTINGTON........137 D5
Hartington Ave S17..85 C7
Hartington CE Prim Sch
SK17.............137 D5
Hartington Cl DE7 . .207 E8
Hartington Ct
Clowne S43.........81 A4
Dronfield S18........57 B2
Hartington Dr
Chinley SK23........34 E1
Creswell S80........81 C1
Hartington Gdns **11**
SK17..............85 B7
Hartington Ind Est
S43..............78 E4
Hartington Pl DE7 . .194 E3
Hartington Rd
Buxton SK17..........85 B7
Chesterfield S41......96 C2
Dronfield S18........57 B2
Hartington St
Derby DE1, DE23 . . .267 B1
Langwith NG20.....119 F8
Hartington View S43..78 F4
Hartington Way
DE3.............217 D2
Hartland Ct **21** S41...95 F8
Hartland Dr DE23...231 E6
Hartland Way S41....77 A1
Hart Lea **1** S40....223 B5
Hartley St S2.........43 A5
Hartopp Ave S2.....43 C6
Hartopp Cl S2........43 C6
Hartopp Dr S2.......43 D6
Hartopp Rd S2......43 D6
Hartshay Cl DE7....194 F5
Hartshay Hill DE5...169 C2
Hartshill Rd DE11...257 A4
HARTSHORNE.......257 A6
Hartshorne CE Prim Sch
DE11.............257 B6
Hartshorne Rd
Derby DE23........231 C5
Repton DE65.......249 E2
Woodville DE11....256 F3
Hartside Cl **16** S40...95 D5
Hartside Gdns **1**
NG10.............236 A8
Hartside Way DE75 . .182 B5
Hartwood Dr NG9...209 D1
Harvester Cl DE55...169 D2
Harvester Way S43....80 D2
Harvest Hill DE11...256 B7
Harvest Way
Chesterfield S40......94 F5
2 Chesterfield S42...95 A5
Derby DE21........206 C3
Harvey Clough Mews
S8................43 B3

Hardwick View Rd
NG19.............134 F7
Hardwick St
Buxton SK17..........85 B8
Chesterfield S41....266 B4
Derby DE24........232 C8
Langwith NG20.....119 F8
Shirebrook NG20....120 A4
Tibshelf DE55......148 A7

Harrier Way DE24...231 E5
Harriet St DE23.....219 A3
Harriet St NG9......223 D7
Harriet Tubman Ho
DE23.............218 F1
Harrimans Dr DE72..235 F8
Harringay Gdns
DE22.............218 C6
Harrington Ave
DE72.............221 C2
Harrington Jun Sch
NG10.............223 B1
Harrington Rd
Derby DE23........218 C1
10 Sheffield S2.........43 A8

Har–Hey 289

Harvey Clough Rd S8 43 B3
Harvey Croft NG9 209 C4
Harvey Ct S44 98 F2
Harvey Pl ST14 210 B1
Harvey Rd
Burton upon Trent
DE14 254 A8
Castle Donington
DE74 247 B2
Chesterfield S41 96 E2
Derby DE24 232 E6
Harwich Rd S2 43 F8
Harwood Ave DE14 253 F8
Harwood Cl
8 Heanor DE75 181 D1
Sheffield S2 43 A8
Harwood St 2 S2 43 A8
Hasgill Cl DE21 206 C3
Haskeys Cl DE22 204 C2
Haslam Cres S8 56 E6
Haslam Ct
Bolsover S44 98 F2
Chesterfield S41 266 B4
Haslam Pl DE56 179 C1
Haslam's La DE21,
DE22 205 B1
HASLAND 115 D7
HASLAND GREEN 115 C7
Hasland Hall Com Sch
S41 115 D7
Hasland Inf Sch
S41 115 C8
Hasland Jun Sch
S41 115 D7
Hasland La S44 97 C1
Hasland Rd S41 115 C8
Haslemere Ct DE23 219 B2
Haslemere Rd NG10 236 B8
Haslin Rd SK17 85 D2
Hassall Rd DE65 227 D1
Hassock Lane N
DE75 194 B7
Hassock Lane S DE7,
DE75 194 C6
Hassocky La S44,
S42 116 B6
HASSOP 90 F5
Hassop Cl
Buxton SK17 85 D6
Chesterfield S41 95 C6
Dronfield S18 57 C2
Hassop Rd
Calver S32 72 B1
Derby DE21 220 A8
Hassop DE45 90 D1
Hassop DE45 90 E4
Staveley S43 78 F3
Hastilar Cl S2 44 B8
Hastilar Rd S2 44 B8
Hastilar Road S S13 44 C7
Hastings Cl
Breedon on the Hill
DE73 252 E2
Chesterfield S41 95 D6
Derby DE23 230 F5
Hastings La DE65 229 C3
Hastings Rd
Buxton SK17 85 C4
Swadlincote DE11 256 B3
Hastings St
1 Derby DE23 218 F8
Derby DE23 219 A1
Hasting St DE74 247 B2
Haston Dr DE55 170 D8
Hatchmere Cl DE21 206 A1
Hatfield Ave NG10 223 B4
Hatfield La 3 DE65 227 D2
Hatfield Rd DE24 232 F5
Hathaway Cl S42 131 B6
Hathern Cl
Calow S43 96 F4
Derby DE23 231 E5
Long Eaton NG10 236 D5
HATHERSAGE 53 B7
Hathersage Ave
Derby DE23 231 E8
Long Eaton NG10 235 F5
Hathersage Cres SK13 9 E2
Hathersage Dr
Glossop SK13 17 F8
Somercotes DE55 170 B7
Hathersage Pk S32 53 A7
Hathersage Rd
Bamford S32, S33 40 B1
Grindleford S32 72 C8
Sheffield S11, S17 54 D6
Hathersage St Michael's
CE (Aided) Prim Sch
S32 53 A8
Hathersage Sta S32 53 A7
HATTON 239 D8
Hatton Cl S18 75 D8
Hatton Crofts NG10 236 C6
Hatton Ct DE73 252 A7
Hatton Dr S40 95 B5
Hatton Mws DE21 220 E3
Haulton Dr DE74 247 A4
HAUNTON 263 B2
Haunton Rd B79 263 A2
Havelock Rd DE23 232 A8
Havelock St
Ilkeston DE7 208 F7
Ripley DE5 169 E2
Haven Baulk Ave
DE23 230 E7
Haven Baulk La
DE23 230 E7
Haven Ct DE24 233 D6
Havenwood Gr
DE23 231 C5
Havercroft Terr S21 60 B7
Havering Close
DE22 218 A5
Hawfield La DE15 248 E4
Hawke Brook Cl S44 99 B3
Hawke St DE22 218 C5
Hawk Green Rd SK6 23 A3
Hawkhill Rd S32 71 D6
Hawkinge Ho 13 S41 95 D5
Hawking La
Stainsby S44 133 A7
Stainsby Common
S44 132 F7
Hawkins Ct DE7 194 F4
Hawkins Dr DE56 168 B3
Hawk Rd SK22 33 E8
Hawksdale Cl DE73 233 A2
Hawk's Dr DE15 248 D3
Hawkshead Ave
Derby DE21 205 D1
Dronfield S18 56 E1
Hawkshead Fold
SK13 10 E3
Hawkshead Rd SK13 10 E3
Hawksley Ave S40 95 E4
Hawksley Dr
Darley Dale DE4 127 B4
Rolleston DE13 240 B4
Hawksway S21 59 B3
Hawleys Cl DE4 143 E6
Hawley St S18 58 A1
Hawthorn Ave
Breaston DE72 235 F8
Derby DE24 233 A7
Mastin Moor S43 79 C4
Netherseal DE12 264 F7
Ripley DE5 180 D8
Stapleford NG9 223 D6
Hawthorn Bank
Glossop SK13 9 F4
New Mills SK22 33 B6
Hawthorn Cl
Ashbourne DE6 185 D8
Chinley SK23 34 E1
Clowne S43 80 D4
Denstone ST14 196 E6
Disley SK12 32 E6
Doveridge DE6 211 B1
Hilton DE65 228 D1
Hope S33 39 A4
Mansfield Woodhouse
NG19 136 E5
Hawthorn Cres
Burton upon Trent
DE15 254 F7
Findern DE65 230 D2
Hawthorn Ct DE1 267 A5
Hawthorn Dr DE4 155 A6
Hawthorne Ave
Borrowash DE72 221 C2
Creswell S80 81 E2
Dronfield S18 57 A3
Glapwell S44 134 B8
Long Eaton NG10 236 C6
Shirebrook NG20 119 D4
Shirland DE55 146 C5
Tibshelf DE55 148 B8
Hawthorne Cl
Ashover DE55 145 D8
Barlborough S43 80 A6
Kilburn DE56 179 F2
Killamarsh S21 60 D5
Hawthorne Rd
Barlborough S43 80 A6
Pinxton NG16 160 D3
Hawthornes Ave
DE55 159 F5
Hawthorne St S40 266 C1
Hawthorn Gr SK14 9 D6
Hawthorn Hill S43 78 F6
Hawthorn Rd
Castle Donington
DE74 247 B5
Chapel-en-le-Frith
SK23 47 B4
Eckington S21 59 B2
Hawthorn Rise
Awsworth NG16 195 B4
Swadlincote DE11 255 F7
Hawthorn St DE24 232 C8
Hawthorns The
Belper DE56 179 D5
Little Eaton DE21 205 D8
Wirksworth DE4 165 F7
Hawthorn Way S42 94 F5
Hawton Cl NG19 135 F1
Hawtrey Gdns DE24 233 A7
Haxby Cl S13 44 E6
Haxby Pl S13 44 E6
Haxby St S13 44 E6
Haybrook Ct S17 55 E5
Haycock Dr 7 DE6 185 D7
Haycroft Cl NG19 135 E2
Haycroft Ct DE23 231 A7
Haycroft Gdns S43 79 B4
Hayden Ct 1 SK13 10 C1
Haydn Fold SK13 16 D7
Haydn Rd DE21 219 F8
Haydock Cl
Burton upon Trent
DE14 254 A7
Kimberley NG16 195 E7
Haydock Park Rd
DE24 232 E8
Hayes Ave
Breaston DE72 235 B7
Hayes Ave *continued*
Derby DE23 231 D8
Hayes Cl
Pinxton NG16 160 C3
West Hallam DE7 207 E8
Hayes Conf Ctr The
DE55 170 A6
Hayes Cres DE55 169 F7
Hayes Ct S20 59 E6
Hayes Dr S20 59 E6
Hayes Farm Ct
DE73 251 A4
Hayes La
Grassmoor S40 115 E4
Swanwick DE55 169 F7
Hayes The DE65 230 C1
Hayes Wood Rd
DE7 193 A1
HAYFIELD 25 C2
Hayfield Cl
Belper DE56 179 B5
Dronfield S18 56 D1
Staveley S43 78 F3
Wingerworth S42 114 F3
Hayfield Cres S12 44 D3
Hayfield Dr
Branston DE14 253 C8
Sheffield S12 44 D3
Hayfield Gdns DE23 231 B6
Hayfield Pl S12 44 D3
Hayfield Prim Sch
SK22 25 C3
Hayfield Rd
Chapel-en-le-Frith
SK23 47 B8
Chinley SK23 35 A3
New Mills SK22 24 E1
New Mills SK22 33 D8
Hayfield Road E
SK23 47 C6
Hayfield View S21 59 C3
Hayfield Visitor Ctr★
SK22 25 C2
Hayford Pl DE22 218 D4
Hayford Way S43 78 E1
Hay La
Ashover S45 145 B7
Holymoorside S45 113 D5
Scropton DE65 226 E5
Spout DE4 166 C5
Haylee La SK23 46 D1
Hayley Cl NG16 195 D6
Hayley Croft DE56 190 F1
Hayling Cl DE7 194 C3
Hayman Cl 3 NG19 136 C3
Haymans Cnr 5
NG19 136 C3
Haynes Ave NG9 209 C5
Hays Cl DE7 194 D2
Haysden La 3 S8 43 A2
Hays La DE6 164 E1
Hays The DE65 227 C2
Hay The S45 145 B6
Hay Wain La DE11 256 B7
Haywards Cl SK13 10 C3
Haywood Cl DE24 233 A5
Haywoods Rd DE11 256 E1
Hayworth Rd NG10 223 B5
Hazel Ave
Derby DE23 231 D6
Killamarsh S21 60 C5
Pilsley S45 132 B3
Hazelbadge Cres S12 44 E3
Hazelby Rd S80 100 F8
Hazel Cl
Ashbourne DE6 185 D8
Dronfield S18 76 B8
Findern DE65 230 E2
Heanor DE75 181 D1
Swadlincote DE11 256 A5
Hazel Cres
Branston DE14 253 E6
Branston DE14 256 E6
Shirebrook NG20 119 D4
Hazel Croft S17 55 C8
Hazel Ct
Dronfield S18 76 B8
Matlock DE4 143 D5
Hazel Dene DE4 143 D5
Hazeldene Cl DE56 190 E5
Hazeldene Cotts
DE56 178 D2
Hazel Dr
Chesterfield S40 114 E8
Derby DE21 221 A6
Wingerworth S42 115 B3
HAZELFORD 53 A5
Hazel Gr
Calver S32 72 C2
Duffield DE56 190 E3
Mansfield Woodhouse
NG19 136 B5
Mastin Moor S43 79 C4
Matlock DE4 143 D5
South Normanton
DE55 160 B5
Hazelhurst S41 115 D6
Hazelhurst Ave S41 96 A5
Hazelhurst La S41 96 A5
Hazelmererd S80 100 B8
Hazelmere Rd S80 81 D2
Hazel Rd S21 59 C2
Hazelrigg Cl DE74 246 F4
Hazeltree Cl DE5 180 C8
HAZELWOOD 190 A8
Hazelwood Cl
5 Dronfield S18 56 C1
1 Glossop SK13 10 A6
Hazelwood Cl *continued*
6 Tibshelf DE55 148 B7
Hazelwood Hill
Hazelwood DE56 178 B1
Hazelwood DE56 190 C8
Hazelwood Rd
Burton upon Trent
DE15 254 E6
Derby DE21 219 F8
Duffield DE56 190 D5
Hazlebarrow Cl S8 57 C6
Hazlebarrow Cres
S8 57 C7
Hazlebarrow Ct S8 57 B7
Hazlebarrow Dr S8 57 B7
Hazlebarrow Gr S8 57 C7
Hazlebarrow Rd S8 57 B7
Hazlehurst Ave S41 96 B5
Hazlehurst La
Chesterfield S41 96 B5
Eckington S8 57 F8
Hazlewood Dr S43 80 B6
Headingley Ct DE23 231 C8
Headland Cl S43 96 E7
Headland Rd S43 96 E7
Headlands Cres 3
DE73 233 A3
Headstock Drive
DE11 255 D1
HEAGE 168 E1
Heage La DE65 229 D8
Heage Prim Sch
DE56 168 D2
Heage Rd DE5 169 C1
Heage Road Ind Est
DE5 169 B1
Heage Windmill★
DE56 168 D2
Healaugh Way S40 115 B8
Heale St S43 80 E3
HEANOR 181 C2
HEANOR GATE 193 C8
Heanor Gate 3
DE75 181 D1
Heanor Gate Ind Est
DE75 193 D8
Heanor Gate Rd
DE75 193 D8
Heanor Gate Science
Coll DE75 181 C1
Heanor Ho DE21 220 E3
Heanor Langley Inf Sch
1 NG16 182 B3
Heanor Rd
Denby DE5 181 A3
Heanor, Heanor Gate
DE75 181 D1
Ilkeston DE7 194 D3
Smalley DE7, DE75 193 B7
Heanor Retail Pk
DE75 181 E2
Heanor Small Bsns Ctr
DE75 193 D8
Hearthcote Rd
DE11 256 A3
HEARTHSTONE 143 D1
Hearthstone La
DE4 143 D1
HEATH 117 B2
Heath Ave
Derby DE23 218 C1
Killamarsh S21 60 D5
Heath Cl DE72 246 B8
Heath Common S44 117 B2
HEATHCOTE
138 B5
SK17 138 B5
Heathcote Cl DE24 233 C5
Heathcote Dr S41 115 E8
Heathcote Ho S41 96 B6
Heath Cross 3
ST14 210 A1
Heath Ct
Chesterfield S40 115 A8
Derby DE24 231 E3
HEATH END 258 D7
Heath End La DE73 258 E8
Heather Ave S44 116 F1
Heather Bank Cl 2
SK13 17 A7
Heather Cl
Burton upon Trent
DE14 254 A8
Calow S44 97 A3
Derby DE24 231 D2
Glossop SK13 10 C3
South Normanton
DE55 160 A3
Swanwick DE55 170 A8
Heather Close DE13 239 D5
Heather Cres
Breaston DE72 235 F7
Derby DE23 231 C6
Heather Ct DE75 182 B1
Heather Falls SK22 33 B8
Heather Gdns S41 115 E7
Heather Gr SK14 9 D6
Heather La S32 53 A6
Heather Lea Ave S17 55 C7
Heather Lea Pl S17 55 C7
Heatherley Dr
NG19 136 E1
Heatherley Prim Sch
NG19 136 E1
Heathermead Cl 2
DE21 205 F1
Heathers Edge S32 53 A6
Heather Vale S41 115 E7
Heather Vale Cl
S41 115 E7
Heather Vale Rd
S41 115 D7
Heather Way
Holymoorside S42 113 D7
Shirebrook NG20 119 D2
Heathfield DE4 143 C7
Heathfield Ave
Chesterfield S40 95 D3
Etwall DE65 229 C3
Ilkeston DE7 209 A8
Heathfield Cl
Dronfield S18 75 F8
Wingerworth S42 115 B4
Heathfield Gdns
Buxton SK17 85 A8
Tibshelf DE55 148 A7
Heathfield Nook Rd
SK17 85 E2
Heathfield Rd S12 44 D4
Heath Fields Prim Sch
DE65 227 C1
Heath Gdns DE72 236 A8
Heath Gr SK17 85 C6
Heath La
Blackfordby DE11 257 C2
Findern DE65 242 D8
Hartshorne DE11 257 E4
Smisby LE65 258 B6
Heathlands Dr ST14 210 B1
Heathlands Grange
DE15 254 E7
Heath Lane SK23 46 F5
Heathley Mews
DE14 254 C8
Heath Park Rd SK17 85 C6
Heath Prim Sch S44 116 F1
Heath Rd
Burton upon Trent
DE15 254 E7
Glossop SK13 10 D2
Holmewood S44 116 E1
Holmewood, Williamthorpe
S42 132 E8
Ripley DE5 169 E1
Uttoxeter ST14 210 B1
Heath St SK17 85 B6
HEATH THE 210 A1
Heath The
Eastwood NG16 195 A8
Glossop SK13 10 C3
HEATHTOP 227 A6
Heath View SK17 85 E1
Heathy Way DE65 227 D1
Heathy Dales SK17 69 B2
Heaton Cl S18 56 D1
Heaton Ct 4 S40 95 C2
Heaton Pl SK17 85 E8
Heaton St S40 95 C2
Heavygate La DE56 177 F8
Hebden Cl DE23 230 F6
Hebden Dr SK13 17 F8
Hebrides Cl DE24 231 D3
Heddon Bar NG19 136 E3
Hedgebank Ct DE21 206 C3
Hedge Gr DE11 256 B7
Hedgerow Gdns
DE21 206 C3
Hedges Dr DE7 209 A5
Hedgevale Cl DE23 231 A7
Hedingham Cl NE7 194 D1
Hedingham Way
DE3 230 D8
Hedley Cl DE55 170 D8
Hedley Dr S43 96 D8
Hedley St DE11 256 F5
HEELEY 43 B6
Heeley Arches S2 43 A7
Heeley Bank Rd S2 43 B7
Heeley City Farm★
S2 43 B7
Heeley Gn S2 43 A8
Heigham Cl DE24 232 D3
Heights of Abraham
The★ DE4 143 A2
Heild End SK11 102 A2
Helmsley Ave S20 59 E7
Helmsley Cl S41 95 C7
Helmton Dr S8 43 A2
Helmton Rd S8 43 A2
Helpston Cl DE55 147 C1
Helston Cl
Chesterfield S41 115 B8
Derby DE24 233 B6
Linton DE12 261 D5
Helvellyn Way 5
NG10 223 B2
Heming Ave S45 132 C2
HEMINGTON 247 D5
Hemington Ct DE74 247 C5
Hemington Hill
DE74 247 C4
Hemington La DE74 247 E5
Hemington Prim Sch
DE74 247 D5
Hemlock Ave
Long Eaton NG10 223 D1
Stapleford NG9 223 E8
Hemlock Cl DE21 206 A3
Hemlock La DE7 208 D5
Hemlock Stone The★
NG9 209 F2
HEMMING GREEN 94 B4
Hemper Gr S8 56 D7
Hemper La S8 56 D7
Hemp Yd DE6 165 B1
Hemsley Dr NG16 182 D3
HEMSWORTH 43 D3
Hemsworth Rd S8,
S14 43 C2
Henderson Cl S45 131 E5
Hendon Way DE22 218 B6
Henley Ave S8 57 C8
Henley Gdns NG9 209 E1
Henley Gn DE22 217 F6
Henley Grove DE11 255 F2
Henley Way DE7 207 D8
HENMOOR 131 A4
Henmore Cres
Derby DE3 217 B1
Derby DE3 230 B8
Henmore Pl 10 DE6 173 C2
Henmore Trad Est
DE6 173 A1
Hennymoor Cl S80 82 A5
Hennymoor La S80 82 C2
Henry Ave
Mansfield Woodhouse
NG19 136 B5
Matlock DE4 143 C6
Henry Bradley Inf Sch
S43 96 F8
Henry Cres DE55 159 C3
Henry St
Chesterfield S41 96 B8
Derby DE1 267 A4
Eckington S21 59 D3
Glossop SK13 10 C1
Grassmoor S42 115 E3
Ripley DE5 169 D2
Henshall Dr DE72 245 B8
Henshall Ho S41 96 B6
Henshaw Ave DE7 208 D5
Henshaw Gardens
DE5 169 C1
Henshaw Pl DE7 194 E4
HEPTHORNE LANE 131 E6
Hepworth Dr NG16 195 B7
Hepworth Rd DE11 256 E1
Herald Gr DE73 244 E8
Herbert Dr DE11 256 F5
Herbert St DE15 248 B3
Herbert Strutt Prim Sch
DE56 179 B2
Herb Garden at
Hardstoft The★
S45 132 E3
HERDINGS 43 F3
Herdings Ct S12 44 A3
Herdings Rd S12 44 A3
Herdings View
Sheffield S12 43 F3
Sheffield S12 44 A3
Hereford Ave NG19 136 D5
Hereford Cl SK17 85 C4
Hereford Cres DE11 256 D6
Hereford Dr S43 96 F8
Hereford Rd
Buxton SK17 85 C4
Derby DE21 219 D8
Hereward's Rd S14 43 D1
Herewood Cl NG20 119 F4
Heritage Ct DE6 201 B7
Heritage Dr S43 80 D5
Heritage High Sch
S43 80 D4
Heritage Rd DE74 246 F2
Heritage St S43 81 E2
Heritage Way DE15 248 A1
Hermitage Ave
Borrowash DE72 221 C2
Somercotes DE55 170 C5
Hermitage Cl DE6 185 C8
Hermitage Ct DE21 206 B1
Hermitage Gdns 1
ST14 210 A1
Hermitage La DE6 184 B6
Hermitage Park Way 7
DE11 256 A7
Hermitage Wlk DE7 208 F6
Hernstone La SK17 49 B2
Heron Cl SK13 17 F8
Heron Dr DE11 256 F3
Heron Grange DE14 253 D7
Heron Rd S43 98 A8
Heronswood Dr
DE21 220 D6
Heron View SK13 16 F8
Heron Way
Derby DE3 218 A2
Mansfield NG19 135 C1
Herriot Dr S40 266 C1
Hesketh Cl DE5 181 A8
Hessey St S13 44 F6
Hetton Drive S45 131 D4
Hewer Cl 4 DE7 194 F8
Hewer Ct S20 60 A6
Hewer Drive DE11 255 D2
Hewers Holt S43 80 B6
Hewett St NG20 120 D5
Hewitt Pl S26 61 E5
Hexham Ave DE7 209 A4
Hexham Wlk DE21 205 E1
Heyden Bank 26 SK13 9 D2
Heyden Fold 27 SK13 9 D2
Heyden Terr 25 SK13 9 D2
Heydon Cl DE56 179 B6
Heyford Ct DE75 182 A1
Heysbank Rd SK12 32 D5
Hey St NG10 236 C4
Heywood St S43 96 E8
Heywood View S43 80 C6

Heywood Villas 5
S43 96 E8
Heyworth Rd SK23 47 C6
Heyworth St DE22 218 D6
Hibbert St SK22 33 B6
Hibbitt Cl DE55 170 B7
Hickings La NG9 223 E8
Hickingwood La S43 81 A5
Hickinwood Cres S43 80 F5
Hickleton Cl DE5 169 C1
Hickleton La S2 44 A7
Hickling Cl
Derby DE24 232 D3
1 Nottingham NG10 236 B5
Hickory Gr 1 DE11 256 B7
Hickton Rd DE55 169 F6
HIDEBANK 33 C8
Hide La SK17 137 E7
Hides Gn S44 99 A2
HIGGENHOLES 109 D8
Higger La S32 52 F8
Higgins Rd DE11 255 F6
Higg La
Alderwasley DE4 166 F5
Alderwasley DE56 167 A6
Higgot La DE15 248 B5
Higgott Cl DE14 254 B8
HIGHAM 146 C3
Higham La
Compstall SK14 15 A7
Stonebroom DE55 146 E4
Highashes La S45 113 E1
Highbank SK13 9 F7
High Bank DE5 180 F2
Highbank Rd SK13 17 F7
High Bank Rd DE15 248 B3
High Bridge La
DE15 241 D3
Highbury Cl DE22 217 F6
Highbury Grove S40 95 F5
Highbury Rd S41 95 F5
High Cliffe S32 71 D7
Highcliffe Ave
NG20 119 D4
Highcroft Cl NG10 236 E5
High Cross
Hartington SK17 137 F5
Linton DE11 261 F7
HIGH CROSS BANK 261 E8
High Ct 1 DE4 143 C6
Highdale Fold 6
S18 57 A1
High Edge Dr DE56 179 E8
High Edge Mews
DE56 179 A5
Higher Albert St
S41 266 B4
Higher Barn Rd SK13 9 F4
HIGHER BIBBINGTON 67 A6
HIGHER BUXTON 85 C6
HIGHER CHISWORTH
SK13 16 B4
Higher Cliffe SK6 23 D2
HIGHER CROSSINGS 46 F6
HIGHER DINTING 10 A2
Higher Dinting SK13 10 A2
HIGHER DISLEY 32 E5
HIGHER GAMESLEY 16 D8
Higher Hallsteads
SK17 47 F3
Higher La SK12 32 E1
Higher Noon Sun
SK22 24 F2
Higher Sq SK13 10 A7
HIGHFIELD 43 A8
Highfield DE45 108 E8
Highfield Ave
Chesterfield S41 95 E6
Dove Holes SK17 47 E1
Mansfield NG19 136 B1
Shirebrook NG20 119 D6
Highfield Cl
Bakewell DE45 109 C5
Heanor DE75 181 B5
Mansfield NG19 136 B1
High Field Cl S44 118 A5
Highfield Cotts
Alfreton DE55 158 D3
Derby DE21 219 E5
Highfield Ct SK14 9 A4
Highfield Dr
Bakewell DE45 109 C5
Ilkeston DE7 208 B5
Matlock DE4 143 D6
South Normanton
DE55 160 B5
Highfield Gdns
Derby DE22 218 F7
Hollingworth SK14 9 D5
Highfield Hall Prim Sch
S41 95 F6
Highfield La
Chesterfield S41 95 E6
Clay Cross SK17 131 F3
Derby DE21 219 F5
Hartington SK17 137 F5
Weston Underwood
DE6 188 F5
Highfield Mews
DE21 219 E5
Highfield Pl S2 43 A8
Highfield Rd
Ashbourne DE6 185 B8
Belper DE56 178 F2

Highfield Rd *continued*
Bolsover S44 99 A1
Chesterfield S41 266 A4
Derby DE22 218 F7
Derby, Littleover
DE23 231 C7
Glossop SK13 17 D8
Hayfield SK22 25 D3
Hulland Ward DE6 175 F3
Kilburn DE56 191 F8
Little Eaton DE21 205 C8
Marple SK6 23 B6
Swadlincote DE11 256 B3
Swanwick DE55 169 D7
HIGHFIELDS 132 C7
Highfields
Buxton SK17 67 B5
Clowne S43 80 D2
Codnor DE5 181 B8
Highfields Cl 5
DE55 158 E3
Highfields Cres S18 76 A8
Highfields Dr
Holmewood S42 132 D8
Linton DE12 261 C6
Highfields Lower Sch
DE4 143 C3
Highfields Park Dr
DE22 204 E1
Highfields Rd S18 76 A8
Highfields Sch DE4 143 E7
Highfields Spencer Acad
DE23 230 E3
Highfield St
Long Eaton NG10 223 C2
Swadlincote DE11 256 B3
Highfields Way S42 132 D8
Highfield Terr
Chesterfield S41 95 F5
New Mills SK22 33 D8
Highfield View Rd
S41 95 F5
Highfield Way DE5 180 C8
HIGHGATE 25 D1
Highgate Cl S43 77 D3
Highgate Dr
Dronfield S18 76 C7
Ilkeston DE7 194 D3
Highgate Gn DE22 218 A5
Highgate La S18 76 C7
Highgate Rd SK22 25 E1
Highgates DE1 267 B2
High Gr
Belper DE56 179 D4
Mansfield NG19 136 E1
High Grange Sch
DE3 230 B7
Highgrove Cl
Burton upon Trent
DE13 240 C1
6 Chesterfield S41 96 A8
Heanor DE75 181 C1
Highgrove Ct DE24 232 F4
Highgrove Dr DE73 232 F2
Highgrove Gdns 4
DE65 227 D2
High Hazel Ct S45 131 D4
High Hazel Dr NG19 136 B1
High Hazels Cl S45 131 E4
High Hazels Rd S43 80 B5
High Hazels Wlk
S45 131 E4
High Hill Rd
New Mills SK22 24 D1
New Mills SK22 33 D8
High Holbeck S80 101 C7
High Holborn DE7 194 E3
High Holborn Rd
DE5 170 B1
High La
Broadbottom SK13 16 E7
Eckington S12 44 E1
Holloway, Dethick Common
DE4 144 E2
Holloway, Upper Holloway
DE4 156 D6
Holymoorside S42 113 E5
Sheffield S12 58 F8
Wigley S42 93 F4
High La East DE7 208 B7
Highland Cl
Buxton SK17 85 C5
Mansfield Woodhouse
NG19 136 D3
Highland Rd
Chesterfield S43 77 D4
Chesterfield S43 77 D5
Highlands Dr DE15 248 A4
Highlands Pl S41 76 F4
HIGH LANE 32 A8
High Lane Central
DE7 193 F1
High Lane E DE7 208 B8
High Lane W DE7 193 E1
High Lea Rd SK22 33 A8
High Leys Rd S43 80 E2
Highlightley La S18 75 C5
HIGH LOW 52 E5
Highlow Cl S40 95 C5
High Mdws SK13 17 B7
High Meadow Cl
DE5 180 D8
High Pavement
DE56 179 A3
High Peak Rd SK17 85 C3
High Peak School
SK12 32 E1
High Rd DE55 157 F4

High Ridge
Mansfield NG19 136 F2
Matlock DE4 143 C7
High Spannia NG16 195 F7
High St
Alfreton DE55 158 F4
Alfreton DE55 159 A4
Apperknowle S18 58 A1
Barlborough S43 80 A7
Belper DE56 179 A4
Bolsover S44 99 A1
Bonsall DE4 142 D1
Brimington S43 96 F7
Brinsley NG16 171 E1
Buxton SK17 85 B7
Calver S32 72 B2
Castle Donington
DE74 247 A2
Chapel-en-le-Frith
SK23 47 B6
Chellaston DE73 233 A1
Chesterfield S41, S43 77 D4
Chesterfield, Stonegravels
S40 266 B3
Clay Cross S45 131 C3
Clowne S43 80 D3
Codnor DE5 181 B8
Derby DE1 267 C1
Doveridge DE6 211 B1
Dronfield S18 57 A1
Eckington S21 59 D3
Ilkeston DE7 208 F8
Kilburn DE56 192 A8
Killamarsh S21 60 D6
Kimberley NG16 195 F6
Linton DE12 261 C6
Long Eaton NG10 236 E8
Longnor SK17 121 C6
Mansfield Woodhouse
NG19 136 C3
Marchington ST14 224 E2
Melbourne DE73 252 A7
New Mills SK22 33 C8
Pilsley DE45 91 C3
Pleasley NG19 135 B5
Repton DE65 242 D2
Ripley DE5 169 D1
Rocester ST14 196 F3
Sheffield, Dore S17 55 D7
Sheffield, Mosborough
S20 59 D7
Somercotes DE55 170 C8
Somercotes, Riddings
DE55 170 D5
South Normanton
DE55 160 A6
Stapleford NG9 223 E7
Staveley S43 78 E2
Stonebroom DE55 147 A4
Stoney Middleton S32 71 F3
Stramshall ST14 210 A4
Swadlincote, Church Gresley
DE11 256 C3
Swadlincote, Newhall
DE11 256 A6
Swanwick DE55 169 F7
Tibshelf DE55 148 A7
Ticknall DE73 251 A4
Tideswell SK17 69 C4
Tutbury DE13 239 C6
Whitwell S80 81 F6
Woodville DE11 256 F2
Highstairs La DE55 146 C8
Highstones Gdns
SK13 10 F2
Highstool La SK17 106 B6
High Street E SK13 10 D1
High Street Mews
S20 59 C7
High Street W SK13 10 B1
High Tor★ DE4 143 B3
High Tor Rd DE4 143 B2
High Trees S17 55 D7
Highview SK13 17 A7
High View Cl S41 96 D2
High View Rd DE55 160 C7
Highway La DE6 151 F2
High Withins La
DE6 149 A3
Highwood Ave
DE56 179 C1
High Wood Bank
DE56 179 C1
Highwood Cl SK13 17 B8
High Wood Fold SK6 23 C8
Highwood La S80 81 D5
Highwood Pl S21 59 C3
High Wood Way
S43 80 C5
Hilary Cl DE56 179 E5
HILCOTE 148 C1
Hilcote La DE55 148 B1
Hilcote St DE55 160 A6
Hilderstone Cl
DE24 233 D6
Hillary Pl DE7 208 B5
Hillberry 1 DE5 170 A1
Hillberry Rise S40 114 F6
Hill Brow DE1 267 B2
Hill Cl
Derby DE21 220 E4
Stanley Common DE7 193 A1
Turnditch DE56 177 B2
Hillcliff La
Hulland Ward DE56 176 F2
Turnditch DE56 177 A3
HILLCLIFFLANE 177 A3
Hill Cotts DE45 125 B5

Hillcrest
Aston-on-Trent
DE72 234 A1
Belper DE56 179 E4
Blackwell DE55 147 E1
2 Matlock DE4 143 A7
Tutbury DE13 239 B5
Hill Crest
Crich DE4 157 A1
Shirebrook NG20 119 D3
Hillcrest Ave
Burton upon Trent
DE15 248 A4
Hulland Ward DE6 175 F3
South Normanton
DE55 160 A4
Hill Crest Ave DE55 157 E8
Hillcrest Close S44 98 F6
Hill Crest Cotts DE4 142 F8
Hillcrest Dr
Codnor DE5 181 B8
Kilburn DE56 192 A8
Hillcreste Dr DE73 232 F3
Hillcrest Gr S43 78 F4
Hillcrest Rd S41 115 D7
Hill Crest Rd DE21 219 D7
Hill Crest Rise S26 61 F5
Hillcroft Dr DE72 221 C4
HILLCROSS 231 C7
Hill Cross DE45 108 F8
Hill Cross Ave DE23 231 C7
Hill Cross Dr DE23 231 B7
Hill Dr SK23 45 D8
Hillend SK14 9 A1
Hillend La SK14 9 A1
Hillfield Cl DE11 262 B7
Hillfield La DE13 240 F1
Hillfield Rd NG9 209 F1
Hill Fields DE55 160 A3
HILLFOOT 55 D5
Hillfoot Ct S17 55 D4
Hillfoot Rd S17 55 D5
Hill Gr S43 78 B4
Hill Green Cl DE12 260 D3
Hill Head S33 51 A7
Hill Head Dr SK17 85 E1
Hillhead La SK17 85 E1
Hillhouses La S42 114 E3
Hillingdon Avenue
DE22 218 A5
Hillingdon Dr DE7 209 A7
Hill La
Hathersage S32 52 F8
Holymoorside S42 113 D6
Hillman Dr S43 97 C7
Hillmoor St NG19 135 C3
Hillmorton DE45 108 F7
Hill Nook Cl DE73 233 A1
Hillock The S32 72 E2
Hill Pond Ave SK22 24 D1
Hill Rd
Ashover S45 129 F4
Heanor DE75 181 D1
Hill Rise NG9 209 C4
Hill Rise Cl DE23 231 D8
HILLS AND HOLES 120 E5
Hillsdale Rd DE15 248 B5
Hillside
Ashover S45 130 A4
Brassington DE4 152 F1
Buxton SK17 85 D3
Castle Donington
DE74 247 B4
Chinley SK23 47 B8
Curbar S32 72 E2
Findern DE65 230 C2
Holloway DE4 156 A6
Langley Mill NG16 182 A3
Middleton DE4 154 D4
Sheffield S20 59 C7
Tutbury DE13 239 C6
Whitwell S80 81 F5
Hillside Ave
Ashbourne DE6 173 C3
Derby DE21 220 A5
Dronfield S18 76 A8
Hillside Cl
Disley SK12 32 E6
Glossop SK13 9 E3
Whitwell S80 81 F5
Hillside Cotts S32 53 B7
Hillside Cres DE21 220 F4
Hillside Ct
Breedon on the Hill
DE73 252 F2
Kirk Langley DE6 202 E4
Hillside Dr
Chesterfield S40 95 D1
Long Eaton NG10 236 B8
Mastin Moor S43 79 C3
Hillside Gdns
4 Matlock DE4 143 A7
Swadlincote DE11 255 F2
Hillside Gr
Marple SK6 15 B1
Sandiacre NG10 223 A6
Hillside Green S26 61 E5
Hillside La DE6 152 F1
Hillside Pk
Alfreton DE55 158 B4
South Wingfield DE55 158 B4
Hillside Rd
Branston DE14 253 C8
Derby DE21 220 F4
Linton DE12 261 D7
Hillside Rise DE56 178 F2
Hillside View SK22 33 A8
Hills La DE73 244 E3

Hillsmede 2 DE55 147 F6
HILL SOMERSAL 212 A2
Hill Sq The DE22 205 A1
Hills Rd DE72 235 C7
Hill St
Burton upon Trent
DE15 254 E8
Clay Cross S45 131 C3
Donisthorpe DE12 262 E1
Ripley DE5 169 D3
Sheffield S2 43 A8
Swadlincote DE11 255 F6
Swadlincote, Church Gresley
DE11 256 C3
Wingerworth S42 115 C4
HILLS THE 51 A6
Hills The S33 51 A6
HILLSTOWN 118 C8
Hillstown Bsns Ctr
S44 118 B7
Hillsview Ct NG19 135 A5
Hillsway
Chellaston DE73 232 F3
Derby DE23 218 B1
Shirebrook NG20 119 D3
Hill The
Cromford DE4 155 A5
Derby DE22 205 A1
Glapwell S44 118 A1
HILLTOP
Chapel-en-le-Frith 46 B6
Flash 103 B5
Hilltop DE56 168 B7
HILL TOP 76 A7
Hill Top
Bolsover S44 99 A2
Castle Donington
DE74 247 A1
Derby DE21 205 E3
Flash SK17 103 B5
Hilltop Ave NG20 119 E4
Hilltop Cl S44 118 B1
Hilltop Dr 3 DE55 158 F1
Hilltop La
Belper DE56 179 E2
Thurvaston DE6 215 D5
Hilltop Rd
Ashover S45 129 F5
Chesterfield S41 77 B2
Dronfield S18 76 B7
Glossop SK13 10 B3
Pinxton NG16 160 C3
Wingerworth S42 114 D4
Hill Top Rd DE55 170 C5
Hill Top Rise SK23 45 D8
Hilltops View DE4 143 D5
Hilltop Way S18 76 A7
Hill View
Duffield DE56 190 D3
Repton DE65 242 E2
Whaley Bridge SK23 45 C8
Hill View Cl DE7 192 B7
Hillview Ct NG19 136 D4
Hill View Gr DE21 220 E5
Hillview Ho 1 DE1 267 B2
Hill View Rd S43 96 E8
Hillwood Dr SK13 17 F8
HILLYFIELDS 132 B7
HILTON 228 C1
Hilton Bsns Pk
DE65 240 E8
Hilton Cl
Derby DE3 217 D1
Long Eaton NG10 235 F4
Pleasley NG19 135 C3
Swadlincote DE11 256 A7
HILTON COMMON 228 F2
Hilton Gdns DE72 246 A7
Hilton Ind Est DE65 228 D3
Hilton Park Dr
DE55 170 C8
Hilton Prim Sch
DE65 228 D2
Hilton Rd
Disley SK12 32 B7
Egginton DE65 241 B7
Etwall DE65 229 B4
Hinckley Ct DE4 110 F1
Hind Ave DE72 235 C8
Hindersitch La DE4 156 D2
Hindlip Cl 4 DE6 211 A1
HIND LOW 105 B7
Hindscarth Cres
DE3 217 E1
Hinton Gr SK14 15 A8
Hipley Cl S40 95 B6
Hipper St S40 266 B2
Hipper Street S S40 266 B2
Hipper Street W S40 95 E2
Hitchen Road NG10 236 B7
Hixon's La DE7 208 B1
Hoades St S42 131 C8
Hoargate La DE6 200 F2
Hobart Cl
Burton upon Trent
DE15 248 C2
Derby DE3 217 F2
Hobart Dr NG9 209 F1
Hob Hill DE56 190 B8
Hob Hill Mdws SK13 17 D7
Hobhouse Rd NG19 135 D2
Hob Hurst's Ho★
DE45 111 F7
Hobkirk Dr DE24 231 E2
Hob La DE6 176 D8
Hobroyd SK13 16 B7
HOBSIC 182 D8
Hobsic Cl NG16 182 D8

Hobsic La NG16 171 E8
Hobson Dr
Derby DE21 220 F2
Derby DE72 221 A2
Ilkeston DE7 208 E6
Hobson Moor Rd SK14 9 A7
Hockerley Ave SK23 45 D8
Hockerley Cl SK23 45 D8
Hockerley La SK23 45 D8
Hockerley New Rd
SK23 45 D8
HOCKLEY 115 A2
Hockley La
Ashover S45 130 A1
Dalebank S45 145 C8
Wingerworth S42 115 A3
Hockley Rise S42 115 A2
Hockleys Yard DE5 181 C8
Hockley Way DE55 159 B2
Hodder Cl DE4 156 F2
Hodding Rd S80 82 C6
Hodge Beck Cl
DE24 233 C6
Hodge Fold SK14 15 F8
Hodge La
Ashover S45 128 E7
Broadbottom SK14 15 F8
Marchington ST14 224 A1
Uppertown S45 128 F7
Hodmire La S44 133 E7
HODTHORPE 82 C6
Hodthorpe Cl DE21 206 B1
Hodthorpe Prim Sch
S80 82 C5
Hogarth Cl NG9 223 E6
Hogarth Rd SK6 23 B8
Hogarth Rise S18 75 F8
Hogbarn La DE75,
NG16 181 D5
Hoggs Field NG16 182 F2
HOGNASTON 164 A1
Hogshaw Dr SK17 66 C1
Hogshaw Villas Rd
Buxton SK17 66 C1
1 Buxton SK17 85 C8
Hoillant Sq DE6 175 E3
Holbeach Dr S40 114 E8
HOLBECK 101 C7
Holbeck Ave S44 99 C2
Holbeck Cl S41 266 C4
Holbeck La S80 101 D8
Holbeck St S80 81 D1
HOLBECK WOODHOUSE 101 E7
Holbein Cl S18 75 F8
Holborn Dr DE22 218 A7
Holborn View DE5 170 B1
HOLBROOK
Belper 191 D6
Sheffield 60 A8
Holbrook Ave
North Wingfield S42 132 A7
Sheffield S20 60 A8
Holbrook CE Prim Sch
DE56 191 C7
Holbrook Cl
Chesterfield S40 114 C8
Pleasley NG19 135 A5
Holbrook Ct 4
DE65 242 E2
Holbrook Dr S13 44 B6
Holbrook Gn S20 60 A8
Holbrook Ind Est
S20 60 A8
HOLBROOK MOOR 191 D7
Holbrook Pl S43 97 C6
Holbrook Rd
Belper DE56 178 F2
Derby DE24 233 B6
Sheffield S13 44 B7
Holbrook Sch For Autism
DE56 191 D5
Holbrook St DE75 182 A2
Holbrook View
DE56 192 A8
Holbrook Way S42 132 A7
Holburn Ave S18 57 A2
Holcombe St DE23 219 B1
Holden Ave DE72 246 A8
Holden Ct DE24 233 A8
Holden Gdns 1
NG9 223 E6
Holderness Cl DE24 231 D2
Holdings The DE11 256 A1
Holdon Croft DE12 260 C6
HOLEHOUSE 16 C5
HOLESTONE 144 C8
Holestone Gate Rd
S45 129 D1
Holker Ave SK17 85 C8
Holker Rd SK17 85 C7
Holkham Cl DE7 194 C3
Holland Cl DE55 146 F5
Holland Mdw NG10 236 D5
Holland Pl 8 S2 43 A8
Holland Rd
Chesterfield S41 76 F2
Sheffield S2 43 A8
Hollbank Cotts
DE55 158 B3
Hollens Way
Chesterfield S40 95 A5
Woodnook S40 94 F5
Hollies Cl
Clifton DE6 184 F6
Dronfield S18 76 C8
Newton Solney DE15 248 E8
Hollies Ct DE65 229 B3

Hollies Dr SK6......23 A5
Hollies Farm Cl
DE73..............244 E3
Hollies Farm Drive
DE7..............192 C7
Hollies La DE5......198 C4
Hollies Rd DE22....204 D3
Hollies The
Eastwood NG16.....182 F2
Repton DE65.......243 A1
Sandiacre NG10....223 A5
Shirebrook NG20...119 E2
Hollin Bank Rd S32...41 B4
Hollin Cl S41......95 C8
Hollincross La SK13..17 C8
Hollindale Dr S12....44 C5
Hollin Dr SK23......47 B5
HOLLINGTON.......200 F4
Hollington Cl DE21..219 E7
Hollington La DE6...260 E7
Hollington Rd ST14..196 D3
Hollingwood Cres
S43..............78 A1
Hollingwood Prim Sch
S43..............78 A1
HOLLINGWORTH.......9 C6
Hollingworth Ave
NG10.............223 B3
Hollingworth Prim Sch
SK14.............9 C5
Hollinhey Terr SK14..9 C5
Hollin Hill Rd S43....81 A3
HOLLINS
94 A4
Wigley S42..........93 F4
Hollins Ave SK17.....85 B7
Hollins Bank 41 SK13..9 D2
Hollins Cl 40 SK13....9 D2
HOLLINSCLOUGH....104 C1
Hollinsclough CE VA
Prim Sch SK17....104 D2
Hollinsclough Rake
Hollinsclough SK17...103 F3
Hollinsclough SK17...104 B2
Hollinsend Ave S12...44 C5
Hollinsend Pl S12....44 C5
Hollinsend Rd S12...44 B5
Hollins Fold 43 SK13..9 D2
Hollins Gdns 46 SK13..9 D2
Hollins Gr 42 SK13....9 D2
HOLLINS GREEN.....130 E3
Hollins Ind Pk
SK13.............10 B5
Hollins La
Chapel-en-le-Frith
SK23.............46 C2
Crich DE4.........157 A4
Marple SK6.........23 C8
Hollins Mews 44 SK13..9 D2
Hollinsmoor Rd SK6,
SK22.............24 D7
Hollins Mount SK6...23 B8
Hollins Spring Ave
S18..............76 A8
Hollins Spring Rd
S18..............76 A8
Hollins St SK17.....85 B7
Hollins The DE4....156 A6
Hollins Way 45 SK13..9 D2
Hollins Wood Cl
DE4..............156 A5
HOLLIN WOOD......34 B1
Hollinwood La S42....23 B2
Hollinwood Rd SK12..32 D6
Hollis La
Chesterfield S40......96 B2
Chesterfield S41.....266 C2
Denstone ST14.....196 B6
Hollis St DE24......233 A8
Hollins Ave 47 SK13..9 D2
HOLLOWAY........156 F6
Holloway DE65.....242 E2
Holloway Rd
Derby DE24........232 F6
Duffield DE56......190 E4
Hollow Cres DE15...248 C4
Hollowford Ctr S33...38 C4
Hollowford Rd S33...38 B4
Hollow Gate
Bradwell S33.......51 A7
Froggatt S32........72 C5
Hollow La
Burton upon Trent
DE15.............248 C4
Mayfield DE6......172 C1
Sheffield, Mosborough
S20..............59 D6
Hollowood Ave
DE23.............231 C8
Hollow O'the Moor
SK17.............87 E4
Hollow Rd DE73....252 E2
Hollows The NG10...237 A8
Hollow The
Bamford S33........40 B3
Castle Donington
DE74.............247 B4
Derby, Littleover
DE23.............231 C8
Derby, Markeaton
DE3..............230 D8
Holloway DE4......156 B5
Roston DE6........197 E7
Holly Ave
Breaston DE72.....222 F1
Creswell S80........81 D2
Ripley DE5.........180 D8
Hollybank S12.......44 B6

Holly Bank
Glossop SK13.......17 E8
Hollingworth SK14....9 D5
Hollybank Ave S12...44 C6
Hollybank Cl
Sheffield S12.......44 D6
Swadlincote DE11..256 A7
Holly Bank Cl
New Houghton
NG19.............135 A6
South Wingfield DE55..158 B3
Hollybank Cres S12...44 C6
Holly Bank Dr DE4...156 F1
Hollybank Dr S12....44 D6
Hollybank Rd S12...44 C6
Hollybank Way S12...44 D6
Hollybrook Way
DE23.............230 F6
Holly Brook Way
DE23.............230 F6
Holly Bush Cl DE12..264 F7
Holly Bush La DE56..191 A6
Holly Cl
Ashbourne DE6.....185 D8
Chesterfield S41.....266 C2
Draycott DE72.....235 A7
Killamarsh S21......60 C5
Holly Croft DE15....248 C2
Holly Ct
Aston-on-Trent
DE72.............246 A7
3 Chesterfield S40....95 C2
Derby DE3........217 D1
2 Mansfield NG19...136 E1
Woodville DE11....256 F2
Holly End Rd 7
DE3..............217 D1
Holly Gdns S12.....44 C6
Holly Gn DE15......254 F8
Holly Gr
Sheffield S12.......44 C6
Swanwick DE55....169 F8
Holly Hill Rd NG16..171 F6
Hollyhock Drive
NG19.............135 F1
Hollyhock Way
DE14.............253 E6
Hollyhouse Dr
DE55.............160 B6
Holly House La
DE56.............178 C4
Holly House Sch S41..77 A3
Hollyhurst La DE6...212 B6
Hollyhurst Row
DE55.............170 F6
Holly La
Alderwasley DE56...167 D4
Glossop SK13.......10 C3
Tansley DE4.......144 A4
Hollymoor Dr DE73..232 F2
Holly Mount 2 SK13..10 D1
Holly Rd
Kimberley NG16....195 F7
Mansfield NG19....136 F2
5 Tutbury DE13....239 C5
Uttoxeter ST14....210 B1
Hollyseat La
Blackbrook DE56...178 A5
Shottle DE56.......177 F6
Holly St DE15......254 F8
Hollythorpe Cl S41..115 D8
Hollythorpe Cres S8..43 A4
Hollythorpe Rd S8...43 B4
Hollywell Ave DE15..181 B7
Hollywell Prim Sch
NG16.............195 F7
Hollywood Rd SK6...23 F8
Holm Ave DE21.....205 B7
Holm Cl S18........56 D2
HOLME.............2 F8
Holme Bank DE6...184 D7
Holmebank Cl S40....95 E4
Holmebank E S40....95 E4
Holmebank View
S40..............95 E4
Holmebank W S40...95 E4
Holmebrook Ct S40..95 D4
Holmebrook View
S41..............95 C6
Holme Cl
Hatton DE65.......227 C1
Holloway DE4......156 A5
Ilkeston DE7......194 D2
Holme Croft DE7....207 E7
Holme Ct DE45.....109 D5
Holme Farm Ave
DE15.............254 F8
Holmefield Cres
DE7..............209 A8
Holmefield Rd S80...82 A6
Holmegate Close
DE21.............219 F8
Holme Hall Cres S40..95 B5
Holme Hall Prim Sch
S40..............95 B5
Holme La
Bakewell DE45.....109 D7
Derby DE21.......220 C3
Holme Lea 2 NG10..223 B6
Holme Mdws S21....60 C5
Holme Park Ave S41..95 C7
Holme Rd
Chesterfield S41.....96 A6
Matlock Bath DE4...143 B1
Holmes Cl NG16....182 A3
Holmes Ct DE11....256 B5
HOLMESDALE.......57 C2
Holmesdale Cl S18...57 C3

Holmesdale Inf Sch
S18..............57 C2
Holmesdale Rd S18...57 C3
HOLMESFIELD......75 A8
Holmesfield Cl DE4..144 A5
HOLMESFIELD
COMMON..........74 C2
Holmesfield Dr
Derby DE3........217 D2
Shipley DE75......194 A8
Holmesfield Rd S18...56 B1
Holmes Rd DE72....235 D8
Holmes St
Derby DE23.......219 A2
Heanor DE75......181 D2
HOLMEWOOD......116 E1
Holmewood Ave
NE7..............194 F5
Holmewood Bsns Pk
S42..............116 C2
Holmewood Dr
NG16.............195 B8
Holmewood Ind Est
S42..............132 F8
Holmewood Ind Pk
S42..............116 D1
Holme Woods La HD9..42 A1
Holmfield
Buxton SK17........84 E6
Derby DE23.......231 E7
HOLMGATE.......130 E4
Holmgate Prim Sch
S45..............131 A4
Holmgate Rd
Clay Cross S45.....131 A4
Clay Cross S45.....131 C3
Holm La DE55......158 A4
Holmley Bank S18....57 A3
HOLMLEY COMMON..57 A3
Holmley La S18......57 A3
Holmoak Cl DE21...206 B3
Holmshaw Dr S13...44 E8
Holmshaw Gr S13...44 E8
Holmwood Terr 2
SK17.............85 C8
Holroyd Circle
NG16.............182 F7
Holt Ave DE24......233 C6
Holt Croft Cl DE72...235 E7
Holt Dr DE4.......142 F7
Holt La
Lea DE4..........156 B7
Matlock DE4.......143 A5
Holtlands Dr DE24...232 F5
Holt Rd DE4.......127 F1
Holt's La
Tutbury DE13......239 B6
Tutbury DE13......239 C6
Holt Way DE76......233 C3
Holyhead Dr DE21...206 B3
Holymoor Rd S42....113 E8
HOLYMOORSIDE....113 D8
Holyoake Ave S13....44 E8
Holyoake Dr NG10...236 F7
Holyrood Cl DE21...221 A5
Holyrood Ho DE24....4 C3
Holy Rosary RC Prim Sch
DE15.............248 A3
Holywell Cl DE45....109 D4
Holywell La DE45...125 B5
Holywell Rd DE7....194 C3
Holywell St S41.....266 B3
Homecroft Dr NG16..171 E7
Home Farm Cl
DE72.............221 C5
Home Farm Cotts
SK17.............105 C2
Home Farm Courtyard
DE74.............246 C3
Home Farm Ct
Castle Gresley
DE11.............255 D1
Selston NG16......171 C6
Home Farm Dr
Derby DE22.......205 A4
Foston DE65......226 D4
Home Farm Ho
DE15.............249 A3
Home Farm Park Homes
DE13.............240 A5
Homefields Prim Sch
DE73.............232 E1
Home La DE55......145 C2
Homemoss Ho SK17...85 A8
Homeport Mews
S41..............266 B4
Homer Dr SK6.......23 B8
Homerton Vale DE3..217 F3
Homestead NG16....182 A4
Homestead Rd SK12..32 C6
Homestead Way
SK23.............47 C5
Honeycroft Cl DE56..179 B2
Honeycroft Ct DE56..160 B4
Honeyfield Dr DE5...180 F8
Honey Pot Cl 4
NG10.............236 F8
Honeysuckle Avenue
DE13.............239 C5
Honeysuckle Cl 1
DE11.............256 A6
Honeysuckle Dr
DE55.............160 B7
Honeysuckle Pl SK13..10 C1
Honeysuckle Road
S41..............115 C2
Honeysuckle View
DE15.............255 A8

Honeywell La DE6...183 E8
Honingham Rd DE7..194 C3
Honiton Ct 11 S41....95 F8
Hoodcroft La S43....80 A4
Hook La ST14......210 B6
Hoole St S41......115 D8
Hooley Cl NG10....236 B6
Hooley St NG16....171 F6
Hoon La DE65......228 A3
Hoon Rd DE65......239 D8
Hoonwell La DE6....175 F5
Hope Ave DE3......217 D2
HOPEDALE.........149 C2
Hopedale Head
DE6..............149 C2
Hopedale Rd S12....44 D4
Hopefield Ave S12...44 D4
Hope Prim Sch S33...39 A4
Hope Rd
Edale S33..........29 B1
Edale S33..........38 A8
Hope S33...........39 D2
Hope St
Chesterfield S40.....95 E3
Derby DE1........219 B4
Derby DE1........267 C2
Glossop SK13.......10 C2
2 Ilkeston DE7....208 F7
Melbourne DE73...252 A7
Hope Sta S33.......39 C3
Hope Terr DE4.....143 B2
Hopetoun St DE23..232 A8
Hope Valley Coll S33..38 F3
Hope Way DE11....255 E1
Hopewell Rd DE4...143 C6
Hop Inge The S26....61 F5
Hopkins Ct
Eastwood NG16....182 F3
5 Holmewood DE4..116 E1
Hopkinson Cl DE55..159 C4
Hopmeadow Way
DE15.............248 A1
Hopping Hill DE56...190 F8
Hopping Hill Terrace E
DE56.............191 A7
Hopping Hill Terrace W
DE56.............191 A7
Hopping La DE45...125 B3
Hop Pl DE3.......217 C4
HOPTON...........164 F7
Hopton Cl
Derby DE21.......206 A1
Ripley DE5.........169 F1
Hopton Dr DE23....231 A5
Hopton La
Wirksworth DE4....154 D1
Wirksworth DE4....165 C8
Hoptonwood Cl
DE4..............154 D4
Hopton Wood Way
SK17.............85 C2
Hopwell Rd DE72...222 A2
Horace Ave NG9....223 D6
Hordern Cl SK13.....10 A4
Horderns La SK23....47 B5
Horderns Park Rd
SK23.............47 B5
Horderns Rd SK23...47 A5
Horeston Cotts DE7..192 B7
Hornbeam Cl
Brimington S43......78 A2
Derby DE21.......205 E2
Ilkeston DE7......209 B7
Hornbeam Dr S42...115 B5
Hornbeam La S42...115 B4
Hornbeams The 2
ST14.............210 A1
Hornby Dr DE72....233 E3
Horncastle Rd DE21..205 D1
Horner Rd 1 S7.....43 A7
Horn Hoo S26.....201 A4
Hornscroft Rd S44...99 A1
Hornsea Rd DE21...205 D1
Hornthorpe Rd S21...59 C2
Horridge St DE7....194 F4
Horse Chestnut Cl
S40..............266 B1
Horse Chestnut Gdns
DE73.............232 F3
Horsecroft Cl DE7...194 C3
Horse Croft La DE4..141 C6
Horsedale DE4.....142 C1
Horsefair Ave SK23...47 A6
Horsehead La S44....99 C2
Horse & Jockey Yd 7
DE6..............173 C2
Horse Mill La SK17...87 F4
Horseshoe Ave SK17..47 F1
Horse Shoes The
DE74.............247 D4
Horsewood Rd S40..114 B8
HORSLEY..........191 F6
Horsley CE (Controlled)
Prim Sch DE21....191 F5
Horsley Cl S40......95 A5
Horsley Cres
Holbrook DE56.....191 C7
Langley Mill NG16...182 A3
HORSLEYGATE.......74 E6
Horsleygate La S18...74 E7
Horsleygate Rd S17,
S18..............74 D4
Horsley La DE21....191 E4
Horsley Rd DE21,
DE56.............191 D4

HORSLEY
WOODHOUSE.....192 D6
Horsley Woodhouse
Prim Sch DE7....192 D6
Horson Moor Rd SK14..4 C1
Horton Cl
Sheffield S20.......59 E7
Swanwick DE55....169 F8
Horton Dr S20.......59 E7
Horton St DE22.....219 C2
Horton's La DE56....98 F3
HORWICH END......45 D5
Horwood Ave DE23..218 D2
Hoselett Field Rd
NG10.............236 E5
Hoskins La DE55....248 B5
Hospital La DE3....230 B7
Houfton Cres S44....98 F3
Houfton Rd S44.....98 F3
Hough Cl S40......266 B1
Houghton Ave DE7..194 C3
Houghton Cl SK22...25 C2
Houghton Ct 7
DE21.............205 F2
Houldsworth Cres
S44..............98 F2
Houldsworth Dr S41..96 F2
Hoult St DE22......218 D4
Houndhill ST14.....224 F1
Hound hill ST14....225 A1
Houndkirk Rd S11,
S17..............42 F2
Hounslow Rd DE22..218 B6
Housley Rd SK32....70 E5
Houston Cl DE21...220 B6
Hoveton Cl DE24....232 D3
Howard Cl
Glossop SK13.......10 B2
11 Long Eaton NG10..223 E1
Howard Dr
Chesterfield S41.....77 A2
North Wingfield S42..131 F5
Howards Mdw SK13..17 B7
Howard St
Derby DE23.......218 F2
Glossop SK13.......10 C1
Howards Way
3 Branston DE14...253 E7
3 Branston DE14...256 E7
Howarth Cl NG10...236 A7
Howden Cl
Derby DE3........217 C1
Staveley S43........78 F2
Swadlincote DE11...256 A5
Howden Rd SK22....24 C1
Howe Grove S45....131 E5
Howells Pl S43......79 B3
Howe St DE22......218 D5
Howitt Cres ST14...210 B2
Howitt Prim Com Sch
DE75.............181 D2
Howitt St
Heanor DE75......181 F2
Long Eaton NG10..236 E7
How La S33.........38 C3
Howth Cl DE21.....220 A4
Hoylake Ave S40....114 C7
Hoylake Cl NG19...136 E6
Hoylake Ct DE3....217 C3
Hoylake Dr DE3....217 C3
Hoyland Ct DE56...179 E5
Hoyle Ct DE45.....109 D5
Hubert Shaw Cl
DE24.............232 E4
Huckerby Rd DE7...194 C2
Hucklow Ave
Chesterfield S40.....266 A1
North Wingfield S42..132 A4
Staveley S43........97 C7
Hucklow Bank 36
SK13.............9 D2
Hucklow Cl 35 SK13..9 D2
Hucklow Ct DE21...206 B3
Hucklow Fold 34 SK13..9 D2
Hucklow Lanes 33
SK13.............9 D2
Hucknall Ave S40....95 C4
Hudson Cl S26.......45 F1
Hudson Mount S44..118 B8
Hudson Pl
Darley Dale DE4....142 E8
7 Holmewood DE4..116 E1
Hudson Way DE24..219 C3
Hufton's Ct DE75...194 A7
Huftons Dr DE75....193 F7
Hufton's Dr DE75...194 A7
Hugh La S33.........51 A7
Hugh St SK13.......10 B1
Hulford Dr S41......76 D2
Hulland CE Prim Sch
DE6..............175 F3
Hulland Moss DE6...175 E1
Hulland St DE1......267 D1
Hulland View DE22..204 D1
HULLAND VILLAGE..175 D2
HULLAND WARD....175 F3
Hull St DE65.......228 E1
Humber Cl
Derby DE24.......233 C6
9 Sheffield S2......43 C8

Hundall La continued
Unstone S18........77 A7
Hungerhill Cl DE21..205 D3
Hungerhill La S42,
S45..............113 B4
Hunger La DE6.....188 E3
Hungry La
Bradwell S33.......51 A6
Hathersage S32......53 B8
Hunloke Ave S40....95 E1
Hunloke Cres S40....95 E1
HUNLOKE ESTATE..115 C2
Hunloke Park Prim Sch
S42..............115 A4
Hunloke Rd S42....132 E8
Hunloke View S42...115 B4
Hunsdon Rd S21.....59 C3
Hunstone Ave S8.....57 A7
Hunt Ave DE75.....181 E2
Hunter Dr DE56....191 F8
Hunter Pk S18......57 C1
Hunter Rd DE56....179 D5
Hunters Chase
NG19.............136 B2
Hunters Croft DE24..231 E2
Hunters Green Cl
SK23.............34 E1
Hunters La SK13....16 F8
Hunter's La S13.....44 C6
Hunters Wlk S41...266 A3
Huntingdon Ave S44..99 B1
Huntingdon Ct
DE73.............252 B8
Huntingdon Dr
DE74.............247 A4
Huntingdon Gn
DE21.............219 C6
Huntingdon Rd
DE15.............254 D7
Huntingdon Way 1
NG9..............223 F2
Huntingdon Wlk 2
NG10.............223 B5
Hunt La S45.......145 B8
Huntley Ave DE21...220 F5
Huntley Cl S43......97 B8
Hunts La DE12......264 E8
Huntsman Rd S43...78 F2
Huntspill Rd DE65..248 E1
Hunts Row DE55...157 E3
Hunt Way S11......256 F4
Hurdlow Gn 10 SK13..9 D1
Hurdlow Lea 11 SK13..9 D1
Hurdlow Mews SK13..9 D1
Hurdlow Way 12 SK13..9 D1
Hurds Hollow DE4...143 A6
Hurker Rise S41....143 C7
Hurl Dr S12.........43 F5
Hurley Ct DE7.....207 E8
HURL FIELD........43 E5
Hurlfield Ct S12.....44 A6
Hurlfield Dr S12.....43 F6
Hurlfield Rd S12.....43 F5
Hurrier Pl S20.......60 A6
Hurstbrook Cl SK13..10 F1
Hurst Cl S13........10 E1
Hurstclough La S32,
S33..............40 D2
Hurst Cres SK13....17 E8
Hurst Ct DE12.....264 F4
Hurst Dr
Burton upon Trent
DE13.............240 E1
Stanley DE7.......207 C6
Hurst La DE55.....146 A5
Hurst Lea Rd SK22...33 C7
Hurst Mills Ind Est 6
SK13.............10 F1
Hurst Rd SK13......10 F1
Hurst Rise DE4.....143 D5
Huss's La NG10....236 F7
Hutchings Cres S43...80 D5
Hutfall The 13 DE56..178 F4
HUTHWAITE........148 E3
Huthwaite All Saints CE
(Aided) Inf Sch
NG17.............148 F2
Huthwaite La DE55..148 C2
Hut La
Ashover S45......129 E6
Killamarsh S21......60 F4
Hutmoor Butts
SK17.............107 A3
Hutton St DE24....232 E6
Huxley Cl DE23....231 F7
Hyde Bank Ct SK22...33 C7
Hyde Bank Rd SK22..33 C8
Hyde Park Rd DE22..218 A6
Hyde Rd SK14........9 A4
Hydro Cl DE45......91 F6
Hylton Cl DE14....254 A7
Hyndley Rd S44.....98 F3

I

Ian Ave DE4.......165 F2
Ians Way S40.......95 C4
Ibbotsons Croft S32..53 A8
Ibbotsons Farm Cotts
S32..............53 A8
Ibble Cl S18.........57 C3
Ibsley Cl DE24.....233 C6
Ida's Rd S21........59 D4
IDRIDGEHAY......176 F6

IDRIDGEHAY
GREEN 176 E7
Idridgehay Sta*
DE56. . . . . .176 F6
Ihub DE24. . . . . .232 B3
Ikea Way NG16 . . . . . 195 C7
Ilam CI S43. . . . . .97 C6
Ilam Ct DE6 . . . . 185 D8
Ilam Moor La DE6 . . 149 D1
Ilam Rd DE6 . . . . 161 C2
Ilam Sq DE7 . . . . 194 E5
Ilford CI DE7 . . . . 194 D3
Ilford Ct S43 . . . . .77 D4
Ilford Rd DE22. . . . . . 218 A5
Ilford Wlk DE22. . . . . 218 A5
Ilfracombe Ct ■ S41 . .95 F8
Ilion St NG19 . . . . 135 F2
ILKESTON 208 E7
Ilkeston Com Hospl
DE7. . . . . 194 D4
Ilkeston Rd
Heanor DE75 . . . . . . .193 F8
Sandiacre DE7, NG10. . 223 C8
Smalley DE7 . . . . .192 F2
Stanton-by-Dale DE7. .208 F3
Stapleford NG9. . . . . . .209 F2
Trowell NG9 . . . . .209 C5
Ilkeston Stn DE7 . . . . 195 A4
Immaculate Conception
RC Prim Sch S21. . . .60 C2
Immingham Grove
S43. . . . . .78 D1
Imperial Ct DE22 . . . .204 D5
Imperial Rd DE4 . . . . 143 B5
Inby CI S43. . . . . 132 A7
Inchwood CI ■
NG9 . . . . .223 F2
Independent Hill
DE55. . . . . .158 F3
Industrial St ■
DE23. . . . . .219 A2
Infinity Park Way
DE24. . . . . .232 C3
Infinity Pk Way
Chellaston DE73. . . . . .244 E8
Derby DE73 . . . . .232 D2
Infirmary Rd S41 . . . .266 C4
Ingham Dr DE3 . . . . .230 D8
Ingham Rd NG10. . . . 223 C2
Ingleborough Gdns ■
NG10 . . . . .236 A8
INGLEBY 243 F2
Ingleby Ave DE23. . . . 231 F7
Ingleby CI
Dronfield S18. . . . . . . .56 C1
Swadlincote DE11 . . . . 256 A3
Ingleby Gall* DE73. . .243 F3
Ingleby La
Ingleby DE65 . . . . .243 F1
Repton DE65. . . . . . . .243 B3
Ticknall DE65 . . . . . . .250 F7
Ticknall DE73 . . . . . . .251 A5
Ingleby Rd
Barrow upon Trent
DE73. . . . . 244 D3
Long Eaton NG10 . . . .235 F4
Ingle CI DE21 . . . . . . .220 E5
Ingledew CI ■
DE21. . . . . .205 F1
Inglefield Rd DE7. . . . 208 B8
Ingleton Rd S41 . . . . . 115 B7
Inglewood Ave DE3 . . 217 B1
Ingliston CI DE24 . . . 233 D6
INGMANTHORPE 94 C7
Inkerman CI NE7 . . . .194 E5
Inkerman Cotts S40 . . .95 C3
Inkerman Rd NG16. . . 171 F5
Inkerman St NG16. . . 171 F5
INKERSALL 97 D7
Inkersall Dr S20 . . . . . .59 E8
INKERSALL GREEN 97 D6
Inkersall Green Rd
S43. . . . . .97 C7
Inkersall Prim Sch
S43. . . . . .97 C7
Inkersall Rd S43 . . . . . .97 F7
Inn La DE22 . . . . .204 B7
Innovation Dr DE24. . 232 B3
Inns La DE55 . . . . 157 E4
Institute La DE55 . . . 159 A4
Instow Dr DE3 . . . . . .231 D6
Intake Ind Est S44. . . .98 E3
Intake La
Bakewell DE45 . . . . . .109 E3
Cromford DE4. . . . . . .155 B6
Holloway DE4 . . . . . . .155 B6
Intake Prim Sch S12. .44 C6
Intake Rd S44 . . . . .98 E3
Intakes La
Hulland Ward DE56 . . .176 D1
Hulland Ward DE56 . . .188 C7
Interchange 25 Bsns Pk
NG10 . . . . .223 A4
Invaders Close
NG10 . . . . .223 A4
Inveraray CI DE24. . . 231 D3
Invernia CI DE23. . . . 231 E5
Iona CI
Derby DE24. . . . . .231 E4
Tibshelf DE55. . . . . . .147 F5
Iona Dr NG9. . . . . 209 D2
Ionian Dr DE24 . . . . . 231 E3
iPro Stad (Derby
County FC) DE24. . .219 E3
Ireland CI S43 . . . . .78 F1

Ireland Ind Est S43 . . .78 F1
Ireland St S43. . . . . . . .78 F2
Ireland Trad Est S43 . .78 F1
Ireton Ct DE56. . . . . . 179 E3
Ireton Ct DE6. . . . . . . 165 B1
IRETON WOOD. 176 D4
Iris Cres DE3 . . . . 217 C5
Iron Cliff Rd S44. . . . . .98 F3
Irongate S40 . . . . .266 B3
Iron Gate DE1 . . . . . . 267 B3
Ironside CI S14. . . . . . .43 D3
Ironside PI S14. . . . . . .43 E3
Ironside Rd S14 . . . . . .43 E3
Ironside Wlk S14. . . . . .43 D2
Ironstone La DE15 . . . 255 C4
IRONVILLE. 170 E4
Ironville & Codnor Park
Prim Sch. 170 F4
Ironwalls La DE13 . . . 239 C5
Irvine CI DE4 . . . . 231 D3
Irving PI DE24 . . . . . . .232 F7
Isaac Grove LE66 . . . . 258 B1
Isaac's La NG9. . . . . . 223 F7
Isis Way DE65 . . . . . . .228 F1
Isla CI DE3 . . . . 217 C1
Island CI DE11 . . . . . . 262 C8
Island The
Castleton S33. . . . . .38 B2
Eastwood NG16. . . . . .182 F1
Islay CI NG9 . . . . 209 D3
Islay Rd DE24. . . . . . . 231 E4
Isleworth Dr DE22 . . . 217 F6
Islington La
Elton DE4 . . . . .140 F6
Winster DE4. . . . . .141 A5
Ismay Rd DE21 . . . . . . 219 F6
Ivan Brook CI ■ S18. .56 C1
Ivanhoe CI S42 . . . . . . 115 D1
Ivanhoe Ct ■ S41 . . . .96 A6
Ivanhoe Ind Est
LE65 . . . . .257 F1
Ivanhoe Pk Way
LE65 . . . . .258 A1
Iveagh Wlk DE55. . . . 170 E5
Ivel Cres S81. . . . . .63 F8
Ivonbrook CI DE4. . . . 142 B8
Ivybridge CI DE21. . . 206 C3
Ivy CI
Chesterfield S41. . . . . . .77 A2
Donisthorpe DE12 . . . .262 E1
Willington DE65. . . . . .242 A5
Ivycroft SK13 . . . . .9 E4
Ivy Ct
Derby DE3 . . . . .217 D1
Egginton DE65 . . . . . . .241 A5
Hilton DE65 . . . . .228 D1
Sheffield S8 . . . . .43 C2
Ivy Farm CI S43. . . . . . .80 E3
Ivy Gr DE5. . . . . 169 D1
Ivy House DE23. . . . . . 231 B7
Ivy La
Eastwood NG16. . . . . .182 E2
Elton DE4 . . . . .140 E6
Ivyleaf Way DE23 . . . . 231 B6
Ivy Lodge CI DE15 . . . 254 E7
Ivy Side CI S21 . . . . . . .60 D6
Ivy Side Gdns S21 . . . .60 D6
Ivy Spring CI S42 . . . . 115 B4
Ivy Spring Close
S42. . . . . 115 B4
Ivy Sq DE23. . . . . 219 C2
Ivywood Gdns S44. . . .98 A5

Jackass La DE56. . . . . 167 B4
Jackdaw CI DE22 . . . . 218 D5
Jacklin CI DE14. . . . . . 254 A6
JACKSDALE. 171 C7
Jacksdale Prim Sch
NG16. . . . . .171 B3
Jack's La ST14 . . . . . . 224 E2
Jackson Ave
Derby DE3. . . . . .218 A2
Ilkeston DE7. . . . . .208 E8
Sandiacre NG10 . . . . . .223 A6
Tupton S42. . . . . .131 C8
Whitwell S43 . . . . .81 F5
Jackson CI DE73. . . . . 245 A1
Jackson Rd
Clay Cross S45. . . . . . .131 E3
Matlock DE4. . . . . . . .143 B6
Jacksons Edge Rd
SK12. . . . . .32 B6
Jacksons La
Belper DE56. . . . . .190 E7
Etwall DE65 . . . . .229 C2
Jackson's La
Heage DE56 . . . . .179 D7
Ripley DE5 . . . . .169 A8
Jacksons Ley DE4 . . . 154 E3
Jackson St
Derby DE22 . . . . .218 E4
Glossop SK13. . . . . .17 C7
Glossop, Padfield SK13 .10 C5
Mottram in Longdendale
SK14. . . . . .9 A3
Jackson Tor Rd
DE4. . . . . .143 B6
Jackys La S26. . . . . .61 E6
Jacobean St DE15 . . . 248 C4
Jacobite CI ■ DE75 193 C8
Jacques Orch DE55. . 160 B6
Jade CI ■ DE11 . . . . . 255 C4
Jaeger CI DE56. . . . . . 179 A4
Jaggers La DE4. . . . . . 128 E5

Jagger's La S32 . . . . . . .52 E8
Jago Ave S43. . . . . .81 A4
James Andrew CI S8 . .56 F7
James Andrew Cres
S8. . . . . .56 E7
James Andrew Croft
S8. . . . . .56 F7
James Ave DE55. . . . . 170 D7
James Brindley Way
Burton upon Trent
DE13. . . . . .240 F1
■ Stretton DE13. . . . . 240 F1
James CI DE1 . . . . 218 E5
James Clarke Rd
DE65. . . . . .242 B6
James's La DE6. . . . . . 215 C1
James's La DE65. . . . . 215 C1
James St
Chesterfield S41. . . . . . .96 A6
■ Glossop SK13. . . . . . .17 C8
Kimberley NG16. . . . . .195 F6
Somercotes DE55. . . . .170 C7
Swadlincote DE11 . . . . 256 D5
James Walton Ct
S20. . . . . .59 F7
James Walton Dr
S20. . . . . .59 F7
James Walton PI
S20. . . . . .59 F7
James Walton View
S20. . . . . .59 F7
Jane La SK23. . . . . .34 B1
Jankyns Croft SK12. . .32 E5
Jap La DE45 . . . . 110 E8
Jardine Ct DE72 . . . . . 235 B7
Jardines La ST14 . . . . 196 D4
Jarnett The SK17 . . . . 107 B8
Jarvey's La DE22 . . . . 217 E8
Jarvis Ct DE24. . . . . . . 231 E2
Jarvis Rd DE24. . . . . . 231 E2
Jasmin CI NG20 . . . . . 119 D6
Jasmine CI
Burton upon Trent
DE15. . . . . 255 A8
Derby DE21 . . . . .220 B5
Swanwick DE55 . . . . . .169 F7
Jasmine Ct DE75 . . . . 182 B1
Jasmine Dr S18 . . . . . 56 B7
Jasper Ave S40. . . . . . 115 E7
Jaspers La DE4 . . . . . . 153 A1
Jaunty Ave S12. . . . . . .44 C4
Jaunty CI S12 . . . . .44 B3
Jaunty Cres S12. . . . . .44 C4
Jaunty Dr S12 . . . . .44 B3
Jaunty La S12 . . . . .44 B4
Jaunty Mount S12 . . .44 C3
Jaunty PI S12 . . . . .44 B3
Jaunty Rd S12 . . . . . . .44 C3
Jaunty View S12. . . . . .44 C3
Jaunty Way S12 . . . . . .44 B4
Java Ct DE24 . . . . 219 E2
Jawbone La DE73. . . . 252 C8
Jaw Bones Hill S40. . 115 A8
Jay Ct DE22 . . . . 218 D5
JCB Acad The ST14 . 197 A3
Jebb Gdns S40 . . . . . . .95 C2
Jebb's La
Idridgehay DE56. . . . . .176 F8
Shottle DE56. . . . . . . .177 B8
Jedburgh CI DE24 . . . 231 E2
Jefferson PI S2. . . . . . .43 B6
Jeffery La S33. . . . . . . .51 A6
Jeffery St ■ S2 . . . . . . .43 B6
Jeffrey Ave DE4. . . . . . 156 F1
Jeffries Close DE7. . . 194 D4
Jeffries La ■ DE4. . . . 156 F1
Jellicoe St NG20. . . . . 101 A2
Jemison CI DE23 . . . . 230 E7
Jenkin CI ■ DE7 . . . . 194 F8
Jennison St NG19. . . . 136 A1
Jenny's Ct DE56. . . . . 179 C5
Jephson Rd DE14. . . . 254 B7
Jepson Rd S41 . . . . . . 115 C7
Jermyn Ave S12 . . . . . .44 F4
Jermyn CI S12. . . . . . . .44 F3
Jermyn Cres S12. . . . . .44 F4
Jermyn Dr S12 . . . . . . .44 F3
Jermyn Way S12 . . . . . .44 F3
Jerram's La DE16. . . . 254 E8
Jersey Rd S2 . . . . .43 A7
Jervis Ct DE7. . . . . 194 F3
Jervis PI S43 . . . . .97 B6
Jesop Dr DE24. . . . . . . 231 E2
Jesses La DE56. . . . . . 178 C7
Jessie La DE7 . . . . 194 E2
Jessop Ave NG16. . . . 170 F4
Jessop Lodge DE5 . . . 181 B7
Jessop St DE5. . . . . . . 181 B7
Jetting St
Ashover S45. . . . . .129 F1
Ashover S45. . . . . .130 A1
Jill Iain Ct ■ NG9 . . . 223 E5
Jinny CI DE65 . . . . 239 C8
Joan Ave DE75 . . . . . . 181 E2
Joan La S33. . . . . .40 C3
Jodrell Ave DE56 . . . . 179 D3
Jodrell Mdw SK23. . . .45 E8
Jodrell Rd SK23 . . . . . .45 D8
Jodrell St SK22. . . . . . .33 B7
Joes La SK17 . . . . 104 B2
John Bank La DE15 . . .97 F7
John Berrysford CI
DE21. . . . . .219 F5
John Dalton St SK13. . .9 E5
John Davies Prim Sch
NG17. . . . . .148 F4
John Davies Workshops
NG17. . . . . .148 F3

John Eaton's
Almshouses S8. . . . .43 B2
John F Kennedy Gdns
DE21. . . . . .220 C6
John Flamsteed Sch
DE5. . . . . .180 B2
John Hett Dr DE5. . . . 170 A4
John Kennedy Rd
SK14. . . . . .9 A3
John King Inf Sch
NG16 . . . . .160 D3
John King Workshop
Mus* NG16 . . . . . . .160 D3
John Lombe Dr
DE1. . . . . .219 A7
Johnnygate La S18. . . .75 A4
John of Rolleston Prim
Sch DE13. . . . . .240 B4
John O'Gaunts Way
DE56. . . . . .179 D4
Johno Wood CI ■
DE55. . . . . .158 E3
John Port CI DE65. . . 229 C4
John Port Sch DE65 . 229 C4
Johnson Ave DE24. . . 232 F6
Johnson CI ■ DE74. 246 E3
Johnson Dr DE75. . . . 181 F2
Johnson La
Idridgehay DE56. . . . . .176 E7
Monyash DE45. . . . . . .107 F6
Johnson Rd ST14 . . . . 210 B1
Johnson St SK23 . . . . .45 E8
Johnson Way SK23 . . .47 D6
John St
Alfreton DE55. . . . . . . .159 A4
Brimington S43. . . . . . .96 E8
Chesterfield S40. . . . . . .95 E3
Clay Cross S45 . . . . . . .131 D4
Clowne S43. . . . . .80 D3
Compstall SK6. . . . . . . .15 B3
Creswell S80 . . . . .81 E1
Derby DE1 . . . . .267 C2
Eckington S21. . . . . . . .59 D3
Glossop SK13. . . . . .17 C8
Heanor DE75 . . . . .181 D2
Ilkeston DE7. . . . . .194 F1
Marple SK6. . . . . .23 A5
Matlock DE4. . . . . . . .143 B6
North Wingfield S42. . .131 E7
Somercotes DE55. . . . .170 C8
Swadlincote DE11 . . . . 255 E6
Swadlincote, Albert Village
DE11. . . . . .256 C2
Swadlincote, Lower Medway
DE11. . . . . .256 C5
Johnstone CI S40. . . . 266 A1
John Taylor Free Sch
DE13. . . . . .256 B8
John Turner Rd
DE4. . . . . .127 C3
John Twells Way
DE5. . . . . .170 A4
John Walton CI
SK13. . . . . .16 C7
Jolly La DE6. . . . . 175 A7
Jones St SK13 . . . . .10 A5
Jordan Ave DE13 . . . . 240 F2
Jordan St SK13. . . . . . .10 E1
JORDANTHORPE. . . .57 B7
Jordanthorpe Ctr
S8. . . . . .57 C8
Jordanthorpe Gn S8. .57 C9
Jordanthorpe Parkway
S8. . . . . .57 C0
Jordanthorpe View
S8. . . . . .57 C7
Joseph Fletcher Dr
S42. . . . . .114 F2
Joseph Roe Dr DE4. . 157 A1
Joseph St
Belper DE56. . . . . .178 F4
Derby DE23 . . . . .219 A1
Eckington S21. . . . . . . .59 D3
Marple SK6. . . . . .23 A6
Joseph Stone Court
S20. . . . . .59 D7
Joseph Wright Terr
DE1. . . . . .267 B4
Joshua Bsns Pk
NG16 . . . . .182 C3
Joules Croft DE4 . . . . 140 F2
Joyce Ave NG9 . . . . . . 223 F3
Jubalton CI DE24 . . . . 232 E6
Jubilee Ave DE5 . . . . . 169 C1
Jubilee Bsns Pk
DE21. . . . . .267 C4
Jubilee CI DE73. . . . . . 252 B7
Jubilee Cotts S44. . . . .97 A1
Jubilee Cres
Clowne S43. . . . . .81 A4
Killamarsh S21. . . . . . .60 E7
Whitwell S80 . . . . .81 E5
Jubilee Ct
Belper DE56. . . . . .179 A2
Burton upon Trent
DE16. . . . . .254 C8
Pinxton NG16. . . . . . . .160 D3
Shirebrook NG20. . . . . .119 F2
West Hallam DE7. . . . .207 D8
Wirksworth DE4. . . . . .165 E7
Jubilee Gdns
New Mills SK22. . . . . . .33 C7
Whitwell S80. . . . . .81 E5
Jubilee Parkway
DE21. . . . . .267 C4
Jubilee Pk DE11 . . . . . 256 F4
Jubilee PI S80. . . . . . . .81 F5

Jubilee Rd
Chapel-en-le-Frith
SK23. . . . . .47 B5
Derby DE24. . . . . .232 F4
Whitwell S80 . . . . .81 F5
Jubilee Rise DE15 . . . 248 C3
Jubilee Sq DE6 . . . . . . 184 D7
Jubilee St
Kimberley NG16. . . . . .195 E7
New Mills SK22. . . . . . . .33 C7
Jubilee Terr DE12 . . . 262 E1
Judd CI S20. . . . . .60 A6
Judson Ave NG9. . . . . 223 F6
Judy Hill DE7. . . . . 127 F1
Julia Cres DE55. . . . . . 146 F3
Julian CI DE7. . . . . 209 B6
Julie Ave DE75 . . . . . . 182 B1
Julius CI NG16. . . . . . . 182 B4
Jumble Rd S17. . . . . . . .42 F1
Junction Rd NG10 . . . 237 A6
Junction St DE1 . . . . . 218 E4
Juniper CI S43 . . . . . . .78 A2
Juniper Ct NG16. . . . . 195 C8
Juniper Rise S21 . . . . .60 C5
Jura Ave S43. . . . . 169 D2
Jury St DE1 . . . . 267 A3

K

Kariba CI
Chesterfield S40. . . . . . .96 B3
Chesterfield S41. . . . . . 266 C3
Katherine Dr NG9. . . . 223 F4
Katrine Wlk DE24. . . . 231 E5
Kay Dr DE11. . . . . 255 F5
Kayes Ct ■ NG9. . . . . 223 D7
Kean PI DE24 . . . . .232 F7
Kearsley Rd S2. . . . . . .43 A8
Keats Ave DE23. . . . . . 218 A1
Keats CI NG10 . . . . . . 236 B5
Keats Dr DE11 . . . . . . 256 C6
Keats Rd
Chesterfield S41. . . . . . .95 F8
Stonebroom DE55. . . . .146 F3
Keats Way S42 . . . . . . 115 E4
Keats Wlk DE55. . . . . 146 F3
Keble CI
Burton upon Trent
DE15. . . . . .248 C2
Derby DE1 . . . . .267 C1
Long Eaton NG10 . . . .236 A5
Ripley DE5 . . . . .169 C3
Kedelston st DE1 . . . . 267 A4
KEDLESTON
203 C7
Kedleston DE22. . . . . . 204 A7
Kedleston CI
■ Belper DE56. . . . . .178 F3
Burton upon Trent
DE13. . . . . .240 C1
Chesterfield S41. . . . . . .95 C6
Derby DE22 . . . . .204 D1
Long Eaton NG10 . . . .236 A5
Staveley S43. . . . . .78 E2
Tibshelf DE55. . . . . . . .148 B6
Kedleston Ct
■ Derby DE22 . . . . . .204 D2
■ Staveley S43. . . . . . .78 E2
Tibshelf DE55. . . . . . . .148 B6
Kedleston Dr
Heanor DE75 . . . . .181 C2
Ilkeston DE7. . . . . .194 D3
Kedlestone CI NG17 . 148 F2
Kedleston Gdns
DE1. . . . . .267 A4
Kedleston Hall* DE22. . . . . .203 E5
Kedleston Old Rd
DE22. . . . . .218 D8
Kedleston Rd
Buxton SK17. . . . . .85 C7
Derby DE22 . . . . .218 E7
Quarndon DE22. . . . . .204 B5
Weston Underwood
DE6. . . . . .189 D1
Weston Underwood
DE22. . . . . .203 D8
Kedleston St DE1 . . . . 267 A4
Keeble CI DE75. . . . . . 193 E8
Keele Dr ■ DE11 . . . . 255 E1
Keeling La DE4 . . . . . . 126 B1
Keeling Terr DE4 . . . . 126 B1
Keepers Corner Rd
NG19 . . . . .118 E1
Keepers Croft ■
DE6. . . . . .185 C8
Keepers La S18. . . . . . .75 C3
Kegworth Ave DE23. . 231 C6
Kegworth Rd NG11. . . 237 F1
Keilder Ct S40. . . . . . . .95 D1
Keith Willshee Way
DE11. . . . . .255 D3
Kelburn Ave S40. . . . . .95 C1
Keldeston CI S41. . . . . .95 C5
Keldholme La DE24. . 233 D6
Kelgate S20 . . . . .59 D6
Kelhams Court
DE74. . . . . .247 D6
Kelham Way NG16. . . 182 E3
Kelmoor Rd DE24. . . . 233 B7
Kelsons Ave SK17. . . . .85 D5
Kelso Wlk DE24. . . . . . 231 E2
KELSTEDGE 129 D4
Kelstedge La S45. . . . 129 D5
Kelvedon Dr DE23 . . . 231 A6
Kelvin CI NG9 . . . . 223 C5
Kemble PI DE24 . . . . . .232 F7
Kemp CI S21. . . . . .60 C5
Kemp Rd SK6. . . . . .23 C7

Kempton CI NG16. . . . 195 E7
Kempton Park Rd
DE24. . . . . .232 D8
Kempton Rd DE15 . . . 248 A5
Kendal CI SK17 . . . . . . .85 C4
Kendal Dr S18. . . . . . . .56 E1
Kendal Rd S41. . . . . . . .95 E8
Kendal Wlk ■
DE21. . . . . .205 D1
Kendon Ave DE3. . . . . 231 E6
Kendray CI DE56. . . . . 179 D5
Kendricks CI DE11. . . 257 A7
Kenilworth Ave
DE23. . . . . .231 F8
Kenilworth Ct ■ S41 .96 A6
Kenilworth Dr S41. . . 208 C5
Kenilworth Rd DE5 . . 169 C1
Kenmere CI S45. . . . . . 131 C2
Kennack CI DE55 . . . . 160 C6
Kennedy Ave
Long Eaton NG10 . . . .236 C5
Mansfield Woodhouse
NG19 . . . . .136 D4
Kennedy CI DE21 . . . . 220 A7
Kennedy Ct ■ DE4 . . 116 C1
Kennedy Dr NG9. . . . . 209 E1
Kennet Paddock
NG19 . . . . .136 D3
Kennett Gr SK17 . . . . . .84 E6
Kennet Vale S40. . . . . . .95 D5
Kenninghall CI S2 . . . .43 D7
Kenninghall Dr S2. . . .43 D7
Kenninghall Rd S2. . . .43 D7
Kenninghall View
S2. . . . . .43 D7
Kenning PI S45. . . . . . 131 C5
Kenning St S45. . . . . . 131 C3
Kensal Rise DE22 . . . . 218 B6
Kensey Rd
Derby DE3. . . . . .217 B1
Derby DE3. . . . . .230 B8
Kensington Ave
DE75. . . . . .181 C1
Kensington Bsns Pk
DE7. . . . . .209 A6
Kensington Chase
S10. . . . . .42 F8
Kensington CI NG19 136 E5
Kensington Dr S10. . . .42 F8
Kensington Gdns
DE7. . . . . .208 F7
Kensington Gr SK13 . .17 A8
Kensington Jun Acad
DE7. . . . . .209 A7
Kensington Pk S10. . . .42 F8
Kensington Rd
Burton upon Trent
DE15. . . . . .248 A3
Sandiacre NG10. . . . . .223 A4
Kensington St
Derby DE1 . . . . .267 A3
Ilkeston DE7. . . . . .208 F6
Kent Ave NG16 . . . . . . 171 B4
Kent CI S41 . . . . .95 F5
Kent Grange ■ S8 . . . .43 B6
Kent House CI S8. . . . 258 E8
Kentish Ct DE1 . . . . . . 219 B7
Kentmere CI S18 . . . . .56 E1
Kentmere Way
Staveley S43. . . . . .78 C1
Staveley S43. . . . . .97 C8
Kent Rd
Burton upon Trent
DE15. . . . . .254 E6
Eastwood NG16. . . . . .195 C8
Glossop SK13. . . . . .10 D1
Sheffield S8 . . . . .43 C8
Kent's Bank Rd SK17. .85 C6
Kent St
Chesterfield S41. . . . . . 115 C8
Derby DE21 . . . . .219 D7
Kent Way DE11 . . . . . . 255 E2
Kenwell Dr S17. . . . . . . .56 B5
Kenyon Rd S41 . . . . . . .96 E1
Keppel Ct DE7. . . . . . . 194 F3
Kepple Gate DE5 . . . . 180 F8
Kernel CI DE23 . . . . . . 231 A8
Kernel Dr NG20. . . . . . 119 D2
Kernel Way NG20 . . . . 119 D2
Kerry Dr DE7. . . . . 192 F6
Kerry St DE21 . . . . 219 D7
Kerry's Yd DE56. . . . . 191 F8
Kershaw St SK13. . . . . .17 C8
Kershope Dr DE21. . . 206 B3
Kerwin CI S17. . . . . .55 C8
Kerwin Dr S17. . . . . . . .55 C8
Kerwin Rd S17. . . . . . . .55 C8
Kesbrook Dr DE12 . . . 262 A3
Kestrel Ave DE11 . . . . 256 F3
Kestrel CI
Bolsover S44. . . . . .98 F3
Burnaston DE3. . . . . . .230 B7
Ilkeston DE7. . . . . .208 F4
Killamarsh S21. . . . . . .60 B7
Marple SK6. . . . . .23 A3
■ Swarkestone
DE73. . . . . .244 E8
Tibshelf DE55. . . . . . . .147 E5
Kestrel Ct S42 . . . . 116 C1
Kestrel Dr S21 . . . . .59 B3
Kestrel Ho DE24 . . . . . 231 E2
Kestrel Hts NG16 . . . . 171 F3
Kestrel Rd S42. . . . . . . 115 F1
Kestrels Croft DE21. . 205 D1
Kestrel View SK13 . . . .16 F8
Kestrel Way DE15. . . . 248 D3
Keswick Ave DE23. . . 231 E6

Keswick Cl
Bolsover S44 . . . . .98 F1
Ilkeston DE7. . . . . .208 D5
Keswick Ct NG10 . . . . 223 B2
Keswick Dr
Chesterfield S41. . . . . .95 C8
Chesterfield S41. . . . . .95 D8
Keswick Pl S18. . . . . . .56 D1
Kettlewell Cl DE24 . . 232 E6
Ketton Ave S8. . . . . . . .43 B3
Kevin Cl DF21 . . . . . . 220 B8
Kew Cres
Heanor DE75 . . . . . . .182 B1
Sheffield S12 . . . . .44 A2
Kew Gdns DE22. . . . . 218 B5
Keyhaven Cl DE21 . . . 219 D8
Keynsham Cl DE24. . 232 E2
Keys Rd DE55. . . . . . . 159 B2
Keys St DE1 . . . . 267 C4
Kibworth Cl
Chesterfield S41. . . . . 115 C7
Derby DE21 . . . . 220 B8
Kidd La SK17. . . . . . . 104 B1
Kidd Rd SK13. . . . . . . .17 E6
Kidsley Cl
7 Chesterfield S40. . . .95 A5
Smalley DE75 . . . . 193 C8
Kilbourne Ct DE56 . . 179 D3
Kilbourne Rd DE56 . . 179 C4
KILBURN 192 A8
Kilburn Dr DE7 . . . . . 194 D3
Kilburn Inf Sch
DE56. . . . . .191 F8
Kilburn Jun Sch
DE56. . . . . 192 A8
Kilburn La DE56 . . . . 179 E8
Kilburn Rd S18. . . . . . .56 C1
Kilburn Toll Bar
DE56. . . . . .179 F1
Kilburn Way DE11 . . . 255 F5
Kilby Ho NG10. . . . . . 236 E7
Kildale Gdns S20 . . . . .59 D7
Kildare Rd DE21 . . . . 220 B4
Kildonan Gr S12. . . . . .44 C3
Kildrummy Cl DE73 . . 232 E1
KILLAMARSH 60 E6
Killamarsh Inf Sch
S21. . . . . .60 E6
Killamarsh Jun Sch
S21. . . . . .60 E7
Killamarsh La S21,
S26 . . . . .61 B6
Killamarsh Sp Ctr
S21. . . . . .60 D7
Killingworth Ave
DE24. . . . . .231 F4
Killis La
Belper DE56 . . . . 179 D1
Holbrook DE56 . . . . . .191 D8
Kilmory Fold SK13. . . .10 E3
Kiln Bent Rd HD9 . . . . . .3 A6
Kiln Cl
Dove Holes SK17 . . . . .47 F2
West Hallam DE7 . . . . 193 E1
Kiln Croft DE65 . . . . . 229 C4
Kiln Hill S18. . . . . .57 C3
Kiln La
Glossop SK13 . . . . .10 A5
Harpur Hill SK17. . . . . .85 B2
Parwich DE6. . . . . 151 D2
Kilnsey Ct DE23. . . . . 230 F6
Kiln Way
Swadlincote DE11 . . . 256 D2
Swadlincote DE11 . . . 256 D3
Kilverston Rd NG10 . . 223 A6
Kilvington Ave S13 . . . .44 B7
Kilvington Cres S13. . . .44 B7
Kilvington St S13 . . . . .44 B7
KIMBERLEY 195 F8
Kimberley Cl NG16. . . 195 E6
Kimberley Dr DE15 . . 248 C3
Kimberley Prim Sch
NG16. . . . . .195 F6
Kimberley Rd DE72 . . 221 B2
Kimbolton Way
DE24. . . . . .233 D4
Kinder Ave DE11. . . . . 256 A5
Kinder Cl SK13 . . . . . . .17 A8
Kinder Cres DE56. . . . 168 B5
Kinder Dr SK6. . . . . . . .23 A6
Kinder Gr SK17. . . . . . .85 A6
Kinderlee Way SK13 . .16 B5
Kinder Rd
Hayfield SK22. . . . . . . .25 C2
Staveley S43. . . . . .97 B6
Kinder Row DE22 . . . . .25 F2
Kinder View SK22. . . . .33 C7
Kinder View Cl SK22. . .33 A6
Kinder Way SK17 . . . . .85 E7
Kinder Wlk DE22 . . . . 218 E4
King Alfred St DE22. . 267 A2
King Charles Ct SK13 .17 D7
King Cup Cl SK13 . . . . .17 E8
King Ecgbert Rd S17. .55 E5
King Ecgbert Sch
S17. . . . . .55 D6
King Edward Ave
SK13. . . . . .10 D1
King Edward Gdns **1**
NG10. . . . . 223 B6
King Edward St
Ashbourne DE6. . . . . .173 B1
Sandiacre NG10 . . . . . 223 B6
Shirebrook NG20 . . . . .119 F4
1 Washgreen DE4 . . . 165 E7
Wirksworth DE4. . . . . 166 A8
Kingfisher Ave
DE11. . . . . .256 F3

Kingfisher Cl DE3. . . 230 B7
Kingfisher Ct
Bolsover S44 . . . . .98 F3
Ilkeston DE7. . . . . . . .208 F4
Kingfisher Gdns
DE14. . . . . .253 D2
Kingfisher Ho S41 . . . .77 B3
Kingfisher La DE65 . . 242 A5
Kingfisher Mews
SK6. . . . . .23 A6
Kingfisher Rd NG19. . 135 D1
Kingfisher Vlew S43 . .80 E4
Kingfisher Way SK13. .16 F8
Kingfisher Wlk
DE24. . . . . .231 E2
King George Ave
DE7. . . . . .208 E8
King George St
Wessington DE55. . . . .145 E1
Wessington DE55. . . . .157 E8
Wirksworth DE4. . . . . .165 E7
Kinglas Dr DE3 . . . . . 217 B1
Kingsbury Cl DE15. . . 248 A4
Kingsbury Rd DE22 . . 218 A6
Kings Cl
Carsington DE4 . . . . . .164 E8
Clowne S43. . . . . .80 F3
Creswell S80 . . . . .81 F1
Heanor DE75. . . . . . . .181 C1
King's Cl SK17. . . . . . . .85 D8
Kingsclere Ave
DE21. . . . . .206 B2
Kingsclere Wlk S40. . 114 F8
Kings Coppice S17 . . . .55 D6
Kings Croft DE22 . . . . 204 F4
Kingscroft Cl S17. . . . .55 E8
Kings Ct
Derby DE1 . . . . .267 B4
5 Glossop SK13 . . . . .17 C8
Kingsdale Cl NG10. . . 236 A5
Kingsdale Gr DE73. . . 244 F8
Kings Dr
Brinsley NG16 . . . . . . .182 E7
Derby DE3, DE23 . . . . .218 B2
Kingsfield Ind Est
DE4. . . . . .165 E6
Kingsfield Rd DE4 . . . 165 E7
Kingsgate S32. . . . . . .72 C2
Kings Gate DE74. . . . .247 F4
Kingsgate Rd DE72 . . 245 B8
Kingshead La DE4 . . . 174 A6
Kings Head La DE6 . . 173 F7
Kings Hill DE4 . . . . . . 153 A2
Kings Hollow Mews
DE6. . . . . .173 F4
Kingsland Cl DE21 . . . 205 F2
Kingsley Ave
Chesterfield S40. . . . . 114 F8
Mansfield Woodhouse
NG19 . . . . .136 D5
Kingsley Cl NG19 . . . . 136 D4
Kingsley Cres
Long Eaton NG10 . . . . 236 B4
Stonebroom DE55 . . . .146 F3
Kingsley Ct NG19 . . . . 136 D5
Kingsley Rd DE22 . . . . 204 D4
Kingsley St DE24 . . . . 231 F5
Kingsmead Ave
NG9 . . . . .209 D2
King's Mead Cl DE1. . 267 A4
King's Mead Ho **1**
DE22. . . . . .218 F7
Kingsmead Ind Est
DE22. . . . . .218 D6
Kingsmead Sch The
DE1. . . . . .267 A4
King's Mead Wlk
DE1. . . . . .267 A4
Kingsmede Ave S40 . . .95 D1
Kings Mews S21 . . . . . .59 E3
King's Mill La DE72. . 245 F5
King's Mills La DE72 . 245 F5
Kingsmoor Fields
SK13. . . . . .10 D3
Kingsmoor Rd SK13. . .10 D2
Kingsmuir Rd DE3 . . . 217 C3
Kings Newton La
DE73. . . . . .244 F1
Kings Rd
Sandiacre NG10. . . . . .223 B6
Swadlincote DE11 . . . 256 B6
King's Rd SK17. . . . . . .85 D8
King St
Alfreton DE55. . . . . . . .158 F4
Ashbourne DE6. . . . . .173 C2
Bakewell DE45 . . . . . .109 D5
Belper DE56 . . . . .178 F3
Brimington S43. . . . . . .77 F1
Broadbottom SK14. . . .16 A8
Burton upon Trent
DE14. . . . . .254 C8
Clay Cross S45 . . . . . .131 C3
Clowne S43. . . . . .80 E3
Creswell S80 . . . . .81 F1
Creswell, Hodthorpe
S80. . . . . .82 C6
Derby DE1 . . . . .267 B4
Duffield DE56 . . . . . . .190 E4
Eastwood NG16 . . . . . .182 F2
Glossop SK13 . . . . .17 C8
Hollingworth SK14. . . . .9 D5
Ilkeston DE7. . . . . .194 F1
Long Eaton NG10 . . . . 236 D8
Mansfield Woodhouse
NG19 . . . . .136 D2
Middleton DE4 . . . . . .154 D5
Pinxton NG16 . . . . 160 D3

King St continued
Shirebrook NG20 . . . . 120 D5
South Normanton
DE55. . . . . 159 F5
Tibshelf DE55 . . . . 148 A7
Youlgreave DE45 . . . . . 125 B5
Kingsthorpe Cl **6**
NG19 . . . . 136 E1
Kingston Ave S41 . . . . .87 A4
Kingston Ct
3 Barrow Hill S43. . . . .78 B3
West Hallam DE7 . . . . 207 D8
Kingston Rd DE15 . . . 248 C2
Kingston St DE1 . . . . . 218 F7
King Street N S41 . . . . .96 A7
King Street S S40. . . . 115 A7
Kingsway
Burton upon Trent
DE14. . . . . .254 B8
Derby DE22 . . . . .218 B5
Heanor DE75 . . . . 181 D2
Ilkeston DE7. . . . . . . .209 A5
Kings Way S80 . . . . . . .82 C6
Kingsway Bvd DE22. . 218 B4
Kingsway Cres
DE56. . . . . .192 A8
Kingsway Hospital
DE22. . . . . .218 B4
Kingsway Ind Pk
DE22. . . . . .218 C5
Kingsway Park Cl
DE22. . . . . .218 C5
Kingsway Ret Pk
DE22. . . . . .218 C5
Kingswood Ave
DE56. . . . . .179 C6
Kingswood Cl
Chesterfield S41. . . . . .95 C8
Derby DE22 . . . . .218 A6
Kingswood Pl DE23. . 218 B2
King William Ctr **2**
NG16. . . . . .170 F4
King William St
NG16. . . . . .170 F4
Kinnaird Gdns SK17. . .85 A7
Kinross Ave DE21 . . . . 219 C8
Kintyre Dr DE24 . . . . . 231 D3
Kinver Cl DE6 . . . . 184 C8
Kinver Rd DE15 . . . . . . 248 A4
Kipling Cl S18. . . . . . . .76 C8
Kipling Dr DE3 . . . . . . 217 D1
Kipling Rd S41 . . . . . . .95 F8
Kiran View DE21. . . . . 206 C3
Kirby Cl S41. . . . . 115 C7
Kirby La DE4 . . . . 142 B7
Kirkby Ave
Ilkeston DE7. . . . . . . .208 B4
Sheffield S12 . . . . .44 A4
Kirkby Dr S12 . . . . .44 A4
Kirkby La NG16. . . . . . 160 F3
Kirkby Rd S12 . . . . .44 A4
Kirkby View S12. . . . . .44 A4
Kirkby Way S12 . . . . . .44 A3
Kirk Cl DE5. . . . . 180 C8
Kirkcroft Ave S21. . . . .60 D7
Kirkcroft Dr S21. . . . . .60 D7
Kirkcroft La S21. . . . . .60 D7
Kirk Dale Ave DE21 . . 220 F3
Kirkdale Cl S40. . . . . . 115 B8
Kirkdale Gdns NG10. . 236 B6
Kirkdale Rd NG10. . . . 236 B6
Kirkewhite Ave
NG10 . . . . 236 D7
Kirkewhite Ho
NG10 . . . . 236 D7
Kirkfield Dr DE72 . . . . 235 D8
KIRK HALLAM. 208 D6
Kirk Hallam Com Acad
DE7. . . . . .208 D5
Kirk Hallam Pupil
Referral Unit DE7 . .208 E5
Kirkham Cl **5** DE75. . 181 D1
Kirkham Dr NG9. . . . . . 223 F2
Kirkham La DE56 . . . . . 168 B7
KIRK IRETON 165 C1
Kirk Ireton CE Prim Sch
DE6. . . . . .165 B1
Kirkistown Cl DE24 . . 233 C6
Kirkland Cl DE74 . . . . 247 A3
Kirkland Way
1 Derby DE24 . . . . . 231 D3
Swadlincote DE11 . . . 256 B1
KIRK LANGLEY 202 F2
Kirk Langley CE Prim
Sch DE6. . . . . .202 F2
Kirkley Dr DE75. . . . . . 181 C1
Kirk Leys Avenue N
DE21. . . . . .220 E4
Kirk Leys Avenue S
DE21. . . . . .220 E4
Kirkman Rd DE75. . . . 181 C4
Kirk's La DE56. . . . . . . 179 B3
Kirk St DE1. . . . . 219 B8
KIRKSTEAD. 160 D3
Kirkstead Cl
Derby DE21 . . . . .206 B1
Pinxton NG16 . . . . . . .160 D3
Kirkstead Jun Sch
NG16. . . . . .160 D3
Kirkstead Rd NG16. . . 160 D3
Kirkstone Ave DE75. . 182 B1
Kirkstone Cl NG10. . . 223 B2
Kirkstone Rd
Buxton SK17. . . . . .85 D3
Chesterfield S41. . . . . .95 D8
Kirton Ave NG10. . . . . 236 D7
Kishfield La SK23. . . . .45 A6

Kissingate L Ctr
NG20 . . . . 119 E4
Kitchener Ave DE23. . 231 F7
Kitchener Terr
NG20 . . . . 101 A2
Kitchen Wood La
S18. . . . . .75 C8
Kitson Ave NG16. . . . . 171 C4
Kiwi Dr DE24 . . . . 232 F7
Knabb Rd DE4. . . . . . . 127 F3
Knabhall La DE4. . . . . 144 C5
Knapp Ave NG16. . . . . 182 F1
Knarr Rd SK17. . . . . . . 102 C5
Knifesmithgate S40. . 266 B3
Knife & Steel Ct
DE7. . . . . .192 C7
Knighton Cl S41. . . . . . 115 B7
Knighton Cl S42. . . . . . 131 E6
Knighton St S42. . . . . . 131 E6
Knightsbridge DE22 . 218 A6
Knights Cl
Beeston NG9 . . . . .223 F2
Derby DE24 . . . . .231 E2
Knights Ct DE13 . . . . . 240 E2
Knight's La DE15 . . . . . 249 B5
Knight's Pl DE15 . . . . . 248 D2
Knights Rd
Chellaston DE73. . . . . .244 E8
Mansfield NG19 . . . . . .135 D1
Knightsyard Ct
NG10 . . . . 236 C5
Knightwake Rd SK22. .33 A4
Knightwood DE12 . . . . 260 D5
Knitters Road DE55. . 160 C6
KNIVETON 163 B1
Kniveton CE Prim Sch
DE6. . . . . .163 C1
Kniveton Close
DE22. . . . . .218 D6
Kniveton La DE6. . . . . 174 C4
Kniveton Pk DE7. . . . . 208 C7
Knob Fields DE11. . . . 261 E8
Knob La DE4 . . . . 166 D5
Knoll Cl DE23. . . . . 231 A8
Knoll St SK22. . . . . .33 B8
Knoll The
Chesterfield S40. . . . . .94 F2
Dronfield S18 . . . . .57 D3
Shirebrook NG20 . . . . .119 D3
Swadlincote DE11 . . . 256 B6
Tansley DE4 . . . . .144 A5
Knotbury 102 F5
Knotbury Edge La
SK17. . . . . .102 F5
Knotcross Rd S45 . . . . 145 B6
Knowl Ave DE56 . . . . . 178 E5
Knowle Ave SK23 . . . . .47 B5
Knowle Gn S17. . . . . . . .55 C7
Knowle Rd SK6. . . . . . . .23 C6
Knowles Cl SK17. . . . . .85 E8
Knowles Cres SK17 . . . .85 E8
Knowles Farm Ct **11**
DE11. . . . . .256 E1
Knowles Hill DE13 . . . 240 B3
Knowles Ind Est
SK23. . . . . .33 D3
Knowleston Pl DE4 . . 143 C4
Knowles View
DE11. . . . . .256 D4
Knowle Top S20. . . . . . .59 E7
Knowsley Hill SK17 . . 126 F4
Knutsford Gn DE21 . . 205 D2
Kraft Gdns DE21. . . . . 220 B5
Kye La S26 . . . . .61 E6
Kyle Cl S21. . . . . .60 B1
Kyle Gr DE21 . . . . 206 B3
Kyle Rd DE65 . . . . 240 D8
Kynance Cl
Derby DE24 . . . . .233 C5
South Normanton
DE55. . . . . 160 C6
Kynnersley Croft
ST14. . . . . 210 B1
Kytes La DE7. . . . . 192 F3
Kyte's La DE7. . . . . 193 A3

L

Laban Dr DE3 . . . . 217 B2
Laburnum Ave
NG20 . . . . 119 E5
Laburnum Cl
Bolsover S44 . . . . .99 C1
Creswell S80 . . . . .81 F1
Darley Dale DE4 . . . . . .127 B3
Sandiacre NG10 . . . . . 223 B6
South Normanton
DE55. . . . . 160 B7
Laburnum Cres
Derby DE22 . . . . .204 D4
Swanwick DE55 . . . . . .170 A8
Swadlincote S44 . . . . . .97 A3
Laburnum Gr
Derby DE22 . . . . .218 B5
Killamarsh S21 . . . . . . .60 C5
Mansfield Woodhouse
NG19 . . . . .136 A4
Laburnum Rd
Burton upon Trent
DE15. . . . . .254 F6
Swadlincote DE11 . . . 256 A6
Laburnum St
Brimington S43. . . . . . .78 A1
Hollingwood S43 . . . . . .97 B8
Laburnum Way
DE65. . . . . .229 C3
Laceby Ct NG19. . . . . . 136 E4

Lace Makers Cl
DE72. . . . . .221 D1
Lacey Cl DE7 . . . . 194 C3
Lacey Fields Rd
DE75. . . . . .182 B1
Ladbroke Gdns
DE22. . . . . .217 F6
Ladies Spring Ct S17 .56 A7
Ladies Spring Dr S17 .56 A7
Ladies Spring Gr S17 .56 A7
Ladle End La DE12. . . 253 D1
LADMANLOW 84 E4
Ladybank Rd
Derby DE3 . . . . .217 C2
Sheffield S20 . . . . .59 D6
Lady Bank View S21. . .59 D4
Ladybower Cl DE11 . . 256 A2
Ladybower Ct
Glossop SK13 . . . . .10 C1
4 Sheffield S17. . . . . .56 A5
Ladybower Dr S32. . . . .53 A7
Ladybower La S43. . . . .97 D8
Ladybower Rd DE21 . 220 F4
Ladybower Way
DE65. . . . . .240 E8
Ladycroft SK17. . . . . . . .66 C1
Ladycroft Paddock
DE22. . . . . .204 E4
Ladycross Inf Sch **3**
NG10 . . . . 223 B6
Lady Field Rd S80 . . . . .62 D8
Ladyfields DE11 . . . . . . 256 D6
Ladyfields Way
DE11. . . . . .255 F6
Ladyflatts Rd DE4. . . . 165 E7
Ladygrove
Bullbridge DE56 . . . . . .168 D5
Sawmills DE56 . . . . . . .168 D5
Ladygrove Cotts
DE23. . . . . .219 B3
Ladygrove Rd DE4. . . 127 E2
Lady Hole La DE6. . . . . 186 B7
Lady Ida's Dr
Eckington S21. . . . . . . .59 C4
Sheffield S20, S21 . . . . .59 C5
Ladylea Rd NG10 . . . . 236 A4
Lady Lea Rd DE21,
DE7. . . . . .192 A6
Lady Ley Hill DE21. . . 192 A6
Lady Manners Sch
DE45. . . . . .109 C4
Lady Mantle Cl
DE73. . . . . .232 E2
Lady Meadow Cl
ST14. . . . . 196 E5
Lady Meadow La
ST14. . . . . 196 E5
Ladypit Rd SK23. . . . . . .33 E4
Ladysmith Rd DE72 . . 246 B1
Ladythorn Ave SK6. . . .23 A5
Ladywell Cl DE13 . . . . 240 E1
Ladywell Ct DE56. . . . 179 A3
Ladywood Ave DE56 . 179 B5
Ladywood Dr S41. . . . . .95 C7
Ladywood Prim Sch
DE7. . . . . .208 D5
Ladywood Rd DE7 . . . 208 C5
Lake Ave DE75. . . . . . . 181 C4
Lake Dr
Derby DE23 . . . . .231 F8
Dronfield S18. . . . . .57 C3
Long Eaton NG10 . . . . 236 A6
Lake Gdns DE75 . . . . . 181 C4
Lake Lands S42. . . . . . . 114 F2
Lakeside
12 Ashbourne DE6. . . 173 C2
Bakewell DE45 . . . . . .109 B7
Wingerworth S42. . . . . 114 F2
Lake Side
Doveridge DE6 . . . . . . .211 A1
Glossop SK13 . . . . .10 A6
Lakeside Bsns Ctr
DE75. . . . . .194 A6
Lakeside Cl S41 . . . . . . .77 C4
Lakeside Community
Prim Sch. 219 F1
Lakeside Com Prim Sch
DE24. . . . . .219 F2
Lakeside Cres NG10 . 236 D5
Lakeside Dr DE23. . . . 231 A7
Lakeside Inf Sch
NG10 . . . . 236 C5
Lakes Rd SK6. . . . . .23 B6
Lake View SK23. . . . . . .33 D4
Lake View Ave S40. . . . .95 C1
Lakin Cl **1** DE11. . . . . 256 B3
Lamb Cres DE5 . . . . . . 169 F1
Lamb Croft DE23 . . . . 267 C1
Lambert St DE22 . . . . 218 B5
Lambeth Cl DE23. . . . . 217 F5
Lambeth Rd DE22 . . . . 217 F5
Lambgates SK13. . . . . . .10 A5
Lambgates La S13. . . . .10 A5
Lamb Hill Cl S13. . . . . . .44 D7
LAMBHOUSE 177 E7
Lambhouse La
DE56. . . . . .177 E5
Lambley Dr DE22 . . . . 204 E2
Lambourn Cl DE22. . . 205 A3
Lambourn Dr DE22 . . 205 A3
Lambourne Ave
DE6. . . . . .185 D8
Lambpart La SK17/
S33. . . . . .50 D5
Lambrook Cl DE23 . . . 217 C2
Lambton Cl DE7 . . . . . 194 C3
Lampad Cl **4** DE73 . . 252 A8
Lampeter Cl DE21 . . . 206 B2

Lamplight Way
DE11. . . . . .255 E2
Lanark St DE21 . . . . . . 219 E2
Lancaster Ave
Sandiacre NG10 . . . . . 223 A4
Stapleford NG9. . . . . . .223 E4
Lancaster Dr
Hilton DE65 . . . . .228 E2
Tutbury DE13 . . . . .239 B5
Lancaster Rd S41. . . . . .95 E8
Lancaster Rise
DE56. . . . . .179 A6
Lancaster St S44. . . . . 117 F1
Lancaster Wlk DE21 . 221 A6
Lancelot Cl S40. . . . . . . 114 C8
Lancelot Dr DE13 . . . . 240 E2
Lancelot Way NG19 . . 135 D1
Lancing Rd S2. . . . . .43 A8
Landau Forte Coll
DE1. . . . . .267 C4
Lander La DE56 . . . . . . 179 A4
Landmere DE24 . . . . . 231 E3
Landmere Cl DE7. . . . . 194 C3
Landon Cl S40. . . . . 114 B7
Landsdowne Ave S41 95 E6
Landsdown Gr
NG10. . . . . 223 F1
Landseer Cl
4 Dronfield S18. . . . . .56 E1
Sheffield S14 . . . . .43 D2
Landseer Dr
Marple SK6. . . . . .23 B7
Sheffield S14 . . . . .43 E2
Landseer Pl S14. . . . . . .43 E2
Landseer Wlk S14 . . . . .43 E2
LANE 2 E8
LANE ENDS
Disley 32 E4
Marple 15 D1
Sutton on the Hill 215 A2
Lane Head
Longnor SK17. . . . . . . .121 B7
Stoney Middleton S32. . .71 C3
Tideswell SK17. . . . . . . .69 D5
LANE HEAD 69 E5
Lane Head Gn S33. . . . .37 C7
Lanehead Rd
Birch Vale SK22. . . . . . .25 B7
Horwich End SK23 . . . . .45 C5
Lane Head Rd S17. . . . .55 C4
Lanesend Cotts SK23 .46 A8
Laneside Ave NG9 . . . . 223 E2
Laneside Cl SK23 . . . . . .47 A5
Laneside Rd
New Mills SK22. . . . . . . .33 E7
New Mills, Rowarth
SK22. . . . . .24 E6
Lanes The DE4 . . . . 155 A3
Lane The
Awsworth NG16. . . . . . .195 C4
Brimington S43. . . . . . .77 F1
Ripley DE5 . . . . .169 C2
Spinkhill S21. . . . . .60 D1
Stanton in Peak DE4. . .126 C3
Laneward Cl DE7 . . . . 194 D4
Langale Cl S40 . . . . .94 F5
Langdale Dr
Derby DE21 . . . . .205 D1
Dronfield S18. . . . . .57 C3
Long Eaton NG10 . . . . 236 A6
Langdale Sq S43 . . . . . .96 D8
Langdon Cl **3**
NG10. . . . . 223 A1
Langen Ct NG10 . . . . . 236 E6
Langer Cl DE14 . . . . . . 254 B6
Langerfield Ave
S40. . . . . 115 A7
Langer La
Wingerworth S40,
S42. . . . . 114 E5
Wingerworth S42. . . . . 114 E3
Langford Croft S40 . . 266 B1
Langford Rd S41 . . . . . 217 D3
Langham Park Ind Est
DE55. . . . . .160 C7
Langhurst Cl S40. . . . . .95 D4
Langhurst Rd S40 . . . . .95 D4
LANGLEY 182 B1
Langley Ave
Ilkeston DE7. . . . . . . .194 D5
Somercotes DE55. . . . .170 C8
Langley Bridge Ind Est
NG16. . . . . .182 C3
Langley Bsns Pk
NG16. . . . . .182 B2
Langley Cl
3 Chesterfield S40. . . .95 A5
Mansfield NG19 . . . . . .135 E1
Langley Close DE24. . 233 D4
LANGLEY
COMMON 217 B8
Langley Ct SK13 . . . . . . .10 A5
Langley Dr
Derby DE3 . . . . .217 D6
Glossop SK13 . . . . .17 F8
LANGLEY GREEN . . . 202 D2
Langley Inf Sch
DE75. . . . . .182 A1
LANGLEY MILL 182 B3
Langley Mill Acad
NG16. . . . . .182 A4
Langley Mill CE Inf Sch
NG16. . . . . .182 B3
Langley Mill Sta
NG16. . . . . .182 B3

Langley Pk NG16 . . . . . .182 B3
Langley Rd DE21. . . . . .220 E3
Langley St DE22 . . . . . .218 D6
Lang Rd DE24 . . . . . .232 F6
Langsett Ave 13 SK13 . .9 D1
Langsett Dr DE73 . . . .233 A2
Langsett Gn 15 SK13. . . .9 D1
Langsett Gr 14 SK13. . . .9 D1
Langsett La SK13 . . . .9 D2
Langsett Lea 25 SK13. . .9 D1
Langsett Terr 24 SK13 .9 D1
Langstone Ave S44 . . . .99 C1
Langton Hollow
NG16 . . . . .171 D6
Langton The 4
DE22. . . . . .218 E5
Langtree Ave S41. . . . . .77 A1
LANGWITH 119 F8
Langwith Bassett Comm
Prim Sch NG20. . . . . .119 E7
Langwith Cl
Derby DE3 . . . . .217 F2
Ilkeston NE7. . . . . . . .194 F5
Langwith Dr NG20 . . . .100 F1
LANGWITH
JUNCTION 119 D6
Langwith Lodge Dr
NG20 . . . . .101 B2
Langwith Maltings
NG20 . . . . .119 F8
Langwith Rd
Bolsover S44 . . . . . . .118 C8
Cuckney NG20 . . . . . .101 L1
Scarcliffe S44. . . . . . .118 F7
Shirebrook NG20 . . . . .119 F5
Langwith-Whaley
Thorns Sta NG20. . . .100 F2
Lansbury Ave
Mastin Moor S43 . . . . .79 B4
Pilsley S45 . . . . .132 C1
Lansbury Ct S21. . . . . . .59 D3
Lansbury Dr DE55 . . . .160 A4
Lansbury Rd S21. . . . . . .59 D2
Lanscombe Park Rd
DE22. . . . . .204 E1
Lansdowne Ave
DE24. . . . . .232 F5
Lansdowne Rd
Branston DE14. . . . . .253 F7
Brimington S43. . . . . . .96 D7
Buxton SK17. . . . . .66 B1
Swadlincote DE11 . . . .256 A3
Lansing Gdns DE21 . . .220 B6
Lantern Gr DE3. . . . . . .217 D4
Lantern Pike View
SK22. . . . . .25 A2
Lantern View SK22 . . . .24 B1
Lant La DE4 . . . . .144 B8
Lapwing Cl
Belper DE56 . . . . .192 A8
Derby DE24 . . . . .231 E2
Lara Croft Way DE1. . .219 A4
Lara Croft Wy DE1. . . .267 B2
Larch Ave
Killamarsh S21. . . . . . .60 C5
Mansfield Woodhouse
NG19. . . . . .136 B5
Ripley DE5. . . . . .169 D1
Shirebrook NG20 . . . . .119 D4
Larch Cl DE22 . . . . . . .204 D3
Larch Cres NG16. . . . . .182 E2
Larchdale Cl DE55 . . . .160 A4
Larch Dr NG10. . . . . . .223 B7
Larch Rd
Eckington S21. . . . . . . .59 B2
Kilburn DE56. . . . . . . .192 B7
Swadlincote DE11 . . . .255 F6
Larch Way
Chesterfield S40. . . . . .95 D5
Glossop SK13. . . . . . . .17 D8
Larges St DE1 . . . . . . .218 E5
Lark Cl
Derby DE23 . . . . .231 C6
3 Mansfield NG19 . . .135 F1
Larkfields Cres
DE55. . . . . .169 F8
Larkhill DE55 . . . . .169 F8
Lark Hill DE3 . . . . .230 B7
Larkhill Cl DE55 . . . . . .169 F8
Lark Hill Cotts SK22. . .33 A8
Larkhill Cres DE24 . . . .231 F4
Larkin Cl DE24. . . . . . .232 A5
LARKLANDS 209 B8
Larkland's Ave DE7. . .209 A7
Larklands Inf Sch
DE7. . . . . .209 A8
Lark Rise DE21 . . . . . .220 B7
Larkspur Cl
Derby DE23 . . . . .231 C3
Mansfield NG19. . . . . .136 D2
South Normanton
DE55. . . . . .160 A4
Larkspur Ct DE21 . . . .206 A3
Larkstone La DE6. . . . .149 A1
Larpit Gn S80 . . . . .82 A5
Lascelles Rd SK17 . . . . .85 B8
Lashley Gdns DE21 . . .205 F2
Latham Cl DE15 . . . . . .248 C2
Lathbury Cl DE21 . . . .205 D1
Lathkil Dr DE55 . . . . . .159 F5
Lathkill Gr
Buxton SK17. . . . . .85 D7
Tibshelf DE55 . . . . . . .147 F6
Lathkill Ave
Derby DE24 . . . . .233 C7
Ilkeston DE7. . . . . . . .194 E5
Staveley S43. . . . . .97 C6
Lathkill Cl
Sheffield S13 . . . . .44 C7
West Hallam DE7 . . . .207 E8
Lathkill Ct S42. . . . . . .132 A7
Lathkilldale Cres
NG10 . . . . .236 A5
Lathkill Dr
Ashbourne DE6. . . . . .185 E8
Ripley DE5. . . . . .180 D6
Selston NG16. . . . . . . .171 F7
Lathkill Gr S45 . . . . . .131 D1
Lathkill La DE4 . . . . . .156 C2
Lathkill Rd
Derby DE21 . . . . .219 F8
Sheffield S13 . . . . .44 C7
Latimer Cl DE23 . . . . .230 E7
Latimer St DE24 . . . . .232 D6
Latrigg Cl DE3 . . . . . . .217 E1
Laud Cl DE12 . . . . .262 E3
Lauder Cl DE24 . . . . . .231 E2
Launceston Rd
DE24. . . . . .233 B5
Laund Ave DE56 . . . . .179 B6
Laund Cl DE56. . . . . . .179 A6
Laund Farm DE56 . . . .179 C6
Laund Farm Mews
DE56. . . . . .179 C6
Laund Hill DE56 . . . . .179 A5
Laund Nook DE56 . . . .179 A5
Launds Ave NG16 . . . .171 D7
Laurel Ave
Arkwright Town S44 . . .97 D3
Mansfield Woodhouse
NG19. . . . . .136 F1
Ripley DE5. . . . . .169 D1
Laurel Cl
Eckington S21. . . . . . . .59 C2
Shirebrook NG20 . . . . .119 D6
Swanwick DE55 . . . . . .170 A8
Laurel Cres
Brimington S43. . . . . . .78 A1
Long Eaton NG10 . . . .236 C6
Smalley DE7 . . . . .192 F5
Laurel Dr
Aston-on-Trent
DE72. . . . . .246 A7
Killamarsh S21. . . . . . .60 C5
Laurel Garth Cl S41. . . .77 B3
Laurel Gr
Burton upon Trent
DE15. . . . . .254 E5
South Normanton
DE55. . . . . .160 A4
Laurel Grove ST14 . . . .210 C1
Laurence Cl S41. . . . . . .77 A2
Lauren Gr 6 NG10 . . . .223 F1
Laurie Pl DE24 . . . . . . .232 E7
Lavant Cl 3 S43. . . . . . .96 E8
Lavender Cl
Burton upon Trent
DE14. . . . . .254 A8
Shirebrook NG20 . . . . .119 D3
Tibshelf DE55 . . . . . . .148 B7
Lavender Gdns
DE75. . . . . .182 B1
Lavender Rd DE55 . . . .170 A8
Lavender Row DE22 . .204 F1
Lavender Way DE13. . .239 C5
Lavender Wlk DE55 . . .157 F5
Laverdene Ave S17 . . . .55 E5
Laverdene Cl S17 . . . . .55 E4
Laverdene Dr S17 . . . . .55 E4
Laverdene Rd S17 . . . . .55 E4
Laverdene Way S17. . . .55 F4
Laver Dr S41 . . . . .96 B5
Laverick Rd NG16. . . . .171 A4
Laverock Cl NG16. . . . .195 F6
Laverstoke Ct DE22 . . .218 E4
Lavinia Ct DE73. . . . . .232 D2
Lawman Gdns DE55. . .158 F4
Lawman Mews
DE55. . . . . .159 A4
Lawn Ave
Derby DE22 . . . . .204 D2
Etwall DE65. . . . . .229 C5
Lawn Cl DE75. . . . . . . .181 F2
Lawnfold SK13 . . . . . . .9 E4
Lawn Heads Ave
DE23. . . . . .218 C2
Lawn La DE45 . . . . . . .126 B6
Lawnlea Cl DE23. . . . . .231 E5
Lawn Mill Rd NG16. . . .195 E7
Lawn Prim Sch
DE22. . . . . .204 D1
Lawns Dr DE11 . . . . . .256 A7
Lawnside DE21 . . . . . .220 F5
Lawns La DE45 . . . . . .125 F5
Lawns The
Aston-on-Trent
DE72. . . . . .246 B8
Rolleston DE13. . . . . .240 A4
Uttoxeter ST14. . . . . .210 A2
Lawnswood Cl
DE23. . . . . .231 C8
Lawnswood Close
DE65. . . . . .229 C5
Lawn The S18. . . . . . . .57 B2
Lawn Villas S44. . . . . . .97 A2
Lawrence Ave
Awsworth NG16. . . . . .195 C4
Breaston DE72. . . . . . .235 E8
Derby DE21 . . . . .220 B7
Eastwood NG16. . . . . .182 F2
Holmewood S42. . . . . .116 D1
Lawrence Ave continued
Mansfield Woodhouse
NG19. . . . . .136 B4
Ripley DE5. . . . . .180 C8
Lawrence Cl NG16. . . . .182 D8
Lawrence St
Derby DE23 . . . . .231 F8
Long Eaton NG10 . . . .236 D8
Sandiacre NG10 . . . . .223 B7
Stapleford NG9. . . . . .223 D6
Lawson Ave NG10. . . . .236 E7
Lawson Cl S44. . . . . . . .99 C1
Lawson Rd S44. . . . . . . .99 C1
Lawton Rd DE11 . . . . .257 B1
Laxfield Cl S40 . . . . . .114 C8
Layton Dr S41. . . . . . . .77 B1
LCPL Steven Bagshaw
Ave SK14. . . . . .9 F6
LEA 156 B7
Lea Bank DE55 . . . . . .160 A4
Leabrook Rd S18 . . . . . .56 C1
LEABROOKS 170 B7
Leabrooks Ave
NG19. . . . . .136 D5
Leabrooks Rd DE55. . . .170 C8
Lea Cl DE22 . . . . .204 E3
Lea Cres DE55 . . . . . . .170 C6
Leacroft Rd
Derby DE23 . . . . .219 B1
Winster DE4 . . . . .141 C6
Lea Ct S41 . . . . .266 B4
Leadale Ave DE55. . . . .170 A7
Leadale Cres NG19 . . .136 E5
Leadbeater Dr S12 . . . .44 A5
Leadbeater Rd
Sheffield S12 . . . . .43 F5
Sheffield S12 . . . . .44 A4
Leaden Knowle SK23 . .34 C1
Leadhill Rd S40. . . . . . .95 A4
LEADMILL 53 B5
Lea Dr
Derby, Chaddesden
DE21. . . . . .219 F6
Derby, Markeaton
DE3. . . . . .217 E3
Leafenden Cl DE22 . . .205 A3
Leafgreen La DE23. . . .231 C6
Leafield Rd SK12 . . . . .32 C6
Leafy La DE75. . . . . . . .181 F1
Leaholme Est S44 . . . . .98 D2
Leake St DE23 . . . . . . .218 D5
Lea La
Matlock DE4 . . . . .156 C2
Selston NG16. . . . . . . .171 F6
LEAM. 53 A3
Lea Main Rd DE4 . . . . .156 B8
Leam Glen NG19. . . . . .136 D2
Leamington Cl
DE23. . . . . .218 D1
Leamington Dr
DE55. . . . . .160 B5
Leamington Rd
DE14. . . . . .253 E7
Leamington St DE5. . . .169 F2
Leamoor Ave DE55 . . .170 B8
Lea Moor Rd DE4 . . . . .156 E8
Leander Cl DE23. . . . . .231 D7
Leander Ct 5 S43. . . .78 F2
Leander Rise DE15. . . .255 A8
Leantown SK13. . . . . . .16 C6
Lean Town SK13. . . . . .17 D6
Leaper St DE1 . . . . . . .218 E6
Leapley La DE6. . . . . . .199 D3
Lea Prim Sch DE4 . . . .156 A7
Lea Rd
Cromford DE4. . . . . . .155 D6
Dronfield S18 . . . . .57 A1
Hayfield SK22. . . . . . . .25 C3
Lea DE4 . . . . .156 A7
Leas Ave NG19 . . . . . .135 A5
Leashaw DE4. . . . . . . .156 C4
Leashaw Rd DE4. . . . . .156 C3
Leas Park Jun Sch
NG19. . . . . .136 C4
Leas Rd NG19 . . . . . . .136 D4
Lea St SK22 . . . . .33 B8
Leathersley La DE6,
DE65. . . . . .226 C2
Lea Vale DE55 . . . . . . .160 A4
Leaway The NG10. . . . .119 D3
Lea Wood Croft
DE4. . . . . .156 A5
Leawood Gdns
DE21. . . . . .206 B3
Leawood Pump Ho *
DE4. . . . . .155 F4
Leawood Rd DE11 . . . .256 D7
Leche Croft DE56. . . . .179 D4
Lechlade Cl DE7. . . . . .207 D8
Lechlade Rd DE24 . . . .231 C3
Ledbury Chase
DE24. . . . . .231 D2
Ledbury Pl 2 DE21 . .205 D1
Leden Cl SK17 . . . . . . .85 D4
Ledo Ave DE5 . . . . . . .169 D2
Leebangs Rd SK14. . . .16 A8
Leech Cl SK16 . . . . . . .195 B7
Lee Cres DE7. . . . . . . .209 B8
Lee Dale SK17. . . . . . . .85 C3
Leedhams Croft
DE12. . . . . .259 D8
Leeds Pl DE1 . . . . .267 D2
Leeds Rd S81. . . . . . . .63 F7
Lee Farm Cl DE73. . . . .232 F1
Leefield Rd SK23 . . . . .47 B5
LEE HEAD 16 C6
Lee Head SK13 . . . . .16 C5
Leek Rd
Buxton SK17. . . . . .84 E5
Longnor SK17. . . . . . .121 B6
Mayfield DE6 . . . . . . .172 B2
Lee La DE75 . . . . .182 B1
Leeming La NG19,
NG20 . . . . .136 E7
Leeming Lane N
NG19. . . . . .136 E5
Leeming Lane S
NG19. . . . . .136 C2
Leeming Pk NG19. . . . .136 C3
Lee Mount SK13. . . . . .17 C7
Leen Valley Dr
NG20 . . . . .119 D3
Lee Rd S41. . . . . .96 E2
LEES 216 B7
Lees Bank DE21 . . . . . .220 A7
Lees Brook Com Sch
DE21. . . . . .220 B8
Lees Brook Ho
DE21. . . . . .220 A7
Lees Hall Ave S8. . . . . .43 B5
Lees Hall Pl S8. . . . . . .43 B5
Lees Hall Rd S8. . . . . . .43 B4
Lees House Ct S8. . . . . .43 A4
Leeside DE24. . . . . . . .220 A1
Lees La DE55. . . . . . . .159 F6
Lees Mill 4 SK22. . . . .33 C7
Lees Nook S8. . . . . . . .43 A4
Lees Rd DE4. . . . . .126 E3
Lees Row S8. . . . . . . .10 C5
Lees The DE72. . . . . . .233 D5
Leeswood Cl S41. . . . . .95 D8
Lee Vale Dr SK13 . . . . .16 D7
Leeway DE21 . . . . . . .220 D4
Leggers Row DE55. . . .170 C3
Legh Rd SK12 . . . . . . .32 A6
Leicester Dr SK13 . . . .17 F8
Leicester Ho 2
NG9. . . . . .223 F8
Leicester St
Burton upon Trent
DE14. . . . . .254 C8
Derby DE22 . . . . .218 E3
Long Eaton NG10 . . . .236 E6
Leigh Rd NG9. . . . . . . .223 F3
Leighton Dr
Marple SK6. . . . . .23 C8
Sheffield S14 . . . . .43 F3
Leighton Pl S14 . . . . . .43 F3
Leighton Rd
Sheffield S12 . . . . .44 A3
Sheffield S14 . . . . .43 F4
Leighton View S14 . . . .43 E5
Leighton Way 6
DE56. . . . . .178 F3
Leigh Way S42 . . . . . . .131 F7
Leisure La SK17 . . . . . .137 E5
Leisure Way DE6 . . . . .173 B1
Leman St DE22 . . . . . .218 E3
Lemon Gr DE11 . . . . . .256 B1
Lemont Rd S17 . . . . . . .55 C4
Leniscar Ave DE75. . . .181 C4
Lens Rd DE21. . . . . . . .220 C2
Lenthall Inf Sch S18. .57 B3
Lenton Ave DE21 . . . . .219 F6
Lenton St NG10. . . . . .223 C7
Leominster Dr
DE21. . . . . .206 B2
Leonard Cheshire Cl
DE75. . . . . .182 B1
Leonard Cl
Derby DE23 . . . . .267 B1
Sheffield S2 . . . . .44 A7
Leonard Gdns 2
DE11. . . . . .256 A6
Leonard St DE1. . . . . .267 C4
Leonard Wlk DE23 . . . .267 B1
Leopold St
Derby DE1 . . . . .267 B2
Long Eaton NG10 . . . .236 D8
Lesley Cres DE5 . . . . . .169 E3
Leslie Ave NG16 . . . . . .195 F6
Leslie Cl DE23 . . . . . . .230 E8
Lesser La
Buxton SK17. . . . . .85 E8
Chapel-en-le-Frith
SK23. . . . . .65 D7
Level La SK17 . . . . .84 D5
Leven Cl DE24 . . . . . . .231 F2
Levens Way S41. . . . . . .95 E8
Leveret Cl DE73 . . . . . .233 B2
Levetts Close DE24 . . .231 C3
Lewcote La DE7 . . . . . .194 A1
Lewisham Drive
DE11. . . . . .255 E1
Lewis Rd S13. . . . . .44 C7
Lewis St DE23 . . . . . . .218 F1
Lewiston Rd DE21 . . . .220 B5
Lexington Rd DE21 . . .220 C6
Ley Ave DE55. . . . . . . .159 B3
Lime Ave
Derby DE1 . . . . .267 A1
Derby, Breadsall Hilltop
DE21. . . . . .205 D2
Duffield DE56. . . . . . .190 E5
Langley Mill NG16. . . .182 C2
New Mills SK22. . . . . . .24 D1
Ripley DE5. . . . . .169 D1
Staveley S43. . . . . .78 E1
Lime Cl
Calow S44. . . . . .97 A3
Doveridge DE6 . . . . . .224 B8
Pinxton NG16. . . . . . .160 D3
Lime Cres
Belper DE56 . . . . .179 B2
Church Warsop NG20. .120 F7
Leyland Cl
Beeston NG9. . . . . . . .223 F2
Bolsover S44 . . . . .99 D1
Leyland Ct DE1 . . . . . .218 E7
Leyland Dr S44. . . . . . .99 D1
Leyland Gdns DE1 . . . .218 E7
Leylands DE22. . . . . . .218 E8
Leylands Cottages
SK14. . . . . .15 F8
Leylands La SK14 . . . . .15 F7
Leyland St DE1 . . . . . .218 E7
LEYS 154 A8
Leys Ct DE56 . . . . . . .179 D4
Leys Field Gdns
DE73. . . . . .233 A2
Leys Jun Sch DE55 . . .159 C4
Leys La DE4 . . . . .154 B7
Leys The
Little Eaton DE21 . . . .191 D2
Swadlincote DE11 . . . .255 E6
Leyton Ct S43 . . . . . . .77 D4
Leytonstone Dr
DE22. . . . . .218 A5
Liberty 4 NG19 . . . . . .135 F1
Lichfield Ave DE11. . . .256 E5
Lichfield Cl NG9 . . . . . .223 E3
Lichfield Dr DE24 . . . .233 A7
Lichfield Rd
Branston DE13,
DE14. . . . . .253 A1
Chesterfield S40. . . . .114 D8
Sudbury ST14 . . . . . . .225 F3
Walton-On-Trent
DE14. . . . . .253 A1
Lichford Rd S2 . . . . . . .43 C6
Lickpenny La
Ashover S45 . . . . .144 E4
Tansley S45. . . . . .144 D5
Lidgate Cl DE3 . . . . . . .217 C1
Lid La
Ashover S45 . . . . .129 A6
Roston DE6. . . . . .197 E7
Lifes Rd SK17. . . . . . . .138 C3
Liffey Ho DE24. . . . . . .232 E5
Liffs Rd DE6, SK17 . . . .137 E4
Light Alders La SK12. .32 A6
Light Alders Lodge
SK12. . . . . .32 A6
Lightfoot Rd ST14 . . . .210 A1
Lightning Lane
DE74. . . . . .246 F4
LIGHTWOOD
Eckington. 58 F2
Sheffield. 57 F6
Lightwood Ave 3
SK17. . . . . .85 C8
Lightwood La
Chesterfield S21. . . . . .77 C8
Eckington S8. . . . . .43 F1
Eckington, Middle Handley
S21. . . . . .58 C1
Lightwood Rd
Buxton SK17. . . . . .66 B1
Eckington S21. . . . . . . .58 E2
Lilac Ave DE22. . . . . . .218 A5
Lilac Cl
Derby DE24 . . . . .233 A6
Holmewood S44. . . . . .116 F2
Lilac Ct DE24 . . . . .233 A6
Lilac Gr
Bolsover S44 . . . . .99 C1
Burton upon Trent
DE15. . . . . .254 F6
Church Warsop NG20. .120 F7
Glapwell S44 . . . . .134 B8
Heanor DE75 . . . . .181 E1
Shirebrook NG20 . . . . .119 E5
South Normanton
DE55. . . . . .160 A4
Lilac Mews DE7 . . . . . .194 D3
Lilac St
Brimington S43. . . . . . .78 B1
Staveley S43. . . . . .97 A8
Lilac Way
Derby DE22 . . . . .204 D2
Shirland DE55. . . . . . .146 D1
Lilian Prime Cl
DE24. . . . . .233 B8
Lilley Cl NG16. . . . . . . .171 E6
Lilley St DE4 . . . . .233 B6
Lilly Ct DE13. . . . . .239 D5
Lillymede Cl S40 . . . . .114 F6
Lilybank Cl S41 . . . . . .143 C5
Lilybank Ct 6 DE4. . . .143 C6
LILYPOOL. 252 D7
Lilypools The DE73 . . .252 B7
Lilystreet Farmway 2
DE55. . . . . .158 F1
Lilywood Cl S44 . . . . . .97 B3
Limbersitch La
DE65. . . . . .227 F6
Limb La S17. . . . . .55 D8
Lime Ave
Derby DE1 . . . . .267 A1
Lime Croft DE22 . . . . .204 F4
Limecroft View S42. . . .115 B3
Lime Ct DE15 . . . . . . .256 E7
Limedale Ave DE21 . . .206 B3
Lime Gate Mews
DE23. . . . . .218 D2
Lime Gr
Burton upon Trent
DE15. . . . . .254 E5
Darley Dale DE4 . . . . .127 C3
Derby DE21 . . . . .220 B5
Draycott DE72. . . . . . .234 F7
Hatton DE65. . . . . . . .227 D1
Long Eaton NG10 . . . .236 D8
Sandiacre NG10 . . . . .223 B6
South Normanton
DE55. . . . . .160 A5
Stapleford NG9. . . . . .223 D5
Lime Grove Ave
DE4. . . . . .143 C5
Lime Grove Wlk
DE4. . . . . .143 B5
Limehouse La S26. . . . .61 E7
LIMEKILN FIELD. 99 A3
Limekiln Fields Rd
S44. . . . . .99 A3
Lime Kiln La
Marple SK6. . . . . .23 A5
Turnditch DE56. . . . . .189 B8
Wensley DE4 . . . . .142 B8
Lime Kilns The
DE73. . . . . .252 F2
Limekiln Way
Barlborough S43 . . . . .80 C6
Shireoaks S81 . . . . .63 F7
Lime Kiln Way SK17 . . .85 D2
Lime La
Derby DE21 . . . . .206 C3
Morley DE7, DE21. . . .206 D5
Lime Rd S21. . . . . .59 B2
Limerick Rd DE21. . . . .220 B4
Limers Rake SK17 . . . .104 D1
Limes Ave
Derby DE3 . . . . .217 D1
Whaley Thorns NG20 . .101 A2
Limes Cl NG16. . . . . . .182 C4
Limes Cl The DE4. . . . .143 C5
Limes Cres NG20 . . . . .119 D5
Limes Ct 8 DE21 . . . .217 D1
Limes Pk DE5 . . . . . . .169 C1
Limes St DE7 . . . . .208 F7
Limes The
Barton in Fabis
NG11. . . . . .237 E6
Duffield DE56. . . . . . .190 D3
Mapperley DE7. . . . . . .193 E3
5 Uttoxeter ST14 . . . .210 B1
Limestone Cft 2
DE4. . . . . .143 A5
Limestone Cl
Hartshorne DE11 . . . . .257 A4
5 Swadlincote DE11. .255 F4
Limestone Ct SK17. . . .47 F2
Limestone Terr
NG19. . . . . .136 B4
Lime Terr NG10. . . . . . .236 D8
Limetree Ave DE11 . . .256 B7
Lime Tree Ave
Darley Dale DE4 . . . . .127 B3
Glapwell S44 . . . . .134 B8
Killamarsh S21. . . . . . .60 C5
Mansfield Woodhouse
NG19. . . . . .136 A5
Lime Tree Bsns Pk
DE4. . . . . .143 C4
Limetree Cl S43 . . . . . .96 F5
Lime Tree Cl
1 Branston DE14 . . . .253 E7
1 Branston DE14 . . . .256 E7
Swadlincote DE11 . . . .256 B2
3 Tibshelf DE55 . . . .147 F6
Limetree Ct DE7. . . . . .208 C6
Lime Tree Gr
Arkwright Town S44 . . .97 D3
Clay Cross S45 . . . . . .131 E5
Lime Tree Pk SK17 . . . .85 D6
Lime Tree Rd DE14 . . .254 C5
Limetree Rise DE7. . . .208 C6
Lime Wlk
Clay Cross S45 . . . . . .131 E5
Derby DE23 . . . . .218 D1
Linacre Ave S45 . . . . . .131 E2
Linacre Rd S40, S42 . . .95 A5
Linacre Reservoirs *
S42. . . . . .94 B5
Linacres Dr DE73 . . . .233 A2
Linacre Way SK13 . . . .17 F7
Linbery Cl DE55 . . . . . .158 B4
Lincoln Ave
Derby DE24 . . . . .233 A8
Derby DE3 . . . . .230 E5
Sandiacre NG10 . . . . .223 A4
Lincoln Cl
Stapleford NG9. . . . . .209 E1
Tibshelf DE55 . . . . . . .148 A6
Lincoln Dr NG19 . . . . .136 D4
Lincoln Gn DE73. . . . . .232 F2
Lincoln Rd DE15 . . . . .254 D7
Lincoln St
Alfreton DE55. . . . . . .158 F3
Chesterfield S40. . . . .115 A8
Tibshelf DE55 . . . . . . .148 A6
Lincoln Way
5 Glossop SK13 . . . .17 F8
North Wingfield S42. . .131 F6
Swadlincote DE11 . . . .256 E5

Lincote Way **9**
DE11 . . . . 256 E1
Lindale Rd S41 . . . . . .76 E1
Lindale Way DE73 . . 233 A2
Linden Ave
Chesterfield S40 . . . . . .95 B1
Clay Cross S45 . . . . . . 131 D2
Dronfield S18 . . . . .57 B3
Linden Cl
Denstone ST14 . . . . . . 196 D6
Kilburn DE56 . . . . 192 B8
Linden Ct S45 . . . . . . 131 D2
Linden Dr S41 . . . . . . 115 D6
Linden Gr
Matlock DE4 . . . . 143 C5
Sandiacre NG10 . . . . . . 223 A7
Shirebrook NG20 . . . . . 119 F4
Stapleford NG9 . . . . . . 223 E6
Linden Park Gr S40 . . .95 D3
Linden Rd S80 . . . . .81 E2
Linden St
Mansfield NG19 . . . . . . 136 A1
Shirebrook NG20 . . . . . 119 F4
Shirebrook NG20 . . . . . 120 A4
Linden Way SK6 . . . . . .32 A7
Lindford Cl DE21 . . . . 205 F3
Lindisfarne Cl **4**
DE24 . . . . 231 D3
Lindisfarne Ct S40 . . . .95 D1
Lindisfarne Rd S18 . . .76 B8
Lindley St NG16 . . . . . 171 D6
Lindon Dr DE24 . . . . . 233 C6
Lindrick Cl
Derby DE3 . . . . 217 F1
Mansfield Woodhouse
NG19 . . . . 136 D6
Lindrick Gdns S40 . . . 114 C8
Lindrick Way S41 . . . . .80 B5
Lindsey Cl DE21 . . . . . 219 E6
Lindup Rd S17 . . . . .56 E2
Lindway La
Brackenfield DE55 . . . . 145 B1
Dethick DE55 . . . . 144 F1
Linear View S43 . . . . . .80 F4
Lingfield Rd DE14 . . . 253 F7
Lingfield Rise DE3 . . . 217 C3
Lingfoot Ave S8 . . . . . .57 B6
Lingfoot Cl S8 . . . . .57 B6
Lingfoot Cres S8 . . . . . .57 C6
Lingfoot Dr S8 . . . . . . .57 C6
Lingfoot Pl S8 . . . . .57 B6
Lingfoot Wlk S8 . . . . . .57 C6
Ling La S44 . . . . 118 C4
Linglongs Ave SK23 . . .45 C5
Linglongs Rd SK23 . . . .45 C5
Ling Rd S40 . . . . 114 D8
Lings Cl DE7 . . . . 194 F5
Lings Cres S42 . . . . . . 132 A8
Lingwell Croft Ave
S21 . . . . .59 D2
Linkmel Rd NG16 . . . . 182 C3
Links Cl DE24 . . . . 231 F4
Links Rd
Chapel-en-le-Frith
SK23 . . . . .46 F5
Dronfield S18 . . . . .76 B8
Links The NG16 . . . . . 171 D6
Links View SK17 . . . . . .66 D1
Linley La S12, S13 . . . . .44 E5
Linnet Cl DE21 . . . . . . 220 F6
Linnet Hill DE3 . . . . . 230 C7
Linnet Ho S41 . . . . .77 A3
Linnet Way S43 . . . . . . .81 E1
Linscott Cl S41 . . . . . . .95 D7
Linshaws Rd HD9 . . . . . .3 E5
Linstock Way DE74 . . . 233 C3
LINTON 261 D6
Linton Heath DE12 . . . 261 E6
Linton Prim Sch
DE12 . . . . 261 D5
Linton Rd
Chesterfield S40 . . . . . 114 C8
Linton DE11 . . . . 261 E7
Rosliston DE12 . . . . . . 260 E5
Linwood Cres NG16 . . 182 F1
Linwood Ct NG19 . . . . 136 E4
Lionheart La DE13 . . . 240 E2
Lipp Ave S21 . . . . .60 C7
Liskeard Dr DE22 . . . . 204 D4
Lismore Ct **6** DE24 . 231 D3
Lismore Gr SK17 . . . . . .85 A7
Lismore Pk SK17 . . . . . .85 A7
Lismore Rd
Buxton SK17 . . . . .85 A7
Sheffield S8 . . . . .43 B5
Lisset Cl S15 . . . . 158 B3
Lissett Ave DE7 . . . . . 208 E7
Lister Ave S12 . . . . .44 B3
Lister Cl
Chesterfield S41 . . . . . 266 B4
Derby DE3 . . . . 218 B3
Sheffield S12 . . . . .44 B3
Lister Cres S12 . . . . . . .44 B3
Lister Dr S12 . . . . .44 B3
Lister Pl S12 . . . . .44 B3
Lister Way S12 . . . . .44 B3
Liston Dr DE22 . . . . . . 218 F8
Litchen Cl DE7 . . . . . . 194 F2
Litchfield Cl NG10 . . . 237 A2
LITCHURCH 219 C3
Litchurch La DE24 . . . 219 C2
Litchurch St DE1 . . . . 267 C1
Little Acre NG19 . . . . . 136 E5
LITTLE BOLEHILL 155 B2
Little Bolehill DE4 . . . 155 A4
Little Breck DE55 . . . . 160 A4
Little Bridge DE13 . . . 239 C7
Little Bridge St DE1 . . 218 F6

Little Brind Rd S40 . . . .95 B7
Littlebrook Cl SK13 . . . .10 A4
LITTLE CHESTER 219 A7
Little Cl DE11 . . . . 256 E1
LITTLE CUBLEY 212 E8
Littledale Cl DE21 . . . 206 C3
Little Debdale La
NG19 . . . . 135 F1
Little Derby Hill
DE3 . . . . 230 B2
LITTLE EATON 205 C8
Little Eaton Prim Sch
DE21 . . . . 205 C7
Little Edge S32 . . . . . . .71 C6
Little Fallows
Belper DE56 . . . . 190 F7
4 Milford DE56 . . . . 191 A7
Little Fen DE55 . . . . . . 147 F5
Littlefield La
Ellastone DE6 . . . . 183 A2
Snelston DE6 . . . . 184 B4
Littlefield Rd DE65 . . . 227 C7
Littlefields SK14 . . . . . . .9 A4
LITTLE HALLAM 208 E5
Little Hallam Hill
DE7 . . . . 208 E6
Little Hallam Hill
DE7 . . . . 209 A6
LITTLE HAYFIELD 25 B5
LITTLE HUCKLOW 50 E2
Little La
Ashford in the Water
DE45 . . . . .89 C1
Bradwell S33 . . . . .51 A7
Heanor DE5 . . . . 181 A3
Kimberley NG16 . . . . . 195 F5
Litton SK17 . . . . .69 E3
Pleasley NG19 . . . . . . 135 B5
Sheffield, Woodthorpe
Estate S12 . . . . .44 B6
Shirebrook NG20 . . . . . 119 D3
Sutton in Ashfield
NG17 . . . . 148 E2
Thorpe Salvin S80 . . . . .63 B6
Little Liverpool
DE12 . . . . 260 C1
Little London DE4 . . . . 156 A6
LITTLE LONGSTONE 89 E4
Little Longstone Cl
DE3 . . . . 217 F2
Little Lunnon NG11 . . 237 E6
LITTLE MATLOCK 135 F7
Little Meadow Close **5**
DE7 . . . . 194 E2
Little Meadow Rd
DE73 . . . . 233 A2
LITTLEMOOR
Chesterfield S41 . . . . . .95 D7
Eckington S21 . . . . .59 E4
Littlemoor Bsns Ctr
S21 . . . . .59 E4
Littlemoor Cres S41 . . .95 D7
Littlemoor Ct **3**
SK13 . . . . .17 C6
Littlemoor Ctr **2**
S41 . . . . .95 E7
Littlemoor La
Matlock Bath DE4 . . . . 143 F1
Newton DE55 . . . . 148 B4
Littlemoor Rd SK14 . . . .9 A2
Little Moorside
DE72 . . . . 246 B8
Little Morton Rd S42,
S45 . . . . 132 A5
LITTLE NORTON 57 A8
Little Norton Ave S8 . .57 A8
Little Norton Dr S8 . . .57 A8
Little Norton La S8 . . .57 A8
Little Norton Way S8 . .57 A7
LITTLEOVER 231 B8
Littleover Com Sch
DE23 . . . . 230 F8
Littleover Cres
DE23 . . . . 218 D1
Littleover La DE23 . . . 231 E8
Little Thorn Ind Est
DE11 . . . . 256 F2
Littlewell La DE7 . . . . 208 F2
Little Woodbury Dr **4**
DE23 . . . . 230 F6
Little Wood Dr S12 . . . .44 A3
Littlewood La
Mansfield Woodhouse
NG19 . . . . 136 A6
Pleasley Vale NG19 . . . 135 F8
Shirebrook NG20 . . . . . 119 F1
Little Wood La S26,
S80 . . . . .62 D4
Little Wood Rd S12 . . . .44 A3
LITTLEWORTH 262 D8
Littleworth La DE6 . . . 213 E6
LITTON 69 F3
Litton Bank SK13 . . . . . .9 E1
Litton CE Prim Sch
SK17 . . . . .69 E3
Litton Cft DE6 . . . . . . 185 D7
Litton Cl
Belper DE56 . . . . 179 B5
Ilkeston DE7 . . . . 194 E4
Staveley S43 . . . . .97 C8
Litton Ct **6** S40 . . . . .95 D5
Litton Dale
Litton SK17 . . . . .69 D2
Tideswell SK17 . . . . . . .69 D2
Litton Dr DE21 . . . . . . 220 F3
Litton Fold **16** SK13 . . .9 E1
Litton Gdns **17** SK13 . . .9 E1

Litton Mews SK13 . . . . . .9 E1
LITTON MILL 88 E7
Litton Rd
Buxton SK17 . . . . .85 E7
Mansfield Woodhouse
NG19 . . . . 136 E4
Littonslack SK17 . . . . . .88 E7
Litton Slack SK17 . . . . .88 E8
Liverpool St **4**
DE21 . . . . 219 E8
Liversage Almshouses
DE1 . . . . 267 C2
Liversage Pl DE1 . . . . 267 C2
Liversage Rd DE1 . . . . 267 C2
Liversage St DE1 . . . . 267 C2
Livingstone Rd
DE23 . . . . 218 E1
Lloyd St DE22 . . . . 218 D5
Loadshead La S42 . . . 112 D8
Loads Rd
Holymoorside S42 . . . . 113 B7
Holymoorside S42 . . . . 113 D7
Loake Ct **1** DE73 . . . 252 A8
Lochinvar Cl DE21 . . . 220 F4
Lock Cl DE7 . . . . 208 C6
Locker Smith La
DE11 . . . . 257 A1
LOCKINGTON 247 F5
Lockington Cl DE73 . . 232 F2
Lockington Rd
DE74 . . . . 247 D5
Lock La
Long Eaton NG10 . . . . 236 C4
Sandiacre NG10 . . . . . . 223 C4
Locko Ct DE21 . . . . . . 220 D5
Lockoford La
Chesterfield, Stonegravels
S41 . . . . .96 A4
Chesterfield, Tapton
S41 . . . . .96 C6
Lockoford Rd S41 . . . . .96 A5
Locko Hall DE7 . . . . . . 206 F2
Locko La S45 . . . . 132 E3
Locko Rd
Derby DE21 . . . . 220 E7
Morley DE21 . . . . 206 D2
Pilsley S45 . . . . 132 C4
Lockside SK6 . . . . .23 A6
Lockton Ave DE75 . . . 193 E8
Lock Up Yd DE1 . . . . . 267 B3
Lockwood Rd DE22 . . . 204 D4
Locomotive Way
DE24 . . . . 219 C3
Lodege La DE6 . . . . . . 202 F3
Lode La DE6 . . . . 149 F4
Lodes La SK17 . . . . .67 C7
Lodes View SK17 . . . . . .47 F2
Lodge Ave DE6 . . . . . . 185 B8
Lodge Bank SK13 . . . . . .10 A6
Lodge Cl
Calow S44 . . . . .97 A4
Duffield DE56 . . . . 190 E3
Etwall DE65 . . . . 229 C4
Lodge Ct SK14 . . . . .9 A4
Lodge Dr
Belper DE56 . . . . 178 E5
Wingerworth S42 . . . . . 115 A4
Lodge Est DE72 . . . . . 246 B7
Lodge Farm Chase
DE6 . . . . 185 B8
Lodge Farm Cl S40 . . . 114 C7
Lodge Hill
Rolleston DE13 . . . . . . 239 E3
Tutbury DE13 . . . . 239 D4
Lodge La
Alstonefield DE6 . . . . . 149 B3
Derby DE1 . . . . 267 A4
Derby, Spondon DE21 . . 220 D4
Heanor DE5 . . . . 181 E6
Mackworth DE6,
DE22 . . . . 203 C5
Shottle DE56 . . . . 177 D8
Lodge Mews DE72 . . . 246 B7
Lodge Moor Rd S10 . . .42 F8
Lodge Pl S43 . . . . .97 C6
Lodge Rd
Eastwood NG16 . . . . . 195 A8
Long Eaton NG10 . . . . 236 D5
Netherseal DE12 . . . . . 261 D1
Lodge Row DE7 . . . . . 193 E3
Lodge St DE72 . . . . . . 235 A7
Lodge The
Glossop SK13 . . . . .10 A6
Tideswell SK17 . . . . . . .69 C3
Lodge Way DE3 . . . . . 217 D1
Lodge Wlk S43 . . . . .97 F8
Loganberry Ct DE24 . 232 E8
Lohengrin Ct DE13 . . 240 E2
Lomas Cotts SK17 . . . .69 E3
Lombard St DE22 . . . . 217 F6
Lomond Ave DE24 . . . 231 F2
London Ho DE45 . . . . 109 D5
London Rd
Buxton SK17 . . . . .85 C6
Castle Donington
DE72 . . . . 247 B8
Derby DE23, DE24 . . . 219 D2
Derby DE24 . . . . 219 E1
Derby DE24 . . . . 233 F4
Shardlow DE72 . . . . . . 234 C2
Shardlow DE72 . . . . . . 234 E1
Sheffield, Heeley S2 . . . .43 A6
Sheffield, Highfield S2 . .43 A6
London Road Com Hospl
DE1 . . . . 267 C1
London Road S S2 . . . .43 A7
London St S43 . . . . .77 D3
Long Acre DE74 . . . . . 247 B6

Longacre Rd S18 . . . . . .76 A7
Long Acre View S20 . . .60 A8
Long Acre Way S20 . . .60 A8
Longbourne Ct
NG19 . . . . 136 F2
Longbow Cl DE13 . . . . 240 C1
Longbow Gr DE13 . . . . 240 C1
Longbridge La
Buxton SK17 . . . . .67 B4
Heanor DE5 . . . . 181 D3
Long Bridge La
DE24 . . . . 232 D8
Long Causeway
Bamford S32 . . . . .40 F5
Hallam Moors S10 . . . . .41 F8
Soughley S10 . . . . .42 A8
LONGCLIFFE 152 F4
Longcliff Wlk **2** S41 . .95 C6
Longclough Dr SK13 . .17 A8
Longcourse La S44 . . . .98 A2
Long Croft DE72 . . . . . 246 A8
Longcroft Ave
Dronfield S18 . . . . .56 C2
Ilkeston NE7 . . . . 194 F8
Longcroft Cl S42 . . . . . 131 D8
Longcroft Cres S18 . . . .56 C2
Longcroft Rd S18 . . . . . .56 C2
Longcroft View S80 . . . .82 A6
Longdale NG19 . . . . . . 136 E5
Longdale Dr S14 . . . . . . .9 A3
Longdale Gdns S14 . . . .9 A3
Longden Cl NG9 . . . . . 209 F2
Longdendale Com
Language Coll SK14 . . .9 C5
Longdons Row
DE21 . . . . 220 D5
LONG
DUCKMANTON 98 A3
LONG EATON 236 C7
Long Eaton Sch The
NG10 . . . . 236 C6
Long Eaton Sta
NG10 . . . . 236 C5
Long Eaton Trade Ctr
NG10 . . . . 236 F8
Longedge Gr S42 . . . . 115 B3
Longedge La S42 . . . . . 114 F3
Longedge Rise S42 . . . 115 A3
Longfield Cres DE7 . . 208 F5
Long Field Grange
S41 . . . . .95 C6
Longfield La DE7 . . . . 208 F5
LONGFORD 214 D8
Longford CE VC Prim
Sch DE6 . . . . 214 D8
Longford Cl
Burton upon Trent
DE15 . . . . 248 B2
Derby DE22 . . . . 204 D1
2 Derby DE23 . . . . 230 F5
Sheffield S17 . . . . .56 A5
Longford Cres S17 . . . .56 A5
Longford Ct S17 . . . . . .55 F4
Longford La
Church Broughton
DE65 . . . . 214 D2
Church Broughton
DE65 . . . . 227 F8
Longford DE6 . . . . 214 F7
Longford DE6, DE65 . . 214 C4
Sutton on the Hill
DE6 . . . . 215 A4
LONGFORDLANE 215 A5
Longford Rd S17 . . . . . .56 A4
Longford Spinney
S17 . . . . .55 F4
Longford St DE22 . . . . 218 E8
Long Gallery DE4 . . . . 110 E6
Longhedge La
Burton upon Trent
DE13 . . . . 239 F1
Pleasley NG19 . . . . . . 134 E5
Long Hill
Darley Dale DE4 . . . . . 127 C4
Whaley Bridge SK17,
SK23 . . . . .65 C5
Longhurst La
1 Marple SK7 . . . . . .24 C7
Marple Bridge SK6 . . . .23 D7
Stockport SK6 . . . . .23 D3
Longhurst View S80 . . .81 F5
Long La
Alkmonton DE6 . . . . . . 199 E2
Alkmonton DE6 . . . . . . 200 A1
Alstonefield DE6 . . . . . 149 B5
Ashover S42 . . . . 130 A6
Broadbottom SK13 . . . .16 C7
Chapel-en-le-Frith
SK23 . . . . .47 B4
Chapel-en-le-Frith, Combs
SK23 . . . . .46 C3
Chesterfield S21 . . . . . .77 C7
Cressbrook SK17 . . . . . .89 B7
Disley SK12 . . . . .32 E4
Holloway DE4 . . . . 156 B6
Killamarsh S21 . . . . . . .60 F6
Kirk Langley DE6 . . . . . 202 B1
Longford DE6 . . . . 214 C8
Shipley DE75 . . . . 194 E7
Shirebrook NG20 . . . . . 119 E3
Taddington SK17 . . . . . .87 E5
Thurvaston DE6 . . . . . . 201 D1
Wardlow SK17 . . . . .70 E2
Longlands S44 . . . . .99 B2
Longlands Dr SK22 . . . .33 B8
Longlands La
DE65 . . . . 230 C1

Longlands Mews
DE65 . . . . 230 C1
Longlands Rd
New Mills SK22 . . . . . . .33 B8
Swadlincote DE11 . . . . 256 D7
Longlands Villas
DE56 . . . . 167 F3
Long Lane CE Prim Sch
DE6 . . . . 201 D1
Long Lea Dr NG16 . . . 182 A5
Longley La DE21 . . . . . 220 D6
Longlieve Gdns S45 . . 132 B2
Longload La DE7 . . . . 154 E5
Long Mdw
Great Cubley DE6 . . . . 198 F1
Mansfield Woodhouse
NG19 . . . . 136 D5
Longmeade Dr SK23 . .47 B4
Long Meadow La
SK17 . . . . .69 E1
Long Meadow Rd
DE55 . . . . 158 F3
Longmoor Gdns **2**
NG10 . . . . 223 A2
Longmoor La
Breaston DE72 . . . . 222 E1
Breaston DE72 . . . . 235 E8
Sandiacre NG10 . . . . . . 223 B4
Longmoor Prim Sch
NG10 . . . . 223 C3
Longmoor Rd
Glossop SK13 . . . . .17 A7
Long Eaton NG10 . . . . 223 B2
LONGNOR 121 A6
Longnor Craft Ctr*
SK17 . . . . 121 B7
Longnor Gn **38** SK13 . .9 D2
Longnor Mews **39**
SK13 . . . . .9 D2
Longnor Way **37** SK13 . .9 D2
Long Rake DE45 . . . . . 123 D4
Longreave La DE45 . . . .90 C4
Longridge La SK17 . . . .66 F7
Longrose La
Kniveton DE6 . . . . 163 B2
Kniveton DE6 . . . . 163 B3
Long Row
Belper DE56 . . . . 178 F4
Shardlow DE72 . . . . . . 235 B2
Long Row Prim Sch
DE56 . . . . 178 F4
Long Shambles S40 . . 266 B3
Longshaw Cl
North Wingfield S42 . . . 131 F6
Staveley S43 . . . . .97 D8
Longshaw Est & Ctry
Pk* S11 . . . . 54 A3
Longshaw Estate Trail*
S11 . . . . .54 A4
Longshaw Estate Visitor
Ctr* S11 . . . . 54 A4
Longshaw Gdns
DE24 . . . . 233 A6
Longshaw Lodge
S11 . . . . .54 A4
Longside Rd
Disley SK12 . . . . .32 F4
Holymoorside S42 . . . . 112 E6
Long Sleets DE55 . . . . 160 B4
Longs Mill **4** DE1 . . 267 A4
Longson Rd SK23 . . . . . .47 C6
Long St DE15 . . . . 254 E7
Longster La NG20,
NG19 . . . . 120 C3
Longstock Cl DE21 . . . 205 E1
Longstone Bsns Pk
DE45 . . . . .90 A4
Longstone CE Prim Sch
DE45 . . . . .89 F4
Longstone Cres S12 . . .44 D4
Longstone La DE45 . . . .89 F2
Longstone Rise
DE56 . . . . 179 B6
Longstone Wlk DE1 . . 267 A2
Longthorpe Cl DE23 . 231 A7
Longthorpe Road
DE24 . . . . 233 D4
Long View La DE6 . . . 185 A4
Longwalls La DE56 . . . 178 C5
Longway Bank DE4 . . 156 A2
Longwood Cl DE75 . . 181 D4
Longwood Hall Rise
DE55 . . . . 159 F4
Longwood Inf Acad
NG16 . . . . 160 C2
Longwood Rd NG16 . . 160 C2
Lonsdale Gr DE4 . . . . 142 F7
Lonsdale Pl DE22 . . . . 218 C4
Lonsdale Rd
Burton upon Trent
DE14 . . . . 254 B8
Pilsley S45 . . . . 132 B2
Lons Inf Sch DE5 . . . . 169 D2
Loom Cl DE56 . . . . . . 179 C5
Loosemore Dr S12 . . . .43 F5
Lord Haddon Rd
DE7 . . . . 194 E1
Lord Roberts Rd
S40 . . . . 266 B1
Lords Cl S44 . . . . .99 A1
Lordsmill St S41 . . . . 266 C2
Lord St
Derby DE24 . . . . 219 E8
Glossop SK13 . . . . .10 D1
Hollingworth SK14 . . . . .9 D4
Lorne Cl S18 . . . . .56 D2

Lornes Dr DE15 . . . . . 248 B3
Lorne St DE22 . . . . . . 218 F3
Lorraine Cl DE24 . . . . 232 E3
LOSCOE 181 C3
Loscoe CE Prim Sch
DE75 . . . . 181 B4
Loscoe Ct **2** S40 . . . .95 D5
Loscoe-Denby La DE5,
DE75 . . . . 181 B4
Loscoe Grange
DE75 . . . . 181 D3
Loscoe Rd
Derby DE21 . . . . 206 A1
Heanor DE75 . . . . 181 D2
Losehill Hall Study
Centre* S33 . . . . .38 C4
Lose Hill La S33 . . . . . .38 F6
Losk Cnr S44 . . . . 118 D2
Losk La
Palterton S44, NG19 . . . 118 C3
Scarcliffe NG20 . . . . . . 119 A2
Lothian Pl
Castle Donington
DE74 . . . . 247 A3
Derby DE21 . . . . 219 D7
Lothlorien Cl DE23 . . . 231 B7
Loudon St DE23 . . . . . 219 A3
Loudoun Pl DE74 . . . . 247 A4
Loundes Rd S18 . . . . . .76 E6
Loundes Wood Ave
S41 . . . . .95 C8
LOUNDSLEY GREEN . . .95 B6
Loundsley Green Rd
S40 . . . . .95 C5
Lount La S13 . . . . 239 E1
Lousie Greaves La
DE21 . . . . 220 E6
Louvain Rd DE22,
DE23 . . . . 218 D2
Louwil Ave NG19 . . . . 136 E5
Lovatt Cl DE13 . . . . . . 240 F2
Lovatt Dr NG16 . . . . . 182 C4
Love La
Flash SK11 . . . . 102 C1
Stonebroom DE55 . . . . 147 C4
Loveys Croft DE73 . . . 252 A4
Lowburn Rd S13 . . . . . .44 C7
Low Cl DE6 . . . . 189 A2
Low Comm S21 . . . . . . .79 D7
Lowcroft SK17 . . . . .66 C2
Lowe Avenue DE7 . . . 193 C8
LOWEDGES 57 A6
Lowedges Cl S8 . . . . . .56 F6
Lowedges Cres S8 . . . .56 F6
Lowedges Dr S8 . . . . . .56 F6
Lowedges Jun Academy
SK13 . . . . .56 F6
Lowedges Pl S8 . . . . . .57 A6
Lowedges Prim Sch
S8 . . . . .56 E6
Lowedges Rd S8 . . . . . .56 E6
Lower Al S44 . . . . .97 A1
Lower Bagthorpe
NG16 . . . . 171 F3
Lower Bank SK13 . . . . .17 D8
Lower Bank St S13 . . . . .9 E4
Lower Barn Rd SK13 . . .9 E4
Lower Birchwood
DE55 . . . . 170 F8
Lower Bloomsgrove Rd
DE7 . . . . 194 F2
LOWER BRADWAY 56 C6
Lower Brook St
NG10 . . . . 236 E7
Lower Burch Pl S32 . . .71 C8
Lower Chapel St
9 Ilkeston DE7 . . . . 194 F1
Stonebroom DE55 . . . . 147 A3
Lower Clara Mount Rd
DE75 . . . . 182 A1
Lower Cliffe SK22 . . . . .23 D3
LOWER CROSSINGS . . .46 F6
Lower Dale Rd
DE23 . . . . 218 F2
LOWER DINTING 10 B1
Lower Dr DE55 . . . . . . 169 D7
Lower Dunstead Rd
Aldercar NG16 . . . . . . 182 B3
Langley Mill NG16 . . . . 182 A3
Lower Eaves View
SK23 . . . . .47 C5
Lower Eley St DE1 . . . 267 A1
LOWER
ELLASTONE 183 C2
Lower Fold SK6 . . . . . . .23 B8
Lower Gladstone St
DE75 . . . . 181 E2
Lower Gn DE65 . . . . . . 230 D1
Lower Granby St
DE7 . . . . 194 F2
Lower Greenhall La
SK12 . . . . .32 F6
Lower Grove Rd
S40 . . . . 266 A3
Lower Hague DE22 . . . .32 E8
Lower Hall DE56 . . . . . 191 C6
Lower Hardwick St **1**
SK17 . . . . .85 B8
LOWER
HARTSHAY 169 C4
Lower Higham Visitor
Ctr* SK14 . . . . .15 A8
Lower High St DE13 . . 239 C7
LOWER KILBURN 191 F7
Lower La SK23 . . . . .34 D1

Lowerlea SK12 . . . . **32** C6
Lower Macclesfield Rd
Horwich End SK23 . . . . . . **45** D6
Horwich End SK23 . . . . . **45** E6
Lower Mantle Cl
S45 . . . . **131** D4
Lower Maples DE75. **194** A8
Lower Market St
SK14 . . . . **16** B8
Lower Meadows Prim
Sch S8 . . . . **57** A5
Lower Middleton St
DE7 . . . . **195** A1
Lower Midland Rd 1
DE11 . . . . **256** B4
LOWER MIDWAY **256** E6
Lower Mill 1 DE5 . . **169** E1
Lower Orchard St 1
NG9 . . . . **223** D7
Lower Park St NG9 . . **223** C6
LOWER PILSLEY **132** B3
Lower Pingle Rd
DE6 . . . . **185** C8
Lower Rd DE22 . . . . . **217** F8
Lower Rock St 2
SK22. . . . . **33** C7
Lower Smithy La
SK17 . . . . **88** A3
Lower Somercotes
DE55 . . . . **170** E7
Lower Sq SK13 . . . . **10** A7
Lower St DE6 . . . . **224** B8
Lower Stanton Rd
DE7 . . . . **208** F4
Lower Strines Rd
SK6 . . . . **23** A5
Lower Terrace Rd
SK17 . . . . **69** B5
LOWER THURVASTON **214** F6
Lowerwhitworth Rd 2
DE7 . . . . **208** F6
Lower Whitworth Rd
DE7 . . . . **208** F6
Lower Wood SK17 . . . . . **89** A7
Lower Wood Cotts
SK17 . . . . **89** A7
Lowes Hill DE5 . . . . . **169** D3
Lowes La DE73 . . . . . . **244** C7
Lowe St DE24. . . . . . . **232** E6
LOWFIELD **43** B8
Lowfield Ave S12 . . . . . **58** E8
Lowfield Com Prim Sch
8 S2 . . . . **43** A7
Lowfield Ct 4 S2. . . . . **43** A7
Lowfields S43 . . . . **79** A2
LOWGATES **78** F3
Lowgates S43 . . . . **79** A2
Lowick Cl 4 DE23 . . **231** E1
Lowlands Lea DE75 . **181** F2
Lowlands Rd DE56. . . **179** B4
Low Lea Rd SK6 . . . . . . **23** B6
Low Leas DE4 . . . . **156** A8
LOW LEIGHTON **33** D8
Low Leighton Rd
SK14 . . . . **33** D8
Lowman Way DE65 . . **240** F8
Low Mdw S43 . . . . **45** D8
Low Mdw Row S81 . . . **63** E7
Low Meadows DE45 . . **91** E6
Low Pavement S40 . . **266** B3
Lowry Ct SK14 . . . . **9** A4
Lowry Dr
Dronfield S18 . . . . **56** F1
Marple S6 . . . . **23** B8
Lows Ct DE73 . . . . . . **233** B2
Lowside S32 . . . . **72** B2
Lowside Cl S32. . . . . . . **72** B2
Low's La DE7 . . . . **209** B2
Loxley Cl
Chesterfield S40. . . . . . **95** B3
Derby DE21 . . . . **206** B2
Loxley La S80 . . . . **82** A5
Loxton Ct DE3 . . . . . . **217** D3
Loyne Cl DE24 . . . . . . **231** F2
Lucas La DE65 . . . . . . **228** E2
Lucas Rd S41 . . . . **95** E5
Lucas Terr SK22 . . . . . . **25** C3
Lucas Works S18 . . . . . **57** A2
Luccombe Dr DE24 . **233** D5
Lucerne Rd DE21 . . . **206** C3
Ludborough Wlk 14
NG19 . . . . **136** E4
Ludburn La SK17 . . . . **121** C1
Ludford Cl NG10 . . . . **236** E4
Ludgate St DE13 . . . . **239** C6
Ludgate Wlk DE22 . . **217** E6
Ludham Cl S41 . . . . **95** F7
Ludlam Ave NG16 . . . **195** E4
Ludlam Ho S2 . . . . **43** E6
Ludlow Cl DE21 . . . . . **220** F5
Ludlow Rd DE23 . . . . **230** F5
Ludworth Prim Sch
SK6 . . . . **23** B8
Luke La DE6 . . . . **201** D8
LULLINGTON **263** E7
Lullington Mews
DE12 . . . . **262** A3
Lullington Rd
Clifton Campville
B79 . . . . **263** E8
Coton in the Elms
DE12 . . . . **260** C2
Edingale DE12 . . . . . . **263** A5

Lullington Rd continued
Overseal DE12 . . . . . **262** A3
Lulworth Cl DE21 . . . **231** D6
Lulworth Ct NG16 . . . **195** F7
Lulworth Rd DE72 . . **233** D3
Lumber La DE6 . . . . . . **176** D2
Lumb La
Belper DE56 . . . . **178** C4
Cowers Lane DE56 . . **177** D2
Hazelwood DE56 . . . **178** B2
Northwood DE4 . . . . . **127** B6
Lumb The SK14 . . . . **9** A6
Lumford Cotts
DE45 . . . . **109** D7
Lumley Close DE24 . **233** D4
LUMSDALE **143** E6
Lumsdale DE4 . . . . **143** E6
Lumsdale Cres DE4 . **143** D5
Lumsdale Rd
Matlock DE4 . . . . **143** D4
Staveley S43 . . . . **97** C8
Lumsdale Terr DE4 . **143** E7
Lum's Hill Rise DE4 . **143** D6
Luna Croft
Sheffield S12 . . . . **43** F2
Sheffield S12 . . . . **44** A3
Lunch Lane SK17 . . . . **88** F8
Lundie Cl DE24 . . . . . **231** D2
Lundy Rd S18 . . . . **76** B8
Lune Mdw NG19 . . . . **136** E3
Lupin Cl
Derby DE24 . . . . **206** C3
Derby DE24 . . . . **231** C3
Shirebrook NG20 . . . . **119** D3
Lupin Way S44 . . . . **97** A3
Lupton Cres S8. . . . . . . **56** F6
Lupton Rd S8 . . . . **56** F6
Lupton St S8 . . . . **56** F6
Lupton Wlk S8 . . . . **57** A6
Luton Rd DE11 . . . . . . **255** E2
Lutyens Court S40 . . . **94** F2
Lychgate Cl DE21 . . . **205** D2
Lydden Cl S43 . . . . **96** E8
Lydford Ave S41 . . . . . . **77** B1
Lydford Rd DE55. . . . . **159** B5
LYDGATE **74** D8
Lydgate S32 . . . . **71** E5
Lydgate Cotts S33 . . . **40** A6
Lydgate Dr S42 . . . . . . **114** E3
Lydgate La S33 . . . . **40** A6
Lydia Gdns NG16 . . . **182** E1
Lydstep Cl DE21 . . . . **206** C2
Lyle Cl NG16 . . . . **195** E7
Lymefield SK14 . . . . **16** A8
Lymefield Terr SK14 . **16** B7
Lymefield Visitor Ctr ✱
SK14 . . . . **16** B8
Lyme Park ✱ SK12 . . **32** B1
Lyme Park Ctry Pk ✱
SK12 . . . . **32** B2
Lyme Pk
Chinley SK23 . . . . **34** E2
Disley SK12 . . . . **32** B2
Lyme Rd SK12 . . . . **32** A4
Lymewood Dr SK12 . . **32** C6
Lynam Rd DE55,
DE56 . . . . **168** D7
Lyncroft Ave DE5 . . . **169** E1
Lyndale Dr DE5 . . . . . **181** B8
Lynden Ave NG10 . . . **236** D5
Lyndhurst Gr DE21 . . **220** A5
Lyndhurst St DE23 . . **219** A2
Lyne Ave SK13 . . . . **17** A8
Lynholmes Rd DE4 . . **143** D5
Lynholmes Rise
DE4 . . . . **143** D5
Lynmouth Dr DE7 . . . **194** D3
Lynmouth Ho DE65 . . **228** C1
Lynne Cl SK13 . . . . **17** F8
Lynton Cl DE5 . . . . **169** D3
Lynton Ct 10 S41 . . . . . **95** F8
Lynton Rd DE56 . . . . . **168** A3
Lynton St DE22 . . . . . **218** E4
Lynwood Cl
Branston DE14 . . . . . . **253** F7
1 Dronfield S18 . . . . . **56** D1
Lynwood Rd
Branston DE14 . . . . . . **253** E8
Derby DE24 . . . . **231** F4
Lysander Dr DE73. . . **232** E1
Lytham Cl DE21 . . . . . **205** D1
Lyttelton St DE22 . . . **218** C5

M

M1 Commerce Pk
S44 . . . . **98** B4
Macaulay St DE24 . . **232** A5
Macclesfield Main Rd
SK17 . . . . **84** D5
Macclesfield Old Rd
SK17 . . . . **84** D6
Macclesfield Rd
Buxton SK17 . . . . **85** A6
Horwich End SK23 . . . . **45** D6
Macdonald Cl S42 . . **115** F3
Macdonald Sq DE7 . **208** D5
Machins Ct S18 . . . . . . **57** A2
Mackenzie St DE22 . **218** D5
Mackinley Ave NG9 . **209** E1
Macklin St DE1 . . . . . **267** B3
MACKWORTH **217** E8
Mackworth Ave
DE3 . . . . **230** E5
Mackworth Cl
5 Sheffield S2 . . . . . . **44** A7
Swadlincote DE11 . . . **256** B7

Mackworth Rd DE1,
DE22 . . . . **218** E6
Macmillan Mews S40 **95** B3
Macnair Cl SK6 . . . . **23** A5
Macnair Mews SK6 . . **23** A5
Macready Pl DE24 . . . **232** F7
Maddock La DE4 . . . . **153** A1
Madehurst Gdns S2 . . **43** B7
Madehurst Rd S2 . . . . . **43** B7
Madehurst Rise S2 . . . **43** B7
Madehurst View S2 . . **43** B7
Madeley Ct DE3 . . . . . **217** F3
Madeley St DE23 . . . . **219** A2
Madin Dr S43 . . . . **97** B6
Madin St
Chesterfield S41 . . . . **266** B4
Tupton S42 . . . . **131** D8
Madison Ave DE21 . . **219** F7
Madras St DE1 . . . . . . **267** C4
Magdala Cotts DE56 **190** E5
Magdalene Drive
DE3 . . . . **217** F3
Magee Ct DE1 . . . . . . **267** C1
Magellan Way DE24 **219** E1
Mag La
Creswell NG20 . . . . . **100** D5
Idridgehay DE56 . . . . **176** D5
Magnolia Close
DE13 . . . . **239** C5
Magnolia St DE55. . . **159** E4
Magnolia Way DE55 **170** A8
Magnus St DE21 . . . . **219** B8
Magpie Way S40 . . . . . **95** D6
Maguire Ave SK13 . . . **10** A6
Maiden Rd NG20 . . . . **119** D2
Maidstone Dr DE24 . **231** C3
Maidwell Cl DE56 . . . **179** C6
Main Ave
Derby DE22 . . . . **204** F5
Sheffield S17 . . . . **55** E4
Main Bright Rd 8
NG19 . . . . **136** B1
Main Bright Wlk
NG19 . . . . **136** B1
Main Dr SK12 . . . . **114** E2
Maine Dr DE21 . . . . . **220** A6
Main Rd
Abney S32 . . . . **51** E3
Abney S33 . . . . **52** A4
Bamford S33 . . . . **40** B3
Barlow S18 . . . . **75** E2
Bradwell S33 . . . . **51** A8
Brailsford DE6 . . . . . . **201** F7
Chesterfield, Ashgate
S42 . . . . **94** F4
Chesterfield, West Handley
S21 . . . . **77** D7
Cressbrook SK17 . . . . . **89** C7
Crich DE4 . . . . **156** D1
Cutthorpe S42 . . . . **94** E8
Darley Bridge DE4 . . . **142** B8
Denstone ST14 . . . . . . **196** E6
Denstone ST14 . . . . . . **197** A8
Earl Sterndale SK17 . . **105** C2
Eckington, Lightwood
S21 . . . . **58** F3
Eckington, Ridgeway
S12 . . . . **58** F3
Ellastone ST14 . . . . . . **183** A1
Elmton S80 . . . . **100** A7
Elvaston DE72 . . . . . . **234** A6
Eyam S32 . . . . **71** C6
Flagg SK17 . . . . **106** E6
Foolow SK17 . . . . **70** D6
Great Hucklow SK17. . . **70** B8
Grindleford S32 . . . . . . **72** C7
Hathersage S32 . . . . . . **53** A8
Haunton B79 . . . . **263** C2
Heath S44 . . . . **117** B2
Holmesfield S18 . . . . . . **75** A8
Hulland Ward DE6 . . . **175** E3
Jacksdale NG16 . . . . . **171** B3
Lea DE4 . . . . **156** B8
Little Hucklow S17 . . . . **50** F2
Lower Hartshay DE5 . . **168** F4
Marsh Lane S21 . . . . . . **58** E4
Mayfield DE6 . . . . **184** D8
Morley Smithy DE7 . . **206** C8
Nell Croft S11 . . . . **54** A5
Renishaw S21 . . . . **79** B8
Ripley DE5 . . . . **169** A3
Ripley, Pentrich DE5 . **169** C5
Shirland DE55 . . . . . . **146** D1
Smalley DE7 . . . . **192** F3
Somercotes, Leabrooks
DE55 . . . . **170** C7
Somercotes, Pye Bridge
DE55 . . . . **170** F6
Stanton in Drive DE4 . **125** D6
Stonebroom DE55 . . . **147** A5
Sudbury DE6 . . . . **225** F4
Sudbury, Aston DE6 . . **226** A4
Taddington SK17 . . . . . **88** A3
Underwood Green
NG16 . . . . **171** F2
Unstone S18 . . . . **76** E7
Upper Padley S32 . . . . . **53** F4
Wadshelf S42 . . . . **93** E4
Wardlow SK17 . . . . **70** C1
Wensley DE4 . . . . **127** C1
Wensley DE4 . . . . **142** A7
Whaley Thorns NG20 . **101** A1
Winster DE4 . . . . **141** E6
Wyaston DE6 . . . . **185** C2
Yeaveley DE6 . . . . **199** D7
Main St
Awsworth NG16 . . . . . **195** C5
Biggin SK17 . . . . **138** C3

Main St continued
Blackfordby DE11 . . . **257** C1
Bolsover S44 . . . . **98** F1
Bolsover S44 . . . . **117** F8
Bradbourne DE6 . . . . . **163** B6
Branston DE14 . . . . . . **253** F7
Breaston DE72 . . . . . . **235** D8
Breedon on the Hill
DE73. . . . . **252** F2
Brinsley NG16 . . . . . . **171** D1
Burnaston DE65 . . . . . **229** F5
Burton upon Trent,
Stapenhill DE15 . . . **254** D5
Burton upon Trent, Stretton
DE13 . . . . **240** E1
Caldwell DE12 . . . . . . **260** F7
Calke LE65 . . . . **251** E1
Calver S32 . . . . **72** C1
Carsington DE4 . . . . . **164** E7
Chelmorton SK17 . . . . **106** A8
Church Broughton
DE65. . . . . **227** B8
Clifton Campville B79 **263** F2
Coton in the Elms
DE12. . . . . **260** D3
Eastwood NG16 . . . . . **182** F1
Edensor DE4 . . . . **110** D8
Eggington DE65 . . . . . **241** B5
Elton DE4 . . . . **140** E6
Elvaston DE72 . . . . . . **234** D6
Etwall DE65 . . . . **229** B4
Etwall DE65 . . . . **229** C5
Findern DE65 . . . . **230** D1
Great Longstone DE45 . **90** A4
Hartshorne DE11 . . . . **257** B6
Hemington DE74 . . . . **247** D5
Hilton DE65 . . . . **228** C2
Hollington DE6 . . . . . **200** F4
Hollington DE6 . . . . . **201** A4
Hopton DE4 . . . . **165** A7
Horsley Woodhouse
DE7. . . . . **192** C6
Ingleby DE56 . . . . **243** F2
Ingleby DE73 . . . . **244** A2
Kimberley NG16 . . . . . **195** F6
King's Newton DE73. . **245** C1
Kirk Ireton DE6 . . . . . **165** B1
Kniveton DE6 . . . . **163** B1
Kniveton DE6 . . . . **174** A8
Linton DE12 . . . . **261** D6
Little Longstone DE45 . **89** D4
Lockington DE74. . . . . **247** F5
Long Eaton NG10 . . . . **236** E7
Longford DE6 . . . . **214** D8
Lullington DE12 . . . . . **263** E7
Mapperley DE7 . . . . . . **193** E3
Middleton DE4 . . . . . . **154** D4
Moira DE11 . . . . **256** C1
Netherseal DE12 . . . . **264** F7
Newton DE55 . . . . **148** A4
Newton Solney DE15 . **248** E8
Over Haddon DE45. . . **109** A1
Overseal DE12 . . . . . . **262** B3
Palterton S44 . . . . **118** A5
Repton DE65 . . . . **242** D1
Rosliston DE12 . . . . . . **260** D6
Roston DE6 . . . . **197** E6
Scarcliffe S44 . . . . **118** E6
Scropton DE65 . . . . . . **226** E1
Sheldon DE45 . . . . **108** A6
Sheldon DE45 . . . . **108** B6
Shirebrook NG20 . . . . **119** E3
Smisby LE65 . . . . **257** F3
South Normanton
DE55. . . . . **160** B6
Stanton-by-Dale DE7 . **222** F8
Sutton in Ashfield
NG17 . . . . **148** F3
Swadlincote DE11 . . . **255** E6
Tatenhill DE13 . . . . . . **253** A8
Ticknall DE73 . . . . **251** B4
Ticknall, Milton DE65 . **243** A1
Walton-on-Trent
DE12. . . . . **253** D1
Weston-on-Trent
DE72. . . . . **245** E5
Whaley Thorns NG20 . **100** F2
Whaley Thorns NG20 . **101** A2
Wilson DE73 . . . . **252** E6
Winster DE4 . . . . **141** C6
Youlgrave DE45 . . . . . **125** B5
Mais Cl DE4 . . . . **144** A5
Maisies Way DE55 . . **160** D6
Maitland DE11 . . . . . . **261** B6
Maize Cl DE23 . . . . . . **231** A6
Majestic Place
DE11 . . . . **256** B3
Majolica Mews
DE11 . . . . **256** F2
MAKENEY **191** A6
Makeney Rd
Belper DE56 . . . . **191** A6
Duffield DE56 . . . . . . **190** F2
Holbrook DE56 . . . . . **191** C6
Makeney Terr DE56. . **191** A6
Malbon's Yd DE6 . . . **173** C1
MALCOFF **35** E2
Malcolm Gr DE23 . . . **230** E8
Malcolm St DE23 . . . **219** B2
Malcote Mws DE11 . . **261** B6
Maldon Close NG10. **236** E5
Malham Cl S40 . . . . **95** D5
Malham Gdns DE21 . . **59** D7
Malham Gr DE23 . . . . **230** F6
Malham Rd DE23 . . . **218** C5
Malia Rd S41 . . . . **96** C6
Malik Way DE75 . . . . **193** F8
Malin Cl DE24 . . . . . . **233** B5

Malinder Cl S21 . . . . . . **60** D6
Malinscommon La
DE56 . . . . **166** C4
Malkin La DE6 . . . . . . **188** E2
Malkin St S41 . . . . **266** C3
Mallard Cl NG20 . . . . **119** E3
Mallard Ct
Mansfield NG19 . . . . **136** A2
6 Staveley S43 . . . . . . **78** F2
Mallard Dr S21 . . . . **60** B7
Mallard Way DE24 . . **219** D3
Mallard Wlk DE3 . . . . **230** C8
Mallatratt Pl NG19 . . **136** B4
Mallory Cl S41. . . . . **76** E3
Mallow Close DE24 . **231** C2
Mall The S45 . . . . **131** C3
Malmesbury Ave
DE11 . . . . **256** D6
Malpas Rd DE41 . . . . **143** B6
Malson Way S41 . . . . . **95** D6
Maltby Ave DE55. . . . **146** E5
Maltby Cl 2 DE22 . . . **204** F2
Malthouse Cl
Eastwood NG16 . . . . . **182** F1
Wirksworth DE4 . . . . . **154** F3
Malthouse Ct
DE56 . . . . **179** B8
Malthouse Drive
DE56 . . . . **179** B8
Malthouse La
Ashover S45 . . . . **129** F3
Boylestone DE6 . . . . . **213** C4
Froggatt S32. . . . . **72** C5
Hatton DE65 . . . . **227** D3
Nether Heage DE56 . . **168** B2
Wingerworth S42. . . . **114** C3
Malthouse Mws
DE4 . . . . **157** F4
Malthouse Rd
Ilkeston DE7. . . . . **208** F4
Whitwell S80 . . . . **82** A6
Malt House Yard
S44 . . . . **118** E6
Maltings The
2 Ashbourne DE6 . . . **173** B2
Burton upon Trent
DE15. . . . . **248** A1
Derby DE1 . . . . **267** B2
Derby DE22 . . . . **218** D6
Shardlow DE72 . . . . . **235** B1
Malton Pl DE21 . . . . . **205** D1
Malton Wlk S40 . . . . . **114** F7
Malvern Ave DE55 . . **248** A1
Malvern Cl DE3 . . . . . **217** D3
Malvern Gdns
5 Long Eaton
NG10 . . . . **236** A4
Matlock DE4 . . . . **143** B6
Malvern Rd S40 . . . . . . **95** E4
Malvern Rise SK13 . . . **10** A5
Malvern Way 3
DE21 . . . . **205** D1
Manchester La
DE11 . . . . **257** C5
Manchester Rd
Buxton SK17 . . . . **65** F1
Chapel-en-le-Frith
SK23 . . . . **46** B5
Glossop SK13, SK14 . . . **9** E7
Tideswell SK17 . . . . . . **50** A1
Tideswell SK17 . . . . . . **69** B5
Manchester St
Derby DE22 . . . . **218** D6
Long Eaton NG10 . . . . **236** D6
Mandalay Rd NG19 . . **135** B4
Mandarin Close
NG19 . . . . **136** E2
Mandarin Way DE24 **232** F8
Manifold Ave
Ashbourne DE6 . . . . . **173** D1
Staveley S43 . . . . **97** D8
Manifold Dr DE24. . . **233** B8
Manitoba Way
NG16 . . . . **171** F7
Manknell Rd S41 . . . . . **96** A8
Manners Ave DE7 . . . **194** D1
Manners Cl SK23 . . . . **34** D2
Manners Ind Est
DE7 . . . . **194** C1
Manners Rd DE7 . . . . **194** E1
Manners St DE7 . . . . **209** A6
Manning View DE7 . . **194** F2
Mannion Cres NG10 **236** B5
Manor S42 . . . . **157** E3
Manor Ave
Brimington S43. . . . . . . **96** F7
Derby DE23 . . . . **218** C3
Stapleford NG9 . . . . . **223** D8
Manor Bglws 4 S18. **56** F1
Manor Cl
Brassington DE4 . . . . **153** A4
Chesterfield S44. . . . . . **80** B1
Newton DE55 . . . . **148** A3
Pilsley S45 . . . . **132** C1
Swadlincote DE15 . . . **255** A6
Manor Coach Ct
DE11 . . . . **256** D3
Manor Court Rd S44 . **98** F3
Manor Cres
Dronfield S18 . . . . **56** F1

Manor Ct
Barrow upon Trent
DE73. . . . . **244** B5
Breaston DE72 . . . . . . **235** E8
Breedon on the Hill
DE73. . . . . **252** F3
Clowne S43. . . . . **80** F3
Risley DE72 . . . . **222** D4
Somercotes DE55. . . . **170** E5
South Wingfield DE55 **157** E3
Manor Dr
Brimington S43. . . . . . . **96** F7
Chesterfield S40. . . . . . **95** D3
Netherseal DE12 . . . . **264** F6
Manor Farm S45 . . . . **132** C1
Manor Farm Barns
DE21 . . . . **205** B3
Manor Farm Cotts
DE45 . . . . **89** C4
Manor Farm Ct
Killamarsh S21 . . . . **60** D5
Whitwell S80 . . . . **81** F6
Manor Farm Mews
Aston-on-Trent
DE72. . . . . **246** B8
Burnaston DE65 . . . . . **229** F5
Long Duckmanton S44 . **98** A3
Manor Farm Rd
DE72 . . . . **246** B8
Manor Fields Dr
DE7 . . . . **208** D7
Manor Gdns DE11 . . **261** C6
Manor Gr S43 . . . . **80** A6
Manor House Court
S41 . . . . **96** A5
Manor House Rd
NG10 . . . . **236** F6
Manor La
Fritchley DE55 . . . . . . **168** F8
South Wingfield DE55 **157** F1
Manorleigh DE72 . . . **235** E8
Manor Leigh DE72 . . **235** E8
Manor Mws 6
NG19 . . . . **136** C3
Manor Park Ct
DE22 . . . . **218** B3
Manor Park Rd SK13. . **10** C1
Manor Park View
SK13 . . . . **10** C1
Manor Park Way
DE3 . . . . **218** B3
Manor Pk DE72 . . . . . **221** B1
Manor Rd
Ashbourne DE6 . . . . . **173** D3
Barlborough S43 . . . . . **80** A7
Barton in Fabis NG11 **237** E6
Belper DE56 . . . . **178** F3
Borrowash DE72 . . . . **221** A1
Calow S43 . . . . **96** F6
Chellaston DE73 . . . . . **232** F1
Chesterfield S40. . . . . . **95** C3
Derby DE23 . . . . **218** C2
Derby DE73 . . . . **233** A1
Eastwood NG16 . . . . . **182** F1
Harthill S26 . . . . **61** F8
Horwich End SK23 . . . . **45** E5
Ilkeston DE7. . . . . **194** E1
Killamarsh S21 . . . . **60** E5
Mansfield Woodhouse
NG19 . . . . **136** A4
South Wingfield DE55. **157** F3
Swadlincote DE15 . . . **255** B6
Manor Rise B79 . . . . . **263** D3
Manor School View
DE12 . . . . **262** B3
Manor Sch The
NG19 . . . . **136** C3
Manor St SK13 . . . . **10** C1
Manor View
Hartshorne DE11 . . . . **257** B6
Sheffield S20 . . . . **59** E7
Manse Ave S80 . . . . . **100** D8
Manse Cl
Creswell S43 . . . . **81** D1
Creswell S80 . . . . **100** D8
Mansfeldt Cres S41. . **95** E6
Mansfeldt Rd S41. . . . **95** E6
MANSFIELD **135** F2
Mansfield Cl DE11 . . **256** D4
Mansfield Dr S12 . . . . **44** C6
Mansfield Rd
Alfreton DE55. . . . . . . **159** B4
Bramley-Vale S44. . . . **117** E1
Brinsley NG16 . . . . . . **182** F4
Chesterfield S41. . . . . **115** F6
Clowne S43. . . . . **80** E2
Creswell S80 . . . . **81** F1
Creswell S80 . . . . **100** F8
Creswell S80 . . . . **101** A8
Derby DE1 . . . . **219** A6
Derby DE1, DE21 . . . . **267** B4
Eastwood NG16 . . . . . **182** F4
Glapwell NG19, S44 . . **134** C8
Heanor DE75 . . . . **182** A2
Heath S44. . . . . **117** A3
Holmewood S42 . . . . . **116** C3
Killamarsh S21 . . . . **60** F6
Mansfield Woodhouse
NG19 . . . . **136** C2
Morley DE7 . . . . **206** B4
Palterton S44 . . . . **118** B6
Scarcliffe S44 . . . . **118** E5
Selston NG16 . . . . **171** F7
Sheffield S12 . . . . **44** B6
Shirebrook NG20 . . . . **120** C1
South Normanton
DE55. . . . . **160** D6
Spion Kop NG19 . . . . **136** F8

Mansfield Rd continued
Tibshelf DE55 . . . . .148 B7
Whitwell S80 . . . . .82 F7
Mansfields Croft
DE65 . . . . .229 B4
Mansfield St
Derby DE1 . . . . .267 B5
Somercotes DE55. . . .170 C8
Mansfield Terr
DE55 . . . . .159 C5
Mansfield View S12 . . .44 B6
**MANSFIELD
WOODHOUSE**. 136 E2
**Mansfield Woodhouse
Sta** NG19. . . . . .136 A3
Manton Cl
2 Burton upon Trent
DE13. . . . . .240 F1
Swadlincote DE11 . . . .255 F6
Manvers Ave **2**
DE5. . . . . .169 E1
Manvers Ct
Chesterfield S41. . . . . .266 B4
Shirebrook NG20 . . . .120 A4
Manvers Rd S44 . . . . . .97 A4
Manvers St
Mansfield Woodhouse
NG19 . . . . .136 A3
Ripley DE5 . . . . .169 E1
Shirebrook NG20 . . . .120 A4
Manystones La
Brassington DE4. . . . . .153 B3
Middleton DE4 . . . . . . .154 B2
Maple Ave
Derby DE23 . . . . .231 D6
Disley SK12 . . . . .33 A6
Ripley DE5 . . . . .180 C8
Sandiacre NG10 . . . . . .223 B7
Maplebeck Ct DE1 . . .267 B5
Maple Cl
Alfreton DE55. . . . . . . .160 B5
Doveridge DE6 . . . . . . .211 B1
Hilton DE65 . . . . .228 D2
Mansfield NG19 . . . . . .136 E1
Maple Dr
Ashbourne DE6. . . . . . .185 D7
Aston-on-Trent DE72 . .246 A7
Belper DE56 . . . . .179 B2
Chellaston DE73. . . . . .233 A2
Creswell S80 . . . . .81 C2
Derby, Boulton DE24. . .233 A6
Killamarsh S21. . . . . . . .60 C5
South Normanton
DE55. . . . . .160 B4
Maple Gdns
1 Heanor DE75. . . . . .181 D1
Langley Mill NG16. . . . .182 B3
Maple Gr
Breaston DE72. . . . . . . .235 F8
Burton upon Trent
DE15. . . . . .254 E5
Derby DE22 . . . . .204 D5
Glapwell S44 . . . . .134 B8
Maple Rd
Castle Donington
DE74. . . . . .247 A5
Swadlincote DE11 . . . .256 B4
Maple St S43 . . . . .97 B8
Maples The DE75 . . . .194 A4
Mapletoft Ave NG19 136 A5
MAPLETON. 172 F4
Mapleton Ave DE21 .205 F1
Mapleton Rd
Ashbourne DE6. . . . . . .173 A2
Draycott DE72 . . . . . . .235 A8
Maple View DE4. . . . .143 C3
Maple Way
Branston DE14. . . . . . . .253 F8
Burton upon Trent
DE14. . . . . .254 A8
Selston NG16. . . . . . . .171 F7
MAPPERLEY. 193 E3
**Mapperley CE
(Controlled) Prim Sch**
DE7. . . . . .193 E3
Mapperley La DE7 . . .193 E2
Mapperley Rd S18. . . .56 C1
Marble Cl DE1 . . . . . . .267 B4
Marble Ct SK17. . . . . . .85 C2
Marble Dr DE11 . . . . . .255 F4
MARCHINGTON 224 E2
Marchington Cl
DE22. . . . . .204 C1
Marchwood Cl S40 . . .95 E4
Marcie Ct DE65. . . . . .242 D2
Marcus St DE1 . . . . . .219 A7
Mardale Cl S41. . . . . . .76 C1
Maree Cl DE24. . . . . . .231 E4
MAREHAY. 180 D6
Marfleet Cl DE3 . . . . .217 D3
Margaret Ave
Derby DE21 . . . . .219 F5
Ilkeston DE7. . . . . .208 F8
Long Eaton NG10 . . . . .223 F1
Sandiacre NG10 . . . . . .223 B4
Margaret St DE1. . . . .267 B5
Margery Cl DE6. . . . . .185 B8
Margreave Rd DE21 .219 F7
Mariana Cl DE73. . . . .232 E2
Marigold Cl DE21 . . . .206 B3
Marigold Pl DE11 . . . .256 F4
Marina Dr
Derby, Allenton
DE24. . . . . .232 E5
Derby, Spondon DE21 .220 D5
Shireoaks S81 . . . . .63 F6
Marina Rd DE7 . . . . . .193 B8
Marine Dr S41. . . . . . . .96 C3

Marion Ct SK17. . . . . . .85 C6
Marisco Cl DE24. . . . .233 D4
Marjoram Gro DE3. . .217 D4
Marjorie Rd DE21. . . .219 F8
Marjory La DE6,
DE65. . . . . .213 C2
MARKEATON 218 B8
Markeaton La
Derby DE22 . . . . .204 C1
Derby DE22 . . . . .218 B8
Markeaton Pk★
DE22. . . . . .218 C7
Markeaton Prim Sch
DE22. . . . . .218 E7
Markeaton St DE22 .218 E6
Market Arc 2 SK13. . .10 C1
Market Cl
Hope S33 . . . . .39 A4
Shirebrook NG20 . . . . .119 F3
South Normanton
DE55. . . . . .160 A6
Market Head DE56. . .179 A3
Market Pl
Alfreton DE55. . . . . . . .158 F4
5 Ashbourne DE6 . . .173 C2
Belper DE56 . . . . .179 A3
Bolsover S44 . . . . .99 A1
7 Buxton SK17. . . . . . .85 B7
Castleton S33. . . . . .38 C2
Chapel-en-le-Frith
SK23. . . . . .47 B6
8 Charlesworth SK13. .16 A4
Chesterfield S40. . . . . .266 B3
Codnor DE5 . . . . .181 B8
Compstall SK6 . . . . .15 A2
Crich DE4. . . . . .156 F1
Cromford DE4. . . . . . . .155 A6
Cromford DE4. . . . . . . .155 B6
Derby DE1 . . . . .219 A5
Derby DE1 . . . . .267 B3
Hartington SK17. . . . . .137 D5
1 Heanor DE5. . . . . . .181 E1
Ilkeston DE7. . . . . .208 E8
Ironville NG16 . . . . . . .170 F4
Long Eaton NG10 . . . . .236 E8
Longnor SK17. . . . . . . .121 B6
Mansfield Woodhouse
NG19 . . . . .136 C3
Melbourne DE73. . . . . .252 B7
Mottram in Longdendale
SK14. . . . . .9 A3
Ripley DE5 . . . . .169 D1
Shirebrook NG20 . . . . .119 F4
Somercotes DE55. . . . .170 C8
Somercotes, Riddings
DE55. . . . . .170 E6
South Normanton
DE55. . . . . .160 A6
South Wingfield DE4. . .157 F4
Staveley S43. . . . . .78 E2
Sutton in Ashfield
NG17. . . . . .148 F3
Tideswell SK17. . . . . . . .69 C4
Wirksworth DE4. . . . . .165 F8
Market Sq SK17 . . . . . .69 C4
Market St
Bakewell DE45 . . . . . . .109 D6
Broadbottom SK14. . . . .16 A8
Buxton SK17. . . . . .85 B7
Castle Donington
DE74. . . . . .247 B3
Chapel-en-le-Frith
SK23. . . . . .47 C6
Clay Cross S45. . . . . . . .131 D4
Disley SK12 . . . . .32 D6
Draycott DE72 . . . . . . .235 A7
Eckington S21. . . . . .59 E3
Glossop SK13. . . . . .10 C1
Hayfield SK22. . . . . .25 D3
Heanor DE75 . . . . .181 E1
Hollingworth SK14. . . . . .9 D5
Ilkeston DE7. . . . . .208 F8
Ironville NG16 . . . . . . .170 F4
Mottram in Longdendale
SK14. . . . . .9 A4
New Mills SK22. . . . . . . .33 B7
Shirebrook NG20 . . . . .119 F4
South Normanton
DE55. . . . . .160 A5
Staveley S43. . . . . .78 E2
Sutton in Ashfield
NG17. . . . . .148 F3
Swadlincote DE11 . . . .256 B4
Whaley Bridge SK23. . . .33 E1
Whaley Bridge SK23. . . .45 E7
Market View 15 SK17 .85 B7
Markham Cres S43 . . .78 F2
Markham Ct
Derby DE21 . . . . .205 F2
Duckmanton S44 . . . . . .98 A5
Markham La S44 . . . . . .98 B4
Markham Quay S41. .266 C2
Markham Rd
Chesterfield S40. . . . . .266 B2
Long Duckmanton S44. .98 B5
Markham Ret Pk
S40. . . . . .266 B2
Markham Rise S45 .131 B4
**Markham Vale
Environment Ctr**
S44. . . . . .98 B4
Markhma La S44 . . . . .98 B6
Markland Ave S43. . . .81 A4
Markland Cres S43. . . .81 A4
Markland La S80, S43 .81 A2
Markland View S80. . .81 D3
Mark's Cl DE23. . . . . .231 D6
Mark St NG10 . . . . . . .223 C5

Marlborough Cres
DE15. . . . . .255 A8
Marlborough Dr
DE56. . . . . .179 C5
Marlborough Rd
Breaston DE72. . . . . . . .235 D7
Buxton SK17. . . . . .85 B8
Derby DE24 . . . . .232 C7
Long Eaton NG10 . . . . .223 F1
Mansfield NG19 . . . . . .135 F1
Marlow Brow SK13. . . .10 A4
Marlow Cres DE7 . . . .207 D8
Marlow Dr DE14. . . . . .254 A8
Marlow Ct DE23 . . . . .231 F6
Marlow St
5 Buxton SK17. . . . . . .85 C8
6 Glossop SK13 . . . . . .10 A5
Marlpit La
Bolsover S44 . . . . .99 C3
Denstone ST14. . . . . . .196 D6
Ellastone DE6. . . . . . . .183 A3
Sutton on the Hill
DE6. . . . . .228 A8
MARLPOOL. 193 F8
Marlpool Inf Sch
DE75. . . . . .194 A8
Marlpool Jun Sch
DE75. . . . . .182 A1
Marl Way DE11 . . . . . .256 A4
MARPLE. 23 A5
Marple Rd SK13 . . . . . .16 B5
MARPLERIDGE. 23 A2
Marples Ave NG19 . . .136 E5
Marple Sta SK6. . . . . . .23 A7
Marquis Cl DE12. . . . .262 E5
Marquis Dr DE12 . . . .262 E5
Marquis Gdns DE73. .244 E8
Marriott S43. . . . . .34 E1
Marrison Dr S21. . . . . .60 C6
Marsden Cl DE56 . . . .190 E3
Marsden Pl
2 Chesterfield S40. . . .95 D2
Chesterfield S41. . . . . .266 B4
Marsden Row S33 . . . .40 B4
Marsden St
Chesterfield S40. . . . . .266 B3
Derby DE24 . . . . .232 E7
Glossop SK13 . . . . .10 A4
Marsden Wood Grove
S45. . . . . .131 E7
Marshall Dr 1
NG9 . . . . .223 F8
Marshall St
Alfreton DE55. . . . . . . .159 A3
Heanor DE75 . . . . .181 F2
Marshall Way DE7 . . .208 C6
Marsham Dr SK6 . . . . .23 A5
Marsh Ave
Dronfield S18 . . . . .57 B3
Hope S33 . . . . .38 F4
Ilkeston NE7. . . . . .194 E6
Marshaw Cl DE3 . . . . .217 E1
Marsh Cl S20. . . . . .59 C6
Marshes The S33. . . . .38 E4
Marsh Green S23. . . . .47 B4
Marshfield Gr S43. . . . .79 A2
Marshgreen Cl
DE24. . . . . .233 D5
Marsh Green La
S45. . . . . .129 F4
Marsh Hall La S23. . . .46 F5
Marsh Hollow DE6. . .200 F5
Marsh La
Belper DE56 . . . . .179 B5
Mayfield DE6 . . . . .183 D8
New Mills SK22, SK23. . .33 D6
MARSH LANE 58 F3
Marsh Lane Cres
DE56. . . . . .179 B4
Marsh Lane Prim Sch
S21. . . . . .58 E3
Marsh Lane Trad Est
S22. . . . . .33 D7
Marsh View S21. . . . . .59 B2
Marsh Way SK23. . . . . .46 F5
Marston SK17 . . . . . . .106 B7
Marston Bank
Marston Montgomery
DE6. . . . . .197 C2
Marston Montgomery
DE6. . . . . .197 D3
Marston Brook
DE65. . . . . .228 E1
Marston Cl
Belper DE56 . . . . .179 C6
Derby DE23 . . . . .231 D5
Dronfield S18 . . . . .75 D8
Marston Common
Marston Montgomery
DE6. . . . . .197 F2
Marston Montgomery
DE6. . . . . .198 A4
Marstone Cres S17 . . .55 F5
Marston La
Doveridge DE6 . . . . . . .211 B1
Doveridge DE6 . . . . . . .211 C2
Hatton DE65 . . . . .239 D8
Marston on Dove
DE65. . . . . .228 B1
Marston on Dove
DE65. . . . . .240 A8
Rolleston DE13. . . . . . .240 A4
**MARSTON
MONTGOMERY**. . . .211 E8
**Marston Montgomery
Prim Sch** DE6 . . . . .211 E8
Marston Old La
DE65. . . . . .239 D8

**MARSTON ON
DOVE** 240 B8
Marston Rd
Somersal Herbert
DE6. . . . . .211 F3
Somersal Herbert
DE6. . . . . .212 A3
Marston Rise DE15 . .254 F8
Martha Rd DE3 . . . . . .217 F6
Martin Ct S21. . . . . . . .59 C3
Martindale Cl S43 . . . .97 C8
Martindale Ct
DE56. . . . . .179 D5
Martin Dr DE21. . . . . .220 A8
Martinet Close
DE74. . . . . .246 F4
Martin Rise S21 . . . . . .59 C3
MARTINSIDE. 47 D3
Martins La S42. . . . . . .131 B8
Martin's La DE13 . . . .238 A4
Martival Court LE66. .258 A1
Martlet Ave S42. . . . . .32 C6
Marx Ct S45. . . . . .131 C3
Mary Ann St S41. . . . . .76 E4
Mary Devonshire Cotts
DE45. . . . . .91 C2
Maryland Ct
Stapleford NG9. . . . . . .209 E1
Swadlincote DE11 . . . .256 A7
Maryland Rd DE21 . . .220 B6
Marylebone Cres
Derby DE22 . . . . .218 A6
3 Derby DE3. . . . . . . .217 F6
Mary St
Eckington S21. . . . . .59 D3
Whaley Thorns NG20 . .101 A2
**Mary Swanwick Com
Prim Sch** S41 . . . . . . .77 A3
Masefield Ave
Derby DE23 . . . . .231 E7
Holmewood S42. . . . . .116 D1
Holmewood S42. . . . . .132 C8
Holmewood S42. . . . . .132 E8
Swadlincote DE11 . . . .256 C6
Masefield Rd S13. . . . .44 C6
Masefield Way S42. . .132 C8
Mason Cres
Sheffield S13 . . . . .44 D6
Swadlincote DE11 . . . .256 C4
Mason Gr S13. . . . . . . .44 D7
Mason Mills Sh Village
DE4. . . . . .155 A7
Mason Rd DE7. . . . . . .194 D2
Masons Cotts S21 . . . .59 A3
Masons Gr SK13 . . . . . .10 A6
Masons Place Bsns Pk
DE21. . . . . .219 D6
Mason St S80 . . . . .81 F6
Masoy Way DE6 . . . . . .184 C4
Masson Cl 12 S40. . . . .95 D5
Masson Hill View
DE4. . . . . .142 F7
Masson Rd DE4. . . . . .143 A5
**Masson Shopping
Village** DE4 . . . . . . .155 A7
Masson Terr DE4. . . . .144 A5
Masson Wlk DE22 . . . .218 E4
Masters View
6 Ripley DE5. . . . . . . .170 A1
Ripley DE5 . . . . .181 A8
Mastin Ave S43. . . . . . .80 D5
MASTIN MOOR. 79 C4
Matcham Way SK17. . .84 E5
MATHERSGRAVE. 145 C3
Mathersgrave La
DE55. . . . . .145 B2
Mather's Way S42. . . .115 D1
MATLOCK. 143 A5
MATLOCK BANK 143 C4
Matlock Bank 8 SK13 .9 E1
MATLOCK BATH 143 C5
Matlock Bath
Aquarium★
DE4. . . . . .143 A1
**Matlock Bath Holy
Trinity CE Prim Sch**
DE4. . . . . .155 A8
Matlock Bath Sta
DE4. . . . . .143 B1
MATLOCK BRIDGE .143 B5
MATLOCK CLIFF 143 D4
MATLOCK DALE. 143 B4
Matlock Ct NG10 . . . .235 F5
Matlock Dr S43. . . . . . .97 C5
Matlock Farm Park★
DE4. . . . . .128 D5
Matlock Gdns 5 SK13 .9 E1
Matlock Gn DE4 . . . . .143 C4
MATLOCK GREEN. . .143 C5
Matlock Ho DE21. . . . .220 E3
Matlock La 7 SK13. . . .9 E1
Matlock Parks Nature
Reserve★ DE4. . . . . . .143 B3
Matlock Pl 6 SK13. . . .9 E1
Matlock Rd
Ambergate DE56 . . . . .167 F4
Ashover S42, S45 . . . . .113 C3
Belper DE56 . . . . .178 F8
Brackenfield DE55 . . . .145 C2
Derby DE21 . . . . .205 F1
Holymoorside S40,
S42. . . . . .114 B7
Wessington DE55. . . . .157 E8
Matlock Riverside Sta★
DE4. . . . . .143 A6

**Matlock St Giles CE (VA)
Prim Sch** DE4 . . . . .143 C3
Matlock Spard DE4 .142 F5
Matlock Spa Rd
DE4. . . . . .143 A5
Matlock St DE45. . . . .109 D5
Matlock Sta DE4 . . . . .143 B5
Mattersey Ct 4
NG19 . . . . .136 B1
Matthew Cl SK13 . . . . .9 F7
Matthew Kirtley Mus★
DE5. . . . . .170 B4
Matthews Ct NG9. . . .209 E1
Matthews Fold S8. . . .43 C1
Matthews La S8. . . . . .43 C1
Matthew St DE24 . . . .232 F6
Matthew Way DE23 . .230 E7
Matt Orch DE55. . . . . .160 B4
Maudesley Ave S41. .266 B1
Maugerhay S8. . . . . . . .43 C1
Maunleigh NG19. . . . .136 E1
Maun Valley Pk Nature
Reserve★ NG19. . . . .136 E2
Mawfa Ave S14. . . . . . .43 D2
Mawfa Cres S14. . . . . .43 D2
Mawfa Dr S14 . . . . .43 D2
Mawfa Rd S14. . . . . . . .43 D2
Mawfa Wlk S14. . . . . . .43 D2
Mawkin La NG16. . . . .160 F5
Maws La NG16. . . . . . .195 E7
Mawstone La
Youlgrave DE45 . . . . . .125 C4
Youlgrave DE45 . . . . . .125 B3
Maxey Pl S8. . . . . .43 A6
Max Rd DE21 . . . . .219 F8
Maxwell Ave DE22 . . .218 D8
Maxwell St DE72. . . . .235 F8
May Ave S41 . . . . .77 C3
Maybank Cl SK23. . . . .35 A1
Mayfair DE11. . . . . . . .255 E6
Mayfair Cres DE7. . . .217 F6
Mayfair Ct DE56 . . . . .190 C4
MAYFIELD. 184 C8
Mayfield Ave
Heanor DE75 . . . . .181 E1
Kilburn DE56. . . . . .192 A8
Mayfield DE6 . . . . .184 C7
Mayfield Dr
Burton upon Trent
DE15. . . . . .255 A8
North Wingfield S42. . .131 F6
Stapleford NG9. . . . . . .209 F2
Mayfield Gr NG10. . . .223 E1
Mayfield Mill DE6. . . .184 B8
Mayfield Pl DE6. . . . . .184 C8
Mayfield Rd
Burton upon Trent
DE15. . . . . .248 A3
Chesterfield S40. . . . . . .95 C2
Derby DE21 . . . . .219 E7
Marple SK6. . . . . .15 B1
Mayfield DE6 . . . . .172 D1
Sheffield S10 . . . . .42 F7
Mayfield Terr
Hathersage S32. . . . . . .53 A8
Mayfield DE6 . . . . .184 D6
Mayflower Cl SK13 . . .17 E8
Mayflower Ct
Sheffield S12 . . . . .44 B6
Shirebrook NG20 . . . . .119 E4
Mayflower Rd NG16. .195 B8
Mayhall Ave NG19 . . .136 A4
Maylands DE72 . . . . . .221 B1
Maylands Ave DE72. .235 E8
Maynard Rd
Chesterfield S40. . . . . .266 A1
Grindleford S32 . . . . . . .53 D1
Maynestone Rd
SK23. . . . . .34 E5
Maypole Cl DE7 . . . . .208 C4
Maypole Hill DE11 . . .256 A6
Maypole La DE23 . . . .230 E7
May South DE7 . . . . . .194 D3
May St
Derby DE22 . . . . .218 F3
Ilkeston DE7. . . . . .194 E4
Maytree Cl DE21. . . . .206 C3
Mayvale Dr DE22 . . . .218 C4
McAdam Cl DE15 . . . .248 B2
McAuley Ct S41 . . . . .267 B4
McDavid Way S44 . . . .98 C5
McGough Mews
DE24. . . . . .232 A5
McGregor's Way
S40. . . . . .115 B7
McMahon Ave S43. . . .97 B4
McNeil Gr DE72. . . . . .235 A7
Mdws The DE4. . . . . . .165 E8
Mead Cl DE24 . . . . . . .231 F4
Mead Cres DE15. . . . .255 A6
Meadow Ave
Buxton SK17. . . . . .67 B5
Codnor DE5 . . . . .181 B8
Meadow Bank
Glossop SK13. . . . . .16 F7
Hollingworth SK14. . . . . .9 D6
Mansfield Woodhouse
NG19 . . . . .136 E6
South Normanton
DE55. . . . . .160 A7
Meadowbank Ct
NG16 . . . . .182 D3
Meadowbank Way
NG16 . . . . .182 D3
**Meadowbank Way Ind
Est** NG16. . . . . .182 D3
Meadow Brook Cl 3
DE23. . . . . .230 F6

Meadowbrook Ind Est
S20. . . . . .60 A8
Meadowbrook Pk
S20. . . . . .60 A8
Meadow Cl
Barlborough S43. . . . . . .80 C6
Bolsover S44 . . . . .118 A8
Chesterfield S43. . . . . . .77 D2
Derby DE21 . . . . .220 E4
Dove Holes SK17 . . . . . .47 E1
Draycott DE72 . . . . . . .235 A7
Dronfield S18 . . . . .57 C4
Eastwood NG16 . . . . . .182 F4
Findern DE65 . . . . .230 D2
Horsley Woodhouse
DE7. . . . . .192 C6
Repton DE65. . . . . .242 E2
Stoney Middleton S32. . .72 B3
Tibshelf DE55 . . . . .148 B3
Whaley Bridge SK23. . . .45 C8
Meadow Cotts
NG19 . . . . .136 C3
Meadow Cres
Castle Donington
DE74. . . . . .247 B2
Sheffield S20 . . . . .59 B7
Meadowcroft SK14. . . .9 A4
Meadow Croft S42. . .132 D8
Meadowcroft Gdns
S20. . . . . .59 E8
Meadowcroft Glade
S20. . . . . .59 E8
Meadowcroft Rise 2
S20. . . . . .59 E8
Meadow Ct
Belper DE56 . . . . .178 F4
Chesterfield S43. . . . . . .77 D4
5 Derby DE3. . . . . . . .217 D1
Elvaston DE72 . . . . . . .234 D6
2 Grassmoor S41. . . .115 F2
Grassmoor S42 . . . . . . .116 A2
Kilburn DE56. . . . . .192 A7
South Normanton
DE55. . . . . .159 F4
Meadow Drive DE7 . .193 B8
Meadow End DE4. . . .165 E2
Meadow Farm Prim Sch
DE21. . . . . .220 A4
Meadowfield SK23. . . .45 D8
Meadowfield Cl SK13 .9 F3
Meadow Fields
DE13. . . . . .240 C4
Meadowgate Pk S21. .60 D7
Meadow Gdns DE75 .182 B1
Meadow Gr
Newton DE55 . . . . .148 A3
Sheffield S17 . . . . .55 E4
Meadowgrass Cl
DE23. . . . . .231 B6
Meadow Grove Rd
S17. . . . . .55 D4
Meadow Head Ave
S8. . . . . .56 F8
Meadow Head Cl S8. .56 F8
Meadow Head Dr S8. .56 F8
Meadow Head Rd S17 .56 F8
Meadowhead Sch S8 .57 A7
Meadowhill Rd S41. .115 D8
Meadow House Way
S44. . . . . .98 C3
Meadow La
Burton upon Trent
DE13. . . . . .248 A8
Derby DE1, DE21 . . . . .267 D3
Derby, Chaddesden
DE21. . . . . .219 D5
Disley SK12 . . . . .32 D6
Dove Holes SK17 . . . . . .47 E2
Hilton DE65 . . . . .228 C1
Long Eaton NG10 . . . . .236 F7
Newton DE55 . . . . .159 F7
Repton DE65. . . . . .243 A4
Roston DE6. . . . . .197 C7
Shirebrook NG19,
NG20 . . . . .119 D2
Swadlincote DE11 . . . .256 A6
Tideswell SK17. . . . . . . .69 B2
Meadowlands S44. . . .99 C2
Meadow Lane Ind Est
DE55. . . . . .159 F6
Meadowlark Gr
DE21. . . . . .206 A1
Meadow Nook
DE24. . . . . .233 C5
Meadow Pl DE4 . . . . .142 F7
Meadow Rd
Awsworth NG16. . . . . .195 C5
Clay Cross S45. . . . . . . .131 A5
Derby DE1 . . . . .267 C3
Derby, Wilmorton DE21,
DE24. . . . . .219 F1
Ripley DE5 . . . . .169 C1
Meadow Rise
Brassington DE4. . . . . .153 A1
Chesterfield S42. . . . . . .94 F4
Church Broughton
DE65. . . . . .227 B8
Glossop SK13. . . . . .16 F7
Meadows Croft
DE56. . . . . .190 D3
Meadows Dr S43. . . . . .97 F6
Meadowside
Disley SK12 . . . . .33 A6
Mayfield DE6 . . . . .184 D6

Meadowside continued
Whaley Bridge SK23. . . .**45** D8
Meadowside Cl
Shirley DE6. . . . . **200** D8
Wingerworth S42. . . . .**115** B4
Meadows Ind Est The
DE21. . . . . **219** D5
Meadows Rd SK22. . . .**25** D2
Meadow St
Ilkeston DE7. . . . .**194** F1
Ironville NG16 . . . . . .**170** F5
New Mills SK22. . . . . . .**33** C8
Meadows The
Awsworth NG16 . . . . .**195** C5
Belper DE56. . . . .**178** E4
Burton upon Trent
DE15. . . . .**248** B2
Chesterfield S42. . . . . .**95** A5
Dove Holes SK17. . . . . .**47** F1
Great Longstone DE45. .**90** A4
3 Heanor DE75. . . . . .**181** E1
Killamarsh S21. . . . . . .**60** D6
Swanwick DE55. . . . . .**169** E7
Uttoxeter ST14. . . . . .**210** A2
Meadows Wlk S43. . . .**80** F4
Meadow Vale DE56 . **190** D3
Meadow View
Belper DE56. . . . .**178** F3
Bolsover S43. . . . .**80** F3
Chesterfield S40. . . . .**114** A8
Darley Dale DE4. . . . .**142** F7
Doveridge DE6 . . . . . .**224** C8
Higham DE55 . . . .**146** C2
Holmewood S42. . . . . .**132** D8
Rolleston DE13. . . . . .**240** C4
Selston NG16 . . . .**171** E6
South Wingfield DE55. .**157** F5
South Wingfield S55. . .**158** A5
Stapleford NG9. . . . . .**223** D8
Meadow View Cl
Derby DE21. . . . .**206** B3
Hanbury DE13. . . . . . .**238** A4
Meadow View Ct
DE72. . . . . **222** F4
Meadow View Rd
Sheffield S8 . . . .**56** F8
Swadlincote DE11. . . . .**255** F5
Meadow Way
Chellaston DE73. . . . . .**233** A1
Swadlincote DE11. . . . .**256** A6
Meads The S8. . . . .**57** B8
Meadway Dr S17 . . . . .**55** D7
Meadway The S17. . . . .**55** D7
Mead Wlk DE15. . . . . .**255** A6
Meakin Drive DE11. . .**256** F1
Meakin St S41. . . . . . .**115** D8
Meal Hill Rd HD9 . . . . . .**2** F8
Meal St SK22. . . . .**33** C8
Mear Dr DE72 . . . .**221** B1
Mear Greaves La
DE15. . . . . **248** B4
Mease La B79 . . . .**263** B2
Mease Spencer Acad
The DE45 . . . .**240** D8
Mease The
Hilton DE65 . . . .**228** C1
Hilton DE65 . . . .**228** E1
Measham Rd
Appleby Magna
DE12. . . . .**265** F1
Donisthorpe DE12 . . . .**265** D6
Moira DE12. . . . .**262** F3
Meath Ave DE21. . . . . .**220** B4
Meden Ave NG19 . . . . .**134** F7
Meden Bank NG19 . . . .**135** B5
Meden Cl NG19. . . . . . .**135** B5
Meden Rd NG19 . . . . . .**136** D4
Meden Sq NG19 . . . . . .**135** B5
Medhave Ave DE11. . . .**261** B6
Medina Cl DE24 . . . . . .**233** D5
Medlock Cl S40. . . . . . .**114** B7
Medlock Rd S40. . . . . .**114** C8
Medway Dr DE22 . . . . .**205** B5
Meerbrook Cl DE21. . . .**206** A1
Meerbrook Dr DE4. . . .**154** F2
Meerbrook Pl DE7. . . .**208** C5
MEERSBROOK. **43** B5
**MEERSBROOK
BANK**. **43** A5
Meersbrook Park Rd
S8. . . . .**43** A5
Meersbrook Rd S8 . . . . .**43** A5
Meersbrook Works [13]
S2. . . . .**43** A6
Meersdale S2. . . . .**43** C6
Megaloughton La
DE21. . . . . **220** C3
Megdale DE4. . . . .**143** A6
Melandra Castle Rd
SK13. . . . .**9** D2
Melandra Ct DE22 . . .**218** E4
Melandra Rd SK13. . . . . .**9** E3
Melanie Cl SK13. . . . . . .**17** A8
Melbourn Cl DE56 . . . .**190** E3
MELBOURNE. **252** B8
Melbourne Ave
Burton upon Trent
DE15. . . . .**248** C3
Dronfield S18. . . . .**56** B1
Melbourne Cl
Belper DE56. . . . .**179** A2
Derby DE22 . . . .**204** D2
Derby, Markeaton
DE3. . . . .**217** F3

Melbourne Ct DE24. .**219** E4
Melbourne Ct
Long Eaton NG10 . . . . .**235** F4
8 Staveley S43 . . . .**78** E2
Melbourne Hall & Gdns ★
DE73. . . . . **252** C2
Melbourne Ho DE21 **220** E3
Melbourne Inf Sch
DE73. . . . . **252** B8
Melbourne Jun Sch
DE73. . . . . **252** B8
Melbourne La
Breedon on the Hill
DE73. . . . .**252** E2
Ticknall DE73 . . . .**251** C5
Melbourne L Ctr
DE73. . . . . **252** B7
Melbourne Rd
Breedon on the Hill
DE73. . . . .**252** A2
Ibstock LE67. . . . .**252** F8
Stapleford NG9. . . . . .**209** E1
Melbourne St
Derby DE1. . . . .**267** B1
Mansfield Woodhouse
NG19 . . . .**136** C6
Melbreak Cl DE3 . . . .**217** E1
Melfort Cl DE24 . . . . .**231** F2
Melling Cl S40. . . . . . .**114** F8
Melling Ct S40. . . . . . .**114** F8
Mellington Cl S8 . . . . . .**43** C2
MELLOR. **23** D5
Mellor Dr ST14 . . . . . .**210** B1
Mellor La
Barlow S18. . . . .**75** E1
Chapel-en-le-Frith
SK23. . . . .**47** A6
Mellor Prim Sch SK6 .**23** C6
Mellor Rd
Burton upon Trent
DE14. . . . .**254** B7
New Mills SK6, SK22. . . .**24** C3
Mellor's La DE56 . . . .**191** C6
Mellors Rd NG19 . . . .**135** D1
Mellor St DE24 . . . . . .**232** E6
Mellor Way S40 . . . . . .**115** A7
Melrose Cl
Chesterfield S40. . . . . .**95** D3
Derby DE24. . . . .**231** E2
Melrose Cl [7] S41. . . . . .**96** A6
Melrose Way S41. . . .**158** B4
Meltham La S41. . . . . . .**96** B6
Melton Ave
Derby DE23. . . . .**231** C6
Melbourne DE73. . . . .**252** A8
Melton Ct
Derby DE22 . . . .**218** E6
Sandiacre NG10 . . . . . .**223** A5
Somercotes DE55. . . . .**170** C6
Melville Cl DE6 . . . . . .**175** F3
Melville Cres S43. . . . . .**96** F4
Melville Ct DE65. . . . . .**229** B3
Melville Dr S2. . . . .**44** A8
Memorial Croft DE4 .**154** F3
Memorial Pl SK17 . . . . .**67** C5
Memorial Rd DE22. . .**204** C3
Memorial View Rd DE4. .**156** F2
Mendip Cl [1] NG10 . . . .**223** A1
Mendip Cres S40 . . . . . .**95** B4
Mendip Ct DE21 . . . . .**205** E2
Menin Rd DE22 . . . . . .**204** C2
Mentmore Cl DE55. . . .**170** A7
Meon Cl DE3 . . . .**217** B1
MERCASTON. **188** B3
Mercaston Cl S40. . . . . .**95** A5
**MERCASTON
GREEN**. **188** B3
Mercaston La
Hulland Ward DE6 . . . .**188** B4
Mackworth DE6,
DE22. . . . .**203** B8
Mercaston DE6. . . . . .**188** C2
Weston Underwood
DE6. . . . .**202** B4
Mercaston Rd DE21. .**219** F8
Mercer Cres DE55 . . .**159** C3
Merchant Ave DE21. **220** D4
Merchant Drive
DE55. . . . . **170** C7
Merchantman Mews
DE74. . . . . **246** F4
Merchants Cnr
DE22. . . . . **218** E6
Merchant St
Derby DE22 . . . .**218** E6
Shirebrook NG20 . . . .**120** A4
Mercia Cl
Eastwood NG16 . . . . . **195** A8
Hatton DE65. . . . .**239** D8
Mercia Dr
Sheffield S17. . . . .**55** E6
Willington DE65 . . . . .**242** B5
Mercian Cl DE7. . . . . .**194** E1
Mercian Mews
DE21. . . . . **220** D4
Mercian Pk DE7. . . . . .**194** E1
Mercian Wy DE1. . . . .**267** A2
Mere Beck DE72 . . . . .**234** D6
Meredith Ct NG9 . . . .**209** E2
Mereoak La DE11,
DE73. . . . . **251** F1
Mereside Gdns SK23. . .**45** D6
Merevale Way DE24 . **231** C3
Meridian Cl DE7 . . . . .**194** E4
Merion Gr DE23 . . . . .**218** A1
Merlin Cl S44. . . . .**98** F3
Merlin Cl DE56 . . . . . .**179** C5

Merlin Cres DE14 . . . .**253** F8
Merlin Gdns [7]
DE73. . . . . **244** E8
Merlin Gn DE24. . . . . .**231** D4
Merlin La DE7 . . . .**192** D6
Merlin Road NG19 . . .**136** B2
Merlin Way
Burnaston DE3 . . . . . .**230** B7
Ilkeston DE7. . . . .**208** F4
Woodville DE11 . . . . . .**256** F3
Merrial Cl S40. . . . .**95** D5
Merrick Cl S40 . . . .**95** D5
Merridale Rd DE23. . .**231** C8
Merrill Coll DE24 . . . .**232** E5
Merrill Way DE24 . . . .**232** D5
Merrybower Cl
DE24. . . . . **231** D3
Merrydale Rd DE15 . .**255** A8
Merryton DE7. . . . .**205** F3
Mersey Bank Rd SK13. .**9** F4
Mersey Way
Hilton Common
DE65. . . . .**228** C1
13 Sheffield S2. . . . .**43** C8
Merthyr Ct DE21. . . . .**206** B2
Merton Cl [2] DE6. . . . .**181** F1
Merton Close DE11 . .**255** E1
Merton Ct NG9 . . . . . .**209** E1
Merton Drive DE22 . .**217** F5
Mervyn Rd DE15. . . . .**248** A3
Mesne La DE45 . . . . . .**109** E7
Messiter Mews
DE24. . . . . **231** D3
Metcalfe Ave S21. . . . .**60** C6
Metcalfe Ct DE24 . . . .**233** B8
Meteor Bsns Pk
DE21. . . . . **205** B4
Meteor Ctr The
DE21. . . . . **205** C1
Methley Cl S12 . . . .**43** F6
Metro Ave DE55 . . . . .**148** A3
Mettesford DE4 . . . . .**143** D5
Meverill Rd SK17 . . . . .**69** D5
Mevril Rd SK23 . . . .**45** E5
Mevril Springs Way
SK23. . . . .**45** E5
Mewies Cl DE12 . . . . .**253** D1
Mews Ct DE3 . . . .**217** D4
Mews The
Burton upon Trent
DE14. . . . .**254** C8
Horsley Woodhouse
DE7. . . . .**192** C7
Little Eaton DE6 . . . . .**191** B2
Melbourne DE73. . . . .**252** B7
New Mills SK22 . . . .**33** D8
Wyaston DE6 . . . .**185** B2
Meynell Cl
Burton upon Trent
DE15. . . . .**248** B1
Chesterfield S40. . . . . .**95** C2
Meynell Ct
Derby DE22 . . . .**204** C2
Kirk Langley DE6. . . . .**202** F2
Meynell Langley
DE6. . . . . **203** C4
Meynell Rd NG10 . . . .**236** D5
Meynell Rise DE6. . . .**173** C4
Meynell St
Derby DE23 . . . .**218** F1
Swadlincote DE11. . . .**256** A1
Meynell Way S21. . . . . .**60** C6
Michael Cl S42. . . . . . .**115** A5
Michael House Sch
DE75. . . . . **194** A6
Michael's La DE6 . . . .**183** C5
Michaels Mdw DE55 .**159** F3
Michaelwood Way
S43. . . . .**98** F6
Michelle Cl DE24 . . . .**231** C3
Michigan Cl DE21. . . .**220** C5
Michlow Cl S33. . . . . . .**51** A8
Michlow Dr S33 . . . . . .**51** A8
Michlow La S33. . . . . . .**51** A8
Micklebring Cl DE5. .**169** C1
Micklecroft Gdns
DE23. . . . . **230** E7
Mickledon Cl [3]
NG10 . . . . **236** B8
MICKLEOVER. **217** E2
Mickleover Ho DE3 . .**230** D8
Mickleover Prim Sch
DE3. . . . . **217** D2
Mickleross Cl DE3 . . .**217** D4
Mickleton Cl DE11. . .**256** B1
MICKLEY. **56** B3
Mickley Inf Sch
DE55. . . . . **146** C4
Mickley La
Sheffield S17, S18 . . . . .**55** F4
Shirland DE55. . . . . . .**146** C5
Middlebeck Cl
DE73. . . . . **232** F2
Middle Cl DE11. . . . . .**256** B4
MIDDLECROFT. **97** C7
Middlecroft Rd S43. .**97** D7
Middlefield Cl
Derby DE22 . . . .**204** D4
Sheffield S17. . . . .**55** C7
Middlefield Croft
S17. . . . .**55** C7
Middlegate Field Dr
S80. . . . .**82** A5
MIDDLE HANDLEY. **77** F8
Middle Hay Cl S14. . . . .**43** E4
Middle Hay Pl S14. . . . .**43** E4
Middle Hay Rise S14 . . .**43** E4
Middle Hay View S14 .**43** E4

Middle La
Clay Cross S45. . . . . . .**131** E3
Crich DE4. . . . .**156** D1
Stanton Lees DE45. . . .**126** E3
MIDDLE MAYFIELD. .**184** B6
Middle Mdw S81 . . . . . .**63** E7
Middle Mill [2] DE1 . .**267** A4
Middle Orchard St
NG9. . . . . **223** D7
Middle Ox Cl S20 . . . . .**59** F6
Middle Ox Gdns S20 . .**59** F6
Middle Pavement
S40. . . . . **266** B3
MIDDLEPEAK. **154** E3
Middle Rd S42. . . . . . .**114** E1
Middle Row SK17. . . . . .**89** A7
Middle Shambles
S40. . . . . **266** B3
Middle St
Bolsover S44. . . . .**99** A1
Bolsover, Hillstown
S44. . . . .**118** C8
Stanton in Peak DE4. . .**126** C5
MIDDLETON
Wirksworth **154** D4
Youlgrave. **124** E3
Middleton Ave
Codnor DE5 . . . .**181** B6
Derby DE23 . . . .**218** C2
Middleton Cl DE11. . .**256** B1
Middleton Com Prim Sch
DE4. . . . . **154** D4
Middleton Dale
Foolow SK32. . . . .**70** F5
Hope Valley S32 . . . . . .**71** A5
Middleton Dr
Derby DE23 . . . .**218** C2
Staveley S43. . . . .**97** B5
Middleton Rd
Ilkeston DE7. . . . .**209** A5
Mansfield Woodhouse
NG19 . . . .**136** C5
Middleton DE4 . . . . . .**154** E2
Middleton St
Awsworth NG16 . . . . .**195** C4
Cossall DE7 . . . .**195** A1
Derby DE23 . . . .**219** A1
Middleton Top DE4 . .**154** C2
**Middleton Top Visitor
Ctr** ★ DE4 . . . .**154** D3
Middleton Way
DE55. . . . . **170** C7
Middletown Mdws
S43. . . . .**80** A6
Midgley La SK11. . . . . .**102** A1
Midhill Cres S2. . . . .**43** B7
Midhill Rd S2 . . . .**43** B7
Midland Ave NG9 . . . .**223** D5
Midland Cotts
Grindleford S32 . . . . . .**53** D2
Pleasley NG19 . . . . . .**135** A6
Rowsley DE4 . . . .**110** F1
Midland Ct
Barlborough S43 . . . . . .**80** A5
5 Chesterfield S41. . . .**115** B7
Midland Ind Est
DE56. . . . . **168** A4
Midland Pl DE1. . . . . .**267** D2
*Midland Railway
Butterley* ★ DE5 . . . . .**169** F4
*Midland Railway Ctr
The* ★ DE5. . . . .**169** F4
Midland Rd
Chapel-en-le-Frith
SK23. . . . .**47** A6
Derby DE1. . . . .**267** D1
Eastwood NG16 . . . . .**182** F2
Heanor DE75 . . . .**181** E2
Swadlincote DE11 . . . .**256** B4
Midland Road Ind Est
DE11. . . . . **256** B4
Midland St NG10 . . . .**236** E8
Midland Terr
Ambergate DE56 . . . .**167** F4
Barrow Hill S43 . . . . . .**78** B4
Blackwell DE55. . . . . .**147** C1
4 Chesterfield S41. . . .**115** B7
New Mills SK22. . . . . . .**33** C7
Midland View
7 Belper DE56. . . . . .**178** F3
North Wingfield S42. . .**131** F7
Midland Way S43. . . . . .**80** A5
Midway DE22 . . . .**204** E2
Midway Ctr S45 . . . . .**131** D4
Midway Rd DE11. . . . .**256** C5
Mikado Rd NG10. . . . .**236** C5
Milborne Ct DE24 . . .**217** E6
Milburn Gdns DE21. .**206** B3
Milbury Cl DE21 . . . . .**205** F2
Mile Ash La DE22. . . .**204** F1
MILEHILL. **115** F5
Milfoil Close DE24 . . .**231** C2
MILFORD. **191** A7
Milford DE45 . . . .**109** D6
Milford Ave NG10. . . .**223** B3
Milford Cl S42. . . . . . .**115** B4
Milford Ct DE45 . . . . .**109** D6
Milford Dr DE7 . . . . . .**194** D3
Milford Prim Sch
DE56. . . . . **190** F7
Milford Rd
Duffield DE56. . . . . . .**190** E4
Staveley S43. . . . .**97** C5
Milford St [4] DE1. . . .**218** F7
Milford The DE22. . . .**218** F5
Milken La S45. . . . .**130** B4
Milking La S43 . . . .**80** B3

Milkings La DE45 . . .**123** D8
Mill DE72. . . . .**235** A1
Mill Acre Cl DE4 . . . . .**194** D2
Millash La S80. . . . .**82** B4
Millbank DE75. . . . . . .**194** A8
Millbank Cl DE7 . . . . .**194** D3
Millbank Ct DE7 . . . . .**194** D3
Mill Bank Ct S32. . . . . .**53** B8
Mill Bank Dr ST14 . . .**197** A3
Millbridge S33 . . . .**38** C3
Mill Bridge S33. . . . . . .**38** C2
Millbrook SK14. . . . .**9** D6
Millbrook Ho SK14. . . . . .**9** E6
MILL BROW. **23** E8
Mill Brow
2 Broadbottom
SK14. . . . .**16** A8
Marple SK6. . . . .**23** D8
Mill Brow Rd SK6. . . . . .**23** E8
Mill Cl
Borrowash DE72 . . . . .**221** C1
Findern DE65 . . . .**230** D2
Kilburn DE56. . . . .**192** A7
Newton Solney DE15 . .**248** E8
Swadlincote DE11 . . . .**256** C5
Swanwick DE55 . . . . .**169** F7
Mill Cliff SK17. . . . .**85** C7
Mill Cres
Whitwell S80 . . . .**82** A6
Wingerworth S42. . . . .**115** C3
Mill Croft DE3 . . . .**217** D4
Millcross La S18. . . . . . .**75** E3
Mill Ct
Chinley SK23. . . . .**34** E1
Glossop SK13. . . . .**10** C1
MILLDALE. **149** F2
Milldale Ave SK17 . . . . .**84** F6
Milldale Cl
Chesterfield S40. . . . . .**95** C5
Ripley DE5 . . . .**180** D6
Milldale Ct
Ashbourne DE6. . . . . .**185** D8
Belper DE56. . . . .**179** B3
Milldale Rd
Derby DE21. . . . .**220** F3
Long Eaton NG10 . . . .**236** B6
Sheffield S17. . . . .**55** F5
Milldam La DE6 . . . . . .**186** E7
Millennium Ave
DE12. . . . . **262** E5
Millennium Cl DE7 . . .**194** E5
Millennium Ct NG19 .**135** E2
Millennium Way
Chesterfield S41. . . . . .**76** F1
Derby DE24 . . . .**219** A4
Whitwell S80 . . . .**82** A6
Miller Ave S43. . . . .**79** C4
Miller Dr DE7. . . . .**194** B5
Millers Ct DE7 . . . .**194** B4
MILLER'S DALE. **88** A2
Millersdale Ave
DE7. . . . . **194** E5
Millersdale Cl DE15. .**248** D5
Millers Dale Cl
DE56. . . . . **179** C5
Millersdale Ct [3]
SK13. . . . .**10** C1
Millersdale Dr
DE55. . . . . **160** A7
Millersdale Way
SK17. . . . .**85** B6
Millers Gn DE4 . . . . . .**165** E6
MILLERS GREEN. **165** E6
Millership Way
Ilkeston DE7. . . . .**194** F2
Ilkeston DE7. . . . .**195** A2
Millers La DE55 . . . . . .**145** E2
Millers Vale S42. . . . . . .**33** C8
Millers Way DE56. . . .**190** F8
Mill Farm Cl S32. . . . . .**72** C1
Mill Farm Dr [2]
DE55. . . . . **148** B7
Mill Fleam DE65 . . . . .**228** C1
Mill Gate DE22 . . . . . .**218** E6
Mill Gn
Shardlow DE72. . . . . .**235** A1
Staveley S43. . . . .**78** E2
Mill Green Way S43. . .**80** E4
Mill Hill
Elvaston DE24 . . . .**233** C4
Long Duckmanton
S44. . . . .**117** B6
Repton DE65. . . . .**242** E1
Mill Hill Cl DE5. . . . . .**169** F1
Mill Hill Dr DE15. . . . .**248** B4
Mill Hill La
Breaston DE72. . . . . . .**222** E1
Burton upon Trent
DE15. . . . .**248** B4
Derby DE1, DE23 . . . .**267** B1
Mill Hill Rd DE23 . . . .**267** A1
Mill Hill Sch DE15 . . .**180** F8
Mill Holme DE55. . . . .**160** B4
Millhouse Ct DE72. . .**235** B7
**MILLINGTON
GREEN**. **176** A4

Mill La
Ashbourne DE6. . . . . .**173** F1
Ashford in the Water
DE45. . . . .**108** F8
Ashover S45. . . . .**129** C5
Atlow DE6. . . . .**175** A7
Ault Hucknall S44 . . . .**133** C8
Barlow S18. . . . .**75** D4
Belper DE56. . . . .**179** B3
Bolsover S44. . . . .**99** A3
Bradbourne DE6 . . . . .**163** B6
Brailsford DE6 . . . . . .**201** C8
Castleton S33 . . . .**38** C3
Chesterfield S40. . . . . .**95** D2
Clay Cross S42, S45 . . .**130** F5
Clay Cross S45 . . . . . .**131** B2
Codnor DE5 . . . .**181** B8
Commonside DE6. . . .**187** D1
Cossall NG16 . . . .**195** C1
Cossall NG16 . . . .**209** C8
Cubley DE6 . . . .**212** E8
Cubley DE6 . . . .**212** F8
Cubley DE6 . . . .**213** A8
Derby DE3 . . . .**217** D4
Doveridge DE6 . . . . . .**211** A1
Dronfield S18 . . . .**57** B1
Ellastone DE6. . . . . . .**183** B2
Eyam S32 . . . .**71** E5
Grassmoor S42 . . . . . .**115** D3
Hartington SK17. . . . .**137** D5
Heath S44. . . . .**117** B1
Hilton DE65 . . . .**228** C2
Holloway DE4. . . . . . .**156** A5
Holmesfield S18. . . . . .**74** F5
Holmewood S42. . . . .**116** B4
Hope Valley S33 . . . . . .**40** B3
Longnor SK17. . . . . . .**121** B5
Old Bolsover S44. . . . . .**79** F1
Pinxton NG16 . . . .**160** D1
Renishaw S21. . . . .**60** A2
Roston DE6. . . . .**197** D7
1 Sandiacre NG10 . . .**223** C6
Scropton DE65. . . . . .**226** F1
Scropton, Foston
DE65. . . . .**226** D7
Sheffield S17. . . . .**55** F5
Shirley DE6. . . . .**200** D7
Shuttlewood S44 . . . . . .**98** F8
Somercotes DE55. . . .**170** C2
Sudbury DE6. . . . .**225** F1
Sutton in Ashfield
NG17. . . . .**148** F1
Tupton S42 . . . .**131** C2
Whitwell S80 . . . .**82** A6
Mill Meadow Way
DE65. . . . . **229** B4
Mill Moor Cl DE73. . . .**232** F2
Millom Pl DE21. . . . . .**205** D1
Millpond SK23. . . . .**34** F1
Mill Pond Ave SK22. . .**24** D1
Millpond Cl DE55 . . . .**158** E3
Mill Pond Cl
Hilton DE65 . . . .**228** C2
Strines SK6. . . . .**23** C2
Mill Pond Cotts
DE4. . . . . **155** A7
Millpool Cl DE11. . . . .**257** A7
Mill Rd
Cromford DE4. . . . . . .**155** B6
Eckington S21. . . . .**59** E4
Heanor DE75 . . . .**194** A8
Stapleford NG9. . . . . .**223** D8
Millrise S44. . . . .**99** A3
Mill Rise S42 . . . .**115** C3
Mill Row DE21 . . . . . .**220** D5
Mills Cl DE72 . . . .**235** A7
Mills Croft DE6 . . . . . .**164** B1
Mills Ct DE4 . . . .**156** F1
Mill St
Alfreton DE55. . . . . . .**159** C1
Bakewell DE45 . . . . . .**109** D6
Barlow S18. . . . .**75** D3
Belper DE56. . . . .**179** A4
Chesterfield S41. . . . .**266** C3
Clowne S43. . . . .**80** E3
Coton in the Elms
DE12. . . . .**260** D3
Derby DE1. . . . .**218** E6
Glossop SK13. . . . .**10** D1
Hayfield SK22. . . . .**25** D3
Ilkeston DE7. . . . .**194** F1
Rocester ST14 . . . . . .**197** A3
Somercotes DE55. . . .**170** C2
Stoney Middleton S32. .**72** A3
Millstone Cl [1] S18. . . .**56** D7
Millstone Ct DE4 . . . .**143** E7
Millstone La
Ashford in the Water
DE45. . . . .**108** F7
Ripley DE5 . . . .**169** F1
Mill Stream Cl S40. . . .**95** C1
Millstream Grange [2]
DE72. . . . . **221** D1
Mill Stream La
DE13. . . . . **241** A1
MILLTHORPE. **74** F5
Millthorpe La S18 . . . . .**75** A6
MILLTOWN. **145** B8
Milltown
Charlesworth SK13. . . . .**16** C8
Glossop SK13. . . . .**10** C1
Mill View DE56 . . . . . .**178** F5
Millward Dr DE3. . . . .**217** B2
Millway NG19. . . . .**136** D1
Millway La DE6. . . . . .**149** F3
Mill Wlk
Bolsover S44. . . . .**99** A3
Whitwell S80 . . . .**82** A6

Mill Wood La S80....82 D4
Mill Yd DE55 ....170 C8
Milnbank Ave SK17...85 D8
Milner Ave
  Codnor DE5 ....181 B8
  Draycott DE72 ......235 A7
Milner Rd NG10 ....236 D8
Milnhay Rd NG16 ...182 C2
MILTON 243 A1
Milton Ave
  Alfreton DE55.......159 C4
  Ilkeston DE7........194 E4
  Shirland DE55.......146 C4
  Swadlincote DE11 ...256 C6
Milton Cl DE3 ....217 C3
Milton Cres S40 .....115 A7
Milton Ct 12 SK17....85 B7
Milton La SK23......46 B5
Milton Pl S43........78 F2
Milton Rd
  Ilkeston DE7........194 E4
  Repton DE65........242 D2
Milton St
  Derby DE22 ....218 D4
  Ilkeston DE7........194 F4
  Long Eaton NG10 ...236 D7
Milton Terr NG10 ...236 D7
Milward Rd DE75 ...181 D2
Mimosa Cres DE23...231 E5
Miners Hill DE4.....153 A1
Minimum Terr S40 ..266 A2
Mining La DE4......164 E7
Minkley Dr NG16 ...182 C4
Minninglow La
  Ballidon DE4.......151 F7
  Ballidon DE4.......152 A6
  Parwich DE4.......151 F8
Minster Court DE24..232 F4
Minster Rd DE21....205 E2
Minster Way DE55 ..169 F7
Mint Gr NG10.......236 A7
Mint Gro DE3.......217 C5
Minton Rd DE74....246 F4
Miracle Ct DE45....109 D6
Mires La
  Great Longstone
    DE45.............90 B4
  Tideswell SK17......70 A3
Mires The
  Birchover DE4 ......126 A1
  Great Longstone DE45..90 B3
  Wetton DE6 ....149 A3
Miriam Ave
  Chesterfield S40.....114 A8
  Holymoorside S40 ...113 F8
Miry La DE65 ....227 C4
Miry Mdw SK23......47 B6
Misterton Cl DE22...204 E2
Misterton Ct 3
  NG19 ....136 B1
Mistletoe Dr DE11 ..256 F2
Mitcham Wlk DE22 ..218 A6
Mitchell Ave NG16..182 A4
Mitchells Cl DE65...229 A4
Mitchell St
  Clowne S43.........80 F4
  Long Eaton NG10....236 E7
Mitchell Terr DE7...209 A5
Mitchell Villas S43...77 E3
Mitchell Way S43....77 E3
Mitford Rd DE72....233 D3
Mitre DE11 ....261 B6
Mitre Dr DE65 ......242 C2
Mizzen Road S43....80 E5
Moat Bank DE15....248 D2
Moat The DE7......247 B4
Model La S80.......100 E8
Model View S80 ....100 E8
Model Village S80...100 E8
Model Village Prim Sch
  NG20 ....119 E3
Mods La S18........75 D3
Moffatt Rd S2 ....43 B7
MOIRA 262 E3
Moira Cl DE21......220 A7
Moira Dale DE74....247 C3
Moira Furnace Mus *
  DE12.............262 E3
Moira Junc Nature
  Reserve * DE12...262 D4
Moira Rd
  Donisthorpe DE12 ...262 F1
  Moira DE11.........262 E8
  Overseal DE12......262 B3
  Woodville DE11.....256 E2
Moira St DE73 ......252 A7
Moisty La
  Marchington ST14 ..224 C3
  Stoney Middleton S32...71 B3
Molineux Ave S43....78 D1
Molineux St DE23...219 B2
Molloy Pl 11 S8.....43 A6
Molloy St 10 S8.....43 A6
Molyneaux Bsns Pk
  DE4...............127 B3
Monarch Dr DE11...206 D3
Monarch Way DE75.181 D2
Moncreiff Dr
  Burton upon Trent
    DE13.............241 A1
  4 Stretton DE13...240 F1
Moncrieff Cres
  DE21.............261 D5
Mondello Dr DE24...233 C6
Moneyash Rd SK17.121 D6
Monk Rd
  Alfreton DE55......159 B2

Monk Rd continued
  Branston DE14......253 D8
Monk Road Ind Est
  DE55.............159 C2
Monks Cl
  Derby DE24 ....231 C3
  Ilkeston DE7........209 A8
Monksdale Cl SK17...69 B4
Monksdale La
  Tideswell SK17......68 F2
  Wheston SK17......68 F4
Monk's Rd SK13.....17 A4
Monk St
  Derby DE22 ....267 A2
  Tutbury DE13 ......239 C7
Monks Way S81......63 F7
Monkton Cl DE7....194 D3
Monkwood Rd S41...95 D8
Monmouth St DE21..219 D6
Monnies End S43.....80 D5
Monsal Ave SK17....85 D7
Monsal Cres
  Staveley S43........97 C6
  Tibshelf DE55......147 F6
Monsaldale Cl
  Burton upon Trent
    DE15.............248 B4
  Long Eaton NG10...236 B6
Monsal Dr
  Derby DE21 ....220 F3
  South Normanton
    DE55.............159 F5
Monsal Gr SK17......85 D7
MONSAL HEAD
  89 D4
Little Longstone DE45..89 D3
Monsall Ave DE7 ...194 E5
Monsdale La DE7...151 E2
Monsom La DE65...242 D3
Montague Way
  DE73.............232 E2
Montagu St S6 ......15 B2
Monteith Pl DE74...247 B4
Montford Mews
  DE74.............247 B4
Montgomery Cl
  DE65.............228 E2
Montpelier DE22 ...204 D7
Montpelier Cl DE14..254 A7
Montpelier Gdns 5
  SK17.............85 D8
Montpelier Pl SK17..66 D1
Montpelier Rd DE56..167 F3
Montrose Cl DE24...231 E4
Montrose Ct NG9 ...209 E1
Montrose Pl S18.....56 D2
Montrose Sq NG19..136 B6
Monument La NG16..170 E3
MONYASH 107 C2
Monyash CE Prim Sch
  DE45.............107 C1
Monyash Cl
  Derby DE21 ....220 A8
  Ilkeston DE7........194 E3
  Staveley S43........97 C7
Monyash Ct 32 SK13....9 D1
Monyash Gr 31 SK13...9 D1
Monyash Lea 33 SK13..9 D1
Monyash Mews 30
  SK13.............9 D1
Monyash Pl 29 SK13...9 D1
Monyash Rd
  Bakewell DE45......109 C5
  Over Haddon DE45...108 D2
  Over Haddon DE45...109 A2
Monyash Way
  Belper DE56........179 B5
  Buxton SK17........85 E7
  1 Gamesley SK13......9 E1
Moonpenny Way S18..57 A1
Moonstone Way
  Chesterfield S40....115 E7
  1 Swadlincote DE11..255 F4
Mooracre La S44....99 D1
Moorbridge La NG9..209 D1
Moorbrook La
  Bradwell S33.......50 F1
  Bradwell S33.......51 A7
Moor Cres S20 ......59 C7
Moor Croft DE4.....143 E7
Moor Dr DE24 ......233 B5
Moore Cl S42........116 D1
Moore St DE23 .....219 A3
Moor Farm Ave S20..59 B8
Moor Farm Cl DE55..148 B4
Moor Farm Garth
  S20..............59 C8
Moor Farm Rise S20..59 B8
Moor Farm Road E
  DE6..............185 F7
Moor Farm Road W
  DE6..............185 E8
MOORFIELD SK13...18 B6
Moorfield DE4......143 C7
Moorfield Ave S44...99 B1
Moorfield Cres 3
  NG10 ....223 B5
Moorfield Ct NG9...209 E1

Moorfield La NG20...100 F4
Moorfield Prec SK14...9 D5
Moorfield Rd DE56 ..191 C7
Moorfields Ave
  NG16.............182 F3
Moorfield Sq S44....99 B1
Moorfield St SK14....9 D5
Moorfield Terr SK14...9 D5
Moor Furlong DE13..240 F1
Moorgate DE22 .....217 E6
Moorgate Ave NG19..134 F7
Moorgate Cres S18...78 D8
MOORHAIGH 135 A3
Moorhaigh Close
  NG19.............134 F7
Moorhaigh La NG19..135 A3
MOORHALL 74 D2
Moorhall DE45 ....109 C5
Moorhay Cl S41 .....95 B7
Moorhead Ave DE24..232 F5
Moorhead Prim Sch
  DE24.............232 F6
Moorhen Dr S43.....98 A8
Moorings The SK12...32 E6
Moor La
  Aston-on-Trent
    DE72.............246 B8
  Barrow upon Trent
    DE73.............244 B8
  Bolsover S44 ....99 B1
  Bonsall DE4 ....142 B2
  Calow S44..........116 C8
  Dale Abbey DE7 ....207 F2
  Darley Dale DE4....127 C4
  Derby DE24 ....232 C6
  Elton DE4 ....140 E5
  Flagg SK17 ....106 E4
  Horsley DE7 ....192 A2
  Kirk Ireton DE6.....165 A3
  Kirk Langley DE6....202 F1
  Little Eaton DE21...191 E1
  Little Eaton DE21...205 D8
  Ockbrook DE72.....221 C6
  Osmaston DE6 .....185 F5
  Scarcliffe S44.......119 A8
  Taddington SK17....87 E1
  Youlgreave DE45....125 C5
Moorland Ave NG9...223 D6
Moorland CtrThe *
  S33..............37 C8
Moorland Dr S44....116 F2
Moorland Rd
  Derby DE3 ....217 D3
  Hathersage S32 .....53 A7
Moorlands Cl NG10..223 B2
Moorlands Dr DE4..184 C7
Moorlands La
  Bonsall DE4 ....142 B3
  Froggatt S32.......72 C5
Moorlands Rd DE56..168 B4
Moorland Terr DE4..144 A4
Moorland View
  Apperknowle S18....58 A1
  Sheffield S12........44 A2
Moorland View Rd
  S40..............95 C1
Moorlawn Ave S42...113 E7
Moorpark Ave S40...114 C8
Moorpool Cres
  DE56.............191 C7
Moor Rd
  Ashover S45........129 F3
  Breadsall DE7, DE21..205 F5
  Brinsley NG16......182 E8
  Fawfieldhead SK17...121 A1
  Great Longstone DE45,
    S32..............89 F6
  Great Longstone S32...90 A7
  Great Longstone SK17..89 F8
  Wardlow SK17......70 E1
Moor Rise DE56 ....191 C8
Moors Cl DE3.......230 B8
MOORSIDE 165 A2
Moorside Cl
  Cromford DE4......155 A5
  Glossop SK13.......17 B7
  Sheffield S20.......59 C8
Moorside Cres
  DE24.............231 F4
Moorside Gdns
  DE72.............234 C1
Moorside La DE56 ..191 C7
Moorspring Way
  S45..............131 B7
Moor St DE21.......220 E5
Moor The
  Brinsley NG16......182 D8
  Middleton DE4 .....154 C4
  Tideswell SK17......69 C5
Moorthorpe Gn S20..44 F2
Moorthorpe Way
  S20..............44 F2
Moortop Rd S18, S21..58 B1
Moor Valley S20......44 F2
Moorview Cl
  Brimington S43......96 D7
  Wingerworth S42....115 B5
Moorview Ct 2 S17...56 B5
Moor View Rd S43...79 A2
Moorway DE21......205 E4
Moorway Croft
  DE23.............231 B7
Moorway La DE23...231 B6
Moorways Sports Ctr
  DE24.............232 D6
Moorwinstow Croft
  S17..............55 E7
Moorwood La S17....55 C1

Moorwoodmoor La
  DE55.............157 D6
Moray Cl DE11......255 F1
Moray Ct NG16.....195 F7
Moray Pl S18........56 D2
Moray Wlk DE21....219 C8
Mordaunt Rd S2.....43 F6
Morden Gn DE22 ...218 A6
Morden Rd NG16....195 C8
Morefern Dr DE21...205 F2
Morel Cl NG16......182 F1
Morcton La ST14 ...225 B1
Morewood Dr DE55..159 B5
Morgana Rd NG19 ..135 D1
Morland Bank S14...43 F3
Morland Cl S14......43 F3
Morland Dr S14.....43 F3
Morland Pl S14......43 F3
Morland Rd
  Hayfield SK22.......25 B2
  Sheffield S14.......43 F3
Morledge
  Derby DE1 ....267 C3
  Matlock DE4 ....142 F6
  1 Matlock DE4 .....143 A7
Morleston St DE23..267 C1
MORLEY 206 C6
Morley Almshouses La
  DE7..............206 B7
Morley Ave S40......95 C4
Morley Cl
  Belper DE56 ....179 E6
  Burton upon Trent
    DE15.............248 B2
  Dronfield S18 ......56 C1
  5 Heanor DE75....181 F1
Morley Dr DE7......194 D3
Morleyfields Cl DE55..169 F1
Morley Gdns DE21...220 B8
Morley Ho
  Derby, Alvaston
    DE24.............233 A7
  1 Derby, Markeaton
    DE3.............217 D1
Morley La
  Little Eaton DE7,
    Morley DE21.......205 E8
  Morley DE21........206 F6
  Stanley DE7 ....207 B6
Morley Mews DE21..220 A7
Morley Pk Rd DE56..179 E6
Morley Prim Sch
  DE7..............206 C7
Morley St
  Derby DE22 ....218 C5
  Glossop SK13.......17 D8
Morlich Dr DE24....231 E5
Morningside Cl
  DE24.............232 D4
Mornington Cl
  NG10.............223 C6
Mornington Cres
  DE22.............218 B6
Mornington Rd S42..132 D8
Mornington Rise
  DE4..............143 C4
Morpeth Gdns
  DE21.............205 D3
Morrells La DE56 ...190 F7
Morrell Wood Dr
  DE56.............179 D5
Morris Ave S41......95 E5
Morris Dr S41.......95 E5
Mortimer Rd S33....43 F6
Mortimer St DE24 ..232 C7
MORTON 146 F5
Morton Ave
  Clay Cross S45......131 B4
  Ilkeston DE7........194 F6
Morton Gdns S20....59 F6
Morton La S18, S21..58 C1
Morton Mount S20...59 F7
Morton Prim Sch
  DE55.............147 A5
Morton Rd
  Pilsley S45.........147 C8
  Shirland DE55......146 D6
Morton St NG19 ....135 E1
Morven Ave
  Bolsover S44 ....99 B1
  Mansfield Woodhouse
    NG19.............136 B2
Morven St S80......100 F8
MOSBOROUGH.....59 D7
Mosborough Hall Dr
  S20..............59 E6
Mosborough Hall Farm
  S20..............59 D6
Mosborough Moor
  S20..............59 B8
Mosborough Parkway
  S13..............44 F7
Mosborough Pkway
  S12..............44 F7
Mosborough Prim Sch
  S20..............59 E6
Mosborough Rd S13..44 B7
Moscow Farm Ct
  DE56.............190 F5
Mosedale Cl DE24 ..232 F8
Moseley St S5......169 D2
Moses La DE7 ......206 E7
Moses View S43......63 F7
Mosley Rd ST14....210 A1
Mosley Mews DE13..240 A4
Mosley Rd SK17.....85 B6
Mossbank Cl SK13....9 E4

Moss Beck Ct S21 ...59 C2
Mossbrook Ct S21...59 C4
Mossbrook Sch S8...57 C8
Mosscar Cl NG20....120 F1
Mosscar La NG20....120 F1
Mossdale Ave S20....59 D7
Moss Dr S21 ....60 D5
Moss Edge Rd HD9...3 C8
Moss House Ct S20...59 D6
Moss La
  Broadbottom SK14....15 F8
  Hulland Ward DE6 ..175 F4
  Ripley DE5 ....169 D3
Moss Rd
  Ilkeston DE7........208 E7
  Sheffield S17 ....55 B4
Moss Rise Pl S21 ...59 C3
Moss St
  Derby DE22 ....218 E3
  Hollingworth SK14....9 D5
Moss The SK17......102 D1
Mossvale Dr DE23 ..231 A6
Moss View S20 ......59 C6
Moss View Rd SK23..47 C5
Moston Wlk S40 ...114 E6
Mostyn Ave S21.....218 D1
Mottistone Cl DE24..233 D5
Mottram CE Prim Sch
  SK14.............9 A4
Mottram Fold SK14...9 A3
MOTTRAM IN
  LONGDENDALE....9 B4
Mottram Moor SK14...9 B4
Mottram Old Rd
  SK14.............15 B8
Mottram Rd SK14...16 A8
Moulbourn Dr DE56..190 D4
Mouldridge La DE4..139 F2
Moult Ave DE21 ....220 E4
Moulton Cl
  Belper DE56 ....179 D5
  Swanwick DE55.....169 F8
Mound Rd S40 .....266 B1
Mountbatten Cl
  DE24.............232 E4
Mountbatten Ct
  DE7..............194 F3
Mount Carmel St
  DE23.............267 A1
Mountcastle St S41...95 F8
Mountcastle Wlk S41..95 F8
Mount Cres DE55 ...160 A3
Mountfield Ave
  NG10.............223 A4
Mountfield Way
  DE24.............233 D4
Mountford Ave DE4..165 E7
Mountford Cl DE21..206 B2
Mountford Croft S17..55 E5
MOUNT PLEASANT
  Belper............178 D6
  Blackwell..........147 F2
  Castle Gresley......261 E7
  Melbourne.........251 F8
  Repton............242 E1
Mount Pleasant
  Ashford in the Water
    DE45.............108 F8
  Buxworth SK23......46 A8
  Castle Donington
    DE74.............247 B3
  Cromford DE4......155 B7
  Ilkeston DE4.......194 E4
  Ripley DE5 ....169 D2
  Somercotes DE55....170 D5
  Youlgreave DE45....125 C5
Mount Pleasant Ct
  S32..............72 C8
Mount Pleasant Dr
  Belper DE56 ....178 E5
  Heage DE56 ....179 E8
Mount Pleasant La
  Nethersoal DE12 ...265 A8
  Overseal DE12......262 B1
Mount Pleasant Rd
  Castle Gresley DE12..262 A2
  Grindleford S32 .....72 C8
  Linton DE11 ....261 E8
  Mount Pleasant DE11..261 F7
  Repton DE65.......242 E1
  Swadlincote DE11 ...256 A1
Mount Pleaseant
  SK6..............15 B3
Mount Rd
  Bretby DE15.......249 A3
  Compstall SK14 ....15 A6
  Hartshorne DE11....257 A4
  Linton DE11 ....261 D8
Mount St Mary's RC Coll
  S21..............60 C2
Mount St
  Breaston DE72.....235 F7
  Burton upon Trent
    DE15.............248 A3
  Derby DE1 ....267 B1
  Glossop SK13.......17 C8
  Heanor DE75.......181 E1
  Mansfield NG19 ....136 A1
  Stapleford NG9.....223 E7
Mount The
  Chesterfield S41.....77 A3
  Stapleford NG9.....223 D6
Mount View Ave S8..43 A4
Mount View Rd S8...43 F3
Mount View Lodge 2
  S8..............43 A3

Mouselow Mews
  SK13.............10 A3
Mowbray Gdns
  DE24.............232 C7
Mowbray St DE24...232 D8
Moy Ave DE24......231 F2
Moyne Gdns
  Chellaston DE73....245 A8
  13 Derby DE73.....244 F8
MUDD 9 A2
Mudhurst La SK12...32 E3
MUGGINTON.......188 F7
Mugginton CE Prim Sch
  DE6..............188 E2
MUGGINTONLANE END
  188 E6
  DE56.............188 E7
Muirfield Cl S41.....96 B6
Muirfield Dr
  Derby DE3 ....217 F2
  Derby DE3 ....218 A2
Muirfield Way
  NG19.............136 E6
Mulberries Ct DE22..204 E4
Mulberry Cl
  Belper DE56 ....179 B3
  Wingerworth S42....115 A4
Mulberry Croft
  Brimington S43......78 A1
  Staveley S43........78 A1
Mulberry Gdns 5
  ST14.............210 A1
Mulberry Grove
  S42..............131 C7
Mulberry Mews
  DE5..............180 C6
Mulberry Rd S21....59 B2
Mulberry Way
  Aston-on-Trent
    DE72.............246 A6
  Branston DE14.....253 E6
  Branston DE14.....256 E6
  Hilton DE65........228 E2
  Killamarsh S21......60 B5
Mulberry Wlk S45...132 C4
Mull Ct 3 DE24....231 D3
Mullion Pl DE24....233 B5
Mumford Dr DE6 ...185 D8
Mundella Pl S8......43 A3
Mundella Prim Sch 5
  S8..............43 A3
Mundy CE Jun Sch
  DE75.............193 F8
Mundy Cl DE1......218 E6
Mundy's Dr DE75...193 F8
Mundy St
  Derby DE1 ....218 E6
  Heanor DE75.......181 E1
  Ilkeston DE7........194 E2
Munro Cl S21.......60 D6
Munro Ct DE24.....231 E4
Murdoch Rd DE24..219 E3
Murrayfield Dr 6
  S20..............59 E6
Murray La S42......115 C2
Murray Park Sch
  DE3..............217 F4
Murray Rd
  Derby DE1 ....217 F4
  Killamarsh S21......60 E7
Murray St DE24.....232 F8
Musard Pl S43......78 E1
Musard Way S21....60 C6
Muse La
  Boylestone DE6 ....213 A2
  Church Broughton
    DE6.............226 B7
Museum of Making *
  DE1..............267 B4
Musgrave Ho S33....40 B3
Mushroom Farm Ct
  NG16.............182 D3
Mushroom La
  Albert Village DE11..256 C1
  Moira DE11........262 D8
Muskham Ave DE4..194 F3
Muskham Ct 1
  S18..............136 B1
Mus of Industry &
  History The (Silk Mill
  Mus) * DE1 .....267 B4
Musters St NG20...120 A4
Muswell Rd DE22 ..217 E5
Mycock La
  Flagg SK17........106 F4
  Flagg SK17........106 F5
Myers Cl DE24.....231 F4
Mynd The NG19 ....136 E6
Myrce Way S17.....55 E6
Myrtle Ave
  Derby DE3 ....217 C4
  Long Eaton NG10 ...236 C6
  Stapleford NG9.....223 E6
Myrtle Cl
  Sheffield S2 ....43 C6
  Shirebrook NG20....119 D6
Myrtle Cres S2......43 C7
Myrtle Gr S43.......78 A1
Myrtle Rd S2........43 B7
Myrtle Springs Dr
  S12..............43 F5
Mytham Bridge S33..40 B1
Mytholme Cl NG10..223 C2

N

Nabb La ST14 196 A4
Naggle Gate Close
DE7 193 B1
Nailers Way DE56 179 C5
Nailor La DE4 142 D3
Nairn Ave DE21 219 D7
Nairn Cl DE24 231 D3
Nairn Dr S18 56 D1
Namur Cl DE22 218 C3
Nan Gell's Hill DE4 155 A3
Napier Cl
Derby DE3 217 E4
Swadlincote DE11 255 E2
Napier Ct S43 80 B5
Napier St DE22 218 C5
Naples Cres NG19 134 F5
Napoleon Pk DE24 232 E7
Narlow La DE6 161 F2
Narrowdale La
Alstonefield SK17 149 C7
Clay Cross SK17 131 D2
Narrowgate La SK17 70 D3
Narrow La
Denstone ST14 196 D6
Donisthorpe DE12 265 E8
Ticknall DE73 250 F4
Narrowleys La S45 129 F3
Naseby Cl DE3 217 C3
Naseby Dr NG10 236 E4
Naseby Rd DE56 179 D4
Nathaniel Rd NG10 236 F7
National Sikh Her Ctr & Holocaust Mus*
DE23 219 B1
National Stone Ctr*
DE4 154 F3
National Tramway Mus*
DE4 156 E2
Natterer Grove
DE23 230 F8
Navigation Home Park
DE24 232 E8
Navigation Way S18 57 D1
Neal Ct NG16 182 A3
Neale Bank S43 96 D7
Neale St
Clowne S43 80 F4
Long Eaton NG10 236 E7
Near Mdw NG10 236 E5
Nearwell Cl SK23 46 F6
Nearwood Dr DE21 205 E3
Needham St DE5 181 B8
Needham Terr DE4 143 A7
Needwood Ave
DE13 240 C4
Need Wood Ave
NG9 209 D2
Needwood Ct DE13 239 C6
Neighwood Cl NG9 223 E2
Neilson St DE24 232 F7
Nelper Cres DE7 209 A5
Nelson Cl DE3 217 F3
Nelson Pl LE65 257 F3
Nelson St
Burton upon Trent
DE15 248 C4
Chesterfield S41 96 A6
Derby DE1 219 C3
Derby DE1 267 D1
1 Heanor DE75 181 D2
Ilkeston DE7 194 F3
Long Eaton NG10 236 D6
Swadlincote DE11 256 B5
Nene Cl DE13 240 C1
Nene Way DE65 240 D8
Nerissa Cl DE73 232 E2
Nesbit St S44 118 B8
Nesfield Cl
Chesterfield S41 95 D8
Derby DE24 233 C7
Nesfield Ct DE7 194 E1
Nesfield Rd DE7 194 E1
Ness Wlk DE22 204 E3
Nestor Cl DE73 232 D2
Nether Ave S21 60 C6
NETHER BIGGIN 175 F5
Nether Blindlow La
SK17 106 B5
NETHER BOOTH 29 A1
NETHER BURROWS 202 C3
Netherby Manor S17 56 A7
NETHER CHANDERHILL 94 C1
Nether Cl
Duffield DE56 190 E5
Eastwood NG16 182 F4
Swanwick DE55 169 F7
Wingerworth S42 115 A2
Netherclose St
DE23 219 A1
Nether Croft Cl S43 96 E7
Nethercroft La S45 131 E3
Nether Croft Rd S43 96 E7
Netherdene Rd S18 57 A1
Nether End
Baslow DE45 91 F5
Baslow DE45 92 A5
Nether Farm Cl S43 96 F5
Netherfield Cl
Ashbourne DE6 185 C8
Netherfield Cl *continued*
Staveley S43 79 A2
Uttoxeter ST14 210 C1
Netherfield Close
DE4 143 C4
Netherfield La
Castle Donington DE72,
DE74 247 F8
Hollins S42 94 A3
Wadshelf S42 93 F2
Netherfield Rd
Chapel-en-le-Frith
SK23 47 D6
Chesterfield S40 114 A8
Long Eaton NG10 236 C4
Sandiacre NG10 223 B4
Netherfields Cres
S18 76 A8
Nether Gdns DE4 165 F8
NETHER GREEN 60 D7
Nethergreen Ave
S21 60 D7
Nethergreen Ct S21 60 D7
Nethergreen Gdns
S21 60 D7
Netherhall Rd DE11 256 F8
NETHER HANDLEY 77 F7
NETHER HEAGE 168 C1
Nether La
Brassington DE4 163 F8
Hazelwood DE56 190 A7
Holbrook DE56 191 D6
Kirk Ireton DE6 176 B8
NETHER LANGWITH 101 B1
Netherleigh Ct S40 95 B3
Netherleigh Rd S40 95 B3
Nether Mill Ct 3
DE4 155 A1
Nethermoor Ave S21 60 D7
Nethermoor Cl S21 60 D7
Nethermoor Cotts
DE55 147 D5
Nethermoor Dr S21 60 D7
Nethermoor La S21 60 D7
Nethermoor Rd
Tupton S42 131 C8
Wingerworth S42 115 A1
NETHER PADLEY 53 E1
Nether Park Dr
DE22 204 C1
NETHER PILSLEY 132 D1
NETHERSEAL 264 E7
Netherseal Rd
Chilcote DE12 264 F4
Clifton Campville B79 263 F2
Clifton Campville
DE12 264 A3
Netherside S33 51 A7
Netherside Dr DE73 233 B2
Nether Slade Road
DE7 194 E2
Nether Springs Rd
S44 98 F3
NETHER STURSTON 173 F1
NETHERTHORPE 79 A2
Netherthorpe S43 79 A2
Netherthorpe Airfield
S80 63 B5
Netherthorpe Cl
Killamarsh S21 60 C7
Staveley S43 78 F2
Netherthorpe La S21 60 C7
Netherthorpe Rd 3
S43 78 F2
Nether Thorpe Rd
S80 63 B5
Netherthorpe Sch
S43 79 A2
Nether View S44 99 B4
Nether Way DE4 127 C3
Nether Wheel Row
S13 44 F5
Netherwood Ct
DE22 204 C3
Netley Rd DE24 233 D4
Nettlefold Cres
DE73 245 B1
Nettleship Rd NG16 195 F6
Nettleton Cl DE23 231 A6
Nettleton La SK17 85 D3
Nettleworth Inf Sch
NG19 136 C4
Networkcentre Barlborough Links
S43 80 A5
Neville Cl DE13 240 B3
Nevinson Ave DE23 231 D7
Nevinson Dr DE23 231 D7
Nevis Cl
Chesterfield S40 95 D4
Derby DE24 231 D2
Newark 8 S20 59 E8
Newark Rd DE21 205 D2
Newark St DE24 233 E4
New Bank St SK13 10 A5
NEW BARLBOROUGH 80 D5
New Barlborough Cl
S43 80 D5
Newbarn Cl NG20 119 D2
New Bath Rd DE4 155 A8
New Beetwell St
Chesterfield S40 95 F3
Chesterfield S40 266 B2
Newbery Ave NG10 236 F6
NEWBOLD 95 E6
Newbold Ave
Borrowash DE72 221 C1
Chesterfield S41 95 E6
Newbold Back La
S40 95 E5
Newbold CE Prim Sch
S41 95 E7
Newbold Cl DE73 232 F2
Newbold Ct 1 S41 95 D7
Newbold Dr
Castle Donington
DE74 247 B5
Chesterfield S41 95 E6
NEWBOLD MOOR 95 F7
Newbold Rd
Chesterfield S40 95 D6
Chesterfield S41 95 B7
NEW BOLSOVER 98 F2
New Bolsover S44 98 F1
New Bolsover Prim Sch
S44 98 F1
Newborough Rd
DE24 233 C6
Newbound La NG17 134 D2
Newboundmill La
NG19 135 A4
New Breck Rd DE56 179 A3
New Bridge S32 72 C3
Newbridge Cl DE7 207 D8
Newbridge Cres
DE24 232 E4
Newbridge Ct S41 77 A1
Newbridge Dr S43 96 D8
Newbridge La
Brimington S43 96 D8
Chesterfield S41 77 B1
Newbridge Rd DE56 168 A2
Newbridge St S41 77 A1
NEW BRIMINGTON 77 F1
NEW BRINSLEY 171 E1
Newburgh Terr S32 72 C2
Newbury Dr DE13 240 C1
Newbury St DE24 232 E8
Newby Cl DE15 248 B1
Newby Rd S41 95 C8
Newcastle St
Mansfield Woodhouse
NG19 136 B3
Sutton in Ashfield
NG17 148 F3
Newchase Bsns Pk
DE23 219 C1
New Chestnut Pl
DE23 231 E7
New Church St S33 51 A7
New City Park Homes
DE24 220 A1
New Cl S32 71 C6
New Cl La DE45 109 B2
New Cotts
Buxton SK17 84 E4
Whaley Thorns NG20 101 F3
Newcrest Cl DE23 218 B1
Newdelves Ct 2
DE75 193 E8
New Derby Rd
NG16 182 D3
Newdigate St
Derby DE23 232 A8
Ilkeston DE7 209 A6
Kimberley NG16 195 F6
West Hallam DE7 207 C8
New Eaton Rd NG9 223 E5
Newell Way DE4 127 C3
New England Way
NG19 135 C3
New Fall St NG17 148 F3
Newfield Cres S17 55 C7
Newfield Croft S17 55 C8
Newfield Farm Cl
S14 43 E5
NEWFIELD GREEN 43 D5
Newfield Green Rd
S2 43 D6
Newfield La S17 55 C7
Newfield Pl S17 55 C7
Newfield Rd DE15 248 B4
Newfields DE12 262 F4
Newfield Secondary Sch
S8 43 C3
New Gardens DE45 109 D5
NEWGATE
75 D1
Newgate S18 75 D1
Newgate Cl DE73 233 B2
NEWHALL 255 F6
Newhall Com Jun Sch
DE11 255 E6
Newhall Inf Sch
DE11 255 F7
Newhall Rd DE11 256 C5
New Hall Rd S40 95 D2
Newham Ave DE5 169 C1
Newham Cl DE75 182 A1
Newham Close
DE22 217 F5
NEWHAVEN 138 F5
Newhaven Ave
NG19 136 B3
Newhaven Cl S40 95 B1
New Haven Gdns
S17 55 E4
Newhaven Rd DE21 220 B6
Newhay
Burton upon Trent
DE13 240 F1
Stretton DE13 241 A1
New High St SK17 85 D8
Newhill Lane S12 44 F4
Newholme Hospl
DE45 109 D7
NEW HORWICH 45 E6
New Horwich Rd
SK23 45 E7
NEW HOUGHTON 134 F7
New Houses
Chesterfield S41 96 C3
Tideswell SK17 88 E8
New Inn La DE21 205 C7
New La
Bradwell S33 50 E6
Hilcote DE55 148 C1
Over Haddon DE45 109 C1
Newland Dale S41 266 B4
Newland Gdns S41 95 E5
NEWLANDS 181 F2
Newlands Ave
Chesterfield S40 95 C3
Sheffield S12 44 A6
Newlands Barns
DE22 189 E3
Newlands Cl
Ripley DE5 169 E2
Swadlincote DE11 256 A2
Newlands Cres
DE55 148 A3
Newlands Dr
Glossop SK13 9 F4
Heanor DE75 181 E3
Sheffield S12 44 A6
Somercotes DE55 170 D5
Newlands Gr S12 44 B6
Newlands Ho DE55 170 D4
Newlands Inn Sta*
DE55 170 C3
Newlands Pk DE55 170 D5
Newlands Rd
Sheffield S12 44 A6
Somercotes DE55 170 C4
Newland St DE1 267 A3
Newlands The DE4 155 A7
New Lane Galleries
DE55 159 A4
New Lawn Rd DE7 208 E8
New Linden St
NG20 120 A4
New Lumford DE45 109 C7
Newlyn Dr
3 Derby DE23 231 F8
South Normanton
DE55 160 C6
Newlyn Pl S8 43 A3
Newman Dr
Burton upon Trent
DE14 254 B8
Swadlincote DE11 255 E2
Newmanleys Rd
NG16 194 F8
Newmanleys Rd (South)
NG16 182 E1
Newmanleys Road S
NG16 194 E8
NEWMARKET 131 A2
Newmarket Ct DE24 219 E1
Newmarket Dr
DE24 232 E8
Newmarket La S45 130 F3
New Market St SK17 85 B6
Newmarket Way
NG9 223 F2
New Mill La NG19 136 E3
NEW MILLS 33 D7
New Mills Adult Com Ed
Ctr SK22 33 C8
New Mills Central Sta
SK22 33 B7
New Mills Her Ctr*
SK22 33 B7
New Mills L Ctr SK22 33 C8
New Mills Newtown Sta
SK22 33 B6
New Mills Prim Sch
SK22 33 B8
New Mills Rd
Broadbottom SK13 16 B4
Hayfield SK22 25 B3
New Mills Sch and Sixth
From Ctr 1 SK22 33 C8
New Mount Cl DE23 231 D5
Newness Ct 4 DE4 143 C6
New Orchard Pl
DE3 217 D2
New Park Ct SK22 33 D7
New Park Pl DE24 219 D3
Newport Cres NG19 135 E1
Newport Ct DE24 233 C5
Newquay Pl DE24 233 C5
New Queen St S41 266 B4
New Rd
Alderwasley DE4 167 B8
Alderwasley DE56 156 B1
Alfreton DE55 170 E5
Apperknowle S18 58 A1
Bamford S33 40 B5
Barlborough S43 80 B7
Barton in Fabis NG11 237 F6
Belper DE56 178 F3
Boylestone DE6 213 B4
Bradwell S33 51 A4
Bradwell, Bradwell Hills
S33 51 B6
Coton in the Elms
DE12 260 D3
Crich DE4 168 A8
Denstone ST14 196 F5
Derby DE22 205 A1
New Rd *continued*
Eyam S32 71 F5
Fawfieldhead SK17 121 B1
Flash SK17 102 F1
Flash SK17 103 A3
Glossop SK13 9 F7
Grindleford S32 72 B5
Heage DE56 179 D8
Hilton DE65 228 E2
Hollinsclough SK17 104 D1
Holmesfield S18 75 A5
Holymoorside S42 113 D7
Horwich End SK23 45 E6
Idridgehay DE56 176 F4
Ironville NG16 170 F3
Middleton DE4 154 B5
Ridgeway DE56 168 B4
Somercotes DE55 170 E7
Somercotes NG16,
DE55 170 D2
Stapleford NG9 209 D1
Swadlincote DE11 255 E6
Uttoxeter ST14 210 A1
Weston Underwood
DE6 188 D1
Whaley Bridge SK23 34 A1
Whaley Bridge, Bridgemont
SK23 33 F1
Wingerworth S42 114 E3
Wirksworth DE4 155 A3
Woodville DE11 256 E2
Youlgreave DE45 125 C5
New Rd (Baslow Rd)
DE45 108 F8
New Road Ind Est
NG9 209 D1
New Row NG16 171 A5
NEW SAWLEY 236 B5
New School Cl S20 59 C7
New School Ct S20 59 C7
New School Rd S20 59 C7
New Scott St NG20 101 A2
Newshaw La SK13 9 F4
NEW SMITHY 35 A1
New Sq S40 266 B3
New St
Alfreton DE55 159 A4
Bakewell DE45 109 D6
Bolsover S44 99 A3
3 Broadbottom SK14 16 A8
Buxton SK17 67 B5
Chesterfield S40 266 B2
Derby DE1 219 B4
Derby DE1 267 C2
Donisthorpe DE12 262 E1
Draycott DE72 235 A7
Grassmoor S42 115 F3
Hilcote DE55 160 C8
Little Eaton DE21 205 C8
Long Eaton NG10 236 E8
Matlock DE4 143 C5
New Mills SK22 33 D7
Newton DE55 148 A4
North Wingfield S42 131 F6
Ockbrook DE72 221 C4
Pilsley S45 132 D1
Ripley DE5 169 E1
Rosliston DE12 260 D6
Sheffield, Holbrook
S20 60 A8
Shirland DE55 146 C2
Somercotes DE55 170 C8
South Normanton
DE55 160 A6
Stanley DE7 207 C6
Stonebroom DE55 147 A5
Sutton in Ashfield
NG17 148 F3
Swadlincote DE11 256 B2
Swanwick DE55 169 E7
Tupton S45 131 C8
Whitwell S80 81 E5
NEW STANTON 208 E3
New Station Rd S44 99 B1
Newstead Ave
Derby DE21 219 F6
Sheffield S12 44 E3
Newstead Cl
Dronfield S18 56 C1
Sheffield S12 44 E3
Newstead Ct SK17 84 F7
Newstead Dr S12 44 E2
Newstead Gr S12 44 E3
Newstead Rd
Long Eaton NG10 223 C3
Sheffield S12 44 F3
Newstead Rise S12 44 F2
Newstead Road N
DE7 194 D3
Newstead Road S
DE7 194 D3
Newstead Terr 3
SK17 85 B6
Newstead Way S12 44 E2
New Street Bus Link
S20 60 A8
New Terr
Pleasley NG19 134 F5
Sandiacre NG10 223 B6
NEWTHORPE 195 A8
Newthorpe Comm
NG16 195 A8
NEWTHORPE COMMON 195 A8
NEWTON 148 B3
Newton Cl
Belper DE56 179 C6
Newton Solney DE15 248 E8
Newton Ct 16 S41 95 F8
Newtondale Ave
NG19 136 E1
Newton Dr
Eastwood NG16 182 A1
Stapleford NG9 223 E6
Newton Gn DE3 217 F2
NEWTON GREEN 148 A4
Newton La
Bretby DE15 249 A5
Newton Solney DE15 248 F7
Tibshelf DE55 147 F6
Newton Leys DE15 248 C4
Newtonmore Dr
DE22 218 B3
Newton Park Cl 2
DE11 256 A7
Newton Pk
Burton upon Trent
DE15 248 D7
Newton Solney DE15 248 D7
Newton Prim Sch
DE55 148 A3
Newton Rd
Burton upon Trent
DE15 248 A5
Tibshelf DE55 147 F4
Newtons Croft Cres
S43 80 B6
Newtons La NG16 195 B4
NEWTON SOLNEY 248 E8
Newton Solney CE (Aided) Infant Sch
DE15 248 E8
Newton's Wlk DE22 218 E8
Newton Wonder Ct
DE73 245 B1
Newtonwood La
Tibshelf DE55 148 B5
Tibshelf DE55, NG17 148 C5
NEW TOTLEY 55 E4
NEWTOWN 33 B6
Newtown Prim Sch
SK22 33 B6
New Tythe St NG10 236 F7
New Victoria Ct
DE24 232 E5
NEW WESTWOOD 171 C4
New Westwood
NG16 171 D4
New Whittington Com Prim Sch S43 77 D3
New Whittington Com Prim Sch (Handley Rd Site) S43 77 D4
New Wye St SK17 85 C8
NEW YORK 252 A7
NEW ZEALAND 218 C5
New Zealand La
DE56 190 E2
New Zealand Sq
DE22 218 C5
Nicholas Cl
Derby DE21 220 E6
3 Ilkeston DE7 208 F6
5 Ilkeston DE7 209 A6
Nicholas St S41 115 D7
Nicholson Ct
9 Sheffield S8 43 B6
Tideswell SK17 69 C4
Nicholson Pl 7 S8 43 B6
Nicholson Rd S8 43 A6
Nicholson's Row
NG20 119 F3
Nicklaus Cl DE14 254 A7
Nicola Gdns DE23 231 D4
Nicolas Cl SK17 85 E8
Nidderdale Ct DE24 233 D6
Nields Way SK6 23 D4
Nightingale Ave
NG19 135 A4
Nightingale Bsns Pk
DE24 232 D8
Nightingale Cl
Chesterfield S41 96 A4
Chesterfield S41 266 B4
Clay Cross S45 131 E2
Holloway DE4 155 F6
Kelstedge S45 129 D4
Ripley DE5 169 D1
Nightingale Dr
Mansfield NG19 135 E1
Woodville DE11 256 F3
Nightingale Gr
DE55 160 C5
Nightingale Mews
DE1 267 D2
Nightingale Rd
DE24 232 C8
Nightingale Way
DE65 229 C3
Nikolas Rd S21 60 B1
Nimbus Way NG16 195 F7
Nine Corners NG16 195 F6
Nine Ladies Stone Circle* DE4 126 D3
Ninelands Rd S32 53 A7
Ninth Ave
Branston DE14 253 E8
Branston DE14 256 E8
NITHEN END 84 F8
Nitticarhill Rd
Barlborough S26 61 D1
Barlborough S43 80 C8
Nix's Hill DE55 159 B2
Noahs Arc ST14 210 E1
Noble Rd S42 131 F7
Noble St DE1 267 D1

Noc–Old 301

Noctule La DE3 230 E8
Nodder Rd S13 44 C7
Nodin Hill La DE56 168 B3
Noe La S33 40 A2
Noel-Baker Acad DE24 233 A4
Noel-Baker Sch DE24 232 F4
Noel St DE22 218 D6
No Mans Heath Rd B79 264 B2
No Man's Heath Rd DE12 264 F3
No Man's La DE7, DE27 222 D7
Nook End Rd DE75 181 D1
Nook La S44 97 B3
Nook The
Barrow upon Trent DE73 244 A6
Eyam S32 71 D6
Heanor DE75 181 C4
Holbrook DE56 191 C7
Shirebrook NG20 119 D3
Stoney Middleton S32 72 A4
Nooning La DE72 234 E8
NORBRIGGS 79 C3
Norbriggs Prim Sch S43 79 B3
Norbriggs Rd S43 79 C2
Norburn Dr S21 60 D6
NORBURY 183 D1
Norbury CE Prim Sch DE6 197 E7
Norbury Cl
Chesterfield S40 95 B5
Derby DE22 204 D1
Dronfield S18 56 D1
Norbury Cres DE23 231 C5
Norbury Ct 2 DE22 204 D2
Norbury Hollow DE6 183 D1
Norbury Way
Belper DE56 179 C6
Sandiacre NG10 223 A6
Norfolk Ave S42 115 F2
Norfolk Cl S40 114 B8
Norfolk Com Prim Sch S2 43 D8
Norfolk Ct NG19 136 E5
Norfolk Gdns DE22 218 F8
Norfolk Park Ave S2 43 D8
Norfolk Park Sch S2 44 A8
Norfolk Rd
Burton upon Trent DE15 254 D7
Long Eaton NG10 223 F1
Norfolk Sq 3 SK13 10 C1
Norfolk St
Derby DE23 219 B2
Glossop SK13 10 D1
Norfolk Wlk NG10 223 B5
Norgreave Way S20 59 E7
Norman Ave DE23 231 E7
Norman Cres DE7 194 E3
Norman Ct LE65 258 A1
Normandy Rd DE65 228 E2
Normanhurst Pk DE4 127 E1
Norman Keep DE13 239 C6
Norman Rd
Ripley DE5 169 C1
Somercotes DE55 170 E7
Tutbury DE13 239 C6
Norman St
Ilkeston DE7 194 E3
Kimberley NG16 195 F7
NORMANTON 231 F7
Normanton Ave DE55 159 C3
Normanton Brook Rd DE55 160 D7
Normanton Gr S13 44 F6
Normanton Hill S13 44 D6
Normanton Ho 3 SK17 85 A7
Normanton House Prim Sch DE23 231 F8
Normanton La DE23 231 C8
Normanton Lodge DE23 231 E8
Normanton Rd DE1 267 B1
Normanton Spring Cl S13 44 F6
Normanton Spring Rd S13 44 F5
Northacre Rd DE21 206 B2
Northam Dr DE5 169 C2
North Ave
Ashbourne DE6 173 B2
Derby DE3 217 E2
Derby, Darley Abbey DE22 205 A3
Sandiacre NG10 223 A6
North Brook Rd SK13 9 E4
North Church St DE45 109 D6
North Cl
Derby DE3 217 E3
Glossop SK13 9 F7
South Normanton DE55 159 F5
Unstone Green S18 76 E6
Willington DE65 242 B5
Northcliffe Rd DE6 173 B2
Northcote Ave S2 43 B6
Northcote Rd S2 43 B6
Northcote St NG10 236 E7
Northcote Way S44 117 D1
North Cres
Duckmanton S44 98 A5
Killamarsh S21 60 E8
NORTHEDGE 130 C6
Northedge Bsns Pk DE21 205 B2
Northedge La S42 130 B7
North End DE4 154 F1
Northern Ave S2 43 E7
Northern Comm S18 56 B2
Northern Dr NG9 209 D3
Northern Rd DE75 181 D2
North Farm Cl S26 61 E7
Northfield
Derby DE24 231 D3
Kilburn DE56 179 F2
Shirland DE55 146 D2
Northfield Ave
Ilkeston DE7 194 E1
Long Eaton NG10 236 B4
Mansfield Woodhouse NG19 136 A4
Rocester ST14 197 A4
Northfield Cl ST14 210 A2
Northfield Cres NG9 223 F4
Northfield Jun Sch S18 57 C3
Northfield La
Mansfield Woodhouse NG19 135 F4
Mansfield Woodhouse NG19 136 A5
Mansfield Woodhouse NG19 136 B5
Palterton S44 118 C6
Northfield Pk NG19 136 B5
Northfield Prim Sch NG19 136 B5
Northfield Rd NG9 223 F4
Northfields
Clowne S43 80 F3
Long Eaton NG10 236 B4
Northgate DE1 267 B4
North Gate S44 98 E3
Northgate Ho S21 59 D3
Northgate St 4 DE7 194 F1
North Gr S44 98 A6
North La
Belper DE56 178 D2
Belper, Milford DE56 190 E7
Brailsford DE6 187 E4
Old Brampton S42 94 D4
Northlands
4 Buxton SK17 85 D8
Harthill S26 61 E7
North Leys DE6 173 B1
Northmead Dr DE3 218 B3
Northmoor Cl S43 96 F7
North Moor View S43 96 F7
North Par
Derby DE1 267 B4
Matlock Bath DE4 143 A1
North Rd
Buxton SK17 66 D1
Calow S44 96 F3
Clowne S43 80 E4
Glossop SK13 10 C3
Hayfield SK22 25 D3
Long Eaton NG10 236 C6
North Row DE22 205 A1
Northside S42 115 D1
North Side S42 115 D1
North St
Alfreton DE55 159 B3
Blackwell DE55 147 F2
Bramley-Vale S44 117 D1
Burton upon Trent DE15 248 B3
Clay Cross S45 131 B5
Cromford DE4 155 A6
Derby DE1 267 B5
Derby DE23 218 C2
7 Ilkeston DE7 194 F1
Langley Mill NG16 182 B3
Melbourne DE73 252 A7
North Wingfield S42 131 E6
Pinxton NG16 160 D3
Shirebrook NG20 120 D4
Somercotes DE55 170 D6
South Normanton DE55 159 F5
Swadlincote DE11 256 B5
Whaley Thorns NG20 101 A2
North Terr 1 S41 115 B7
Northumberland Rd DE15 254 D7
Northumberland St DE23 218 F2
North View
Crich DE4 168 A8
Derby DE23 218 C1
North View St S44 98 F1
Northway Dr DE1 218 E4
NORTH WINGFIELD 132 B8
North Wingfield Prim Sch
North Wingfield S42 131 F7
North Wingfield S42 131 F8
North Wingfield Rd S42 115 E3
NORTHWOOD 127 B5
Northwood Ave
Derby DE21 219 E7
Northwood Ave *continued*
Temple Normanton DE4 116 C3
Northwood La
Ellastone DE6 183 C5
Northwood DE4 127 A6
Northwood Rise DE6 185 B8
Northwood St NG9 223 D8
NORTON 57 B8
Norton Ave
Chesterfield S40 114 A8
Sheffield S14 43 E2
Shuttlewood S44 98 F6
Shuttlewood S44 99 A6
Norton Church Glebe S8 43 C1
Norton Church Rd S8 43 B1
Norton Free CE Prim Sch S8 43 C1
Norton Green Cl S8 43 C1
Norton Hall S8 43 B1
Norton Hall Ct S8 43 B1
Norton La S8 43 C1
Norton Lawns S8 43 C1
NORTON LEES 43 A4
Norton Lees Cl S8 43 A3
Norton Lees Cres S8 43 A4
Norton Lees Glade S8 43 A4
Norton Lees La S8 43 A4
Norton Lees Rd S2 43 A3
Norton Lees Sq S8 43 A3
Norton Mews S8 43 C1
Norton Park Ave S8 57 B8
Norton Park Cres S8 57 A8
Norton Park Dr S8 57 A8
Norton Park Rd S8 57 B8
Norton Park View S8 57 B8
NORTON WOODSEATS 43 A2
Norwell Ct 2 NG19 136 B1
Norwich Cl NG19 136 D5
Norwich St DE21 219 D7
NORWOOD 60 F8
Norwood Ave S41 115 E6
Norwood Cl
Chesterfield S41 115 E6
Derby DE22 218 A5
Ilkeston DE7 194 F5
Norwood Cres S21 60 F7
Norwood Ind Est S21 60 E8
Norwood La NG20 100 E5
Norwood Pl S21 60 F7
Noskwith St DE7 209 A5
Nothill Rd DE65 228 E1
Nothills Cl DE73 233 A1
Nottingham 26 Bus Pk (under development) NG16 182 D3
Nottingham Canal Nature Reserve* DE7, NG16 195 C1
Nottingham Cl
10 Castle Gresley DE11 255 E1
Wingerworth S42 115 B3
Nottingham Dr
Derby DE3 230 E5
Wingerworth S42 115 B3
Nottingham La
Ironville NG16 170 F5
Pye Hill NG16 171 A5
Nottingham Rd
Alfreton DE55 159 B2
Ashby-de-la-Zouch LE65 258 F1
Belper DE56 179 B4
Borrowash DE72 221 D2
Breedon on the Hill DE73 252 D1
Codnor DE5, NG16 181 C8
Derby DE1, DE21 267 C4
Derby DE21 220 E2
Derby, Chaddesden DE21 219 E6
Derby, Spondon DE21 220 E3
Eastwood, Bailey Grove NG16 182 E2
Eastwood, Giltbrook NG16 195 C8
Ilkeston DE7 209 A6
Long Eaton NG10 236 F8
Ripley DE5 169 E2
Selston NG16 171 F6
Stapleford NG9 223 E7
Tansley DE4 144 B4
Trowell NG9 209 E5
Nowill Ct 2 S8 43 A6
Nowill Pl 3 S8 43 A6
Nuffield Health Derby Hospl DE23 230 F6
Nunbrook Gr SK17 85 C8
Nunn Brook Rd NG17 148 E2
Nunn Brook Rise NG17 148 E2
Nunn Cl NG17 148 E1
Nunsfield Dr DE24 233 B7
Nunsfield Rd SK17 66 C1
Nun's St DE1 218 E6
Nursery Ave
Sandiacre NG10 222 F5
West Hallam DE7 207 E7
Nursery Cl
Borrowash DE72 221 B2
4 Glossop SK13 17 C8
Nursery Cl *continued*
Swadlincote DE11 256 B6
Nursery Croft DE4 165 E6
Nursery Dr
Bolsover S44 98 F2
Buxton SK17 66 C2
Nursery Gdns DE55 160 C4
Nursery Hollow DE7 208 E6
Nursery La SK17 84 E6
Nutbrook Cres DE7 208 D4
Nuthall Circ DE7 208 C4
Nuttall Cl DE55 158 F3
Nuttall St DE55 158 F3
Nuttall Terr S44 117 D1
NUTTALS PARK 169 E1
Nutwood Cl DE22 205 A3
Nutwood/Darley Tip Nature Reserve* DE56 205 A2

O

Oadby Dr S41 115 C7
Oadby Rise DE23 231 E6
Oakamoor Cl S40 95 A5
Oak Apple Cres DE7 208 E6
Oak Ave
Aldercar NG16 182 B5
Disley SK12 33 A6
Ripley DE5 180 D7
Sandiacre NG10 223 A7
Shirebrook NG20 119 D4
Oak Bank SK12 33 A6
Oak Bank Ave S41 77 B2
Oakbank Ct S17 55 E5
Oak Cl
Brimington S43 96 D7
Chapel-en-le-Frith SK23 47 C5
Derby DE22 204 E4
Duffield DE56 190 E2
Killamarsh S21 60 C5
Linton DE11 261 E7
Mottram in Longdendale SK14 9 A4
Ockbrook DE72 221 C5
Pinxton NG16 160 C3
Oak Cres
Ashbourne DE6 185 C7
Derby DE23 231 C8
Wingerworth S42 114 F3
Oakdale Cl S45 131 E2
Oakdale Gdns DE21 206 B3
Oakdale Rd DE55 160 A4
Oakdell S18 57 D3
Oak Dr
Alfreton DE55 159 B4
Derby DE23 218 C1
Derby DE3 217 E2
Derby, Boulton DE24 233 A6
Doveridge DE6 211 B1
Eastwood NG16 182 E2
Hilton DE65 228 D2
Mansfield Woodhouse NG19 136 E2
Oakenthorpe Nature Reserve* DE55 158 C3
Oaker Terr DE4 142 A7
OAKERTHORPE 158 C3
Oakerthorpe Rd
Bolehill DE4 154 F4
Bolehill DE4 155 B2
Wirksworth DE4 155 B2
Oakes Cl
Langley Mill NG16 182 A5
Somercotes DE55 170 C7
Oakes Park View S14 43 D1
Oakes The S8 43 D1
Oakfield Ave S40 95 B1
Oakfield Ct DE7 193 A2
Oakfield Dr NG10 223 B3
Oakfield Rd
Glossop SK13 9 E3
Stapleford NG9 223 D7
Oakfields DE13 238 A4
Oakfields Gr DE21 220 D3
Oak Grove Gn S17 55 E4
Oakham Cl DE21 205 D1
Oakham Rd 5 DE23 230 F6
Oakham Way DE7 194 E3
Oakhill Rd S18 57 C3
Oakhurst Cl DE56 178 D6
Oak La DE6 212 D4
Oakland Ave
Long Eaton NG10 236 C5
Sutton in Ashfield NG17 148 F2
Oakland Cres DE55 170 D5
Oakland Croft NG17 148 F3
Oakland Dr DE12 262 F3
Oaklands SK22 25 C3
Oaklands Ave
Derby DE23 231 C5
Heanor DE75 182 A2
Marple Bridge SK6 23 C8
Oaklands Cl DE5 180 D1
Oaklands Dr 1 DE7 193 A6
Oaklands Drive DE7 192 F6
Oaklands Rd DE65 229 C4
Oakland St DE55 159 B4
Oaklands The DE55 160 A4
Oaklands Way DE73 252 B8
Oakland Terr NG10 236 C5
Oaklea SK17 85 C5
Oaklea Way S42 131 B6
Oakleigh Ave
Derby DE21 219 F6
Mansfield Woodhouse NG19 136 E4
Swadlincote DE11 255 F5
Oakley Ave S40 95 E4
Oakley Cl DE55 159 C4
Oakley's Rd NG10 236 E7
Oakley's Road W NG10 236 D6
Oak Lodge Dr NG16 195 F7
Oakmeadows DE55 160 B4
Oakover Dr DE22 204 D2
Oak Rd
Denstone ST14 196 D5
Elvaston DE72 233 F4
Grassmoor S42 115 F3
Matlock DE4 143 C5
Shardlow DE72 234 A5
Sheffield, Gleadless Townend S12 44 A2
Oakridge DE21 220 B7
Oakridge Cl NG19 136 F1
Oakridge Pk DE74 247 A5
Oaks Ave
Creswell S80 100 C8
Hayfield SK22 25 D2
Oaks Barn DE45 109 A2
Oaksedge La
Tansley DE4 143 F6
Tansley DE4 144 A5
Oaksetts Dr S43 82 E2
Oaks Farm La S44 97 A2
OAKS GREEN 225 D7
Oakside Way DE21 206 B3
Oaks La
Ashover S45 129 C5
Cutthorpe S18, S42 94 A8
Oak Sq DE11 255 F2
Oaks Rd DE65 242 B5
Oak St
Brimington S43 78 A1
Derby DE23 219 A2
Glossop SK13 10 C1
Sheffield S20 59 C8
Sheffield, Heeley S8 43 A7
Swadlincote DE11 256 A2
Oakstedge La S45 145 B7
Oaks The
Glossop SK13 17 A7
Little Eaton DE21 205 C8
OAKTHORPE 265 F5
Oaktree Ave DE24 232 B7
Oak Tree Ave S44 134 B8
Oaktree Bsns Pk DE11 255 E3
Oak Tree Cl
Arkwright Town S44 97 D3
Ripley DE5 180 C8
Swanwick DE55 170 A8
Oak Tree Close DE12 260 D4
Oak Tree Cotts S44 97 A1
Oak Tree Cres NG19 136 B4
Oak Tree Ct DE72 221 D1
Oak Tree Gdns DE4 144 A4
Oaktree Rd DE55 160 C8
Oak Tree Rd S43 80 E2
Oak Trees Cl DE13 240 B3
Oakvale Ho DE23 219 A2
Oakview S17 55 E5
Oak View Gardens DE55 146 E5
Oakway Dr DE11 256 F1
Oakwell Cres DE7 208 E8
Oakwell Dr
Crich DE4 156 F1
Ilkeston DE7 208 E8
OAKWOOD 206 A2
Oakwood SK13 16 F8
Oakwood Cl
Derby DE65 231 D2
Hatton DE65 239 C8
Oakwood District Ctr DE21 206 A1
Oakwood Dr
Bolsover S44 98 F3
Darley Dale DE4 142 E8
Derby DE21 206 B2
Oakwood Inf Sch DE24 233 A6
Oakwood Jun Sch DE24 233 A6
Oakwood Rd SK12 32 D6
Oakwood Way S43 79 B4
Oakworth Cl 1 S20 59 E6
Oakworth Dr S20 59 D6
Oakworth Gr S20 59 D6
Oakworth View S20 59 D6
Oat Hill DE4 165 F7
Oats Orch S20 59 D6
Oberon Cl DE73 232 E1
Oberon Ret Pk DE56 178 F3
Occupation Cl S43 80 A6
Occupation La
North Wingfield S42 131 E7
Sheffield, Birley S12 44 F3
Woodville DE11 256 D1
Occupation Rd
Chesterfield S41 95 F8
Moira DE11 262 C8
New Houghton NG19 134 F7
Ocean Ct DE24 219 E1
Ochbrook Ct DE7 194 F3
OCKBROOK 221 D5
Octavia Cl DE73 232 E2
Octavia Ct S40 266 B1
Oddfellows Cotts 16 SK17 85 B7
Oddfellows Rd S32 53 A7
Oddfellows Row S32 53 A7
Oddfellows Terr S32 53 A7
Oddfellow Terr DE45 109 D6
Oddford La DE4 127 D2
Odom Ct S2 43 B6
Odridgehay Sta* DE56 176 F6
Offcote Cres 1 DE6 173 D3
OFFERTON 52 D7
Offerton Ave DE23 231 F8
Offerton La S33 52 C7
Offridge Cl S43 80 F2
Off Spring Bank SK22 33 C8
Ogden St SK14 16 B8
OGSTON 146 A4
Ogston La DE55 146 B4
Ogston New Rd DE55 145 E4
Okeover Ave DE6 173 D1
OKER 142 D7
Oker Ave DE4 127 B3
Oker Dr DE4 127 B3
Oker La DE4 142 D6
Oker Rd DE4 142 B7
Old Ashbourne Rd ST14 210 B3
Old Bakery Cl
Chesterfield S41 77 A2
Hognaston DE6 164 B1
Old Bakery Way NG18 136 C1
Old Bank DE6 184 D8
Old Barn Cl DE21 205 D8
OLD BRAMPTON 94 D4
Old Brampton Rd DE45 92 D5
Old Brick Works La S41 96 A6
Oldbury Cl DE21 206 A2
Old Buxton Rd SK11 83 A6
Old Chester Rd DE1 219 A8
Old Church Cl DE22 204 C5
Old Coach Rd DE4 143 F4
Old Coalpit La
Chelmorton SK17 86 F1
Chelmorton SK17 105 D8
Old Colliery La S42 132 E8
Old Coppice Side DE75 193 E7
Old Court House Shops 4 SK17 85 B8
Old Cross SK13 10 E2
OLD DAM 49 B4
Old Dam SK17 49 A4
Old Dam La SK17 49 C4
Old Denstone Rd ST14 196 E4
Old Derby Rd
Ashbourne DE6 173 C1
Eastwood NG16 182 D3
Olde Derwent Ave DE4 143 B4
Olde English Rd DE4 143 B4
Old End DE12 265 F1
Olders Valley DE11 256 E4
Old Etwall Rd DE3 230 C8
Old Fall St NG17 148 F3
Old Farm Ct NG11 237 E6
Old Farm Gdns DE12 262 F4
Old Farmhouse The DE45 109 D6
Oldfield Dr DE11 256 C5
Oldfield La
Egginton DE65 241 A8
Hognaston DE6 164 B2
Kirk Ireton DE6 164 F2
Snelston DE6 184 B3
Warrencarr DE45 126 F2
Wensley DE4 142 A8
Old Forge Bsns Pk 5 S2 43 A7
Old Forge Cl DE65 241 A5
Old Gate HD9 2 F7
Old Gate Ave DE72 245 E5
Old Gate Cl 6 DE5 170 B1
OLD GLOSSOP 10 E2
Old Green Close S80 82 A6
Old Hackney La DE4 142 F8
Old Hall Ave
Derby DE23 218 B1
Derby, Alvaston DE24 233 B7
Duffield DE56 190 E3
Old Hall Cl
Darley Dale DE4 127 C3
Glossop SK13 10 D2
Pilsley S45 132 C2
Old Hall Ct DE55 169 E7
Old Hall Dr
Horwich End SK23 45 E4
Willington DE65 242 B5
Old Hall Gdns
Stoney Middleton S32 72 A4
Swadlincote DE11 256 A2
Old Hall Jun Sch S40 95 C2

Old Hall La
Church Broughton
 DE65.................227 B8
Marple SK6............23 C5
Mottram in Longdendale
 SK14................9 A5
Whitwell S80..........81 F6
Old Hall Mews S8.....56 F7
Old Hall Mills Bsns Pk
 DE21................205 C7
Old Hall Rd
 Chesterfield S40.......95 D3
 Derby DE23.........218 C1
Old Hall Sq 3 SK13....10 A5
Old Hartshay Hill
 DE5................169 C2
Oldhay Cl S17.........55 D6
Old Hay Gdns S17.....55 C6
Old Hay La S17.......55 C6
Old Hill
 Ashbourne DE6.......173 C1
 Ashbourne DE6......185 C8
Old Hillcliff La
 DE56...............177 A3
Old House Mus★
 DE45...............109 C6
Old House Rd S40......95 D6
Old Houses S41........96 C3
Oldicote La DE15....248 E3
Oldikes SK17.........102 E1
Oldknow Rd SK6.......23 A6
Old La
 Cubley DE6.........198 E1
 Derby DE22.........205 A2
 Idridgehay DE56.....176 F3
 Sheffield S20.........60 A7
 Shottle DE56.......177 A5
 Tintwistle SK13.......6 E3
 Wirksworth DE4.....154 F2
Old Lime Ct DE4.....143 C5
Old Lodge Cl ST14...210 A1
Old Longhill Rd
 SK17................65 B4
Old Manor Rd NG19..136 C3
Old Mansfield Rd
 DE21...............205 C1
Old Market Pl DE55..160 A6
OLD MATLOCK.....143 C4
Old Mill Cl
 Duffield DE56........190 E3
 Mansfield NG19......136 E1
Old Mill Dr S40........95 A8
Old Mill La
 Calver S32...........72 D2
 Mansfield NG19.....136 E1
Old Mill Lane Ind Est
 NG19...............136 C1
Old Nurseries Cl
 DE56...............179 E5
Old Nursery Gdns
 DE4................144 A5
Old Oak Cl DE4......157 A1
Old Orchard DE5......56 D7
Old Park Ave S8.......56 D7
Old Park Rd S8.......56 D7
Old Parks La LE65...258 C3
Old Peveril Rd S44....98 A5
Old Pheasant Ct S40..95 A2
Old Pit La
 Clay Cross S45......131 F3
 Smalley DE7.........193 A6
Old Pk DE56..........187 D6
Old Plough Close
 DE72...............245 F5
Old Pond The DE75..194 A8
Old Porter La DE4...154 F3
Old Post Office Row
 S33.................40 B4
Old Printworks 2
 DE11...............256 B3
Old Quarry Cl S43....80 C6
Old Railway Mws
 DE11...............256 C4
Old Rd
 Branston DE14......253 E7
 Buxton SK17, SK23....65 C5
 Chesterfield S40......95 C3
 Darley Dale DE4.....127 C1
 Furness Vale SK23....33 D4
 Glossop SK13........10 A7
 Heage DE56.........179 E8
 Horwich End, New Horwich
  SK23................45 E6
 Mottram in Longdendale
  SK14................9 A5
Oldridge Cl S40.......95 B6
Old School Cl
 Bramley-Vale S44....117 D1
 Holymoorside S42....113 D7
 Tideswell SK17.......69 C4
Old School Close
 DE4................127 E1
Old School Ct DE56..168 E1
Old School Ho The
 S42................113 D7
Old School La
 Awsworth NG16.....195 C5
 Chesterfield S44......96 F2
 Creswell S80.........81 F1
 Pleasley NG19.......135 A5
Old School Mews
 DE72...............246 B8
Old School The
 DE65...............228 C2
Old Ship La S40.....266 B3

Old Smithy Row
 SK22................33 C7
Old St SK14...........16 A8
Old Station Cl
 Etwall DE65.........229 B4
 Rowsley DE4.........126 F8
Old Station Yd S43....96 C8
Old Stone La DE4....143 E7
Old Storth La DE55..160 B4
Old Swanwick Colliery
 Rd DE55...........158 F1
Old Tennis Courts The
 SK17................85 B8
Old Terr NG19.......134 F4
OLD TUPTON.......131 C7
Old Turnpike Dr
 DE4................157 A1
Old Uttoxeter Rd
 Crakemarsh ST14....210 C6
 Rocester ST14......196 D1
Old Vicarage Cl
 DE23...............218 C1
Old Vicarage La
 DE22...............204 C5
Old Vicarage Sch
 DE22...............205 A3
Old Water La NG19..135 D1
Old Waterworks The
 DE73...............243 A4
Oldwell Cl S17.........55 D4
OLD WHITTINGTON..77 B1
Old Whittington La
 S18.................76 E6
Old Works La S44.....97 B3
Olive Ave
 Long Eaton NG10....223 E1
 Shirebrook NG20....119 D6
Olive Cl
 Branston DE14......253 E6
 Branston DE14......256 E6
Olive Cres S12........44 A2
Olive Gdns S41........95 F6
Olive Gr DE21.......219 F5
Olive Grove Rd S2....43 B8
Oliver Cl DE75.......182 B2
Oliver Close DE72....235 E8
Olive Rd S20..........59 D7
Oliver Ho S41.......266 C3
Oliver Rd DE7.......208 C6
Olive St DE22........218 E4
Olive Terr 1 SK14....16 A8
Olivier St DE23......219 B1
OLLERBROOK
 BOOTH.............37 D8
Ollersett Ave
 New Mills SK22.......24 D1
 New Mills SK22.......33 D8
Ollersett Dr SK22.....33 D8
Ollersett Ho SK22....33 D8
Ollersett La SK22......24 C1
Olton Dr DE65.......240 E8
Olton Rd DE3........217 C4
Olympian Way DE4..127 B4
Onslow Rd DE3......217 E4
Onward Cotts SK17....85 E8
Opal Cl DE21........206 A2
Opal Gdns DE11.....255 F4
Opal St S40..........115 E6
Openacre NG16......170 F4
OPENWOODGATE..179 D3
Openwoodgate
 DE56...............179 D3
Openwood Rd DE56..179 E3
Optimum Rd DE11...255 E3
Orange Birch Cl S43..80 D2
Orange Cl NG20.....119 E6
Orange St DE55.....159 B4
Orchard Ave
 Castle Donington
  DE74...............247 A3
 Whaley Bridge SK23...45 D7
Orchard Bsns Pk
 DE7................194 D1
Orchard Cl
 Barlborough S43......80 A7
 Belper DE56........191 B8
 Bolsover S44.........99 B1
 Breadsall DE21......205 D4
 Breaston DE72......235 F8
 Clowne S43...........80 E3
 Derby DE23.........231 C7
 Elvaston DE24......233 D4
 Hilton DE65.........228 D1
 Melbourne DE73.....252 A7
 Moira DE12.........262 F4
 Ockbrook DE72......221 C4
 Ripley DE5..........181 A7
 Shirebrook NG20....119 E5
 Sudbury DE6........225 E5
 1 Uttoxeter ST14....210 B1
 Walton-on-Trent
  DE12...............253 D1
 West Hallam DE7....207 E7
 Willington DE65......242 B6
Orchard Com Prim Sch
 DE74...............247 A3
Orchard Cotts DE56..190 E4
Orchard Cres
 Glapwell S44........134 B8
 Swanwick DE55.....169 D7
Orchard Ct
 Derby DE21.........220 E5
 Doveridge DE6.......211 B1
 Langley Mill NG16...182 B3
 South Normanton
  DE55...............159 F4

Orchard Ct continued
 Sutton-in-Ashfield
  NG17...............148 E2
Orchard Dr
 1 Creswell S43........81 E2
 Creswell S80.........81 E2
 Gamesley SK13........9 E1
Orchard Gr DE5.....181 B6
Orchard La DE6.....185 D1
Orchard Lee S26......61 E6
Orchard Mews S18....56 E2
Orchard Mws NG10..160 E3
Orchard Park Ind Est
 NG10...............223 C6
Orchard Pl S21........60 D6
Orchard Rd
 Compstall SK6........15 B2
 Darley Dale DE4.....142 E8
 Matlock Bath DE4...143 A1
 Somercotes DE55....170 C6
 Whaley Bridge SK23...45 D7
Orchard Rise
 Alfreton DE55.......159 C3
 Heanor DE75........181 F2
Orchard Sq S18........56 D2
Orchard St
 5 Derby DE3.........230 D8
 Derby, Markeaton
  DE3................217 D1
 Eastwood NG16.....195 A8
 Ilkeston DE7........208 F7
 Kimberley NG16.....195 F6
 Langley Mill NG16...182 B3
 Long Eaton NG10....236 E7
 Mansfield NG19.....136 B1
 Swadlincote DE11...255 F6
Orchards The
 Derby DE22.........204 D3
 Jacksdale NG16.....171 B4
 Orchards Way S40....95 D1
Orchard The
 Belper DE56........179 A4
 Chesterfield S40......80 E5
 Codnor DE5.........170 B1
 Disley SK12..........32 D6
 Horsley Woodhouse
  DE7................192 D6
 Morton DE55........147 A5
 Stanton-by-Dale DE7..222 F8
 Uttoxeter ST14.....210 A4
 Youlgreave DE45....125 C5
Orchard View
 Bolsover S44.........117 F8
 Mansfield Woodhouse
  NG19...............136 B3
 North Wingfield S45..131 F5
Orchard View Rd
 S40.................95 C4
Orchard Way
 Chellaston DE73....232 F2
 Clay Cross S45......131 B3
 Donisthorpe DE12...265 E8
 Sandiacre NG10.....223 A3
Orchid Cl
 Burton upon Trent
  DE15...............255 A8
 Calow S44............97 A3
Orchid Court DE24..231 C3
Orchid Dr SK23........46 F5
Orchid Gr
 Pleasley NG19......134 F5
 Pleasley NG19.......135 A5
Orchid Gro NG20....119 D2
Orchid Way
 Shirebrook NG20....119 D3
 Wingerworth S40....115 D2
Orchil Street NG16..195 B8
Ordish Ave DE21.....219 F5
Ordley La DE6.......183 F8
Ordley Wlk DE65....228 D1
Oregano Cl DE3.....217 C5
Oregon Way DE21...220 C6
Ore St S45...........131 C5
Orford Ave SK14......32 D6
Organ Way SK14......9 D5
Oriel Ct DE1.........267 C1
Orient Way DE24....219 E2
Orkney Cl DE24......231 D3
Orlando Ct DE73.....232 E2
Orly Ave DE74......247 A2
Ormesby Cl S18.......56 C1
Ormiston Enterprise
 Acad DE7...........194 F4
Ormond Cl
 Chesterfield S40.....114 B7
 Sheffield S8...........57 B6
Ormond Dr S8........57 B6
Ormonde Dr DE5....180 D5
Ormonde St NG16...182 B4
Ormonde Terr
 NG16...............182 B4
Ormond Rd S8........57 B7
Ormond Way S8......57 B7
Ormsby Rd S41.......95 F7
Ormskirk Rise
 DE21...............220 F4
Orpean Way NG9....223 E2
Orpen Dr S14..........43 D2
Orpen Ho S8...........43 D2
Orpen Way S14........43 E2
Orton Way DE56.....179 B6
Orwell Road DE65...228 E1
Orwins Cl 5 S41......95 D7
Osborne Cl NG10....223 B4
Osborne Croft S26....61 F6
Osborne Pl SK13......10 A5
Osborne Rd DE23....219 C3

Osborne St
 Burton upon Trent
  DE15...............248 A3
 Derby DE23.........267 D1
Osborne Gdns
 DE15...............248 A3
Oscar Ct S43..........77 D3
Osiers Cl DE22.......204 C1
OSLESTON..........215 D7
Osleston La
 Longlane DE6........201 C1
 Thurvaston DE6.....215 D7
OSMASTON
 Ashbourne.........185 F4
 Derby...............232 C8
Osmaston CE (VC) Prim
 Sch DE6............185 F4
Osmaston Cl NG10..235 F5
Osmaston Park Ind Est
 DE24...............232 E8
Osmaston Park Rd DE23,
 DE24...............232 C7
Osmaston Prim Sch
 DE24...............232 C7
Osmaston Rd
 Derby DE23, DE24...219 B2
 Derby DE24.........232 B6
Osmaston St NG10..223 C6
Osmaton Park Ind Est
 DE24...............219 D1
Osmund Ct S21........59 C3
Osmund Rd S21.......59 C3
Osprey Cl
 Burton upon Trent
  DE15...............248 D4
 Derby DE24.........231 E2
Osprey Dr
 Branston DE14......253 E6
 Branston DE14......256 E6
Osterly Gn DE22.....218 A5
Ostrich La DE6.......163 B1
Oswestry Cl DE21....206 B3
Othello Dr DE73.....232 D2
Otterburn Dr DE22..204 C2
Otterhole Cl SK17.....84 F7
Otter St
 Derby DE1...........219 A7
 Hilton DE65.........228 D1
Otter Way NG19.....135 D1
Oulton Cl DE24......232 D4
Oundle Dr
 Ilkeston DE7........209 B7
 Mansfield NG19.....135 D1
Ousley La DE56.......183 C5
Outfield Rd DE15....254 F8
Outgang La
 Mansfield Woodhouse
  NG19...............136 D4
 Pleasley NG19.......135 C6
Out La S42, S44.....132 F6
Outlands Rd S33......50 F6
Outram Cl DE72.....221 B1
Outram Ct DE5......169 E2
Outram Dr DE11.....256 D4
Outram Rd S41........95 F6
Outram St S45......169 E2
Outrams Wharf
 DE21...............205 C6
Outram Way DE24..231 E2
Outram Wy S21.......34 E1
Outseats Dr DE55....159 B3
Outwood Acad City
 S13.................44 F6
Outwood Acad Newbold
 S41.................95 F6
Oval Ct DE23........231 C3
OVER BURROWS....202 A4
Over Croft La DE4...168 A3
Overcroft Rise S17....55 D4
Overdale S33.........143 D5
Overdale Ave SK17....85 C8
Overdale Cl NG10....236 A6
Overdale Dr SK13.....17 B8
Overdale Gdns S17....55 D6
Overdale Rd
 Derby DE23.........218 E2
 New Mills SK12........32 F6
Overdale Rise S17....55 C6
Overend Cl S14.......43 D4
Overend Dr S14......43 D4
Overend Rd S14......43 D4
Overend Way S14....43 D4
OVERGREEN.........94 B8
OVER HADDON.....109 B1
Over Hill Rd SK22,
 SK23................34 A5
Over La
 Baslow DE45..........91 E6
 Belper DE56........179 F4
 Hazelwood DE56....178 A2
Overlees S18..........75 D3
OVER LEIGH.........45 F6
Overmoor View
 DE55...............148 B7
Over Rd DE45.........91 E6
OVERSEAL...........262 A3
Overseal Prim Sch
 DE12...............262 B4
OVERSETTS.........255 E5
Oversetts Cl DE11...255 F6
Oversetts Rd DE11...255 E5
Overstone Cl DE56...179 D4
Overton Cl S43.........78 C3
Overtown DE6........164 B4
OVER WOODHOUSE..98 E3
Owen Ave NG10.....237 A6
Owen Falls Ave S41...96 C3
OWEN'S BANK.....239 B6

Owers Ave DE75.....193 F7
OWLCOTES.........117 A4
Owlcotes View S44...118 A8
OWLER BAR..........55 B1
Owler Bar Rd S11.....54 B4
Owler Car La S18......57 F5
Owlers La DE23.....218 C2
Owlers The SK23......45 E6
Owlston Cl NG16.....182 F3
Owlswick Cl DE23....231 A8
OWLTHORPE.........59 B8
Owlthorpe Ave S20...59 B8
Owlthorpe Cl S20......59 B8
Owlthorpe Dr S20.....59 B8
Owlthorpe Gr S20....59 B8
Owlthorpe La S20.....59 B8
Owlthorpe Rise S20...59 B8
Oxbury Rd NG16.....195 F8
Ox Cl S45.............131 D3
Oxclose Dr 2 S18.....56 C1
Oxclose La
 Alsop en le Dale
  DE6................150 C2
 Dronfield S18.........56 C1
 Mansfield Woodhouse
  NG19...............136 A3
Oxclose Park Gdns
 S20.................59 F6
Oxclose Park Rise
 S20.................59 F6
Oxclose Park View
 S20.................59 F6
Oxclose Park Way
 S20.................59 F6
Oxcroft Est S44.......99 D7
Oxcroft Ind Est S44..99 A8
Oxcroft La
 Bolsover S44.........99 A2
 Bolsover S44.........99 B6
 Elmton S44..........99 E8
Oxcroft View S44.....99 B8
Oxcroft Way S43......80 B5
Oxenhope Cl DE23...230 E7
Oxcroft Cl S43........96 F8
Oxford Rd S43........96 F6
Oxford St
 Blackwell DE55.....147 E1
 Bramley-Vale S44...117 D1
 Derby DE1..........267 C1
 Derby, Spondon DE21..220 E5
 Eastwood NG16.....182 F2
 Long Eaton NG10...236 D8
 Mansfield Woodhouse
  NG19...............136 C1
 Ripley DE5..........169 D1
 Swadlincote DE11...256 A1
Oxhay Gdns DE4.....157 A1
Ox Hill S20............60 A5
Oxley Rd DE15.......248 A3
Oxmead Dr DE4......184 D7
Oxpasture La NG20..100 B5
Oxton Rake Rd S18...94 A4
OXTON RAKES.......94 A8
Oxwich Ct DE21......206 B2
Oyster Cl DE14......254 E7
Oyster Rd NG16.....182 C4
Ozier Holt NG10.....236 C6

P

Pacific Way DE24....219 E2
Packenham Bvd
 DE65...............227 A4
Packer's Row S40....266 B3
Pack Horse Rd
 DE73...............252 B8
Packington Rd
 DE65...............240 E8
Packman La S26, S80...62 C6
Paddington Ct S43....78 B4
Paddock Cl
 Castle Donington
  DE74...............246 F3
 Sheffield S2...........43 E6
 Wingerworth S42....114 F3
Paddock Cres S2.....43 E5
Paddock Croft 9
 DE21...............205 F2
Paddock Ct ST14....196 E5
Paddock Dr DE75....193 C8
Paddock La S43.......45 F5
Paddocks Cl NG16...160 C4
Paddocks The
 Mansfield Woodhouse
  NG19...............136 D4
 Pilsley S45..........132 C2
 Ripley DE5..........180 F8
 Sandiacre NG10.....223 A5
 Staveley S43.........79 C3
 Sutton in Ashfield
  NG17...............148 F2
 Swadlincote DE11...255 F5
Paddocks View
 NG10...............236 B8
Paddock The
 Alfreton DE55.......157 F3
 Blackwell DE55.....147 F1
 Burton upon Trent
  DE15...............248 A4
 Buxton SK17..........84 F7

Paddock The continued
 Elvaston DE24......233 D4
 Glossop SK13..........9 E5
 Holbrook DE56.......191 C6
 Hollingworth SK14....9 F5
 Horwich End SK23....45 F6
 Ockbrook DE72......221 C4
 Pleasley NG19.......135 A5
 Rolleston DE13.....240 A4
 Shirebrook NG20....119 D4
Paddock Way S18.....57 B3
PADFIELD............10 C5
Padfield Com Prim Sch
 SK13................10 B5
Padfield Gate SK13...17 D7
Padfield Main Rd
 SK13................10 C5
Padley Cl
 Derby DE22.........205 A5
 Ripley DE5..........169 C3
Padley Hill S32........53 E1
Padley Rd S32........53 D1
Padley Way S42.....131 F5
Padley Wood La
 S45................147 B8
Padley Wood Rd
 S45................132 C2
Padstow 13 DE24...231 D3
Padstow Rd DE24...233 C5
Paget High Sch
 DE14...............254 A7
Paget Road DE73....245 A1
Paige Gardens
 NG10...............223 A5
Paignton Ct 16 S41..95 F8
Painters La DE6.....187 A1
Painter's La DE6.....186 B5
Painters Way
 Darley Dale DE4.....127 D3
 Winster DE4.........141 C6
Paisley Cl S43.........97 C8
Palace La DE6........166 D1
Palace Rd SK17........85 B8
Palatine Gr DE23....230 F7
Palerow La DE56.....166 E3
Palissy Cl DE11......256 D4
Palladium Dr DE23..231 A6
Pall Mall DE21......205 E4
Palm Cl DE23........218 A1
Palmer Cl DE14......254 B8
Palmer Cres 3 S18...57 B1
Palmer Dr
 Stapleford NG9.....223 D5
 Swanwick DE55.....169 E7
PALMER MOOR.....224 E7
Palmersgate S40....266 B3
4 Ilkeston DE7.......208 F7
Palmerston Ct DE73..252 B7
Palmerston Rd 4
 DE7................208 F8
Palmerston St
 Derby DE23.........218 E1
 Underwood Green
  NG16...............171 F2
 Westwood NG16.....171 C4
PALTERTON.........118 A5
Long Duckmanton
  S44................117 D7
 Palterton S44........118 C5
Palterton Prim Sch
 S44................118 B5
Panama Circle
 DE24...............219 F2
Pankhurst Pl S45....131 C3
Panthers Place S41...96 A5
Parade The
 4 Derby DE3.........217 D1
 Sheffield S12.........44 A6
Paradise St SK13......10 A5
Parcel Terr DE22....218 D5
Pares Way DE72.....221 C5
Pares Way Cl DE72..221 C5
Pargate Cl DE5.......180 D6
Park Ave
 Ashbourne DE6......173 D1
 Awsworth NG16.....195 B5
 Castle Donington
  DE74...............246 F3
 Darley Dale DE4....127 C3
 Dronfield S18.........57 B2
 Eastwood NG16.....182 E3
 Furness Vale SK23...33 D3
 Glapwell S44........118 C1
 Holmesfield S18......75 A8
 Ilkeston DE7........208 F8
 Mansfield Woodhouse
  NG19...............136 C4
 Ripley DE5..........169 F1
 Scropton DE65......227 A5
 Shirebrook NG20....119 E4
 Stanley DE7.........207 C6
 Uttoxeter ST14.....210 B2
Park Cl
 Burton upon Trent
  DE16...............254 D6
 Chesterfield S40.....115 A7
 Glossop SK13........10 D2
 Kilburn DE56........192 A8
 Linton DE12........261 C6
 Little Eaton DE21...205 B8
 Matlock DE4........143 D4
 Pinxton NG16.......160 C2
 Shirland DE55......146 E1
 Stanton-by-Dale DE7..222 F8
Park Cotts DE4.......127 A4
Park Cres
 Chapel-en-le-Frith
  SK23................47 B5

Park Cres *continued*
Doveridge DE6 . . . . . . 211 B1
Eastwood NG16 . . . . . . 182 F4
Furness Vale SK23 . . . .33 D3
Glossop SK13 . . . . .10 B3
Heage DE56 . . . . 179 E8
Ilkeston DE7 . . . . 209 A8
Park Ct DE75 . . . . . . 181 F1
Park Dene Dr SK13 . .10 C2
Park Dr
Chesterfield S41 . . . . . 266 C1
Derby DE23 . . . . 218 C1
Ilkeston DE7 . . . . 208 F7
Sandiacre NG10 . . . . . 223 A3
Swanwick DE55 . . . . . 169 F6
Park Edge S32 . . . . . . .52 F8
Parker Ave S44 . . . . . . .96 F3
Park Cl DE1 . . . . 267 A4
Parker Ctr DE21 . . . . 219 B8
Parke Rd SK17 . . . . . . .69 C4
Parker Gdns NG9 . . . 223 F8
Parker Ind Est DE21 . 205 B1
Parkers La S17 . . . . . . .55 D8
Parker St DE1 . . . . . . 218 F7
Park Farm S18 . . . . . . .56 C2
Park Farm Ctr DE22 . 204 D2
Park Farm Dr DE22 . 204 D2
Park Farm Mews
S21 . . . . .60 D1
Parkfield Cres DE12 .265 F1
Parkfield Ct SK17 . . . . .85 A7
Parkfield La DE6 . . . . 184 D4
Parkfield Pl S2 . . . . . . .43 A8
Parkfields S43 . . . . . . .80 E3
Parkfields Dr DE22 . . 218 E8
Parkfields View
DE56 . . . . 179 E8
Parkgate
Derby DE23 . . . . .219 B2
Dronfield S18 . . . . .57 C2
Parkgate Cl S20 . . . . . .59 A8
Parkgate Croft S20 . . .59 A8
Parkgate Dr S20 . . . . . .59 A8
Parkgate La S21, S43 . .77 E5
Park Gr DE22 . . . . 218 E7
Park Grange Croft Sta
S2 . . . . .43 C8
Park Grange Ct S2 . . . .43 C8
Park Grange Dr S2 . . . .43 C8
Park Grange Mount
S2 . . . . .43 C8
Park Grange Rd S2 . . . .43 C8
Park Grange Rise S2 .43 C8
Park Grange View
S2 . . . . .43 D8
Park Hall SK17 . . . . . . .85 B8
Park Hall Ave S40,
S42 . . . . 114 B8
Park Hall Cl S40 . . . . 114 B7
Park Hall Gdns
Chesterfield S40 . . . . .114 B7
Mansfield Woodhouse
NG19 . . . . 136 C5
Parkhall La S21 . . . . . . .60 D2
Park Hall La
Mapperley DE7 . . . . . 193 D2
West Hallam DE7 . . . . 207 C8
Park Hall Rd
Denby Village DE5 . . . 180 A3
Mansfield Woodhouse
NG19 . . . . 136 C5
Parkham Rd NG16 . . 195 F7
PARK HEAD 157 C2
Park Head Rd DE4 . . 143 B5
Park Hill
Awsworth NG16 . . . . .195 B5
Eckington S21 . . . . .59 E3
Park Hill Cl SK22 . . . . .24 C1
Park Hill Dr DE23 . . . 231 F7
Park Ho DE56 . . . . 179 A2
Parkhouse Cl S45 . . . 131 B4
Parkhouse Dr DE55 . 159 C6
Park House Prim Sch
S45 . . . . .132 B4
Parkhouse Rd S42,
S45 . . . . 132 A4
Parkin St DE55 . . . . . 159 B4
Park Jun & Inf Schs The
NG20 . . . . .119 E5
Park La
Baslow DE45 . . . . .91 F5
Baslow DE45 . . . . .92 A5
Castle Donington
DE74 . . . . 246 E3
Chesterfield S41 . . . . . .95 F7
Darley Dale DE4 . . . . 127 D2
Derby, Allestree DE22 . 204 F4
Derby, Normanton Park
DE23 . . . . 218 C1
Hayfield SK22 . . . . .25 D5
Heage DE56 . . . . 179 E8
Holbeck NG20, S80 . . 101 C6
Over Haddon DE45,
DE4 . . . . 110 C1
Pinxton NG16 . . . . . . 160 C2
Ripley DE5 . . . . 169 A7
Rodsley DE6 . . . . 200 B3
Shirland DE55 . . . . . . 159 A8
Shirley DE6 . . . . 200 D8
South Wingfield
DE55 . . . . 157 D1
Stanton in Peak DE4 . 126 C5
Tutbury DE13 . . . . . . .239 B6
Weston-on-Trent
DE72 . . . . 245 E4
Parkland Ave SK22 . .24 C1

Parkland Cres S12 . . . .44 E2
Parkland Dr S42 . . . . 115 A2
Parkland Mews
NG10 . . . . 236 D8
Parklands Dr DE73 . . 245 A8
Parklands Inf Sch
NG10 . . . . 223 B1
Park Leys Ct DE21 . . 220 E4
Park Lodge Rd
NG16 . . . . 195 A7
Park Mews
Derby DE22 . . . . .218 F8
Mansfield Woodhouse
NG19 . . . . 136 C4
Somercotes DE55 . . . . 170 D6
Park Mill Dr DE55 . . 159 C7
Park Nook Cl DE73 . . 233 A3
Park Pale The DE13 . 239 C5
Park Rd
Ashbourne DE6 . . . . . 173 C2
Bakewell DE45 . . . . . . 109 D5
Bakewell DE45 . . . . . . 109 F3
Belper DE56 . . . . 179 A2
Buxton SK17 . . . . .85 A7
Buxton SK17 . . . . .85 A8
Chapel-en-le-Frith
SK23 . . . . .47 B6
Chesterfield S40 . . . . . 266 A2
Derby DE3 . . . . 217 D2
Donisthorpe DE12 . . . 262 E2
Duffield DE56 . . . . 190 D3
Glossop SK13 . . . . .10 A4
Heage DE56 . . . . 179 E8
High Lane SK12 . . . . . . .32 A6
Holmewood S42 . . . . . 116 E1
Horwich End SK23 . . . .45 D6
Ilkeston DE7 . . . . 208 F7
Mansfield Woodhouse
NG19 . . . . 136 B3
New Mills SK22 . . . . . .33 C7
Over Haddon DE45 . . . 110 B2
Overseal DE11 . . . . . . 261 F6
Overseal DE12 . . . . . . 262 A6
Ripley DE5 . . . . 169 E1
Shirebrook NG20 . . . . 119 E5
Stapleford NG9 . . . . . 223 F8
Swadlincote DE11,
DE15 . . . . 256 A1
Swadlincote, Church Gresley
DE11 . . . . 256 C2
Tupton S42 . . . . 131 C7
Park Rise S18 . . . . .75 A8
Park Row
Bretby DE15 . . . . 249 B1
Clay Cross S45 . . . . . . 131 D4
Parks Ave DE55 . . . . . 157 F3
Parkside
Belper DE56 . . . . 179 A3
Buxton SK17 . . . . .85 A8
Chesterfield S41 . . . . . .96 A7
Heage DE56 . . . . 179 E8
Renishaw S21 . . . . .60 B1
Park Side DE55 . . . . . 170 D7
Parkside Ave NG10 . 236 B8
Parkside Cl NG16 . . . 170 F4
Parkside Close S12 . . . .44 F2
Parkside Com Sch
S40 . . . . 266 A1
Parkside Dr
Ironville NG16 . . . . . . 170 F4
Long Eaton NG10 . . . . 236 B8
Parkside La S36 . . . . . .23 C6
Parkside Mews S12 . . . .44 F3
Parkside Rd DE21 . . . 220 D6
Parkside Sh Ctr S21 . .60 D7
Parkside Shopping Ctr
S20 . . . . .60 D7
Parkside View S40 . . . .95 B6
Park Spring Dr 10 S2 . .43 C8
Park Spring Dr S2 . . . .43 C8
Park Spring Grove
S2 . . . . .43 C8
Park Spring Pl S2 . . . .43 C8
Park Spring Way S2 . .43 C8
Park St
Alfreton DE55 . . . . . . .158 F3
Barlborough S43 . . . . . .80 B7
Breaston DE72 . . . . . . 235 F8
Chesterfield S40 . . . . . 115 A7
Derby DE1 . . . . 267 D2
Heanor DE75 . . . . 181 D2
Long Eaton NG10 . . . . 223 C1
Mansfield Woodhouse
NG19 . . . . 136 B3
Ripley DE5 . . . . 169 E1
Stapleford NG9 . . . . . 223 D6
Swadlincote DE11 . . . . 256 A6
Uttoxeter ST14 . . . . . . 210 C1
Wessington DE55 . . . . 145 E1
Wessington DE55 . . . . 157 E8
Parkstone Ct DE3 . . . 217 C2
Parkstone Delph S12 . 44 A2
Park Studios S40 . . . 266 A2
Park Terr
Charlesworth SK13 . . . .16 C8
Northwood DE4 . . . . . 127 A5
Park The
Bakewell DE45 . . . . . . 109 D5
Darley Dale DE4 . . . . . 127 D3
Duffield DE56 . . . . 190 E3
Ironville NG16 . . . . . . 170 E3
Mansfield Woodhouse
NG19 . . . . 136 C1
Mayfield DE6 . . . . 184 C8
Parkview DE21 . . . . . 205 C8
Park View
9 Ashbourne DE6 . . . 173 C2

Park View *continued*
Aston-on-Trent DE72 .246 B7
Bakewell DE45 . . . . . . 109 D5
Barlborough S43 . . . . . .80 B7
Burton upon Trent
DE15 . . . . 248 B3
Chesterfield S41 . . . . . 115 D7
Clowne S43 . . . . .80 F5
Hadfield SK14 . . . . .9 F5
Heanor DE75 . . . . 181 D1
Northwood DE4 . . . . . 127 A5
Pleasley NG19 . . . . . . 135 A5
Somercotes DE55 . . . . 170 D5
Whaley Thorns NG20 . 100 F2
Park View Cl DE22 . .204 F4
Park View Ct S8 . . . . . .43 A2
Park View Dr SK23 . . . .47 B6
Park View Ho DE21 . 219 C6
Parkview Prim Sch
DE21 . . . . 206 A2
Park View Rise S42 . .24 C1
Parkville Cl SK17 . . . .85 D5
Parkway
Branston DE14 . . . . . . .253 E7
Branston DE14 . . . . . . 256 F7
Chellaston DE73 . . . . . 232 E1
New Mills SK22 . . . . . .24 C1
Whitwell S80 . . . . .82 B6
Parkway Cl S8 . . . . .56 F7
Parkway The DE4 . . . 127 C3
Parkwood Cl 2
DE55 . . . . 158 E3
Park Wood Close
DE22 . . . . 204 F3
Parkwood Sch DE55 158 F4
Parliament Cl DE22 . 218 E4
Parliament St
Derby DE22 . . . . .218 E4
Swadlincote DE11 . . . . 255 F6
PARSLEY HAY 123 B4
Parsonage Cl S20 . . . .59 D6
Parsonage Croft
DE45 . . . . 109 C5
Parsonage Gdns SK6 .23 A4
Parson House Outdoor
Pursuit Ctr S11 . . . .54 B6
Parsons Cl
Hartington SK17 . . . . . 137 D5
Swadlincote DE11 . . . . 256 A1
Parsons Gate S33 . . . .40 A6
Parsons Gn DE3 . . . . 217 E6
Parsons Gr DE55 . . . . 180 D2
Parsons Way SK16 . . 254 D5
Parson's Wlk B79 . . . 263 F2
Parthenon Cl NG19 . .134 F5
Partington Ct 2
SK13 . . . . .10 F1
Partington Pk SK13 . .10 C3
Partington Theatre ★ 7
SK13 . . . . .10 C1
Partridge Cl S21 . . . . . .59 B3
Partridge Dr DE11 . . .256 F3
Partridge Way DE3 . 218 A3
PARWICH 151 E1
Parwich Cl S40 . . . . . . .95 A5
Parwich Dale
Hartington Nether Quarter
SK17 . . . . .150 F8
Parwich DE6 . . . . .151 B4
Parwich La DE6 . . . . . 151 E7
PARWICH LEES 151 A2
Parwich Prim Sch
DE6 . . . . 151 D2
Parwich Rd S42 . . . . . 131 F5
Pasteur Ave DE5 . . . . 169 D2
Pasture Gr S21 . . . . . . .59 C3
Pasture La
Brassington DE4 . . . . . 152 D1
Flagg SK17 . . . . 106 D6
Hilcote DE55 . . . . 148 C1
Long Eaton NG10 . . . . 237 A5
Stonebroom DE55 . . . 147 A3
Pasture Rd NG9 . . . . 209 D1
Pastures Ave DE23 . . 230 F7
Pastures Drive DE7 . 193 B8
Pastures Hill DE23 . . 218 B1
Pastures The
Duffield DE56 . . . . 190 E4
Eastwood NG16 . . . . . 195 B8
Mansfield Woodhouse
NG19 . . . . 136 E5
Repton DE65 . . . . 242 C2
Swadlincote DE11 . . . . 255 F5
Weston-on-Trent
DE72 . . . . 245 F5
Patchwork Row
NG20 . . . . 119 F4
Paterson Ave DE21 . 220 B6
Pathfinder Way 7
DE74 . . . . 246 E3
Patina Way DE11 . . . 256 A4
Patmore Sq DE23 . . . 231 F7
Paton Gr S43 . . . . .96 D8
Patrick Cl DE12 . . . . . 261 D5
Patten Ct DE24 . . . . . .232 A8
Patterdale Cl 2 S18 . .56 E1
Patterdale Rd DE24 . 220 A1
Pattison St S44 . . . . . . .98 F6
Paulet High Sch
DE15 . . . . 254 F7
Paulet Sch Dr DE15 . 254 F7
Pavements The (Sh Ctr)
S40 . . . . .266 B3
Pavilion Cl S43 . . . . . . .80 E2
Pavilion Ct DE7 . . . . . 207 D7

Pavilion Drive S43 . . . .97 E8
Pavilion Gdns NG19 . .134 F8
Pavilion Gdns The ★
SK17 . . . . .85 B7
Pavilion La SK6 . . . . . . .23 C2
Pavilion Mans 3
SK17 . . . . .85 B7
Pavilion Rd DE23 . . . 231 C8
Pavilion Workshops
S42 . . . . .116 D1
Paxton Cl
Derby DE3 . . . . 217 C1
Matlock DE4 . . . . 143 A6
Paxton Ct S14 . . . . .43 F4
Paxton Pl SK17 . . . . . . .84 E5
Paxton Rd S41 . . . . .96 C5
Payler Cl S2 . . . . .44 A8
Payne St DE22 . . . . . . 218 D6
Peacehaven 3
DE65 . . . . 242 B6
Peach Ave
Selston NG16 . . . . . . .171 F6
South Normanton
DE55 . . . . 160 B7
Peach St
Derby DE22 . . . . 218 D5
Heanor DE75 . . . . 181 D1
Peacock Cl
Glossop SK13 . . . . .9 E4
Killamarsh S21 . . . . . . .60 D6
Peacock Dr NG16 . . . 182 E1
Peacock Gr DE23 . . . 231 B6
Peacock Pl DE7 . . . . . 194 D4
Peacock Way DE55 . 169 F8
Peacroft Ct DE65 . . . 228 D2
Peacroft La DE65 . . . 228 D2
Peafield La NG19 . . . 136 F4
Peafield Lane Prim Sch
NG19 . . . . .136 F3
Peak Ave DE55 . . . . . 170 B6
Peak Cavern ★ S33 . . .38 B2
Peak Cavern Rd S33 . .38 B2
Peak Cl
Belper DE56 . . . . 179 A4
Pilsley S45 . . . . 132 C1
PEAK DALE 67 B5
Peakdale Cl
Long Eaton NG10 . . . . 236 A6
Ripley DE5 . . . . 180 D6
Peakdale Cres S12 . . . .44 E5
Peak Dale Prim Sch
SK17 . . . . .67 B5
Peakdale Rd
Glossop SK13 . . . . .9 E3
Marple SK6 . . . . .23 A4
Peak District Mining
Mus ★ DE4 . . . . 143 A1
Peak Dr DE23, DE24 . 232 A7
PEAK FOREST 49 B3
Peak Forest CE Prim Sch
SK17 . . . . .49 A3
Peak Ho SK13 . . . . .10 A5
Peaklands Pk S32 . . . . .71 F3
Peakland View DE4 . 127 C3
PEAKLEY HILL 75 C6
Peaknaze Cl SK13 . . . .17 B8
Peak Pl S43 . . . . .97 D7
Peak Railway ★ DE4 . 143 A5
Peak Rd SK23 . . . . .33 D8
Peak Sch DE55 . . . . . . .34 F2
Peaks The SK23 . . . . . .46 C5
Peak The NG20 . . . . . 119 E3
Peaktor La DE4 . . . . . 126 E7
Peak View
Buxton SK17 . . . . . . .105 E6
Clowne S43 . . . . .80 D5
Glossop SK13 . . . . .9 F4
South Normanton
DE55 . . . . 159 F5
Peak View Cl S32 . . . . .72 B2
Peak View Dr DE6 . . . 173 C1
Peak View Rd S40 . . . .95 D5
Peak Village Outlet Sh
Ctr DE4 . . . . 110 F1
Pearce La S42 . . . . . . 114 D3
Pearl Bank DE6 . . . . . 211 F8
Pearl Cl DE21 . . . . 206 B1
Pearl Gdns 4 DE11 . .255 F4
Pearl Way SK14 . . . . . . .9 A2
Pearson Croft S41 . . . .95 C6
Pearson Gdns S44 . . 117 E8
Pearson Trad Est
S41 . . . . .96 B8
PEAR TREE 232 B8
Pear Tree S45 . . . . . . 129 F3
Pear Tree Ave
Ripley DE5 . . . . 180 D8
Swadlincote DE11 . . . . 255 F7
Wingerworth S42 . . . . 114 E3
Peartree Cl DE74 . . . 247 A3
Pear Tree Cl
Brimington S43 . . . . . . .97 A8
Glossop SK13 . . . . .9 F4
Hartshorne DE11 . . . . 257 A7
Killamarsh S21 . . . . . . .60 C5
Marple SK6 . . . . .23 B8
Pear Tree Cres
DE23 . . . . 232 A8
Peartree Ct
Derby DE21 . . . . 205 D1
Etwall DE65 . . . . 229 B4
Pear Tree Dr
Linton DE12 . . . . 261 C6
Shirebrook NG20 . . . . 119 E6
Pear Tree Inf Sch
Derby DE23 . . . . 219 A1
Derby DE23 . . . . .232 B8
Peartree La NG17 . . . 134 B1

Pear Tree Mews
DE73 . . . . 252 F2
Pear Tree Rd
Derby DE23 . . . . 219 A1
Pilsley S45 . . . . 132 C1
Peartree Sta DE23 . . 232 B7
Pease Cl
Alfreton DE55 . . . . . . .159 B3
Clay Cross S45 . . . . . . 131 C5
PEASEHILL 180 F8
Peasehill DE5 . . . . 180 F8
Pease Hill DE55 . . . . . 159 D3
Peasehill Rd DE5 . . . 180 E8
Peaslows La
Bagshaw SK17 . . . . .47 F6
Sparrowpit SK23 . . . . . .48 A6
Peasunhurst La
Ashover S45 . . . . 113 A1
Ashover S45 . . . . 112 F1
Peatburn Ave DE75 . 181 C1
Peatfield Ct NG9 . . . . 209 D1
Peatfield Rd
Killamarsh S21 . . . . . . .60 F7
Stapleford NG9 . . . . . 209 D1
Peat La
Chapel-en-le-Frith
SK23 . . . . .35 F2
Spout DE4, DE56 . . . . 166 D4
Peats Cl DE6 . . . . 165 B1
Peckham Gdns
DE23 . . . . 218 A5
Pedley Ave 4 S20 . . . .59 E8
Pedley Dr S20 . . . . .59 E8
Pedley St DE7 . . . . . . 208 F7
Peebles Cl DE24 . . . . 231 E2
Peel Cres NG19 . . . . . 135 D2
Peel Gdns S18 . . . . .56 F1
Peel St
Derby DE22 . . . . 218 D6
Glossop SK13 . . . . .10 C5
Langley Mill NG16 . . . .182 B3
Long Eaton NG10 . . . . 236 D8
South Normanton
DE55 . . . . 160 B6
Peeres Cl SK6 . . . . .23 C1
Peers Cl DE21 . . . . . . 206 B2
Peet St DE22 . . . . 218 E4
Pegasus Ct S44 . . . . . . .99 B1
Pegasus Sch DE12 . . 260 F7
Pegasus Way DE65 . 228 E2
Peggars Cl S43 . . . . . . .80 B6
Peggs Wlk DE21 . . . . 231 E7
Peggy La DE55 . . . . . . 146 B6
Pegwell Cl DE21 . . . . 231 D7
Pelham Ave DE7 . . . . 194 E1
Pelham St
Derby DE22 . . . . 218 F4
Ilkeston DE7 . . . . 194 E1
Pemberton Pl 3
NG16 . . . . 182 F2
Pemberton The
DE55 . . . . 160 B4
Pembleton Dr NG19 135 D1
Pembrey Cl NG9 . . . . 209 D2
Pembroke Cl S40 . . . . .95 C1
Pembroke Ct S41 . . . . .95 F7
Pembroke Rd
Dronfield S18 . . . . .76 A8
Shireoaks S81 . . . . .63 F7
Pembroke St DE21 . . 219 D8
Penallton Cl DE24 . . 232 E6
Pencroft Gr DE23 . . . 231 C5
Pendean Cl DE55 . . . 147 E1
Pendennis Cl DE24 . 233 B6
Pendine Cl DE55 . . . . 160 C6
Pendlebury Dr DE3 . 217 C1
Pendleside Way
DE23 . . . . 230 E7
Pendleton La DE56 . 166 F7
Pendragon Dr DE72 . 245 A8
Penfold Way DE55 . . 147 B5
Penge Rd DE22 . . . . . 218 A7
Penhaligan's Cl
DE73 . . . . 232 F1
Penistone Gdns
S45 . . . . 131 D2
Peniston Rise DE73 . 252 A7
Penkridge Rd DE11 . 256 B1
Pen La S45 . . . . 131 E3
Penmore Cl S41 . . . . . 115 C8
Penmore Gdns 4
S41 . . . . .96 C1
Penmore La S41 . . . . 115 C8
Penncroft Dr S45 . . . 131 D2
Penncroft La S45 . . . 131 D3
Pennie Cl NG10 . . . . . 236 D4
Penniment La NG19 . 135 B2
Pennine Ave DE55 . . 170 C7
Pennine Cl
Long Eaton NG10 . . . . 223 A1
Mansfield Woodhouse
NG19 . . . . 136 C4
Newton DE55 . . . . 148 A3
Sutton in Ashfield
NG17 . . . . 148 E4
Tibshelf DE55 . . . . 147 F6
Pennine Dr
Selston NG16 . . . . . . .171 F7
South Normanton
DE55 . . . . 159 F5
Pennine Rd SK13 . . . . .17 A8
Pennine View
Heage DE56 . . . . .179 E8
Palterton S44 . . . . 118 A5
Pennine Way
Chesterfield S40 . . . . . .95 C5
Grassmoor S42 . . . . . . 115 F3

Pennine Way *continued*
Swadlincote DE11 . . . 256 A3
Pennine Way Jun Sch
DE11 . . . . 256 A2
Pennine Wlk S42 . . . 115 F3
Penn La DE73 . . . . 252 B7
Penn Moor Cl NG10 . 236 A6
Penns Rd S2 . . . . .43 C6
Pcnn St DE56 . . . . 179 A4
Penny Acres Prim Sch
S18 . . . . .74 F8
Pennycress Cl DE23 . 231 A7
Pennycroft La ST14 . 210 C1
Pennycroft Rd ST14 . 210 A1
Penny Engine La S21 . 59 E4
Pennyfields Bvd
NG10 . . . . 236 B7
Penny Gn S80 . . . . .82 A5
Penny La S17 . . . . .55 C5
Penny Long La
DE22 . . . . 218 E8
Pennytown Ct DE55 . 159 C1
Pennytown Ponds
Nature Reserve ★
DE55 . . . . 159 D1
Pennyunk La DE45 . . .89 C1
Pennywell Dr S42 . . . 113 D7
Penrhyn Ave DE23 . . 218 D1
Penrith DE23 . . . . .230 F5
Penrith Pl DE21 . . . . 205 D2
Penrose Cres S44 . . . . .97 D3
Penryn Cl DE55 . . . . . 160 C6
Pentagon The DE21 . 219 C6
Pentewen Cl DE22 . . 204 E2
Penthorpe Cl S12 . . . . .44 B6
Pentland Cl
5 Chesterfield S40 . . . .95 C5
Derby DE21 . . . . 206 A2
Pentland Gdns
NG10 . . . . 223 A1
Pentland Rd S18 . . . . . .56 D1
PENTRICH 169 B5
Pentrich Ct 1 S40 . . . .95 D5
Pentrich Rd
Giltbrook NG16 . . . . . . 195 C7
Ripley DE5 . . . . 169 D2
Swanwick DE55 . . . . . 169 D7
Pentridge Dr DE7 . . . 194 C3
Penzance Rd DE24 . . 233 B5
Pepper La
Stanton-by-Dale
DE7 . . . . 208 E1
Stanton-By-Dale DE7 . 222 E8
Percival Cl SK17 . . . . 138 D3
Percy St
Derby DE22 . . . . .218 E3
Ilkeston DE7 . . . . 208 F7
Percy Wood Cl
DE65 . . . . 228 C2
Peregrine Cl
Burton upon Trent
DE15 . . . . 248 D3
Derby DE24 . . . . 231 D4
Peregrine Way
Harthill S26 . . . . .61 E5
Tibshelf DE55 . . . . 147 E5
Periwinkle Road
S42 . . . . 115 A2
Perlethorpe Ave
NG19 . . . . 136 A1
Perrydale
Peak Forest SK17 . . . . .49 A5
Perryfoot SK17 . . . . . . .48 E7
PERRYFOOT 48 E7
Perry Gdns NG16 . . . 182 D6
Pershore Dr DE14 . . . 254 A8
Perth Cl
Burton upon Trent
DE15 . . . . 248 C2
Derby DE3 . . . . 217 E4
Mansfield Woodhouse
NG19 . . . . 136 C5
Perth Dr NG9 . . . . 209 F1
Perth St DE21 . . . . . . 205 D1
Peter Baines Ind Est
DE22 . . . . 267 A4
Peterborough St
DE21 . . . . 219 E8
Peterdale Cl S43 . . . . . .96 E8
Peterdale Rd S43 . . . . .96 E8
Peterhouse Terr 1
DE23 . . . . 219 A2
Peterlees The DE12 . 262 E1
Peterlee Pl DE24 . . . 233 A4
Peter More Hill S80 . .81 E4
Peters Ave S45 . . . . . 131 B4
Peters Ct DE65 . . . . . 227 D1
Petersgate NG10 . . . 223 A1
Petersgate Cl NG10 . 223 A2
Petersham Ct 7
NG10 . . . . 223 B2
Petersham Dr DE24 . 233 C6
Petersham Rd
NG10 . . . . 223 A1
Peters St DE11 . . . . . 256 C1
Peter St
Ashbourne DE6 . . . . . . 173 C1
Glossop SK13 . . . . .10 A6
Petcrway DE55 . . . . . 170 C8
Pettifor Terr DE55 . . 147 C1
Pettyclose La S41,
S43 . . . . .96 D5
Petty Close La DE6 . 202 C1
Petworth Ave NG9 . . 223 F3
Pevensey Ave S41 . . . .95 E6

Pevensey Ct S41. . . . . . . .95 E7
Peverel House DE5. .181 B8
Peveril Ave
　Borrowash DE72 . . . . 221 C2
　New Mills SK22. . . . . . . .24 C1
Peveril Castle ★ S33 . .38 C2
Peveril Cl
　Castleton S33. . . . . .38 C2
　Darley Dale DE4 . . . . . 127 C3
　Somercotes DE55. . . . . 170 C6
Peveril Cres
　Long Eaton NG10 . . . . .235 F5
　West Hallam DE7 . . . . .207 E8
Peveril Ct
　❶ Glossop SK13. . . . . . .17 F8
　Ripley DE5 . . . . 169 C1
Peveril Dr
　Ilkeston DE7. . . . . 194 D2
　Somercotes DE55. . . . . 170 C6
Peveril Gdns SK12. . . .33 A6
Peveril Ho SK17 . . . . . .85 A6
Peveril Mews SK12. . . .33 A6
Peveril Rd
　Bolsover S44. . . . . .98 F3
　Buxton SK17. . . . . .85 C7
　Castleton S33. . . . . .38 C2
　Chesterfield S41. . . . . . .95 F7
　Eckington S21. . . . . . . .59 E3
　Tibshelf DE55. . . . . . . .147 F6
Peveril St DE24 . . . . . . 232 D6
Pewit Cl S42 . . . . 132 D8
Pewit La DE55 . . . . 147 C6
*Pewitt Carr Nature
　Reserve* ★ DE7. . . . . . 208 C8
Pheasant Field Dr
　DE21. . . . . 221 A6
Pheasant Hill DE6. . . 136 A1
Phildock Wood Rd
　DE3. . . . . 217 D6
Philip Howard Rd
　SK13. . . . . .17 C8
Philips Croft DE56 . . 190 E4
Philipway DE55. . . . . . 170 D8
Phoenix Ct S12. . . . . . .44 E1
Phoenix Rd S12 . . . . . .44 E1
Phoenix Rise NG19 . . 135 A5
Phoenix St DE1. . . . . . 267 B4
Phoenix Ri NG19. . . . . 134 F5
Phyllis Gr NG10. . . . . . 236 F7
Piccadilly Cl NG19 . . 136 C6
Piccadilly La
　Mayfield DE6 . . . . 172 C1
　Mayfield DE6 . . . . 184 B8
Piccadilly Rd S41. . . . .96 C3
Pickard Cres S13. . . . .44 D8
Pickard Dr S13 . . . . . . .44 D8
Pickard La DE56 . . . . . 168 D1
Pickburns Gdns
　Belper DE56. . . . . 191 F8
　Kilburn DE56. . . . . 191 F8
Pickerell Cl DE6. . . . . 203 A2
Pickering Ave NG16 .182 F2
Pickering Dr DE11 . . 257 B1
Pickering Rise
　DE21. . . . . 205 D1
Pickford Gr ❶ DE6 . 211 A1
Pickford Pl SK23 . . . . .47 B6
Pickford's House (Mus) ★
　DE1. . . . . .218 F5
Pickleys La DE6 . . . . 224 C8
Pickton Cl S40 . . . . . . .95 D2
Picory Corner DE45. 126 C7
Pictor Gr SK17. . . . . . .85 D7
Pic Tor La DE4 . . . . . 143 B4
Pictor Rd SK17. . . . . . .85 D7
Piddocks Rd DE15 . . 255 B5
Pighills La S18 . . . . . . .57 F4
Pig La DE4 . . . . 111 B4
Pike Cl
　Chesterfield S40. . . . . . .95 B5
　Hayfield SK22. . . . . .25 C3
PIKEHALL. 139 E3
Pike Hall La DE6. . . . 151 E4
Pike's La SK13. . . . . . . .17 B8
Pike View Cl SK23 . . . .34 E2
Pilgrim Ct S81. . . . . . .63 F7
Pilgrims Way DE24 . 231 C3
PILHOUGH. 126 E7
Pilhough La DE4. . . . 126 C6
Pilhough Rd DE4 . . . . 126 E5
Pillar Butts DE4 . . . . 165 E8
PILSLEY
　Baslow 91 C3
　Clay Cross 132 D1
**Pilsley CE (Aided) Prim
　Sch** DE45. . . . . .91 C2
Pilsley Cl
　Belper DE56. . . . . 179 C6
　Clay Cross S45. . . . . . . 131 E3
PILSLEY GREEN. . . . 147 C8
Pilsley La DE45 . . . . . .91 D3
Pilsley Prim Sch
　S45. . . . . 132 C1
Pilsley Rd
　Clay Cross S45 . . . . 131 E3
　Lower Pilsley S45. . . . . 132 A4
　Stonebroom DE55. . . . .147 B6
Pimlico
　Derby DE22 . . . . .218 B6
　Ilkeston DE7. . . . . .208 E8
Pimm's Rd DE6. . . . . . 217 A8
Pinchom's Hill Rd
　DE56. . . . . 179 B3
Pinch The DE6 . . . . . 150 B2
Pindale Ave S43. . . . . .97 C7

Pindale Rd
　Castleton S33. . . . . . . .38 D1
　Hope S33 . . . . .38 E1
Pinders La DE6. . . . . 152 D4
Pine Ave NG16. . . . . . 182 A3
Pine Cl
　Burton upon Trent
　　DE14. . . . . 254 A8
　Creswell S80 . . . . .81 F1
　Derby DE21 . . . . 220 B4
　Etwall DE65. . . . . 229 C4
　Killamarsh S21. . . . . . .60 C5
　Mansfield Woodhouse
　　NG19 . . . . 136 C5
　Ripley DE5 . . . . 169 D1
　Shirebrook NG20. . . . . 119 E6
　Smalley DE7. . . . . 192 F5
Pine Croft DE6 . . . . . 185 D7
Pinecroft Ct DE21 . . . 206 B1
Pine Gr DE11. . . . . . . .255 F6
Pines Cl NG16. . . . . . . 171 F7
Pine St S43. . . . . .97 A8
Pines The DE72. . . . . 235 B7
Pine Tree Wlk
　NG16. . . . . 182 E2
Pine View
　Chesterfield S40. . . . . . .95 B3
　Clay Cross S45 . . . . 131 E3
Pineview Gdns
　DE23. . . . . 218 B1
Pine Wlk DE11. . . . . . 261 E7
Pinewood DE6. . . . . . 181 B7
Pinewood Cl
　Alfreton DE55. . . . . 159 C3
　Shirland DE55. . . . . . . .146 F2
Pinewood Dr DE55. . . 146 D2
Pinewood Rd
　Belper DE56. . . . . .178 E6
　Burton upon Trent
　　DE15. . . . . .254 F6
　Matlock DE4. . . . . .143 B7
Pinfold SK13. . . . . .9 E4
Pinfold Cl
　Holymoorside S42. . . . .113 E8
　Repton DE65. . . . . 242 D2
　Tutbury DE13 . . . . 239 C5
Pinfold Cres SK17 . . . .69 C3
Pinfold Gdns NG19 . .136 F2
Pinfold Hill S32 . . . . . .72 E2
Pinfold La
　Bradley DE6 . . . . 187 A8
　Repton DE65. . . . . 242 D2
　Stapleford NG9. . . . . . .223 E7
　Pinfold St SK17 . . . . . .69 C3
　Pinfold St S21. . . . . . . .59 D3
Pinfold The
　Belper DE56. . . . . .179 C5
　Elvaston DE72 . . . . 233 F4
　Glapwell S44 . . . . 118 B1
　Middleton DE45. . . . . . 124 E3
Pinfold Trad Est
　NG9. . . . . .223 E7
Pinfold View DE45. . 109 C5
Pingle DE22. . . . . 204 E4
Pingle Cl S81. . . . . . . .63 E7
Pingle Cres DE56 . . . .178 F5
Pingle Farm Rd
　Swadlincote DE11. . . . .255 F5
　❸ Swadlincote DE11. . 256 A5
Pingle Grange S43 . . . .96 E7
Pingle Hill DE73. . . . .252 F5
Pinglehill Way
　DE73. . . . . 233 B2
Pingle La
　Belper DE56. . . . . .178 F5
　Carsington DE4 . . . . . .164 E7
　Heage DE56. . . . . .168 F2
　Swarkestone DE73. . . . 244 E7
Pingle Rd S21. . . . . . . .60 E7
Pingle Rise DE4 . . . . 143 D6
Pingle Sch The
　DE11. . . . . 256 A5
Pingle The
　Derby DE12 . . . . .57 C3
　Long Eaton NG10 . . . . 236 D8
　Melbourne DE73. . . . . . 252 A7
　Sheffield S21 . . . . .59 E7
Pingot Rd SK22. . . . . . .33 D8
Pingott La S33 . . . . . . .10 A5
Pingreaves Dr DE73 233 A2
Pinhole Pl ❸ S43. . . . .81 E2
Pinnacle Way DE24 . 219 D3
PINXTON. 160 C2
Pinxton Gn NG16. . . . .160 F3
Pinxton La
　Kirkby-in-Ashfield
　　NG17 . . . . .160 F6
　South Normanton
　　DE55. . . . . 160 C5
**Pioneer Meadows
　Nature Reserve** ★
　DE7. . . . . 208 C4
Pioneer Way DE24 . . 232 B3
Piper Ave S45 . . . . . . 131 E4
Piper Avenue DE74 . 246 F3
Piper Close NG19. . . . 136 B2
Piper Gro NG20. . . . . . 119 F2
Piper La S42 . . . . .94 E3
Piper Rd S44 . . . . .97 D3
Pipers Ct NG16. . . . . . 170 F3
Piper St SK13. . . . . . . .10 A5
Pipeyard La S21. . . . . .59 C2
Pipistrelle Pl DE3. . . 230 E8
Pippenwell Rd
　SK17. . . . . 106 A7
Pippin Gdns DE24 . . .232 F7
Pippin Hill DE5. . . . . 180 E1

Pipworth La S21. . . . . .59 F4
Pirelli Cl DE74. . . . . . 246 E2
Pitch Cl S43. . . . . .80 E2
Pitch Close NG16. . . . 195 C8
Pit Close La DE73. . . 233 A1
Pit La
　Codnor DE5 . . . . 181 A7
　Crich DE4, DE55. . . . . .157 B6
　Mansfield NG19 . . . . . 135 A5
　Pleasley NG19 . . . . . . .134 F5
　Ripley DE5 . . . . .169 E1
　Sheffield S12 . . . . .44 A8
　Shipley DE75 . . . . .194 B6
　Shirland DE55. . . . . . . 158 D8
　Stonebroom DE55 . . . . 147 A5
Pit Lane DE6. . . . . 209 E3
Pits La
　Parwich DE6. . . . . .151 E1
　Parwich DE6. . . . . .162 E8
Pittar St DE22 . . . . . . 267 A2
Pitt Hill NG20. . . . . . . 100 F2
Pittlemere La SK17 . . .50 A1
Pitt St S21. . . . . .59 C2
Pittywood Rd DE4 . . . 165 E7
Pk Cres DE4. . . . . 143 A5
Pk House Ct S45. . . . 131 E3
Pk La S44 . . . . .98 A3
Pk Rd DE45. . . . . .109 F4
Pk View Mws S8. . . . . .43 B2
Placket La DE4. . . . . . 141 B6
Plackett Cl
　Breaston DE72. . . . . . . 235 D8
　Stapleford NG9. . . . . . .223 F8
Plains La DE56 . . . . . 178 B4
Plainspot Rd NG16. . 171 E2
Plain The DE6 . . . . . . 201 F8
PLAISTOW. 156 F6
Plaistow Gn Rd DE4 157 A4
PLAISTOW GREEN. . 156 F4
Plaistow Green Rd
　Crich DE4 . . . . .156 F2
　Plaistow Green DE4 . . .156 F4
Plantain Gdns DE23. 231 C5
Plantation Cl
　Chesterfield S40. . . . . . .95 A5
　Whitwell S80 . . . . .81 E5
Plantation Rd ❼ S8 . .43 A6
Plantations The ❾
　NG10. . . . . 236 A8
Plantation The
　DE23. . . . . 218 B1
Plantin Rise S20. . . . . .59 E7
Plantin The S20. . . . . .59 E7
Plant La NG10 . . . . . . 236 A4
Platchetts The DE73 .252 F4
Platform Ct DE21 . . . 220 D3
Platts Ave DE75. . . . . 181 C1
Platt St
　Glossop SK13. . . . . . . .10 B5
　Pinxton NG16. . . . . . . 160 D2
Platts Yard DE4. . . . . .157 F4
Pleasant Ave S44. . . . 118 B7
Pleasant Cl S12 . . . . . .44 B6
Pleasant Pl S40 . . . . . .95 D3
Pleasant Rd S12. . . . . .44 B6
Pleasant View SK6. . . .15 B3
PLEASLEY. 135 B6
PLEASLEYHILL. 135 C4
Pleasley Hill Way
　NG19 . . . . 135 B4
*Pleasley Pit and Country
　Pk* ★ NG19. . . . . .134 E6
Pleasley Rd NG17. . . 134 C1
Pleasley Springs
　NG19 . . . . 135 B5
*Pleasley Vale Nature
　Reserve* ★ NG19 . . . 135 D7
**Pleasley Vale Outdoor
　Activity Ctr** NG19. 135 D6
Plimsoll Ct DE22. . . . 267 A1
Plimsoll St DE22. . . . 218 C6
Plough Croft DE16 . . 254 E7
Ploughfield Cl DE23 231 B6
Plough Gate DE22 . . .204 F2
Plover Ave DE4 . . . . . .156 F3
Plover Cl SK13. . . . . . . .17 F8
Plover Ct DE3 . . . . . . 230 B7
Plover Way S44. . . . . . .96 F3
Plowman Ct NG9 . . . . 223 D6
Plowright Cl S14 . . . . .43 D5
Plowright Dr S14 . . . . .43 D5
Plowright Mount
　S14. . . . . .43 D5
Plowright Way S14 . . .43 D5
Plucksbridge Rd SK6 .23 B3
Plumbley Hall Mews
　S20. . . . . .59 C6
Plumbley Hall Rd
　S20. . . . . .59 C6
Plumbley La S20 . . . . . .59 B6
Plumbleywood La S12,
　S20. . . . . .58 F6
Plummer Rd DE11 . . . 256 A5
Plumptre Cl NG16. . . .182 F1
Plumptre Gdns ❷
　NG16. . . . . .182 F2
Plumptre Rd NG16. . .182 F2
Plumptre Way NG16 .182 F1
Plymouth Ave NG16. 160 E2
Plymouth Ct ❼ S41. . .95 F8
Pochard Close
　NG19 . . . . .136 F2
Pocknedge La S42. . . 113 D8
Podmore View ST14 .196 F3
Podnor La SK6 . . . . . . .24 A6
Poets Cl S42 . . . . 132 C8
Pole La SK6. . . . . .24 B4
Pole's Rd DE6 . . . . 217 A8

Pollards Oaks DE72. 221 C1
Pollard Way ❸ DE4. 116 E1
Polly Froggatt La
　S32. . . . . .72 B2
Polyfields La S44 . . . . 118 B8
Pomegranate Rd
　S40. . . . . .95 D6
Pomegranite Theatre ★
　S41. . . . . 266 C3
Pomeroy Cotts
　SK17. . . . . 106 B4
Pond Cotts DE4. . . . . 143 E6
Pond End DE74. . . . . . 247 B6
Pond La
　Tupton S42 . . . . 131 D8
　Wingerworth S42. . . . . 114 E4
Pond Rd DE56 . . . . . . 191 C7
Pond St S40. . . . . 266 B2
Pondwell Cnr S43 . . . .96 F7
Pondwell Dr S43. . . . . .96 F7
Ponsonby Terr DE1. 218 E5
Pontefract St DE24 . 232 D7
Pontypool Cl DE21. . 206 B2
Pool Cl
　Elvaston DE24 . . . . . . 233 C4
　Pinxton NG16. . . . . . . 160 D2
Poolclose Row
　NG16. . . . . 160 D2
Poole's Cavern ★
　SK17. . . . . .85 A6
Poole St DE24 . . . . . . 232 E6
Pool Rd DE73. . . . . . . 252 D6
POOLSBROOK. 98 A7
Poolsbrook Ave S43 . .98 A8
Poolsbrook Cres S43 .98 A8
Pools Brook Ctry Pk ★
　S43. . . . . .79 B1
Poolsbrook Sq S43 . . .98 A8
Poolsbrook View
　S43. . . . . .98 A8
Pools Head La DE6 . .201 F6
Pool's La S21. . . . . . . .77 C7
Pool St DE11 . . . . 256 D2
Pope Carr Rd DE4 . . 143 C5
Poplar Ave
　Chesterfield S40. . . . . . .95 B2
　Derby DE21 . . . . 220 E5
　Moira DE12. . . . . 262 E2
　New Mills SK22. . . . . . .24 D1
　Ripley DE5 . . . . 180 D8
　Sandiacre NG10 . . . . . 223 A7
　Swadlincote DE11 . . . . 256 B6
Poplar Cl
　Derby DE24 . . . . 233 B7
　Dronfield S18 . . . . .76 C7
　Killamarsh S21. . . . . . .60 C5
　Overseal DE12 . . . . . . 262 B3
Poplar Cres DE56 . . . 185 D8
Poplar Dr
　Chesterfield S42. . . . . . 115 C1
　Glapwell S44 . . . . 134 B8
　Pleasley NG19 . . . . 135 B4
Poplar Grange
　DE21. . . . . 206 C3
Poplar Grove S45. . . 132 A4
Poplar Heights S44. . .98 A4
Poplar Nook DE22 . . .204 F4
Poplar Rd
　Breaston DE72. . . . . . . 235 F8
　Eckington S21. . . . . . . .59 C2
　South Normanton
　　DE55. . . . . 160 B7
Poplar Row DE22 . . . 205 A1
Poplar St ❷ NG19 . . 136 C3
Poplars The
　Derby DE22 . . . . .204 F4
　Whitwell S80 . . . . .82 A5
Poplar Terr
　Chapel-en-le-Frith
　　SK23. . . . . .47 B7
　Selston NG16. . . . . . . .171 E6
Poplar Way
　High Lane SK6 . . . . .32 A7
　Ilkeston DE7. . . . . .208 D5
Poppleton Croft S40 . .96 F4
Poppy Cl NG20 . . . . . . 119 D3
Poppy Close DE13 . . 239 D5
Poppy Cres S40 . . . . . .96 C7
Poppy Ct S42. . . . . . . 116 C1
Poppyfields
　Clowne S43. . . . . .80 D2
　❺ Denstone ST14 . . . 196 C6
　Ripley DE5 . . . . 180 D7
Poppy Fields Close
　DE4. . . . . .142 F7
Poppyfields Dr DE3. 217 C2
Poppyfields Mdw
　DE22. . . . . 204 C2
Poppy Mws DE7 . . . . .262 F4
Porlock Cl ❷ NG10. 236 A8
Porlock Ct DE21 . . . . 206 A2
Portaway La ST14 . . . 183 B3
Portchester Leys ❶
　DE11. . . . . 255 E6
Porteous Cl DE4. . . . 127 D3
Porter Dr DE5 . . . . . . 159 C4
Porter Ho ❾ S43. . . . .78 E2
PORTERHOUSE. 169 F1
Porterhouse Rd
　DE5. . . . . .169 F1
Porter La DE4 . . . . . . 154 E3
Porter Pl DE21 . . . . . 220 D5
Porter Rd DE24. . . . . .218 F2
Porters Farm Ct
　ST14. . . . . 224 C2
Porters La DE21 . . . . 205 F3

Porter's La
　Derby DE21 . . . . 205 F3
　Findern DE65 . . . . 230 D1
Porter St S43. . . . . .78 E2
Porthcawl Pl DE21. . 206 C2
Portico Rd DE23. . . . . 231 A6
Portis Ct DE21. . . . . . 220 D3
Portland Ave
　Bolsover S44. . . . . .99 B1
　Burton upon Trent
　　DE14. . . . . 254 A7
　Creswell S80 . . . . .81 E1
Portland Cl
　Chesterfield S41. . . . . . 266 B4
　Derby DE3 . . . . 217 D2
Portland Court Mews
　NG19 . . . . 136 C4
Portland Cres
　Bolsover S44. . . . . .99 B1
　Mansfield Woodhouse
　　NG19 . . . . 136 D3
　Stapleford NG9. . . . . . .223 E6
Portland Dr NG20. . . . 119 F3
Portland Heights
　DE55. . . . . 148 E4
Portland La DE72. . . . 245 A8
Portland Rd
　Beeston NG9 . . . . 223 F1
　Eastwood NG16 . . . . . .195 B8
　Ilkeston DE7. . . . . .194 F3
　Long Eaton NG10 . . . . 236 B4
　New Mills SK22. . . . . . .24 D1
　Shirebrook NG20. . . . . 119 F4
　Whaley Thorns NG20 . 101 A3
Portland Sq DE45. . . 109 D6
Portland St
　Clowne S43. . . . . .81 A4
　Derby DE23 . . . . 232 A8
　Etwall DE65. . . . . 229 B4
　Mansfield Woodhouse
　　NG19 . . . . 136 C4
　New Houghton NG19 . . 135 A7
　Whitwell S80 . . . . .81 F6
Portland Terr NG20. 101 A2
Portman Chase
　DE24. . . . . 231 D2
Porton La DE55. . . . . 160 A7
Portreath Dr DE22. . 204 E3
Portsmouth Cl
　DE11. . . . . 255 E2
Port Way
　Branston DE14. . . . . . 253 D8
　Holbrook DE56, DE56. 191 D5
Portway Cl DE22. . . . 205 A4
Portway Close S12 . . .44 E5
Portway Dr
　Matlock DE4. . . . . 143 D6
　Tutbury DE13 . . . . 239 C5
Portway Inf Sch
　DE22. . . . . 204 E4
Portway Jun Sch
　DE22. . . . . 204 E4
Portwood Ind Est
　DE11. . . . . 256 A1
Posthill Cl S80 . . . . . . .82 A6
Postmans La S42. . . . 116 C1
Post Office La DE6. . .201 F7
Post Office Rd DE6 . 149 E4
Post Office Row
　SK17. . . . . .69 E3
Post St SK13. . . . . .10 B5
Posy La DE72 . . . . 246 A7
Potato Pit La
　Dale Abbey DE7 . . . . . 208 A1
　Stanton-by-Dale DE7. 222 A8
Potlocks The DE65. . 242 C6
Potter Rd SK13. . . . . . . .9 E3
Potters Cl S41. . . . . . . .77 C2
Potters La DE4,
　DE55. . . . . 157 B5
Potters Nook S81. . . . .63 E7
**POTTER
　SOMERSAL**. 212 A4
Potter St
　Derby DE21 . . . . 220 D4
　Melbourne DE73. . . . . .252 B7
Potters Way DE7 . . . . 209 A8
Potters Yd DE73 . . . . 252 B7
Pottery Cl DE56. . . . . 179 C5
Pottery Lane E S41 . . .96 B8
Pottery Lane W S41 . .96 A7
Pottery Prim Sch
　DE56. . . . . 179 C4
Poulter Ctry Pk ★
　NG20. . . . . 100 E2
Poulter St NG20 . . . . 100 F1
Pounder La DE4 . . . . 142 D2
Powell Dr S21. . . . . . . .60 C6
Powell St DE23 . . . . . 218 E2
Pown St SK17 . . . . 137 A6
Powtrell Pl DE7 . . . . 209 B6
Poynter Cl DE75 . . . . 181 C1
Poynton Wood Cres
　S17. . . . . .56 A6
Poynton Wood Glade
　S17. . . . . .56 A6
Poyser Ave DE21 . . . 220 A7

Poyser La
　Kirk Langley DE6. . . . . 203 A1
　Langley Common DE6. .202 F1
Pratt Cl NG19. . . . . . . 135 D1
PRATTHALL. 94 B7
Pratthall La DE4 . . . . 166 A6
Premier Ave DE6 . . . 185 B8
Prescot Cl DE3 . . . . . 217 C1
Press La S42 . . . . 130 D6
Prestbury Ct DE21 . . 206 B1
Preston Ave DE55. . . 159 B4
Preston Rd ❸ DE23. 230 F1
Preston St S8 . . . . .43 A7
Prestwick Way
　DE73. . . . . 232 E2
Prestwold Way S41. . 115 C7
Prestwood La ST14 . .196 F8
Prestwood Park Dr
　DE11. . . . . 256 D5
Pretoria St S44. . . . . . .98 C5
Pride Park DE24. . . . . 219 D3
Pride Parkway
　DE24. . . . . 219 D3
Pride Pl DE21 . . . . 219 D3
Pride Point Dr
　DE24. . . . . 219 D2
PRIESTCLIFFE. 87 F5
**PRIESTCLIFFE
　DITCH**. 87 D4
*Priestcliffe Lees (Nature
　Reserve)* ★ SK17. . . . .88 B7
Priestcliffe Rd
　Priestcliffe SK17 . . . . . .88 A5
　Taddington SK17. . . . . .87 F4
Priestfield Gdns S41. .95 B7
Priest La SK23. . . . . . . .45 A6
Priestland Ave
　DE21. . . . . 220 D4
Priestley Ave DE55. . 146 C5
Primary Cl DE56 . . . . 179 A4
Prime Enterprise Pk
　DE1. . . . . 267 C4
Prime Ind Est DE23 . 219 C2
Prime Ind Pk DE23 . . 219 C2
Prime Parkway DE1 . 267 B3
Primrose Ave NG16. .171 F2
Primrose Bank
　DE65. . . . . 229 C5
Primrose Bsns Pk
　DE55. . . . . .147 F1
Primrose Cl
　Derby DE21 . . . . 205 F3
　Killamarsh S21. . . . . . .60 E7
　South Normanton
　　DE55. . . . . .160 B7
Primrose Cotts
　Hazelwood DE56 . . . . . 190 C7
　Risley DE72 . . . . 222 D3
Primrose Cres ❶
　SK13. . . . . .17 B8
Primrose Ct
　Hayfield SK22. . . . . .25 D3
　Mansfield Woodhouse
　　NG19 . . . . 136 F4
Primrose Dr
　Burton upon Trent
　　DE14. . . . . 254 A8
　Morley DE7. . . . . 206 C8
　Tutbury DE13 . . . . 239 C5
Primrose Hill
　Blackwell DE55. . . . . . .147 F1
　Glossop SK13. . . . . . . .17 B8
　Ilkeston NE7. . . . . .194 E3
Primrose La
　Glossop SK13. . . . . . . .17 B8
　Hayfield SK22. . . . . .25 C5
　Killamarsh S21. . . . . . .60 E7
　Marple SK6. . . . . .24 A4
　Tideswell SK17. . . . . . . .69 C3
Primrose Mdw
　DE11. . . . . 256 B7
Primrose Rise NG16 195 B8
Primrose St DE7. . . . 194 E3
Primrose Terr ❷
　SK13. . . . . .17 B8
Primrose Vale Cotts
　SK22. . . . . .25 C4
Primrose Way NG20 .119 F6
Primula Cl NG20. . . . . 119 D3
Primula Way DE23 . . 231 D4
Prince Charles Ave
　DE22. . . . . 218 A6
Prince Edward Drive
　DE22. . . . . 218 B3
Prince Edward Prim Sch
　S12. . . . . .44 A7
Prince George Drive
　DE22. . . . . 218 B3
Prince of Wales Rd
　S2. . . . . .44 B7
Princes Dr DE23 . . . . 218 B2
Princes Rd SK23. . . . . .34 E2
Prince's Rd SK17 . . . . .85 C7
Princess Ave
　Linton DE12 . . . . 261 C6
　South Normanton
　　DE55. . . . . 160 A5
Princess Cl
　Heanor DE75 . . . . 181 D2
　Woodville DE11 . . . . . .256 F2
Princess Ct S2 . . . . . . .44 B8
Princess Dr
　Borrowash DE72 . . . . . 221 A2
　Sandiacre NG10 . . . . . 223 B4
Princess Pl S45. . . . . . 131 C2
Princess Rd
　Dronfield S18 . . . . .57 B2
　Uttoxeter ST14. . . . . . . 210 A1

Princess St
Brimington S43. . . . . . . **96** F8
Chesterfield S40. . . . . **266** A4
Glossop SK13. . . . .**17** C8
Long Eaton NG10 . . . . **236** D8
Swadlincote DE11 . . . .**261** F8
Princes St
Derby DE23 . . . .**232** D8
Eastwood NG16. . . . . .**182** F3
Prince's St DE23. . . . . **219** B1
Princess Way DE13 . **240** E1
Prince St
Ilkeston DE7. . . . .**194** E4
Long Eaton NG10 . . . . **236** D8
Prince William Drive
DE22. . . . . **218** B3
Pringle La S41. . . . .**76** F4
Printers Brow SK14. . . .**9** D5
Printers Dr SK15. . . . . . .**4** A6
Printers Drive SK6. . . .**23** C2
Printers Fold SK14. . . . .**9** D5
Printers Pk SK14 . . . . . .**9** E5
Priors Barn Cl DE72. **221** D2
Priorway Ave DE72 . **221** D2
Priorway Gdns
DE72. . . . . **221** C1
Priory Cl
Breedon on the Hill
DE73. . . . .**252** E2
Chellaston DE73. . . . **245** A8
Ilkeston DE7. . . . . **208** C6
Swadlincote DE11 . . . **256** A6
Tutbury DE13 . . . .**239** B5
Yeaveley DE6 . . . . **199** D5
Priory Ct S26. . . . .**61** E5
Priory Gdns
Derby DE21 . . . .**205** F3
Swanwick DE55 . . . . . **170** A8
Priory Lands DE13 . .**240** F2
Priory Rd
Alfreton DE55. . . . . . .**159** B5
Eastwood NG16 . . . . . **182** F1
Mansfield Woodhouse
NG19. . . . .**136** B3
Priory Sq NG19 . . . . . **136** B3
Priory Way
Newton DE55 . . . . **148** A3
Ripley DE5. . . . . **180** E8
Pritchard Dr NG9. . . **223** E6
Pritchett Dr DE23. . . **230** E8
Private Dr S43. . . . .**78** A1
Privet Cl S44 . . . .**99** D1
Proact Stad
(Chesterfield FC)
S40. . . . .**96** A7
Progress Ct DE45. . . **109** D6
Prospect Ave DE55 . .**159** F5
Prospect Cotts S43 . .**80** E5
Prospect Ct
[1] Sheffield S17. . . . . . .**56** B5
Sutton in Ashfield
NG17 . . . .**148** E1
Prospect Dr
Belper DE56 . . . .**178** F2
Matlock DE4. . . . . **143** A6
Sheffield S17 . . . .**55** F5
Shirebrook NG20 . . . .**119** C3
Prospect Gdns
DE55. . . . . **169** E7
Prospect Ho S43. . . . . .**78** F1
Prospect Pl
Derby DE21 . . . .**219** E4
Sheffield S17 . . . .**56** A5
Prospect Rd
Chesterfield S41. . . . . .**76** F2
Denby Village DE5 . . . **180** A1
Dronfield S18. . . . .**57** C3
Heanor DE75 . . . . **194** A8
Pilsley S45 . . . . **132** C1
Sheffield, Bradway Bank
S17. . . . .**56** A5
Sheffield, Lowfield S2. . .**43** A8
Prospect St DE55 . . . **159** B4
Prospect Terr
Bakewell DE45. . . . . . **109** C6
Chesterfield S40. . . . . .**95** E4
Crich DE4 . . . . **168** A8
Providence Ct DE11. .**256** F7
Providence Pl
Alfreton DE55. . . . . . .**158** F3
[5] Ilkeston DE7. . . . . . .**194** E1
Providence Rd
NG16 . . . . **171** A4
Providence St DE5. . **180** E8
Provident St [4]
DE23. . . . . **219** A2
Pryor Mede S26. . . . . .**61** E5
Pryor Nook S26 . . . . . .**61** E5
Pudding Bag La
S45. . . . . **129** F4
Pudding Plate Cl [8]
DE7. . . . . **208** E5
Puddle Hill
Bonsall DE4 . . . .**142** C1
Slaley DE4 . . . . **154** C8
Pulborough Gdns
DE23. . . . . **231** A6
Pullman Cl S43. . . . . . .**78** F3
Pullman Rd DE21. . . .**219** F4
Pump Cl DE4 . . . . **143** C3
Pump La
Doveridge DE6 . . . . . .**224** B8
Wyaston DE6 . . . . **185** D1
Pump Yd DE56 . . . . . .**177** B2
Punch Bowl Pk SK17. .**85** A8
Purbeck Ave S40 . . . . .**95** D4
Purbeck Cl
Long Eaton NG10 . . . .**236** A8

Purbeck Cl continued
Mansfield Woodhouse
NG19. . . . .**136** C6
Purchase Ave DE75. **181** C2
Purdy Mdw NG10 . . . .**235** F5
Pursglove Dr SK17. . . .**69** D4
Pursglove Rd SK17 . . .**69** C4
Putney Cl DE22. . . . . . **217** E5
Pybus St DE22. . . . . . .**218** D6
PYE BRIDGE **170** F6
Pye Bridge Ind Est
DE55. . . . .**170** F6
Pyegrove SK13 . . . .**10** F1
Pyegrove Rd SK13 . . . .**10** F1
PYE HILL **171** A5
Pye Hill Rd NG16 . . . . **171** A4
Pykestone Cl [6]
DE21. . . . . **205** F2
Pym Chair Rd SK23 . .**64** F6
Pym Leys NG10 . . . . . .**235** F5
Pynot Rd S41. . . . .**77** B2
Pytchley Cl DE56 . . . . **179** D4

Q

Quad DE1 . . . .**267** B3
Quadrant Mews [5]
SK17. . . . .**85** B8
Quadrant The
Buxton SK17. . . . .**85** B8
Sheffield S17 . . . .**55** E5
Quaker Cl DE73. . . . . . **252** D8
Quaker Way DE1 . . . . .**267** A4
Quantock Cl DE24 . . .**231** D2
Quantock Rd NG10 . .**223** A1
Quantock Way S40 . . .**95** B5
QUARNDON. **204** D6
Quarndon Hts DE22. **204** C3
Quarndon View
DE22. . . . . **204** C2
Quarn Dr DE22 . . . . . .**204** C3
Quarn St
Derby DE1 . . . .**218** E6
Derby DE1 . . . .**218** F7
Quarn Way DE1. . . . . . **218** F6
Quarry Bank
Clowne S43. . . . .**80** D4
Matlock DE4. . . . . **143** B7
Quarrybank La
DE11. . . . . **256** A4
Quarry Bank Rd S41 . .**96** C2
Quarry Berry La
DE12. . . . . **264** F1
Quarry Cl SK13 . . . .**10** D1
Quarry Gro S45. . . . . **131** C5
Quarry Hill
Eckington S21. . . . .**58** D2
Sheffield S20 . . . .**59** A8
Stanton-by-Dale DE7 . **223** A8
Quarry Hill Ind Est
DE7. . . . . **208** F5
Quarry Hill Rd DE7. . **208** F5
Quarry La
Alton S42 . . . . **130** C5
Brackenfield DE55 . . . **145** D6
Chesterfield S40. . . . . .**95** C2
Matlock DE4. . . . . **143** E7
Northedge S42. . . . . . **130** C6
Stonebroom DE55 . . .**146** F3
Quarry Rd
Apperknowle S18. . . . . .**58** A1
Belper DE56 . . . .**178** F2
Bolsover S44 . . . .**99** A3
Hayfield SK22. . . . .**24** F2
Killamarsh S21. . . . . . .**60** C7
Morley DE7. . . . . **192** B1
New Mills SK22. . . . . . .**33** D7
Sheffield, Totley Brook
S17. . . . .**55** E5
Somercotes DE55. . . .**170** C7
Whaley Bridge SK23. . .**33** D3
Quarry Vale Gr S12 . . .**44** C4
Quarry Vale Rd S12. . .**44** C4
Quarry Way [4]
DE55. . . . .**170** D8
Quartz Dr SK17 . . . .**85** D2
Queen Anne Ct S14. . .**43** E3
Queen Elizabeth Ct
[8] Ashbourne DE6. . . .**173** B2
Sheffield S14 . . . .**43** E3
Queen Elizabeth's Acad
NG19 . . . . **136** A1
Queen Elizabeths Cl
[2] Washgreen DE4 . . **155** A1
Wirksworth DE4 . . . . . **166** A8
Queen Elizabeths Close
DE4. . . . . **155** A1
Queen Elizabeth's Gram
Sch DE6. . . . . **173** C3
Queen Elizabeth Way
DE7. . . . . **208** C5
Queen Mary Cl S2 . . . .**44** A7
Queen Mary Cres [1]
S2. . . . .**44** A8
Queen Mary Ct
Derby DE1 . . . .**218** F7
Sheffield S2 . . . .**44** A8
Queen Mary Gr S2. . . .**43** F7
Queen Mary Mews
S2. . . . .**44** A7
Queen Mary Rd
Chesterfield S40. . . . . .**95** B1
Sheffield S2 . . . .**44** B8
Queen Mary Rise [3]
S2. . . . .**44** A8
Queens Ave
Heanor DE75 . . . . **181** D2

Queens Ave continued
Ilkeston DE7. . . . . **209** A5
Stanley DE7. . . . . **207** C6
Queen's Ave SK17 . . . .**85** D8
Queensbury Chase
DE23. . . . . **231** A6
Queensbury Park Drive
DE24. . . . . **232** F4
Queens Cl S80. . . . .**82** C5
Queens Ct
Burton upon Trent
DE14. . . . .**254** B8
Buxton SK17. . . . .**85** D8
Creswell S80 . . . .**81** F2
Derby DE22 . . . .**218** E8
Draycott DE72 . . . . . . **235** A7
Queen's Ct
Chesterfield S41. . . . . **266** A4
Marple SK6. . . . .**23** A6
Queens Dr
Brinsley NG16 . . . .**182** E7
Derby DE23 . . . .**218** C2
Sandiacre NG10 . . . . .**223** B4
Queen's Dr
Belper DE56 . . . .**178** E5
Glossop SK13 . . . .**10** F1
Ilkeston DE7. . . . . **208** E8
Swadlincote DE11 . . . **256** B6
Queensferry Gdns
DE24. . . . . **232** E4
Queensgate Dr
DE73. . . . . **244** F8
Queens Gdns S2. . . . . .**43** C8
Queensland Cl DE3 . .**217** E4
Queensland Cres
DE15. . . . . **248** C2
Queen's L Ctr DE1. . . .**267** B4
Queens Mews S2. . . . .**43** C8
Queen's Park Sports Ctr
S40. . . . . **266** A2
Queens Rd
Creswell S80 . . . .**82** C6
Sheffield, Lowfield S2. . .**43** B8
Queen's Rd SK17 . . . . .**85** D8
Queens Ret Pk S2. . . . .**43** B8
Queens Rise DE13 . . .**239** C6
Queens Road N
NG16 . . . . **182** F2
Queens Road S
NG16 . . . . **182** F1
Queen's Sq NG16. . . . .**182** F2
Queens Stables S2 . . .**43** C8
Queen St
Belper DE56 . . . .**179** A3
Brimington S43. . . . . . .**77** F1
Chesterfield S40. . . . . **266** A4
Clay Cross S45 . . . . . . **131** C3
Creswell S80 . . . .**81** F1
Derby DE1 . . . .**267** B4
Eckington S21. . . . .**59** E3
Glossop SK13 . . . .**17** B8
Hadfield SK13. . . . .**10** A4
Ilkeston DE7. . . . . **208** E8
Ironville NG16 . . . .**170** F4
Langley Mill NG16. . . .**182** C3
Long Eaton NG10 . . . .**236** E7
Longnor SK17. . . . . . . **121** B6
Marple SK6. . . . .**23** A6
Middleton DE4 . . . . . . **154** D5
Pilsley S45 . . . . **132** D1
Pinxton NG16 . . . . **160** C3
Ripley DE5. . . . . **181** A7
Sheffield, Mosborough
S20. . . . .**59** C7
Somercotes DE55. . . .**170** D8
South Normanton
DE55. . . . .**159** F5
Staveley S43. . . . .**97** D8
Swadlincote DE11 . . . **256** A1
Tideswell SK17 . . . .**69** C4
Queen Street Mews
S20. . . . .**59** C7
Queen Street N S41. . .**96** A8
Queens View S2 . . . . . .**43** C8
Queensview Dr DE5. **181** A7
Queensway
Castle Donington
DE74. . . . .**246** F4
Castle Donington
DE74. . . . .**247** A4
Derby DE22 . . . .**204** F2
Holmewood S42. . . . . .**116** E1
Holmewood S42. . . . . .**132** E8
Melbourne DE73. . . . .**252** B8
Pilsley S45 . . . . **132** C1
Stonebroom DE55 . . .**146** F3
Queen's Way S42. . . . .**115** D1
Queens Wlk S42. . . . . . **116** E1
Queen's Wlk
Tupton S42. . . . . **115** D1
Whaley Thorns NG20 . **101** A1
Queen Victoria Dr
DE11. . . . . **256** B5
Queen Victoria Rd
Sheffield S17 . . . .**55** F5
Tupton S42. . . . . **115** C1
Quenby La DE5 . . . . . . **169** E1
Quentin Rd SK23 . . . . .**47** C6
Quick Cl DE73 . . . .**252** A7
Quick Hill Rd DE24 . .**231** D2
Quillings Way DE72 . .**221** D1
Quilow La DE6. . . . . . . **185** E3
Quintin Rd DE24 . . . . .**233** A8
QUIXHILL. **196** E7
Quixhill Bank
Denstone ST14. . . . . . .**196** F8
Denstone ST14. . . . . . .**197** A8
Quixhill Cl DE6 . . . . . . **185** B8

Quixhill La ST14 . . . . .**196** D8
Quoit Gn S18. . . . .**57** B1
QUOIT GREEN. **57** B1
Quoin Cl DE15. . . . . . . **248** A1
Quorndon Cres
NG10 . . . . **236** D5
Quorn Dr [5] S40. . . . . .**95** A5
Quorn Rise DE23 . . . **231** E6

R

Rabbit La
Eckington S21. . . . .**60** A2
Hyde SK14 . . . .**9** A6
Rabown Ave DE23 . . .**231** D8
Racecourse Ind Est
DE21. . . . . **219** C8
Racecourse Mount
S41. . . . .**95** F8
Racecourse Park
DE21. . . . . **219** C7
Racecourse Rd S41. . .**76** F1
RADBOURNE. **216** F5
Radbourne Comm [4]
S18. . . . .**56** D1
Radbourne Common
DE6. . . . . **216** F6
Radbourne Gate
DE3. . . . . **217** D5
Radbourne La DE22. **217** E6
Radbourne St
Derby DE22 . . . .**218** C6
Mansfield Woodhouse
NG19. . . . .**136** E4
Radburn Ct NG9. . . . .**209** E1
Radcliffe Ave DE21 . .**219** F7
Radcliffe Dr DE22. . . **218** D3
Radcliffe Way DE23. .**230** F5
Radford Mdw
Castle Donington
DE74. . . . .**246** F3
Castle Donington
DE74. . . . .**247** A2
Radford Rd
Smalley DE7 . . . .**192** F6
[3] Smalley DE7 . . . . .**193** A6
Radford St DE24. . . . .**232** F7
Radleigh Gr DE11. . . .**257** A2
Radleigh Grange
DE11. . . . . **257** A2
RADMANTHWAITE . . .**135** D3
Radmanthwaite La
NG19 . . . . **135** B5
Radmanthwaite Rd
NG19 . . . . **135** D3
Rad Mdws NG10 . . . .**236** C6
Radnor Pl NG19 . . . . . **135** C4
Radnor St DE21. . . . . .**219** D7
Radstock Gdns
DE21. . . . . **205** E1
Radstone Cl DE21. . . .**206** B2
Raeburn Cl S14. . . . . . .**43** E2
Raeburn Dr
Beeston NG9 . . . .**223** E2
Marple SK6. . . . .**23** B8
Raeburn Pl S14. . . . . . .**43** E3
Raeburn Rd S14 . . . . . .**43** E3
Raeburn Way S14 . . . . .**43** E2
Raglan Ave DE22 . . . **218** C5
Raglan St DE55 . . . . . . **159** A4
Railway Ave S80. . . . . **100** D8
Railway Cottages
S44. . . . .**98** C2
Railway Cotts
Derby DE24 . . . .**232** A6
Derby, Stenson DE73 . **243** A8
Egginton DE65 . . . . . .**241** B7
Holmewood S42. . . . . .**116** F1
Kimberley NG16 . . . . . **195** F6
Temple Normanton
S41. . . . .**116** A5
Railway Row NG16 . . .**170** F4
Railway Side
Denby Bottles DE5 . . . **180** A2
Rawson Green DE56. . .**179** F2
Swadlincote DE11 . . . .**256** B1
Railway St
Glossop SK13 . . . .**10** C1
Hadfield SK13. . . . .**10** A5
Railway Terr
Buxton SK17. . . . .**85** C8
[3] Chesterfield S41. .**115** B7
Derby DE1 . . . .**267** D2
Disley SK12 . . . .**32** D6
Railway View S45. . . .**131** F4
Rainham Gdns
DE24. . . . . **233** A5
Rainier Dr DE21 . . . . .**220** A6
Rain's La DE4 . . . . **154** C4
Rake Head Rd HD9 . . . .**2** E7
Rake La DE45. . . . .**124** D3
Rakes La DE6. . . . . **162** A6
Rakes Rd DE45 . . . . . . **107** C1
Rakes The
Alstonefield DE6. . . . . **149** D4
Alstonefield DE6. . . . . **149** D5
Rake The DE45 . . . . . . **123** B6
Raleigh Cl DE7. . . . . . .**194** F3
Raleigh Gr S2 . . . .**43** B6
Raleigh St DE22 . . . . . **218** C6
Ralley Cl S42. . . . . **132** D8
Ralph Dr DE55. . . . . . . **170** D7
Ralph Rd S43. . . . .**79** A2
Ralston Croft S20. . . . .**59** E6
Ralston Ct S20 . . . .**59** D6
Ralston Gr S20 . . . .**59** D6
Ralston Pl S20. . . . .**59** D6

Pri–Red 305

Rambler Cl DE11 . . . .**256** A5
Ramblers Dr DE21. . . **206** C3
Ramcroft S44 . . . . **117** D3
Ramper Ave S43. . . . . .**80** E2
Ramscliff Ave
Donisthorpe DE12 . . .**262** F1
Donisthorpe DE12 . . .**265** F8
Ramsdean Cl DE21 . .**219** D8
Ramsden Cl SK13. . . . . .**10** D2
Ramsden La HD9 . . . . . .**3** B7
Ramsden Rd HD9. . . . . . .**3** C7
Ramsey Ave S40. . . . . .**95** D1
Ramsey Cl NG9 . . . . . .**209** E2
Ramshaw Cl S41. . . . . .**95** C7
Ramshaw Rd S18. . . . . .**76** E6
Ramshaw Way
DE22. . . . . **218** B7
Ramsley Ct [17] S40. . .**95** D5
Ramson Close DE24 .**231** C3
Randal Cres SK23. . . . .**45** C5
Randall Dr DE11 . . . . .**256** B4
Randall Pl [1] S2. . . . . . .**43** A8
Randall St S21. . . . .**59** B2
Randolph Rd DE23. . . .**231** F8
Ranelagh Gdns
DE22. . . . . **218** B7
Raneld Mount S40. . . **114** C8
Rangemoor La DE6 . . **183** D6
Rangemore Cl DE3 . .**217** E4
Rangewood Rd
DE55. . . . . **159** F4
Ranmoor Cl S41. . . . . .**115** C8
Ranmoor Hill S32. . . . .**52** E8
Ranmoor La S32. . . . . .**52** F8
Rannoch Cl
Derby DE22 . . . .**204** E3
Derby, Spondon DE21. .**220** F5
Ranworth Cl DE24 . . .**232** D3
Ratcliffe Ave DE14. . .**254** B8
Ratcliffe Cl S41. . . . . .**115** C7
Ratcliffe La S80 . . . . . .**82** D6
Ratcliffe St NG16 . . . .**182** F2
Ratcliff Mews DE15 . .**248** B5
Rauche Ct DE23 . . . . .**267** C1
Raven Ave DE55. . . . . .**147** F5
Ravencar Rd S21 . . . . .**59** B3
Raven Cl DE55. . . . . . .**170** C6
Raven Ct DE75. . . . . . .**181** E2
Raven Oak Cl DE56 . .**179** A3
Ravens Cl SK13 . . . .**16** F8
Ravenscourt Rd
DE22. . . . . **218** C6
Ravenscroft Ave S13. .**44** E8
Ravenscroft Cl S13 . . .**44** E8
Ravenscroft Cres
S13. . . . .**44** E8
Ravenscroft Ct S13 . . .**44** E8
Ravenscroft Dr
Derby DE21 . . . .**219** F6
Sheffield S13 . . . .**44** E7
Ravenscroft Oval
S13. . . . .**44** E8
Ravenscroft Pl S13 . . .**44** E8
Ravenscroft Rd S13. . .**44** E7
Ravenscroft Way S13 .**44** E8
Ravensdale Ave
NG10 . . . . **223** B2
Ravensdale Cl S43. . . . .**97** C5
Ravensdale Cotts
SK17. . . . .**89** A8
Ravensdale Inf &
Nursery Sch DE3. . .**217** E1
Ravensdale Rd
Derby DE22 . . . .**204** C3
Dronfield S18. . . . .**56** D1
Ravenshorn Way S21 .**79** C8
Ravenside Ret Pk
S40. . . . . **266** B2
RAVENSNEST. **144** F7
Raven St DE22. . . . . . .**218** E3
Ravenstor Rd DE4 . . .**154** F2
Ravenstor Sta ★
DE4. . . . . **154** F2
Ravenswood Rd S40. .**95** A5
Ravensworth Cl [4]
S2. . . . .**44** A7
Ravenwood DE11. . . . **256** C3
Rawdon Bsns Pk
DE12. . . . . **262** E5
Rawdon Cl DE74. . . . . **247** A4
Rawdon Rd DE12. . . . **262** E5
Rawdon Side DE11. . .**256** B4
Rawdon St DE23. . . . . **218** F2
Rawlins Ct S18 . . . .**57** C4
Rawlinson Ave
DE23. . . . . **232** A7
Rawson Cl DE3 . . . . . .**217** B3
Rawson Gn DE56 . . . .**179** F1
RAWSON GREEN. **179** F1
Rawson Way S2 . . . . . .**43** E8
Rayleigh Ave S43. . . . . .**96** D8
Raymond Way
NG19 . . . . **136** D1
Raynald Rd S2. . . . .**44** A8
Rayneham Rd DE7. . . **194** C4
Raynesway
Derby DE21 . . . .**220** A2
Derby, Alvaston DE21. .**233** D8
Raynesway Park Dr
DE21. . . . . **220** A2
Ray Rushin Bsns Pk The
DE5. . . . . **180** E7
Ray's Ave DE75 . . . . . .**181** E1
Ray St DE75 . . . .**181** E1
Reader St DE21. . . . . . **220** E5
Reading Ave [11]
DE11. . . . . **255** E1
Realm Cl DE73. . . . . . .**244** E8

Rebecca Court
LE66 . . . . **258** A1
Rebecca Ho DE1. . . . . **218** E5
Recreation Cl
Blackwell DE55. . . . . .**147** E1
Clowne S43. . . . .**80** E4
Recreation Dr NG20 .**119** F2
Recreation Rd
Calow S43. . . . .**96** F5
New Houghton NG19 . **134** F7
Sandiacre NG10 . . . . .**223** B6
Shirebrook NG20 . . . .**119** C6
Tideswell SK17. . . . . . .**69** C4
Wirksworth DE4. . . . . **165** E7
Recreation St NG10. .**236** F7
Recreation Terr
NG9 . . . . **223** D6
Recreation View
NG20 . . . . **119** E6
Rectory Cl
Breedon on the Hill
DE73. . . . .**252** E2
Eckington S21. . . . .**59** E4
Long Duckmanton S44 . .**98** A3
Rectory Dr S42. . . . . . **114** C4
Rectory Farm Mews
DE72. . . . . **245** E4
Rectory Gdns
Aston-on-Trent
DE72. . . . .**246** A7
Harthill S26 . . . .**61** E6
Killamarsh S21. . . . . . .**60** D5
Long Duckmanton S44 . .**98** A3
Rectory Gro S44. . . . . .**98** A3
Rectory La
Appleby Magna
DE12. . . . .**265** E1
Breadsall DE21. . . . . . **205** D5
Kirk Ireton DE6. . . . . . **165** B1
Stretton en le Field
DE12. . . . .**265** D4
Rectory Mews
DE65. . . . . **241** B4
Rectory Pl NG11. . . . . **237** E6
Rectory Rd
Breaston DE72. . . . . . .**235** E8
Clowne S43. . . . .**80** E4
Killamarsh S21. . . . . . .**60** D5
Langwith NG20. . . . . . **119** D7
Long Duckmanton S44 . .**98** A4
Staveley S43. . . . .**78** E2
Reculver Cl DE23 . . . .**231** D7
Redacre Cl S44. . . . .**99** C2
Red Barn Cl DE55. . . . **148** B3
Redbarn La DE55 . . . . **148** B3
Red Brick Cl DE55 . . . **147** A5
Redbrick Gdns
DE11. . . . . **256** A4
Red Brick La DE55. . . **147** A5
Redbridge Cl
[6] Derby DE22. . . . . .**218** A5
Ilkeston DE7. . . . . **209** A7
Shirebrook NG20 . . . .**119** F2
Redbrook Ave S41. . . **115** B8
Redbrow Hollow
SK6. . . . .**15** A2
Redbury Cl DE1. . . . . . **218** E4
Redcar Gdns [6]
DE21. . . . . **205** D1
Reddie Cl ST14 . . . . . . **196** F4
Reddish Ave SK23 . . . .**45** D6
Reddish La SK23. . . . . .**45** D6
Reddish Rd SK23 . . . . .**45** D6
Redens The NG10. . . .**236** B4
Redfearn La SK17. . . .**104** B2
Redfern Ave DE5 . . . . **169** E2
Redfern Cl SK13 . . . . . .**10** A6
Redfern La SK17. . . . . **104** C1
Redfern Rd ST14 . . . . .**210** A1
Redfern St S42 . . . . . . **131** C7
Redgap La SK17. . . . . . .**86** A8
Redgate SK13 . . . .**10** C4
Redgate St NG16 . . . . **160** D2
Redground Way S40 . **114** C8
Red Hill ST14 . . . .**196** E3
Redhill Ct DE56. . . . . . **179** B2
Redhill Foundation Prim
Sch DE72. . . . .**221** C5
Redhill La DE13. . . . . . **239** B5
Red Hill La DE4. . . . . . **144** D3
Redhill Lodge Rd [6]
DE11. . . . . **256** A7
Redhouse Cl S43 . . . . .**77** D4
Redhouse La SK12. . . .**32** E7
Redhouse Stables
Working Carriage
Mus ★ DE4 . . . .**127** D1
Red La
Belper DE56 . . . .**191** B6
Brinsley NG16 . . . .**171** E1
Chesterfield S41. . . . . .**77** C1
Chesterfield S41. . . . . .**96** B8
Disley SK12 . . . .**32** C5
Repton DE65. . . . .**249** F6
South Normanton
DE55. . . . .**159** F3
Redland Cl
Derby DE24 . . . .**231** F4
Ilkeston DE7. . . . . **194** F3
Red Lion Hill DE4. . . . **153** A1
Red Lion Row S32. . . . .**72** C8
Red Lion Sq DE75. . . . **181** E1
Red Lodge SK12 . . . . . .**32** A6
Redmires Dr DE73. . . **233** A2
Redmires Rd S10. . . . . .**42** B8

Redmoor Cl
Burton upon Trent
DE15............248 B3
Codnor DE5.........170 B1
Redmoor La
Disley SK12..........33 A4
New Mills SK22........33 B6
Rednall Cl S40.......95 A5
Red Pine Cl S43.......80 D2
Red River Nature
Reserve★ DE75... 181 C3
Red Rose Ct DE15 ... 254 E7
Redruth Pl DE24.....233 C5
Redshaw St DE1 ....218 E2
Redstart Cl DE21 ....220 F6
Redthorn Rd S13.....44 F8
Redvers Buller Rd
S40.............266 B1
Redway SK17........131 A5
Redway Croft 3
DE73............252 A8
Redwing Croft
DE23............231 D7
Redwood Ave S21....60 C5
Redwood Cl S43......97 B8
Redwood Dr DE15 ... 255 A6
Redwood Prim Sch
DE24............231 F3
Redwood Rd DE24 ... 231 E3
Reedman Rd NG10... 236 B4
Reeves Ave S45......132 C1
Reeves Rd DE23 ....219 B1
Regal Gate DE73...244 F8
Regency Cl
Derby DE23 ....231 D7
4 Glossop SK13......10 D1
Regent Ct
Ironville NG16.......170 F4
Swadlincote DE11...256 B2
Regent Gdns S41 ....266 B4
Regents Dr DE3.....217 B1
Regents Gn 6 S41..115 C7
Regents Ho 3 DE14 .253 F7
Regents Park Rd
DE14.............254 B8
Regent St
Clowne S43...........80 D4
Derby DE1 ....267 C1
Glossop SK13.........10 D1
Glossop, Padfield SK13..10 B5
Ilkeston DE7........208 F7
Kimberley NG16......195 F6
Langley Mill NG16...182 B3
Long Eaton NG10 ...236 D8
Stapleford NG10....223 C5
Swadlincote DE11...256 B2
Reginald Road N
DE21............219 F7
Reginald Road S
DE21............219 F6
Reginald St DE23 ... 219 B2
Regis Cl DE21 ......206 B2
Reigate Dr DE22 ... 218 A7
Reigate Park Prim Sch
DE22............218 A7
Reliant Cl 2 DE11..256 E1
Rembrandt Dr S18...56 E1
Remembrance Way
Brimington S40........96 C7
Thrumpton NG11 ....237 D2
Rempstone Dr S41..115 C7
Renals St DE23 ....267 B1
Reney Ave
Sheffield S17.........56 D6
Sheffield S8.........56 D6
Reney Cres S8......56 D6
Reney Dr S8.........56 D6
Reney Rd S8.........56 D6
Reney Wlk
Sheffield S17.........56 D6
Sheffield S8.........56 D6
Renfrew St DE21 ... 219 E7
RENISHAW.........79 B8
Renishaw Hall & Gdns★
S21.............59 F2
Renishaw Pk
Eckington S21........59 F2
Eckington S21........60 A2
Renishaw Prim Sch
S21.............79 B8
Renshaw Rd S43.....79 C4
Renshaw Dr DE11...255 F5
Rensons Way DE75 .181 E4
REPTON..........242 E2
Repton Ave DE23 ...218 D1
Repton Cl S40........95 A5
Repton Ct 8 NG19 .136 E4
Repton Dr DE7 ......209 B7
Repton Pl S18........56 C1
Repton Prep Sch
DE65............243 C2
Repton Prim Sch
DE65............242 E2
Repton Rd
Appleby Magna
DE12............265 F5
Hartshorne DE11...256 F8
Long Eaton NG10 ...235 F4
Newton Solney DE15 .241 F1
Newton Solney DE15 .248 F8
Repton DE65........242 A1
Ticknall DE73......250 E5
Willington DE65 ....242 A5
Reservoir Hill DE12. 262 D6
Reservoir Hos DE55. 146 A5

Reservoir Rd SK23...45 D7
Reservoir Terr S40...95 E4
Reservoir Way 6
DE11............256 E1
Resthaven DE11 ... 256 B5
Retford Cl DE21 ....205 D2
Revell Close DE55 . 160 A7
Revill Cl DE7 ......194 C2
Revill Cres NG9......223 F8
Revolution Ho (Mus)★
S41.............77 A2
Rewley Ct DE73.....233 A3
Reynard Cres S21....79 B8
Reynards La SK17 ... 137 E4
Reynolds Ave DE5 ...169 F1
Reynolds Cl S18......75 E8
Reynolds Dr SK6.....23 B8
Rhein O' Thorns
NG20............120 E5
Rhodes Ave S41......95 F5
Rhodes Cotts S43.....80 F4
Rhodes Ho DE15.....248 C3
Rhodesia Rd S40.....95 C2
Rhodes St S13........10 B5
Rhodes Top SK13.....10 B5
Rhodeswood Ave
SK14.............9 F6
Rhodeswood Cl 2
DE65............240 E8
Rhodeswood Dr
SK13.............10 A6
Rhuddlan Pl SK23 ...34 D1
Ribble Cl DE45 .....240 D8
Ribblesdale DE7 ... 208 C5
Ribblesdale Cl
DE22............204 C2
Ribblesdale Dr S12...44 F1
Ribblesdale Rd
NG10............236 A5
RIBER..........143 E3
Riber Ave DE55......170 D8
Riber Bank 14 SK13...9 E1
Riber Cl
Long Eaton NG10 ...236 D6
Staveley S43.........97 C5
West Hallam DE7 ...207 E8
Riber Cres S42......131 B5
Riber Ct 11 S40......95 D5
Riber Dr
Derby DE72 ....245 A8
12 Derby DE73......244 F8
Riber Fold 18 SK13...9 E1
Riber Gn 19 SK13....9 E1
Riber Rd
Lea DE4 ....156 A8
Matlock DE4 ......143 C2
Riber Terr S40......266 A2
Riber View Cl DE4 ...144 A5
Richard La SK17......69 C3
Richards Ct 2 S2....43 B6
Richardson Dr DE7 ..192 D4
Richardson Endowed
Prim Sch DE7 ....192 F6
Richardsons La
DE55............170 C5
Richardson St DE22. 218 D6
Richardson Way
DE22............217 E6
Richards Rd S2.......43 B6
Richard Wakefield CE
(VC) Prim Sch
DE13............239 C6
Richmond Ave
Derby DE23 ....231 C8
Ilkeston DE7........194 F4
Long Eaton DE72 ...236 A8
Sandiacre NG10.....223 A4
Sheffield S13........44 F8
Richmond Cl
Chesterfield S40.....114 E8
Derby DE23 ....231 A7
Glossop SK13........10 A5
West Hallam DE7 ...207 D8
Richmond Ct
5 Barrow Hill S43...78 B3
Repton DE65........242 D2
Sheffield S13........44 D7
Richmond Dr
2 Aston-on-Trent
DE72............246 A6
Duffield DE56 .....190 D5
Mansfield Woodhouse
NG19............136 E4
Richmond Farm Mews
S13.............44 D7
Richmond Gdns
S41.............266 B4
Richmond Gr S13....44 E8
Richmond Hall Ave
S13.............44 D8
Richmond Hall Cres
S13.............44 D7
Richmond Hall Dr
S13.............44 D8
Richmond Hall Rd
S13.............44 D8
Richmond Hall Way
S13.............44 D7
Richmond Hill Ho
S13.............44 D7
Richmond Hill Rd
S13.............44 D7
Richmond Ho DE65. 228 C1
Richmond La DE72. 245 A8
Richmond Pk Rd
3 Derby DE22......218 A5
Derby DE3.........217 F5

Richmond Pk Rd *continued*
Sheffield S13........44 E8
Richmond Pl S13.....44 D7
Richmond Rd
Derby, Chaddesden
DE21............219 F6
Derby, Rose Hill
DE23............219 A1
Sheffield S13........44 D7
Richmond Terr SK6...23 B1
Richworth Rd S13....44 F8
Ricroft Rd SK6........15 B3
RIDDINGS
Denstone..........196 B4
Somercotes........170 D5
Riddings DE22......204 E4
Riddings Cl S2.......44 A7
Riddings Croft S41 ...95 C6
Riddings Inf Sch
DE55............170 D6
Riddings Jun Sch
DE55............170 D6
Riddings La S32......72 D4
Riddings St DE22...218 F3
Ridd Way S42.......115 A3
Ridge Ave SK6........23 A4
Ridge Cl S13.........9 E3
Ridge Cres SK6.......23 A4
Ridgedale Rd S44 ...118 A8
Ridgedale View
DE5.............169 D2
Ridge End Fold SK6..23 A2
Ridgehill Ave S12....44 B5
Ridgehill Gr S12......44 B5
Ridge La
Chapel-en-le-Frith, Combs
SK23.............46 E1
Marple SK6.........23 A2
Ridge Rd
Eckington S21........58 E2
Marple SK6.........23 A3
Ridge The
Blackwell DE55.......147 E1
Blackwell DE55.......159 E8
Marple SK6.........23 A2
Marple SK6.........23 A3
Newton Solney DE15 .248 B6
Totley Top La SK22...25 C2
RIDGEWAY
Bullbridge........168 C4
Sheffield...........58 E8
Ridgeway
Chellaston DE73......245 A8
Clowne S43..........80 F2
Clowne S43..........81 A3
Dronfield S18........57 D3
Heanor DE75.......193 F8
Shirebrook NG20.....119 F5
Ridgeway Ave
Bolsover S44.........99 C2
Derby DE23 ....231 D6
Ridgeway Courtyard
S12.............58 E8
Ridgeway Craft Ctr★
S12.............58 E8
Ridgeway Cres S12...44 A6
Ridgeway Ct DE23 . 218 D2
Ridgeway Dr
Ilkeston DE7........208 B5
Sheffield S12........44 A6
Ridgeway Inf Sch
DE23............231 D6
Ridgeway La S13....58 C4
RIDGEWAY MOOR...58 E7
Ridgeway Moor S12..58 E6
Ridgeway Moor Farm Ct
S20.............58 E6
Ridgeway On The Hill
DE56............168 A1
Ridgeway Prim Sch
S12.............58 E8
Ridgeway Rd
Burton upon Trent
DE15............254 E7
Sheffield S12........44 A5
Ridgeways The SK22..25 C2
Ridgway W S43.......80 E2
Ridgewood Ct DE21. 205 E2
Ridgewood Dr DE4 . 155 C6
Ridgway The SK12....32 C6
Riding Bank DE73 ...251 F6
Riding Hill Ave
NG20............119 D3
Ridings Rd SK13......9 F5
Ridings The
Mansfield NG19.......136 F1
Ockbrook DE72.......221 D5
Rigga La DE56.......191 B1
Riggotts La S42......114 D7
Riggotts Way S42.....94 E5
Riggs La
Marston Montgomery
DE6.............211 F8
Marston Montgomery
DE6.............212 A7
Rigley Ave 10 DE7 ..194 F1
Rigsby Ct S13.......217 C3
Riley Ave DE55 .....157 D8
Riley Back La S32....71 E6
Riley La
Ripley DE5 ....169 A6
Stoney Middleton S32..71 F5
Stoney Middleton S32..72 A5
Rimsdale Cl DE24...231 E3
Ringer Ct S43........80 E3
Ringer Gdns S43......80 E3

Ringer La
Clowne S43..........80 E3
Clowne S43..........80 E1
Clowne S80..........99 F8
Elmton S80.........100 A8
Ringer Way S43.......80 E3
RINGINGLOW.......42 F4
Ringinglow Rd S10,
S11.............42 E4
Ring-o-Bells La
SK12.............32 D6
Ringstone Rise SK23..33 E2
Ringstone Way SK23 .45 D8
Ringwood Ave
Chesterfield S41......95 E7
Compstall SK14.......15 A8
Staveley S43.........97 C8
Ringwood Cl 3
DE21............204 E4
Ringwood Mdws S43..77 E3
Ringwood Rd S43.....96 F8
Ringwood View S43 ..96 F7
Rink Dr DE11........256 B3
Rinkway Bsns Pk
DE11............256 B3
RIPLEY..........169 C2
Ripley Ave DE72....245 B8
Ripley Ho DE21 .....220 E3
Ripley Hospl DE5....169 D1
Ripley Inf Sch DE5..180 D8
Ripley Jun Sch DE5..180 D8
Ripley L Ctr DE5....169 D1
Ripley Rd
Bullbridge DE56......168 D5
Heage DE56 ......169 A1
Ripley DE5 ....169 B4
Ripon Cres DE21....219 E8
Ripon Gdns SK17.....85 D5
Ripple Wlk S40.......96 C7
Risborrow Cl DE65 ..229 D4
RISE END........154 E3
Rise End DE4 ......154 D3
Rises The SK13.......9 F5
Rise The
Derby DE22 ....204 E2
Horwich End SK23 ...45 C6
Swadlincote DE11...255 F5
Risings The S12......24 B1
RISLEY..........222 E3
Risley Ct DE7 ......194 F3
Risley La DE72......222 D2
Risley Lower Gram CE
Prim Sch DE72...222 E4
Risley Way S42......115 B4
Rivenhall Cl DE23...230 F7
Riverbank DE4 ......110 F1
Riverbank The DE65 242 B5
Riverbank Way SK13..17 F7
Rivercroft Cl ST14...197 A3
River Ct S17.........56 A7
Riverdale S32........72 C7
Riverdale Cl DE15 ...248 B5
Riverdale Rd S18.....68 B4
Riversdale Dr ST14...196 F3
Riverside
Baslow DE45........91 D6
Walton-on-Trent
DE12............253 C1
Riverside Bsns Pk
DE45............109 C7
Riverside Cl
Calver S32.........72 D1
Glossop SK13........10 C1
Riverside Court SK17 .84 F7
Riverside Cres
Bakewell DE45......109 D6
Holymoorside S42....113 C7
Riverside Ct
Ambergate DE56 ....167 F3
Baslow DE45........91 E6
Calver S32.........72 D2
Derby DE24 ....219 C4
Riverside Dr
Branston DE14.......253 F7
Calver S32.........72 D1
Riverside Park Bsns Ctr
DE21............220 B2
Riverside Rd DE1 ...219 D4
Riverside Studios
S18.............57 B1
Riverside Way
Bolsover S44.........98 C2
Mansfield Woodhouse
NG19............136 D5
River St S43........267 B4
Riversvale SK17......84 F7
RIVER'S VALE......84 F7
River View
Aldercar DE55 .....171 A6
Belper DE56.......190 F7
Chesterfield S40......115 A8
Long Eaton NG10 ...236 A3
Longnor SK17.......121 B6
Tideswell SK17.......88 D7
Riverview Cotts 2
SK13.............17 C7
Riverview Court
DE1.............267 A4
Riverview Prim Sch
DE15............254 E7
Rivington Rd 3
NG9.............223 E2
Rivoli Dr 8 DE11...256 E1
Roadmeadow Cl
DE6.............185 D8
Robert Bakewel Way
ST14............210 C2

Robert Cl S18........76 E5
Robert Rd S8.........57 A7
Roberts Ave NG17 ...148 F2
Roberts Cl S2........43 D8
Roberts Dr DE55 ....159 B4
Robertson Rd SK17...85 B6
Robertson's Ave S44..98 A4
Roberts St DE7 .....209 A6
Robert St DE1 ......267 C4
Robey Dr NG16......182 F3
Robey Vale S81.......63 F8
Robian Way DE11 ...256 A4
Robina Dr NG16.....195 C8
Robin Court S21......60 D7
Robin Croft S40 ....114 F7
Robincroft Rd S42...114 D4
Robin Croft Rd
DE22............204 D4
Robinettes La
Cossall NG16.......195 D1
Cossall NG16.......195 E2
ROBIN HOOD.......92 D5
Robin Hood Cl
NG16............182 F1
Robin Hood Pl
DE11............256 C2
Robin Hood Prim Sch 1
NG19............136 B3
Robin Hood Rd DE4. 156 C2
Robinia Cl DE21 ....206 C3
Robinlands La S33....38 B4
Robin Rd DE1 ......218 F7
Robins Cl DE72 .....233 D5
Robinscross DE72 ...221 B1
Robin's Cross La
DE65............249 F7
Robinson Ct 4 DE4. 116 C1
Robinson Ind Est
S43.............219 B2
Robinson Rd DE11 ..256 A6
Robinson's Hill
DE73............251 F6
Robinson Way S21....60 C6
Robinwood Lodge 30
SK13.............9 E1
Robridding Rd S45. 129 A4
Robson Cl DE24 .....233 A7
Roby Lea DE74......246 F4
ROCESTER.......197 A3
Rocester Bypass
Rocester ST14.......196 F4
Rocester ST14.......197 A5
Rocester Way S42...131 F6
Roche S20.........59 E8
Rochester Cl
Derby DE24 ....233 A5
Long Eaton NG10 ...236 A7
Rochley Cl DE21....205 F2
Rock Art Cl 4 S43...81 E2
Rock Bank
Buxton SK17.........85 C3
Horwich End SK23 ...45 E6
Rockbourne Cl
DE24............233 D6
Rock Cres S45......131 A5
Rockcliffe Cl DE11...256 B1
Rockford Ct NG9 ...209 C4
Rockhall Terr SK22...25 E2
Rock Ho DE4 ......155 B6
Rock House Cl
DE55............147 F5
Rockhouse Rd DE24. 233 A6
Rockingham 11 S20 ..59 E8
Rockingham Cl
Chesterfield S40......95 C3
Derby DE22 ....205 A4
3 Dronfield S18 ....56 C1
Rockingham Way
DE15............255 C6
Rockland The
NG20............119 E4
Rockley Cl S40 .....114 F7
Rockley Way NG20...119 E4
Rockmay Ho DE55 .. 170 E6
Rock Mill Bsns Pk
S32.............71 E4
Rock Mill La SK22....33 B7
Rock Side NG16.....195 F6
Rockside Cotts S43...80 E4
Rockside Hall DE4 ...143 C6
Rockside Hydro
DE4.............143 C6
Rockside Steps DE4. 143 C6
Rockside View DE4. 143 C7
Rock Sq S32.........71 D6
Rock St S32.........33 C7
Rocks The DE4 .....144 A5
Rockstone Way
NG19............136 B2
Rock Terr
Bakewell DE45......109 D6
Buxton SK17.........85 B6
Rock The DE45 .....109 C6
Rockvale Terr DE4. 143 B1
Rockvale Villas DE4. 143 B1
Rock View SK17......88 A7
Rodge Croft S41......77 A3
Rodger's La DE55 ...159 A5
Rodknoll La S42......93 D2
Rod Moor Rd S17,
S18.............56 B4
Rodney Cl DE65 ....228 E2
Rodney Ho DE24.....232 E6
Rodney Way DE7 ....194 F3
Rodney Wlk DE23...230 E7

RODSLEY..........200 A5
Rodsley Cl
Chesterfield S40......95 B5
Yeaveley DE6 .....199 D5
Rodsley Cres DE23. 231 D5
Rodsley La
Rodsley DE6.........199 F7
Rodsley DE6.........200 A2.
Rodsley DE6.........200 A5
Yeaveley DE6 .....199 E5
Rodwood Ave S43....80 A7
Roebuck Pl SK23.....47 B6
Roecar Cl S41........77 B2
Roe Cross Ind Est
SK14.............9 A5
Roe Cross Rd SK14....9 A5
Roe Farm La DE21 ..219 E7
Roe Farm Prim Sch
DE21............219 E6
Roehampton Dr
Derby DE22 ....218 A7
Stapleford NG9.....209 D2
Roe's Ct DE4 ......157 A2
Roe's La DE4 ......157 A1
Roe Wlk DE23 .....219 A1
Rogers Ave S80......81 D1
Rogers Ct DE65 ....227 D1
Rolaine Cl NG19 ... 136 C4
ROLLESTON.......240 A4
Rolleston Cres
NG16............195 F8
Rolleston Dr NG16. 195 B8
ROLLESTONE......43 D5
Rolleston La DE13 ..239 D5
ROLLESTON ON
DOVE.........240 C3
Rolleston Rd DE13 ..240 B1
Rollins La S45........15 A1
Roman Bank NG19 ..136 D3
Roman Cl 3 DE11 ..256 C5
Roman Cres DE16...254 F7
Roman Dr DE14.....253 D8
Roman Rd DE1 .....219 B7
Roman Way
Borrowash DE72 ....221 C1
Moira DE12.........262 E4
Romeley Cres S43....80 B2
Romeley La S43.......80 B2
Romford Way 4 S43 .78 B3
Romney Dr S18.......56 E1
Romney Gdns S2.....43 B6
Romorantin Pl
NG10............236 E7
Romsley Cl DE3.....217 D4
Rona Cl DE24........231 E4
Ronald Cl DE23.....230 E7
Rood La
Clowne S43..........80 E3
Idridgehay DE56 ....176 F6
Idridgehay DE56 ....177 A6
Rookery Close
DE56............179 D5
Rookery Farm La
DE56............177 A7
Rookery The DE11 ..256 F2
Roosevelt Ave
Derby DE21 ....220 B6
Long Eaton NG10 ...236 C5
Roost The S32........53 A6
Roper Ave DE75 ....193 F7
Roper Hill S10.......42 D7
Ropewalk Ind Ctr
DE7.............195 A1
Ropewalk The
Heanor DE75 .....193 F8
Ilkeston DE7........195 A1
Stanley Common DE7..193 B1
Walton-on-Trent
DE12............253 D1
Rosamond Ave S17...56 A6
Rosamond Cl S17....56 A6
Rosamond Ct S17....56 A5
Rosamond Dr S17....56 A6
Rosamond Glade
S17.............56 A6
Rosamond Pl S17....56 A6
Rosamond's Ride
DE23............231 D8
Rose Ave
Borrowash DE72 ....221 C1
Burton upon Trent
DE13............241 A2
Calow S44..........97 A3
Clowne S43..........81 A5
Ilkeston DE7........194 E2
Rose Bank Cl SK14....9 F3
Rosebay Gdns SK23...47 B4
Roseberry Ct DE21. 206 B1
Rose Ct DE73 ......232 E1
Rose Cottage Dr
NG17............148 F2
Rose Cotts
Bonsall DE4 ....142 C1
Chesterfield S41......96 C2
Rose Cres S43........79 C4
Rosecroft Gdns
DE11............256 C3
Rose Ct
Clay Cross S45 ....131 A4
Long Eaton NG10 ...223 D1
Rosedale Ave
Chesterfield S40......115 B8
Rosedale Cl NG10... 236 B6
Rosedale View S40 ..114 B2
Rosedale NG19 .136 F2
Rosedene View
DE12............262 C4

Rose End Ave DE4 . . 155 A6
Rosefinch Way
NG19 . . . . .136 F2
Rose Garth Cl S41 . . . .96 C1
Rose Gdns S44 . . . . . . .97 D2
Roseheath Cl DE23 . 231 E5
ROSE HILL 219 B2
Rose Hill
Chesterfield S40. . . . .266 B3
Sheffield S20 . . . . .59 B8
Woodville DE11 . . . . .256 F3
Rose Hill Ave S20. . . .59 B8
Rosehill Bsns Ctr
DE23. . . . . 219 A2
Rose Hill Cl S20 . . . . .59 B8
Rosehill Ct S44 . . . . . .99 A1
Rose Hill Dr S20. . . . .59 B8
Rose Hill E S40 . . . . 266 B3
Rose Hill Mews S20. . .59 B8
Rose Hill St DE23 . . 219 A2
Rose Hill View S20 . . .59 B8
Rose Hill W S40 . . . . 266 A3
Rose La
Mansfield Woodhouse
NG19 . . . . 136 C3
Ticknall DE73 . . . . . . 251 A4
Roseland La NG20 . . 119 C3
Roseleigh Cres
DE11. . . . . 255 F6
Rosemary Ct **1** S8 . . .43 A3
Rosemary Dr DE4 . . 233 A5
ROSEMARYHILL 171 F7
Rosemeyer La **2**
DE74. . . . . 246 E3
Rosemoor La DE21 . 206 B1
Rosemount Ct DE22 204 C3
Rosengrave St DE1 . 267 B2
Rose Tree La DE11 . . 255 F7
Rosette Ct DE21 . . . 206 C3
Rose Valley DE11 . . 256 A5
Rose Way S21 . . . . . . .60 D5
Rosewood SK14 . . . . . .9 D5
Rosewood Ave S44 . . .98 F3
Rosewood Cl
Derby DE24 . . . . 233 B7
South Normanton
DE55. . . . . 160 B7
Rose Wood Cl S41 . . .95 D8
Rosewood Cres
DE75. . . . . 182 B2
Rosewood Rd DE15 . 254 F6
Roseybank SK23 . . . . .34 B1
Rosier Cres DE55 . . 170 A8
Rosling Way S44 . . . . .97 D2
ROSLISTON 260 D6
Rosliston CE Prim Sch
DE12. . . . . 260 C8
Rosliston Forestry Ctr★
DE12. . . . . 260 C8
Rosliston Rd
Burton upon Trent
DE15. . . . . 254 D3
Walton-on-Trent
DE12. . . . . 259 E8
Rosliston Road S
DE15. . . . . 254 E5
Roslyn Cres S32 . . . . .53 A7
Roslyn Rd S32 . . . . . . .53 A7
Ross Ct S21 . . . . .60 D4
Rossell Dr NG9 . . . . 223 E5
Rossendale DE7 . . . . 194 E4
Rossendale Cl S40. . 114 E8
Rosser Ave S12. . . . . . .43 F2
Rossington Dr DE23 .230 F6
Rosslyn Gdns DE24 . 233 A6
Ross Wlk DE21 . . . . 205 E1
ROSTON 197 E2
Roston Cl **3** S18 . . . . .56 D1
Roston Common
DE6. . . . . 198 B6
Roston Court DE21 . 220 E3
Rosyth Cres DE73. . . 232 E1
Rothay Cl S18 . . . . . . .75 E8
Rothbourne Croft
DE6. . . . . 151 D2
Rothbury Ave NG9 . . 209 D2
Rothbury Pl DE21 . . 205 E1
Rother Ave S43 . . . . . .96 D8
Rother Cl S40 . . . . . . 114 E8
Rother Close DE65. . 228 E1
Rother Croft S42 . . . 131 D8
Rotherham Cl S21 . . .60 F8
Rotherham Rd
Bolsover S44 . . . . .99 E2
Eckington S20, S21. . . .59 F6
Killamarsh S21 . . . . . . .60 F8
New Houghton NG19 .134 F7
Pleasley NG19 . . . . . .134 F6
Scarcliffe S44 . . . . . . 118 D7
Shirebrook S44,
NG19 . . . . 118 D3
Spinkhill S43 . . . . .61 D2
Rotherham Road N
S20. . . . . .59 F8
Rotherside Rd S21. . . .59 F4
Rother St S45 . . . . . 132 C2
Rothervale Rd S40. . 115 A8
Rother Valley Ctry Pk★
S21. . . . . .60 C8
Rother Valley Way
S20. . . . . .60 B8
Rother Way S41 . . . . .96 B6
Rother Wlk S45. . . . . 131 E4
Rotherwood Rd S21 . .60 E7
Rothesay Cl DE24 . . 231 E4
Rothey Gr S40 . . . . . . .94 F5
Rothwell Ho DE65 . . 228 D1
Rothwell La DE56. . . 179 B4

Rothwell Rd DE3 . . . 217 D3
Rough Heanor Rd
DE3. . . . . 218 A2
Rough La DE6 . . . . . . 186 E4
Roughlow La DE6. . . 183 D1
Roughpiece La DE4. 166 D5
Roughton Cl DE3 . . . 230 D8
Round Hill Cl SK13. . . .9 F3
Round House Cl
DE21. . . . . 193 C8
Roundhouse Gall★
DE65. . . . . 226 D4
Roundhouse Rd
DE24. . . . . 219 C4
Round Way SK22 . . . . .33 D8
Rouse St S45 . . . . . . 132 D1
Rousseau Ct DE6. . . 173 D1
Routh Ave DE74 . . . . 247 B2
Rovings Dr DE21. . . . 220 F7
Rowallan Way DE73. 232 E1
Rowan Ave
Ripley DE5 . . . . 180 D8
Stapleford NG9. . . . . .209 E2
Rowan Cl
Creswell S80 . . . . .81 E2
Darley Dale DE4 . . . . .127 B3
Denstone ST14. . . . . .196 D6
Derby, Cherrytree Hill
DE21. . . . . .220 B5
Derby, Sinfin DE24 . . .231 D3
Ilkeston DE7. . . . . . . .208 F5
Mansfield NG19 . . . . .136 D1
Rowan Croft NG17. . 148 F4
Rowan Ct ST14 . . . . 196 F4
Rowan Dr
Branston DE14. . . . . .253 E6
Branston DE14. . . . . .256 E6
Kilburn DE56. . . . . . . .192 B8
Selston NG16 . . . . . . .171 D6
Shirebrook NG20 . . . .119 D5
Shirland DE55. . . . . . .146 D1
Swadlincote DE11 . . .256 B7
Wingerworth S42. . . . .115 C4
Rowan Gdns **1**
DE72. . . . . 246 A6
Rowan Grove S42 . . 115 C4
Rowan Park Cl
DE23. . . . . 231 D7
Rowan Rd
Clowne S43. . . . . .80 D2
Eckington S21. . . . . . . .59 C1
Mastin Moor S43 . . . . .79 C2
Rowan Sch The S17 . .55 E6
Rowan Tree Cl
Ashbourne DE6. . . . . .185 D8
Killamarsh S21 . . . . . . .60 C5
Rowan Tree Dell S17 .55 E3
Rowan Tree Rd S21. .60 C5
Rowan Wlk SK13 . . . . .9 E4
ROWARTH 24 E7
Rowarth Ave **13** SK13 . .9 D2
Rowarth Bank 9
SK13. . . . . .9 D2
Rowarth Cl **10** SK13. . . .9 D2
Rowarth Dr SK22 . . . . .33 D7
Rowarth Fold **12** SK13 .9 D2
Rowarth Way **11** SK13. .9 D2
Rowbury Dr DE15. . . 248 B2
Rowdale Cres S12 . . . .44 D5
Rowditch Ave DE22. 218 D4
Rowditch Cotts
DE1. . . . . 218 D4
Rowditch Pl DE22. . 218 D4
Rowena Cl DE24 . . . 232 F7
Rowen Ct DE56 . . . . 179 B2
Rowfields La DE6. . . 173 F7
ROWLAND 90 C5
Rowland Cl DE55 . . 158 F4
Rowland Rd **3** S32. . .43 A8
Rowland St
Alfreton DE55. . . . . . .159 A4
Derby DE24 . . . . .232 E6
Rowleston Cl **2**
DE6. . . . . 201 E8
Rowley Cl DE11. . . . 256 D5
Rowley Ct DE11. . . . 256 B4
Rowley Gdns DE23. . 231 C7
Rowley La DE23 . . . 231 C7
Rowleys Mill **3**
DE1. . . . . 218 E5
ROWSLEY 111 A1
Rowsley Ave
Derby DE23 . . . . .231 D8
Long Eaton NG10 . . . .236 A5
Rowsley CE (Controlled)
Prim Sch DE4 . . . . 126 F8
Rowsley Cl SK13. . . . . .9 E2
Rowsley Cres S43 . . . .97 C8
Rowsley Gn SK13 . . . . .9 E2
Rowsley Gr SK13 . . . . .9 E2
Rowsley Mews SK13. . .9 E2
Rowsley South Sta★
DE4. . . . . 127 A5
Rowsley Wlk SK13 . . . .9 E2
Row The
Great Cubley DE6. . . .198 E1
Lea DE4 . . . . .156 B8
ROWTHORNE 134 C6
Rowthorne Ave
DE55. . . . . 170 A8
Rowthorne La DE4. . 134 B7
Rowthorne Trail Nature
Reserve★ NG17 . . 134 D3
Rowton Grange Rd
SK23. . . . . .47 B5
Rowton Way DE72 . . 233 D3
Roxburgh Ave DE21. 219 E7

Roxton Ave **2** S8. . . . .56 F8
Roxton Ct NG16. . . . 195 F7
Royal App DE73 . . . . 244 F8
Royal Ave NG10. . . . 223 D1
Royal Cl DE72 . . . . . 221 B1
Royal Court Bsns Pk
S41. . . . . 266 B3
Royal Croft Dr DE45 .91 E6
Royal Crown Derby
Visitor Ctr★ DE23. 267 C1
Royal Derby Hospl
DE23. . . . . 218 B2
Royale Cl S21 . . . . . . .59 E3
Royal Gate DE56. . . 179 D3
Royal Gr DE21 . . . . . 206 D3
Royal Hill Rd DE21. 220 D6
Royal La DE12 . . . . . 262 B4
Royal Oak Ct S43 . . . .79 D4
Royal Oak Pl DE45 . 109 D5
Royal Park Drive
DE24. . . . . 232 F4
Royal Rd SK12. . . . . . .32 D5
Royal Sch for the Deaf
(Derby) DE22 . . . . 218 D6
Royal Scot Rd DE24. 219 E2
Royal Way DE24 . . . 219 E3
Royce Cl DE65 . . . . . 229 C3
Roydon Cl DE3 . . . . 217 C3
Royle Ave SK13 . . . . . .10 D1
Royle Bsns Pk DE15 254 E3
Royston Cl
Ashbourne DE6. . . . . .185 C8
Chesterfield S40. . . . .114 B7
Royston Dr DE56. . . 179 D5
RTC Bsns Pk DE24 . 219 D2
Rubens Cl
Dronfield S18. . . . . . . .56 F1
Marple SK6. . . . . .23 C8
Ruby Dr S40. . . . . . . 115 E6
Ruby Ho S8 . . . . .43 B5
Ruby Paddocks
NG16 . . . . 195 F5
Ruby Way DE11. . . . . 255 F4
Rudyard Ave DE21 . . 220 E6
Rufford Cl S40 . . . . . .95 E1
Rufford Dr NG19. . . . 136 E3
Rufford Rd NG10 . . . 236 B4
Ruffstone Cl DE56 . 191 C7
Rugby Ave DE55 . . . 159 C3
Rugby Cl DE14. . . . . 254 C8
Rugby Drive S41. . . . .96 A5
Rugby Pk View
NG20 . . . . 120 E4
Rugby St DE24 . . . . . 219 E1
Rugeley Ave NG10 . . 237 A7
Ruislip Cl NG16. . . . 195 E7
Runway Bsns Pk
DE6. . . . . 185 E8
Rupert Rd DE21 . . . . 220 A7
Rupert St
Ilkeston DE7. . . . . . . .195 A1
Pilsley S45 . . . . .132 B3
Rushcliffe Ave DE21 219 F6
Rushcliffe Gdns
DE21. . . . . 219 F6
Rushdale Ave
Derby DE23 . . . . .231 D6
Sheffield S8 . . . . .43 B5
Rushdale Mount **4**
S8. . . . . .43 A5
Rushdale Rd S8. . . . . .43 B5
Rushdale Terr **3** S8. .43 A5
Rushen Mount S40 . 114 F6
Rushes The
Glossop SK13 . . . . .9 F4
Mansfield Woodhouse
NG19 . . . . .136 D5
Rush La SK6. . . . . .24 A6
Rushleigh Ct S17 . . . .55 D7
Rushley Ave S17. . . . . .55 C8
Rushley Cl S17 . . . . . . .55 D8
Rushley Dr S17. . . . . . .55 C7
Rushley Rd S17. . . . . . .55 D7
Rush Leys NG10 . . . 236 D5
Rushmere SK13 . . . . . .17 E8
Rushpool Ave NG19 . .16 F2
Rushpool Cl NG19 . . 136 F2
Rushton Cl DE13. . . 239 C6
Rushton Dr SK6 . . . . . .23 A5
Rushup Cl DE22 . . . 205 A5
Rushup La SK17,
SK23. . . . . .48 D8
Rushycroft SK14. . . . . .9 A4
Rushy La NG10,
DE72. . . . . 222 E6
Ruskin Ave NG10 . . . 236 B5
Ruskin Rd
Derby DE1 . . . . .218 F7
Mansfield NG19 . . . . .135 D1
Ruskin Sq S8. . . . . . . .43 A6
Ruskin Way DE23 . . 231 B8
Rusk The S43. . . . . . . .80 B6
Russell Ct **1** NG10. . 223 E7
Russell Gdns S42 . . 131 B6
Russell St
Compstall SK6. . . . . . . .15 B3
Derby DE24 . . . . .219 C1
Long Eaton NG10 . . . .223 D1
Swadlincote DE11 . . .256 C3
Russet Cl
Derby DE21 . . . . .206 B1
Hatton DE65. . . . . . . .227 C1
Russet Ct DE23 . . . . 218 E2
Ruston Cl
Chesterfield S40. . . . . .95 B6
Swadlincote DE11 . . .256 B4
Rutherford Rise 8
DE21. . . . . 205 F2

Ruthyn Ave S43 . . . . . .80 A7
Rutland Ave
Bolsover S44 . . . . .99 A1
Borrowash DE72 . . . . .221 C2
Matlock DE4 . . . . .143 C6
Ripley DE5 . . . . .181 A7
Rutland Cl
Burton upon Trent
DE15. . . . . 254 D6
Hilton DE65 . . . . 240 E8
Rutland Ct
Ilkeston DE7. . . . . . . .194 D1
3 Matlock DE4 . . . . .143 C6
Rutland Dr DE3. . . . . 217 E3
Rutland Gate Cl 7
DE4. . . . . 143 C6
Rutland Gr NG10. . . . 223 C5
Rutland Mews DE45 109 E6
Rutland Pl DE56 . . . 168 B6
Rutland Rd
Chesterfield S40. . . . .266 A3
Westwood NG16 . . . . .171 C4
Rutland Sports Pk
DE75. . . . . 208 D8
Rutland Sq DE45. . . 109 D6
Rutland St
Chesterfield S41. . . . . .77 A2
Derby DE23 . . . . .219 A1
Ilkeston DE7. . . . . . . .194 F2
Matlock DE4 . . . . .143 C6
Rutland Terr
Barlow S18. . . . . .75 E3
Ilkeston DE7. . . . . . . .194 F2
Rutland Way SK23 . . . .34 D2
Ryal Cl DE21 . . . . . . 221 C5
Ryan Cl DE24 . . . . . . 231 E3
Rycroft Cl DE11 . . . . 255 E2
Rycroft Rd DE74 . . . 247 D6
Rydal Ave NG10. . . . 223 B2
Rydal Cl
Derby DE22 . . . . .204 E4
Dronfield S18. . . . . . . .56 D1
Rydal Cres S41 . . . . . .95 E8
Rydal Way S45 . . . . . 131 B3
Ryde Ho DE24 . . . . . 233 C7
Ryder Cl DE11. . . . . 255 E2
Ryder Point Rd DE4. 154 A4
Rye Butts DE73 . . . . 232 E1
Rye Cl DE21 . . . . . . 205 E3
Rye Cres S45 . . . . . . 131 D3
Rycroft DE4 . . . . 127 D2
Ryecroft CE Mid Sch
ST14. . . . . 196 E4
Ryecroft Glen Rd
S17. . . . . .56 A8
Ryecroft St NG9 . . . 223 E8
Ryecroft View S17. . . .55 D8
Rye Ct S45 . . . . 131 D3
Rye Flatt La S40 . . . . .95 C2
Rye Flatts La DE65. . 227 C5
Ryegrass Cl DE56. . . 179 D4
Ryegrass Rd DE21 . . 206 C2
Ryehill Ave S40. . . . . .95 A2
Ryemere Cl NG16. . . 182 E2
Ryemere Ct NG16. . . 182 E2
Rykneld Cl DE23 . . . 230 E6
Rykneld Ct S45 . . . . 131 C3
Rykneld Dr DE23. . . 230 F7
Rykneld Prim Sch
DE14. . . . . 253 E7
Rykneld Rd DE23 . . . 230 E6
Rykneld Rise S42. . . 115 A3
Rykneld St S40. . . . . 266 B3
Rykneld Way DE23. . 230 E6
Rykneld Hill DE5. . . 180 B2
Rykneld Rd DE56,
DE7. . . . . 192 B8
RYLAH 117 F5
Rylah Hill S44 . . . . . 118 A5
Rymill Dr DE21 . . . . 205 F1
Ryton Way DE65 . . . 228 D1

S

Sacheveral La DE4. . 140 F4
Sacheverall Ave
NG16 . . . . 160 D3
Sacheverel St S8 . . . . .43 B5
Sackerville Terr S21. .60 B7
Sackville Cl S40 . . . . 114 B8
Sackville St DE23. . . 231 F8
Saddlers Cl NG19 . . 136 F1
Saddlers Croft S42 . 131 F7
Saddletree
View S43. . . . . .79 B4
Saddleworth Wlk
DE24. . . . . 232 E3
Sadler Dr **3** DE6 . . . 211 C1
Sadler Gate DE1. . . . 267 B3
Saffron Dr DE21 . . . 206 A1
Saffron St NG19 . . . 136 F2
Sage Ct DE3 . . . . 217 C5
Sage Dr DE11. . . . . . 256 F4
Sage Mews SK23 . . . . .47 B8
Sail Cl S41 . . . . .76 C5
St Agnes Ave DE22. . 204 D4
St Aidan's Ave S2 . . . .43 E8
St Aidan's Dr S2. . . . . .43 E8
St Aidan's Pl S2 . . . . . .43 E8
St Aidan's Rd S2 . . . . .43 E8
St Aidan's Rise S2 . . . .43 E8
St Aidan's Way S2 . . . .43 E8
St Albans Cl
Holmewood S42. . . . . .132 E8
Long Eaton NG10 . . . .236 E5

St Alban's RC Prim Sch
DE21. . . . . 219 F6
St Albans St DE22 . . 218 D3
St Albans St S22. . . . .33 C8
St Alkmund's Cl
DE56. . . . . 190 E4
St Alkmunds Way
DE56. . . . . 190 E4
St Alkmund's Way
DE1. . . . . 267 B4
St Andrew's CE
(Controlled) Prim Sch
B79. . . . . 263 E2
St Andrew's CE Jun Sch
Glossop SK13 . . . . .9 F4
Glossop SK13 . . . . . . .10 A4
St Andrew's CE
Methodist (Aided) Prim
Sch **5** S18. . . . . . . .56 D1
St Andrew's CE Inf Sch
DE7. . . . . 207 B5
St Andrews Cl DE55. 170 A7
St Andrew's Cl B79 . 263 F2
St Andrews Ct
Glossop SK13 . . . . . . .10 A4
Swadlincote DE11 . . .255 E2
St Andrew's Ct
DE7. . . . . 194 D1
St Andrew's Dr
Ilkeston DE7. . . . . . . .208 E8
Swanwick DE55 . . . . .169 F7
St Andrews Rise
S40. . . . . 114 C8
St Andrew's Sch
DE21. . . . . 205 E1
St Andrews View
DE21. . . . . 205 E1
St Andrews Wlk
S22. . . . . .33 D8
St Anne's CE Prim Sch
DE45. . . . . .91 E5
St Anne's Cl
Baslow DE45 . . . . .91 E5
Derby DE1 . . . . .218 E6
Staveley S43. . . . . .97 E8
St Anne's La DE74 . . 247 B3
St Anne's RC Prim Sch
SK17. . . . . .66 B1
St Annes St **4** SK14 . .16 A4
St Anne's Well★
SK17. . . . . .85 B8
St Ann's Cl SK23. . . . . .46 F6
St Anselms Preparatory
Sch DE45. . . . . 109 C6
ST AUGUSTINES 115 B7
St Augustines Ave
S40. . . . . 115 A8
St Augustines Cres
S40. . . . . 115 A8
St Augustines Dr
S40. . . . . 266 B1
St Augustines Mount
S40. . . . . 266 B1
St Augustines Rd
S40. . . . . 115 A8
St Augustines Rise
S40. . . . . 115 A8
St Augustine St
DE23. . . . . 218 F1
St Barnabas Ho **12**
S2. . . . . .43 A8
St Barnabas La **4**
S2. . . . . .43 A8
St Barnabas Rd **5**
S2. . . . . .43 A8
St Bartholomew's CE
Controlled Sch
SK17. . . . . 121 B7
St Benedict RC Sch &
Performing Arts Coll
DE22. . . . . 204 E1
St Benedicts Ct S2. . .43 B8
St Bride's Wlk DE22 218 B6
St Catherine's Rd
DE11. . . . . 255 F5
St Chad's CE Inf Sch
DE23. . . . . 218 F2
St Chad's Cl
Denstone ST14. . . . . .196 D6
Draycott DE72 . . . . . .235 A7
St Chad's Rd DE23 . 218 F2
St Chad's Water Nature
Reserve★ DE72 . . 235 A4
St Chad's Way S41. . . .96 A8
St Charles Cl SK13. . . .9 F5
St Charles's RC Prim Sch
SK13. . . . . .9 E5
St Christopher's Way
DE24. . . . . 219 D3
St Clare's Cl DE22 . . 218 D2
St Clare's Sch DE3 . 218 A2
St Cuthberts Rd 1
DE6. . . . . 211 C1
St Cuthbert's Rd
DE22. . . . . 218 F3
St Davids Cl NG16 . . 170 F3
St David's Cl DE22 . 218 D3
St Davids Rd B79 . . 263 F2
St David's Rise S40 . 114 D8
St Edmund's Ave
NG19 . . . . 136 C3
St Edmund's CF Prim
Sch NG19 . . . . 136 C3
St Edmund's Cl
DE22. . . . . 204 F4
St Edward's CE Prim Sch
DE74. . . . . 247 B3
St Edwards Ct DE11. 255 E5

St Edward's RC Prim Sch
DE11. . . . . 256 B5
St Edward's Rd
DE74. . . . . 247 B2
St Elizabeth Cl S2 . . . .43 B8
St Elizabeth's RC Prim
Sch DE56. . . . . 178 F5
St Elphins House 6
DE4. . . . . 116 C1
St George's
CE(Controlled)Prim Sch
DE11. . . . . 256 B1
St George's CE Prim Sch
S22. . . . . .33 C8
St George's Cl DE22 204 F3
St Georges Dr **3**
NG9 . . . . 223 D7
St George's Ho
DE22. . . . . 204 F3
St George's Pl **1**
DE56. . . . . 178 F4
St George's RC Prim Sch
DE23. . . . . 231 C7
St Georges Rd S22. . .33 C8
St Giles CE Prim Sch
S21. . . . . .60 C6
St Giles Cl S40 . . . . . 115 B8
St Giles Rd DE23. . . 218 F1
St Giles' Sch DE21 . 205 C1
St Giles Sch the Hive
DE1. . . . . 267 D5
St Giles Wlk DE4. . . 143 C4
St Hardulph's Prim Sch
DE73. . . . . 252 F2
St Helena Centre Univ of
Derby Chesterfield
Campus S41 . . . . . 266 B4
St Helens Ave NG16. 160 C4
St Helen's Cl
Chesterfield S41. . . . .266 B4
Darley Dale S32 . . . . .127 B3
Grindleford S32 . . . . . .72 C8
St Helen's Cres NG9 209 C4
St Helen's Croft S32 .72 D8
St Helen's Dr NG16 . 171 D7
St Helen's La DE4. . 166 A7
St Helen's St
Chesterfield S41. . . . .266 B4
Derby DE1 . . . . .267 A4
St Hugh's Cl DE22 . . 205 A2
St Ives Dr **4** S8 . . . . . .43 A2
St James' CE Inf Sch
DE23. . . . . 267 C1
St James' CE Prim Sch
7 SK13 . . . . .17 B8
St James Cl
Belper DE56 . . . . .179 D4
2 Chesterfield S41. . . .96 C1
Glossop SK13 . . . . . . .17 C7
Swadlincote DE11 . . .256 B6
Willington DE65 . . . . .242 C5
St James' Court S8. .43 B1
St James Cl
Ashbourne DE6. . . . . .173 D3
Sandiacre NG10 . . . . .223 B3
St James' Dr NG16. . 182 D8
St James Gdns
NG19 . . . . 136 E6
St James's Rd DE23 . 218 F1
St James's CE Jun Sch
DE23. . . . . 219 B3
St James's Ct SK17. . .85 C3
St James Sq S40 . . . 266 B3
St James's St **3**
NG9 . . . . 223 C6
St James' St
14 Buxton SK17 . . . . .85 B7
Derby DE1 . . . . .267 B3
Derby, Rose Hill
DE23. . . . . 219 A1
St James Terr **1**
NG9 . . . . 223 C6
St James' Terr SK17 . .85 B7
St John Fisher RC Prim
Sch DE24. . . . . 233 C4
St John Houghton Cath
Voluntary Acad Sch
DE7. . . . . 208 C6
St John's **4** SK17 . . . .85 A7
St John's Ave DE21 . 220 B5
St John's CE Prim Sch
Belper DE56 . . . . .179 B5
Ripley DE5 . . . . .169 F1
Stapleford NG9. . . . . .223 E7
St Johns Cl
Bamford S33 . . . . .40 B3
Chesterfield S40. . . . .114 B7
Ripley DE5 . . . . .169 F2
St John's Cl
Brinsley NG16 . . . . . .171 D1
Derby DE22 . . . . .204 D3
St John's Cres S43 . . .80 C3
St John's Dr
Derby DE21 . . . . .220 B5
Kilburn DE56. . . . . . . .192 A8
Swadlincote DE11 . . .255 E5
St Johns Mount S41 .95 F8
St Johns Pl S43 . . . . .78 C1
St Johns Rd
29 Chesterfield S41. . . .95 F8
Staveley S43. . . . . .78 D1
St John's Rd
Belper DE56 . . . . 179 A4

St John's Rd continued
Buxton SK17 . . . . .85 A7
Chesterfield S41 . . . . . . .95 F8
Dronfield S18 . . . . .76 E7
Ilkeston DE7 . . . . .209 A7
Matlock Bath DE4 . . . . .143 B3
Smalley DE7 . . . . .192 F5
Tideswell SK17 . . . . . . .69 C4
St Johns Road Bsns Ctr
S41 . . . . .95 F8
St John's St
Long Eaton NG10 . . . . 236 D7
Wirksworth DE4 . . . . .165 F8
St John St
Hayfield SK22 . . . . .25 D2
7 Middlepeak DE4 . .154 F1
St John's Terr DE1 . .218 F6
St Joseph's Cath Prim
Sch DE23 . . . . .267 A1
St Joseph's RC & CE VA
Prim Sch S43 . . . . . . .97 D8
St Joseph's RC Prim Sch
Matlock DE4 . . . . 143 D6
Shirebrook NG20 . . . . .119 F5
St Joseph's St DE4 . 143 C5
St Katherines Cl
DE4 . . . . 110 E1
St Katherine's Ct
DE22 . . . . 218 D6
**St Laurence CE
(Voluntary Aided) Prim**
Sch NG10 . . . . .236 E6
St Laurence Ct
NG10 . . . . 236 E6
St Laurence Gdns 10
DE56 . . . . .178 F4
St Lawrence Ave
S44 . . . . 118 C8
St Lawrence Cl
DE75 . . . . .181 F2
St Lawrence Rd S42 .131 F6
St Lawrence View
S80 . . . . .81 F5
St Leonards Dr S41 . .96 C1
St Leonards Pl
DE55 . . . . .146 E1
ST LUKE'S 218 E3
St Luke's CE Prim Sch
Glossop SK13 . . . . .10 C1
Shireoaks S81 . . . . . . .63 F7
St Lukes Cl DE22 . . .218 E4
St Lukes Ct 27 S41 . . .95 F8
St Lukes View S81 . . .63 F7
St Margaret's Dr
S40 . . . . 266 A3
St Margaret's RC Prim
Sch SK13 . . . . .16 D8
St Marks Cl DE4 . . . .155 A6
St Mark's Rd
Chesterfield S40 . . . . . .95 E3
Derby DE21 . . . . 219 D6
St Martins Cl 12
DE11 . . . . .255 E1
St Martin's Cl S41 . . .95 D6
St Martins Ct DE55 . .158 F4
St Martin's Rd SK6 . . .23 A6
St Martins Sch
Derby DE23 . . . . .232 F5
Derby DE24 . . . . 233 A4
St Martin's Sch
DE24 . . . . .232 F8
**St Mary & All Saints
Church (Crooked
Spire)** ★ S40 . . . . . . .266 B3
St Mary's Ave DE72 . 235 A7
St Marys Bridge
DE1 . . . . 219 A6
St Mary's Cath Prim Sch
DE22 . . . . .204 F1
St Mary's Cath Voluntary
Acad DE1 . . . . .267 C4
St Mary's CE (Aided) Fst
Sch 4 ST14 . . . . .210 B1
St Mary's Cl
Chinley SK23 . . . . .34 E2
Derby DE24 . . . . 233 A6
Newton Solney DE15 . .248 E8
St Mary's Cres ST14 210 B1
St Mary's Ct
Derby DE1 . . . . .267 B4
Hollingworth SK14 . . . . .9 C5
St Mary's Dr DE13 . .240 F2
St Mary's Gate
Chesterfield S41 . . . . .266 C3
Derby DE1 . . . . .267 B3
4 Wirksworth DE4 . .165 F8
St Mary's Pl S41 . . . .266 C3
St Mary's RC High Sch
S41 . . . . .95 C1
St Mary's RC Prim Sch
Chesterfield S40 . . . . .266 A4
Derby DE1 . . . . .267 B4
Glossop SK13 . . . . .17 D8
Marple SK6 . . . . .23 B7
New Mills SK22 . . . . . .33 B8
St Mary's Rd
Disley SK12 . . . . .32 D5
Glossop SK13 . . . . .17 C8
New Mills SK22 . . . . . .33 B8
St Mary St DE7 . . . . 208 E8
St Mary's View DE4 . 142 B7
St Marys Wharf Rd
DE1 . . . . 219 B7
St Mary's Wlk NG16. 171 B3

St Matthew's Cl S21 . .60 B1
St Matthew's St
DE14 . . . . .254 C8
St Matthew's Wlk 4
DE22 . . . . .204 F2
St Mawes Cl DE22 . . 204 D4
St Mellion Cl DE3 . . .217 F1
St Michaels Cl
Crich DE4 . . . . .156 F2
Derby DE24 . . . . 233 C7
St Michael's Cl
Holbrook DE56 . . . . . .191 C6
Shirley DE6 . . . . 200 D8
Willington DE65 . . . . .242 B5
St Michael's Dr
Appleby Magna
DE12 . . . . .265 F1
South Normanton
DE55 . . . . .160 A7
St Michael's La DE1 267 B4
St Michaels Rd 3
ST14 . . . . .210 A4
St Michaels View
Derby DE24 . . . . 233 C7
Selston NG16 . . . . . . .171 F5
St Monicas Way
DE6 . . . . .173 C3
**St Morden's Catholic
Primary School**
DE13 . . . . .240 B1
St Nicholas Cl DE22 . 204 D2
St Nicholas Pl DE1 . .267 A5
St Norbert Dr DE7 . .208 D4
St Oswald Cres DE6 . 173 C1
St Oswald's CE Inf Sch
DE6 . . . . .173 B1
St Oswald's Hospl
DE6 . . . . .173 B1
St Pancras Way
Derby DE1 . . . . .267 C5
Ripley DE5 . . . . .169 E4
St Pauls Ave S41 . . .115 D6
St Pauls Ct NG16 . . .195 F6
St Paul's Rd DE1 . . . 219 A7
St Peter & St Paul's
S41 . . . . .96 D3
St Peter's CE(Aided) Jun
Sch DE23 . . . . .218 C1
**St Peter's CE
(Controlled) Prim Sch**
DE12 . . . . .264 F6
St Peter's CE VA Fst Sch
ST14 . . . . .224 F2
St Peter's Churchyard
DE1 . . . . 267 B3
St Peters Cl
Hartshorne DE11 . . . . .257 B6
Long Duckmanton S44 . .98 A4
St Peter's Cl DE56 . . 179 A4
St Peters Croft
DE56 . . . . .179 A4
St Peters Ct DE24 . . 233 A8
St Peter's Rd
Buxton SK17 . . . . .66 B1
Chellaston DE7 . . . . . .233 A1
Thorpe Salvin S80 . . . . .62 E7
St Peter's St
Derby DE1 . . . . 219 A5
Derby DE1 . . . . .267 B3
St Peter's Way DE1 . 267 B2
**St Philip Howard
Catholic Voluntary**
Acad 6 SK13 . . . . . . .17 B8
St Philip's Dr S41 . . .115 B8
St Quentin Cl
Derby DE22 . . . . 218 C3
Sheffield S17 . . . . .56 B5
St Quentin Dr S17 . . .56 B5
St Quentin Mount
S17 . . . . .56 B5
St Quentin Rise S17 .56 B5
St Quentin View S17. .56 B5
St Ronan's Ave
DE56 . . . . .190 E2
St Stephen's Cl
DE23 . . . . .231 D6
St Stephen's Ct
DE11 . . . . .256 E3
St Swithin's Cl
DE22 . . . . .218 D3
St Swithuns Ct
DE56 . . . . .179 A2
St The DE6 . . . . 162 B5
StTheresa's RC Prim
Sch S2 . . . . .44 B7
St Thomas Cl DE55 . 147 E5
**StThomas More Cath
Sch** Buxton SK17 . . . .85 B8
**StThomas of Canterbury
RC Prim Sch** 5 S8 . .56 F8
StThomas RC Prim Sch
DE7 . . . . .208 E6
St Thomas Rd DE23 . 219 A1
St Thomas' St S40 . . . .95 C1
St Vincent Cl NG10 . 236 E4
**St Werburgh's CE (VA)
Prim Sch** DE21 . . . . 220 D5
St Werburghs View
DE55 . . . . .148 A3
St Werburgh's View
DE21 . . . . .220 D5
St Wilfrid's Rd
11 Sheffield S2 . . . . . .43 A8
West Hallam DE7 . . . . .207 E8
St Wystan's Rd
DE22 . . . . .218 C3
St Wystans Sch
DE65 . . . . .242 C2

Salcey Cl DE55 . . . . .169 F7
Salcey Rd NG9 . . . . . 209 D2
Salcey Sq S40 . . . . . . .95 D1
Salcombe Ct 12 S41 . .95 F8
Salcombe Rd DE55 . 159 C5
Salcombe Rd Ind Units
DE55 . . . . .159 C5
Salcombe Way
NG19 . . . . .136 F2
Sale & Davys CE Prim
Sch DE73 . . . . .244 A6
Sales Ave S42 . . . . . 131 C8
Sales La DE15 . . . . . 248 C4
Sale St DE23 . . . . . . 219 B2
Salestune Mews
NG16 . . . . .171 F6
Salford Way DE11 . . 255 E2
Salisbury Ave
Burton upon Trent
DE15 . . . . .248 D3
Chesterfield S41 . . . . . .95 F7
Dronfield S18 . . . . .76 A7
Salisbury Cl NG19 . . 136 D4
Salisbury Cres S41 . . .95 F7
Salisbury Dr
Belper DE56 . . . . .179 D5
Swadlincote DE11 . . . .256 E5
Salisbury Ho SK17 . . .85 C7
Salisbury La DE73 . . 252 B7
Salisbury Rd S18 . . . .76 B8
Salisbury St
Derby DE1 . . . . 219 A3
Derby DE23 . . . . .267 B1
Glossop SK13 . . . . .10 A5
Long Eaton NG10 . . . . 236 E7
Sallyfield La DE6 . . .183 E8
Sallywood Cl DE24 . .231 D2
Saltburn Cl DE21 . . . 205 C1
Salter Cl DE74 . . . . .246 F4
Saltergate S40 . . . . 266 B3
Saltergate La S33 . . .40 B2
Salters La
Matlock DE4 . . . . .142 F3
Matlock DE4 . . . . .143 A2
Matlock Bath DE4 . . . .142 F4
Salvin Cres S43 . . . . .80 E4
Samantha Ct DE11 . . 206 B1
Samara Cl 2 DE11 . .256 B7
Samphire Cl DE3 . . . 217 C4
Sampson's La NG19 . 135 B3
Sampsons Yd NG17 . .148 F3
Samuel Cl S2 . . . . . . .43 D7
Samuel Ct DE5 . . . . .180 D8
Samuel Dr S2 . . . . . . .43 D7
Samuel Pl S2 . . . . . . .43 D7
Samuel Rd S2 . . . . . . .43 D8
Samuel Road DE22 . 217 E6
Samuel St SK14 . . . . . .9 C4
Samuel Wood Cl
SK13 . . . . .16 C8
Sancroft Ave DE21 . 220 F6
Sancroft Rd DE21 . . 220 F6
*Sanctuary Nature
Reserve The* ★
DE24 . . . . .219 E3
Sandal Cl DE72 . . . . 233 D3
Sandalwood Cl
DE24 . . . . .233 C7
Sandalwood Rd
DE15 . . . . .254 E6
Sandbach Cl DE21 . . 206 A1
Sandbed La
Belper DE56 . . . . .179 C2
Belper DE56 . . . . .179 D3
Sandby Croft S14 . . . .43 E2
Sandby Cl S14 . . . . . . .43 E2
Sandby Dr
Marple SK6 . . . . .23 B8
Sheffield S14 . . . . .43 E2
Sandcliffe Pk DE11 . .256 D7
Sandcliffe Rd DE11 . 256 D6
Sandcroft Cl DE11 . . 256 D5
Sanderling Heath
DE3 . . . . 230 B7
Sanderling Way
NG19 . . . . .136 E2
Sanderman Ho
DE11 . . . . .256 E3
Sanders Cl DE7 . . . . 194 C2
Sanderson Dr DE14 . 253 C8
Sanderson Rd DE21 . 220 B8
Sandfield Cl DE21 . . 220 B8
Sandfield Rd 1
NG9 . . . . 223 E2
Sandford Ave NG10 . 236 E7
Sandford Brook
DE65 . . . . .228 E1
Sandgate Ave NG19 . 136 D4
Sandgate Cl DE24 . . 233 A6
Sandgate Rd
Derby DE72 . . . . 245 A8
Mansfield Woodhouse
NG19 . . . . .136 D4
Sandhall La
Alderwasley DE56 . . . .167 A5
Spout DE56 . . . . .166 F5
Sandham La DE5 . . . 169 C1
Sandhill La
Broadbottom SK6 . . . . .16 A2
Marple SK6 . . . . .16 E1
Sandhills Rd S44 . . . . .99 C1
SANDIACRE 223 A6
Sandiacre Friesland Sp
Ctr NG10 . . . . .222 F5
Sandiacre Rd NG9 . . 223 C6
Sandiway
Chesterfield S40 . . . . . 114 C8
Glossop SK13 . . . . .17 F7

Sand La DE6 . . . . 211 B1
Sandlands The
DE11 . . . . .256 D6
Sandlands Way
NG19 . . . . .136 F2
Sandown Ave DE3 . . 217 C3
Sandown Cl
Burton upon Trent
DE14 . . . . .254 A7
Eckington S21 . . . . . . .59 B2
Sandown Rd
Beeston NG9 . . . . .223 F2
Derby DE24 . . . . .232 E8
Sandpiper La DE3 . . 230 B6
Sandpiper Place
NG20 . . . . .120 D5
Sandringham Ave
DE15 . . . . .248 A1
Sandringham Cl
Calow S44 . . . . .97 A4
5 Chesterfield S41 . . .96 A8
5 Hatton DE65 . . . . .227 D2
Swadlincote DE11 . . . .256 B5
Sandringham Ct
13 Buxton SK17 . . . . .85 B7
Mansfield Woodhouse
NG19 . . . . .136 B6
Sandringham Dr
Derby DE21 . . . . .220 F5
Heanor DE75 . . . . .181 C2
Mansfield Woodhouse
NG19 . . . . .136 B6
Sandringham Ho
DE24 . . . . .219 D1
Sandringham Pl
Ilkeston DE7 . . . . .208 D5
Sheffield S10 . . . . .42 F8
Sandringham Rd
Calow S44 . . . . .97 A4
Derby DE21 . . . . .205 E1
Mansfield Woodhouse
NG19 . . . . .136 C5
Sandiacre NG10 . . . . .223 B4
Sands Cl S14 . . . . .43 E4
Sandstone Ave
Chesterfield S40 . . . . . .95 B1
Chesterfield S40 . . . . . 114 B8
Sandwell Cl NG10 . . 236 A6
Sandwood Cl DE55 . 148 A3
Sandybank Cl SK13 . . .9 E4
Sandybrook Cl DE6 . 173 C4
Sandybrook Country Pk
DE6 . . . . .173 B5
Sandybrook Hall
DE6 . . . . .173 B5
Sandy Cl S80 . . . . . . .81 F5
Sandycliffe Cl NG19 .136 F1
Sandyford La DE56 . .166 F4
Sandyhill Cl DE73 . . 233 A2
Sandy La
Broadbottom SK13 . . . .16 A4
Caldwell DE12 . . . . . . .261 A8
Chinley SK23 . . . . .35 B3
Crich DE4 . . . . .167 F8
Farley DE4 . . . . 128 D1
Grangewood DE12 . . . 261 C1
Hartington upper Quarter
SK23 . . . . .65 A3
Hollingsclough SK17 . . 104 A4
Hollingsclough SK17 . . 104 B2
Horsley DE21, DE7 . . .192 A3
Matlock DE4 . . . . .143 D8
Netherseal DE12 . . . . .264 B6
Rainow SK17 . . . . .64 A4
Whitwell S80 . . . . .81 F5
Sandypits La DE65 . . 229 C4
Sanforth St S41 . . . . . .96 A6
Sankey Dr DE11 . . . . 256 C1
Santolina Dr DE21 . . 205 F1
SAPPERTON 213 C1
Sapperton Cl DE23 . 231 D5
Sapperton La DE65 . .213 E1
Sapperton Rd
DE65 . . . . .213 D3
Sapphire Dr DE5 . . . 180 B2
Saracens Court DE6 . 201 F7
Sarah Cl DE55 . . . . . .170 C7
Sark Rd S2 . . . . .43 A7
Saundby Ave NG19 . 135 D1
Saundersfoot Way
DE21 . . . . .206 C2
Savage La S17 . . . . . . .55 D7
Save Penny La
DE56 . . . . .191 A5
Saville Cl NG9 . . . . . .223 E8
Saville House Sch 2
NG19 . . . . .136 B3
Savoy The 2 SK17 . . .85 B7
SAWLEY 236 A4
Sawley Inf and Nursery
Sch NG10 . . . . .236 A4
Sawley Jun Sch
Long Eaton NG10 . . . . 236 A4
Long Eaton NG10 . . . . 236 A5
Sawley Rd
Breaston DE72 . . . . . .235 E6
Draycott DE72 . . . . . . .235 B7
Sawmand Cl NG10 . . 236 C6
Sawmill Mws S41 . . . . .96 B5
Sawmills Ind Pk
DE75 . . . . .181 D3
Saw Pit Ind Est
DE55 . . . . .148 C6
Sawpit La DE65 . . . . 227 C2
Saw Pit La DE55 . . . .148 B5
Saxelby Cl DE55 . . . 170 D6
Saxelbye Ave DE1 . . .267 C2
Saxon Ave S17 . . . . . . .55 D6

Saxon Cl
2 Ashbourne DE6 . . 185 C8
Breedon on the Hill
DE73 . . . . .252 F2
Burton upon Trent
DE15 . . . . .254 F7
Saxon Close DE6 . . . 185 C7
Saxon Croft DE65 . . .242 D3
Saxon Ct DE21 . . . . . .94 F6
Saxondale Ave DE3 . 217 C4
Saxon Gr DE65 . . . . .242 A5
Saxon Rd S2 . . . . .43 A6
Saxon St DE15 . . . . . .254 F7
Saxton Ave DE75 . . . .181 F2
Saxton Cl S41 . . . . . .115 C8
Scaddows La DE73 . .250 E3
Scalby Cl NG16 . . . . .182 D2
Scaliot Cl SK22 . . . . .33 B8
Scalpcliffe Rd DE15. .248 A2
Scarborough Ave
DE7 . . . . 208 E8
Scarborough Rise
DE21 . . . . .205 D1
SCARCLIFFE 118 E6
Scarcliffe Cl DE24 . . 232 E3
Scarcliffe Lanes
NG20 . . . . .119 C7
Scarcliffe Prim Sch
S44 . . . . 118 F6
Scarcliffe Terr
NG20 . . . . .101 A2
Scargill CE (Aided) Prim
Sch DE7 . . . . .207 D7
Scargill Rd DE7 . . . . 207 E8
Scargill Wlk NG16 . . .182 F3
Scarlet Way NG20 . . 119 D2
Scarsdale Ave
Derby, Allestree
DE22 . . . . 204 D3
Derby, Littleover
DE23 . . . . .218 C2
Scarsdale Cl S18 . . . .76 B8
Scarsdale Cres S43. . .96 D7
Scarsdale Cross 1
S18 . . . . .57 B1
Scarsdale Pl 8 SK17 .85 B7
Scarsdale Rd
2 Chesterfield S41 . . .96 A8
2 Dronfield S18 . . . . .57 B1
Dronfield S18 . . . . .76 B8
Duffield DE56 . . . . 190 E3
Scarsdale St S44 . . . . 117 E8
Schofield Ct DE4 . . . . 110 F1
Scholar Cl 1 DE7 . . 208 F6
School Ave S20 . . . . . .59 F7
School Board La
S40 . . . . .95 E3
School Cl
Blackwell DE55 . . . . . .147 C1
Darley Dale DE4 . . . . .127 C3
Fenny Bentley DE6 . . . 162 A1
Glossop SK13 . . . . .9 E5
Moira DE11 . . . . .256 C1
Newton DE55 . . . . .148 B3
Sheffield S20 . . . . .59 F7
Shirland DE55 . . . . . . .146 D2
Stonebroom DE55 . . . .146 F4
School Croft DE55 . . 170 D6
Schoolfield Cl S44 . . . .99 C1
School House Hill
DE56 . . . . .168 D1
School La
Arkwright Town S44 . . . .97 D3
Ashbourne DE6 . . . . . .173 B1
Baslow DE45 . . . . .91 E5
Beeley DE4 . . . . 111 B4
Brackenfield DE55 . . . .145 C2
Carsington DE4 . . . . . .164 E7
Castle Donington
DE74 . . . . .247 A4
Chellaston DE7 . . . . . .233 A2
Compstall SK14 . . . . . .15 A4
Compstall SK6 . . . . . . .15 B4
Crich DE4 . . . . 157 A1
Cuckney NG20 . . . . . . .101 F3
Dronfield S18 . . . . .57 A1
Eckington S21 . . . . . . .58 C3
Fawfieldhead SK17 . . .121 A2
Great Hucklow SK17. . .70 B8
Hassop DE45 . . . . .90 F5
Hassop DE45 . . . . .91 A5
Hathersage S32 . . . . . .53 A8
Heage DE56 . . . . .168 D2
Hope Valley S33 . . . . .39 A3
Ingmanthorpe S18 . . . .94 D7
Mansfield Woodhouse
NG19 . . . . .136 C3
Old Brampton S42 . . . .93 F3
Over Haddon DE45 . . . 109 B1
Ripley DE5 . . . . .169 D1
Rolleston DE13 . . . . . .240 A3
Rowsley DE4 . . . . .126 F8
Rowsley DE45 . . . . . . .126 F8
Sheffield S8 . . . . .43 C1
Sheffield, Greenhill S8 . .56 F7
South Normanton
DE55 . . . . .160 B4
Stanton-by-Dale DE7,
NG10 . . . . .222 F8
Stanton in Peak DE4 . .126 C5
Sudbury DE6 . . . . .225 E4
Taddington SK17 . . . . .87 F3
School Lane Cl S8 . . . .43 C1
School Meadow
DE6 . . . . .197 D6
School Piece La
DE65 . . . . .227 F7

School Rd
Buxton SK17 . . . . .67 B5
Chesterfield S41 . . . . . .96 A7
Matlock DE4 . . . . .143 D5
Uttoxeter ST14 . . . . . .210 A1
School Rise DE6 . . . . 201 B8
School Sq DE7 . . . . . 207 F8
School St
Eckington S21 . . . . . . .59 D3
Moira DE12 . . . . .262 F2
Sheffield, Mosborough
S20 . . . . .59 D7
Swadlincote DE11 . . . .256 B2
School View S42 . . . .132 A7
School Woods Cl
DE75 . . . . .194 A6
School Yd The 1 DE7 . 267 B4
Schooner Dr S41 . . . . .76 E5
Scollins Court 1
DE7 . . . . 194 E2
Scotches The DE56 .178 F5
Scotia Cl S43 . . . . . . .43 F8
Scotia Dr S43 . . . . . . .43 F8
Scotland St S80 . . . . .81 F6
Scotswood Rd
NG19 . . . . .136 B6
Scott Cl S42 . . . . 115 E3
Scott Cres DE55 . . . .146 F3
Scott Dr
Belper DE56 . . . . .179 E5
Marple SK6 . . . . .23 B8
Somercotes DE55 . . . .170 D8
Scott St DE23 . . . . . . 218 F1
Scotts The DE11 . . . .261 D8
Scotty Brook Cres
SK13 . . . . .17 E8
Scout La
Hulland Ward DE56 . . .188 A6
Hulland Ward DE6 . . . .187 F7
Scowerdons Cl S12 . . .44 F5
Scowerdons Dr S12 . .44 F5
Scratta La S80 . . . . . .63 C2
Screetham La DE4 . . 112 C1
SCROPTON 226 E1
Scropton Old Rd
DE65 . . . . .239 C8
Scropton Rd DE65 . . 239 B8
Scropton Wlk DE24 . 232 E3
Sea Breeze Terr
S13 . . . . .44 D8
Seaburn Rd NG9 . . . .223 E2
Seagrave Ave S12 . . . .44 B4
Seagrave Cl DE21 . . 220 B8
Seagrave Cres S12 . . .44 B4
Seagrave Dr
Chesterfield S41 . . . . . 115 C7
Sheffield S12 . . . . .44 B4
Seagrave Rd S12 . . . . .44 B4
Seale St DE1 . . . . . . 267 B5
Sealey Cl DE65 . . . . .242 C5
Seals Rd DE12 . . . . . .262 E1
Seal View DE12 . . . . .261 C6
Sealwood La DE12 . . 261 F5
Seal Wood La DE12 . 261 F5
Seamer Rd NG16 . . . .195 F7
Seanor La S45 . . . . . .132 B4
Searl St DE1 . . . . .218 F6
Searson Ave S44 . . . . .99 A1
Searston Ave S42 . . . 132 D8
Seascale Cl 5
DE21 . . . . .205 D1
Seaton Cl DE3 . . . . . 217 C3
Seaton Ct 9 S41 . . . . .95 F8
Sebastian Cl SK6 . . . .23 B7
Second Ave
Branston DE14 . . . . . .253 E8
Chellaston DE73 . . . . . 245 A8
Risley DE72 . . . . .222 F5
Sedbergh Cres S41 . .95 D8
Sedgebrook Cl 2
DE21 . . . . .205 D2
Sedgebrook St
NG19 . . . . .136 E3
Sedgefield Gn DE3 . . 217 C1
Sedgefield Rd
Branston DE14 . . . . . .253 F7
Burton upon Trent
DE14 . . . . .254 A8
Sedgemoor Cl S40. . .95 B4
Sedgemoor Rd
NG10 . . . . .236 C5
Sedgemoor Way
DE23 . . . . .231 A5
Sedgwick Cl NG16 . . 160 D2
Sedgwick St
Jacksdale NG16 . . . . .171 B3
Langley Mill NG16 . . . .182 B3
Seely La S42 . . . . 115 C2
Sefton Ave NG9 . . . . 223 E8
Sefton Cl DE15 . . . . . 248 B1
Sefton Rd DE21 . . . . .219 F6
Sefton St SK13 . . . . . .17 C8
Sefton Way DE56 . . . 190 D4
Selborne St DE24 . . . 219 D2
Selby Cl
Beeston NG9 . . . . .223 E8
Chesterfield S40 . . . . . 114 C8
Selby Dr DE3 . . . . . . 217 B1
Selhurst Rd S41 . . . . . .95 F5
Selig Par S12 . . . . .44 C2
Selina Cl DE74 . . . . . 247 A4
Selina St DE73 . . . . . .252 A7
Selkirk St DE21 . . . . . 219 E7
Sellers Yard 3 DE6 . 173 C1
Selly Oak Gr S8 . . . . . .57 C6
Selly Oak Rd S8 . . . . .57 C6
Selmer Ct S43 . . . . . . .96 D8
SELSTON 171 E7

Selston CE Inf Sch
  NG16 . . . . 171 E6
SELSTON GREEN . . . 171 D7
Selston High Sch
  NG16 . . . . 171 F7
Selston L Ctr NG16 . . 171 F7
Selston Rd NG16 . . . . 171 B5
Selworthy Cl DE21 . . . 206 A4
Selwyn St
  Bolsover S44 . . . . 118 C8
  Derby DE22 . . . . 218 C6
Senners La SK17 . . . . . .87 A2
Sepycoe La DE6 . . . . . 214 D2
Serina Ave DE23 . . . . 231 D8
Serlby Dr S26 . . . . .61 F5
Serlby La S26 . . . . .61 F6
Serpentine Wlk S8 . . .57 B8
Service Rd DE24 . . . . 232 E5
Setcup La S21 . . . . .59 D2
Sett Cl SK22 . . . . .33 B8
Settlement Dr S43 . . . .80 F7
Settlement The
  DE72 . . . . 221 C5
Setts Way S42 . . . . . . 115 B4
Sevenlands Dr
  DE24 . . . . 233 C4
Sevenoaks Ave
  DE22 . . . . 217 F6
Seven Oaks Rd DE7 . 209 A4
Severals NG9 . . . . 223 F7
Severnale Cl DE22 . . 205 B5
Severn Cl
  Burton upon Trent
    DE13 . . . . 240 C1
  Ripley DE5 . . . . 181 A8
Severn Cres S42 . . . . 132 A5
Severn Dr DE65 . . . . . 240 D8
Severn Sq DE55 . . . . 159 A4
Severn St DE24 . . . . . 232 F8
Sewell Rd S20 . . . . .59 F6
Sexton St SK13 . . . . .9 F7
Seymour Cl
  Derby DE22 . . . . 218 C5
  Ilkeston DE7 . . . . 194 F5
Seymour La S43 . . . . . .79 C1
Seymour Link Rd
  Woodthorpe S43 . . . . .79 C2
  Woodthorpe S43 . . . . .98 C7
Seymour Rd NG16 . . 182 F1
SHACKLECROSS . . . 221 D1
Shacklecross Cl
  DE72 . . . . 221 C1
Shady Gr DE65 . . . . . 228 C2
Shaef Cl DE65 . . . . . . 228 E2
Shaftesbury Ave
  Chesterfield S40 . . . . . .95 D3
  Long Eaton NG10 . . . . 236 B4
  Mansfield NG19 . . . . . 135 E2
  Sandiacre NG10 . . . . . 223 A5
Shaftesbury Cres
  DE23 . . . . 219 B1
Shaftesbury Sp Ctr
  DE23 . . . . 219 B1
Shaftesbury St
  DE23 . . . . 219 B2
Shaftesbury Street
  South DE23 . . . . 219 B1
Shafton Cl S45 . . . . . 131 E4
Shafton Wlk S45 . . . . 131 E4
Shakespeare Ave
  Creswell S80 . . . . .81 C1
  Mansfield Woodhouse
    NG19 . . . . 136 B4
  Shirland DE55 . . . . . . 146 C4
Shakespeare Cl
  Clay Cross S42 . . . . . 131 B6
  Repton DE65 . . . . 242 D1
  Swadlincote DE11 . . . 256 C6
Shakespeare Cres
  S18 . . . . .76 C7
Shakespeare Ct 4
  DE6 . . . . 173 B2
Shakespeare Dr
  DE55 . . . . 159 B4
Shakespeare Mdws
  DE65 . . . . 242 D1
Shakespeare Rd
  NG16 . . . . 195 C5
Shakespeare St
  Derby DE24 . . . . 232 A5
  Grassmoor S42 . . . . . 115 E3
  Holmewood S42 . . . . . 116 D1
  Long Eaton NG10 . . . . 223 D1
Shaldon Dr DE21 . . . 218 D1
Shalfleet Dr DE24 . . . 233 C5
Shallcross Ave
  SK23 . . . . .45 F4
Shallcross Cres
  High Peak SK23 . . . . . .45 E4
  Horwich End SK23 . . . . .45 E4
Shallcross Hall Barns
  SK23 . . . . .45 E4
Shallcross Mill Rd
  SK23 . . . . .45 E5
Shallcross Rd SK23 . . .45 E4
Shambles The S40 . . 266 B3
Shamrock Pl S43 . . . . .79 C4
Shamrock St DE23 . . 218 E1
Shandwick Ct 10
  DE24 . . . . 231 D3
Shanklin Dr NG9 . . . . 223 D7
Shanklin Ho DE24 . . 233 C7
Shannon Cl DE23 . . . 231 D6
Shannon Ho DE24 . . 232 E4
Shannon Sq DE21 . . 220 B4
Shap Cl 7 S40 . . . . . . .95 C5
Sharcote Dr DE15 . . . 255 C4
SHARDLOW 234 E2

Shardlow Bsns Pk
  DE72 . . . . 234 D1
Shardlow Hall
  Workshops & Offices
  DE72 . . . . 234 E2
Shardlow Her Ctr ★
  DE72 . . . . 235 A1
Shardlow Prim Sch
  DE72 . . . . 234 E2
Shardlow Rd
  Aston-on-Trent
    DE72 . . . . 246 B7
  Derby DE24, DE74 . . . 233 C6
Sharley Park Com Prim
  Sch S45 . . . . 131 E3
Sharley Pk L Ctr
  S45 . . . . 131 D4
Sharman Cl S18 . . . . . .58 A1
Sharman Wlk S18 . . . .58 A1
Sharp Cl
  Ilkeston DE7 . . . . 208 C6
  Long Eaton NG10 . . . . 236 C6
Sharpe Ave S8 . . . . . . .56 E8
Sharpes Ind Est
  DE11 . . . . 256 B4
Sharpes La DE55 . . . . 170 C6
Sharpe's Pottery Mus ★
  DE11 . . . . 256 B4
Sharpswood Manor
  DE11 . . . . 256 A4
Sharrard Cl S12 . . . . . .44 B5
Sharrard Dr S12 . . . . . .44 B5
Sharrard Gr S12 . . . . . .44 B6
Sharrard Rd S12 . . . . . .44 B5
SHATTON 39 F1
Shatton La
  Bamford S33 . . . . .40 A1
  Thornhill S32, S33 . . . .51 E7
Shawcroft 8 DE6 . . . 173 C2
Shawcroft Ave
  DE55 . . . . 170 C5
Shawcross Cl DE55 . . 170 C6
Shawfield Rd SK13 . . . .9 F3
Shaw La
  Belper DE56 . . . . 191 B7
  Glossop SK13 . . . . .9 F3
  Holloway DE4 . . . . . . 156 C8
  Marston Montgomery
    DE6 . . . . 198 A1
Shaws Gn DE22 . . . . 218 D6
Shaws Hill
  Crich DE4 . . . . 156 D1
  Wirksworth DE4 . . . . 166 D8
Shaw's Row S40 . . . . . .95 D2
Shaw St
  Charlesworth SK13 . . . .11 A2
  Chesterfield S40 . . . . . .95 D2
  Glossop SK13 . . . . .10 F2
  Hadfield SK13 . . . . .9 E3
Shepley's Yd S40 . . . . 266 B3
Shepton Cl DE7 . . . . . 194 D3
Sheraton Way SK17 . . .66 E1
Sherbourne Ave S41 . .95 E8
Sherbourne Dr
  Belper DE56 . . . . 179 D5
  Burton upon Trent
    DE14 . . . . 254 A7
  Hilton DE65 . . . . 228 C1
Sherbrooke Rd SK12 . .32 D6
Sherbrook Gr SK17 . . . .85 C5
Sherholt Rd DE13 . . . 240 D4
Sheridan Ct
  Stapleford NG9 . . . . . 209 F1
  4 Uttoxeter ST14 . . . 210 A1
Sheridan St DE24 . . . 231 F5
Sheriff Dr DE4 . . . . . . 143 B6
Sherman Cl DE65 . . . 228 E2
Sheroside Cl DE22 . . 204 D4
Sherroside Cl DE22 . . 204 D4
Sherston Cl DE21 . . . 206 B2
Sherwin Rd
  Stapleford NG9 . . . . . 209 F1
  4 Stapleford NG9 . . . 223 F8
Sherwin St DE22 . . . . 218 E8
Sherwood Ave
  Borrowash DE72 . . . . 221 D2
  Creswell S80 . . . . .81 D1
  Derby, Chaddesden
    DE21 . . . . 219 F7
  Derby, Littleover
    DE23 . . . . 231 D5
  Hope S33 . . . . .39 A3
  Pinxton NG16 . . . . . . 160 D3
  Shirebrook NG20 . . . . 119 E4
Sherwood Chase S17 . 55 E5
Sherwood Copse
  SK17 . . . . .69 C4
Sherwood Ct
  Bolsover S44 . . . . 117 F8
  Mansfield NG19 . . . . . 136 B2
Sherwood Dr
  Crich DE4 . . . . 157 A1
  Shirebrook NG20 . . . . 119 E3
Sherwood Fold SK13 . .16 D7
Sherwood Foresters
  Regiment Meml ★
  DE4 . . . . 156 E3
Sherwood Hall L Ctr
  DE4 . . . . 156 E3
Sherwood Pl 2 S18 . .56 D1
Sherwood Rd
  Buxton SK17 . . . . .85 C5
  Dronfield S18 . . . . .56 D1
  Killamarsh S21 . . . . . . .60 E7
  Matlock DE4 . . . . 143 C4
  Tideswell SK17 . . . . . . .69 C3
Sherwood Rise
  Eastwood NG16 . . . . . 182 F1
  Mansfield Woodhouse
    NG19 . . . . 136 A1
Sherwood St
  Bolsover S44 . . . . 117 F8

Sheffield Rd continued
  Owler Bar S17 . . . . .74 A8
  Ramsley Moor S17 . . . .73 E4
  Renishaw S21, S43 . . . .79 D8
  Sheepbridge S41 . . . . . .76 E3
  Sheffield S20 . . . . .44 F2
  Unstone S18, S41 . . . . .76 E4
Sheffield Transport
  Sports Club S8 . . . . . . .56 F7
Shelden Cl 4 SK13 . . . .9 D1
Shelden Fold 3 SK13 . .9 D1
Shelden Mews SK13 . . .9 D1
Shelden Pl 5 SK13 . . . .9 D1
SHELDON 108 A6
Sheldon Cl NG10 . . . . 223 B3
Sheldon Ct DE24 . . . . 232 E3
Sheldon Gdns DE4 . . 156 F1
Sheldon La
  Bakewell DE45 . . . . . 108 C5
  Bakewell DE45 . . . . . 109 A5
Sheldon Moor SK17 . 107 D6
Sheldon Rd
  Buxton SK17 . . . . .85 D7
  Chesterfield S40 . . . . . .95 B5
  Heanor DE75 . . . . 181 C5
Shelford Cl DE3 . . . . . 217 C3
Shelford La DE4 . . . . . 156 B7
Shelley Ave NG19 . . . 136 B4
Shelley Dr
  Derby DE24 . . . . 232 A5
  Dronfield S18 . . . . .76 C7
Shelley Gr DE55 . . . . 146 F3
Shelley Rd DE11 . . . . 256 C5
Shelley St S42 . . . . . . 116 D1
Shelmory Cl DE24 . . . 232 E5
Shelton Cl NG19 . . . . 135 E1
Shelton Dr DE24 . . . . 232 F3
Shelton Gate Cl
  DE24 . . . . 232 E5
Shelton Jun Sch
  DE24 . . . . 232 D4
SHELTON LOCK 232 F3
Shenington Way
  DE21 . . . . 206 B2
Shepherds Cl S43 . . . . .80 A6
Shepherd's La DE73 . 251 D6
Shepherd St DE23 . . 218 C1
Shepley St
  Charlesworth SK13 . . . .11 A2
  Chesterfield S40 . . . . . .95 D2
  Glossop SK13 . . . . .10 F2
  Hadfield SK13 . . . . .9 E3
Shepley's Yd S40 . . . . 266 B3

Sherwood St continued
  Chesterfield S40 . . . . 266 C1
  Derby DE22 . . . . 218 E3
  Mansfield Woodhouse
    NG19 . . . . 136 B2
  Newton DE55 . . . . 148 B4
  Shirland DE55 . . . . . . 146 C5
  Somercotes DE55 . . . . 170 C8
Sherwood St
  NG17 . . . . 148 F3
Shetland Cl
  Derby DE21 . . . . 219 C7
  Mansfield NG19 . . . . . 136 F1
  Shirebrook NG20 . . . . 119 D2
Shetland Rd
  Dronfield S18 . . . . .76 B8
  Tibshelf DE55 . . . . . . 147 F5
Shibden Cl S8 . . . . . . .43 B2
Shields Cres
  Castle Donington
    DE74 . . . . 246 F3
  Castle Donington
    DE74 . . . . 247 A3
Shields La DE45 . . . . 197 D5
Shieling The DE65 . . 227 C2
Shilling Way NG10 . . 236 A7
Shiloh Cl DE11 . . . . . 256 C3
Shiloh Rd SK22, SK6 . .24 B6
Shilo Way NG16 . . . . 195 B4
Shiners Way DE55 . . . 159 F6
Shiner Way DE55 . . . . 160 A6
Shinwell Ave S43 . . . . .97 B7
SHIPLEY 194 B6
Shipley Cl DE14 . . . . 254 B6
SHIPLEY COMMON . 194 C4
Shipley Common La
  DE7 . . . . 194 D4
Shipley Country Park ★
  DE7 . . . . 194 A4
Shipley Country Park
  Visitor Ctr ★ DE75 . 193 E7
Shipley Ct DE7 . . . . . 194 D1
Shipley Gate DE7 . . . 194 D1
Shipley La DE7,
  DE75 . . . . 193 F5
Shipley Pk Gdns
  DE75 . . . . 193 E7
Shipley View DE7 . . . 192 F6
Shipley Wlk DE24 . . . 232 E3
Shipman Ct S20 . . . . . .59 D7
Shippen Rural Bsns Ctr
  The S18 . . . . .75 E2
Shippon La S32 . . . . . .72 B2
SHIREBROOK 119 F3
Shirebrook Acad
  NG20 . . . . 119 D5
Shirebrook Bsns Pk
  NG20 . . . . 120 A3
Shirebrook Cl NE7 . . 194 F6
Shirebrook Ct S2 . . . . .43 A6
Shirebrook Dr SK13 . .17 E8
Shirebrook Rd S8 . . . . .43 A6
Shirebrook Sta
  NG20 . . . . 120 A4
Shiregate Gdns
  DE23 . . . . 231 A5
Shire Hill Hospl SK13 10 E3
Shire La
  Holmewood S44 . . . . . 116 F4
  Sutton Scarsdale S44 . 117 A6
SHIREOAKS 63 E6
Shireoaks DE56 . . . . 178 F5
Shireoaks Cl DE23 . . 231 C7
Shireoaks Comm
  S81 . . . . .63 F7
Shireoaks Rd
  Dronfield S18 . . . . .57 C2
  Shireoaks S81 . . . . .63 F6
Shireoaks Row S81 . . .63 E7
Shireoaks Sta S81 . . . .63 E7
Shires The NG19 . . . . 136 F1
Shire Way SK13 . . . . . .10 E3
SHIRLAND 146 D2
Shirland Cl DE7 . . . . 194 D3
Shirland Ct DE24 . . . 232 E3
Shirland Prim Sch
  DE55 . . . . 146 D2
Shirland St S41 . . . . . 266 B4
SHIRLEY 200 E8
Shirley Cl
  Castle Donington
    DE74 . . . . 247 A4
  Chesterfield S40 . . . . . .95 B5
  Hope S33 . . . . .39 A4
Shirley Common
  DE6 . . . . 186 D3
Shirley Cres DE72 . . 235 D8
Shirley La
  Hollington DE6 . . . . . 200 F6
  Rodsley DE6 . . . . 200 B6
Shirley Pk DE72 . . . . 246 B7
Shirley Rd
  Derby DE21 . . . . 205 F1
  Ripley DE5 . . . . 169 D1
  Swanwick DE55 . . . . . 169 F7
Shirley St NG10 . . . . 236 A4
Shop La DE56 . . . . . . 168 C2
Shop Stones DE72 . . 221 C5
Shoreham St S2 . . . . . .43 A8
Short Ave DE22 . . . . . 204 F5
Shortbrook Bank 10
  S20 . . . . .59 E8
Shortbrook Cl S20 . . . .59 E8
Shortbrook Com Prim
  Sch S20 . . . . .59 E8
Shortbrook Croft 6
  S20 . . . . .59 E8
Shortbrook Dr S20 . . . .59 E8

Shortbrook Rd S20 . . . .59 E8
Shortbrook Way 13
  S20 . . . . .59 E8
Shortbrook Wlk 12
  S20 . . . . .59 E8
Short Cl S42 . . . . 113 D7
Shortheath DE12 . . . 262 C3
SHORT HEATH 262 D2
Shortheath Rd
  DE12 . . . . 262 E3
Short Hill DE73 . . . . . 252 E6
Short La DE74 . . . . . . 246 F4
Short Lands DE56 . . . 179 A4
Shortlands The DE4 . 143 B3
Short Row 4 DE56 . . 178 F4
Shorts La S17 . . . . .55 B6
Short St
  Belper DE56 . . . . 179 B4
  Burton upon Trent
    DE15 . . . . 254 E7
Shorwell Gdns
  DE24 . . . . 233 C5
SHOTTLE 177 E8
SHOTTLEGATE 177 F3
Shottle Wlk DE24 . . . 232 E3
Shotwood Cl DE13 . . 240 A4
Shotwoodhill La
  DE13 . . . . 240 C5
Shrewsbury Cl
  DE21 . . . . 206 C2
Shrewsbury Mws
  SK13 . . . . .10 C1
Shrewsbury Rd
  DE13 . . . . 240 F2
Shrewsbury St SK13 . .10 C1
Shrewsbury Terr
  S17 . . . . .55 D4
Shropshire Ave
  Derby DE21 . . . . 219 E7
  Westwood NG16 . . . . . 171 C4
Shropshire Dr SK13 . . .17 F8
Shrovetide Wlk DE4 . 173 C2
Shrubbery The
  DE11 . . . . 257 A2
Shuckstone La DE4 . 156 F6
Shudehill Cl SK22 . . . .25 D3
Shunters Drift S43 . . . .80 B6
SHUTTLEWOOD 98 F7
Shuttlewood Rd S44 . .99 A4
Shuttleworth Cl 3
  DE74 . . . . 246 E3
Shutts La
  Bakewell DE45 . . . . . 109 C3
  Bakewell DE45 . . . . . 109 C3
Sicklebrook La S18 . . .57 F4
Sickleholme S33 . . . . .40 B1
Sidcup Ct S43 . . . . .78 B4
Siddalls St DE15 . . . . 248 B3
Siddals La DE22 . . . . 204 F4
Siddals Rd DE1 . . . . . 267 C2
Siddons St DE24 . . . . 233 A7
Side End La SK23 . . . . .45 A2
Sides La DE6 . . . . 184 B5
Sidings Dr DE16 . . . . 254 E5
Sidings The
  Chinley SK23 . . . . .34 E2
  Derby DE21 . . . . 220 A4
  Kimberley NG16 . . . . . 195 F6
  Mansfield NG19 . . . . . 136 A3
  Whaley Bridge SK23 . . .45 E8
Sidings Way DE55 . . . 147 C1
Siding The S43 . . . . . . .80 E4
Sidlaw Cl 6 S40 . . . . . .95 C5
Sidmouth Cl DE24 . . 233 C7
Sidmouth Ct 17 S41 . .95 F8
Sidney Robinson Bsns Pk
  DE24 . . . . 219 D1
Sidney St
  Derby DE1 . . . . 219 B3
  Kimberley NG16 . . . . . 195 F6
  Long Eaton NG10 . . . . 236 D6
Siggate S33 . . . . .38 D1
Signal Way NG19 . . . 136 B2
Silken Holme DE55 . . 160 B4
Silk Hill SK23 . . . . .45 F8
Silk Mill La DE1 . . . . 267 B4
Silk St SK13 . . . . .10 E1
Silkstone Cl
  Sheffield S13 . . . . .44 E4
  Swadlincote DE11 . . . 256 B1
Silkstone Cres S12 . . .44 E4
Silkstone Dr S12 . . . . .44 E4
Silkstone Pl S12 . . . . .44 E4
Silkstone Rd S12 . . . . .44 E4
Sills Rd DE74 . . . . . . 247 A6
Silver Birch Cres
  DE55 . . . . 159 C8
Silver Birch Way
  S42 . . . . 115 B4
Silverburn Dr DE21 . 206 A2
Silverdale NG9 . . . . . 223 E5
Silverdale Ave
  NG19 . . . . 136 B4
Silverdale Cl
  Chellaston DE73 . . . . . 233 A2
  Chesterfield S41 . . . . . .76 E1
Silverhill Cl DE13 . . . 240 C1
Silverhill La NG17 . . . 148 E5
Silverhill Prim Sch
  DE3 . . . . 217 C3
Silverhill Rd DE21 . . 220 D3
Silver Hill Rd DE23 . 219 A2
Silverhill Wood Cl
  DE3 . . . . 217 D6
Silver La
  Elvaston DE72 . . . . . . 234 A5
  Marchington ST14 . . . 224 F1
Silverlands SK17 . . . . .85 C7

Silverlands Cl SK17 . . .85 C7
Silverlands Pk SK17 . . .85 C7
Silver Mill Rd S2 . . . . .43 A8
Silver Springs SK14 . .15 A8
Silverton Dr DE24 . . . 231 C2
Silver Well Dr S43 . . . .97 D8
Silvey Gr DE21 . . . . . 220 D4
Simcoe Leys DE73 . . 233 A2
Simcrest Ave S21 . . . . .60 D5
Simkin Walk NG10 . . 236 B/
SIMMONDLEY 17 A7
Simmondley La SK13 .17 A8
Simmondley New Rd
  SK13 . . . . .17 A7
Simmondley Prim Sch
  SK13 . . . . .17 A8
Simmondley Village
  SK13 . . . . .16 A7
Simons Cl SK13 . . . . . .17 A7
Simons Wlk SK13 . . . .17 A8
Sims Ave DE1 . . . . . . 218 E5
Sims Croft S41 . . . . . . .77 C3
Sinclair Cl
  Derby DE24 . . . . 231 E4
  Heanor DE75 . . . . 193 D8
SINFIN 231 F4
Sinfin Ave DE24 . . . . 232 D3
Sinfin Central Bsns Pk
  DE23, DE24 . . . . 231 F5
Sinfin District Ctr
  DE24 . . . . 231 E3
Sinfin Fields Cres
  DE24 . . . . 232 D5
Sinfin La
  Barrow upon Trent
    DE73 . . . . 244 A6
  Derby DE23, DE24 . . . 231 F4
Sinfin Moor La
  Chellaston DE73 . . . . . 232 E2
  Derby DE24 . . . . 231 F3
Sinfin Prim Sch
  DE24 . . . . 231 F5
Sir Francis Ley Ind Pk
  DE23 . . . . 219 C1
Sir Frank Whittle Rd
  DE21 . . . . 219 C7
Sir Henry's La DE73 . 252 A4
Sir Herbert Wragg Way
  DE11 . . . . 256 C1
Sir John Hurt Pl
  DE11 . . . . 256 E3
Sirjohn Warren Way
  DE75 . . . . 181 D3
Sir Joseph's La DE4 . 127 B4
Sir William Hill Rd
  Eyam S32 . . . . .71 C8
  Great Hucklow SK17 . . . .70 C1
  Grindleford S32 . . . . . .53 B1
Sir William Terr S32 . .72 C8
Siskin Cl DE3 . . . . . . 230 B7
Siskin Dr DE24 . . . . . 231 D4
Sisley Ave NG9 . . . . . 223 E6
Sister's La DE72 . . . . 221 C5
Sitch La
  Hayfield SK22 . . . . .24 C3
  Kirk Ireton DE4 . . . . . 165 A4
  Wensley DE4 . . . . 142 D7
Sitwell 14 S20 . . . . . . .59 E8
Sitwell Ave S40 . . . . . 266 A1
Sitwell Cl
  Derby DE21 . . . . 220 D4
  Smalley DE7 . . . . 192 F5
Sitwell Dr DE56 . . . . 192 A4
Sitwell Grange La
  S45 . . . . 147 D8
Sitwell Mus ★ S21 . . . .59 F2
Sitwell St
  Derby DE1 . . . . 267 B2
  Derby, Spondon DE21 . 220 E4
  Eckington S21 . . . . .59 C3
Sitwell Villas S45 . . . 146 E5
Skeavington's La
  DE7 . . . . 194 E5
Skeldale Dr S40 . . . . 115 B8
Skellow Cl 2 S2 . . . . .44 A7
Skelton Cl DE24 . . . . 233 D4
Skelton Rd S8 . . . . . . .43 A5
Skelwith Cl S41 . . . . . .95 D8
Skiddaw Cl 2 S40 . . . .95 C6
Skiddaw Dr DE3 . . . . 217 E1
Skimmer St S42 . . . . 132 C8
Skinner St S80 . . . . . . .81 D2
Skinners Way
  Swadlincote DE11 . . . 256 D5
  Swadlincote DE11 . . . 256 E5
Skipness Cl DE73 . . . 232 E2
Skipper Dr 7 S41 . . . 115 F2
Skipsea Rd S13 . . . . . .44 B7
Skipton Cl DE7 . . . . . 194 D3
Skipton Dr DE21 . . . . 205 C1
Skye Gdns DE55 . . . . 147 F5
Skylark Rise 3 NG9 . 209 E2
Skylark Way DE24 . . . 231 D4
Slackey La DE12 . . . . 262 C4
SLACKHALL 47 F8
Slack La
  Ashover S45 . . . . 129 C2
  Brailsford DE6 . . . . . . 187 D1
  Chesterfield S40 . . . . . .95 B3
  Derby, Allestree DE22 . 204 F2
  Derby, New Zealand
    DE22 . . . . 218 D5
  Hartshorne DE11 . . . . 257 B6
  Heath S44 . . . . 116 F2
  Mayfield DE6 . . . . 184 C8

Slack La *continued*
Nether Heage DE56 . . 168 C3
Ripley DE5 . . . . 169 D1
Shipley DE75 . . . . .193 E8
Somercotes DE55. . . . .170 B5
Wessington DE55. . . . 157 D8
Slack Rd
Ilkeston DE7. . . . . 194 A3
Mapperley DE7. . . . . . .193 F3
Slacks Cotts SK17 . . . .84 E4
Slacks La SK22 . . . . . . .25 C5
Slack's La S45. . . . . . 132 C2
Slade Cl
Etwall DE65 . . . . 229 C4
Ilkeston DE7. . . . . 209 A5
South Normanton DE55. . . . . .160 B4
Slade Farm DE73 . . . 251 A4
Slade Fields ST14. . . 210 B1
Slade Hollow La DE6. . . . . 201 A3
Slade La
Weston Underwood DE6. . . . . .202 E7
Wilson DE73. . . . . .252 F6
Slade Lands Dr DE73. . . . . 233 A2
Slag La S43 . . . . .77 D6
Slaidburn Cl DE3 . . . 217 E1
SLALEY. 154 C7
Slaley La DE4. . . . . . . 154 C8
Slancote La SK17 . . . . .69 A2
Slaney Cl DE24 . . . . . 232 E7
Slant Cl SK13. . . . . .17 E8
Slant La
Mansfield Woodhouse NG19 . . . . .136 B4
Shirebrook NG20 . . . . 119 D4
Slatelands Ave SK13 . .17 B8
Slatelands Rd SK13 . . .17 B8
Slate Pit Dale S42 . . 113 E4
Slatepit La S18, S42 . . .93 C8
Slater Ave DE22 . . . . 218 E6
Slater Cres DE4 . . . . .165 F7
Slater St S45 . . . . 131 D3
Slater Way DE7. . . . . 208 E5
Slate St S2. . . . . .43 B8
Slayley Hill S43. . . . . . .80 C4
Slayley View S43 . . . . .80 C5
Slayley View Rd S43 . .80 B6
Slaypit La S80 . . . . .62 D6
SLEAT MOOR 170 B8
Sledgegate La DE4 . 156 B7
Sledmere Cl DE24 . . 233 C7
Sleepy La DE73. . . . . 245 C1
Sleetmoor La DE55 . 170 B8
Sleights La NG16 . . . 160 C2
Slindon Croft DE24 . 233 D6
Slipperlow La SK17 . . .87 F2
Sloade La
Eckington S12. . . . . .58 D7
Ridgeway S12. . . . . .58 D6
Sloane Rd DE22 . . . . 218 A6
SMALLDALE
Bradwell. 50 F8
Peak Dale. 67 D7
Smalldale Cotts SK17. . . . . .67 D7
Smalldale Head Rd S33. . . . . .50 F7
Smalldale Rd
Buxton SK17. . . . . .67 C7
Sheffield S12 . . . . .44 D4
SMALLEY 192 F5
SMALLEY COMMON. 193 A2
Smalley Dr DE21. . . . 206 B3
Smalley Farm Cl 5 DE75. . . . . 193 C8
SMALLEY GREEN. . . .192 F3
Smalley Manor Dr 1 DE7. . . . . 193 C8
Smalley Manor Drive DE7. . . . . 193 C8
Smalley Mill Rd DE21, DE7. . . . . 192 B4
Small Gate NG19 . . . 136 E6
Small Knowle End
Buxton SK17. . . . . .67 C6
Peak Dale SK17 . . . . . . .67 D5
Small Meer Cl DE73. .232 F1
Small Thorn Pl DE11. . . . . 256 E1
Smeath Rd NG16 . . . .171 F2
Smeckley Wood Cl S41. . . . . .76 C3
Smedley Ave
Ilkeston DE7. . . . . 209 A7
Somercotes DE55. . . . 159 D1
Smedley Ct DE65 . . . 241 B5
Smedley Pl SK13 . . . . .10 E2
Smedley's Ave NG10 . . . . 223 B5
Smedley St DE4 . . . . 143 B6
Smedley Street E DE4. . . . . 143 C5
Smedley Street W DE4. . . . . 143 B7
Smeeton St DE75 . . . 182 B1
Smelter Wood Ave S13. . . . . .44 E7
Smelter Wood Cl S13. . . . . .44 E7
Smelter Wood Cres S13. . . . . .44 F7
Smelter Wood Ct S13. . . . . .44 E7
Smelter Wood Dr S13. . . . . .44 E7
Smelter Wood La S13. . . . . .44 E7
Smelter Wood Pl S13. . . . . .44 F7
Smelter Wood Rd S13. . . . . .44 E7
Smelter Wood Rise S13. . . . . .44 F7
Smelter Wood Way S13. . . . . .44 E7
Smeltinghouse La S18. . . . . .75 E3
SMISBY 257 F3
Smisby Rd LE65 . . . . 258 A1
Smisby Way DE24. . . 232 E3
Smith Ave
Codnor DE5 . . . . .170 B1
King's Newton DE73. . .245 B1
Staveley S43. . . . . .97 C7
Smithbrook Cl SK23 . .47 C6
Smith Cres S41. . . . . . .96 D1
Smith Dr NG16 . . . . . 182 A3
SMITHFIELD 47 C6
Smithfield Ave
Chesterfield S41. . . . . 115 C7
Trowell NG9 . . . . 209 D4
Smithfield Rd S12 . . . .44 A3
Smith-Hall La DE6. . 176 A1
Smith Hall La DE6 . . 188 A7
Smith La S42. . . . . . . 115 C2
Smith Rd DE4 . . . . . . 143 B6
Smiths La
Bakewell DE45 . . . . . . .109 E6
Shirland DE55. . . . . . . 146 C7
Smithson Ave S44 . . . .99 B1
Smiths Yard 9 DE6. 173 B1
Smithurst Rd NG16 . 195 B7
Smithy Ave S45. . . . . 131 C4
Smithy Brook Fold SK23. . . . . .47 B7
Smithy Brook Rd S21. . . . . .79 C8
Smithy Cl
Glossop SK13. . . . . .10 D1
Parwich DE6. . . . . 151 D1
Smithy Croft S18 . . . . .56 D2
Smithy Fold SK13. . . . .10 D1
SMITHY-HILL 51 A7
Smithy Hill S33. . . . . . .51 A7
Smithy House DE45. . .91 C2
Smithy Knoll Rd S32. .72 C2
Smithy La
Clifton Campville B79. . . . . .263 E2
Marple SK6. . . . . .15 F1
Marple Bridge, SK6 . . . .24 A8
Parwich DE6. . . . . 151 D2
Taddington SK17 . . . . . .88 A3
Smithy Mdws S32 . . . .53 A8
SMITHY MOOR. 146 B7
Smithy Pl S42 . . . . . . .115 F2
Smuse La DE4. . . . . . 143 E4
Snake La DE56 . . . . . 190 E4
Snake Pass SK13 . . . . .11 B1
Snake Rd
Bamford S33 . . . . .29 D6
Derwent S33. . . . . .30 B2
High Peak S33 . . . . .28 D8
Snake Woodland Forest Walk* S33. . . . . .19 F3
SNAPE HILL. 57 A2
Snape Hill S18 . . . . . . .57 A2
Snapehill Cl S18. . . . . .57 A3
Snape Hill Cl S18. . . . .57 A3
Snape Hill Cres S18 . .57 A3
Snape Hill Dr S18. . . . .57 B3
Snape Hill Gdns S18 . .57 B3
Snape Hill La S18. . . . .57 A2
Snapes La DE6 . . . . . 184 B1
Snelsmoor La
Chellaston DE73. . . . . .233 B2
Derby DE24 . . . . 233 D4
Derby DE72 . . . . 233 D3
SNELSTON. 184 C3
Snelston Cl S18 . . . . . .56 D1
Snelston Cres DE23. 218 D2
Snelston La DE6. . . . 184 E6
Snipe Cl S42 . . . . 113 D7
Snipesmoor La DE6. .185 F7
SNITTERTON. 142 D5
Snitterton Rd
Matlock DE4. . . . . 143 A5
Snitterton DE4 . . . . . . 142 D6
Snowberry Ave DE56. . . . . 179 B3
Snowberry Close S41. . . . . 115 E7
Snowdon La
Apperknowle S21. . . . . .58 B2
Unstone S18. . . . . .57 F3
Snowdrop Dr NG19 . .136 F4
Snowdrop Valley DE4. . . . . 168 A8
Snowfield View DE4. . . . . 165 E6
Soaper La S18. . . . . . . .57 A2
Soarbank Cl NG16 . . . 195 E7
Soar Cl DE56 . . . . 179 C6
Soar Way DE65 . . . . . 228 D1
Society Pl DE23. . . . . 219 A2
Soft Water La S33 . . . .51 A7
Soldier's Croft DE45. . . . . 107 C2
Solent Rd DE11. . . . . 255 E1
Solney Cl
Swadlincote DE11 . . . .255 F3
1 Swadlincote DE11. . 256 A3
Soloman Pk NG16 . . 195 B2
Soloman Rd DE7 . . . 195 B2
Solomans Ct SK17 . . . .85 D2
Solomons View SK17 .85 C7
Solway Cl DE21. . . . . 206 A2
Solway Rise S18. . . . . .56 D2
Somerby Way 3 DE21. . . . . .205 F2
SOMERCOTES 170 C7
Somercotes Hill DE55. . . . . 170 D8
Somercotes Inf Sch 1 DE55. . . . . 170 C8
Somercotes Rd S12. . .44 D5
Somerlea Park Jun Sch DE55. . . . . 170 C8
Somerleyton Dr DE7. . . . . 209 A4
Somersal Cl DE24. . . 232 E3
SOMERSAL HERBERT. 211 E3
Somersal La
Marston Montgomery DE6. . . . . .211 F6
Somersal Herbert DE6. . . . . 212 A1
Sudbury DE6. . . . . 225 C7
Somersall Cl S40 . . . . .95 A1
Somersall Halldr S40 .95 A1
Somersall La S40. . . . .95 A1
Somersall Park Rd S40. . . . . .95 A1
Somersall Willows S40. . . . . .95 A1
Somersby Ave S40. . 114 B8
Somerset Cl
Buxton SK17. . . . . .85 C4
Derby DE22 . . . . .218 B4
Long Eaton NG10 . . . . 237 A8
Somerset Dr S43 . . . . .97 A8
Somerset Rd DE15. . 254 D6
Somerset St DE21 . . 219 D7
Somerton Cl 8 DE23. . . . . .230 F5
Somme Rd DE22. . . . 204 B3
Songbird Cl DE22. . . .204 F1
SOOKHOLME 120 D2
Sookholme Cl NG20 .119 F3
Sookholme La NG20 . . . . 120 E3
Sorchestun La 11 DE73. . . . . .244 F8
Soresby St S40 . . . . . 266 B3
Sorrel Dr DE11 . . . . . 256 E4
Sough La
Calver S32 . . . . .72 B2
Taddington SK17 . . . . . .87 D2
Wirksworth DE4. . . . . .154 F2
Wirksworth, Steeple Grange DE4. . . . . .155 B2
Soughley La S10. . . . . .42 C8
Sough Rd DE55. . . . . 160 B7
Sough Wood Cl DE75. . . . . 181 C2
Southall St 9 S8. . . . .43 A6
Southard's La S80 . . . .62 E5
South Ave
Buxton SK17. . . . . .85 B7
Chellaston DE73. . . . . .232 F3
Derby DE23 . . . . 218 D1
Derby, Darley Abbey DE22. . . . . 205 A2
Derby, Spondon DE21. .220 E4
Shirebrook NG20 . . . . .119 F3
Southbourne Ct S17 . .55 D6
South Brae Cl DE23. 231 D7
South Broadway St DE14. . . . . 254 C8
Southbrook Cl SK13 . . . 9 E4
South Church St DE45. . . . . 109 D5
South Cl
Glossop SK13. . . . . 9 F7
Unstone Green S18 . . . .76 E6
Southcote Dr S18. . . . .56 D1
South Cres
Bolsover S44 . . . . .99 B1
Duckmanton S44 . . . . . .98 A5
Killamarsh S21. . . . . . . .60 E7
Southcroft
Alfreton DE55. . . . . . . 159 A3
1 Buxton SK17. . . . . . . .85 A7
Derby DE23 . . . . 231 D4
South Ct S17 . . . . .55 E7
South Darley CE Prim Sch DE4. . . . . .142 B7
Southdown Ave S40 . .95 C5
Southdown Cl DE24. 231 C2
Southdown Close S44. . . . . 117 D1
South Dr
Chellaston DE73. . . . . .232 F3
Derby, Cherrytree Hill DE21. . . . . 220 A5
Derby, Littleover DE3 . .218 F7
Swadlincote DE11 . . . .255 F5
South East Derbyshire Coll DE75 . . . . .181 F1
Southend S42 . . . . . . .115 F2
South End DE4 . . . . . 155 A7
South Farm Ave S26 . .61 E6
Southfield Ave S41 . 115 D6
Southfield Cl S80. . . . .81 F5
Southfield Dr
Dronfield S18. . . . . .76 C8
Southfield Dr *continued*
South Normanton DE55. . . . . 160 C5
Southfield Ind Site S80. . . . . .82 A4
Southfield La S80 . . . .82 A4
Southfield Mount S18. . . . . .76 C8
Southfields
Clowne S43. . . . . .80 F3
Long Eaton NG10 . . . . .236 E7
Southfields Ave NG16 . . . . 160 D4
Southgate S21 . . . . . . .59 E3
Southgate Bglws S80. . . . . .81 C7
Southgate Cl DE3. . . 217 C3
Southgate Cres S43 . .80 F5
Southgate Ct S21. . . . .59 E3
Southgate Dr DE15 . 248 B2
Southgate Innovation Ctr DE23. . . . . .267 B1
Southgate Ret Pk DE23. . . . . .267 B1
Southgate Way S43. . .78 B4
South Head Dr SK23 . .47 C7
South Hill
Ashover DE55. . . . . . . .145 F7
Rolleston DE13. . . . . . . 240 D4
Stretton DE55. . . . . . . 146 A7
South Hill La DE55. . .145 F6
South Lodge Ct S40 . .95 B3
South Lodge Mws DE11. . . . . 256 E5
South Marlow St SK13. . . . . .10 A4
Southmead Way DE3. . . . . 218 B3
South Mews 10 SK17. .85 B7
Southmoor Cl S43 . . . .96 F4
SOUTH NORMANTON. 160 A7
South Oak St DE14. . 254 B8
South Par DE4. . . . . . 143 A1
South Park Ave DE4. . . . . 127 C3
South Pl
Chesterfield, Brampton S40. . . . . .95 D2
Chesterfield, Stonegravels S40. . . . . .266 B2
Ripley DE5 . . . . 169 D1
South St
Ashbourne DE6. . . . . . 173 C1
Blackwell DE55. . . . . . .147 F2
Buxton SK17. . . . . .85 B7
Chesterfield S40. . . . . .266 B2
Derby DE1 . . . . .218 E5
Draycott DE72 . . . . . . 235 A7
Eastwood, Bailey Grove NG16 . . . . .182 E2
Eastwood, Giltbrook NG16 . . . . 195 C8
Ilkeston DE7. . . . . .208 F8
Long Eaton NG10 . . . . .236 F7
Melbourne DE73. . . . . 252 A7
Pilsley S45 . . . . 132 D1
Sheffield S20 . . . . .59 D6
Somercotes DE55. . . . 170 D5
South Normanton DE55. . . . . .160 B6
Swanwick DE55 . . . . . .169 E7
Woodville DE11 . . . . . 257 A1
South Street N S43 . . .77 D3
South Terr S18 . . . . . . .94 C7
South Uxbridge St DE14. . . . . 254 B8
South View
Bamford S33 . . . . .40 B4
Chesterfield S41. . . . . . .95 D7
Derby DE23 . . . . 218 C1
Mayfield DE6 . . . . 184 D6
New Mills SK22. . . . . . . .33 B8
Pilsley DE45 . . . . .91 C2
Sheffield S20 . . . . .60 A7
Whitwell S80 . . . . .81 F5
Whitwell S80 . . . . .82 A5
South View Rd SK13 . .17 F7
South View Wlk ST14. . . . . .196 F3
Southwark Cl DE22 . 218 B5
Southwell Rise NG16 . . . . 195 B7
SOUTH WINGFIELD. 157 E3
South Wingfield Prim Sch DE55. . . . . .157 F4
SOUTHWOOD. 258 B7
Southwood 2 SK17 . .85 A7
Southwood Ave S18 . .76 B7
Southwood Dr S43 . . .80 F3
Southwood St DE24. .232 F8
Southworth Rd DE73. . . . . 252 E2
Sovereign Dr DE14 . 254 B8
Sovereign Gr NG10 . 236 B7
Sovereign Way
Chapel-en-le-Frith SK23. . . . . .47 B7
Derby DE21 . . . . 206 D3
Heanor DE75 . . . . 181 D1
Sowbrook Brook DE7. . . . . 208 D4
Sowbrook La DE7. . . 208 E3
Sowter Rd DE1 . . . . . 267 B4
Sowters Row S40. . . 266 B3
Spa Brook Cl S12. . . . .44 F4
Spa Brook Dr S12 . . . .44 F5
Spa Croft DE55 . . . . . 147 E5
Spa Ct DE1 . . . . 267 A1
Spa La
Chesterfield, Hady S41. . . . . 266 C2
Derby DE1 . . . . 267 A1
Mansfield Woodhouse NG19 . . . . .136 F4
Spalden Ave DE6 . . . 173 C3
Spang La NG17 . . . . . 148 E4
Spanker La DE56 . . . 168 B2
Spanker Terr DE56 . 168 C2
Sparkbottom La SK23. . . . . .46 C5
Sparrowbusk Cl S43 . .80 B6
Sparrow Cl
Derby DE24 . . . . 231 D4
Ilkeston DE7. . . . . 209 A5
SPARROWPIT. 48 B6
SPATH 210 A3
Spa View Ave S12 . . . . .44 F3
Spa View Dr S12. . . . . .44 F3
Spa View Pl S12. . . . . .44 F3
Spa View Rd S12 . . . . .44 F3
Spa View Terr S12. . . . .44 F3
Spa View Way S12. . . . .44 F3
Speedway Close NG10 . . . . .236 F8
Speedwell SK13 . . . . 9 F7
Speedwell Cavern* S33. . . . . .37 F2
Speedwell Cl
Derby DE21 . . . . 206 C3
Glossop SK13. . . . . 9 F7
Woodville DE11 . . . . . .256 F4
Speedwell Ind Est S43. . . . . .78 F2
Speedwell Inf Sch S43. . . . . .78 E1
Speedwell La
Kimberley NG16 . . . . . .195 E6
Nottingham NG16. . . . .195 E6
Speetley View S43. . . .80 B7
Speighthill Cres S42. . . . . 114 E4
Spenbeck Dr DE22 . . 205 A5
Spencer Ave
Belper DE56. . . . . .179 B4
Derby DE24 . . . . 232 D4
Sandiacre NG10 . . . . . .223 B6
Staveley S43. . . . . .79 B2
Spencer Cl
Ashbourne DE6. . . . . . 185 C8
Burton upon Trent DE13. . . . . 240 D1
Spencer Cres NG9 . . .223 F8
Spencer Dr DE55 . . . 170 D7
Spencer Gr SK17 . . . . .85 B6
Spencer Ho
Derby, Crewton DE24. . . . . 233 A8
Derby, Spondon DE21. 220 D3
Spencer Rd
Belper DE56. . . . . .179 B4
Buxton SK17. . . . . .85 B6
Chapel-en-le-Frith SK23. . . . . .46 F6
Sheffield S2 . . . . .43 A7
Spencer St
Bolsover S44 . . . . .117 F8
Chesterfield S40. . . . . .266 B4
Derby DE24 . . . . 233 A8
Stanley Common DE7 . 193 A1
Spend La DE6 . . . . . . 161 E2
Sperry Cl NG16 . . . . . .171 F6
Spey Dr DE22. . . . . . . 218 B3
Spilsbury Cl DE65. . . 242 C5
Spinaker Close DE5. 169 E4
Spindle Drive S42 . . 115 A2
Spindletree Dr DE21. . . . . .205 F2
SPINKHILL. 60 D2
Spinkhill Ave S13. . . . .44 C8
Spinkhill Dr S13. . . . . .44 D8
Spinkhill La S21 . . . . . .60 B2
Spinkhill Rd
Killamarsh S21. . . . . . . .60 E4
Sheffield S13 . . . . .44 D8
Spinkhill View S21 . . .60 B1
Spinnaker Road S43 . .80 E5
Spinnerbottom SK22. .24 F2
Spinner Croft
Chesterfield S40. . . . . . .96 A1
Chesterfield S40. . . . . .266 B1
Spinners Close DE55. . . . . 160 C6
Spinners Way DE56. 179 C5
Spinneybrook Way DE3. . . . . 217 D4
Spinney Cl
Derby DE22 . . . . 205 A2
Glossop SK13. . . . . .10 C2
Mansfield Woodhouse NG19 . . . . .136 E6
Spinney Cres NG9 . . .223 F3
Spinney Dr NG10 . . . 223 C2
Spinney Hill DE73. . . 252 A7
Spinney La DE16. . . . 254 D5
Spinney Lodge
Repton DE65. . . . . 242 C2
Tutbury DE13 . . . . .238 E6
Spinney Rd
Branston DE14 . . . . . . .253 F8
Derby DE22 . . . . .218 E3
Derby, Chaddesden DE21. . . . . .219 F7
Ilkeston DE7. . . . . .208 E6
Long Eaton NG10 . . . . 223 C2
Spinney Rise NG9 . . 223 E3
Spinney The
Belper DE56. . . . . 179 A6
Borrowash DE72 . . . . 221 C1
Brailsford DE6 . . . . . . .201 E8
Castle Donington DE74. . . . . 247 A4
Ilkeston DE7. . . . . .208 E6
Ripley DE5 . . . . 169 D3
Sheffield S17 . . . . .55 C7
Shirebrook NG20 . . . . 119 D3
Stanton-by-Dale NG10 . . . . .222 F8
SPION KOP 120 F2
Spion Pk Mws NG20 .120 F2
Spire Close DE6 . . . . 173 A1
Spire Heights S40 . . 266 A3
Spire Hollin SK13. . . . .10 C2
Spire Hollin Ho SK13 .10 C2
Spire Inf Sch S40. . . 115 A7
Spire Jun Sch S40. . 115 A8
Spire La S44 . . . . 118 B6
Spire Valley S45. . . . 131 D5
Spire View NG10. . . . 236 B4
Spire Walk Bsns Pk S40. . . . . .266 B1
Spire Wlk S40. . . . . . . .96 B2
SPITAL 96 C1
Spital Brook Cl S41. . .96 C1
Spital Gdns S41 . . . . . .96 C2
SPITALHILL. 185 C8
Spital La
Chesterfield S40. . . . . . .96 B2
Chesterfield S41. . . . . . .96 C1
Spital Rise DE74. . . . 247 A4
SPITEWINTER. 113 D1
Spitewinter La S18, S42. . . . . .93 D8
Spitfire Road DE74 . .246 F3
Spittal DE74. . . . . 247 A4
Spittal Gn S44. . . . . . . 118 A8
Spittal Hill DE74 . . . . 247 A4
Spittal The 3 DE74. .246 F4
Spode Drive DE11 . . .256 F1
SPONDON 220 E4
Spondon Rd
Dale Abbey DE7 . . . . . 207 D2
Ilkeston DE7. . . . . .208 F5
Spondon Sta DE21. . 220 D3
Spooner Dr S21 . . . . . .60 C6
Spooner La S32 . . . . . .72 C5
Spoonley Wood Ct DE23. . . . . .230 F7
Sporton Cl DE55 . . . . 160 A7
Sporton La DE55. . . . 160 B7
Spotswood Cl S14 . . . .43 E4
Spotswood Dr S14. . . .43 E5
Spotswood Mount S14. . . . . .43 E4
Spotswood Pl S14 . . . .43 D4
Spotswood Rd S14 . . .43 D5
SPOUT 166 C3
Spout La
Spout DE56. . . . . 166 C3
Tansley DE4 . . . . 144 A4
Spridgeon Cl 2 NG10 . . . . 223 B2
Springbank
Glossop SK13. . . . . 9 F5
Unstone S18. . . . . .76 E8
Spring Bank
Buxton SK17. . . . . .67 C4
Great Longstone DE45 . .90 A4
New Mills SK22. . . . . . . .33 C8
Springbank Gdns SK22. . . . . .33 B8
Springbank Prim Sch
Eastwood NG16 . . . . . .182 E2
1 Eastwood NG16 . . . .182 F2
Spring Bank Rd S40. . . . . 266 A3
Spring Cl
Belper DE56. . . . . .178 E6
Breaston DE72 . . . . . . 235 C8
Renishaw S21. . . . . .79 C7
Swadlincote DE11 . . . . 256 A1
Wirksworth DE4. . . . . .154 F2
Spring Close Dell S14. . . . . .43 F4
Spring Close Mount S14. . . . . .43 F4
Spring Close View S14. . . . . .43 F4
SPRING COTTAGE. . 262 D5
Spring Cottage Rd DE12. . . . . 262 D5
Spring Ct 4 NG9. . . . 223 E7
Spring Ct Mews SK14. . 9 D5
Springdale SK17. . . . . . .84 F7
Springdale Ct DE3. . 217 E1
Spring Dale Gdns NG9 . . . . 209 D3
Springfarm Rd DE15. . . . . 248 A1
Springfield
Broadbottom SK13. . . . .16 C6
Derby DE23 . . . . .218 B2
Springfield Ave
Ashbourne DE6. . . . . . 185 D8
Chesterfield S40. . . . . . .95 D3
Heanor DE75 . . . . .181 B5
Long Eaton NG10 . . . . .236 F8
Sandiacre NG10 . . . . . .223 B3
Shirebrook NG20 . . . . .119 E5
Springfield Cl
Bradwell S33 . . . . .51 A7
Clowne S43. . . . . .80 E3
Crich DE4 . . . . 157 A1

Springfield Cl *continued*
Eckington S21. . . . . .59 C3
Glossop SK13. . . . . .9 E4
Swadlincote DE11. . . .256 B6
Springfield Cres
Bolsover S44. . . . . .98 F3
Somercotes DE55. . . . .170 D7
Springfield Ct NG9 . . 209 E1
Springfield Dr DE56 . 190 D3
Springfield Gdns
DE7. . . . . .194 F2
Springfield Jun Sch
DE11. . . . . .256 C5
**SPRINGFIELD
PARK**. 223 A3
Springfield Prim Sch
DE21. . . . . .220 D5
Springfield Rd
Barlow S18. . . . . .75 D3
Bradwell S33. . . . . .51 A8
Chellaston DE73. . . . . .232 F2
Derby, Cherrytree Hill
DE21. . . . . .220 B5
Etwall DE65 . . . . .229 B3
Holmewood S42. . . . . . .132 E8
Repton DE65. . . . . .242 D2
Swadlincote DE11 . . . .256 B6
Springfield Rise
DE4. . . . . 143 C6
Springfield Terr
Burton upon Trent
DE15. . . . . .248 A1
Hayfield SK22. . . . . . . .25 D2
Ripley DE5. . . . . .169 E1
Springfield View
DE5. . . . . 169 D2
Spring Gardens
DE55. . . . . .157 D8
Spring Gardens Ctr The
SK17. . . . . .85 B8
Spring Garden Terr
DE7. . . . . .194 F2
Spring Gdns
Buxton SK17. . . . . .85 C8
Derby DE21 . . . . .219 F7
Glossop SK13. . . . . .10 A5
Springhill DE11. . . . .257 A8
Spring Hill
Kimberley NG16. . . . . .195 F5
Mansfield Woodhouse
NG19 . . . . .136 B3
Whitwell S80 . . . . .82 A6
Springhill Way DE5 . 181 A8
Spring Hollow DE56 190 C8
Spring House Cl S42. .94 F5
Spring La
Elmton S80. . . . . .99 F6
Heanor DE75 . . . . .181 E1
Renishaw S21. . . . . . . .79 C7
Sheffield S2. . . . . .43 E8
Shireoaks S80, S81. . . . .63 F5
Warsop NG20. . . . . . . .120 C6
Spring Mdw 4
DE55. . . . . .148 B7
Springmeadow SK13. .16 D7
Spring Mount SK22 . . .33 C8
Spring Pl S40 . . . . . . .266 C3
Spring Rd DE55. . . . . 170 E6
Spring Rise SK13 . . . . .16 F7
Springs L Ctr S21. . . . .43 F6
Spring St
Broadbottom SK14. . . . .16 A8
Derby DE22 . . . . .267 A2
Glossop SK13. . . . . .10 B1
Hollingworth SK14. . . . . .9 C5
Swadlincote DE11 . . . . .262 A8
Whitwell S80 . . . . .82 A6
Spring The NG10 . . . .236 D5
Spring Vale SK22. . . . .24 E3
Springvale Cl S45 . . 131 D2
Springvale Gdns
S45. . . . . 131 E2
Springvale Rd S45. .131 D2
Spring Vale Rd
Brimington S43. . . . . . . .96 E8
Hayfield SK22. . . . . . . .25 E2
Spring Water Ave
S12. . . . . .44 F3
Springwater Cl S12. . .44 F3
Spring Water Dr
Glossop SK13. . . . . .9 E3
Sheffield S12. . . . . .44 F3
Spring Way S2 . . . . . . .44 A8
Springwell Com Coll
S43. . . . . .97 D7
Springwell Hill
Middle Handley S21. . . .78 A8
Unstone S21. . . . . .77 F6
Springwell Park Dr
S43. . . . . .97 C7
Springwell St NG17 . .148 F2
Springwood SK13. . . . .16 F8
Spring Wood Cl S41. . .95 D8
Springwood Ct S43 . . .77 D4
Springwood Dr
Derby DE21 . . . . .206 B2
Mansfield Woodhouse
NG19 . . . . .136 C2
Springwood Farm Rd
DE11. . . . . .256 B7
Springwood Gdns
DE56. . . . . .179 A4
Springwood L Ctr
DE21. . . . . .206 A2
Springwood St S8 . . .43 A6
Springwood St S42. .116 B4
Sprinkswoods La
DE6. . . . . .184 E5

Spruce Ave NG16 . . . 171 D6
Spruce Cl S40. . . . . . . .95 B2
Spruce Rise S21. . . . .60 C5
Spurr St S2 . . . . .43 B8
Sq The DE4. . . . . .142 A7
Square The
Boylestone DE6 . . . . . .213 C4
Bretby DE15. . . . . .249 B3
8 Buxton SK17. . . . . . . .85 B8
Clay Cross S45 . . . . . . .131 E3
Derby DE3 . . . . .217 D1
Derby, Darley Abbey
DE22. . . . . .205 A1
Elmton S80. . . . . .100 A7
Eyam S32. . . . . .71 E5
Hartington SK17. . . . . .137 D5
Marchington ST14 . . . .224 E2
Middleton DE45. . . . . .124 F3
Monyash DE45 . . . . . . .107 C2
Whitwell S80 . . . . .81 F6
Squashley Bank
Roston DE6. . . . . .197 F6
Roston DE6. . . . . .198 B6
Squires La S33 . . . . . .38 C3
Squires Way DE23 . . 231 A6
Squirrel La DE73. . . . .252 E4
Squirrel Wlk
Duffield DE56 . . . . . . .191 A2
Overseal DE12 . . . . . . .262 B3
Stable Cl DE4. . . . . . . .156 B5
Stable Cotts DE4 . . . 155 A6
Stable La
Alstonefield DE6. . . . . .149 B1
Buxton SK17. . . . . .84 E5
Stable Mews DE11. . .256 F2
Stables Cl S44. . . . . . .99 C1
Stables La SK17 . . . . .85 C4
Stables St DE22. . . . . 218 D5
Stables The DE65 . . .228 F1
Stacey Rd NG19 . . . 135 D2
Stackyard The DE7 . .207 F2
STADEN. 85 E5
Staden Bsns Pk SK17 85 E5
Staden La SK17. . . . . .85 E4
Stadium Bsns Ct
DE24. . . . . .219 E4
Stadium Ind Pk
NG10 . . . . .236 F8
Stadium View DE24. 219 E3
Stadmoor Ct DE73 . . 232 F1
Staffa Dr DE55. . . . . .147 F5
Stafford Cl
Dronfield S18 . . . . .56 C2
6 Glossop SK13 . . . . . .17 F8
Melbourne DE73. . . . . .252 B8
Smalley DE7 . . . . .192 F6
Stafford Cres DE4 . . .165 E2
Stafford Dr DE23 . . . .230 F5
Stafford Ho DE24 . . . 232 E6
Stafford St
Derby DE1 . . . . .267 A3
Long Eaton NG10 . . . . .236 F8
New Mills SK22. . . . . . .24 C1
Staines Cl DE3. . . . . .217 C2
Stainforth St NG19. . 136 C2
Stainsbro' La DE4,
DE6. . . . . .165 B6
STAINSBY. 133 B7
Stainsby Ave
Heanor DE75 . . . . .193 E8
Horsley Woodhouse
DE7. . . . . .192 E6
Stainsby Cl S42. . . . . .132 F8
Stainsby Gr NG17. . . .148 F2
Stainsby Mill ★ S44 . 133 D7
Staithes Wlk DE21 . . 205 C1
Staker La DE3 . . . . . .230 D6
Staley Close DE11 . . 256 B2
Staley Dr
Glapwell S44 . . . . 118 C1
Glapwell S44 . . . . .134 B8
Stalybridge Ctry Pk ★
SK15. . . . . .4 A2
Stalybridge Rd SK14 . . .9 A4
Stamford Cl NG10 . . 236 E4
Stamford Ct 5
DE75. . . . . .181 D2
Stamford St
Awsworth NG16 . . . . . .195 C4
Derby DE24 . . . . .232 D6
Heanor DE75 . . . . .181 E2
2 Ilkeston DE7 . . . . . . .194 E1
Stamps Cl DE15 . . . . .248 C3
Stanage Gn DE3 . . . .217 F1
Stanage Rise S12. . . . .44 E5
Stanage Way S40. . . . .94 F5
Stancliffe Ave DE4. . .127 C3
Stancliffe View
DE4. . . . . .127 B3
Standall Close S18 . . .56 B3
Standing Butts Cl
DE12. . . . . .259 D8
Standlow La DE6. . . . 163 C2
Stand Park Ind Est
S41. . . . . .96 A7
Stand Rd S41. . . . . . . .95 F7
Standedge Rd
Bakewell DE45. . . . . . .109 B6
Bakewell DE45. . . . . . .109 C6
Stanford Rd S18. . . . . .56 C1
Stanford Way S40 . . . 114 B8
STANFREE. 99 B8
**STANHOPE
BRETBY**. 248 F1
Stanhope Cl DE65 . . .229 C3
Stanhope Glade
DE15. . . . . .256 A8
Stanhope Gn DE15. . .248 F1

Stanhope Rd
Derby DE3 . . . . .217 E3
Sheffield S12. . . . . .44 C5
Swadlincote DE11 . . . .256 B3
Stanhope St
Bramley-Vale S44. . . . .117 C1
Burton upon Trent
DE15. . . . . .248 B3
Derby DE23 . . . . .218 F8
Derby DE23 . . . . .219 A2
Ilkeston DE7 . . . . .209 A6
Long Eaton NG10 . . . . .236 D8
Stanton-by-Dale
NG10 . . . . .222 E8
Stanier Ct S41. . . . . . 115 C7
Stanier Dr DE11 . . . .256 F4
Stanier Way
Derby DE21 . . . . 220 A3
Renishaw S21. . . . . . . .60 B1
Staniforth Ave S21. . .59 B3
Stanleigh Gdns
DE12. . . . . .265 E8
Stanleigh Ho DE12. . 265 E8
Stanleigh Rd DE12. . 262 B4
STANLEY
Tibshelf 133 D1
West Hallam. 207 C5
Stanley Ave
Ripley DE5 . . . . .169 E2
Staveley S43. . . . . .97 B7
Stanley Cl
Derby DE22 . . . . .218 F8
Ilkeston DE7 . . . . .208 E7
Netherseal DE12 . . . . .264 F7
Woodville DE11 . . . . . .256 F3
**STANLEY
COMMON**. 193 B1
**Stanley Common CE
Prim Sch** DE7 . . . . .193 B1
Stanley Cres DE7. . . 210 A2
Stanley Ct NG16 . . . .182 F1
Stanley Dr
Beeston NG9 . . . . .209 F1
5 Stapleford NG9 . . . .223 F8
Stanley Hall SK12. .32 C6
Stanley La S44,
NG17 . . . . 133 D2
Stanley Mws NG16. . 195 D7
Stanley Rd
Derby, Allenton
DE24. . . . . .232 F6
Derby, Cherrytree Hill
DE21. . . . . 220 A5
Sheffield S8 . . . . .43 B5
Stanley St
Chesterfield S41. . . . . . .96 C2
Derby DE22 . . . . 218 D5
Ilkeston DE7. . . . . .208 F7
Killamarsh S21. . . . . . . .60 D7
Long Eaton NG10 . . . . .236 E7
Somercotes DE55. . . . . 170 D8
Swadlincote DE11 . . . . .256 C4
STANSHOPE. 149 D1
Stanshope La DE6 . . 149 C2
Stanstead Rd DE3 . . 217 C3
STANTON
Mayfield 183 D8
Swadlincote 255 C4
Stanton Ave DE56. . . 179 B4
**STANTON BY
BRIDGE**. 244 D3
**STANTON-BY-
DALE**. 222 E8
Stanton Cl
Alfreton DE55. . . . . . . .159 A3
Darley Dale DE4 . . . . . .127 B3
Stanton Cres S12. . . .44 D4
STANTON GATE. . . . 209 C1
Stanton Gate DE7. . . 209 C1
Stantonhall La
DE4. . . . . 126 D7
Stanton Hill DE73. . . 251 C5
STANTON IN PEAK. 126 C5
**Stanton in Peak
CE Prim Sch** DE4 . . 126 C5
Stanton La
Ellastone DE6. . . . . . . .183 C4
Mayfield DE6 . . . . 172 A4
STANTON LEES. 126 F3
Stanton Moor View
DE4. . . . . .142 F7
Stanton Pl NG19. . . . .134 F7
Stanton Prim Sch
DE15. . . . . .255 B5
Stanton Rd
Ashbourne DE6. . . . . . .185 D8
Burton upon Trent
DE15. . . . . .254 F7
Ilkeston DE7. . . . . .208 F7
Sandiacre NG10 . . . . . .223 A7
Stanton St
Derby DE23 . . . . .218 F1
New Houghton NG19 . .134 F7
Stanton Vale Sch
NG10 . . . . .236 C7
Stanton View DE45 . 109 C4
Stanwood Dr S40. . . . 114 B8
Stanyforth St SK13. . .10 A4
STAPENHILL. 254 F8
STAPLEFORD. 223 C4
Stapleford La NG9. . .223 F1
Stapleford Rd NG9. . 209 D3
Stapleton Rd DE7. . . 194 E4
Starch La NG10 . . . . .223 C7
Starcross Ct DE3 . . . 217 C3
Starflower Way
DE3. . . . . .217 D5
STARKHOLMES 143 C2

Starkholmes Rd
DE4. . . . . .143 C2
Starkie Ave DE74 . . .246 F3
Starkie St SK13. . . . . .10 E3
Starling Rd SK17 . . . .85 D2
Starthe Bank DE75. .181 F1
Starthe View DE75. .181 F1
Starth La DE4. . . . . . . 144 A3
Start La SK23. . . . . . . .45 B7
Statham Ave S42 . . . 131 C8
Statham Cl DE3. . . . . 217 B3
Statham St DE22. . . . 218 E7
Station App
Ambergate DE56 . . . . .167 F4
Buxton SK17. . . . . .85 B8
Derby DE1 . . . . .267 B4
Duffield DE56. . . . . . . .190 F4
Hathersage S32. . . . . . .53 A7
Station Back La
S41. . . . . .266 C3
Station Cl
Burton upon Trent
DE16. . . . . .254 E5
Chellaston DE73. . . . . .232 F1
Kilburn DE56. . . . . . . .179 F1
Station Cotts DE6. . . 225 E2
Station Cres 6
DE11. . . . . .256 C4
Station Ct 3 DE7. . . 194 E1
Station Dr
Elvaston DE72 . . . . . . .234 A8
Moira DE12. . . . . .262 F4
Station Hill NG19 . . . 136 B3
Station La
Chesterfield S41, S43. . .77 C2
Codnor DE5 . . . . .181 B6
Walton-on-Trent
DE12. . . . . .253 D1
Station La Ind Est
S41. . . . . .77 B2
Station New Rd
S42. . . . . 131 D7
Station Rd
Ashbourne DE6. . . . . . .173 B1
Awsworth NG16 . . . . . .195 C5
Bakewell DE45. . . . . . .109 E6
Bamford S33 . . . . .40 B2
Barrow Hill S43 . . . . . . .78 B3
Bolsover S44 . . . . .98 F2
Borrowash DE72 . . . . . .221 B1
Breadsall DE21. . . . . . .205 E4
Brimington S43. . . . . . . .96 D8
Brimington, Hollingwood
S43. . . . . .78 A2
Burton upon Trent
DE13. . . . . .253 A1
Buxton SK17. . . . . .85 B7
Castle Donington
DE74. . . . . .247 C5
Chapel-en-le-Frith
SK23. . . . . .47 B6
Chellaston DE73. . . . . .232 F1
Chesterfield S41. . . . . . .96 A7
Chesterfield S41. . . . . . 266 C3
Chesterfield, Old Whittington
S41. . . . . .77 A1
Chinley SK23. . . . . .34 D2
Clowne S43. . . . . .80 E4
Creswell S43 . . . . .81 C1
Darley Dale DE4 . . . . . .127 C2
Denby Village DE5 . . . .180 B3
Derby DE3 . . . . .217 D3
Derby, Spondon DE21. . 220 D3
Dove Holes SK17 . . . . . .47 F1
Draycott DE72 . . . . . . .235 B7
Draycott in the Clay
ST14. . . . . .225 E1
Duffield DE56 . . . . .190 F4
Furness Vale SK23. . . . .33 D4
Glossop SK13 . . . . .10 A5
Great Longstone DE45 . .89 F3
Hathersage S32. . . . . . .53 A7
Hatton DE65 . . . . .239 D8
Hayfield SK22. . . . . .25 D2
Hayfield, Birch Vale
SK22. . . . . .25 A2
Hope S33 . . . . .39 B3
Ilkeston DE7. . . . . .194 F1
Ironville NG16 . . . . . . .170 F3
Killamarsh S21. . . . . . . .60 B6
Kimberley NG16. . . . . .195 F6
Langley Mill NG16. . . . .182 B2
Little Eaton DE21. . . . . 205 C7
Long Eaton NG10 . . . . .236 F8
Marchington ST14 . . . .224 E3
Marple SK6. . . . . .23 A7
Marple, Strines SK6,
SK22. . . . . .23 D1
Melbourne DE73. . . . . .252 C8
New Mills SK22. . . . . . .33 B7
North Wingfield S42. . .131 E6
North Wingfield S45. . .131 E7
Pilsley S45 . . . . .132 D1
Renishaw S21. . . . . .60 A2
Rocester ST14 . . . . . . .196 E3
Rolleston DE13. . . . . . .240 C4
Sandiacre NG10 . . . . . .223 C5
Scarcliffe S44. . . . . .118 F6
Scarcliffe S44. . . . . . . .119 A5
Selston NG16. . . . . . . .160 E1
Selston NG16. . . . . . . .171 F8
Shelton S20 . . . . .59 E7
Shirebrook NG20 . . . . .119 E6
Spinkhill S21. . . . . .60 D2
Stanley DE7 . . . . .207 C6
Stonebroom DE55 . . . .147 B5
Tibshelf DE55. . . . . . . .147 F6
Upper Padley S11. . . . . .53 E2

Station Rd *continued*
West Hallam DE7 . . . . .207 C8
Whaley Bridge SK23. . . .34 A1
Whitwell S80 . . . . .82 A5
8 Wirksworth DE4 . . . .154 F1
Woodville DE11 . . . . . .256 F2
Station Road Ind Est
S43. . . . . .80 E4
Station St
Ashbourne DE6. . . . . . .173 B1
Cossall DE7 . . . . .195 A1
Glossop SK13 . . . . .10 C1
Long Eaton NG10 . . . . .236 E7
Mansfield Woodhouse
NG19 . . . . .136 B3
Swadlincote DE11 . . . .261 F8
Station Vw NG20. . . . 119 E4
Station Wlk 1 SK17. .85 D8
Station Yard SK22 . . .33 A6
Station Yd DE73 . . . . .252 C8
Staton La
Apperknowle S18. . . . . .58 A1
Apperknowle S18. . . . . .77 A8
Staunton Ave DE23 . 231 E6
Staunton Cl
Castle Donington
DE74. . . . . .247 A4
Chesterfield S40. . . . . . 115 A6
Staunton Harold
DE73. . . . . .258 E7
*Staunton Harold Resr
Visitor Ctr* ★ DE73. . .251 F5
Staunton La
DE73. . . . . .258 B8
STAVELEY. 78 D1
Staveley Cl DE24. . . .232 E3
Staveley Jun Sch
S43. . . . . .78 E1
Staveley La
Barrow Hill S21, S43. . . .78 A5
Eckington S21. . . . . . . .59 E2
Staveley S43. . . . . .78 E7
Staveley Rd
Chesterfield S43. . . . . . .77 E3
Long Duckmanton S44 . .97 E4
Poolsbrook S43 . . . . . . .98 A8
Sheffield S8 . . . . .43 A7
Staverton Dr DE3 . . .217 D4
Stead Mews S21. . . . .59 D3
Stead St S21. . . . . .59 D3
Steam Mill La DE5 . .170 A1
Steele Ave S43 . . . . . .97 B6
Steele St SK17. . . . . . .85 A8
Steel La S44. . . . . .99 B2
Steel's La S44. . . . . . . 118 B6
Steelyard Cl DE5 . . . .169 E4
Steeping Cl S43 . . . . .96 E8
Steep La S42 . . . . 114 A4
Steeple Cl DE21 . . . . 205 E2
Steeple Dr DE5 . . . . . 180 E8
Steeple End Fold
SK22. . . . . .25 D2
Steeplegate S40. . . . 266 B3
STEEPLE GRANGE. . 155 A3
Steeple Grange
Chesterfield S41. . . . . . .96 D1
Wirksworth DE4. . . . . . .154 F3
*Steeple Grange Light
Rly* ★ DE4 . . . . 154 F4
Steep Turnpike
DE4. . . . . 143 C5
Steetley La S80. . . . . . .63 E3
STENSON. 243 B8
Stenson Ave DE23 . . 231 E6
Stenson Ct DE5. . . . . 169 F1
**Stenson Fields Prim
Com Sch** DE24 . . . . 231 D2
Stenson Rd DE23,
DE24. . . . . .231 D4
Stenton Rd S8. . . . . . .56 F7
Stephenson Cl S45 . . 131 B4
Stephenson Ct S40 . . .95 B2
Stephenson La S45. . 131 C5
Stephenson Pl
Chesterfield S40. . . . . .266 B3
Clay Cross S45 . . . . 131 A4
Stephenson Rd
1 Eastwood DE7. . . . .194 E8
Staveley S43. . . . . .78 E1
Stephensons Way
DE21. . . . . 220 A3
Stephens Rd DE14. . . 254 B8
Stephouses SK6 . . . . .23 F8
Stepping Cl DE22. . . . 218 E5
Stepping La DE22. . . . 218 E5
Sterland St S40. . . . . .95 E3
Sterling Cl DE5 . . . . . 180 B2
Sterndale Cl SK17 . . . .69 E3
Sterndale Ho 4
DE1. . . . . .267 B2
Sterndale La SK17 . . .69 E3
Sterndale Moor
SK17. . . . . 105 E6
Sterndale Rd NG10 . 236 B6
Sterry Cl S43. . . . . .80 E2
Stevenage Cl DE24. .232 F5
Steven Cl NG9 . . . . . . .223 F4
Steven Mangle Close
S12. . . . . .44 E2
Stevens La DE72. . . . 235 D8
Stevenson Ave
DE72. . . . . .235 B8
Stevenson Ho S41. . . .96 B6
Stevenson Pl DE23. . 231 B8
Stevenson Rd DE6. . .224 D8
Stevenson Way
DE56. . . . . .168 B5

Stevens Rd NG10 . . .223 A5
Steward Gate S33 . . . .40 A6
Stewart Cl
Burton upon Trent
DE14. . . . . .254 A6
Derby DE21. . . . . 220 E6
Stewart St DE55 . . . . 170 D5
Stichill Ave DE23 . . . 231 E1
Stile Croft DF4 . . . . . 154 D5
Stiles Cl SK13. . . . . .9 E5
Stiles Rd DE24. . . . . . 233 B8
Stillman Cl S41. . . . . . 115 C8
Stinting La
Mansfield NG19 . . . . . .136 E2
Shirebrook NG20 . . . . .119 D3
Stirland St DE5 . . . . . 170 B1
Stirling Cl
Castle Gresley DE11. . .255 F1
Derby DE21 . . . . .219 C8
Stirling Ct S41. . . . . . 266 E4
Stirling Gr NG16. . . . .195 E7
Stirling Way
Swadlincote DE11 . . . .256 E5
Woodville DE11 . . . . . .257 A5
Stockbrook Rd
DE22. . . . . .218 D3
Stockbrook St DE22 218 E4
Stockdove Cl DE24. .218 F1
Stocker Ave DE24. . . 233 D7
Stock La ST14 . . . . . .224 C1
STOCKLEY. 117 E4
Stockley La S44. . . . . . 117 F1
Stockley View S44. . . 118 B8
Stockport Rd
Broadbottom SK14. . . . .15 D8
Marple SK6. . . . . .23 A6
Stocks Brow S13. . . . .10 A7
Stocks Green Ct S17. .55 D4
Stocks Green Dr S17. .55 D4
Stocks La SK23 . . . . . .45 A4
Stocks Rd NG16 . . . . .195 E7
Stocks The SK13. . . . . .10 A7
Stockton Close
DE11. . . . . .255 F2
Stockton Dr SK23. . . . .34 C1
Stockwell Cl S40 . . . . 114 F7
Stockwell Dr
4 Derby DE22. . . . . . .218 A5
Derby DE23 . . . . .217 F5
Stoddard Dr DE75. . .181 F2
Stodhart Flats SK23. . .47 C8
STOKE. 72 C6
Stoke Cl DE56 . . . . . .179 E5
Stoke La S32 . . . . .72 C5
Stollard St S45. . . . . . 131 D4
Stone Ave NG16 . . . . .182 A1
Stone Bank Ct S18. . . .57 B1
Stonebench La
SK17. . . . . 106 C3
Stone Bench Way
SK17. . . . . .85 E8
Stonebridge La
NG20 . . . . .120 F4
STONEBROOM. 146 F4
Stonebroom Ind Est
DE55. . . . . .147 B4
Stonebroom La
DE55. . . . . 147 B5
Stonebroom Prim Sch
DE55. . . . . 147 A4
Stonebroom Wlk
DE24. . . . . 232 E3
Stonechat Cl DE3. . . 218 A3
Stone Cl
Derby DE21. . . . . 220 E6
Dronfield S18. . . . . .57 C3
Stonecliff Terr SK17 . .35 D8
Stone Cotts DE6. . . . .184 E8
Stonecroft S80 . . . . . .82 C6
Stonecroft Rd S17. . . .55 F5
Stonedale Cl S20 . . . .59 D7
Stone Fronts DE73. . .251 A4
Stone Gr NG20 . . . . . . 101 A1
STONEGRAVELS. 96 A5
Stonegravels Croft 7
S20. . . . . .59 F6
Stonegravels La S41. .96 A5
Stonegravels Way
S20. . . . . .59 F6
Stoneheads
Whaley Bridge SK23. . . .33 B1
Whaley Bridge SK23. . . .45 B8
Whaley Bridge SK23. . . .45 C8
Stoneheads Rise
SK23. . . . . .45 B8
Stonehill DE74. . . . . .247 B2
Stone Hill Rd DE23. . 218 F2
Stoneholes Dr S45. . . 131 E2
Stone La
Chesterfield S43. . . . . . .77 D4
Sheffield S13. . . . . .44 F5
Stoneleigh Way
DE55. . . . . .169 F8
Stoneley Cl S12. . . . . .44 B1
Stoneley Cres S12. . . .44 B1
Stoneley Dell S12 . . . .44 B1
Stoneley Dr S12. . . . . .44 B1
Stonelow
Baslow DE45 . . . . .92 F4
Wadshelf S42. . . . . .93 B5
Stonelow Cres S18 . . .57 C2
Stonelow La S18 . . . . .57 B2
Stonelow Jun Sch
S18. . . . . .57 C2
Stonelow Rd S18 . . . .57 C2

Stone Mdws NG10 . . 236 E5
Stonepit La DE6 . . . . 164 A3
Stone Rd S18. . . . . . . .57 C3
Stoneridge SK13. . . . . . 9 F5
Stone Row
　Chesterfield S40. . . . . .95 D2
　Marple SK6. . . . . .23 A6
Stone Row Pl DE12 . .262 F4
Stonerows La S45 . . . 145 C6
Stonesby Cl DE21. . .205 F2
Stonesdale Ct 1
　DE24. . . . . .233 C6
Stones La DE4. . . . . .156 F1
Stone St S20 . . . . .59 D7
Stones The S33. . . . . . .38 B2
Stonewell La SK17. . .137 D5
Stoney Cl DE45 . . . . .109 D4
Stoneycroft La S42 . .114 A5
Stoney Cross DE21. .220 E3
Stoney Cross Ind Est
　DE21. . . . . .220 D3
Stoneydale Cl DE11. .255 F5
Stoneyfield Bank
　DE56. . . . . .179 A5
Stoney Flatts Cres
　DE21. . . . . .220 A8
STONEYFORD 182 A7
Stoneyford Rd
　DE12. . . . . .262 A3
Stoney Furlong Rd
　DE45. . . . . .91 E6
Stoney Gate Rd
　DE21. . . . . .220 D3
Stoney Hill DE4. . . . .155 B2
Stoney La
　Appleby Magna
　DE12. . . . . .265 F1
　Ashover S42. . . . . . . .130 C3
　Brinsley NG16. . . . . . .182 D6
　Derby DE21. . . . . .220 E5
　Hognaston DE6. . . . . . .164 A2
　Selston NG16. . . . . . . .171 E7
　Thorpe DE6. . . . . .161 E1
　Trowell NG9 . . . . .209 B5
Stoneyland Dr SK22 . .33 B8
STONEY
　MIDDLETON 72 A4
Stoney Middleton CE
　Prim Sch S32 . . . . . . .71 F3
Stoneyside DE45. . . .125 C5
Stoney View
　5 Creswell S43. . . . . . .81 E2
　Langley Mill NG16. . . . .182 D5
Stoney Way DE4. . . . .143 C4
Stoney Wood Dr
　DE4. . . . . .156 C1
Stony Clouds Nature
　Reserve* NG10 . . . . .223 B8
STONY
　HOUGHTON 118 F1
Stonyhurst Ct DE24 . .232 E4
Stony La DE56 . . . . . .191 D6
Stony Ridge M11. . . . .54 C5
Stoodley Pike Gdns
　DE22. . . . . .204 C2
Stoops Cl S40 . . . . . . .95 D6
Stoppard Cl DE7. . . .194 D2
Storer La DE4 . . . . . .166 B3
Stores Rd DE21. . . . .267 D4
Storey Road SK12 . . . .32 A6
Storforth La S41. . . . .115 B7
Storforth Lane Terr
　S41. . . . . .115 C8
Storforth Lane Trad Est
　S40. . . . . .115 B8
Stormont Cl DE55. . . .160 B4
Stormont Gr S43 . . . . .97 C7
Stornoway Cl 9
　DE24. . . . . .231 D3
Storrs Rd S40 . . . . . . .95 B2
Storth Bank S13. . . . . .16 A7
Storth Brook Ct S13 .16 A7
Storthfield Way
　DE55. . . . . .160 B4
Storth La DE55 . . . . .160 B4
Storth Meadow Rd
　Charlesworth SK13. . . . .16 A7
　Glossop SK13. . . . . . . .16 F7
Stort Sq NG19 . . . . . .136 C2
Stour Cl
　Brimington S43. . . . . . .96 E8
　4 Hilton DE65. . . . . . .240 E8
Stourdale Cl NG10 . . .236 A6
Stourport Dr DE73. . .233 A3
Stow Ct 6 NG19. . . . .136 E3
Stowmarket Dr
　DE21. . . . . .219 D8
Stradbroke Ave S13 . .44 D7
Stradbroke Cl S13 . . .44 E7
Stradbroke Cres S13 .44 E7
Stradbroke Dr S13. . .44 E7
Stradbroke Pl S13. . .44 E7
Stradbroke Prim Sch
　S13. . . . . .44 D7
Stradbroke Rd S13 . . .44 E6
Stradbroke Rise
　S40. . . . . .114 C8
Stradbroke Way S13. .44 E7
Stradbroke Wlk S13 . .44 D7
STRAMSHALL 210 A4
Stramshall Rd ST14. .210 B3
Strand Arc DE1. . . . .267 B3
Strand The DE1. . . . .267 B3
Stranfaer Cl DE55. . .170 A7
Stranraer Cl NG19 . .136 C6

Stratford Cl DE65 . . .242 D1
Stratford Rd DE21 . . .205 D2
Stratford St DE7. . . .194 F4
Strathallan Cl DE4. .127 C4
Strathaven Ct DE21. .220 E5
Strathglen Cl NG16 .195 E7
Strathmore Ave
　DE24. . . . . .233 A6
Stratton Rd S44. . . . . .99 A2
Strawberry Bank
　NG17. . . . . .148 E4
Strawberry La
　Blackfordby DE11. . . . . .257 B1
　Rosliston DE12. . . . . . .260 D5
Strawberry Lee La
　S17. . . . . .55 B5
Straw La
　Clay Cross DE55 . . . . .146 D8
　Shirland DE55. . . . . . .146 D8
Streatham Rd DE22. .218 B6
Street Farm La S26 . . .61 E6
Streetfield Cres S20 .59 D6
Streetfields S20. . . . .59 E6
Street La
　Ripley DE5. . . . . .169 B1
　Ripley DE5. . . . . .180 B6
Street Lane Prim Sch
　DE5. . . . . .180 B5
Street The SK10,
　SK17. . . . . .64 C5
StreetThe* SK17. . . . .64 E4
Strelley Ave DE5. . . .180 C8
Stretfield Rd S33 . . . .39 B1
Strettea La DE55. . . .146 C2
STRETTON
　Clay Cross 146 C7
　Rolleston on Dove 240 D1
Stretton Cl DE5. . . . .217 D1
STRETTON EN LE
　FIELD 265 D4
Stretton Handley CE
　Prim Sch DE55 . . . . .145 D7
STRETTON
　HILLSIDE 146 B5
Stretton Rd
　Clay Cross S45 . . . . . .131 C1
　Shirland DE55. . . . . . .146 C8
　Stonebroom DE55 . . . .146 E5
　Tansley DE4 . . . . .144 C4
Stretton View DE12. .265 F6
Striding Edge Cl 4
　NG10 . . . . .223 B2
STRINES. 23 C2
Strines Rd
　Marple SK6. . . . . .23 B4
　Marpleridge SK6 . . . . . .23 B2
　New Mills SK6. . . . . . . .32 D8
Strines SK6. . . . . .23 D1
Strines Sta SK6 . . . . .23 D1
Stringer Cl DE7. . . . .194 E2
Stringer Dr DE55 . . .170 C8
Stroma Cl DE24. . . . .231 F4
Strouts Way S2. . . . . .43 E8
Strutt Close DE55. . .148 A3
Strutts Cl DE55. . . . .159 F4
Strutt's North Mill*
　DE56. . . . . .178 F5
Strutt's Park Ho 2
　DE22. . . . . .218 F7
Strutt St
　Belper DE56 . . . . .178 F3
　Derby DE23. . . . . .219 A2
Stuart Cl
　Ashbourne DE6. . . . . . .173 D1
　Chesterfield S41. . . . . . .96 C6
Stuart St
　Derby DE1 . . . . .219 A6
　Derby DE1 . . . . .267 B4
Stubben Edge La
　S45. . . . . .130 C2
Stubbing Rd S40 . . . .114 F7
Stubbins La S23 . . . . .34 D2
Stubbins Wood
　NG20 . . . . .119 E6
Stubbins Wood La
　NG20 . . . . .119 E5
Stubbin Wood Sch
　NG20 . . . . .119 F6
Stubby La ST14. . . . .224 E1
Stuble Dr DE21. . . . .205 D3
Stubley Cl S18. . . . . . .56 E2
Stubley Croft S18. . . .56 D2
Stubley Dr S18 . . . . . .56 E2
Stubley Hollow S18. . .56 F3
Stubley La S18. . . . . . .56 D2
Stubley Pl S18. . . . . . .56 E2
STUBWOOD 196 D4
Stubwood Hollow
　ST14. . . . . .196 D5
Stubwood La ST14. . .196 D4
Studbrook Cl DE74. .246 F3
Studfarm Cl DE73. . .252 E2
Studios The S40 . . . . .95 E3
Studland Cl NG19. . .136 D6
Stunstead La DE4. . .141 A2
Stupenhill Post 16 Ctr
　DE15. . . . . .255 A7
Sturge Croft 3 S2. . . .43 B6
Sturges La DE7. . . . .233 F4
Sturston Close
　DE24. . . . . .231 C3
Sturston Rd DE6. . . .173 C1
SUDBURY 225 E4
Sudbury Ave
　Ilkeston DE7. . . . . . . .209 B7
　Sandiacre NG10. . . . . .223 A6
Sudbury Cl
　Chesterfield S40. . . . . . .95 B5

Sudbury Cl continued
　Derby DE1. . . . . .218 E5
Sudbury Ct NG10 . . . .235 F4
Sudbury Dr NG17. . . .148 E2
Sudbury Hall* DE6 . .225 D5
Sudbury Mews
　NG16. . . . . .182 E1
Sudbury Pk DE6 . . . .225 D7
Sudbury Prim Sch
　DE6. . . . . .225 E4
Sudbury St DE1. . . . .218 E5
Sudhall Cl S41. . . . . . .95 D8
Suff La NG16 . . . . . . .160 C3
Suffolk Ave DE21 . . . .219 E7
Suffolk Rd DE15 . . . .254 D7
Suffolk Way DE11. . .255 E1
Sugworth Rd S6. . . . . .31 F6
Sulleys Field DE22. .204 D7
Summerbottom
　SK14. . . . . .16 A8
Summerbrook Ct
　DE22. . . . . .218 F4
Summer Cross
　Tideswell SK17. . . . . . .69 B4
　Wheston SK17. . . . . . . .68 F3
Summer Dr DE4 . . . . .165 E7
Summerfield Cres
　S43. . . . . .96 E8
Summerfield Rd
　Chesterfield S40. . . . . .266 A1
　Dronfield S18 . . . . .57 B3
Summer Fields Dr
　DE11. . . . . .256 D6
Summerfields Way
　DE7. . . . . .194 D1
Summerfields Way S
　DE7. . . . . .194 D2
Summerhill La
　SK17. . . . . .103 C4
Summerhouse Drive
　S8. . . . . .43 C1
Summer La
　Sheffield S17 . . . . .55 D4
　Wirksworth DE4. . . . . . .165 E8
SUMMERLEY. 57 E2
Summerley Lower Rd
　S18. . . . . .57 F2
Summerley Rd S18. . .57 F2
Summerskill Gn S43. .97 C7
Summerville Cl
　DE23. . . . . .231 B6
Summerwood Croft
　S18. . . . . .56 F2
Summer Wood Ct
　DE23. . . . . .231 D7
Summerwood La
　S18. . . . . .56 F3
Summerwood Pl S18 .56 F2
Summit Dr NG20. . . .119 E4
Sumners Pl SK13. . . . .10 B1
Sumner St S13. . . . . . .17 C8
Sunart Cl DE24 . . . . .231 F2
Sunday School La
　SK23. . . . . .47 B6
Sunderland Close 4
　DE11. . . . . .255 E1
Sundew Cl DE21. . . . .220 F4
Sundew Court DE24 .231 B3
Sundial Cl S18. . . . . .201 E8
Sundial Wlk DE6. . . .201 E8
Sundown Ave DE23 .231 D6
Sundown Cl SK22. . . . .33 A8
Sundown Pl S13. . . . . .44 F8
Sundown Rd S13 . . . . .44 F8
Sunflower Cl
　Derby DE24 . . . . .220 A1
　Shirebrook NG20 . . . . .119 D3
Sunflower Gr DE12 . .262 F3
Sun La DE4. . . . . . . .156 F1
Sunlaws St SK13. . . . .17 B8
Sunlaws St S13. . . . . .17 B8
Sunlea Cres NG9 . . . .223 F5
Sunlight DE56 . . . . . .190 F1
Sunningdale Ave
　Derby DE21. . . . . .220 D5
　Heanor DE75 . . . . .193 F8
Sunningdale Cl
　Burton upon Trent
　DE13. . . . . .240 C1
　Chesterfield S40. . . . . .114 E8
Sunningdale Dr
　Glossop SK13. . . . . . . .10 E1
　Ilkeston DE7 . . . . .208 B5
Sunningdale Pk
　S42. . . . . .115 C1
Sunningdale Rise
　S40. . . . . .114 C8
Sunninghill Cl DE7. .207 D8
Sunnybank DE4 . . . . .110 F1
Sunny Bank
　Great Longstone
　DE45. . . . . .90 A4
　Mayfield DE6 . . . . .184 C7
　Tibshelf DE55 . . . . . . .147 F5
Sunny Bank Gdns
　DE56. . . . . .178 F2
Sunny Bank La S17 . .69 C4
Sunny Banks 3 SK13 .17 B8
Sunny Brook Cl S43 . .80 E3
Sunnydale Park Nature
　Reserve* DE23. . . . . .231 C7
Sunnyfield SK17. . . . . .85 F1
Sunny Gr DE21. . . . . .220 A5
SUNNY HILL 231 D5
Sunny Hill DE56 . . . .190 F7
Sunnyhill Ave DE23 .231 E6
Sunny Hill Gdns 1
　DE56. . . . . .190 F7

Sunnyside
　Swadlincote DE11 . . . .255 E7
　Whitwell S80 . . . . .82 A6
Sunnyside Ct DE11. .255 F7
Sunnyside Rd ST14 .210 B1
Sunnyside Terr DE4 .143 A8
Sunny Springs S41 . .266 B4
Sunnyvale Ave S17 . . .55 E4
Sunnyvale Rd S17 . . . .55 D4
Sunset DE7. . . . . . . .265 F1
Sunset Gdns DE12 . .262 F3
Sunshine Cl NG16 . . .160 D4
Sun St
　Derby DE22 . . . . .267 A2
　Woodville DE11 . . . . . .256 F7
Surbiton Cl DE22 . . .218 A6
Surbiton Ct DE7 . . . .207 D8
Surgery La DE4. . . . .157 A1
Surprise Villas S32. . .53 A7
Surrey St
　Derby DE22 . . . . .218 D6
　Glossop SK13. . . . . . . .10 C1
Sussex Cir DE21 . . . .219 E8
Sussex Cl NG16. . . . .195 A8
Sussex Rd DE15 . . . .254 E6
Sussex Way NG10. . .223 B5
Sustainability Dr
　DE21. . . . . .220 C8
Sutherland Farm View
　S44. . . . . .99 B4
Sutherland Rd
　3 Derby DE23. . . . . . .218 F8
　Derby DE23 . . . . .219 A1
Sutton Ave DE73. . . .232 F4
Sutton Cl DE22 . . . . .218 D6
Sutton Cres S43. . . . . .97 C7
Sutton Ct DE7 . . . . . .194 E2
Sutton Dr DE24. . . . .232 F4
Sutton Hall Rd S44 . .117 E8
Sutton Ho DE24. . . . .233 C5
SUTTON IN
　ASHFIELD 148 F1
Sutton La
　Burntheath DE65 . . . . .228 C4
　Etwall DE65 . . . . .229 B5
　Hatton DE65. . . . . . . .227 C4
　Hilton DE65 . . . . .228 D2
　Hilton DE65 . . . . .228 D3
　Long Duckmanton
　S44. . . . . .116 F7
　Longford DE6 . . . . . . .214 C5
　Sutton on the Hill DE6,
　DE65. . . . . .228 B6
　Sutton Scarsdale S44. .117 A6
SUTTON ON THE
　HILL. 228 B8
Sutton Rd
　Church Broughton
　DE65. . . . . .227 D7
　Sutton in Ashfield
　NG17. . . . . .148 F3
Suttons Ave 5
　DE11. . . . . .256 E1
Suttons Bsns Pk
　DE11. . . . . .256 E3
Sutton Scarsdale Hall*
　S44. . . . . .117 A6
Suttons La S6. . . . . . . .23 A5
SUTTON SPRINGS
　WOOD. 116 C6
Sutton View
　Bolsover S44 . . . . .118 B8
　Temple Normanton
　S42. . . . . .116 A4
Sutton Way S13. . . . . .10 A5
Swaddale Ave S41. . . .96 B6
Swaddale Cl S41 . . . . .96 B6
SWADLINCOTE. 256 D4
Swadlincote La
　DE11. . . . . .255 E2
Swadlincote Rd
　DE11. . . . . .256 E3
Swadlincote Ski &
　Snowboard Ctr
　DE11. . . . . .256 D6
Swaines Mdw DE4. . .165 D8
Swains Cl DE12. . . . .262 C5
SWAINSPARK 262 B7
Swainspark Ind Est
　DE12. . . . . .262 B6
Swalebank Cl S40 . . .115 B8
Swaledale Ct 2
　DE24. . . . . .233 C6
Swallow Cl DE3. . . . .218 A3
Swallow Cl DE5 . . . . .180 D6
Swallowdale Rd
　DE24. . . . . .231 D4
Swallow Fold SK13 . .16 F8
Swallow Ho DE1. . . . .218 E5
Swallow House Cres
　SK22. . . . . .25 C3
Swallow House La
　SK22. . . . . .25 C3
Swallow Rd DE11. . . .256 F3
Swanbourne Cl 1
　S41. . . . . .96 C1
Swan Dr DE14. . . . . .253 D7
Swan Hill DE3 . . . . . .230 B6
Swan La NG19 . . . . . .136 B3
Swanmore Rd DE23 .231 A8
Swann Yd NG17. . . . .148 F3
Swan Rake SK17. . . . .104 C1
Swanson Ave NG17 . .148 F3
Swans Rest DE11. . . .255 F6
Swan St S43 . . . . .98 A7
SWANWICK 169 E6
Swanwick Ave
　NG20 . . . . .119 F3

Swanwick Ct DE55. . .158 F2
Swanwick Gdns
　DE55. . . . . .206 A1
Swanwick Hall Sch
　DE55. . . . . .169 F7
Swanwick Hill
　Swanwick DE55. . . . . .169 E6
　Swanwick DE55. . . . . .169 E7
Swanwick Junc Sta*
　DE55. . . . . .170 A5
Swanwick Prim Sch
　DE55. . . . . .169 D6
Swanwick Rd
　Ilkeston DE7. . . . . . . .194 F5
　Somercotes DE55. . . . .170 D7
Swanwick Sch & Sports
　Coll DE55. . . . . .169 F7
Swanwick St S41. . . . .77 A2
Swanwick Way S45. . .131 F5
SWARKESTONE 244 D6
Swarkestone Bridge
　DE73. . . . . .244 E4
Swarkestone Dr
　DE23. . . . . .231 C5
Swarkestone Rd
　Barrow upon Trent
　DE73. . . . . .244 B6
　Chellaston DE73. . . . . .244 F8
　Swarkestone DE73. . . .244 D6
Swartling Dr DE11. . .256 D4
SWATHWICK 114 D4
Swathwick Cl S42 . . .114 E4
Swathwick La S42 . . .114 D4
Swayfield Cl DE3 . . . .217 C3
Sweeney Dr DE7 . . . .194 E4
Sweetbriar Cl DE24. .233 A5
Sweethill DE12 . . . . .262 F5
Sweet Leys Way
　DE73. . . . . .252 C8
Swift Bank SK13. . . . .16 F8
Swift Cl
　Bradwell S33 . . . . .51 A7
　Derby DE3 . . . . .218 A3
　Woodville DE11 . . . . . .256 F7
Swift Ct NG16 . . . . . .182 F2
Swinburne St DE1 . . .267 B1
Swindells Yard SK22. .33 C7
Swinderby Dr DE21 .206 B1
Swindon Cl NG16 . . .195 C7
Swiney Way NG9 . . . .223 F2
SWINGATE. 195 F5
Swing Bridge Wharf
　DE12. . . . . .262 F3
Swinger La S45. . . . . .129 C7
Swinney Bank DE56. .179 A5
Swinney La DE56 . . . .179 A5
Swinscoe Hill DE6 . .172 B2
Swinscoe Ho 3
　DE1. . . . . .267 B2
Swinscoe Way S40 . . .95 A5
Swinson Cl ST14. . . .197 A3
Swithland Cl S41 . . . .115 C7
Sycamore Ave
　Chesterfield S40. . . . . . .95 E2
　Creswell S80 . . . . .81 E2
　Derby DE22 . . . . .204 D3
　Dronfield S18 . . . . .57 A3
　Findern DE65 . . . . . . .230 E1
　Glapwell S44 . . . . . . .134 B8
　Ripley DE5 . . . . .180 D8
　Swadlincote DE11 . . . .256 A7
Sycamore Cl
　Bolsover S44 . . . . .99 C2
　3 Borrowash DE72. . . .221 A1
　Burton upon Trent
　DE15. . . . . .254 E5
　Buxton SK17. . . . . .66 B1
　Etwall DE65 . . . . .229 C4
　Linton DE12 . . . . .261 D5
　Mapperley DE7. . . . . . .193 F3
　New Mills SK22. . . . . . .24 C1
　Pinxton NG16. . . . . . . .160 D3
　Selston NG16. . . . . . . .171 D7
　Shirland DE55. . . . . . .146 C4
Sycamore Cotts
　DE6. . . . . .151 D6
Sycamore Cres
　NG10 . . . . .223 A7
Sycamore Croft
　DE56. . . . . .179 B2
Sycamore Ct
　Belper DE56 . . . . .179 F1
　Derby DE21 . . . . .220 E5
　Willington DE65 . . . . . .242 B5
Sycamore Dr
　Calow S44 . . . . .96 E3
　Ilkeston DE7. . . . . . . .209 B7
　Killamarsh S21. . . . . . .60 C5
Sycamore Gdns 7
　DE75. . . . . .181 D7
Sycamore La
　Barlborough S43 . . . . . .80 B6
　Brimington S43. . . . . . .78 A1
Sycamore Rd
　Awsworth NG16. . . . . .195 C5
　Brimington S43. . . . . . .78 A1
　Burton upon Trent
　DE15. . . . . .254 F6
　Castle Donington
　DE74. . . . . .247 B5
　Chapel-en-le-Frith
　SK23. . . . . .47 B4
　Hayfield SK22. . . . . . . .24 F7
　Long Eaton NG10 . . . .236 C5
　Mansfield Woodhouse
　NG19 . . . . .136 C5
　Matlock DE4. . . . . . . .143 B6
　Mayfield DE6 . . . . .184 C7

Sycamore St
　Church Warsop
　NG20 . . . . .120 F6
　Sheffield S20 . . . . .59 C8
Sycamores The
　Eastwood NG16 . . . . . .182 E1
　Glossop SK13. . . . . .9 F1
　Sheffield S13 . . . . .44 C6
　South Normanton
　DE55. . . . . .160 B5
　Tutbury DE13. . . . . . . .239 E6
Sycamore Terr S25 . .25 D3
Sycamore Way DE6 . .201 F8
Syda La
　Old Brampton S42. . . . .93 E1
　Upper Loads S42 . . . . .112 D7
Sydall Rise S45. . . . . .131 D5
Syday La S21. . . . . . . .60 D1
Sydenham Rd DE22. .218 A7
Sydney Cl
　Derby DE3 . . . . .217 F3
　Mansfield Woodhouse
　NG19 . . . . .136 C6
Sydney Rd DE72 . . . .235 A7
Sydney St S40 . . . . . . .95 E3
Sydnope Hall DE4 . . .128 A5
Sydnope Hill DE4 . . .128 A5
Syerscote La
　Clifton Campville
　B79. . . . . .263 B2
　Haunton B79. . . . . . . .263 B2
Sylvan Cl S41. . . . . . .266 C1
Sylvan Cliff SK17 . . . .85 C2
Sylvan Dr S42 . . . . . .131 A6
Sylvan Pk SK17. . . . . .85 C8
Sylvester Cl DE1. . . .267 C2
Sylvia Rd S18. . . . . . . .76 D5
Sywell Cl DE55. . . . . .169 F8

T

Tabley Gdns SK6. . . . .23 A4
TADDINGTON. 88 B3
Taddington Cl 2
　DE21. . . . . .219 E8
Taddington Pl 31
　SK13. . . . . .9 E1
Taddington &
　Priestcliffe Sch
　SK17. . . . . .87 F3
Taddington Rd
　Chesterfield S40. . . . . . .95 B5
　Derby DE21 . . . . .205 F1
Taft Ave NG10 . . . . . .223 B6
Tagg La
　Crowdecote SK17. . . . .121 E7
　Moneyash SK17. . . . . .122 C8
　Monyash DE45 . . . . . . .107 A1
Taggs Knoll S33 . . . . .40 B4
Taghole La DE14. . . .188 E2
Tailby Dr DE65 . . . . .242 A5
Talbot Cres S41 . . . . .115 D7
Talbot Dr NG9 . . . . . .209 D2
Talbot Meadows
　DE65. . . . . .228 D2
Talbot Pl DE12. . . . . .265 E8
Talbot Rd SK13. . . . . .10 C2
Talbot St
　Buxton SK17. . . . . .85 D4
　Chesterfield S41. . . . . .115 D7
　Derby DE1 . . . . .267 A3
　Glossop SK13. . . . . . . .10 C1
　Pinxton NG16. . . . . . . .160 C2
　Swadlincote DE11 . . . .256 A7
Talgarth Cl DE21 . . .206 C2
Tallys End S43. . . . . . .80 A6
Tamar Ave DE22 . . . .204 D4
Tamworth Rd
　Appleby Magna
　DE12. . . . . .265 E2
　Castle Donington DE72,
　NG10 . . . . .235 E1
　Long Eaton NG10 . . . .236 C5
Tamworth Rise
　DE56. . . . . .190 E4
Tamworth St DE56. . .190 E3
Tamworth Terr
　DE56. . . . . .190 E4
Tanglewood DE56 . . .179 A6
Tanner's La DE65 . . .242 C3
TANSLEY 144 B4
Tansley Ave DE7. . . .193 A1
Tansley Ct S41 . . . . . .95 C6
Tansley Dr S40 . . . . . .95 A5
Tansley House Gdns
　DE4. . . . . .144 A4
TANSLEY KNOLL . . .144 A5
Tansley Prim Sch
　DE4. . . . . .144 A4
Tansley Rd S42. . . . . .131 F5
Tansley Rise 4
　DE21. . . . . .205 F1
Tansley Way S43 . . . . .97 C6
Tansley Wood Ho
　DE4. . . . . .143 E5
Tansy Ct DE24. . . . . .231 C3
Tants Mdw DE56. . . .191 F8
Tantum Ave DE75. . .181 C4
Tanyard Ct DE74. . . .247 B8
Tapestry Wlk S45. . . .131 E5
Tap La S40. . . . . .266 A3
Taplow Cl DE3. . . . . .217 C2
TAPTON 96 C6
Tapton Bsns Pk
　S41. . . . . .266 C4
Tapton La S41. . . . . .266 C3
Tapton Lock Hill S41 .96 B6

Tapton Lock Visitor Ctr ★
  S41 . . . . .96 B6
Tapton Park Bsns Pk **11**
  DE11 . . . . .256 C6
Tapton Park Ind Est **10**
  DE11 . . . . .256 C6
Tapton Terr S41 . . . . . . 266 C4
Tapton Vale S41 . . . . .96 C5
Tapton View Rd S41 . . .95 F5
Tapton Way S44 . . . . . . .96 F3
Tarina Cl DE73 . . . . 233 A1
Tarmac Way NG20 . . 120 D8
Tarn Cl NG16 . . . . 182 B4
Tarnside Fold **1**
  SK13 . . . . .17 A7
Tarquin Cl DE13 . . . . . 240 E2
Tarragon Cl DE3 . . . . . 217 D4
Tarrat Street **3**
  DE7 . . . . 194 E2
Tasman Cl DE3 . . . . . . .217 F3
TATENHILL 253 A8
Tatenhill La
  Branston DE14 . . . . . . 253 D7
  Tatenhill DE13 . . . . . . 253 A8
Tatham's La DE7 . . . . . 194 E3
Tattersall Wlk **5**
  NG19 . . . . 136 E4
Tattle Hill DE7 . . . . . . .207 F2
Tatwin Cl DE73 . . . . . . .252 F2
Taunton Cl DE24 . . . . . 233 C8
Tavern Cl **10** DE7 . . . . 194 E1
Taverners Cres
  DE23 . . . . 231 C8
Tavern Rd SK13 . . . . .9 E3
Tavistock Ave DE5 . . . 169 D2
Tavistock Cl **14**
  DE24 . . . . 231 D3
Tavistock Ct **14** S41 . . .95 F8
Tavistock Sq DE55 . . . 159 B5
Tawney Cl DE4 . . . . . . 144 A4
Tawny Way DE23 . . . . 231 A7
TAXAL 45 D6
Taxal & Fernilee CE Prim
  Sch SK23 . . . . .45 D6
Taxal Mews SK23 . . . . .45 D6
Taxal Moor Rd SK23 . .45 C3
Taxhall Rd SK13 . . . . .9 E3
Tayberry Cl DE24 . . . . 232 E7
Tay Cl
  Derby DE24 . . . . 231 D2
  Dronfield S18 . . . . .56 D2
Taylor Cres
  Chesterfield S41 . . . . . .96 D1
  Stapleford NG9 . . . . . . 223 F8
Taylor Ct DE6 . . . . 173 C1
Taylor La DE75 . . . . . . 181 D4
Taylors La ST14 . . . . . 196 D4
Taylor's La
  Spout DE4 . . . . 166 B4
  Trusley DE6 . . . . .215 E6
Taylor St
  Derby DE24 . . . . .219 E2
  Hollingworth SK14 . . . . . .9 D4
  Ilkeston DE7 . . . . 194 E1
Taylor Way DE55 . . . . .158 F1
Tayside Cl DE24 . . . . . 231 D3
Tay Wlk DE22 . . . . 204 E3
Tealby Wlk **18** NG19 . 136 E4
Teal Cl NG20 . . . . 119 D3
Tean Cl DE15 . . . . 248 A1
Teasel Dr DE11 . . . . . . 256 C6
Teasel Gro **3** DE3 . . . 217 C4
Tedder Ave SK17 . . . . . .85 D3
Tedgness Rd S32 . . . . . .53 E1
Tedworth Ave DE24 . . 231 D2
Teesdale Rd
  Long Eaton NG10 . . . . 236 A6
  Sheffield S12 . . . . .58 F8
Telford Cl DE3 . . . . 217 E1
Telford Cres S43 . . . . . .78 F2
Telford Rd SK6 . . . . .23 A4
Telmah Cl DE13 . . . . . 240 E1
Temperance Hill
  DE55 . . . . .145 E7
Temperance Sq SK14 . . .9 A4
Temperance St **5**
  SK14 . . . . .16 A8
Templar Cl DE24 . . . . . 231 C3
Templar Road LE66 . . 258 A1
Temple Ave SK13 . . . . .10 C5
Templebell Cl DE23 . 236 A6
Temple Ct SK17 . . . . . . .85 A6
TEMPLE
  NORMANTON 116 B3
Temple Normanton Bsns
  Pk S41 . . . . 116 A4
Temple Normanton Prim
  Sch S42 . . . . 116 C4
Temple Rd
  Buxton SK17 . . . . .85 A6
  Matlock Bath DE4 . . . . 143 A1
Temple St
  6 Derby DE23 . . . . 218 F3
  Derby DE23 . . . . .219 A3
  Glossop SK13 . . . . .10 C5
Templeton Close
  DE3 . . . . .217 F3
Temple View SK17 . . . .85 C7
Temple Wlk DE4 . . . . . 143 A1
Tenant St DE1 . . . . 267 B3
Tenby Dr DE21 . . . . . . 206 C2
Ten Foot Cl SK13 . . . . . .10 B2
Tennessee Rd DE21 . . 220 B7
Tennyson Ave
  Chesterfield S40 . . . . . 266 A3
  Mansfield Woodhouse
    NG19 . . . . 136 C2
  Swadlincote DE11 . . . . 256 C6

Tennyson Rd S80 . . . . .81 D1
Tennyson Sq NG16 . . . 195 C4
Tennyson St
  Derby DE24 . . . . 232 D7
  Holmewood S42 . . . . . 116 D1
  Ilkeston DE7 . . . . 194 E3
  Shirland DE55 . . . . 146 C5
Tennyson Way S42 . . . 115 E3
Tenter Cl NG10 . . . . . . 236 D5
Tenter La DE56 . . . . . . 168 D1
Terminus Dr DE5 . . . . .180 F7
Tern Ave DE11 . . . . 256 F3
Terrace La NG19 . . . . . 134 F5
Terrace Rd
  Buxton SK17 . . . . .85 B7
  Chapel-en-le-Frith
    SK23 . . . . .47 B6
  Tideswell SK17 . . . . . . .69 C4
Terret Gr SK17 . . . . .84 D5
Terrey Rd S17 . . . . .55 C5
Terr The DE21 . . . . 219 E7
Terry Pl DE24 . . . . 232 F6
Tetford Wlk **13**
  NG19 . . . . 136 E4
Tetron Point DE11 . . . 255 E3
Tetron Way DE11 . . . . 255 D3
Teversal Ave NG19 . . . 135 B4
Tevery Cl NG9 . . . . 223 E8
Teviot Pl DE21 . . . . . . 206 A2
Tewkesbury Ave
  NG19 . . . . 136 D4
Tewkesbury Cres
  DE21 . . . . 219 D8
Tewkesbury Dr
  NG16 . . . . 195 E7
Tewkesbury Rd
  NG10 . . . . 236 E4
Thackeray Rd DE55 . .146 F3
Thackeray St DE24 . . . 232 A5
Thame Ct **2** S43 . . . . .96 E8
Thames Ave **8** S2 . . .43 C8
Thames Cl DE22 . . . . . .217 F5
Thames Way DE65 . . . 228 D1
Thanet Dr DE24 . . . . . . 233 A6
Thanet St S45 . . . . 131 D3
Thatch Cl DE22 . . . . . . 204 F2
Thatchers Croft
  DE4 . . . . 144 A3
Thatchers La DE4 . . . . 144 A3
Thatchmarsh Cl
  NE7 . . . . .194 F6
Theatre La DE1 . . . . . . 266 C3
Theatre Wlk DE1 . . . . . 267 C3
Theatre Yd S40 . . . . . . 266 B3
Thickley Bank NG20 . .119 F4
Thimble Hill DE6 . . . . 189 A2
Thirlmere Ave DE22 . . 204 E3
Thirlmere Cl **3**
  NG10 . . . . 223 B2
Thirlmere Dr S18 . . . . .57 A2
Thirlmere Rd
  Chesterfield S41 . . . . . .95 C7
  Long Eaton NG10 . . . . 223 B2
Thirlwell Rd S8 . . . . .43 A6
Thirsk Pl DE24 . . . . . . 232 D7
Thirteen Row S44 . . . . 118 A6
Thistle Bank NG19 . . . 136 F4
Thistle Cl
  Eastwood NG16 . . . . . .195 B8
  Woodville DE11 . . . . . . 256 F4
Thistledown Cl
  DE22 . . . . 205 A2
Thistle Gr DE73 . . . . . . 232 E1
Thistlegreen Cl
  DE75 . . . . 182 B1
Thistle Rd DE7 . . . . . . 209 A4
Thomas Chambers **3**
  SK13 . . . . .17 C7
Thomas Cl NG16 . . . . . 170 F3
Thomas Cook Cl
  DE73 . . . . 252 A7
Thomas Cl DE1 . . . . . . 218 E4
Thomas Mdws SK23 . .47 A5
Thomas Meadows
  SK23 . . . . .47 A5
Thomas St
  Compstall SK6 . . . . .15 B2
  Glossop SK13 . . . . .10 E1
Thompson Cl
  4 Chesterfield S41 . . .96 A8
  Derby DE3 . . . . .217 B3
  Swadlincote DE11 . . . . 256 E4
Thompson St
  Chesterfield S41 . . . . . .96 A1
  Langley Mill NG16 . . . . 182 B3
Thomson Dr DE5 . . . . 181 B7
Thomson Wlk DE5 . . . 181 A8
Thoresby Ave
  Clowne S43 . . . . .81 A4
  Shirebrook NG20 . . . . .119 E4
Thoresby Cl
  Derby DE21 . . . . 206 B1
  Ripley DE5 . . . . 169 E1
Thoresby Cres DE72 . 234 F7
Thoresby Pl S43 . . . . . .97 C6
Thoresby Rd
  Long Eaton NG10 . . . . 236 C6
  Mansfield Woodhouse
    NG19 . . . . 136 A3
Thorn Ave NG19 . . . . . .135 F1
Thornborough Cl S2 . .43 C7
Thornborough Pl S2 . .43 C7
Thornborough Rd S2 .43 C7
Thornbridge Ave
  S12 . . . . .44 D3
Thornbridge Cl S12 . . .44 D3
Thornbridge Cres
  Chesterfield S40 . . . . . 115 A6

Thornbridge Cres
  continued
  Sheffield S12 . . . . .44 E3
Thornbridge Dr S12 . .44 E3
Thornbridge Gr S12 . .44 E3
Thornbridge La S12 . .44 E3
Thornbridge Pl S12 . .44 E3
Thornbridge Rd S12 . .44 E3
Thornbridge Rise
  S12 . . . . .44 E3
Thornbridge Way
  S12 . . . . .44 E3
Thornbrook Cl SK23 . .47 C5
Thornbrook Rd SK23 . .47 C6
Thorn Cl
  Buxton SK17 . . . . .85 E8
  Derby DE22 . . . . 204 D4
Thorncliffe Ave
  DE4 . . . . 127 A6
Thorncliffe Rd SK13 . . .9 F4
Thorncliffe Terr
  SK17 . . . . .69 C3
Thorncliffe Vale SK14. .9 C6
Thorndene Cl S41 . . . . .96 A6
Thorndike Ave
  DE24 . . . . 233 A7
Thorndon Cl DE3 . . . . 230 D8
Thorndon Way S40 . . 114 C8
Thorn Dr NG16 . . . . . . 195 B8
Thorne Cl S42 . . . . .94 F4
Thorncliffewood
  SK14 . . . . .9 D5
Thornell Cl SK23 . . . . . .47 C5
Thornescroft Gdns
  DE14 . . . . 254 B8
Thorness Cl DE24 . . . . 233 C5
Thornewill Dr DE13 . .240 F1
Thorneywood Rd
  NG10 . . . . 236 F8
Thornfield Ave DE4 . . . .95 B1
Thornfield Ct S41 . . . . .96 A5
Thornfield Pl S43 . . . . .80 D2
Thornfield Sq NG10 . . 236 E8
THORNHILL 39 F3
Thornhill Ave DE56 . . 179 B2
Thornhill Dr DE55 . . . 160 B6
Thornhill La S33 . . . . . .39 F4
Thornhill Rd DE23 . . . 218 C1
Thornley Pl DE6 . . . . . 173 C1
THORNSETT 24 E3
Thornsett SK22 . . . . . . .24 E2
Thornsett Ave SK17 . . .85 E8
Thornsett Cl SK17 . . . .85 E8
Thornsett Gdns S17 . . .55 F8
Thornsett La SK22 . . . .25 B3
Thornsett Prim Sch
  SK22 . . . . .24 E3
Thornsett Trad Est
  SK22 . . . . .24 E2
Thornsett Trading Estate
  SK22 . . . . .24 F2
Thorn St
  Derby DE23 . . . . .218 F2
  Woodville DE11 . . . . . . 256 F2
Thorn Street Mews
  DE11 . . . . 256 F2
Thornton Dr DE65 . . . 240 E8
Thornton Pl **11** S8 . . .56 C1
Thornton Way DE56 . . 179 C6
Thorntree Cl
  Breaston DE72 . . . . . . 222 F1
  Breaston DE72 . . . . . . 235 E8
Thorntree Cotts
  DE4 . . . . 154 F1
Thorntree Ct S40 . . . . 114 F7
Thorn Tree Gdns
  NG16 . . . . 182 F4
Thorntree La
  2 Branston DE14 . . 253 E7
  2 Branston DE14 . . 256 E7
  Derby DE1 . . . . 267 B3
Thorn Tree La DE11,
  DE15 . . . . 255 F7
Thorn Tree Rd **1**
  DE6 . . . . 201 B8
Thornway SK6 . . . . .32 A7
Thornwood Ct SK17 . .85 A8
Thorp Cl S2 . . . . .43 A8
THORPE 161 C1
Thorpe Ave
  Dronfield S18 . . . . .57 C4
  Whitwell S80 . . . . .81 F5
Thorpe Cl
  Burton upon Trent
    DE15 . . . . 248 C2
  26 Chesterfield S41 . .95 F8
  Stapleford NG9 . . . . . . 223 D7
Thorpe Croft DE4 . . . . 156 B5
Thorpe Downs Rd
  DE11 . . . . 256 B1
Thorpe Dr DE3 . . . . . . 217 E3
Thorpe Hill Dr DE75 193 E8
Thorpe House Ave
  S8 . . . . .43 B4
Thorpe House Rd S8. .43 B4
Thorpe House Rise
  S8 . . . . .43 B4
Thorpe La
  Clifton Campville
    B79 . . . . 263 E1
  Shireoaks S80, S81 . . . . .63 D4
Thorpelands Ave
  NG19 . . . . 136 E1
Thorpelands Dr
  DE22 . . . . 204 E1
Thorpe Leys NG10 . . 236 D5
Thorpe Rd
  Eastwood NG16 . . . . . .182 F4

Thorpe Rd continued
  Harthill S26 . . . . .62 A7
  Ilam DE6 . . . . 161 A2
THORPE SALVIN 62 F6
Thorpe's Rd
  Heanor DE75 . . . . 181 D1
  Shipley DE75 . . . . 193 D8
Thorpe's Rd Ind Est
  DE75 . . . . 193 D8
Thorpe St
  Glossop SK13 . . . . .10 E2
  Ilkeston DE7 . . . . 194 E3
Thorpe View DE6 . . . . 185 C8
Thorpe Way DE56 . . . 179 B5
Thorpleigh Rd S43 . . . .79 B2
Three Gates DE56 . . . 178 F2
Threeshires Rd
  SK11 . . . . 102 D5
Thrift Cl DE3 . . . . 217 C5
Thrift Rd DE14 . . . . . . 254 B8
Throstle Nest Way
  DE56 . . . . .201 F8
THRUMPTON 237 C3
Thrumpton Ave
  NG10 . . . . 237 A7
Thrumpton Hall ★
  NG11 . . . . .237 B3
Thrushton Cl DE65 . . 230 C2
Thruxton Cl DE24 . . . . 233 C5
THULSTON 233 F4
Thunderpit La S21 . . . .71 A3
Thurgarton Ct DE6. . . 173 D1
Thurgaton Way
  DE55 . . . . 148 A3
Thurlby St **9** NG19 . 136 E4
Thurlow Booth DE4. . 167 E7
Thurlow Ct DE21 . . . . 206 A1
Thurman St DE7 . . . . . 209 A6
Thurrows Way
  DE73 . . . . 233 B2
Thurstan Ave S8 . . . . . .56 E8
Thurston Ave DE55 . . 170 D8
Thurstone Furlong
  DE73 . . . . 232 E1
THURVASTON
  Longford 215 C8
  Marston Montgomery 197 F1
Thurvaston La
  Lower Thurvaston
    DE6 . . . . .214 F6
  Thurvaston DE6 . . . . . 215 A8
Thurvaston Rd DE6 . .197 F1
Thyme Cl DE23 . . . . . . 231 D4
Thyme St
  Branston DE14 . . . . . . 253 E6
  Branston DE14 . . . . . . 256 E6
Tiber Cl DE24 . . . . 233 D5
Tib Meadow Cl **7**
  DE7 . . . . 208 E5
TIBSHELF 148 A6
Tibshelf Bsns Pk
  DE55 . . . . 148 C6
Tibshelf Com Sch
  DE55 . . . . .147 E5
Tibshelf Inf Sch
  DE55 . . . . 148 A7
Tibshelf Rd
  Blackwell DE55 . . . . . . 147 C1
  Holmewood S42 . . . . . 132 E7
TIBSHELF WHARF . . 148 D7
Tickham Ave DE24 . . . 231 C2
Tickhill Dr **1** S2 . . . . .44 A7
TICKNALL 251 A4
Ticknall La DE5,
  DE56 . . . . 180 B1
Ticknall Rd
  Hartshorne DE11 . . . . 250 C1
  Hartshorne DE11 . . . . 257 B7
  Repton DE65 . . . . 250 B6
Ticknall Wlk DE23 . . . 231 E6
Ticknal DE65 . . . . 243 A1
TIDESWELL 69 C4
Tideswell Bank **15**
  SK13 . . . . .9 E1
Tideswell Cl S43 . . . . . .97 C8
Tideswell Ct **5** S40. . .95 D5
Tideswell Gn DE11 . . 255 E5
Tideswell La S32 . . . . . .71 C6
Tideswell Moor
  Tideswell SK17 . . . . . . .50 A3
  Tideswell SK17 . . . . . . .69 A8
  Wheston SK17 . . . . .68 F8
Tideswell Rd DE21 . . 205 F1
Tideswell Wlk **13**
  SK13 . . . . .9 E1
Tiger Yd **6** DE6 . . . . 173 B2
Tilbury Pl DE24 . . . . . 233 A5
Tilford Gdns NG9 . . . 223 F6
Tiller Cl DE23 . . . . 231 B6
Tilley Gn DE11 . . . . . . 255 F6
Tillotson Cl **1** S8 . . . .43 A6
Tillotson Rise S8 . . . . . .43 A6
Tilton Gr DE7 . . . . 208 C5
Timber La S45 . . . . 132 D5
Timbersbrook Cl
  DE21 . . . . 206 A1
Timor Ct DE24 . . . . 219 E2
Timsbury Ct DE21 . . . 205 E2
Tinderbox La DE65 . . 229 F5
Tinker Croft DE7 . . . . 208 E7
Tinkerley La DE6 . . . . 165 D1
Tinkley La S42 . . . . 130 D4
Tinsell Brook
  Hilton DE65 . . . . 228 C1
  5 Hilton DE65 . . . . . 240 E8
Tinsell La DE6 . . . . 183 A8
Tinsley Rd DE756,
  NG16 . . . . 182 D1

Tintagel Cl
  Burton upon Trent
    DE13 . . . . 240 E2
  2 Derby DE23 . . . . . .219 B2
Tintagel Way NG19 . . 135 D1
TINTWISTLE 10 B8
Tintwistle CE (Aided)
  Prim Sch SK13 . . . . .9 F6
Tipnall Rd DE74 . . . . . 247 A3
Tipper's La DE65 . . . . 227 A8
Tip Tree Cl NG16 . . . . 195 F7
Tiree Cl
  Derby DE24 . . . . 231 F4
  Stapleford NG9 . . . . . . 209 D2
  Tibshelf DE55 . . . . .147 F5
TISSINGTON 162 B6
Tissington Bank **27**
  SK13 . . . . .9 D1
Tissington Cl S40 . . . . .95 B5
Tissington Dr DE21 . 206 B3
Tissington Gn **26** SK13 .9 D1
Tissington Terr **28**
  SK13 . . . . .9 D1
Titchfield Ave NG19 . 136 D3
Titchfield St
  Creswell S80 . . . . .81 F1
  Whitwell S80 . . . . .81 F6
Tithe Barn Cl SK17 . . . .69 C3
Tithebarn Dr DE12 . . 262 B3
Tithe Barn Gdns
  DE65 . . . . 242 D2
Tithebarn La DE6 . . . 215 C5
Titterton La
  Alstonefield SK17 . . . . 149 A8
  Clay Cross SK17 . . . . . 131 A2
Tiverton Cl DE3 . . . . . 217 D4
Tiverton Ct **22** S41 . . .95 F8
Tivey Rd S21 . . . . .59 D2
Tivey Way S43 . . . . 252 C8
Tivoli Gdns DE1 . . . . . 218 E7
Toad Hole Cl **4**
  DE7 . . . . 208 C6
TOADHOLE
  FURNANCE 158 C6
Toad La DE21 . . . . 191 E2
TOADMOOR 167 F3
Toadmoor La DE56 . .167 F3
Tobermory Way
  DE24 . . . . 231 D3
Todbrook Cl SK23 . . . .45 D6
Todd St SK13 . . . . .17 D8
Toll Bar Ave S12 . . . . . .43 E5
Toll Bar Cl S12 . . . . .43 E5
Toll Bar Dr S12 . . . . . . .43 E5
Toll Bar Rd S12 . . . . . . .43 E5
Tollbridge Rd S43 . . . .79 B2
Tollemache Cl SK14 . . .9 A5
Tollemache Rd SK14. . .9 A5
Tollgate Cotts DE6 . . 184 E8
Toll House Mead
  S20 . . . . .59 C7
Tom Brads Croft
  SK23 . . . . .45 E8
Tom La
  Chapel-en-le-Frith
    SK23 . . . . .46 D5
  Staveley S44 . . . . .97 F5
Tomlinson Bsns Pk
  DE65 . . . . 226 F4
Tomlinson Ct DE24 . . 232 F7
Tomlinson Ind Est
  DE21 . . . . 205 B8
Tomlinsons Cotts
  DE21 . . . . 205 C2
Tom Mead Cl **3**
  DE11 . . . . 255 F5
TOMTHORN 66 E4
Tom Will Way LE65 . . 258 A1
Tomwood Rise SK13. .16 C6
Tonbridge Dr DE24 . . 233 A5
Tonge La DE73 . . . . . . 252 F3
Tongue La S17 . . . . .85 E7
Tongue Lane Ind Est
  SK17 . . . . .85 E7
Tooth St **3** DE11 . . . 256 E1
Top Cotts SK17 . . . . . . .88 F7
Top Farm Ct DE56 . . . 191 F8
Top Farm Mws S21 . . .60 C1
Top Hagg La DE56 . . 168 A6
Tophill La DE4 . . . . 153 D8
Tophole Rd S33 . . . . . . .50 F4
Top La
  Crich DE4 . . . . 156 D1
  Mansfield NG19 . . . . . . 135 A1
  Old Brampton S42 . . . . .93 E3
  Shottle DE56 . . . . 166 C1
  Tideswell SK17 . . . . . . .69 B5
  Wadshelf S42 . . . . .93 D5
Topley Gdns DE21 . . . 205 F2
Top Lons DE6 . . . . 176 B8
Top Manor Cl DE72 . . 221 C5
Top Mdw DE11 . . . . . . 256 B7
Top of Hope DE6 . . . . 149 D3
Top o' th' Edge La
  SK17 . . . . 121 C7
Toppham Dr S8 . . . . . . .56 F7
Toppham Rd S8 . . . . . . .56 F7
Toppham Way S8 . . . . .56 F7
Top Pingle Cl S43 . . . . .96 E7
Top Rd
  Calow S44 . . . . .97 A3
  Pilsley DE45 . . . . .91 C2
  Wingerworth S42 . . . . 114 D1
Top Row
  Pilsley NG19 . . . . .135 F4
  Pilsley DE45 . . . . .91 C2
  Somercotes NG16 . . . 171 A5
Topshill La DE6 . . . . . . 165 B2

Tor Ave DE55 . . . . 170 C6
Tor Cl DE4 . . . . 143 B2
Torfield Cotts DE4 . . . 127 B3
Torksey Wlk **11**
  NG19 . . . . 136 E4
Torquay Ct **6** S41 . . . .95 F8
Torrance Cl DE14 . . . . 254 A6
Torrani Way S42 . . . . .131 F2
Torridon Cl DE24 . . . . 231 E4
Tor Rise DE4 . . . . 143 B3
Torr St SK17 . . . . .85 B7
Torrs Valley SK22 . . . . .33 C7
TORR TOP 33 C8
Torr Top St SK22 . . . . . .33 C7
Torrvale Rd SK22 . . . . . .33 B7
Torr View SK17 . . . . . . .85 E1
Torside Mews SK13. . . .10 A6
Torside St
  Tintwistle SK13 . . . . . . .10 A6
  Tintwistle SK14 . . . . .9 F6
Torside Visitor Ctr ★
  SK13 . . . . .6 D1
Torside Way SK13 . . . .10 A5
Tors Spring DE4 . . . . . 168 A3
Tors The DE4 . . . . .156 F1
Tor View Rise DE4 . . . 155 A6
Torwood Dr S8 . . . . . . .56 E7
TOTLEY 55 E4
Totley All Saints CE VA
  Prim Sch S17 . . . . .55 D4
Totley Ave **42** SK13 . . .9 D1
TOTLEY BROOK 55 E5
Totley Brook Cl S17 . .55 D5
Totley Brook Croft
  S17 . . . . .55 D5
Totley Brook Glen
  S17 . . . . .55 D5
Totley Brook Gr S17 . .55 D5
Totley Brook Rd S17 . .55 E5
Totley Brook Way
  S17 . . . . .55 D5
Totley Cl **47** SK13 . . . . .9 D1
Totley Gdns **46** SK13 . .9 D1
Totley Gn **23** SK13 . . . .9 D1
Totley Grange Cl
  S17 . . . . .55 D4
Totley Grange Dr
  S17 . . . . .55 D4
Totley Grange Rd
  S17 . . . . .55 D4
Totley Hall Croft S17 .55 D3
Totley Hall Dr S17 . . . .55 D4
Totley Hall La S17 . . . .55 D4
Totley Hall Mead
  S17 . . . . .55 D3
Totley La S17 . . . . .56 A5
Totley Lanes **48** SK13 . .9 D1
Totley Mews **20** SK13 . .9 D1
Totley Mount S43 . . . . .96 D8
Totley Mws S17 . . . . . .55 D4
Totley Pl **45** SK13 . . . . .9 D1
Totley Prim Sch S17 . .55 D4
TOTLEY RISE 55 F5
TOTON 223 E2
Toton Bispham Drive
  Jun Sch NG9 . . . . 223 E3
Toton La NG9 . . . . 223 E6
Touchstone Ct
  DE73 . . . . 232 D2
Toulmin Dr DE11 . . . . 256 B4
Tower Bsns Pk S45 . . 131 C4
Tower Cl
  Sheffield S2 . . . . .43 C8
  Somercotes DE55 . . . . 170 C8
Tower Cres S44 . . . . . . 118 B8
Tower Dr DE3 . . . . 217 D6
Tower Ho S2 . . . . .43 C8
Tower La
  Bonsall DE4 . . . . 141 F3
  Bonsall DE4 . . . . 142 A3
Tower Rd
  Burton upon Trent
    DE15 . . . . 248 B2
  Hartshorne DE11 . . . . 257 A6
Tower Rise **11** S2 . . . .43 C8
Towers La S32 . . . . .40 E1
Tower St DE24 . . . . . . 232 D7
Tower View Prim Sch
  DE15 . . . . 248 C3
Towle Cl DE72 . . . . . . 221 C1
Towles Pastures
  DE74 . . . . 247 A3
Towle St NG10 . . . . . . 236 A4
Town Cres NG16 . . . . 160 D4
TOWNEND 47 C7
TOWN END
  Eyam 71 E6
  Tideswell 69 C3
Town End
  Apperknowle S18 . . . . . .58 A1
  Bolsover S44 . . . . .99 A1
  Buxton SK17 . . . . .66 E1
  Crich DE4 . . . . .156 F2
  Kirk Ireton DE6 . . . . . . 165 B1
  Shirland DE55 . . . . 146 D2
  Taddington SK17 . . . . . .88 B2
Town End Jun Sch
  DE55 . . . . .147 E5
Town End La DE7 . . . . 172 A4
Town End Rd DE72 . . 235 B7
Townfield La S33 . . . . . .39 E1
Town Fold S6 . . . . .23 B7
Town Gate S33 . . . . . . .51 A7
Town Hall Yd **3**
  DE6 . . . . 173 C2

TOWNHEAD 55 C7
Townhead S32 .....71 C6
TOWN HEAD
Eyam.............71 C6
Tideswell........69 C5
Town Head
Ashbourne DE6....173 C3
Bonsall DE4 ......142 D2
Townhead La S33 ...39 F4
Townhead Rd S17 ..55 C7
Town La
Bradwell S33 ......51 A7
Broadbottom SK13..16 D6
Newton DE55......148 A3
Townscliffe La SK6..23 C6
Townsend Gr DE73 .233 A2
Townside Cl NG10 .236 B4
Town St
Brassington DE4....153 A1
Duffield DE56......190 F3
Holbrook DE56.....191 C6
Marple SK6.........23 B7
Pinxton NG16......160 E3
Sandiacre NG10...223 B5
Town The DE21......205 C7
Town View NG16....195 F7
Towpath Way DE21.220 D3
Towson Ave NG16..182 C2
Trafalgar Parkway
DE24.............232 B6
Trafalgar Rd NG10..236 D6
Trafalgar Sq NG10..236 F7
Trafalgar Terr NG10.236 F7
Trafalgar Way
NG19.............136 C7
Traffic St DE1......267 C2
Traffic Terr
Barrow Hill S43.....78 B4
2 Chesterfield S41...115 B7
Trafford Way DE23 .231 C8
Trail View
Alfreton DE55.....147 F6
Glossop SK13......10 B5
Tramway The DE11..255 F7
Tranmere Ave S45..131 D3
Transport Way
4 Ironville NG16...170 F4
Ironville NG16......171 A5
Transvaal Terr S44 .118 B5
Trapper Way S20...60 A6
Traso Bsns Pk S18...57 C1
Travellers Cl S44 ...98 F6
Traversgate S44.....97 B3
Travers Rd NG10...223 B6
Travey Rd S2........44 A7
Treak Cliff Cavern ★
S33.............37 E3
Tredcroft St SK13...17 B8
Tredegar Dr DE21 .206 B2
Treeneuk Cl S40....95 B3
Treeneuk Gardens
S40.............95 B3
Trefoil Cl S21......133 A7
Tregaron Cl DE21..206 C2
Tregony Way DE24..231 D3
Trelawney Rd S45..131 D3
Trenchard Dr SK17..85 D3
Trent Ave
Buxton SK17........85 C4
Willington DE65....242 C5
Trent Bridge Ct
DE23.............231 C8
Trent Bsns Ctr
NG10.............223 C2
Trent Cl
Derby DE24.......231 D2
Willington DE65....242 C5
Trent Coll NG10....236 C8
Trent Cotts NG10...236 F6
Trent Dr DE73......231 D6
Trent Gr
Alfreton DE55.....159 A2
Dronfield S18.......57 B3
Trent Ho NG10.....236 A4
Trent La
Castle Donington
DE74.............247 A5
King's Newton DE73..245 C1
Long Eaton NG10...236 F5
Newton Solney DE15.248 E8
Weston-on-Trent
DE72.............245 F4
Trent Lane Ind Est
DE74.............247 B5
TRENTLOCK 236 E3
Trenton Dr
Derby DE21.......220 B4
Long Eaton NG10...237 A8
Trenton Gn DE21...220 B6
Trent Rd DE7......208 D4
Trent Rise DE21....220 F4
Trent Side
Barrow upon Trent
DE73.............244 D6
Barton In Fabis NG11..237 D6
Trent St
Derby DE24.......233 A7
Long Eaton NG10...236 E8
Trent Way DE24.....217 B1
Trent Wlk **1** NG19..136 E4
Tresillian Cl DE22..204 E2
Tressall Cl DE7.....209 A8
Trevelyn Cl DE15...248 C2
Treveris Cl DE21...220 E4
Trevone Ave NG9...223 E6

Trevone Ct DE24.....233 C5
Trevorrow Cres S40 .266 B1
Trevose Cl S40......114 C7
Triangle The
Belper DE56.......178 F4
Ilkeston DE7.......209 A6
Trickett Cl S33.......38 C3
Trinity Cl
Ashford in the Water
DE45.............108 F8
Chesterfield S40....266 A4
Ilkeston DE7.......194 E3
Trinity Ct S41......266 A4
Trinity Gr DE11....256 B3
Trinity Mews S41...266 A4
Trinity Passage **6**
SK17..............85 C7
Trinity St DE1......267 C2
Trinity Way NG10..236 E8
Trinity Way
3 Heanor DE75.....181 F1
4 Heanor DE75.....193 E8
Trinity Wlk DE1....267 C2
Trinkey La S32......72 A3
Tristram Gr DE13...240 E2
Trocadero Ct DE23.267 B1
Troon Cl
Burton upon Trent
DE13.............240 C1
Chesterfield S40....114 C8
Derby DE23.......231 A8
Kimberley NG16....195 E7
Trot La
Great Hucklow SK17..69 F7
Great Hucklow SK17..70 A5
Troughbrook Hill
S43.............97 B8
Troughbrook Rd S43 .78 B1
Trough La
Hulland Ward DE6 ..175 D2
Kimberley NG16....195 F8
Trough Rd NG16....195 F8
Troutbeck Gr DE23 .231 A7
TROWAY 58 B4
Trowbridge Cl DE21.205 E2
TROWELL 209 C5
Trowell Ave DE7...209 A5
Trowell CE Prim Sch
NG9 ....209 D4
Trowell Gr
Long Eaton NG10...223 C1
Stapleford NG9....209 D3
Trowell Marsh Nature
Reserve ★ DE7....209 B4
Trowell Park Dr
NG9 ....209 D2
Trowell Rd NG9....209 D2
Trowels La DE22...218 C4
Trueblue La DE45...108 B5
Trueman St DE7....194 F4
Truman St
Cossall DE7.......195 A1
Kimberley NG16....195 E7
Truro Cl DE11......256 E5
Truro Cres DE21...219 E8
TRUSLEY 215 F4
Trusley Brook DE65.228 D1
Trusley Gdns DE23..231 D5
Trusley Wlk **7**
NG19.............136 E4
Trustley Cl DE14...254 B7
Tudor Cl NG10.....223 E1
Tudor Court DE13...239 B6
Tudor Ct
Borrowash DE72....221 E1
3 Derby DE22....204 F3
Selston NG16......171 D6
Tudor Falls DE75...181 E3
Tudor Field Cl DE73.233 A1
Tudor Gdns **6**
DE13.............239 C5
Tudor House Cl
DE11.............256 A7
Tudor Pl DE7.......208 C5
Tudor Rd DE21....220 A6
Tudor Rise B79....263 E2
Tudor St **2** S43....78 F2
Tudor Way NG11...256 A6
Tufnell Gdns DE22..218 B7
Tulip Rd
Awsworth NG16....195 B5
Tutbury DE13......239 C5
Tulla Cl DE24......231 E2
Tumbling Hill DE56..168 E1
Tuniscliffe Ct DE11 .256 D4
Tunnel Yd **7** DE6...173 B2
Tunstall Gn S40.....95 C1
Tunstall Way S40....95 C1
TUNSTEAD 67 F2
Tunstead Dr DE72 .245 B8
TUNSTEAD MILTON..46 C5
Tuphall Cl DE73....233 B2
TUPTON 131 D8
Tupton Hall Sch
S42.............131 D7
Tupton Moor Cl
S42.............115 D1
Tupton Prim Sch
S42.............115 D1
Tupton Rd S45.....131 C5
Tupton Way S42...116 D1
Turf Lea Fold SK6...23 B1
Turf Lea Rd
Disley SK6..........32 B8
Marple SK6.........23 B1
TURLOW FIELDS ...175 C7
Turlowfields La
Hognaston DE6....164 B1

Turlowfields La continued
Hognaston DE6.....175 C7
Turnberry Cl
Chesterfield S40....114 C8
Ilkeston DE7.......194 C2
Turnbull Cl S40.....266 A1
Turnbury Cl DE14...254 A7
Turncliffe Cl SK17...84 F6
TURNDITCH 177 B1
Turnditch CE Prim Sch
DE56.............177 B2
Turner Ave NG16...182 A3
Turner Cl
Dronfield S18.......56 F1
Stapleford NG9....223 E6
Turner Dr
Eastwood NG16....195 B7
Staveley S43........97 B7
Turner Rd
Buxton SK17........84 E5
Long Eaton NG10..236 C4
Turner's Almshouses
DE22.............218 D6
Turners Cl **1** DE55..158 F1
Turners La DE55...170 A7
Turner St DE24....232 E6
TURNERWOOD S81..63 B7
Turnlee Cl SK13.....17 C7
Turnlee Dr SK13.....17 C7
Turnlee Rd SK13....17 C7
Turnley Rd DE55...160 C6
Turnoak Ave NE7...194 F5
Turnoaks Bsns Pk
S40.............115 A6
Turnoaks La S40...115 A7
Turnpike Bsns Pk
DE55.............158 F2
Turnpike Cl
Alfreton DE55.....158 F2
Matlock DE4......143 C5
Turnpike Way DE6..185 E7
Turton Cl NG16....182 A3
TUTBURY 239 C5
Tutbury Ave DE3...230 E5
Tutbury Bypass
DE13.............239 D7
Tutbury Castle ★
DE13.............239 D7
Tutbury Dr **4**
DE15.............248 A1
TUTBURY, FAULD ..238 C6
Tutbury & Hatton Sta
DE65.............239 D8
Tutbury Hollow
1 Ashbourne DE6..185 C8
Spitalhill DE6......185 C7
Tutbury Rd DE13...240 A1
Tutbury Rd Rural
DE13.............239 F2
Tuxford Cl DE21...206 B1
Twayblade DE14....254 B8
Twayblade Cres
SK23..............46 F6
Tweeds Muir Cl **5**
DE21.............205 F2
Twentylands DE13 .240 D4
Twentywell Ct S17...56 A7
Twentywell Dr S17...56 B6
Twentywell La S17...56 B6
Twentywell Rd S17..56 B5
Twentywell Rise
S17.............56 B6
Twentywell View
S17.............56 B6
Twickenham Cl **11**
S20.............59 E6
Twickenham Cres
S20.............59 E6
Twickenham Ct **8**
S20.............59 E6
Twickenham Dr
DE22.............218 A6
Twickenham Glade **10**
S20.............59 E6
Twickenham Glen
S20.............59 F5
Twickenham Gr **9**
S20.............59 E6
Twiggs Row DE4...143 A7
Twin Oaks Cl DE23..230 F7
Twisses Bank DE6 ..213 A2
TWO DALES 127 E3
TWYFORD 243 B6
Twyford Cl
Heanor DE75......193 C8
Swadlincote DE11...255 F2
West Hallam DE7...207 D8
Willington DE65....242 C5
Twyford Rd
Barrow upon Trent
DE73.............244 A6
Long Eaton NG10...235 D2
Twyford DE73......243 C6
Willington DE65....242 B6
Twyford St DE23...267 B1
Tylney Rd S40......114 B8
Tyndale Chase
DE24.............231 C2
Tynedale Cl NG10...236 A6
Tynefield Ct DE65...229 B2
Tynefield Mews
DE65.............229 B2
Tynsel Parkes (VC) CE
Fst Sch **4** ST14...210 A1
Tyrian Street
NG16.............195 B8
Tythe Barn La DE6..215 C5
Tythe The DE11....256 B7

U

Uffa Magna DE3....217 C1
Uldale Gr DE11.....256 C1
Ulley Cres S13.......44 B7
Ulley Rd S13........44 B7
Ullswater Ave S20...59 E6
Ullswater Cl
Derby DE21.......205 D2
Dronfield S18.......56 E2
Sheffield S20........59 E6
Ullswater Dr
Derby DE21.......220 E5
Dronfield S18.......56 E2
Ullswater Pk S18....56 E2
Ullswater Pl
Chesterfield S41....95 C7
Dronfield S18.......56 E2
Ulverston Rd S41...95 D7
Undercliffe DE45...109 D6
Underhall DE4......127 D2
Underhill Ave DE23.231 F7
Underhill Cl DE23...231 E6
Underhill Rd S43....80 B6
Underpass The DE1..267 C4
Undertown La DE6..197 D6
Underwood CE Prim Sch
NG16.............171 F1
UNDERWOOD
GREEN 171 F2
Underwood Terr
Chelmorton SK17....106 A8
Darley Dale DE4....143 A7
Union Rd
Ilkeston DE7.......208 F1
New Mills SK22.....33 C7
Swadlincote DE11...256 B5
Union St
Ashbourne DE6.....173 B2
Glossop SK13.......17 C8
Harthill S26.........61 E6
Long Eaton NG10...236 E8
Melbourne DE73...252 A7
South Normanton
DE55.............159 F5
Unistates Bsns Pk
S41.............77 B2
Unity Cl DE11......256 A1
Unity Wlk SK13.....17 C7
Univ of Derby (Britannia
Mill) DE22........218 E6
Univ of Derby (Buxton
Campus) SK17.....85 B8
Univ of Derby (Kedleston
Rd) DE22.........204 D1
Univ of Derby
(Markeaton St)
DE22.............218 D6
Univ of Sheffield
(Research Labs)
SK17..............85 B1
UNSTONE 76 E8
Unstone Dronfield By-
Pass S18..........56 F3
UNSTONE GREEN ..76 E6
Unstone Hill S18....76 D7
Unstone Jun Sch
S18.............76 E7
Unstone Rd S41.....76 A3
Unstone St Mary's Inf
Sch S18...........76 F7
UNTHANK 74 D5
Unthank La S18.....74 C4
Upchurch Cl DE3...217 C3
Upland Dr DE4.....143 A7
Upland Rise S40.....95 D1
Uplands Ave DE23..231 C6
Uplands Gdns DE23..218 E2
Uplands Rd
Compstall SK14.....15 A6
Glossop SK13.......17 D8
Upper Albert Rd S2...43 B4
Upper Bainbrigge St
5 Derby DE23....218 F3
Derby DE23.......219 A3
Upper Barn Cl DE75..181 F2
UPPER BIGGIN ...175 C4
Upper Blindlow La
SK17.............106 A5
UPPER BOOTH 36 E7
Upper Boundary Rd
DE22.............218 E4
UPPER BRADWAY..56 B5
Upper Croft
Clay Cross S45....131 E3
Tupton S42........131 D8
Upper Croft Cl S43...96 B7
UPPERDALE 89 B5
Upper Dale Rd
DE23.............218 F1
Upper Derwent Visitor
Ctr ★ S33.........30 A7
Upper Dunstead Rd
NG16.............182 B4
UPPER
ELLASTONE.....183 B4
UPPER END.........67 C7
Upper End Rd
Buxton SK17........67 C4
Peak Dale SK17.....67 B5
Upper Greenhill Gdns **5**
DE4.............143 C6
UPPER HACKNEY . 143 B4
Upper Hall Cl DE56 .191 C6
UPPER HARTSHAY .169 A2
Upper Hartshay
Heage DE56.......168 F1

Upper Hartshay continued
Heage DE56 ....169 A1
Upper Hollow DE23..218 C1
UPPER
HOLLOWAY 156 C5
Upper King St S43...77 F1
Upper La DE6......175 E4
UPPER LANGWITH .119 D8
Upper Lum Cl S41...96 D2
Upper Lumsdale
DE4.............143 E7
Upper Mantle Cl
S45.............131 C4
Upper Marehay Rd
DE5.............180 D6
UPPER MAYFIELD .172 B1
UPPER MIDWAY ...256 C7
Upper Moor Rd
DE24.............232 E6
Upper Moor St S40...95 B2
Upper Nelson St **3**
DE75.............181 D2
UPPER NEWBOLD...95 A8
Upper Newbold Cl
S40.............95 B7
Upper Northfield Cl **6**
DE56.............178 F5
Upper Orchard St **2**
NG9.............223 E7
UPPER PADLEY 53 D2
UPPER PILSLEY ...132 E6
Upper School La
5 Dronfield S18....57 A1
Dronfield S18.......76 B8
UPPERTHORPE 60 D4
Upperthorpe Rd S21..60 D4
Upperthorpe Villas
S21.............60 D5
UPPERTOWN 129 A7
UPPER TOWN
Birchover 141 C8
Bonsall 142 C1
Hognaston 164 B4
Uppertown La DE4..142 C1
Upper Town La DE4..126 B1
Upper Valley Rd S8...43 B5
Upper Wellington St
NG10.............223 C1
UPPERWOOD 155 A8
Upper Wood Cl **6**
DE7.............208 E5
Upperwood Rd DE4..143 A1
Upton Cl
Castle Donington
DE74.............247 B4
Heanor DE75......182 A1
Upton Mount NG19..135 E1
Upwood Cl S40......95 A5
Upwoods La DE6 ...211 B3
Upwoods Rd
Doveridge DE6.....210 F4
Doveridge DE6.....211 A1
Utah Cl DE65......228 E2
UTTOXETER 210 C1
Uttoxeter New Rd
DE22.............218 C3
Uttoxeter Old Rd
DE22.............218 E5
Uttoxeter Rd
Birch Cross ST14....224 A2
Derby DE3........217 E1
Hatton DE65......227 B2
Hilton DE65.......228 C2
Scropton DE65....226 C4
Scropton, Foston
DE65.............226 F3
Uxbridge St DE14...254 C8

V

Vale Cl
Bolsover S44........99 A1
Dronfield S18.......57 B1
Vale Ct NG19......136 B3
Vale Dr NG20......119 F2
Valehouse Cl **7**
DE65.............240 E8
Vale House Dr SK13...10 A5
Valehouse Way SK14...9 F6
Vale Mills DE22....218 F3
Valemount SK13....10 A5
Valentine Ave NG16..171 E7
Vale Rd
Hartshorne DE11....257 A3
Mansfield Woodhouse
NG19.............136 B4
Swadlincote DE11...256 B6
Valerian Cl SK17....85 C7
Valerie Rd DE72....246 A7
Vale Rise
Matlock DE4......142 F7
3 Matlock DE4....143 A7
Vale The DE4......194 E3
Vallance St NG19...136 B4
Valley Cl S45......132 B4
Valley Cres S41.....96 C5
Valley Dr
Chapel-en-le-Frith
SK23.............47 C6
Killamarsh S21.....60 D5
Valley Gdns SK14...15 E8
Valley Park Com Prim
Sch S14...........43 D7
Valley Rd
Barlow S18.........75 D3
Bolsover S44......118 A8
Broadbottom SK14....15 E8

Valley Rd continued
Chesterfield S41....96 C2
Clay Cross S45....131 A4
Derby DE23.......218 D1
Derby, Cherrytree Hill
DE21.............220 B5
Glossop SK13.......16 F8
Hayfield SK22......25 E2
Ilkeston DE7.......208 E5
Killamarsh S21.....60 D7
Kimberley NG16....195 D7
Mastin Moor S43....79 C4
Overseal DE12....262 A3
Sheffield, Heeley S8...43 A6
Shirebrook NG20...119 C5
Valley Rise
Barlow S18.........75 D3
Swadlincote DE11...256 B5
Valley View
Alton S42.........130 C5
Belper DE56......179 A2
Ilkeston DE7.......208 E5
Valley View Cl
Chesterfield S41....115 E7
Eckington S21......59 C2
Valley View Dr DE7 .193 B1
Valley View Rd
DE55.............170 D4
Valley View Wlk
ST14.............197 A3
Vancouver Ave
DE21.............220 D4
Vancouver Dr DE15..248 C3
Vanguard Rd NG10 .236 D5
Vanguard Trad Est
S40.............115 B7
Varley Cl NG16....182 A2
Varley Ho S41......96 B6
Varley St DE24....232 D6
Vaughan Pl NG20...119 E4
Vaughan Rd SK23...45 E5
Vauxhall Ave DE22..218 A7
Velvet Mill SK17.....69 B4
Venice Cl DE73....232 E2
Ventnor Ho DE24..233 C7
Ventura Ct SK22....24 D1
Venture Ave NG17..160 F8
Venture Cres DE55..159 A2
Venture Ho S41.....76 F1
Venture Way S41....76 F1
Verbena Dr DE23...231 D4
Vere Cl DE65......242 B5
Vermont Dr DE21...220 C6
Verney St NG19.....134 F7
Verney Way NG19..134 F7
Vernon Cotts DE4..154 F1
Vernon Ct
Bakewell DE45.....109 D5
Shirebrook NG20...120 A4
Vernon Dr
Bakewell DE45.....109 B7
Derby DE21.......220 B7
Vernongate DE1....218 E5
Vernon Gn DE45...109 B7
Vernon La S45.....129 D4
Vernon Oaks La
DE6.............212 C5
Vernon Rd
Chesterfield S40....95 D3
Sheffield S17.......55 F6
Vernon Rise S42....115 F2
Vernon St
Derby DE1........218 E5
Ilkeston DE7.......194 F4
Shirebrook NG20...120 A4
Vernon Street Ind Est
NG20.............120 A4
Verona Way DE73...232 E2
Veronica Dr NG16...195 C8
Vestry Rd DE21....205 E3
Vetchfield Cl DE24..231 F2
Viadevana DE12....262 E3
Via Gellia Rd
Bonsall DE4......154 C7
Upperwood DE4....155 A7
Vicarage Ave
Derby DE23.......218 E2
Ilkeston DE7.......194 D4
Vicarage Cl
Belper DE56......179 A4
Blackfordby DE11...257 C1
Burton upon Trent
DE15.............248 B4
Heath S44........117 B2
Holmesfield S18....75 A8
Shirebrook NG20...119 E3
Smalley DE7.......192 F6
Swanwick DE55...169 E7
Vicarage Croft DE4 .110 E1
Vicarage Ct
Derby DE3........217 D1
Mansfield NG19....135 E1
Vicarage Dr
Derby DE21.......220 A7
Uttoxeter ST14....210 A4
Vicarage Gdns
Clay Cross S45....131 C2
Heanor DE75......181 F1
Swadlincote DE11...256 C4
Vicarage La
Ashford in the Water
DE45.............89 E1
Ashford in the Water
DE45.............108 E8
Duffield DE56......190 E4
Hayfield SK22......25 D2
Ironville NG16......170 F4
Little Eaton DE21...205 C8

Vicarage La continued
Sheffield S17 . . . . .55 D7
Vicarage Mews
DE55. . . . . 170 E6
Vicarage Rd
Belper DE56 . . . . .190 F8
Chellaston DE73. . . .232 F2
Derby DE3 . . . . .217 C2
Swadlincote DE11 . . .256 C4
Woodville DE11 . . . . .256 C4
Vicarage St DE7 . . . . 194 D4
Vicarage Wlk
Clowne S43. . . . . .80 E4
Rosliston DE12. . . . . .260 C6
Vicar La
Chesterfield S40. . . . .266 B3
Tibshelf DE55 . . . . 148 A6
Vicarwood Ave
Derby DE22 . . . . .204 F1
Holbrook DE56. . . . . .191 C7
Victor Ave DE22 . . . . .218 F8
Victor Cres NG10 . . . 223 C4
Victoria Ave
Borrowash DE72 . . . .221 B2
2 Buxton SK17. . . . . . .85 D8
Draycott DE72 . . . . . .235 A7
Glossop SK13. . . . . . . .10 A5
Heanor DE75 . . . . . . .181 D1
Ilkeston DE7. . . . . .207 B3
Staveley S43. . . . . .79 A3
Victoria Cl DE3 . . . . . 217 E4
Victoria Cotts DE45. 109 D6
Victoria Cres NG16 . .170 F4
Victoria Ct
6 Glossop SK13. . . . . . .17 C8
Long Eaton NG10 . . . .236 D7
Matlock DE4. . . . . 143 C6
Overseal DE12 . . . . . .262 A5
Victoria Dr
Blackwell DE55. . . . . .147 E1
Woodville DE11 . . . . .256 E1
Victoria Gr S43. . . . . .96 F5
Victoria Hall Gdns
DE4. . . . . 143 C6
Victoria Ho S80 . . . . .81 F1
Victoria Mews 2
SK13. . . . . .17 C8
Victoria Park L Ctr
DE7. . . . . 194 E1
Victoria Park Rd
Buxton SK17. . . . . .85 D7
Calow S43. . . . . .96 F5
Victoria Rd
Bamford S33 . . . . .40 B3
Draycott DE72 . . . . . .235 A7
Pinxton NG16 . . . . . . .160 D3
Ripley DE5 . . . . .169 D2
Sandiacre NG10 . . . . .223 B6
Selston NG16 . . . . 171 F6
Victoria Sq 13 DE6. . 173 C2
Victoria St
Alfreton DE55. . . . . . . 159 B4
Bolsover S44 . . . . 118 B8
Brimington S43. . . . . . .77 F1
Castle Donington
DE74. . . . . .247 B5
Chesterfield S41. . . . .266 B4
Clay Cross S45 . . . . . .131 C3
Creswell S80 . . . . .81 F1
Derby DE1 . . . . .267 B3
Dronfield S18. . . . . . . .56 F2
Glossop SK13. . . . . . . .17 C8
Ilkeston DE7. . . . . .194 F3
Ironville NG16 . . . . . .170 F4
Langley Mill NG16. . . .182 C3
Long Eaton NG10 . . . .236 B5
Melbourne DE73. . . . .252 A7
New Mills SK22. . . . . . .33 B6
Pye Hill NG16. . . . . . .171 A4
Ripley DE5 . . . . .169 F2
Shirebrook NG20 . . . . 119 F4
Somercotes DE55. . . .170 C8
South Normanton
DE55. . . . . .160 A6
Stapleford NG9. . . . . .223 D7
**Victoria Street
North** S41. . . . . .76 F2
**Victoria Street
West** S40 . . . . .95 C2
Victoria Terr
Great Longstone
DE45. . . . . .89 F4
Selston NG16 . . . . . . .160 E1
Tibshelf DE55 . . . . 148 B7
Victoria Way DE24 . .219 E3
Victoria Wlk S42 . . . 115 D1
Victor Rd S17 . . . . . . .55 F7
Victory Ave DE5 . . . .169 F1
Victory Cl NG10. . . . .236 E5
Victory Dr NG19 . . . .136 F1
Victory Park Way
DE24. . . . . .232 B6
Victory Rd
Derby DE24 . . . . .232 B6
Derby DE24 . . . . .232 C5
Viewdales Cl DE56 . .175 F2
View Rd S2. . . . . .43 A7
Viking Bsns Ctr
DE11. . . . . .256 F3
Vikinglea Cl S2. . . . . .44 B8
Vikinglea Dr S2. . . . . .44 B8
Village Ct DE56. . . . . .190 F3
Village Prim Sch
DE23. . . . . .231 F7
Village St DE23 . . . . .231 F8
Village The
Dale Abbey DE7 . . . . .207 F2
West Hallam DE7 . . . .207 E7

Villas Rd
Ambergate DE56 . . . .167 F3
Bolsover S44 . . . . .98 E2
Villa St DE72 . . . . . . .235 B7
Villas The
Bolsover S44 . . . . .99 B3
Burton upon Trent
DE16. . . . . .254 E7
Whaley Thorns NG20 . 101 A2
Villa The SK14 . . . . . . .9 A5
Villiers Cl S2. . . . . . . .43 E6
Villiers Dr S2. . . . . . . .43 E6
Vincent Ave
Derby DE21 . . . . .220 E3
Ilkeston DE7. . . . . .208 F8
Vincent Cl DE56 . . . . 192 A8
Vincent Cres S40 . . . .95 B2
Vincent La S40 . . . . . .95 B2
Vincent St DE23 . . . . 218 F1
Vine Cl DE23 . . . . 231 B7
Vine Cres NG10. . . . . .223 B6
Vine Farm Cl DE7. . . .208 D5
Vine Gr Ct S20. . . . . . .59 D7
Vine Gr Gdns S20. . . .59 D7
Vine Wlk Pk NG19 . . .136 C6
Vineyard Terr DE4 . . . 127 C4
Viola Cl DE21. . . . . . . .206 C3
Violet Ave NG16 . . . . 195 B8
Violet Cl
Donisthorpe DE12 . . .262 E1
Shirebrook NG20 . . . . 119 D3
Violet La
Burton upon Trent
DE15. . . . . .254 F8
Burton upon Trent
DE15. . . . . 255 A7
Violet St
Derby DE23 . . . . 218 F1
Derby DE23 . . . . 219 A1
Violet Way DE15. . . . 255 A8
Violet Way Acad
DE15. . . . . .254 F8
Virginsalley La DE6. 184 D2
Virtue Cl DE3. . . . . . . 217 D1
Vista The NG9 . . . . . .223 E5
Vivian St
Derby DE1 . . . . .219 B8
Shuttlewood S44. . . . . .98 F6
Vulcan St DE23 . . . . . 219 B1
Vulcan Way DE74. . . .246 F4
Vyse Dr NG10. . . . . . .236 C6

W

Wade Ave
Derby DE23 . . . . 218 C2
Ilkeston DE7. . . . . .209 B7
Wadebridge Gr
DE24. . . . . .233 C5
Wade Dr DE3. . . . . 217 E2
Wade St DE23 . . . . . . 218 C1
Wadham Close DE3. .217 D1
WADSHELF 93 E3
Wadsworth Ave S12. .44 D5
Wadsworth Cl S12. . . .44 D5
Wadsworth Dr S12. . . .44 D5
**Wadsworth Fields Prim
Sch** NG9. . . . . .223 B8
Wadsworth Rd
Sheffield S12 . . . . .44 C5
Stapleford NG9. . . . . .223 B8
Wagon La
Bretby DE11. . . . . .256 A8
Bretby DE15 . . . . .249 A1
Wagstaff La NG16 . . . 171 B3
Wagtail Cl
Derby DE24 . . . . 231 D4
1 Stapleford NG9. . . .209 E2
Wain Ave
Chesterfield S41. . . . .266 C3
North Wingfield S42. . 132 A7
Wainfleet Cl DE7 . . . . 194 C3
WAINGROVES. 181 A7
Waingroves Prim Sch
DE5. . . . . 181 A7
Waingroves Rd
Codnor DE5 . . . . 181 B8
Ripley DE5 . . . . 181 A8
Wainhouse Brow
SK22. . . . . .25 D3
Wains Cl SK17. . . . . . . .47 F1
Wain Way S42. . . . . . . 132 A7
Wainwright Ave
Mansfield NG19 . . . . .135 D1
Sheffield S13 . . . . .44 D8
Wainwright Cres
S13. . . . . .44 D8
Wainwright Dr
DE11. . . . . .256 F4
Wakami Cres DE73 . .233 A3
WAKEBRIDGE 156 D3
Wakefield Ave DE13 .239 B6
Wakefield Croft
DE7. . . . . 194 C3
Wakefield Ct
Castle Donington
DE74. . . . . .247 C4
Derby DE74 . . . . .247 B4
Wakelyn Cl
Hilton DE65 . . . . .228 C2
Shardlow DE72. . . . . .234 F1
Walbrook Rd DE23. . 218 F1
Walcote Cl DE56. . . . .179 D5
Walden Cl DE7 . . . . . .245 A8
Waldene Dr DE24. . . .233 A6
Walden Rd S2. . . . . . . .43 B7
WALDLEY. 211 C7

Waldley La DE6. . . . . 211 D7
Waldorf Ave DE24 . . .233 A7
Waldorf Cl DE24 . . . .233 A7
Walford Rd
Killamarsh S21. . . . . . .60 C6
Rolleston DE13. . . . . .240 D3
Walgrave Cl DE56. . . .179 B6
Walgrove Ave S40 . . . .95 E1
Walgrove Rd S40. . . . .95 D1
Walk Cl DE72. . . . . . . .235 A7
Walkdale Brow SK13. .17 R7
Walker Ave DE5 . . . . .169 E2
Walker Brow SK17. . . .47 F1
Walker Brow Rd
SK23. . . . . .45 C5
Walker La DE7. . . . . . .209 A4
Walker Gr 2 NG9. . . .223 E6
Walker La DE1. . . . . . .267 A4
Walkers La S21. . . . . . .60 D6
Walker St SK13. . . . . . .10 A4
Wallace Gdns NG9. . .223 F1
Wallace St DE22 . . . . 218 C5
WALLASH 184 C7
Wall Ditch DE6. . . . . .149 B2
Wallef Rd DE6. . . . . . .201 E8
Wallfields Cl DE65. . .230 D2
Wallis Cl
Draycott DE72 . . . . . .235 A7
4 Ripley DE5. . . . . . . .180 E8
Wallis Ho DE11. . . . . .256 E3
Wall Rd DE14. . . . . . . .254 A7
Wallsend Cl DE7. . . . .194 F4
Walls La S80 . . . . .81 A8
Wall St
Buxton SK17. . . . . .85 D8
Ripley DE5 . . . . .169 D2
Walmsley Cl S45 . . . . 131 C5
Walnut Ave
Derby DE24 . . . . .233 B7
Shireoaks S81 . . . . .63 F7
Walnut Cl
Aston-on-Trent
DE72. . . . . .246 B8
Barrow upon Trent
DE73. . . . . .244 A6
Burnaston DE65 . . . . .229 F5
Chellaston DE73. . . . .245 A8
Ilkeston DE7. . . . . .209 A7
Repton DE65. . . . . . . .242 F2
Repton DE65. . . . . . . .243 A2
Swadlincote DE11 . . .256 A5
Walnut Dr
Hilton DE65 . . . . .228 D2
Killamarsh S21. . . . . . .60 C5
Walnut Rd DE6 . . . . . .179 B3
Walnut St DE24. . . . . .232 C7
Walpole St DE7. . . . . .219 D6
Walseker La S26. . . . . .61 C7
Walsham Ct DE21. . . .205 D1
**Walter Evans CE (Aided)
Prim Sch** DE22 . . . .204 F2
**Walter Evans CE (Aided)
Prim Sch** DE22 . . . .205 A2
Walters Ave NG16 . . . 182 E6
Walters Cres NG16. . . 171 D6
Walter St
Derby DE1 . . . . .218 E7
Draycott DE72 . . . . . .234 F8
Walters Wood SK23. . .45 F5
Waltham Ave DE24 . . 231 F4
Waltham Croft S41. . 115 C7
Walthamstow Dr
DE22. . . . . 218 B6
Waltheof Rd S2. . . . . . .44 A8
WALTON 114 D8
Walton Ave DE24 . . . .232 E4
Walton Back La
Chesterfield S40. . . . .114 B7
Holymoorside S42 . . .113 F7
Walton Cl
Chesterfield S40. . . . .114 B8
Dronfield S18. . . . . . . .56 C2
Swadlincote DE11 . . .256 A3
Walton Cres
Ashbourne DE6. . . . . .173 C1
Chesterfield S40. . . . . .95 E1
Walton Ct
Sheffield S8 . . . . .56 E8
West Hallam DE7 . . . .207 D8
Walton Dr
Chesterfield S40. . . . . .95 E1
Derby DE23 . . . . 231 E7
Walton Drive Ct S40. .95 E1
Walton Fields Rd
S40. . . . . .95 D2
Walton Hill
4 Castle Donington
DE74. . . . . .246 F4
Castle Donington
DE74. . . . . .247 A4
**Walton Holymoorside
Prim Sch** S42 . . . . .113 E4
Walton Hospl S40 . . .114 E8
Walton La DE14 . . . . . 253 C1
**WALTON-ON-
TRENT** 253 D1
**Walton-on-Trent
CE Sch** DE12 . . . . . .259 D8
Walton Rd
Burton upon Trent
DE15. . . . . .254 D7
Chesterfield S40. . . . . .95 D1
Derby DE21 . . . . 219 F5
Walton St NG10 . . . . .223 D1
Walton Way S42. . . . . 114 E4
Walton Wlk S40 . . . . .266 A2

Wansfell Cl DE3 . . . . . 217 E1
Wapentake La DE6 . . 165 C2
Warburton Cl S2 . . . . .43 C7
Warburton Gdns S2 . .43 C7
Warburton Rd S2. . . . .43 C7
Ward Cl DE4. . . . . .165 E6
Ward Dr DE55 . . . . . . .170 D7
Wardgate Way S40 . . . .95 A5
Ward La
Barlborough S43 . . . . . .80 B8
Disley SK12. . . . . .32 F4
WARDLOW. 70 C2
Wardlow Ave
Derby DE21 . . . . .220 A8
17 Gamesley SK13. . . . . .9 D1
Wardlow Cl S40. . . . . .114 F8
Wardlow Fold 21
SK13. . . . . .9 D1
Wardlow Gdns 19
SK13. . . . . .9 D1
Wardlow Gr 22 SK13. . .9 D1
Wardlow Mews 18
SK13. . . . . .9 D1
WARDLOW MIRES. . .70 C4
Wardlow Rd
Ilkeston DE7. . . . . .194 E3
Sheffield S12 . . . . .44 D5
Wardlow Wlk 18 SK13 .9 D1
WARDS END 143 C2
Ward's La
Barrow upon Trent
DE73. . . . . .244 F3
Breaston DE72 . . . . . .235 D8
King's Newton DE73. .245 A2
Ward St
Derby DE22 . . . . .218 E4
Tupton S40 . . . . 115 D1
Tupton S42 . . . . 131 D8
Wards Yd S18. . . . . . . .57 A1
Wardwick DE1. . . . . . .267 B3
Warehouse La S33. . . .38 D4
WARHILL 9 A3
Warhurst Fold 2
SK13. . . . . .10 A5
Warke Flatt DE74 . . . .247 B6
WARMBROOK. 165 E3
Warmbrook Rd SK23. .47 C6
Warminster Cl S8 . . . . .43 A4
Warminster Cres S8. . .43 B4
Warminster Dr S8. . . . .43 B3
Warminster Gdns S8 .43 A3
Warminster Pl S8 . . . . .43 B3
Warminster Rd S8. . . . .43 B4
Warmwells La DE5. . .180 D6
Warner St
Chesterfield S41. . . . .266 C1
Derby DE22 . . . . .267 A1
Derby, Markeaton
DE3. . . . . 217 D1
Warney Rd DE4. . . . . .127 D2
Warren Ave NG9. . . . .223 D7
Warren Ave Extension
NG9 . . . . .223 D7
Warren Cl
Burton upon Trent
DE13. . . . . .240 E1
Pilsley NG19 . . . . .132 C2
Warren Cres S21. . . . . .58 E2
Warren Ct NG9 . . . . . .223 D7
Warrendale Ct
DE73. . . . . .233 A2
Warren Dr DE22 . . . . . 261 C6
Warren Hill 7 DE11 . 255 E5
Warren La
Branston DE14. . . . . .253 F7
Castle Donington DE74,
NG10 . . . . .236 B2
Warren Lea SK6. . . . . . .15 B2
Warren Rd 6 DE5 . . . .170 A1
Warren Rise S18 . . . . . .57 C3
Warren St DE24 . . . . .232 F8
Warren Wlk S21. . . . . . .58 E2
Warslow Rd SK17. . . . 121 B4
Warsop Rd NG19 . . . . 136 D3
WARSOP VALE. 120 D4
Warwick Ave DE23. . . 218 D1
Warwick Cl
Branston DE14. . . . . .253 F8
Glossop SK13. . . . . . . .17 F8
Swadlincote DE11 . . .256 E5
Warwick Ct
Somercotes DE55. . . .170 C8
Swanwick DE55. . . . . .170 B8
Warwick Dr DE7. . . . .194 C3
Warwick Gdns
DE56. . . . . 179 D5
Warwick Rd
Long Eaton NG10 . . . .237 A7
Somercotes DE55. . . .159 C1
Warwick St
Chesterfield S40. . . . .115 B7
Derby DE23 . . . . 219 D2
Warwick Street Ind Est
S40. . . . . 115 B7
Wasdale Ave 5 S20. .59 E6
Wasdale Cl S20. . . . . . .59 E6
WASH. 35 C1
Washbrook La DE6. . .161 F4
Washford Rd DE65. . .240 E8
Washgate La SK17. . . . 104 C6
Wash Gn DE4. . . . . . . .166 B8
WASHGREEN. 155 A1
Wash Hills Cl DE4. . . . 153 A1
Washhouse Bottom
SK17. . . . . .69 E8
Wash House Bottom
SK17. . . . . .50 E1

Wash House La S40. . . .95 C2
Washington Ave
DE21. . . . . .220 B6
Washington Cl
DE73. . . . . .252 A7
Washington Cotts
DE72. . . . . .221 D1
Washington Dr NG9 .209 F1
Washington Terr
DE4. . . . . 143 E7
Wash Meadow Cl 5
DE7. . . . . .208 C5
Watburn Rd SK22. . . . .24 D1
Watchorn Cl DE11 . . .256 D5
Watchorn Cotts
DE55. . . . . .158 F3
Watchorn La DE55. . .158 F2
Watchorn Lawns
DE55. . . . . .158 F2
Watercress La S45. . . 131 D2
Waterdown Cl
NG19 . . . . 136 D5
Waterfall Cl S8. . . . . . .43 C1
Waterfoot Cotts SK14. .9 A4
Waterfoot La SK23. . . .45 C6
Waterford Dr DE21 . . .220 B4
Watergo La DE3 . . . . .230 C7
Wateringbury Gr 1
S43. . . . . .78 F2
Watering La DE56 . . . 191 D6
Water La
Bakewell DE45 . . . . . .109 D6
Bamford S33 . . . . .40 A3
Bolsover S44 . . . . 117 E8
Cromford DE4. . . . . . .155 A6
Eyam S32 . . . . .71 E6
Hollingworth SK14. . . . .9 D5
Middleton DE4 . . . . . .154 C5
Pleasley NG19 . . . . . . .135 B3
Sheffield S17 . . . . .55 F7
Shirebrook NG19 . . . . 118 C1
South Normanton
DE55. . . . . .160 B6
Tideswell SK17. . . . . . .68 F6
Wirksworth DE4. . . . .165 F7
Waterlagg La
Hulland Ward DE56 . .188 D8
Hulland Ward DE6 . . .176 C1
Water Lily Gdns S80. .81 E3
WATERLOO 132 C3
Waterloo Cotts DE55. 160 C8
Waterloo Ct
Derby DE1 . . . . .267 C5
Waterloo S45 . . . . 132 B2
Waterloo La NG9 . . . .209 F6
Waterloo Pl DE11. . . .256 B4
Waterloo Rd
Mansfield NG19 . . . . .136 B2
Matlock Bath DE4. . . .143 A1
Waterloo St
Clay Cross S45 . . . . . .131 C4
Doe Lea S44 . . . . 117 F1
Watermede S21 . . . . . .59 B2
Watermeadow Rd
DE24. . . . . .233 A5
Watermeadows The
NG10 . . . . .236 A8
Watermint Cl DE23 . . 231 B6
Watermint Rd S40. . . . 115 D2
Waterpark Rd DE6. . .224 B8
Waters Edge SK6. . . . .23 B8
Waters Edge La SK23 .47 C5
Waterside
Burton upon Trent
DE15. . . . . .254 E7
Disley SK12. . . . . .32 E7
Glossop SK13. . . . . . . .10 A6
Waterside Ave SK6. . . .23 A5
Waterside Bsns Pk
SK13. . . . . .9 F6
Waterside Cl
Derby DE22 . . . . .205 A2
Sandiacre NG10 . . . . .223 B3
Waterside Ho DE1 . . .267 B4
Waterside Rd
Ashbourne DE6. . . . . .185 A8
Burton upon Trent
DE15. . . . . .254 D7
Disley SK12, SK22 . . . .32 E7
Waterside Ret Pk
DE7. . . . . 195 A1
Water St
Bakewell DE45 . . . . . .109 D5
Buxton SK17. . . . . .85 B8
Glossop SK13. . . . . . . .10 E2
WATER SWALLOWS. .67 A3
**WATERSWALLOWS
GREEN** 66 F3
Waterswallows Ind Pk
SK17. . . . . .67 A3
Waterswallows La
SK17. . . . . .66 F4
Waterswallows Mews
SK17. . . . . .66 E1
Waterswallows Rd
Buxton SK17. . . . . .66 C1
Peak Dale SK17 . . . . . .67 C3
Waterthorpe Cl 4
S20. . . . . .59 F8
Waterthorpe Cres
S20. . . . . .59 F8

Waterthorpe Gdns 3
S20. . . . . .59 F8
Waterthorpe Glade 5
S20. . . . . .59 F8
Waterthorpe Glen 2
S20. . . . . .59 F8
Waterthorpe Rise 1
S20. . . . . .59 F8
Waterton Cl DE13. . . .241 A1
Waterway The
NG10 . . . . .223 C4
Watery La
Bretby DE15 . . . . .249 C3
Clifton DE6 . . . . .184 E7
Ellastone DE6. . . . . . .183 B4
Holme HD9. . . . . .2 F8
Scropton DE65 . . . . . .226 E2
Scropton DE65 . . . . . .227 A3
Swadlincote DE11 . . .255 D5
Thurvaston DE6. . . . . .215 D5
Watford Bridge Ind Est
SK22. . . . . .24 C1
Watford Bridge Rd
SK22. . . . . .24 D1
Watford La SK22. . . . . .24 C2
Watford Lodge SK22. .24 C1
Watford Rd
Buxton SK17. . . . . .84 F8
New Mills SK22. . . . . . .24 C2
Watkin Ave SK13 . . . . . .9 E4
Watkinson St DE75. . . 181 D2
Watson Ave DE75. . . .181 F2
Watson La S42 . . . . 114 C3
Watson Rd DE7. . . . . .194 C2
Watson St
Derby DE1 . . . . .218 E6
Derby DE22 . . . . 218 E7
Watten Cl DE24 . . . . . 231 F2
Watts Gn DE45 . . . . . .108 F8
Waveney Cl DE22 . . . .205 B5
Waverley Ct 2 S41. . .96 A6
Waverley St
Derby DE24 . . . . .232 D7
Long Eaton NG10 . . . .236 E8
Tibshelf DE55 . . . . 148 A7
Wayfaring Rd DE21. . .206 A1
Wayford Ave S41 . . . .266 C1
Wayside S43 . . . . .96 D8
Wayside Cl S42 . . . . . .132 A7
Wayside Ct S43. . . . . . .96 D8
Wayzgoose Dr
DE21. . . . . 219 C6
Weaddow La
Middleton DE45 . . . . .124 F2
Middleton DE45 . . . . .140 A8
Weakland Cl S12. . . . . .44 F3
Weakland Cres S12. . . .44 F3
Weakland Dr S12. . . . . .44 F3
Weakland Way S12. . . .44 F3
Weather Hill La HD9. . .3 E8
Weathern Field
DE12. . . . . 261 D5
Weaver Cl
Ashbourne DE6. . . . . .185 C8
Crich DE4. . . . . 156 F1
Weaver Rd ST14. . . . . .210 B2
Weavers Cl
Belper DE56 . . . . 179 C5
Borrowash DE72 . . . .221 D1
Weavers Court
DE55. . . . . 148 A3
Weavers Croft DE5 . . 180 E8
Weavers Ct SK14 . . . . . .9 A4
Weavers Gn DE3. . . . . 217 C1
Weavers The ST14. . . 196 D6
Weavers Way DE55 . . 160 B6
Weaving Ave S33. . . . . .38 C2
Webb Dr DE74. . . . . . .246 E3
Webbs Orch SK23 . . . . .45 D8
Webster Ave NG16. . . 182 F1
Webster Croft S41. . . . .77 B2
Webster Ct S40. . . . . . .95 E5
Webster St DE1. . . . . .267 A2
Webster's Terr DE4. . 143 D4
Wedgewood Cl
DE15. . . . . .248 B1
Wedgewood Way
DE11. . . . . .256 F1
Wedneshough SK14. . .9 C5
Wedneshough Green
SK14. . . . . .9 C5
Weighbridge Rd
NG20 . . . . 119 F2
Weightman Dr
NG16 . . . . 195 B7
Weir Bank DE15 . . . . .254 E6
Weirfield Rd DE22. . . .205 A2
Weirside DE6. . . . . 184 D7
Welbeck Ave
Buxton SK17. . . . . .85 C6
Ilkeston DE7. . . . . .208 D5
Welbeck Cl
Alfreton DE55. . . . . . . 170 D7
Dronfield S18. . . . . . . .56 C2
Staveley S43. . . . . .97 D6
Welbeck College La
S80. . . . . .82 F1
Welbeck Ct
1 Chesterfield S40. . . .95 C2
Clowne S43. . . . . .80 F3
7 Staveley S43. . . . . . .78 E2
Welbeck Dr S42 . . . . . 114 E4
Welbeck Gdns
Beeston NG9 . . . . .223 F3
Bolsover S44 . . . . .99 C2

Welbeck Glade S44....99 B2
Welbeck Gr DE22... 204 D3
Welbeck Rd
　Bolsover S44 ....99 B2
　Long Eaton NG10 .. 223 C3
　Mansfield Woodhouse
　NG19 .... 136 C3
Welbeck St
　Creswell S80 ....81 E1
　Whitwell S80 ....82 B6
Welburn Cl NG19 ... 136 F2
Welbury Gdns S20....59 E6
Welch Ave NG9.... 223 E8
Welfare Ave S40.....95 D3
Welfare Cl NG20.... 119 E3
Welfitt Gr NG20.... 101 B2
Welland Cl
　Burton upon Trent
　DE15.............. 248 A5
　Derby DE3 .... 217 D4
Welland Rd DE65 ... 228 D1
Well Banks
　Kirk Ireton DE6.....165 B1
　Kirk Ireton DE6.....176 B8
Wellcarr Rd S8......43 A2
Well Cl DE6 .... 175 E3
Wellcroft DE4 ..... 126 B1
Wellcroft Grange
　DE6............... 183 B8
Welldon St S41..... 181 A4
Wellesley Ave DE23. 231 D7
Wellfield DE4 ...... 143 C6
Wellfield Cl S12......44 E1
Wellfield Ct **2** DE4. 143 C6
Well Gate SK13......10 E2
Wellgate La DE45... 109 B1
Well Green S32......72 C1
Wellhead Rd DE4 .. 142 B2
Wellhead Rd **4** S8 ..43 A6
Wellington Cl DE43.. 143 D7
Wellington Court
　DE74..............246 F4
Wellington Cres
　DE1............... 267 D2
Wellington Ct
　1 Belper DE56....178 F3
　Eastwood NG16.....182 F2
Wellington Mews
　DE55.............. 146 D2
Wellington Pk
　Burton upon Trent
　DE16.............. 254 A8
　Shirland DE55......146 D2
Wellington Pl NG16. 182 F2
Wellington Rd DE14 253 E8
Wellington St
　Chesterfield S43......77 D3
　Derby DE1 .... 267 D2
　Eastwood NG16.....182 F2
　Heanor DE75 ...... 181 D3
　Long Eaton NG10 .. 223 C2
　Matlock DE4...... 143 C6
　Ripley DE5 .... 169 E1
　Stapleford NG9.... 223 C6
Well La
　Belper DE56........190 F7
　Blackfordby DE11...257 B2
　Holymoorside S42... 112 F7
　Repton DE65....... 242 C1
　Shirland DE55......146 C3
Well Rd S8........43 A6
Well Row SK14......16 A8
Wells Cl NG19 ..... 136 D4
Wells Ct DE23 ..... 230 E7
Wellspring Cl
　Barlborough S43 .....80 B6
　Wingerworth S42.....115 B4
Well Spring Cl S43...96 E7
Wellspring Dale
　NG9............... 223 E5
Wells Rd DE3...... 217 E2
Wells St S44....... 118 C8
Well St
　Brassington DE4.....152 F1
　Derby DE1 ....267 B5
　Elton DE4 ....140 E7
　New Mills SK22......33 B8
　Ripley DE5 .... 169 D1
Wellwood Rd DE11 . 256 A6
Well Yd
　Belper DE56 ...... 179 A5
　Holbrook DE56...... 191 C6
Welney Cl DE55.... 179 B6
Welshpool Pl S40.....95 D3
Welshpool Rd DE21. 205 D1
Welsted Rd DE74... 246 E2
Welton Ave DE56 ... 179 B6
Welwyn Ave
　Derby DE22 ...... 204 D3
　Derby, Allenton DE24 .232 E4
　Mansfield Woodhouse
　NG19............136 E4
Welwyn Cl
　Chesterfield S40......95 D3
　Sheffield S12 ....44 B4
Welwyn Ct S12......44 B4
Welwyn Rd S12......44 B4
Wembley Gdns
　DE22............. 218 A6
Wendover Cl DE3 .. 217 C1
Wenham La NG17...148 F4
Wenlock Cl
　Chesterfield S40......95 D4
　Derby DE3 ....217 E1
　Eastwood NG16.... 195 C8

Wenlock Cres S40....95 D4
Wenlock Dr S42.....115 F3
Wenlock Wlk S42....115 F3
Wenslees DE4...... 116 C1
WENSLEY.......... 142 A7
WENSLEY DALE .. 142 B6
Wensleydale Cl
　NG19 .... 136 E1
Wensleydale Rd
　NG10 .... 236 B6
Wensleydale Wlk
　DE24.............. 233 C7
Wensley Dr DE21...220 F3
Wensley Rd
　North Wingfield S42..131 F5
　Winster DE4 ...... 141 D6
Wensley Way S41.....97 C8
Wentworth Ave S40 114 E8
Wentworth Cl
　Derby DE3 ....217 F2
　Mansfield NG19 .....136 F2
Wentworth Croft
　DE75.............. 182 A3
Wentworth Dr DE13 240 D1
Wentworth Ho **1**
　DE1............... 267 B5
Wentworth Pl ST14. 197 A3
Wentworth Rd S18 ..56 C1
Wentworth St DE7.. 195 A2
Werburgh St DE21.. 220 D4
Werburgh St DE22... 267 A2
Werneth Low Ctry Pk ★
　SK14...............15 A7
Werneth Low Rd
　SK14...............15 B6
Werneth Rd SK13....17 A7
Wesleyan Chapel La
　SK17...............88 A3
Wesleyan Chapel Wlk
　NG9 .... 223 D7
Wesley Cl **2** DE6... 211 C1
Wesley Ct SK23......47 C6
Wesley Ho **3** SK17 ..85 D8
Wesley La DE72 .... 221 C5
Wesley Pl NG9...... 223 D7
Wesley Rd
　Ambergate DE56 ....167 F3
　Derby DE24 ....233 B5
　Stonebroom DE55...146 F3
Wesley St
　Glossop SK13........10 E2
　Hadfield SK13.......10 A5
　Ilkeston DE7.......194 E4
　Langley Mill NG16...182 C3
Wessex Cl **5** S43....96 F8
Wessex Dr NG16.... 195 A8
Wessex Gdns S17....55 D5
WESSINGTON...... 157 C8
Wessington Bank **9**
　SK13................9 E2
Wessington Dr S43...97 C8
Wessington Fold **12**
　SK13................9 E2
Wessington Gn **11**
　SK13................9 E2
*Wessington Green
　Nature Reserve ★*
　DE55..............157 E8
Wessington La
　DE55.............. 158 A6
Wessington Mews
　Derby DE22 ......204 E1
　Gamesley SK13 ....9 E2
Wessington Prim Sch
　DE55..............157 E8
Westacre Dr DE11...255 F2
Westanes Gn DE55.. 145 D1
West Ave
　Chellaston DE73.....232 E3
　Derby DE1 ....267 A4
　Draycott DE72.....234 F8
　Hilton DE65 ......228 C2
　Ripley DE5 ....169 C1
　Sandiacre NG10.... 223 A6
　Stapleford NG9..... 223 E8
West Ave S DE73 .. 232 E2
West Bank
　Matlock Bath DE4...143 A1
　Toadmoor DE56 ....168 A2
　Winster DE4 ......141 B5
West Bank Ave
　Crich DE4 ....156 F1
　Derby DE22 ......218 F8
　Mansfield NG19 .....136 B1
Westbank Cl S18.....57 B4
West Bank Cl DE22 . 218 E8
Westbank Cl S18.....57 C4
West Bank Lea
　NG19 .... 136 B1
West Bank Link
　NG19 .... 136 B1
West Bank Rd DE22. 204 E5
West Bars S40....... 266 A3
Westbourne Ave
　DE55..............147 A4
Westbourne Cl
　NG19 .... 136 E4
Westbourne Ct
　NG9 .... 209 F1
Westbourne Gr S40...95 B3
Westbourne Pk
　DE22.............217 F7
Westbridge Rd S43...80 A7
Westbrook Cl
　Chapel-en-le-Frith
　SK23................47 C5
　Chesterfield S40.....94 F2
Westbrook Dr S40....94 F2

West Brook La **1**
　DE55..............147 F6
WEST
　BROUGHTON 225 A6
Westbury Ct DE22.. 218 E3
Westbury Gdns
　DE56.............. 179 C5
Westbury St DE22 .. 218 E3
Westby La NG16.... 195 B3
West Cl DE22...... 204 E2
West Cres
　Duckmanton S44 .....98 A5
　Matlock DE4 ...... 143 A6
West Croft Ave
　DE23............. 231 D5
West Croft Cl DE45. 125 B5
Westcroft Cres S20....59 E8
West Croft Ct S43....97 B5
Westcroft Dr S20.....59 E7
West Croft Dr S43....97 B5
Westcroft Gdns S20 ..59 E8
Westcroft Glen S20....59 E7
West Croft Gr S20....59 E7
Westcross Ave
　NG9 .... 223 E8
Westdale Cl NG10 .. 236 A5
Westdale Rd
　Mansfield NG19 .....136 B1
　Westwood NG16 .....171 C4
Westdene Ave
　DE24............. 232 D5
West Dr
　Derby DE3 ....217 D2
　Doveridge DE6 .....211 B1
　Glossop SK13..........9 E7
West Edge Cl S45... 129 D4
West End
　Alfreton DE55.......159 A3
　Barlborough S43 .....80 A7
　Baslow DE45 ....91 E5
　Brassington DE4.....152 F1
　Broadbottom SK14...15 F8
　Elton DE4 ....140 E6
　Pinxton NG16.......160 C4
　Wirksworth DE4.....165 E8
West End Cl DE55.. . 159 A3
West End Cres DE7 . 208 D8
West End Dr
　Ilkeston DE7.......208 D8
　Shardlow DE72.....234 E1
West End St NG9 ... 223 D7
West End View S21....59 C2
West End Way SK14 ..15 F8
Westerlands NG9.... 223 F6
Western Ave DE55 . 169 D7
Western Dr DE75... 193 F8
Western La SK23.....46 A8
Western Mere Cl
　DE72............. 235 C7
Western Rd
　7 Derby DE23...218 F3
　Derby DE3 ....217 E2
　Derby, Rose Hill
　DE23.............. 219 A3
Western View DE45...90 A4
Western Villas DE56 .167 F3
WESTFIELD.........59 F8
Westfield Ave
　Chesterfield S40......95 B1
　5 Heanor DE75......181 F1
West Field Bank S43..80 A7
Westfield Cl
　Chesterfield S40......95 B8
　Ilkeston DE7.......208 C6
Westfield Cres S20....59 C8
Westfield Ctr S20.....59 E8
Westfield Derby (Sh Ctr)
　DE1............... 267 C2
Westfield Dr
　Blackwell DE55......147 E1
　Ilkeston DE7.......194 D2
Westfield Gdns S20...95 B2
Westfield Gr DE22 .. 218 D4
Westfield Inf Sch
　S40................95 B2
Westfield La
　Barlborough S43 .....79 F7
　Chesterfield S21......77 E8
Westfield Northway
　S20................59 E8
Westfield Rd
　Dronfield S18.......76 C8
　Killamarsh S21.......60 C5
　Swadlincote DE11 ...256 B6
Westfield Southway
　S20................59 E8
Westgate DE1...... 218 E6
West Gate
　Holme HD9..........3 F8
　Long Eaton NG10 ...236 E7
Westgate St ST14...196 F3
West Gr DE24...... 232 D5
Westgreen Ave
　DE24............. 232 D5
WEST HALLAM.....207 F8
WEST HALLAM
　COMMON.......... 207 D8
West Hallam Ind Est
　DE7...............207 E6
Westhall Rd DE4....217 D3
WEST HANDLEY.....77 D7
West Hill DE5 ..... 181 B7
Westhill La S42..... 115 E3
West Hill Pk NG19 . 136 B3
West Ho S8 ....43 A4
West Horderns SK23..47 B5
Westhorpe Dr NG10 236 C8
WESTHOUSES 159 C8

Westhouses Prim Sch
　DE55..............147 C1
Westland Dr NG16... 160 C3
Westland Gdns S20...59 D8
Westland Gr **3** S20...59 E8
Westland Rd **1** S20 ..59 E8
Westlands The
　ST14.............. 196 D6
West Lawn DE65....230 D2
Westlea DE4 ...... 143 D6
West Lea
　Chesterfield S40......95 B2
　Clowne S43.........80 D4
West Lea Cotts S43...80 D4
Westlea View S43.....80 D4
West Lees Rd S33 ....40 B4
Westleigh NG16..... 136 D6
Westleigh Ave DE22 218 C6
Westleigh Cl S40.....95 E5
Westley Cres DE21.. 191 D2
West Meadow Rise
　DE74............. 246 E4
Westminster Ave **1**
　NG10 .... 223 C5
Westminster Dr
　DE11.............. 255 E1
Westminster St
　DE24.............. 232 F8
Westmoor Rd S43....96 F4
Westmoreland Rd
　S41................76 D1
Westmorland Cl
　DE21............. 219 C6
Westmorland Way
　NG16............. 171 B3
Weston Bank DE6 .. 197 F1
Weston Cl S40........95 A5
Weston Cres NG10.. 235 F4
Weston Ct DE72 ... 245 E4
Weston Hall Dr
　DE72............. 245 E5
Westonhill Chalet Pk
　DE72............. 245 C4
WESTON-ON-
　TRENT.......... 245 F5
Weston-on-Trent CE
　(Aided) Prim Sch
　DE72.............245 F5
Weston Park Ave
　DE24.............. 232 E3
Weston Park Gdns
　DE24.............. 232 D3
Weston Rd
　Aston-on-Trent
　DE72............. 246 A7
　Weston-on-Trent
　DE72.............245 F6
Weston Rise DE73 .. 245 A8
Weston Spot Cl
　DE5............... 180 D7
Weston St
　Heanor DE75 ..... 194 A8
　Swadlincote DE11 ...256 B3
WESTON
　UNDERWOOD..... 189 A2
West Park Sch SK10 . 236 D7
West Park L Ctr
　NG10 .... 236 D6
*West Park Mdw Nature
　Reserve ★ DE21... 220 C5*
West Park Rd DE22 . 218 E8
West Park Sch
　DE21............. 220 D5
West Rd
　Buxton SK17........85 B6
　Derby DE21 ...... 220 D5
West Road Ho **2**
　SK17...............85 B6
West Row DE22.... 205 A1
West Service Rd
　DE21............. 220 B3
West St
　Bramley-Vale S44... 117 D1
　Burton upon Trent
　DE15.............248 B3
　Chesterfield S40... 266 A4
　Clay Cross S45 .... 131 A4
　Clowne S43.........81 A5
　Creswell S80 ....81 D1
　Dronfield S18.......56 F2
　Eckington S21.......59 C2
　Glossop SK13..........9 F7
　Heanor DE75 ..... 181 D2
　Ilkeston DE7.......208 E7
　Langley Mill NG16...182 B3
　Shirebrook NG20 ....120 D4
　Somercotes DE55... 170 C6
　South Normanton
　DE55..............159 F5
　Stonebroom DE55...146 F3
　Swadlincote DE11 ...256 B4
　Whaley Thorns NG20 101 A3
West Terr **6** DE7....194 F1
WESTTHORPE.......60 D4
Westthorpe Fields Rd
　S21................60 C4
Westthorpe Rd S21...60 D5
West Towers Mews
　SK6................23 A4
West View
　Barlborough S43 .....80 A6
　Bolsover S44 ......118 B8
　Hulland Village DE6..175 E2
　Mayfield DE6 ......184 D6
　Parwich DE6.......151 E1
　Rocester ST14 .....197 A3
　Staveley S43.........78 D1
　Tibshelf DE55.......147 F6

West View Ave
　DE23............. 231 B7
West View Cl S17.....55 F6
West View La
　Sheffield S17 ....55 F6
　Sheffield S17 ....56 A6
West View Rd S41....95 E6
Westward Cl ST14 . 210 B1
Westwell Ct S21......59 C6
Westwell Pl S20......59 D6
Westwick Cres S8 ....56 D7
Westwick Gr S8 .....56 E7
Westwick La S42.....94 D2
Westwick Pk S41.....76 D3
Westwick Rd S8......56 E7
Westwick St DE7 ... 209 B6
WESTWOOD....... 171 C3
Westwood Ave S43...97 C8
Westwood Cl S43.....97 C5
Westwood Dr
　Derby DE24 ...... 232 D5
　Staveley S43........97 C5
Westwood Drive Gdns
　S43................97 B5
Westwood Gdns
　DE55..............147 B5
Westwood Inf Sch
　NG16............. 171 C4
Westwood La S43.....96 F4
Westwood Pk DE11.. 255 F5
Westwood Rd S44.....97 A4
Wetherby Cl NG16.. 195 C7
Wetherby Ct DE14 . 253 F7
Wetherby Rd DE24.. 232 E7
Wetherel Rd DE15 .. 248 C2
Wetlands La S43, S44 .96 E4
Wetsough La DE4.... 141 D6
WETTON........... 149 A3
Wetton La DE55 ... 148 A6
Weyacres DE72..... 221 C1
Weybridge Cl DE7 . 207 D8
WHALEY........... 100 D4
WHALEY BRIDGE....45 D7
Whaley Bridge Prim Sch
　SK23................45 E7
Whaley Bridge Sta
　SK23................45 E8
Whaley Common
　NG20 .... 100 D4
Whaley La SK23......45 C8
Whaley Rd
　Bolsover S44 ....99 F3
　Holbeck NG20.......101 B5
　Whaley S44.........100 B3
　Whaley Thorns NG20 .100 C2
WHALEY THORNS .. 101 A2
Whaley Thorns Her Ctr ★
　NG20 .... 101 A3
Whaley Thorns Ind Est
　NG20.............100 F2
Whaley Thorns Prim Sch
　NG20 .... 101 A3
Wharf Ct SK23......45 E7
Wharfedale Cl DE22 205 B4
Wharfedale Rd
　NG10 .... 236 A6
Wharf Hos DE13 ... 253 A1
Wharf La
　Chesterfield S41.....266 B4
　Staveley S43........78 F3
　Tibshelf DE55 ..... 148 C7
Wharf Rd
　Pinxton NG16.......160 D2
　Whaley Bridge SK23...45 E7
Wharf Road Ind Est
　NG16............. 160 D2
WHARF THE 210 C1
Wharf The DE72 ... 235 B7
Wharmby Ave NG19. 135 D3
Wharncliffe Cl SK13 ..9 E4
Wharncliffe Rd DE7. 208 E8
Wharton Dr S41.... 266 C3
WHATSTANDWELL. 156 C1
Whatstandwell Sta
　DE4............... 156 C1
Wheal La SK17 .... 107 D7
Wheatbridge Rd
　S40............... 266 A3
Wheatbridge Ret Pk
　S40............... 266 A2
WHEATCROFT 157 A7
Wheatcroft SK13 .....9 E4
Wheatcroft Cl
　Clay Cross S45 .... 131 D2
　Wingerworth S42.....115 A4
　Wirksworth DE4.....165 F6
Wheatcroft Dr DE56 168 B5
Wheatcroft La
　1 Castle Donington
　DE74..............246 E3
　Crich DE4 ....157 A7
Wheatcroft Way
　DE21............. 205 C2
Wheatfield Cres
　NG19 .... 136 E5
Wheatfield Ct DE65. 242 D5
Wheatfields SK23.....47 C7
Wheatfield Way S42..94 F5
Wheathill Cl
　Calow S43..........96 A5
Wheathill Gr DE23.. 231 A6
Wheatland Cl DE24 . 231 C2
Wheatlands DE11.... 256 B7
Wheatlands La DE45 .91 C5

Wheatlands Rd
　Burton upon Trent
　DE15..............254 E7
　Wingerworth S42....114 E4
Wheatley Ave DE55 . 159 C1
Wheatley Cl NG19 .. 136 F1
Wheatley Gdns DE4. 127 D2
Wheatley La DE15 .. 248 C4
Wheatley Rd DE4 .. 127 D3
Wheatsheaf Cl
　Derby DE21 ...... 206 C2
　Horwich End SK23 ...45 E6
Wheatsheaf La DE4. 156 F1
Wheatsheaf Rd SK23. 45 E6
Wheatsheaf Way
　S43................80 D2
Wheeldon Ave
　Belper DE56.......179 B4
　Derby DE22 ...... 218 E8
Wheeldon Cl NE7... 194 F6
Wheeldon Cres S43...96 D7
Wheeldon Manor
　DE22............. 218 E8
Wheeldon Way DE6. 175 E3
Wheelton Farming
　Office Buildings
　DE12..............259 B7
Wheelwright Way
　DE24............. 219 D3
Whenby Cl DE3.... 217 C2
Whernside Cl DE24 . 233 D6
WHESTON...........68 F5
Wheston Bank
　Tideswell SK17......69 B4
　Wheston SK17 .....68 F5
Wheston Ct **7** S40 ..95 D5
Wheston La
　Peak Forest SK17.....49 D1
　Wheston SK17 .....68 E7
Whetmorhurst La
　SK6................23 E4
Whilton Cres DE7... 207 D8
Whilton Ct DE56.... 179 D4
Whinacre Cl S8......57 B6
Whinacre Pl S8......57 A6
Whinacre Wlk S8.....57 A6
Whinbush Ave DE24 232 E5
Whinfell Rd
　Chesterfield S41......76 D1
　Chesterfield S41.....95 C8
Whinney Bank
　NG19 .... 136 D4
Whinney Hill NG19.. 136 D4
Whippet Way S40 ....96 C7
Whisperwood Cl S44 .98 A5
Whistlestop Cl DE3 . 217 D4
Whiston St DE23.... 219 A2
Whitaker Gdns
　DE23............. 218 E2
Whitaker Mews
　ST14.............. 196 F3
Whitaker Rd DE23.. 218 E2
Whitaker St DE23... 219 A2
Whitburn Rd NG9... 223 E3
Whitby Ave DE21... 205 C1
Whitcombe Pl DE5 . 169 D4
White Ash Rd DE55 . 159 E4
Whitebank Cl S41 .. 266 C1
Whitecarr La DE55,
　S45............... 145 B4
White Carr La DE55...145 B4
Whitecotes Cl S40... 114 E8
Whitecotes La S40.. 114 E8
Whitecotes Pk S40 . 114 F8
Whitecotes Prim Sch
　S40............... 114 F8
Whitecroft Rd SK6....23 C1
Whitecross Ave SK17 .69 D4
Whitecross Gdns
　DE1............... 218 E7
Whitecross Ho DE1. 218 E7
Whitecross Ind Est
　SK17................69 D5
Whitecross Rd SK17 .69 D5
Whitecross St DE1... 218 E6
White Edge Cl S40....95 D5
White Edge Dr DE45 .91 E6
Whitefield La
　Ashover S45........129 A5
　Chelmorton SK17....106 E8
White Gate Rd HD9 ...3 D7
Whitegates SK14 .....9 A1
White Gates DE5 ... 181 B8
Whitegates Way
　NG17..............148 F2
Whitehall Terr SK23 ..34 D1
White Hart Cl DE7 . 207 D7
White Hart Cnr S21...59 E4
White Hart Yd DE56..179 F1
Whitehaven Gr
　DE73.............. 233 A3
Whitehead Cl DE7.. 194 D2
Whitehead Dr NG16. 182 D3
Whitehead St **4**
　S43................78 D1
White Horse La
　DE55.............. 145 D7
WHITEHOUGH.......46 D8
WHITEHOUGH
　HEAD.............46 E8
Whitehough Head La
　SK23................46 A6
Whitehouse Cl
　DE24.............. 232 D1
Whitehouse Rise
　DE56.............. 178 E6
Whitehouses S41... 266 C1
Whitehurst St DE24. 232 D1

White Knowle Cl
 SK17 . . . . .85 C5
White Knowle Pk
 SK17 . . . . .85 C5
White Knowle Rd
 SK17 . . . . .85 C5
White La
 Eckington S12 . . . . .44 C2
 Shottle DE56 . . . . .177 D4
Whitelands Cl DE72 . 246 A7
Whitclca DE4 . . . . 144 B6
White Leas S40 . . . . .95 B4
White Leas Ave S42 . 132 A7
Whiteleas Rd SK23 . . . .45 D3
WHITELEY 180 F6
Whiteley Rd DE5 . . . .180 F7
White Lion Sq DE7 . . .208 F7
White Lodge La DE45 .91 E6
Whitelow La
 Ible DE4 . . . . .153 E7
 Sheffield S17 . . . . .55 B7
Whitely Ave DE7 . . .194 F5
Whitely Cl 3 NG9 . . 223 E8
WHITE MOOR 179 C5
Whitemoor Hall
 DE56 . . . . .179 D5
Whitemoor La DE56 179 D5
White Rd
 New Mills SK22 . . . . . . .24 C2
 Staveley S43 . . . . .79 A3
White Rock Ct DE4 . 143 D6
Whites Cl DE55 . . . .159 A2
Whites Croft View
 S43 . . . . .80 B6
Whites La
 Blackwell DE55 . . . . . .147 F1
 Somercotes DE55 . . . . .170 B8
Whitesmead Cl SK12 .32 D5
White St DE22 . . . . .218 C4
White Thorns Cl S8 . .57 B5
White Thorns Dr S8 . .57 B6
White Thorns View
 S8 . . . . .57 B6
White Tor Rd DE4 . . 143 C2
Whiteway DE22 . . . . .204 E2
Whitewell Gdns
 DE24 . . . . .233 C5
Whitewells La DE56 . 178 C8
Whitewells Rd DE56 167 E2
Whitewood Way
 DE4 . . . . .143 B3
WHITFIELD 17 C8
Whitfield Ave SK13 . . . .17 C7
Whitfield Cross SK13 . .17 D7
Whitfield La DE45 . . .124 E2
Whitfield Pk SK13 . . . .17 C7
Whitfield Wells SK13 . .17 D7
Whiting Ave 2 NG9 .223 F2
Whiting St 8 S8 . . . .43 A6
Whitle Bank Rd SK22 .24 B2
Whitle Rd SK22 . . . . . .24 C1
Whitley Way DE6 . . . .185 E8
Whitley Wlk SK13 . . . . .16 F8
Whitmore Ave S42 . . 115 E2
Whitmore Rd DE21 . .219 F6
Whitsome Rd DE23 . 231 E1
Whitstable Cl DE23 . 231 D7
Whittaker La DE21 . . 191 D2
Whitt Cl DE72 . . . . . . .221 C1
Whittinglands Cl
 DE73 . . . . .233 A3
Whitting Mews S41 . .76 F2
Whittington Green Sch
 S41 . . . . .77 B3
Whittington Hill S41 . .77 A2
Whittington La S18 . .76 F5
WHITTINGTON
 MOOR 96 A7
Whittington Moor Inf
 Acad 9 S41 . . . . .96 A8
Whittington Rd S43 . . .77 F4
Whittington St
 DE24 . . . . .232 D6
Whittington Way
 S41 . . . . .77 A1
Whitting Valley Rd
 S41 . . . . .77 B1
Whittlebury Dr
 DE23 . . . . .230 F7
Whitton Pl S44 . . . . . .98 A6
WHITWELL 81 E6
Whitwell S80 . . . . .82 A5
Whitwell Bank 5
 SK13 . . . . .9 D2
Whitwell Cl
 4 Gamesley SK13 . . . . .9 D2
 Ilkeston NE7 . . . . .194 E6
Whitwell Fold 1 SK13 .9 D2
Whitwell Gn 2 SK13 . .9 D2
Whitwell Lea 3 SK13 . .9 D2
Whitwell Prim Sch
 S80 . . . . .82 A5
Whitwell Rd S80 . . . . .63 A4
Whitwell Sta S80 . . . . .82 A5
Whitworth Ave DE4 . 127 C3
Whitworth Cl DE12 . 262 E4
Whitworth Hospl
 DE4 . . . . .142 F8
Whitworth Rd
 Chesterfield S41 . . . . . . .95 F6
 1 Chesterfield S41 . . . . .96 A6
 Darley Dale DE4 . . . . . .127 B4
 Ilkeston DE7 . . . . .208 F7
Wholey Pl S45 . . . . . .131 C3
Whysall Rd NG10 . . . .236 B7
Whysall St DE75 . . . .181 E2
Whyteleafe Gr DE21 . 206 B1
Whytes La SK14 . . . .196 F5

Wibben Cl DE21 . . . .205 F3
Wichal Farm Cl
 DE5 . . . . .180 D7
Wicken La SK23 . . . . . .35 A4
Wickenlow La SK17 . 103 D1
Wickersley Cl 1
 DE22 . . . . .204 F2
Wickets The DE15 . . .254 F8
Wickfield Cl S12 . . . . . .44 F5
Wickfield Dr S12 . . . . . .44 F5
Wickfield Gr S12 . . . . . .44 F5
Wickfield Pl S12 . . . . . .44 F5
Wickfield Rd S12 . . . . . .44 F5
Wickins Pl S43 . . . . . .79 B3
Wicksteed Cl DE56 . .179 D5
Widdop Cl S13 . . . . . . .44 D8
Widdop Croft S13 . . . .44 D8
 NG10 . . . . .236 B5
Widdybank Cl DE22 . 204 C2
Widecombe Ct 24
 S41 . . . . .95 F8
Wideshaft DE11 . . . . 256 C4
Widmerpool St
 NG16 . . . . .160 C2
Wifel Green DE73 . . .252 E5
WIGLEY 93 F4
Wigley Prim Sch S42 . .93 F4
Wigley Rd S43 . . . . . . .97 C6
Wigmore Cl DE3 . . . 217 C3
Wikeley Way S43 . . . .96 D7
Willow Rd
 NG19 . . . . .135 D2
Wilcock Ho DE21 . . .219 C6
Wilcox Ave NG19 . . .136 B5
WILDAY GREEN 75 A2
Wildaygreen La S18 . .75 B2
Wilday Green La S17 .74 F3
Wilden Croft S43 . . . . .96 C8
Wilderbrook La
 DE56 . . . . .178 A8
Wilders Lea Ct
 DE56 . . . . .179 A2
Wildersley Rd DE56 . 179 A1
Wilders Way DE74 . . 247 E2
Wildflower Cl S44 . . . .97 A3
Wildhay Brook
 DE65 . . . . .228 C1
Wildhay La DE6 . . . . .183 C7
Wild Hill NG17 . . . . . .148 E7
Wild La DE4, DE55 . . .157 B4
Wildpark La DE6 . . . .202 D6
Wildsmith St DE24 . . 233 A8
Wild St DE22 . . . . . . .218 D5
Wilfred St DE23 . . . . .219 B2
Wilhallow La NG16 . . 171 E2
Wilkin Hill S18 . . . . . . .75 E2
Wilkins Dr DE24 . . . .232 E7
Wilkinson Cl
 Chesterfield S40 . . . . . .115 A6
 Pleasley NG19 . . . . . . .135 A5
Wilkinson Dr S43 . . . . .97 B7
Willbury Dr S12 . . . . . .44 A6
Willcock Rd DE14 . . .254 A7
 DE4 . . . . .155 B7
Willersley Castle *
Willersley Ct 3 S41 .95 C7
Willersley Ho NG10 . 236 A5
Willersley La
 Matlock DE4 . . . . .143 C1
 Matlock Bath DE4 . . . . .155 C8
Willesden Ave DE22 . 218 A7
Willetts Rd DE11 . . . .220 A7
William Allitt Sch The
 DE11 . . . . .255 E7
William Ave NG16 . . .182 F2
William Brown Square
 S40 . . . . .266 B1
William Cl
 Duffield DE56 . . . . .190 D4
 Sheffield S20 . . . . .59 D6
William Cres S20 . . . . .59 D6
William Gilbert CE
 Endowed Prim Sch
 DE56 . . . . .190 E4
William Gregg VC L Ctr
 DE75 . . . . .181 F1
William Holmes
 Almshouses DE5 . .169 F2
William Levick Prim Sch
 S18 . . . . .56 C2
William Lilley Inf Sch
 NG9 . . . . .223 D6
William Nadin Way
 DE11 . . . . .255 F4
William Newton Cl
 DE65 . . . . .241 B6
William Rd NG9 . . . .223 D7
William Rhodes Prim
 Sch S40 . . . . .266 A2
Williams Cl DE55 . . . 170 D6
William Shrewsbury
 County Prim Sch
 DE13 . . . . .240 E1
Williamson Ave SK17 .66 C1
Williamson Cres
 SK23 . . . . .45 D8
Williamson Gdns
 NG16 . . . . .182 A2
Williamson Rd SK23 . .45 D8
William St
 Belper DE56 . . . . .178 F4
 Chesterfield S41 . . . . . . .96 A4
 Derby DE1 . . . . .218 E6
 Eckington S21 . . . . .59 D3
 Long Eaton NG10 . . . . .223 D2
William Street N S41 .76 F2
WILLIAMTHORPE . . 132 C8

Williamthorpe Cl
 S42 . . . . .132 A7
Williamthorpe Ind Pk
 S42 . . . . .116 D2
Williamthorpe Ponds *
 S42 . . . . .116 E2
Williamthorpe Rd
 S42 . . . . .132 B7
William Wood La
 NG20 . . . . .120 C5
WILLINGTON 242 A6
Willington Prim Sch
 DE65 . . . . .242 B5
Willington Rd
 Etwall DE65 . . . . .229 D3
 Findern DE65 . . . . . . .242 D8
 Repton DE65 . . . . .242 B4
Willington Sta DE65 242 A6
Willn St DE23 . . . . . .218 F1
Willoughby Almshouses
 NG16 . . . . .195 C1
Willoughby Ave
 NG10 . . . . .223 C3
Willoughby Cl DE72 .235 F8
Willoughby Ct DE72 .222 D4
Willoughby Ho
 DE11 . . . . .256 C4
Willow Ave
 Long Eaton NG10 . . . . .223 D1
 Ripley DE5 . . . . .180 D7
 Shirebrook NG20 . . . . .119 D5
 Stapleford NG9 . . . . . .223 D6
Willow Bank
 Somersal Herbert
 DE6 . . . . .211 F3
 Somersal Herbert
 DE6 . . . . .212 A2
Willowbath La DE4 . .165 F7
Willowbrook Cl
 DE65 . . . . .228 C2
Willowbrook Grange
 DE73 . . . . .233 A1
Willow Cl
 Aldercar NG16 . . . . . . .182 B4
 Alfreton DE55 . . . . . . .159 B5
 Aston-on-Trent DE72 . . .246 B7
 Creswell S80 . . . . .81 F1
 Derby DE72 . . . . .204 F2
 Pilsley S45 . . . . .132 C1
 South Normanton
 DE55 . . . . .160 B5
 Stanley Common DE7 . .193 A2
Willow Croft DE24 . . 233 C4
Willowcroft Rd
 DE21 . . . . .220 E4
Willow Ct
 Ashbourne DE6 . . . . . .185 D7
 Calow S44 . . . . .97 A3
 Swadlincote DE11 . . . . .256 C4
Willow Dr
 Chapel-en-le-Frith
 SK23 . . . . .47 B5
 Mastin Moor S43 . . . . . .79 C4
 Swadlincote DE11 . . . . .255 F7
Willow Farm Bsns Pk
 DE74 . . . . .247 B6
Willow Farm Ct
 DE65 . . . . .230 D2
Willowfields DE65 . . 228 D2
Willow Garth Rd S41 .95 C8
Willow Gr
 Belper DE56 . . . . .179 A2
 Willington DE65 . . . . . .242 A6
Willow Grove DE73 . .232 F1
Willowherb Cl DE24 .231 F2
Willow Ho DE21 . . . .219 C6
Willow Meadow Rd
 DE6 . . . . .185 D7
Willow Park Way
 DE72 . . . . .246 A7
Willowpit La DE65 . . 228 E5
Willow Pl DE15 . . . . 254 E7
Willow Rd
 Castle Donington
 DE74 . . . . .247 B5
 Killamarsh S21 . . . . . . .60 C5
Willow Rise NG10 . . .223 B5
Willow Row DE1 . . . .267 A4
Willows Ave DE55 . . .159 B5
Willows Ct DE5 . . . . .169 C1
Willowsend Cl
 DE65 . . . . .230 D1
Willowside Gn
 DE21 . . . . .220 D3
Willow Sq S42 . . . . . 115 C1
Willows Sports Ctr
 DE1 . . . . .267 A4
Willow St DE55 . . . . 146 C1
Willows The
 Chesterfield S40 . . . . . . .95 B1
 Hulland Ward DE6 . . . .175 F3
 Pleasley NG19 . . . . . . .135 A6
 Shirland DE55 . . . . . . .146 C4
Willow Stream SK22 . .33 D8
Willow Tree Cl DE3 . 217 D2
Willowtree Dr DE21 . 220 B7
Willow Tree Dr S43 . . .80 F2
Willow Way DE4 . . . .127 B3
Willridding La DE6 . .183 C7
Will Shore's La DE4 . 142 D6
Willson Ave DE23 . . .231 D8
Willson Dr DE55 . . . .170 C7
Willson Rd DE23 . . . .231 C8
Wilmans Wlk SK13 . . . .10 A6
Wilmington Ave
 DE24 . . . . .233 B5
Wilmore Rd DE24 . . .232 B5
WILMORTON 219 E2

Wilmot Ave
 Derby DE21 . . . . .219 F5
 Weston-on-Trent
 DE72 . . . . .245 E5
Wilmot Dr DE7 . . . . .192 F6
Wilmot Rd
 Belper DE56 . . . . .179 A4
 Swadlincote DE11 . . . . .256 B3
Wilmot St
 Derby DE1 . . . . .267 B2
 Heanor DE75 . . . . . . .181 E1
 3 Heanor DE75 . . . . .193 E8
 Ilkeston DE7 . . . . .194 E1
 Long Eaton NG10 . . . . .236 A5
 Matlock DE4 . . . . .143 B6
Wilmslow Dr DE21 . . 206 B1
Wilne Ave NG10 . . . .236 A4
Wilne Cl NG10 . . . . .235 F4
Wilne La
 Breaston DE72 . . . . . . .235 D4
 Shardlow DE72 . . . . . . .235 B2
Wilne Rd
 Draycott DE72 . . . . . . .235 B5
 Long Eaton NG10 . . . . .235 F4
Wilshaw Bottom La
 SK17 . . . . .104 B2
Wilshaw Cl SK23 . . . .47 C5
WILSON 252 F6
Wilson Ave
 Blackwell DE55 . . . . . .147 E1
 Clowne S43 . . . . .80 F5
 Heanor DE75 . . . . . . .181 B4
Wilson Cl
 Burnaston DE3 . . . . . .230 C8
 Clay Cross S45 . . . . . .131 D2
Wilson La S44 . . . . . .117 B2
Wilson Pl 6 S8 . . . . .43 A7
Wilson Rd
 Derby DE21 . . . . .219 F8
 Dronfield S18 . . . . .57 C4
 Eastwood NG16 . . . . . .182 F1
Wilson Rise DE73 . . .252 E6
Wilson St
 Alfreton DE55 . . . . . . .159 B4
 Derby DE1 . . . . .267 B2
 Dronfield S18 . . . . .76 B8
 Mansfield NG19 . . . . . .135 D2
 Pinxton NG16 . . . . . . .160 D3
Wilson's Terr SK13 . .17 B8
WILSTHORPE 236 B7
Wilsthorpe Rd
 Breaston DE72 . . . . . . .235 F8
 Derby DE21 . . . . .220 A7
 Long Eaton NG10 . . . . .236 B7
Wilsthorpe Sch
 NG10 . . . . .223 B1
Wilton Cl DE24 . . . . 231 C2
Wilton Pl DE7 . . . . . .194 F1
Wilton St DE7 . . . . . .194 F1
Wiltra Gr DE56 . . . . .190 F3
Wiltshire Ave NG16 . 171 B4
Wiltshire Dr SK13 . . . .17 F8
Wiltshire Rd DE21 . . 219 E7
Wimbledon Rd
 DE22 . . . . .218 A7
Wimborne Cres S41 . .95 F7
Wimbourne Cl
 DE73 . . . . .233 A2
Wimpole Gdns
 DE22 . . . . .218 B6
Wimsey Way DE55 . .159 B2
Wincanton Cl DE24 . 219 D1
Winchcombe Dr
 DE15 . . . . .248 B1
Winchcombe Way
 DE21 . . . . .206 B2
Winchester Cl S42 . .131 F6
Winchester Cres
 DE7 . . . . .209 A8
Winchester Dr
 Burton upon Trent
 DE14 . . . . .254 C8
 Linton DE12 . . . . .261 D5
 Mansfield Woodhouse
 NG19 . . . . .136 D4
 Swadlincote DE11 . . . . .256 D6
Winchester Rd S41 . . .95 E7
Wincobank Way
 DE55 . . . . .160 C7
Winder Ave
 Killamarsh S20 . . . . . . .60 A6
 Sheffield S21 . . . . .59 F6
Windermere Ave
 Dronfield S18 . . . . .56 E1
 Ilkeston DE7 . . . . .208 D5
Windermere Cl
 NG10 . . . . .136 C2
Windermere Cres
 DE22 . . . . .204 E5
Windermere Dr
 DE21 . . . . .220 C5
Windermere Drive
 DE65 . . . . .228 E1
Windermere Gdns
 NG10 . . . . .223 B2
Windermere Rd
 Chesterfield S41 . . . . . . .95 D7
 Clay Cross S45 . . . . . .131 B3
 Long Eaton NG10 . . . . .223 B2
Winders Cnr S43 . . . . .80 B5
Windgather Rd
 Kettleshulme SK23 . . . . .45 A1
 Oldfield SK23 . . . . .64 E8
Winding Wheel The *
 S41 . . . . .266 C3
Windlass Way DE21 . .220 F2
Windlea Rd DE55 . . .170 C6

WINDLEY 189 D7
Windley Cres
 DE22 . . . . .204 F1
Windley Dr DE7 . . . . 194 D3
Windley La
 Idridgehay DE56 . . . . . .176 E5
 Turnditch DE56 . . . . . .177 A1
 Windley DE56 . . . . . . .189 E7
WINDMILL 70 A8
Windmill Ave
 DE56 . . . . .192 A8
Windmill Cl
 4 Albert Village DE11 256 F1
 Bolsover S44 . . . . .99 A3
 Castle Donington DE74 247 B2
 Elvaston DE24 . . . . . . .233 D4
 Ockbrook DE72 . . . . . .221 C5
 Ripley DE5 . . . . .181 A8
 3 Uttoxeter ST14 . . . .210 B1
Windmill Dr ST14 . . .224 E3
Windmill Greenway
 S20 . . . . .59 C2
Windmill Hill La
 DE22 . . . . .218 C6
Windmill La
 Alderwasley DE56 . . . . .166 F6
 Ashbourne DE6 . . . . . .173 C4
 Belper DE56 . . . . .179 A4
 Eyam S32 . . . . .71 C6
 Snelston DE6 . . . . .184 E2
 Unstone S18 . . . . .77 A6
Windmill Mdw
 DE21 . . . . .220 D5
Windmill Pl DE21 . . .205 D3
Windmill Rd DE65 . . .229 B3
Windmill Rise
 Belper DE56 . . . . .179 A5
 Somercotes DE55 . . . . .170 D7
 South Normanton
 DE55 . . . . .159 F5
Windmill St DE11 . . .256 A1
Windmill View
 DE56 . . . . .179 E8
Windmill Way
 S43 . . . . .96 C8
Windrush Cl DE22 . . 205 B5
 S43 . . . . .96 C8
Windrush Ct 4
 S43 . . . . .96 E8
Windrush Rd DE65 . . 240 D8
Windses Est S32 . . . .53 D2
Windsmoor Rd
 NG16 . . . . .182 C8
Windsor Ave
 Derby DE23 . . . . .231 B8
 Hatton DE65 . . . . .227 D2
 Melbourne DE73 . . . . . .252 A8
Windsor Cl
 6 Ashbourne DE6 . . . .173 D3
 Borrowash DE7 . . . . . .221 C1
 Chesterfield S40 . . . . . . .95 C1
 Heanor DE75 . . . . . . .181 E3
 Swadlincote DE11 . . . . .256 A6
 Swanwick DE55 . . . . . .170 A7
 Trowell NG9 . . . . .209 B5
Windsor Cres
 Ilkeston DE7 . . . . .208 E4
 Stapleford NG9 . . . . . .223 E7
Windsor Ct
 Derby DE3 . . . . .217 D3
 Long Eaton NG10 . . . . .236 E7
 Sandiacre NG10 . . . . . .223 B4
 West Hallam DE7 . . . . .207 D8
Windsor Dr
 Derby DE21 . . . . .221 A6
 Dronfield S18 . . . . .56 C1
 Wingerworth S42 . . . . .114 E4
Windsor Park Rd
 SK17 . . . . .85 D8
Windsor Rd
 Buxton SK17 . . . . .85 C8
 Linton DE12 . . . . .261 D5
 Uttoxeter ST14 . . . . . .210 A1
Windsor St NG9 . . . .223 E7
Windsor Wlk 7
 S41 . . . . .96 C1
Windwhistle Dr 4
 S41 . . . . 115 F2
Windy Arbour DE6 . .202 D5
Windy Fields Rd
 S42 . . . . .113 D7
Windy House La S2 . .44 A8
Windy Knowle SK22 . .25 A3
Windy La DE21 . . . . .191 C1
Windyridge SK17 . . .121 B6
Winfield Gr SK6 . . . . .15 B1
Winfield Way DE11 . .257 B1
WINGERWORTH 114 F4
Wingerworth Ave
 S8 . . . . .56 D8
Wingerworth Cotts
 S42 . . . . 115 E3
Wingerworth Park Rd
 DE21 . . . . .220 E5
Wingerworth St
 S42 . . . . 115 E3
Wingerworth Way
 S40 . . . . .114 F7
Wingfield Cl 6
 S18 . . . . .56 C1
Wingfield Cres
 Harpur Hill SK17 . . . . . .85 D1
 Sheffield S12 . . . . .44 C5
Wingfield Dr
 Derby DE21 . . . . .205 F1
 Ilkeston DE7 . . . . .194 D3
Wingfield Gr SK13 . . . .17 F7
Wingfield Hall
 DE55 . . . . .157 F1

Whi–Wol 317

Wingfield Manor
 House * DE55 . . . . .157 E2
Wingfield Pk
 Crich Common DE55 . . .168 C8
 Fritchley DE56 . . . . . . .168 F5
Wingfield Rd
 Alfreton DE55 . . . . . . .158 E3
 Tupton S42 . . . . .131 D8
Wingfield View S45 . 131 E4
Winhill Rd SK22 . . . . . .24 C1
Winkpenny La DE55 .147 F5
Winnat Pl S43 . . . . . . .97 C7
Winnats Cl
 Chesterfield S40 . . . . . . .95 D5
 Glossop SK13 . . . . .17 E8
Winnats Pass S33 . . . .38 A2
Winnats Rd S33 . . . . . .37 E2
Winney Hill S26 . . . . . .61 E5
Winney La S26 . . . . . . .61 E3
Winnings The S80 . . 101 E8
Winnington Rd SK6 . .23 A7
Winn La DE6 . . . . .174 F7
WINSHILL 248 B3
Winshill Village Prim
 Sch DE15 . . . . .248 C3
WINSICK 115 E6
Winslow Ave SK14 . . . .9 A2
Winslow Gn DE21 . . .220 C6
WINSTER 141 C6
Winster CE Prim Sch
 DE4 . . . . .141 D6
Winster Cl
 Belper DE56 . . . . .179 B5
 Clay Cross S42 . . . . . .131 A5
Winster Ct S41 . . . . . .96 A5
Winster Gn 3 DE11 . 255 C6
Winster Gr SK17 . . . . .85 E7
Winster La DE4 . . . . .140 F7
Winster Market House *
 DE4 . . . . .141 C6
Winster Mews SK13 . .9 E2
Winster Rd
 Derby DE21 . . . . .205 E1
 Staveley S43 . . . . .97 C8
Winster Sq SK17 . . . .85 E7
Winster Way NG10 . .235 F5
Winston Cl NG9 . . . .223 E8
Winterbourne Dr
 NG9 . . . . .209 E1
Winter Closes NG16 . 171 F1
Wintercroft La DE4 . .161 E1
Wintergreen Dr
 DE23 . . . . .230 F6
Winyard Ct 9 S40 . . .95 D5
Wire La DE55 . . . . . .148 B3
Wirestone La
 Ashover S45 . . . . .128 D7
 Ashover S45 . . . . .129 A3
Wirksmoor Rd SK22 . .33 D7
WIRKSWORTH 165 E8
Wirksworth CE Inf Sch
 DE4 . . . . .154 F1
Wirksworth Dale
 DE4 . . . . .153 B2
Wirksworth Hall Gdns
 DE4 . . . . .165 F8
Wirksworth Heritage
 Ctr * DE4 . . . . .154 F1
Wirksworth Ind Ctr
 DE4 . . . . .154 F3
Wirksworth Inf Sch
 DE4 . . . . .154 F1
Wirksworth Jun Sch
 DE4 . . . . .155 A1
Wirksworth L Ctr
 DE4 . . . . .165 F8
Wirksworth Rd
 Duffield DE56 . . . . .190 B4
 Holloway DE4 . . . . . . .156 B2
 Idridgehay DE56 . . . . . .176 D2
 Ilkeston DE7 . . . . .208 C2
 Kirk Ireton DE6 . . . . . .165 B2
 Shottle DE56 . . . . .177 C3
 Windley DE56 . . . . . . .189 F6
Wirksworth Sta *
 DE4 . . . . .155 A1
Wisbech Cl S40 . . . . 114 E8
Wisgreaves Rd
 DE24 . . . . .232 F8
Wishing Stone Way
 DE4 . . . . .143 E6
Wistanes Gn DE55 . .145 D1
Wisteria Way SK13 . . .10 C3
Wiston Way S41 . . . . 115 C7
Witham Cl
 Chesterfield S41 . . . . . . .96 C6
 Hilton DE65 . . . . .228 E2
Witham Ct S40 . . . . . .95 C3
Witham Dr DE23 . . . 231 D6
Witney Cl DE24 . . . .232 C8
Witney St S8 . . . . .43 A8
Wittering Cl NG10 . . 236 E5
Witton Cl DE24 . . . . 231 D4
Woburn Cl
 Blackwell DE55 . . . . . .147 E4
 Swanwick DE55 . . . . . .169 F7
Woburn Cotts DE4 . . 143 B8
Woburn Croft NG10 . 223 A4
Woburn Ho DE55 . . .147 E1
Woburn La NG19 . . . 135 C4
Woburn Pl
 Derby DE22 . . . . .218 B5
 Pleasley NG19 . . . . . . .135 C4
Woburn Rd NG19 . . . 135 C4
Wolds Rd DE4 . . . . .143 D7

Wolds Rise DE4 .... 143 C7
Wolfa St DE22 ...... 267 A2
Wolfcote Cl S45 ... 131 D1
Wolfe Cl S40 .... 95 D1
Wolfscote Cl DE21...205 F3
Wolfscote Dale DE11 255 F2
Wollaton Ave S17 ....56 A5
Wollaton Dr S17......56 A5
Wollaton Rd
  Derby DE21 ....219 F8
  Sheffield S17 ....56 A5
Wollaton Road N 5
  DE21................205 F1
Wollen Cl S80 ....81 F1
Wolseley Rd 2 S8...43 A7
Wolverley Grange
  DE24...............233 D6
Woodale Cl DE23 ...230 F6
WOODALL.............61 C6
Woodall La S26......61 D6
Woodall Rd S21 ......60 F5
Woodall Way S21.....60 F5
Wood Ave
  Creswell S80 ....81 D1
  Sandiacre NG10 .....223 A6
Woodbank Ct S17.....56 A7
Woodbeck Ct DE21 .206 B2
Woodbine Cl DE14...156 B6
Woodbine Terr SK23..47 A6
Woodborough Rd
  NG19 ....135 E1
Woodbourne Rd
  SK22................33 A5
Woodbridge Cl
  Chellaston DE73......232 F1
  Heanor DE75........182 B1
Woodbridge Jun Sch
  DE55...............159 A3
Woodbridge Rise
  S40................114 B8
Woodbrook SK23......45 E8
Woodbrook Ct SK23 ..45 E7
Woodbrook Rd SK6...23 C6
Woodchester Dr
  DE24...............233 D6
Wood Cl S42 ....114 D4
Woodcock Gr SK13....10 E1
Woodcock Sq DE3 ..230 C8
Woodcote Way
  Chesterfield S42......114 E8
  Derby DE23 ....231 A7
Wood Croft DE23 ...231 D8
Wood Cutters Way
  SK23................46 F5
WOODEND
  Disley...............32 E8
  Hanbury 238 A1
Wood End DE4 ......156 B6
Wood End La DE73..244 D1
Wood End Rd DE75..181 E2
Woodfall La
  Duffield DE56.......190 A1
  Windley DE22.......189 E3
Wood Farm Ct
  NG11 ....237 D2
Wood Farm La
  DE11...............237 D2
Woodfield Cl SK13.....9 F5
Woodfield Dr
  4 Ripley DE5........170 A1
  Swadlincote DE11 ...256 C5
Woodfield Rd
  Pinxton NG16 ......160 D4
  South Normanton
  DE55...............159 F4
Woodfield The SK17 ..85 D4
Woodford Rd DE22 ..218 A7
Woodford Way S43...78 B4
Woodgate Dr DE73 ..233 A1
Woodhall Dr DE23...230 E8
Woodhall House Farm
  S26................61 C6
WOODHEAD
  Crowden..............7 C4
  Littlemoor..........130 E2
Woodhead La S45 ..130 D1
Woodhead Rd
  Charlesworth SK13......6 C1
  Charlesworth SK13 ....11 A8
  Glossop SK13 ....10 D5
  Holme HD9 ....2 E6
  Sheffield, Highfield S2 ..43 A8
  Tintwistle SK13 ....5 E1
  Tintwistle SK13 ......10 B8
Woodhead Way 6
  DE65..............240 E8
Woodhouse Ct
  NG19 ....136 C2
Woodhouse La
  Barlborough S43......79 E5
  Bolsover S44 ....98 E3
  Heathtop DE65 .....227 A6
  Mastin Moor S43 .....79 C5
  Scropton DE65......226 F7
  South Normanton
  DE55..............159 E5
  Winster DE4........141 C6

Woodhouse Rd
  Kilburn DE56, DE7 ... 192 A7
  6 Mansfield NG19 ...136 B1
  Rowsley DE4.........126 F7
  Sheffield S12 ....44 B6
WOODHOUSES.......252 A5
Woodhouse St
  DE11...............256 D3
Woodhouse Station Ent
  Ctr NG19 ....136 B3
Woodhouse West Prim
  Sch S13............44 B6
Woodhurst Cl DE21. 219 D8
Wood La
  Belper DE56.........190 F7
  Church Warsop NG20..120 F7
  Creswell S80 ....100 C8
  Crich DE4 ....157 B3
  Hanbury DE13 ......238 A4
  Hayfield SK22........25 C3
  Holloway DE4.......144 A1
  Horsley Woodhouse
  DE7................192 D5
  Ible DE4............153 E6
  Idridgehay DE6, DE56.176 E8
  Kniveton DE4 ....163 A1
  Nether Langwith
  NG20...............101 D1
  Pleasley NG19 ......119 D1
  Ripley DE5 ....169 A4
  Scarcliffe S44........118 F6
  Shirebrook NG20.....119 E1
  Swadlincote DE11 ...256 A7
Woodland Ave
  Borrowash DE72 .....221 C2
  Breaston DE72.......235 F8
  Ilkeston DE7........194 D4
  Sutton in Ashfield
  NG17 ....148 E4
Woodland Cl
  Hodthorpe S80.......82 C6
  4 Smalley DE75....193 C8
Woodland Dr
  Rocester ST14.......196 F3
  Scropton DE6 ......226 D4
  Sheffield S12........44 B2
Woodland Gr
  Barlborough S43......80 A6
  Clay Cross S42.......131 B6
  Clowne S43...........81 A4
  Mansfield Woodhouse
  NG19 ....136 C4
Woodland Gro
  NG20 ....119 D2
Woodland Pl S17.....55 F5
Woodland Rd
  Derby DE22 ....218 E8
  Mansfield NG19......136 F1
  Sheffield S8 ....43 B3
  Swadlincote DE15 ...255 B4
Woodlands
  Brimington S43.......96 D7
  Great Longstone DE45..89 F3
  Wirksworth DE4......165 E8
Woodlands Ave
  Breaston DE72.......235 F8
  Derby DE24.........232 E4
Woodlands Brow
  DE6................173 D4
Woodlands Cl
  Castle Gresley DE11..255 E2
  Glossop SK13..........9 F6
  Little Eaton DE21 ....205 B8
  Melbourne DE73......252 A8
  Thorpe DE6..........161 D1
Woodlands Cres
  DE12...............262 B4
Woodlands La
  Chellaston DE73......245 A8
  Quarndon DE22 .....204 D6
Woodlands Rd
  Chapel-en-le-Frith
  SK23................47 B4
  Derby DE22 ....204 E5
  High Lane SK12 ......32 A6
  New Mills SK22.......33 A8
  Overseal DE12 ......262 B4
Woodlands Sch
  DE22...............204 D4
Woodlands The
  5 Mansfield NG19 ..136 B1
  Melbourne DE73......252 B8
  Tatenhill DE13 ......253 A8
  Whaley Thorns NG20..101 A3
Woodlands View
  DE7................193 A2
Woodlands Way
  Melbourne DE73......252 B8
  Spion Kop NG20 .....120 F1
Woodlands Yd DE73 245 A8
Woodland View
  Buxton SK17.........85 C8
  Chilcote DE12.......264 F3
  Crich DE4...........167 E8
  Hathersage S32.......53 A7
  Horwich End SK23....45 F2
  Sheffield, Abbeydale Park
  S17................56 A7
  Sheffield, Charnock Hill
  S12................44 B2
  Whaley Thorns NG20..101 A3

Woodland Views
  ST14..............224 E2
Woodland Way
  Clay Cross S42.......131 B6
  Eastwood NG16......182 E2
Woodland Wlk S40 ...94 F5
Woodlark Cl SK17 ....85 D2
Woodlea Gr DE21 ...205 C8
Woodlea Rd SK13.....17 B7
Woodleigh Cl S40 ...94 F5
WOODLINKIN 181 E6
Woodmans Croft
  DE65...............227 C1
Woodmere Dr S41....77 C4
Woodminton Dr
  DE73...............232 F3
WOODNOOK..........94 E5
Woodnook Cl S42....95 A4
Wood Nook Cl
  NG16...............171 F6
Woodnook Gr S21....58 E2
Woodnook La
  Chesterfield S42......94 F5
  Ingmanthorpe S18...94 C7
Woodnook Way S42...94 F4
Woodpecker Hill
  DE7................208 A2
Woodpigeon Ct S43 ..98 A7
Wood Rd
  Derby, Chaddesden
  DE21...............220 A8
  Derby, Oakwood
  DE21...............205 F1
  Derby, Spondon DE21. 221 A6
Woodridge The
  DE56...............190 F6
Woodrising Cl DE21 206 B3
Woodroffe Wlk
  DE23...............231 E7
Woodrove Ave S13 ...44 B7
Woodrove Cl S13......44 B7
Woods Cl DE15 ......248 A1
Woodsea Level
  ST14..............210 D8
Woodseat Gr ST14...197 A4
Woodseat Level
  ST14..............196 E2
WOODSEATS..........16 A6
Woodseats La SK13...16 B6
Woodsford Drive
  DE24...............233 D4
Woodshop La DE73..244 D6
WOODSIDE...........192 D4
Woodside
  Buxton SK17.........85 C7
  Carsington DE4 .....164 E7
  Crich DE4 ....168 A7
  Eastwood NG16......182 E3
  Horsley DE7 ....192 D3
Woodside Ave
  Holmesfield S18.......75 A8
  Killamarsh S21.......60 F7
  Ripley DE5 ....180 D8
Woodside Cl
  Bakewell DE45......109 D5
  Chesterfield S40......95 B4
Woodside Cres
  Ilkeston DE7........194 D5
  Long Eaton NG10 ...236 B8
Woodside St S45.....131 B4
Woodside Dr
  Bakewell DE45......109 D5
  Derby DE22 ....205 A4
Woodside La S17.....56 E2
Woodside Pl S45 ....131 B4
Woodside Rd
  Sandiacre NG10......223 B5
  Shirebrook NG20.....119 E5
  Shireoaks S81........63 F7
Woodside St S45.....33 B6
Woodside View S18 ..75 A8
Woods La
  Burton upon Trent,
  Stapenhill DE15......254 F8
  Derby DE22 ....267 A1
Woods Mdw DE72...233 D5
Woodsome Pk S42 ..116 D1
Woodsorrel Dr
  DE21...............206 B3
Wood St
  Alfreton DE55.......159 C5
  Codnor DE5 ....181 B8
  Derby DE1 ....267 C4
  Eastwood NG16......182 F3
  Glossop SK13 ....17 C8
  Hollingworth SK14......9 D5
  Holmewood S42......116 E1
  Ilkeston DE7........194 F1
  New Mills SK22.......33 B7
  Ripley DE5 ....169 D2
  Somercotes DE55....170 C8
  Swadlincote DE11 ...256 B2
  Wirksworth DE4......165 F8
Woodstock Cl
  DE22...............204 D4
Woodstock Ct 5
  S41................96 A6
Woodstock Dr S41...115 C8
Woodstock Rd NG9..223 F3
Woodstock Rise 2
  S41................115 C8

Wood Street North
  DE55...............159 C5
Woodthorne Ave
  DE24...............232 E4
WOODTHORPE.........79 C2
Woodthorpe Ave
  Clay Cross S45 ......131 A4
  Derby, Chaddesden
  DE21...............219 F6
Woodthorpe CE Prim
  Sch S43.............79 C1
Woodthorpe Cl S44...98 F7
Woodthorpe Com Prim
  Sch S13.............44 C7
Woodthorpe Cres
  S13.................44 C8
Woodthorpe Rd
  Sheffield S13........44 C7
  Shuttlewood S44 .....98 F8
  Staveley S43.........79 C2
Woodvale Cl S40 ....114 A8
Wood View S21 ......79 A8
Woodview Cl S42....114 F2
Woodview Gdns
  DE22...............218 F8
Wood View Ho S21...59 C3
Woodview Rd
  Swadlincote DE11 ...255 E4
  Swadlincote DE11 ...255 E5
WOODVILLE 256 E3
Woodville CE Jun Sch
  DE11...............256 F2
Woodville Inf Sch
  DE11...............256 F2
Woodville Rd
  Hartshorne DE11 ....257 A5
  Overseal DE12 ......262 B4
  Woodville DE11 .....257 A4
Woodwards Cl
  DE72...............221 D1
Woodward's Pl
  DE11...............256 C3
Woodward Way
  DE11...............256 D4
Woodyard Ave S41...96 B5
Woodyard Ct DE11...255 F1
Woodyard La
  Church Broughton
  DE65...............227 C6
  Scropton DE65......226 F5
Wooley Cl S42......131 B7
Wooliscroft Cl DE7 .194 C2
Woollaton La SK17 ..138 D2
WOOLLEY 145 E5
Woolley Bridge Rd
  Glossop SK13..........9 F5
  Hadfield SK13..........9 F5
Woolley Cl SK14......9 D4
Woolley La SK14......9 D4
Woolley Mill La SK13 .9 E7
WOOLLEY MOOR...145 D7
Woolley Rd DE4 ....143 B6
Woolley's Yd DE4 ...141 C6
Woolrych St DE23 ..218 F2
Woolsthorpe Cres
  DE7................208 D4
Woolstitch Pk DE12. 264 E7
Woosnam Cl DE14 ..254 A6
Wootton Cl DE55 ....170 C7
Wootton Rd DE6.....183 A4
Worcester Ave
  NG19 ....136 C6
Worcester Cl S45....131 E4
Worcester Cres
  DE21...............219 E8
Worcester Gr SK13...17 F3
Worcester Mews
  NG19 ....136 C6
Worcester Rd DE15. 254 E6
Wordsworth Ave
  Derby DE24 ....231 F5
  Mansfield Woodhouse
  NG19 ....136 B4
  Swadlincote DE11 ...256 C6
Wordsworth Dr
  DE24...............232 A5
Wordsworth Pl S18...76 C7
Wordsworth Rd
  Awsworth NG16......195 C5
  Chesterfield S41......95 F8
Works La S44.........97 B3
Worksop Rd
  Barlborough S43......80 D7
  Belph S80...........82 D2
  Darfoulds S80 ....63 C1
  Holbeck Woodhouse
  S80...............101 E7
  Mastin Moor S43 .....79 D4
  Thorpe Salvin S80....62 E7
  Whitwell S43 ....81 C7
  Whitwell S80 ....81 F6
  Whitwell S80 ....82 A8
  Works S43 ....78 B2
WORMHILL...........68 C1
Worrall Ave NG10...223 E1
Worthington La
  DE73...............252 F1
Wortley Ave NG9 ...209 D3
Wortley Cl DE7 .....209 A8
Wortley Ct S33 ......51 B7
Wragley Way DE24. 231 D2

Wreakes La S18......56 F2
Wren Cl DE11 ......256 F3
Wren Nest Cl SK13...17 B8
Wren Nest Rd SK13 .10 B1
Wren Nest Ret Pk
  SK13................10 B1
Wren Nest Terr SK13 .10 C1
Wren Park Cl
  Belper DE56.........178 E5
  Chesterfield S40......114 F7
  Eckington S12........58 E8
  Findern DE65 ....230 D1
Wren Park Prim Sch
  DE3................218 A2
Wrenpark Rd S42....114 D4
Wren Way DE3 ......230 B7
Wretham Cl DE3.....230 D8
Wright Ave DE5......169 F1
Wright Cres DE6.....185 D8
Wright St DE5 ......181 B8
Wroxham Cl DE24 ..232 D4
Wulfric Cl S2........43 F8
Wulfric Pl S2........43 F8
Wulfric Rd
  Eckington S21........59 C3
  Sheffield S2 ....44 A8
WYASTON 185 D2
Wyaston Cl DE22 ...204 E1
Wyaston Ct DE6.....185 D1
Wyaston Gdns DE6 .185 D1
Wyaston Rd
  Ashbourne DE6.......185 C6
  Yeaveley DE6 ....199 D6
Wyatts Way DE5 ....169 F3
Wyatville Ave SK17...84 E5
Wybersley Rd SK6....32 A8
Wychwood Dr NG9 .209 D2
Wycliffe Rd DE55 ...159 A4
Wycombe Grange
  NG19 ....136 F2
Wye Bank DE45......109 E4
Wye Bank Gr DE45..109 E4
Wye Cl
  Hilton DE65 ....228 D1
  Hilton DE65 ....240 D8
Wye Croft Ct DE45..109 D5
Wye Dale
  Castle Gresley DE11..255 F2
  Swadlincote DE11 ...255 F2
Wyedale Cl
  Bakewell DE45......109 E4
  Buxton SK17.........85 B6
Wyedale Cres DE45 .109 E4
Wyedale Ct 5 S41...95 E7
Wyedale Dr DE45 ...109 E4
Wyedale View DE45. 109 E4
Wye Gr SK17.........85 A7
Wye Head Cl SK17 ...84 F7
Wye Ho SK17.........66 B1
Wyelands Cl SK17 ...84 F7
Wye Mill SK17........89 A6
Wye St
  Buxton SK17.........85 C8
  Derby DE24 ....233 A8
Wye Terr DE4 ......126 F8
Wylam Cl S45 ......131 D5
Wyming Brook Dr
  S10.................42 B8
Wyndale Dr DE7.....208 C6
Wyndham Cres
  DE15...............248 C3
Wyndham Prim Acad
  DE24...............233 A6
Wyndham St DE24 ..233 A7
Wyndham Way
  NG19 ....135 B4
Wynd The S21.......79 C7
Wynton Ave DE24...232 F8
Wyntor Ave DE4 ....141 C6
Wynyard Cl DE7 ....194 C3
Wysall Cl NG19 .....135 E1
Wystan Ct DE65 ....242 D2
Wyston Brook DE65. 228 D1
Wythburn Rd S41....95 C7
Wyver La DE56 .....178 F6
Wyvern Ave NG10...236 D5
Wyvern Bsns Pk
  DE21...............220 A4
Wyvern Cl
  Eastwood NG16......195 A8
  Matlock DE4........143 A6
Wyvern Gdns S17....55 E6
Wyvernside DE21 ...219 F4
Wyvern Way DE21 ..220 A4
Wyvil Close LE66 ...258 B1

Y

Yard Cl DE11 ...... 256 B4
Yardley Cl DE55 ....169 E4
Yardley Way DE56 ..179 D4
Yard The 4 SK13 ....10 C1
Yarmouth Ho DE24. 233 C7
Yarncliff Cl S40 .....95 D5
Yarrow Cl
  Burton upon Trent
  DE15...............248 B2
  Derby DE24 ....231 E2
Yarwell Cl DE21 ....205 D1

Yates Ave DE72......246 A7
Yates Rd SK22........33 C7
Yates St DE23 ......219 A1
Yeardsley Ave SK23...33 D3
Yeardsley Gn SK23....45 D8
Yeardsley La SK23.....33 D3
Yeats La DE4 ....155 A5
Yeldersley Cl S40......95 B5
YELDERSLEY
  HOLLIES...........186 F4
Yeldersley La
  Brailsford DE6.......187 B2
  Ednaston DE6 ......201 C8
  Osmaston DE6 ......186 E6
Yeld Rd
  Bakewell DE45......109 C4
  Bakewell DE45......109 D4
  Bakewell DE45......109 D5
Yeld The DE45......109 C5
Yelt La
  Doveridge DE6 .....224 D6
  Doveridge DE6 .....224 D8
Yeoman Park Sch
  NG19 ....136 C4
Yeoman St DE4......142 D1
Yeovil Cl DE24......233 C7
Yerley Hill DE6 .....172 C6
Yewdale Gr DE21 ...206 C3
Yews Cl DE73 ....233 A1
Yews The ST14......197 A3
Yew Tree Ave DE72. 221 D5
Yew Tree Cl
  Ashover S45........129 F3
  Darley Dale DE4.....127 B3
  Derby DE24 ....233 C7
  3 Smalley DE75 ...193 C8
Yew Tree Cottages
  SK6................15 B3
Yew Tree Cotts
  DE73...............222 E3
Yewtree Cres DE15..254 F7
Yew Tree Ct DE65 ..227 C2
Yew Tree Dr
  Chesterfield S40.....114 A8
  Clay Cross S42.......131 B6
  Killamarsh S21........60 C5
  Shirebrook NG20 ...119 D5
  Sutton in Ashfield
  NG17 ....148 F2
Yew Tree Gdns
  DE12...............260 C6
Yew Tree Hill DE4 ..156 B5
Yew Tree La
  Bradley DE6 ....186 E8
  Elvaston DE72 ......233 F4
Yewtree Rd DE11....255 F7
Yew Tree Rd
  Hatton DE65.........227 D1
  Rosliston DE12......260 C6
Yokecliffe Ave DE4 .165 E8
Yokecliffe Cres DE4 165 E8
Yokecliffe Dr DE4 ..165 E8
Yokecliffe Hill DE4 .165 E8
Yokecliffe La DE4....165 E8
York Ave
  Jacksdale NG16......171 B4
  Sandiacre NG10 .....223 A5
York Cl DE11 ....256 D6
York Cres S44 ......117 E1
Yorke St NG19......136 B2
York Pl
  North Wingfield S42...132 B7
  Shireoaks S81........63 F7
York Rd
  Derby DE21 ....219 F7
  Long Eaton NG10 ...223 C1
  Shirebrook NG20 ...119 E3
  Swadlincote DE11 ...256 B2
Yorkshire Way SK13 .17 F8
York St
  Chesterfield S41......115 C7
  Derby DE1 ....218 E5
  Glossop SK13 ....10 E1
York Terr
  Glossop SK13........17 C8
  Pinxton NG16........160 C1
Youlgrave Rd
  Over Haddon DE45 ..109 D1
  Over Haddon DE45...125 C8
YOULGREAVE 125 B5
Youlgreave Cl DE21. 205 F1
Youlgreave Cres SK13 .9 D1
Youlgreave Dr S12 ...44 D5
Young St DE23 .....218 F1
Yoxall Dr DE22 .....218 C4
Ypres Rd DE22......204 C2

Z

Zetland Cres DE24.. 231 C2
Zion Ho DE11 ......256 C1
Zouche Cl DE75 .... 181 C2